THE
PREACHER'S
OUTLINE & SERMON
BIBLE®

ISAIAH I

(CHAPTERS 1–35)

THE PREACHER'S OUTLINE & SERMON BIBLE®

OLD TESTAMENT
_____
_____

KING JAMES VERSION

Leadership Ministries Worldwide
Chattanooga, TN

THE PREACHER'S OUTLINE & SERMON BIBLE® - ISAIAH I

KING JAMES VERSION

Copyright © 2005 by ALPHA-OMEGA MINISTRIES, INC.

Published by Leadership Ministries Worldwide, Chattanooga, Tennessee

All other Bible study aids, references, indexes, reference materials
Copyright © 1991 by Alpha-Omega Ministries, Inc.

Previous Editions of **The Preacher's Outline & Sermon Bible®**,
New International Version NT   Copyright © 1998
King James Version NT   Copyright © 1991, 1996, 2000
by Alpha-Omega Ministries, Inc.

Please address all requests for information or permission to:
Leadership Ministries Worldwide
Ph.# (800) 987-8790   E-Mail: info@lmw.org
Web: lmw.org

Library of Congress Catalog Card Number: 96-75921
ISBN Softbound Edition: 978-1-57407-203-7

Printed in the United States of America

DEDICATED

To all the men and women of the world
who preach and teach the Gospel of
our Lord Jesus Christ and
to the Mercy and Grace of God

- Demonstrated to us in Christ Jesus our Lord.

  "In whom we have redemption through His blood, the forgiveness of sins, according to the riches of His grace." (Ep.1:7)

- Out of the mercy and grace of God, His Word has flowed. Let every person know that God will have mercy upon him, forgiving and using him to fulfill His glorious plan of salvation.

  "For God so loved the world, that he gave His only begotten Son, that whosoever believeth in Him should not perish, but have everlasting life. For God sent not his son into the world to condemn the world, but that the world through him might be saved." (Jn.3:16-17)

  "For this is good and acceptable in the sight of God our Saviour; who will have all men to be saved, and to come unto the knowledge of the truth." (1 Ti.2:3-4)

10/22

The Preacher's Outline & Sermon Bible®

is written for God's servants to use in their study, teaching, and preaching of God's Holy Word...

- to share the Word of God with the world.
- to help believers, both ministers and laypersons, in their understanding, preaching, and teaching of God's Word.
- to do everything we possibly can to lead men, women, boys, and girls to give their hearts and lives to Jesus Christ and to secure the eternal life that He offers.
- to do all we can to minister to the needy of the world.
- to give Jesus Christ His proper place, the place the Word gives Him. Therefore, no work of Leadership Ministries Worldwide will ever be personalized.

ACKNOWLEDGMENTS AND BIBLIOGRAPHY

Every child of God is precious to the Lord and deeply loved. And every child as a servant of the Lord touches the lives of those who come in contact with him or his ministry. The writing ministries of the following servants have touched this work, and we are grateful that God brought their writings our way. We hereby acknowledge their ministry to us, being fully aware that there are many others down through the years whose writings have touched our lives and who deserve mention, but whose names have faded from our memory. May our wonderful Lord continue to bless the ministries of these dear servants—and the ministries of us all—as we diligently labor to reach the world for Christ and to meet the desperate needs of those who suffer so much.

THE REFERENCE WORKS

Aharoni, Yohanan, Michael Avi-Yonah, Anson F. Rainey and Ze'ev Safrai, Editors. *The MacMillan Bible Atlas*, 3rd Ed. Jerusalem: Carta, The Israel Map and Publishing Company, 1993.

Albright, W.F. *History, Archaeology and Christian Humanism.* New York: McGraw Hill, 1964.

Archer, Gleason L. *A Survey of Old Testament Introduction.* Chicago, IL: Moody Bible Institute of Chicago, 1974.

_____. *Encyclopedia of Bible Difficulties.* Grand Rapids, Michigan: Zondervan Publishing House, 1982.

Atlas of the World. Hammond Concise Edition. Maplewood, NJ: Hammond Inc., 1993.

Baker's Dictionary of Theology. Everett F. Harrison, Editor-in-Chief. Grand Rapids, MI: Baker Book House, 1960.

Barker, William P. *Everyone in the Bible.* Westwood, NJ: Fleming H. Revell Co., 1966.

Benware, Paul N. *Survey of the Old Testament.* "Everyman's Bible Commentary." Chicago, IL: Moody Bible Institute of Chicago, 1993.

Bromiley, Geoffrey W., Editor, et. al. *David.* "The International Standard Bible Encyclopedia." Grand Rapids, MI: Eerdmans Publishing Co., 1988.

Brown, Francis. *The New Brown-Driver-Briggs-Gesenius Hebrew-English Lexicon.* Peabody, MA: Hendrickson Publishers, 1979.

Cruden's Complete Concordance of the Old & New Testament. Philadelphia, PA: The John C. Winston Co., 1930.

Dake, Finis Jennings. *Dake's Annotated Reference Bible, The Holy Bible.* Lawrenceville, GA: Dake Bible Sales, Inc., 1963.

Douglas, J.D. Editor. *New Bible Dictionary.* Wheaton, IL: Tyndale House Publishers, Inc., 1982.

Easton's 1897 Bible Dictionary. Database NavPress Software, 1996.

Elwell, Walter A., Editor. *The Evangelical Dictionary of Theology.* Grand Rapids, MI: Baker Book House, 1984.

Enhanced Nave's Topics. Database NavPress Software, 1991, 1994.

Frank, Harry Thomas, ed. *Atlas of the Bible Lands.* Maplewood, NJ: Hammond Incorporated, 1977.

Freedman, David Noel, Editor, et. al. *The Anchor Bible Dictionary.* New York: Doubleday, 1992.

Funk & Wagnalls Standard Desk Dictionary. Lippincott & Crowell, Publishers, 1980, Vol.2.

Geisler, Norman. *A Popular Survey of the Old Testament.* Grand Rapids, MI: Baker Book House, 1977.

Gill, Dr. A.L., Compiler. *God's Promises For Your Every Need.* Dallas, TX: Word Publishing, 1995.

Good News Bible. Old Testament: © American Bible Society, 1976. New Testament: © American Bible Society, 1966, 1971, 1976. Collins World.

Good News for Modern Man, The New Testament. New York, NY: American Bible Society, 1971.

Goodrick, Edward W. and John R. Kohlenberger, III. *The NIV Exhaustive Concordance.* Grand Rapids, MI: Zondervan Publishing House, 1990.

Grun, Bernard. *The Timetables of History.* 3rd Edition. New York: Simon & Schuster, 1991.

Harrison, Roland Kenneth. *Introduction to the Old Testament.* Grand Rapids, MI: Eerdmans Publishing Co., 1969.

Holman Bible Dictionary. Nashville, TN: Broadman & Holman Publishers, 1991. Database NavPress Software.

Hooper, Jerry L., Editor. *The Holman Bible Atlas.* Philadelphia, PA: A.J. Holman Company, 1978.

ISBE. Grand Rapids, MI: Eerdmans Publishing Co., 1988.

Josephus, Flavius. *Complete Works.* Grand Rapids, MI: Kregel Publications, 1981.

Kaiser, Walter C. *A History of Israel.* Nashville, Tennessee: Broadman and Holman Publishers, 1998.

Kipfer, Barbara Ann, Ph.D. *Roget's 21st Century Thesaurus.* New York, NY: Dell Publishing, 1992.

Kohlenberger, John R. III. *The Interlinear NIV Hebrew-English Old Testament.* Grand Rapids, MI: Zondervan Publishing House, 1987.

Kouffman, Donald T. *The Dictionary of Religious Terms.* Westwood, NJ: Fleming H. Revell Co., 1967.

Life Application® Bible. Wheaton, IL: Tyndale House Publishers, Inc., 1991.

Life Application® Study Bible. New International Version. Tyndale House Publishers, Inc.: Wheaton, IL 1991, and Zondervan Publishing House: Grand Rapids, MI, 1984.

Lindsell, Harold and Woodbridge, Charles J. *A Handbook of Christian Truth.* Westwood, NJ: Fleming H. Revell Company, A Division of Baker Book House, 1953.

Living Quotations For Christians. Edited by Sherwood Eliot Wirt and Kersten Beckstrom. New York, NY: Harper & Row, Publishers, 1974.

Lockyer, Herbert. *All the Books and Chapters of the Bible.* Grand Rapids, MI: Zondervan Publishing House, 1966.

_____. *All the Kings and Queens of the Bible.* Grand Rapids, MI: Zondervan Publishing House, 1961.

_____. *All the Men of the Bible.* Grand Rapids, MI: Zondervan Publishing House, 1958.

_____. *All the Miracles of the Bible.* Grand Rapids, MI: Zondervan Publishing House, 1961.

_____. *All the Parables of the Bible.* Grand Rapids, MI: Zondervan Publishing House, 1963.

_____. *The Women of the Bible.* Grand Rapids, MI: Zondervan Publishing House, 1967.

Luckenbill, Daniel David. *Ancient Records of Assyria and Babylonia*, 2 Vols. (ARAB) London: Histories and Mysteries of Man Ltd., 1989.

ACKNOWLEDGMENTS AND BIBLIOGRAPHY

Martin, Alfred. *Survey of the Scriptures*, Part I, II, III. Chicago, IL: Moody Bible Institute of Chicago, 1961.

McDowell, Josh. *Evidence That Demands a Verdict*, Vol.1. San Bernardino, CA: Here's Life Publishers, Inc., 1979.

Miller, Madeleine S. & J. Lane. *Harper's Bible Dictionary*. New York, NY: Harper & Row Publishers, 1961.

Nave, Orville J. *Nave's Topical Bible*. Nashville, TN: The Southwestern Company. Copyright © by J.B. Henderson, 1921.

Nelson's Complete Book of Bible Maps & Charts. Nashville, TN: Thomas Nelson Publishers, Inc., 1996.

New American Standard Bible, Updated Edition. La Habra, CA: The Lockman Foundation, 1995.

New Bible Dictionary, 3rd Edition. Leicester, England: Universities & Colleges Christian Fellowship, 1996.

New Living Translation, Holy Bible. Wheaton, IL: Tyndale House Publishers, Inc., 1996.

NIV Thompson Student Bible. Jauchen, John S., Editor, et. al. Indianapolis, IN: Kirkbride Bible Company, 1999.

Orr, James, Editor. *The International Standard Bible Encyclopaedia*, Grand Rapids, MI: Eerdmans Publishing Co., 1939.

Orr, William. *How We May Know That God Is*. Wheaton, IL: Van Kampen Press, n.d.

Owens, John Joseph. *Analytical Key to the Old Testament*, Vols.1, 2, 3. Grand Rapids, MI: Baker Book House, 1989.

Payne, J. Barton. *Encyclopedia of Biblical Prophecy*. New York, NY: Harper & Row, Publishers, 1973.

Pilgrim Edition, Holy Bible. New York, NY: Oxford University Press, 1952.

Ridout, Samuel. *Lectures on the Tabernacle*. New York, NY: Loizeaux Brothers, Inc., 1914.

Silverman, David P. ed. *Ancient Egypt*. New York: Oxford University Press, 1997.

Smith, William. *Smith's Bible Dictionary*. Peabody, MA: Hendrickson Publishers, n.d.

Stone, Nathan J. *Names of God*. Chicago, IL: Moody Press, 1944.

Strong, James. *Strong's Exhaustive Concordance of the Bible*. Nashville, TN: Thomas Nelson, Inc., 1990.

———. *The Tabernacle of Israel*. Grand Rapids, MI: Kregel Publications, 1987.

Strong's Greek and Hebrew Dictionary as compiled by iExalt Software. Database NavPress Software, 1990-1993.

The Amplified Bible. Scripture taken from THE AMPLIFIED BIBLE, Old Testament copyright © 1965, 1987 by the Zondervan Publishing House. The Amplified New Testament copyright © 1958, 1987 by The Lockman Foundation. Used by permission.

The Holy Bible in Four Translations. Minneapolis, MN: Worldwide Publications. Copyright © The Iversen-Norman Associates: New York, NY, 1972.

The Illustrated Bible Atlas, with Historical Notes by F. F. Bruce. Grand Rapids, MI: Kregel Publications, 1994.

The Interlinear Bible, Vols.1, 2, 3. Translated by Jay P. Green, Sr. Grand Rapids, MI: Baker Book House, 1976.

The Interpreter's Bible, 12 Vols. New York, NY: Abingdon Press, 1956.

The NASB Greek/Hebrew Dictionary and Concordance. La Habra, CA: The Lockman Foundation, 1988.

The Nelson Study Bible, New King James Version. Earl D. Radmacher, General Editor. Nashville, TN: Thomas Nelson Publishers, Inc., 1997.

The New Compact Bible Dictionary. Edited by T. Alton Bryant. Grand Rapids, MI: Zondervan Publishing House, 1967. Used by permission of Zondervan Publishing House.

The New Scofield Reference Bible. Edited by C.I. Scofield. New York, NY: Oxford University Press, 1967.

The New Testament-English, PI-RHO. "The Complete Biblical Library." Springfield, MO: World Library Press Inc, 1991.

The New Thompson Chain Reference Bible. Indianapolis, IN: B.B. Kirkbride Bible Co., Inc., 1964.

The New Unger's Bible Dictionary. Chicago, IL: Moody Press, 1998. Database NavPress Software, 1997.

The NIV Study Bible, New International Version. Grand Rapids, MI: Zondervan Publishing House, 1985.

The Old Testament Hebrew-English Dictionary, NUN—AYIN. "The Complete Biblical Library." Springfield, MO: World Library Press Inc., 1999.

The Open Bible. Nashville, TN: Thomas Nelson Publishers, 1977.

The Quest Study Bible. New International Version. Grand Rapids, MI: Zondervan Publishing House, 1994.

The Zondervan Pictorial Encyclopedia of the Bible, Vol.1. Merrill C. Tenney, Editor. Grand Rapids, MI: Zondervan Publishing House, 1982.

Theological Wordbook of the Old Testament. Edited by R. Laird Harris. Chicago, IL: Moody Bible Institute of Chicago, 1980.

Unger, Merrill F. & William White, Jr. *Nelson's Expository Dictionary of the Old Testament*. Nashville, TN: Thomas Nelson Publishers, 1980.

Vine, W.E., Merrill F. Unger, William White, Jr. *Vine's Complete Expository Dictionary of Old and New Testament Words*. Nashville, TN: Thomas Nelson Publishers, 1985.

Walton, John H. *Chronological and Background Charts of the Old Testament*. Grand Rapids, MI: Zondervan Publishing House, 1978.

Webster's Seventh New Collegiate Dictionary. Springfield, MA: G. & C. Merriam Company, Publishers, 1971.

Wilmington. Harold L. *The Outline Bible*. Wheaton, IL: Tyndale House Publishers, Inc., 1999.

Wilson, William. *Wilson's Old Testament Word Studies*. McLean, VA: MacDonald Publishing Company, n.d.

Wood, Leon. *A Survey of Israel's History*. Grand Rapids, MI: Zondervan Publishing House, 1982.

Young, Edward J. *An Introduction to the Old Testament*. Grand Rapids, MI: Eerdmans Publishing Co., 1964.

Young, Robert. *Young's Analytical Concordance to the Bible*. Grand Rapids, MI: Eerdmans Publishing Co., n.d.

Zodhiates, Spiros, Th.D., Executive Editor. *The Hebrew-Greek Key Study Bible, New International Version*. Chattanooga, TN: AMG Publishers, 1996.

Zondervan NIV Bible Library. Version 2.5. Grand Rapids, MI: Zondervan Publishing House.

ACKNOWLEDGMENTS AND BIBLIOGRAPHY

THE COMMENTARIES

Alexander, Joseph Addison. *The Prophecies of Isaiah.* "The Zondervan Commentary Series." Grand Rapids, MI: Zondervan Publishing House, 1981.

Bultema, Harry. *Isaiah.* Grand Rapids, MI: Kregel Publications, 1981.

Burroughs, P.E., D.D. *Old Testament Studies.* Nashville, TN: Sunday School Board, Southern Baptist Convention, 1915.

Clements, R.E. *Isaiah 1-39.* "The New Century Bible Commentary." Grand Rapids, MI: Eerdmans Publishing Co., 1980.

Criswell, W.A. *Isaiah an exposition.* Grand Rapids, MI: Zondervan Publishing House, 1977.

Elwell, Walter A., Editor. *Topical Analysis of the Bible.* (Grand Rapids, MI: Baker Book House, 1991.

Evans, Mary J. *1 and 2 Samuel.* "New International Biblical Commentary." Peabody, MA: Hendrickson Publishers, Inc., 2000.

Griffin, Gilbert L. *The Gospel in Isaiah.* Nashville, TN: Convention Press, 1968.

Grogan, G.W. *Isaiah.* "The Expositor's Bible Commentary," Vol.6. Grand Rapids, MI: Zondervan Publishing House, 1988.

Henry, Matthew. *Matthew Henry's Commentary*, 6 Vols. Old Tappan, NJ: Fleming H. Revell Co., n.d.

Holladay, William L. *Isaiah: Scroll of a Prophetic Heritage.* Grand Rapids, MI: Eerdmans Publishing Co., 1978.

Horton, Stanley M. *Isaiah.* "The Complete Biblical Library: The Old Testament," Vol.9. Springfield, MO: World Library Press Inc., 1995.

Ironside, H.A. *The Prophet Isaiah.* Neptune, NJ: Loizeaux Brothers, Inc., 1952.

Jennings, F.C. *Studies in Isaiah.* Neptune, NJ: Loizeaux Brothers, Inc., n.d..

Kaiser, Walter C., Jr. *A History of Israel.* Nashville, TN: Broadman & Holman Publishers, 1998.

Keil-Delitzsch. *Commentary on the Old Testament*, Vol.8. Grand Rapids, MI: Eerdmans Publishing Co., n.d.

Kirkpatrick, A.F., General Editor. *The Book of the Prophet Isaiah Chapters I-XXXIX.* "The Cambridge Bible for Schools and Colleges." New York, NY: Cambridge University Press, 1958.

_____. *The Book of the Prophet Isaiah Chapters XL-LXVI.* "The Cambridge Bible for Schools and Colleges." New York, NY: Cambridge University Press, 1960.

Leupold, H.C. *Exposition of Isaiah,* Vol.1. Baker Book House, Grand Rapids, Michigan, 1968.

Maclaren, Alexander. *Expositions of Holy Scripture*, 11 Vols. Grand Rapids, MI: Eerdmans Publishing Co., 1952-59.

Martin, Alfred. *Isaiah, The Salvation of Jehovah.* "Everyman's Bible Commentary." Chicago, IL: Moody Bible Institute of Chicago, 1956.

McGee, J. Vernon. *Thru the Bible*, Vol.3. Nashville, TN: Thomas Nelson Publishers, 1982.

McKenna, David. *Isaiah 1-39.* "Mastering the Old Testament," Vol.16A. Dallas, TX: Word Publishing, 1994.

Morgan, G. Campbell. *Living Messages of the Books of the Bible*, Vol.1. Old Tappan, NJ: Fleming H. Revell, 1912.

Morris, Henry M. *The Genesis Record.* Grand Rapids, MI., 1996.

Motyer, J. Alec. *Isaiah* ."The Tyndale Old Testament Commentaries." Downers Grove, IL: Inter-Varsity Press, 1999.

_____. *The Prophecy of Isaiah.* Downers Grove, IL: Inter-varsity Press, 1993.

Oswalt, John N. *Isaiah 1-39.* "The New International Commentary on the Old Testament," Grand Rapids, MI: Eerdmans Publishing Co. 1982.

Poole, Matthew. *Matthew Poole's Commentary on the Holy Bible*, Vol.2. Peabody, MA: Hendrickson Publishers, n.d.

Redpath, Alan. *Victorious Christian Service.* Westwood, NJ: Fleming H. Revell Co., 1958.

Schulz, Samuel J. *The Old Testament Speaks*, 4th Edition. San Francisco, CA: Harper Collins Publishers, 1990.

Smith, James E. *What the Bible Teaches about the Promised Messiah.* Nashville, TN: Thomas Nelson Publishers, 1993.

Spurgeon, C.H. *Spurgeon's Sermon Notes. Genesis to Malachi.* Westwood, NJ: Fleming H. Revell Co., n.d.

The Pulpit Commentary. 23 Vols. Edited by H.D.M. Spence & Joseph S. Exell. Grand Rapids, MI: Eerdmans Publishing Co., 1950.

Walvoord, John F. and Roy B. Zuck, Editors. *The Bible Knowledge Commentary, Old Testament.* Colorado Springs, CO: Chariot Victor Publishing, 1985.

Wiersbe, Warren W. *Be Comforted.* Wheaton, IL: Victor Books, 1992.

Willis, John T. *Isaiah.* "The Living Word Commentary on the Old Testament." Abilene, TX: ACU Press, 1984.

Wright, G. Ernest. *Isaiah.* "The Layman's Bible Commentary," Vol.11. Atlanta, GA: John Knox Press, 1964.

Young, Edward J. *The Book of Isaiah,* Vol.1. Grand Rapids, MI: Eerdmans Publishing Co., 1965.

THE ARTWORK

Isaiah. Art Resource. New York, NY. www.artres.com; The Jewish Museum, New York, NY.

ABBREVIATIONS

&	= and		O.T.	= Old Testament
Bc.	= because		p./pp.	= page/pages
Concl.	= conclusion		Pt.	= point
Cp.	= compare		Quest.	= question
Ct.	= contrast		Rel.	= religion
e.g.	= for example		Rgt.	= righteousness
f.	= following		Thru	= through
Illust.	= illustration		v./vv.	= verse/verses
N.T.	= New Testament		vs.	= versus

THE BOOKS OF THE OLD TESTAMENT

Book	Abbreviation	Chapters	Book	Abbreviation	Chapters
GENESIS	Gen. or Ge.	50	Ecclesiastes	Eccl. or Ec.	12
Exodus	Ex.	40	The Song of Solomon	S. of Sol. or Song	8
Leviticus	Lev. or Le.	27	Isaiah	Is.	66
Numbers	Num. or Nu.	36	Jeremiah	Jer. or Je.	52
Deuteronomy	Dt. or De.	34	Lamentations	Lam.	5
Joshua	Josh. or Jos.	24	Ezekiel	Ezk. or Eze.	48
Judges	Judg. or Jud.	21	Daniel	Dan. or Da.	12
Ruth	Ruth or Ru.	4	Hosea	Hos. or Ho.	14
1 Samuel	1 Sam. or 1 S.	31	Joel	Joel	3
2 Samuel	2 Sam. or 2 S.	24	Amos	Amos or Am.	9
1 Kings	1 Ki. or 1 K.	22	Obadiah	Obad. or Ob.	1
2 Kings	2 Ki. or 2 K.	25	Jonah	Jon. or Jona.	4
1 Chronicles	1 Chron. or 1 Chr.	29	Micah	Mic. or Mi.	7
2 Chronicles	2 Chron. or 2 Chr.	36	Nahum	Nah. or Na.	3
Ezra	Ezra or Ezr.	10	Habakkuk	Hab.	3
Nehemiah	Neh. or Ne.	13	Zephaniah	Zeph. or Zep.	3
Esther	Est.	10	Haggai	Hag.	2
Job	Job or Jb.	42	Zechariah	Zech. or Zec.	14
Psalms	Ps.	150	Malachi	Mal.	4
Proverbs	Pr.	31			

THE BOOKS OF THE NEW TESTAMENT

Book	Abbreviation	Chapters	Book	Abbreviation	Chapters
MATTHEW	Mt.	28	1 Timothy	1 Tim. or 1 Ti.	6
Mark	Mk.	16	2 Timothy	2 Tim. or 2 Ti.	4
Luke	Lk. or Lu.	24	Titus	Tit.	3
John	Jn.	21	Philemon	Phile. or Phm.	1
The Acts	Acts or Ac.	28	Hebrews	Heb. or He.	13
Romans	Ro.	16	James	Jas. or Js.	5
1 Corinthians	1 Cor. or 1 Co.	16	1 Peter	1 Pt. or 1 Pe.	5
2 Corinthians	2 Cor. or 2 Co.	13	2 Peter	2 Pt. or 2 Pe.	3
Galatians	Gal. or Ga.	6	1 John	1 Jn.	5
Ephesians	Eph. or Ep.	6	2 John	2 Jn.	1
Philippians	Ph.	4	3 John	3 Jn.	1
Colossians	Col.	4	Jude	Jude	1
1 Thessalonians	1 Th.	5	Revelation	Rev. or Re.	22
2 Thessalonians	2 Th.	3			

HOW TO USE
The Preacher's Outline & Sermon Bible®
Follow these easy steps to gain maximum benefit from The POSB.

1 SUBJECT HEADING

2 MAJOR POINTS

3 SUBPOINTS
&
SCRIPTURE

4 COMMENTARY

---

1 CORINTHIANS 13:1-13

CHAPTER 13

D. The Most Excellent Quality of Life: Love, Not Gifts, 13:1-13[DS1]

1. The great importance of love
a. Verdict 1: Tongues without love are meaningless
b. Verdict 2: Gifts without love are nothing
   1) Prophecy is nothing
   2) Understanding all mysteries & knowledge are nothing
   3) Faith is nothing
c. Verdict 3: Giving without love profits nothing
   1) Giving one's goods
   2) Giving one's life—martyrdom

2. The great acts of love

Though I speak with the tongues of men and of angels, and have not charity, I am become *as* sounding brass, or a tinkling cymbal.
2 And though I have *the gift of* prophecy, and understand all mysteries, and all knowledge; and though I have all faith, so that I could remove mountains, and have not charity, I am nothing.
3 And though I bestow all my goods to feed *the poor*, and though I give my body to be burned, and have not charity, it profiteth me nothing.
4 Charity suffereth long, *and* is kind; charity envieth not; charity vaunteth not itself, is not puffed up,
5 Doth not behave itself unseemly, seeketh not her own, is not easily provoked, thinketh no evil;

6 Rejoiceth not in iniquity, but rejoiceth in the truth;
7 Beareth all things, believeth all things, hopeth all things, endureth all things.
8 Charity never faileth: but whether *there be* prophecies, they shall fail; whether *there be* tongues, they shall cease; whether *there be* knowledge, it shall vanish away.
9 For we know in part, and we prophesy in part.
10 But when that which is perfect is come, then that which is in part shall be done away.
11 When I was a child, I spake as a child, I understood as a child, I thought as a child: but when I became a man, I put away childish things.
12 For now we see through a glass, darkly; but then face to face: now I know in part; but then shall I know even as also I am known.
13 And now abideth faith, hope, charity, these three; but the greatest of these *is* charity.

3. The great permanence of love
a. It never fails, never ceases, never vanishes
b. It is perfect & complete
c. It is maturity—mature behavior
d. It is the hope of being face-to-face with God—possessing perfect consciousness & knowledge

4. The great supremacy of love

DIVISION VII
THE QUESTIONS CONCERNING SPIRITUAL GIFTS, 12:1–14:40

D. The Most Excellent Quality of Life: Love, Not Gifts, 13:1-13

(13:1-13) **Introduction:** there is no question, what the world needs more than anything else is love. If people loved each other, really loved each other, there would be no more war, crime, abuse, injustice, poverty, hunger, starvation, homelessness, deprivation, or immorality. Love is the one ingredient that could revolutionize society. Love is the greatest quality of human life. Love is the supreme quality, the most excellent way for a man to live.
1. The great importance of love (vv.1-3).
2. The great acts of love (vv.4-7).
3. The great permanence of love (vv.8-12).
4. The great supremacy of love (v.13).

DEEPER STUDY # 1
(13:1-13) **Love:** throughout this passage, the word used for love or charity is the great word *agape*. (See DEEPER STUDY # 4, *Love*—Jn.21:15-17 for more discussion.) The meaning of *agape love* is more clearly seen by contrasting it with the various kinds of love. There are essentially four kinds of love. Whereas the English language has only the word *love* to describe all the affectionate experiences of men, the Greek language had a different word to describe each kind of love.
1. There is *passionate love* or *eros love*. This is the physical love between sexes; the patriotic love of a person for his nation; the ambition of a person for power, wealth, or fame. Briefly stated, *eros love* is the base love of a man that arises from his own inner passion. Sometimes *eros love* is focused upon good and other times it is focused upon bad. It should be noted that *eros love* is never used in the New Testament.
2. There is *affectionate love* or *storge love*. This is the kind of love that exists between parent and child and between loyal citizens and a trustworthy ruler. *Storge love* is also not used in the New Testament.
3. There is an *endearing love*, the love that cherishes. This is *phileo love*, the love of a husband and wife for each other, of a brother for a brother, of a friend for the dearest of friends. It is the love that cherishes, that holds someone or something ever so dear to one's heart.
4. There is *selfless and sacrificial love* or *agape love*. Agape love is the love of the mind, of the reason, of the will. It is the love that goes so far…
• that it loves a person even if he does not deserve to be loved
• that it actually loves the person who is utterly unworthy of being loved

---

1 Glance at the **Subject Heading**. Think about it for a moment.

2 Glance at the **Subject Heading** again, and then the **Major Points** (1, 2, 3, etc.). Do this several times, reviewing them together while quickly grasping the overall subject.

3 Glance at **both** the **Major Points** and **Subpoints** together while reading the **Scripture**. Do this slower than Step 2. Note how these points sit directly beside the related verse and simply restate what the Scripture is saying—in Outline form.

4 Next read the **Commentary**. Note that the *Major Point Numbers* in the Outline match those in the Commentary. A small raised number (**DS1, DS2, etc.**) at the end of a Subject Heading or Outline Point, directs you to a related **Deeper Study** in the Commentary.

Finally, read the **Thoughts** and **Support Scripture** (not shown).

As you read and re-read, pray that the Holy Spirit will bring to your attention exactly what you should preach and teach. May God bless you richly as you study and teach His Word.

The POSB contains everything you need for sermon preparation:

1. **The Subject Heading** describes the overall theme of the passage, and is located directly above the Scripture (keyed *alphabetically*).

2. **Major Points** are keyed with an outline *number* guiding you to related commentary. Note that the Commentary includes "*Thoughts*" (life application) and abundant Supporting Scriptures.

3. **Subpoints** explain and clarify the Scripture as needed.

4. **Commentary** is fully researched and developed for every point.

• **Thoughts** (in bold) help apply the Scripture to real life.

• **Deeper Studies** provide in-depth discussions of key words.

"Woe is unto me, if I preach not the gospel"
(1 Co.9:16)

TABLE OF CONTENTS
ISAIAH I

PAGE

INTRODUCTION TO ISAIAH I — 1

HISTORICAL AND PRACTICAL BACKGROUND — 3

A TIMELINE OF KINGS, PROPHETS, AND HISTORY — 52

GENERAL OUTLINE OF ISAIAH I — 55

DIVISION I.   THE PROPHECIES OF REBUKE AND HOPE GIVEN TO JUDAH AND JERUSALEM: AN OVERVIEW OF THE PRESENT AND FUTURE OF GOD'S PEOPLE, 1:1–12:6 — 57

DIVISION II.   THE PROPHECIES CONCERNING GOD'S JUDGMENT OF THE NATIONS AND HIS TRIUMPH OVER THE WORLD, 13:1–27:13 — 154

DIVISION III.   THE PROPHECIES OF WOE: GOD'S WARNING TO HIS PEOPLE, 28:1–35:10 — 242

PRACTICAL BIBLE HELPS AND RESOURCES – ISAIAH I — 297
MAP 1: The Assyrian Empire — 298
MAP 2: The Babylonian Empire — 299
CHART 1: A Timeline of Kings, Prophets, and History — 300
CHART 2: Sacred Days in the Hebrew Calendar — 302
CHART 3: The Prophets: Their Message—Then and Now — 304
    ➢ Chronological Listing of the Prophets — 305
    ➢ Alphabetical Listing of the Prophets — 306
    ➢ The Prophets — 307

TYPES IN ISAIAH I
    ➢ Alphabetical Outline — 375
    ➢ Chronological Outline — 377

OUTLINE AND SUBJECT INDEX – ISAIAH I — 379

THE BOOK OF
ISAIAH

AUTHOR: the very first words of this great book declare that Isaiah is the author. Almost the entire book consists of the visions and sermons of Isaiah the prophet, the son of Amoz. Such has been the clear position down through church history. During the eighteenth century, however, many liberal theories arose disputing the authorship. Nevertheless the following evidence strongly supports the position that Isaiah the prophet is the author:

1. The book of *Isaiah* states in the very first verse that the prophet Isaiah is the author.
2. The book of *Isaiah* was written from the perspective of a prophet. Set in the time after the fall of the Northern Kingdom, Isaiah preached for many years to the Southern Kingdom of Judah, warning them time and again to turn to the LORD for help. The author has one distinct purpose in mind: to declare, as his name reveals, that salvation is of the LORD and Him alone. Over and over Isaiah challenged Judah to be faithful in worshipping the only living and true God. These facts point to a prophet being the author of the great book of *Isaiah*.
3. The book of *Isaiah* was apparently written no later than 680 B.C., in keeping with the time of Isaiah's ministry.
4. The historical facts contained in the book were known to Isaiah personally.
5. Jewish and Christian tradition have always stated that Isaiah is the author of the book.
6. Throughout the book of *Isaiah*, the style, words, and thinking of the author match that of a prophet.

Although the evidence points strongly to the prophet Isaiah's being the author, it is far more important to know the Divine Author. The Holy Spirit of God *breathed* or *inspired* the great book of *Isaiah*. Through His inspiration, the Holy Spirit has given to the world a clear warning against sin and a graphic picture of the saving power of God. The inspiring prophecies in the book of *Isaiah* were written both as a warning and a promise to every reader.

DATE: completed no later than 680 B.C. and perhaps not long after 701 B.C. when the Assyrian army was destroyed. Since tradition strongly suggests that Isaiah was martyred by being sawed in two, it is reasonable to believe that he wrote down his messages *during* his ministry. The time of Isaiah's ministry was during the great Babylonian and Assyrian Empires, after the Northern Kingdom had fallen and gone into captivity. All that was left of the great kingdom of Israel was the small territory of Judah, which included only the tribes of Judah and Benjamin. These were desperate times, when God's people lived under the constant and threatening shadow of great foreign powers.

The Judean kings reigning during Isaiah's ministry were:
⇒ Uzziah (792–740 B.C.)
⇒ Jotham (750–731 B.C.)
⇒ Ahaz (735–715 B.C.)
⇒ Hezekiah (729–686 B.C.)

TO WHOM WRITTEN: the Southern Kingdom of Judah in particular and to the human race in general. The book of *Isaiah* was first written to the small nation of Judah:
⇒ to present God's wonderful salvation to all who would listen
⇒ to warn people of the penalty of sin if they continued to disobey and reject God
⇒ to comfort those who trusted in the LORD
⇒ to paint a graphic picture of the Messiah, both of His suffering for the sins of the world and of His coming reign over the world

PURPOSE:
1. The *Historical* Purpose:
   a. To record God's prophecies concerning Judah and Jerusalem (chs.1–12).
   b. To record God's judgment of the nations and His triumph over the world (chs.13–27).
   c. To record God's warnings to His people (chs.28–35).
   d. To document the reign of Hezekiah and his deliverance from Assyria, showing how his reign marked a shift from the threat of Assyria to the captivity of Judah by Babylon (chs.36–39).
   e. To record God's prophecies concerning Israel's deliverance, comfort, and glorious future (chs.40–64).
   f. To record God's prophecies that give a glimpse into the millennial reign of Christ on earth and the fulfillment of human history (chs.65–66).
2. The *Doctrinal* or *Spiritual* Purpose:
   a. To call God's people back to salvation and faithfulness (chs.1–6).
   b. To prophesy of the coming Messiah (chs.7–12).
   c. To warn other nations of the futility of trying to stand against the sovereign LORD (chs.13–35).
   d. To illustrate through the life of Hezekiah the tremendous delivering power of the LORD, no matter what the circumstances (chs.36–39).
   e. To give comfort to the people of God, assuring them that they will never be forgotten (chs.40–48).
   f. To paint a graphic picture of the Messiah, the Suffering Servant of the LORD (chs.49–53).
   g. To share the prophecies concerning the reign of Christ—His ability to avenge His people and restore all things (chs.54–66).
3. The *Christological* or *Christ-Centered* Purpose: prophecies concerning Christ are more clearly seen in the book of *Isaiah* than in any other Old Testament book except for *Psalms*. Isaiah foresaw at least twenty prophecies about the Messiah. (For a complete list of Old Testament prophecies fulfilled by Christ, see Is.9:1-7, DEEPER STUDY #3).

The richest passage in Isaiah concerning Jesus Christ is 52:13–53:12, where Isaiah describes in detail the passion (sacrificial death) of the Savior. In this beloved section of Scripture, we see Christ fulfilling the sacrificial work of the Law on the cross. This is vitally important to Isaiah, because he understood that Christ would do more than *cover* sin—He would actually *cleanse* from sin all who would believe. Jesus Christ, the Savior of the world, came through David's family line (11:1) and died for the sins of the world, just as Isaiah foretold (53:4-5).

INTRODUCTION TO ISAIAH

SPECIAL FEATURES:
1. *Isaiah* is "The Great Book That Offers Hope to a Rebellious People" (1:1–5:30).
2. *Isaiah* is "The Great Book That Tells of the Great Vision of the LORD on His Throne" (6:1–7).
3. *Isaiah* is "The Great Book That Records the Call of Isaiah" (6:8–13).
4. *Isaiah* is "The Great Book That Warns of Coming Judgment but Promises a Wonderful Savior" (7:1–9:7).
5. *Isaiah* is "The Great Book That Warns That God Will Not Tolerate Pride" (9:8–10:34).
6. *Isaiah* is "The Great Book That Paints a Glorious Picture of the Coming Messiah, the Son of David" (11:1–12:6).
7. *Isaiah* is "The Great Book That Prophesies Judgment on the Heathen Nations" (13:1–24:23).
8. *Isaiah* is "The Great Book That Tells of God's Unswerving Faithfulness to His People and His Triumph Over the World" (25:1–27:13).
9. *Isaiah* is "The Great Book That Gives Prophecy After Prophecy of Judgment but Assures the Restoration of God's People" (28:1–35:10).
10. *Isaiah* is "The Great Book That Records God's Great Deliverances of King Hezekiah" (36:1–39:8).
11. *Isaiah* is "The Great Book That Promises Comfort and Deliverance to God's People" (40:1–48:22).
12. *Isaiah* is "The Great Book That Prophesies the Coming Messiah, the Suffering Servant Who Would Die for the Sins of the World" (49:1–53:12).
13. *Isaiah* is "The Great Book That Tells of the New Covenant to Come" (54:1–55:13).
14. *Isaiah* is "The Great Book That Warns of God's Judgment upon Idolators" (56:1–58:14).
15. *Isaiah* is "The Great Book That Assures the Restoration of Zion" (59:1–60:22).
16. *Isaiah* is "The Great Book That Prophesies Good News to Be Brought by the Messiah" (61:1–11).
17. *Isaiah* is "The Great Book That Tells of the Coming Salvation of Zion" (62:1–64:12).
18. *Isaiah* is "The Great Book That Predicts Time and Again the Coming Kingdom of the Messiah and the Consummation of Human History" (65:1–66:24).

AN EXTENSIVE HISTORICAL AND PRACTICAL BACKGROUND TO THE TIMES OF ISAIAH

THE FOUR KINGS WHO RULED DURING ISAIAH'S MINISTRY

The voice of one crying in the wilderness, "Prepare ye the way of the Lord" (Is.40:3).

UZZIAH—792-740 B.C.

JOTHAM—750-731 B.C.

AHAZ—735-715 B.C.

HEZEKIAH—729-686 B.C.

Isaiah by Duccio di Buoninsegna (1308-1311)

AN EXTENSIVE HISTORICAL AND PRACTICAL BACKGROUND TO THE TIMES OF ISAIAH

THE FOUR KINGS WHO RULED DURING ISAIAH'S MINISTRY

OVERVIEW: to gain a proper understanding of the book of *Isaiah*, a person should be aware of the historical background in which his prophecies were first preached. The most accurate history book in the world is, of course, the Bible. And there is a large section in the book of *Second Chronicles* revealing much of what happened during the reigns of the four kings to whom Isaiah ministered (Uzziah [*also called Azariah*], Jotham, Ahaz and Hezekiah).

Take a look at the outline below. As you glance at the practical outline points, you will immediately begin to see what a tremendous resource this overview can be. The reign of each king is outlined in detail including thoughts for application and deeper studies. The outlines in the following pages will be a great help to your study of the great book of *Isaiah* the prophet.

BACKGROUND TO ISAIAH'S DAY

I. **THE REIGN OF UZZIAH (AZARIAH): A CLEAR WARNING AGAINST PRIDE AND ARROGANCE, 2 CHR.26:1-23**

II. **THE REIGN OF JOTHAM: A PICTURE OF HOLDING FAST UNTIL THE END OF LIFE, 2 CHR.27:1-9**

III. **THE REIGN OF AHAZ: A PICTURE OF UTTER WICKEDNESS AND TOTAL DEPRAVITY, 2 CHR.28:1-27**

IV. **THE REIGN OF HEZEKIAH (PART 1)—THE CLEANSING OF THE TEMPLE FOR WORSHIP: A LESSON ON THE GREAT NEEDS OF THE CHURCH, 2 CHR.29:1-36**

V. **THE REIGN OF HEZEKIAH (PART 2)—A MEANINGFUL CELEBRATION OF THE PASSOVER: A PICTURE OF TRUE REVIVAL, 2 CHR.30:1-27**

VI. **THE REIGN OF HEZEKIAH (PART 3)—HIS RELIGIOUS REFORMS: THE PICTURE OF A REVIVED, ORDERLY CHURCH, 2 CHR.31:1-21**

VII. **THE REIGN OF HEZEKIAH (PART 4)—HIS DELIVERANCE FROM ASSYRIA, TERMINAL ILLNESS, AND DEATH: A PICTURE OF GOD'S UNLIMITED, SOVEREIGN POWER, 2 CHR.32:1-33**

BACKGROUND TO ISAIAH'S DAY

(The Four Kings Who Ruled During Isaiah's Ministry)

I. THE REIGN OF UZZIAH (AZARIAH): A CLEAR WARNING AGAINST PRIDE AND ARROGANCE, 2 CHR.26:1-23

OUTLINE	SCRIPTURE	SCRIPTURE	OUTLINE
1. Uzziah's early years—his righteousness & achievements: Rewarded for seeking God a. Uzziah's background 1) He was crowned at age 16 2) He was known for recapturing & rebuilding Elath, an important seaport at the eastern tip of the Red Sea 3) He had a long reign as king: 52 years 4) He was the son of Amaziah & Jecoliah 5) He had a strong spiritual life • Lived a righteous life, pleasing the LORD • Sought God & was instructed in the fear of God (His Word)—by a man named Zechariah • Was prosperous, successful as long as he sought God b. Uzziah's important & far-reaching achievements 1) He achieved success in battle • Warred against the Philistines, thereby extending Judah's territory • Warred against the Arabs & Meunites • Warred against the Ammonites who paid him tribute • Became so powerful, his fame spread all the way to Egypt 2) He achieved success in construction projects • Built fortress towers on the great wall surrounding Jerusalem • Built forts in the desert of southern Judah • Built cisterns to catch rain water 3) He achieved success in ranching & agriculture • Had large livestock herds • Had many farms, vineyards, & workers 4) He achieved success in building a strong, well-	Then all the people of Judah took Uzziah, who *was* sixteen years old, and made him king in the room of his father Amaziah. 2 He built Eloth, and restored it to Judah, after that the king slept with his fathers. 3 Sixteen years old *was* Uzziah when he began to reign, and he reigned fifty and two years in Jerusalem. His mother's name also *was* Jecoliah of Jerusalem. 4 And he did *that which was* right in the sight of the LORD, according to all that his father Amaziah did. 5 And he sought God in the days of Zechariah, who had understanding in the visions of God: and as long as he sought the LORD, God made him to prosper. 6 And he went forth and warred against the Philistines, and brake down the wall of Gath, and the wall of Jabneh, and the wall of Ashdod, and built cities about Ashdod, and among the Philistines. 7 And God helped him against the Philistines, and against the Arabians that dwelt in Gur-baal, and the Mehunims. 8 And the Ammonites gave gifts to Uzziah: and his name spread abroad *even* to the entering in of Egypt; for he strengthened *himself* exceedingly. 9 Moreover Uzziah built towers in Jerusalem at the corner gate, and at the valley gate, and at the turning *of the wall,* and fortified them. 10 Also he built towers in the desert, and digged many wells: for he had much cattle, both in the low country, and in the plains: husbandmen *also,* and vine dressers in the mountains, and in Carmel: for he loved husbandry. 11 Moreover Uzziah had an host of fighting men, that	went out to war by bands, according to the number of their account by the hand of Jeiel the scribe and Maaseiah the ruler, under the hand of Hananiah, *one* of the king's captains. 12 The whole number of the chief of the fathers of the mighty men of valour *were* two thousand and six hundred. 13 And under their hand *was* an army, three hundred thousand and seven thousand and five hundred, that made war with mighty power, to help the king against the enemy. 14 And Uzziah prepared for them throughout all the host shields, and spears, and helmets, and habergeons, and bows, and slings *to cast* stones. 15 And he made in Jerusalem engines, invented by cunning men, to be on the towers and upon the bulwarks, to shoot arrows and great stones withal. And his name spread far abroad; for he was marvellously helped, till he was strong. 16 But when he was strong, his heart was lifted up to *his* destruction: for he transgressed against the LORD his God, and went into the temple of the LORD to burn incense upon the altar of incense. 17 And Azariah the priest went in after him, and with him fourscore priests of the LORD, *that were* valiant men: 18 And they withstood Uzziah the king, and said unto him, *It appertaineth* not unto thee, Uzziah, to burn incense unto the LORD, but to the priests the sons of Aaron, that are consecrated to burn incense: go out of the sanctuary; for thou hast trespassed; neither *shall it be* for thine honour from the LORD God. 19 Then Uzziah was wroth, and *had* a censer in his hand	trained military • Was organized by Jeiel, secretary of the army, & his assistant Maaseiah • Was led by 2,600 officers from the clan leaders of Judah • Was an elite force of 307,500 troops • Was well-equipped by the king • Developed a special machine that was placed on the corners of the wall of Jerusalem: Shot arrows & hurled stones like a catapult 5) He achieved great fame & power through God's mighty hand **2. Uzziah's latter years—his slide into sin & his fall: Judged for personal pride** a. Uzziah's sin: Exalted himself & boldly burned incense in the temple 1) The High Priest & eighty other brave priests confronted the king in the temple • They informed him of his lawless act: Burning incense was to be performed only by a priest, God's appointed intercessor (the priest was a type of Christ the High Priest, who alone could make prayer [incense] acceptable to God) • They asked him to leave the sanctuary 2) The king reacted in anger & broke out in a verbal

OUTLINE	SCRIPTURE	SCRIPTURE	OUTLINE
rage against the priests: Refused to put down the censer	to burn incense: and while he was wroth with the priests, the leprosy even rose up in his forehead before the priests in the house of the LORD, from beside the incense altar.	house, *being* a leper; for he was cut off from the house of the LORD: and Jotham his son *was* over the king's house, judging the people of the land.	Le.13:46; Nu.5:1-14; 12:15; 2 K.7:3 5) He was excluded from the temple 6) He put his son in charge of the government
b. Uzziah's judgment: Leprosy suddenly broke out on his forehead 1) He was rushed out of the temple by the priests: A symbol of defilement, Le.22:2-6; Nu.12:10, 15 2) He was afflicted by God 3) He had leprosy until the day he died 4) He lived in isolation,	20 And Azariah the chief priest, and all the priests, looked upon him, and, behold, he *was* leprous in his forehead, and they thrust him out from thence; yea, himself hasted also to go out, because the LORD had smitten him. 21 And Uzziah the king was a leper unto the day of his death, and dwelt in a several	22 Now the rest of the acts of Uzziah, first and last, did Isaiah the prophet, the son of Amoz, write. 23 So Uzziah slept with his fathers, and they buried him with his fathers in the field of the burial which *belonged* to the kings; for they said, He *is* a leper: and Jotham his son reigned in his stead.	c. Uzziah's death & burial 1) His achievements: Were recorded by the prophet Isaiah, Is.1:1; 6:1 2) His death & burial: Was not buried with the kings due to his leprosy but was buried in a nearby field

(26:1-23) **Introduction**: pride is often thought of only in positive terms, not as a negative trait, and certainly not as a sin. People must have a healthy self-image and strong self-esteem in order to be successful in life. If all a person does is focus upon his weaknesses and lack of skills, he will never be successful or achieve anything of significance. It is absolutely essential to recognize our strengths and skills in order to plow through life capably and productively. We should take pride in who we are and in the abilities God has given us, acknowledging that it has all come from God and has been given to us to make a worthwhile contribution to society. This is an acceptable pride, a humble pride.

But pride becomes sinful when we exalt who we are and esteem our abilities over the abilities of others. When we use our appearance, authority, or skills to degrade, humiliate, shame, dominate, or enslave others—this kind of pride is evil. It is wicked arrogance and will cause us to face the terrifying judgment of God.

In the present Scripture, we first see King Uzziah as a man who achieved great success. But, tragically, when he looked at his achievements, he began to feel *overly* important, to become prideful, exalting himself before the LORD and over others. Just as his father Amaziah and his grandfather Josiah had experienced strong and righteous beginnings, so did Uzziah. But also like his father and grandfather, he had ended his life in a weak, sinful condition. Early in their reigns all three kings ruled over the Southern Kingdom in righteousness and justice, faithfully serving the LORD and the people. But in the end, all three kings failed both the LORD and the people.

In reading this account about Uzziah, the returning exiles under Ezra could see a clear warning. They must guard against pride and arrogance. The task laying out before them was enormous, the task of restoring *true worship* in the temple and of rebuilding their nation. Nevertheless, success was assured if they would seek the LORD and remain faithful to Him. As they went about their day-to-day duties, the LORD would give them confidence and support, enabling them to achieve their goals. But as God blessed them, they would need to guard against vanity and over-confidence, against thinking they were better than others because God was blessing them so much more than others. Being alert to the seduction of pride was the great lesson they needed to learn from the reign of Uzziah. And it is the much-needed lesson we too need to learn. This is, *The Reign of Uzziah (Azariah): A Clear Warning Against Pride and Arrogance*, 26:1-23.

    1. Uzziah's early years—his righteousness and achievements: rewarded for seeking God (vv.1-15).
    2. Uzziah's latter years—his slide into sin and his fall: judged for personal pride (vv.16-23).

1 (26:1-15) **Seeking, God, Example of—God, Seeking, Example of—Uzziah, King of Judah, Reign of—Kings, of the Southern Kingdom of Judah—Uzziah, Achievements of—Uzziah, Spiritual Life**: in the early years of Uzziah's reign, he lived a life of righteousness and made many significant contributions to the nation. Remember that Uzziah's father, King Amaziah, had left the city of Jerusalem in utter ruin (25:21-24). In a war he had launched against Israel, he was totally defeated and forced to surrender the capital city. In attacking Jerusalem, the forces of Israel had broken down a major section of the wall and looted the temple and palace. They also took as hostages many of the skilled and wealthy of the land and exiled them to Samaria. It was during this time, right after the exile of his father Amaziah, that Uzziah was crowned king. Throughout Scripture, Uzziah is also called "Azariah." Most likely "Azariah" was his personal name and "Uzziah" his throne name. Uzziah ruled over Judah at the same time that Jeroboam II ruled over the Northern Kingdom. Both of these kings had long, successful reigns, and they surprisingly were able to restore the boundaries of Israel to those achieved under David and Solomon (6-7; 2 K.14:25).

    a. The basic facts about Uzziah's background are given first (vv.1-5). Although he was only 16 years old, Uzziah was crowned king by the people right after his father Amaziah was taken captive and deported to Samaria, the capital of the Northern Kingdom (25:23-24). Thus he ruled in a co-regency with his father until his father's death. After Amaziah died, Uzziah recaptured and rebuilt Elath, an important seaport at the eastern tip of the Red Sea (v.2). Decades earlier it had been conquered by Solomon (8:17-18), but it was lost during the reign of Jehoram (21:8-10). Now, Elath is once again brought under the control of Judah, which gave the nation an important seaport for commerce and economic growth.

    Uzziah had a long reign as king, ruling for 52 years (v.3). Keep in mind that many of these years, from about 792 to 767, were spent in a co-regency with his father. Uzziah's mother's name was Jecoliah.

    Uzziah had a strong spiritual life, living righteously and pleasing the LORD (v.4). In the early days of his life, he was placed under the care of a man named Zechariah who instructed him in the *visions* or *fear* of God (v.5). Most likely, this means that he was instructed in the Word of God, taught the commandments of God as well as the duties of the king. As long as Uzziah sought the LORD, he was successful and prosperous.

 b. The LORD blessed King Uzziah richly and enabled him to accomplish one thing after another. Five noteworthy and far-reaching achievements are given by Scripture (vv.6-15). Keep in mind that all these achievements were gifts of God, blessings poured out upon Uzziah because he was seeking the LORD.

  1) Uzziah achieved success in war and in extending Judah's territory (vv.6-8). To secure peace in the west, he subdued the Philistines by conquering three of their major cities. He rebuilt these cities and some other towns and established fortresses throughout the conquered territory (vv.6-7). These cities included Gath, Jabneh, and Ashdod. After securing peace in the west, he marched southeastward in order to secure peace along the eastern border. The LORD enabled him to overpower the Arabs and the Meunites, most likely nomadic tribes who constantly raided Judean settlements along the eastern border of the nation.

   Uzziah was also able to subject the Ammonites under his rule, for they paid an annual tribute or tax to the Southern Kingdom of Judah. Because of his military power and achievements, his fame spread throughout all the surrounding nations, including Egypt.

  2) Uzziah achieved success in several major construction projects (vv.9-10). Remember that much of Jerusalem—including a large section of the wall—had been destroyed when Jehoash of Israel defeated Uzziah's father (25:23-24). Uzziah constructed not only the wall of Jerusalem but also built the towers on top of the wall and then fortified them all. In addition, he constructed forts in the desert of southern Judah and built many cisterns to catch rainwater for the great herds of livestock throughout the desert regions of the nation.

  3) Uzziah achieved success in ranching and in agriculture, for he was a man who loved the soil (v.10). Without question he was unusually blessed by God. He owned large herds of livestock and a great number of farms. He also employed many workers to handle his various business enterprises.

  4) Uzziah also achieved success in building a strong, well-trained military (v.11). It was organized by the secretary of the army Jeiel and his assistant Maaseiah and was led by 2,600 officers from the clan leaders of Judah (vv.11-12). Under their command was an elite force of 307,500 troops (v.13). These troops were well-equipped by the king with shields, spears, body armor, bows, and slings used to hurl stones. Interestingly, Uzziah developed a special machine that was placed on the corners of the wall of Jerusalem, a machine that shot arrows and hurled stones like a catapult (v.15).

  5) Uzziah achieved great fame, a fame that spread far and wide (v.15). But it must be remembered, his fame and power were due to the help of the LORD.

Thought 1. In looking at the life of Uzziah, we must remember the crisis this young man faced. The very city in which he was living was destroyed in a major war. At only 16 years old. In addition, the young man witnessed thousands of people being killed, injured, and maimed, others being taken captive and exiled to a foreign land. He even witnessed his father being taken prisoner and exiled. Once his father was removed from power, the people obviously turned to the young man and crowned him king, laying the burden of the devastated city and nation upon his young shoulders. Having just experienced and witnessed so much, he was no doubt gripped with a spirit of apprehension and fear. The young man could do but one thing: seek the LORD for His help. And, thankfully, Uzziah did seek the LORD—a practice that became the dominant trait of his early life.

No matter what we may face in life, the answer is to do just what Uzziah did: seek the LORD. When we seek the LORD, He hears and answers our prayers. He meets our needs. He helps us wherever we need help. No matter what the problem may be—any hardship, trial, misfortune, temptation, seduction, enticement—the LORD will help us if we will only seek Him. Listen to what God says about seeking Him:

> "But seek ye first the kingdom of God, and his righteousness; and all these things shall be added unto you" (Mt.6:33).
>
> "Ask, and it shall be given you; seek, and ye shall find; knock, and it shall be opened unto you" (Mt.7:7).
>
> "For every one that asketh receiveth; and he that seeketh findeth; and to him that knocketh it shall be opened" (Lu.11:10).
>
> "And he spake a parable unto them *to this end,* that men ought always to pray, and not to faint" (Lu.18:1).
>
> "That they should seek the Lord, if haply they might feel after him, and find him, though he be not far from every one of us" (Ac.17:27).
>
> "Is any among you afflicted? let him pray. Is any merry? let him sing psalms. Is any sick among you? let him call for the elders of the church; and let them pray over him, anointing him with oil in the name of the Lord" (Js.5:13-14).
>
> "But if from thence thou shalt seek the LORD thy God, thou shalt find *him,* if thou seek him with all thy heart and with all thy soul" (De.4:29).
>
> "Seek the LORD and his strength, seek his face continually" (1 Chr.16:11).
>
> "This poor man cried, and the LORD heard *him,* and saved him out of all his troubles" (Ps.34:6).
>
> "This *is* the generation of them that seek him, that seek thy face, O Jacob. Selah" (Ps.24:6).
>
> "*When thou saidst,* Seek ye my face; my heart said unto thee, Thy face, LORD, will I seek" (Ps.27:8).
>
> "From the end of the earth will I cry unto thee, when my heart is overwhelmed: lead me to the rock *that* is higher than I" (Ps.61:2).
>
> "He shall call upon me, and I will answer him: I *will be* with him in trouble; I will deliver him, and honour him" (Ps.91:15).
>
> "Seek the LORD, and his strength: seek his face evermore" (Ps.105:4).

BACKGROUND TO ISAIAH'S DAY

(The Four Kings Who Ruled During Isaiah's Ministry)

"With my whole heart have I sought thee: O let me not wander from thy commandments" (Ps.119:10).

"Seek ye the LORD while he may be found, call ye upon him while he is near" (Is.55:6).

"And it shall come to pass, that before they call, I will answer; and while they are yet speaking, I will hear" (Is.65:24).

"And ye shall seek me, and find *me*, when ye shall search for me with all your heart" (Je.29:13).

"And I [Daniel] set my face unto the Lord God, to seek by prayer and supplications, with fasting, and sackcloth, and ashes" (Da.9:3).

"Sow to yourselves in righteousness, reap in mercy; break up your fallow ground: for *it is* time to seek the LORD, till he come and rain righteousness upon you" (Ho.10:12).

"For thus saith the LORD unto the house of Israel, Seek ye me, and ye shall live" (Am.5:4).

"Seek ye the LORD, all ye meek of the earth, which have wrought his judgment; seek righteousness, seek meekness: it may be ye shall be hid in the day of the LORD'S anger" (Zep.2:3).

2 (26:16-23) **Pride, Example of—Self-Exaltation, Example of—Uzziah, Sin and Failure of—Judgment, Caused by, Sin**: in Uzziah's latter years, he slipped into sin and suffered the judgment of God. His sin was the fatal flaw of pride and self-exaltation. So far as is known, this was the only blot and blemish in the life of Uzziah. But as Matthew Henry says, it was a very serious blot and blemish. Other kings were guilty of sexual immorality, murder, oppression, persecution and idolatry.[1] Although Uzziah was not guilty of these gross sins, he was guilty of the horrible sin of pride and of exalting himself before the LORD and over others.

a. Uzziah became *puffed up* with pride and a sense of self-importance. Note exactly what Scripture says: it was when he had achieved so much, when he became so powerful, successful, prosperous, and famous—that he began to feel prideful. And his pride was to lead to his downfall. Exalting himself as a God-appointed priest, he actually entered the temple and burned incense before the LORD—a function that was to be performed only by the priest, God's appointed intercessor. Obviously, in his own eyes he had achieved great things for the LORD and was important to the LORD; therefore, he felt he could personally approach God without the help of the priest. But Uzziah was mistaken, for the LORD had long ago commanded that only the priest was to burn incense within the temple. When the priest burned the incense, he was symbolizing the need for an intercessor to stand between the LORD and His people and their prayers. This pointed to the Lord Jesus Christ as the Perfect Intercessor, the Mediator who alone could stand between God and His people. After the coming of Christ, people were to approach God through Christ, the Perfect Intercessor. Thereafter, prayer was to be offered through Christ, and people were to be accepted only through Christ. Down through history it was important for this symbolism to be protected and kept pure, for the burning of incense was symbolizing God's appointed intercessor who was yet to come, the Lord Jesus Christ. For this reason, Uzziah committed a horrible sin when he usurped the role of the priest in burning the incense.

Soon after Uzziah entered the temple, the High Priest and eighty other brave priests confronted the king to rebuke and stop him from committing this terrible violation. When they asked him to leave the sanctuary, he reacted in anger and broke out in a verbal rage against the priests.

b. Because of Uzziah's *puffed up* pride and self-exaltation, God chastised and disciplined him (vv.20-21). As soon as the king broke out in a verbal rage against the priests, he was instantly stricken with leprosy—even while he was standing there spouting out his rage. The priest immediately noticed the leprosy breaking out on Uzziah and rushed him out of the temple. Leprosy was a symbol of defilement; and no matter the consequences or cost to them personally, the priests had to protect the temple from becoming defiled (Le.22:2-6; Nu.12:10, 15). However, Uzziah was not about to retaliate against them, for he knew that the affliction was due to the LORD's hand of judgment against him. He was afflicted with leprosy because he had sinned. And note, he had leprosy until the day he died (v.21). Because of his affliction, he was forced to live in isolation and to step aside from public ruling (Le.13:46; Nu.5:1-14; 12:15; 2 K.7:3). He was also excluded from worshipping in the temple. Left with no choice, he put his son in charge of the government, allowing father and son to rule in a co-regency until Uzziah's death (v.21).

c. A summary of Uzziah's achievements and life were recorded by the prophet Isaiah (v.22-23). But just where Isaiah recorded these is not known, for they are not included in the biblical book of *Isaiah*. The only information given in the biblical book *Isaiah* concerns Uzziah's death (Is.1:1; 6:1; 7:1). Thus, the information must have come from some other writing by the prophet Isaiah. After Uzziah's death and burial in Jerusalem, he was succeeded on the throne by his son Jotham. With the death of Uzziah, the Southern Kingdom experienced one of its last peaceful and prosperous periods. Although the people were unaware of the fact at the time, never again would they enjoy such success and prosperity as a nation. Other than for a few years during Josiah's reign (640–609 B.C.), they would always be suffering from the oppression of another nation or else facing the threat and pressure of being attacked. The Northern Kingdom of Israel would fall first, but soon thereafter the Southern Kingdom of Judah would follow and the people would be taken into exile by the Babylonians. The patience of the LORD would soon run out. The day of His longsuffering and mercy would soon be over. Judgment would soon come.

Thought 1. Pride and self-exaltation are serious blemishes upon the life of any person. Personal pride exalts oneself over others and degrades them. Pride says, "I am better than someone else, more worthy of attention, recognition, and honor." A person who is prideful declares that he or she is more attractive or appealing, more knowledgeable or skillful, better able to do things. Of course, we must acknowledge and give thanks for who we are and for the knowledge and skills we do have. But we must never exalt our appearance, personality, position, wealth or abilities over others by degrading, shaming, embarrassing, or lording ourselves over them. Being attractive or talented or skillful is a blessing from God and must never be used to demean or degrade others. Listen to what God's Holy Word says about the terrible sins of pride and self-exaltation:

---

[1] Matthew Henry. *Matthew Henry's Commentary*, Vol.4. (Old Tappan, NJ: Fleming H. Revell Co., n.d.), p.988.

"And whosoever shall exalt himself shall be abased; and he that shall humble himself shall be exalted" (Mt.23:12).

"Love not the world, neither the things *that are* in the world. If any man love the world, the love of the Father is not in him. For all that *is* in the world, the lust of the flesh, and the lust of the eyes, and the pride of life, is not of the Father, but is of the world" (1 Jn.2:15-16).

"The wicked in *his* pride doth persecute the poor: let them be taken in the devices that they have imagined" (Ps.10:2).

"Therefore pride compasseth them about as a chain; violence covereth them *as* a garment" (Ps.73:6).

"Thou hast rebuked the proud *that are* cursed, which do err from thy commandments" (Ps.119:21).

"Be not wise in thine own eyes: fear the LORD, and depart from evil" (Pr.3:7).

"The fear of the LORD *is* to hate evil: pride, and arrogancy, and the evil way, and the froward mouth, do I hate" (Pr.8:13).

"*When* pride cometh, then cometh shame: but with the lowly *is* wisdom" (Pr.11:2).

"Pride *goeth* before destruction, and an haughty spirit before a fall" (Pr.16:18).

"He loveth transgression that loveth strife: *and* he that exalteth his gate seeketh destruction" (Pr.17:19).

"An high look, and a proud heart, *and* the plowing of the wicked, *is* sin" (Pr.21:4).

"Seest thou a man wise in his own conceit? *there is* more hope of a fool than of him" (Pr.26:12).

"*As* a roaring lion, and a ranging bear; *so is* a wicked ruler over the poor people" (Pr.28:15).

"And I will punish the world for *their* evil, and the wicked for their iniquity; and I will cause the arrogancy of the proud to cease, and will lay low the haughtiness of the terrible" (Is.13:11).

"For thou hast said in thine heart, I will ascend into heaven, I will exalt my throne above the stars of God: I will sit also upon the mount of the congregation, in the sides of the north: I will ascend above the heights of the clouds; I will be like the most High. Yet thou shalt be brought down to hell, to the sides of the pit" (Is.14:13-15).

"Though thou exalt *thyself* as the eagle, and though thou set thy nest among the stars, thence will I bring thee down, saith the LORD" (Obad.4).

BACKGROUND TO ISAIAH'S DAY

(The Four Kings Who Ruled During Isaiah's Ministry)

II. THE REIGN OF JOTHAM: A PICTURE OF HOLDING FAST UNTIL THE END OF LIFE, 2 CHR. 27:1-9

OUTLINE	SCRIPTURE	SCRIPTURE	OUTLINE

1. Jotham's very successful life: A godly, righteous walk that pleased the LORD
a. His background
  1) He reigned 16 years
  2) He was the son of Jerusha
b. His spiritual life
  1) He lived a righteous life
  2) He did not abuse the temple, exalt himself as his father had done
  3) He had little influence on the people: They continued in false worship
c. His building projects
  1) He rebuilt the Upper Gate of the Temple
  2) He repaired part of the wall of Jerusalem
  3) He built towns, forts, & towers
d. His war with Ammon
  1) He conquered the nation
  2) He forced them to pay an
	Jotham *was* twenty and five years old when he began to reign, and he reigned sixteen years in Jerusalem. His mother's name also *was* Jerushah, the daughter of Zadok. 2 And he did *that which was* right in the sight of the LORD, according to all that his father Uzziah did: howbeit he entered not into the temple of the LORD. And the people did yet corruptly. 3 He built the high gate of the house of the LORD, and on the wall of Ophel he built much. 4 Moreover he built cities in the mountains of Judah, and in the forests he built castles and towers. 5 He fought also with the king of the Ammonites, and prevailed against them. And	the children of Ammon gave him the same year an hundred talents of silver, and ten thousand measures of wheat, and ten thousand of barley. So much did the children of Ammon pay unto him, both the second year, and the third. 6 So Jotham became mighty, because he prepared his ways before the LORD his God. 7 Now the rest of the acts of Jotham, and all his wars, and his ways, lo, they *are* written in the book of the kings of Israel and Judah. 8 He was five and twenty years old when he began to reign, and reigned sixteen years in Jerusalem. 9 And Jotham slept with his fathers, and they buried him in the city of David: and Ahaz his son reigned in his stead.	annual tribute for 3 years
			• 7,500 pounds of silver
			• 50,000 bushels of wheat
			• 50,000 bushels of barley
			
			2. Jotham's very powerful reign: An obedient, steadfast rule that was blessed by the LORD
			a. His achievements: Recorded in *The Book of the Kings of Israel & Judah*
			
			b. His reign: Was 25 years old when he was crowned & ruled for 16 years
			
			c. His death & burial: In Jerusalem
			
			d. His successor: Ahaz, his son

(27:1-9) Introduction: holding fast, persevering, being steadfast—these are traits that are lacking in so many lives today. Far too many people begin something—a project, a task, a program, a job, a relationship—and then never finish what they started. How many of us have begun projects and never finished them? Or have taken entirely too long to complete them? How many of us make promises and fail to keep them? How many children fail to do the tasks or chores assigned by parents? How many husbands and wives fail to keep their promise to be faithful to one another? How many workers fail to be diligent, loyal, and conscientious in their responsibilities? How many of us have made a commitment to the LORD and then slacked off, failing to be steadfast and dedicated? How many of us no longer hold fast to the profession of faith we have made?

The present Scripture is the story of King Jotham, a man who held fast to the end of his life. He persevered and followed the LORD through all the years of his life. When reading this account about Jotham, the returning exiles would have a dynamic example of the kind of life they needed to live. If they persevered in following the LORD, the LORD would bless them and help them to restore *true worship* to the temple and rebuild their nation. Just as the LORD had blessed King Jotham, so He would bless them if they continued to be faithful in following the LORD. This is, *The Reign of Jotham: A Picture of Holding Fast Until the End of Life*, 27:1-9.

1. Jotham's very successful life: a godly, righteous walk that pleased the LORD (vv.1-5).
2. Jotham's very powerful reign: an obedient, steadfast rule that was blessed by the LORD (vv.6-9).

1 (27:1-5) **Walk, Spiritual, Example of—Spiritual Walk, Example of—Righteous, Walk, Example of—Jotham, King of Judah, Reign of—Judah, Kingdom of, Kings**: Jotham, Uzziah's son, had a very successful life. He was greatly blessed because of his righteous walk before the LORD.

Jotham was only 25 years old when he was crowned king, and he reigned for 16 years, 11 of which were apparently spent as co-regent with his father Uzziah (26:21). Remember, his father had been stricken with leprosy because he failed to worship God as instructed. Because a person with leprosy was isolated, not able to carry on public functions, Jotham had to step in and rule with his father, managing the government while his father served behind the scenes. Jotham's mother was Jerusha, the daughter of the priest Zadok, which gives some indication that she lived a righteous life just as her husband King Uzziah had done prior to his downfall (26:4-5).

With a godly father and mother as examples, Jotham lived a righteous life before the LORD. He was strong and faithful in worship, proving to be even more faithful than his father. Uzziah had allowed his power to go to his head and committed the terrible sin of exalting himself before the LORD and over other people (the priests). But not Jotham. He always approached the LORD just as instructed. And he apparently always walked righteously before the LORD, executing true justice throughout the nation. However, his righteous reign seemed to have little influence on the people, for many of them continued to walk in their corrupt ways and to worship false gods. If he failed in any area, it was in this, that he failed to remove the high places of false worship. By not removing them, he became a stumbling block to the people, allowing them to continue to worship at the very site where false gods had formerly been worshiped. Down through the years, many of the people had allowed some of the false worship to seep into their worship of the LORD. As a result, much of the people's worship was now corrupted, nothing more than the worship of idols and false gods. Jotham allowed the people to continue their false worship at the high places. He failed to launch a reformation to turn the people back to the LORD. Thus Jotham stood guilty before the LORD and no doubt cut the heart of God. The *sins of omission* make a person just as guilty as the *sins of commission.* Therefore, failing to do right made Jotham just as guilty as the kings before him who had done wrong.

While serving as co-regent with his father Uzziah, Jotham continued the public works projects launched by his father. Then after his father's death, he completed several major building projects of his own. These included rebuilding the *upper gate* of the temple that stood near the palace. This was the major gate used by the king and his royal officials. He also repaired part of the wall of Jerusalem in addition to building towns, forts, and military lookout towers (vv.3-4). These were necessary for military defense and for storing food, supplies, and weapons. Maintaining a standing army and building fortresses and supply centers throughout the nation was an unending project for the kings of Judah (8:2, 4-6; 11:5-12; 14:6-8; 17:12-19; 26:9-15).

At some point during Jotham's reign, the Ammonites rebelled against Judah and refused to pay their annual tribute or tax. Losing this tax base would have seriously affected the economy of Judah. For this reason, Jotham was forced to march against the Ammonites, to conquer and reinstate the annual tax. The annual payments amounted to 7,500 pounds of silver, 50,000 bushels of wheat, and 50,000 bushels of barley. For a period of three years, the Ammonites faithfully paid the tribute, but the tribute then stopped, suggesting that the Ammonites were finally able to break free from Judean domination and gain their independence.

Thought 1. A godly, righteous life pleases the LORD. If we follow the LORD day by day and keep His commandments, He promises to bless us. If we obey Him, He will be present with us, guiding and meeting our every need. God promises to look after and take care of the faithful, obedient believer. When we are faithful, God gives us the power to conquer all the trials and temptations of life. No matter what the hardship or misfortune, the seduction or enticement, God will give us the strength to triumphantly overcome the problem or to victoriously walk through it. Through the presence and power of Christ, we are given a victorious life. But to receive the presence and power of Christ we must live godly, righteous lives. We must obey the LORD, keep His holy commandments. Listen to what God's Holy Word says:

"For I say unto you, That except your righteousness shall exceed *the righteousness* of the scribes and Pharisees, ye shall in no case enter into the kingdom of heaven" (Mt.5:20).

"But seek ye first the kingdom of God, and his righteousness; and all these th *his* to your shame" (1 Co.15:34).

"Wherefore take unto you the whole armour of God, that ye may be able to withstand in the evil day, and having done all, to stand. Stand therefore, having your loins girt about with truth, and having on the breastplate of righteousness" (Ep.6:13-14).

"And this I pray, that your love may abound yet more and more in knowledge and *in* all judgment; That ye may approve things that are excellent; that ye may be sincere and without offence till the day of Christ; Being filled with the fruits of righteousness, which are by Jesus Christ, unto the glory and praise of God" (Ph.1:9-11).

"I exhort therefore, that, first of all, supplications, prayers, intercessions, *and* giving of thanks, be made for all men; For kings, and *for* all that are in authority; that we may lead a quiet and peaceable life in all godliness and honesty" (1 Ti.2:1-2).

"But refuse profane and old wives' fables, and exercise thyself *rather* unto godliness" (1 Ti.4:7).

"For bodily exercise profiteth little: but godliness is profitable unto all things, having promise of the life that now is, and of that which is to come" (1 Ti.4:8).

"But godliness with contentment is great gain" (1 Ti.6:6).

"But thou, O man of God, flee these things; and follow after righteousness, godliness, faith, love, patience, meekness. Fight the good fight of faith, lay hold on eternal life, whereunto thou art also called, and hast professed a good profession before many witnesses" (1 Ti.6:11-12).

"Teaching us that, denying ungodliness and worldly lusts, we should live soberly, righteously, and godly, in this present world; Looking for that blessed hope, and the glorious appearing of the great God and our Saviour Jesus Christ" (Tit.2:12-13).

"*This is* a faithful saying, and these things I will that thou affirm constantly, that they which have believed in God might be careful to maintain good works. These things are good and profitable unto men" (Tit.3:8).

"But whoso looketh into the perfect law of liberty, and continueth *therein,* he being not a forgetful hearer, but a doer of the work, this man shall be blessed in his deed" (Js.1:25).

"But the day of the Lord will come as a thief in the night; in the which the heavens shall pass away with a great noise, and the elements shall melt with fervent heat, the earth also and the works that are therein shall be burned up. *Seeing* then *that* all these things shall be dissolved, what manner *of persons* ought ye to be in *all* holy conversation [behavior, conduct] and godliness, Looking for and hasting unto the coming of the day of God, wherein the heavens being on fire shall be dissolved, and the elements shall melt with fervent heat? Nevertheless we, according to his promise, look for new heavens and a new earth, wherein dwelleth righteousness. Wherefore, beloved, seeing that ye look for such things, be diligent that ye may be found of him in peace, without spot, and blameless" (2 Pe.3:10-14).

"Blessed *are* they that do his commandments, that they may have right to the tree of life, and may enter in through the gates into the city" (Re.22:14).

"Now therefore, if ye will obey my voice indeed, and keep my covenant, then ye shall be a peculiar treasure unto me above all people: for all the earth *is* mine" (Ex.19:5).

"Thou shalt keep therefore his statutes, and his commandments, which I command thee this day, that it may go well with thee, and with thy children after thee, and that thou mayest prolong *thy* days upon the earth, which the LORD thy God giveth thee, for ever" (De.4:40).

"Keep therefore the words of this covenant, and do them, that ye may prosper in all that ye do" (De.29:9).

"And if thou wilt walk in my ways, to keep my statutes and my commandments, as thy father David did walk, then I will lengthen thy days" (1 K.3:14).

"Then shalt thou prosper, if thou takest heed to fulfil the statutes and judgments which the LORD charged Moses with concerning Israel: be strong, and of good courage; dread not, nor be dismayed" (1 Chr.22:13).

"And he sought God in the days of Zechariah, who had understanding in the visions of God: and as long as he sought the LORD, God made him to prosper" (2 Chr.26:5).

"And in every work that he began in the service of the house of God, and in the law, and in the commandments, to seek his God, he did *it* with all his heart, and prospered" (2 Chr.31:21).

"Blessed *is* the man that walketh not in the counsel of the ungodly, nor standeth in the way of sinners, nor sitteth in the seat of the scornful. But his delight *is* in the law of the LORD; and in his law doth he meditate day and night. And he shall be like a tree planted by the rivers of water, that bringeth forth his fruit in his season; his leaf also shall not wither; and whatsoever he doeth shall prosper" (Ps.1:1-3).

"Though a sinner do evil an hundred times, and his *days* be prolonged, yet surely I know that it shall be well with them that fear God, which fear before him" (Ec.8:12).

"Say ye to the righteous, that *it shall be* well *with him:* for they shall eat the fruit of their doings" (Is.3:10).

"Sow to yourselves in righteousness, reap in mercy; break up your fallow ground: for *it is* time to seek the LORD, till he come and rain righteousness upon you" (Ho.10:12).

---

2 (27:6-9) **Obedience, Example of—Steadfastness, Example of—Jotham, Power of—Blessings, of God, Source of—Success, Source of—Obedience, Results of, God's Blessings—Steadfastness, Results of—Perseverance, Results of**: King Jotham was greatly blessed by God and grew more and more powerful throughout the years of his reign. God blessed him because he remained faithful to the LORD, obeying and keeping the LORD's commandments. He was steadfast in following the LORD, persevering to the very end of his life. Unlike so many in the past who had started out well but ended up forsaking the LORD, Jotham stayed true to the LORD all his days. He was faithful from beginning to end.

Jotham's life and achievements were recorded in *The Book of the Kings of Israel and Judah* (v.7). As mentioned earlier, he began to reign when he was 25 years old and ruled for 16 years (v.8). After his death, he was buried in Jerusalem and succeeded by his son Ahaz.

A significant fact needs to be noted about the people of Judah during these days. Under Uzziah's and Jotham's rule, Judah became very prosperous. The nation was strong both economically and militarily. The people became comfortable, so comfortable that they eventually became complacent and ignored the LORD and His commandments. In forgetting and neglecting the LORD, they set the stage for a king who would be utterly wicked and totally depraved. This man was to be the very next king, King Ahaz the son of Jotham. Just how complacent and wicked the people became is vividly described by the prophet Isaiah (see Isaiah chs.1–5). But for now, the lesson for us to note is the obedience and faithfulness of Jotham.

Thought 1. As believers, we are to obey the LORD, to be steadfast in following after Him. We are to persevere to the end, for all who persevere will be saved (Mt.10:22). Listen to what God's Holy Word says:
(1) We must obey the LORD.

"Not every one that saith unto me, Lord, Lord, shall enter into the kingdom of heaven; but he that doeth the will of my Father which is in heaven. Many will say to me in that day, Lord, Lord, have we not prophesied in thy name? and in thy name have cast out devils? and in thy name done many wonderful works? And then will I profess unto them, I never knew you: depart from me, ye that work iniquity" (Mt.7:21-23).

"Therefore whosoever heareth these sayings of mine, and doeth them, I will liken him unto a wise man, which built his house upon a rock: And the rain descended, and the floods came, and the winds blew, and beat upon that house; and it fell not: for it was founded upon a rock. And every one that heareth these sayings of mine, and doeth them not, shall be likened unto a foolish man, which built his house upon the sand: And the rain descended, and the floods came, and the winds blew, and beat upon that house; and it fell: and great was the fall of it" (Mt.7:24-27).

"Jesus answered and said unto him, If a man love me, he will keep my words: and my Father will love him, and we will come unto him, and make our abode with him" (Jn.14:23).

"If ye keep my commandments, ye shall abide in my love; even as I have kept my Father's commandments, and abide in his love" (Jn.15:10).

"Ye are my friends, if ye do whatsoever I command you" (Jn.15:14).

"Blessed *are* they that do his commandments, that they may have right to the tree of life, and may enter in through the gates into the city" (Re.22:14).

"Now therefore, if ye will obey my voice indeed, and keep my covenant, then ye shall be a peculiar treasure unto me above all people: for all the earth *is* mine" (Ex.19:5).

"Ye shall not tempt the LORD your God, as ye tempted *him* in Massah" (De.6:16).

BACKGROUND TO ISAIAH'S DAY

(The Four Kings Who Ruled During Isaiah's Ministry)

"This book of the law shall not depart out of thy mouth; but thou shalt meditate therein day and night, that thou mayest observe to do according to all that is written therein: for then thou shalt make thy way prosperous, and then thou shalt have good success" (Jos.1:8).

"And Samuel said, Hath the LORD *as great* delight in burnt offerings and sacrifices, as in obeying the voice of the LORD? Behold, to obey *is* better than sacrifice, *and* to hearken than the fat of rams" (1 S.15:22).

(2) We must be faithful, steadfast, persevering to the very end.

"And ye shall be hated of all *men* for my name's sake: but he that endureth to the end shall be saved" (Mt.10:22).

"As the Father hath loved me, so have I loved you: continue ye in my love" (Jn.15:9).

"Therefore, my beloved brethren, be ye stedfast, unmovable, always abounding in the work of the Lord, forasmuch as ye know that your labour is not in vain in the Lord" (1 Co.15:58).

"Stand fast therefore in the liberty wherewith Christ hath made us free, and be not entangled again with the yoke of bondage" (Ga.5:1).

"And let us not be weary in well doing: for in due season we shall reap, if we faint not" (Ga.6:9).

"Only let your conversation [conduct, behavior] be as it becometh the gospel of Christ: that whether I come and see you, or else be absent, I may hear of your affairs, that ye stand fast in one spirit, with one mind striving together for the faith of the gospel" (Ph.1:27).

"Prove all things; hold fast that which is good. Abstain from all appearance of evil. And the very God of peace sanctify you wholly; and *I pray God* your whole spirit and soul and body be preserved blameless unto the coming of our Lord Jesus Christ" (1 Th.5:21-23).

"Seeing then that we have a great high priest, that is passed into the heavens, Jesus the Son of God, let us hold fast *our* profession" (He.4:14).

"Let us hold fast the profession of *our* faith without wavering; (for he is faithful that promised;)" (He.10:23).

"Wherefore seeing we also are compassed about with so great a cloud of witnesses, let us lay aside every weight, and the sin which doth *so* easily beset us, and let us run with patience the race that is set before us" (He.12:1).

"Blessed *is* the man that endureth temptation: for when he is tried, he shall receive the crown of life, which the Lord hath promised to them that love him" (Js.1:12).

"Behold, we count them happy which endure. Ye have heard of the patience of Job, and have seen the end of the Lord; that the Lord is very pitiful, and of tender mercy" (Js.5:11).

"Wherefore gird up the loins of your mind, be sober, and hope to the end for the grace that is to be brought unto you at the revelation of Jesus Christ" (1 Pe.1:13).

"Be sober, be vigilant; because your adversary the devil, as a roaring lion, walketh about, seeking whom he may devour: Whom resist stedfast in the faith, knowing that the same afflictions are accomplished in your brethren that are in the world" (1 Pe.5:8-9).

"Ye therefore, beloved, seeing ye know *these things* before, beware lest ye also, being led away with the error of the wicked, fall from your own stedfastness. But grow in grace, and *in* the knowledge of our Lord and Saviour Jesus Christ. To him *be* glory both now and for ever. Amen" (2 Pe.3:17-18).

"Remember therefore how thou hast received and heard, and hold fast, and repent. If therefore thou shalt not watch, I will come on thee as a thief, and thou shalt not know what hour I will come upon thee" (Re.3:3).

"Behold, I come quickly: hold that fast which thou hast, that no man take thy crown" (Re.3:11).

"But cleave unto the LORD your God, as ye have done unto this day" (Jos.23:8).

"If iniquity *be* in thine hand, put it far away, and let not wickedness dwell in thy tabernacles. For then shalt thou lift up thy face without spot; yea, thou shalt be stedfast, and shalt not fear" (Jb.11:14-15).

"The righteous also shall hold on his way, and he that hath clean hands shall be stronger and stronger" (Jb.17:9).

(The Four Kings Who Ruled During Isaiah's Ministry)

III. THE REIGN OF AHAZ: A PICTURE OF UTTER WICKEDNESS AND TOTAL DE-PRAVITY, 2 CHR.28:1-27

OUTLINE	SCRIPTURE	SCRIPTURE	OUTLINE

1. Ahaz's shameful & devastating evil: The awful depth of wickedness & false worship
a. He began to rule at age 20 & ruled for 16 years
b. He was wicked: Did not live righteously as David had
c. He followed the sinful ways of Israel's kings
d. He promoted & led the people in false worship
e. He committed the detestable sin of *human sacrifice*, even sacrificing his own sons
 	
f. He was totally committed to false worship
 	
2. Ahaz's defeat by a Syrian & Israelite alliance (the Syro-Ephraimite War): A picture of God's justice & judgment
a. The defeat by Syria
  1) The defeat was allowed by God
  2) The defeat resulted in many prisoners' being exiled to Damascus
 	
b. The defeat by Israel
  1) The Israelite king, Pekah, killed 120,000 soldiers in one day of the battle: Allowed by God as a just judgment for Judah's terrible evil
  2) The Israelite warrior Zicri killed three royal officials
  • Maaseiah, the king's son
  • Azrikam, palace manager
  • Elkanah, second in command
  3) The Israelites ransacked the cities of Judah
  • Exiled 200,000 women & children
  • Took a large amount of plunder
 	
c. The warning of God to victorious Israel: Sent by the prophet Obed
  1) They were guilty of excessive cruelty
  • Had been allowed to de-
	Ahaz *was* twenty years old when he began to reign, and he reigned sixteen years in Jerusalem: but he did not *that which was* right in the sight of the LORD, like David his father:
	2 For he walked in the ways of the kings of Israel, and made also molten images for Baalim.
	3 Moreover he burnt incense in the valley of the son of Hinnom, and burnt his children in the fire, after the abominations of the heathen whom the LORD had cast out before the children of Israel.
	4 He sacrificed also and burnt incense in the high places, and on the hills, and under every green tree.
	5 Wherefore the LORD his God delivered him into the hand of the king of Syria; and they smote him, and carried away a great multitude of them captives, and brought *them* to Damascus. And he was also delivered into the hand of the king of Israel, who smote him with a great slaughter.
	6 For Pekah the son of Remaliah slew in Judah an hundred and twenty thousand in one day, *which were* all val-iant men; because they had forsaken the LORD God of their fathers.
	7 And Zichri, a mighty man of Ephraim, slew Maaseiah the king's son, and Azrikam the governor of the house, and Elkanah *that was* next to the king.
	8 And the children of Israel carried away captive of their brethren two hundred thousand, women, sons, and daughters, and took also away much spoil from them, and brought the spoil to Samaria.
	9 But a prophet of the LORD was there, whose name *was* Oded: and he went out before the host that came to Samaria, and said unto them, Behold, because the LORD God of
		your fathers was wroth with Judah, he hath delivered them into your hand, and ye have slain them in a rage *that* reacheth up unto heaven.
		10 And now ye purpose to keep under the children of Judah and Jerusalem for bondmen and bondwomen unto you: *but are there* not with you, even with you, sins against the LORD your God?
		11 Now hear me therefore, and deliver the captives again, which ye have taken captive of your brethren: for the fierce wrath of the LORD *is* upon you.
		12 Then certain of the heads of the children of Ephraim, Azariah the son of Johanan, Berechiah the son of Meshil-lemoth, and Jehizkiah the son of Shallum, and Amasa the son of Hadlai, stood up against them that came from the war,
		13 And said unto them, Ye shall not bring in the captives hither: for whereas we have offended against the LORD *already,* ye intend to add *more* to our sins and to our trespass: for our trespass is great, and *there is* fierce wrath against Israel.
		14 So the armed men left the captives and the spoil before the princes and all the congregation.
		15 And the men which were expressed by name rose up, and took the captives, and with the spoil clothed all that were naked among them, and arrayed them, and shod them, and gave them to eat and to drink, and anointed them, and carried all the feeble of them upon asses, and brought them to Jericho, the city of palm trees, to their brethren: then they returned to Samaria.
		16 At that time did king Ahaz send unto the kings of Assyria to help him.
		17 For again the Edomites had come and smitten Judah, and carried away captives.
		18 The Philistines also had
			feat Judah because of God
			• Had gone too far in their cruelty: Their rage reached & disturbed all heaven
			2) They were guilty of enslaving the men & women—guilty of sin against God, Le.25:39-46
			
			3) They must return the slaves, for God's fierce wrath had turned against them (was ready to strike out with a just anger & judgment)
			
			d. The confrontation by some of Israel's leaders with the army
			  1) The leadership appointed a delegation of four to confront the army commanders
			
			  2) The delegation negotiated the release of the prisoners
			  • Pointed out Israel's sin & guilt
			  • Argued that God's fierce wrath had turned against them
			
			  3) The delegation convinced the army to turn over the prisoners & the plunder to them
			  4) The delegation ministered to the prisoners & personally escorted them back home to Judah
			  • Clothed & fed them
			  • Took care of the injured & wounded
			  • Provided transportation for the weak
			  • Escorted them back as far as Jericho
			
			3. Ahaz's failed alliance with Assyria: A man who looked for a savior other than the LORD[DS1]
			a. The reason for Ahaz's appeal for help from Assyria
			  1) Because of constant danger & the threat of raids &

BACKGROUND TO ISAIAH'S DAY

(The Four Kings Who Ruled During Isaiah's Ministry)

OUTLINE	SCRIPTURE	SCRIPTURE	OUTLINE
attacks by surrounding nations • The Edomites on the east, 17 • The Philistines on the west & south 2) Because God was humbling (disciplining) Ahaz & Judah: Due to their sin & continued unfaithfulness b. The response of Tiglath-Pileser of Assyria: He oppressed Ahaz instead of helping him 1) Ahaz paid a large fee to secure the help of the Assyrians: Taken from the treasuries of the palace, the temple, & the leaders 2) Ahaz's bribe failed to help him **4. Ahaz's utter apostasy & his death: A total rejection of God** a. His apostasy, 2 K.16:10-18 1) He offered sacrifices to the Syrian false gods • The reason: He believed	invaded the cities of the low country, and of the south of Judah, and had taken Beth-shemesh, and Ajalon, and Gederoth, and Shocho with the villages thereof, and Timnah with the villages thereof, Gimzo also and the villages thereof: and they dwelt there. 19 For the LORD brought Judah low because of Ahaz king of Israel; for he made Judah naked, and transgressed sore against the LORD. 20 And Tilgath-pilneser king of Assyria came unto him, and distressed him, but strengthened him not. 21 For Ahaz took away a portion *out* of the house of the LORD, and *out* of the house of the king, and of the princes, and gave *it* unto the king of Assyria: but he helped him not. 22 And in the time of his distress did he trespass yet more against the LORD: this *is that* king Ahaz. 23 For he sacrificed unto the gods of Damascus, which smote him: and he said, Be-	cause the gods of the kings of Syria help them, *therefore* will I sacrifice to them, that they may help me. But they were the ruin of him, and of all Israel. 24 And Ahaz gathered together the vessels of the house of God, and cut in pieces the vessels of the house of God, and shut up the doors of the house of the LORD, and he made him altars in every corner of Jerusalem. 25 And in every several city of Judah he made high places to burn incense unto other gods, and provoked to anger the LORD God of his fathers. 26 Now the rest of his acts and of all his ways, first and last, behold, they *are* written in the book of the kings of Judah and Israel. 27 And Ahaz slept with his fathers, and they buried him in the city, *even* in Jerusalem: but they brought him not into the sepulchres of the kings of Israel: and Hezekiah his son reigned in his stead.	they had helped Syria defeat him: If he worshipped them, perhaps they would help him also • The result: Led to his downfall 2) He closed the temple • Plundered & destroyed the furnishings • Barricaded the doors 3) He set up altars for the worship of false gods at every street corner of Jerusalem 4) He built false worship centers in every town of Judah 5) He provoked, aroused the anger of God b. His reign & death 1) His reign was recorded in *The Book of the Kings of Judah & Israel* 2) His death & burial were in Jerusalem, but he was dishonored by the public who refused to bury him in the cemetery of the kings 3) His successor was Hezekiah, his son

(28:1-27) **Introduction**: one of the most *unpopular subjects* to discuss with people is the depravity of the human heart. The reason is that it is quite difficult for some to accept that the human heart is depraved, wicked. Within all of us there is some good. Every human being, no matter how wicked, will sometimes act kindly, helping other people and doing good deeds. But the truth is, no matter how good we may be, there are times when everyone of us acts selfishly or thinks evil thoughts, even times when we become unjustly upset or disturbed or angry with another person. Not one of us is without sin. As Scripture declares, "all have sinned and come short of the glory of God" (Ro.3:23). We are all short of God's perfection, of His perfect glory and holiness. Moreover, the light of God's glory and perfection shines forth so brilliantly that it will consume any imperfect thing that stands in His presence.

The present passage of Scripture paints the picture of a man who was utterly wicked and totally depraved. This man was Ahaz, a ruler who was to bring devastation upon the kingdom of Judah. In the history of the Southern Kingdom, no king had plunged the nation into the depths of depravity as much as King Ahaz.

In reading this account of King Ahaz's rule, the returning exiles under Ezra's leadership would see a strong warning against turning away from the LORD. When Ahaz assumed the throne, the nation of Judah had reached a summit of prosperity and success seldom experienced by any nation. Yet within just 16 years, Ahaz brought the nation to total ruin. He bankrupted the economy and decimated the military, causing indescribable suffering for the citizens of the nation. This is, *The Reign of Ahaz: A Picture of Utter Wickedness and Total Depravity*, 28:1-27.

1. Ahaz's shameful and devastating evil: the awful depth of wickedness and false worship (vv.1-4).
2. Ahaz's defeat by a Syrian and Israelite alliance (the Syro-Ephramite War): a picture of God's justice and judgment (vv.5-15).
3. Ahaz's failed alliance with Assyria: a man who looked for a savior other than the LORD (vv.16-21).
4. Ahaz's utter apostasy and his death: a total rejection of God (vv.22-27).

1 (28:1-4) **False Worship, Example of—Human Sacrifice, Example of—Wickedness, Depth of, Example—Worship, False, Example of—Ahaz, King, of Judah—Judah, Kings of—Evil, Depths of, Example**: now begins the reign of King Ahaz of Judah, a disgraceful reign, a reign of devastating evil. His appalling reign can be matched only by the evil reign of Jeroboam I in the Northern Kingdom (1 K.12:25–13:34). Ahaz set loose a stream of wickedness that rushed madly to its inevitable end, total destruction under the hand of God's judgment. Glance quickly at the outline, noting how the author simply introduces Ahaz and then immediately launches into a detailed record of his gross offenses within the nation (see outline and note—2 K.16:1-20 for more discussion).

BACKGROUND TO ISAIAH'S DAY

(The Four Kings Who Ruled During Isaiah's Ministry)

Ahaz began to rule at age 20 and ruled for 16 years (v.1). Based upon his age and the years of his rule, he must have served as co-regent with his father Jotham for some years.

Rejecting the righteous example of his father Jotham and his grandfather Uzziah, Ahaz instead followed the path of wickedness. He failed to walk in the righteous steps of his ancestor King David (v.1). Remember, David had a heart that was just like the heart of God (1 S.13:14). For this reason, he was held up as the ideal righteous king whose example was to be followed by all who succeeded him.

To his disgrace, Ahaz walked in the sinful ways of Israel's kings instead of following the righteous examples set by Judah's kings (v.2). And even more tragic, he promoted and led the people in the worship of the false god Baal. In the most revolting pagan practice imaginable, Ahaz committed the abominable sin of human sacrifice, even sacrificing his own sons to a false god. The false god was either Molech or another god associated with the Baal worship that was conducted in the valley of Ben Hinnom (2 K.23:10). By committing this atrocity, he was following a contemptible religious practice of the Canaanites, a people who had become so depraved that God had commanded their extermination, dooming them to eternal death (Le.18:28-30; 20:22-23; De.7:22-26; 12:2-4; 18:9-14).

Ahaz obviously became totally committed to idol worship at various high places throughout the nation (v.4). Note how Scripture describes his participation: as though he rushed from high place to high place, on the hilltops and under every spreading tree where an altar or worship center had been built. He was zealous—even fanatical—over the worship of false gods.

> **Thought 1**. Sadly, far too many people today are living in the depths of sin and false worship just as Ahaz did. Think of all those who commit repeated acts of lawlessness, violence, and immorality. How many are committing illicit acts of sex day after day, time after time, disobeying the clear commandment of God? How many people are lying and stealing over and over again? How many fail to be diligent, working hard at their employment, committing the sins of slothfulness, indulgence, and complacency? How many continue living in the sin of unbelief, either denying or refusing to accept the Lord Jesus Christ as the Savior of the world? No sin is any greater or more dangerous than the wickedness of unbelief. And tragically, most people have never trusted the Lord Jesus Christ as their Savior. As a result, most people are not worshipping the only living and true God but, rather, false gods. The living and true God is the Father of the Lord Jesus Christ, the Lord God who so loved the world that He gave His only Son to save the world. Listen to what God's Holy Word says:
>
> (1) The human heart is corrupt, depraved, and most people are living in the depths of sin.
>
> > **"For from within, out of the heart of men, proceed evil thoughts, adulteries, fornications, murders" (Mk.7:21).**
> >
> > **"For the invisible things of him from the creation of the world are clearly seen, being understood by the things that are made, *even* his eternal power and Godhead; so that they are without excuse: Because that, when they knew God, they glorified *him* not as God, neither were thankful; but became vain in their imaginations, and their foolish heart was darkened. Professing themselves to be wise, they became fools, And changed the glory of the uncorruptible God into an image made like to corruptible man, and to birds, and fourfooted beasts, and creeping things. Wherefore God also gave them up to uncleanness through the lusts of their own hearts, to dishonour their own bodies between themselves: Who changed the truth of God into a lie, and worshipped and served the creature more than the Creator, who is blessed for ever. Amen" (Ro.1:20-25).**
> >
> > **"This know also, that in the last days perilous times shall come. For men shall be lovers of their own selves, covetous, boasters, proud, blasphemers, disobedient to parents, unthankful, unholy, Without natural affection, trucebreakers, false accusers, incontinent, fierce, despisers of those that are good, Traitors, heady, highminded, lovers of pleasures more than lovers of God; Having a form of godliness, but denying the power thereof: from such turn away" (2 Ti.3:1-5).**
> >
> > **"And God looked upon the earth, and, behold, it was corrupt; for all flesh had corrupted his way upon the earth" (Ge.6:12).**
> >
> > **"They are all gone aside, they are *all* together become filthy: *there is* none that doeth good, no, not one" (Ps.14:3).**
> >
> > **"And judgment is turned away backward, and justice standeth afar off: for truth is fallen in the street, and equity cannot enter" (Is.59:14).**
> >
> > **"But we are all as an unclean *thing,* and all our righteousnesses *are* as filthy rags; and we all do fade as a leaf; and our iniquities, like the wind, have taken us away" (Is.64:6).**
> >
> > **"The good *man* is perished out of the earth: and *there is* none upright among men: they all lie in wait for blood; they hunt every man his brother with a net" (Mi.7:2).**
>
> (2) The corruption and depravity of the human heart can be cleansed away through the shed blood of the Lord Jesus Christ.
>
> > **"What then? are we better *than they?* No, in no wise: for we have before proved both Jews and Gentiles, that they are all under sin; As it is written, There is none righteous, no, not one: There is none that understandeth, there is none that seeketh after God. They are all gone out of the way, they are together become unprofitable; there is none that doeth good, no, not one. Their throat *is* an open sepulchre; with their tongues they have used deceit; the poison of asps *is* under their lips: Whose mouth *is* full of cursing and bitterness: Their feet *are* swift to shed blood: Destruction and misery *are* in their ways: And the way of peace have they not known: There is no fear of God before their eyes. Now we know that what things soever the law saith, it saith to them who are under the law: that every mouth may be stopped, and all the world may become guilty before God. Therefore by the deeds of the law there shall no flesh be**

justified in his sight: for by the law *is* the knowledge of sin. But now the righteousness of God without the law is manifested, being witnessed by the law and the prophets; Even the righteousness of God *which is* by faith of Jesus Christ unto all and upon all them that believe: for there is no difference: For all have sinned, and come short of the glory of God; Being justified freely by his grace through the redemption that is in Christ Jesus: Whom God hath set forth *to be* a propitiation through faith in his blood, to declare his righteousness for the remission of sins that are past, through the forbearance of God; To declare, *I say,* at this time his righteousness: that he might be just, and the justifier of him which believeth in Jesus" (Ro.3:9-26).

"Much more then, being now justified by his blood, we shall be saved from wrath through him" (Ro.5:9).

"In whom we have redemption through his blood, the forgiveness of sins, according to the riches of his grace" (Ep.1:7).

"Neither by the blood of goats and calves, but by his own blood he entered in once into the holy place, having obtained eternal redemption *for us.* For if the blood of bulls and of goats, and the ashes of an heifer sprinkling the unclean, sanctifieth to the purifying of the flesh: How much more shall the blood of Christ, who through the eternal Spirit offered himself without spot to God, purge your conscience from dead works to serve the living God?" (He.9:12-14).

"Forasmuch as ye know that ye were not redeemed with corruptible things, *as* silver and gold, from your vain conversation *received* by tradition from your fathers; But with the precious blood of Christ, as of a lamb without blemish and without spot" (1 Pe.1:18-19).

"Who his own self bare our sins in his own body on the tree, that we, being dead to sins, should live unto righteousness: by whose stripes ye were healed" (1 Pe.2:24).

"For Christ also hath once suffered for sins, the just for the unjust, that he might bring us to God, being put to death in the flesh, but quickened by the Spirit" (1 Pe.3:18).

---

2 (28:5-15) **Judgment, Example of—God, Judgment of—Ahaz, Wars of—Judah, Wars of—Israel, Northern Kingdom of, Wars—Syro-Ephraimite War, Discussed—Syria, War Against Judah**: because of Ahaz's terrible evil, the LORD allowed him to be defeated in a war with the Syrians and Israelites. For some reason, Syria and Israel had formed an alliance and attacked the Southern Kingdom of Judah in what is known as the Syro-Ephraimite war. A detailed description of the bloody battle and the suffering brought upon the people of Judah is given by Scripture. Apparently, two campaigns or two different battalions, one under the command of Syria and the other under the command of Israel, were launched against Judah:

a. First, the Syrian attack against Judah was extremely successful (v.5). The LORD was using Syria and Israel to execute judgment against Judah because of Ahaz's and the people's sin. Defeating the Judean army, the Syrians captured and exiled large numbers of the soldiers and citizens of Judah, deporting them to Damascus.

b. Second, Israel's attack against Judah was also successful (vv.6-8). In just one day, Israel's King Pekah killed over 120,000 Judean soldiers. Scripture clearly says that behind the scenes God was executing a just judgment because of Judah's terrible evil of forsaking Him (v.6). Among the enormous number of casualties were three royal officials killed by a warrior named Zicri. These three officials included Maaseiah, the king's son, Azrikam, the palace manager, and Elkanah, second in command to the king (v.7). But the devastation of its army was not the only loss suffered by Judah. Marching throughout the countryside, Israel's army ransacked the cities of Judea, taking captive over 200,000 women and children and carrying them back to Samaria as exiles (v.8). In addition, they took a large amount of plunder from the towns and villages they had raided.

c. When Israel's army returned to Samaria, to their surprise they were immediately confronted by the prophet Oded who issued a strong warning to them (vv.9-11). His forceful warning included three points.

   1) They were guilty of brutality, excessive cruelty (v.9). They were not victorious...
- because of their military power
- because of racial merit or value
- because they were more favored by God
- because they were more righteous and the Judeans more wicked

They were victorious because the LORD was executing justice upon Judah; for that reason, the LORD had allowed Israel to conquer King Ahaz and the Judean citizens. However, Israel's army had gone too far. They had used excessive force and given in to a spirit of brutality and cruelty. They had slaughtered the Judean army in a rage that had reached up and disturbed all of heaven. They had shown no mercy to the Judean soldiers, not even to those who had been captured.

   2) The army had been guilty of enslaving the men and women, a serious violation of God's commandment. No Jew was allowed to enslave one of his fellow countrymen (Le.25:39-46). The victorious army of Israel needed to remember a fact: they themselves were guilty of sin before the LORD. Just as the LORD had executed judgment against Judah, so He would execute judgment against the Northern Kingdom unless they repented of their sins (v.10).

   3) The leaders of Israel must return the Judean slaves, for God's fierce wrath had turned against them and was ready to strike in an act of *just* punishment (v.11). If they failed to show mercy, they would immediately face the judgment of God. But if they showed compassion and returned the slaves to their homeland, God would have compassion on them.

d. In response to the prophecy of Oded, a delegation of four political leaders confronted the military commanders (vv.12-15). They pointed out Israel's sin and guilt before the LORD and negotiated the release of the prisoners (v.13). Arguing that God's fierce wrath had turned against Israel, the delegation convinced the army to turn over the prisoners and return the plunder they had taken (v.14). In a remarkable demonstration of mercy, the army released the prisoners to the delegation. The delegation then immediately clothed and fed the prisoners, taking care of the injured and wounded (v.15). Finally, the delegation had the prisoners—all 200,000 women and children—taken back to their homeland. They even provided transportation for the weak and escorted some as far back as Jericho.

Thought 1. The very depth of wickedness and human depravity is seen in the life of Ahaz. He personally turned completely away from the LORD and then tragically led the people into false worship, even the atrocious practice of human sacrifice. His life stands as a strong warning to us: we must turn away from wickedness and false worship. If we continue to live sinful, wicked lives and reject the LORD, we will be doomed. God's judgment will fall upon us. Because God loves the world, He will not always tolerate behavior that causes suffering upon this earth. When we commit wickedness, we bring loss and suffering upon other people. When we steal, we cause a loss for one or more individuals; and if the theft involves a large item like an automobile or a huge sum of money, we can cause terrible suffering for those involved. Even if we shoplift, we cause loss for companies, who in turn have to raise their prices, which causes loss for all of us. Stated simply, all unrighteousness causes suffering and loss for someone.

So it is with false worship. None of us lives in isolation, which means that we all influence other people. Consequently, when we reject the LORD and participate in false worship—whether it is an actual idol or the idolization of fame, wealth, possessions, position, authority, sex, sports, television, a celebrity, or an any other physical token or ideal—we set a bad example for other people. We become stumbling blocks to our friends and to other children and adults, giving our stamp of approval to false worship. We mislead other people into idolatry and away from the LORD. All worship other than the worship of the LORD—the Father of the Lord Jesus Christ—is idolatry.

Again, committing wickedness and engaging in false worship will not always be tolerated by the LORD. God loves the world too much to allow the suffering to go on forever. If we mislead people and cause them to suffer, we will face the hand of God's judgment. Listen to what God's Holy Word says about His just and holy judgment:

> "For the wrath of God is revealed from heaven against all ungodliness and unrighteousness of men, who hold the truth in unrighteousness….Being filled with all unrighteousness, fornication, wickedness, covetousness, maliciousness; full of envy, murder, debate, deceit, malignity; whisperers, Backbiters, haters of God, despiteful, proud, boasters, inventors of evil things, disobedient to parents, Without understanding, covenantbreakers, without natural affection, implacable, unmerciful: Who knowing the judgment of God, that they which commit such things are worthy of death, not only do the same, but have pleasure in them that do them" (Ro.1:18, 29-32).

> "Know ye not that the unrighteous shall not inherit the kingdom of God? Be not deceived: neither fornicators, nor idolaters, nor adulterers, nor effeminate, nor abusers of themselves with mankind, Nor thieves, nor covetous, nor drunkards, nor revilers, nor extortioners, shall inherit the kingdom of God" (1 Co.6:9-10).

> "Now the works of the flesh are manifest, which are *these;* Adultery, fornication, uncleanness, lasciviousness, Idolatry, witchcraft, hatred, variance, emulations, wrath, strife, seditions, heresies, Envyings, murders, drunkenness, revellings, and such like: of the which I tell you before, as I have also told *you* in time past, that they which do such things shall not inherit the kingdom of God" (Ga.5:19-21).

> "But fornication, and all uncleanness, or covetousness, let it not be once named among you, as becometh saints; Neither filthiness, nor foolish talking, nor jesting, which are not convenient: but rather giving of thanks. For this ye know, that no whoremonger, nor unclean person, nor covetous man, who is an idolater, hath any inheritance in the kingdom of Christ and of God. Let no man deceive you with vain words: for because of these things cometh the wrath of God upon the children of disobedience" (Ep.5:3-6).

> "But the fearful, and unbelieving, and the abominable, and murderers, and whoremongers, and sorcerers, and idolaters, and all liars, shall have their part in the lake which burneth with fire and brimstone: which is the second death" (Re.21:8).

---

3 (28:16-21) **Salvation, Source, Example—Deliverance, Source, Example—Savior, False, Seeking—Deliverer, False, Seeking—Ahaz, Alliances of—Assyria, Alliance with Israel—Ahaz, Evil of**: right after his devastating defeat, Ahaz turned to Assyria for help (vv.17-19). With his nation torn apart and his army diminished, Ahaz and the Judeans were entirely helpless to defend themselves. Consequently, the cities and towns of the nation were under constant attack by the surrounding nations and marauders. Almost immediately the Edomites struck from the east, plundering and taking captives, while the Philistines raided various cities in the west and south (v.18). Having captured six cities, they then occupied them and added them to the territory of Philistia. No doubt these were dark, terrible days of suffering for the surviving Judeans. But remember why they were suffering so much: because God was humbling and disciplining them for their gross sins and continued unfaithfulness. King Ahaz had not only lived a life of wickedness before the nation, but he had also promoted wickedness among the people. And tragically, the people had followed in his footsteps, pursuing the path of unfaithfulness to the LORD.

When the Assyrian king Tiglath-Pileser received Ahaz's appeal for help, he did respond, but his actions ended up oppressing Ahaz instead of helping him (v.20). As the book of *Kings* explains, Assyria attacked Syria and conquered Damascus, the capital of Syria. This removed the Syrians as a threat. But this did not help Ahaz, for he was forced to pay a large fee to the Assyrians for their help. In doing so, Ahaz apparently bankrupted the nation by raiding the treasuries of the palace and temple and demanding huge sums of wealth from the princes of the nation. Obviously, there was little wealth left in the nation after his actions. King Ahaz had inherited a strong nation both economically and militarily, but he had foolishly brought defeat and devastation to the land. He had wrecked the economy and caused incomprehensible suffering for the people. By seeking help from the Assyrian king, a human savior, Ahaz was not helped but, rather, hurt (v.21).

BACKGROUND TO ISAIAH'S DAY

(The Four Kings Who Ruled During Isaiah's Ministry)

Thought 1. Ahaz was a man who looked for a savior other than the LORD. In seeking deliverance from trouble, he turned to a man, Tiglath-Pileser, not to God. But there is only one true Savior, the LORD Himself. And the LORD has proven His power to deliver His people down through the centuries. Still, Ahaz rejected the lessons of history and sought salvation in mortal man instead of turning to the eternal LORD.

However, Ahaz is not the only person to make this mistake. How many of us seek salvation in someone or some thing other than the Lord Jesus Christ? Only the Lord can save us. Only He has the power to deliver us from the sin and bondages of this life. When trials, temptations, hardships, misfortunes, or any other bitter enemy confronts us, there is only one living Savior—the Lord Jesus Christ Himself—who can deliver us. Only He has the power to carry us victoriously through this life and on into the eternity of heaven. Listen to what God's Holy Word says:

> **"For God so loved the world, that he gave his only begotten Son, that whosoever believeth in him should not perish, but have everlasting life" (Jn.3:16).**
> **"For the Son of man is come to seek and to save that which was lost" (Lu.19:10).**
> **"Him hath God exalted with his right hand *to be* a Prince and a Saviour, for to give repentance to Israel, and forgiveness of sins" (Ac.5:31).**
> **"There hath no temptation taken you but such as is common to man: but God *is* faithful, who will not suffer you to be tempted above that ye are able; but will with the temptation also make a way to escape, that ye may be able to bear *it*" (1 Co.10:13).**
> **"Now unto him that is able to do exceeding abundantly above all that we ask or think, according to the power that worketh in us" (Ep.3:20).**
> **"And the Lord shall deliver me from every evil work, and will preserve *me* unto his heavenly kingdom: to whom *be* glory for ever and ever. Amen" (2 Ti.4:18).**
> **"Forasmuch then as the children are partakers of flesh and blood, he also himself likewise took part of the same; that through death he might destroy him that had the power of death, that is, the devil; And deliver them who through fear of death were all their lifetime subject to bondage" (He.2:14-15).**
> **"For Christ also hath once suffered for sins, the just for the unjust, that he might bring us to God, being put to death in the flesh, but quickened by the Spirit" (1 Pe.3:18).**
> **"The Lord knoweth how to deliver the godly out of temptations, and to reserve the unjust unto the day of judgment to be punished" (2 Pe.2:9).**

DEEPER STUDY #1

(2 Chr.28:16) **Assyria**: of all the enemies Israel faced, Assyria was the most terrifying. Assyria not only fought fiercely but also with unbelievable cruelty. The powerful enemy knew how to inflict shocking pain and horror. Their gruesome war tactics included such devices as placing an enemy on a sharp stake and flaying him alive and ripping open pregnant women with a sword. These devices were used to strike fear among the people and to force them into submission. Their lust for war and power knew no limits. There was simply nothing they would *not* do in their pursuit of victory and world domination.

Despite their brutality and savagery, the LORD used Assyria to punish Israel. Because the people of Israel and Judah insisted on committing idolatry, God allowed the Assyrians to conquer Israel. As a result, the people of Israel lived in fear and trepidation of Assyria from the 9th century B.C. until late in the 7th century B.C., when Assyria was finally conquered by the Scythians. In 722 B.C., the prophecy of judgment against Israel was fulfilled when Sargon II took Samaria. In that year, the Northern Kingdom fell, opening the way for more pressure on Jerusalem and the Southern Kingdom.

Foolishly, King Ahaz of Judah made an alliance with the Assyrian king Tiglath-Pileser, trusting in the former enemy to give him protection. The prophet Isaiah had clearly warned against forming a close agreement with such an evil nation, but King Ahaz would not listen. Soon Assyria demanded tribute from Judah. But even worse than that, Assyria insisted that Judah worship the false gods of Assyria. Out of fear, Ahaz had made the alliance. Now again out of fear, he was forced to agree to the tribute and to worship Assyria's false gods. In failing to fully trust in the LORD for protection, Judah's sin of idolatry led to a flood of terrible tragedy.

The teaching of Scripture is unmistakable: close alliances with unbelievers will result in tragedy. The believer simply cannot hold hands with the world and with God at the same time. We must trust in God and God alone for our needs. He is the only One who can provide for and protect us.

Note the kings of Assyria mentioned in the Bible:

⇒ Tiglath-Pil(n)eser III (or Pul) reigned from 745 to 727 B.C. (2 K.15:29; 16:7, 10). Tiglath-Pileser attacked Azariah in Judah and left behind a burning path of destruction. He easily smashed the fortified cities, just as a person would smash an ordinary dish (ARAB 1:770[2]). He forced the terrified King Ahaz and King Menahem to pay tribute to him (ARAB 1:815). Tiglath-Pileser also conquered city after city during the days of King Pekah of Israel (2 K.15:29). He was later hired by Ahaz, king of Judah, to attack the Northern Kingdom, which he did, assassinating King Rezin (2 K.16:7-10). During his invasion, he captured and deported many of the citizens to Assyria (1 Chr.5:26).

⇒ Shalmaneser V reigned from 727 to 722 B.C. (2 K.17:3; 18:9). He also expanded the Assyrian territory far beyond the kings who ruled Assyria before him (ARAB 1:830). When Hoshea, king of Israel, refused to pay the tribute demanded, Shalmaneser marched and set siege against Samaria for three years (2 K.17:5). Finally, after conquering the capital, he took all but a few people of the Northern Kingdom of Israel into exile (2 K.18:9-11).

---

2 Daniel David Luckenbill. *Ancient Records of Assyria and Babylonia*, 2 vols. (ARAB) (London: Histories and Mysteries of Man Ltd., 1989).

BACKGROUND TO ISAIAH'S DAY

(The Four Kings Who Ruled During Isaiah's Ministry)

⇒ Sargon II reigned from 722 to 705 B.C. (Is.20:1) He took the control of Assyria away from Shalmaneser (ARAB 1:132). Sargon trampled across the land of Israel all the way to Ashdod, the Philistine coastal city. Iamani, the king of Ashdod, delayed paying tribute to Sargon. As a result, Sargon sent a field marshal to attack and capture the city. Iamani fled for his life, barely escaping by sea to Egypt, and leaving his family behind (ARAB 2:79, 92).

⇒ Sennacherib reigned from 705 to 681 B.C. (2 K.18:13; 19:16, 20, 36; 2 Chr.32:1-2, 9-10, 22; Is.36:1; 37:17, 21, 37). Sennacherib marched against Jerusalem but was unsuccessful. He recorded that he took away spoils of war; and, "like a caged bird, I shut up [Hezekiah] in Jerusalem, his royal city," and that "the terrifying splendor of my royalty overcame him" (ARAB 2:240, 312). But he did not record anything about the 185,000 soldiers being killed in one day by God. After this great miracle, Sennacherib was forced to lift the siege and withdraw from the city (2 K.19:35-36; 2 Chr.32:22). Sennacherib only wrote, "On Hezekiah [Judah's king], I laid my yoke" (ARAB 2:347), letting the reader assume that Sennacherib won the battle.

⇒ Esarhaddon reigned from 681 to 669 B.C. (2 K.19:37; Ezr.4:2; Is.37:38). He was the son of Sennacherib. Esarhaddon recorded that he summoned Manasseh, along with twenty-one other kings, and forced them into slave labor (ARAB 2:690).

---

4 **(28:22-27) Apostasy, Example of—Rejection, of God, Example—Turning Away, from God, Example—Forsaking, of God, Example—Ahaz, Rejection of God—Ahaz, Summary of His Reign**: Ahaz totally rejected God. He reached a depth of unfaithfulness seldom seen in men. When Ahaz was confronted by trouble, suffering or deep distress, he became even more unfaithful to the LORD. In the very times he should have been turning to the LORD, he turned elsewhere, seeking the help of men and of false gods. After his defeat by Syria, he even began to worship the gods of the Syrians. Foolishly, he held the belief that these false gods had helped Syria defeat him. He reasoned that if he worshipped these idols, perhaps the false gods would help him also (v.23). But the result was the exact opposite, for his idolatry and false worship led to the downfall of all Israel. Ahaz became totally immersed in false worship and idolatry. He even closed the doors of the temple to those who continued to worship the LORD. Plundering and destroying the temple's furnishings, he barricaded the doors and encouraged the people to worship the false gods he had adopted. He even set up altars for the worship of false gods on every street corner of Jerusalem and built false worship centers in every town of Judah. Steeped in wickedness and immersed in idol worship, he provoked and aroused the anger of the LORD (v.25).

Ahaz's life and reign were recorded in *The Book of the Kings of Judah and Israel* (v.26). After his death he was buried in Jerusalem. But he was dishonored by the public who refused to bury him in the cemetery of the kings. His successor was his son Hezekiah.

In evaluating his life and reign, it is evident that few men have lived such a wicked life and brought so much evil upon a nation and its people as did King Ahaz. In the midst of their suffering Ahaz sought a deliverer in mere man, King Tiglath-Pileser of Assyria. He placed his confidence in a human being, not in the LORD. Thus, he never received the help he needed, not the help of a permanent Savior and Deliverer. Neither he nor his people were rescued.

> **Thought 1**. Ahaz forsook the LORD and fell into the depths of unbelief. The same is true with so many of us all around the world. Many of us have rejected the LORD either by denying Him or by refusing to accept Him as our personal Savior. The results of such a decision are, in this life, most tragic, for a person who rejects the LORD has only the arm of the flesh to help him. When a day of trouble or distress comes, God is not present to help or deliver, for unbelief and rejection pushes away the LORD and separates Him from us. Thus, when a severe accident or disease strikes, we are left all alone, in a state of separation. No help is available except what medicine and technology can give us. And as helpful as medicine and technology are, they are limited in what they can offer us. They can only delay death, not eliminate or erase it.
>
> When the severe trials of life strike us and we need the LORD's help, He wants to help us. But if we continue in our unbelief and rejection, we cut ourselves off from His help. Yet in the midst of our hardships and misfortunes, if we will cry out for help, the LORD will hear and help us. This is His wonderful promise. But again, He cannot—nor will He—help us if we reject Him. Listen to what God says about unbelief and the rejection of Him:
>
> > "He came unto his own, and his own received him not. But as many as received him, to them gave he power to become the sons of God, *even* to them that believe on his name" (Jn.1:11-12).
> >
> > "He that believeth on the Son hath everlasting life: and he that believeth not the Son shall not see life; but the wrath of God abideth on him" (Jn.3:36).
> >
> > "I am come in my Father's name, and ye receive me not: if another shall come in his own name, him ye will receive" (Jn.5:43).
> >
> > "I said therefore unto you, that ye shall die in your sins: for if ye believe not that I am *he,* ye shall die in your sins" (Jn.8:24).
> >
> > "He that rejecteth me, and receiveth not my words, hath one that judgeth him: the word that I have spoken, the same shall judge him in the last day" (Jn.12:48).
> >
> > "Now the Spirit speaketh expressly, that in the latter times some shall depart from the faith, giving heed to seducing spirits, and doctrines of devils" (1 Ti.4:1).
> >
> > "For the time will come when they will not endure sound doctrine; but after their own lusts shall they heap to themselves teachers, having itching ears; And they shall turn away *their* ears from the truth, and shall be turned unto fables" (2 Ti.4:3-4).
> >
> > "Harden not your hearts, as in the provocation, in the day of temptation in the wilderness: When your fathers tempted me, proved me, and saw my works forty years. Wherefore I was grieved with that generation, and said, They do alway err in *their* heart; and they have not known my ways. So I sware in

my wrath, They shall not enter into my rest.) Take heed, brethren, lest there be in any of you an evil heart of unbelief, in departing from the living God" (He.3:8-12).

"Take heed, brethren, lest there be in any of you an evil heart of unbelief, in departing from the living God. But exhort one another daily, while it is called To day; lest any of you be hardened through the deceitfulness of sin. For we are made partakers of Christ, if we hold the beginning of our confidence stedfast unto the end; While it is said, To day if ye will hear his voice, harden not your hearts, as in the provocation. For some, when they had heard, did provoke: howbeit not all that came out of Egypt by Moses. But with whom was he grieved forty years? *was it* not with them that had sinned, whose carcases fell in the wilderness? And to whom sware he that they should not enter into his rest, but to them that believed not? So we see that they could not enter in because of unbelief" (He.3:12-19).

"Let us therefore fear, lest, a promise being left *us* of entering into his rest, any of you should seem to come short of it. For unto us was the gospel preached, as well as unto them: but the word preached did not profit them, not being mixed with faith in them that heard *it.* For we which have believed do enter into rest, as he said, As I have sworn in my wrath, if they shall enter into my rest: although the works were finished from the foundation of the world" (He.4:1-3).

"Let us labour therefore to enter into that rest, lest any man fall after the same example of unbelief" (He.4:11).

"I will therefore put you in remembrance, though ye once knew this, how that the Lord, having saved the people out of the land of Egypt, afterward destroyed them that believed not. And the angels which kept not their first estate, but left their own habitation, he hath reserved in everlasting chains under darkness unto the judgment of the great day. Even as Sodom and Gomorrha, and the cities about them in like manner, giving themselves over to fornication, and going after strange flesh, are set forth for an example, suffering the vengeance of eternal fire" (Jude 5-7).

"For my people have committed two evils; they have forsaken me the fountain of living waters, *and* hewed them out cisterns, broken cisterns, that can hold no water" (Je.2:13).

BACKGROUND TO ISAIAH'S DAY

(The Four Kings Who Ruled During Isaiah's Ministry)

IV. THE REIGN OF HEZEKIAH (PART 1)— THE CLEANSING OF THE TEMPLE FOR WORSHIP: A LESSON ON THE GREAT NEEDS OF THE CHURCH, 2 CHR.29:1-36

OUTLINE	SCRIPTURE	SCRIPTURE	OUTLINE
1. Hezekiah's background: A godly, righteous man a. His reign: Began at age 25 b. His mother, Abijah, & grandfather, Zechariah: Were most likely believers c. His righteous life: Followed the godly example of David **2. Hezekiah's reformation, his cleansing of the temple: A need for ministers & churches to be holy, pure** a. The temple doors were quickly opened b. The religious leaders were all summoned to a meeting c. The order for much-needed change was immediately given to the religious leaders: Must sanctify, cleanse themselves & the temple (church)—removing all rubbish & every defiling thing 1) Because they & their fathers had sinned & done evil, forsaking the Lord 2) Because they & their fathers had forsaken His temple (church) 3) Because they & their fathers had shut the doors of the temple (church): Had stopped the public worship services 4) Because God's anger & judgment had been aroused • He had given them up to trouble, horror, & ridicule, Je.19:8; 25:9, 18; 51:37 • He had given up their families to be conquered & exiled by Syria, Israel, Edom, & Philistia, 28:5-10, 17-18 d. The only answer to revival was clearly stated 1) The king & people must make a renewed covenant with the LORD 2) The priests & Levites	Hezekiah began to reign *when he was* five and twenty years old, and he reigned nine and twenty years in Jerusalem. And his mother's name *was* Abijah, the daughter of Zechariah. 2 And he did *that which was* right in the sight of the LORD, according to all that David his father had done. 3 He in the first year of his reign, in the first month, opened the doors of the house of the LORD, and repaired them. 4 And he brought in the priests and the Levites, and gathered them together into the east street, 5 And said unto them, Hear me, ye Levites, sanctify now yourselves, and sanctify the house of the LORD God of your fathers, and carry forth the filthiness out of the holy *place.* 6 For our fathers have trespassed, and done *that which was* evil in the eyes of the LORD our God, and have forsaken him, and have turned away their faces from the habitation of the LORD, and turned *their* backs. 7 Also they have shut up the doors of the porch, and put out the lamps, and have not burned incense nor offered burnt offerings in the holy *place* unto the God of Israel. 8 Wherefore the wrath of the LORD was upon Judah and Jerusalem, and he hath delivered them to trouble, to astonishment, and to hissing, as ye see with your eyes. 9 For, lo, our fathers have fallen by the sword, and our sons and our daughters and our wives are in captivity for this. 10 Now *it is* in mine heart to make a covenant with the LORD God of Israel, that his fierce wrath may turn away from us. 11 My sons, be not now	negligent: for the LORD hath chosen you to stand before him, to serve him, and that ye should minister unto him, and burn incense. 12 Then the Levites arose, Mahath the son of Amasai, and Joel the son of Azariah, of the sons of the Kohathites: and of the sons of Merari, Kish the son of Abdi, and Azariah the son of Jehalelel: and of the Gershonites; Joah the son of Zimmah, and Eden the son of Joah: 13 And of the sons of Elizaphan; Shimri, and Jeiel: and of the sons of Asaph; Zechariah, and Mattaniah: 14 And of the sons of Heman; Jehiel, and Shimei: and of the sons of Jeduthun; Shemaiah, and Uzziel. 15 And they gathered their brethren, and sanctified themselves, and came, according to the commandment of the king, by the words of the LORD, to cleanse the house of the LORD. 16 And the priests went into the inner part of the house of the LORD, to cleanse *it,* and brought out all the uncleanness that they found in the temple of the LORD into the court of the house of the LORD. And the Levites took *it,* to carry *it* out abroad into the brook Kidron. 17 Now they began on the first *day* of the first month to sanctify, and on the eighth day of the month came they to the porch of the LORD: so they sanctified the house of the LORD in eight days; and in the sixteenth day of the first month they made an end. 18 Then they went in to Hezekiah the king, and said, We have cleansed all the house of the LORD, and the altar of burnt offering, with all the vessels thereof, and the showbread table, with all the vessels thereof.	must not neglect their duties any longer • Must represent the LORD & serve Him • Must minister & burn incense (symbolized prayer) e. The obedience of the Levites & priests was immediate: They went to work as charged 1) The leaders of the Levites were appointed • Two leaders were appointed from each of the three major clans: Kohath, Merari, & Gershon • Two leaders were appointed from a fourth clan, Elizaphan • Other leaders were appointed from three clans of the Levitical musicians: Asaph, Zechariah, & Mattaniah, 13 2) The Levites first sanctified themselves 3) The Levites then sanctified, cleansed the temple: Just as the king charged & as the LORD's Word instructed, 1 Chr.28:12, 19 • The priests removed all rubbish & every defiled thing from the sanctuary, taking them out to the courtyard • The Levites then carted out all the unclean items to the Kidron Valley • The cleansing took sixteen days: Eight days to clean the courts up to the portico or porch & then eight more days to cleanse the temple itself 4) The Levites & priests reported to the king • They had cleansed the entire temple, the altar, the table for sacred bread, & all the utensils

22

OUTLINE	SCRIPTURE	SCRIPTURE	OUTLINE

• They had recovered & sanctified all the items & utensils taken by King Ahaz when he closed the temple
 	
3. Hezekiah's rededication of the temple: A new beginning in worship
  a. The civic leaders were summoned to attend
  1) The leaders brought animals to be sacrificed as a sin offering, Le.4:1–5:13
    • The purpose: To make atonement for the sins of the kingdom (royal court), the sanctuary (priest & Levites), & Judah (people)
    • The priests offered the sacrifices to the LORD, sprinkling the blood on the altar: The blood of the bulls, rams, & lambs
 	
    • The king & the assembly (leaders) laid their hands on the goats (designated them as the substitute sacrifice for sin)
    • The priests then sacrificed the goats & sprinkled their blood on the altar: Was a sin offering to atone for *all Israel*, as was the burnt offering
 	
  2) The king stationed the Levite musicians in the temple for the dedication service
    • They were placed just as David, Gad the king's seer, & Nathan the prophet had instructed
    • They stood ready with their instruments
 	
  3) The king ordered the burnt offering to be sacrificed & presented to the LORD
    • The musicians sang & the instruments played throughout the sacrifice of the burnt offering
	19 Moreover all the vessels, which king Ahaz in his reign did cast away in his transgression, have we prepared and sanctified, and, behold, they *are* before the altar of the LORD.
	20 Then Hezekiah the king rose early, and gathered the rulers of the city, and went up to the house of the LORD.
	21 And they brought seven bullocks, and seven rams, and seven lambs, and seven he goats, for a sin offering for the kingdom, and for the sanctuary, and for Judah. And he commanded the priests the sons of Aaron to offer *them* on the altar of the LORD.
	22 So they killed the bullocks, and the priests received the blood, and sprinkled *it* on the altar: likewise, when they had killed the rams, they sprinkled the blood upon the altar: they killed also the lambs, and they sprinkled the blood upon the altar.
	23 And they brought forth the he goats *for* the sin offering before the king and the congregation; and they laid their hands upon them:
	24 And the priests killed them, and they made reconciliation with their blood upon the altar, to make an atonement for all Israel: for the king commanded *that* the burnt offering and the sin offering *should be made* for all Israel.
	25 And he set the Levites in the house of the LORD with cymbals, with psalteries, and with harps, according to the commandment of David, and of Gad the king's seer, and Nathan the prophet: for *so was* the commandment of the LORD by his prophets.
	26 And the Levites stood with the instruments of David, and the priests with the trumpets.
	27 And Hezekiah commanded to offer the burnt offering upon the altar. And when the burnt offering began, the song of the LORD began *also* with the trumpets, and with the instruments *ordained* by
		David king of Israel.
		28 And all the congregation worshipped, and the singers sang, and the trumpeters sounded: *and all this continued* until the burnt offering was finished.
		29 And when they had made an end of offering, the king and all that were present with him bowed themselves, and worshipped.
		30 Moreover Hezekiah the king and the princes commanded the Levites to sing praise unto the LORD with the words of David, and of Asaph the seer. And they sang praises with gladness, and they bowed their heads and worshipped.
		31 Then Hezekiah answered and said, Now ye have consecrated yourselves unto the LORD, come near and bring sacrifices and thank offerings into the house of the LORD. And the congregation brought in sacrifices and thank offerings; and as many as were of a free heart burnt offerings.
		32 And the number of the burnt offerings, which the congregation brought, was threescore and ten bullocks, an hundred rams, *and* two hundred lambs: all these *were* for a burnt offering to the LORD.
		33 And the consecrated things *were* six hundred oxen and three thousand sheep.
		34 But the priests were too few, so that they could not flay all the burnt offerings: wherefore their brethren the Levites did help them, till the work was ended, and until the *other* priests had sanctified themselves: for the Levites *were* more upright in heart to sanctify themselves than the priests.
		35 And also the burnt offerings *were* in abundance, with the fat of the peace offerings, and the drink offerings for *every* burnt offering. So the service of the house of the LORD was set in order.
		36 And Hezekiah rejoiced, and all the people, that God had prepared the people: for the thing was *done* suddenly.
			• The whole assembly bowed & worshipped while the singers sang & the burnt offering was sacrificed
			
			4) The king & everyone present knelt & worshipped after all the offerings had been presented
			
			5) The king commanded the Levites to sing songs from the psalms of David & of Asaph the seer
			
			b. The invitation was issued for the congregation to bring their individual offerings
			1) The people's response was wholehearted
			  • Many brought their sacrifices & thanksgiving offerings
			  • Those with willing hearts brought burnt offerings
			2) The offerings sacrificed were enormous in number
			  • The burnt offerings: 70 bulls, 100 rams, 200 male lambs
			
			  • The other offerings: 600 bulls & 3,000 sheep & goats
			3) The priests were too few to handle all the work involved in the sacrificing of animals
			  • They were not yet sanctified, cleansed: Had been lax, slow to respond to the revival
			  • The Levites stepped in to help
			
			4) The burnt offerings presented by the people were surprisingly numerous, as were the accompanying drink offerings & the large amount of fat from the fellowship offerings
			c. The temple was restored for worship: The king & the people rejoiced over what God had done & done so quickly

23

(29:1-36) **Introduction**: commitment, steadfastness, perseverance, endurance, holding fast, faithfulness—this is the great need of the church, not buildings and not money. A place for a body of believers to meet is essential. But the place can be a home, a hut, or out in the open air, as well as a magnificent structure.

Money is also essential to carry on the mission of the church, for the gospel of Christ must be carried not only to our own communities but also to the whole world. Therefore, the church is responsible not only to take the gospel to its own community and to meet the needs of its neighbors but also to meet the needs of everyone everywhere.

Yet as necessary as a meeting place and money are, these two resources are not the major needs of the church. The primary need is the resource of people, people who are wholeheartedly committed, dedicated, loyal, devoted, steadfast, persevering, enduring, and who are strong witnesses for Him. This is the greatest need of the church.

A *new reformation* is heralded, proclaimed in this present Scripture. After King Ahaz brought ruin upon Judah through war and the closing of the temple, the nation of Judah was in desperate need. Its economy was wrecked and its military was decimated. There was no courageous, godly leadership to restore the nation, not as long as King Ahaz lived and continued to reign. But God knew the catastrophic devastation that had swept over the nation, and even while Ahaz was still ruling, the LORD was preparing his son Hezekiah to take the throne and to restore the nation. The present passage covers the story of Hezekiah, a godly man who was to rule the nation in righteousness and justice. When he ascended to the throne, a renewed hope was aroused within the hearts of the people, a hope for the restoration of the nation to its former glory. Keep in mind that the Northern Kingdom of Israel had collapsed under the assault of Assyria during the reign of Ahaz, Hezekiah's father. The year of the Northern Kingdom's collapse and exile was 722 B.C. In His sovereignty, God knew that a strong and righteous king would need to be upon the throne of Judah following the fall of Israel. And though Hezekiah was reared in one of the most ungodly environments imaginable, he came to know the LORD in a very personal way, committing his life wholeheartedly to the LORD. His godly reign would not stop the tide of wickedness from flowing throughout Judah, but it would significantly delay the hand of God's judgment from falling upon the Southern Kingdom. Due much to Hezekiah's righteous reign, Judah would not fall to Babylon for over 100 years. Scripture records more on the history of Hezekiah than on any king other than David and Solomon.

In studying the history of Hezekiah, the returning exile would be aroused to recommit his life to the LORD and to make sure that the temple was kept pure for the worship of the LORD. Remember that the exiles were returning to Judah to achieve the very same goals that had challenged Hezekiah, those of restoring *true worship* in the temple and of rebuilding the nation. This is, *The Reign of Hezekiah (Part 1)—the Cleansing of the Temple for Worship: A Lesson on the Great Needs of the Church*, 29:1-36.

1. Hezekiah's background: a godly, righteous man (vv.1-2).
2. Hezekiah's reformation, his cleansing of the temple: a need for ministers and churches to be holy, pure (vv.3-19).
3. Hezekiah's rededication of the temple: a new beginning in worship (vv.20-36).

---

1 (29:1-2) **Godliness, Example of—Righteousness, Example of, Hezekiah—Character, Good, Example of—Commitment, Example of—Dedication, Example of—Devotion, to the LORD, Example of—Hezekiah, King of Judah—Kings, of the Southern Kingdom of Judah**: the major feature of Hezekiah's life and reign was his godly, righteous life before the LORD. He was totally devoted to God and committed to launching a reformation throughout the nation, a reformation that would reestablish *true worship* and rebuild the nation economically, politically, and militarily.

Hezekiah began his independent rule when he was 25 years old, and he reigned as an independent king for 29 years. Apparently, 14 years of his reign were spent serving as co-regent with his father Ahaz. Then he reigned 18 years alone and another 11 years as co-regent with his son Manasseh.[3] Considering that Hezekiah's father was Ahaz, one of history's most wicked kings, it is surprising that Hezekiah made a deep, genuine commitment to the LORD. Nevertheless, he did, and he had one of the most successful reigns among all the kings. His mother was Abijah, the daughter of a man named Zechariah. Perhaps Zechariah was the godly man who had advised King Uzziah (26:5) and served as a witness for the prophet Isaiah (8:2). If so, then Hezekiah's mother was probably a genuine believer who had a righteous influence upon him.

Whatever the case, at some point in his life, Hezekiah made a deep commitment to the LORD. He lived righteously, following the godly example of David (v.2).

> **Thought 1**. Hezekiah's godliness and righteousness are dynamic examples for us. Against all odds, he chose to follow the LORD. With a father steeped in wickedness who had fallen into the very depths of depravity, Hezekiah stood little chance of ever making a commitment to the LORD. Nevertheless, he defied the odds, seeking to follow and to give his life over to the LORD. Likewise, no matter how bad or terrible our upbringing, we can break the cycle. We too can trust the LORD and become successful in life. Through the power of Christ, we can overcome the negative impact of alcoholic, abusive, or profane parents.
> - If we were reared in a divisive, broken, or single-parent home, we can break the trend through the power of Christ.
> - If we were reared in an uneducated or poverty-stricken environment, we can break the trend through the power of Christ.
>
> Even an immoral, wicked, depraved, or corrupt environment can be overcome through the power of Christ. In Christ, God has given us the Savior, the Deliverer who can rescue us from bad parents, bad childhoods, and bad environments—no matter how dreadful or appalling they may be. In Christ, there is power to rise above the enslavements and bondages of our past. Therefore, if we reject Christ, it is *our* choice; we are without excuse. The power of Christ is available to all of us. Christ can enable us to live righteous and godly lives, lives free of all the bondages and enslavements of this life. Listen to what God's Holy Word says:

---

3 John F. Walvoord and Roy B. Zuck, Editors. *The Bible Knowledge Commentary.* (Colorado Springs, CO: Chariot Victor Publishing, 1985), p.572.

"That it might be fulfilled which was spoken by Esaias the prophet, saying, Himself took our infirmities, and bare *our* sicknesses" (Mt.8:17).

"For God so loved the world, that he gave his only begotten Son, that whosoever believeth in him should not perish, but have everlasting life" (Jn.3:16).

"The thief cometh not, but for to steal, and to kill, and to destroy: I am come that they might have life, and that they might have *it* more abundantly" (Jn.10:10).

"Neither is there salvation in any other: for there is none other name under heaven given among men, whereby we must be saved" (Ac.4:12).

"For when we were yet without strength, in due time Christ died for the ungodly" (Ro.5:6).

"There hath no temptation taken you but such as is common to man: but God *is* faithful, who will not suffer you to be tempted above that ye are able; but will with the temptation also make a way to escape, that ye may be able to bear *it*" (1 Co.10:13).

"Awake to righteousness, and sin not; for some have not the knowledge of God: I speak *this* to your shame" (1 Co.15:34).

"[Christ] Who gave himself for our sins, that he might deliver us from this present evil world, according to the will of God and our Father" (Ga.1:4).

"Wherefore take unto you the whole armour of God, that ye may be able to withstand in the evil day, and having done all, to stand. Stand therefore, having your loins girt about with truth, and having on the breastplate of righteousness" (Ep.6:13-14).

"And this I pray, that your love may abound yet more and more in knowledge and *in* all judgment; That ye may approve things that are excellent; that ye may be sincere and without offence till the day of Christ; Being filled with the fruits of righteousness, which are by Jesus Christ, unto the glory and praise of God" (Ph.1:9-11).

"And the Lord shall deliver me from every evil work, and will preserve *me* unto his heavenly kingdom: to whom *be* glory for ever and ever. Amen" (2 Ti.4:18).

"Teaching us that, denying ungodliness and worldly lusts, we should live soberly, righteously, and godly, in this present world; Looking for that blessed hope, and the glorious appearing of the great God and our Saviour Jesus Christ" (Tit.2:12-13).

"Who gave himself for us, that he might redeem us from all iniquity, and purify unto himself a peculiar people, zealous of good works" (Tit.2:14).

"Forasmuch then as the children are partakers of flesh and blood, he also himself likewise took part of the same; that through death he might destroy him that had the power of death, that is, the devil; And deliver them who through fear of death were all their lifetime subject to bondage" (He.2:14-15).

"Who his own self bare our sins in his own body on the tree, that we, being dead to sins, should live unto righteousness: by whose stripes ye were healed" (1 Pe.2:24).

"The Lord knoweth how to deliver the godly out of temptations, and to reserve the unjust unto the day of judgment to be punished" (2 Pe.2:9).

"But the day of the Lord will come as a thief in the night; in the which the heavens shall pass away with a great noise, and the elements shall melt with fervent heat, the earth also and the works that are therein shall be burned up. *Seeing* then *that* all these things shall be dissolved, what manner *of persons* ought ye to be in *all* holy conversation [conduct, behavior] and godliness, Looking for and hasting unto the coming of the day of God, wherein the heavens being on fire shall be dissolved, and the elements shall melt with fervent heat? Nevertheless we, according to his promise, look for new heavens and a new earth, wherein dwelleth righteousness. Wherefore, beloved, seeing that ye look for such things, be diligent that ye may be found of him in peace, without spot, and blameless" (2 Pe.3:10-14).

"And he said, The LORD *is* my rock, and my fortress, and my deliverer" (2 S.22:2).

"But I *am* poor and needy; *yet* the Lord thinketh upon me: thou *art* my help and my deliverer; make no tarrying, O my God" (Ps.40:17).

"Surely he shall deliver thee from the snare of the fowler, *and* from the noisome pestilence" (Ps.91:3).

"They reel to and fro, and stagger like a drunken man, and are at their wit's end. Then they cry unto the LORD in their trouble, and he bringeth them out of their distresses. He maketh the storm a calm, so that the waves thereof are still. Then are they glad because they be quiet; so he bringeth them unto their desired haven. Oh that *men* would praise the LORD *for* his goodness, and *for* his wonderful works to the children of men!" (Ps.107:27-31).

"Fear not: for I have redeemed thee, I have called *thee* by thy name; thou *art* mine. When thou passest through the waters, I *will be* with thee; and through the rivers, they shall not overflow thee: when thou walkest through the fire, thou shalt not be burned; neither shall the flame kindle upon thee" (Is.43:1-2).

"Be not afraid of their faces: for I *am* with thee to deliver thee, saith the LORD" (Je.1:8).

"Sow to yourselves in righteousness, reap in mercy; break up your fallow ground: for *it is* time to seek the LORD, till he come and rain righteousness upon you" (Ho.10:12).

---

2 (29:3-19) **Churches, Needs of, to Be Pure—Ministers, Needs of, to Be Sanctified—Sanctification, Duty—Ministers, Duty—Churches, Duty—Hezekiah, Reformation of—Temple, Cleansing of, Example**: right after his father's death, in the very first month of his independent rule, Hezekiah launched a reformation throughout the nation. Under Ahaz's leadership, the nation had been devastated by war, resulting in a wrecked economy, military, and political administration. All three branches of government desperately needed to be strengthened. Thus, as soon as Hezekiah could fully take over the nation's command, he embarked on a strategy to rebuild the economy and the military and to strengthen the political base. But note this significant fact: the focus of the author is the *spiritual reformation* that Hezekiah initiated. He focused solely upon the basic need of the people, that of returning to the LORD and of serving Him. If the people would return to the LORD, they would have the blessings of God as they sought to rebuild the nation economically and militarily.

a. Hezekiah's very first act as sole ruler of Judah was to reopen the doors of the temple (v.3). His wicked father had closed the temple and barricaded the doors in an attempt to irradicate the worship of the LORD.

b. As soon as the doors were opened and repaired, Hezekiah summoned all the religious leaders of the nation to a meeting at the temple in Jerusalem. He then drew them together in the courtyard just east of the temple.

c. Once they were assembled, Hezekiah challenged the religious workers to sanctify and cleanse themselves as well as the temple of the LORD. By this, he meant that they were to remove all sin and every defiling thing from their lives and from the temple (v.5). Both they and the temple needed to be sanctified, cleansed, and recommitted to the LORD. They needed to be totally set apart to His service. Four reasons were given for their sanctification.

    1) First, they needed to be cleansed because they and their forefathers had sinned and done evil. They had forsaken the LORD (v.6). Note that Hezekiah does not say "my father" but "our fathers." It was not just Ahaz who had been guilty of forsaking the LORD but the entire nation. For that reason, Hezekiah laid the guilt of apostasy at the feet of all the people.

    2) Second, they needed to be cleansed because they and their fathers had forsaken the LORD's temple, turning their backs upon Him and the worship of His Holy Name.

    3) Third, they needed to be cleansed because they and their fathers had shut the doors of the temple and put out the lamps, plunging the temple into total darkness. They had disallowed any worship there. In addition, they had not burned incense to symbolize the offering up of prayers to the LORD, nor had they presented any burnt offerings at the sanctuary. Simply stated, they had failed to seek atonement and reconciliation with the LORD, failed to offer up public worship to Him.

    4) Fourth, they needed to be cleansed because God's anger and judgment had been aroused. He had given them up to trouble, horror, and ridicule. He had given up their families to be conquered and exiled, enslaved by Syria, Samaria, Edom, and Philistia (28:5-10, 17-18).

d. There was only one answer for Judah: revival (vv.10-11). Hezekiah declared that he personally was going to make a renewed covenant, recommitment to the LORD. His purpose was to secure the favor of the LORD so the LORD would turn His fierce anger away from the nation.

After declaring his own intentions, Hezekiah with tenderness of heart addressed the religious workers as "my sons," calling upon them not to be negligent in their duty. They too needed to recommit their lives and renew their covenant with the LORD. As God's ministers, they represented Him and served Him. Therefore, they must sanctify and cleanse themselves in order to minister and burn incense before Him. Remember that incense symbolized prayer. It was necessary for the priests and Levites to be cleansed of all sin before they could pray and worship the LORD in purity of heart and life.

e. The Levites and priests immediately obeyed after Hezekiah's address. They went to work exactly as he had charged (vv.12-19).

    1) The Levites appointed leaders to supervise their work (vv.12-14). Two leaders were appointed from each of the three major clans: Kohath, Merari, and Gershon. Two leaders were also appointed from a fourth clan, Elizaphan (v.13). Other leaders were appointed from three clans of the Levitical musicians, the clans of Asaph, Zechariah, and Mattaniah (vv.13-14).

    2) After selecting their leadership, the Levites then sanctified themselves (v.15). This was a public service of sanctification, a service when they all assembled together as brothers, fellow servants of the LORD. Just picture the scene: a mass of priests and Levites gathered together in a service of recommitment to the LORD, sanctifying and setting themselves apart to serve the LORD with renewed devotion.

    3) Once the Levites had personally recommitting their lives to the LORD, they then sanctified and cleansed the temple (vv.15-17). Just as the king had charged and as the LORD's Word instructed, they carried out their tasks (1 Chr.28:12, 19). The Levites removed all the rubbish and every defiled thing from the sanctuary and piled it all out in the courtyard. They then carted all the rubbish out through the Kidron Valley (v.16). The cleansing of the temple took sixteen days altogether (v.17). Eight days were needed to clean the courts up to the portico or porch, and then eight more days were needed to cleanse the temple itself.

    4) After completing the cleansing of the temple, the Levites and priests went to the king and gave him their report (vv.18-19). They had cleansed the entire temple, the altar, the Table of Showbread, and all the utensils and articles used with each. Furthermore, they had recovered and sanctified (cleansed) all the items and utensils taken by King Ahaz when he closed the temple.

Thought 1. Ministers and churches have a responsibility to be holy and pure, for the LORD has set them apart to proclaim His Holy Word to the world and to minister to people. If the minister is slothful or living in sin, he becomes defiled and unclean before the LORD. As a result, the power of God does not rest upon his life, neither in preaching nor in ministering. He preaches and ministers without power, being empty and nothing more than sounding brass and tinkling cymbals (1 Co.13:1). As a poor, even bad, representative of the LORD, he is to face a far more severe judgment from the LORD. Why? Because the sinful, unclean, and defiled minister was given the unique privilege of proclaiming the unsearchable riches of Christ to a lost and dying world. For this reason, every minister of the gospel must be sanctified every day of his life, daily cleansed from sin and set apart anew to the LORD.

Similarly, the church must be sanctified, cleansed from all defilement and kept holy, set apart as a lighthouse for the LORD. Sitting on the streets of our cities and villages, the church building becomes a symbol of our need to worship and of the LORD's presence among us when we worship faithfully. For this reason, the church building is to be maintained and never abused. Unclean and shameful activities are not to be allowed in the church. Churches are not to be defiled by any behavior that dishonors or pollutes the air within the church or that damages the human body such as smoking, drinking alcoholic beverages, immoral or indecent activities, or any other pursuit that could arouse sinful behavior. The holy church is to be kept holy. It is to remain an atmosphere set apart for the worship of the LORD and the blessing of the people through the presence and health that God gives to his worshippers—both spiritual and physical health.

The sanctification or purity of the minister and of the church is an absolute essential. Listen to what God says about sanctification and holiness:

"Know ye not that ye are the temple of God, and *that* the Spirit of God dwelleth in you? If any man defile the temple of God, him shall God destroy; for the temple of God is holy, which *temple* ye are" (1 Co.3:16-17).

"Know ye not that the unrighteous shall not inherit the kingdom of God? Be not deceived: neither fornicators, nor idolaters, nor adulterers, nor effeminate, nor abusers of themselves with mankind, Nor thieves, nor covetous, nor drunkards, nor revilers, nor extortioners, shall inherit the kingdom of God. And such were some of you: but ye are washed, but ye are sanctified, but ye are justified in the name of the Lord Jesus, and by the Spirit of our God" (1 Co.6:9-11).

"What? know ye not that your body is the temple of the Holy Ghost *which is* in you, which ye have of God, and ye are not your own? For ye are bought with a price: therefore glorify God in your body, and in your spirit, which are God's" (1 Co.6:19-20).

"Having therefore these promises, dearly beloved, let us cleanse ourselves from all filthiness of the flesh and spirit, perfecting holiness in the fear of God" (2 Co.7:1).

"Husbands, love your wives, even as Christ also loved the church, and gave himself for it; That he might sanctify and cleanse it with the washing of water by the word, That he might present it to himself a glorious church, not having spot, or wrinkle, or any such thing; but that it should be holy and without blemish" (Ep.5:25-27).

"For this is the will of God, *even* your sanctification, that ye should abstain from fornication" (1 Th.4:3).

"And the very God of peace sanctify you wholly; and *I pray God* your whole spirit and soul and body be preserved blameless unto the coming of our Lord Jesus Christ" (1 Th.5:23).

"Follow peace with all *men,* and holiness, without which no man shall see the Lord" (He.12:14).

"But as he which hath called you is holy, so be ye holy in all manner of conversation; Because it is written, Be ye holy; for I am holy" (1 Pe.1:15-16).

"And let the priests also, which come near to the LORD, sanctify themselves, lest the LORD break forth upon them" (Ex.19:22).

"And ye shall be holy unto me: for I the LORD *am* holy, and have severed you from *other* people, that ye should be mine" (Le.20:26).

"And said unto them, Hear me, ye Levites, sanctify now yourselves, and sanctify the house of the LORD God of your fathers, and carry forth the filthiness out of the holy *place*" (2 Chr.29:5).

"Wash you, make you clean; put away the evil of your doings from before mine eyes; cease to do evil" (Is.1:16).

---

3 (29:20-36) **Beginning, New, Example of—Fresh Start, Example of—Worship, Duty, to Be Renewed—Rededication, of the Temple—Temple, Rededication of**: early in the morning on the day after receiving the report, Hezekiah led the people in a great rededication service for the newly sanctified temple. He and the people rededicated both their own lives and the temple to the LORD. No time was wasted in launching this new beginning, this fresh new start for worshipping of the LORD.

a. Rising earlier than usual, Hezekiah summoned all the city officials to join him in a rededication service in honor of the temple's being reopened and prepared for the worship of the LORD. Obviously, many of these officials had served in the evil and corrupt administration of King Ahaz. Therefore, they were just as guilty as Ahaz was of rejecting the LORD and misleading the people in the worship of idols. By summoning the officials to join him in a worship service of rededication, Hezekiah was taking a major stand for the LORD. He expected his officials to follow his example and to set a pattern for the people to follow. Also, by arising earlier than usual to summon the leaders, he demonstrated both excitement and devotion for the LORD, a fact that could not be missed by the royal officials.

1) Challenged by the example of their king, the leaders brought animals to be sacrificed as sin offerings to make atonement for their sins (see outline and notes—Le.4:1–5:13 for more discussion). Their purpose was to seek atonement...

- for the kingdom, which probably refers to the royal court, including the royal family and the royal officials of the nation
- for the sanctuary, which refers to the priests and Levites
- for Judah, which refers to the people or citizens of the nation

Seven of each kind of animal to be sacrificed were brought by the royal officials: seven bulls, seven rams, seven lambs, and seven male goats—all 28 animals to be presented as sin offerings for the personal sins of the officials as well as for the sins of the nation. Remember that the basic meaning of atonement is *covering* and *reconciliation*. By presenting these sin offerings to the LORD, the leaders were asking God to cover their sins and to reconcile them to the LORD through the substitute sacrifice of the animal. Also remember that the number seven symbolized perfection, completion. Thus, by bringing seven of each animal, the leaders were declaring a whole-hearted, complete recommitment to the LORD.

Taking the animals, the priests offered the sacrifices to the LORD and sprinkled the blood on the altar (v.22). When the king and the leaders laid their hands on the goats, they identified them as the substitute sacrifice. By this act, they were declaring their faith in the LORD and in His promise to free them from sin through the substitute sacrifice. Of course, the substitute sacrifice was a type of the coming Savior and Messiah of the world, the Lord Jesus Christ Himself, who was the *Perfect Sacrifice* for sin. After sacrificing the goats, the priests sprinkled their blood on the altar. Thus, atonement was made for all Israel through the sin offering. Note also that sacrifices were made for the burnt offering, which was a symbol of reconciliation with God (v.24).

2) The king stationed the Levite musicians in the temple for the dedication service (v.25). They were placed there just as David, Gad the king's seer, and Nathan the prophet had instructed. And they stood ready to sing and play their instruments and trumpets at the appropriate time (v.26).

3) As soon as the king ordered the burnt offering to be sacrificed and presented to the LORD, the musicians began to sing and play their instruments. They continued with their music throughout the sacrifice of the burnt offering (vv.27-28). While the singers sang and the priests presented their offerings to the LORD, the entire assembly bowed and worshipped the LORD (v.28).

4) The king and all the royal officials also knelt and worshipped the LORD after the offerings were made (v.29). Just picture the scene, the mass of people seeking forgiveness for their sins and reconciliation with God—everyone kneeling and worshipping the LORD. They were seeking Him with all their hearts. Even the city officials who had been a stumbling block, guilty of trying to exterminate the true worship of the LORD, were now kneeling, asking for forgiveness and reconciliation with the LORD.

5) While the people were worshipping, the Levites were singing praises to the LORD. Note what they sang: the psalms of David and of Asaph the seer, the very same songs that we find in the Holy Bible (v.30).

b. After the leadership of the nation sought forgiveness and reconciliation with God, King Hezekiah invited the congregation to bring their sacrifices and thanksgiving offerings (see outline and notes—Le.3:1-17 for more discussion). The people needed to personally seek the LORD for forgiveness and reconciliation just as the leadership had individually sought the LORD.

1) Many people responded positively, bringing their sacrifices and thanksgiving offerings to the LORD. When making the thanksgiving offering, a person was allowed to eat some of the meat as a meal. However, some of the people—those with willing hearts—brought burnt offerings in which the entire animal was sacrificed. The person received none of the meat. The point being made is that some of the people—those who gave whole animals for the burnt offerings—were more willing to follow the LORD than others were. In other words, some were seeking forgiveness and reconciliation more wholeheartedly, completely, or sincerely than others.

2) The offerings sacrificed were enormous in number:
   ⇒ the burnt offerings numbered 70 bulls, 100 rams, and 200 male lambs
   ⇒ the other offerings totaled 600 bulls and 3,000 sheep and goats (v.33)

3) As the scores of people brought their offerings, the line began to back up and become congested. The number of priests was insufficient to handle all the work involved in sacrificing the animals (v.34). There were just too few priests who had responded to Hezekiah's challenge to sanctify and cleanse themselves. Sadly, too many of the priests had been lax, complacent, slow to respond to the revival. But not so with the Levites. Many more of them had been conscientious about sanctifying and purifying themselves. For this reason, they stepped in to help, taking the place of the priests and presenting the sacrifices to the LORD.

4) Hezekiah was very encouraged by the outcome of his restoration of the temple worship service. The burnt offerings presented by the people were surprisingly numerous, as were the accompanying drink offerings and the sizeable amount of fat offered from the fellowship offerings (v.35). The large number of offerings indicated a tremendous response to the reopening of the temple, and a wonderful spirit of revival broke out among the people.

c. Within the very first month of Hezekiah's reign, he restored the temple and swung its doors wide open for worship. In concluding their first worship service in the newly restored temple, the king and the people rejoiced over what God had done—rejoicing especially because it had been accomplished so quickly (v.36).

Thought 1. The lesson for us is most challenging, that of getting a *new beginning in worship*. How many of us need a fresh start, a revitalization of our worship? For many of us, worship has become dull, uninteresting, irrelevant, impractical, having little to do with day-to-day life. Perhaps, the lessons and sermons come across as little more than stories about ancient history or as typical self-esteem, ego-boosting seminars or speeches. Maybe little is said or done that seems to make a difference in life. Many of us get little or nothing out of worship, little motivation or enthusiasm, guidance or direction, provision or supply, assurance or security. There appears to be a lack of true godly power—the power of salvation and deliverance—in the worship so many of us participate in, as well as our own personal worship.

A new beginning, a fresh start is desperately needed in our worship. We must take two steps to renew it, the very same steps taken by Hezekiah and the people of his day:

(1) First, the leaders of God's people must approach the LORD through the *substitute sacrifice* of the Lord Jesus Christ, the only Perfect Sacrifice that is acceptable to God. This was exactly what Hezekiah led his people to do. They first sought forgiveness of sins and reconciliation with God. And they sought forgiveness and reconciliation through the *substitute sacrifice* (vv.21-30).

(2) Second, after the leaders have recommitted their lives to the LORD, the invitation must be extended to the congregation to approach the LORD through the *substitute sacrifice* of the Lord Jesus Christ (vv.31-36).

BACKGROUND TO ISAIAH'S DAY

(The Four Kings Who Ruled During Isaiah's Ministry)

Approaching God through the Lord Jesus Christ will bring forgiveness of sins and reconciliation, for God forgives the sins of all who come to Him through the death of His Son. And when a person comes, God reconciles that person to Himself.

Reemphasizing the fact, a new beginning in worship can be achieved if, first, the leadership of God's people will recommit their lives to the LORD and, second, the people will follow the example of the leadership in recommitting their lives to the LORD. When we seek the LORD through Christ, the substitute sacrifice, God guarantees a new beginning in worship—whether corporately as a church body or individually. Listen to what God's Holy Word says:

"And that repentance and remission of sins should be preached in his name among all nations, beginning at Jerusalem" (Lu.24:47).

"God *is* a Spirit: and they that worship him must worship *him* in spirit and in truth" (Jn.4:24).

"Jesus saith unto him, I am the way, the truth, and the life: no man cometh unto the Father, but by me" (Jn.14:6).

"I beseech you therefore, brethren, by the mercies of God, that ye present your bodies a living sacrifice, holy, acceptable unto God, *which is* your reasonable service. And be not conformed to this world: but be ye transformed by the renewing of your mind, that ye may prove what is that good, and acceptable, and perfect, will of God" (Ro.12:1-2).

"For it is written, *As* I live, saith the Lord, every knee shall bow to me, and every tongue shall confess to God" (Ro.14:11).

"To wit, that God was in Christ, reconciling the world unto himself, not imputing their trespasses unto them; and hath committed unto us the word of reconciliation. Now then we are ambassadors for Christ, as though God did beseech *you* by us: we pray *you* in Christ's stead, be ye reconciled to God" (2 Co.5:19-20).

"And walk in love, as Christ also hath loved us, and hath given himself for us an offering and a sacrifice to God for a sweetsmelling savour" (Ep.5:2).

"Wherefore God also hath highly exalted him, and given him a name which is above every name: That at the name of Jesus every knee should bow, of *things* in heaven, and *things* in earth, and *things* under the earth; And *that* every tongue should confess that Jesus Christ *is* Lord, to the glory of God the Father" (Ph.2:9-11).

"Who gave himself for us, that he might redeem us from all iniquity, and purify unto himself a peculiar people, zealous of good works" (Tit.2:14).

"Who his own self bare our sins in his own body on the tree, that we, being dead to sins, should live unto righteousness: by whose stripes ye were healed" (1 Pe.2:24).

"For Christ also hath once suffered for sins, the just for the unjust, that he might bring us to God, being put to death in the flesh, but quickened by the Spirit" (1 Pe.3:18).

"That which we have seen and heard declare we unto you, that ye also may have fellowship with us: and truly our fellowship *is* with the Father, and with his Son Jesus Christ" (1 Jn.1:3).

"And they sing the song of Moses the servant of God, and the song of the Lamb, saying, Great and marvellous *are* thy works, Lord God Almighty; just and true *are* thy ways, thou King of saints" (Re.15:3).

"Look unto me, and be ye saved, all the ends of the earth: for I *am* God, and *there is* none else. I have sworn by myself, the word is gone out of my mouth *in* righteousness, and shall not return, That unto me every knee shall bow, every tongue shall swear" (Is.45:22-23).

V. THE REIGN OF HEZEKIAH (PART 2)—A MEANINGFUL CELEBRATION OF THE PASSOVER: A PICTURE OF TRUE REVIVAL, 2 CHR.30:1-27

OUTLINE	SCRIPTURE	SCRIPTURE	OUTLINE
1. The plans for a great Passover Feast: A picture of witnessing, inviting people to Christ, the Lamb of God a. The decision to celebrate the Passover 　1) The invitation was sent to *all Israel* & Judah 　2) The decision was made to celebrate the Passover in the second month, not as it usually was in the first month, Ex.12:1-2 　　• Due to the priests: Not enough of them had yet turned back—consecrated themselves—to the LORD 　　• Due to the people: They had not had time to travel to Jerusalem 　3) The king & his officials were pleased & in agreement about the decision b. The invitation to attend the Passover proclaimed throughout the entire nation 　1) The proclamation was sent from Beersheba to Dan: The farthest cities in the Southern & Northern Kingdoms 　2) The Passover had been neglected for a long time: Not many had observed it c. The message of the invitation, the proclamation, 2 Chr.7:14; 29:6-9; Zec.1:2-6 　1) Return to the LORD 　　• The LORD identified: The God of Abraham, Isaac, & Israel (Jacob) 　　• The promise made: He will return to you who have escaped death & exile 　2) Do not follow the sinful examples of your fathers & brothers 　　• They forsook the LORD 　　• God judged them, gave them up to desolation 　3) Do not be stubborn, unresponsive to God: Submit to Him 　4) Come to the temple (church) 　　• The place God has sanctified (set apart, made holy) forever 　　• The reason: God will turn His anger away	And Hezekiah sent to all Israel and Judah, and wrote letters also to Ephraim and Manasseh, that they should come to the house of the LORD at Jerusalem, to keep the passover unto the LORD God of Israel. 2 For the king had taken counsel, and his princes, and all the congregation in Jerusalem, to keep the passover in the second month. 3 For they could not keep it at that time, because the priests had not sanctified themselves sufficiently, neither had the people gathered themselves together to Jerusalem. 4 And the thing pleased the king and all the congregation. 5 So they established a decree to make proclamation throughout all Israel, from Beer-sheba even to Dan, that they should come to keep the passover unto the LORD God of Israel at Jerusalem: for they had not done *it* of a long *time in such sort* as it was written. 6 So the posts went with the letters from the king and his princes throughout all Israel and Judah, and according to the commandment of the king, saying, Ye children of Israel, turn again unto the LORD God of Abraham, Isaac, and Israel, and he will return to the remnant of you, that are escaped out of the hand of the kings of Assyria. 7 And be not ye like your fathers, and like your brethren, which trespassed against the LORD God of their fathers, *who* therefore gave them up to desolation, as ye see. 8 Now be ye not stiffnecked, as your fathers *were,* but yield yourselves unto the LORD, and enter into his sanctuary, which he hath sanctified for ever: and serve the LORD your God, that the fierceness of his wrath may turn away from you.	9 For if ye turn again unto the LORD, your brethren and your children *shall find* compassion before them that lead them captive, so that they shall come again into this land: for the LORD your God *is* gracious and merciful, and will not turn away *his* face from you, if ye return unto him. 10 So the posts passed from city to city through the country of Ephraim and Manasseh even unto Zebulun: but they laughed them to scorn, and mocked them. 11 Nevertheless divers of Asher and Manasseh and of Zebulun humbled themselves, and came to Jerusalem. 12 Also in Judah the hand of God was to give them one heart to do the commandment of the king and of the princes, by the word of the LORD. 13 And there assembled at Jerusalem much people to keep the feast of unleavened bread in the second month, a very great congregation. 14 And they arose and took away the altars that *were* in Jerusalem, and all the altars for incense took they away, and cast *them* into the brook Kidron. 15 Then they killed the passover on the fourteenth *day* of the second month: and the priests and the Levites were ashamed, and sanctified themselves, and brought in the burnt offerings into the house of the LORD. 16 And they stood in their place after their manner, according to the law of Moses the man of God: the priests sprinkled the blood, *which* they received of the hand of the Levites. 17 For *there were* many in the congregation that were not sanctified: therefore the Levites had the charge of the killing of the passovers for every one *that was* not clean,	from you 　5) Repent & God will have compassion upon you 　　• He will move the captors to release your families to return home 　　• The reason: He is gracious & compassionate 　　• The condition: He will not turn His face from you—if you repent d. The response to the invitation 　1) The vast majority of the Northern Kingdom scorned & ridiculed the messengers & the invitation 　2) Some men from three tribes did humble themselves & make the pilgrimage: Asher, Manasseh, & Zebulun 　3) Judah responded very favorably: Was stirred by the hand of God to obey the Word of God & to keep the Passover **2. The celebration of the Passover: A picture of genuine revival** a. The people assembled b. The people turned away from false worship: They arose & destroyed all the altars to false gods, throwing them into the Kidron Valley, 28:24 c. The people believed God's promise of salvation through the substitute sacrifice: They slaughtered the Passover lambs d. The religious workers consecrated themselves anew: They were shamed & stirred by the people's zeal 　1) They brought burnt offerings 　2) They then took their places at the temple & began to serve as God's law instructs 　　• They sprinkled the blood on the altar 　　• They helped the worshippers who were not ritually, ceremonially clean: Killed & sanctified the lambs, set them apart for the LORD

BACKGROUND TO ISAIAH'S DAY

(The Four Kings Who Ruled During Isaiah's Ministry)

OUTLINE	SCRIPTURE	SCRIPTURE	OUTLINE
e. The priests & Levites judged people by the intent of their hearts, not by ritual & ceremony 1) Most of the people from the Northern Kingdom were not supposed to eat the Passover meal: Because they were unfit, had not gone through the required ritual, Ex.12:43-49 2) Hezekiah prayed for them: Asked God to forgive & accept them 3) The LORD heard Hezekiah's prayer & healed them: Forgave & accepted them f. The people were filled with joyful praise 1) The people celebrated the Feast of Unleavened Bread for seven days: A symbol of the need & urgency to leave Egypt (the world) 2) The musicians sang & played music every day 3) The king encouraged the religious workers daily 4) The people continued the feast for seven days, sacrificing their peace or	to sanctify *them* unto the LORD. 18 For a multitude of the people, *even* many of Ephraim, and Manasseh, Issachar, and Zebulun, had not cleansed themselves, yet did they eat the passover otherwise than it was written. But Hezekiah prayed for them, saying, The good LORD pardon every one 19 *That* prepareth his heart to seek God, the LORD God of his fathers, though *he be* not *cleansed* according to the purification of the sanctuary. 20 And the LORD hearkened to Hezekiah, and healed the people. 21 And the children of Israel that were present at Jerusalem kept the feast of unleavened bread seven days with great gladness: and the Levites and the priests praised the LORD day by day, *singing* with loud instruments unto the LORD. 22 And Hezekiah spake comfortably unto all the Levites that taught the good knowledge of the LORD: and they did eat throughout the feast seven days, offering peace offerings, and making	confession to the LORD God of their fathers. 23 And the whole assembly took counsel to keep other seven days: and they kept *other* seven days with gladness. 24 For Hezekiah king of Judah did give to the congregation a thousand bullocks and seven thousand sheep; and the princes gave to the congregation a thousand bullocks and ten thousand sheep: and a great number of priests sanctified themselves. 25 And all the congregation of Judah, with the priests and the Levites, and all the congregation that came out of Israel, and the strangers that came out of the land of Israel, and that dwelt in Judah, rejoiced. 26 So there was great joy in Jerusalem: for since the time of Solomon the son of David king of Israel *there was* not the like in Jerusalem. 27 Then the priests the Levites arose and blessed the people: and their voice was heard, and their prayer came *up* to his holy dwelling place, *even* unto heaven.	fellowship offerings & confessing their sins g. The people decided to continue the festival for seven additional days 1) The king provided 1,000 bulls & 7,000 sheep & goats for sacrifice 2) The royal officials donated 1,000 bulls & 10,000 sheep & goats 3) The priests—a great number—renewed their commitment & returned to the ministry, 3 4) The people & religious workers—including the foreigners—rejoiced greatly in the LORD 5) The rejoicing was greater than any since the days of Solomon & David h. The priests & Levites prayed for the people, & their prayers were heard by God, 7:12

(30:1-27) **Introduction**: in observing people today, we see that far too many are lax, complacent, slothful, self-satisfied, overly comfortable, and too easygoing. There is a lack of ambition and diligence, an inner motivation that drives a person to do a good job, to complete the task, to succeed and to achieve. Far too many people are indulging themselves, living lives of extravagance, hoarding wealth instead of giving to meet the needs of the world. In addition, wickedness, immorality and violence are sweeping the earth. Righteousness and godliness seem to be on the decline.

If there has ever been a day when revival—a renewed spirit of righteousness and godliness is needed, it is today. A true revival is the subject of the present Scripture. As soon as King Hezekiah assumed the throne of Judah, he did all he could to launch a spiritual revival throughout the nation. For years the temple had been shut down and its doors barricaded there in an attempt to eliminate the worship of the LORD from the land. But within a period of one month, King Hezekiah had reestablished worship within the temple and the people experienced the first taste of genuine revival. Longing to see the revival continue, Hezekiah called the leadership of the nation together to discuss ways to strengthen the people's recommitment to the LORD.

In reading this account, the exiles returning with Ezra would be stirred to seek true revival among themselves. As they sought to restore *true worship* in the temple and to rebuild their nation, they desperately needed a continued spirit of renewal and new life filling their hearts and flowing among them. This is, *The Reign of Hezekiah (Part 2)—a Meaningful Celebration of the Passover: A Picture of True Revival*, 30:1-27.

    1. The plans for a great Passover Feast: a picture of witnessing, inviting people to Christ, the Lamb of God (vv.1-12).
    2. The celebration of the Passover: a picture of genuine revival (vv.13-27).

1 (30:1-12) **Witnessing, Example of—Passover, Celebration of—Hezekiah, Reformation of—Hezekiah, Attempt to Reunite Israel and Judah**: longing to keep the fires of revival burning within the hearts of his people, Hezekiah laid the plans for a great Passover Feast. The temple had been closed for years and no worship allowed within its sacred walls. But now the temple was restored and a great worship service had been held to celebrate its restoration. Many of the people had made recommitments to the LORD and their commitments needed to be strengthened, reinforced so they would remain faithful to the LORD. It was the season for the Passover, the most meaningful feast or festival of the Jews, for it celebrated their liberation from Egyptian slavery and the wonderful hope of the promised land. Hezekiah saw in this the opportunity to use

31

the Passover to strengthen the recommitment of the people and also to reinstate the annual celebration of this important feast. Scripture gives the details of the plans laid out by Hezekiah:

a. Once the decision to celebrate the Passover was made, the invitation to attend was sent to *all Israel* as well as to Judah (vv.1, 5). In celebrating the Passover, Hezekiah saw the opportunity to reach out in an attempt to reunite "*all Israel.*" Remember that the Northern Kingdom had earlier been conquered by the Assyrians and most of the people exiled and taken to Assyria as slaves (see outline and note—2 K.17:1-41 for more discussion). In ancient times, when a ruler conquered a nation and then deported its citizens, he left a few citizens behind to maintain the land and to provide some tribute to the conquering nation. In addition, the ruler usually replaced the conquered population with refugees from other nations. When the Assyrians conquered the northern kingdom of Israel, they did just this: they left a few Israelites behind and transported foreign refugees to Israel to maintain the land as a vassal state of Assyria. Thus Hezekiah saw an opportunity to reach out to the people of the Northern Kingdom. The potential for spiritually reuniting *all Israel* now existed. The Passover celebration could be used to call *all Israel* together in the worship of the LORD. If spiritual unity could be achieved and the people of both the Northern and Southern Kingdoms would recommit their lives to the LORD, perhaps the LORD would bless, reuniting and restoring the entire nation of Israel.

Hezekiah involved all the royal officials in the decision to celebrate the Passover (vv.2-3). Together they decided to celebrate it in the second month, not as it usually was in the first month (Ex.12:1-2; De.16:1-8). Bear in mind that Hezekiah had assumed the throne in the first month of the year and that he had immediately ordered the temple to be reopened and restored for worship. The Passover was ordinarily celebrated in the first month of the year, but preparing the temple for worship had taken sixteen days (29:17). This meant that Hezekiah would have to wait another year to celebrate the Pass-over or else make the decision to celebrate it in the second month. God's law did make allowances for the celebration date to be changed, in particular for people who were ritually defiled or absent due to being out of town traveling (Nu.9:9-14). Two reasons are given for Hezekiah's delaying the Passover:

⇒ The Passover needed to be delayed due to the priests. Not enough of them had yet been recruited, contacted, and challenged to recommit themselves to the LORD (v.3). More time was needed to spread the word of the restored temple to the priests throughout the nation. Once they heard and were challenged to sanctify themselves, many of them would respond.

⇒ Second, the Passover needed to be delayed in order to give people time to travel to Jerusalem. Delaying the Passover one month satisfied both the king and his officials (v.4). They were all in full agreement about the decision they were making.

b. Once the decision had been made to delay the feast, the invitation to attend the Passover was proclaimed throughout the entire nation (v.5). A proclamation was sent from Beersheba to Dan, which represented the farthest cities in the Southern and Northern Kingdoms. For over 200 years, since the days of Solomon, the Passover had been neglected as a national celebration at the temple (v.5). Very few of the people had been faithful in celebrating it.

c. Hezekiah sent letters of invitation and proclamation to all the people throughout both Judah and Israel (vv.6-9). In reality, the proclamation was a written sermon that included five points.

1) First, Hezekiah called upon the people to return to the LORD (v.6). He unmistakably identified the LORD as the true God in contrast to the false gods being worshipped by so many of the people. They must return to the God of Abraham, Isaac and Israel (Jacob). Note that Hezekiah was basing his call to the people upon the Abrahamic covenant, (see outline and note—Ge.12:1-3 for more discussion). It was in the Abrahamic covenant that the LORD had given the wonderful promise of the *promised land.* Because of the terrible oppression by the Assyrians, the people would have their hearts stirred with renewed hope when they were reminded of God's promises. Obviously Hezekiah mentioned Abraham for this very purpose, to arouse the people's hope for the restoration and reunification of the nation (promised land). In fact, Hezekiah declared that the LORD would return to all who had escaped death and exile at the hand of the Assyrians, if the people would just return to the LORD.

2) Second, Hezekiah warned the people: they must not follow the sinful example of their fathers and brothers (v.7). Their forefathers forsook the LORD, and the LORD judged them by allowing various nations to conquer and exile them, devastating the land and enslaving many of the people (28:5-10, 17-18; 2 K.17:1-41).

3) Third, Hezekiah challenged the people not to be stubborn, unresponsive to God (v.8). They must not continue to be stiff-necked, rejecting the LORD and refusing to obey His commandments. They must submit, yield to Him.

4) Fourth, Hezekiah challenged the people to come to the temple, the very place God had sanctified, set apart, and made holy forever (v.8). Note the wonderful hope Hezekiah held out for the people: if they would return to the LORD, worshipping and serving Him, God would turn His anger away from them. The implication is that He would restore and reunify them as a people as well as their nation, the promised land.

5) Fifth, Hezekiah challenged the people to repent, to turn away from their sin and return to the LORD (v.9). If they returned to Him, God would have compassion upon them. He would move upon the captors to release their families to return home to the promised land. God would do this because He is gracious and compassionate. But note, there was a condition: repentance. If they repented, He would not turn His face from them.

d. The response to the couriers' proclamation to the people was mixed (vv.10-12). The vast majority of the Northern Kingdom scorned and ridiculed the messengers and the invitation (v.10). However, some of the people from three tribes did humble themselves and make the pilgrimage to the temple in Jerusalem (v.11). Those who responded favorably were from the northern tribes of Asher, Manasseh, and Zebulun.

In the Southern Kingdom of Judah, the hand of the LORD was moving mightily upon the people, so a great number of them responded very positively (v.12). They obeyed the Word of the LORD and made the pilgrimage to keep the Pass-over.

Thought 1. This is a vivid picture of witnessing and of bearing strong testimony for the LORD, inviting people to Christ, the Lamb of God. If the world has ever needed to hear the message of the *Lamb* of God, it is today. Never has the gospel of Christ been so desperately needed. Witnesses for Christ—dynamic witnesses—are needed. If we are followers of Christ, we need to be proclaiming the wonderful salvation He has provided for people, for He is the Perfect *Lamb* of God. By His sacrificial death upon the cross, He bore the judgment of God against all hatred, brutality, savagery, enslavement, murder, rape, sexual abuse—all the sins of violence, lawlessness, and immorality. The Perfect *Lamb* of God—the Lord Jesus Christ—bore the penalty of death for our sins. He died for you and for me. Therefore, if we ask God to allow the death, the blood of Christ, to cover us, God's judgment will *pass over* us. God's judgment will never fall upon us, for Christ covered and bore our sins for us. This is the meaning of the *Passover*. If we trust Christ as our personal Savior to save us from sin through His death on the cross, we are spared from God's hand of judgment. It *passes over* us. His death, His blood covers our sins.

This wonderful, glorious message of salvation and deliverance must be proclaimed to the world. Listen to what God's Holy Word says:

(1) Jesus Christ is the Perfect Lamb of God. His blood cleanses us from all sin and removes the judgment of God from us.

"The next day John seeth Jesus coming unto him, and saith, Behold the Lamb of God, which taketh away the sin of the world" (Jn.1:29).

"For this is my blood of the new testament, which is shed for many for the remission of sins" (Mt.26:28).

"Take heed therefore unto yourselves, and to all the flock, over the which the Holy Ghost hath made you overseers, to feed the church of God, which he hath purchased with his own blood" (Ac.20:28).

"Much more then, being now justified by his blood, we shall be saved from wrath through him" (Ro.5:9).

"Purge out therefore the old leaven, that ye may be a new lump, as ye are unleavened. For even Christ our passover is sacrificed for us" (1 Co.5:7).

"How much more shall the blood of Christ, who through the eternal Spirit offered himself without spot to God, purge your conscience from dead works to serve the living God?" (He.9:14).

"Forasmuch as ye know that ye were not redeemed with corruptible things, *as* silver and gold, from your vain conversation [conduct, behavior] *received* by tradition from your fathers; But with the precious blood of Christ, as of a lamb without blemish and without spot" (1 Pe.1:18-19).

"But if we walk in the light, as he is in the light, we have fellowship one with another, and the blood of Jesus Christ his Son cleanseth us from all sin" (1 Jn.1:7).

"And from Jesus Christ, *who is* the faithful witness, *and* the first begotten of the dead, and the prince of the kings of the earth. Unto him that loved us, and washed us from our sins in his own blood" (Re.1:5).

"He was oppressed, and he was afflicted, yet he opened not his mouth: he is brought as a lamb to the slaughter, and as a sheep before her shearers is dumb, so he openeth not his mouth" (Is.53:7).

(2) We must bear strong witness and testimony to the Lamb of God, the Lord Jesus Christ.

"Whosoever therefore shall confess me before men, him will I confess also before my Father which is in heaven. But whosoever shall deny me before men, him will I also deny before my Father which is in heaven" (Mt.10:32-33).

"Go ye therefore, and teach all nations, baptizing them in the name of the Father, and of the Son, and of the Holy Ghost: Teaching them to observe all things whatsoever I have commanded you: and, lo, I am with you alway, *even* unto the end of the world. Amen" (Mt.28:19-20).

"And he said unto them, Go ye into all the world, and preach the gospel to every creature" (Mk.16:15).

"Also I say unto you, Whosoever shall confess me before men, him shall the Son of man also confess before the angels of God: But he that denieth me before men shall be denied before the angels of God" (Lu.12:8-9).

"And ye also shall bear witness, because ye have been with me from the beginning" (Jn.15:27).

"Then said Jesus to them again, Peace *be* unto you: as *my* Father hath sent me, even so send I you" (Jn.20:21).

"But ye shall receive power, after that the Holy Ghost is come upon you: and ye shall be witnesses unto me both in Jerusalem, and in all Judaea, and in Samaria, and unto the uttermost part of the earth" (Ac.1:8).

"And they were all filled with the Holy Ghost, and began to speak with other tongues, as the Spirit gave them utterance" (Ac.2:4).

"For we cannot but speak the things which we have seen and heard" (Ac.4:20).

"Go, stand and speak in the temple to the people all the words of this life. And when they heard *that*, they entered into the temple early in the morning, and taught. But the high priest came, and they that were with him, and called the council together, and all the senate of the children of Israel and sent to the prison to have them brought" (Ac.5:20-21).

"For thou shalt be his witness unto all men of what thou hast seen and heard" (Ac.22:15).

"We having the same spirit of faith, according as it is written, I believed, and therefore have I spoken; we also believe, and therefore speak" (2 Co.4:13).

"Be not thou therefore ashamed of the testimony of our Lord, nor of me his prisoner: but be thou partaker of the afflictions of the gospel according to the power of God" (2 Ti.1:8).

"These things speak, and exhort, and rebuke with all authority. Let no man despise thee" (Tit.2:15).

(The Four Kings Who Ruled During Isaiah's Ministry)

"But sanctify the Lord God in your hearts: and *be* ready always to *give* an answer to every man that asketh you a reason of the hope that is in you with meekness and fear" (1 Pe.3:15).

"Come *and* hear, all ye that fear God, and I will declare what he hath done for my soul" (Ps.66:16).

"I will mention the lovingkindnesses of the LORD, *and* the praises of the LORD, according to all that the LORD hath bestowed on us, and the great goodness toward the house of Israel, which he hath bestowed on them according to his mercies, and according to the multitude of his lovingkindnesses" (Is.63:7).

"Then they that feared the LORD spake often one to another: and the LORD hearkened, and heard *it*, and a book of remembrance was written before him for them that feared the LORD, and that thought upon his name" (Mal.3:16).

---

2 (30:13-27) **Revival, Example of—Renewal, Spiritual, Example of—Reawakening, Example of—Passover, Celebration**: at last, the long-awaited day arrived for the celebration of the Passover. And following immediately upon the heels of the Passover was the Feast of Unleavened Bread. Remember that the Festival of Unleavened Bread was tied to the Passover and that it was celebrated for seven full days. The Festival of Unleavened Bread symbolized the sudden and hasty flight of Israel from Egyptian slavery and their need to be *spiritually separated* from Egypt, a symbol of the world (see outline and note—Le.23:4-14, pt.2 for more discussion). Scripture paints an exciting picture of the joyful occasion:

a. People flooded into Jerusalem from all over the Northern and Southern Kingdoms, from both Israel and Judah. Those from the Northern Kingdom of Israel came primarily from the three tribes mentioned above, Asher, Manasseh, and Zebulun (v.11). People from Judah flooded in from all over the nation, being moved by the Spirit of God to respond favorably to Hezekiah's proclamation (v.13). Moreover, many of the people from Jerusalem and the surrounding villages had still recommitted their lives to the LORD and were already gripped by a spirit of revival.

b. In preparation for the Passover, the people continued their spiritual reformation. Before celebrating the Passover, they tore down and removed the altars in Jerusalem that had been set up by the wicked King Ahaz (28:24). They took the altars that had been built to the false gods, destroyed them, and threw them into the Kidron Valley. By destroying all the altars of the false gods, the people demonstrated the sincerity of their hearts in seeking the LORD, Him and Him alone.

c. The people were now ready to celebrate the Passover Feast with their hearts fully prepared (v.15). Believing God's promise of salvation through the *substitute sacrifice,* they slaughtered the Passover lambs (v.15).

d. Interestingly, the religious workers—priests and Levites—were put to shame by the renewed dedication and zeal of the laypersons. Keep in mind that many of the religious workers had been slow to respond to Hezekiah's call for spiritual renewal (v.3; 29:34). They had been lax and complacent in responding to the revival that was sweeping the nation, in particular among the laypersons. But when they witnessed the spirit of revival, the zeal that was gripping the laypeople, they obviously began to sense guilt and to be convicted by God's Spirit. They began to feel uneasy, embarrassed, and were aroused to recommit themselves anew to the LORD. Bringing their burnt offerings to the temple, the priests and Levites confessed their sins and approached the LORD through the *substitute sacrifice.* Now cleansed from their sins and consecrated before the LORD, they took their places at the temple and began to serve the people as they brought their sacrifices to be offered to the LORD. The priests sprinkled the blood of the sacrifice on the altar, just as God's law had instructed. Both the priests and Levites helped the worshippers who were not ritually, ceremonially clean (v.17). According to the law, it was the duty of family heads to kill the Passover lamb. But so many family heads had forsaken the LORD for so long, they also were not spiritually clean. For this reason, the Levites had to step in to kill the lambs for the family heads, sanctifying and setting them apart for the LORD.

e. Because such a large number of the people were spiritually unclean, the priests and Levites began to judge people by the intent of their heart, not by ritual and ceremony (vv.18-20). Most of the people from the Northern Kingdom were not supposed to eat the Passover meal because they were unfit; that is, they had not gone through the required ritual of cleans-ing (Ex.12:43-49). Remember that the Passover itself lasted only one day. Apparently, there were far too many people for the priests to handle within the time frame allowed. Therefore, Hezekiah and the priests allowed these people to par-ticipate in the *Passover meal.* Offering a special prayer in their behalf, Hezekiah asked God to forgive them for not following the strict *letter of the law,* beseeching the LORD to accept them because their hearts were set on seeking God (v.19). Scripture clearly states that the LORD heard Hezekiah's prayer and healed the people. That is, the LORD forgave and accepted them.

f. After offering the Passover sacrifice to the LORD, the people were filled with joyful praise and celebrated the Feast of Unleavened Bread for seven days (vv.21-22). Each day was filled with music as the musicians sang and played their instruments. Meanwhile the king encouraged the religious workers, in particular the Levites. For seven wonderful days the people continued to celebrate the festival. They sacrificed their peace or fellowship offerings and confessed their sins.

g. So great was the spirit of revival that swept over the people, they decided to continue the festival for seven additional days (vv.23-26). Due to the multitude of people seeking the LORD, there were not enough sacrificial animals available to meet the need. As a result, the king himself provided 1,000 bulls and 7,000 sheep and goats for sacrifice during this second week of services (v.24). Even the royal officials generously donated 1,000 bulls and 10,000 sheep and goats.

The spirit of revival sweeping across the land was so great that a large number of priests had renewed their commitment to the LORD and returned to the ministry (v.3, 15). Thus, all the people from both Judah and Israel, and all the priests and Levites, and all the foreigners who attended the festival rejoiced enthusiastically in the LORD (v.25). Not since the days of Solomon and David had there been such joy and rejoicing (v.26).

h. As the people came, either to make their sacrifices or for other reasons, the priests and Levites blessed and prayed for them (v.27). And their prayers reached up to heaven, the holy dwelling place of God Himself. Their prayers was heard by the LORD (7:12).

Thought 1. What a picture of genuine revival! A picture that shows us just how critically important it is today. God's church and people need to be renewed and revitalized. Revival must sweep this earth, revival that sees multitudes of believers recommitting their lives and unbelievers turning to the Lord Jesus Christ for salvation. Too many believers are lax, complacent, and comfortable, being *at ease in Zion*. Far too many have become worldly, fleshly, lusting after the pleasures and possessions of this world. Many have given in to the enticements of immorality, greed, fortune, and fame. Too few of us are obeying the commandment of God to assemble ourselves together in worship. Too few of us are living righteous and holy lives, bearing strong witness and testimony for the LORD. Only some of us are even trying to turn others to Christ or are faithful to the church, supporting it through our tithes and service.

And yet revival is necessary not only among the laypersons but also among the ministers of the church. Far too many ministers are living complacent, indulgent, worldly, and carnal lives. Many have given themselves over to lives of comfort and ease and to all the other sins listed in God's Holy Word, sins too terrible to mention when dealing with ministers of the gospel.

Wherever we look today, revival is needed. Every nation, as well as every community and church, need to be revived and led to make recommitments to the LORD. For this reason, God's people must be about the business of the LORD, working to bring about revival and renewal. Listen to what God's Holy Word says:

"For as the Father raiseth up the dead, and quickeneth *them;* even so the Son quickeneth whom he will" (Jn.5:21).

"It is the spirit that quickeneth; the flesh profiteth nothing: the words that I speak unto you, *they* are spirit, and *they* are life" (Jn.6:63).

"Then they that gladly received his word were baptized: and the same day there were added *unto them* about three thousand souls" (Ac.2:41).

"And the people with one accord gave heed unto those things which Philip spake, hearing and seeing the miracles which he did" (Ac.8:6).

"And all that dwelt at Lydda and Saron saw him, and turned to the Lord" (Ac.9:35).

"And the hand of the Lord was with them: and a great number believed, and turned unto the Lord" (Ac.11:21).

"I beseech you therefore, brethren, by the mercies of God, that ye present your bodies a living sacrifice, holy, acceptable unto God, *which is* your reasonable service. And be not conformed to this world: but be ye transformed by the renewing of your mind, that ye may prove what is that good, and acceptable, and perfect, will of God" (Ro.12:1-2).

"For which cause we faint not; but though our outward man perish, yet the inward *man* is renewed day by day. For our light affliction, which is but for a moment, worketh for us a far more exceeding *and* eternal weight of glory; While we look not at the things which are seen, but at the things which are not seen: for the things which are seen *are* temporal; but the things which are not seen *are* eternal" (2 Co.4:16-18).

"For godly sorrow worketh repentance to salvation not to be repented of: but the sorrow of the world worketh death" (2 Co.7:10).

"That ye put off concerning the former conversation [conduct, behavior] the old man, which is corrupt according to the deceitful lusts; And be renewed in the spirit of your mind; And that ye put on the new man, which after God is created in righteousness and true holiness" (Ep.4:22-24).

"And have put on the new *man,* which is renewed in knowledge after the image of him that created him" (Col.3:10).

"Not by works of righteousness which we have done, but according to his mercy he saved us, by the washing of regeneration, and renewing of the Holy Ghost" (Tit.3:5).

"Then the children of Israel did put away Baalim and Ashtaroth, and served the LORD only" (1 S.7:4).

"The LORD *is* nigh unto them that are of a broken heart; and saveth such as be of a contrite spirit" (Ps.34:18).

"Create in me a clean heart, O God; and renew a right spirit within me" (Ps.51:10).

"Restore unto me the joy of thy salvation; and uphold me *with thy* free spirit. *Then* will I teach transgressors thy ways; and sinners shall be converted unto thee" (Ps.51:12-13).

"The sacrifices of God *are* a broken spirit: a broken and a contrite heart, O God, thou wilt not despise" (Ps.51:17).

"Turn us again, O God of hosts, and cause thy face to shine; and we shall be saved" (Ps.80:7).

"So will not we go back from thee: quicken us, and we will call upon thy name" (Ps.80:18).

"Wilt thou not revive us again: that thy people may rejoice in thee?" (Ps.85:6).

"My soul cleaveth unto the dust: quicken thou me according to thy word" (Ps.119:25).

"Behold, I have longed after thy precepts: quicken me in thy righteousness" (Ps.119:40).

"Quicken me, O LORD, for thy name's sake: for thy righteousness' sake bring my soul out of trouble" (Ps.143:11).

"Until the spirit be poured upon us from on high, and the wilderness be a fruitful field, and the fruitful field be counted for a forest. Then judgment shall dwell in the wilderness, and righteousness remain in the fruitful field. And the work of righteousness shall be peace; and the effect of righteousness quietness and assurance for ever" (Is.32:15-17).

"But they that wait upon the LORD shall renew *their* strength; they shall mount up with wings as eagles; they shall run, and not be weary; *and* they shall walk, and not faint" (Is.40:31).

"Blessed *is* the man *that* doeth this, and the son of man *that* layeth hold on it; that keepeth the sabbath from polluting it, and keepeth his hand from doing any evil" (Is.56:2).

BACKGROUND TO ISAIAH'S DAY

(The Four Kings Who Ruled During Isaiah's Ministry)

"A new heart also will I give you, and a new spirit will I put within you: and I will take away the stony heart out of your flesh, and I will give you an heart of flesh" (Eze.36:26).

"And rend your heart, and not your garments, and turn unto the LORD your God: for he *is* gracious and merciful, slow to anger, and of great kindness, and repenteth him of the evil" (Joel 2:13).

"O LORD, I have heard thy speech, *and* was afraid: O LORD, revive thy work in the midst of the years, in the midst of the years make known; in wrath remember mercy" (Hab.3:2).

VI. THE REIGN OF HEZEKIAH (PART 3)—HIS RELIGIOUS REFORMS: THE PICTURE OF A REVIVED, ORDERLY CHURCH, 2 CHR.31:1-21

OUTLINE	SCRIPTURE	SCRIPTURE	OUTLINE
1. The people rejected false worship: Realizing the powerlessness & hopelessness of false worship a. They destroyed the false worship centers throughout Judah when they left the Passover: Destroyed both the idols & the sites (high places) throughout Judah, Benjamin, Ephraim, & Manasseh b. They were totally committed: Would not return home until all gods & sites were destroyed **2. The king reestablished regular worship services: Worshipping the LORD** a. Hezekiah reorganized the priests & Levites into divisions: Based upon their duties, 1 Chr.23:1–26:28 1) To present the offerings 2) To minister & serve 3) To give thanks & praise b. Hezekiah personally provided for the temple from his own wealth: Gave the burnt offerings for the regular worship services **3. The king commanded the people to support the religious workers: Giving to support the LORD's work** a. The purpose: So the workers could devote themselves to God's Word b. The response of the people 1) The people gave • Gave the firstfruits (very first) of their produce • Gave a tithe of their livestock • Gave over a period of five months	Now when all this was finished, all Israel that were present went out to the cities of Judah, and brake the images in pieces, and cut down the groves, and threw down the high places and the altars out of all Judah and Benjamin, in Ephraim also and Manasseh, until they had utterly destroyed them all. Then all the children of Israel returned, every man to his possession, into their own cities. 2 And Hezekiah appointed the courses of the priests and the Levites after their courses, every man according to his service, the priests and Levites for burnt offerings and for peace offerings, to minister, and to give thanks, and to praise in the gates of the tents of the LORD. 3 *He appointed* also the king's portion of his substance for the burnt offerings, *to wit,* for the morning and evening burnt offerings, and the burnt offerings for the sabbaths, and for the new moons, and for the set feasts, as *it is* written in the law of the LORD. 4 Moreover he commanded the people that dwelt in Jerusalem to give the portion of the priests and the Levites, that they might be encouraged in the law of the LORD. 5 And as soon as the commandment came abroad, the children of Israel brought in abundance the firstfruits of corn, wine, and oil, and honey, and of all the increase of the field; and the tithe of all *things* brought they in abundantly. 6 And *concerning* the children of Israel and Judah, that dwelt in the cities of Judah, they also brought in the tithe of oxen and sheep, and the tithe of holy things which were consecrated unto the LORD their God, and laid *them* by heaps. 7 In the third month they began to lay the foundation of	the heaps, and finished *them* in the seventh month. 8 And when Hezekiah and the princes came and saw the heaps, they blessed the LORD, and his people Israel. 9 Then Hezekiah questioned with the priests and the Levites concerning the heaps. 10 And Azariah the chief priest of the house of Zadok answered him, and said, Since *the people* began to bring the offerings into the house of the LORD, we have had enough to eat, and have left plenty: for the LORD hath blessed his people; and that which is left *is* this great store. 11 Then Hezekiah commanded to prepare chambers in the house of the LORD; and they prepared *them,* 12 And brought in the offerings and the tithes and the dedicated *things* faithfully: over which Cononiah the Levite *was* ruler, and Shimei his brother *was* the next. 13 And Jehiel, and Azaziah, and Nahath, and Asahel, and Jerimoth, and Jozabad, and Eliel, and Ismachiah, and Mahath, and Benaiah, *were* overseers under the hand of Cononiah and Shimei his brother, at the commandment of Hezekiah the king, and Azariah the ruler of the house of God. 14 And Kore the son of Imnah the Levite, the porter toward the east, *was* over the freewill offerings of God, to distribute the oblations of the LORD, and the most holy things. 15 And next him *were* Eden, and Miniamin, and Jeshua, and Shemaiah, Amariah, and Shecaniah, in the cities of the priests, in *their* set office, to give to their brethren by courses, as well to the great as to the small: 16 Beside their genealogy of males, from three years old and upward, *even* unto every one that entereth into the	2) The king & his officials visited the High Priest to get a report on the offerings • Saw huge piles of gifts & praised the LORD • Asked the High Priest for a report on the offerings 3) The High Priest Azariah gave a wonderful report to the king & his officials • The religious workers had plenty to eat & to spare since the people began to bring their offerings • The balance—what was left over—was lying there in huge piles 4) The king, after hearing the report, immediately issued an order for the temple storerooms to be prepared 5) The offerings & gifts were then locked in the storerooms—faithfully c. The assignment of supervisors to oversee the collection & distribution of the offerings 1) The chief supervisor was Conaniah, & his brother Shimei was his assistant: Ten other deputy supervisors served under them 2) The chief supervisor of the freewill offerings & their distribution was Kore: He was assisted by six deputy Levites • They distributed the offerings to the priests who lived outside of Jerusalem, Jos.21:18-19 • They distributed to all males three years old & older who had been dedicated to the

BACKGROUND TO ISAIAH'S DAY

(The Four Kings Who Ruled During Isaiah's Ministry)

OUTLINE	SCRIPTURE	SCRIPTURE	OUTLINE
ministry & the temple by their parents	house of the LORD, his daily portion for their service in their charges according to their courses;	fields of the suburbs of their cities, in every several city, the men that were expressed by name, to give portions to	Certain men were appointed to deliver adequate portions to them
• They distributed to all priests who were listed in the genealogical records by families & to all who were 21 years old & older	17 Both to the genealogy of the priests by the house of their fathers, and the Levites from twenty years old and upward, in their charges by their courses;	all the males among the priests, and to all that were reckoned by genealogies among the Levites.	
• They did not neglect the families: They distributed to the families of all the priests	18 And to the genealogy of all their little ones, their wives, and their sons, and their daughters, through all the congregation: for in their set office they sanctified themselves in holiness:	20 And thus did Hezekiah throughout all Judah, and wrought *that which was* good and right and truth before the LORD his God. 21 And in every work that he began in the service of the house of God, and in the law, and in the commandments, to	**4. The king served the LORD faithfully: Being totally committed** a. He did what was good & right before God b. He sought God wholeheartedly in everything 1) In the service of God's house
• They did not forget the priest in rural areas:	19 Also of the sons of Aaron the priests, *which were* in the	seek his God, he did *it* with all his heart, and prospered.	2) In obedience to God's Word & commandments

(31:1-21) **Introduction**: despite the wretched state that the world is in, the tragic condition and the outright wickedness and immorality, the church today seems lethargic, sluggish, apathetic, somewhat drowsy and sleepy-eyed. A spirit of slumber, unconcern, and inactivity has crept into the lives of countless believers. Many have become indifferent, forgetting the mission of the LORD to reach the world for Christ. Too few are witnessing and sharing the gospel of Christ. Many believers have even forsaken the church, failing to consistently worship the LORD, the LORD whom they profess has saved them. A concern for lost family members is lacking in the hearts of many believers. Far too many have made promises to serve the LORD and His church, but they have broken their promises. Many believers served in the past, but now they have resigned their positions of service and are inactive.

Even more tragic is the apostasy being committed by so-called believers. Untold numbers have turned away from the LORD. They no longer follow Him. They have turned to sin and wickedness. Slipping into immorality, lawlessness, and sometimes violence, believers are dishonoring the LORD. The very name of God is discredited and shamed when a believer…

- looks at pornography
- curses or uses profanity
- tells off-colored jokes
- becomes intoxicated
- commits immorality
- abuses a spouse or child verbally, mentally, or physically
- becomes bitter or vengeful
- gives in to covetousness or greed
- fails to study the Scripture and pray
- fails to worship and bear witness for the LORD

If there has ever been a day when revival within the church is needed, it is today. God's people need to be broken over their sins. They need to confess and repent by turning from their wicked ways and coming back to the LORD. A spirit of revival needs to flood the hearts of God's people and sweep throughout the church and the world.

God's people in both Judah and Israel had just experienced a marvelous revival. A summons had been sent throughout all the land by King Hezekiah, inviting the people to celebrate the Passover and the Festival of Unleavened Bread. In response, thousands of people had flooded to the temple in Jerusalem to seek the LORD with renewed hearts and to celebrate the Passover festival. As soon as the celebration began, God poured out a spirit of revival upon the people. A desire to reform the nation, to turn the nation back to the LORD, filled the hearts of both Hezekiah and the people. As a result, a number of major reforms were launched. Several of these are discussed in the present Scripture. In reading about these reforms, the returning exiles under Ezra would be encouraged to reinstitute the very same changes and improvements. For just as the LORD blessed Hezekiah and his people in carrying out their reforms, so the LORD would bless the exiles as they sought to reinstitute *true worship* within the temple and rebuild their nation. And just as it took both clergy and laypersons during the days of Hezekiah, so the returning exiles needed everyone helping them in their restoration task. This is, *The Reign of Hezekiah (Part 3)—His Religious Reforms: The Picture of a Revived, Orderly Church*, 31:1-21.

1. The people rejected false worship: realizing the powerlessness and hopelessness of false worship (v.1).
2. The king reestablished regular worship services: worshipping the LORD (vv.2-3).
3. The king commanded the people to support the religious workers: giving to support the LORD'S work (vv.4-19).
4. The king served the LORD faithfully: being totally committed (vv.20-21).

1 (31:1) **Idolatry, Rejection of, Example—Worship, False, Rejection of—Idols, Powerlessness and Hopelessness of—Powerlessness, of Idols, Example of—Hopelessness, of False Worship, Example—Hezekiah, Reformation of—Revival, Results of—Reformation, Results of**: continuing his religious reform, Hezekiah led the people to reject false worship, for he knew the powerlessness and hopelessness of worshipping false gods.

For fourteen days the people had been celebrating the Passover and the Festival of Unleavened Bread. A powerful spirit of revival now gripped their hearts. Prior to leaving Jerusalem, the people apparently made the decision to destroy all their idols and false worship centers when they got back home. Therefore, while traveling and as the caravans of pilgrims reached one city after another, the people would join together to destroy the idols and false worship centers of that particular city. They destroyed all the sites of false worship throughout Judah and Benjamin and in the former Northern Kingdom, particularly in Ephraim and Manasseh. The people had been genuinely revived, making renewed commitments to the LORD. A righteous anger against sin and a holy zeal for the LORD were flooding their hearts. The LORD and the LORD alone is the only living and true God. Thus He and He alone is to be worshipped. All other gods are nothing more than the creation of man's mind. They are false gods, powerless to help people in the hour of their need. False gods leave people hopeless, without any possibility of help whatsoever. Consequently, all the images of false gods and all the sites of false worship were to be utterly destroyed. None were to be spared. No matter how ancient the false religion was, or how costly, attractive, or popular, the false worship centers were, they were all to be destroyed.

Note the depth of the people's revived spirit, the sincerity of their renewed commitment. They would not return home until all false worship centers were destroyed. They were totally devoted to the worship of the LORD, to worshipping Him and Him alone.

Thought 1. False worship is to be deliberately and totally rejected, for it dooms a person to a tragic end. First, if we engage in false worship, our spirits become helpless, powerless. The living and true LORD is not with us if we are worshipping false gods. His presence and power are not available to help us when we face the crises, trials, and temptations of life. We are left to ourselves and to what help other people can give us. Why? Because false gods are nothing more than the creation of people's thoughts and ideas, nothing more than what a person imagines god to be.

Second, false gods doom us to an eternity of hopelessness. Only the living and true God can deliver us from death and give us eternal life. And, as important, only He can deliver us from the judgment and hell that God's Holy Word says are coming. False gods are empty, vacant, blank. Therefore, if our hope is in false gods, then our hope is false, misplaced, and empty. For a false god is not living and is utterly helpless to give us hope. A non-existent god has no power to impart hope or anything else to us.

Again, false gods are non-existent; they are powerless and helpless. Consequently, worshipping false gods leaves us powerless to conquer the trials and temptations of this life. Worshipping false gods also leaves us powerless to conquer death and to be delivered from the judgment and hell to come. Listen to what God says about idolatry and false worship:

"Forasmuch then as we are the offspring of God, we ought not to think that the Godhead is like unto gold, or silver, or stone, graven by art and man's device" (Ac.17:29).

"For the wrath of God is revealed from heaven against all ungodliness and unrighteousness of men, who hold the truth in unrighteousness; Because that which may be known of God is manifest in them; for God hath showed *it* unto them. For the invisible things of him from the creation of the world are clearly seen, being understood by the things that are made, *even* his eternal power and Godhead; so that they are without excuse: Because that, when they knew God, they glorified *him* not as God, neither were thankful; but became vain in their imaginations, and their foolish heart was darkened. Professing themselves to be wise, they became fools, And changed the glory of the uncorruptible God into an image made like to corruptible man, and to birds, and fourfooted beasts, and creeping things. Wherefore God also gave them up to uncleanness through the lusts of their own hearts, to dishonour their own bodies between themselves: Who changed the truth of God into a lie, and worshipped and served the creature more than the Creator, who is blessed for ever. Amen" (Ro.1:18-25).

"As concerning therefore the eating of those things that are offered in sacrifice unto idols, we know that an idol *is* nothing in the world, and that *there is* none other God but one. For though there be that are called gods, whether in heaven or in earth, (as there be gods many, and lords many,) But to us *there is but* one God, the Father, of whom *are* all things, and we in him; and one Lord Jesus Christ, by whom *are* all things, and we by him" (1 Co.8:4-6).

"Ye know that ye were Gentiles, carried away unto these dumb idols, even as ye were led" (1 Co.12:2).

"Little children, keep yourselves from idols. Amen" (1 Jn.5:21).

"Thou shalt have no other gods before me. Thou shalt not make unto thee any graven image, or any likeness *of any thing* that *is* in heaven above, or that *is* in the earth beneath, or that *is* in the water under the earth: Thou shalt not bow down thyself to them, nor serve them: for I the LORD thy God *am* a jealous God, visiting the iniquity of the fathers upon the children unto the third and fourth *generation* of them that hate me" (Ex.20:3-5).

"Ye shall make you no idols nor graven image, neither rear you up a standing image, neither shall ye set up *any* image of stone in your land, to bow down unto it: for I *am* the LORD your God" (Le.26:1).

"The graven images of their gods shall ye burn with fire: thou shalt not desire the silver or gold *that is* on them, nor take *it* unto thee, lest thou be snared therein: for it *is* an abomination to the LORD thy God" (De.7:25).

"Take heed to yourselves, that your heart be not deceived, and ye turn aside, and serve other gods, and worship them" (De.11:16).

"There shall no strange god be in thee; neither shalt thou worship any strange god" (Ps.81:9).

"Not unto us, O LORD, not unto us, but unto thy name give glory, for thy mercy, *and* for thy truth's sake. Wherefore should the heathen say, Where *is* now their God? But our God *is* in the heav-ens: he hath done whatsoever he hath pleased. Their idols *are* silver and gold, the work of men's hands. They have mouths, but they speak not: eyes have they, but they see not: They have ears, but they hear not: noses have they, but they smell not: They have hands, but they handle not: feet have they, but they walk not: neither speak they through their throat. They that make them are like unto them; *so is* every one that trusteth in them" (Ps.115:1-8).

(The Four Kings Who Ruled During Isaiah's Ministry)

"To whom then will ye liken God? or what likeness will ye compare unto him? The workman melteth a graven image, and the goldsmith spreadeth it over with gold, and casteth silver chains. He that *is* so impoverished that he hath no oblation chooseth a tree *that* will not rot; he seeketh unto him a cunning workman to prepare a graven image, *that* shall not be moved. Have ye not known? have ye not heard? hath it not been told you from the beginning? have ye not understood from the foundations of the earth? *It is* he that sitteth upon the circle of the earth, and the inhabitants thereof *are* as grasshoppers; that stretcheth out the heavens as a curtain, and spreadeth them out as a tent to dwell in: That bringeth the princes to nothing; he maketh the judges of the earth as vanity. Yea, they shall not be planted; yea, they shall not be sown: yea, their stock shall not take root in the earth: and he shall also blow upon them, and they shall wither, and the whirlwind shall take them away as stubble. To whom then will ye liken me, or shall I be equal? saith the Holy One. Lift up your eyes on high, and behold who hath created these *things,* that bringeth out their host by number: he calleth them all by names by the greatness of his might, for that *he is* strong in power; not one faileth. Why sayest thou, O Jacob, and speakest, O Israel, My way is hid from the LORD, and my judgment is passed over from my God? Hast thou not known? hast thou not heard, *that* the everlasting God, the LORD, the Creator of the ends of the earth, fainteth not, neither is weary? *there is* no searching of his understanding. He giveth power to the faint; and to *them that have* no might he increaseth strength. Even the youths shall faint and be weary, and the young men shall utterly fall: But they that wait upon the LORD shall renew *their* strength; they shall mount up with wings as eagles; they shall run, and not be weary; *and* they shall walk, and not faint" (Is.40:18-31).

"I *am* the LORD: that *is* my name: and my glory will I not give to another, neither my praise to graven images" (Is.42:8).

"Assemble yourselves and come; draw near together, ye *that are* escaped of the nations: they have no knowledge that set up the wood of their graven image, and pray unto a god *that* cannot save" (Is.45:20).

"They *are* upright as the palm tree, but speak not: they must needs be borne, because they cannot go. Be not afraid of them; for they cannot do evil, neither also *is it* in them to do good" (Je.10:5).

2 (31:2-3) **Worship, Duty—Ministers, Duty—Priests, Duty—Levites, Duty—Worship, Services of, Organized—Hezekiah, Religious Reforms—Reformation, Religious, of Hezekiah**: right after celebrating the Passover, Hezekiah reestablished regular worship services within the temple. To do this he had to reorganize the priests and Levites, reassigning them to their tasks (1 Chr.23:1-26:28). Remember, his father had closed the temple, barricading the doors in an attempt to eliminate the worship of the LORD throughout the land. As a result, the various responsibilities of the religious workers and of worship itself had fallen into utter chaos. In reestablishing regular worship within the temple, Hezekiah needed to reassign the priests and Levites to their various divisions of service and to spell out their duties. Their duties were threefold:

⇒ to present the burnt offerings daily to the LORD as well as the special offerings brought by the people
⇒ to serve and minister to both the LORD and the people
⇒ to offer thanksgiving and praise to the LORD within the gates of the temple

As David and Solomon had been faithful in worship and in supporting the temple and Hezekiah followed their example (1 Chr.29:1-5; 2 Chr.9:10-11). He set a dynamic example of personal worship and of supporting the temple from his own wealth (v.3). He personally gave all the animals for both the morning and evening burnt offerings as well as for the burnt offerings on the Sabbath, special holidays, and festivals.

Thought 1. Hezekiah is a dynamic example for us. He established regular worship services for the people and was personally faithful in worshipping the LORD, likewise must we be. Worship is due the LORD. He is the Creator and Sustainer of the universe, the Maker of heaven and earth and all that is therein. He is the Sovereign LORD, having established and overseen all the laws that control the universe and human life. All glory and majesty belong to Him, and all dominion and power are His forever and ever.

Who the LORD is—His person, His being—demands that we worship Him. In addition, what the LORD has done demands that we worship Him. The LORD has not only given us life upon this earth, but He has also provided salvation for us. And no greater provision could be given us than to be saved from sin with all its bondages; from death with all its apprehension, dread, and fear; and from hell with all its torment and horror. Salvation from sin, death, and hell—no greater gift could ever be granted us. This is what the LORD has done for us: redeemed us from all the entrapments of this life. Through His salvation we can live victoriously, conquering all the crises and temptations that confront us. Furthermore, the LORD has made it possible for us never to experience death but instead to live with Him eternally.

Because of who the LORD is and what He has done for us, He is to be worshipped. Listen to what God's Holy Word says about worship:

"Then saith Jesus unto him, Get thee hence, Satan: for it is written, Thou shalt worship the Lord thy God, and him only shalt thou serve" (Mt.4:10).

"Let your light so shine before men, that they may see your good works, and glorify your Father which is in heaven" (Mt.5:16).

"And he came to Nazareth, where he had been brought up: and, as his custom was, he went into the synagogue on the sabbath day, and stood up for to read" (Lu.4:16).

"And they worshipped him, and returned to Jerusalem with great joy: And were continually in the temple, praising and blessing God. Amen" (Lu.24:52-53).

"And they, continuing daily with one accord in the temple, and breaking bread from house to house, did eat their meat with gladness and singleness of heart, Praising God, and having favour with all the people. And the Lord added to the church daily such as should be saved" (Ac.2:46-47).

"Now the God of patience and consolation grant you to be likeminded one toward another according to Christ Jesus: That ye may with one mind *and* one mouth glorify God, even the Father of our Lord Jesus Christ" (Ro.15:5-6).

"What? know ye not that your body is the temple of the Holy Ghost *which is* in you, which ye have of God, and ye are not your own? For ye are bought with a price: therefore glorify God in your body, and in your spirit, which are God's" (1 Co.6:19-20).

"Giving thanks unto the Father, which hath made us meet to be partakers of the inheritance of the saints in light" (Col.1:12).

"In every thing give thanks: for this is the will of God in Christ Jesus concerning you" (1 Th.5:18).

"*Let your* conversation *be* without covetousness; *and be* content with such things as ye have: for he hath said, I will never leave thee, nor forsake thee" (He.13:5).

"But ye *are* a chosen generation, a royal priesthood, an holy nation, a peculiar people; that ye should show forth the praises of him who hath called you out of darkness into his marvellous light" (1 Pe.2:9).

"Fear God, and give glory to him; for the hour of his judgment is come: and worship him that made heaven, and earth, and the sea, and the fountains of waters" (Re.14:7).

"Then saith he unto me, See *thou do it* not: for I am thy fellowservant, and of thy brethren the prophets, and of them which keep the sayings of this book: worship God" (Re.22:9).

"But unto the place which the LORD your God shall choose out of all your tribes to put his name there, *even* unto his habitation shall ye seek, and thither thou shalt come" (De.12:5).

"Sing praises to the LORD, which dwelleth in Zion: declare among the people his doings" (Ps.9:11).

"LORD, I have loved the habitation of thy house, and the place where thine honour dwelleth" (Ps.26:8).

"One *thing* have I desired of the LORD, that will I seek after; that I may dwell in the house of the LORD all the days of my life, to behold the beauty of the LORD, and to enquire in his temple" (Ps.27:4).

"Praise the LORD with harp: sing unto him with the psaltery *and* an instrument of ten strings" (Ps.33:2).

"And my tongue shall speak of thy righteousness *and* of thy praise all the day long" (Ps.35:28).

"Let the people praise thee, O God; let all the people praise thee" (Ps.67:3).

"Blessed *are* they that dwell in thy house: they will be still praising thee. Selah" (Ps.84:4).

"For a day in thy courts *is* better than a thousand. I had rather be a doorkeeper in the house of my God, than to dwell in the tents of wickedness" (Ps.84:10).

"O come, let us worship and bow down: let us kneel before the LORD our maker" (Ps.95:6).

"O worship the LORD in the beauty of holiness: fear before him, all the earth" (Ps.96:9).

"Enter into his gates with thanksgiving, *and* into his courts with praise: be thankful unto him, *and* bless his name" (Ps.100:4).

"Seven times a day do I praise thee because of thy righteous judgments" (Ps.119:164).

"I was glad when they said unto me, Let us go into the house of the LORD" (Ps.122:1).

"Let them give glory unto the LORD, and declare his praise in the islands" (Is.42:12).

---

3 (31:4-19) **Support, of the Church—Support, of the LORD's Work—Stewardship, Duty—Giving, to the Church, Example of—Reformation, of Stewardship—Hezekiah, Reforms of, Stewardship—Ministers, Duty, to Study and Administer God's Word**: Hezekiah's reformation also restored the offerings that supported the priests and Levites (see outline and notes—Le.6:8–7:38; Nu.18:8-32; De.14:22-29; 18:1-8; 26:1-11). The offerings had long been neglected, especially during the years when the worship services were stopped by King Ahaz (28:24). Without support, the priests and Levites would not have time to conduct the worship services and minister to the people. They would have to be out working at secular employment. Thus, reinstating the offerings to support the LORD's work was an absolute essential.

a. The purpose for reinstating the offerings is stated in a very clear and straightforward manner: the priests and their associates needed to devote themselves to God's law, His Holy Word (v.4). If they had to be out working for a livelihood, they would not have the time to prepare and conduct the worship services nor to minister to the people. Support was an absolute essential for them to fulfill their calling and responsibilities.

b. As soon as King Hezekiah's decree was circulated among the citizens of the nation, the people immediately responded with willing, overflowing hearts (vv.5-12). Generously, even excitedly, they gave abundant offerings to the priests and Levites who had recommitted their lives to serve the LORD and His people (vv.5-7):

⇒ They gave the first fruits (very first) of their produce, freely giving large amounts of grain, wine, oil, honey, and all their other produce.

⇒ They also gave a tithe of their livestock, bringing large herds to the priests and Levites (v.6).

⇒ They continued to give liberally for a period of five months (v.7). Remember that the first month of Hezekiah's reign had been spent in preparing the temple for worship. The second month had been spent in a special worship service and in celebrating the Passover and the Festival of Unleavened Bread. It was in the third month that Hezekiah issued his decree that reinstituted the offerings. Thus, the people began tithing in the third month and continued to bring an abundance of offerings until the seventh month.

At the end of the seventh month, the king and his officials visited the High Priest to secure reports on the offerings (v.8). When they arrived, they saw huge piles of gifts, whereupon Hezekiah immediately praised the LORD and pronounced a blessing upon His people.

In response to the king's request for a report on the offerings, the High Priest Azariah gave an astounding and marvelous account (v.10). Demonstrating a true spirit of revival, the people had willingly and generously responded. They had brought more than enough food and money to take care of the priests and Levites and their families. Thus the piles of supplies now being seen by the king were the remainder, what was left over from the offering.

After hearing the report and seeing the piles heaped up, Hezekiah immediately issued an order for the temple storerooms to be prepared and for the offerings to be faithfully locked in the storerooms (vv.11-12).

c. With such huge offerings being brought to the temple, it became necessary for Hezekiah to appoint supervisors to oversee the collection and distribution of the gifts (vv.12-19). If the overseers left the grain and other perishable gifts exposed, they were apt to rot or be wasted or stolen. For this reason, it was absolutely essential for storage rooms to be prepared and for supervisors to watch over and manage all the contributions.

1) The chief supervisor was Conaniah. His brother Shimei was his assistant (vv.12-13). Ten other deputy supervisors were appointed to serve under them. Note that these twelve men were in charge of supervising the offerings within the temple itself.

2) Another chief supervisor was appointed to oversee the freewill or volunteer offerings (Le.7:11-21). His name was Kore, and he had six deputy Levites to assist him (vv.14-19). Their particular responsibility was to distribute the offerings to the priests who lived outside of Jerusalem (Jos.21:18-19). Even young boys three years old received a distribution of the offerings, for they had been dedicated to the ministry and the temple by their parents. Some day they would become the priests ministering in the temple, serving the LORD and the people (v.16).

All priests listed in the genealogical records of priests shared in the distribution of the offerings (v.17). The genealogical records of Levites were also used for their distribution.

No family listed in the genealogical records of the priests and Levites was neglected. All the little babies, the wives, the sons and daughters—all received their share of the offerings. They had been faithful in recommitting their lives to the LORD, setting themselves apart to live holy and righteous lives and to faithfully serving Him. Even the priests—the descendants of Aaron—who lived on distant farms in distant towns received their portion of the offerings; certain men were appointed to deliver the offerings throughout the entire nation. All who were recorded in the genealogies, no matter where they lived, were to receive their portion.

Thought 1. Supporting the church and the ministers of the gospel is an absolute essential, for the laborer deserves wages. When the minister is serving the LORD and His people, he deserves to be compensated. Think for a moment about the work of the minister:

⇒ preaching and teaching an average of three or more times every week: reading, studying, preparing, and praying
⇒ visiting not only church members in the hospital but also relatives and friends of church members
⇒ visiting and ministering to church members when serious problems arise
⇒ counseling church members and occasionally non-church members
⇒ visiting and comforting family members when a death occurs, conduct funerals
⇒ marriage counseling and conducting marriage ceremonies
⇒ meeting with major committees
⇒ planning and managing the ministry of the church including its employees, business, missions, work, committees, schedules, finances, building programs, outreach program, and whatever else may come up—along with all the unique problems that come with each.
⇒ visiting and reaching new people for the LORD and the church.
⇒ constantly facing the scrutiny of church members and handling any and all criticisms, grumblings, and divisions that arise.

Imagine all the duties listed above and then picture this: at the top of the list is the primary responsibility of preparing at least three sermons or lessons—challenging, interesting, and new lessons—every week, week after week and year after year. How can a person conceivably carry out all these duties? Only by the strength and empowering of the Lord Jesus Christ Himself. So when a person serves the Lord and His church, he deserves to be compensated for his work and ministry.

In addition, the church must be supported financially, for the church has been given the greatest mission in all the world, that of proclaiming the good news of God's very own Son. Through the Lord Jesus Christ and Him alone, the world can be saved from sin, death, and judgment to come. Without Christ, people will die and face the judgment of God. They will be eternally separated from God and destined to live forever in a place Jesus Christ called *hell*, a place that He says is filled with torment and anguish.

The gospel cannot be carried to the world without finances. Without the necessary funds, missionaries, evangelists, and ministers cannot be sent around the world to proclaim the gospel. We must give sacrificially to take the gospel around the world and to meet the desperate needs of people who are crying for help. Listen to what God's Holy Word says about giving in order to support His church and work around the world:

> **"Give, and it shall be given unto you; good measure, pressed down, and shaken together, and running over, shall men give into your bosom. For with the same measure that ye mete withal it shall be measured to you again" (Lu.6:38).**

> **"And he looked up, and saw the rich men casting their gifts into the treasury. And he saw also a certain poor widow casting in thither two mites. And he said, Of a truth I say unto you, that this poor widow hath cast in more than they all: For all these have of their abundance cast in unto the offerings of God: but she of her penury hath cast in all the living that she had" (Lu.21:1-4).**

> **"Neither was there any among them that lacked: for as many as were possessors of lands or houses sold them, and brought the prices of the things that were sold, And laid *them* down at the apostles' feet: and distribution was made unto every man according as he had need" (Ac.4:34-35).**

> **"Then the disciples, every man according to his ability, determined to send relief unto the brethren which dwelt in Judaea" (Ac.11:29).**

BACKGROUND TO ISAIAH'S DAY

(The Four Kings Who Ruled During Isaiah's Ministry)

"Upon the first *day* of the week let every one of you lay by him in store, as *God* hath prospered him, that there be no gatherings when I come" (1 Co.16:2).

"How that in a great trial of affliction the abundance of their joy and their deep poverty abounded unto the riches of their liberality" (2 Co.8:2).

"For if there be first a willing mind, *it is* accepted according to that a man hath, *and* not according to that he hath not" (2 Co.8:12).

"But this *I say,* He which soweth sparingly shall reap also sparingly; and he which soweth bountifully shall reap also bountifully. Every man according as he purposeth in his heart, *so let him give;* not grudgingly, or of necessity: for God loveth a cheerful giver" (2 Co.9:6-7).

"For even in Thessalonica ye sent once and again unto my necessity" (Ph.4:16).

"And they came, both men and women, as many as were willing hearted, *and* brought bracelets, and earrings, and rings, and tablets, all jewels of gold: and every man that offered *offered* an offering of gold unto the LORD" (Ex.35:22).

"And they spake unto Moses, saying, The people bring much more than enough for the service of the work, which the LORD commanded to make" (Ex.36:5).

"And all the tithe of the land, *whether* of the seed of the land, *or* of the fruit of the tree, *is* the LORD'S: *it is* holy unto the LORD" (Le.27:30).

"Every man *shall give* as he is able, according to the blessing of the LORD thy God which he hath given thee" (De.16:17).

"Blessed *is* he that considereth the poor: the LORD will deliver him in time of trouble" (Ps.41:1).

"Honour the LORD with thy substance, and with the firstfruits of all thine increase: So shall thy barns be filled with plenty, and thy presses shall burst out with new wine" (Pr.3:9-10).

"The liberal soul shall be made fat: and he that watereth shall be watered also himself" (Pr.11:25).

"He that hath a bountiful eye shall be blessed; for he giveth of his bread to the poor" (Pr.22:9).

"And *if* thou draw out thy soul to the hungry, and satisfy the afflicted soul; then shall thy light rise in obscurity, and thy darkness *be* as the noonday" (Is.58:10).

"Bring ye all the tithes into the storehouse, that there may be meat in mine house, and prove me now herewith, saith the LORD of hosts, if I will not open you the windows of heaven, and pour you out a blessing, that *there shall* not *be room* enough *to receive it*" (Mal.3:10).

---

4 (31:20-21) **Commitment, Example of—Dedication, Example of—Wholehearted, Example of—Faithful, Example of—Hezekiah, Example of, Wholehearted Commitment**: in everything Hezekiah did, he was faithful to the LORD. He was committed wholeheartedly. Hezekiah reformed the temple and reestablished regular worship services for the people. But he was also personally faithful in worshipping the LORD and in obeying the commandments of the LORD. As a result, the LORD made him successful and gave him prosperity.

Thought 1. Once we have made a commitment to the LORD, we must be true to that commitment. Whether the commitment is a profession of faith or a commitment to serve the LORD in some capacity, God expects us to be faithful. Scripture says, "a double-minded man is unstable in all his ways" (Js.1:8). Only the person who perseveres, who follows through with his commitment will be saved and receive the reward. A lukewarm, halfhearted commitment is like water that is neither hot nor cold and is spewed out of God's mouth (Re.3:15-16). Success and prosperity can only be achieved through wholehearted commitment and diligent labor. Conquering or overcoming the trials and temptations of this life with all their pitfalls can be achieved only if we are totally committed to the LORD. Only the committed receive the conquering power of Christ. If we are fully devoted to the LORD, He gives us the power to overcome any obstacle that confronts us, no matter the severity of the problem or situation. Christ's power is available to any person who is totally dedicated to Him. A heart that is wholly devoted to the LORD will be blessed by the LORD. Listen to what God says about total commitment to Him:

"Jesus said unto him, If thou wilt be perfect, go *and* sell that thou hast, and give to the poor, and thou shalt have treasure in heaven: and come *and* follow me" (Mt.19:21).

"Jesus said unto him, Thou shalt love the Lord thy God with all thy heart, and with all thy soul, and with all thy mind. This is the first and great commandment" (Mt.22:37-38).

"Then Peter began to say unto him, Lo, we have left all, and have followed thee" (Mk.10:28).

"And after these things he went forth, and saw a publican, named Levi, sitting at the receipt of custom: and he said unto him, Follow me. And he left all, rose up, and followed him" (Lu.5:27-28).

"And he said to *them* all, If any *man* will come after me, let him deny himself, and take up his cross daily, and follow me" (Lu.9:23).

"So likewise, whosoever he be of you that forsaketh not all that he hath, he cannot be my disciple" (Lu.14:33).

"And he said unto them, Verily I say unto you, There is no man that hath left house, or parents, or brethren, or wife, or children, for the kingdom of God's sake, Who shall not receive manifold more in this present time, and in the world to come life everlasting" (Lu.18:29-30).

"For if ye live after the flesh, ye shall die: but if ye through the Spirit do mortify the deeds of the body, ye shall live" (Ro.8:13).

"I beseech you therefore, brethren, by the mercies of God, that ye present your bodies a living sacrifice, holy, acceptable unto God, *which is* your reasonable service. And be not conformed to this

43

world: but be ye transformed by the renewing of your mind, that ye may prove what *is* that good, and acceptable, and perfect, will of God" (Ro.12:1-2).

"But I keep under my body, and bring *it* into subjection: lest that by any means, when I have preached to others, I myself should be a castaway" (1 Co.9:27).

"I am crucified with Christ: nevertheless I live; yet not I, but Christ liveth in me: and the life which I now live in the flesh I live by the faith of the Son of God, who loved me, and gave himself for me" (Ga.2:20).

"And they that are Christ's have crucified the flesh with the affections and lusts" (Ga.5:24).

"But what things were gain to me, those I counted loss for Christ. Yea doubtless, and I count all things *but* loss for the excellency of the knowledge of Christ Jesus my Lord: for whom I have suffered the loss of all things, and do count them *but* dung, that I may win Christ, And be found in him, not having mine own righteousness, which is of the law, but that which is through the faith of Christ, the righteousness which is of God by faith: That I may know him, and the power of his resurrection, and the fellowship of his sufferings, being made conformable unto his death; If by any means I might attain unto the resurrection of the dead" (Ph.3:7-11).

"Nevertheless the foundation of God standeth sure, having this seal, The Lord knoweth them that are his. And, Let every one that nameth the name of Christ depart from iniquity. But in a great house there are not only vessels of gold and of silver, but also of wood and of earth; and some to honour, and some to dishonour. If a man therefore purge himself from these, he shall be a vessel unto honour, sanctified, and meet for the master's use, *and* prepared unto every good work" (2 Ti.2:19-21).

"For Moses had said, Consecrate yourselves to day to the LORD, even every man upon his son, and upon his brother; that he may bestow upon you a blessing this day" (Ex.32:29).

"And thou shalt love the LORD thy God with all thine heart, and with all thy soul, and with all thy might. And these words, which I command thee this day, shall be in thine heart: And thou shalt teach them diligently unto thy children, and shalt talk of them when thou sittest in thine house, and when thou walkest by the way, and when thou liest down, and when thou risest up. And thou shalt bind them for a sign upon thine hand, and they shall be as frontlets between thine eyes. And thou shalt write them upon the posts of thy house, and on thy gates" (De.6:5-9).

"Blessed *are* they that keep his testimonies, *and that* seek him with the whole heart" (Ps.119:2).

"Trust in the LORD with all thine heart; and lean not unto thine own understanding. In all thy ways acknowledge him, and he shall direct thy paths" (Pr.3:5-6).

"My son, give me thine heart, and let thine eyes observe my ways" (Pr.23:26).

"And ye shall seek me, and find *me,* when ye shall search for me with all your heart" (Je.29:13).

"Therefore also now, saith the LORD, turn ye *even* to me with all your heart, and with fasting, and with weeping, and with mourning" (Joel 2:12).

(The Four Kings Who Ruled During Isaiah's Ministry)

VII. THE REIGN OF HEZEKIAH (PART 4)— HIS DELIVERANCE FROM ASSYRIA, TERMINAL ILLNESS, AND DEATH: A PICTURE OF GOD'S UNLIMITED, SOVEREIGN POWER, 2 CHR.32:1-33

OUTLINE	SCRIPTURE	SCRIPTURE	OUTLINE
1. Hezekiah's deliverance from the Assyrian invasion: God's power to deliver His people a. The invasion by Assyria's king, Sennacherib: He laid siege to the fortified cities of Judah b. The preparations for war by Hezekiah 1) He stopped up the springs outside the city: To block or conceal the water supply from the Assyrians • The project took a large force of men • The project included blocking all the springs & stopping the major stream flowing through the land 2) He reinforced the city's fortifications • Repaired the city's wall • Built additional towers • Built a second wall at strategic locations • Reinforced the Millo, the supporting terraces 3) He made more weapons for the army 4) He organized the citizens into an army & appointed officers over them 5) He assembled the people & encouraged them • They must be strong & courageous • They must not fear nor be discouraged by the huge army of the Assyrians • They must know this one fact: They have a greater power, for the Assyrians have only men—only the arm of the flesh • They must trust the LORD to help & to fight their battles for them c. The threat by the Assyrian king & his demand for Hezekiah to surrender: The Assyrian king sent a large ar-	After these things, and the establishment thereof, Sennacherib king of Assyria came, and entered into Judah, and encamped against the fenced cities, and thought to win them for himself. 2 And when Hezekiah saw that Sennacherib was come, and that he was purposed to fight against Jerusalem, 3 He took counsel with his princes and his mighty men to stop the waters of the fountains which *were* without the city: and they did help him. 4 So there was gathered much people together, who stopped all the fountains, and the brook that ran through the midst of the land, saying, Why should the kings of Assyria come, and find much water? 5 Also he strengthened himself, and built up all the wall that was broken, and raised *it* up to the towers, and another wall without, and repaired Millo *in* the city of David, and made darts and shields in abundance. 6 And he set captains of war over the people, and gathered them together to him in the street of the gate of the city, and spake comfortably to them, saying, 7 Be strong and courageous, be not afraid nor dismayed for the king of Assyria, nor for all the multitude that *is* with him: for *there be* more with us than with him: 8 With him *is* an arm of flesh; but with us *is* the LORD our God to help us, and to fight our battles. And the people rested themselves upon the words of Hezekiah king of Judah. 9 After this did Sennacherib king of Assyria send his servants to Jerusalem, (but he *himself laid siege* against	Lachish, and all his power with him,) unto Hezekiah king of Judah, and unto all Judah that *were* at Jerusalem, saying, 10 Thus saith Sennacherib king of Assyria, Whereon do ye trust, that ye abide in the siege in Jerusalem? 11 Doth not Hezekiah persuade you to give over yourselves to die by famine and by thirst, saying, The LORD our God shall deliver us out of the hand of the king of Assyria? 12 Hath not the same Hezekiah taken away his high places and his altars, and commanded Judah and Jerusalem, saying, Ye shall worship before one altar, and burn incense upon it? 13 Know ye not what I and my fathers have done unto all the people of *other* lands? were the gods of the nations of those lands any ways able to deliver their lands out of mine hand? 14 Who *was there* among all the gods of those nations that my fathers utterly destroyed, that could deliver his people out of mine hand, that your God should be able to deliver you out of mine hand? 15 Now therefore let not Hezekiah deceive you, nor persuade you on this manner, neither yet believe him: for no god of any nation or kingdom was able to deliver his people out of mine hand, and out of the hand of my fathers: how much less shall your God deliver you out of mine hand? 16 And his servants spake yet *more* against the LORD God, and against his servant Hezekiah. 17 He wrote also letters to rail on the LORD God of Israel, and to speak against him, saying, As the gods of the nations of *other* lands have not delivered their people out of	my to Jerusalem to intimidate Hezekiah & to demand his surrender, 2 K.18:17-18 d. The Assyrian officer's address to Jerusalem's officials & the citizens standing near the wall: He questioned their confidence in the tactics of Hezekiah 1) He declared that Hezekiah was only deceiving them by persuading them to trust the LORD: They would die of hunger & thirst due to the Assyrian siege 2) He charged Hezekiah with displeasing the LORD by destroying the high places & altars of worship (a misunderstanding of God & idolatry) 3) He sought to intimidate the people through propaganda: Threatened them with the power of Assyria • No nation had ever been delivered from Assyria, not by any god • No people had ever been saved from the Assyrians by any god • Their God would be powerless against Assyria: Equated the LORD with false gods 4) He again charged Hezekiah with deceiving the people: Claimed the evidence was clear • No god of any nation had been able to save its people from Assyria • How much less would their God be able to deliver them? He would be powerless against Assyria 5) He continued on & on in his propaganda, speaking against the LORD & Hezekiah • He presented letters from the Assyrian king scorning & denying the power of the LORD to rescue His people

BACKGROUND TO ISAIAH'S DAY

(The Four Kings Who Ruled During Isaiah's Ministry)

OUTLINE	SCRIPTURE	SCRIPTURE	OUTLINE
• He spoke loudly in Hebrew to strike terror in the hearts of the people standing on the wall of Jerusalem e. The fallacy of the Assyrian argument: Did not understand the difference between the LORD & false gods that were only creations of people's minds, the works of their hands f. The wonderful deliverance by God's mighty power 1) The king & Isaiah cried out to God in prayer 2) The LORD sent an angel who utterly annihilated the Assyrian army: Executed 185,000 soldiers during the night, 2 K.19:35 3) The Assyrian king Sennacherib withdrew his army: He was later assassinated by his sons g. The continued deliverance & blessings of God 1) The LORD saved Hezekiah & the people from Assyria & from all others, giving them peace 2) The people expressed their appreciation by bringing gifts both to the LORD & to King Hezekiah 3) The surrounding nations highly esteemed Hezekiah after the Assyrian victory 2. **Hezekiah's terminal illness & prosperity: God's power to answer prayer & to heal** a. Hezekiah's fatal illness: God healed him in answer to prayer b. Hezekiah's pride: His heart was lifted up & he did not acknowledge the LORD as he should have 1) The LORD'S wrath began to loom over & convict him	mine hand, so shall not the God of Hezekiah deliver his people out of mine hand. 18 Then they cried with a loud voice in the Jews' speech unto the people of Jerusalem that *were* on the wall, to affright them, and to trouble them; that they might take the city. 19 And they spake against the God of Jerusalem, as against the gods of the people of the earth, *which were* the work of the hands of man. 20 And for this *cause* Hezekiah the king, and the prophet Isaiah the son of Amoz, prayed and cried to heaven. 21 And the LORD sent an angel, which cut off all the mighty men of valour, and the leaders and captains in the camp of the king of Assyria. So he returned with shame of face to his own land. And when he was come into the house of his god, they that came forth of his own bowels slew him there with the sword. 22 Thus the LORD saved Hezekiah and the inhabitants of Jerusalem from the hand of Sennacherib the king of Assyria, and from the hand of all *other,* and guided them on every side. 23 And many brought gifts unto the LORD to Jerusalem, and presents to Hezekiah king of Judah: so that he was magnified in the sight of all nations from thenceforth. 24 In those days Hezekiah was sick to the death, and prayed unto the LORD: and he spake unto him, and he gave him a sign. 25 But Hezekiah rendered not again according to the benefit *done* unto him; for his heart was lifted up: therefore there was wrath upon him, and upon Judah and Jerusalem.	26 Notwithstanding Hezekiah humbled himself for the pride of his heart, *both* he and the inhabitants of Jerusalem, so that the wrath of the LORD came not upon them in the days of Heze-kiah. 27 And Hezekiah had exceeding much riches and honour: and he made himself treasuries for silver, and for gold, and for precious stones, and for spices, and for shields, and for all manner of pleasant jewels; 28 Storehouses also for the increase of corn, and wine, and oil; and stalls for all manner of beasts, and cotes for flocks. 29 Moreover he provided him cities, and possessions of flocks and herds in abundance: for God had given him substance very much. 30 This same Hezekiah also stopped the upper watercourse of Gihon, and brought it straight down to the west side of the city of David. And Hezekiah prospered in all his works. 31 Howbeit in *the business of* the ambassadors of the princes of Babylon, who sent unto him to enquire of the wonder that was *done* in the land, God left him, to try him, that he might know all *that was* in his heart. 32 Now the rest of the acts of Hezekiah, and his goodness, behold, they *are* written in the vision of Isaiah the prophet, the son of Amoz, *and* in the book of the kings of Judah and Israel. 33 And Hezekiah slept with his fathers, and they buried him in the chiefest of the sepulchres of the sons of David: and all Judah and the inhabitants of Jerusalem did him honour at his death. And Manasseh his son reigned in his stead.	2) The king repented of his pride & the people humbled themselves 3) The LORD delayed His hand of judgment against Judah during Hezekiah's lifetime c. Hezekiah's prosperity 1) He built treasuries to store his wealth 2) He built storage buildings for his farms 3) He built stalls for his livestock 4) He built towns for the nation 5) He acquired vast flocks & herds with the great wealth given by God d. Hezekiah's major building project: The construction of a water tunnel for Jerusalem, 2 K.20:20 e. Hezekiah's test by God 1) The Babylonian ruler sent envoys to ask about his healing by God[DS1] 2) The LORD tested Hezekiah: To expose what was in his heart (vv.24-26). f. Hezekiah's reign & acts of devotion: Recorded in *The Vision of the Prophet Isaiah Son of Amoz*—included in *The Book of the Kings of Judah & Israel* g. Hezekiah's death & burial in Jerusalem 1) He was greatly honored by the people 2) He was succeeded by his son Manasseh

(32:1-33) Introduction: at any given time within any country, government, or ruling body, a crisis can arise, a critical situation that has to be handled. The crisis can be the threat of war or war itself, a broken treaty, terrorist actions, an uprising, or a natural disaster such as an earthquake, a hurricane, a forest fire, or a flash flood.

On a personal level, every one of us also faces crises in life, critical situations such as: serious illness, disease, accidents, financial difficulties, loss of a job, divisive relationships, and a host of other potentially serious problems.

But no matter what confronts us, there is wonderful news. Unlimited, sovereign power is available to *carry us through* the crisis. That power is the power of God Himself. We are the creation of God's hand; therefore, God loves us and cares about what happens to us. Thus He makes His power available to us, a power that has the strength to *carry us through* any crisis.

BACKGROUND TO ISAIAH'S DAY

(The Four Kings Who Ruled During Isaiah's Ministry)

God's unlimited, sovereign power is the subject of this Scripture. God's power delivered Hezekiah from an invasion by the oppressive Assyrians, who were the terror and scourge of the world during that particular period of history. In reading this account, the returning exiles would learn that God could also deliver them through any crisis, no matter how critical the situation. The same power that God had used to deliver Hezekiah and the people of his day was available to deliver the returning exiles if they remained faithful. This is, *The Reign of Hezekiah (Part 4)—His Deliverance from Assyria, Terminal Illness, and Death: A Picture of God's Unlimited, Sovereign Power*, 32:1-33.

1. Hezekiah's deliverance from the Assyrian invasion: God's power to deliver His people (vv.1-23).
2. Hezekiah's terminal illness and prosperity: God's power to answer prayer and to heal (vv.24-33).

1 **(32:1-23) Power, of God, Example of—Deliverance, Source, God's Power—Assyria, Wars of, Against Judah—Judah, Wars of, Invaded by Assyria—Hezekiah, Wars of, Invaded by Assyria**: Hezekiah was mightily delivered from an Assyrian invasion, the superpower of that day. Assyria was a terrifying and bothersome nuisance to her neighbors in the world, but God's mighty power would deliver His people. Earlier, Hezekiah's father Ahaz had willingly subjected Judah to Assyria, which meant that they were paying a heavy annual tribute or tax to the domineering nation (28:16-21). Nevertheless, the LORD filled Hezekiah with inner strength, giving him the courage to resist the oppression of the Assyrians. Rebelling against the king of Assyria and refusing to pay the tax took enormous courage. But God filled Hezekiah's heart with an inner strength, a strength seldom seen in rulers. As a result, Hezekiah broke the heavy yoke of Assyrian oppression.

However, Hezekiah went on to make a very unwise decision. Rejecting the warning of the LORD through His prophet Isaiah, Hezekiah formed an alliance with Egypt, and together they marched against the Philistines and others who were *vassal states* of Assyria (Is.30:1-5; 31:1-3). In battle after battle, the coalition defeated the Philistines as far as Gaza and its territory (2 K.18:7-8). It was these two reasons that aroused the Assyrian King Sennacherib to invade Judah.

a. The invasion by Assyria took place in the fourteenth year of Hezekiah's reign. Seeking to subject Hezekiah under Assyria's yoke again, Sennacherib launched a major military campaign by laying siege to all the fortified cities of Judah (v.1).

b. Knowing that Assyria would soon be attacking Jerusalem, Hezekiah began to make preparations for the expected battle (vv.2-8). Five major preparations were made:

1) First, Hezekiah had the military block off and conceal all the streams, that is, the water supply, outside the city (vv.3-4). A large force of men was needed for this defensive measure, for there were apparently a large number of springs surrounding the city. No doubt working at a feverish pace, they quickly concealed the springs and somehow cut off the major spring that ran through the land. By doing this, water would not be available for the Assyrian troops.

2) Second, Hezekiah reinforced the city's fortifications (v.5). These construction projects included…
   - repairing the city's wall
   - building additional towers on the wall
   - building a second wall outside the main wall at strategic locations
   - reinforcing the millo, that is, the supporting terraces

3) Third, Hezekiah had a substantial number of additional weapons manufactured for the army (v.5).

4) Fourth, Hezekiah organized the citizens into an army and appointed officers over them (v.6).

5) Fifth, Hezekiah assembled the people in the square at the city gate and encouraged them in the LORD. The LORD was to be their only hope of deliverance against the cruel Assyrian army (vv.6-8). Drawing on the great strength and courage that God had instilled within him, Hezekiah shouted out four exhortations to his people:
   ⇒ They must be strong and courageous, rejecting any thought of surrendering the city. They must be resolved, determined to stand against the enemy to the last person, standing boldly and bravely, side by side, holding their posts and not giving a foothold to the enemy (v.7).
   ⇒ They must not fear nor be discouraged by the massive size or might of the well-equipped Assyrian forces (v.7).
   ⇒ They, God's people, must know this one fact: they had a greater power than the Assyrians. The Assyrians had only men—only the arm of the flesh—but God's people had the LORD (vv.7-8). His unlimited power would protect His people and conquer any enemy who attacked them.
   ⇒ They must, therefore, trust the LORD to help fight their battles for them (v.8). Not only would the LORD help them in their conflict, but He would also actually fight the battle for them.

c. Sometime later, the Assyrian king sent an envoy and a large army to Jerusalem to intimidate Hezekiah and to demand his surrender (v.9; 2 K.18:17-18). *Second Kings* tells us that a large number of Assyrian troops laid siege to Jerusalem (2 K.18:17). With this action, the Assyrian king was launching a propaganda war of intimidation, threatening and demanding that Hezekiah surrender Jerusalem to the Assyrians.

d. After the officials set up siege around the capital, the Assyrian officer appointed by King Sennacherib approached the city. He addressed Jerusalem's officials and the citizens standing nearby on the wall (vv.10-18). Shouting out, he questioned their confidence in Hezekiah and in his tactics.

1) He declared that Hezekiah was only misleading them by persuading them to trust the LORD (v.11). If they continued to listen to the deception of Hezekiah, they would die of hunger and thirst due to the Assyrian siege.

2) The Assyrian spokesman charged Hezekiah with displeasing the LORD by destroying the high places and altars of the gods (v.12). Note that he put his charge in the form of a question, attempting to arouse the people to question Hezekiah's dependence on the LORD. How could the LORD bless Hezekiah since the king had destroyed the worship centers of the gods? Of course, this was a complete misunderstanding of the LORD since He is the only living and true God and all other gods are false.

3) The Assyrian spokesman then sought to intimidate the Judean officials and people who were standing on the walls listening to the negotiations. Being a skilled negotiator, the Assyrian spokesman continued to argue his case in the form of questions. He aroused the Judeans to think about the power of Assyria, arguing…

- that no nation had ever been delivered from Assyria, not by any god (v.13)
- that no people had ever been saved from the Assyrians by any god (v.14)
- that the Judean God would be powerless against Assyria (v.14)

Note how he equated the LORD with false gods, which was the fallacy of his argument. The LORD is not just one god among many. He is the only living and true God.

4) Again, the Assyrian spokesman charged Hezekiah with deceiving the people. Moreover any thinking people could easily recognize the deception (v.15). No god of any nation had been able to save its people from Assyria. How much less would the Judean God be able to deliver them? The Judean god would be powerless against Assyria.
5) Continuing on in his propaganda, the Assyrian commander railed against the LORD and Hezekiah (vv.16-18). Remember that Sennacherib had remained behind in Lachish (v.9), but he sent letters that were to be presented to Hezekiah (v.17). These letters scorned and denied the power of the LORD to rescue His people. Shouting out as loudly as he could, the spokesman shared the letters in Hebrew in order to strike terror in the hearts of the people standing on the wall of Jerusalem (v.18).

e. The Assyrians did not understand the difference between the LORD and the false gods that were only creations of people's minds. There was a fallacy, a serious illusion, a fatal misconception (v.19). There is only one true and living God, the LORD Himself. All other gods are false, the fabrication of people's overactive imaginations, the busywork of people's hands.

f. Facing the fierce, overwhelming Assyrians, Hezekiah and Isaiah did the only thing they could do: they cried out to the LORD in prayer (vv.20-21). That very night the hand of God's mighty power and judgment fell upon the Assyrian invaders. The LORD sent an angel into the Assyrian camp sometime during the night, and the angel executed 185,000 soldiers (v.21; 2 K.19:35-37). Stunned, horrified, dismayed, and confused about what had happened, the Assyrian survivors broke camp and withdrew, returning to Ninevah. And in disgrace they remained there. Soon thereafter, Assyria's King Sennacherib was assassinated by his own son as he went into the temple of his false god to worship.

g. As a result of this great and miraculous deliverance, Hezekiah and his people had a long period of peace (vv.22-23). Other nations were now obviously afraid to attack Judah, for the LORD was protecting His people on every side, giving them peace throughout the land.

In an expression of appreciation, the people brought offerings for the LORD and valuable gifts for Hezekiah. Hezekiah was even highly respected by all the surrounding nations after the victory over Assyria.

Thought 1. God has the power to deliver His people. No matter what we may be facing…
- disappointment
- discouragement
- depression
- loneliness
- emptiness
- purposelessness
- disease
- accident
- financial difficulty
- broken relationships
- unfaithfulness
- tragedy
- the loss of a loved one
- unemployment

The LORD's power is more than sufficient to meet our every need. God's power is always available to…
- deliver us
- set us free
- rescue us
- save us
- strengthen us
- provide for us
- lift us up
- walk with us
- carry us
- care for us
- love us
- watch over us
- protect us
- shield us
- comfort us

Even in death, God delivers us. So that we never have to taste or experience death, He transfers us immediately—quicker than the eye can blink—into the spiritual world or dimension of being. And there we live forever in the LORD's presence.

If we will trust the LORD in all that we do, crying out to Him for deliverance, nothing will ever be able to conquer or defeat us. The LORD will empower us to stand up and *walk through* any trial or temptation, no matter how terrifying or seductive. Listen to what God's Holy Word says:

> **"Who shall separate us from the love of Christ? *shall* tribulation, or distress, or persecution, or famine, or nakedness, or peril, or sword?…Nay, in all these things we are more than conquerors through him that loved us. For I am persuaded, that neither death, nor life, nor angels, nor principalities, nor powers, nor things present, nor things to come, Nor height, nor depth, nor any other creature, shall be able to separate us from the love of God, which is in Christ Jesus our Lord" (Ro.8:35, 37-39).**

> **"There hath no temptation taken you but such as is common to man: but God *is* faithful, who will not suffer you to be tempted above that ye are able; but will with the temptation also make a way to escape, that ye may be able to bear *it*" (1 Co.10:13).**

> **"For we would not, brethren, have you ignorant of our trouble which came to us in Asia, that we were pressed out of measure, above strength, insomuch that we despaired even of life: But we had the sentence of death in ourselves, that we should not trust in ourselves, but in God which raiseth the dead: Who delivered us from so great a death, and doth deliver: in whom we trust that he will yet deliver *us*" (2 Co.1:8-10).**

> **"And he said unto me, My grace is sufficient for thee: for my strength is made perfect in weakness. Most gladly therefore will I rather glory in my infirmities, that the power of Christ may rest upon me.**

Therefore I take pleasure in infirmities, in reproaches, in necessities, in persecutions, in distresses for Christ's sake: for when I am weak, then am I strong" (2 Co.12:9-10).

"That he would grant you, according to the riches of his glory, to be strengthened with might by his Spirit in the inner man" (Ep.3:16).

"Now unto him that is able to do exceeding abundantly above all that we ask or think, according to the power that worketh in us" (Ep.3:20).

"Henceforth there is laid up for me a crown of righteousness, which the Lord, the righteous judge, shall give me at that day: and not to me only, but unto all them also that love his appearing" (2 Ti.4:8).

"Forasmuch then as the children are partakers of flesh and blood, he also himself likewise took part of the same; that through death he might destroy him that had the power of death, that is, the devil; And deliver them who through fear of death were all their lifetime subject to bondage" (He.2:14-15).

"Who through faith subdued kingdoms, wrought righteousness, obtained promises, stopped the mouths of lions, Quenched the violence of fire, escaped the edge of the sword, out of weakness were made strong, waxed valiant in fight, turned to flight the armies of the aliens" (He.11:33-34).

"So that we may boldly say, The Lord *is* my helper, and I will not fear what man shall do unto me" (He.13:6).

"The Lord knoweth how to deliver the godly out of temptations, and to reserve the unjust unto the day of judgment to be punished" (2 Pe.2:9).

"For whatsoever is born of God overcometh the world: and this is the victory that overcometh the world, *even* our faith. Who is he that overcometh the world, but he that believeth that Jesus is the Son of God?" (1 Jn.5:4-5).

"And he said, The LORD *is* my rock, and my fortress, and my deliverer" (2 S.22:2).

"For thou hast girded me with strength to battle: them that rose up against me hast thou subdued under me" (2 S.22:40).

"He shall deliver thee in six troubles: yea, in seven there shall no evil touch thee" (Jb.5:19).

"The LORD *is* my strength and my shield; my heart trusted in him, and I am helped: therefore my heart greatly rejoiceth; and with my song will I praise him" (Ps.28:7).

"But I *am* poor and needy; *yet* the Lord thinketh upon me: thou *art* my help and my deliverer; make no tarrying, O my God" (Ps.40:17).

"Through thee will we push down our enemies: through thy name will we tread them under that rise up against us" (Ps.44:5).

"Surely he shall deliver thee from the snare of the fowler, *and* from the noisome pestilence" (Ps.91:3).

"They reel to and fro, and stagger like a drunken man, and are at their wit's end. Then they cry unto the LORD in their trouble, and he bringeth them out of their distresses. He maketh the storm a calm, so that the waves thereof are still. Then are they glad because they be quiet; so he bringeth them unto their desired haven. Oh that *men* would praise the LORD *for* his goodness, and *for* his wonderful works to the children of men!" (Ps.107:27-31).

"But they that wait upon the LORD shall renew *their* strength; they shall mount up with wings as eagles; they shall run, and not be weary; *and* they shall walk, and not faint" (Is.40:31).

"Fear thou not; for I *am* with thee: be not dismayed; for I *am* thy God: I will strengthen thee; yea, I will help thee; yea, I will uphold thee with the right hand of my righteousness" (Is.41:10).

"Fear not: for I have redeemed thee, I have called *thee* by thy name; thou *art* mine. When thou passest through the waters, I *will be* with thee; and through the rivers, they shall not overflow thee: when thou walkest through the fire, thou shalt not be burned; neither shall the flame kindle upon thee" (Is.43:1-2).

"And *even* to *your* old age I *am* he; and *even* to hoar [gray] hairs will I carry *you*: I have made, and I will bear; even I will carry, and will deliver *you*" (Is.46:4).

"Be not afraid of their faces: for I *am* with thee to deliver thee, saith the LORD" (Je.1:8).

"He delivereth and rescueth, and he worketh signs and wonders in heaven and in earth, who hath delivered Daniel from the power of the lions" (Da.6:27).

---

2 (32:24-33) **Prayer, Power of—Power, of Prayer—Sickness, Healed by—Illness, Healed by—Disease, Healed by—Healing, Source of, Prayer—Hezekiah, Terminal Illness of—Prosperity, Example of—Hezekiah, Prosperity of—Tests - Testing, of God, Example of**: in closing out Hezekiah's reign, the author discusses the king's terminal illness and his prosperity. The account given here is more abbreviated than the story given in *Second Kings* (2 K.20:1-21).

a. Shockingly, right after the deliverance of Jerusalem from the Assyrian threat, Hezekiah became deathly sick and was soon to die. Yet in faith he prayed to the LORD. Out of compassion, the LORD immediately answered the king's prayer and miraculously healed him.

b. But Hezekiah let pride fill his heart, and he did not acknowledge the LORD as he should have (vv.25-26). As a result, God pronounced judgment upon Hezekiah and the nation. But during the pronouncement, Hezekiah repented of his pride. Both he and the people humbled themselves before the LORD. Because of their sincere repentance and humility, the LORD delayed His hand of judgment during Hezekiah's lifetime (v.26).

But what had stirred pride within his heart? When the crown prince of Babylon heard about the miraculous healing of Hezekiah, his curiosity was aroused (v.31; 2 K.20:12). So he sent several envoys to inquire about the healing. While entertaining the ambassadors, Hezekiah pridefully showed them his vast wealth (2 K.20:12-21). Obviously, this included the strength of his military as well as the wealth found in the palace, the temple treasuries, and the storage cities throughout the nation. Immediately, the LORD sent the prophet Isaiah to rebuke the king. With the authority of God Himself, Isaiah pronounced God's judgment upon Hezekiah and Judah due to the king's pride and the people's sins down through the centuries (1 K.16–18). Some day in the near future, Babylon would conquer Judah and carry off all the wealth of the nation, the very wealth Hezekiah had so readily shown to the Babylonian ambassadors. Unsurprisingly, the ambassadors would not forget what they had seen. Future leaders of Babylon would covet the wealth, all because of Hezekiah's self-exaltation and vanity.

c. In summarizing Hezekiah's reign, the author tells of the LORD's great blessings upon his life. He gave him great wealth and prosperity. So much wealth was accumulated that he had to build several treasury buildings to store his silver, precious stones, spices, shields, and all the other valuable items (v.27).

Hezekiah also built storage buildings to harvest the grain, wine, and oil from his farms (v.28). He had barns, stalls, and pens erected for his livestock. In addition, he built a large number of towns throughout the nation as well as acquiring a vast number of flocks and herds. All this was a sign of God's blessing upon Hezekiah.

d. Hezekiah's major building project was the construction of a water tunnel for Jerusalem (2 K.20:20). Cutting a tunnel beneath Jerusalem, he was able to provide a permanent water supply for the capital city. As Scripture says, Hezekiah succeeded and prospered in all the works he undertook.

e. In the midst of God's blessings upon his life, the LORD tested Hezekiah (v.31). The LORD had used the ambassadors sent by the Babylonian ruler to test the heart of the king. Knowing that Hezekiah was taking personal pride in his wealth, the LORD sought to expose the arrogance of his heart. As noted above, Hezekiah repented of his pride and the LORD delayed the pronounced judgment upon him and the nation.

f. A summary of Hezekiah's righteous reign and his acts of devotion were recorded in *The Vision of the Prophet Isaiah Son of Amoz*. Note that this particular writing of Isaiah was included in *The Book of the Kings of Judah and Israel* (v.32).

g. After Hezekiah's death, he was buried in Jerusalem and greatly honored by the people (v.33). His successor was his son Manasseh.

Thought 1. The power of prayer is indescribable and too wonderful for words. Why? Because there is no limit to God's power. God is omnipotent, all-powerful, possessing perfect and unlimited power to do anything He desires. And yet, God is not only omnipotent but also omniscient, knowing all things. Nothing is hid from God nor out of His sight. God sees and knows all things. The fact of God's omnipotence and omniscience is the most glorious news, for God knows when a serious illness strikes us or a crisis confronts us. God then has the power to handle our serious illness or the severe crisis. When we face these seemingly insurmountable problems, our responsibility is to pray, turning our face toward the LORD and crying out to Him. If we are sincere and willing to turn our lives totally over to Him, God will hear and answer our prayer. In some cases, He will miraculously heal us. In other cases, He will give us the strength to *walk through* the illness or crisis victoriously, even conquering death itself. Through prayer, there is nothing, absolutely nothing, that can conquer and overcome us, for God knows the very number of hairs on our head—everything about us—and God has the power to help us. Listen to what God's Word says about the *power of prayer*.

"**Ask, and it shall be given you; seek, and ye shall find; knock, and it shall be opened unto you**" (Mt.7:7).

"**Therefore I say unto you, What things soever ye desire, when ye pray, believe that ye receive *them*, and ye shall have *them***" (Mk.11:24).

"**If ye abide in me, and my words abide in you, ye shall ask what ye will, and it shall be done unto you**" (Jn.15:7).

"**Hitherto have ye asked nothing in my name: ask, and ye shall receive, that your joy may be full**" (Jn.16:24).

"**For this thing I besought the Lord thrice, that it might depart from me. And he said unto me, My grace is sufficient for thee: for my strength is made perfect in weakness. Most gladly therefore will I rather glory in my infirmities, that the power of Christ may rest upon me. Therefore I take pleasure in infirmities, in reproaches, in necessities, in persecutions, in distresses for Christ's sake: for when I am weak, then am I strong**" (2 Co.12:8-10).

"**Now unto him that is able to do exceeding abundantly above all that we ask or think, according to the power that worketh in us**" (Ep.3:20).

"**And the prayer of faith shall save the sick, and the Lord shall raise him up; and if he have committed sins, they shall be forgiven him. Confess *your* faults one to another, and pray one for another, that ye may be healed. The effectual fervent prayer of a righteous man availeth much. Elias was a man subject to like passions as we are, and he prayed earnestly that it might not rain: and it rained not on the earth by the space of three years and six months. And he prayed again, and the heaven gave rain, and the earth brought forth her fruit**" (Js.5:15-18).

"**And whatsoever we ask, we receive of him, because we keep his commandments, and do those things that are pleasing in his sight**" (1 Jn.3:22).

"**Call unto me, and I will answer thee, and show thee great and mighty things, which thou knowest not**" (Je.33:3).

DEEPER STUDY #1

(2 Chr.32:31) **Babel/Babylon**: the capital city of Babylon was 80km or 50 miles south of the modern Baghdad, the capital of Iraq.[4] Babylon was also southeast of and right next to Assyria. Although Assyria became the dominant world power of its time and Babylon was not far away, Assyria could never keep Babylon completely subject to them. Eventually, Babylon became the strongest power in the world.

In the Old Testament, Babylon is a name that refers to several different categories: a city, a nation, a people and, symbolically, a civilization or society that man builds in defiance of God. From the beginning of human history, ever since the Tower of Babel (Ge.11:9), Babylon has represented a civilization that is devoted to materialism and sensual pleasure. In addition, the wicked, oppressive, rebellious pride of governments and nations—the very worst of human government—is symbolized in the name Babylon. Babylon further represents the power of darkness that seeks to enslave and oppress people. Therefore, any world power that rises up in willful rebellion against God—against establishing a truly free, just, and righteous society—is following in the footsteps of Babylon. The notorious city of Babylon was characterized by its self-inflating, hostile defiance toward God and its brutal oppression of all other peoples. Even when the end time comes and Babylon is once again rebuilt, it will stand as a symbol of rebellion and enmity against the LORD. Babylon will be the capital of an apostate civilization that rebels against the LORD (see outline and notes—Re.14:8; 17:1–18:24 for more discussion).

The Hebrew word for Babel and Babylon is the same. And just as pride and wickedness were in the hearts of the people who tried to build the Tower of Babel (Ge.11:4), great pride and wickedness were in the people of Babylon—so much so that the final empire that will take its stand against God will also be called Babylon (Re.16:19). In the same way that the people of Babel stood together against God, so it will be in the last days of world history. The ungodly and greedy of this world will unite, believing that nothing and no one will be able to tear apart their united political system.

A less talked about but equally significant fact to note about Babylon is this: while the Bible paints the picture of pride in the Babylonians of Old Testament times, we also see that God used the Babylonians to execute judgment against other wicked nations of that day and to discipline the people of Judah for their idolatry. Nebuchadnezzar conquered Jerusalem and led away all but a few of the people of Judah (2 K.24:11-16). Additionally, he took the temple treasures and put them in his own palace (2 Chr.36:7), but he did not recognize the one true God as the source of his success. Instead, Nebuchadnezzar became so full of pride that he claimed all credit for what he had done in life, giving no honor the LORD at all. But note carefully what happened to Nebuchadnezzar, who was considered at that time the most powerful man in the world:

> **"The king spake, and said, Is not this great Babylon, that I have built for the house of the kingdom by the might of my power, and for the honour of my majesty? While the word *was* in the king's mouth, there fell a voice from heaven, *saying*, O king Nebuchadnezzar, to thee it is spoken; The kingdom is departed from thee. And they shall drive thee from men, and thy dwelling *shall be* with the beasts of the field: they shall make thee to eat grass as oxen, and seven times shall pass over thee, until thou know that the most High ruleth in the kingdom of men, and giveth it to whomsoever he will. The same hour was the thing fulfilled upon Nebuchadnezzar: and he was driven from men, and did eat grass as oxen, and his body was wet with the dew of heaven, till his hairs were grown like eagles' *feathers*, and his nails like birds' *claws*." (Da.4:30-33).**

Nebuchadnezzar was not restored to his right mind or his throne until he gave all honor and glory to the LORD. Despite Nebuchadnezzar's experience, his grandson Belshazzar desecrated the vessels from the temple of the LORD by using them in a pagan feast. Belshazzar and the Babylonian leaders could not have been more arrogant against the living God! For this awful pride, Belshazzar and the nation suffered the terrifying judgment of God. God Himself wrote on the wall of the palace, declaring the immediate defeat and death of Belshazzar and the end of the Babylonian kingdom once and for all (Da.5:5-6, 18-30). God brought them down as He did Sodom and Gomorrah (Is.13:19). There was nothing left of the once mighty Babylonian empire.

The lesson for us today is clear: God judges individuals as well as nations. God will not put up with pride, not for long. If we do not put away pride and walk humbly before the LORD, judgment will come. No one can be prideful in the face of God, proclaiming his own greatness. No one…

- no matter who he is
- no matter how much power or wealth he has
- no matter what position or authority he has
- no matter what others think of him
- no matter how feared or respected he is

The world is going to face a day of final judgment. All the nations, governments, civilizations, cultures, societies, cities, and communities will stand before God to give an account for what they have done. God is going to execute perfect justice upon this earth, correcting all the wrongs that have ever been done. No mistreatment of other people has ever escaped the eye of God. Every act, including every word and thought, has been seen and heard by the Sovereign LORD and Majesty of the universe. Scripture even declares that a record is being kept of every word and thought ever conceived or spoken by a person (Mt.12:36; 2 Co.10:3-5). Everything we have ever done, whether inside or outside of our bodies, will face the judgment of God. There is to be a final day of judgment upon this earth, a day when all injustices and evil deeds will be corrected. Exactly as God's predicted, judgment fell upon Babylon. Likewise, it will fall upon this earth and upon every human being who has lived on this earth. The hand of God will bring down the prideful. Judgment is certain. Babylon is a clear picture of pride and the need for every person to repent.

> **"Pride goeth before destruction, and an haughty spirit before a fall" (Pr.16:18).**
> **"Alas, alas, that great city Babylon, that mighty city! for in one hour is thy judgment come" (Re.18:10).**
> **"And I will break the pride of your power; and I will make your heaven as iron, and your earth as brass" (Le.26:19).**

---

[4] J.D. Douglas, Editor. *New Bible Dictionary*. (Wheaton, IL: Tyndale House Publishers, Inc., 1982), p. 111.

TIMELINE OF KINGS, PROPHETS AND HISTORY*

HISTORY

DATE BC	FOREIGN KINGS	WORLD EVENTS
1000	Ashur-Rabi II (1010–970) *(Assyria)*; Hiram (1003–966) *(Tyre)*; Tiglath-Pileser II (960–935) *(Assyria)*	David captures Jerusalem (1004); Foundation for the Temple (966); 22ⁿᵈ Egyptian Dynasty (945)
950		
930		Kingdom Divided (930)
	Shishak I (945–924) *(Egypt)*	Assyria makes peace with Babylon (915); Jehoshaphat leads a revival (865)
900	Ben-Hadad I (900) *(Syria)*; Eth-Baal (887–856) *(Sidon)*	Elijah's contest with prophets of Baal (857); Elijah's mantle passed to Elisha (845)
850	Hazael (840) *(Syria)*	Carthage established (814); Joash repairs Temple (812); 23ʳᵈ Egyptian dynasty (800)
800	Ben-Hadad II (798) *(Syria)*; Ben-Hadad III (773) *(Syria)*	Olympic games begin (776); Rome founded (753)
750	Rezin (750) *(Syria)*	Babylonian and Chinese calendar (750)

THE UNITED KINGDOM

BIBLE REF.	KINGS (Years Reigned)	PROPHETS
1 S.16:1-1 K.2:11; 1 Chr.11:1-30	David (40) (1011–971)	Samuel (1095–1015); Gad (1015–950); Asaph (1004); Nathan (1003–931); Heman (971)
1 K.2:12-11:43; 1 Chr. 28:1-2 Chr.9:31	Solomon (40) (971–931)	

THE DIVIDED KINGDOM

NORTHERN KINGDOM OF ISRAEL

PROPHETS	KINGS (Years Reigned)	BIBLE REF.
Ahijah (931–910); Man from Judah (930); Shemaiah (927)	Jeroboam I (22) (931–910)	1 K.12:1-24; 12:25-14:20; 2 Chr.10:1-16
Jehu (886)	Nadab (2) (910–909)	1 K.15:25-31
	Baasha (24) (909–886)	1 K.15:16-16:7; 2 Chr.16:1-6
	Elah (2) (886–885)	1 K.16:6-14
	Zimri (7 days) (885)	1 K.16:9-20
Hanani (870)	Omri (12) (885–874)	1 K.16:21-28
Elijah (860–845)	Ahab (22) (874–853)	1 K.16:28-22:40; 2 Chr.18:1-34
Micaiah (853); Elisha (850–795); Eliezer (849–48)	Ahaziah (2) (853–852)	1 K.22:49-51; 2 K.1:1-18
	Joram/Jehoram (12) (852–841)	1 K.22:1-17; 3:1-8:15; 2 Chr.20:35-37; 22:1-11
	Jehu (28) (841–814)	2 K.9:1-10:36; 2 Chr.22:7-9
	Jehoahaz (17) (814–798)	2 K.13:1-9
Zechariah (797)	Jehoash (16) (798–782)	2 K.13:9-25; 14:8-16
Jonah (780–765); Amos (750)	Jeroboam II (41) (793–753)	2 K.14:23-29
	Zechariah (6 mos) (753)	2 K.15:8-12
	Shallum (1 mo) (752)	2 K.15:13-15
	Menahem (10) (752–742)	2 K.15:16-22

SOUTHERN KINGDOM OF JUDAH

BIBLE REF.	KINGS (Years Reigned)	PROPHETS
1 K.12:1-24; 14:21-31; 2 Chr.9:31-12:16	Rehoboam (17) (931–913)	
1 K.15:1-8; 2 Chr.12:16-14:1	Abijah (3) (913–911)	
1 K.15:9-24; 2 Chr.14:1-16:14	Asa (3) (911–870)	Iddo (910); Azariah (896)
1 K.22:41-50; 2 K.3:6-14; 2 Chr.17:1-21:1	Jehoshaphat (25) (873–848)	
2 K.8:16-24; 2 Chr.21:1-20	Jehoram (8) (853–841)	Obadiah (845)
2 K.8:25-29; 9:27-29; 2 Chr.22:1-10	Ahaziah (2) (841)	
2 K.11:1-16; 2 Chr.22:10-23:21	Athaliah (7) (841–835)	
2 K.11:17-12:21; 2 Chr.22:11-12; 24:1-27	Joash/Jehoash (40) (835–796)	Joel (830)
2 K.14:1-20; 2 Chr.24:27-25:28	Amaziah (29) (796–767)	
2 K.14:21-22; 15:1-7; 2 Chr.26:1-23	Azariah/Uzziah (52) (792–740)	Hosea (788–723); Jonah (780–765)
2 K.15:32-38; 2 Chr.26:23-27:9	Jotham (16) (750–731)	

THE DIVIDED KINGDOM

	SOUTHERN KINGDOM OF JUDAH		NORTHERN KINGDOM OF ISRAEL		DATE BC	FOREIGN KINGS	HISTORY
BIBLE REF.	KINGS (YEARS REIGNED)	PROPHETS	BIBLE REF. — KINGS (YEARS REIGNED) / PROPHETS				WORLD EVENTS

SOUTHERN KINGDOM OF JUDAH

BIBLE REF.	KINGS (YEARS REIGNED)	PROPHETS
2 K.15:38-16:20; 2 Chr.27:9-27; Is.7:1-9:1	**Ahaz** (16) (735–715)	**Isaiah** (740–690)
2 K.18:1-20:21; 2 Chr.28:27-32:33; Pr.25:1; Is.36:1-39:8	**Hezekiah** (29) (729–686)	**Micah** (735–725) **Oded** (733)
2 K.20:21-21:18; 2 Chr.32:33-33:20	**Manasseh** (55) (696–642)	**Nahum** (663–612)
2 K.21:18-26; 2 Chr.33:20-25	**Amon** (2) (642–640)	**Zephaniah** (640–609)
2 K.21:26-23:30; 2 Chr.33:25-35:27	**Josiah** (31) (640–609)	**Jeremiah** (627–562)
2 K.23:31-33; 2 Chr.36:1-4	**Jehoaz/Jehoahaz** (3 mos) (609)	**Habakkuk** (615–598)
2 K.23:34-24:7; 2 Chr.36:5-8	**Jehoiakim** (11) (608–598)	**Daniel** (605–535)
2 K.24:8-17; 25:27-30; 2 Chr.36:8-10;	**Jehoiachin** (3 mos) (598–597)	**Ezekiel** (593–571)
2 K.24:18-25:21; 2 Chr.36:10-14; Je.21:1-52:11	**Zedekiah/Mattaniah** (11) (597–586)	
2 K.25:22-26; Je.40:5-41:18	**Gedaliah** (2 mos) (Appointed by Nebuchadnezzar) (586)	**Haggai** (520) **Zechariah** (520–518)
		Malachi (430)

NORTHERN KINGDOM OF ISRAEL

BIBLE REF.	KINGS (YEARS REIGNED)	PROPHETS
2 K.15:23-26	**Pekahiah** (2) (742–740)	
2 K.15:27-31	**Pekah** (20) (752–732) (752–740) (ruled only in Gilead) (740–732) (ruled in Samaria)	
2 K.17:1-23	**Hoshea** (9) (732–722)	

DATE BC / FOREIGN KINGS / WORLD EVENTS

DATE BC	FOREIGN KINGS	WORLD EVENTS
	Tiglath-Pil[n]eser III [or Pul] (745–727) (Assyria)	Assyria takes control of Northern Kingdom (745–627)
	Shalmaneser V (727–722) (Assyria)	Assyria invades Northern Israel (732)
	So (727–716) (Egypt) **Sargon II** (710–705) (Assyria)	Fall of Northern Kingdom (722)
700	**Sennacherib** (705–681) (Assyria) **Merodach-Baladan** (721–710, 705–704) (Assyria) **Tirhakah** (690–664) (Egypt)	Sennacherib defeats Egypt (701) Hezekiah's tunnel (701) 185,000 Assyrians killed by God (701)
650	**Esarhaddon** (681–669) (Assyria) **Nabopolassar** (626–605) (Assyria) **Neco** (610–595) (Egypt)	Sennacherib destroys Babylon (689) Josiah's reform (621) Nineveh destroyed (612) Battle of Carchemish (605) 1st group of exiles from Judah taken to Babylon (605)
600	**Nebuchadnezzar II** (605–562) (Babylon)	2nd group of exiles from Judah taken to Babylon (597) Fall of Judah—Third group of exiles from Judah taken to Babylon (586)
550	**Evil-Merodach** (562–560) (Babylon) **Cyrus II** (559–530) (Medo-Persia) **Belshazzar** (552–539) (Babylon)	Fall of Babylon to Medo-Persian Empire (539) Cyrus II decrees that the Jews may return to the Holy Land (538) 1st exiles return to Holy Land with Zerubbabel (537)
500	**Darius I** (521–486) (Medo-Persia)	1st Temple foundation laid (536) 2nd Temple foundation laid (520) Temple completed (516) Republic of Rome est. (509)
450	**Artaxerxes** (465–425) (Persia)	2nd return under Ezra (458) 3rd return under Nehemiah (445)

*Some dates are approximate.

The resources used for the timeline in addition to the Bible are as follows:

1 Archer, Gleason L. *Encyclopedia of Bible Difficulties.* (Grand Rapids, Michigan: Zondervan Publishing House), 1982.
2 Freedman, David Noel, et. al. *The Anchor Bible Dictionary.* (New York: Doubleday), 1992.
3 Grun, Bernard. *The Timetables of History.* 3rd ed. (New York: Simon & Schuster), 1991.
4 Kaiser, Walter C. *A History of Israel.* (Nashville, Tennessee: Broadman & Holman Publishers), 1998.
5 Silverman, David P., ed. *Ancient Egypt.* (New York: Oxford University Press), 1997.

OUTLINE OF ISAIAH

THE PREACHER'S OUTLINE AND SERMON BIBLE® is *unique*. It differs from all other Study Bibles and Sermon Resource Materials in that every Passage and Subject is outlined right beside the Scripture. When you choose any *Subject* below and turn to the reference, you have not only the Scripture but also an outline of the Scripture and Subject *already prepared for you—verse by verse.*

For a quick example, choose one of the subjects below and turn over to the Scripture; you will find this to be a marvelous help for more organized and streamlined study.

In addition, every point of the Scripture and Subject is *fully developed in a Commentary with supporting Scripture* at the end of each point. Again, this arrangement makes sermon preparation much simpler and more efficient.

Note something else: the Subjects of *Isaiah* have titles that are both Biblical and *practical*. The practical titles are often more appealing to people. This *benefit* is clearly seen for use on billboards, bulletins, church newsletters, etc.

A suggestion: for the *quickest* overview of *Isaiah*, first read *all the Division titles* (I, II, III, etc.), then come back and read the individual outline titles.

OUTLINE OF ISAIAH

PART I: THE PROPHECIES OF CONDEMNATION, 1:1–35:10

I. **THE PROPHECIES OF REBUKE AND HOPE GIVEN TO JUDAH AND JERUSALEM: AN OVERVIEW OF THE PRESENT AND FUTURE OF GOD'S PEOPLE, 1:1–12:6**

   A. The LORD's Indictment of His People, 1:1-31
   B. The Future Kingdom and Temple of God, the Day of the LORD, and the Restoration of Israel: Three Key Events in the Future, 2:1–4:6
   C. The LORD's Condemnation of His Wayward Nation: Three Major Warnings to God's People, 5:1-30
   D. The Call of God's Prophet Isaiah: Three Elements Necessary to Serve God, 6:1-13
   E. The Deliverance from Threatening Enemies (Syria and Israel): Hope Given Through Five Clear Signs, 7:1–9:7
   F. The Sure Judgment of Unrepentant and Wicked Enemies (Israel and Assyria): Hope Given Through God's Assurance of Victory, 9:8–10:34
   G. The Coming Savior and the Establishment of God's Kingdom on Earth: Hope Given Through the Messiah, the Lord Jesus Christ, 11:1–12:6

II. **THE PROPHECIES CONCERNING GOD'S JUDGMENT OF THE NATIONS AND HIS TRIUMPH OVER THE WORLD, 13:1–27:13**

   A. God's Judgment of Babylon: A Picture of God's Judgment upon Evil Governments, 13:1–14:23
   B. God's Judgment of Assyria, Philistia, and Moab: A Picture of God's Plan for Judgment and of His Protection and Compassion, 14:24–16:14
   C. God's Judgment of Damascus (Syria), Ephraim (Israel), and Ethiopia: A Picture of Distrust and of Hope in the Face of Judgment, 17:1–18:7
   D. God's Judgment of Egypt: A Picture on God's Just Punishment, His Enduring Mercy, and His Clear Warning, 19:1–20:6
   E. God's Judgment of Babylon (the Persian Gulf Region), Edom, and Arabia: A Need to Watch, Repent, and Turn to the LORD, 21:17
   F. God's Judgment of Judah and Jerusalem: A Picture of God's Coming Judgment and Grace, 22:1-25
   G. God's Judgment of Tyre (Phoenicia): A Picture of the Proud Being Humbled Yet Given Hope, 23:1-18
   H. God's Judgment of the Whole World, His Universal Judgment: A Time of Great Tribulation, 24:1-23
   I. God's Plan for the Whole World and for His People: God's Seven-Step Plan for the World, 25:1-12
   J. God's Works and the Protection of His Vineyard, His People: God's Great Care for His People, 26:1–27:13

OUTLINE OF ISAIAH

III. THE PROPHECIES OF WOE: GOD'S WARNING TO HIS PEOPLE, 28:1–35:10

    A. Woe—A Strong Warning to Ephraim and Judah: Sins that Destroy a Nation and Its People, 28:1-29

    B. Woe—A Strong Warning to Ariel (Jerusalem): God's Unusual Dealings with Jerusalem, 29:1-24

    C. Woe—A Strong Warning to the Rebellious, the Stubborn, and the Hard-Hearted: A Message to All Who Rebel Against God, 30:1-33

    D. Woe—A Strong Warning to Those Who Ignore God and Place Their Trust in Egypt (the World): A Message to All Who Foolishly Misplace Their Trust, 31:1–32:20

    E. Woe—A Strong Warning to the Destroyer: A Message to All Who Commit Acts of Violence, 33:1-24

    F. Woe—A Strong Warning to the Whole World: The LORD's Day of Wrath and His Coming Kingdom, 34:1–35:10

DIVISION I

THE PROPHECIES OF REBUKE AND HOPE GIVEN TO JUDAH AND JERUSALEM: AN OVERVIEW OF THE PRESENT AND FUTURE OF GOD'S PEOPLE, 1:1–12:6

(1:1–12:6) **DIVISION OVERVIEW**: the book of *Isaiah* begins with a number of serious charges against God's people, indictments issued by the LORD Himself. The people of Judah were guilty of terrible sins, including acts of rebellion, false worship and injustice. As followers of God, they were supposed to be witnesses to the nations, but they had failed miserably. Yet, in the middle of the charges, there was a *great ray of hope*. The very name of Isaiah, which means *Jehovah saves*, pointed to the salvation offered by God to all who would turn from sin and be cleansed (1:1-31).

After leveling these serious charges against the people, Isaiah revealed the future of the kingdom of God, including the terrifying judgment and the glorious restoration of Israel (2:1–4:6). Isaiah strongly condemned the sins of Judah. Whereas the people should have been doing the work of the LORD, they were busy with their own interests. As a result, judgment would come to the nation at the hand of foreigners. But each time God condemned sin, He immediately offered hope (5:1-30).

The first five chapters introduce the major themes of the book. Following in chapter six is the record of Isaiah's call. Isaiah saw a powerful vision of God sitting upon His throne in all the radiant glory and majesty of His person. Deeply sensing the holiness of God, as well as his own terrible sinfulness, Isaiah fell prostrate before the LORD. He cried out, "Woe is me! for I am undone! My destruction is set!" But again hope was offered to the sinful. God forgave Isaiah of his sins and then called him to preach His Word to the world. It was a difficult message, a message of judgment that Isaiah was to take to the masses of the world. But a great hope lay in the future. A Messiah would come—a Savior, a Deliverer—who would offer salvation to the world (6:1-13).

As Isaiah took God's message to the world, the names of his own family served as living illustrations of the coming judgment. Their names, as well as the messages of Isaiah, called people to trust in the LORD completely for the salvation of their souls (7:1–9:7).

The LORD promised great victory over all the wicked and unrepentant enemies who opposed true believers (9:8–10:34). Most importantly, a remnant would survive and there would always be a people who would follow the LORD. The ultimate purpose of salvation would be accomplished, for the Messiah would come and salvation would be purchased for every human being. The coming Savior would pay the price for all who believed. And the good news of salvation would be taken to the world. The first major division of the book of *Isaiah* ends with a glorious song of praise to the LORD for what He would do through Jesus Christ, the Son of David (11:1–12:6).

THE PROPHECIES OF REBUKE AND HOPE GIVEN TO JUDAH AND JERUSALEM: AN OVERVIEW OF THE PRESENT AND FUTURE OF GOD'S PEOPLE, 1:1–12:6

A. The LORD's Indictment of His People, 1:1-31

B. The Future Kingdom and Temple of God, the Day of the LORD, and the Restoration of Israel: Three Key Events in the Future, 2:1–4:6

C. The LORD's Condemnation of His Wayward Nation: Three Major Warnings to God's People, 5:1-30

D. The Call of God's Prophet Isaiah: Three Elements Necessary to Serve God, 6:1-13

E. The Deliverance from Threatening Enemies (Syria and Israel): Hope Given Through Five Clear Signs, 7:1–9:7

F. The Sure Judgment of Unrepentant and Wicked Enemies (Israel and Assyria): Hope Given Through God's Assurance of Victory, 9:8–10:34

G. The Coming Savior and the Establishment of God's Kingdom on Earth: Hope Given Through the Messiah, the Lord Jesus Christ, 11:1–12:6

CHAPTER 1

PART I—THE PROPHECIES OF CONDEMNATION, 1:1–35:10

I. THE PROPHECIES OF REBUKE & HOPE GIVEN TO JUDAH & JERUSALEM: AN OVERVIEW OF THE PRESENT & FUTURE OF GOD'S PEOPLE, 1:1–12:6

A. The LORD's Indictment of His People, 1:1-31

1. God's prophet Isaiah: He was a man given a very special vision by God
a. Concerned Judah & Jerusalem
b. Touched the reigns of four kings

2. God's first charge: They were rebellious
a. The picture of a court trial: Called on heaven & earth to witness the charges

b. The charge: Rebellion
1) They had less knowledge & understanding than an ox or donkey

2) They had become a sinful people, loaded down with guilt: Were evil & corrupt children
3) They had forsaken the LORD, despised the Holy One, turned their backs on Him
c. The folly of rebellion: Continued chastisement
1) They were like victims, attacked & injured in both head & heart
• With the whole body beaten, bruised, & cut
• With wounds left untreated & allowed to fester & rot

2) They were to witness their country ravaged
• Their cities burned
• Their farms plundered & destroyed

• Their capital Jerusalem, the Daughter of Zion, besieged & destroyed: Would be nothing more than a shattered hut
3) They were to be judged like Sodom & Gomorrah,

The vision of Isaiah the son of Amoz, which he saw concerning Judah and Jerusalem in the days of Uzziah, Jotham, Ahaz, *and* Hezekiah, kings of Judah.

2 Hear, O heavens, and give ear, O earth: for the LORD hath spoken, I have nourished and brought up children, and they have rebelled against me.

3 The ox knoweth his owner, and the ass his master's crib: *but* Israel doth not know, my people doth not consider.

4 Ah sinful nation, a people laden with iniquity, a seed of evildoers, children that are corrupters: they have forsaken the LORD, they have provoked the Holy One of Israel unto anger, they are gone away backward.

5 Why should ye be stricken any more? ye will revolt more and more: the whole head is sick, and the whole heart faint.

6 From the sole of the foot even unto the head *there is* no soundness in it; *but* wounds, and bruises, and putrifying sores: they have not been closed, neither bound up, neither mollified with ointment.

7 Your country *is* desolate, your cities *are* burned with fire: your land, strangers devour it in your presence, and *it is* desolate, as overthrown by strangers.

8 And the daughter of Zion is left as a cottage in a vineyard, as a lodge in a garden of cucumbers, as a besieged city.

9 Except the LORD of hosts had left unto us a very small remnant, we should have been as Sodom, *and* we should have been like unto Gomorrah.

10 Hear the word of the LORD, ye rulers of Sodom; give ear unto the law of our God, ye people of Gomorrah.

11 To what purpose *is* the multitude of your sacrifices unto me? saith the LORD: I am full of the burnt offerings of rams, and the fat of fed beasts; and I delight not in the blood of bullocks, or of lambs, or of he goats.

12 When ye come to appear before me, who hath required this at your hand, to tread my courts?

13 Bring no more vain oblations; incense is an abomination unto me; the new moons and sabbaths, the calling of assemblies, I cannot away with; *it is* iniquity, even the solemn meeting.

14 Your new moons and your appointed feasts my soul hateth: they are a trouble unto me; I am weary to bear *them.*

15 And when ye spread forth your hands, I will hide mine eyes from you: yea, when ye make many prayers, I will not hear: your hands are full of blood.

16 Wash you, make you clean; put away the evil of your doings from before mine eyes; cease to do evil;

17 Learn to do well; seek judgment, relieve the oppressed, judge the fatherless, plead for the widow.

18 Come now, and let us reason together, saith the LORD: though your sins be as scarlet, they shall be as white as snow; though they be red like crimson, they shall be as wool.

19 If ye be willing and obedient, ye shall eat the good of the land:

20 But if ye refuse and rebel, ye shall be devoured with the sword: for the mouth of the LORD hath spoken *it.*

21 How is the faithful city become an harlot! it was full of judgment; righteousness lodged in it; but now murderers.

22 Thy silver is become

utterly decimated: BUT, God would leave a remnant, a few survivors
d. The call to hear God's Word: Rejected God's Word like Sodom and Gomorrah

3. God's second charge: They were insincere, unacceptable in their worship
a. The scathing accusation: Their worship was phony, empty, ritualistic
1) They worshipped, but hypocritically (vv.4,10): Were rejected by God
2) They came to God, but their coming was worthless, nothing more than trampling His courts
b. The strong command: They must stop their formal, false worship
1) Their meaningless offerings
2) Their detestable incense
3) Their evil assemblies
4) Their special services: Festivals & feasts
• Were hated by God
• Had become a weary burden to Him
5) Their formal prayers: Were not heard by God because their hands were as murderers, guilty of treating the needy unfairly, unjustly

c. The astounding offer of clemency, a full pardon: Through spiritual cleansing
1) They must repent: Turn from evil & learn to do right
• Seek justice
• Help the oppressed
• Defend the fatherless
• Plead for the widow
2) They must come to the LORD & reason with Him: Face His convincing arguments
• They were sinful, 2-4
• They could be forgiven

d. The warning: Two possibilities
1) If they obeyed, would be rewarded
2) If they kept turning away & rebelling, they would be destroyed: Judgment was certain, declared by God's Word

4. God's third charge: They were unjust, deceitful
a. The picture of a faithful, just, & righteous city: Became unfaithful—full of murderers
1) Had been like pure silver

& wine but were now impure & worthless

2) Had corrupt leaders
- Were covetous, like thieves who sought bribes
- Refused to help & defend the fatherless & widows

b. The verdict & sentence: Pronounced by the LORD, the LORD of hosts, the Mighty One of Israel

1) He will judge, get rid of all His enemies

2) He will purge away all the impurities of the city

3) He will restore righteous & just leaders: Jerusalem will be called *The City*

---

dross, thy wine mixed with water:

23 Thy princes *are* rebellious, and companions of thieves: every one loveth gifts, and followeth after rewards: they judge not the fatherless, neither doth the cause of the widow come unto them.

24 Therefore saith the Lord, the LORD of hosts, the mighty One of Israel, Ah, I will ease me of mine adversaries, and avenge me of mine enemies:

25 And I will turn my hand upon thee, and purely purge away thy dross, and take away all thy tin:

26 And I will restore thy judges as at the first, and thy counsellors as at the beginning: afterward thou shalt be

---

called, The city of righteousness, the faithful city.

27 Zion shall be redeemed with judgment, and her converts with righteousness.

28 And the destruction of the transgressors and of the sinners *shall be* together, and they that forsake the LORD shall be consumed.

29 For they shall be ashamed of the oaks which ye have desired, and ye shall be confounded for the gardens that ye have chosen.

30 For ye shall be as an oak whose leaf fadeth, and as a garden that hath no water.

31 And the strong shall be as tow, and the maker of it as a spark, and they shall both burn together, and none shall quench *them*.

---

of Righteousness, the Faithful City

4) He will place the repentant people in the new, redeemed city of Jerusalem

5) He will execute true justice against all rebels & sinners, all who forsake Him

- They will be ashamed & disgraced: Due to their false worship

- They will suffer the fate of the things in which they trusted: Fade away

- They & their works will be burned, suffer in an unquenchable fire

DIVISION I

THE PROPHECIES OF REBUKE AND HOPE GIVEN TO JUDAH AND JERUSALEM: AN OVERVIEW OF THE PRESENT AND FUTURE OF GOD'S PEOPLE, 1:1–12:6

A. The LORD's Indictment of His People, 1:1-31

(1:1-31) **Introduction**: the scene is a courtroom trial. The presiding judge is the LORD Himself. The accused are the citizens of Judah and Jerusalem, the very people God had chosen to be His witnesses to the unbelieving nations of the earth. However, Isaiah's message in this passage is applicable to all who know the LORD, for all believers are called to be His witnesses. Thus as His professed followers, we are all standing before the bar of the Judge of the universe. We are on trial, defending ourselves against some serious charges. And the LORD's case against us is as strong as it was against Judah and Jerusalem.

God's case is presented by the great prophet Isaiah, who makes a powerful, dramatic presentation of God's charges. But even as he pronounces the LORD's indictment, the love of God shines forth. With each charge, the LORD offers His people the hope of salvation. Even Isaiah's name offers hope, for it means *the LORD saves*.

Only the redeemed—those who have been set free from sin and judgment—will live in the Holy City of God, the New Jerusalem. God will create New Jerusalem when Jesus Christ returns to set up God's kingdom on earth (see outline and notes—Re.21:9-23 for more discussion). Through Isaiah, God tells His people that if they will repent of their sins, He will forgive them. Furthermore, He assures them that they will live in this Holy City of righteousness where there will be no evil or injustice. This is, *The LORD's Indictment of His People*, 1:1-31.

1. God's prophet Isaiah: he was a man given a very special vision by God (v.1).
2. God's first charge: they were rebellious (vv.2-10).
3. God's second charge: they were insincere, unacceptable in their worship (vv.11-20).
4. God's third charge: they were unjust, deceitful (vv.21-31).

1 (1:1) **Prophets, List of, Isaiah—Isaiah the Prophet, Prophecies Concerning, Judah and Jerusalem; Ministry of, Spanned the Reign of Four Kings**: Isaiah was one of God's great prophets, a man who received a very special vision from the LORD. The word *vision* means to see, to grasp and understand some truth or future event. It is not the same as an insight that comes from human reasoning or from the opinions of people. A vision is a *revelation* from God.

> **"For the Prophecy came not in old time by the will of man: but holy men of God spake *as they were* moved [led along] by the Holy Ghost" (2 Pe.1:21).**

In a clear and dramatic way, God gave Isaiah a special revelation into events yet to come. Isaiah clearly saw…
- the future of Judah and Jerusalem (1:1–12:6)
- the future judgment of God on the nations and His triumph over the world (13:1–27:13)
- the future *woe* (condemnation) that would fall upon God's people because of their continued sin and refusal to repent (28:1–35:10)
- the future shift of world power from Assyria to Babylon and the impact upon Judah and Jerusalem (36:1–39:8)
- the future captivity of the Jews in Babylon and their release by King Cyrus of Persia (40:1–48:22)
- the future coming of the Lord Jesus Christ (49:1–59:21)
- the future consummation of history: the glorious destiny of God's people and the terrifying fate of unbelievers (60:1–66:24)

ISAIAH 1:1-31

In addition to learning that the LORD gave Isaiah very special visions, we glean two other significant facts from the opening verse of Isaiah:

OUTLINE	SCRIPTURE
1. God's prophet Isaiah: He was a man given a very special vision by God a. Concerned Judah & Jerusalem b. Touched the reigns of four kings	The vision of Isaiah the son of Amoz, which he saw concerning Judah and Jerusalem in the days of Uzziah, Jotham, Ahaz, *and* Hezekiah, kings of Judah.

a. Isaiah's ministry focused on Judah and Jerusalem, and he preached and proclaimed the prophecies given by God. But in truth, Isaiah ministry is to the whole world. As the above outline shows, God gave him visions that concerned the future of the nations and of world history itself. His visions included the coming of the Savior, which lay some 700 years in the future. Furthermore, God revealed to Isaiah the glorious consummation of human history. Thus he is definitely a prophet to minister to the whole world. His prophecies and messages are to be heard and obeyed by all people of all times. They are the Word of God, God's clear warning to the world.

b. Isaiah's visions and ministry touched the reigns of four kings. He began his ministry in the year that King Uzziah died (6:1). Uzziah lived a righteous life that pleased the LORD, but later in life pride and self-exaltation caused him to slide into sin. As a result, God disciplined him by afflicting him with leprosy, a disease he had until the day he died. As a leper, he was forced to live in isolation and to put his son, the Crown Prince Jotham, in charge of the government (see outline and notes—2 Chr.26:1-23 for more discussion).

King Jotham was also a godly king, and he ruled over Judah for 16 years. Apparently he and Isaiah had a close relationship, for the prophet seems to have had unrestricted access to the royal court and the freedom to preach without fear of persecution (see outline and notes—2 Chr.27:1-9 for more discussion).

However, when Jotham's son Ahaz took the throne, the godly environment throughout the nation changed dramatically. Ahaz was a very wicked king, totally depraved. Throughout his 16 year rule, he promoted and led the people in false worship, even committing the detestable sin of human sacrifice. Shockingly, he sacrificed his own sons to false gods. It was during his reign that the famous Syro-Ephraimite War took place, a war that utterly devastated Judah. The nation lost 120,000 soldiers in battle and 200,000 women and children were taken captive. King Ahaz was also guilty of seeking an alliance with the evil and brutal Assyrians, looking to them as Judah's savior. He sought the help of Assyria rather than the help of the LORD.

No doubt, Isaiah faced a difficult time during the reign of Ahaz, for the king led the entire nation down the path of secular living and false worship. People who live wicked lives and engage in false worship want nothing to do with the LORD and His claims of righteousness. Although Scripture says nothing about Isaiah facing the threat of persecution, he was most likely under constant pressure to stop preaching the coming judgment of God. As a prophet of God during the reign of an evil king, he most certainly faced ridicule, contempt, and threats upon his life. (See outline and notes—2 Chr.28:1-27 for more discussion.)

Whatever the case, when Ahaz's son Hezekiah took the throne, the situation throughout Judah again changed dramatically. Although Hezekiah had been reared in one of the most wicked environments imaginable, he somehow came to know the LORD in a very personal way, and he wholeheartedly committed his life to the LORD. Hezekiah's godly reign would not stop the tide of wickedness flowing through the Southern Kingdom, but it would stay the hand of God's judgment for a long time. Judah would not fall to Babylon until more than one hundred years had passed. Under Hezekiah's leadership, a spiritual reformation took place and revival broke out among the people (see outline and notes—2 Chr.29:1–32:33 for more discussion). Apparently Isaiah had a close relationship with Hezekiah, for he devoted four complete chapters to him, covering his entire reign (see outline and notes—Is.36:1–39:8 for more discussion).

Violence, immorality, and the constant threat of war—these were the problems facing society in Isaiah's day. Assyria, the most powerful nation of that day, was determined to build a world empire, and the Assyrians were among the most brutal people to ever come upon the stage of world history. Seldom before or since have there been days so turbulent, so gripped by a spirit of lawlessness. These were the days in which Isaiah was called to minister and proclaim God's Word to the world.

> **Thought 1.** People today desperately need a spiritual vision—a clear insight into spiritual matters—yet millions seem to be blinded to spiritual truth. They are complacent, disinterested, and even closed-minded to the truth that only those who approach God through His Son Jesus Christ are acceptable to God. Down through history prophets have courageously proclaimed this truth. The vast majority of people reject prophetic visions of Christ and of God's warnings to the world. They want nothing to do with a message that proclaims the truth of righteousness and of the judgment to come.
>
> But not Isaiah, the great prophet of God. He wanted clear insight into the future. He wanted to know what God's people faced. He undoubtedly sought the LORD often for clear insight into the future so he could face whatever was coming and do all he could to prepare God's people.
>
> As believers, we should all seek clear insight as we study the prophecies in God's Word. Understanding what He says about the future strengthens our faith and better prepares us to face the terrible trials of life. Listen to what God's Holy Word says about spiritual vision and insight:
>
> **"And their eyes were opened, and they knew him [Christ]; and he vanished out of their sight"** (Lu.24:31).
> **"He shall glorify me: for he shall receive of mine, and shall show *it* unto you. All things that the Father hath are mine: therefore said I, that he shall take of mine, and shall show *it* unto you"** (Jn.16:14-15).

60

"For God, who commanded the light to shine out of darkness, hath shined in our hearts, to *give* the light of the knowledge of the glory of God in the face of Jesus Christ" (2 Co.4:6).

"The eyes of your understanding being enlightened; that ye may know what is the hope of his calling, and what the riches of the glory of his inheritance in the saints" (Ep.1:18).

"By faith he forsook Egypt, not fearing the wrath of the king: for he endured, as seeing him who is invisible" (He.11:27).

"And God opened her eyes, and she saw a well of water; and she went, and filled the bottle with water, and gave the lad drink" (Ge.21:19).

"And Elisha prayed, and said, LORD, I pray thee, open his eyes, that he may see. And the LORD opened the eyes of the young man; and he saw: and, behold, the mountain *was* full of horses and chariots of fire round about Elisha" (2 K.6:17).

"For thou wilt light my candle: the LORD my God will enlighten my darkness" (Ps.18:28).

"The entrance of thy words giveth light; it giveth understanding unto the simple" (Ps.119:130).

"And in that day shall the deaf hear the words of the book, and the eyes of the blind shall see out of obscurity, and out of darkness" (Is.29:18).

---

2 (1:2-10) **Rebellion, Example of, Israel—Rebellion, Discussed—Judah, Indictment Against, Rebellion—Jerusalem, Indictment Against, Rebellion—Forsaking God, Example of, Judah—Turning Away, From God, Example—Apostasy, Example of, Judah—Discipline, Example of—Chastisement, Example of—Remnant, of Israel, Promised—Court Trial, of Whom, Judah and Jerusalem**: God's first charge against His people was a strong one: they were rebellious children. God's relationship with His people is like that of a father with his children. God's Father-son relationship with Israel began when the LORD called Abraham to trust Him. From the time God chose him, Abraham and his descendants were to follow and obey the LORD just as children follow and obey their fathers. Down through the generations, God nurtured His people, caring for and looking after them. He always guided them, taught them, and met their needs. And when they sinned, He disciplined them and did all He could to bring them back into fellowship with Him.

God chose the Israelites to be His special witnesses on earth, to proclaim that the LORD Himself (Jehovah, Yahweh) is the only true and living God (Ge.12:1-3). He gave them two wonderful gifts: His Word, which they were to share with the world, and His Son, the Savior, who was to rescue the world from the bondage of sin and death.

But down through the generations, the Israelites rebelled against the LORD. Like rebellious children, they rejected His love and His Word and broke all of His commandments. Forsaking the LORD, they lived wicked lives characterized by immorality, lawlessness, and violence, and they corrupted the society and land God had so freely given them. Note God's first charge against His people, the charge of rebellion.

OUTLINE	SCRIPTURE	SCRIPTURE	OUTLINE

2. God's first charge: They were rebellious children
a. The picture of a court trial: Called on heaven & earth to witness the charges
b. The charge: Rebellion
  1) They had less knowledge & understanding than an ox or donkey
 	
  2) They had become a sinful people, loaded down with guilt: Were evil & corrupt children
  3) They had forsaken the LORD, despised the Holy One, turned their backs on Him
c. The folly of rebellion: Continued chastisement
  1) They were like victims, attacked & injured in both head & heart
  • With the whole body beaten, bruised, & cut
	2 Hear, O heavens, and give ear, O earth: for the LORD hath spoken, I have nourished and brought up children, and they have rebelled against me.
	3 The ox knoweth his owner, and the ass his master's crib: *but* Israel doth not know, my people doth not consider.
	4 Ah sinful nation, a people laden with iniquity, a seed of evildoers, children that are corrupters: they have forsaken the LORD, they have provoked the Holy One of Israel unto anger, they are gone away backward.
	5 Why should ye be stricken any more? ye will revolt more and more: the whole head is sick, and the whole heart faint.
	6 From the sole of the foot even unto the head *there is* no
		soundness in it; *but* wounds, and bruises, and putrifying sores: they have not been closed, neither bound up, neither mollified with ointment.
		7 Your country *is* desolate, your cities *are* burned with fire: your land, strangers devour it in your presence, and *it is* desolate, as overthrown by strangers.
		8 And the daughter of Zion is left as a cottage in a vineyard, as a lodge in a garden of cucumbers, as a besieged city.
		9 Except the LORD of hosts had left unto us a very small remnant, we should have been as Sodom, *and* we should have been like unto Gomorrah.
		10 Hear the word of the LORD, ye rulers of Sodom; give ear unto the law of our God, ye people of Gomorrah.
			• With wounds left untreated & allowed to fester & rot
			
			2) They were to witness their country ravaged
			  • Their cities burned
			  • Their farms plundered & destroyed
			
			  • Their capital Jerusalem, the Daughter of Zion, besieged & destroyed: Would be nothing more than a shattered hut
			3) They were to be judged like Sodom & Gomorrah, utterly decimated: BUT God would leave a remnant, a few survivors
			
			d. The call to hear God's Word: Like Sodom & Gomorrah, they had rejected God's Word

a. The picture is that of a court trial (v.2). The great judge is the LORD Himself. He sits upon His sovereign throne of judgment, ready to indict the accused and to execute justice. The defendants are God's own people, the very ones He had chosen to be His special witnesses. In a deep, thunderous voice, the LORD calls upon heaven and earth to witness the charges against His people. Heaven and earth had witnessed not only the birth of Israel, but also its rebellion against the LORD. Therefore, all creation would agree with the charges God was now leveling against them. Choosing heaven and earth as witnesses showed just how solemn and serious the judgment of God's people would be.

b. The charge of rebellion revealed three facts about God's people (vv.3-4):

1) It showed they had less knowledge and understanding than an ox or donkey. These animals know their owners. They know the person who feeds them and looks after them. They even know who holds them responsible to work. But not God's people, not the Israelites. Their rebellion proved they did not really know the LORD. They did not understand His love or why He had chosen them to be His people. They simply did not comprehend that they were to be His witnesses to the other peoples of the earth.

2) It showed they had sinful hearts. God's people had become loaded down with a heavy burden of guilt (v.4). They were evil children, not only corrupt themselves, but corruptors who led others to imitate their evil behavior.

3) It showed they had forsaken the LORD, despised the Holy One of Israel, and turned their backs on Him (v.4). The title *The Holy One of Israel* is used about 25 times in the book of *Isaiah*, but only six times elsewhere in the Old Testament. The word *holy* emphasizes the character of God and contrasts His righteous acts with the sins of Israel. God's holiness stresses the necessity of their living pure and righteous lives. As *The Holy One of Israel,* God had a very special claim on the nation. But Israel totally rejected Him and His claims on their lives. They refused to be His witnesses to the unbelieving nations and peoples of the earth.

c. The rebellion of God's people was sheer folly, for it led to continued chastisement by God (vv.5-9). Their rebellion down through the years had caused God to discipline the Israelites. Other nations had been allowed to attack, conquer, and devastate them. In addition to war, the nation had suffered all of the consequences that sin brings upon a people: it had become an immoral, lawless, and violent society. As long as Judah persisted in its rebellion, it would continue to feel the hand of God's discipline.

When Isaiah announced this prophecy, the nation was apparently still experiencing some prosperity. The judgment predicted here still lay in the future; therefore, the people still had time to repent of their rebellion and turn back to the LORD. Seeking to focus their attention on God's judgment, Isaiah asked two questions: Why would they choose to be stricken by God's judgment again? Why would they force Him to discipline them? Then he made three comparisons to show what the nation would be like when God's judgment fell:

1) The nation would be like a wretched victim that had been attacked and beaten (vv.5-6). No part of the nation's body would escape injury, and the wounds would be severe. The head, heart, and entire body of the nation, from the sole of the foot to the top of the head, would be bruised and cut. Left untreated, the wounds would become infected and open sores allowed to fester and rot.

2) The nation would be ravaged (vv.7-8). Cities would be burned and the people's farms plundered and destroyed. Jerusalem, the daughter of Zion, would be besieged, destroyed, and abandoned (v.8). The capital would look like a crumbling hut that had been left to deteriorate in a field long after the melons had been harvested.

3) The nation would suffer the same fate as Sodom and Gomorrah: it would be decimated (v.9). In His mercy, God would save some people, but they would be few—just a small remnant. Although the vast number of Israelites would continue to rebel against God, there would be a few genuine believers who would obey God's commandments and live righteously. God would spare those few so that His purpose for the Jewish people could be fulfilled. He would still give His Word to the world through the believers of Israel, and His Son, the promised Messiah, would come through the Jewish people. The promise of the *remnant* is one of the great promises of Holy Scripture (Is.1:9; 4:3; 6:13; 10:20-23; 11:11, 16; 46:3; Je.6:9; 23:3; 31:7; Mi.2:12; Zec.8:12; Ro.9:27-29; 11:5).

d. Because of the people's sin, they had become just like Sodom and Gomorrah: totally depraved. Their only hope was to hear the Word of the LORD and to listen to His law (v.10). *Hear* and *listen* mean to heed, give attention to, and obey God's commandments. This was the only hope for the rebellious children of Jerusalem and Judah.

Thought 1. How many of us have rebelled against God, turning away from Him and His Holy Word? To *rebel* means to disobey God. People who refuse to keep God's commandments live as they please, doing their own thing. How many of us are living immoral and unrighteous lives, engaging in sex outside of marriage, oppressing the weak, and cheating others? A person who rebels is defiant. How many of us are defiant toward parents, employers, teachers, or any other person in authority? A person who rebels can cause divisiveness and sometimes rebellion. Think of the turmoil when athletes rebel against a coach, when students rebel against teachers, when employees rebel against employers, when children rebel against parents, and when people rebel against governments. But as serious as rebellion is within society, the gravest offense is rebellion against God. When we rebel against Him, we contribute to the immorality, lawlessness, and violence of society. And we doom ourselves to suffer the punishment of God's judgment. Listen to what God's Holy Word says about rebellion:

"But after thy hardness and impenitent heart treasurest up unto thyself wrath against the day of wrath and revelation of the righteous judgment of God" (Ro.2:5).

"But fornication, and all uncleanness, or covetousness, let it not be once named among you, as becometh saints; Neither filthiness, nor foolish talking, nor jesting, which are not convenient: but rather giving of thanks. For this ye know, that no whoremonger, nor unclean person, nor covetous man, who is an idolater, hath any inheritance in the kingdom of Christ and of God. Let no man deceive you with vain words: for because of these things cometh the wrath of God upon the children of disobedience" (Ep.5:3-6).

"And to you who are troubled rest with us, when the Lord Jesus shall be revealed from heaven with his mighty angels, In flaming fire taking vengeance on them that know not God, and that obey not the gospel of our Lord Jesus Christ: Who shall be punished with everlasting destruction from the presence of the Lord, and from the glory of his power" (2 Th.1:7-9).

"For if the word spoken by angels was stedfast, and every transgression and disobedience received a just recompence of reward; How shall we escape, if we neglect so great salvation; which at the first began to be spoken by the Lord, and was confirmed unto us by them that heard *him*" (He.2:2-3).

"Take heed, brethren, lest there be in any of you an evil heart of unbelief, in departing from the living God. But exhort one another daily, while it is called To day; lest any of you be hardened through the deceitfulness of sin" (He.3:12-13).

"I will therefore put you in remembrance, though ye once knew this, how that the Lord, having saved the people out of the land of Egypt, afterward destroyed them that believed not. And the angels which kept not their first estate, but left their own habitation, he hath reserved in everlasting chains under darkness unto the judgment of the great day. Even as Sodom and Gomorrha, and the cities about them in like manner, giving themselves over to fornication, and going after strange flesh, are set forth for an example, suffering the vengeance of eternal fire" (Jude 1:5-7).

"And a curse, if ye will not obey the commandments of the LORD your God, but turn aside out of the way which I command you this day, to go after other gods, which ye have not known" (De.11:28).

"But if ye will not obey the voice of the LORD, but rebel against the commandment of the LORD, then shall the hand of the LORD be against you, as *it was* against your fathers" (1 S.12:15).

"Happy *is* the man that feareth alway: but he that hardeneth his heart shall fall into mischief" (Pr.28:14).

"He, that being often reproved hardeneth *his* neck, shall suddenly be destroyed, and that without remedy" (Pr.29:1).

"Woe to the rebellious children, saith the LORD, that take counsel, but not of me; and that cover with a covering, but not of my spirit, that they may add sin to sin" (Is.30:1).

"I have spread out my hands all the day unto a rebellious people, which walketh in a way *that was* not good, after their own thoughts"(Is.65:2).

"And he said unto me, Son of man, I send thee to the children of Israel, to a rebellious nation that hath rebelled against me: they and their fathers have transgressed against me, *even* unto this very day" (Eze.2:3).

"Son of man, thou dwellest in the midst of a rebellious house, which have eyes to see, and see not; they have ears to hear, and hear not: for they *are* a rebellious house"(Eze.12:2).

3 (1:11-20) **Worship, False, Formal and Ritualistic—Worship, Formal and Ritualistic—Ritual, Danger of, Formal Worship—Ceremony, Dangers of, Formal Worship—Worship, Dangers of, Insincere and Formal—Temple, Abuse of, Formal Worship; Insincere Worship—Cleansing, Spiritual, Steps to—Spiritual Cleansing, Steps to—Reason, Invitation to—Reason, True and Honest, Results of—Forgiveness of Sins, Secured by, Honest Reasoning—Prayers, Kinds of, Formal and Insincere—Offerings, Kinds of, Formal and Insincere**: God's second charge against His people was sad and tragic. Their worship was insincere; thus it was unacceptable to God. The people of Judah and Jerusalem were worshipping, but their worship was false. Isaiah used strong language to express God's disgust with false worship.

OUTLINE	SCRIPTURE	SCRIPTURE	OUTLINE
3. **God's second charge: Their worship was insincere, unacceptable** a. The scathing accusation: The worship was phony, empty, ritualistic 　1) They worshipped, but hypocritically (vv.4,10): Were rejected by God 　2) They came to God, but their coming was worthless, nothing more than trampling His courts b. The strong command: They must stop their formal, false worship 　1) Their meaningless offerings 　2) Their detestable incense 　3) Their evil assemblies 　4) Their special services: Festivals & feasts 　• Were hated by God 　• Had become a weary burden to Him 　5) Their formal prayers: Were not heard by God because their hands were	11 To what purpose *is* the multitude of your sacrifices unto me? saith the LORD: I am full of the burnt offerings of rams, and the fat of fed beasts; and I delight not in the blood of bullocks, or of lambs, or of he goats. 12 When ye come to appear before me, who hath required this at your hand, to tread my courts? 13 Bring no more vain oblations; incense is an abomination unto me; the new moons and sabbaths, the calling of assemblies, I cannot away with; *it is* iniquity, even the solemn meeting. 14 Your new moons and your appointed feasts my soul hateth: they are a trouble unto me; I am weary to bear *them.* 15 And when ye spread forth your hands, I will hide mine eyes from you: yea, when ye	make many prayers, I will not hear: your hands are full of blood. 16 Wash you, make you clean; put away the evil of your doings from before mine eyes; cease to do evil; 17 Learn to do well; seek judgment, relieve the oppressed, judge the fatherless, plead for the widow. 18 Come now, and let us reason together, saith the LORD: though your sins be as scarlet, they shall be as white as snow; though they be red like crimson, they shall be as wool. 19 If ye be willing and obedient, ye shall eat the good of the land: 20 But if ye refuse and rebel, ye shall be devoured with the sword: for the mouth of the LORD hath spoken *it.*	as murderers, guilty of treating the needy unfairly, unjustly c. The astounding offer of clemency, a full pardon: Through spiritual cleansing 　1) They must repent: Turn from evil & learn to do right 　• Seek justice 　• Help the oppressed 　• Defend the fatherless 　• Plead for the widow 　2) They must come to the LORD & reason with Him: Face His convincing arguments 　• They were sinful, 2-4 　• They could be forgiven d. The warning: Two possibilities 　1) If they obeyed, would be rewarded 　2) If they kept turning away & rebelling, they would be destroyed: Judgment was certain, declared by God's Word

a. God charged His people with phony, empty, ritualistic worship (vv.11-12). Note that the people were worshipping the LORD. They were faithfully attending worship services and offering their sacrifices to the LORD. But their worship was hypocritical, for in their hearts they were rebelling against God (vv.2-4, 10). They refused to obey His Word and were living sinful lives. As soon as they left the worship services, they returned to their immoral, lawless, and selfish ways.

Remember that the burnt offering was sacrificed in order to bring about reconciliation with God (see outline and notes—Le.1:1-17 for more discussion). Thus in making their offerings, the people were seeking to be reconciled with God. However, they were unwilling to turn from their sins and turn back to God. They were unwilling to keep His commandments, unwilling to live righteous lives, unwilling to commit all they were and had to Him. As a result, God rejected their offerings. He took no delight in them.

The people's coming before Him to worship amounted to nothing but trampling His courts. They were hypocrites—people who professed to know God, but whose hearts were far from Him. Their worship was nothing but outward show. Their sacrifices had become nothing more than a ritual, a formal and insincere ceremony that God hated. They had become a weary burden to Him. Keep in mind what God wanted: obedience. To obey is better than sacrifice, that is, worship (1 S.15:22).

b. God issued a strong warning through Isaiah: His people must immediately stop their false worship (vv.13-15).
⇒ They must stop making meaningless offerings.
⇒ They must stop bringing detestable incense. Remember that incense was a symbol of prayer ascending to the LORD.
⇒ They must stop their evil assemblies—not only their regular worship services, but also their special festivals, feasts, and gatherings (v.14).
⇒ They must stop their formal prayers. God did not hear their prayers because their hands were as murderers who treated the needy unfairly and unjustly and in some cases murdered them (v.15).

c. Surprisingly, despite the people's hollow and hypocritical worship, God made the astounding offer of full pardon. The people could be spiritually cleansed from their sin (vv.16-18). But three steps were necessary:
1) They must first repent, turn from their evil ways, and learn to do right (vv.16-17). They must...
• seek justice
• help the oppressed
• defend the fatherless and orphans
• plead and fight for the rights of widows

2) They must come to the LORD and reason with Him (v.18). They must admit that their sins were as scarlet, the deepest color of red, and that they were as guilty as murderers who shed the blood of innocent people.
3) They must come to the LORD for forgiveness. Believing the promise of God, they must confess their sins and ask God to forgive them. Though their sins have stained them as red as scarlet, the LORD can make them as white as snow, as white as wool.

d. Isaiah warned God's people of two possible verdicts (vv.19-20). If they were willing to be cleansed and to obey God, they would be rewarded (v.19). The people would once again eat the very best fruit of the land and live fruitful and productive lives.

However, if the people continued to turn away from the LORD, they would be destroyed. Judgment was certain, for the LORD Himself had declared it. His Word was the guarantee that judgment would fall on all who continued to rebel against Him and disobey His holy commandments.

Thought 1. False worship is unacceptable to God. When people truly believe and obey God's Word, their worship is acceptable; but when they continue in sin, their worship is unacceptable. No matter how much they worship, their worship is meaningless, for they are just going through the motions. They are insincere and hypocritical. As soon as they leave the worship service, they continue in their sinful ways. They profess one thing, but live another. In truth, their hearts are far from God.

Think of the millions of churches and worship sites throughout the world. There is one within walking distance of almost every person living in a major city of the world. Yet crime, immorality, and greed flood these same cities. Churches and organized religion seem to make little difference. It is as though they have become irrelevant to society.

Why? Because the worship of so many people is insincere. Think of the number of people who own a Bible and claim to be religious, but whose behavior exposes them as hypocrites. Many attend worship services, but as soon as they walk out the church doors, they return to their sinful ways. In God's eyes their worship is meaningless. Listen to what God's Holy Word says about false worship:

"Not every one that saith unto me, Lord, Lord, shall enter into the kingdom of heaven; but he that doeth the will of my Father which is in heaven. Many will say to me in that day, Lord, Lord, have we not prophesied in thy name? and in thy name have cast out devils? and in thy name done many wonderful works?" (Mt.7:21-22).

"Woe unto you, scribes and Pharisees, hypocrites! for ye devour widows' houses, and for a pretence make long prayer: therefore ye shall receive the greater damnation" (Mt.23:14).

"Even so ye also outwardly appear righteous unto men, but within ye are full of hypocrisy and iniquity" (Mt.23:28).

"He answered and said unto them, Well hath Esaias prophesied of you hypocrites, as it is written, This people honoureth me with *their* lips, but their heart is far from me" (Mk.7:6).

"And why call ye me, Lord, Lord, and do not the things which I say? Whosoever cometh to me, and heareth my sayings, and doeth them, I will show you to whom he is like: He is like a man which built an house, and digged deep, and laid the foundation on a rock: and when the flood arose, the stream beat vehemently upon that house, and could not shake it: for it was founded upon a rock. But he that heareth, and doeth not, is like a man that without a foundation built an house upon the earth; against which the stream did beat vehemently, and immediately it fell; and the ruin of that house was great" (Lu.6:46-49).

"For the kingdom of God is not meat and drink; but righteousness, and peace, and joy in the Holy Ghost" (Ro.14:17).

"Ye observe days, and months, and times, and years. I am afraid of you, lest I have bestowed upon you labour in vain" (Ga.4:10-11).

"This know also, that in the last days perilous times shall come. For men shall be lovers of their own selves, covetous, boasters, proud, blasphemers, disobedient to parents, unthankful, unholy, Without natural affection, trucebreakers, false accusers, incontinent, fierce, despisers of those that are good, Traitors, heady, highminded, lovers of pleasures more than lovers of God; Having a form of godliness, but denying the power thereof: from such turn away. For of this sort are they which creep into houses, and lead captive silly women laden with sins, led away with divers lusts" (2 Ti.3:1-6).

"They profess that they know God; but in works they deny *him*, being abominable, and disobedient, and unto every good work reprobate" (Tit.1:16).

"My little children, let us not love in word, neither in tongue; but in deed and in truth" (1 Jn.3:18).

"For thou desirest not sacrifice; else would I give *it:* thou delightest not in burnt offering. The sacrifices of God *are* a broken spirit: a broken and a contrite heart, O God, thou wilt not despise" (Ps.51:16-17).

"And they remembered that God *was* their rock, and the high God their redeemer. Nevertheless they did flatter him with their mouth, and they lied unto him with their tongues" (Ps.78:35-36).

"Burning lips and a wicked heart *are like* a potsherd covered with silver dross" (Pr.26:23).

"Keep thy foot when thou goest to the house of God, and be more ready to hear, than to give the sacrifice of fools: for they consider not that they do evil" (Ecc.5:1).

"Wherefore the Lord said, Forasmuch as this people draw near *me* with their mouth, and with their lips do honour me, but have removed their heart far from me, and their fear toward me is taught by the precept of men" (Is.29:13).

"Hear ye this, O house of Jacob, which are called by the name of Israel, and are come forth out of the waters of Judah, which swear by the name of the LORD, and make mention of the God of Israel, *but* not in truth, nor in righteousness" (Is.48:1).

"Cry aloud, spare not, lift up thy voice like a trumpet, and show my people their transgression, and the house of Jacob their sins. Yet they seek me daily, and delight to know my ways, as a nation that did righteousness, and forsook not the ordinance of their God: they ask of me the ordinances of justice; they take delight in approaching to God. Wherefore have we fasted, *say they,* and thou seest not? *wherefore* have we afflicted our soul, and thou takest no knowledge? Behold, in the day of your fast ye find pleasure, and exact all your labours. Behold, ye fast for strife and debate, and to smite with the fist of wickedness: ye shall not fast as *ye do this* day, to make your voice to be heard on high. Is it such a fast that I have chosen? a day for a man to afflict his soul? *is it* to bow down his head as a bulrush, and to spread sackcloth and ashes *under him?* wilt thou call this a fast, and an acceptable day to the LORD? *Is* not this the fast that I have chosen? to loose the bands of wickedness, to undo the heavy burdens, and to let the oppressed go free, and that ye break every yoke? *Is it* not to deal thy bread to the hungry, and that thou bring the poor that are cast out to thy house? when thou seest the naked, that thou cover him; and that thou hide not thyself from thine own flesh?" (Is.58:1-7).

"And they come unto thee as the people cometh, and they sit before thee *as* my people, and they hear thy words, but they will not do them: for with their mouth they show much love, *but* their heart goeth after their covetousness. And, lo, thou *art* unto them as a very lovely song of one that hath a pleasant voice, and can play well on an instrument: for they hear thy words, but they do them not" (Eze.33:31-32).

"For I desired mercy, and not sacrifice; and the knowledge of God more than burnt offerings" (Ho.6:6).

4 (1:21-31) **Injustice, Caused by, Corrupt Leaders and People—Jerusalem, Described as, a Harlot; an Unjust City—Jerusalem, Sins of, Injustice—Society, Sins of, Injustice—Jerusalem, Titles of, the City of Righteousness—Promises, Restoration of Jerusalem—Jerusalem, New, Assured by God—Judgment, Against Whom, God's Enemies—Justice, of God, Will Be Executed**: God's third charge against His people was heart-rending: they were unjust and deceitful. Wickedness, lawlessness, and violence ran rampant throughout Judah and Jerusalem. Even so, God had not given up on His people. There was still a remnant, a small number of true believers scattered here and there across the land. For the sake of these few who were righteous, and because of His own promise to Abraham, the LORD would restore Jerusalem and the promised land.

Note the charge of injustice leveled against the city of Jerusalem and its citizens (representing all Judah). Note also God's wonderful promise that some day in the future He would restore the great city and free its citizens from all enemies and oppressors.

OUTLINE	SCRIPTURE	SCRIPTURE	OUTLINE
4. God's third charge: They were unjust, deceitful a. The picture of a faithful, just, & righteous city: Became unfaithful—full of murderers 　1) Had been like pure silver & wine but were now impure & worthless 　2) Had corrupt leaders 　　• Were covetous, like thieves who sought bribes 　　• Refused to help & defend the fatherless & widows b. The verdict & sentence: Pronounced by the LORD, the LORD of hosts, the Mighty One of Israel 　1) He will judge, get rid of all His enemies 　2) He will purge away all the impurities of the city 　3) He will restore righteous	21 How is the faithful city become an harlot! it was full of judgment; righteousness lodged in it; but now murderers. 22 Thy silver is become dross, thy wine mixed with water: 23 Thy princes *are* rebellious, and companions of thieves: every one loveth gifts, and followeth after rewards: they judge not the fatherless, neither doth the cause of the widow come unto them. 24 Therefore saith the Lord, the LORD of hosts, the mighty One of Israel, Ah, I will ease me of mine adversaries, and avenge me of mine enemies: 25 And I will turn my hand upon thee, and purely purge away thy dross, and take away all thy tin: 26 And I will restore thy	judges as at the first, and thy counsellors as at the beginning: afterward thou shalt be called, The city of righteousness, the faithful city. 27 Zion shall be redeemed with judgment, and her converts with righteousness. 28 And the destruction of the transgressors and of the sinners *shall be* together, and they that forsake the LORD shall be consumed. 29 For they shall be ashamed of the oaks which ye have desired, and ye shall be confounded for the gardens that ye have chosen. 30 For ye shall be as an oak whose leaf fadeth, and as a garden that hath no water. 31 And the strong shall be as tow, and the maker of it as a spark, and they shall both burn together, and none shall quench *them.*	& just leaders: Jerusalem will be called *The City of Righteousness, the Faithful City* 4) He will place the repentant people in the new, redeemed city of Jerusalem 5) He will execute true justice against all rebels & sinners, all who forsake Him 　• They will be ashamed & disgraced: Due to their false worship 　• They will suffer the fate of the things in which they trusted: Fade away 　• They & their works will be burned, suffer in an unquenchable fire

a. Under David's leadership and during the early part of Solomon's reign, Jerusalem had been a faithful city, a just and righteous city. But since that time, Jerusalem and its citizens had become as unfaithful as harlots who had turned away from the LORD. Now the city was full of murderers! In its early years, Jerusalem had been like pure silver, but now it had become like dross, like worthless scum (v.22). Because of the unrighteousness of its citizens, Jerusalem had become like watered-down wine. The leaders of the city were corrupt, filled with a spirit of covetousness. Many of their associates were thieves, so the leaders often took bribes to keep silent. Ignoring their duty to serve the citizens of the land, the leaders refused to help and defend the orphans and widows when their cases were brought before them.

b. Isaiah predicted the verdict and sentence of God (vv.24-31). And what he predicted would take place, for the LORD Himself was pronouncing it. To emphasize the certainty of God's verdict, Isaiah used three divine titles in making this declaration: it is the LORD, the LORD of hosts (LORD Almighty), the Mighty One of Israel who pronounces this verdict and sentence. The people could rest assured that what was now being declared would take place. Isaiah proclaimed five startling judgments:

1) The LORD will judge and get rid of all His enemies (v.24). Vengeance will be executed upon all who oppose and rebel against Him. The profession and worship attendance of people will not matter. If they have lived sinful lives and engaged in false worship, they will face God's judgment.
2) The LORD will purge Jerusalem of all impurities (v.25). Although He will execute judgment upon all who rebel and engage in false worship, His purpose is to purify the city so that no evil will dwell within its boundaries. The future capital of the world will be the New Jerusalem, the city of God in which the throne of the Lord Jesus Christ will sit. Thus the city must be cleansed.
3) The LORD will restore righteous and just leaders to serve His people (v.26). Someday in the future, Jerusalem will be restored and called *The City of Righteousness, the Faithful City.*
4) The LORD will place all repentant people in the redeemed city of Jerusalem (v.27). All who repent of their sins—turn away from their rebellion, false worship, and injustice and return to the LORD—will be the citizens of the New Jerusalem. They will be the redeemed, the people set free from sin and the judgment of God.
5) The LORD will execute true justice against all rebels and sinners who forsook Him (v.28). Having turned away from the LORD, the Creator of the universe, they turned to false worship. Now they must stand face-to-face with the LORD of the universe. In that day they will bear the judgment of God's hand. They will be ashamed and disgraced because of their false worship, and they will perish. They had trusted and worshipped false gods; as a result, they will suffer the same fate as the things in which they trusted. Just as the leaves of an oak tree fade away, so they also will fade away. They will be like a garden without water: the ground soon turns to dust and blows away. Even the strong and mighty—they and their works—will be burned with unquenchable fire (v.31). They will be consumed along with their wicked works.

Thought 1. Treating people unfairly is an injustice and it involves all kinds of sins and acts of wickedness. Abusing or sexually assaulting children is an act of injustice, for children are unable to defend themselves. Verbally abusing a spouse is an injustice, for it is lashing out unfairly and unkindly. Far too many of us mistreat other people, committing all kinds of injustices against them, such as…
• committing criminal acts
• showing favoritism

- spreading rumors and malicious gossip
- lying, stealing and cheating
- oppressing others
- encroaching upon the property or rights of others
- holding prejudices and discriminating against people
- abusing the trust and responsibility placed in us by people

Covetous, corrupt leaders ruled the government in Isaiah's day. They were companions of thieves and willingly took bribes. Helping to meet the needs of their citizens was the farthest thing from their thoughts. They even neglected the fatherless and widows. Single mothers had to fend for themselves, no matter how many children they had. Few people in the community offered to help any of the needy. Each person was out for himself, living a selfish and self-centered life. As a result, injustice ruled supreme. The innocent and defenseless were discriminated against, treated unfairly, and often oppressed. Listen to what God's Holy Word says about injustice and oppression:

"He that is faithful in that which is least is faithful also in much: and he that is unjust in the least is unjust also in much" (Lu.16:10).

"Know ye not that the unrighteous shall not inherit the kingdom of God? Be not deceived: neither fornicators, nor idolaters, nor adulterers, nor effeminate, nor abusers of themselves with mankind, Nor thieves, nor covetous, nor drunkards, nor revilers, nor extortioners, shall inherit the kingdom of God" (1 Co.6:9-10).

"For this ye know, that no whoremonger, nor unclean person, nor covetous man, who is an idolater, hath any inheritance in the kingdom of Christ and of God" (Ep.5:5).

"I charge *thee* before God, and the Lord Jesus Christ, and the elect angels, that thou observe these things without preferring one before another, doing nothing by partiality" (1 Ti.5:21).

"Also thou shalt not oppress a stranger: for ye know the heart of a stranger, seeing ye were strangers in the land of Egypt" (Ex.23:9).

"Ye shall do no unrighteousness in judgment: thou shalt not respect the person of the poor, nor honour the person of the mighty: *but* in righteousness shalt thou judge thy neighbour" (Le.19:15).

"Thou shalt not oppress an hired servant *that is* poor and needy, *whether he be* of thy brethren, or of thy strangers that *are* in thy land within thy gates" (De.24:14).

"Thou shalt not pervert the judgment of the stranger, *nor* of the fatherless; nor take a widow's raiment to pledge" (De.24:17).

"He will surely reprove you, if ye do secretly accept persons" (Jb.13:10).

"Trust not in oppression, and become not vain in robbery: if riches increase, set not your heart *upon them*" (Ps.62:10).

"How long will ye judge unjustly, and accept the persons of the wicked? Selah" (Ps.82:2).

"He that oppresseth the poor reproacheth his Maker: but he that honoureth him hath mercy on the poor" (Pr.14:31).

"A poor man that oppresseth the poor *is like* a sweeping rain which leaveth no food" (Pr.28:3).

"An unjust man *is* an abomination to the just: and *he that is* upright in the way *is* abomination to the wicked" (Pr.29:27).

"*It is* not for kings, O Lemuel, *it is* not for kings to drink wine; nor for princes strong drink: Lest they drink, and forget the law, and pervert the judgment of any of the afflicted" (Pr.31:4-5).

"And moreover I saw under the sun the place of judgment, *that* wickedness *was* there; and the place of righteousness, *that* iniquity *was* there" (Ec.3:16).

"If thou seest the oppression of the poor, and violent perverting of judgment and justice in a province, marvel not at the matter: for *he that is* higher than the highest regardeth; and *there be* higher than they" (Ec.5:8).

CHAPTER 2

B. The Future Kingdom & Temple of God, the Day of the LORD, & the Restoration of Israel: Three Key Events in the Future, 2:1–4:6

1. **The future kingdom & temple of God: A picture of Christ's rule on earth**[DS1]
   a. The era: *The last days* [DS2]
   b. The exaltation of God's kingdom
      1) Established on Mt. Zion: Governed from the temple
      2) Made the most vital & important place on earth: People will stream to it
   c. The purpose of God's kingdom
      1) To attract & invite people to the LORD
      2) To arouse people to hear & heed God's Word

      3) To bring peace to the earth

   d. The appeal to believers: To walk in the light, the righteousness of the LORD
2. **The future *Day of the LORD*, His terrifying judgment** [DS3]
   a. The reason for God's judgment
      1) People followed the world of the occult & sorcery
      2) People formed evil alliances with unbelievers
      3) People placed their confidence in money & weapons (the nation's economy & military)

      4) People engaged in idolatry & false worship: Idols & false gods were worshipped everywhere
      5) People were beyond repentance & forgiveness: Had hard, stubborn hearts
   b. The reaction of the people to the wrath of God
      1) The people will seek to escape, flee, hide

The word that Isaiah the son of Amoz saw concerning Judah and Jerusalem.

2 And it shall come to pass in the last days, *that* the mountain of the LORD'S house shall be established in the top of the mountains, and shall be exalted above the hills; and all nations shall flow unto it.

3 And many people shall go and say, Come ye, and let us go up to the mountain of the LORD, to the house of the God of Jacob; and he will teach us of his ways, and we will walk in his paths: for out of Zion shall go forth the law, and the word of the LORD from Jerusalem.

4 And he shall judge among the nations, and shall rebuke many people: and they shall beat their swords into plowshares, and their spears into pruninghooks: nation shall not lift up sword against nation, neither shall they learn war any more.

5 O house of Jacob, come ye, and let us walk in the light of the LORD.

6 Therefore thou hast forsaken thy people the house of Jacob, because they be replenished from the east, and *are* soothsayers like the Philistines, and they please themselves in the children of strangers.

7 Their land also is full of silver and gold, neither *is there any* end of their treasures; their land is also full of horses, neither *is there any* end of their chariots:

8 Their land also is full of idols; they worship the work of their own hands, that which their own fingers have made:

9 And the mean man boweth down, and the great man humbleth himself: therefore forgive them not.

10 Enter into the rock, and hide thee in the dust, for fear of the LORD, and for the glory of his majesty.

11 The lofty looks of man shall be humbled, and the haughtiness of men shall be bowed down, and the LORD alone shall be exalted in that day.

12 For the day of the LORD of hosts *shall be* upon every one that *is* proud and lofty, and upon every *one that is* lifted up; and he shall be brought low:

13 And upon all the cedars of Lebanon, *that are* high and lifted up, and upon all the oaks of Bashan,

14 And upon all the high mountains, and upon all the hills *that are* lifted up,

15 And upon every high tower, and upon every fenced wall,

16 And upon all the ships of Tarshish, and upon all pleasant pictures.

17 And the loftiness of man shall be bowed down, and the haughtiness of men shall be made low: and the LORD alone shall be exalted in that day.

18 And the idols he shall utterly abolish.

19 And they shall go into the holes of the rocks, and into the caves of the earth, for fear of the LORD, and for the glory of his majesty, when he ariseth to shake terribly the earth.

20 In that day a man shall cast his idols of silver, and his idols of gold, which they made *each one* for himself to worship, to the moles and to the bats;

21 To go into the clefts of the rocks, and into the tops of the ragged rocks, for fear of the LORD, and for the glory of his majesty, when he ariseth to shake terribly the earth.

22 Cease ye from man, whose breath *is* in his nostrils: for wherein is he to be accounted of?

CHAPTER 3

For, behold, the Lord, the LORD of hosts, doth take away from Jerusalem and from Judah the stay and the staff, the whole stay of bread, and the whole stay of water,

2 The mighty man, and the man of war, the judge, and the prophet, and the prudent,

2) The arrogant & prideful will be humbled *in that day*: The LORD alone will be exalted

3) The whole world will be humbled *in that day*, 2:11-12; 3:7, 18; 4:1-2
   • All the proud & lofty

   • All the towering trees of earth in their natural beauty

   • All the towering mountains & high hills of the earth
   • All the world's military power & defenses

   • All the economies & businesses

   • All the arrogance & pride of people

   • All the idols & false worship: Destroyed
4) The idolater will be stricken with terror
   • Will seek to hide, escape

   • Will cast away all idols in seeking to escape God's wrath

   • Will seek to escape the glory of God's majesty

   • Will seek to escape when God rises to *shake the earth*, 19, 21
   c. The only way to escape God's wrath: Must separate from the wicked & idolatrous

   d. The description of the approaching judgment: To be executed by the LORD, the LORD of hosts
      1) A loss of the basic necessities of life: Water & food
      2) A removal of all leaders: Military, legal, religious, civil, business, & social

leaders

3) A government of weak, inexperienced leaders

4) A society of oppression, lawlessness, & anarchy

5) A people with no answer to their problems & no desire or willingness to serve

- People will feel hopeless & helpless

- People will refuse to serve as leaders

e. The reason for such a destructive judgment reemphasized
1) Because their tongues & deeds defy the LORD

2) Because they sin openly, brazenly just as Sodom did
- Woe to them! How terrible their judgment will be
- They have brought judgment on themselves

f. The duty of believers in light of the coming judgment
1) To assure the righteous: They will be rewarded
2) To warn the wicked: They will be judged

- Immature rulers will oppress them
- Unwise women will rule, lead them astray, 1 K.18:4; 21:5; 2 K.11:1

g. The LORD's case against the leaders: A betrayal of trust

1) They had oppressed, ruined the vineyard (Israel)
2) They had taken advantage of the people
- Stolen, plundered their property
- Oppressed, crushed them, grinding their faces into the ground

h. The LORD's case against the

and the ancient,
3 The captain of fifty, and the honourable man, and the counsellor, and the cunning artificer, and the eloquent orator.
4 And I will give children *to be* their princes, and babes shall rule over them.
5 And the people shall be oppressed, every one by another, and every one by his neighbour: the child shall behave himself proudly against the ancient, and the base against the honourable.
6 When a man shall take hold of his brother of the house of his father, *saying,* Thou hast clothing, be thou our ruler, and *let* this ruin *be* under thy hand:
7 In that day shall he swear, saying, I will not be an healer; for in my house *is* neither bread nor clothing: make me not a ruler of the people.
8 For Jerusalem is ruined, and Judah is fallen: because their tongue and their doings *are* against the LORD, to provoke the eyes of his glory.
9 The show of their countenance doth witness against them; and they declare their sin as Sodom, they hide *it* not. Woe unto their soul! for they have rewarded evil unto themselves.
10 Say ye to the righteous, that *it shall be* well *with him:* for they shall eat the fruit of their doings.
11 Woe unto the wicked! *it shall be* ill *with him:* for the reward of his hands shall be given him.
12 *As for* my people, children *are* their oppressors, and women rule over them. O my people, they which lead thee cause *thee* to err, and destroy the way of thy paths.
13 The LORD standeth up to plead, and standeth to judge the people.
14 The LORD will enter into judgment with the ancients of his people, and the princes thereof: for ye have eaten up the vineyard; the spoil of the poor *is* in your houses.
15 What mean ye *that* ye beat my people to pieces, and grind the faces of the poor? saith the LORD GOD of hosts.
16 Moreover the LORD saith,

Because the daughters of Zion are haughty, and walk with stretched forth necks and wanton eyes, walking and mincing *as* they go, and making a tinkling with their feet:
17 Therefore the LORD will smite with a scab the crown of the head of the daughters of Zion, and the LORD will discover their secret parts.
18 In that day the Lord will take away the bravery of *their* tinkling ornaments *about their feet,* and *their* cauls, and *their* round tires like the moon,
19 The chains, and the bracelets, and the mufflers,
20 The bonnets, and the ornaments of the legs, and the headbands, and the tablets, and the earrings,
21 The rings, and nose jewels,
22 The changeable suits of apparel, and the mantles, and the wimples, and the crisping pins,
23 The glasses, and the fine linen, and the hoods, and the vails.
24 And it shall come to pass, *that* instead of sweet smell there shall be stink; and instead of a girdle a rent; and instead of well set hair baldness; and instead of a stomacher a girding of sackcloth; *and* burning instead of beauty.
25 Thy men shall fall by the sword, and thy mighty in the war.
26 And her gates shall lament and mourn; and she *being* desolate shall sit upon the ground.

CHAPTER 4

And in that day seven women shall take hold of one man, saying, We will eat our own bread, and wear our own apparel: only let us be called by thy name, to take away our reproach.
2 In that day shall the branch of the LORD be beautiful and glorious, and the fruit of the earth *shall be* excellent and comely for them that are escaped of Israel.
3 And it shall come to pass, *that he that is* left in Zion, and *he that* remaineth in

haughty, worldly women of society
1) Their sins
- Pride, arrogance
- Flirting with men
- Immodest behavior & dress
2) Their judgment
- Will have sores on their heads
- Will be uncovered, stripped naked (raped)
- Will lose all their jewelry, wardrobe, perfume, gowns, & all else of value that had been coveted

- Will stink instead of smelling sweet
- Will wear a rope, not a sash
- Will be bald
- Will wear sackcloth, not fine clothing
- Will be branded with shame, not beauty
- Will be widowed

- Will be exiled, led away from Jerusalem into captivity

- Will face fierce competition for husbands due to so few men surviving the war

3. The future restoration of Israel: Assured by the *Branch of the LORD* (Christ)
a. The LORD will save some: *In that day,* 2:2, 11-12, 17, 20; 3:7, 18; 4:1-2
1) Provide a fruitful earth, 2
2) Make them holy

OUTLINE	SCRIPTURE	SCRIPTURE	OUTLINE
3) Cleanse them from moral filth, sin • The filth of the women • The lawlessness & violence of everyone	Jerusalem, shall be called holy, *even* every one that is written among the living in Jerusalem: 4 When the Lord shall have washed away the filth of the daughters of Zion, and shall have purged the blood of Jerusalem from the midst thereof by the spirit of judgment, and by the spirit of burning.	upon every dwelling place of mount Zion, and upon her assemblies, a cloud and smoke by day, and the shining of a flaming fire by night: for upon all the glory *shall be* a defence. 6 And there shall be a tabernacle for a shadow in the daytime from the heat, and for a place of refuge, and for a covert from storm and from	with His glory 1) The canopy of His presence & provision
b. The LORD will cover Israel	5 And the LORD will create	rain.	2) The shelter of His protection: Will provide a refuge & security

DIVISION I

THE PROPHECIES OF REBUKE AND HOPE GIVEN TO JUDAH AND JERUSALEM: AN OVERVIEW OF THE PRESENT AND FUTURE OF GOD'S PEOPLE, 1:1–12:6

B. The Future Kingdom and Temple of God, the Day of the LORD, and the Restoration of Israel: Three Key Events in the Future, 2:1–4:6

(2:1–4:6) **Introduction**: the future is, for the most part, unknown. No person can know all that lies out in the future except God Himself. However, if the future could be known, it could prove very beneficial for many people. For example, if businesses could predict the acceptance of new products, they could net far greater profit. If young people could see future unfaithfulness in the persons they were about to marry, they could immediately break the engagements. If employees could foresee a company's going bankrupt, they could seek employment elsewhere. If we could see the future diseases we were going to suffer through due to our way of eating, some of us could immediately change our diets. The same is true with smoking, drinking, taking drugs, and a host of other damaging and sinful habits. If we could see into the future, some of us would take dramatic steps to change our behavior.

In the present Scripture, the LORD gives Isaiah a glimpse into the future. Three astounding and major events are revealed to him. And because the revelation is by God Himself, believers of all generations can know with certainty that they will take place. All three major events will take place in *the last days* of human history. Therefore, any believer still alive should heed the warnings given and act before it is too late. These events are, *The Future Kingdom and Temple of God, the Day of the LORD, and the Restoration of Israel: Three Key Events in the Future, 2:1–4:6.*

1. The future kingdom and temple of God: a picture of Christ's rule on earth (2:1-5).
2. The future *Day of the LORD*, His terrifying judgment (2:6–4:1).
3. The glorious restoration of Israel: assured by the *Branch of the LORD* (Christ) (4:2-6).

[1] (2:1-5) **Kingdom of God, Established on Earth, Promised; Purpose of—God, Kingdom of, Promised—Temple, Future, Promised—Christ, Rule on Earth, Purpose—Peace, Promised, Coming to Earth—Messiah, Kingdom on Earth, Promised—Millennium, Discussed—Age, Messianic, Description**: in the future, God's kingdom will be established on earth. Jerusalem will become the center of the worldwide government and the worship of the LORD. Note how clearly this is stated in the Scripture and outline:

OUTLINE	SCRIPTURE	SCRIPTURE	OUTLINE
1. The future kingdom & temple of God: A picture of Christ's rule on earthDS1 a. The era: *The last days*DS2 b. The exaltation of God's kingdom 1) Established on Mt. Zion: Governed from the temple 2) Made the most vital & important place on earth: People will stream to it c. The purpose of God's kingdom 1) To attract & invite people to the LORD 2) To arouse people to hear & heed God's Word	The word that Isaiah the son of Amoz saw concerning Judah and Jerusalem. 2 And it shall come to pass in the last days, *that* the mountain of the LORD's house shall be established in the top of the mountains, and shall be exalted above the hills; and all nations shall flow unto it. 3 And many people shall go and say, Come ye, and let us go up to the mountain of the LORD, to the house of the God of Jacob; and he will teach us of his	ways, and we will walk in his paths: for out of Zion shall go forth the law, and the word of the LORD from Jerusalem. 4 And he shall judge among the nations, and shall rebuke many people: and they shall beat their swords into plowshares, and their spears into pruninghooks: nation shall not lift up sword against nation, neither shall they learn war any more. 5 O house of Jacob, come ye, and let us walk in the light of the LORD.	3) To bring peace to the earth d. The appeal to believers: To walk in the light, the righteousness of the LORD

a. God's government will be established in *the last days* (v.2). This is a clear reference to the era of the Messiah, the promised Messianic age that lies out in the future for Isaiah and God's people. *The last days* point to the future days that involve the end of human history. Isaiah's glimpse into the future reached forward to the events that will take place after the return of Christ. (See Deeper Study #1—Is.2:1-5 for more discussion.)

b. God's kingdom and His temple will be exalted above all the kingdoms and temples that have ever existed. Throughout Scripture, *mountains* often refer to governments, to their authority and power (Da.2:35; Am.4:1). In *the last days,* the mountain of the LORD's kingdom, His government, will be established and exalted above all the mountains or governments down through history. And the center of His government will be the new temple that will be built on Mount Zion (see Eze. chs.40–43). The *mountain of the LORD* or Mount Zion is a common theme running throughout *Isaiah.* It is pictured as being the place to which all the nations and people who live in *the last days* will stream and flow. Why? Because the LORD Himself will be ruling the earth, with the center of government being the temple that has been rebuilt on Mount Zion. The leaders who live in *the last days* will naturally travel to the capital of the world, the political and economic center of world government and commerce (Is.11:9; 25:6-7; 27:13; 30:29; 56:7; 57:13; 65:11, 25; 66:20; see also Zec.14:16). Likewise, all people will attempt to make pilgrimages to God's temple to worship the LORD.

c. God will have three primary purposes for establishing His kingdom on earth (vv.3-4). First, God's purpose will be to attract people to the LORD and to invite people to worship the LORD (v.3). The LORD deserves to be honored above all who have ever existed, for the LORD is not only the Creator of the universe but also the Savior of the world. Securing salvation for mankind cost Him the ultimate price. The penalty for sin is death, and Christ paid the penalty with His life. God the Father has determined that every knee will bow and worship the LORD in *the last days.* Thus, when the LORD establishes His kingdom on earth, it will be for the purpose of attracting and inviting people to worship Christ. Note that many people will worship Him and enthusiastically invite others to go to the mountain of the LORD to do the same.

Second, the LORD's purpose will be to arouse people to hear and heed His Word (v.3). Those who come to the LORD will be taught His ways and they will walk in His path of righteousness, morality, and justice. The law of God will be executed from Zion, and the Word of God will be proclaimed by the LORD Himself from Jerusalem. Many people will hear the Word of God and obey His commandments. No longer will most people hear and reject God's Word, refusing to be obedient. Unlike generations before, in *the last days, many people* (a significant percentage of the entire world's population) will live righteous and moral lives. They will keep the two greatest commandments, those of loving the LORD first and then loving their neighbors as themselves. They will follow the golden rule, doing to others what they want done to themselves.

Note this fact: there has been a partial fulfillment of these first two purposes since Christ's death and resurrection. The gospel has been carried to the world, attracting and inviting people to accept the Lord. Since Christ, people have been aroused to hear and heed God's Word. The ways of the LORD have been taught, and some are walking in His path of righteousness, morality, and justice. But, significantly, only a small percentage of people are true followers of the LORD. Only a few sincerely study His Word, obey His commandments, and live righteous lives. Only a few bear strong testimony to His saving power. Only a few have really turned their lives over to the LORD. But this will not be true in the future foreseen by Isaiah. Many people will give their lives to the LORD and faithfully study His Word, living righteously. Since Christ, there has been a partial fulfillment in the church age, but the complete fulfillment will be in *the* (very) *last days,* that is, the millennial reign of Christ. Verse four definitely indicates this fact. Universal peace has not come to the earth through the preaching of the gospel. No person or group of people has the power to bring peace to this earth. Only the LORD Himself can fulfill the prophecy of universal peace. For this reason, God will send His Son back to the earth to rule over the nations and peoples of the earth. The Lord Jesus Christ Himself will sit upon the throne of God on Mount Zion in Jerusalem. From the Holy City of Jerusalem, He will execute justice among the nations and will lead the rulers to settle their international disputes. All of this will take place during the period of human history known as the Millennium (see Deeper Study #2—Is.2:1-5 for more discussion).

Third, God's purpose for establishing His kingdom on earth will be to bring peace to the world (v.4). Note that this Scripture actually states this fact: the LORD Himself will serve as judge between nations and will settle whatever international disputes arise among them. This is one of the most well-known verses in the book of *Isaiah.* Universal peace will sweep the world and there will be no more war. All wars will be stopped. Military weapons will be recycled into machines and tools for commercial purposes. No nation will take up a sword against another nation, nor will they call upon their people to train for war. All military training will come to an end.

d. Isaiah made a strong appeal to the people of his day, an appeal that speaks to our hearts (v.5). Since the LORD is going to bring His kingdom of righteousness and peace to earth, the house of Jacob (all believers) should walk in the *light* of the LORD. We should let the *light* of His Word shine upon us, the wisdom of His commandments and instructions. We should obey God's Word, living righteous, moral, and honest lives. We should love the LORD, worshipping Him daily and then coming together as a church to worship Him as the living LORD. We also should love one another as neighbors, reaching out to help and encourage one another when needed. We should fellowship and rejoice together in the wonderful promises God has given us. Furthermore, as we walk day by day, we should follow the golden rule, treating others as we wish to be treated.

> **"Therefore all things whatsoever ye would that men should do to you, do ye even so to them: for this is the law and the prophets" (Mt.7:12).**
>
> **"Master, which *is* the great commandment in the law? Jesus said unto him, Thou shalt love the Lord thy God with all thy heart, and with all thy soul, and with all thy mind. This is the first and great commandment. And the second *is* like unto it, Thou shalt love thy neighbour as thyself. On these two commandments hang all the law and the prophets" (Mt.22:36-40).**
>
> **"Love worketh no ill to his neighbour: therefore love *is* the fulfilling of the law" (Ro.13:10).**
>
> **"We then that are strong ought to bear the infirmities of the weak, and not to please ourselves. Let every one of us please *his* neighbour for *his* good to edification" (Ro.15:1-2).**
>
> **"Awake to righteousness, and sin not; for some have not the knowledge of God: I speak *this* to your shame" (1 Co.15:34).**
>
> **"For all the law is fulfilled in one word, *even* in this; Thou shalt love thy neighbour as thyself" (Ga.5:14).**

"And this I pray, that your love may abound yet more and more in knowledge and *in* all judgment; That ye may approve things that are excellent; that ye may be sincere and without offence till the day of Christ; Being filled with the fruits of righteousness, which are by Jesus Christ, unto the glory and praise of God" (Ph.1:9-11).

"But thou, O man of God, flee these things; and follow after righteousness, godliness, faith, love, patience, meekness. Fight the good fight of faith, lay hold on eternal life, whereunto thou art also called, and hast professed a good profession before many witnesses" (1 Ti.6:11-12).

"If ye fulfil the royal law according to the scripture, Thou shalt love thy neighbour as thyself, ye do well" (Js.2:8).

"Keep yourselves in the love of God, looking for the mercy of our Lord Jesus Christ unto eternal life" (Jude 1:21).

"And now, Israel, what doth the LORD thy God require of thee, but to fear the LORD thy God, to walk in all his ways, and to love him, and to serve the LORD thy God with all thy heart and with all thy soul?" (De.10:12).

DEEPER STUDY # 1

(2:1-5) **Millennium—Jesus Christ, Millennial Reign—Kingdom, of Christ on Earth—Rule, of Christ, on Earth:** Due to the length of this Deeper Study, it is being placed at the end of the commentary for Is.2:1—4:6.

DEEPER STUDY # 2

(2:2) **Days, Last—Last Times—End Times—History, Last Days of—World, End of:** What does the term *the last days* mean? What period of human history launched *the last days*? When Isaiah used the term some seven hundred years before Christ, *the last days* were out in the future. Scripture says the following about *the last days*:

1. The prophets referred to a future period of human history that would be known as *the last days*.

    "And it shall come to pass in the last days, *that* the mountain of the LORD'S house shall be established in the top of the mountains, and shall be exalted above the hills; and all nations shall flow unto it. And many people shall go and say, Come ye, and let us go up to the mountain of the LORD, to the house of the God of Jacob; and he will teach us of his ways, and we will walk in his paths: for out of Zion shall go forth the law, and the word of the LORD from Jerusalem. And he shall judge among the nations, and shall rebuke many people: and they shall beat their swords into plowshares, and their spears into pruninghooks: nation shall not lift up sword against nation, neither shall they learn war any more" (Is.2:2-4).

    "Afterward shall the children of Israel return [from captivity], and seek the LORD their God, and David their king; and shall fear the LORD and his goodness in the latter days" (Ho.3:5).

    "But in the last days it shall come to pass, *that* the mountain of the house of the LORD shall be established in the top of the mountains, and it shall be exalted above the hills; and people shall flow unto it. And many nations shall come, and say, Come, and let us go up to the mountain of the LORD, and to the house of the God of Jacob; and he will teach us of his ways, and we will walk in his paths: for the law shall go forth of Zion, and the word of the LORD from Jerusalem. And he shall judge among many people, and rebuke strong nations afar off; and they shall beat their swords into plowshares, and their spears into pruninghooks: nation shall not lift up a sword against nation, neither shall they learn war any more. But they shall sit every man under his vine and under his fig tree; and none shall make *them* afraid: for the mouth of the LORD of hosts hath spoken *it*" (Mic.4:1-4).

2. The disciples of Christ and Christ Himself discussed *the end times* of human history. The disciples actually asked Christ, "What will be the sign of your coming and of the end of the world?" In answering their question, Christ used the occasion to reveal some of the events that are to take place on earth during *the last days*. (These events are outlined and discussed in detail in *The Preacher's Outline and Sermon Bible, Matthew, Vol.2.* See outline and notes—Mt.24:1–25:46 for discussion.)

The point to note is that the timeframe of *the last days* being discussed by Christ stretched from His day up to the very end of the world. His answer to the apostles suggests this fact: Christ was saying that His coming launched *the last days*. The signs and events the apostles were to experience would be duplicated in the lives of believers down through the generations. These signs and events—at least many of them—would lead right up to the end of the world. Note the beginning of Christ's discussion in Mt. chs.24–25:

"And as he sat upon the mount of Olives, the disciples came unto him privately, saying, Tell us, when shall these things be? and what *shall be* the sign of thy coming, and of the end of the world? And Jesus answered and said unto them, Take heed that no man deceive you. For many shall come in my name, saying, I am Christ; and shall deceive many. And ye shall hear of wars and rumours of wars: see that ye be not troubled: for all *these things* must come to pass, but the end is not yet. For nation shall rise against nation, and kingdom against kingdom: and there shall be famines, and pestilences, and earthquakes, in divers places. All these *are* the beginning of sorrows. Then shall they deliver you up to be afflicted, and shall kill you: and ye shall be hated of all nations for my name's sake. And then shall many be offended, and shall betray one another, and shall hate one another. And many false prophets shall rise, and shall deceive many. And because iniquity shall abound, the love of many shall wax cold. But he that shall endure unto the end, the same shall be saved. And this gospel of the kingdom shall be preached in all the world for a witness unto all nations; and then shall the end come [note the end]" (Mt.24:3-14).

3. The New Testament definitely says that *the last days* began when Christ came to earth. Since Jesus Christ's coming, history is in its last stage. Right now, the time between Christ's first coming and the day of final judgment is called the age of *grace*—the age when God's mercy and grace are flowing out to the world through His Son, the Lord Jesus Christ. How long *these last days* will last is not known. The point to remember is this fact: from God's perspective, this period of history from the sending of His Son to the world right up to the end of human history is known as…

- *these last days* (He.1:2)
- *the last time* (1 Pe.1:5; 1 Jn.2:18; Jude 1:18)
- *the last days* (Ac.2:17; 2 Ti.3:1; 2 Pe.3:3)

---

2 (2:6–4:1) **Judgment, Described As,** *Day of the LORD*—**Prophecy, Listed,** *Day of the LORD*—**Women, Worldly, Judgment of**—**Judgment, Reason for, Fivefold Reason**—**Believers, Duty, Twofold Duty**—**Leaders, Sins of, Oppression**—**Women, Worldly, God's Case Against**—**Judgment, in the Last Days, Discussed**: in the future, God's terrifying judgment will fall upon the earth, a period of time known as the *Day of the LORD* (2:11, 20; 3:7, 18; 4:1-2). This whole section of Scripture gives an excellent description of God's coming judgment upon the world. The *Day of the LORD* refers to a period of time when God's judgment will fall upon the nations, and the LORD will be exalted as the sovereign ruler over the entire universe. Right before His kingdom is established on earth, as discussed above (vv.1-5), the darkest night of God's judgment will cover the earth. All of nature, the very environment of the earth, will be devastated, and millions upon millions of people will die. (See DEEPER STUDY #3—Is.2:6–4:1 for more discussion.)

a. God's terrifying judgment—the *Day of the LORD*—will sweep across the earth for five reasons. Note the Scripture actually says that God will forsake His people during the *Day of the LORD*. He will not abandon His people because He no longer loves them but because they are forsaking and abandoning Him. They are turning away from the LORD and turning to the world. In the last days of human history, people in general—including those who falsely profess to be God's people—will become guilty of five serious offenses against the LORD. Because of these offences, God's terrifying judgment will move swiftly over the earth.

OUTLINE	SCRIPTURE	SCRIPTURE	OUTLINE

2. The future *Day of the LORD*, His terrifying judgment DS3
a. The reason for God's judgment
  1) People followed the world of the occult & sorcery
  2) People formed evil alliances with unbelievers
  3) People placed their confidence in money & weapons (the nation's
	6 Therefore thou hast forsaken thy people the house of Jacob, because they be replenished from the east, and *are* soothsayers like the Philistines, and they please themselves in the children of strangers.
	7 Their land also is full of silver and gold, neither *is there any* end of their treasures; their land is also
		full of horses, neither *is there any* end of their chariots:
		8 Their land also is full of idols; they worship the work of their own hands, that which their own fingers have made:
		9 And the mean man boweth down, and the great man humbleth himself: therefore forgive them not.
			economy & military)
			
			4) People engaged in idolatry & false worship: Idols & false gods were worshipped everywhere
			
			5) People were beyond repentance & forgiveness: Had hard, stubborn hearts

1) People will follow the world of the occult and sorcery (v.6). They will practice the superstitions of the east, their religions, magic, and forms of meditation and relaxation. In addition, they will practice the divination and sorcery of the west. Participating in the world of the occult and sorcery is expressly forbidden by the LORD.

> **"And it came to pass, as we went to prayer, a certain damsel possessed with a spirit of divination met us, which brought her masters much gain by soothsaying: The same followed Paul and us, and cried, saying, These men are the servants of the most high God, which show unto us the way of salvation. And this did she many days. But Paul, being grieved, turned and said to the spirit, I command thee in the name of Jesus Christ to come out of her. And he came out the same hour" (Ac.16:16-18).**

> **"Ye shall not eat *any thing* with the blood: neither shall ye use enchantment, nor observe times" (Le.19:26).**

> **"There shall not be found among you *any one* that maketh his son or his daughter to pass through the fire, or that useth divination, *or* an observer of times, or an enchanter, or a witch....For these nations, which thou shalt possess, hearkened unto observers of times, and unto diviners: but as for thee, the LORD thy God hath not suffered thee so *to do*" (De.18:10, 14).**

> **"And he made his son pass through the fire, and observed times, and used enchantments, and dealt with familiar spirits and wizards: he wrought much wickedness in the sight of the LORD, to provoke *him* to anger" (2 K.21:6).**

> **"And I will cut off witchcrafts out of thine hand; and thou shalt have no *more* soothsayers" (Mi.5:12).**

2) People will form evil alliances with unbelievers (v.6). Believers and unbelievers will clasp hands, forming business partnerships, seeking more and more money. They will also join hands in marriage, believers marrying unbelievers. Believers will ignore God's commandment that demands *spiritual separation*. They will fellowship and participate with unbelievers in their worldly activities. Living holy, righteous lives and morally pure lives will be ignored by believers. They will become as worldly as the sinful, wicked unbelievers they associate with. They will pay little attention to God's commandment against forming evil alliances with unbelievers.

"I wrote unto you in an epistle not to company with fornicators: Yet not altogether with the fornicators of this world, or with the covetous, or extortioners, or with idolaters; for then must ye needs go out of the world. But now I have written unto you not to keep company, if any man that is called a brother be a fornicator, or covetous, or an idolater, or a railer, or a drunkard, or an extortioner; with such an one no not to eat" (1 Co.5:9-11).

"Be ye not unequally yoked together with unbelievers: for what fellowship hath righteousness with unrighteousness? and what communion hath light with darkness? And what concord hath Christ with Belial? or what part hath he that believeth with an infidel? And what agreement hath the temple of God with idols? for ye are the temple of the living God; as God hath said, I will dwell in them, and walk in *them;* and I will be their God, and they shall be my people" (2 Co.6:14-16).

"Love not the world, neither the things *that are* in the world. If any man love the world, the love of the Father is not in him. For all that *is* in the world, the lust of the flesh, and the lust of the eyes, and the pride of life, is not of the Father, but is of the world" (1 Jn.2:15-16).

"Thou shalt not follow a multitude to *do* evil; neither shalt thou speak in a cause to decline after many to wrest *judgment*" (Ex.23:2).

"Take heed to thyself, lest thou make a covenant with the inhabitants of the land whither thou goest, lest it be for a snare in the midst of thee" (Ex.34:12).

"Blessed *is* the man that walketh not in the counsel of the ungodly, nor standeth in the way of sinners, nor sitteth in the seat of the scornful" (Ps.1:1).

"Enter not into the path of the wicked, and go not in the way of evil *men*" (Pr.4:14).

"Make no friendship with an angry man; and with a furious man thou shalt not go: Lest thou learn his ways, and get a snare to thy soul" (Pr.22:24-25).

"Be not thou envious against evil men, neither desire to be with them" (Pr.24:1).

3) God will judge people because they place their confidence and money in the things of this world, in a nation's economy, weapons, or military (v.7). We must always remember that God does not always condemn wealth but, rather, the placing of our trust in wealth instead of in Him. This will be a widespread trait of people in the last days. Rather than seeking God, people will seek wealth. Religion will be mainly for social acceptance or for securing and maintaining business contacts. People will clamor for more and more riches and possessions, and nations will struggle to maintain economic strength. Militarily, there will be constant war, and there will be no end to the production of weapons. The result will be constant conflict, one war after another, and a relentless barrage of terrorist actions. Only the LORD Himself will be able to bring peace to earth and execute true justice and judgment upon the nations and peoples of the earth.

4) Fourth, God's terrifying judgment will fall because people engage in idolatry and false worship (v.8). In *the last days,* the earth will be full of false gods and false worship. False gods are only the creation of people's imaginations, whether they be tangible or intangible idols or merely an idea of what God is like. Any so-called god other than the LORD Himself is simply false, a fabrication of the individual himself or of an individual who conceived it before him. By having a god created by one's own desires or needs, a person can live as he wishes. No restraint is put upon his behavior. He can oppress others, lie, steal, cheat, drink, smoke, have illicit sex, and still be acceptable to *his* god. The person worships a god created by sinful man who allows him to live sinfully, a god who accepts him regardless of his sin. This will be a characteristic of *the last days*. People will engage in all forms of idolatry and worship gods that allow them to live as they wish. But as Isaiah describes in this verse, they are only false gods created by their own hands and fingers, false gods that are stirred from their own ideas and imaginations.

"For the wrath of God is revealed from heaven against all ungodliness and unrighteousness of men, who hold the truth in unrighteousness; Because that which may be known of God is manifest in them; for God hath showed *it* unto them. For the invisible things of him from the creation of the world are clearly seen, being understood by the things that are made, *even* his eternal power and Godhead; so that they are without excuse: Because that, when they knew God, they glorified *him* not as God, neither were thankful; but became vain in their imaginations, and their foolish heart was darkened. Professing themselves to be wise, they became fools, And changed the glory of the uncorruptible God into an image made like to corruptible man, and to birds, and fourfooted beasts, and creeping things. Wherefore God also gave them up to uncleanness through the lusts of their own hearts, to dishonour their own bodies between themselves: Who changed the truth of God into a lie, and worshipped and served the creature more than the Creator, who is blessed for ever. Amen" (Ro.1:18-25).

"Little children, keep yourselves from idols. Amen" (1 Jn.5:21).

"Thou shalt have no other gods before me. Thou shalt not make unto thee any graven image, or any likeness *of any thing* that *is* in heaven above, or that *is* in the earth beneath, or that *is* in the water under the earth: Thou shalt not bow down thyself to them, nor serve them: for I the LORD thy God *am* a jealous God, visiting the iniquity of the fathers upon the children unto the third and fourth *generation* of them that hate me" (Ex.20:3-5).

"And there ye shall serve gods, the work of men's hands, wood and stone, which neither see, nor hear, nor eat, nor smell" (De.4:28).

"Take heed to yourselves, that your heart be not deceived, and ye turn aside, and serve other gods, and worship them" (De.11:16).

"There shall no strange god be in thee; neither shalt thou worship any strange god" (Ps.81:9).

"I *am* the LORD: that *is* my name: and my glory will I not give to another, neither my praise to graven images" (Is.42:8).

5) The *Day of the LORD*—His execution of justice and judgment—is coming because people will be beyond repentance and forgiveness (v.9). Their hearts will be hard, stubborn against God and His Holy Word. No matter how much people hear the gospel and the warning of coming judgment, they still continue in their sin. They love pleasure, recreation, power, wealth, and possessions—the things of this world—more than they love God. Consequently, they harden their hearts against God and stubbornly reject Him time and again. Finally, they become so hardened that they are beyond repentance. They will never give up their worldly pleasures, never surrender to the LORD and seek His forgiveness. Thus, God is left with no choice: justice and judgment must be executed against the hard-hearted and stubborn of this earth.

> **"Ye stiffnecked and uncircumcised in heart and ears, ye do always resist the Holy Ghost: as your fathers *did*, so *do* ye" (Ac.7:51).**
> **"But after thy hardness and impenitent heart treasurest up unto thyself wrath against the day of wrath and revelation of the righteous judgment of God; Who will render to every man according to his deeds: To them who by patient continuance in well doing seek for glory and honour and immortality, eternal life: But unto them that are contentious, and do not obey the truth, but obey unrighteousness, indignation and wrath, Tribulation and anguish, upon every soul of man that doeth evil, of the Jew first, and also of the Gentile" (Ro.2:5-9).**
> **"Take heed, brethren, lest there be in any of you an evil heart of unbelief, in departing from the living God. But exhort one another daily, while it is called To day; lest any of you be hardened through the deceitfulness of sin" (He.3:12-13).**
> **"He, that being often reproved hardeneth *his* neck, shall suddenly be destroyed, and that without remedy" (Pr.29:1).**

b. When the *Day of the LORD* comes, the reaction of the people will be that of terror and panic (vv.10-21).

OUTLINE	SCRIPTURE	SCRIPTURE	OUTLINE
b. The reaction of the people to the wrath of God 1) The people will seek to escape, flee, hide 2) The arrogant & prideful will be humbled in that day: The LORD alone will be exalted 3) The whole world will be humbled *in that Day*, 2:11-12; 3:7, 18; 4:1-2 • All the proud & lofty • All the towering trees of earth in their natural beauty • All the towering mountains & high hills of the earth • All the world's military power & defenses • All the economies & businesses	10 Enter into the rock, and hide thee in the dust, for fear of the LORD, and for the glory of his majesty. 11 The lofty looks of man shall be humbled, and the haughtiness of men shall be bowed down, and the LORD alone shall be exalted in that day. 12 For the day of the LORD of hosts *shall be* upon every *one that is* proud and lofty, and upon every *one that is* lifted up; and he shall be brought low: 13 And upon all the cedars of Lebanon, *that are* high and lifted up, and upon all the oaks of Bashan, 14 And upon all the high mountains, and upon all the hills *that are* lifted up, 15 And upon every high tower, and upon every fenced wall, 16 And upon all the ships of Tarshish, and upon all pleasant pictures.	17 And the loftiness of man shall be bowed down, and the haughtiness of men shall be made low: and the LORD alone shall be exalted in that day. 18 And the idols he shall utterly abolish. 19 And they shall go into the holes of the rocks, and into the caves of the earth, for fear of the LORD, and for the glory of his majesty, when he ariseth to shake terribly the earth. 20 In that day a man shall cast his idols of silver, and his idols of gold, which they made *each one* for himself to worship, to the moles and to the bats; 21 To go into the clefts of the rocks, and into the tops of the ragged rocks, for fear of the LORD, and for the glory of his majesty, when he ariseth to shake terribly the earth.	• All the arrogance & pride of people • All the idols & false worship: Destroyed 4) The idolater will be stricken with terror • Will seek to hide, escape • Will cast away all idols in seeking to escape God's wrath • Will seek to escape the glory of God's majesty • Will seek to escape when God rises to *shake the earth,* see 19, 21

People will seek to escape, hiding in the rocks and caves of the earth, fleeing from the majestic glory and splendor of the LORD. Having denied and rebelled against the LORD all of their lives, they will finally see that Jesus Christ is the Lord God of the universe. His majestic glory will humble the arrogant and prideful of this earth, and they will be brought low. The LORD alone will be exalted in the day of His majestic glory and judgment (v.11).

In fact, the whole world will be humbled in the *Day of the LORD* (vv.12-18):
⇒ All the proud and lofty—all who have exalted themselves—will be humbled.
⇒ All the exalted beauty of creation, such as the cedars of Lebanon and the oaks of Bashan, will be humbled before the majestic glory of the LORD.
⇒ All the towering mountains and high hills of the earth in their splendid, natural beauty will be humbled before the LORD's majestic glory.
⇒ All the world's military power and defenses, every lofty tower and fortified wall will be humbled in the face of the LORD's terrifying judgment.

⇒ All the businesses and economies of this earth, every great commercial ship and every small commercial and recreational boat will be humbled before the glory of the LORD.

⇒ All the arrogance and pride of man will be brought low and humbled, and the LORD alone will be exalted in the day of his terrifying judgment.

⇒ All the idols and false worship will be totally destroyed in that great *Day of the LORD* (v.18).

When the LORD returns to earth in His majestic glory, the idolater will be especially stricken with terror and seek to hide from the coming wrath of God. Note that His wrath will actually shake and turn the world of mankind upside down or, more accurately, right side up (v.19). The LORD alone will be acknowledged as the true and living God. The idolater will cast away all idols, leaving them as hiding places for the rats and bats. Whereas the idolater had placed his welfare in the trust of these idols, now the rats and bats could place their welfare in the shelter of the idols. In that day, every idolater on earth will flee into the caverns and jagged rocks of the earth, seeking to escape the glory of the LORD's majesty. In contrast, the LORD will rise up and return to *shake the earth* by executing justice and judgment upon every human being.

c. Again, Isaiah issues the strong challenge to the people of his day as well as to the people of our day. There is only one way to escape God's wrath: spiritual separation.

OUTLINE	SCRIPTURE
c. The only way to escape God's wrath: Must separate from the wicked & idolatrous	22 Cease ye from man, whose breath *is* in his nostrils: for wherein is he to be accounted of?

We must not participate in the behavior of the wicked and idolatrous of this earth (v.22). It is utterly insane to trust the humanistic, materialistic philosophy of the world. Man is not the supreme being of the universe. He merely possesses the breath of life, breath that can be ever so quickly snuffed out. Standing in his humanistic, secular philosophy and living a selfish and sinful life, man is of no account, no importance. He has value only as he stands in the LORD and lives a life of righteousness, love, and service to mankind. If he rejects the LORD, he will face the terrifying judgment of the LORD. The only way he can escape God's wrath is to set himself apart from those who are evil or who worship false gods. He must not put his trust in man, nor in humanistic, secular philosophy.

d. A description of the approaching judgment of God is next given by the prophet Isaiah (3:1-7).

OUTLINE	SCRIPTURE	SCRIPTURE	OUTLINE
d. The description of the approaching judgment: To be executed by the LORD, the LORD of hosts 1) A loss of the basic necessities of life: Water & food 2) A removal of all leaders: Military, legal, religious, civil, business, & social leaders	**CHAPTER 3** For, behold, the Lord, the LORD of hosts, doth take away from Jerusalem and from Judah the stay and the staff, the whole stay of bread, and the whole stay of water, 2 The mighty man, and the man of war, the judge, and the prophet, and the prudent, and the ancient, 3 The captain of fifty, and the honourable man, and the counsellor, and the cunning artificer, and the eloquent orator.	shall rule over them. 5 And the people shall be oppressed, every one by another, and every one by his neighbour: the child shall behave himself proudly against the ancient, and the base against the honourable. 6 When a man shall take hold of his brother of the house of his father, *saying,* Thou hast clothing, be thou our ruler, and *let* this ruin *be* under thy hand: 7 In that day shall he swear, saying, I will not be an healer; for in my house *is*	4) A society of oppression, lawlessness, & anarchy 5) A people with no answer to their problems & no desire or willingness to serve • People will feel hopeless & helpless
3) A government of weak, inexperienced leaders	4 And I will give children *to be* their princes, and babes	neither bread nor clothing: make me not a ruler of the people.	• People will refuse to serve as leaders

Note that the truth spelled out in these verses is a universal truth; that is, it applies to all people of all ages at all times. If a person turns away from the LORD and trusts the things of this world, he eventually loses everything. The things of this world are not lasting. At best, they are temporary, and the security they bring is limited. Thus, if we trust the things of the world, we eventually face collapse, failure, emptiness, loneliness, purposelessness, and insecurity. The things of the world have no future beyond this life. This was the situation being faced by the people of Jerusalem and Judah in the days of Isaiah. Isaiah wanted them to understand that their trust must be placed in the LORD, not in the leadership and things of this world. As he had just pointed out, man and the things he has made in this world are only temporary (2:22). Because the people had placed their trust in sinful man and false gods, the LORD Almighty was about to execute judgment upon the nation. Since the penalty of sin is a universal truth, what was about to take place in Jerusalem and Judah will also take place in *the last days* during the *Day of the LORD.* Five specific judgments are to fall.

⇒ There will be a loss of the basic necessities of life, including both food and water (v.1). All the supplies needed to support human life and to maintain a stable government will be used up or lost.

⇒ There will be a removal of all leaders: military, legal, religious, civil, business and social leaders (vv.2-3). The very backbone of the nation—all capable and wise leaders—will be crushed.

⇒ There will be a government of weak, inexperienced leaders (v.4). Political and military leadership will be so inexperienced that it will be as if children were leading the nation.

⇒ There will be oppression, lawlessness, and anarchy sweeping throughout society (v.5). Neighbor will rise up against neighbor, children against their parents and the elderly, the base against the honorable. Respect for people will cease to exist. Disrespect, lawlessness, and violence will run rampant throughout society.

⇒ There will be a spirit of hopelessness gripping people, and nobody will have the answer to the world's problems (vv.6-7). Moreover, no one will desire or be willing to serve in a position of leadership. Utter chaos and depravation will prevail. People will be so hungry and their clothing so ragged that anyone wearing good clothing will be constrained to take a leadership position. However, because of the spirit of hopelessness gripping people, no one will be willing to take the reigns of leadership.

e. Isaiah again emphasized the reasons for such a destructive judgment coming upon Jerusalem and Judah (vv.8-9). Keep in mind that this passage has a double meaning, referring both to the Jews of Isaiah's day and to the people of succeeding generations, the people of *the last days*.

OUTLINE	SCRIPTURE	SCRIPTURE	OUTLINE
e. The reason for such a destructive judgment reemphasized 1) Because their tongues & deeds defy the LORD 2) Because they sin openly,	8 For Jerusalem is ruined, and Judah is fallen: because their tongue and their doings *are* against the LORD, to provoke the eyes of his glory. 9 The show of their counte-	nance doth witness against them; and they declare their sin as Sodom, they hide *it* not. Woe unto their soul! for they have rewarded evil unto themselves.	brazenly just as Sodom did • Woe to them! How terrible their judgment will be • They have brought judgment on themselves

Jerusalem will stagger and Judah will fall for two reasons: first, because the people's words and deeds defied the LORD (v.8). People refused to heed and obey God's Word, His holy commandments. With their tongues they used foul language, cursed the LORD's name, mocked true believers and prophets of the LORD, lied and deceived people and praised their false gods. In their deeds they committed all forms of sin, wickedness, and evil. They simply rebelled against the LORD, committing apostasy against Him.

Second, God's judgment was to fall because the people sinned openly, brazenly, just as Sodom had done (v.9). They denied God so much that He became meaningless to them. To them, sin was not sin, so they could live as they wished. They sensed no need to preserve any appearance of godliness before the public. Sin and sinful activity were openly talked about and shamefully practiced for all to see. But note the sharp warning given by Isaiah: woe to their souls! How terrible their judgment would be! They had brought disaster upon themselves.

f. In light of the coming judgment, the believer had two very specific duties (vv.10-12).

OUTLINE	SCRIPTURE	SCRIPTURE	OUTLINE
f. The duty of believers in light of the coming judgment 1) To assure the righteous: They will be rewarded 2) To warn the wicked: They will be judged • Immature rulers will	10 Say ye to the righteous, that *it shall be* well *with him:* for they shall eat the fruit of their doings. 11 Woe unto the wicked! *it shall be* ill *with him:* for the reward of his hands shall be	given him. 12 *As for* my people, children *are* their oppressors, and women rule over them. O my people, they which lead thee cause *thee* to err, and destroy the way of thy paths.	oppress them • Unwise women will rule, lead them astray, 1 K.18:4; 21:5; 2 K.11:1

Despite the rampant wickedness sweeping the world of Isaiah's day, there was a remnant or small number of true believers. These believers had a specific task to carry out for the LORD. First, they were to assure the righteous that all believers would be rewarded (v.10). It would go well for them. They would receive a wonderful reward, reaping the fruits of their righteous deeds.

Second, the believer was to warn the wicked that they would be judged. Disaster was coming upon them! They would be judged for exactly what they have done, nothing more and nothing less. God's judgment would be fair. Perfect justice would be executed upon the wicked. Two examples are given:

⇒ The people had turned away from the LORD and placed their trust totally in their leaders. As a result, righteous and capable leaders had been removed from the nation. Now, only young, inexperienced rulers were governing, and many of those were oppressing the people.

⇒ Unwise women were in some cases exercising strong influence over the inexperienced rulers, leading the young astray.

In all cases, these young, inexperienced rulers were leading the people down the path of disobedience to the LORD. Failing to warn people of the righteous judgment of God, they actually encouraged the worship of false gods and led the people to reject the LORD and His Holy commandments (see 1 K.18:4; 21:5; 2 K.11:1).

g. Again, Isaiah painted the scene of a courtroom, presenting the LORD's case against the leaders of Jerusalem and Judah. However, remember, this is a picture of God's case against all leaders who rebel against Him, no matter the generation. It is definitely a picture of God's case against the leaders who will hold positions of authority in *the last days*. The charge is a strong indictment: they have betrayed the trust, the responsibility given them (vv.13-15).

OUTLINE	SCRIPTURE	SCRIPTURE	OUTLINE
g. The LORD's case against the leaders: A betrayal of trust 1) They had oppressed, ruined the vineyard (Israel) 2) They had taken advantage of the people	13 The LORD standeth up to plead, and standeth to judge the people. 14 The LORD will enter into judgment with the ancients of his people, and the princes thereof: for ye have eaten up	the vineyard; the spoil of the poor *is* in your houses. 15 What mean ye *that* ye beat my people to pieces, and grind the faces of the poor? saith the LORD GOD of hosts.	• Stolen, plundered their property • Oppressed, crushed them, grinding their faces into the ground

The leaders had oppressed and ruined the vineyard of God, which is Israel or God's people. Whereas they should have tended—looked after and guarded—the vineyard, they had neglected God's people. They had taken advantage of the people under their care, stealing and plundering their property. In some cases the leaders had actually crushed and trampled the faces of the people—even the poor and helpless—into the ground. Note that this charge is a declaration of the LORD, the LORD of hosts or the LORD Almighty (v.15).

h. The LORD not only had a case against the leaders but also against the haughty, worldly women of society (3:16–4:1).

OUTLINE	SCRIPTURE	SCRIPTURE	OUTLINE
h. The LORD's case against the haughty, worldly women of society 1) Their sins • Pride, arrogance • Flirting with men • Immodest behavior & dress 2) Their judgment • Will have sores on their heads • Will be uncovered, stripped naked (raped) • Will lose all their jewelry, wardrobe, perfume, gowns, & all else of value that had been coveted	16 Moreover the LORD saith, Because the daughters of Zion are haughty, and walk with stretched forth necks and wanton eyes, walking and mincing *as* they go, and making a tinkling with their feet: 17 Therefore the LORD will smite with a scab the crown of the head of the daughters of Zion, and the LORD will discover their secret parts. 18 In that day the Lord will take away the bravery of *their* tinkling ornaments *about their feet,* and *their* cauls, and *their* round tires like the moon, 19 The chains, and the bracelets, and the mufflers, 20 The bonnets, and the ornaments of the legs, and the headbands, and the tablets, and the earrings, 21 The rings, and nose jewels, 22 The changeable suits of apparel, and the mantles, and the wimples, and the crisping	pins, 23 The glasses, and the fine linen, and the hoods, and the vails. 24 And it shall come to pass, *that* instead of sweet smell there shall be stink; and instead of a girdle a rent; and instead of well set hair baldness; and instead of a stomacher a girding of sackcloth; *and* burning instead of beauty. 25 Thy men shall fall by the sword, and thy mighty in the war. 26 And her gates shall lament and mourn; and she *being* desolate shall sit upon the ground. **CHAPTER 4** And in that day seven women shall take hold of one man, saying, We will eat our own bread, and wear our own apparel: only let us be called by thy name, to take away our reproach.	• Will stink instead of smelling sweet • Will wear a rope, not a sash • Will be bald • Will wear sackcloth, not fine clothing • Will be branded with shame, not beauty • Will be widowed • Will be exiled, led away from Jerusalem into captivity • Will face fierce competition for husbands due to so few men surviving the war

Note that these women were "the daughters or women of Zion (Jerusalem)." They were professing believers, women who claimed to know and follow the LORD. But their lives and behavior exposed their *false profession.* In truth they professed one thing and lived another. They were hypocrites. God's case against these women was strong. They were guilty of *pride* and *arrogance.* As they walked throughout the day, they looked down on other people, thinking themselves better, more attractive, more intelligent, and more capable than others. As they walked about, they also flirted with men, using their eyes to get the attention of men. They craved to be recognized as attractive in the eyes of men and to be desired by men. Accordingly, they dressed and behaved immodestly at times.

Remember, these women declared they were followers of the LORD. Because they focused their lives and attention upon themselves and the lust of the flesh, they were to face the severe judgment of God. They were to experience deep distress and suffering. A quick glance at the judgment coming upon them shows how horrible their sufferings would be:

⇒ They would have sores break out on their heads, somewhat like leprosy (v.17).
⇒ They would be uncovered, stripped naked, which probably refers to being raped by invading armies (v.17).
⇒ They would lose all their jewelry, wardrobe, perfume, party clothes, gowns, and all else of value (vv.18-23).
⇒ They would stink instead of smelling sweet (v.24).
⇒ They would wear the rope of a captive around their waist, not a sash.
⇒ They would be bald.
⇒ They would wear sackcloth, not fine clothing.
⇒ They would be branded with shame, not beauty.
⇒ They would be widowed, because their husbands would be killed in battle (v.25).

⇒ They would be exiled, led away from Jerusalem into captivity (v.26).

⇒ They would face fierce competition for a husband due to so few men surviving the war (4:1).

Thought 1. The *Day of the LORD* is coming, the day of His terrifying judgment. No person will escape the judgment of God. Perfect justice will be executed on earth. All the oppression and mistreatment of people, the injustices and unfair dealings that have been committed—all wrong behavior—will be judged. We will be punished for the wrong we have done, but only for the wrong we have done. We will never be punished for something we did not do or for something someone else did. Perfect justice will be executed. Whatever judgment we face in the future will be exactly what we deserve.

But the wonderful news is the gospel of Jesus Christ. Christ has taken our wrong, our sins upon Himself. He has already paid the penalty for our sins, which is death. Christ died for our sins. If we will place our trust in Him, surrender our lives to believe and follow Him, God will accept us. He will forgive our sins and count us *righteous* before Him. Our sins will be forgiven, erased, never remembered nor brought up at the judgment seat. Standing before the throne of God's judgment, we will claim only the righteousness of Jesus Christ. When we claim His righteousness—not our own, but His righteousness—God will accept us.

Nevertheless, the thrust of Isaiah's message is not the redemption, not the forgiveness of sins that we have in Christ. The thrust of his message is judgment, because most people refuse to come to the LORD for forgiveness. Most people are still rebelling against God, turning away from Him and walking in the sin and shame of this world. Thus, Isaiah issues a strong warning to all who continue in sin: they will face the judgment of God. Listen to the warning of God's Holy Word:

> **"When the Son of man shall come in his glory, and all the holy angels with him, then shall he sit upon the throne of his glory: And before him shall be gathered all nations: and he shall separate them one from another, as a shepherd divideth *his* sheep from the goats: And he shall set the sheep on his right hand, but the goats on the left" (Mt.25:31-33).**

> **"Whosoever therefore shall be ashamed of me and of my words in this adulterous and sinful generation; of him also shall the Son of man be ashamed, when he cometh in the glory of his Father with the holy angels" (Mk.8:38).**

> **"He that believeth on the Son hath everlasting life: and he that believeth not the Son shall not see life; but the wrath of God abideth on him" (Jn.3:36).**

> **"For the wrath of God is revealed from heaven against all ungodliness and unrighteousness of men, who hold the truth in unrighteousness" (Ro.1:18).**

> **"But unto them that are contentious, and do not obey the truth, but obey unrighteousness, indignation and wrath" (Ro.2:8).**

> **"But fornication, and all uncleanness, or covetousness, let it not be once named among you, as becometh saints; Neither filthiness, nor foolish talking, nor jesting, which are not convenient: but rather giving of thanks. For this ye know, that no whoremonger, nor unclean person, nor covetous man, who is an idolater, hath any inheritance in the kingdom of Christ and of God. Let no man deceive you with vain words: for because of these things cometh the wrath of God upon the children of disobedience" (Ep.5:3-6).**

> **"And to you who are troubled rest with us, when the Lord Jesus shall be revealed from heaven with his mighty angels, In flaming fire taking vengeance on them that know not God, and that obey not the gospel of our Lord Jesus Christ" (2 Th.1:7-8).**

> **"And as it is appointed unto men once to die, but after this the judgment" (He.9:27).**

> **"The Lord knoweth how to deliver the godly out of temptations, and to reserve the unjust unto the day of judgment to be punished" (2 Pe.2:9).**

> **"But the heavens and the earth, which are now, by the same word are kept in store, reserved unto fire against the day of judgment and perdition of ungodly men" (2 Pe.3:7).**

> **"And Enoch also, the seventh from Adam, prophesied of these, saying, Behold, the Lord cometh with ten thousands of his saints, To execute judgment upon all, and to convince all that are ungodly among them of all their ungodly deeds which they have ungodly committed, and of all their hard *speeches* which ungodly sinners have spoken against him" (Jude 14-15).**

> **"Behold, he cometh with clouds; and every eye shall see him, and they *also* which pierced him: and all kindreds of the earth shall wail because of him. Even so, Amen" (Re.1:7).**

> **"Kiss the Son, lest he be angry, and ye perish *from* the way, when his wrath is kindled but a little. Blessed *are* all they that put their trust in him" (Ps.2:12).**

DEEPER STUDY # 3

(2:6–4:1) **Day of the LORD (Jehovah)**: in the simplest of terms, the *Day of the LORD* is a dramatic period of time when God executes swift judgment on the wicked and saves the righteous. Throughout history the *Day of the LORD* has fallen time and again to save God's people. But the *Day of the LORD* in the latter days of human history refers to the day when Christ will return to execute judgment on earth. It is a definite *day* that is coming to earth, and it is coming at the end of the *last days*, at the end of the present age. (See outlines and notes—Mt.24:1-25:46 for more discussion.) Note two points:

1. The *Day of the LORD* is to be characterized by several things.
   a. *Wonders* (terata): signs and events in heaven above (outer space) that point to something unusual about to happen (Ac.2:19-20).
   b. *Signs* (semeia): events and happenings on earth given by God to warn that the end is at hand.
   c. *Blood and fire and vapor of smoke*: terrible bloodshed and an explosive fire that causes...
      • mushrooming vapors of smoke
      • the sun to be turned into darkness and blotted out
      • the moon to be turned to blood red

Thought 1. It is thought provoking when we consider how closely the language resembles atomic warfare.

2. The events that will happen in the *Day of the LORD* (as revealed by the whole of Scripture) seem to be fourfold. Note: no attempt whatsoever is made to put these events in a specific order. There are two reasons for this.
   ⇒ There are so many different opinions about the matter.
   ⇒ More importantly, Scripture does not give a complete list of events in *the last days*.

Throughout Scripture, at least four events are discussed as happening on the *Day of the LORD*: the terrible tribulation, the return of Christ as Sovereign Lord, judgment, and the remaking of the universe.
   a. A terrible period of tribulation (7 years): this includes the last half of the period known as the great tribulation (3½ years). This is the fulfillment of Daniel's *seventieth week* (Da.9:27). (See outline and notes—Mt.24:15-28; Mk.13:1-37; Lu.21:20-24; Re.6:1–19:21. Also see Is.13:6-16; Eze.30:1-26; Joel 1:15; 2:1-11; Zep.1:7-18; Zec.14:1-15.)
   b. The return of Christ as sovereign Lord: He will rule and reign in glory upon earth (the millennial reign of God's Son, Re.20:4-6).
   c. The resurrection and final judgment of all: this will include...
      • men who are described as sheep and goats (Mt.25:31-46; Re.20:11-15)
      • the Beast or the antichrist, the false prophet, and their followers (Re.19:11-21)
      • Satan and his angels (Re.20:10)

   d. The destruction and remaking of the earth and heavens (the universe) (2 Pe.3:3-15; Re.21:1; see Is.65:17; 66:22).

3 (4:2-6) **Jesus Christ, Names – Titles of, Branch of the LORD—Branch of the LORD, Meaning, a Title of Christ—Israel, Restoration of, Promised; Assured—Millennium, Description of**: in the future, Israel will be restored. *In that day*, the *Day of the LORD,* a remnant of Israel will be saved. Judgment is never the end of God's message. Rather, His message always ends with the hope of salvation. Isaiah now looks beyond the judgment of God to the event that will take place right after the terrible battle of Armageddon. Note the Scripture and outline:

OUTLINE	SCRIPTURE	SCRIPTURE	OUTLINE
3. The future restoration of Israel: Assured by the *Branch of the LORD* (Christ)	2 In that day shall the branch of the LORD be beautiful and glorious, and the fruit of the earth *shall be* excellent and comely for them that are escaped of Israel.	thereof by the spirit of judgment, and by the spirit of burning.	
a. The LORD will save some: *In that day*, 2:2, 11-12, 17, 20; 3:7, 18; 4:1-2	3 And it shall come to pass, *that he that is* left in Zion, and *he that* remaineth in Jerusalem, shall be called holy,	5 And the LORD will create upon every dwelling place of mount Zion, and upon her assemblies, a cloud and smoke by day, and the shining of a flaming fire by night: for upon all the glory *shall be* a defence.	b. The LORD will cover Israel with His glory
1) Provide a fruitful earth, 2			1) The canopy of His presence & provision
2) Make them holy	*even* every one that is written among the living in Jerusalem:		
3) Cleanse them from moral filth, sin	4 When the Lord shall have washed away the filth of the daughters of Zion, and shall have purged the blood of Jerusalem from the midst	6 And there shall be a tabernacle for a shadow in the daytime from the heat, and for a place of refuge, and for a covert from storm and from rain.	2) The shelter of His protection: Will provide a refuge & security
• The filth of the women			
• The lawlessness & violence of everyone			

a. Right after the terrible *Day of the LORD*, the LORD will save a remnant of Israel (vv.2-4). And He will save them by the *Branch of the LORD*, which is a direct reference to the Messiah Himself, even the Lord Jesus Christ. The Messiah is the *Branch* who came as a *sprout* or *shoot* from the stump of David's dynasty, a dynasty that seemed to be dead (11:1; 53:2; Je.23:5; 33:15; Zec.3:8; 6:12). Note that the *Branch* will be beautiful and glorious in the eyes of the people. He will be the vine in whom the people will find their nourishment and strength (Jn.15:1). As the *Branch of the LORD*, the Messiah will do three wonderful things for the people:
   ⇒ He will provide a fruitful land for them (v.2). All the necessities of life—food, water, shelter, and whatever else is needed—will be provided for them in the promised land.
   ⇒ He will make them holy, totally set apart and consecrated to God, to worship and serve Him (v.3). Following the future day of judgment, the only people who will survive will be genuine believers, those who have set their lives apart to God. At that time the LORD will perfect the holiness of all believers, purifying them and making them acceptable to live with Him eternally. This verse must be referring to the millennial reign of Christ and to eternity in the new heavens and earth. Why? Because the survivors left behind after the Assyrian and Baby-lonian invasions were not called holy. As Ezra, Nehemiah, and the prophets describe, they were anything but holy.
   ⇒ The LORD will cleanse the people from moral filth and sin (v.4). The filth of the women of Zion will be washed away, as will the lawlessness and violence of everyone who is to live in the Holy City of Jerusalem.

b. After the people are perfectly cleansed and made holy, the LORD will cover His people with the glory of His presence (vv.5-6). In fact, the canopy of His presence and provision will cover all of Mount Zion (Jerusalem). During the Exodus, the very presence of God was seen in a cloud by day and a pillar of fire by night (Ex.13:21-22; 40:34-38; see also 16:10). So it will be in the millennium and in the new heavens and earth: God's very presence will cover the New Jerusalem and be visible to all who travel and assemble there. The very shelter of God's protection will provide a refuge and security for the people. His presence will provide a perfect safe haven. There will be no stifling heat from hot summer days or danger from violent storms.

Thought 1. The LORD is our shelter, our overshadowing protection from the storms of life. When tempted and lured to participate in some sinful behavior, the LORD's presence will be with us. He will protect and deliver us. If we will flee to Him for shelter and protection, He will deliver us from the temptation. When trials strike us—distressing circumstances, hardships, or misfortunes—the LORD will protect us. If we will flee into His Being, calling out to Him, He will be a refuge for us. He will overshadow us with His presence. No matter the strain, pressure, distress, or grief, the LORD will grant His protective Spirit.

(1) The LORD is our overshadowing protection. He will shelter us in His presence.

> "O Jerusalem, Jerusalem, *thou* that killest the prophets, and stonest them which are sent unto thee, how often would I have gathered thy children together, even as a hen gathereth her chickens under *her* wings, and ye would not!" (Mt.23:37).
> "Be merciful unto me, O God, be merciful unto me: for my soul trusteth in thee: yea, in the shadow of thy wings will I make my refuge, until *these* calamities be overpast" (Ps.57:1).
> "For thou hast been a strength to the poor, a strength to the needy in his distress, a refuge from the storm, a shadow from the heat, when the blast of the terrible ones *is* as a storm *against* the wall" (Is.25:4).
> "And I have put my words in thy mouth, and I have covered thee in the shadow of mine hand, that I may plant the heavens, and lay the foundations of the earth, and say unto Zion, Thou *art* my people" (Is.51:16).

(2) The LORD is our shelter, our hiding place.

> "Keep me as the apple of the eye, hide me under the shadow of thy wings" (Ps.17:8).
> "For in the time of trouble he shall hide me in his pavilion: in the secret of his tabernacle shall he hide me; he shall set me up upon a rock" (Ps.27:5).
> "Thou shalt hide them in the secret of thy presence from the pride of man: thou shalt keep them secretly in a pavilion from the strife of tongues" (Ps.31:20).
> "Thou *art* my hiding place; thou shalt preserve me from trouble; thou shalt compass me about with songs of deliverance. Selah" (Ps.32:7).
> "Hide me from the secret counsel of the wicked; from the insurrection of the workers of iniquity" (Ps.64:2).
> "Thou *art* my hiding place and my shield: I hope in thy word" (Ps.119:114).
> "Deliver me, O LORD, from mine enemies: I flee unto thee to hide me" (Ps.143:9).

(3) The LORD is our refuge.

> "The eternal God *is thy* refuge, and underneath *are* the everlasting arms: and he shall thrust out the enemy from before thee; and shall say, Destroy *them*" (De.33:27).
> "For in the time of trouble he shall hide me in his pavilion: in the secret of his tabernacle shall he hide me; he shall set me up upon a rock" (Ps.27:5).
> "Thou shalt hide them in the secret of thy presence from the pride of man: thou shalt keep them secretly in a pavilion from the strife of tongues" (Ps.31:20).
> "Be thou my strong habitation, whereunto I may continually resort: thou hast given commandment to save me; for thou *art* my rock and my fortress" (Ps.71:3).
> "The name of the LORD *is* a strong tower: the righteous runneth into it, and is safe" (Pr.18:10).
> "For thou hast been a strength to the poor, a strength to the needy in his distress, a refuge from the storm, a shadow from the heat, when the blast of the terrible ones *is* as a storm *against* the wall" (Is.25:4).

DEEPER STUDY # 1

(2:1-5) Millennium—Jesus Christ, Millennial Reign—Kingdom, of Christ on Earth—Rule, of Christ, on Earth: the word *millennium* simply means 1,000 years. There is only one section of Scripture in the whole Bible that tells us *how long* the reign of Jesus Christ will be (Re.20:2-7). When we speak of the Millennium, we mean the 1,000-year rule of Jesus Christ on earth. God's Holy Word reveals that just prior to the millennial reign of Christ two great events will take place.

First, Jesus Christ is going to return to earth as conqueror. He is going to destroy the Antichrist and all the war machines and armies of the world in a battle known as Armageddon (see outline and notes—Re.19:17-21 for more discussion). Not a single shot will be fired against Christ at Armageddon. When Jesus Christ appears in the heavens, He will give one explosion of His glory and the most powerful beam of light the world has ever known will destroy the armies and nations of the world. (See outline and note—2 Th.2:8 for more discussion.)

Second, Christ will bind and remove Satan from the earth for 1,000 years, the period of the Millennium. For 1,000 years Satan will not be able to tempt or deceive people on earth. This does not mean that people cannot sin or do wrong, for man will still have his human disposition that comes short of God's glory *by its very nature*. Man will still have choices to make:

to follow Christ or not to follow Christ. But with Satan bound and removed, there will be far less evil and ungodliness in the world. Government and society will be under the control of Christ Himself. This means...

- that no more war or killing will take place
- that no more assaults, abuse, or crimes will go unpunished
- that no more hunger, homelessness, or unemployment will exist
- that no more laziness, lethargy, or unconcern will be allowed
- that no selling or taking drugs or drunkenness will be tolerated

When Jesus Christ rules over the earth in the future, He will govern both the nations and the people of the earth.

⇒ The following Scripture reference makes this clear.

> "I saw in the night visions, and, behold, *one* like the Son of man came with the clouds of heaven, and came to the Ancient of days, and they brought him near before him. And there was given him dominion, and glory, and a kingdom, that all people, nations, and languages, should serve him: his dominion *is* an everlasting dominion, which shall not pass away, and his kingdom *that* which shall not be destroyed" (Da.7:13-14).

⇒ Peter definitely said that the Millennium was coming and that it referred to a future time.

> "Repent ye therefore, and be converted, that your sins may be blotted out, when the times of refreshing shall come from the presence of the Lord; and he shall send Jesus Christ, which before was preached unto you: whom the heaven must receive until the times of restitution of all things, which God hath spoken by the mouth of all his holy prophets since the world began" (Ac.3:19-21).

Although this is the only mention of 1,000 years (Re.20:2-7), the coming of Jesus Christ to rule this earth is mentioned numerous times in Scripture, as will be seen in the verses given below. But why is Christ coming back to rule over this earth for 1,000 years? Why is a Millennium necessary? Why does Jesus Christ not just end everything when He comes back to earth? There are at least three reasons.

1. Why must the earth be ruled over by Christ in its present form? Because the earth belongs to Christ; it belongs to Him by *right*. Jesus Christ created the world and placed man in charge of the world. But man gave the world to Satan. Man obeyed Satan instead of God. When he did, he brought evil to earth. Therefore, Jesus Christ has to reclaim the earth and bring righteousness to the earth, and He has to do it while the earth is in its present form. To destroy the earth would be giving up this earth and dooming it to destruction; it would mean that God failed with the present earth. Of course, God cannot fail. Therefore, the Lord Jesus Christ must reclaim this earth and rule over it before He moves the world and believers into the perfect world.

2. Why is the Millennium necessary? Because God has to fulfill all the promises to man that are in His Holy Word. In order to fully bless the few who really believe in Him, Jesus Christ has to come back to earth while it is in its present form. God made a number of wonderful promises in Scripture that have not yet been fulfilled, and they cannot be fulfilled without Christ Himself ruling and bringing them about. Therefore, He is coming back to carry out the promises while the earth exists as it is now.

3. Why does Christ not end everything when He returns? Because God is love. God wants to see more people saved despite the terrible evil of mankind and the atrocious acts yet to come during the last days. Moreover, God is still merciful. Therefore, He is going to give man the very presence of His Son in His majestic glory ruling and reigning from Jerusalem. God is going to give man his utopia upon earth—peace and prosperity—give man every opportunity in the world to receive Jesus Christ as Lord and Savior. In summary, the Millennium is necessary because of the love of God for man, a love that longs for more and more people to be saved.

Now, what will the Millennium be like? A good way to gain an understanding of the Millennium is to ask questions and then to answer the questions by giving Scriptural support. Any minister, teacher, or lay believer can do the same study that we are doing, and it is advantageous because there are so many erroneous ideas about the Millennium. We give just a brief study so the reader will have an idea of what the Millennium will be like. Note four questions and points about the Millennium:

1. What are some verses that tell us that Christ is coming back in glory to rule and reign over the earth?

⇒ Christ will rule over and govern the nations.

> "For the kingdom *is* the LORD's: and he *is* the governor among the nations" (Ps.22:28).
> "O let the nations be glad and sing for joy: for thou shalt judge the people righteously, and govern the nations upon earth. Selah" (Ps.67:4).
> "And he shall judge among the nations, and shall rebuke many people: and they shall beat their swords into plowshares, and their spears into pruninghooks: nation shall not lift up sword against nation, neither shall they learn war any more" (Is.2:4).
> "Of the increase of *his* government and peace *there shall be* no end, upon the throne of David, and upon his kingdom, to order it, and to establish it with judgment and with justice from henceforth even for ever. The zeal of the LORD of hosts will perform this" (Is.9:7).
> "Behold, I have given him *for* a witness to the people, a leader and commander to the people" (Is.55:4).

⇒ Christ will rule over and judge the ends of the earth.

"The adversaries of the LORD shall be broken to pieces; out of heaven shall he thunder upon them: the LORD shall judge the ends of the earth; and he shall give strength unto his king, and exalt the horn of his anointed" (1 S.2:10).

"He shall have dominion also from sea to sea, and from the river unto the ends of the earth" (Ps.72:8).

"And I will cut off the chariot from Ephraim, and the horse from Jerusalem, and the battle bow shall be cut off: and he shall speak peace unto the heathen: and his dominion *shall be* from sea *even* to sea, and from the river *even* to the ends of the earth" (Zec.9:10).

⇒ Christ is coming to rule over the earth.

"Before the LORD: for he cometh, for he cometh to judge the earth: he shall judge the world with righteousness, and the people with his truth" (Ps.96:13).

"Before the LORD; for he cometh to judge the earth: with righteousness shall he judge the world, and the people with equity" (Ps.98:9).

⇒ Christ will be made higher than the kings of the earth.

"His name shall endure for ever: his name shall be continued as long as the sun: and *men* shall be blessed in him: all nations shall call him blessed" (Ps.72:17).

"[The LORD]…cometh to judge the earth: with righteousness shall he judge the world, and the people with equity" (Ps.98:9).

⇒ All nations will come to see Christ's glory and every knee will bow.

"For I *know* their works and their thoughts: it shall come, that I will gather all nations and tongues; and they shall come, and see my glory" (Is.66:18).

⇒ Christ will be exalted over all rule and authority in this world and in the world to come.

"Far above all principality, and power, and might, and dominion, and every name that is named, not only in this world, but also in that which is to come" (Ep.1:21).

⇒ God will subject the world to Christ.

"For unto the angels hath he not put in subjection the world to come, whereof we speak. But one in a certain place testified, saying, What is man, that thou art mindful of him? or the son of man, that thou visitest him? Thou madest him a little lower than the angels; thou crownedst him with glory and honour, and didst set him over the works of thy hands: thou hast put all things in subjection under his feet. For in that he put all in subjection under him, he left nothing *that is* not put under him. But now we see not yet all things put under him" (He.2:5-8).

⇒ The kingdoms of the world will become the kingdoms of God.

"And the seventh angel sounded; and there were great voices in heaven, saying, The kingdoms of this world are become *the kingdoms* of our Lord, and of his Christ; and he shall reign for ever and ever" (Re.11:15).

⇒ Christ the Stone will fill and rule over the whole earth.

"Then was the iron, the clay, the brass, the silver, and the gold, broken to pieces together, and became like the chaff of the summer threshingfloors; and the wind carried them away, that no place was found for them: and the stone that smote the image became a great mountain, and filled the whole earth" (Da.2:35).

⇒ Christ alone has the right to the crown.

"I will overturn, overturn, overturn, it [the crown]: and it shall be no more, until he come whose right it is; and I will give it him" (Eze.21:27).

⇒ Kings will bring gifts to Christ and serve Him.

"The kings of Tarshish and of the isles shall bring presents: the kings of Sheba and Seba shall offer gifts. Yea, all kings shall fall down before him: all nations shall serve him" (Ps.72:10-11).

⇒ Christ's enemies will be made His footstool.

"The LORD said unto my Lord, Sit thou on my right hand, till I make thine enemies thy foot-stool?" (Mt.22:44).

"Till I make thine enemies thy footstool" (Lu.20:43).

"But to which of the angels said he at any time, Sit on my right hand, until I make thine enemies thy footstool?" (He.1:13).

"From henceforth expecting till his enemies be made his footstool" (He.10:13).

⇒ The people will obey Christ.

"The scepter shall not depart from Judah, nor a lawgiver from between his feet, until Shiloh come; and unto him *shall* the gathering of the people *be*" (Ge.49:10).

⇒ The people will serve Christ.

"And there was given him dominion, and glory, and a kingdom, that all people, nations, and languages, should serve him: his dominion is an everlasting dominion, which shall not pass away, and his kingdom that which shall not be destroyed" (Da.7:14).

⇒ The people will glorify and fear Christ.

"Therefore shall the strong people glorify thee, the city of the terrible nations shall fear thee" (Is.25:3).

⇒ Christ will be given the throne of David.

"He shall be great, and shall be called the Son of the Highest: and the Lord God shall give unto him the throne of his father David" (Lu.1:32).

⇒ Christ will rule in Zion (Jerusalem) upon His throne.

"Yet have I set my king upon my holy hill of Zion" (Ps.2:6).

"Even he shall build the temple of the LORD; and he shall bear the glory, and shall sit and rule upon his throne; and he shall be a priest upon his throne: and the counsel of peace shall be between them both" (Zec.6:13).

⇒ Jerusalem will be the place of the LORD's throne.

"At that time they shall call Jerusalem the throne of the LORD; and all the nations shall be gathered unto it, to the name of the LORD, to Jerusalem: neither shall they walk any more after the imagination of their evil heart" (Je.3:17).

"Behold, the days come, saith the LORD, that the city shall be built to the LORD from the tower of Hananeel unto the gate of the corner. And the measuring line shall yet go forth over against it upon the hill Gareb, and shall compass about to Goath" (Je.31:38-39).

"*It was* round about eighteen thousand *measures*: and the name of the city from *that* day *shall be*, the LORD is there" (Eze.48:35).

"So shall ye know that I *am* the LORD your God dwelling in Zion, my holy mountain: then shall Jerusalem be holy, and there shall no strangers [unbelievers] pass through her any more" (Joel 3:17).

"Thus saith the LORD; I am returned unto Zion, and will dwell in the midst of Jerusalem: and Jerusalem shall be called a city of truth; and the mountain of the LORD of hosts the holy mountain" (Zec.8:3).

⇒ The kingdom of Israel will be the LORD's.

"And saviors shall come up on mount Zion to judge the mount of Esau; and the kingdom shall be the LORD's" (Obad.21).

⇒ The millennial kingdom will be centered in Jerusalem, and the Shekinah glory will dwell there.

"And the LORD will create upon every dwelling place of mount Zion, and upon her assemblies, a cloud and smoke by day, and the shining of a flaming fire by night: for upon all the glory *shall be* a defence. And there shall be a tabernacle for a shadow in the daytime from the heat, and for a place of refuge, and for a covert from storm and from rain" (Is.4:5-6).

"At that time they shall call Jerusalem the throne of the LORD; and all the nations shall be gathered unto it, to the name of the LORD, to Jerusalem: neither shall they walk any more after the imagination of their evil heart" (Je.3:17).

"Behold, the days come, saith the LORD, that the city shall be built to the LORD from the tower of Hananeel unto the gate of the corner. And the measuring line shall yet go forth over against it upon the hill Gareb, and shall compass about to Goath" (Je.31:38-39).

"*It was* round about eighteen thousand *measures*: and the name of the city from *that* day *shall be*, The LORD *is* there" (Eze.48:35).

"So shall ye know that I *am* the LORD your God dwelling in Zion, my holy mountain: then shall Jerusalem be holy, and there shall no strangers [unbelievers] pass through her any more" (Joel 3:17).

"The LORD hath taken away thy judgments, he hath cast out thine enemy: the king of Israel, *even* the LORD, *is* in the midst of thee: thou shalt not see evil any more....The LORD thy God in the midst of thee *is* mighty; he will save, he will rejoice over thee with joy; he will rest in his love, he will joy over thee with singing" (Zep.3:15, 17).

"Thus saith the LORD; I am returned unto Zion, and will dwell in the midst of Jerusalem: and Jerusalem shall be called a city of truth; and the mountain of the LORD of hosts the holy mountain" (Zec.8:3).

⇒ Christ will bring peace and security to the world.

"And he shall judge among the nations, and shall rebuke many people: and they shall beat their swords into plowshares, and their spears into pruninghooks: nation shall not lift up sword against nation, neither shall they learn war any more" (Is.2:4).

"Of the increase of *his* government and peace *there shall be* no end, upon the throne of David, and upon his kingdom, to order it, and to establish it with judgment and with justice from henceforth even for ever. The zeal of the LORD of hosts will perform this" (Is.9:7).

"And he shall judge among many people, and rebuke strong nations afar off; and they shall beat their swords into plowshares, and their spears into pruninghooks: nation shall not lift up a sword against nation, neither shall they learn war any more" (Mi.4:3).

"And the streets of the city shall be full of boys and girls playing in the streets thereof" (Zec.8:5).

"In that day, saith the LORD of hosts, shall ye call every man his neighbor under the vine and under the fig tree" (Zec.3:10).

⇒ Christ will begin to reign immediately after the victory at Armageddon.

"And I heard as it were the voice of a great multitude, and as the voice of many waters, and as the voice of mighty thunderings, saying, Alleluia: for the Lord God omnipotent reigneth" (Re.19:6; see Re.19:11-21).

⇒ Christ, the seed of Abraham, will be given the land of Canaan forever.

"And the LORD appeared unto Abram, and said, Unto thy seed [Christ] will I give this land: and there builded he an altar unto the LORD, who appeared unto him" (Ge.12:7, see Gal.3:16).

"For all the land which thou seest, to thee will I give it, and to thy seed [Christ] for ever" (Ge.13:15).

"And I will give unto thee, and to thy seed [Christ] after thee, the land wherein thou art a stranger, all the land of Canaan, for an everlasting possession; and I will be their God" (Ge.17:8).

"The LORD God of heaven, which took me from my father's house, and from the land of my kindred, and which spake unto me, and that sware unto me, saying, Unto thy seed will I give this land; he shall send his angel before thee, and thou shalt take a wife unto my son from thence" (Ge.24:7).

"Sojourn in this land, and I will be with thee, and will bless thee; for unto thee, and unto thy seed [Christ], I will give all these countries, and I will perform the oath which I sware unto Abraham thy father; and I will make thy seed to multiply as the stars of heaven, and will give unto thy seed all these countries; And in thy seed shall all the nations of the earth be blessed" (Ge.26:3-4).

"And give thee the blessing of Abraham, to thee, and to thy seed with thee; that thou mayest inherit the land wherein thou art a stranger, which God gave unto Abraham....And, behold, the LORD stood above it, and said, I *am* the LORD God of Abraham thy father, and the God if Isaac: the land whereon thou liest, to thee will I give it, and to thy seed [Christ]" (Ge.28:4, 13; see Ga.3:16).

"And the land which I gave Abraham and Isaac, to thee I will give it, and to thy seed after thee will I give the land" (Ge.35:12).

"And said unto me, Behold, I will make thee fruitful, and multiply thee, and I will make of thee a multitude of people; and will give this land to thy seed after thee *for* an everlasting possession" (Ge.48:4).

⇒ The whole earth was given to Israel's seed (Christ) forever.

"Thou shalt keep therefore his statutes, and his commandments, which I command thee this day, that it may go well with thee, and with thy children after thee, and that thou mayest prolong thy days upon the earth, which the LORD thy God giveth thee, for ever" (De.4:40).

"For the promise, that he should be the heir of the world [the whole world], was not to Abraham, or to his seed [Christ], through the law, but through the righteousness of faith" (Ro.4:13).

⇒ The borders of Israel will be enlarged.

"Thus saith the Lord GOD; This *shall be* the border, whereby ye shall inherit the land according to the twelve tribes of Israel: Joseph *shall have two* portions. And ye shall inherit it, one as well as another: *concerning* the which I lifted up mine hand to give it unto your fathers: and this land shall fall unto you for inheritance. And this *shall be* the border of the land toward the north side, from the great sea, the way of Hethlon, as men go to Zedad; Hamath, Berothah, Sibraim, which *is* between the border of Damascus and the border of Hamath; Hazar-hatticon, which *is* by the coast of Hauran. And the border from the sea shall be Hazar-enan, the border of Damascus, and the north northward, and the border of Hamath. And *this is* the north side. And the east side ye shall measure from Hauran, and from Damascus, and from Gilead, and from the land of Israel *by* Jordan, from the border unto the east sea. And *this is* the east side. And the south side southward, from Tamar *even* to the waters of strife *in* Kadesh, the river to the great sea. And *this is* the south side southward. The west side also *shall be* the great sea from the border, till a man come over against Hamath. This *is* the west side. So shall ye divide this land unto you according to the tribes of Israel" (Eze.47:13-21).

"Now these *are* the names of the tribes. From the north end to the coast of the way of Hethlon, as one goeth to Hamath, Hazar-enan, the border of Damascus northward, to the coast of Hamath; for these are his sides east *and* west; a *portion for* Dan. And by the border of Dan, from the east side unto the west side, a *portion for* Asher. And by the border of Asher, from the east side even unto the west side, a *portion for* Naphtali. And by the border of Naphtali, from the east side unto the west side, a *portion for* Manasseh. And by the border of Manasseh, from the east side unto the west side, a *portion for* Ephraim. And by the border of Ephraim, from the east side even unto the west side, a *portion for* Reuben. And by the border of Reuben, from the east side unto the west side, a *portion for* Judah" (Eze.48:1-7).

"And for them, *even* for the priests, shall be *this* holy oblation; toward the north five and twenty thousand *in length,* and toward the west ten thousand in breadth, and toward the east ten thousand in breadth, and toward the south five and twenty thousand in length: and the sanctuary of the LORD shall be in the midst thereof. *It shall be* for the priests that are sanctified of the sons of Zadok; which have kept my charge, which went not astray when the children of Israel went astray, as the Levites went astray. And *this* oblation of the land that is offered shall be unto them a thing most holy by the border of the Levites. And over against the border of the priests the Levites *shall have* five and twenty thousand in length, and ten thousand in breadth: all the length *shall be* five and twenty thousand, and the breadth ten thousand. And they shall not sell of it, neither exchange, nor alienate the firstfruits of the land: for *it is* holy unto the LORD" (Eze.48:10-14).

"All the oblation *shall be* five and twenty thousand by five and twenty thousand: ye shall offer the holy oblation foursquare, with the possession of the city. And the residue *shall be* for the prince, on the one side and on the other of the holy oblation, and of the possession of the city, over against the five and twenty thousand of the oblation toward the east border, and westward over against the five and twenty thousand toward the west border, over against the portions for the prince: and it shall be the holy oblation; and the sanctuary of the house *shall be* in the midst thereof. Moreover from the possession of the Levites, and from the possession of the city, *being* in the midst *of that* which is the prince's, between the border of Judah and the border of Benjamin, shall be for the prince. As for the rest of the tribes, from the east side unto the west side, Benjamin *shall have* a *portion.* And by the border of Benjamin, from the east side unto the west side, Simeon *shall have* a *portion.* And by the border of Simeon, from the east side unto the west side, Issachar a *portion.* And by the border of Issachar, from the east side unto the west side, Zebulun a *portion.* And by the border of Zebulun, from the east side unto the west side, Gad a *portion.* And by the border of Gad, at the south side southward, the border shall be even from Tamar *unto* the waters of strife *in* Kadesh, *and* to the river toward the great sea. This *is* the land which ye shall divide by lot unto the tribes of Israel for inheri-tance, and these *are* their portions, saith the Lord GOD" (Eze.48:20-29).

⇒ The city of Jerusalem will be laid out by very fixed and precise measurements.

"And the five thousand, that are left in the breadth over against the five and twenty thousand, shall be a profane *place* for the city, for dwelling, and for suburbs: and the city shall be in the midst thereof. And these *shall be* the measures thereof; the north side four thousand and five hundred, and the south side four thousand and five hundred, and on the east side four thousand and five hundred, and the west side four thousand and five hundred. And the suburbs of the city shall be toward the north two hundred and fifty, and toward the south two hundred and fifty, and toward the east two hundred and fifty, and toward the west two hundred and fifty. And the residue in length over against the oblation of the holy *portion shall be* ten thousand eastward, and ten thousand westward: and it shall be over against the oblation of the holy *portion;* and the increase thereof shall be for food unto them that serve the city. And they that serve the city shall serve it out of all the tribes of Israel" (Eze.48:15-19).

"And these *are* the goings out of the city on the north side, four thousand and five hundred measures. And the gates of the city *shall be* after the names of the tribes of Israel: three gates northward; one gate of Reuben, one gate of Judah, one gate of Levi. And at the east side four thousand and five hundred: and three gates; and one gate of Joseph, one gate of Benjamin, one gate of Dan. And at the south side four thousand and five hundred measures: and three gates; one gate of Simeon, one gate of Issachar, one gate of Zebulun. At the west side four thousand and five hundred, *with* their three gates; one gate of Gad, one gate of Asher, one gate of Naphtali. *It was* round about eighteen thousand *measures:* and the name of the city from *that* day *shall be,* The LORD *is* there" (Eze.48:30-35).

2. Who is going to be in the Millennium? (See outline and notes—Re.20:4; pt.1—Re.20:7-10 for discussion.)
3. What will life be like in the Millennium?
   a. Life in the Millennium will be blessed.
      ⇒ There will be a covenant, a treaty establishing worldwide peace and security. Imagine 1,000 years of harmony, safety, and stability!

"And I will give peace in the land, and ye shall lie down, and none shall make you afraid: and I will rid evil beasts out of the land, neither shall the sword go through your land" (Le.26:6).

"For the mountains shall depart, and the hills be removed; but my kindness shall not depart from thee, neither shall the covenant of my peace be removed, saith the LORD that hath mercy on thee" (Is.54:10).

"Violence shall no more be heard in thy land, wasting nor destruction within thy borders; but thou shalt call thy walls Salvation, and thy gates Praise" (Is.60:18).

"In his days Judah shall be saved, and Israel shall dwell safely: and this is his name whereby he shall be called, THE LORD OUR RIGHTEOUSNESS" (Je.23:6).

"And in that day will I make a covenant for them with the beasts of the field, and with the fowls of heaven, and *with* the creeping things of the ground: and I will break the bow and the sword and the battle out of the earth, and will make them to lie down safely" (Ho.2:18).

"And he shall judge among many people, and rebuke strong nations afar off; and they shall beat their swords into plowshares, and their spears into pruninghooks: nation shall not lift up a sword against nation, neither shall they learn war any more. But they shall sit every man under his vine and under his fig tree; and none shall make *them* afraid: for the mouth of the LORD of hosts hath spoken *it*" (Mi.4:3-4).

⇒ There will be no evil done by one nation against another.

"The remnant of Israel shall not do iniquity, nor speak lies; neither shall a deceitful tongue be found in their mouth: for they shall feed and lie down, and none shall make *them* afraid" (Zep.3:13).

"The LORD hath taken away thy judgments, he hath cast out thine enemy: the king of Israel, *even* the LORD, *is* in the midst of thee: thou shalt not see evil any more" (Zep.3:15).

⇒ There will be no sickness.

"And ye shall serve the LORD your God, and he shall bless thy bread, and thy water; and I will take sickness away from the midst of thee. There shall nothing cast their young, nor be barren, in thy land: the number of thy days I will fulfill" (Ex.23:25-26).

"Then the eyes of the blind shall be opened, and the ears of the deaf shall be unstopped. then shall the lame *man* leap as a hart, and the tongue of the dumb sing: for in the wilderness shall waters break out, and streams in the desert" (Is.35:5-6).

⇒ There will be no more barrenness or miscarriages, but a fruitful population.

"There shall nothing cast their young, nor be barren, in thy land: the number of thy days I will fulfill" (Ex.23:26).

"For I will have respect unto you, and make you fruitful, and multiply you, and establish my covenant with you" (Le.26:9).

"Thou shalt be blessed above all people: there shall not be male or female barren among you, or among your cattle" (De.7:14).

"Blessed *shall be* the fruit of thy body, and the fruit of thy ground, and the fruit of thy cattle, the increase of thy kine [oxen, livestock], and the flocks of thy sheep....And the LORD shall make thee plenteous in goods, in the fruit of thy body, and in the fruit of thy cattle, and in the fruit of thy ground, in the land which the LORD sware unto thy fathers to give thee" (De.28:4, 11).

"Thou hast multiplied the nation, *and*...increased the joy: they joy before thee according to the joy in harvest, *and* as *men* rejoice when they divide the spoil" (Is.9:3).

⇒ There will be bread, water, and all the necessities of life for everyone on earth.

"And ye shall serve the LORD your God, and he shall bless thy bread, and thy water; and I will take sickness away from the midst of thee" (Ex.23:25).

"Blessed *shall be* thy basket and thy store. Blessed *shalt* thou be when thou comest in and blessed *shalt* thou *be* when thou goest out....The LORD shall command the blessing upon thee in thy store-houses, and in all that thou settest thine hand unto; and he shall bless thee in the land which the LORD thy God giveth thee....The LORD shall open unto thee his good treasure, the heaven to give the rain unto thy land in his season, and to bless all the work of thine hand: and thou shalt lend unto many nations, and thou shalt not borrow" (De.28:5-6, 8, 12).

"And the LORD thy God will make thee plenteous in every work of thine hand, in the fruit of thy body, and in the fruit of thy cattle, and in the fruit of thy land, for good: for the LORD will again rejoice over thee for good, as he rejoiced over thy fathers" (De.30:9).

"He shall come down like rain upon the mown grass: as showers *that* water the earth. In his days shall the righteous flourish; and abundance of peace so long as the moon endureth....There shall be an handful of corn in the earth upon the top of the mountains; the fruit thereof shall shake like Lebanon: and *they* of the city shall flourish like grass of the earth" (Ps.72:6-7, 16).

"In that day shall the branch of the LORD be beautiful and glorious, and the fruit of the earth *shall* be excellent and comely for them that are escaped of Israel" (Is.4:2).

"And I will make them and the places round about my hill a blessing; and I will cause the shower to come down in his season; there shall be showers of blessing. And the tree of the field shall yield her fruit, and the earth shall yield her increase, and they shall be safe in their land, and shall know that I *am* the LORD, when I have broken the bands of their yoke, and delivered them out of the hand of those that served themselves of them....And I will raise up for them a plant of renown, and they shall be no more consumed with hunger in the land, neither bear the shame of the heathen any more" (Eze.34:26-27, 29).

"And it shall come to pass in that day, I will hear, saith the LORD, I will hear the heavens, and they shall hear the earth; And the earth shall hear the corn, and the wine, and the oil; and they shall hear Jezreel" (Ho.2:21-22).

"And it shall come to pass in that day, *that* the mountains shall drop down new wine, and the hills shall flow with milk, and all the rivers of Judah shall flow with waters, and a fountain shall come forth of the house of the LORD, and shall water the valley of Shittim" (Joel 3:18).

"Behold, the days come, saith the LORD, that the plowman shall overtake the reaper, and the treader of grapes him that soweth seed; and the mountains shall drop sweet wine, and all the hills shall melt. And I will bring again the captivity of my people of Israel, and they shall build the waste cities, and inhabit *them*, and they shall plant vineyards, and drink the wine thereof; they shall also make gardens, and eat the fruit of them" (Am.9:13-14).

⇒ There will be food and security, no fear of enemies or criminals.

"And it shall come to pass in the day that the LORD shall give thee rest from thy sorrow, and from thy fear, and from the hard bondage wherein thou wast made to serve" (Is.14:3).

"In righteousness shalt thou be established: thou shalt be far from oppression; for thou shalt not fear: and from terror; for it shall not come near thee" (Is.54:14).

"I will feed them in a good pasture, and upon the high mountains of Israel shall their fold be: there shall they lie in a good fold, and *in* a fat pasture shall they feed upon the mountains of Israel" (Eze.34:14).

"They shall feed and lie down, and none shall make *them* afraid" (Zep.3:13).

"In that day it shall be said to Jerusalem, Fear thou not: *and to* Zion, Let not thine hands be slack" (Zep.3:16).

⇒ There will be long and full life spans.

"There shall nothing cast their young, nor be barren, in thy land: the number of thy days I will fulfill" (Ex.23:26).

"He will swallow up death in victory; and the Lord GOD will wipe away tears from off all faces; and the rebuke of his people shall he take away from off all the earth: for the LORD hath spoken *it*" (Is.25:8).

"There *shall be* no more thence an infant of days, nor an old man that hath not filled his days: for the child shall die a hundred years old; but the sinner *being* a hundred years old shall be accursed" (Is.65:20).

"Thus saith the LORD of hosts; There shall yet old men and old women dwell in the streets of Jerusalem, and every man with his staff in his hand for very age" (Zec.8:4).

⇒ It will be a day of no tears, but of joy and praise.

"Now unto him that is able to keep you from falling, and to present *you* faultless before the presence of his glory with exceeding joy" (Jude 24).

"And in that day shall ye say, Praise the LORD, call upon his name, declare his doings among the people, make mention that his name is exalted" (Is.12:4).

"He will swallow up death in victory; and the Lord GOD will wipe away tears from off all faces; and the rebuke of his people shall he take away from off all the earth: for the LORD hath spoken *it*" (Is.25:8).

"And the ransomed of the LORD shall return, and come to Zion with songs and everlasting joy upon their heads: they shall obtain joy and gladness, and sorrow and sighing shall flee away" (Is.35:10).

"Therefore the redeemed of the LORD shall return, and come with singing unto Zion; and everlasting joy shall be upon their head: they shall obtain gladness and joy; and sorrow and mourning shall flee away" (Is.51:11).

"Sing, O daughter of Zion; shout, O Israel; be glad and rejoice with all the heart, O daughter of Jerusalem" (Zep.3:14).

⇒ Shame and guilt will be removed.

"In that day shalt thou not be ashamed for all thy doings, wherein thou hast transgressed against me: for then I will take away out of the midst of thee them that rejoice in thy pride, and thou shalt no more be haughty because of my holy mountain" (Zep.3:11).

"And ye shall eat in plenty, and be satisfied, and praise the name of the LORD your God, that hath dealt wondrously with you: and my people shall never be ashamed. And ye shall know that I am in the midst of Israel, and *that I am* the LORD your God, and none else: and my people shall never be ashamed" (Joel 2:26-27).

⇒ There will be recognition and honor for God's people, and they will have strong self-esteem, healthy egos, and emotions.

"**Behold, at that time I will undo all that afflict thee: and I will save her that halteth, and gather her that was driven out; and I will get them praise and fame in every land where they have been put to shame. At that time will I bring you** *again*, **even in the time that I gather you: for I will make you a name and a praise among all people of the earth, when I turn back your captivity before your eyes, saith the LORD**" (Zep.3:19-20).

⇒ Everyone will be a neighbor to everyone else.

"**In that day, saith the LORD of hosts, shall ye call every man his neighbor under the vine and under the fig tree**" (Zec.3:10).

⇒ There will no longer be any slavery.

"**For it shall come to pass in that day, saith the LORD of hosts,** *that* **I will break his [the oppressor's] yoke from off thy neck, and will burst thy bonds, and strangers shall no more serve themselves of him; But they shall serve the LORD their God, and [the descendent, the Lord Jesus Christ of] David their king, whom I will raise up unto them**" (Je.30:8-9).

⇒ People will be able to trust the LORD's strong arm.

"**My righteousness** *is* **near; my salvation is gone forth, and mine arms shall judge the people; the isles shall wait upon me, and on mine arm shall they trust**" (Is.51:5).

⇒ It will be a day of mercy.

"**And in mercy shall the throne be established: and he shall sit upon it in truth in the tabernacle of David, judging, and seeking judgment, and hasting righteousness**" (Is.16:5).

⇒ All things will be restored.

"**Whom the heaven must receive until the times of restitution of all things, which God hath spoken by the mouth of all his holy prophets since the world began**" (Ac.3:21).

⇒ Destroyed cities will be rebuilt. (Remember: most of the major cities of the world will have been destroyed, (Is.2:6–4:1).

"**And they shall build the old wastes, they shall raise up the former desolations, and they shall repair the waste cities, the desolations of many generations**" (Is.61:4).
"**And they shall build houses, and inhabit** *them*; **and they shall plant vineyards, and eat the fruit of them**" (Is.65:21).
"**Behold, the days come, saith the LORD, that the plowman shall overtake the reaper, and the treader of grapes him that soweth seed; and the mountains shall drop sweet wine, and all the hills shall melt. And I will bring again the captivity of my people of Israel, and they shall build the waste cities, and inhabit** *them*; **and they shall plant vineyards, and drink the wine thereof; they shall also make gardens, and eat the fruit of them**" (Am.9:13-14).

⇒ All animals will live in peace. There will be no savagery.

"**The wolf and the lamb shall feed together, and the lion shall eat straw like the bullock: and dust** *shall be* **the serpent's meat. They shall not hurt nor destroy in all my holy mountain, saith the LORD**" (Is.65:25).

⇒ Israel will be established as a nation forever.

"**Thus saith the LORD, which giveth the sun for a light by day,** *and* **the ordinances of the moon and of the stars for a light by night, which divideth the sea when the waves thereof roar;** *the* **LORD of hosts** *is* **his name: If those ordinances depart from before me, saith the LORD,** *then* **the seed of Israel also shall cease from being a nation before me for ever. Thus saith the LORD; If heaven above can be measured, and the foundations of the earth searched out beneath, I will also cast off all the seed of Israel for all that they have done, saith the LORD**" (Je.31:35-37).

⇒ The Gentiles will receive the inheritance and blessings of Israel.

"**The princes of the people [from all nations] are gathered together,** *even* **the people of the God of Abraham: for the shields of the earth** *belong* **unto God: he is greatly exalted**" (Ps.47:9).
"**And it shall come to pass,** *that* **ye shall divide it by lot for an inheritance unto you, and to the strangers that sojourn among you, which shall beget children among you: and they shall be unto you as born in the country among the children of Israel; they shall have inheritance with you among the**

tribes of Israel. And it shall come to pass, *that* in what tribe the stranger sojourneth, there shall ye give *him* his inheritance, saith the Lord GOD" (Eze.47:22-23).

⇒ The Feast of Tabernacles will be celebrated on a yearly basis.

"And it shall come to pass, *that* every one that is left of all the nations which came against Jerusalem shall even go up from year to year to worship the King, the LORD of hosts, and to keep the feast of tabernacles" (Zec.14:16; see Ex.23:16. See note—Jn.7:37 for discussion.)

b. Life in the Millennium will be governed by righteousness.
⇒ Christ is going to judge the earth in righteousness and truth.

"The God of Israel said, the Rock of Israel spake to me, He that ruleth over men *must be* just, ruling in the fear of God. And he *shall be* as the light of the morning, *when* the sun riseth, *even* a morning without clouds; *as* the tender grass *springing* out of the earth by clear shining after rain" (2 S.23:3-4).
"O let the nations be glad and sing for joy: for thou shalt judge the people righteously, and govern the nations upon earth" (Ps.67:4).
"Before the LORD: for he cometh, for he cometh to judge the earth: he shall judge the world with righteousness, and the people with his truth" (Ps.96:13).
"Before the LORD; for he cometh to judge the earth: with righteousness shall he judge the world, and the people with equity" (Ps.98:9).
"And in mercy shall the throne be established: and he shall sit upon it in truth in the tabernacle of David, judging, and seeking judgment, and hasting righteousness" (Is.16:5).
"Behold, the days come, saith the LORD, that I will raise unto David a righteous Branch, and a King shall reign and prosper, and shall execute judgment and justice in the earth" (Je.23:5).
"In those days, and at that time, will I cause the Branch of righteousness to grow up unto David; and he shall execute judgment and righteousness in the land" (Je.33:15).

⇒ Christ is going to appoint the apostles as rulers over kingdoms.

"And I appoint unto you a kingdom, as my Father hath appointed unto me" (Lu.22:29).

⇒ Christ will prevent evil from being done by one nation to another nation.

"The remnant of Israel shall not do iniquity, nor speak lies; neither shall a deceitful tongue be found in their mouth: for they shall feed and lie down, and none shall make *them* afraid" (Zep.3:13).
"The LORD hath taken away thy judgments, he hath cast out thine enemy: the king of Israel, *even* the LORD, *is* in the midst of thee: thou shalt not see evil [from any nation] any more" (Zep.3:15).

⇒ God's commandments will be kept by the nations. There will be national obedience.

"But I said, How shall I put thee among the children, and give thee a pleasant land, a goodly heritage of the hosts of nations? and I said, Thou shalt call me, My father; and shalt not turn away from me" (Je.3:19).
⇒ The citizens of Jerusalem will be called holy.

"And it shall come to pass, that *he that is* left in Zion, and *he that* remaineth in Jerusalem, shall be called holy, *even* every one that is written among the living in Jerusalem: When the Lord shall have washed away the filth of the daughters of Zion, and shall have purged the blood of Jerusalem from the midst thereof by the spirit of judgment, and by the spirit of burning" (Is.4:3-4).

⇒ Believers will call God, "My Father."

"But I said, How shall I put thee among the children, and give thee a pleasant land, a goodly heritage of the hosts of nations? and I said, Thou shalt call me, My father; and shalt not turn away from me" (Je.3:19).

c. Life in the Millennium will be a life of true worship.
⇒ All nations—kings and citizens alike—will worship Christ.

"All the ends of the world shall remember and turn unto the LORD: and all the kindreds of the nations shall worship before thee" (Ps.22:27).
"All the earth shall worship thee, and shall sing unto thee; they shall sing *to* thy name" (Ps.66:4).
"And he shall live, and to him shall be given of the gold of Sheba: prayer also shall be made for him continually; *and* daily shall he be praised" (Ps.72:15).
"All nations whom thou hast made shall come and worship before thee, O Lord; and shall glorify thy name" (Ps.86:9).

"So the heathen shall fear the name of the LORD, and all the kings of the earth thy glory....To declare the name of the LORD in Zion, and his praise in Jerusalem; when the people are gathered together, and the kingdoms, to serve the LORD" (Ps.102:15, 21-22).

"All the kings of the earth shall praise thee, O LORD, when they hear the words of thy mouth. Yea, they shall sing in the ways of the LORD: for great *is* the glory of the LORD" (Ps.138:4-5).

"And thou shalt swear, The LORD liveth, in truth, in judgment, and in righteousness; and the nations shall bless themselves in him, and in him shall they glory" (Je.4:2).

"Thus saith the LORD of hosts; In those days *it shall come to pass*, that ten men shall take hold out of all languages of the nations, even shall take hold of the skirt of him that is a Jew, saying, We will go with you: for we have heard *that* God *is* with you" (Zec.8:23).

⇒ All nations will seek instruction from Christ. Gentiles will become the multiplied seed of David and members of the priesthood of God's true people, the true Israel.

"And it shall come to pass in the last days, *that* the mountain of the LORD'S house shall be established in the top of the mountains, and shall be exalted above the hills; and all nations shall flow unto it. And many people shall go and say, Come ye, and let us go up to the mountain of the LORD, to the house of the God of Jacob; and he will teach us of his ways, and we will walk in his paths: for out of Zion shall go forth the law, and the word of the LORD from Jerusalem" (Is.2:2-3).

"And I will also take of them [Gentiles] for priests *and* for Levites [the priesthood], saith the LORD" (Is.66:21).

"Neither shall the priests the Levites [the tribe of the priesthood] want a man before me to offer burnt offerings, and to kindle meat offerings, and to do sacrifice continually....As the host of heaven cannot be numbered, neither the sand of the sea measured: so will I multiply the seed of David my servant, and the Levites [the priests] that minister unto me" (Je.33:18, 22).

"But in the last days it shall come to pass, *that* the mountain of the house of the LORD shall be established in the top of the mountains, and it shall be exalted above the hills; and people shall flow unto it. And many nations shall come, and say, Come, and let us go up to the mountain of the LORD, and to the house of the God of Jacob; and he will teach us of his ways, and we will walk in his paths: for the law shall go forth of Zion, and the word of the LORD from Jerusalem" (Mi.4:1-2).

⇒ There will be a covenant of peace between God and Israel, even the forgiveness of sin.

"And so all Israel shall be saved: as it is written, There shall come out of Sion the Deliverer, and shall turn away ungodliness from Jacob: For this *is* my covenant unto them, when I shall take away their sins" (Ro.11:26-27).

"I will seek that which was lost, and bring again that which was driven away, and will bind up *that which was* broken, and will strengthen that which was sick: but I will destroy the fat and the strong; I will feed them with judgment" (Eze.34:16).

"For the mountains shall depart, and the hills be removed; but my kindness shall not depart from thee, neither shall the covenant of my peace be removed, saith the LORD that hath mercy on thee" (Is.54:10).

⇒ All of God's people will be purified.

"And he shall sit *as* a refiner and purifier of silver: and he shall purify the sons of Levi [the priests], and purge them as gold and silver, that they may offer unto the LORD an offering in righteousness. Then shall the offering of Judah and Jerusalem be pleasant unto the LORD, as in the days of old, and as in former years" (Mal.3:3-4).

⇒ The nations will bless Christ and glory in Him.

"All the ends of the world shall remember and turn unto the LORD: and all the kindreds of the nations shall worship before thee" (Ps.22:27).

"And thou shalt swear, The LORD liveth, in truth, in judgment, and in righteousness; and the nations shall bless themselves in him, and in him shall they glory" (Je.4:2).

4. Scripture gives many verses stating that resurrected believers will rule and reign during the Millennium.
   ⇒ The kingdom and dominion of the world will be given to believers.

"And the kingdom and dominion, and the greatness of the kingdom under the whole heaven, shall be given to the people of the saints of the most High, whose kingdom *is* an everlasting kingdom, and all dominions shall serve and obey him" (Da.7:27).

⇒ The apostles will rule and reign over the twelve tribes of Israel.

"And Jesus said unto them, Verily I say unto you, That ye which have followed me, in the regeneration when the Son of man shall sit in the throne of his glory, ye also shall sit upon twelve thrones, judging the twelve tribes of Israel" (Mt.19:28).

"And he saith unto them, Ye shall drink indeed of my cup, and be baptized with the baptism that I am baptized with: but to sit on my right hand, and on my left, is not mine to give, but it shall *be given to them* for whom it is prepared of my Father" (Mt.20:23).

"I beheld till the thrones were cast down, and the Ancient of days did sit, whose garment *was* white as snow, and the hair of his head like the pure wool: his throne *was like* the fiery flame, *and* his wheels *as* burning fire....And the kingdom and dominion, and the greatness of the kingdom under the whole heaven, shall be given to the people of the saints of the most High, whose kingdom *is* an everlasting kingdom, and all dominions shall serve and obey him" (Da.7:9, 27).

⇒ God's people will be heirs of the world (universe).

"And to make thee high above all nations which he hath made, in praise, and in name, and in honor; and that thou mayest be a holy people unto the LORD thy God, as he hath spoken" (De.26:19).

"For the promise, that he should be heir of the world, *was* not to Abraham, or to his seed, through the law, but through the righteousness of faith" (Ro.4:13).

⇒ God's people will rule as princes.

"Behold, a king shall reign in righteousness, and princes shall rule in judgment" (Is.32:1).

⇒ All believers will rule and reign with Christ.

"And he that overcometh, and keepeth my works unto the end, to him will I give power over the nations: And he shall rule them with a rod of iron; as the vessels of a potter shall they be broken to shivers: even as I received of my Father" (Re.2:26-27).

"To him that overcometh will I grant to sit with me in my throne, even as I also overcame, and am set down with my Father in his throne" (Re.3:21).

"And hast made us unto our God kings and priests: and we shall reign on the earth" (Re.5:10).

"And I saw thrones, and they sat upon them, and judgment was given unto them: and *I saw* the souls of them that were beheaded for the witness of Jesus, and for the word of God, and which had not worshipped the beast, neither his image, neither had received *his* mark upon their foreheads, or in their hands; and they lived and reigned with Christ a thousand years....Blessed and holy *is* he that hath part in the first resurrection: on such the second death hath no power, but they shall be priests of God and of Christ, and shall reign with him a thousand years" (Re.20:4, 6).

"If we suffer, we shall also reign with him: if we deny him, he also will deny us" (2 Ti.2:12).

⇒ The LORD will set up shepherds (leaders) over His people.

"And I will set up shepherds over them which shall feed them: and they shall fear no more, nor be dismayed, neither shall they be lacking, saith the LORD" (Je.23:4).

⇒ God's people will judge or rule over angels. (This may not take place until the new heavens and earth are created.)

"Know ye not that we shall judge angels? how much more things that pertain to this life?" (1 Co.6:3).

⇒ God's people will be put in charge of Christ's possessions.

"Blessed *is* that servant, whom his LORD when he cometh shall find so doing. Of a truth I say unto you, that he will make him ruler over all that he hath" (Lu.12:43-44).

⇒ Believers will rule over unbelieving Jews.

"Behold, I will make them of the synagogue of Satan, which say they are Jews, and are not, but do lie; behold, I will make them to come and worship before thy feet, and to know that I have loved thee" (Re.3:9).

Remember: believers will be in their resurrected bodies and people on earth in their physical bodies. There apparently will be mingling between the two (see verses under point 4 above). What we must keep in mind is this: heaven and eternity are not like what most people think—a spirit floating around on a cloud playing a harp or else a spirit that appears as a ghost or gas-like substance. We will have bodies in heaven and eternity. In fact, we will have our present bodies with one difference:

they will be perfected. This is the very purpose for the resurrection: to raise up the very elements of our bodies in order to perfect them for eternal life in the perfect environment of heaven and earth. Therefore, during the Millennium, it will be just like it was when Christ fellowshipped with the disciples after His resurrection. He was in His resurrected body and the disciples were in their earthly bodies. During the Millennium, it will be a common thing for the resurrected Lord and resurrected believers to fellowship with people in their earthly bodies. All will have bodies, some earthly bodies and others heavenly, that is, perfected bodies. Remember: the Millennium will be a new age for the earth. Life upon earth will be entirely different from what it is now. As has been seen in the study above, when Jesus Christ returns to earth, His presence and power will change everything.

CHAPTER 5

C. The LORD's Condemnation of His Wayward Nation: Three Major Warnings to God's People, 5:1-30

1. The warning to Israel, God's disappointing vineyard: Terrible sin will be exposed
a. God planted His vineyard
  1) Chose a very fertile hill
  2) Cultivated & removed all stones
  3) Planted the choicest vine
  4) Built a watchtower to protect it
  5) Built a winepress
b. God was utterly disappointed: Vineyard bore *wild grapes*

c. God appealed to the people to consider the case themselves

  1) What more could He have done for His vineyard?
  2) Why would a vine so cared for yield *wild grapes*?

d. God judged the vineyard
  1) He will remove its protection, hedge, & wall: It will be destroyed, trampled upon

  2) He will make it a wasteland
    • Not prune or cultivate it
    • Let it grow briers & thorns
    • Stop the rain
e. God identified the vineyard & *wild grapes*
  1) The vineyard: Israel & Judah
  2) The *wild grapes*: God expected justice & righteousness but saw violence & lawlessness, oppression & distress
2. The warning to Israel concerning *wild grapes* (sins): Six *woes* or warnings are given
a. *Woe* to the greedy & covetous
  1) Their houses, mansions, & buildings will become desolate, without occupants
  2) Their property & farms will be unproductive

b. *Woe* to the drunkards (all addicts)

Now will I sing to my wellbeloved a song of my beloved touching his vineyard. My wellbeloved hath a vineyard in a very fruitful hill: 2 And he fenced it, and gathered out the stones thereof, and planted it with the choicest vine, and built a tower in the midst of it, and also made a winepress therein: and he looked that it should bring forth grapes, and it brought forth wild grapes. 3 And now, O inhabitants of Jerusalem, and men of Judah, judge, I pray you, betwixt me and my vineyard. 4 What could have been done more to my vineyard, that I have not done in it? wherefore, when I looked that it should bring forth grapes, brought it forth wild grapes? 5 And now go to; I will tell you what I will do to my vineyard: I will take away the hedge thereof, and it shall be eaten up; *and* break down the wall thereof, and it shall be trodden down: 6 And I will lay it waste: it shall not be pruned, nor digged; but there shall come up briers and thorns: I will also command the clouds that they rain no rain upon it. 7 For the vineyard of the LORD of hosts *is* the house of Israel, and the men of Judah his pleasant plant: and he looked for judgment, but behold oppression; for righteousness, but behold a cry. 8 Woe unto them that join house to house, *that* lay field to field, till *there be* no place, that they may be placed alone in the midst of the earth! 9 In mine ears *said* the LORD of hosts, Of a truth many houses shall be desolate, *even* great and fair, without inhabitant. 10 Yea, ten acres of vineyard shall yield one bath, and the seed of an homer shall yield an ephah. 11 Woe unto them that rise up early in the morning, *that*

they may follow strong drink; that continue until night, *till* wine inflame them! 12 And the harp, and the viol, the tabret, and pipe, and wine, are in their feasts: but they regard not the work of the LORD, neither consider the operation of his hands. 13 Therefore my people are gone into captivity, because *they have* no knowledge: and their honourable men *are* famished, and their multitude dried up with thirst. 14 Therefore hell hath enlarged herself, and opened her mouth without measure: and their glory, and their multitude, and their pomp, and he that rejoiceth, shall descend into it. 15 And the mean man shall be brought down, and the mighty man shall be humbled, and the eyes of the lofty shall be humbled: 16 But the LORD of hosts shall be exalted in judgment, and God that is holy shall be sanctified in righteousness. 17 Then shall the lambs feed after their manner, and the waste places of the fat ones shall strangers eat. 18 Woe unto them that draw iniquity with cords of vanity, and sin as it were with a cart rope: 19 That say, Let him make speed, *and* hasten his work, that we may see *it*: and let the counsel of the Holy One of Israel draw nigh and come, that we may know *it*! 20 Woe unto them that call evil good, and good evil; that put darkness for light, and light for darkness; that put bitter for sweet, and sweet for bitter! 21 Woe unto *them that are* wise in their own eyes, and prudent in their own sight! 22 Woe unto *them that are* mighty to drink wine, and men of strength to mingle strong drink: 23 Which justify the wicked for reward, and take away the righteousness of the righteous from him! 24 Therefore as the fire devoureth the stubble, and the flame consumeth the chaff, *so* their root shall be as rottenness, and their blossom

  1) Their lifestyle described
    • They drink all day & late into the night
    • They engage in drunken parties with seductive music, immoral revelry, & carousing
    • They ignore & never think about the LORD & His wonderful works
  2) Their doom foretold
    • They will be spewed out of the land, exiled: Because they do not know God
    • They will suffer hunger & thirst
    • They will face the wide-open mouth of death, even the grave itself: The leaders, crowds, and revelers will all die

    • They will be humbled, all classes of people: The lowly, the great, & the arrogant

    • They will witness a demonstration of God's justice & holiness: He will be exalted
    • They will suffer the utter devastation of their land: Only sheep will graze among the ruins
c. *Woe* to deceivers & mockers
  1) They are seduced: They deceive themselves & entice others to sin
  2) They mock God, in particular the issue of His judgment (the *Day of the LORD*)

d. *Woe* to those with perverted values who call evil good: Examples are those who justify illicit sex, the worship of false gods, materialism, thievery, & violence
e. *Woe* to the prideful & arrogant

f. *Woe* to the unjust & bribe-takers
  1) They are heroes in their sins of drinking & covetous behavior
  2) They take bribes & pervert justice, oppressing people
3. The warning to all: God's judgment is coming
a. The picture of God's judgment: Will be quick, sudden, & complete

OUTLINE	SCRIPTURE	SCRIPTURE	OUTLINE
b. The reason for God's judgment: The people have rejected God's law & despised the Word of the *Holy One of Israel*	shall go up as dust: because they have cast away the law of the LORD of hosts, and despised the word of the Holy One of Israel.	stumble among them; none shall slumber nor sleep; neither shall the girdle of their loins be loosed, nor the latchet of their shoes be broken:	• Well rested & conditioned • Well dressed in battle clothes
c. The picture of God's anger 1) His anger was aroused 2) His hand stretched out & struck His people • The mountains trembled • The bodies were left in the streets	25 Therefore is the anger of the LORD kindled against his people, and he hath stretched forth his hand against them, and hath smitten them: and the hills did tremble, and their carcases *were* torn in the midst of the	28 Whose arrows *are* sharp, and all their bows bent, their horses' hoofs shall be counted like flint, and their wheels like a whirlwind:	• Well equipped with weapons
3) His anger against evil is persistent	streets. For all this his anger is not turned away, but his hand *is* stretched out still.	29 Their roaring *shall be* like a lion, they shall roar like young lions: yea, they shall roar, and lay hold of the prey, and shall carry *it* away safe, and none shall deliver *it*.	• Well trained & frightening in their attack: Will growl like young lions & roar like the sea
d. The agents of God's judgment: He will use nations such as Assyria, 2 K.17:1-41 & Babylon, 25:1-30 1) They will come swiftly	26 And he will lift up an ensign to the nations from far, and will hiss unto them from the end of the earth: and, behold, they shall come with speed swiftly:	30 And in that day they shall roar against them like the roaring of the sea: and if *one* look unto the land, behold darkness *and* sorrow, and the light is darkened in the heav-	e. The results of God's impending judgment: A dark, gloomy distress will hang over the land
2) They will be well prepared	27 None shall be weary nor	ens thereof.	

DIVISION I

THE PROPHECIES OF REBUKE AND HOPE GIVEN TO JUDAH AND JERUSALEM: AN OVERVIEW OF THE PRESENT AND FUTURE OF GOD'S PEOPLE, 1:1–12:6

C. The LORD's Condemnation of His Wayward Nation: Three Major Warnings to God's People, 5:1-30

(5:1-30) **Introduction**: guilt can be a healthy experience. When we fail or do wrong, guilt gnaws at our souls, causing us to sense conviction, shame, failure, and self-condemnation. In this respect, guilt is a protective mechanism that warns us to correct our behavior before we hurt or damage ourselves. Because of guilt, we know that we have slipped, been irresponsible, done wrong, or committed an offense. Unless we handle or correct our irresponsible behavior, we can seriously damage ourselves and others. Furthermore, depression and other neurotic (or even psychotic) conditions can creep into our lives and take hold of us. For this reason, we must be sure to deal with the guilt in our lives. When we make a mistake, we must correct the irresponsible behavior. Correcting our mistakes is absolutely essential.

This is the reason God has given us His Holy Word: to reveal how we should live, the path we should take, and the things we should do to live victorious, conquering lives. But God's Holy Word also tells us the path not to take. His Word spells out the sins and the misbehavior that will cause problems for us, defeating and dooming us. Thus, when we misbehave, God's Word condemns us and His Spirit convicts us, arousing a sense of guilt within our hearts. Guilt then causes us to correct our behavior before we bring disorder to our lives and doom ourselves to failure.

In the present Scripture, we see the people of Israel and Judah guilty of the most outrageous and evil behavior imaginable. They stood guilty before God and were condemned. Sensing the seriousness of the situation, Isaiah changed his tactical approach to the people. Hoping to stir a renewed interest in the Word of God, he sang a song or parable about the vineyard of God. In his message he issued three major warnings to God's people. This is, *The LORD's Condemnation of His Wayward Nation: Three Major Warnings to God's People*, 5:1-30.

1. The warning to Israel, God's disappointing vineyard: terrible sin will be exposed (vv.1-7).
2. The warning to Israel concerning *wild grapes* (sins): Six *woes* or warnings are given (vv.8-23).
3. The warning to all: God's judgment is coming (vv.24-30).

1 (5:1-7) **Warning, to God's People—Israel, Warning to, Guilty of Terrible Sin—Israel, Names – Title, God's Vineyard—Parable, of God's Vineyard—Vineyard, of God, Symbol of Israel—Wild Grapes, Described As, Sins of the Corrupt Nature—Isaiah, Song of, God's Vineyard**: the first warning was to Israel, which is identified as God's disappointing vineyard. Israel was guilty of terrible sin; therefore, God issued a strong warning to them through His prophet Isaiah. But in this third prophecy, a different approach was used with the people. Before directly condemning the people for their gross sinfulness, Isaiah sang the following parable to them at a public gathering:

OUTLINE	SCRIPTURE	SCRIPTURE	OUTLINE
1. The warning to Israel, God's disappointing vineyard: Terrible sin will be exposed a. God planted His vineyard 1) Chose a very fertile hill	Now will I sing to my wellbeloved a song of my beloved touching his vineyard. My wellbeloved hath a vineyard in a very fruitful hill:	2 And he fenced it, and gathered out the stones thereof, and planted it with the choicest vine, and built a tower in the midst of it,	2) Cultivated & removed all stones 3) Planted the choicest vine 4) Built a watchtower to protect it

ISAIAH 5:1-30

OUTLINE	SCRIPTURE	SCRIPTURE	OUTLINE
5) Built a winepress b. God was utterly disappointed: Vineyard bore *wild grapes* c. God appealed to the people to consider the case themselves 1) What more could He have done for His vineyard? 2) Why would a vine so cared for yield *wild grapes*? d. God judged the vineyard 1) He will remove its protection, hedge, & wall: It	and also made a winepress therein: and he looked that it should bring forth grapes, and it brought forth wild grapes. 3 And now, O inhabitants of Jerusalem, and men of Judah, judge, I pray you, betwixt me and my vineyard. 4 What could have been done more to my vineyard, that I have not done in it? wherefore, when I looked that it should bring forth grapes, brought it forth wild grapes? 5 And now go to; I will tell you what I will do to my vineyard: I will take away the	hedge thereof, and it shall be eaten up; *and* break down the wall thereof, and it shall be trodden down: 6 And I will lay it waste: it shall not be pruned, nor digged; but there shall come up briers and thorns: I will also command the clouds that they rain no rain upon it. 7 For the vineyard of the LORD of hosts *is* the house of Israel, and the men of Judah his pleasant plant: and he looked for judgment, but behold oppression; for righteousness, but behold a cry.	will be destroyed, trampled upon 2) He will make it a wasteland • Not prune or cultivate it • Let it grow briers & thorns • Stop the rain e. God identified the vineyard & *wild grapes* 1) The vineyard: Israel & Judah 2) The *wild grapes*: God expected justice & righteousness but saw violence & lawlessness, oppression & distress

a. The beginning of the song declared that the One whom Isaiah loved had planted a vineyard (vv.1-2). Of course, the One whom Isaiah loved was the LORD, and the vineyard was Israel (see v.7). In planting His vineyard, the LORD was very careful. He even went to the extreme, making sure that the vineyard had every opportunity to produce the highest quality fruit. He took five important steps.

1) The most wonderful land had been given to the Israelites, the promised land of God that flowed with milk and honey, a symbol of heaven. (See outline and note—Ge.12:1ᶜ for more discussion.) Thus the LORD chose a very fertile hill for His vineyard, a hill that had the richest soil and that sat high above the surrounding land. It had constant, unobstructed sunlight (v.1).
2) The LORD cultivated and removed all stones from the land so that nothing would obstruct the growth of the vines (v.2). He did everything He could to prepare the land for the Israelites. As long as they were faithful to Him, they could live in peace and lead victorious lives that bore the choicest fruits (Ga.5:22-23).
3) The LORD then planted the choicest vine in His vineyard (v.2). He gave His people His very own Word, His law. His commandments were to govern their lives. His law would also enable the people to build a just, caring, and secure society.
4) Next, the LORD built a watchtower to protect His field (v.2). The watchtower probably refers to the temple, for it symbolized God's very own presence dwelling among the people. It was His presence that protected them.
5) Finally, the LORD built a winepress, expecting a rich harvest of the finest grapes (v.2). In the days of Isaiah, a winepress had two troughs. The upper trough was used for trampling grapes, and the lower one was used to catch the juice of the grapes as it flowed down into it. The harvest represented the fruitful life God expected His people to produce (Ga.5:22-23).

b. Although the LORD had done everything possible to make sure His vineyard (Israel) produced the finest grapes for the choicest wine, the results were utterly disappointing. When the LORD looked for a crop of good, sweet grapes, He found only *wild grapes* (v.2). The term *wild grapes* actually means *stinking grapes*. However, Isaiah did not identify the *wild grapes* until the end of this parable.

c. God Himself appealed to the people: He wanted them to consider the case of the vineyard (vv.3-4). He asked two very straightforward questions:
⇒ What more could He have done for His vineyard?
⇒ Why would a vine so cared for yield *wild grapes*?

d. Having aroused the people to objectively judge the situation themselves, God then pronounced judgment against the vineyard (vv.5-6). He removed the protection of the vineyard, its hedge and wall. The vineyard would be destroyed and trampled upon by others. Of course, this is a clear reference to the invasion of foreign nations. The LORD actually said that He would make His vineyard a wasteland (v.6). Since it produced only *wild grapes*, there was no need for Him to prune or cultivate it any more. The LORD would stop the rain and the vineyard would become unproductive. Consequently, it would become overgrown with briars and thorns.

e. So that no one could misinterpret or fail to understand the parable, God identified the vineyard and the *wild grapes*. As pointed out above, the vineyard was Israel and Judah. Both the Northern and Southern Kingdoms were named so the listeners would know that all Jews stood accountable before the LORD. The *wild grapes* were identified as the fruit of the corrupt nature, the fruit of a hypocritical life that professed to know the LORD but that exhibited wickedness. Several sins in particular are mentioned. Whereas the LORD looked for the fruit of justice and righteousness among His people, He found only violence, lawlessness, oppression, and distress. Instead of bearing good fruit they were guilty of producing corrupt fruit that stunk in the nostrils of the LORD. The whole vineyard of Israel had become an unjust society, guilty of the worst acts of violence and lawlessness as well as oppression of the innocent and defenseless.

Thought 1. Far too many of us continually engage in sinful behavior. For example, how many of us are guilty of violent acts? Violence includes more heinous acts than just murder, the shedding of innocent blood. It also includes acts of abuse—verbal, physical, mental, or sexual—acts of coercion, of forcing others to do something against their will. Violence also includes acts of cruelty, brutality, and terrorism.

How many of us are guilty of lawless behavior, of breaking not only God's law but also the laws of society? How many of us are guilty of shoplifting, of stealing from our employers, schools, churches, neighbors or even our customers? How many of us cheat, lie, or destroy property?

How many of us are guilty of oppressing other people and causing undue distress for them? Judges, attorneys, and juries oppress the innocent when they rule against them and do not give them the full benefit of the law. Businesses oppress people when they overwork their employees or do not pay fair wages. Any of us oppress people when we do not pay fair wages for work done in our behalf. We oppress people when we mistreat them, whether at school, work, home, or out in public. We oppress people when we put them down, abuse, harass, overload, suppress, trample, pick on, or persecute them.

God warns us against bearing sinful fruit, against producing a harvest of sin. Listen to what God's Holy Word says:

"Even so every good tree bringeth forth good fruit; but a corrupt tree bringeth forth evil fruit" (Mt.7:17).

"For the wrath of God is revealed from heaven against all ungodliness and unrighteousness of men, who hold the truth in unrighteousness....Being filled with all unrighteousness, fornication, wickedness, covetousness, maliciousness; full of envy, murder, debate, deceit, malignity; whisperers, Backbiters, haters of God, despiteful, proud, boasters, inventors of evil things, disobedient to parents, Without understanding, covenantbreakers, without natural affection, implacable, unmerciful: Who knowing the judgment of God, that they which commit such things are worthy of death, not only do the same, but have pleasure in them that do them" (Ro.1:18, 29-32).

"Now the works of the flesh are manifest, which are *these;* Adultery, fornication, uncleanness, lasciviousness, Idolatry, witchcraft, hatred, variance, emulations, wrath, strife, seditions, heresies, Envyings, murders, drunkenness, revellings, and such like: of the which I tell you before, as I have also told *you* in time past, that they which do such things shall not inherit the kingdom of God" (Ga.5:19-21).

"Be not deceived; God is not mocked: for whatsoever a man soweth, that shall he also reap. For he that soweth to his flesh shall of the flesh reap corruption; but he that soweth to the Spirit shall of the Spirit reap life everlasting" (Ga.6:7-8).

"And another angel came out of the temple, crying with a loud voice to him that sat on the cloud, Thrust in thy sickle, and reap: for the time is come for thee to reap; for the harvest of the earth is ripe" (Re.14:15).

"Even as I have seen, they that plow iniquity, and sow wickedness, reap the same" (Jb.4:8).

"In the day shalt thou make thy plant to grow, and in the morning shalt thou make thy seed to flourish: *but* the harvest *shall be* a heap in the day of grief and of desperate sorrow" (Is.17:11).

"They have sown wheat, but shall reap thorns: they have put themselves to pain, *but* shall not profit: and they shall be ashamed of your revenues because of the fierce anger of the LORD" (Je.12:13).

"Let the heathen be wakened, and come up to the valley of Jehoshaphat: for there will I sit to judge all the heathen round about. Put ye in the sickle, for the harvest is ripe: come, get you down; for the press is full, the fats overflow; for their wickedness *is* great" (Joel 3:12-13).

2 (5:8-23) **Woe, Warnings of God, Six Woes or Warnings—Sins, List of, Six Listed—Greed, Warning Against—Covetousness, Warning Against—Drunkenness, Warning Against—Deception, Warning Against—Mockery, Warning Against—Values, Perverted, Warning Against—Perversion, of Values, Warning Against—Cover Up, of Sin, Warning Against—Excuses, for Sin, Warning Against—Calling Evil Good, Warning Against—Pride, Warning Against—Arrogance, Warning Against—Injustice, Warning Against—Bribe-Taking, Warning Against:** the second warning concerned the *wild grapes,* the terrible sins of Israel. Instead of good, sweet grapes of justice and righteousness, the people produced *wild grapes* that were sour and had a repulsive smell to them, the *wild grapes* of disobedience and corruption. As a result, God pronounced six woes or severe warnings to the people:

OUTLINE	SCRIPTURE	SCRIPTURE	OUTLINE
2. The warning to Israel concerning *wild grapes* (sins): Six *woes* or warnings are given	8 Woe unto them that join house to house, *that* lay field to field, till *there be* no place, that they may be placed alone in the midst of the earth!	wine inflame them! 12 And the harp, and the viol, the tabret, and pipe, and wine, are in their feasts: but they regard not the work of the LORD, neither	late into the night • They engage in drunken parties with seductive music, immoral revelry, & carousing
a. *Woe* to the greedy & covetous		consider the operation of his hands.	• They ignore & never think about the LORD & His wonderful works
1) Their houses, mansions, & buildings will become desolate, without occupants	9 In mine ears *said* the LORD of hosts, Of a truth many houses shall be desolate, *even* great and fair, without inhabitant.	13 Therefore my people are gone into captivity, because *they have* no knowledge: and their honourable men *are* famished, and their multitude dried up with thirst.	2) Their doom foretold • They will be spewed out of the land, led into captivity: Because they do not know God
2) Their property & farms will be unproductive	10 Yea, ten acres of vineyard shall yield one bath, and the seed of an homer shall yield an ephah.		• They will suffer hunger & thirst
b. *Woe* to the drunkards (all addicts)	11 Woe unto them that rise up early in the morning, *that* they may follow strong drink;	14 Therefore hell hath enlarged herself, and opened her mouth without measure:	• They will face the wide-open mouth of death,
1) Their lifestyle described • They drink all day &	that continue until night, *till*	and their glory, and their	

OUTLINE	SCRIPTURE	SCRIPTURE	OUTLINE
even the grave itself: The leaders, crowds, and revelers will all die • They will be humbled, all classes of people: The lowly, the great, & the arrogant • They will witness a demonstration of God's justice & holiness: He will be exalted • They will suffer the utter devastation of their land: Only sheep will graze among the ruins c. *Woe* to deceivers & mockers 1) They are seduced: They deceive themselves & entice others to sin 2) They mock God, in particular the issue of His	multitude, and their pomp, and he that rejoiceth, shall descend into it. 15 And the mean man shall be brought down, and the mighty man shall be humbled, and the eyes of the lofty shall be humbled: 16 But the LORD of hosts shall be exalted in judgment, and God that is holy shall be sanctified in righteousness. 17 Then shall the lambs feed after their manner, and the waste places of the fat ones shall strangers eat. 18 Woe unto them that draw iniquity with cords of vanity, and sin as it were with a cart rope: 19 That say, Let him make speed, *and* hasten his work,	that we may see *it*: and let the counsel of the Holy One of Israel draw nigh and come, that we may know *it!* 20 Woe unto them that call evil good, and good evil; that put darkness for light, and light for darkness; that put bitter for sweet, and sweet for bitter! 21 Woe unto *them that are* wise in their own eyes, and prudent in their own sight! 22 Woe unto *them that are* mighty to drink wine, and men of strength to mingle strong drink: 23 Which justify the wicked for reward, and take away the righteousness of the righteous from him!	judgment, (the *Day of the LORD*) d. *Woe* to those with perverted values who call evil good: Examples are those who justify illicit sex, the worship of false gods, materialism, thievery, & violence e. *Woe* to the prideful & arrogant f. *Woe* to the unjust & bribe-takers 1) They are heroes in their sins of drinking & covetous behavior 2) They take bribes & pervert justice, oppressing people

a. *Woe*—a strong warning was issued to the greedy and covetous (vv.8-10). Some persons sought to amass fortunes by buying up all the rental property and land they could. Even if it meant crowding out poorer and weaker home owners, they sought to control entire blocks of houses for rental purposes.[1] Others tried to acquire land in order to build up huge, profitable farms. Sadly, the land barons and property owners were not accumulating wealth for the purpose of helping the needy or for carrying the Word of God to the unbelievers of the world. Rather, they were amassing wealth from a spirit of greed and covetousness, glorying in the mere possession of wealth. They wanted to be recognized as the rich, famous, and powerful of their communities. Frankly, unless a person is going to use his money to benefit society, to help the needy, or to carry the gospel to the world, he does not even need to possess wealth.

The LORD of hosts—He who is God Almighty—issued a strong warning to the greedy and covetous: their houses, mansions, and buildings would be deserted, without occupants (v.9). In addition, their property and farms would be unproductive (v.10). A ten-acre vineyard would produce only about six gallons of wine, and ten measures of seed would yield only about one measure of grain.

Apparently, the LORD was predicting the ravages of war that would sweep across the land when the Assyrians and Babylonians launched their invasions. But whatever the case, the LORD is clearly predicting coming judgment upon the greedy and covetous of this earth.

"And he said unto them, Take heed, and beware of covetousness: for a man's life consisteth not in the abundance of the things which he possesseth. And he spake a parable unto them, saying, The ground of a certain rich man brought forth plentifully: And he thought within himself, saying, What shall I do, because I have no room where to bestow my fruits? And he said, This will I do: I will pull down my barns, and build greater; and there will I bestow all my fruits and my goods. And I will say to my soul, Soul, thou hast much goods laid up for many years; take thine ease, eat, drink, *and* be merry. But God said unto him, *Thou* fool, this night thy soul shall be required of thee: then whose shall those things be, which thou hast provided? So *is* he that layeth up treasure for himself, and is not rich toward God" (Lu.12:15-21).

"Know ye not that the unrighteous shall not inherit the kingdom of God? Be not deceived: neither fornicators, nor idolaters, nor adulterers, nor effeminate, nor abusers of themselves with mankind, Nor thieves, nor covetous, nor drunkards, nor revilers, nor extortioners, shall inherit the kingdom of God" (1 Co.6:9-10).

"But fornication, and all uncleanness, or covetousness, let it not be once named among you, as becometh saints; Neither filthiness, nor foolish talking, nor jesting, which are not convenient: but rather giving of thanks. For this ye know, that no whoremonger, nor unclean person, nor covetous man, who is an idolater, hath any inheritance in the kingdom of Christ and of God. Let no man deceive you with vain words: for because of these things cometh the wrath of God upon the children of disobedience" (Ep.5:3-6).

"Thou shalt not covet thy neighbour's house, thou shalt not covet thy neighbour's wife, nor his manservant, nor his maidservant, nor his ox, nor his ass, nor any thing that *is* thy neighbour's" (Ex.20:17).

"For from the least of them even unto the greatest of them every one *is* given to covetousness; and from the prophet even unto the priest every one dealeth falsely" (Je.6:13).

"And they come unto thee as the people cometh, and they sit before thee as my people, and they hear thy words, but they will not do them: for with their mouth they show much love, *but* their heart goeth after their covetousness" (Eze.33:31).

---

[1] H.C. Leupold. *Exposition of Isaiah,* Vol.1. (Grand Rapids, Michigan: Baker Book House, 1968), p.114.

> "And they covet fields, and take *them* by violence; and houses, and take *them* away: so they oppress a man and his house, even a man and his heritage" (Mi.2:2).
> "Woe to him that coveteth an evil covetousness to his house, that he may set his nest on high, that he may be delivered from the power of evil!" (Hab.2:9).

b. *Woe*—God issued a severe warning to all drunkards, which today would include all substance abusers (vv.11-17). Obviously, heavy drinking was common in the days of Isaiah, just as it is today. Note two points about the drunkards or addicts:

1) Their behavior and lifestyle are described in a colorful way (vv.11-12). Arising early in the morning, they drank all day up until late at night. They engaged in drunken parties, with seductive music, immoral revelry, and carousing. Moreover, they never thought about the LORD or His wonderful works.

2) In descriptive and graphic language, their doom is foretold (vv.13-17). God's people who indulged in strong drink and addictive behavior would face the severe judgment of God. Six specific punishments are spelled out:

a) They would be spewed out of the land, led into captivity and exile—all because they did not know God (v.13). Note what it is that brought about the captivity: it was ignorance of God, disregarding and failing to know Him. Those who engaged in drunken parties and immoral revelry seldom turned their thoughts to the LORD. They were blind to the movement of His Spirit and the works of His hands (see v.12).

b) The drunkard and addict would suffer hunger and thirst (v.13). This meant that a siege would be set up around Jerusalem. Eventually, all the supplies of food and water would be used up and the people would lack the basic necessities of life. But note: when dealing with alcoholics and other addicts, think how many would crave their addiction more than they would food and water. Think how many of them would ignore their health, even to the point of depriving their body of food, in order to feed their addiction.

c) The drunkard and addict would face the large appetite and wide-open mouth of death (v.14). They would doom themselves to death and the grave. Whether leader or commoner—all drunkards and addicts would die. They all face and bear the judgment of God.

d) The drunkard and addict would also be humbled (v.15). No matter what class of society the person represented, the individual would be brought low. The lowly, the high, the indifferent, and the arrogant who abused alcohol or any other substance would be shamed.

e) The drunkard and drug abuser would witness a demonstration of God's justice and holiness (v.16). God's righteousness would be exalted by His executing judgment upon those who, sadly, rebelled against the LORD and refused to obey His Word.

f) The drunkard and addict would suffer the utter devastation of their land (v.17). The judgment of God would bring foreign nations sweeping across the area, destroying everything that lay in the path of the invading army, including houses, buildings, and crops. Utterly ruined, the land would be good only for sheep to graze upon.

> "And take heed to yourselves, lest at any time your hearts be overcharged with surfeiting, and drunkenness, and cares of this life, and *so* that day come upon you unawares" (Lu.21:34).
> "Let us walk honestly, as in the day; not in rioting and drunkenness, not in chambering and wantonness, not in strife and envying" (Ro.13:13).
> "Know ye not that the unrighteous shall not inherit the kingdom of God? Be not deceived: neither fornicators, nor idolaters, nor adulterers, nor effeminate, nor abusers of themselves with mankind, Nor thieves, nor covetous, nor drunkards, nor revilers, nor extortioners, shall inherit the kingdom of God. And such were some of you: but ye are washed, but ye are sanctified, but ye are justified in the name of the Lord Jesus, and by the Spirit of our God" (1 Co.6:9-11).
> "Now the works of the flesh are manifest, which are *these;* Adultery, fornication, uncleanness, lasciviousness, Idolatry, witchcraft, hatred, variance, emulations, wrath, strife, seditions, heresies, Envyings, murders, drunkenness, revellings, and such like: of the which I tell you before, as I have also told *you* in time past, that they which do such things shall not inherit the kingdom of God" (Ga.5:19-21).
> "And be not drunk with wine, wherein is excess; but be filled with the Spirit" (Ep.5:18).
> "Wine *is* a mocker, strong drink *is* raging: and whosoever is deceived thereby is not wise" (Pr.20:1).
> "Who hath woe? who hath sorrow? who hath contentions? who hath babbling? who hath wounds without cause? who hath redness of eyes? They that tarry long at the wine; they that go to seek mixed wine. Look not thou upon the wine when it is red, when it giveth his colour in the cup, *when* it moveth itself aright" (Pr.23:29-31).
> "Woe unto them that rise up early in the morning, *that* they may follow strong drink; that continue until night, *till* wine inflame them!" (Is.5:11).
> "Woe unto him that giveth his neighbour drink, that puttest thy bottle to *him,* and makest *him* drunken also, that thou mayest look on their nakedness!" (Hab.2:15).

c. *Woe*—God issued a strong warning to the deceivers and mockers throughout the land (vv.18-19). Most of the people were so steeped in sin and wickedness that they were utterly deceived. Wherever they went or traveled, they hauled their sins along with them. Note the colorful description of this fact: they used *large cart ropes* to drag their sins along with them. A spirit of deception gripped the people's hearts. As a result, they mocked God, in particular the issue of His judgment. They refused to accept the fact that a day of judgment was coming. How applicable to so many who deny the truth of God's judgment today! But as it was for Israel, so it will be for us: the hand of God's judgment will fall upon all deceivers and mockers.

> "And Jesus answered and said unto them, Take heed that no man deceive you" (Mt.24:4).
> "Or despisest thou the riches of his goodness and forbearance and longsuffering; not knowing that the goodness of God leadeth thee to repentance? But after thy hardness and impenitent heart treasurest

up unto thyself wrath against the day of wrath and revelation of the righteous judgment of God; Who will render to every man according to his deeds" (Ro.2:4-6).

"Know ye not that the unrighteous shall not inherit the kingdom of God? Be not deceived: neither fornicators, nor idolaters, nor adulterers, nor effeminate, nor abusers of themselves with mankind, Nor thieves, nor covetous, nor drunkards, nor revilers, nor extortioners, shall inherit the kingdom of God" (1 Co.6:9-10).

"Be not deceived: evil communications [behavior, conduct] corrupt good manners" (1 Co.15:33).

"For this ye know, that no whoremonger, nor unclean person, nor covetous man, who is an idolater, hath any inheritance in the kingdom of Christ and of God. Let no man deceive you with vain words: for because of these things cometh the wrath of God upon the children of disobedience" (Ep.5:5-6).

"Let no man deceive you by any means: for *that day shall not come,* except there come a falling away first, and that man of sin be revealed, the son of perdition" (2 Th.2:3).

"He that despised Moses' law died without mercy under two or three witnesses" (He.10:28).

"The Lord knoweth how to deliver the godly out of temptations, and to reserve the unjust unto the day of judgment to be punished: But chiefly them that walk after the flesh in the lust of uncleanness, and despise government. Presumptuous *are they,* selfwilled, they are not afraid to speak evil of dignities" (2 Pe.2:9-10).

"Knowing this first, that there shall come in the last days scoffers, walking after their own lusts, And saying, Where is the promise of his coming? for since the fathers fell asleep, all things continue as *they were* from the beginning of the creation. For this they willingly are ignorant of, that by the word of God the heavens were of old, and the earth standing out of the water and in the water: Whereby the world that then was, being overflowed with water, perished: But the heavens and the earth, which are now, by the same word are kept in store, reserved unto fire against the day of judgment and perdition of ungodly men" (2 Pe.3:3-7).

"And ye know that he was manifested to take away our sins; and in him is no sin. Whosoever abideth in him sinneth not: whosoever sinneth hath not seen him, neither known him. Little children, let no man deceive you: he that doeth righteousness is righteous, even as he is righteous. He that committeth sin is of the devil; for the devil sinneth from the beginning. For this purpose the Son of God was manifested, that he might destroy the works of the devil. Whosoever is born of God doth not commit sin; for his seed remaineth in him: and he cannot sin, because he is born of God. In this the children of God are manifest, and the children of the devil: whosoever doeth not righteousness is not of God, neither he that loveth not his brother" (1 Jn.3:5-10).

"And they say, How doth God know? and is there knowledge in the most High?" (Ps.73:11).

"For that they hated knowledge, and did not choose the fear of the LORD: They would none of my counsel: they despised all my reproof. Therefore shall they eat of the fruit of their own way, and be filled with their own devices" (Pr.1:29-31).

"Judgments are prepared for scorners, and stripes for the back of fools" (Pr.19:29).

"Behold, they say unto me, Where *is* the word of the LORD? let it come now"(Je.17:15).

d. *Woe*—the LORD issued a strong warning to those with perverted values, who called evil good and good evil (v.20). Confusion about morality prevailed during the days of Isaiah even as it does today. Moral values no longer controlled the lives of people. Sinking deeper and deeper into sin, they became morally insensitive. The darkness of sin was substituted for the light of righteousness, and they claimed their right to enjoy the pleasures of life as they wished. In their minds, no person, not even God, had the right to put restraints upon their behavior. Consequently, certain illicit sexual acts were called good despite the fact that God said they were evil. Furthermore, the pronouncement of God's Word against the sin was called irrelevant and outdated (evil), not good. The same was true with false worship and materialism, even with stealing and violent behavior. Whatever a person desired to do, he felt he had the freedom to do it. He could worship as he wished and covet what he wished, and no one had the right to rebuke or restrain him. As a result, there was a complete breakdown of morality and justice within society. People's values became totally twisted and polluted. Evil was called good and good evil.

"Who knowing the judgment of God, that they which commit such things are worthy of death, not only do the same, but have pleasure in them that do them" (Ro.1:32).

"Perverse disputings of men of corrupt minds, and destitute of the truth, supposing that gain is godliness: from such withdraw thyself" (1 Ti.6:5).

"The integrity of the upright shall guide them: but the perverseness of transgressors shall destroy them" (Pr.11:3).

"A man shall be commended according to his wisdom: but he that is of a perverse heart shall be despised" (Pr.12:8).

"A wholesome tongue *is* a tree of life: but perverseness therein *is* a breach in the spirit" (Pr.15:4).

"He that justifieth the wicked, and he that condemneth the just, even they both *are* abomination to the LORD" (Pr.17:15).

He that saith unto the wicked, Thou *art* righteous; him shall the people curse, nations shall abhor him" (Pr.24:24).

"They that forsake the law praise the wicked: but such as keep the law contend with them" (Pr.28:4).

"Evil men understand not judgment: but they that seek the LORD understand all *things.* Better *is* the poor that walketh in his uprightness, than *he that is* perverse *in his* ways, though he *be* rich" (Pr.28:5-6).

"Woe unto them that call evil good, and good evil; that put darkness for light, and light for darkness; that put bitter for sweet, and sweet for bitter!" (Is.5:20).

"Then said he unto me, The iniquity of the house of Israel and Judah *is* exceeding great, and the land is full of blood, and the city full of perverseness: for they say, The LORD hath forsaken the earth, and the LORD seeth not. And as for me also, mine eye shall not spare, neither will I have pity, *but* I will recompense their way upon their head" (Eze.9:9-10).

"Because with lies ye have made the heart of the righteous sad, whom I have not made sad; and strengthened the hands of the wicked, that he should not return from his wicked way, by promising him life" (Eze.13:22).

"Ye have wearied the LORD with your words. Yet ye say, Wherein have we wearied *him?* When ye say, Every one that doeth evil *is* good in the sight of the LORD, and he delighteth in them; or, Where *is* the God of judgment?" (Mal.2:17).

e. *Woe*—the LORD issued a strong warning to the prideful and arrogant throughout the nation (v.21). The conceited were condemned to suffer the punishment of God. Think of the people who are absolutely sure they are right in their opinions about the LORD and His Word. In their own eyes they are wise and prudent; therefore, they feel they do not have to accept the Word of God in what they call a *literal translation*. Instead of accepting God's Word, they use their own wisdom and opinions to formulate their personal religion. Thus, their god becomes only a creation of their own imagination and ideas. They reject the fact that the LORD has revealed Himself and the truth about how to live a fruitful and vic-torious life.

Think about the people who feel they are more intelligent, more attractive, more moral, and more valuable, deserving more attention and honor than others. They even look down upon others. But note what Holy Scripture says: the feelings of being better and superior are only in their own eyes. In reality they are mere human beings on the same level as the most lowly. The prideful and arrogant will bear the judgment and the punishment of God.

"But he giveth more grace. Wherefore he saith, God resisteth the proud, but giveth grace unto the humble" (Js.4:6).

"Love not the world, neither the things *that are* in the world. If any man love the world, the love of the Father is not in him. For all that *is* in the world, the lust of the flesh, and the lust of the eyes, and the pride of life, is not of the Father, but is of the world" (1 Jn.2:15-16).

"The wicked in *his* pride doth persecute the poor: let them be taken in the devices that they have imagined" (Ps.10:2).

"Thou hast rebuked the proud *that are* cursed, which do err from thy commandments" (Ps.119:21).

"These six *things* doth the LORD hate: yea, seven *are* an abomination unto him: A proud look, a lying tongue, and hands that shed innocent blood, An heart that deviseth wicked imaginations, feet that be swift in running to mischief, A false witness *that* speaketh lies, and he that soweth discord among brethren" (Pr.6:16-19).

"*When* pride cometh, then cometh shame: but with the lowly *is* wisdom" (Pr.11:2).

"Pride *goeth* before destruction, and an haughty spirit before a fall" (Pr.16:18).

"An high look, and a proud heart, *and* the plowing of the wicked, *is* sin" (Pr.21:4).

"Seest thou a man wise in his own conceit? *there is* more hope of a fool than of him" (Pr.26:12).

"A man's pride shall bring him low: but honour shall uphold the humble in spirit" (Pr.29:23).

f. *Woe*—the LORD pronounced a severe warning to the unjust and the bribe-takers (v.22). For the second time, Isaiah mentioned those who were guilty of heavy drinking (see vv.11-17). Apparently, this was a reference to the leaders and judges of the nation. Despite their drunken, unjust, and crooked behavior, they were looked upon as heroes in their sins. When it came to drinking and greedy behavior, they could hold their own against anyone. They could drink as much as the next person, and they could deal just as dishonestly in taking bribes as the next leader.

But they were overlooking one fact: the judgment of God. By accepting bribes, acquitting the guilty, and denying justice to the innocent, they were oppressing people. A perversion of justice was taking place. The innocent were being mistreated, severely exploited. But God knew about the sins, and He pronounced His coming judgment upon the unjust oppressors.

"He that is faithful in that which is least is faithful also in much: and he that is unjust in the least is unjust also in much" (Lu.16:10).

"And thou shalt take no gift: for the gift blindeth the wise, and perverteth the words of the righteous" (Ex.23:8).

"Ye shall do no unrighteousness in judgment: thou shalt not respect the person of the poor, nor honour the person of the mighty: *but* in righteousness shalt thou judge thy neighbour" (Le.19:15).

"Thou shalt not oppress an hired servant *that is* poor and needy, *whether he be* of thy brethren, or of thy strangers that *are* in thy land within thy gates" (De.24:14).

"Thou shalt not pervert the judgment of the stranger, *nor* of the fatherless; nor take a widow's raiment to pledge" (De.24:17).

"Trust not in oppression, and become not vain in robbery: if riches increase, set not your heart *upon them*" (Ps.62:10).

"He that oppresseth the poor reproacheth his Maker: but he that honoureth him hath mercy on the poor" (Pr.14:31).

"An unjust man *is* an abomination to the just: and *he that is* upright in the way *is* abomination to the wicked" (Pr.29:27).

"If thou seest the oppression of the poor, and violent perverting of judgment and justice in a province, marvel not at the matter: for *he that is* higher than the highest regardeth; and *there be* higher than they" (Ecc.5:8).

"Thy princes *are* rebellious, and companions of thieves: every one loveth gifts, and followeth after rewards: they judge not the fatherless, neither doth the cause of the widow come unto them. Therefore saith the Lord, the LORD of hosts, the mighty One of Israel, Ah, I will ease me of mine adversaries, and avenge me of mine enemies" (Is.1:23-24).

"The sinners in Zion are afraid; fearfulness hath surprised the hypocrites. Who among us shall dwell with the devouring fire? who among us shall dwell with everlasting burnings? He that walketh righteously, and speaketh uprightly; he that despiseth the gain of oppressions, that shaketh his hands from holding of bribes, that stoppeth his ears from hearing of blood, and shutteth his eyes from seeing evil; He shall dwell on high: his place of defence *shall be* the munitions of rocks: bread shall be given him; his waters *shall be* sure. Thine eyes shall see the king in his beauty: they shall behold the land that is very far off" (Is.33:14-17).

"For I know your manifold transgressions and your mighty sins: they afflict the just, they take a bribe, and they turn aside the poor in the gate *from their right*" (Am.5:12).

3 (5:24-30) **Warning, of Judgment, Against the Israelites (God's People)—Believers, Warnings to, of Judgment—Judgment, Warning of, Discussed—Israel, Warning, of God's Judgment**: the third warning given by the LORD to His people concerned coming judgment. Because of their *wild grapes*, their terrible sins, the Israelites were to face the reproach and discipline of God. Impending judgment lay just over the horizon.

OUTLINE	SCRIPTURE	SCRIPTURE	OUTLINE

3. The warning to all: God's judgment is coming
a. The picture of God's judgment: Will be quick, sudden, & complete
b. The reason for God's judgment: The people had rejected God's law & despised the Word of the *Holy One of Israel*
c. The picture of God's anger
  1) His anger was aroused
  2) His hand stretched out & struck His people
    • The mountains trembled
    • The bodies were left in the streets
  3) His anger against evil is persistent
 	
d. The agents of God's judgment: He will use nations such as Assyria (2 K.17:1-41) & Babylon (25:1-30)
  1) They will come swiftly
	24 Therefore as the fire devoureth the stubble, and the flame consumeth the chaff, *so* their root shall be as rottenness, and their blossom shall go up as dust: because they have cast away the law of the LORD of hosts, and despised the word of the Holy One of Israel.
	25 Therefore is the anger of the LORD kindled against his people, and he hath stretched forth his hand against them, and hath smitten them: and the hills did tremble, and their carcases *were* torn in the midst of the streets. For all this his anger is not turned away, but his hand *is* stretched out still.
	26 And he will lift up an ensign to the nations from far, and will hiss unto them from the end of the earth: and, behold, they shall come with
		speed swiftly:
		27 None shall be weary nor stumble among them; none shall slumber nor sleep; neither shall the girdle of their loins be loosed, nor the latchet of their shoes be broken:
		28 Whose arrows *are* sharp, and all their bows bent, their horses' hoofs shall be counted like flint, and their wheels like a whirlwind:
		29 Their roaring *shall be* like a lion, they shall roar like young lions: yea, they shall roar, and lay hold of the prey, and shall carry *it* away safe, and none shall deliver *it*.
		30 And in that day they shall roar against them like the roaring of the sea: and if *one* look unto the land, behold darkness *and* sorrow, and the light is darkened in the heavens thereof.
			2) They will be well-prepared
			  • Well rested & conditioned
			  • Well dressed in battle clothes
			  • Well equipped with weapons
			
			  • Well trained & frightening in their attack: Like the roar of young lions & the roar of the sea
			
			e. The results of God's impending judgment: A dark, gloomy distress will hang over the land

a. God's judgment would be quick, sudden, and complete (v.24). The sins covered in point two (vv.8-23) were as combustible as dried straw and grass that had been set ablaze. In the same way, the blazing judgment of God would consume those who sowed *wild grapes*. And the destruction would be complete, as complete as the roots of a bush that had decayed or flowers that had blown away like dust.

b. The reason for God's judgment is unmistakable: the people had rejected God's law and despised the Word of the *Holy One of Israel* (v.24). They had been given God's Word as a guide to their lives, and they were to share God's Word with the world. But they failed to share the Word with the other nations of the world, for they themselves rejected it. They wanted nothing to do with the commandments of God and refused to heed them. Rather, they chose to live as they wished, "doing their own thing" when and how they wished. Thus, they can rightly be said to have *despised* God's Word. Having received the Word of the Holy God, they should have lived holy lives and produced fruits of righteousness. Instead, they produced *wild grapes*; consequently, their evil fruit was to be consumed by the judgment of God.

c. Because of the people's *wild grapes,* God's anger was aroused against them (also see 9:12, 17, 21; 10:4). God's judgment was so near, so imminent that it was as though His hand were stretched out and ready to strike (v.25). Realizing this fact, nature itself began to feel the weight of God's judgment. Some commentators feel that an earthquake was definitely being predicted or had already taken place when Isaiah preached this message. The very mountains began to shake. And God's enemies, all who rebelled against Him by turning to a sinful lifestyle, were doomed. Their dead bodies would lie like refuse in the streets.

Whatever the case, note that God's anger against evil is said to be persistent. Even after the judgment predicted here, His anger was still not turned away. His hand is still upraised to judge every generation that sows *wild grapes.*

d. In a vivid picture, God described the agents of His judgment. He would use nations such as Assyria and Babylon as instruments to execute judgment against His people (see outline and notes—2 K.17:1-41; 25:1-30 for more discussion). Because of the people's terrible sins, these wicked nations would be allowed to invade the nation of Israel. But note, God

Himself controlled these nations and the judgment they would execute upon His people. It was God who *whistles* for them to mobilize and march.

The judgment seemed to be right over the horizon, for Isaiah said that the armies would come swiftly and be well prepared (vv.26-30). Furthermore, the invaders would be successful, for they would be...

- well rested and conditioned (v.27)
- well dressed and protected in the latest battle clothes and gear
- well equipped with the latest weapons (v.28)
- well trained in military strategies and psychological warfare, growling like young lions and roaring like the sea (vv.29-30)

e. The results of the attacks would be the overrunning of the land by the invading armies (v.30). A dark, gloomy distress would hang over the land. No matter where a person looked, he would see nothing but despair and darkness hanging over the heads of the people.

Thought 1. The warning has been issued: God's judgment is coming to this earth. Every one of us will have to give an account for what we have done. No person will escape the impending judgment of God. Each person is destined to die, and after death, to face judgment (He.9:27). Death is a reality we are all aware of. We know that we will die; the appointed day is coming. However, most of us choose to ignore the impending day. To be honest, considering how swiftly time flies, death lies right over the horizon for every one of us. Life is but a vapor that appears and then quickly vanishes. It scarcely lasts longer than a leaf that appears in the spring and quickly drops to the ground in the fall. As the leaf faces decay and ruin when it falls to the ground, so we will face destruction and ruin if we have continued to walk in sin. If we have never accepted Jesus Christ as our Savior, we will face the coming judgment of God. Listen to God's warning about the impending judgment:

"**For the Son of man shall come in the glory of his Father with his angels; and then he shall reward every man according to his works**" (Mt.16:27).

"**And then shall appear the sign of the Son of man in heaven: and then shall all the tribes of the earth mourn, and they shall see the Son of man coming in the clouds of heaven with power and great glory**" (Mt.24:30).

"**Whosoever therefore shall be ashamed of me and of my words in this adulterous and sinful generation; of him also shall the Son of man be ashamed, when he cometh in the glory of his Father with the holy angels**" (Mk.8:38).

"**And to you who are troubled rest with us, when the Lord Jesus shall be revealed from heaven with his mighty angels, In flaming fire taking vengeance on them that know not God, and that obey not the gospel of our Lord Jesus Christ**" (2 Th.1:7-8).

"**Behold, he cometh with clouds; and every eye shall see him, and they** *also* **which pierced him: and all kindreds of the earth shall wail because of him. Even so, Amen**" (Re.1:7).

"**And I saw a great white throne, and him that sat on it, from whose face the earth and the heaven fled away; and there was found no place for them. And I saw the dead, small and great, stand before God; and the books were opened: and another book was opened, which is** *the book* **of life: and the dead were judged out of those things which were written in the books, according to their works. And the sea gave up the dead which were in it; and death and hell delivered up the dead which were in them: and they were judged every man according to their works. And death and hell were cast into the lake of fire. This is the second death. And whosoever was not found written in the book of life was cast into the lake of fire**" (Re.20:11-15).

"**And, behold, I come quickly; and my reward** *is* **with me, to give every man according as his work shall be**" (Re.22:12).

"**Also unto thee, O Lord,** *belongeth* **mercy: for thou renderest to every man according to his work**" (Ps.62:12).

"**I the LORD search the heart,** *I* **try the reins, even to give every man according to his ways,** *and* **according to the fruit of his doings**" (Je.17:10).

CHAPTER 6

D. The Call of God's Prophet Isaiah: Three Elements Necessary to Serve God, 6:1-13

1. A vision of the LORD
   a. His exaltation & majesty
      1) Isaiah saw Him on His throne
      2) Isaiah saw the LORD's flowing robe fill the temple
   b. His holiness & glory
      1) Isaiah saw the seraphim above God's throne
         • They were like humans: Had faces, feet, & voices
         • They had six wings
      2) Isaiah witnessed the seraphim's fervent, unbroken praise of God's holiness & glory
   c. His power & presence: Isaiah saw the power of the seraphim's voices & saw smoke—God's presence—fill the temple

2. A conviction of unworthiness: All are sinners & need cleansing
   a. Isaiah felt deep anguish & confessed his sin & the sins of the human race
   b. Isaiah was cleansed: By a hot coal from *the altar* being placed on his lips
      1) This symbolized the

mouth, and said, Lo, this hath touched thy lips; and thine iniquity is taken away, and thy sin purged.
8 Also I heard the voice of the Lord, saying, Whom shall I send, and who will go for us? Then said I, Here *am* I; send me.
9 And he said, Go, and tell this people, Hear ye indeed, but understand not; and see ye indeed, but perceive not.
10 Make the heart of this people fat, and make their ears heavy, and shut their eyes; lest they see with their eyes, and hear with their ears, and understand with their heart, and convert, and be healed.
11 Then said I, Lord, how long? And he answered, Until the cities be wasted without inhabitant, and the houses without man, and the land be utterly desolate,
12 And the LORD have removed men far away, and *there be* a great forsaking in the midst of the land.
13 But yet in it *shall be* a tenth, and *it* shall return, and shall be eaten: as a teil tree, and as an oak, whose substance *is* in them, when they cast *their leaves: so* the holy seed *shall be* the substance thereof.

purifying blood of the sacrifice (a type of Christ)
      2) This symbolized God's atonement for his sins
3. A surrender to the LORD, to His call & commission
   a. Isaiah heard God's call & responded: A spirit of readiness, resolve, & trust
   b. Isaiah was commissioned by God: To go & warn the people
      1) Against hearing God's Word but never understanding it
      2) Against hard hearts, deaf ears, & blind eyes, 29:9; 42:18; 43:8; Mt.13:13-15
      3) Against continuing to resist to the point of no return, never being able to repent & escape the coming judgment
   c. Isaiah was called to persevere in a difficult ministry: He asked how long the people would resist the truth
      1) Until the hand of God's judgment fell
         • Until the nation was destroyed, 11
         • Until the people were exiled
      2) Until only a remnant remained, but even they would be destroyed by the Babylonians, 2 K.25:1-30
      3) Until the *holy seed* arose from the stump that was left (the few survivors)

In the year that king Uzziah died I saw also the Lord sitting upon a throne, high and lifted up, and his train filled the temple.
2 Above it stood the seraphims: each one had six wings; with twain he covered his face, and with twain he covered his feet, and with twain he did fly.
3 And one cried unto another, and said, Holy, holy, holy, *is* the LORD of hosts: the whole earth *is* full of his glory.
4 And the posts of the door moved at the voice of him that cried, and the house was filled with smoke.
5 Then said I, Woe *is* me! for I am undone; because I *am* a man of unclean lips, and I dwell in the midst of a people of unclean lips: for mine eyes have seen the King, the LORD of hosts.
6 Then flew one of the seraphims unto me, having a live coal in his hand, *which* he had taken with the tongs from off the altar:
7 And he laid *it* upon my

DIVISION I

THE PROPHECIES OF REBUKE AND HOPE GIVEN TO JUDAH AND JERUSALEM: AN OVERVIEW OF THE PRESENT AND FUTURE OF GOD'S PEOPLE, 1:1–12:6

D. The Call of God's Prophet Isaiah: Three Elements Necessary to Serve God, 6:1-13

(6:1-13) **Introduction**: many are called but few are chosen (Mt.20:16; 22:14). What exactly does this mean? Simply that many individuals have been called by God to minister to people, but few have ever responded to the call. Far more have rejected the call to service than have responded positively. When an opportunity to minister crosses our path, we should grasp the opportunity. We should meet whatever need there is lying in our path. We should never neglect a person or persons in need—whether hungry, impoverished, sick, hurting or otherwise, not if the person is truly in need. No matter what the call to service may be, if the call comes from God, we should surrender to the call.

In the year that King Uzziah died, the LORD gave Isaiah an extraordinary vision of Himself. Obviously, young Isaiah needed this very special encounter with the LORD. Why this was necessary is not specifically stated, but several reasons can be gleaned from Scripture. First, Isaiah's faith needed to be strengthened. He needed to know beyond any doubt who the LORD is and the extreme importance of the message being given to him. It was the LORD of hosts, the sovereign Creator and Majesty of the universe who was calling the young man to proclaim God's message to the world.

Second, Isaiah evidently needed to be humbled. He needed to be shown just what terrible sinners he and the people were, especially when seen in the light of God's glory and holiness (vv.3, 5).

Third, Isaiah needed to be stirred with a renewed sense of urgency to proclaim God's warning of coming judgment. It was absolutely essential that the people repent, turn back to the LORD if they were to escape the coming judgment. If they failed to repent, God's execution of justice was sure to sweep down upon them.

Fourth, Isaiah evidently needed to be prepared for a challenging and difficult ministry. The people's hearts were hard, their ears deaf, and their eyes blinded to the truth of God's Word that He alone is the only living and true God. Therefore, they had to be charged to worship Him alone and to obey Him, living righteous and holy lives as His commandments stipulate.

Fifth, this was a critical time in the history of the nation. King Uzziah was either dying or else already dead. Under Uzziah's leadership the nation had flourished economically and militarily. The king had launched a massive program of public works and construction projects in addition to strengthening the military. As a result, there was little or no unemployment. The people were very successful in their businesses, agriculture, and ranching ventures. Almost everyone had a prosperous lifestyle. However, in the latter years of Uzziah's reign, he slipped into sin and exposed a terrible flaw in his character. He was seen to be full of pride and self-importance. Shockingly, he had forced his way into the temple and assumed the role of a priest, God's appointed intercessor. Usurping the position of a priest was a very serious offense in the eyes of the LORD. For that reason the LORD had afflicted Uzziah with leprosy, and he was forced to live in isolation until his death. Left with no choice, King Uzziah had to put his son Jotham in charge of the government as his co-regent upon the throne.

Although unknown to Isaiah and the people of his day, Uzziah's death was to mark a major change in the history of the Jews. Following the reign of King Uzziah, the prosperity and peace that the nation had known began to decline. His son Jotham was a good king, but Jotham's son Ahaz was a terrible ruler. He led the nation in a downward spiral of wickedness and false worship. Although the tide was turned back to righteousness under Hezekiah's rule, Isaiah was to have a very difficult ministry. The prophet's ministry was launched in the year that King Uzziah died, the very period in which the utter disintegration of the nation began. Of course, the LORD knew the significance of the historical change that was taking place. He knew the desperate need of the people for a prophet who would courageously stand before them and proclaim the Word of the living LORD. To this end, Isaiah was being called. He was to minister to a nation that was declining, marching ever so rapidly down the spiral of utter disintegration and ruin. The people were given over to greed and covetousness, indulgence and drunkenness, lies and deception, pride and arrogance, and the mockery and persecution of the righteous. In fact, throughout Isaiah's entire ministry he faced a people with perverted values, a people who called evil good and good evil. Sadly, the society of his day turned away from the LORD and to false gods and false worship. The people were given over to sin and wickedness. Facing the death of King Uzziah and the resulting shift in government, Isaiah felt a desperate need to seek the face of the LORD. As always, when any genuine believer seeks the LORD, the LORD meets the believer's need. In Isaiah's case, the LORD gave him a very special vision of Himself. Isaiah actually saw the LORD sitting on the throne of God, high and exalted in the heavenly temple. Through this encounter with the LORD, Isaiah was set apart for the very special ministry to which he was being called. This is, *The Call of God's Prophet, Isaiah: Three Elements Necessary to Serve God,* 6:1-13.

1. A vision of the LORD (vv.1-4).
2. A conviction of unworthiness: all are sinners and need cleansing (vv.5-7).
3. A surrender to the LORD, to His call and commission (vv.8-13).

1 (6:1-4) **Vision, of the Lord, Essential for Service—Call – Called, Essential, to See the Lord—Ministers, Call of, Three Essentials—Exaltation, of God, Vision of—Majesty, of God, Vision of—Holiness, of God, Vision of—Glory, of God, Vision of—Power, of God, Vision of—Presence, of God, Vision of—Temple, Heavenly, Vision of—Jesus Christ, Vision of, by Isaiah**: in order to serve the Lord, a person needs a vision of the Lord. A person must know the Lord and understand who He is before he can adequately serve Him. This was true of Isaiah and it is true of every genuine believer, especially the ministers and teachers of God's Holy Word.

OUTLINE	SCRIPTURE	SCRIPTURE	OUTLINE
1. A vision of the LORD	In the year that king Uzziah died I saw also the Lord sitting upon a throne, high and lifted up, and his train filled the temple.	twain he did fly.	• They had six wings
a. His exaltation & majesty		3 And one cried unto another, and said, Holy, holy, holy, *is* the LORD of hosts: the whole earth *is* full of his glory.	2) Isaiah witnessed the seraphim's fervent, unbroken praise of God's holiness & glory
1) Isaiah saw Him on His throne			
2) Isaiah saw the LORD's flowing robe fill the temple			
b. His holiness & glory	2 Above it stood the seraphims: each one had six wings; with twain he covered his face, and with twain he covered his feet, and with	4 And the posts of the door moved at the voice of him that cried, and the house was filled with smoke.	c. His power & presence: Isaiah saw the power of the seraphim's voices & saw smoke—God's presence—fill the temple
1) Isaiah saw the seraphim above God's throne			
• They were like humans: Had faces, feet, & voices			

a. The LORD gave Isaiah a vision of His exaltation and majesty (v.1). Isaiah actually saw the LORD sitting on His heavenly throne, high and exalted. Obviously, this was the highest, most elevated throne Isaiah had ever seen or imagined. It was the throne of the King of kings Himself, the Lord Jesus Christ. The *Gospel of John* confirms this fact, for he clearly says that it was Christ sitting on the heavenly throne in all His glory and majesty (Jn.12:41). The LORD was exalted as the sovereign God over all the universe: above, before, and over all that exists. Transcending everything, He was exalted above all rulers and governments throughout the universe. He held dominion, ruled and reigned, over all powers and principalities, both in this world and the spiritual world.

Isaiah also saw the LORD's flowing robes fill the heavenly sanctuary. Because of His majesty and royalty, no person was able to stand in His immediate presence or to gaze into His holy face. The train of His robe filled the entire temple.

b. The LORD gave Isaiah a vision of His holiness and glory (vv.2-3). Flying above the LORD's throne were a number of spectacular creatures called *seraphim*, who are not mentioned anywhere else in Scripture. The word *seraphim* (*sarap*) means burning ones, suggesting a burning purity and zeal for the LORD. Perhaps their presence suggests the burning, consuming fire of God's holiness in executing His justice and judgment. In appearance, the seraphim were apparently like humans in that they had faces, feet, and voices. But they were unlike humans in that they had six wings.

⇒ With two wings they covered their faces, indicating their unworthiness and humility. They were not worthy to gaze upon the face of the Holy One.

⇒ With two other wings they covered their feet, perhaps indicating their reverence for the LORD. They are not worthy to stand before the LORD.

⇒ With the other two wings they flew or hovered above the throne of God, possibly signifying their continued ministry of proclaiming God's holiness and glory. However, their flying could also signify a readiness to undertake any task assigned by the LORD.

Isaiah saw and heard the seraphim's fervent, unbroken praise of God's holiness and glory (v.3). Obviously, this was their primary ministry. With the deepest fervency possible, the seraphim called back and forth to each other: "Holy, holy, holy, is the LORD of hosts [LORD Almighty]: the whole earth is full of his glory."

The threefold repetition of *holy* emphasizes that holiness is the most essential characteristic of the LORD.[1] Holiness is the very essence of God's being. *Holy* (*qadosh*) means to be set apart, separated, distinctive, different, transcendent. It also has the idea of perfection, purity, and moral cleanness.[2] The LORD is totally set apart, entirely different from all beings throughout the universe, including mankind. From the very presence of God flows the blazing light of perfection and purity. The very nature of God is light, the brilliance and splendor of light, the most pure light imaginable. As Scripture says, "God is light, and in Him is no darkness at all" (1 Jn.1:5).

Being holy—the very essence and energy of pure light—God can have no part with evil or things associated with evil. Thus anyone who wishes to be associated with God must be holy even as He is holy. But since no person can achieve such holiness or perfection, a person must come to the LORD and beg for cleansing. This will be dealt with in the next point. For now, God's holiness is the focus. God's holiness shines forth as a witness to His perfection. In fact, the blazing glory of God's presence (His holiness and light) shines so brightly that there will be no need for a sun in the New Jerusalem (Re.21:23).

Note the second part of the seraphim's song: they declare "the whole earth is full of His glory." Creation—the heavens and earth—declare the glory of God. Wherever we look, whether at the starry sky at night or the astounding beauty of nature, the incomprehensible glory of God is evident.

c. The LORD gave Isaiah a vision of His power and presence (v.4). As the seraphim cried out, the power of their deep voices shook the very foundation of the temple. Even the huge doorposts and thresholds trembled. Witnessing this would remind Isaiah of God's awesome power and of the angelic agents who were available to execute God's justice upon the earth.

Isaiah also saw smoke fill the temple. Most likely, this smoke was a cloud of glory that symbolized the LORD's holy presence. His cloud of glory, His presence, had led the Israelites through the wilderness journeys and had also filled Solomon's temple on the day it was dedicated (Ex.13:21; 16:10; 1 K.8:10-13).[3]

Thought 1. Any person who truly desires to serve the LORD must have a clear vision of the Lord. The individual must know the Lord and know who He is before he can serve Him as Lord. This is true for all genuine believers, but especially for those in leadership positions such as ministers and teachers of God's Holy Word.

(1) To serve the Lord, we must see the Lord exalted, sitting upon the throne of the universe in all His majestic glory. If we do not know that Christ is Lord, how can we lead people to honor and worship Him, to surrender their lives to Him and obey His Holy Word? Unless we know that Jesus Christ is Lord, we waste our time trying to serve Him. Of what value is any ministry in His Name unless He is Lord? If Jesus Christ were not truly Lord, He would not deserve the worship or service of any person. Therefore, God's Holy Word declares to us time and again the wonderful truth that Jesus Christ is the exalted, sovereign Lord of the universe.

"So then after the Lord had spoken unto them, he was received up into heaven, and sat on the right hand of God" (Mk.16:19).

"Hereafter shall the Son of man sit on the right hand of the power of God" (Lu.22:69).

"This Jesus hath God raised up, whereof we all are witnesses. Therefore being by the right hand of God exalted, and having received of the Father the promise of the Holy Ghost, he hath shed forth this, which ye now see and hear. For David is not ascended into the heavens: but he saith himself, The LORD said unto my Lord, Sit thou on my right hand, Until I make thy foes thy footstool. Therefore let all the house of Israel know assuredly, that God hath made that same Jesus, whom ye have crucified, both Lord and Christ" (Ac.2:32-36).

"The God of our fathers raised up Jesus, whom ye slew and hanged on a tree. Him hath God exalted with his right hand *to be* a Prince and a Saviour, for to give repentance to Israel, and forgiveness of sins" (Ac.5:30-31).

"That if thou shalt confess with thy mouth the Lord Jesus, and shalt believe in thine heart that God hath raised him from the dead, thou shalt be saved. For with the heart man believeth unto righteousness; and with the mouth confession is made unto salvation" (Ro.10:9-10).

"For to this end Christ both died, and rose, and revived, that he might be Lord both of the dead and living" (Ro.14:9).

"God *is* faithful, by whom ye were called unto the fellowship of his Son Jesus Christ our Lord" (1 Co.1:9).

---

1 Stanley M. Horton. *Isaiah.* "The Complete Biblical Library: The Old Testament." (Springfield, MO: World Library Press, Inc., 1995), p.57.
2 James Strong. *The New Strong's Exhaustive Concordance of the Bible.* (Nashville, TN: Thomas Nelson Publishers, 1990), #6918, 6942. Also see Edward J. Young's, *The Book of Isaiah*, Vol.1, (Grand Rapids, MI: Eerdmans Publishing Co., 1965), pp.242-243, footnote 19.
3 John F. Walvoord and Roy B. Zuck, Editors. *The Bible Knowledge Commentary, Old Testament*, p.1045.

"Wherefore I give you to understand, that no man speaking by the Spirit of God calleth Jesus accursed: and *that* no man can say that Jesus is the Lord, but by the Holy Ghost" (1 Co.12:3).

"[God's mighty power] Which he wrought in Christ, when he raised him from the dead, and set *him* at his own right hand in the heavenly *places,* Far above all principality, and power, and might, and dominion, and every name that is named, not only in this world, but also in that which is to come: And hath put all *things* under his feet, and gave him *to be* the head over all *things* to the church" (Ep.1:20-22).

"Wherefore God also hath highly exalted him, and given him a name which is above every name: That at the name of Jesus every knee should bow, of *things* in heaven, and *things* in earth, and *things* under the earth" (Ph.2:9-10).

"[Jesus Christ] Who is gone into heaven, and is on the right hand of God; angels and authorities and powers being made subject unto him" (1 Pe.3:22).

"Saying with a loud voice, Worthy is the Lamb that was slain to receive power, and riches, and wisdom, and strength, and honour, and glory, and blessing" (Re.5:12).

(2) To serve the Lord, we must see the holiness and glory or Christ. If Jesus Christ were not the holy and sinless Son of God, He could not be the Savior of the world. He would be as short of God's glory as we are and as guilty of sin as we are. He would need a Savior as much as we do. But the wonderful truth is this: Jesus Christ is the Son of God, holy and sinless, the Savior of the world. If we do not know Him as our Redeemer, how can we proclaim His salvation? If we believe Jesus Christ is only another man, guilty of sin, there is no value in lifting Him up as the Savior of the world. He would be nothing more than a mere human being. But the un-equivocal declaration of God's Holy Word is this wonderful truth: Jesus Christ is the holy, sinless Son of God.

"Which of you convinceth me of sin? And if I say the truth, why do ye not believe me?" (Jn.8:46).

"For he hath made him *to be* sin for us, who knew no sin; that we might be made the righteousness of God in him" (2 Co.5:21).

"Thou hast loved righteousness, and hated iniquity; therefore God, *even* thy God, hath anointed thee with the oil of gladness above thy fellows" (He.1:9).

"For we have not an high priest which cannot be touched with the feeling of our infirmities; but was in all points tempted like as *we are, yet* without sin" (He.4:15).

"And being made perfect, he became the author of eternal salvation unto all them that obey him" (He.5:9).

"Wherefore he is able also to save them to the uttermost that come unto God by him, seeing he ever liveth to make intercession for them. For such an high priest became us, *who is* holy, harmless, undefiled, separate from sinners, and made higher than the heavens" (He.7:25-26).

"For the law maketh men high priests which have infirmity; but the word of the oath, which was since the law, *maketh* the Son, who is consecrated for evermore" (He. 7:28).

"Forasmuch as ye know that ye were not redeemed with corruptible things, *as* silver and gold, from your vain conversation [behavior, conduct] *received* by tradition from your fathers; But with the precious blood of Christ, as of a lamb without blemish and without spot" (1 Pe.1:18-19).

"Who did no sin, neither was guile found in his mouth: Who, when he was reviled, reviled not again; when he suffered, he threatened not; but committed *himself* to him that judgeth righteously: Who his own self bare our sins in his own body on the tree, that we, being dead to sins, should live unto righteousness: by whose stripes ye were healed" (1 Pe.2:22-24).

"And ye know that he was manifested to take away our sins; and in him is no sin" (1 Jn.3:5).

"All we like sheep have gone astray; we have turned every one to his own way; and the LORD hath laid on him the iniquity of us all....And he made his grave with the wicked, and with the rich in his death; because he had done no violence, neither *was any* deceit in his mouth" (Is.53:6, 9).

(3) To serve the Lord, we must know His power and presence. We must know that He has the power to deliver us from the bondage of sin and death, the power to deliver us through all trials and temptations. In addition, we must know that the Lord's presence is always with us, guiding and leading us victoriously throughout life. Listen to what God's Holy Word says about the Lord's power:

"But that ye may know that the Son of man hath power on earth to forgive sins, (then saith he to the sick of the palsy,) Arise, take up thy bed, and go unto thine house. And he arose, and departed to his house" (Mt.9:6-7).

"For where two or three are gathered together in my name, there am I in the midst of them" (Mt.18:20).

"And Jesus came and spake unto them, saying, All power is given unto me in heaven and in earth" (Mt.28:18).

"Teaching them to observe all things whatsoever I have commanded you: and, lo, I am with you alway, *even* unto the end of the world. Amen" (Mt.28:20).

"As thou hast given him power over all flesh, that he should give eternal life to as many as thou hast given him" (Jn.17:2).

"How God anointed Jesus of Nazareth with the Holy Ghost and with power: who went about do-ing good, and healing all that were oppressed of the devil; for God was with him" (Ac.10:38).

"And declared *to be* the Son of God with power, according to the spirit of holiness, by the resurrection from the dead" (Ro.1:4).

"Now unto him that is able to do exceeding abundantly above all that we ask or think, according to the power that worketh in us" (Ep.3:20).

"Who being the brightness of *his* glory, and the express image of his person, and upholding all things by the word of his power, when he had by himself purged our sins, sat down on the right hand of the Majesty on high" (He.1:3).

"And, behold, I *am* with thee, and will keep thee in all *places* whither thou goest, and will bring thee again into this land; for I will not leave thee, until I have done *that* which I have spoken to thee of" (Ge.28:15).

"And he said, My presence shall go *with thee,* and I will give thee rest" (Ex.33:14).

"When thou goest out to battle against thine enemies, and seest horses, and chariots, *and* a people more than thou, be not afraid of them: for the LORD thy God *is* with thee, which brought thee up out of the land of Egypt" (De.20:1).

"But I *am* poor and needy; *yet* the Lord thinketh upon me: thou *art* my help and my deliverer; make no tarrying, O my God" (Ps.40:17).

"But they that wait upon the LORD shall renew *their* strength; they shall mount up with wings as eagles; they shall run, and not be weary; *and* they shall walk, and not faint" (Is.40:31).

"Fear thou not; for I *am* with thee: be not dismayed; for I *am* thy God: I will strengthen thee; yea, I will help thee; yea, I will uphold thee with the right hand of my righteousness" (Is.41:10).

"Fear not: for I have redeemed thee, I have called *thee* by thy name; thou *art* mine. When thou passest through the waters, I *will be* with thee; and through the rivers, they shall not overflow thee: when thou walkest through the fire, thou shalt not be burned; neither shall the flame kindle upon thee" (Is.43:1-2).

2 (6:5-7) **Conviction, of Sin—Unworthiness, Conviction of—Cleansing, Need for, Example—Sin, Universal—Confession, of Sin, Example—Isaiah, Confession of, Sin—Man, Nature of, a Sinner—Guilt, of Sin, All Men—Man, State of – Present State, a Sinner**: a deep conviction of unworthiness is necessary to serve the LORD. Confronted with the vision of the LORD in all His majesty and holiness, Isaiah was stricken with a profound sense of unworthiness. He suddenly realized the horrible nature of sin when contrasted with the majestic light of God's glory and holiness. How filthy, polluted, defiled, dishonorable, and corrupt sin is. Because the LORD is so high and exalted, so pure and righteous, sin stinks within His nostrils. Thus, when Isaiah saw the holiness of God, he realized just how impure and unclean he was. Although he had placed his trust in the LORD years before, in this renewed call to the ministry Isaiah saw how utterly undeserving he was to serve the LORD. Feeling deep anguish within his soul, he cried out, "*Woe*" (v.5). This is a cry of alarm, a sense that some terrible calamity is about to happen. Obviously he sensed that God's brilliant holiness was about to strike him dead. He cried out in distress, "I am undone" (*nidmeyti*). This word means to be ruined, cut off, destroyed, doomed to die. If God dealt with Isaiah in strict justice, he was a doomed man.

Flooding Isaiah's spirit was a deep consciousness of how far short of the glory of God he was. The LORD sat in all His glory and majesty high above the earth, ruling over the entire universe. All sorts of memories no doubt flashed through Isaiah's mind. He thought about his *sins of omission*—the times he had failed to do what he should or to be as diligent as he should—as well as his *sins of commission*—the times he had disobeyed the LORD's Word, His holy commandments. Sensing a desperate need to confess his failures, he cried out that he was a sinful man, a man of "unclean lips." Why did Isaiah refer to his "unclean lips" instead of simply saying that he was a *man of sin*? Probably because he was deeply aware of some recent sin he had committed with his tongue and knew that the root of sin went much deeper. Perhaps he had failed to speak a kind word when it was needed or perhaps he had been silent when he had been given an opportunity to witness for the LORD. Or perhaps Isaiah had recently spoken words that were…

- harsh
- combative, argumentative
- rude
- rash
- divisive
- degrading

Whatever the case, Isaiah knew that his lips were guilty of failing the LORD, guilty of serious sin. An overpowering conviction of sin burned within his soul. And he felt the heavy weight, the total mass of sin that was exposed before the pure holiness and power of God. Having seen the *King*, the LORD of hosts (God Almighty), Isaiah knew that the LORD could strike out at any moment and destroy the human race. Thus he confessed the sins of the whole world, crying out that he lived among a people of "unclean lips" who constantly used language that was…

- foul or filthy
- profane
- irreverent
- scornful toward God or other people
- threatening, full of malice and hate
- bitter or contemptuous
- off-colored or immoral

Obviously, Isaiah was very aware that the sins of the lips or tongue actually flowed from a sinful heart. Later in his-tory, Christ was to express the truth as well as it could be stated.

"A good man out of the good treasure of the heart bringeth forth good things: and an evil man out of the evil treasure bringeth forth evil things. But I say unto you, That every idle word that men shall speak, they shall give account thereof in the day of judgment. For by thy words thou shalt be justified, and by thy words thou shalt be condemned" (Mt.12:35-37).

"But those things which proceed out of the mouth come forth from the heart; and they defile the man. For out of the heart proceed evil thoughts, murders, adulteries, fornications, thefts, false witness, blasphemies" (Mt.15:18-19).

"And he said, That which cometh out of the man, that defileth the man. For from within, out of the heart of men, proceed evil thoughts, adulteries, fornications, murders, Thefts, covetousness, wickedness, deceit, lasciviousness, an evil eye, blasphemy, pride, foolishness: All these evil things come from within, and defile the man" (Mk.7:20-23).

Having fallen prostrate upon the ground in utter anguish of soul, Isaiah was crushed with a deep conviction of his sin. But the wonderful truth is this fact: the LORD never leaves His people bearing the weight of guilt and sin, not when they confess and turn away from their sins. Knowing the genuineness of Isaiah's heart, the LORD met his need. Isaiah was cleansed from his sins. One of the seraphim performed the function of a priest. Flying over to the altar, he picked up a burning coal with a pair of tongs. Then flying over to Isaiah, he touched the lips of the prophet with a hot coal and pronounced that he was cleansed from sin. The hot, burning coal symbolized the burning away of sin, the purifying and cleansing of sin. The fact that the hot coal was taken from the altar was a reminder that sin was forgiven through the blood of the sacrifice, the sacrifice that was always offered upon the altar. The seraphim actually pronounced that Isaiah's sin had been atoned for.

This act definitely symbolized God's atonement for sin. Sometime in the future, Christ was going to die to provide atonement for the sins of every human being. But for now, because Isaiah had confessed his sins, the LORD had the seraphim symbolize the cleansing of Isaiah's sin. Remember that a sensor full of burning coals had always been taken into the Most Holy Place on the Day of Atonement. It was taken before the LORD by the High Priest when the substitute sacrifice was offered to God on behalf of His people (see outline and note—Le.16:11-14 for more discussion).

OUTLINE	SCRIPTURE	SCRIPTURE	OUTLINE
2. A conviction of unworthiness: All are sinners & need cleansing a. Isaiah felt deep anguish & confessed his sin & the sins of the human race b. Isaiah was cleansed: By a	5 Then said I, Woe *is* me! for I am undone; because I *am* a man of unclean lips, and I dwell in the midst of a people of unclean lips: for mine eyes have seen the King, the LORD of hosts. 6 Then flew one of the ser-	aphims unto me, having a live coal in his hand, *which* he had taken with the tongs from off the altar: 7 And he laid *it* upon my mouth, and said, Lo, this hath touched thy lips; and thine iniquity is taken away, and thy sin purged.	hot coal from *the altar* being placed on his lips 1) This symbolized the purifying blood of the sacrifice (a type of Christ) 2) This symbolized God's atonement for his sins

Thought 1. A deep conviction of unworthiness is necessary for us to serve the LORD. We must not measure ourselves against one another, for we are all of the same flesh and blood. We are all guilty of giving in to temptation, sinning through acts of *commission* or *omission*. Therefore, when we measure ourselves against one another, we are as *good* as everyone else. But to learn the truth about ourselves, we must measure ourselves against the LORD. When we see the LORD high and exalted, dwelling in the blazing holiness of His being, then we see the truth. We see just how far short of God's glory we are, how terrible our sin is when contrasted with His perfection and glory (Ro.3:23). The result of this comparison is just what we need: a deep conviction of sin and of unworthiness. Hence, we are driven—or *should be driven*—to seek forgiveness from the LORD, the only source of true forgiveness. And when the LORD pardons us, we are truly freed. Guilt is erased, and our spirits are set free from depression, discour-agement, self-accusation, and the sense of failure. We are set free from the heavy weight of guilt that causes so many emotional problems, problems that far too often crush us and make us helpless, unable to function. Jesus Christ—He and He alone—can and will set us free if we will confess and repent of our sins. In addition, confession and repentance are absolutely essential before we can genuinely serve the Lord. Listen to what God's Holy Word says:

"Blessed *are* they that mourn: for they shall be comforted" (Mt.5:4).

"I tell you, Nay: but, except ye repent, ye shall all likewise perish" (Lu.13:3).

"Now when they heard *this,* they were pricked in their heart, and said unto Peter and to the rest of the apostles, Men *and* brethren, what shall we do? Then Peter said unto them, Repent, and be baptized every one of you in the name of Jesus Christ for the remission of sins, and ye shall receive the gift of the Holy Ghost" (Ac.2:37-38).

"Repent ye therefore, and be converted, that your sins may be blotted out, when the times of refreshing shall come from the presence of the Lord" (Ac.3:19).

"And as he reasoned of righteousness, temperance, and judgment to come Felix trembled, and answered, Go thy way for this time; when I have a convenient season, I will call for thee" (Ac.24:25).

"In whom we have redemption through his blood, the forgiveness of sins, according to the riches of his grace" (Ep.1:7).

"If we confess our sins, he is faithful and just to forgive us *our* sins, and to cleanse us from all unrighteousness" (1 Jn.1:9).

"For mine iniquities are gone over mine head: as an heavy burden they are too heavy for me" (Ps.38:4).

"For I acknowledge my transgressions: and my sin *is* ever before me" (Ps.51:3).

"He that covereth his sins shall not prosper: but whoso confesseth and forsaketh *them* shall have mercy" (Pr.28:13).

"Let the wicked forsake his way, and the unrighteous man his thoughts: and let him return unto the LORD, and he will have mercy upon him; and to our God, for he will abundantly pardon" (Is.55:7).

"Take with you words, and turn to the LORD: say unto him, Take away all iniquity, and receive *us* graciously: so will we render the calves of our lips" (Ho.14:2).

3 (6:8-13) **Surrender, to the LORD's Call, by Isaiah—Call, of the Lord, Surrender to—Commission, of Isaiah—Ministry, of Isaiah—Warning, Threefold—Ministry, Difficult, Example**: Isaiah surrendered to the LORD'S call and commission, an absolute essential in order to serve the LORD. A person must first hear God's call and then respond favorably before he can truly serve the LORD. This was true of Isaiah, and it is true of every genuine believer, but especially the ministers and teachers of God's Word.

OUTLINE	SCRIPTURE	SCRIPTURE	OUTLINE

3. A surrender to the LORD, to His call & commission
a. Isaiah heard God's call & responded: A spirit of readiness, resolve, & trust
b. Isaiah was commissioned by God: To go & warn the people
  1) Against hearing God's Word but never understanding it
  2) Against hard hearts, deaf ears, & blind eyes, 29:9; 42:18; 43:8; Mt.13:13-15
  3) Against continuing to resist to the point of no return, never being able to repent & escape the coming judgment
	8 Also I heard the voice of the Lord, saying, Whom shall I send, and who will go for us? Then said I, Here *am* I; send me.
	9 And he said, Go, and tell this people, Hear ye indeed, but understand not; and see ye indeed, but perceive not.
	10 Make the heart of this people fat, and make their ears heavy, and shut their eyes; lest they see with their eyes, and hear with their ears, and understand with their heart, and convert, and be healed.
		11 Then said I, Lord, how long? And he answered, Until the cities be wasted without inhabitant, and the houses without man, and the land be utterly desolate,
		12 And the LORD have removed men far away, and *there be* a great forsaking in the midst of the land.
		13 But yet in it *shall be* a tenth, and *it* shall return, and shall be eaten: as a teil tree, and as an oak, whose substance *is* in them, when they cast *their leaves*: so the holy seed *shall be* the substance thereof.
			c. Isaiah was called to persevere in a difficult ministry: He asked how long the people will resist the truth
			  1) Until the hand of God's judgment fell
			   • Until the nation was destroyed
			   • Until the people were exiled
			  2) Until only a remnant remained, but even they will be destroyed by the Babylonians, 2 K.25:1-30
			  3) Until the *holy seed* arose from the stump that was left (the few survivors)

a. Isaiah heard God's call and responded favorably (v.8). As soon as Isaiah had been cleansed from his sins, he immediately heard the booming voice of the LORD calling for a volunteer to go forth to minister to His people. Without hesitation—not leaving time for the seraphim or anyone else to respond—Isaiah courageously offered himself: "Here am I! Send me." Having been forgiven his sins and sensing deeply that the LORD accepted him, Isaiah was filled with joy and thanksgiving. Therefore with no reservation, Isaiah leapt at the opportunity to serve his LORD. His immediate surrender reveals...

- a spirit of *readiness*, both a desire and a willingness to serve the LORD
- a spirit of *resolve*, a determination to go and bear witness despite the difficulties
- a spirit of *trust*, leaving the success and results up to the LORD

Unlike so many who hesitate or even reject God's call, Isaiah readily, willingly surrendered to serve the LORD. Whereas Moses and Jeremiah both fought against the call of God, Isaiah offered himself without reservation or qualification.

b. Isaiah was commissioned by God, instructed to go and issue a threefold warning to the people (vv.9-10). First, he was to warn the people about hearing God's Word but never understanding it. Obviously, many of the people were faithful in their worship attendance. They regularly heard the Word of God. But their repeated hearing was not leading to understanding. Instead of truly listening, their minds were wandering about, focused upon their own affairs or problems. They occasionally witnessed God working in the lives of other people, yet they never perceived that they themselves needed a work of God in their own hearts. Simply stated, when they attended worship service or heard the Word of God being taught, they became sleepy eyed, groggy, and inattentive.

Second, Isaiah was to warn the people against having hard hearts, deaf ears, and blind eyes (v.10). Repeatedly rejecting the Word of God and His work in their hearts had a terrible impact upon the people. It hardened them and rendered them incapable of receiving and responding to God's Word. Time and again the people refused to hear the Word of God. Consequently, the more they rejected God's Word, the harder their hearts became and the more deaf and blind they became. Constant resistance resulted in less interest in the LORD. Thus the people were less able to receive Him. They became more and more callous toward God. Note that this experience is so common and so tragic that it is quoted six times in the New Testament (Mt.13:13-15; Mk.4:12; Lu.8:10; Jn.12:40; Ac.28:25-28; Ro.11:8).

Third, Isaiah was to warn the people against continuing to resist to the point of no return. The people could reach a point of never being able to repent, the point of never being able to escape the coming judgment (v.10). People must be warned: the LORD is not playing a game with the human race. His Word must be taken seriously, not trifled with, ignored, neglected, and certainly not disobeyed. Yet despite God's warnings, history has shown that people do harden themselves toward the LORD and His Word. They even deny God's existence and exalt man as lord over his own destiny. These individuals often harden their consciences to the point that they no longer sense conviction of wrongdoing. In doing so, they reach a point of ultimate resistance, a point of never being able to return to the LORD. In other words, a person can become so hardened toward the LORD that he will never repent. The result is sad and tragic, for the person will never be able to escape the coming judgment. He has doomed himself to spending eternity separated from God. It is not God who deliberately hardens the hearts of people, making their ears deaf and their eyes closed. Rather, it is the people who continually resist God's truth. It is the stubbornness of people's hearts, their repeated refusal to hear the Word of God and to surrender their lives to Him that dooms them to never accept the wonderful salvation God offers.

These were the three warnings Isaiah was commissioned to proclaim to the people. No matter how the people responded, he was to continue proclaiming the Holy Word of God.

c. Isaiah sensed that he was being called to persevere in a difficult, unpopular ministry (vv.11-13). Therefore, he asked the LORD how long the people would resist the truth. God's answer was threefold, indicating that the situation was to get much worse before it would get better.

1) The people would resist the truth until the hand of God's judgment fell. Because of their hard hearts, the nation was to be destroyed and the people deported to a far land (vv.11-12). The situation would not get better until the Northern and Southern Kingdoms had been conquered and the people taken into captivity and exiled by the conquerors. (See outline and notes—2 K.17:1-41; 25:1-30 for more discussion.)

2) The people would continue to resist the truth until only a remnant remained, but even this remnant would see the land invaded and wasted again (v.13). Note that the remnant would be only about a tenth of the population. However, they too would experience further destruction due to the hardness of their hearts toward the LORD. This is a clear reference to the future destruction of Jerusalem by the Babylonians under Nebuchadnezzar (See outline and notes—2 K.25:1-30 for more discussion).

3) The people would go on resisting the truth until the *holy seed* arose from the stump. The "stump" represents the few survivors that will be left (v.13). This is a wonderful promise, that a *holy seed*—a small number of true believers—will survive the coming judgment. It will be like the stump of a fallen tree that gives rise to shoots of growth. So it would be with the population of Judah and Jerusalem. There would be a stump, a few survivors of true believers, who would escape the coming judgment. People would continue to resist the truth until these days, so the warning must be issued by Isaiah and then others who follow him. So long as people continue to resist the truth, the warning of God was to be issued against them.

Thought 1. Before we can serve the LORD, we must first surrender to the Him. We must acknowledge Him as the LORD, as the high and exalted Creator of the universe, the Holy One who is to be worshipped and served. Second, we must confess and repent of our sins before we can truly serve the LORD. And then, thirdly, we must surrender to the LORD's call and commission.

We are not called to be successful, but we are called to be available. A spirit of surrender must grip our hearts. No matter the difficulty or hardship of the call, we must be ready and resolved to step forth for the LORD, trusting Him for strength and guidance. If we surrender to the LORD—show Him that our spirits are ready and resolved—He will send us forth in the power of His Spirit. Every step of the way will be directed by His Spirit, and we will be empowered to face any difficulty. No matter how hard the people's hearts may be or how strong the opposition, the LORD will overshadow us with His presence and empower us to complete the task. The one request of us is not that of intelligence, ability, or skill but that of surrender. God simply calls us to be available, surrendered to His call and commission.

"Then Peter began to say unto him, Lo, we have left all, and have followed thee" (Mk.10:28).

"And after these things he went forth, and saw a publican, named Levi, sitting at the receipt of custom: and he said unto him, Follow me. And he left all, rose up, and followed him" (Lu.5:27-28).

"And he said to *them* all, If any *man* will come after me, let him deny himself, and take up his cross daily, and follow me" (Lu.9:23).

"So likewise, whosoever he be of you that forsaketh not all that he hath, he cannot be my disciple" (Lu.14:33).

"And he said unto them, Verily I say unto you, There is no man that hath left house, or parents, or brethren, or wife, or children, for the kingdom of God's sake, Who shall not receive manifold more in this present time, and in the world to come life everlasting" (Lu.18:29-30).

"I beseech you therefore, brethren, by the mercies of God, that ye present your bodies a living sacrifice, holy, acceptable unto God, *which is* your reasonable service. And be not conformed to this world: but be ye transformed by the renewing of your mind, that ye may prove what is that good, and acceptable, and perfect, will of God" (Ro.12:1-2).

"I am crucified with Christ: nevertheless I live; yet not I, but Christ liveth in me: and the life which I now live in the flesh I live by the faith of the Son of God, who loved me, and gave himself for me" (Ga.2:20).

"But what things were gain to me, those I counted loss for Christ. Yea doubtless, and I count all things *but* loss for the excellency of the knowledge of Christ Jesus my Lord: for whom I have suffered the loss of all things, and do count them *but* dung, that I may win Christ, And be found in him, not having mine own righteousness, which is of the law, but that which is through the faith of Christ, the righteousness which is of God by faith: That I may know him, and the power of his resurrection, and the fellowship of his sufferings, being made conformable unto his death; If by any means I might attain unto the resurrection of the dead" (Ph.3:7-11).

"My son, give me thine heart, and let thine eyes observe my ways" (Pr.23:26).

1. Deliverance through believing in God's mercy: A sign given in the name of Isaiah's child Shear-Jeshub
a. The situation taking place: Syria & Israel invaded Judah
  1) They failed to take Jerusalem but inflicted heavy losses, 2 K.16:5; 2 Chr.28:5-15
  2) They struck terror in the hearts of Ahaz & his people: They were shaken like trees struck by a fierce wind
b. The sign of God's deliverance
  1) Isaiah was told to take his son & go to Ahaz
  2) Isaiah's son's name, Shear-Jeshub, gave great hope, for it means *a remnant will return*
c. The assurance of God's deliverance
  1) They must take heed, be calm, not fear nor lose heart: The two enemies were only burned out firewood
  2) They must know that the enemies (Syria & Israel) had plotted evil: They were planning to conquer & split Judah's territory between them & to set up a puppet king
  3) They must rest assured: The enemies would fail, for the LORD would stop them
    • Because Syria & its capital Damascus were led by a mere man, King Rezin
    • Because Ephraim (Israel) would be completely destroyed—within 65 years
    • Because a mere man was also the head of Ephraim (Israel) & Samaria
d. The warning: Ahaz & his people must trust God or else face destruction
2. Deliverance through God's presence: A sign given in a virgin's child named Immanuel, *God with us*
a. God's offer to give Ahaz a

CHAPTER 7

E. The Deliverance from Threatening Enemies (Syria & Israel): Hope Given Through Five Clear Signs, 7:1–9:7

And it came to pass in the days of Ahaz the son of Jotham, the son of Uzziah, king of Judah, *that* Rezin the king of Syria, and Pekah the son of Remaliah, king of Israel, went up toward Jerusalem to war against it, but could not prevail against it.
2 And it was told the house of David, saying, Syria is confederate with Ephraim. And his heart was moved, and the heart of his people, as the trees of the wood are moved with the wind.
3 Then said the LORD unto Isaiah, Go forth now to meet Ahaz, thou, and Shear-jashub thy son, at the end of the conduit of the upper pool in the highway of the fuller's field;
4 And say unto him, Take heed, and be quiet; fear not, neither be fainthearted for the two tails of these smoking firebrands, for the fierce anger of Rezin with Syria, and of the son of Remaliah.
5 Because Syria, Ephraim, and the son of Remaliah, have taken evil counsel against thee, saying,
6 Let us go up against Judah, and vex it, and let us make a breach therein for us, and set a king in the midst of it, *even* the son of Tabeal:
7 Thus saith the Lord GOD, It shall not stand, neither shall it come to pass.
8 For the head of Syria *is* Damascus, and the head of Damascus *is* Rezin; and within threescore and five years shall Ephraim be broken, that it be not a people.
9 And the head of Ephraim *is* Samaria, and the head of Samaria *is* Remaliah's son. If ye will not believe, surely ye shall not be established.
10 Moreover the LORD spake again unto Ahaz, saying,
11 Ask thee a sign of the LORD thy God; ask it either in the depth, or in the height

above.
12 But Ahaz said, I will not ask, neither will I tempt the LORD.
13 And he said, Hear ye now, O house of David; *Is it* a small thing for you to weary men, but will ye weary my God also?
14 Therefore the Lord himself shall give you a sign; Behold, a virgin shall conceive, and bear a son, and shall call his name Immanuel.
15 Butter and honey shall he eat, that he may know to refuse the evil, and choose the good.
16 For before the child shall know to refuse the evil, and choose the good, the land that thou abhorrest shall be forsaken of both her kings.
17 The LORD shall bring upon thee, and upon thy people, and upon thy father's house, days that have not come, from the day that Ephraim departed from Judah; *even* the king of Assyria.
18 And it shall come to pass in that day, *that* the LORD shall hiss for the fly that *is* in the uttermost part of the rivers of Egypt, and for the bee that *is* in the land of Assyria.
19 And they shall come, and shall rest all of them in the desolate valleys, and in the holes of the rocks, and upon all thorns, and upon all bushes.
20 In the same day shall the Lord shave with a razor that is hired, *namely,* by them beyond the river, by the king of Assyria, the head, and the hair of the feet: and it shall also consume the beard.
21 And it shall come to pass in that day, *that* a man shall nourish a young cow, and two sheep;
22 And it shall come to pass, for the abundance of milk *that* they shall give he shall eat butter: for butter and honey shall every one eat that is left in the land.
23 And it shall come to pass in that day, *that* every place shall be, where there were a thousand vines at a thousand silverlings, it shall *even* be for briers and thorns.
24 With arrows and with bows shall *men* come thither; because all the land shall become briers and thorns.

sign: To stir belief
1) Ahaz's rejection: Had decided to trust Assyria instead of God, 2 K.16:5-7
2) Isaiah's rebuke: Ahaz had exhausted God's patience—due to his unbelief & rejection of God
b. God's sign—a virgin would bear a son named Immanuel, which means *God with us*: Fulfilled in Jesus Christ. Mt.1:22:23*DS1*
1) The child would be reared in poverty, in time of national crisis
2) The enemies—both Syria & Israel—would be destroyed while the child was still young, before he could discern right from wrong
c. God's warning of future judgment: Judah would face crises & the most severe suffering since its birth as a nation

1) *In that day*, the LORD would whistle for Egypt & Assyria to attack Judah
  • Would be like swarms of flies & bees
  • Would swarm over the whole countryside

2) *In that day*, the LORD would use Assyria to execute His judgment: Assyria would be like a razor, shaving off all hair—totally humiliating the people
3) *In that day*, a farmer would struggle to have one cow & two goats
  • The animals would produce milk
  • The milk (curds) & wild honey found would be enough to feed the few survivors remaining
4) *In that day*, the cultivated land would go to waste
  • The fruitful vineyards would be only briers & thorns
  • The land would become wild, good only for hunting wild game

- The cultivated farms would be overtaken by briers & thorns: Animals would graze in the fields, trampling down the soil

3. Deliverance through heeding God's warning of impending judgment: Symbolized in the name of Isaiah's child Maher-Shalal-Hash-Baz

a. The instructions of God to Isaiah: Was to publicly record (display) his son's name & to verify it by two witnesses

b. The sign of God's judgment: Isaiah's newborn son was to be named Maher-Shalal-Hash-Baz, which means *quick to plunder, swift to the spoil*

1) The child was a sign of coming judgment on Syria & Israel: Were to be destroyed by Assyria before the child could even speak (about two years)

2) The child was a sign of coming judgment on Judah: Had rejected the flowing waters of *Shiloah*, God's care & provision, 7:11-12; 2 K.16:5-7

c. The description of the coming judgment on Judah

1) Assyria would sweep across the land like the mighty floodwaters of the Euphrates River: Reach up to the neck (Jerusalem), but not totally drown the people

2) Assyria would be like a mighty bird of prey spreading its destructive power over all the land

d. The assurance of deliverance

1) The nations of the world would raise their war cry against Judah, but they would be broken, shattered

2) The reason destruction would take place: Because of Immanuel, *God with us* (7:14), & because the promised land is His, 8:8

4. Deliverance through spiritual separation: Symbolized in the

25 And *on* all hills that shall be digged with the mattock, there shall not come thither the fear of briers and thorns: but it shall be for the sending forth of oxen, and for the treading of lesser cattle.

CHAPTER 8

Moreover the LORD said unto me, Take thee a great roll, and write in it with a man's pen concerning Maher-shalal-hash-baz.
2 And I took unto me faithful witnesses to record, Uriah the priest, and Zechariah the son of Jeberechiah.
3 And I went unto the prophetess; and she conceived, and bare a son. Then said the LORD to me, Call his name Maher-shalal-hash-baz.
4 For before the child shall have knowledge to cry, My father, and my mother, the riches of Damascus and the spoil of Samaria shall be taken away before the king of Assyria.
5 The LORD spake also unto me again, saying,
6 Forasmuch as this people refuseth the waters of Shiloah that go softly, and rejoice in Rezin and Remaliah's son;
7 Now therefore, behold, the Lord bringeth up upon them the waters of the river, strong and many, *even* the king of Assyria, and all his glory: and he shall come up over all his channels, and go over all his banks:
8 And he shall pass through Judah; he shall overflow and go over, he shall reach *even* to the neck; and the stretching out of his wings shall fill the breadth of thy land, O Immanuel.
9 Associate yourselves, O ye people, and ye shall be broken in pieces; and give ear, all ye of far countries: gird yourselves, and ye shall be broken in pieces; gird yourselves, and ye shall be broken in pieces.
10 Take counsel together, and it shall come to nought; speak the word, and it shall not stand: for God *is* with us.
11 For the LORD spake thus to me with a strong hand, and

instructed me that I should not walk in the way of this people, saying,
12 Say ye not, A confederacy, to all *them to* whom this people shall say, A confederacy; neither fear ye their fear, nor be afraid.
13 Sanctify the LORD of hosts himself; and *let* him *be* your fear, and *let* him *be* your dread.
14 And he shall be for a sanctuary; but for a stone of stumbling and for a rock of offence to both the houses of Israel, for a gin and for a snare to the inhabitants of Jerusalem.
15 And many among them shall stumble, and fall, and be broken, and be snared, and be taken.
16 Bind up the testimony, seal the law among my disciples.
17 And I will wait upon the LORD, that hideth his face from the house of Jacob, and I will look for him.
18 Behold, I and the children whom the LORD hath given me *are* for signs and for wonders in Israel from the LORD of hosts, which dwelleth in mount Zion.
19 And when they shall say unto you, Seek unto them that have familiar spirits, and unto wizards that peep, and that mutter: should not a people seek unto their God? for the living to the dead?
20 To the law and to the testimony: if they speak not according to this word, *it is* because *there is* no light in them.
21 And they shall pass through it, hardly bestead and hungry: and it shall come to pass, that when they shall be hungry, they shall fret themselves, and curse their king and their God, and look upward.
22 And they shall look unto the earth; and behold trouble and darkness, dimness of anguish; and *they shall be* driven to darkness.

CHAPTER 9

Nevertheless the dimness *shall* not *be* such as *was* in her vexation, when at the first

names of Isaiah & his children

a. God's warning to Isaiah: Must not follow unbelievers

1) Isaiah (& true believers) must not fear the false accusations, criticisms, plots, & fears of unbelievers

2) Isaiah (& true believers) must fear only the LORD of hosts: He alone is holy

- Because He would be a sanctuary (refuge) for believers
- Because He would be a rock & a trap for unbelievers upon which they would stumble & fall & be captured

b. Isaiah's response to the LORD: He would record & share God's Word

c. Isaiah's strong personal testimony: He & his children were set apart to God

1) He trusted God, not man

2) He & his children were witnesses for the Lord: Their names were signs of God's salvation (Isaiah's name, 1:1), & of hope (7:3), & of judgment, 8:3-6

d. Isaiah's strong warning: The people must not seek counsel from the world of the occult but from God

1) The key question: How could the dead reveal the future for the living?

2) The occult—all counselors & prophets—must be tested by God's Word

3) The occult would lead people to a hopeless end, God's judgment: Assyria would conquer them

- They would suffer terribly
- They would become enraged, cursing the king & God
- They would be hopeless: See only distress, darkness, & gloom
- They would be cast into utter darkness, 2 Pe.2:17

5. Deliverance through God's light shining in the darkness of this world: Fulfilled in

God's child of redemption, Jesus Christ[DS2]

a. The promise of a bright, glorious future, Mt.4:13-16
  1) All gloom would be erased
  2) All the land (Galilee) would be honored
b. The hope for this glorious future: Found in a great light (Christ), Jn.8:12
  1) He would give light to all held in darkness & death
  2) He would enlarge or protect the nation of believers & increase their joy
  3) He would deliver all who were under the yoke of bondage or oppression
  4) He would bring peace to

he lightly afflicted the land of Zebulun and the land of Naphtali, and afterward did more grievously afflict *her by* the way of the sea, beyond Jordan, in Galilee of the nations.
2 The people that walked in darkness have seen a great light: they that dwell in the land of the shadow of death, upon them hath the light shined.
3 Thou hast multiplied the nation, *and* not increased the joy: they joy before thee according to the joy in harvest, *and* as *men* rejoice when they divide the spoil.
4 For thou hast broken the yoke of his burden, and the staff of his shoulder, the rod of his oppressor, as in the day of Midian.
5 For every battle of the

warrior *is* with confused noise, and garments rolled in blood; but *this* shall be with burning *and* fuel of fire.
6 For unto us a child is born, unto us a son is given: and the government shall be upon his shoulder: and his name shall be called Wonderful, Counsellor, The mighty God, The everlasting Father, The Prince of Peace.
7 Of the increase of *his* government and peace *there shall be* no end, upon the throne of David, and upon his kingdom, to order it, and to establish it with judgment and with justice from henceforth even for ever. The zeal of the LORD of hosts will perform this.

people & to the world

c. The Person who would bring this glorious future to earth: Jesus Christ
  1) He would come first as the God-Man
    • Humanity: *A child is born*
    • Deity: *A son is given*
  2) He would come to govern
  3) He would have four names
  4) He would return to establish God's kingdom on earth
    • Would rule in peace
    • Would rule on David's throne forever, fulfilling God's promise
    • Would establish perfect justice & righteousness
    • Would rule eternally
  5) His Word would be guaranteed by God's zeal

DIVISION I

THE PROPHECIES OF REBUKE AND HOPE GIVEN TO JUDAH AND JERUSALEM: AN OVERVIEW OF THE PRESENT AND FUTURE OF GOD'S PEOPLE, 1:1–12:6

E. The Deliverance from Threatening Enemies (Syria and Israel): Hope Given Through Five Clear Signs, 7:1–9:7

(7:1–9:7) **Introduction**: hope—having a great expectation within the heart—is one of the strongest forces on earth. Hope can bring about marvelous and unbelievable results. Great achievements are accomplished by people who have dreams and who are stirred to action by the hope that they can fulfill those dreams. Now think about the opposite of hope, about a person who is gripped by a sense of hopelessness. When hopelessness sets in, a person feels there is no future for him, no reason to dream, to aspire, to achieve, or to solve problems. Hopelessness demoralizes a person, makes him pessimistic, cynical, despondent, discouraged and often throws him into despair and depression. But not hope. Hope is the very opposite. When strong hope fills the heart of a person, the person looks to the future and believes that dreams can be accomplished. A longing within the person's soul is aroused to tackle the task, solve the problem, finish the project, and experience the joy of the dream.

Hope, having a dream of a bright and glorious future—this is the thrust of the present Scripture. The people of Judah and Jerusalem were facing a severe crisis, that of being attacked by Syria and the Northern Kingdom of Israel. For years these two nations had been bitter enemies, but the threat by Assyria aroused them to form an alliance. Apparently Syria and Israel strongly urged King Ahaz of Judah to join the alliance, but Ahaz refused. As a result, the coalition launched an invasion against Judah and set up a siege around the capital Jerusalem. Their purpose was to conquer the nation and to set up a puppet king who would support their rebellion against the Assyrian Empire. This is, *The Deliverance from Threatening Enemies (Syria and Israel): Hope Given Through Five Clear Signs*, 7:1–9:7.

1. Deliverance through believing in God's mercy: a sign given in the name of Isaiah's child Shear-Jeshub (7:1-9).
2. Deliverance through God's Presence: a sign given in a virgin's child named Immanuel, *God with us* (7:10-24).
3. Deliverance through heeding God's warning of impending judgment: symbolized in the name of Isaiah's child Maher-Shalal-Hash-Baz (8:1-10).
4. Deliverance through spiritual separation: symbolized in the names of Isaiah and his children (8:11-22).
5. Deliverance through God's light shining in the darkness of this world: fulfilled in God's child of redemption, Jesus Christ (9:1-7).

1 (7:1-9) **Deliverance, Source of, God's Promise—Mercy, Results of, Deliverance—Promise, to Israel, a Remnant—Hope, Given to Believers, a Remnant—Jews, Promises to, a Remnant—Signs, to Israel, a Remnant—Shear-Jeshub, Isaiah's Child, Meaning of Name—Isaiah, Children of—Israel, Alliances of, Syria—Northern Kingdom of Israel, Wars of, Invaded Judah**: when enemies threaten God's people, they can be delivered by God's mercy. God is by nature compassionate and caring, so when intimidating or frightening situations confront any of His people, He wants to deliver them. But He cannot act in their behalf unless they trust Him. In the present Scripture, a most serious threat confronted Judah

and King Ahaz, a threat that could result in the total collapse of the government and nation unless the people placed their complete trust in the LORD. Note the Scripture and outline:

OUTLINE	SCRIPTURE	SCRIPTURE	OUTLINE

1. **Deliverance through believing in God's mercy: A sign given in the name of Isaiah's child Shear-Jeshub**
a. The situation taking place: Syria & Israel invaded Judah
  1) They failed to take Jerusalem but inflicted heavy losses (2 K.16:5; 2 Chr.28:5-15)
  2) They struck terror in the hearts of Ahaz & his people: They were shaken like trees struck by a fierce wind
 	
b. The sign of God's deliverance
  1) Isaiah was told to take his son & go to Ahaz
  2) Isaiah's son's name, Shear-Jeshub, gave great hope, for it means *a remnant will return*
c. The assurance of God's deliverance
  1) They must take heed, be calm, not fear nor lose
	And it came to pass in the days of Ahaz the son of Jotham, the son of Uzziah, king of Judah, *that* Rezin the king of Syria, and Pekah the son of Remaliah, king of Israel, went up toward Jerusalem to war against it, but could not prevail against it.
	2 And it was told the house of David, saying, Syria is confederate with Ephraim. And his heart was moved, and the heart of his people, as the trees of the wood are moved with the wind.
	3 Then said the LORD unto Isaiah, Go forth now to meet Ahaz, thou, and Shear-jashub thy son, at the end of the conduit of the upper pool in the highway of the fuller's field;
	4 And say unto him, Take heed, and be quiet; fear not, neither be fainthearted for the two tails of these smoking
		firebrands, for the fierce anger of Rezin with Syria, and of the son of Remaliah.
		5 Because Syria, Ephraim, and the son of Remaliah, have taken evil counsel against thee, saying,
		6 Let us go up against Judah, and vex it, and let us make a breach therein for us, and set a king in the midst of it, *even* the son of Tabeal:
		7 Thus saith the Lord GOD, It shall not stand, neither shall it come to pass.
		8 For the head of Syria *is* Damascus, and the head of Damascus *is* Rezin; and within threescore and five years shall Ephraim be broken, that it be not a people.
		9 And the head of Ephraim *is* Samaria, and the head of Samaria *is* Remaliah's son. If ye will not believe, surely ye shall not be established.
			heart: The two enemies were only burned out firewood
			2) They must know that the enemies (Syria & Israel) had plotted evil: They were planning to conquer & split Judah's territory between them & to set up a puppet king
			
			3) They must rest assured: The enemies would fail, for the LORD would stop them
			• Because Syria & its capital Damascus were led by a mere man, King Rezin
			• Because Ephraim (Israel) would be completely destroyed—within 65 years
			• Because a mere man was also the head of Ephraim (Israel) & Samaria
			d. The warning: Ahaz & his people must trust God or else

a. The current situation involved an invasion of Judah by Syria and the Northern Kingdom of Israel (vv.1-2). Down through the centuries Israel and Syria (Aram) had been enemies, but they were now facing a very serious threat from the Assyrians who were seeking to build a worldwide empire. Therefore, to stand against the threat of Assyria, Israel and Syria formed a new alliance. Apparently, they encouraged Judah to join the alliance, but King Ahaz refused. When he rejected their proposal, they made the decision to march against Jerusalem to force the Jews to support their cause against Assyria. Although they failed in their attempt to conquer Jerusalem, they did inflict heavy losses on the army of Judah (see outline and notes—2 Chr.28:5-15 for more discussion. Also see 2 K.16:5.) Note that Egypt supported this alliance because it would provide a buffer zone between Egypt and the Assyrian Empire.

When news of the invasion reached King Ahaz and his people, they were stricken with terror and panic (v.2). Like trees shaken by a fierce wind, their hearts were churning. Anxiously running about, the people were in complete disorder and confusion, wavering and questioning their plans for defense. Ahaz, in a state of total fear himself, sent messengers to Tiglath-Pileser, king of Assyria, appealing for help to go up against the Syro-Ephramite alliance (see outline and notes—2 K.16:5-9 for more discussion). Instead of trusting God for deliverance, Ahaz was trusting *political power* and a human savior, the military might of the Assyrian king.

b. Aware of Ahaz's move to secure *political power,* the LORD commanded Isaiah to go to the King with a very special message concerning God's power to deliver His people (v.3). As a sign of God's power, Isaiah was told to take his son Shear-Jeshub with him. His son's name, Shear-Jeshub means *a remnant will return.* Thus God's power will always make sure that His people, even if only a small number, will survive any attack against them. A remnant will always live in the promised land of God. When Isaiah confronted King Ahaz, the king was inspecting the city's water supply, probably trying to figure out how to protect it from the enemy invaders. The king naturally saw Isaiah's son standing with his father. The son was the sign of God's deliverance, the wonderful promise of the LORD that "a remnant will return." But the sign was not the only message Isaiah was to deliver to the king.

c. God instructed Isaiah to assure the king of His deliverance if the people would just trust Him (vv.4-9). A threefold assurance was to be given:

  1) King Ahaz and the people must take heed, watch them and not worry. They were to be calm and not fear nor lose heart. In God's eyes the two enemies were like burned out firewood (v.4).

  2) King Ahaz and the people must know that the enemies had plotted evil against them (v.5). The Northern Kingdom and Syria were planning to conquer and split Judah's territory between themselves. They were actually plotting to eliminate the dynasty of David and to set up a puppet king who would join their alliance against Assyria. This puppet king was to be the son of Tibeel, probably a relative of King Rezin of Syria.

  3) King Ahaz and the people must rest assured that the two enemies would fail. The attack would not take place. First, it would not happen because Syria and its capital Damascus were led by a mere man, King Rezin (vv.7-9). The LORD Himself would stop them. In fact, King Rezin would be Syria's (Aram's) last king, for Assyria would conquer Syria soon thereafter.

Second, the LORD would stop them because Ephraim (Israel) would be completely destroyed within 65 years (v.8). Isaiah was proclaiming this prophecy in 734 B.C., so 65 years later would be 669 B.C. And exactly as Isaiah predicted, the Northern Kingdom was completely destroyed in 669 B.C. In 722 B.C. Assyria conquered the Northern Kingdom of Israel and deported many of the captives, scattering them throughout the empire (2 K.17:24). However, it was later when more foreigners were moved into Israel (669 B.C.) by the Assyrian king Ashurbanipal (Ezr.4:10) that the demise of the Northern Kingdom was sealed. These settlers naturally intermarried with the few Israelites who had been left behind to maintain the economy for Assyria. The results of the intermarriage were a people who became known as the *Samaritans* (see outline and note—2 K.17:24-41 for more discussion).

Isaiah's prediction was a startling prophecy. Just think! He had predicted Israel's total demise within 65 years, which was the exact time that Ephraim or Israel was so shattered they could never again be a distinct people.

Third, the LORD would stop them because a mere man was also the head of Ephraim (Israel and Samaria), the capital of Israel (v.9). God was promising that the king of Judah would never belong to the Northern Kingdom of Israel. Of course, this meant that the alliance of Syria and Israel would not conquer Jerusalem.

Isaiah was also to deliver a clear warning to King Ahaz and his people (v.9b): they must trust God or else face destruction. Their destiny was to be determined by their faith in the LORD. If Ahaz and the people believed the LORD, they would be delivered by the LORD. But if they did not believe Him, they would be doomed to destruction.

Thought 1. God is merciful. Therefore when enemies attack us, God wants to have mercy upon us and deliver us. When His mercy is showered upon us, we will be delivered from the threat of enemies. But if His mercy is withheld, we are left on our own, without His help. His supernatural power and His deliverance will not be available. His mercy will be withheld.

What determines whether or not God's mercy is poured out upon us? What is it that determines whether or not God delivers us? It is our faith, our believing and trusting Him to deliver us. When enemies attack us, if we will call out to the LORD for mercy, He will deliver us. God will pour out His compassion upon us.

⇒   If an enemy dislikes, ridicules, mocks, hates, opposes, degrades, or does evil things against us, God will have mercy and deliver us.

⇒   If accidents, diseases, financial difficulties, unemployment, divorce, the death of a loved one, or a host of other hardships or misfortunes attack us, God will have mercy and deliver us.

No matter who or what the enemy is that threatens us, God longs to have mercy upon us. He longs to deliver us. This is the promise of His Holy Word:

"As he spake by the mouth of his holy prophets, which have been since the world began: That we should be saved from our enemies, and from the hand of all that hate us; To perform the mercy *promised* to our fathers, and to remember his holy covenant; The oath which he sware to our father Abraham, That he would grant unto us, that we being delivered out of the hand of our enemies might serve him without fear, In holiness and righteousness before him, all the days of our life" (Lu.1:70-75).

"Not by works of righteousness which we have done, but according to his mercy he saved us, by the washing of regeneration, and renewing of the Holy Ghost; Which he shed on us abundantly through Jesus Christ our Saviour; That being justified by his grace, we should be made heirs according to the hope of eternal life" (Tit.3:5-7).

"For if ye turn again unto the LORD, your brethren and your children *shall find* compassion before them that lead them captive, so that they shall come again into this land: for the LORD your God *is* gracious and merciful, and will not turn away *his* face from you, if ye return unto him" (2 Chr.30:9).

"My mercy will I keep for him for evermore, and my covenant shall stand fast with him" (Ps.89:28).

"But the mercy of the LORD *is* from everlasting to everlasting upon them that fear him, and his righteousness unto children's children" (Ps.103:17).

"For a small moment have I forsaken thee; but with great mercies will I gather thee" (Is.54:7).

"Go and proclaim these words toward the north, and say, Return, thou backsliding Israel, saith the LORD; *and* I will not cause mine anger to fall upon you: for I *am* merciful, saith the LORD, *and* I will not keep *anger* for ever" (Je.3:12).

"*It is of* the LORD's mercies that we are not consumed, because his compassions fail not. *They are* new every morning: great *is* thy faithfulness" (La.3:22-23).

"Who *is* a God like unto thee, that pardoneth iniquity, and passeth by the transgression of the remnant of his heritage? he retaineth not his anger for ever, because he delighteth *in* mercy" (Mi.7:18).

2 (7:10-25) **Deliverance, Source, God's Presence—Promise, to Believers, the Messiah—Messiah, Prophecy Concerning, Virgin Birth—Virgin Birth, Predicted—Immanuel, Predicted—Deliverance, Source, Christ—Prophecy, Concerning Christ, Virgin Birth—Enemies, Deliverance from, by Christ**: when enemies threaten God's people, they can be delivered by God's presence. King Ahaz refused to believe God's promise. If he had trusted the LORD, he would have broken his alliance with Assyria and led the people to seek the LORD for deliverance. But Ahaz was an unbeliever, a leader who put his total trust in the arm of the flesh, the power of military alliances. Thus the LORD determined to send a second sign to King Ahaz, a sign that is one of the great promises of Holy Scripture. This sign would be that a child would be born to a virgin. The name of the child would be Immanuel, which means *God with us* (v.14).

OUTLINE	SCRIPTURE	SCRIPTURE	OUTLINE

2. Deliverance through God's presence: A sign given in a virgin's child named Immanuel, *God with us*
 a. God's offer to give Ahaz a sign: To stir belief
  1) Ahaz's rejection: Had decided to trust Assyria instead of God, 2 K.16:5-7
  2) Isaiah's rebuke: Ahaz had exhausted God's patience—due to his unbelief & rejection of God
 	
 b. God's sign—a virgin would bear a son named Immanuel, which means *God with us*: Fulfilled in Jesus Christ (Mt.1:22:23)^DS1
  1) The child would be reared in poverty, in time of national crisis
 	
  2) The enemies—both Syria & Israel—would be destroyed while the child was still young, before he could discern right from wrong
 c. God's warning of future judgment: Judah would face devastating crises & the most severe suffering since its birth as a nation
 	
  1) *In that day*, the LORD would whistle for Egypt & Assyria to attack Judah
  • Would be like swarms of flies & bees
  • Would swarm over the
	10 Moreover the LORD spake again unto Ahaz, saying,
	11 Ask thee a sign of the LORD thy God; ask it either in the depth, or in the height above.
	12 But Ahaz said, I will not ask, neither will I tempt the LORD.
	13 And he said, Hear ye now, O house of David; *Is it* a small thing for you to weary men, but will ye weary my God also?
	14 Therefore the Lord himself shall give you a sign; Behold, a virgin shall conceive, and bear a son, and shall call his name Immanuel.
	15 Butter and honey shall he eat, that he may know to refuse the evil, and choose the good.
	16 For before the child shall know to refuse the evil, and choose the good, the land that thou abhorrest shall be forsaken of both her kings.
	17 The LORD shall bring upon thee, and upon thy people, and upon thy father's house, days that have not come, from the day that Ephraim departed from Judah; *even* the king of Assyria.
	18 And it shall come to pass in that day, *that* the LORD shall hiss for the fly that *is* in the uttermost part of the rivers of Egypt, and for the bee that *is* in the land of Assyria.
		19 And they shall come, and shall rest all of them in the desolate valleys, and in the holes of the rocks, and upon all thorns, and upon all bushes.
		20 In the same day shall the Lord shave with a razor that is hired, *namely*, by them beyond the river, by the king of Assyria, the head, and the hair of the feet: and it shall also consume the beard.
		21 And it shall come to pass in that day, *that* a man shall nourish a young cow, and two sheep;
		22 And it shall come to pass, for the abundance of milk *that* they shall give he shall eat butter: for butter and honey shall every one eat that is left in the land.
		23 And it shall come to pass in that day, *that* every place shall be, where there were a thousand vines at a thousand silverlings, it shall *even* be for briers and thorns.
		24 With arrows and with bows shall *men* come thither; because all the land shall become briers and thorns.
		25 And *on* all hills that shall be digged with the mattock, there shall not come thither the fear of briers and thorns: but it shall be for the sending forth of oxen, and for the treading of lesser cattle.
			whole countryside
			
			 2) *In that day*, the LORD would use Assyria to execute His judgment: Assyria would be like a razor, shaving off all hair—totally humiliating the people
			
			 3) *In that day*, a farmer would struggle to have one cow & two goats
			
			  • The animals would produce milk
			  • The milk (curds) & wild honey found would be enough to feed the few survivors remaining
			 4) *In that day*, the cultivated land would go to waste
			  • The fruitful vineyards would be only briers & thorns
			
			  • The land would become wild, good only for hunting wild game
			
			  • The cultivated farms would be overtaken by briers & thorns: Animals would graze in the fields, trampling down the soil

a. Because Ahaz had continued in unbelief, the LORD soon sent Isaiah with a second message for the king (vv.11-13). In a last attempt to stir belief within Ahaz, the LORD made an unusual offer to the king. Ahaz could ask the LORD for a supernatural sign. No matter what the sign was, God would grant the king's request. But Ahaz rejected the offer, using the excuse that he would not put the LORD to a test. In this statement, the king was exposing a wicked, hypocritical heart. Although God's Word forbids putting the LORD to a test (De.6:16), this offer was being made by God Himself. When God makes a promise to a person, that individual is not putting God to a test by claiming the promise. Ahaz's refusal was not due to his concern for obeying God's Word. Ahaz was an evil ruler, a man who wanted nothing to do with God. He had even barricaded the door of the temple, disallowing worship therein (2 Chr.28:24). His real reason for rejecting the offer of the LORD was that he had already decided to trust Assyria, not the LORD (2 K.16:5-7). When Ahaz rejected God's offer, righteous anger surged through Isaiah's body and he immediately rebuked the king. Ahaz had exhausted God's patience because of his unbelief and rejection of the LORD.

b. Whether Ahaz wanted a sign or not, the LORD was going to give a sign and the sign would be supernatural. Furthermore, the sign would not be for Ahaz's benefit but, rather, for the benefit of the whole "house of David." Note that this sign would be given by the LORD Himself. The sign would be that of a virgin who would bear a son named Imman-uel, meaning *God with us*. (vv.14-16). Of course, we may assume that this sign had an *immediate fulfillment* for the king and the people of that day. Most likely Isaiah's wife was a virgin before she conceived her first son, or else some other virgin woman would get married and bear a son whom she and the father would name "God with us." Throughout the years while the child grew into manhood, people would be reminded of God's promise to always be with them if they would simply trust Him. Note that the child would be reared in poverty, reared during a time when only the curds of milk and honey were available for food. It would be a time of national crisis. Notice, too, the promise of God: when the child was old enough to know right from wrong, approximately a two-year period, both Syria and Israel would be destroyed. What a wonderful promise from the LORD to King Ahaz and the people of Judah.

But even more wonderful is the *ultimate fulfillment* of this prophecy, which is given to the people of all succeeding generations. The prophecy finds its ultimate fulfillment in Jesus Christ, who was born of the virgin Mary (Mt.1:22-23; see DEEPER STUDY #1—Is.7:14 for more discussion).

c. After explaining this second sign, the prophet Isaiah warned King Ahaz of God's future judgment (vv.17-25). Although Judah would escape destruction by Syria and Israel, the nation would face the most severe crises of its history. The people would soon suffer the worst enemy attacks they had ever known, the worst suffering since the birth of the nation when the ten tribes broke away.

   1) *In that day*—the day of God's judgment—the LORD would whistle for Egypt and Assyria to attack Judah (vv.18-19). Like swarms of flies and bees, enemy soldiers would cover the whole countryside of Judah. Throughout Ahaz's reign, he continued to trust Assyria for help during raids and attacks by surrounding nations. Assyria responded to Ahaz's appeal, accepting a large fee for Assyrian protection. However, the Assyrian king Tiglath-Pileaser ended up oppressing Ahaz instead of helping him (see outline and note—2 Chr.28:16-21 for more discussion). Throughout the days of Ahaz, the Assyrians caused enormous problems for Judah. And in the days of Hezekiah, Assyria finally invaded Judah because the king sought to make an alliance with Egypt against Assyria (see outline and notes—Is.30:1-14 for more discussion).

   2) *In that day*—the day of God's judgment—the LORD would use Assyria to execute His judgment against Judah (v.20). The people would suffer utter humiliation at the hands of the Assyrians. The enemy would be like a razor, shaving off the hair of their captives, totally humiliating them.

   3) *In that day*—the day of God's judgment—the people would also suffer utter depravation at the hands of the Assyrians (vv.21-22). A farmer would struggle to have one cow and two sheep. The milk they produce will be enough to sustain the survivors remaining in the land. They would have only a small amount of milk curds and wild honey to eat.

   4) *In that day*—the day of God's judgment—the cultivated land would be utterly wasted (vv.23-25). Fruitful vineyards would be overtaken by briars and thorns. The land would become wild, good only for honey and wild game. As for the cultivated farms, they too would be overtaken by briars and thorns. Only animals would graze in the fields, trampling down the soil.

Thought 1. When enemies attack us, we have the most wonderful promise. The LORD's *presence* will deliver us. If we trust Jesus Christ as our Savior and walk in His righteousness, we can call upon Him for deliverance. And He will deliver us. No matter how fierce the enemy attack may be, the Lord Jesus Christ has the power to rescue us. He can empower us to walk through the most terrifying danger, the power to conquer and overcome any enemy. A victorious life—triumphing over all enemies—is the promise given us through Jesus Christ.

   "For where two or three are gathered together in my name, there am I in the midst of them" (Mt.18:20).
   "Go ye therefore, and teach all nations, baptizing them in the name of the Father, and of the Son, and of the Holy Ghost: Teaching them to observe all things whatsoever I have commanded you: and, lo, I am with you alway, *even* unto the end of the world. Amen" (Mt.28:19-20).
   "*Let your* conversation [behavior, conduct] *be* without covetousness; *and be* content with such things as ye have: for he hath said, I will never leave thee, nor forsake thee. So that we may boldly say, The Lord *is* my helper, and I will not fear what man shall do unto me" (He.13:5-6).
   "And, behold, I *am* with thee, and will keep thee in all *places* whither thou goest, and will bring thee again into this land; for I will not leave thee, until I have done *that* which I have spoken to thee of" (Ge.28:15).
   "And he said, My presence shall go *with thee*, and I will give thee rest" (Ex.33:14).
   "When thou goest out to battle against thine enemies, and seest horses, and chariots, *and* a people more than thou, be not afraid of them: for the LORD thy God *is* with thee, which brought thee up out of the land of Egypt" (De.20:1).
   "The LORD *is* my strength and my shield; my heart trusted in him, and I am helped: therefore my heart greatly rejoiceth; and with my song will I praise him" (Ps.28:7).
   "But I *am* poor and needy; *yet* the Lord thinketh upon me: thou *art* my help and my deliverer; make no tarrying, O my God" (Ps.40:17).
   "Fear thou not; for I *am* with thee: be not dismayed; for I *am* thy God: I will strengthen thee; yea, I will help thee; yea, I will uphold thee with the right hand of my righteousness" (Is.41:10).
   "Fear not: for I have redeemed thee, I have called *thee* by thy name; thou *art* mine. When thou passest through the waters, I *will be* with thee; and through the rivers, they shall not overflow thee: when thou walkest through the fire, thou shalt not be burned; neither shall the flame kindle upon thee" (Is.43:1-2).

DEEPER STUDY # 1

(7:14) **Virgin Birth, of Christ, Discussed—Jesus Christ, Virgin Birth—Deity, of Christ, Importance—Divine Nature, of Christ, Virgin Birth—Deity, of Christ—Immanuel, Name of Christ—Prophecy, of Christ, Virgin Birth**: the virgin birth of the Messiah or Savior, the Lord Jesus Christ, is one of the major doctrines of the Bible. Because of its importance, it cannot be overstressed. Note these facts about the prophecy of the virgin birth:

1. The Lord Himself was to give *the sign. The sign* did not refer to the prophecy but to the *given Child*. Scripture is saying that the Lord Himself would send the Child to the world. Or, to state it another way, the child would come to the people as a *sign* or *gift* from God Himself.

2. The *coming* of the Child would be a *sign*. That is, His coming was to be very significant for the people. Therefore, the people must pay attention, for God was sending the Child to earth for the very purpose of being a *gift*, a *sign* for the people.

3. The word *behold* (*hinneh*) grabs the attention of the reader, stressing the importance of what is being said. *Behold* means to look closely, to pay close attention, to watch carefully. What was being predicted is of utmost importance. What was the prediction? The most significant birth of all times was being announced.

4. The *sign* was given to the whole house of David, which means everyone (see v.13). The word "you" in verse 14 is plural, indicating that every person throughout the nation was to pay attention to the sign. By strong implication, the sign was being given to the *house of humanity*.

5. The virgin was to *conceive and bear a son*. First, note the definite article "the" (NIV) before "virgin" (*ha almah*). This indicates that "the virgin" or unmarried woman was a person formerly referred to or promised. Henry Morris suggests that she is the mother of the "promised seed" who was to crush the head of the serpent or devil (Ge.3:15).[1] Of course, the *promised seed* is a clear reference to Jesus Christ, the promised Messiah who destroyed the works of the devil (Ga.3:16, 19; also see Jn.12:30-31; He.2:14-15; 1 Jn.3:8). Of extreme significance is this fact: if Jesus Christ had not been born of a virgin, He would have been a mere man who needed a savior as much as any other person. Consequently, He could not have died for the sins of mankind nor destroyed him who held the power of death, that is, the devil.

6. In his excellent commentary *The Book of Isaiah*, Edward J. Young states that the definite article "the" used with the word '*almah* is used in a generic sense, pointing to a particular yet unknown person. He says:

> Isaiah's purpose is to distinguish the '*almah* from some other kind of woman. As though he were to say, "It is not an old woman or a married woman which I behold in vision, not a bride or a girl necessarily, but an '*almah*." Hence, in our English translation we may best bring out Isaiah's force by the indefinite article. By this means the prophet focuses the attention upon the '*almah*.
>
> At the outset we may confidently assert that the word '*almah* is never employed of a married woman. At least one of these occurrences makes it clear that the word may designate one who is truly a virgin (Gen.24:43). Rebekah is called an '*almah*, but she is furthermore designated a b^ethulah, and it is said of her that a man had not known her. In one passage, namely, Proverbs 30:19, the word '*almah* may signify an immoral girl, but it does not indicate a married girl. Perhaps the closest equivalent in English is the word damsel or maiden. Neither of these is generally employed of a married woman. Yet even these words may not be precise equivalents, for whereas they could possibly refer to married women, '*almah* does not do so. For these reasons it may be wisest, after all, to render '*almah* in English by "virgin."[2]

7. In the six usages of the Hebrew word '*almah*, H.C. Leupold points out the following facts:

Ge.24:43— The whole context surrounding this verse clearly indicates that Rebecca is a virgin.
Ex.2:8— Again, the whole context surrounding this verse implies that Miriam, Moses' sister, is a virgin.
Ps.68:25— This verse refers to women with honorable reputations. They are women who are worthy or qualified to participate in religious services.
Song of S.1:3— This woman is worthy to be desired by King Solomon. Her reputation is not questionable.
Song of S.6:8— These women stand over queens and concubines in moral purity; therefore the fact that they are virgins is implied.
Pr.30:19— This passage includes the expression, "the way of a man with a maiden." But then immediately there is a contrast with the adulteress (v.20), which places the maiden in the category of the un-blemished.

Mr. Leupold concludes his position with this comment: "Adding up the results of this investigation we conclude that '*almah* in Hebrew signifies a marriageable young lady of unblemished reputation. It cannot be denied that such a one is to be classified as a virgin."[3] Note the scholarly strength of Mr. Leupold's position.

8. The Messiah or Savior had to be born of a virgin, completely apart from a human father. If He had not been, He simply would have been another man. As a mere man, He would have needed a Savior as much as any other person. But since Jesus Christ was given birth by the Holy Spirit of God (the divine nature) through Mary (the human nature), He is the God-Man. His nature is perfect, the divine-human nature. Christ's nature is totally different from the nature of any other created being. He is the Perfect Being, the sinless Person who has been raised from the dead (due to His sinless, holy nature) and given the perfect body. As the perfect, sinless Person, Jesus Christ stands before the human race as the Ideal Man. He is the *Pattern* of what all people should be. As the Ideal Man, He could pay the penalty for the sins of every person. His death would thereby become the Ideal Death and cover the penalty for everyone. Through His death, every person can be set free from the penalty of rebellion against God and become acceptable to God.

Again, this is the critical importance of the virgin birth. If Jesus Christ had been *mere man*, He would have needed a Savior as much as any of us do. But since He was born of a virgin by the Spirit of God coming upon Mary, He is the God-Man. As the God-Man, he was able to live as a human being and to secure righteousness—a sinless perfection—for us. Because He kept His divine nature and entered the world through a virgin, He was able to live a sinless life *and* to die for us. Thereby, He is able to save us from our sins and make us acceptable to God. The words of Warren W. Wiersbe state it well.

> Of course, the ultimate fulfillment of this prophecy is in our Lord Jesus Christ, who is "God with us" (Matt.1:18-25; Luke 1:31-35). The virgin birth of Christ is a key doctrine; for if Jesus Christ is not God come in sinless human flesh, then we have no Savior. Jesus had to be born of a virgin, apart from human generation, because He existed before his mother. He was not just born in this world; he came down from heaven into the world (John 3:13; 6:33; 41-42, 50-51, 58). Jesus was sent by the Father and therefore came into the world having a human mother but not a human father (4:34; 5:23-24, 30; 9:4).[4]

---

1 Henry M. Morris, *The Genesis Record*. (Grand Rapids, MI: Baker Book House, 1996), p.122.
2 Edward J. Young. *The Book of Isaiah*, Vol.1. (Grand Rapids, MI: Eerdmans Publishing Co., 1965), p.287.
3 H.C. Leupold, *Exposition of Isaiah*, Vol. 1, p.156.
4 Warren W. Wiersbe. *Be Comforted*. (Wheaton, IL: Victor Books, 1992), p.33.

9. The Son was to be named Immanuel, meaning *God with us*. As long as this particular Son was known by people, they would be reminded that God was always present with them and caring for them. When a person is honest as well as skilled in studying and understanding the Scripture, it is difficult to understand how he can deny that the clear meaning of *'almah* in Isaiah's mind (and the LORD God of Scripture) is *virgin*.

> *While, technically, virgin is not required, the context clearly necessitates the usage as it suggests something extraordinary....In the New Testament, both Matt. 1:23 and Luke 1:27 have* parthenos *(GED #3795), making it clear that the Messiah was born of a* virgin.*"5*

> **"Behold, a virgin [parthenos] shall be with child, and shall bring forth a son, and they shall call his name Emmanuel, which being interpreted is, God with us" (Mt.1:23).**
> **"To a virgin [parthenon] espoused to a man whose name was Joseph, of the house of David; and the virgin's name *was* Mary" (Lu.1:27).**

> *Primarily "parthenos" [virgin] denotes "an unmarried girl" in secular greek. Gradually through usage, the word's range of meaning narrowed and it came to refer specifically to a young girl who had not had sexual relations. Another term for any young woman, married or not, is neanis. Parthenos, however, was usually reserved for "virgin."6*

---

[3] **(8:1-10) Judgment, Symbols of, Isaiah's Child—Judgment, Deliverance from, by God—Deliverance, Source, Heeding God's Word**: when enemies threaten God's people, they can be delivered by heeding God's warnings of impending judgment. After King Ahaz's second refusal to heed God's warning, God gave the people a third sign. However, this time the sign was a fourfold warning that judgment lay just over the horizon. Again, this sign was symbolized in the name of one of Isaiah's children, a son named Maher-Shalal-Hash-Baz. Note the Scripture and outline:

OUTLINE	SCRIPTURE	SCRIPTURE	OUTLINE
	CHAPTER 8	son; 7 Now therefore, behold, the Lord bringeth up upon them the waters of the river, strong and many, *even* the king of Assyria, and all his glory: and he shall come up over all his channels, and go over all his banks:	ing judgment on Judah 1) Assyria would sweep across the land like the mighty floodwaters of the Euphrates River: Reach up to the neck (Jerusalem), but not totally drown the people
3. Deliverance through heeding God's warning of impending judgment: Symbolized in the name of Isaiah's child Maher-Shalal-Hash-Baz a. The instructions of God to Isaiah: Was to publicly record (display) his son's name & to verify it by two witnesses	Moreover the LORD said unto me, Take thee a great roll, and write in it with a man's pen concerning Maher-shalal-hash-baz. 2 And I took unto me faithful witnesses to record, Uriah the priest, and Zechariah the son of Jeberechiah.		
b. The sign of God's judgment: Isaiah's newborn son was to be named Maher-Shalal-Hash-Baz, which means *quick to plunder, swift to the spoil*	3 And I went unto the prophetess; and she conceived, and bare a son. Then said the LORD to me, Call his name Maher-shalal-hash-baz.	8 And he shall pass through Judah; he shall overflow and go over, he shall reach *even* to the neck; and the stretching out of his wings shall fill the breadth of thy land, O Immanuel.	2) Assyria would be like a mighty bird of prey spreading its destructive power over all the land
1) The child was a sign of coming judgment on Syria & Israel: Were to be destroyed by Assyria before the child could even speak (about two years)	4 For before the child shall have knowledge to cry, My father, and my mother, the riches of Damascus and the spoil of Samaria shall be taken away before the king of Assyria.	9 Associate yourselves, O ye people, and ye shall be broken in pieces; and give ear, all ye of far countries: gird yourselves, and ye shall be broken in pieces; gird yourselves, and ye shall be broken in pieces.	d. The assurance of deliverance 1) The nations of the world would raise their war cry against Judah, but they would be broken, shattered
2) The child was a sign of coming judgment on Judah: Had rejected the flowing waters of *Shiloah*, God's care & provision, see 7:11-12; 2 K.16:5-7 c. The description of the com-	5 The LORD spake also unto me again, saying, 6 Forasmuch as this people refuseth the waters of Shiloah that go softly, and rejoice in Rezin and Remaliah's	10 Take counsel together, and it shall come to nought; speak the word, and it shall not stand: for God *is* with us.	2) The reason destruction would take place: Because of Immanuel, *God with us* (7:14), & because the promised land is His (8:8)

a. Even before this particular son of Isaiah was born, God instructed the prophet to record the child's name on a large scroll. He was to take the scroll to Uriah the priest and Zechariah the father-in-law of King Ahaz (2 Chr.29:1). They were to witness that the name had been written down before the child was born. These two witnesses were unbelievers who served as chief officials to King Ahaz. Uriah the priest (a false priest) had helped Ahaz build a heathen altar in the temple area (2 K.16:10-16). By having these two unbelieving officials sign the document, their signatures would prove once the judgment of God actually fell that God had forewarned the people. His Word would be proven true. Therefore, the people needed to heed His warnings when they were issued.

---

5 *The Old Testament Hebrew-English Dictionary*, NUN—AYIN. "The Complete Biblical Library." (Springfield, MO: World Library Press Inc., 1999), #6183, p.516.
6 *The New Testament-English, PI-RHO*. "The Complete Biblical Library." (Springfield, MO: World Library Press Inc, 1991), #3795, p.91.

b. In mercy, God gave a third sign, a third warning to the people of Judah. Judgment was at hand unless they heeded His Word, repented and turned back to Him (vv.3-6). In fulfillment of the sign, when Isaiah slept with his wife (a prophetess) she conceived and gave birth to a son. As the LORD had instructed, Isaiah named his son Maher-Shalal-Hash-Baz, which is the longest name in the Bible. The child's name means quick to plunder, swift to the spoil. The child was a sign of coming judgment upon Syria and Israel. Even before the child could speak—about one or two years old—these two nations were to be destroyed by Assyria. As pointed out above, Assyria attacked both Damascus (Syria) and Samaria (Israel), plundering the wealth of both nations. This means that Isaiah's prophecy was given somewhere around 734 B.C.[7]

But the child also served as a sign of coming judgment upon the people of Judah (vv.5-6). They had rejected the gentle waters of *Shiloah*, apparently a small stream somewhere around Jerusalem. The descriptive phrase *flowing waters* is a picture of God's care and provision for His people down through the centuries. Instead of trusting the LORD's care and provision, they were focused on rejoicing over the deaths of the Syrian king Rezin and the Israelite king Pekah. Both men died in defense of their country against Assyria.

c. Because the people rejected the LORD, Isaiah described the coming judgment (vv.7-8). God would send upon them the mighty army of Assyria because they rejected the gentle flowing waters of *Shiloah*—the LORD's care and provision. Like the mighty floodwaters of the Euphrates River, the war machine of Assyria would sweep across the land of Judah. And note, the floodwaters would reach all the way up to the neck (that is, Jerusalem), meaning that the waters would nearly, but not totally, drown the people. Assyria would be like a mighty bird of prey: its outspread wings would spread its destructive power over all the land. Only Jerusalem would escape the coming devastation. However, the people behind its walls would experience terrible suffering. Note the reference to the land, that it belonged to Immanuel (v.8). Despite the judgment and devastation, the Lord still possessed the land. Immanuel—God's presence—guaranteed that God had not forgotten His people. Even in the midst of judgment, the LORD would be with the true believer, strengthening him to walk through the judgment.

d. God gave great assurance of deliverance to His people, to the genuine believers (vv.9-10). The nations of the world would raise their war cry against Judah; but these nations would be broken, shattered, and destroyed. They would plan their strategies, yet their plans would prove futile. Immanuel (the LORD) would be with His people (7:14) and the promised land was His (8:8).

Thought 1. God warns us of His wrath to come. The terrifying Day of Judgment is imminent for all who oppose God's people and stand against them. When a person threatens us—whether verbally or physically—he will face the terrifying judgment of God. No mistreatment or injustice escapes the eye of God, especially the abuse of people and, in particular, genuine believers. If we refuse to heed God's warnings, we will not escape. Listen to His warning of terrifying judgment:

"The Lord knoweth how to deliver the godly out of temptations, and to reserve the unjust unto the day of judgment to be punished" (2 Pe.2:9).

"But the heavens and the earth, which are now, by the same word are kept in store, reserved unto fire against the day of judgment and perdition of ungodly men" (2 Pe.3:7).

"Behold, the Lord cometh with ten thousands of his saints, To execute judgment upon all, and to convince all that are ungodly among them of all their ungodly deeds which they have ungodly committed, and of all their hard *speeches* which ungodly sinners have spoken against him" (Jude 14-15).

"Behold, he cometh with clouds; and every eye shall see him, and they *also* which pierced him: and all kindreds of the earth shall wail because of him. Even so, Amen" (Re.1:7).

"And I saw a great white throne, and him that sat on it, from whose face the earth and the heaven fled away; and there was found no place for them. And I saw the dead, small and great, stand before God; and the books were opened: and another book was opened, which is *the book* of life: and the dead were judged out of those things which were written in the books, according to their works. And the sea gave up the dead which were in it; and death and hell delivered up the dead which were in them: and they were judged every man according to their works. And death and hell were cast into the lake of fire. This is the second death. And whosoever was not found written in the book of life was cast into the lake of fire" (Re.20:11-15).

---

4 (8:11-22) **Deliverance, Source, Spiritual Separation—Spiritual Separation, Results, Deliverance—Isaiah, Children, Witnesses for the LORD—Isaiah, Name, a Witness for the LORD—Warning, of God, Given to Isaiah—Believers, Warning, to Be Spiritually Separate—Occult, World of, Warning Against**: when enemies threaten God's people, they are delivered by *spiritual separation*. This truth was clearly symbolized in the name of Isaiah and in the names of his children, for he and his children were *set apart* to serve God. Despite the wonderful promise of the LORD to be with His people, the vast majority still refused to turn their lives over to the LORD. King Ahaz and his leaders still looked to Assyria instead of to the LORD for protection from the threat by Syria and Israel. Sadly, most of the population supported the pro-Assyrian party. But not Isaiah. He opposed all foreign alliances, placing his full trust in the LORD and encouraging the people to trust the LORD as well. He alone could deliver them (7:9; 28:16; 30:15).

---

7 John F. Walvoord and Roy B. Zuck, Editors. *The Bible Knowledge Commentary*, p.1050.

OUTLINE	SCRIPTURE	SCRIPTURE	OUTLINE
4. Deliverance through spiritual separation: Symbolized in the names of Isaiah & his children a. God's warning to Isaiah: Must not follow unbelievers 1) Isaiah (& true believers) must not fear the false accusations, criticisms, plots, & fears of unbelievers 2) Isaiah (& true believers) must fear only the LORD of hosts: He alone is holy • Because He would be a sanctuary (refuge) for believers • Because He would be a rock & a trap for unbelievers upon which they would stumble & fall & be captured b. Isaiah's response to the LORD: He would record & share God's Word c. Isaiah's strong personal testimony: He & his children were set apart to God 1) He trusted God, not man	11 For the LORD spake thus to me with a strong hand, and instructed me that I should not walk in the way of this people, saying, 12 Say ye not, A confederacy, to all *them to* whom this people shall say, A confederacy; neither fear ye their fear, nor be afraid. 13 Sanctify the LORD of hosts himself; and *let* him *be* your fear, and *let* him *be* your dread. 14 And he shall be for a sanctuary; but for a stone of stumbling and for a rock of offence to both the houses of Israel, for a gin and for a snare to the inhabitants of Jerusalem. 15 And many among them shall stumble, and fall, and be broken, and be snared, and be taken. 16 Bind up the testimony, seal the law among my disciples. 17 And I will wait upon the LORD, that hideth his face from the house of Jacob, and I will look for him.	18 Behold, I and the children whom the LORD hath given me *are* for signs and for wonders in Israel from the LORD of hosts, which dwelleth in mount Zion. 19 And when they shall say unto you, Seek unto them that have familiar spirits, and unto wizards that peep, and that mutter: should not a people seek unto their God? for the living to the dead? 20 To the law and to the testimony: if they speak not according to this word, *it is* because *there is* no light in them. 21 And they shall pass through it, hardly bestead and hungry: and it shall come to pass, that when they shall be hungry, they shall fret themselves, and curse their king and their God, and look upward. 22 And they shall look unto the earth; and behold trouble and darkness, dimness of anguish; and *they shall be* driven to darkness.	2) He & his children were witnesses for the Lord: Their names were signs of God's salvation (Isaiah's name (1:1), hope (7:3), & judgment (8:3-6) d. Isaiah's strong warning: The people must not seek counsel from the world of the occult but from God 1) The key question: How could the dead reveal the future for the living? 2) The occult—all counselors & prophets—must be tested by God's Word 3) The occult would lead people to a hopeless end, God's judgment: Assyria would conquer them • They would suffer terribly • They would become enraged, cursing the king & God • They would be hopeless: See only distress, darkness, & gloom • They would be cast into utter darkness, 2 Pe.2:17

a. Isaiah stated that God issued a strong warning to him: he must not walk in the path of unbelievers (vv.11-15). Apparently there was a danger that the pro-Assyrian party might attempt to convince Isaiah of the reasonableness of their position. Assyria was unquestionably the strongest power in the world at that time. If Israel formed an alliance with Assyria, they could seemingly be assured of Assyria's support when facing a threat from other nations. But the leadership and citizens were failing to trust the LORD. They had forsaken the LORD, living unrighteous lives and engaging in false worship. Despite the LORD's pleas and warnings, they had ignored Him and were placing their complete trust in Assyria. Thus it would have been a tragic mistake for Isaiah to join the pro-Assyrian party. To prevent any chance of this happening, the LORD issued this strong warning to His dear prophet. Three specific charges were included in this warning, and all are applicable to believers of all generations.

1) Isaiah (and all true believers) must not fear the false accusations, criticisms, plots, and fears of unbelievers (v.12). Evidently, the leaders of the pro-Assyrian party were plotting against Isaiah, either to put undue pressure upon him to join their cause or else to silence him through threats or perhaps even assassination. Whatever the case, Isaiah was not to fear this conspiracy against him.

2) Isaiah (and true believers) must fear only the LORD of hosts (v.15). Isaiah was to remember that the LORD is the Holy One, the One who is high and exalted above the universe, including all governments and rulers. Therefore, He was the One to be feared, not the earthly leaders who were secretly laying plots against God's prophet. The LORD would be a sanctuary, a refuge for believers. For any believer who fled to the LORD in times of trouble, the LORD would provide a protective shelter for him. And He would be a rock, a trap for unbelievers. Upon Him, unbelievers would stumble, fall, and be snared like captured animals.

b. Isaiah's response to the LORD was strikingly positive (v.16). He stated that he would rededicate his life to the LORD. He would record and share God's Word with the people. The furthest thought from his mind was that of turning away from the LORD and walking in the path of unbelievers.

c. To the contrary, he would maintain a strong testimony for the LORD (vv.17-18). He and his children were *set apart* to God. He had personally put his trust in the LORD, not in man. He and his children were witnesses for the LORD. Even their names stood as signs to the people, symbols that had been given by the LORD of hosts Himself. Remember that Isaiah's name means *the LORD is salvation*, reminding the people that their deliverance could only come from the LORD. Shear-Jeshub's name means *a remnant will return*, reminding the people that the LORD would lead a remnant of believers out of captivity back to the promised land. The child named Immanuel, *God with us*, reminded the people that God was always with those who put their trust in Him. And Isaiah's child Maher-Shalal-Hash-Baz means *quick to plunder, quick to the spoil*. This child's name reminded the people that they must trust the LORD or else face His judgment.

Apparently some of the pro-Assyrian leaders were encouraging people to consult the world of the occult instead of God. As a result, Isaiah issued a strong warning to them (vv.19-22). Living in a world with so much national and international disorder, the people were seeking help from any source recommended to them, that is, any source except the LORD Himself.

Three of the sources were diviners, fortune-tellers, and mediums. Some people claimed that they found refuge in the words of these false teachers. Thus they sought help from the spirits of those who had already died.

But note that Isaiah asked the key question: How can the dead reveal the future for the living? Why do you seek the future by consulting mediums and psychics? Why do you turn to these false prophets, listening to their whisperings and mutterings instead of turning to the Word of the true and living God? What is it that makes you turn to the dead to reveal the future for the living?

Forcefully, Isaiah shouted out: "Go to the law and to the testimony of God's Word! If a teacher does not speak according to this Word, they have no life in themselves." Simply stated, the LORD was declaring that the world of the occult—all their counselors and prophets—must be tested by God's Holy Word (v.20). Isaiah then issued a strong warning to the people (vv.21-22). The occult would lead them to a hopeless end, God's judgment. If they continued in their rebellion against God, Assyria would rise up against them and conquer them. Four terrible consequences would fall upon them:

⇒ They would suffer terribly.
⇒ They would become so enraged, so disappointed, they will curse the king and God.
⇒ They would become gripped with a spirit of hopelessness and experience only distress, despair, and misery.
⇒ They would ultimately be cast into utter darkness (2 Pe.2:17).

What a terrible picture of darkness and gloom! A picture of people going through such horrible suffering that they become infuriated, cursing their government and even the LORD Himself. Hopelessness grips their hearts and lives, as they experience only distress, darkness, and gloom. Eventually they are taken into captivity, banished to a life of utter darkness. Although this was probably a reference to the siege and captivity of the Babylonians, the picture is that of unbelievers facing the terrible judgment of God and being cast into utter darkness at the final judgment (Mt.8:12; 22:13; 2 Pe.2:1; Jude 6; Jb.18:5).

Thought 1. *Spiritual separation* is a command of the LORD. A true follower of the LORD is not to walk in the paths of unbelievers, for unbelievers reject the LORD. They rebel against His Word and His holy commandments. Most unbelievers live selfish, greedy, and covetous lives. They seek the possessions and pleasures of this life, often spending far beyond their financial resources and ending up in debt. Others seek to amass riches and property, hoarding wealth when multitudes of needs throughout the community go unmet. Still others seek the sensual pleasures of this world, pleasures that arouse and stimulate the flesh such as illicit sex, immoral partying, pornography, and so on. Others overeat, shoplift, or become addicted to recreation, sports, or a host of other fleshly cravings. The majority of unbelievers selfishly ignore or neglect the LORD's demand that we help and serve others.

No true believer is to follow or walk in the path of unbelievers, those who live unbalanced lives and in many cases, wicked lives. We are not to participate in their evil associations. Listen to what God's Holy Word says about *spiritual separation*:

"And with many other words did he testify and exhort, saying, Save yourselves from this untoward generation" (Ac.2:40).

"I wrote unto you in an epistle not to company with fornicators: Yet not altogether with the fornicators of this world, or with the covetous, or extortioners, or with idolaters; for then must ye needs go out of the world. But now I have written unto you not to keep company, if any man that is called a brother be a fornicator, or covetous, or an idolater, or a railer, or a drunkard, or an extortioner; with such an one no not to eat" (1 Co.5:9-11).

"Be ye not unequally yoked together with unbelievers: for what fellowship hath righteousness with unrighteousness? and what communion hath light with darkness? And what concord hath Christ with Belial? or what part hath he that believeth with an infidel? And what agreement hath the temple of God with idols? for ye are the temple of the living God; as God hath said, I will dwell in them, and walk in *them*; and I will be their God, and they shall be my people" (2 Co.6:14-16).

"Wherefore come out from among them, and be ye separate, saith the Lord, and touch not the unclean *thing*; and I will receive you, And will be a Father unto you, and ye shall be my sons and daughters, saith the Lord Almighty" (2 Co.6:17-18).

"Thou shalt not follow a multitude to *do* evil; neither shalt thou speak in a cause to decline after many to wrest *judgment*" (Ex.23:2).

"Take heed to thyself, lest thou make a covenant with the inhabitants of the land whither thou goest, lest it be for a snare in the midst of thee" (Ex.34:12).

"Blessed *is* the man that walketh not in the counsel of the ungodly, nor standeth in the way of sinners, nor sitteth in the seat of the scornful" (Ps.1:1).

"My son, if sinners entice thee, consent thou not....My son, walk not thou in the way with them; refrain thy foot from their path" (Pr.1:10, 15).

"Enter not into the path of the wicked, and go not in the way of evil *men*" (Pr.4:14).

"Make no friendship with an angry man; and with a furious man thou shalt not go: Lest thou learn his ways, and get a snare to thy soul" (Pr.22:24-25).

"Eat thou not the bread of *him that hath* an evil eye, neither desire thou his dainty meats" (Pr.23:6).

5 (9:1-7) **Deliverance, Source, God—Light, of God, Results—Darkness, Overcome, by God's Light—Christ, Prophecies Concerning, Blessings—Christ, Blessings of, Fourfold—Blessings, of Christ, Fourfold—Kingdom, of Christ, Predicted—Millennium, Established by, Christ—Millennium, Described—Future, Described, to Be Glorious—Darkness, Overcome by, Christ—Galilee, Prophecy Concerning, to Be Honored—Zebulon, Prophecy Concerning—Naphtali, Prophecy Concerning—Gloom, Deliverance from, by Christ—Distress, Deliverance from**: when enemies threaten God's people, they are delivered by God's light shining in the gloomy darkness of this world. In the previous chapter everything looked black and ominous. A spirit of anguish and distress gripped the hearts of people. They felt completely helpless, for they were living in a war-torn nation. Most of the nation had already fallen to the Assyrians, who had swept across the land like the mighty flood waters of the Euphrates River (8:7-8). It was indeed a dark, dismal, and hopeless day for the people of Judah.

Remember that this devastating invasion by Assyria was a prophecy being predicted by Isaiah. It had not yet happened. Rather, he was warning the people that their sin, their rebellion against God, would bring this terrible judgment upon them. Their wickedness would be the cause of these terrible days of anguish and distress. Nevertheless, Isaiah closed his prophecy with a most wonderful promise: the people would be delivered by God's light, His presence, shining in the agonizing despair of this world.

OUTLINE	SCRIPTURE	SCRIPTURE	OUTLINE
	CHAPTER 9	of his oppressor, as in the day of Midian.	
5. Deliverance through God's light shining in the darkness of this world: Fulfilled in God's child of redemption, Jesus ChristDS2	Nevertheless the dimness *shall* not *be* such as *was* in her vexation, when at the first he lightly afflicted the land of Zebulun and the land of Naphtali, and afterward did more grievously afflict *her by* the way of the sea, beyond Jordan, in Galilee of the nations.	5 For every battle of the warrior *is* with confused noise, and garments rolled in blood; but *this* shall be with burning *and* fuel of fire.	4) He would bring peace to people & to the world
a. The promise of a bright, glorious future, Mt.4:13-16		6 For unto us a child is born, unto us a son is given: and the government shall be upon his shoulder: and his name shall be called Wonderful, Counsellor, The mighty God, The everlasting Father, The Prince of Peace.	c. The Person who would bring this glorious future to earth: Jesus Christ
1) All gloom would be erased			1) He would come first as the God-Man
2) All the land (Galilee) would be honored			• Humanity: *A child is born*
b. The hope for this glorious future: Found in a great light (Christ), Jn.8:12	2 The people that walked in darkness have seen a great light: they that dwell in the land of the shadow of death, upon them hath the light shined.		• Deity: *A son is given*
1) He would give light to all held in darkness & death		7 Of the increase of *his* government and peace *there shall be* no end, upon the throne of David, and upon his kingdom, to order it, and to establish it with judgment and with justice from henceforth even for ever. The zeal of the LORD of hosts will perform this.	2) He would come to govern
			3) He would have four names
2) He would enlarge or protect the nation of believers & increase their joy	3 Thou hast multiplied the nation, *and* not increased the joy: they joy before thee according to the joy in harvest, *and* as *men* rejoice when they divide the spoil.		4) He would return to establish God's kingdom on earth
			• Would rule in peace
			• Would rule on David's throne forever, fulfilling God's promise
			• Would establish perfect justice & righteousness
3) He would deliver all who were under the yoke of bondage or oppression	4 For thou hast broken the yoke of his burden, and the staff of his shoulder, the rod		• Would rule eternally
			5) His Word would be guaranteed by God's zeal

a. In spite of the people's fear and apprehension, a bright and glorious future lay ahead (v.1). A day would come when all darkness and gloom, anguish and despair would be erased. The extreme devastation and suffering caused by the Assyrians (and others down through history) would never again happen, not *in that day*. In the past the LORD had been forced to discipline His people due to their terrible evil. And soon He would allow Assyria to invade the promised land to humble His people. When the Assyrians launched their invasion, the first to feel the brunt of their attack would be the land of Zebulon and Naphtali, which thereafter would become known as Galilee of the Gentiles.

Although Isaiah referred only to these two tribal territories, he obviously was using these as examples of what the LORD was going to do for all oppressed lands and people. A glorious, dramatic change was coming to the promised land and to the world. One day in the future, this land that had been so devastated would be greatly honored by the LORD. All the land of Galilee would be honored. This is a clear prophecy concerning Jesus Christ, a prophecy that was fulfilled when Christ chose His disciples and carried on a large part of His ministry in Galilee (Mt.4:13-16). The Messiah, the Son of God Himself, honored this land by His very presence and ministry.

b. The hope for this bright, glorious future would be found in a *great light*. This is a clear reference to Jesus Christ, for He is the *great light* of the world (vv.2-5; Jn.8:12). Amazingly, Isaiah was making this prediction about the Messiah some 700 years before Christ came to earth. When the Messiah came, four wonderful blessings would be poured out upon the world.

1) The Messiah would give light to all who were held in the bondage of darkness and death, all who were living constantly under the shadow of death (v.2). A person who walks in darkness is a person who cannot see where he is, where he is going, or where he has come from. Darkness causes a person to stumble and fall, sometimes causing injury to self or others. Darkness is a symbol of sin, evil, and ignorance. Thereby, a person who walks in darkness is ignorant of...

• God the Father
• Jesus Christ who came to earth to reveal God the Father and the world's alienation from Him
• the real purpose and objective of life

Natural man, that is, the sinful nature of man, stumbles and gropes about in the darkness of this world. He is blinded to anything beyond this physical world; therefore, he knows nothing of the spiritual realm or dimension. His only hope is the hope of living a long life before death overtakes him. His hope is limited to what man can do for him, limited to the capability of other sinful human beings. Thus he walks in darkness, ignorant of the truth about life now and hereafter. He walks continually in the shadow of death. However, the message proclaimed by Isaiah offered wonderful hope for a glorious future. He declared that God was going to give a *great light* to the world, the light of the coming Messiah and Savior, the Lord Jesus Christ. Moreover, all who walk in darkness and live in the land of the shadow of death will have the opportunity to see a great light. No longer will they be forced to live in darkness nor under the shadow of death, for a *great light* will come to the people.

"In him was life; and the life was the light of men" (Jn.1:4).

"Then spake Jesus again unto them, saying, I am the light of the world: he that followeth me shall not walk in darkness, but shall have the light of life" (Jn.8:12).

"Then Jesus said unto them, Yet a little while is the light with you. Walk while ye have the light, lest darkness come upon you: for he that walketh in darkness knoweth not whither he goeth" (Jn.12:35).

"I am come a light into the world, that whosoever believeth on me should not abide in darkness" (Jn.12:46).

"For God, who commanded the light to shine out of darkness, hath shined in our hearts, to *give* the light of the knowledge of the glory of God in the face of Jesus Christ" (2 Co.4:6).

"Wherefore he saith, Awake thou that sleepest, and arise from the dead, and Christ shall give thee light" (Ep.5:14).

"This then is the message which we have heard of him, and declare unto you, that God is light, and in him is no darkness at all" (1 Jn.1:5).

"The LORD *is* my light and my salvation; whom shall I fear? the LORD *is* the strength of my life; of whom shall I be afraid?" (Ps.27:1).

2) The Messiah would enlarge (protect) the nation of believers and increase their joy (v.3). Due to the ravages of war, the population had been drastically diminished. But the promise was that the population would thrive, even be multiplied, when the Messiah came. The Messiah would also bring great joy to the people. This joy would flood their hearts as much as their rejoicing over a great harvest or when they divided plunder among themselves. Such joy is deep down within the soul. Note that the people would rejoice before the LORD, obviously praising Him for the light, the salvation He brought to them. Again, keep in mind that this is a prophecy being predicted by Isaiah some 700 years before the Messiah (Christ) ever came. Isaiah proclaimed that when the Savior came, He would provide protection for His people and fill them with the fullness of joy.

a) The LORD does protect His people.

"And now I am no more in the world, but these are in the world, and I come to thee. Holy Father, keep through thine own name those whom thou hast given me, that they may be one, as we *are*" (Jn.17:11).

"For the which cause I also suffer these things: nevertheless I am not ashamed: for I know whom I have believed, and am persuaded that he is able to keep that which I have committed unto him against that day" (2 Ti.1:12).

"And the Lord shall deliver me from every evil work, and will preserve *me* unto his heavenly kingdom: to whom *be* glory for ever and ever. Amen" (2 Ti.4:18).

"And, behold, I *am* with thee, and will keep thee in all *places* whither thou goest, and will bring thee again into this land; for I will not leave thee, until I have done *that* which I have spoken to thee of" (Ge.28:15).

"The angel of the LORD encampeth round about them that fear him, and delivereth them" (Ps.34:7).

"He shall cover thee with his feathers, and under his wings shalt thou trust: his truth *shall be thy* shield and buckler" (Ps.91:4).

"*As* the mountains *are* round about Jerusalem, so the LORD *is* round about his people from henceforth even for ever" (Ps.125:2).

b) The LORD does fill us with the fullness of joy.

"And when he hath found *it* [a lost sheep], he layeth *it* on his shoulders, rejoicing" (Lu.15:5).

"These things have I spoken unto you, that my joy might remain in you, and *that* your joy might be full" (Jn.15:11).

"Hitherto have ye asked nothing in my name: ask, and ye shall receive, that your joy may be full" (Jn.16:24).

"And now come I to thee; and these things I speak in the world, that they might have my joy fulfilled in themselves" (Jn.17:13).

"For the kingdom of God is not meat and drink; but righteousness, and peace, and joy in the Holy Ghost" (Ro.14:17).

"Thou wilt show me the path of life: in thy presence *is* fulness of joy; at thy right hand *there are* pleasures for evermore" (Ps.16:11).

"For his anger *endureth but* a moment; in his favour *is* life: weeping may endure for a night, but joy *cometh* in the morning" (Ps.30:5).

125

"They that sow in tears shall reap in joy" (Ps.126:5).

"I will also clothe her priests with salvation: and her saints shall shout aloud for joy" (Ps.132:16).

"Therefore with joy shall ye draw water out of the wells of salvation" (Is.12:3).

"And the ransomed of the LORD shall return, and come to Zion with songs and everlasting joy upon their heads: they shall obtain joy and gladness, and sorrow and sighing shall flee away" (Is.35:10).

3) The Messiah will deliver all who are under the yoke of bondage or oppression (v.4). Just as God gave Gideon victory over the Midianites, so He will give victory to any who trust Him. No matter what the bondage is that enslaves a person, the LORD will infuse the person with enough power to overcome it. And if enslavement is being forced upon a believer by others, the LORD will give the power to endure the suffering being inflicted upon him. Even if the believer is being oppressed to the point of death, the believer will be given the power to conquer death. Quicker than the eye can blink, the believer will be escorted into the very presence of the LORD Himself. Isaiah was proclaiming that the Messiah will set the people free from the enslavement being forced upon them by their enemies. The Messiah will have the power to break any oppression or bondage weighing His people down. He will deliver those who put their trust in Him, breaking the yokes, bars, or chains of those who persecute His people.

"There hath no temptation taken you but such as is common to man: but God *is* faithful, who will not suffer you to be tempted above that ye are able; but will with the temptation also make a way to escape, that ye may be able to bear *it*" (1 Co.10:13).

"For we would not, brethren, have you ignorant of our trouble which came to us in Asia, that we were pressed out of measure, above strength, insomuch that we despaired even of life: But we had the sentence of death in ourselves, that we should not trust in ourselves, but in God which raiseth the dead: Who delivered us from so great a death, and doth deliver: in whom we trust that he will yet deliver *us*" (2 Co.1:8-10).

"And the Lord shall deliver me from every evil work, and will preserve *me* unto his heavenly kingdom: to whom *be* glory for ever and ever. Amen" (2 Ti.4:18).

"Forasmuch then as the children are partakers of flesh and blood, he also himself likewise took part of the same; that through death he might destroy him that had the power of death, that is, the devil; And deliver them who through fear of death were all their lifetime subject to bondage" (He.2:14-15).

"The Lord knoweth how to deliver the godly out of temptations, and to reserve the unjust unto the day of judgment to be punished" (2 Pe.2:9).

"Surely he shall deliver thee from the snare of the fowler, *and* from the noisome pestilence" (Ps.91:3).

4) The Messiah will bring peace to the people and nations of the world (v.5). All military equipment and uniforms that are so often covered with blood will be cast aside and burned. Never again will the military equipment or uniforms be produced. Peace will sweep the earth, both peace within the human soul and peace among nations. Universal harmony will exist everywhere. Of course, this is a clear reference to the future kingdom of the Messiah, the messianic kingdom known as the Millennium.

Some of the predictions in this passage were obviously fulfilled when God defeated Assyria and delivered Jerusalem (see outline and notes—Is.37:1-38 for more discussion). And as the apostle Matthew clearly states, other events found their fulfillment when Christ Himself came to earth (Mt.4:13-16). But the ultimate fulfillment of the prophecy regarding the bright and glorious future will be in the last days of human history, during the millennial reign of Christ upon earth. (See outline and note—Is.2:1-5.) Also see DEEPER STUDY #2—Is.2:1-5.) For now, however, the emphasis is upon the peace that the Messiah will bring to human hearts and to the nations of the world.

"Peace I leave with you, my peace I give unto you: not as the world giveth, give I unto you. Let not your heart be troubled, neither let it be afraid" (Jn.14:27).

"These things I have spoken unto you, that in me ye might have peace. In the world ye shall have tribulation: but be of good cheer; I have overcome the world" (Jn.16:33).

"The word which *God* sent unto the children of Israel, preaching peace by Jesus Christ: (he is Lord of all:)" (Ac.10:36).

"Therefore being justified by faith, we have peace with God through our Lord Jesus Christ" (Ro.5:1).

"For to be carnally minded *is* death; but to be spiritually minded *is* life and peace. Because the carnal mind *is* enmity against God: for it is not subject to the law of God, neither indeed can be" (Ro.8:6-7).

"For the kingdom of God is not meat and drink; but righteousness, and peace, and joy in the Holy Ghost" (Ro.14:17).

"But the fruit of the Spirit is love, joy, peace, longsuffering, gentleness, goodness, faith, Meekness, temperance: against such there is no law" (Ga.5:22-23).

"For he is our peace, who hath made both one, and hath broken down the middle wall of partition *between us*" (Ep.2:14).

"Be careful for nothing; but in every thing by prayer and supplication with thanksgiving let your requests be made known unto God. And the peace of God, which passeth all understanding, shall keep your hearts and minds through Christ Jesus" (Ph.4:6-7).

"And, having made peace through the blood of his cross, by him to reconcile all things unto himself; by him, *I say,* whether *they be* things in earth, or things in heaven" (Col.1:20).

"And let the peace of God rule in your hearts, to the which also ye are called in one body; and be ye thankful" (Col.3:15).

"Let him eschew evil, and do good; let him seek peace, and ensue it" (1 Pe.3:11).

"Depart from evil, and do good; seek peace, and pursue it" (Ps.34:14).

"But he *was* wounded for our transgressions, *he was* bruised for our iniquities: the chastisement of our peace *was* upon him; and with his stripes we are healed" (Is.53:5).

c. The person who will bring this glorious future to earth will be the Messiah, Jesus Christ Himself (vv.6-7). Isaiah predicted five startling facts about the coming Messiah:

1) The Messiah will come first as the God-Man (v.6). Both His humanity and deity are predicted by the prophet. The words *a child is born* refer to the Messiah's humanity. He will come to earth as a child, born through the conception of a woman. The words *a son is given* point to the deity of the Messiah. The child's being *given* indicate that in some special way God Himself will send the child into the world. The words *a son* refer back to Isaiah 7:14, which indicates that Immanuel Himself—*God with us*—will come to earth as the Messiah. Of course, all of this points to the coming of God's Son, the Lord Jesus Christ—to earth (Jn.3:16). The very thought of such a miraculous event staggers the human mind. Nevertheless, it was the clear prophecy of Isaiah, and the prediction was made some 700 years before Christ actually came. Yet come He did. And today we are actually looking back upon this historic event, this pivotal point of human history. On the night that Christ was born, the very angel who appeared to the shepherds seems to refer to these words spoken by Isaiah: "For unto you is born this day in the city of David a Savior, which is Christ the Lord" (Lu.2:11). As Matthew Henry says:

> Christ's being born and given to us is the great foundation of our hopes, and fountain of our joys, in times of greatest grief and fear."[8]

2) The Messiah will come to govern. He will rule over the whole world, executing perfect righteousness and justice among the people (v.6; Mi.5:2; Zec.14:9). The government will be upon His shoulders, which means that He will have the indisputable right to govern. He will set His shoulder to the task of ruling His people and the world. He will not shrink from the duty given Him by the Father. As the exalted Lord, He will rule as the King of kings and Lord of lords.

3) The Messiah will have four very famous and descriptive names. Note that these names are compound. Single names are simply inadequate to express the extent of the Messiah's excellence or superiority. Even the compound titles are inadequate to describe Christ's supremacy, but they do convey the author's intent to wholly glorify the Savior.

a) The Messiah will be called *Wonderful Counselor*. Since Christ has come, we have a far better idea of just what this name means. Christ lived as a man, bearing all the trials and temptations of humanity. He even suffered incomprehensible persecution and was eventually executed as a criminal. Due to His intense suffering, He is able to be the most empathetic counselor imaginable. He knows what it is like to endure pain, to feel hunger and thirst, to experience poverty and homelessness. He knows the feeling of being rejected—even by His own family—and of being forsaken and left all alone. Such are the experiences that confront so many of us as we live out our lives. Thus when we need a counselor, Christ is the one Person who can feel what we feel, and He stands before us as the *Wonderful Counselor*. He is the one Person who can comfort us, who can give us solid guidance about how to handle the problems facing us. As the *Wonderful Counselor*, Christ can guide, encourage, and strengthen us to conquer whatever trial or temptation confronts us. As the *Wonderful Counselor*, He will teach us how to walk victoriously throughout life.

> "For we have not an high priest which cannot be touched with the feeling of our infirmities; but was in all points tempted like as *we are, yet* without sin. Let us therefore come boldly unto the throne of grace, that we may obtain mercy, and find grace to help in time of need" (He.4:15-16).
> "But I *am* poor and needy; *yet* the Lord thinketh upon me: thou *art* my help and my deliverer; make no tarrying, O my God" (Ps.40:17).
> "Like as a father pitieth *his* children, *so* the LORD pitieth them that fear him" (Ps.103:13).
> "Fear thou not; for I *am* with thee: be not dismayed; for I *am* thy God: I will strengthen thee; yea, I will help thee; yea, I will uphold thee with the right hand of my righteousness" (Is.41:10).
> "In all their affliction he was afflicted, and the angel of his presence saved them: in his love and in his pity he redeemed them; and he bare them, and carried them all the days of old" (Is.63:9).

b) The Messiah will be called the *Mighty God*. As predicted earlier in this verse (v.6), the Messiah will be divine. So here He is actually called the *Mighty God*. As God, He will do things that no one else could conceivably do, for example, the very things that are covered in this passage (9:2-5, 7). In addition, as God, He is omnipotent (all-powerful), omniscient (all-knowing), and omnipresent (present everywhere). He is able to save any who cry out to Him for salvation. As the *Mighty God*, He has the power and knowledge to rescue people from all trials and temptations. He has the power to deliver people from any bondage or oppression, whether due to some enemy or to a personal addiction. In the words of Matthew Henry:

---

8 Matthew Henry. *Matthew Henry's Commentary,* Vol.4, p.59.

He is the Mighty God—God, the mighty One. As he has wisdom, so he has strength, to go through with His undertaking: he is able to save to the utmost; and such is the work of the mediator that no less a power than that of the mighty God could accomplish it. [9]

c) The Messiah will be called the *Everlasting Father*. Although He is eternal, this is not the major thrust of this name. The emphasis lies upon the fact that the Messiah will love His people as a father loves His children. He will care for His people: nurture and nourish, comfort and assure, instruct and inform, lead and guide, correct and discipline them. He will do anything His people may need out of a deep, loving concern for them.

A question might be asked about this title: How can the Messiah, the Son, be called the *Everlasting Father*? *The Nelson Study Bible* says this:

Everlasting Father describes a King and Father who provides for and protects His people forever (40:9-11; Mt.11:27-30). Thus the word Father is used here of the Savior's role as an ideal king. [10]

The Bible Knowledge Commentary makes three comments about this title:

First, the Messiah, being the second Person of the Trinity, is in His essence, God. Therefore He has all the attributes of God including eternality. Since God is One (even though He exists in three Person), the Messiah is God. Second, the title "Everlasting Father" is an idiom used to describe the Messiah's relationship to time, not His relationship to the other Members of the Trinity. He is said to be everlasting, just as God (the Father) is called "the Ancient of Days" (Dan. 7:9). The Messiah will be a "fatherly" ruler. Third, perhaps Isaiah had in mind the promise to David (2 Sam. 7:16) about the "foreverness" of the kingdom which God promised would come through David's line. The Messiah, a Descendant of David, will fulfill this promise for which the nation had been waiting. [11]

Matthew Henry says the following:

He is the Everlasting Father, or the Father of eternity: he is God, one with the Father, who is from everlasting to everlasting. His fatherly care of His people and tenderness towards them are everlasting. He is the author of everlasting life and happiness to them, and so is the Father of a blessed eternity to them. He is the Father of the world to come…the father of the gospel-state, which is put in subjection to him, not to the angels (Heb.2:5). He was, from eternity, Father of the great work of redemption: his heart was upon it; it was the product of his wisdom as the counsellor of His love as the everlasting Father. [12]

d) The Messiah will be called the *Prince of Peace*. He is the promised Savior of the world, the One who will bring peace to the human heart and peace among the nations. Note the word *Prince*, which indicates that the Messiah will be a ruler who governs in peace. He will achieve His purposes through methods of peace and carry on His work in a peaceful spirit. The people over whom He rules will be a people of peace. While the Messiah rules upon the earth, there will be no more war, brutality, divisiveness, prejudice, hatred, or bitterness. Peace will reign throughout the world.

But even more important, because the Messiah will bring peace to the human heart, He will solve the problem of mankind's alienation from God. He will reconcile people to God. And when people are reconciled to God, they have *peace with God*, and the *peace of God* floods their hearts. They walk through life with the full assurance that their sins are forgiven and they are accepted by God. Confidence floods their souls, the confidence that they will live eternally with the Father and with the Son, the Lord Jesus Christ, the promised Messiah.

4) The Messiah will return to this world to establish God's kingdom on earth (v.7). As God promised, the Messiah will rule in peace, sitting on David's throne; and He will rule forever (see outline and note—2 S.7:11-17, esp.v.13 for more discussion). The great promise given to David concerning the Messiah was already well-known throughout Israel when Isaiah made this prophecy. Sitting eternally upon the throne of David, the Messiah will establish perfect justice and righteousness on earth. Imagine a world in which there is no lawlessness or violence, no prejudice or intolerance, no injustice or unrighteousness whatsoever. This will be the world ushered in by the coming of the Messiah, when He comes to sit upon the throne of David forever.

5) The Messiah's work will be guaranteed by God's zeal. A burning passion floods the heart of God, a passion to make absolutely sure the promise of the coming Messiah is fulfilled. Nothing could have prevented the fulfillment of Isaiah's prophecy. Some 700 years after the prophet's prediction, the Messiah came into the world and died. He rose again and ascended into heaven, returning to the Father—all in order to save mankind. As we now look to the future, the promise that Christ will return to establish God's kingdom on earth is yet to be fulfilled. But it will be fulfilled. Just as the Messiah came the first time to save the world, so He will come a second time to sit upon the eternal throne of David and to judge the world. This prophecy is guaranteed by God's holy zeal. Jesus Christ is the promised Child of God's redemption. [13]

---

9 *Matthew Henry's Commentary*, Vol.4, p.60.
10 *Nelson Study Bible, New King James Version.* (Nashville, TN; Thomas Nelson Publishers, Inc., 1997), Is.9:6.
11 John F. Walvoord and Roy B. Zuck, Editors. *The Bible Knowledge Commentary*, p.1053.
12 *Matthew Henry's Commentary*, Vol.4, p.60.
13 *John.* "The Preacher's Outline & Study Bible," Vol.5. (Chattanooga, TN: Leadership Ministries Worldwide, 1996), Jn.1:45, DEEPER STUDY #2.

DEEPER STUDY # 3
(9:1-7) **Scripture, Fulfilled—Prophecy, Fulfilled**:

OLD TESTAMENT PROPHECIES ABOUT JESUS AND THEIR FULFILLMENT IN THE NEW TESTAMENT

SCRIPTURE REFERENCE	PROPHECY	FULFILLMENT
Ge.3:15	The Promised Seed of a Woman	Lu.2:7; Ga.4:4; Re.12:5
Ge.12:3; 18:18; 22:18	The Promised Seed of Abraham	Ac.3:25; Ga.3:8 (Mt.1:1; Lu.3:34)
Ge.17:19; 21:12; 22:16-17 26:2	The Promised Seed of Isaac	Mt.1:2; Lu.1:55, 72-74
Ge.28:14 (Nu.24:17)	The Promised Seed of Jacob	Lu.3:34 (Mt.1:2)
Ge.49:10ᵃ	Will Spring from the Royal Tribe of Judah	Lu.3:33; He.7:14
De.18:15, 18	Will Be a Prophet	Jn.6:14; Ac.3:22-23
2 S.7:13ᵇ (Is.9:1, 7; 11:1-5)	Will Be the Eternal Heir to David's Throne	Mt.1:1 (Mt.1:6; Lu.1:32-33)
2 S.7:14ᵃ	Will Be God's Son	Mk.1:1
Jb.17:3	Will Ransom Men	Ep.1:7 (1 Jn.2:1-2)
Ps.2:1-2	Will Be Rejected by the Nations	Lu.23:36ᵃ, 38
Ps.2:7	The Son of God	Ac.13:33; He.1:5; 5:5
Ps.8:2	Is to Be Praised	Mt.21:16
Ps.16:8-11	Will Be Resurrected	Ac.2:25-28, 31; 13:34-35 (Mt.28:1-2; Mk.16:6, 12, 14; Lu.24:1-53)
Ps.22:1	Will Be Forsaken by God	Mt.27:46; Mk.15:34
Ps.22:6-8	People Will Mock, Wag Their Heads at the Cross	Mt.27:39
Ps.22:16	Hands and Feet Will Be Pierced	Mt.27:35
Ps.22:18	Clothes Gambled for	Mt.27:35; Mk.15:24; Lu.23:34; Jn.19:24
Ps.22:22	To Secure Many Brothers	He.2:12
Ps.27:12	Accused by False Witnesses	Mk.14:56
Ps.31:5	Commends His Spirit to God	Lu.23:46
Ps.34:20	No Bones Broken	Jn.19:32-36
Ps.40:6-8	Fulfills God's Will	He.10:5-7
Ps.41:9	Is Betrayed by Judas	Jn.13:18; Ac.1:16
Ps.45:6, 7	Is Eternal and Preeminent	He.1:8, 9
Ps.68:18	Will Lead Captivity Captive and Return to Heaven	Ep.4:8-10
Ps.69:4	Hated Without a Cause	Mt.27:22-23
Ps.69:21	Offered Drugs on the Cross	Mt.27:48; Mk.15:36; Lu.23:36; Jn.19:28, 29
Ps.69:25; 109:8	Judas' Fate	Ac.1:20
Ps.78:1-2; Is.6:9-10	Will Speak in Parables	Mt.13:13; Mk.4:11-13
Ps.89:26-27	Exaltation	Ph.2:9 (Re.11:15)
Ps.95:7-11	Hearts Hardened Against	He.3:7-11; 4:3, 5-7
Ps.102:25-27	Is Creator and Is Eternal	He.1:10-12
Ps.110:1	To Be Exalted	Mt.22:44; Mk.12:36; Lu.20:42; Ac.2:34, 35; He.1:13
Ps.110:4	The High Priest	He.5:6
Ps.118:22, 23	The Stone	Mt.21:42; Mk.12:10; Lu.20:17; Ac.4:11
Ps.118:25, 26	The Triumphal Entry	Mt.21:9; Mk.11:9; Jn.12:13
Ps.132:11, 17	The Son of David	Lu.1:69; Ac.2:30
Is.7:14	The Virgin Birth	Mt.1:23
Is.9:1, 2	A Light to Those in Darkness	Mt.4:15, 16
Is.11:1	Will Be from Nazareth	Mt.2:23
Is.11:2	The Spirit Rests Upon in a Special Way	Lu.4:18-21 (Mt.12:18; Jn.3:34)
Is.11:10	To Save the Gentiles	Ro.15:12
Is.25:8	To Conquer Death	1 Co.15:54
Is.28:16	The Stone	Ro.9:33; 1 Pe.2:6
Is.35:5-6	Do Miracles	Mt.11:4-6; 15:30; 21:14; Jn.6:1-2; 20:30-31

SCRIPTURE REFERENCE (continued)	PROPHECY (continued)	FULFILLMENT (continued)
Is.35:6; 61:1-2 (Ps.72:2; 146:8; Zec.11:11)	Will Meet the Desperate Needs of Men	Mt.11:4-6
Is.42:1-4	To Minister to the Gentiles	Mt.12:17-21
Is.49:6-7; 52:15	A Light to the Gentiles	Lu.2:32; Ac.13:47, 48; 26:23
Is.50:4-9	Obedient to the Father	Lu.22:42; Ph.2:8
Is.50:6	Smitten and Spat Upon	Mt.26:67; 27:30
Is.50:6; Mi.5:1	Hit in the Face	Mt.26:67; 27:30
Is.52:13	Exalted	Ac.1:9; 2:33-35; Ph.2:9-10
Is.52:14; 53:2	Disfigured	Mk.15:15-19
Is.53:1-3	Would Not Be Believed	Jn.12:38; Ro.10:16
Is.53:3-6; Ps.16:10	To Die and Arise	Ac.26:22, 23; 2:27
Is.53:4-6, 11	To Die for Man's Sins	1 Pe.2:24, 25
Is.53:4	To Heal and Bear Man's Sickness	Mt.8:17
Is.53:7	Silent When Accused	Mk.14:61
Is.53:9	To Be Sinless and Buried with the Rich	1 Pe.2:22
Is.53:12	To Be Counted a Sinner	Mk.15:28; Lu.22:37
Is.54:13	To Teach As God	Jn.6:45
Is.55:3	To Be Raised	Ac.13:34
Is.59:20, 21	To Save Israel	Ro.11:26, 27
Is.61:1-2	Proclaim the Year of the Lord	Lu.4:18-19
Je.31:15	Herod Tries to Kill Christ	Mt.2:16-18
Je.31:31-34	To Make a New Covenant with Man	He.8:8-12; 10:16, 17
Je.32:6-9	Betrayal Money Used to Buy Field	Mt.27:9-10
Da.9:25	Would Be Rejected 483 Years After Cyrus' Declaration to Rebuild the Temple	Mt.21:42
Hos.1:10-11	To Bring About the Restoration of Israel	Ro.9:26; 11:1-36
Hos.2:23	The Conversion of the Gentiles	Ro.9:25; 1 Pe.2:10
Hos.11:1	Will Flee to Egypt	Mt.2:13
Joel 2:28-32	The Promise of the Spirit	Ac.2:16-21
Amos 9:11, 12	The LORD's Return and David's Kingdom Reestablished	Ac.15:16, 17
Mic.5:2	The Birthplace of Messiah	Mt.2:5, 6; Jn.7:42
Hab.1:5	The Jews' Unbelief	Ac.13:40, 41
Hag.2:6	The Return of Christ	He.12:26
Zec.9:9	The Triumphal Entry	Mt.21:4, 5; Jn.12:14, 15
Zec.11:12-13	Judas' Betrayal	Mt.27:9, 10
Zec.12:10	The Spear Pierced in Side	Jn.19:37
Zec.13:7	The Scattering of the Disciples at the Cross	Mt.26:31, 56; Mk.14:27, 50
Mal.3:1	The Forerunner, John the Baptist	Mt.11:10; Mk.1:2; Lu.7:27
Mal.4:5, 6	The Forerunner, John the Baptist	Mt.11:13, 14; 17:10-13; Mk.9:11-13; Lu.1:16, 17

1. God's judgment of Israel, the betrayer: Forsaking the LORD (note four sections—9:8, 13, 18; 10:1)
a. Judgment due to pride & arrogance
  1) They had rejected God's warning (sent through Amos, Hosea, & Isaiah)
  2) They suffered a calamity
    • Were not humbled: Still failed to turn to God
    • Were totally self-reliant: Planned to build bigger & better
  3) They were to face God's judgment: An invasion from Assyria (foes of the Syrian king Rezin, 7:1)
  4) They were to be squeezed by other Syrian & Philistine forces
  5) They were to face God's continued judgment (repeated 9:12, 17, 21; 10:4)
b. Judgment due to hardness of heart, a refusal to repent & seek the LORD

  1) The head & tail—leaders & false prophets—were to be cut off

    • Because they misled the people, leading them down the path of destruction
    • Because everyone was wicked, a hypocrite—the youth, the fatherless, & the widows: Every mouth was vile, lying & cursing
  2) The intense anger & judgment of God was to continue: Due to their hard hearts
c. Judgment due to the devouring & destructive force of sin & wickedness
  1) They would be consumed with wickedness: Would be like a raging fire
  2) They would suffer the flaming wrath of God
    • Allowed to suffer civil strife & war

F. The Sure Judgment of Unrepentant & Wicked Enemies (Israel & Assyria): Hope Given Through God's Assurance of Victory, 9:8–10:34

8 The Lord sent a word into Jacob, and it hath lighted upon Israel.
9 And all the people shall know, *even* Ephraim and the inhabitant of Samaria, that say in the pride and stoutness of heart,
10 The bricks are fallen down, but we will build with hewn stones: the sycomores are cut down, but we will change *them into* cedars.
11 Therefore the LORD shall set up the adversaries of Rezin against him, and join his enemies together;
12 The Syrians before, and the Philistines behind; and they shall devour Israel with open mouth. For all this his anger is not turned away, but his hand *is* stretched out still.
13 For the people turneth not unto him that smiteth them, neither do they seek the LORD of hosts.
14 Therefore the LORD will cut off from Israel head and tail, branch and rush, in one day.
15 The ancient and honourable, he *is* the head; and the prophet that teacheth lies, he *is* the tail.
16 For the leaders of this people cause *them* to err; and *they that are* led of them *are* destroyed.
17 Therefore the Lord shall have no joy in their young men, neither shall have mercy on their fatherless and widows: for every one *is* an hypocrite and an evildoer, and every mouth speaketh folly. For all this his anger is not turned away, but his hand *is* stretched out still.
18 For wickedness burneth as the fire: it shall devour the briers and thorns, and shall kindle in the thickets of the forest, and they shall mount up *like* the lifting up of smoke.
19 Through the wrath of the LORD of hosts is the land darkened, and the people shall be as the fuel of the fire: no man shall spare his

brother.
20 And he shall snatch on the right hand, and be hungry; and he shall eat on the left hand, and they shall not be satisfied: they shall eat every man the flesh of his own arm:
21 Manasseh, Ephraim; and Ephraim, Manasseh: *and* they together *shall be* against Judah. For all this his anger is not turned away, but his hand *is* stretched out still.

CHAPTER 10

Woe unto them that decree unrighteous decrees, and that write grievousness *which* they have prescribed;
2 To turn aside the needy from judgment, and to take away the right from the poor of my people, that widows may be their prey, and *that* they may rob the fatherless!
3 And what will ye do in the day of visitation, and in the desolation *which* shall come from far? to whom will ye flee for help? and where will ye leave your glory?
4 Without me they shall bow down under the prisoners, and they shall fall under the slain. For all this his anger is not turned away, but his hand *is* stretched out still.
5 O Assyrian, the rod of mine anger, and the staff in their hand is mine indignation.
6 I will send him against an hypocritical nation, and against the people of my wrath will I give him a charge, to take the spoil, and to take the prey, and to tread them down like the mire of the streets.
7 Howbeit he meaneth not so, neither doth his heart think so; but *it is* in his heart to destroy and cut off nations not a few.
8 For he saith, *Are* not my princes altogether kings?
9 *Is* not Calno as Carchemish? *is* not Hamath as Arpad? *is* not Samaria as Damascus?
10 As my hand hath found the kingdoms of the idols, and whose graven images did excel them of Jerusalem and of Samaria;
11 Shall I not, as I have done unto Samaria and her idols, so do to Jerusalem and her

• Allowed to give themselves over to a consuming greed & selfishness

• Allowed to suffer terrible famine & hunger
• Allowed to suffer conflict as tribes, states, people
  3) Were to face God's continued judgment: Due to their continued & destructive wickedness

d. Judgment due to injustice
  1) The sins of the leaders: Writing unfair, unjust laws that supported evil
    • They deprived the poor, weak, & oppressed of justice
    • They preyed on widows & the fatherless

  2) The inevitable day of God's judgment
    • The leaders needed to ponder three questions (as do people of all generations)
    • The leaders could only expect to reap what they had sown: To cringe as captives or be killed
    • The anger & judgment of God were to continue

2. God's judgment of Assyria, the boastful: Exalting oneself as God
a. The use of Assyria as God's rod, His agent of judgment
b. The reasons for God's judgment: God used Assyria to discipline Judah

  1) Assyria sought world domination
    • Sought to destroy many nations throughout the world
    • Sought to rule through its mighty officers
  2) Assyria felt all-powerful, unstoppable

  3) Assyria was an idolatrous people
    • They believed nations were overseen by different gods
    • They felt they could easily take Jerusalem with its inferior gods

4) Assyria was a prideful people: The king exalted himself—his power & wisdom—above all else: "I" & "my" used nine times

- "I" have conquered other nations, plundered their wealth, & subdued their leaders & people

- "I" am so powerful & wise that it was as easy as snatching eggs out of a nest: No one was able to oppose "my" power

5) Assyria was a boastful people
  - They felt they controlled their own fate & events
  - They were, in reality, under God's control, functioning as His agents

c. The judgment of God described
  1) The Assyrian soldiers would be stricken with a plague: Like a blazing, flaming fire
  2) The judgment would fall in a single day, 37:36-37; 2 K.19:35

  3) The glory of Assyria would be destroyed

  4) The army would have so few soldiers that a child could count them

3. **God's wonderful promise of a small number of survivors (a remnant) in Israel despite Assyria's brutality: Returning to the LORD**
a. The promise of a remnant
  1) They would no longer trust men but God

  2) They would return to the Mighty God

idols?
12 Wherefore it shall come to pass, *that* when the Lord hath performed his whole work upon mount Zion and on Jerusalem, I will punish the fruit of the stout heart of the king of Assyria, and the glory of his high looks.
13 For he saith, By the strength of my hand I have done *it,* and by my wisdom; for I am prudent: and I have removed the bounds of the people, and have robbed their treasures, and I have put down the inhabitants like a valiant *man:*
14 And my hand hath found as a nest the riches of the people: and as one gathereth eggs *that are* left, have I gathered all the earth; and there was none that moved the wing, or opened the mouth, or peeped.
15 Shall the axe boast itself against him that heweth therewith? *or* shall the saw magnify itself against him that shaketh it? as if the rod should shake *itself* against them that lift it up, *or* as if the staff should lift up *itself, as if it were* no wood.
16 Therefore shall the Lord, the Lord of hosts, send among his fat ones leanness; and under his glory he shall kindle a burning like the burning of a fire.
17 And the light of Israel shall be for a fire, and his Holy One for a flame: and it shall burn and devour his thorns and his briers in one day;
18 And shall consume the glory of his forest, and of his fruitful field, both soul and body: and they shall be as when a standardbearer fainteth.
19 And the rest of the trees of his forest shall be few, that a child may write them.
20 And it shall come to pass in that day, *that* the remnant of Israel, and such as are escaped of the house of Jacob, shall no more again stay upon him that smote them; but shall stay upon the LORD, the Holy One of Israel, in truth.
21 The remnant shall return, *even* the remnant of Jacob, unto the mighty God.

22 For though thy people Israel be as the sand of the sea, *yet* a remnant of them shall return: the consumption decreed shall overflow with righteousness.
23 For the Lord GOD of hosts shall make a consumption, even determined, in the midst of all the land.
24 Therefore thus saith the Lord GOD of hosts, O my people that dwellest in Zion, be not afraid of the Assyrian: he shall smite thee with a rod, and shall lift up his staff against thee, after the manner of Egypt.
25 For yet a very little while, and the indignation shall cease, and mine anger in their destruction.
26 And the LORD of hosts shall stir up a scourge for him according to the slaughter of Midian at the rock of Oreb: and *as* his rod *was* upon the sea, so shall he lift it up after the manner of Egypt.
27 And it shall come to pass in that day, *that* his burden shall be taken away from off thy shoulder, and his yoke from off thy neck, and the yoke shall be destroyed because of the anointing.
28 He is come to Aiath, he is passed to Migron; at Michmash he hath laid up his carriages:
29 They are gone over the passage: they have taken up their lodging at Geba; Ramah is afraid; Gibeah of Saul is fled.
30 Lift up thy voice, O daughter of Gallim: cause it to be heard unto Laish, O poor Anathoth.
31 Madmenah is removed; the inhabitants of Gebim gather themselves to flee.
32 As yet shall he remain at Nob that day: he shall shake his hand *against* the mount of the daughter of Zion, the hill of Jerusalem.
33 Behold, the Lord, the LORD of hosts, shall lop the bough with terror: and the high ones of stature *shall be* hewn down, and the haughty shall be humbled.
34 And he shall cut down the thickets of the forest with iron, and Lebanon shall fall by a mighty one.

3) They would no longer be numerous but merely a remnant
  - Because God's righteous judgment would destroy them—in perfect justice
  - Because the LORD of hosts would judge the whole land—all the Israelites

b. The yoke (bondage, siege) of Assyria would be broken
  1) The people of Zion (Jerusalem) were not to fear Assyria, who threatened & oppressed Judah in the same way Egypt had

  - Because the LORD's anger against them was to end & be turned against Assyria
  - Because the LORD would destroy the Assyrians as He did the Midianites (through Gideon, 9:4-7, Jud.7:1-24) & the Egyptians (in the Red Sea, Ex.14:1-31)
  2) The Assyrian yoke that threatened Jerusalem would be broken—*in that day*

  - Their conquest of city after city would carry their yoke right up to the gates of Jerusalem

  - Their army & yoke would be broken at Nob, about two miles north of Jerusalem

c. The yoke of Assyria would be broken because God is all-powerful & in control
  1) The LORD of hosts would chop down the mighty trees: The king & army of Assyria
  2) The Mighty One would cut down the enemy with the ax of His judgment

DIVISION I

THE PROPHECIES OF REBUKE AND HOPE GIVEN TO JUDAH AND JERUSALEM: AN OVERVIEW OF THE PRESENT AND FUTURE OF GOD'S PEOPLE, 1:1–12:6

F. The Sure Judgment of Unrepentant and Wicked Enemies (Israel and Assyria): Hope Given Through God's Assurance of Victory, 9:8–10:34

(9:8–10:34) **Introduction**: the unrepentant and wicked of the world will often oppose us as true believers. Unbelievers can become upset with us, perhaps hate or despise us. Even if we have showered attention and care upon an individual, that person can turn against us because of our testimony for Christ. Hatred can evolve into persecution in the form of verbal, mental, or physical assaults. Sometimes, the law may be twisted to silence our testimony for the LORD or to threaten imprisonment or bodily harm. At other times the enemy may be a religious person, either someone who worships false gods or a true believer who has turned away from the LORD. Whatever the case, as true believers we are often persecuted, called upon to suffer for the name of Christ. The suffering may range all the way from mild ridicule or mockery to im-prisonment or martyrdom. But there is wonderful hope for the genuine believer. Victory is assured by God. The LORD will give victory over all wicked and unrepentant enemies.

This is the message of the present Scripture. Remember that Syria and the Northern Kingdom of Israel had formed an alliance to withstand the threat of Assyria (Is.7:1-9; see outline and notes—2 Chr.28:5-15 for more discussion). They approached King Ahaz of Judah to join their alliance, knowing that three nations would present a more formidable opposition to the Assyrian war machine. However, King Ahaz refused to join the alliance. As a result, the coalition invaded Judah. This meant that the Northern Kingdom of Israel, along with Syria, was invading the land of their brothers, their fellow Israelites. Instead of turning to the LORD for help against the threatening enemies, Ahaz and his people placed their trust in Syria, relying on them in their hour of crisis. Because of their distrust, their unbelieving hearts, and their wicked lives, God's hand of judgment was raised against them. He allowed the Assyrians to conquer and exile the people of Judah. But Isaiah the prophet predicted that Assyria would go too far in their savage treatment of the Israelites and other conquered nations. As a result, God would execute His judgment upon the brutal Assyrians. This is, *The Sure Judgment of Unrepentant and Wicked Enemies (Israel and Assyria): Hope Given Through God's Assurance of Victory*, 9:8–10:34.

1. God's judgment of Israel, the betrayer: forsaking the LORD (Note four sections—9:8, 13, 18; 10:1) (9:8–10:4).
2. God's judgment of Assyria, the boastful: exalting oneself as God (10:5-19).
3. God's wonderful promise of a small number of survivors (a remnant) in Israel despite Assyria's brutality: returning to the LORD (10:20-34).

1 (9:8–10:4) **Judgment, Reasons for, Fourfold—Israel, Judgment of, Caused by—Betrayal – Betrayer of the LORD, Example—Forsaking, the LORD, by Israel—Sins, Guilty of, Israel—Guilty, of Sin, Israel**: God's judgment was to fall upon Israel because they had betrayed the LORD. They had forsaken both the LORD and their fellow Israelites in the Southern Kingdom of Judah. Remember that the Northern Kingdom of Israel had formed an alliance with Syria and attacked the Southern Kingdom, inflicting heavy losses upon the army of Judah (7:1-9; see outline and notes—2 Chr.28:5-15 for more discussion). The Northern Kingdom had proven itself to be a callous and vindictive enemy. As a result, God raised His hand of judgment against them. Note that this prophecy is divided into four sections (9:8, 13, 18; 10:1). Each section is followed by a refrain stating that God's anger is not yet turned away and that His hand is still stretched out, ready to strike the wicked (9:12, 17, 21; 10:4).

OUTLINE	SCRIPTURE	SCRIPTURE	OUTLINE

1. **God's judgment of Israel, the betrayer: Forsaking the LORD (note four sections—9:8, 13, 18; 10:1)**
a. Judgment due to pride & arrogance
  1) They had rejected God's warning (sent through Amos, Hosea, & Isaiah)
  2) They suffered a calamity
  • Were not humbled: Still failed to turn to God
  • Were totally self-reliant: Planned to build bigger & better
  3) They were to face God's judgment: An invasion from Assyria (foes of the Syrian king Rezin, 7:1)
  4) They were to be squeezed
	8 The Lord sent a word into Jacob, and it hath lighted upon Israel.
	9 And all the people shall know, *even* Ephraim and the inhabitant of Samaria, that say in the pride and stoutness of heart,
	10 The bricks are fallen down, but we will build with hewn stones: the sycomores are cut down, but we will change *them into* cedars.
	11 Therefore the LORD shall set up the adversaries of Rezin against him, and join his enemies together;
	12 The Syrians before, and
		the Philistines behind; and they shall devour Israel with open mouth. For all this his anger is not turned away, but his hand *is* stretched out still.
		13 For the people turneth not unto him that smiteth them, neither do they seek the LORD of hosts.
		14 Therefore the LORD will cut off from Israel head and tail, branch and rush, in one day.
		15 The ancient and honourable, he *is* the head; and the prophet that teacheth lies, he *is* the tail.
		16 For the leaders of this people cause *them* to err; and
			by other Syrian & Philistine forces
			5) They were to face God's continued judgment (repeated 9:12, 17, 21; 10:4)
			b. Judgment due to hardness of heart, a refusal to repent & seek the LORD
			
			1) The head & tail—leaders & false prophets—were to be cut off
			
			• Because they misled the people, leading them

OUTLINE	SCRIPTURE	SCRIPTURE	OUTLINE
down the path of destruction • Because everyone was wicked, a hypocrite—the youth, the fatherless, & the widows: Every mouth was vile, lying & cursing 2) The intense anger & judgment of God was to continue: Due to their hard hearts c. Judgment due to the devouring & destructive force of sin & wickedness 1) They would be consumed with wickedness: Will be like a raging fire 2) They would suffer the flaming wrath of God • Allowed to suffer civil strife & war • Allowed to give themselves over to a consuming greed & selfishness • Allowed to suffer terrible famine & hunger • Allowed to suffer conflict as tribes, states, people	*they that are* led of them *are* destroyed. 17 Therefore the Lord shall have no joy in their young men, neither shall have mercy on their fatherless and widows: for every one *is* an hypocrite and an evildoer, and every mouth speaketh folly. For all this his anger is not turned away, but his hand *is* stretched out still. 18 For wickedness burneth as the fire: it shall devour the briers and thorns, and shall kindle in the thickets of the forest, and they shall mount up *like* the lifting up of smoke. 19 Through the wrath of the LORD of hosts is the land darkened, and the people shall be as the fuel of the fire: no man shall spare his brother. 20 And he shall snatch on the right hand, and be hungry; and he shall eat on the left hand, and they shall not be satisfied: they shall eat every man the flesh of his own arm:	21 Manasseh, Ephraim; and Ephraim, Manasseh: *and* they together *shall be* against Judah. For all this his anger is not turned away, but his hand *is* stretched out still. **CHAPTER 10** Woe unto them that decree unrighteous decrees, and that write grievousness *which* they have prescribed; 2 To turn aside the needy from judgment, and to take away the right from the poor of my people, that widows may be their prey, and *that* they may rob the fatherless! 3 And what will ye do in the day of visitation, and in the desolation *which* shall come from far? to whom will ye flee for help? and where will ye leave your glory? 4 Without me they shall bow down under the prisoners, and they shall fall under the slain. For all this his anger is not turned away, but his hand *is* stretched out still.	3) Were to face God's continued judgment: Due to their continued & destructive wickedness d. Judgment due to injustice 1) The sins of the leaders: Writing unfair, unjust laws that supported evil • They deprived the poor, weak, & oppressed of justice • They preyed on widows & the fatherless 2) The inevitable day of God's judgment • The leaders needed to ponder three questions (as do people of all generations) • The leaders could only expect to reap what they had sown: To cringe as captives or be killed • The anger & judgment of God were to continue

a. God's hand of judgment was raised against Israel because of their *pride and arrogance* (vv.9-12). Time and again the LORD had sent prophets to warn Israel: they must repent of their sin or else face His judgment. These prophets were Amos, Hosea, Isaiah, and others. But in each case the people rejected God's warning, and the hand of God's judgment was raised against them. As an example, a calamity of some sort had apparently just happened in the Northern Kingdom, possibly an earthquake or an attack by a neighboring nation. This is known because some of the buildings and city walls had been destroyed as well as some of their crops and fruit-bearing trees (v.10). The LORD had allowed this disaster to take place, hoping it would cause them to humble themselves and turn to Him for help. Yet the very opposite happened. Acting totally independent of God, the people exposed a deep seed of self-sufficiency. They felt they needed no one but themselves. With hearts full of pride and arrogance, they announced plans to build bigger and better buildings and farms. At no time during or after the upheaval did the people turn from their sins back to the LORD.

In mercy, the LORD used Isaiah to warn the Northern Kingdom: they were to face God's judgment (v.11). He would allow the Assyrians—the ruthless people who stood as staunch foes of Syria's King Rezin (7:1)—to launch an invasion against Israel. In addition, he would allow the Israelites to be squeezed by other Syrian and Philistine forces (v.12). And these would not be minor skirmishes. They would be major disasters, for the LORD would allow these nations to devour Israel with open mouths.

Now, note the refrain: despite all this punishment, the people would still not repent or turn to the LORD. Consequently, the LORD's anger would not be turned away. His hand would still be upraised, ready to strike in judgment.

Thought 1. This point is a strong warning to us. We must guard against pride and arrogance and self-sufficiency. We must not live independent of God, ignoring and denying Him. Just as we need each other as friends and neighbors, so we need the LORD. God is not only our Creator, but He is also the only One who can help us through the crises of life. Furthermore, He is the only One who can empower us to walk righteously and victoriously throughout life, conquering all the temptations and trials that confront us. Because of our desperate need for the LORD, we must never walk independent of Him. We must guard against an evil spirit of pride, arrogance, and self-sufficiency.

"**And whosoever shall exalt himself shall be abased; and he that shall humble himself shall be exalted**" (Mt.23:12).

"**Wherefore let him that thinketh he standeth take heed lest he fall**" (1 Co.10:12).

"**But he giveth more grace. Wherefore he saith, God resisteth the proud, but giveth grace unto the humble**" (Js.4:6).

"**For all that *is* in the world, the lust of the flesh, and the lust of the eyes, and the pride of life, is not of the Father, but is of the world**" (1 Jn.2:16).

"**The wicked in *his* pride doth persecute the poor: let them be taken in the devices that they have imagined**" (Ps.10:2).

"**Thou hast rebuked the proud *that are* cursed, which do err from thy commandments**" (Ps.119:21).

"These six *things* doth the LORD hate: yea, seven *are* an abomination unto him: A proud look, a lying tongue, and hands that shed innocent blood, An heart that deviseth wicked imaginations, feet that be swift in running to mischief, A false witness *that* speaketh lies, and he that soweth discord among brethren" (Pr.6:16-19).

"*When* pride cometh, then cometh shame: but with the lowly *is* wisdom" (Pr.11:2).

"Pride *goeth* before destruction, and an haughty spirit before a fall" (Pr.16:18).

"An high look, and a proud heart, *and* the plowing of the wicked, *is* sin" (Pr.21:4).

"He that is of a proud heart stirreth up strife: but he that putteth his trust in the LORD shall be made fat" (Pr.28:25).

"A man's pride shall bring him low: but honour shall uphold the humble in spirit" (Pr.29:23).

"For thou hast said in thine heart, I will ascend into heaven, I will exalt my throne above the stars of God: I will sit also upon the mount of the congregation, in the sides of the north: I will ascend above the heights of the clouds; I will be like the most High. Yet thou shalt be brought down to hell, to the sides of the pit" (Is.14:13-15).

"Though thou exalt *thyself* as the eagle, and though thou set thy nest among the stars, thence will I bring thee down, saith the LORD" (Ob.4).

b.   God's hand of judgment was raised against Israel because of their *hardness of heart*. Despite the LORD's allowing one disaster after another to strike them, the people still refused to repent and seek Him (v.13-17). Their hearts were simply too hard, stubborn, and stiff-necked against God. So the LORD warned them for a second time: He would cut off their head and tail, that is, their leaders and false prophets. And they would be cut off in a single day, which probably means that they would be cut off in one simple attack when the capital Samaria fell in 722 B.C.

Note the reference to the false prophets' teaching lies. They should have been teaching the truth of God's Word, seeking to turn people back to the LORD and establishing them in the faith. Instead, they were twisting God's Word and teaching their own thoughts and philosophies. They were lying to the people and encouraging them to focus their service and money in the social and political arenas instead of in the LORD and His cause. Scripture clearly says that they misled the people, leading them down the path of destruction (v.16). Sadly, the vast majority of the people in the Northern Kingdom were wicked and hypocritical. Isaiah warned the people: the LORD takes no pleasure in those who lives wicked lives (v.17). Even the youth, the fatherless, and the widows were accused of being hypocritical. They were all evildoers whose mouths were full of lying and cursing. Hence, the intense anger of God was to continue falling upon the Israelites (v.17). Due to their hard hearts, God's hand of judgment remained upraised.

Thought 1. We must not harden our hearts toward the LORD. If we are continuing in sin, we must repent and seek the LORD. When we refuse to turn back to Him, we expose a deep-seated stubbornness against the LORD. We stiffen our necks against Him. God warns us against hardness of heart:

"For the heart of this people is waxed gross, and their ears are dull of hearing, and their eyes have they closed; lest they should see with *their* eyes, and hear with *their* ears, and understand with *their* heart, and should be converted, and I should heal them" (Ac.28:27).

"But after thy hardness and impenitent heart treasurest up unto thyself wrath against the day of wrath and revelation of the righteous judgment of God; Who will render to every man according to his deeds: To them who by patient continuance in well doing seek for glory and honour and immortality, eternal life: But unto them that are contentious, and do not obey the truth, but obey unrighteousness, indignation and wrath, Tribulation and anguish, upon every soul of man that doeth evil, of the Jew first, and also of the Gentile" (Ro.2:5-9).

"This I say therefore, and testify in the Lord, that ye henceforth walk not as other Gentiles walk, in the vanity of their mind, Having the understanding darkened, being alienated from the life of God through the ignorance that is in them, because of the blindness of their heart: Who being past feeling have given themselves over unto lasciviousness, to work all uncleanness with greediness" (Ep.4:17-19).

"Now the Spirit speaketh expressly, that in the latter times some shall depart from the faith, giving heed to seducing spirits, and doctrines of devils; Speaking lies in hypocrisy; having their conscience seared with a hot iron" (1 Ti.4:1-2).

"Take heed, brethren, lest there be in any of you an evil heart of unbelief, in departing from the living God. But exhort one another daily, while it is called To day; lest any of you be hardened through the deceitfulness of sin" (He.3:12-13).

"So I spake unto you; and ye would not hear, but rebelled against the commandment of the LORD, and went presumptuously up into the hill [false worship]" (De.1:43).

"Be ye not as the horse, *or* as the mule, *which* have no understanding: whose mouth must be held in with bit and bridle, lest they come near unto thee. Many sorrows *shall be* to the wicked: but he that trusteth in the LORD, mercy shall compass him about" (Ps.32:9-10).

"For thus saith the Lord GOD, the Holy One of Israel; In returning and rest shall ye be saved; in quietness and in confidence shall be your strength: and ye would not" (Is.30:15).

"Hearken unto me, ye stouthearted, that *are* far from righteousness" (Is.46:12).

"Because I knew that thou *art* obstinate, and thy neck *is* an iron sinew, and thy brow brass....*There is* no peace, saith the LORD, unto the wicked" (Is.48:4, 22).

"If ye will not hear, and if ye will not lay *it* to heart, to give glory unto my name, saith the LORD of hosts, I will even send a curse upon you, and I will curse your blessings: yea, I have cursed them already, because ye do not lay *it* to heart" (Mal.2:2).

c. God's hand of judgment was raised against Israel because of the flaming and destructive force of their *wickedness* (vv.18-21). While the nation was certainly suffering from enemies outside its borders, it was also being destroyed from within. The people's iniquity was feeding upon itself, ever increasing and eating away at the very spirit of the people. Increasing lawlessness and discord were destroying the nation. Like a raging fire engulfing a huge forest, so this wickedness was engulfing the people. As a result, the people would suffer the flaming wrath of God (vv.19-20). God allowed them to suffer civil strife and war and to give themselves over to consuming greed and selfishness. The more they engaged in immorality and lawlessness the more they would crave illicit sex and lust after the wealth and possessions of this world. For this reason they would be allowed to suffer terrible famine and to undergo conflict within their own borders. One tribe (Manasseh) would feed upon another (Ephraim) through discrimination and constant conflict.

But despite the rampage of lawlessness and wickedness and the terrible sufferings of civil strife and war, the people would still not repent or turn back to the LORD. Therefore God's anger toward Israel continued, and His hand stayed raised in judgment.

Thought 1. This point is a strong warning to us. We must not live wicked, disobedient, sinful lives. If we engage in behavior such as immorality, lawlessness, violence, greed, or discrimination, the hand of God's judgment will be raised against us. This is the clear teaching of God's Holy Word:

"For the wrath of God is revealed from heaven against all ungodliness and unrighteousness of men, who hold the truth in unrighteousness....Being filled with all unrighteousness, fornication, wickedness, covetousness, maliciousness; full of envy, murder, debate, deceit, malignity; whisperers, Backbiters, haters of God, despiteful, proud, boasters, inventors of evil things, disobedient to parents, Without understanding, covenantbreakers, without natural affection, implacable, unmerciful: Who knowing the judgment of God, that they which commit such things are worthy of death, not only do the same, but have pleasure in them that do them" (Ro.1:18, 29-32).

"Know ye not that the unrighteous shall not inherit the kingdom of God? Be not deceived: neither fornicators, nor idolaters, nor adulterers, nor effeminate, nor abusers of themselves with mankind, Nor thieves, nor covetous, nor drunkards, nor revilers, nor extortioners, shall inherit the kingdom of God. And such were some of you: but ye are washed, but ye are sanctified, but ye are justified in the name of the Lord Jesus, and by the Spirit of our God" (1 Co.6:9-11).

"Now the works of the flesh are manifest, which are *these*; Adultery, fornication, uncleanness, lasciviousness, Idolatry, witchcraft, hatred, variance, emulations, wrath, strife, seditions, heresies, Envyings, murders, drunkenness, revellings, and such like: of the which I tell you before, as I have also told *you* in time past, that they which do such things shall not inherit the kingdom of God" (Ga.5:19-21).

d. God's hand of judgment was raised against Israel due to their *injustice* (10:1-4). Note the word *woe*, which stresses that a special judgment is going to fall upon the leaders who write unfair, unjust laws (vv.1-2). These particular leaders included the politicians, judges, lawyers, and military officers throughout the nation. Instead of serving the people, they were using the law to oppress the people. They were actually depriving the poor, weak, and oppressed of justice. They were even preying upon the widows and fatherless of the nation. Consequently, the day of God's judgment was inevitable and would soon come upon them (vv.3-4). The leaders naturally claimed that they had the law on their side. Therefore the public was forced to support their rulings even if they disagreed or protested.

Confronting the leaders head-on, Isaiah challenged them to ponder three questions, questions that every generation needs to consider:

⇒ What would they do on the day of reckoning, the day disaster struck? This is a clear reference to the invasion and conquest of Israel by Assyria. The Assyrians would execute most of Israel's leaders and deport the majority of the people.

⇒ *In that day*, to whom would the leaders flee for help? They could not expect help from the citizens they had oppressed. To the contrary, in a crisis, the oppressed would probably rise up against the leaders.

⇒ Where would the leaders leave their wealth in the coming crisis? Their wealth would be of no value to them, for they would not be able to take it with them. The leaders could expect to reap only what they had sown: they would either cringe as captives or be killed (v.4). Without question, when the Assyrians attacked, it would be a day of disaster. Remember that the Assyrians were known for their cruelty and brutality. Thus the Israelites could expect very few survivors from an Assyrian invasion. Most of the population would be killed, and the land and its wealth would be plundered. Nevertheless, even after this terrible experience of being utterly devastated and exiled by the Assyrians, the people of Israel would still not repent and turn back to the LORD. In their terrible distress the LORD stood ready to receive and help them, but they had no interest in the LORD. In spite of everything, they continued on in their unbelief and rebellion against God, further provoking the anger of the LORD. His hand of judgment was still lifted and set to fall.

Thought 1. The lesson is clear: the hand of God's judgment falls upon all who treat others unfairly, unjustly—whether politician, judge, attorney, military officer, or any other person in an official capacity. Every individual who oppresses others will face God's judgment. Suppressing people or depriving the poor, weak, widows, or fatherless of true justice will not be tolerated by the LORD. Listen to what God's Holy Word says:

"Nay, ye do wrong, and defraud, and that *your* brethren. Know ye not that the unrighteous shall not inherit the kingdom of God? Be not deceived: neither fornicators, nor idolaters, nor adulterers, nor effeminate, nor abusers of themselves with mankind, Nor thieves, nor covetous, nor drunkards, nor revilers, nor extortioners, shall inherit the kingdom of God" (1 Co.6:8-10).

"Now the works of the flesh are manifest, which are *these;* Adultery, fornication, uncleanness, lasciviousness, Idolatry, witchcraft, hatred, variance, emulations, wrath, strife, seditions, heresies, Envyings, murders, drunkenness, revellings, and such like: of the which I tell you before, as I have also told *you* in time past, that they which do such things shall not inherit the kingdom of God" (Ga.5:19-21).

"But fornication, and all uncleanness, or covetousness, let it not be once named among you, as becometh saints; Neither filthiness, nor foolish talking, nor jesting, which are not convenient: but rather giving of thanks. For this ye know, that no whoremonger, nor unclean person, nor covetous man, who is an idolater, hath any inheritance in the kingdom of Christ and of God. Let no man deceive you with vain words: for because of these things cometh the wrath of God upon the children of disobedience" (Ep.5:3-6).

"Thou shalt not oppress an hired servant *that is* poor and needy, *whether he be* of thy brethren, or of thy strangers that *are* in thy land within thy gates" (De.24:14).

"Thou shalt not pervert the judgment of the stranger, *nor* of the fatherless; nor take a widow's raiment to pledge" (De.24:17).

"He will surely reprove you, if ye do secretly accept persons" (Jb.13:10).

"Trust not in oppression, and become not vain in robbery: if riches increase, set not your heart *upon them*" (Ps.62:10).

"He that oppresseth the poor reproacheth his Maker: but he that honoureth him hath mercy on the poor" (Pr.14:31).

"When goods increase, they are increased that eat them: and what good *is there* to the owners thereof, saving the beholding *of them* with their eyes?" (Ecc.5:11).

---

2 (10:5-19) **Judgment, Reasons for—Assyria, Judgment of—Self-Exaltation, Results of—Nations, Judgment of, Caused by—Pride, Results of, Judgment—Pride, Example of, Assyria's King—Boasting, Example of, Assyria's King—God, Sovereignty of, Uses Nations As His Agent—Nations, Fact, Are Agents of God**: God's hand of judgment was to fall upon Assyria because of its boastful pride. The Assyrian people—the king, the leaders, and the citizens—exalted themselves over others. They acted as though they were gods, as though their nation was superior to other nations. Swelled with pride and arrogance, Assyria felt it had the right to treat people and nations as it wished. In view of this, the hand of God's judgment was destined to fall upon them:

OUTLINE	SCRIPTURE	SCRIPTURE	OUTLINE
2. God's judgment of Assyria, the boastful: Exalting oneself as God a. The use of Assyria as God's rod, His agent of judgment b. The reasons for God's judgment: God used Assyria to discipline Judah	5 O Assyrian, the rod of mine anger, and the staff in their hand is mine indignation. 6 I will send him against an hypocritical nation, and against the people of my wrath will I give him a charge, to take the spoil, and to take the prey, and to tread them down like the mire of the streets.	idols? 12 Wherefore it shall come to pass, *that* when the Lord hath performed his whole work upon mount Zion and on Jerusalem, I will punish the fruit of the stout heart of the king of Assyria, and the glory of his high looks.	4) Assyria was a prideful people: The king exalted himself—his power & wisdom—above all else: "I" & "my" used nine times
1) Assyria sought world domination • Sought to destroy many nations throughout the world • Sought to rule through its mighty officers	7 Howbeit he meaneth not so, neither doth his heart think so; but *it is* in his heart to destroy and cut off nations not a few. 8 For he saith, *Are* not my princes altogether kings?	13 For he saith, By the strength of my hand I have done *it,* and by my wisdom; for I am prudent: and I have removed the bounds of the people, and have robbed their treasures, and I have put down the inhabitants like a valiant *man:*	• "I" have conquered other nations, plundered their wealth, & subdued their leaders & people
2) Assyria felt all-powerful, unstoppable	9 *Is* not Calno as Carchemish? *is* not Hamath as Arpad? *is* not Samaria as Damascus?	14 And my hand hath found as a nest the riches of the people: and as one gathereth eggs *that are* left, have I gathered all the earth; and there was none that moved the wing, or opened the mouth, or peeped.	• "I" am so powerful & wise that it was as easy as snatching eggs out of a nest: No one was able to oppose "my" power
3) Assyria was an idolatrous people • They believed nations were overseen by different gods • They felt they could easily take Jerusalem with its inferior gods	10 As my hand hath found the kingdoms of the idols, and whose graven images did excel them of Jerusalem and of Samaria; 11 Shall I not, as I have done unto Samaria and her idols, so do to Jerusalem and her	15 Shall the axe boast itself against him that heweth therewith? *or* shall the saw magnify itself against him	5) Assyria was a boastful people • They felt they controlled their own fate & events

137

OUTLINE	SCRIPTURE	SCRIPTURE	OUTLINE
• They were, in reality, under God's control, functioning as His agents	that shaketh it? as if the rod should shake *itself* against them that lift it up, *or* as if the staff should lift up *itself, as if it were* no wood.	Holy One for a flame: and it shall burn and devour his thorns and his briers in one day;	2 K.19:35
c. The judgment of God described	16 Therefore shall the Lord, the Lord of hosts, send among his fat ones leanness; and under his glory he shall kindle a burning like the burning of a fire.	18 And shall consume the glory of his forest, and of his fruitful field, both soul and body: and they shall be as when a standardbearer fainteth.	3) The glory of Assyria would be destroyed
1) The Assyrian soldiers would be stricken with a plague: Like a blazing, flaming fire			
2) The judgment would fall in a single day, 37:36-37;	17 And the light of Israel shall be for a fire, and his	19 And the rest of the trees of his forest shall be few, that a child may write them.	4) The army would have so few soldiers that a child would be able to count them

a. Note a very significant fact: the LORD had chosen Assyria to be His rod, His agent of judgment (v.5). He used Assyria's insane desire to dominate the world as a means to carry out His judgment upon the Northern Kingdom of Israel. Because of Israel's rebellion and betrayal, the LORD was going to allow Assyria to conquer the Northern Kingdom. However, because of the heathen nation's brutality in assaulting Israel, the LORD issued a very stern warning to the cruel invaders. Note the word *woe*. The warning was to be a severe judgment.

b. Although God was going to use Assyria to discipline Judah, He gave five reasons why He would eventually execute judgment on Assyria itself (vv.6-15). These five reasons are clearly spelled out:

1) The Assyrians were to be destroyed because they had sought world domination (v.7). In their drive to build a worldwide empire, the Assyrians had maliciously destroyed the nations they had invaded. This they did through a strategy of deporting all citizens to foreign nations and then repopulating the conquered nation with foreigners. Under the Assyrians, a major shift of world population took place as well as the elimination of many people's identity and nationality. Once a conquered nation had been stripped of its government and population, an Assyrian leader or military officer was set up as ruler over the territory.

2) As Assyria sought world domination, the king began to feel that his nation was all powerful, unstoppable (v.9). When he thought about the other nations of the world, he considered them easy prey for capture. It even appeared that no nation could stop the war machine of Assyria. As this verse says, Calno was expected to fare no better than Carchemish; Hamath would be no different than Arpad, and Samaria would fall just as quickly as Damascus (v.9).

3) The Assyrians were an idolatrous people, worshippers of false gods (vv.10-11). They were steeped in idolatry and false worship. One of the major beliefs of ancient society was that a people's gods empowered them to conquer other nations. A victory meant that the gods of a particular people were stronger than the gods of the conquered foe. Apparently, the Assyrians became convinced that no kingdom could stand against their military power because their gods were far superior than the gods of other nations. The point to note is the depth of idolatry to which the Assyrians had sunk. As they planned their strategy to conquer Jerusalem, they felt they could take the city as easily as they had conquered Samaria, the capital of the Northern Kingdom. Again, note why: the Assyrians believed their gods were stronger than the images or gods of Jerusalem.

4) The Assyrians were a prideful people, a people who exalted themselves above others. Note the reference to the king who exalted himself—his power and wisdom—above all others on earth (vv.13-14). He used the word "I" and "my" at least eight times. In essence he was saying…
   • "I" have conquered other nations, plundered their wealth, and subdued their leaders and people (v.13).
   • "I" have proven my power and wisdom, through my brilliant military strategy and conquests. Conquering other nations was as easy as snatching eggs out of a nest. No one was able to oppose my power (v.14).

5) Assyria was a boastful people who felt they controlled their own fate, controlled the affairs and events concerning their nation and the building of their worldwide empire (v.15). But in their boasting they exposed the very folly of their arrogance. What could be more preposterous than for an ax or saw to boast in itself, to think that it is controlling the chopping or sawing instead of the person using the tool? The Assyrians felt that they were manipulating God Himself. Yet in reality, it was the LORD who was using them as a tool to execute His judgment upon the wicked of this earth, including Israel.

c. Because of Assyria's sins, God's hand of judgment would fall upon them and destroy the mighty nation (vv.16-19). The prideful and boastful would be shown how frail even the strongest people and nations were. And the lesson would be taught by the LORD of hosts Himself. Note the double title given to the LORD, emphasizing His enormous power and control over the world. There was no question about the humbling of Assyria that was to take place, for *the LORD, the LORD of Hosts,* could do it. He had the power to strike the Assyrian soldiers with a plague, and the plague would be like a blazing, flaming fire that consumed the glory of their prideful troops (v.16). The LORD's power was so great that the judgment of the plague would fall in a single day (37:36-37; 2 K.19:35). Even the glory of Assyria's harvest and fertile fields would be completely destroyed (v.18). Assyrian land would waste away and become a desert just like a sick man who wastes away. So few soldiers would remain that a child would be able to count them (v.19).

Thought 1. Boasting in self and exalting self over others are sins that will merit terrible judgment in the day of the LORD. When we exalt ourselves over others, we degrade, shame, and humiliate them.

It is an overblown sense of self-importance that causes us to consider ourselves better than others. Feelings of being more appealing, more personable, more intelligent, more valuable, or of more worth than other people cause us to elevate ourselves and demean others. Self-exaltation causes rulers to stifle freedom, threaten war, and even enslave people. Deeming ourselves superior to others leads to all kinds of wicked and perverted behavior. Therefore God warns us against degrading people and tearing them down. God loves people, and He expects us to build up and help one another that we might all live fruitful and victorious lives. Listen to what God's Holy Word says about boasting and exalting ourselves over other people:

"And whosoever shall exalt himself shall be abased; and he that shall humble himself shall be exalted" (Mt.23:12).

"There was a certain rich man, which was clothed in purple and fine linen, and fared sumptuously every day: And there was a certain beggar named Lazarus, which was laid at his gate, full of sores, And desiring to be fed with the crumbs which fell from the rich man's table: moreover the dogs came and licked his sores. And it came to pass, that the beggar died, and was carried by the angels into Abraham's bosom: the rich man also died, and was buried; And in hell he lift up his eyes, being in torments, and seeth Abraham afar off, and Lazarus in his bosom. And he cried and said, Father Abraham, have mercy on me, and send Lazarus, that he may dip the tip of his finger in water, and cool my tongue; for I am tormented in this flame" (Lu.16:19-24; also see vv.25-31).

"But now ye rejoice in your boastings: all such rejoicing is evil" (Js.4:16).

"They that trust in their wealth, and boast themselves in the multitude of their riches; None *of them* can by any means redeem his brother, nor give to God a ransom for him" (Ps.49:6-7).

"He loveth transgression that loveth strife: *and* he that exalteth his gate seeketh destruction" (Pr.17:19).

"Whoso boasteth himself of a false gift *is like* clouds and wind without rain" (Pr.25:14).

"Boast not thyself of to morrow; for thou knowest not what a day may bring forth" (Pr.27:1).

"For thou hast said in thine heart, I will ascend into heaven, I will exalt my throne above the stars of God: I will sit also upon the mount of the congregation, in the sides of the north: I will ascend above the heights of the clouds; I will be like the most High. Yet thou shalt be brought down to hell, to the sides of the pit" (Is.14:13-15).

"Though thou exalt *thyself* as the eagle, and though thou set thy nest among the stars, thence will I bring thee down, saith the LORD" (Ob.4).

3 (10:20-34) **Remnant, Promise of, to Israel—Israel, Promises to, a Remnant—Promises, the Remnant, of Israel—Assyria, Prophecies Concerning, Defeated by the LORD—Returning to the LORD, Promised, a Remnant of Israel**: despite Assyria's savagery toward Israel, a small number of Israelites (a remnant) would survive. This passage explains what happened to the people of the Northern Kingdom after the Assyrians destroyed the nation and deported the people to foreign lands.

OUTLINE	SCRIPTURE	SCRIPTURE	OUTLINE
3. God's wonderful promise of a small number of survivors (a remnant) in Israel despite Assyria's brutality: Returning to the LORD a. The promise of a remnant 1) They would no longer trust men but God 2) They would return to the Mighty God 3) They would no longer be numerous but merely a remnant • Because God's righteous judgment would destroy them—in perfect justice • Because the LORD of hosts would judge the whole land—all the Israelites b. The yoke (bondage, siege) of Assyria would be broken 1) The people of Zion (Jerusalem) were not to fear Assyria, who threatened & oppressed Judah in the	20 And it shall come to pass in that day, *that* the remnant of Israel, and such as are escaped of the house of Jacob, shall no more again stay upon him that smote them; but shall stay upon the LORD, the Holy One of Israel, in truth. 21 The remnant shall return, *even* the remnant of Jacob, unto the mighty God. 22 For though thy people Israel be as the sand of the sea, *yet* a remnant of them shall return: the consumption decreed shall overflow with righteousness. 23 For the Lord GOD of hosts shall make a consumption, even determined, in the midst of all the land. 24 Therefore thus saith the Lord GOD of hosts, O my people that dwellest in Zion, be not afraid of the Assyrian: he shall smite thee with a rod, and shall lift up his staff	against thee, after the manner of Egypt. 25 For yet a very little while, and the indignation shall cease, and mine anger in their destruction. 26 And the LORD of hosts shall stir up a scourge for him according to the slaughter of Midian at the rock of Oreb: and *as* his rod *was* upon the sea, so shall he lift it up after the manner of Egypt. 27 And it shall come to pass in that day, *that* his burden shall be taken away from off thy shoulder, and his yoke from off thy neck, and the yoke shall be destroyed because of the anointing. 28 He is come to Aiath, he is passed to Migron; at Michmash he hath laid up his carriages: 29 They are gone over the passage: they have taken up their lodging at Geba; Ramah	same way Egypt had • Because the LORD's anger against them was to end & be turned against Assyria • Because the LORD would destroy the Assyrians as He did the Midianites (through Gideon, 9:4-7; Jud.7:1-24) & the Egyptians (in the Red Sea, Ex.14:1-31) 2) The Assyrian yoke that threatened Jerusalem would be broken—*in that day* • Their conquest of city after city would carry their yoke right up to

OUTLINE	SCRIPTURE	SCRIPTURE	OUTLINE

the gates of Jerusalem	is afraid; Gibeah of Saul is fled.
	30 Lift up thy voice, O daughter of Gallim: cause it to be heard unto Laish, O poor Anathoth.
	31 Madmenah is removed; the inhabitants of Gebim gather themselves to flee.
	32 As yet shall he remain at Nob that day: he shall shake his hand *against* the mount of
		the daughter of Zion, the hill of Jerusalem.
		33 Behold, the Lord, the LORD of hosts, shall lop the bough with terror: and the high ones of stature *shall be* hewn down, and the haughty shall be humbled.
		34 And he shall cut down the thickets of the forest with iron, and Lebanon shall fall by a mighty one.
			north of Jerusalem
			
			c. The yoke of Assyria would be broken because God is all-powerful & in control
			   1) The LORD of hosts would chop down the mighty trees: The king & army of Assyria
			   2) The Mighty One would cut down the enemy with the ax of His judgment

• Their army & yoke would be broken at Nob, about two miles			

a. Isaiah shared the wonderful promise of God: a remnant of believers would survive the ferocious onslaught by Assyria (vv.20-23). Apparently when Assyria invaded the Northern Kingdom, some of the people fled to Judah to become citizens of the Southern Kingdom. These survivors from northern Israel and their descendants became part of the remnant promised by God. Through them, the names of the northern tribes were preserved among God's people down through the centuries.

Note that these few survivors, this remnant of Israelites, would learn a very important lesson. They would no longer trust men and the arm of the flesh, leaning upon nearby nations to help them in times of crisis (such as Syria, 7:1-9). Rather, they would return to the Mighty God, trusting Him to aid them (vv.20-21). Note also that a remnant of Jacob would return to the Mighty God, for they would learn that He is all powerful. He is more than able to save them from whatever crisis confronts them. Note the emphasis on their returning, that is, repenting.

The end result of the Assyrian captivity would be most tragic. Although Israel had once been numbered as the sand by the sea, only a very small remnant would return to the LORD and the promised land (vv.22-23). Two reasons are given for the small number:

⇒ Because God's righteous judgment would destroy them in an execution of perfect justice.
⇒ Because the LORD of hosts—the One who possesses all power and controls all rulers—would judge the entire land, including the Israelites.

b. A wonderful assurance is given in these verses to the people of Zion (Jerusalem): the yoke or threat of Assyria will be broken (vv.24-32). In its ambition for world domination, the Assyrians had intended to destroy Judah. But Isaiah proclaimed God's wonderful news to the Southern Kingdom: they were not to fear Assyria's threats and oppression (vv.24-26). Their threats and oppression would soon amount to no more than Egypt's had when God dealt with them at the Red Sea. Two reasons are given why the Jews of Judah were not to fear the Assyrians:

⇒ Because the LORD's anger against Judah was to end very soon. At that time, His anger would be turned against Assyria, and the vicious enemy would be destroyed (v.25).
⇒ Because the LORD would destroy the Assyrians as He did the Midianites by empowering His servant Gideon (9:4-7; also see outline and notes—Jdg.7:1-24 for more discussion). The Assyrians would be destroyed by the LORD as the Egyptians had been in the Red Sea (see outline and notes—Ex.14:1-31 for more discussion).

In that day—the day of God's judgment upon Assyria—the Assyrian yoke or siege that had been threatening to starve the people into subjection would be broken (vv.27-32). Although their conquest of city after city had carried their yoke of oppression right up to the gates of Jerusalem, their siege of the capital would fail (vv.28-32). In one day's time their army and yoke (siege) would be broken at Nob, which was about two miles north of Jerusalem. Although the Assyrian army would shake their fists at Mt. Zion (Jerusalem), their threats and self-confidence would be meaningless.

c. The yoke or siege of Assyria would be broken because the LORD of hosts is in control (vv.33-34). It is He who possesses all power and who controls the nations of the earth. Thus the LORD of hosts would chop down the mighty trees, the powerful king and army of Assyria. The Mighty One would cut down the enemy with the ax of His judgment (v.34).

Thought 1. In comparison to the total population of the earth, there is only a small remnant who are genuine believers. Scripture says, broad is the way that leads to destruction and narrow is the way that leads to life (Mt.7:13-14). Few of us are willing to turn from our sins. Sin looks too good, feels too good, and tastes too good. Frankly, we enjoy the sensual pleasures and comforts of life too much. Therefore, giving these up seldom if ever crosses our minds. Thus we continue to walk through life in unbelief, living like we want and doing our own thing when we want. The commandments of God, the restraints upon our sinful behavior, are ignored. In many cases, we even deny the truth of God's Word, claiming that His commandments should not be taken literally or that they don't apply to us today. We think that going after the most comfortable life possible could not be wrong, not if we occasionally give of our time or finances to help meet the desperate needs of the world. We never consider that we keep most of our time and finances for our own personal pleasures while many in the world are suffering terribly and are without adequate provisions.

As stated, there is only a small percentage of people in this world who are genuine believers. There are only a few who deny themselves and take up the cross daily to follow Christ. There are only a few who truly give all they are and have to the cause of Christ, to proclaim the gospel and meet the desperate needs of the world.

Still, the message of the prophet Isaiah is this: return to the LORD. Give your life totally to Him. Deny yourself and take up the cross daily to follow Christ. Turn away from your sinful behavior and false worship. Repent! Turn back to the LORD. Listen to God's Holy Word:

"I tell you, Nay: but, except ye repent, ye shall all likewise perish" (Lu.13:3).

"And he arose, and came to his father. But when he was yet a great way off, his father saw him, and had compassion, and ran, and fell on his neck, and kissed him" (Lu.15:20).

"Repent ye therefore, and be converted, that your sins may be blotted out, when the times of refreshing shall come from the presence of the Lord" (Ac.3:19).

"Repent therefore of this thy wickedness, and pray God, if perhaps the thought of thine heart may be forgiven thee" (Ac.8:22).

"And the times of this ignorance God winked at; but now commandeth all men every where to repent" (Ac.17:30).

"For ye were as sheep going astray; but are now returned unto the Shepherd and Bishop of your souls" (1 Pe.2:25).

"If my people, which are called by my name, shall humble themselves, and pray, and seek my face, and turn from their wicked ways; then will I hear from heaven, and will forgive their sin, and will heal their land" (2 Chr.7:14).

"Let the wicked forsake his way, and the unrighteous man his thoughts: and let him return unto the Lord, and he will have mercy upon him; and to our God, for he will abundantly pardon" (Is.55:7).

"Come, and let us return unto the Lord: for he hath torn, and he will heal us; he hath smitten, and he will bind us up" (Ho.6:1).

"O Israel, return unto the Lord thy God; for thou hast fallen by thine iniquity" (Ho.14:1).

Thought 2. The Lord may use other people to discipline us, just as He used Assyria to discipline Israel and Judah. Even evil men may be used by God to stir our hearts, to turn us away from sin and false worship, to bring us to repentance, and to turn us back to God. God loves His people; therefore when we sin, He will use anything and everything He can to help us turn our lives around. He knows that if we continue in sin we will damage our bodies and relationships. Our sins often wreck our own families and even destroy the lives of other people. Yet because of His love, God seeks to correct us even as a father corrects his child. Thus when we are disciplined by God, we must always know that God disciplines us only in love. Listen to what God's Holy Word says:

"Every branch in me that beareth not fruit he taketh away: and every *branch* that beareth fruit, he purgeth it, that it may bring forth more fruit" (Jn.15:2).

"For this cause many *are* weak and sickly among you, and many sleep. For if we would judge ourselves, we should not be judged. But when we are judged, we are chastened of the Lord, that we should not be condemned with the world" (1 Co.11:30-32).

"And ye have forgotten the exhortation which speaketh unto you as unto children, My son, despise not thou the chastening of the Lord, nor faint when thou art rebuked of him: For whom the Lord loveth he chasteneth, and scourgeth every son whom he receiveth. If ye endure chastening, God dealeth with you as with sons; for what son is he whom the father chasteneth not? But if ye be without chastisement, whereof all are partakers, then are ye bastards, and not sons. Furthermore we have had fathers of our flesh which corrected *us,* and we gave *them* reverence: shall we not much rather be in subjection unto the Father of spirits, and live? For they verily for a few days chastened *us* after their own pleasure; but he for *our* profit, that *we* might be partakers of his holiness. Now no chastening for the present seemeth to be joyous, but grievous: nevertheless afterward it yieldeth the peaceable fruit of righteousness unto them which are exercised thereby" (He.12:5-11).

"As many as I love, I rebuke and chasten: be zealous therefore, and repent" (Re.3:19).

"Thou shalt also consider in thine heart, that, as a man chasteneth his son, *so* the Lord thy God chasteneth thee" (De.8:5).

"Blessed *is* the man whom thou chastenest, O Lord, and teachest him out of thy law" (Ps.94:12).

"My son, despise not the chastening of the Lord; neither be weary of his correction: For whom the Lord loveth he correcteth; even as a father the son *in whom* he delighteth" (Pr.3:11-12).

"O Lord, I know that the way of man *is* not in himself: *it is* not in man that walketh to direct his steps. O Lord, correct me, but with judgment; not in thine anger, lest thou bring me to nothing" (Je.10:23-24).

1. The coming of the Savior: From the Branch of Jesse, David's father, 4:2; 53:2; 2 S.7:16; Mt.1:1; Ac.2:29-30; Ro.1:1-3; Re.5:4-5

2. The qualification of the Savior: God's Spirit rests on Him
   a. In wisdom & in understanding
   b. In counsel & in power
   c. In knowledge & in the fear of God

3. The future work of the Savior
   a. He will establish true righteousness & justice on earth
      1) He will not judge by appearance or hearsay
      2) He will execute perfect righteousness & justice for the poor & the meek, the needy & oppressed
      3) He will execute judgment against the wicked, slaying them with the breath of His mouth, Re.19:15
      4) He will wear righteousness & faithfulness as a belt
   b. He will restore creation itself & bring peace to the earth, 30:23-26; 65:25; Eze.34:25-29; Ho.2:20-22
      1) The nature of animals will be radically changed: From wild & ferocious to tame & peaceful
      2) The nature of man—even that of a child—will be totally changed: Fear & danger will be erased
      3) The destruction of life & property will cease: Because the knowledge of God (His love & peace) will fill the earth
   c. He will save the Gentiles
      1) He will be a *banner* to rally all people, 49:22
      2) He will live in a glorious place of *rest*

CHAPTER 11

G. The Coming Savior & the Establishment of God's Kingdom on Earth: Hope Given Through the Messiah, the Lord Jesus Christ, 11:1–12:6

And there shall come forth a rod out of the stem of Jesse, and a Branch shall grow out of his roots:
2 And the spirit of the LORD shall rest upon him, the spirit of wisdom and understanding, the spirit of counsel and might, the spirit of knowledge and of the fear of the LORD;
3 And shall make him of quick understanding in the fear of the LORD: and he shall not judge after the sight of his eyes, neither reprove after the hearing of his ears:
4 But with righteousness shall he judge the poor, and reprove with equity for the meek of the earth: and he shall smite the earth with the rod of his mouth, and with the breath of his lips shall he slay the wicked.
5 And righteousness shall be the girdle of his loins, and faithfulness the girdle of his reins.
6 The wolf also shall dwell with the lamb, and the leopard shall lie down with the kid; and the calf and the young lion and the fatling together; and a little child shall lead them.
7 And the cow and the bear shall feed; their young ones shall lie down together: and the lion shall eat straw like the ox.
8 And the sucking child shall play on the hole of the asp, and the weaned child shall put his hand on the cockatrice' den.
9 They shall not hurt nor destroy in all my holy mountain: for the earth shall be full of the knowledge of the LORD, as the waters cover the sea.
10 And in that day there shall be a root of Jesse, which shall stand for an ensign of the people; to it shall the Gentiles seek: and his rest shall be glorious.

11 And it shall come to pass in that day, *that* the Lord shall set his hand again the second time to recover the remnant of his people, which shall be left, from Assyria, and from Egypt, and from Pathros, and from Cush, and from Elam, and from Shinar, and from Hamath, and from the islands of the sea.
12 And he shall set up an ensign for the nations, and shall assemble the outcasts of Israel, and gather together the dispersed of Judah from the four corners of the earth.
13 The envy also of Ephraim shall depart, and the adversaries of Judah shall be cut off: Ephraim shall not envy Judah, and Judah shall not vex Ephraim.
14 But they shall fly upon the shoulders of the Philistines toward the west; they shall spoil them of the east together: they shall lay their hand upon Edom and Moab; and the children of Ammon shall obey them.
15 And the LORD shall utterly destroy the tongue of the Egyptian sea; and with his mighty wind shall he shake his hand over the river, and shall smite it in the seven streams, and make *men* go over dryshod.
16 And there shall be an highway for the remnant of his people, which shall be left, from Assyria; like as it was to Israel in the day that he came up out of the land of Egypt.

CHAPTER 12

And in that day thou shalt say, O LORD, I will praise thee: though thou wast angry with me, thine anger is turned away, and thou comfortedst me.
2 Behold, God *is* my salvation; I will trust, and not be afraid: for the LORD JEHOVAH *is* my strength and *my* song; he also is become my salvation.
3 Therefore with joy shall ye draw water out of the wells of salvation.
4 And in that day shall ye say, Praise the LORD, call upon his name, declare his

d. He will save a remnant of Jewish believers, free His people for a second time, 16 (see Ex.12:1–13:16 for the first Exodus)
   1) He will bring His people back from all nations

   2) He will raise a *banner* to rally His people from all over the earth: To free them from their bondage & exile

   3) He will heal the division between Israel & Judah, Eze.37:15-28; Ho.1:11
      • They will no longer be jealous or hostile to one another
      • They will unite, defeat, & be victorious over all their enemies

   4) He will remove all obstacles that hinder the return of His people to the promised land
      • He will carry out a second Exodus, drying the Gulf of Suez & breaking up the great Euphrates River into seven shallow streams, Ex.14:21-22
      • He will make a great highway for His people to leave Assyria, their enslavers

4. The song of praise for the Savior: True reasons to praise the LORD *in that day*
   a. God will turn away from wrath & comfort His people

      1) Because God is their salvation, strength, & song

      2) Because God will provide water, that is, the basic necessities of life
   b. God will flood His people with joy & the desire to proclaim His name

| 1) To share with the nations what He has done for them, 11:11-16
2) To exalt His name
3) To make known all His | doings among the people, make mention that his name is exalted.
5 Sing unto the LORD; for he hath done excellent things: | this *is* known in all the earth.
6 Cry out and shout, thou inhabitant of Zion: for great *is* the Holy One of Israel in the midst of thee. | glorious works
c. God—the Holy One of Israel—will dwell among them |

DIVISION I

THE PROPHECIES OF REBUKE AND HOPE GIVEN TO JUDAH AND JERUSALEM: AN OVERVIEW OF THE PRESENT AND FUTURE OF GOD'S PEOPLE, 1:1–12:6

G. The Coming Savior and the Establishment of God's Kingdom on Earth: Hope Given Through the Messiah, the Lord Jesus Christ, 11:1–12:6

(11:1–12:6) **Introduction**: conflict, strife, war, terrorist attacks, murder, abuse—we live in a world of lawlessness and violence. No community escapes the criminal, wicked behavior of sinful hearts. Despite the peace and comfort that we experience at times, the world is full of crime, corruption, wickedness, and evil. Disorder and disturbance occur within every community and they occur often. How many families are ripped apart by divorce? How many neighbors are alienated from one another due to petty differences? How many co-workers are jealous of each other or prejudiced and discriminatory toward fellow workers? How many people are envious of others or feel slighted by them and begin to slander their names? When we consider all the disturbances that take place every day, we must acknowledge that we live in a world that knows very little peace or tranquility. Disturbance and disorder—ranging from mild agitation to major conflict and war—affect every one of us.

Within society and within the heart of every human being is a longing for peace and tranquility. The *good news* is that there is great hope and a wonderful promise for the world. The LORD promises a day in which there will be no more war or conflict, a day in which the human heart will rest in peace and tranquility. This day will be when the Lord Jesus Christ returns and sets up His kingdom on earth. This is the wonderful message of the present Scripture. The Savior is returning to establish God's kingdom on earth, a kingdom of perfect righteousness and justice.

As we study this passage, we must keep in mind that it is a prophecy about the coming Messiah, the Savior of the world, the Lord Jesus Christ. With this prophecy Isaiah closes the first section of his great book, entitled by us: "The Prophecies of Rebuke and Hope Given to Judah and Jerusalem." No more *fitting climax* could be chosen for closing this first section. Once God has rebuked and judged His people for their terrible sins, He reaches out to offer them the wonderful hope of God's kingdom coming to earth. This is, *The Coming Savior and the Establishment of God's Kingdom on Earth: Hope Given Through the Messiah, the Lord Jesus Christ*, 11:1–12:6.

1. The coming of the Savior: a Branch from Jesse, David's father, 4:2; 53:2; 2 S.7:16; Mt.1:1; Ac.2:29-30; Ro.1:1-3; Re.5:4-5 (11:1).
2. The qualification of the Savior: God's Spirit rests on Him (11:2).
3. The future work of the Savior (11:3-16).
4. The song of praise for the Savior: true reasons to praise the LORD *in that day* (12:1-6).

1 (11:1) **Christ, Symbolized by, a Branch—Branch, Symbol of, Christ—Savior, Prophecy Concerning, Will Bear Fruit—Christ, Roots of, David's Father Jesse—Messiah, Prophecy Concerning, Descendant of David**: the coming of the Savior is promised and the Scripture identifies Him. Closely note who Scripture says He is.

OUTLINE	SCRIPTURE
1. The coming of the Savior: A Branch from Jesse, David's father, 4:2; 53:2; 2 S.7:16; Mt.1:1; Ac.2:29-30; Ro.1:1-3; Re.5:4-5	And there shall come forth a rod out of the stem of Jesse, and a Branch shall grow out of his roots:

a. Scripture says that the Savior (Messiah) is a *rod* or *shoot* that comes from the *stem* or *stump of Jesse*. The *stump* is the line of Jesse, his descendants. Remember that King David was the youngest son of Jesse, and that David's royal kingdom reached the summit of righteousness and justice. But the word *stump* also indicates that the towering tree of David's royal power would be cut off. No longer would the descendants of Jesse rule on a throne. Their rule and royal line would be cut so much that only a stump would remain. Most of the descendants would be cut off, and none of them would hold a position of authority. Even the few who would still be alive when the Savior came would be living in poverty and obscurity. The illustrious family of David would lose its glory and become an average, undistinguished family (see Am.9:11).[1] Remember the poverty of Mary and Joseph and the lowly birth of Christ (Lu.2:7, 24).

b. Although only a stump of descendants would remain, the Savior would come forth from the descendants of Jesse, like a small *shoot* growing out of a stem or a stump. The idea is that the Savior would come as a small and tender child—a totally unexpected entrance into the world. Who would ever think that the promised Messiah—the Prince of Peace who was to come from the royal line of David—would come as a lowly child in such humble surroundings from a poor and obscure family?

---

[1] H.C. Leupold. *Exposition of Isaiah*, Vol. 1, p.216.

c. Nevertheless, the small *shoot*, the Savior, will grow into a strong branch that bears fruit. Jeremiah also refers to the Savior as *a righteous Branch*. He says, "Behold, the days come, saith the LORD, that I will raise unto David a righteous Branch, and a king shall reign and prosper [bear fruit], and shall execute judgment and justice in the earth" (Je.23:5).

This reference to the Savior's being a Branch always means at least two things: first, as a strong Branch growing from the root of Jesse, the Savior will restore David's kingdom. He will sit on the throne of David and fulfill all the wonderful promises God had given David. These promises include the establishment of God's kingdom on earth, which is now being prophesied by Isaiah in this present passage (see outline and note—2 S.7:11-17 for more discussion).

Second, as a strong branch, the Savior will bear fruit, much fruit. Other Scriptures tell us why the Savior came and what the fruit will be:

1) The Savior came to minister and to give His life as a ransom to set people free from the bondage of sin and death.

> **"Even as the Son of man came not to be ministered unto, but to minister, and to give his life a ransom for many" (Mt.20:28).**
> **"In whom we have redemption through his blood, the forgiveness of sins, according to the riches of his grace" (Ep.1:7).**
> **"Forasmuch then as the children are partakers of flesh and blood, he also himself likewise took part of the same; that through death he might destroy him that had the power of death, that is, the devil; And deliver them who through fear of death were all their lifetime subject to bondage" (He.2:14-15).**

2) The Savior came to seek and to save the lost, all who were alienated from God because of their sin.

> **"For the Son of man is come to seek and to save that which was lost" (Lu.19:10).**
> **"Therefore if any man *be* in Christ, *he is* a new creature: old things are passed away; behold, all things are become new. And all things *are* of God, who hath reconciled us to himself by Jesus Christ, and hath given to us the ministry of reconciliation; To wit, that God was in Christ, reconciling the world unto himself, not imputing their trespasses unto them; and hath committed unto us the word of reconciliation. Now then we are ambassadors for Christ, as though God did beseech *you* by us: we pray *you* in Christ's stead, be ye reconciled to God. For he hath made him *to be* sin for us, who knew no sin; that we might be made the righteousness of God in him" (2 Co.5:17-21).**

3) The Savior came that we might have life and have it abundantly.

> **"The thief cometh not, but for to steal, and to kill, and to destroy: I am come that they might have life, and that they might have *it* more abundantly" (Jn.10:10).**
> **"Jesus said unto her, I am the resurrection, and the life: he that believeth in me, though he were dead, yet shall he live" (Jn.11:25).**
> **"Jesus saith unto him, I am the way, the truth, and the life: no man cometh unto the Father, but by me" (Jn.14:6).**
> **"That as sin hath reigned unto death, even so might grace reign through righteousness unto eternal life by Jesus Christ our Lord" (Ro.5:21).**
> **"But is now made manifest by the appearing of our Saviour Jesus Christ, who hath abolished death, and hath brought life and immortality to light through the gospel" (2 Ti.1:10).**
> **"Whereby are given unto us exceeding great and precious promises: that by these ye might be partakers of the divine nature, having escaped the corruption that is in the world through lust....For so an entrance shall be ministered unto you abundantly into the everlasting kingdom of our Lord and Saviour Jesus Christ" (2 Pe.1:4, 11).**
> **"He that hath the Son hath life; *and* he that hath not the Son of God hath not life" (1 Jn.5:12).**

4) The Savior came to do the will of God, which was to die for the sins of people.

> **"But we see Jesus, who was made a little lower than the angels for the suffering of death, crowned with glory and honour; that he by the grace of God should taste death for every man. For it became him, for whom *are* all things, and by whom *are* all things, in bringing many sons unto glory, to make the captain of their salvation perfect through sufferings. For both he that sanctifieth and they who are sanctified *are* all of one: for which cause he is not ashamed to call them brethren, Saying, I will declare thy name unto my brethren, in the midst of the church will I sing praise unto thee. And again, I will put my trust in him. And again, Behold I and the children which God hath given me. Forasmuch then as the children are partakers of flesh and blood, he also himself likewise took part of the same; that through death he might destroy him that had the power of death, that is, the devil" (He.2:9-14).**

d. The Savior or Messiah is definitely Jesus Christ, and the picture of the *Branch* (*netser*) definitely identifies Christ as the Branch. The Hebrew word *netser* became the name of Nazareth (*netsereth*). Christ became known as Jesus of Nazareth, which Scripture says was a fulfillment of prophecy: "And He [Jesus Christ] came and dwelt in a city called Nazareth: that it might be fulfilled which was spoken by the prophets, He shall be called a Nazarene" (Mt.2:23).[2]

---

2 Stanley M. Horton. *Isaiah*, p.97.

Time and again throughout Scripture Jesus Christ is called *The Son of David* and referred to as the *shoot* or the Branch. Without question Jesus Christ is the promised Messiah, the descendant of Jesse and David who is to bring God's kingdom to earth. Note these few Scriptures among many to support the messiahship of Christ:

"And thine house and thy kingdom shall be established for ever before thee: thy throne shall be established for ever" (2 S.7:16).

"In that day shall the branch of the LORD be beautiful and glorious, and the fruit of the earth *shall be* excellent and comely for them that are escaped of Israel" (Is.4:2).

"For unto us a child is born, unto us a son is given: and the government shall be upon his shoulder: and his name shall be called Wonderful, Counsellor, The mighty God, The everlasting Father, The Prince of Peace. Of the increase of *his* government and peace *there shall be* no end, upon the throne of David, and upon his kingdom, to order it, and to establish it with judgment and with justice from henceforth even for ever. The zeal of the LORD of hosts will perform this" (Is.9:6-7).

"And there shall come forth a rod out of the stem of Jesse, and a Branch shall grow out of his roots" (Is.11:1).

"For he shall grow up before him as a tender plant, and as a root out of a dry ground: he hath no form nor comeliness; and when we shall see him, *there is* no beauty that we should desire him" (Is.53:2).

"Behold, the days come, saith the LORD, that I will raise unto David a righteous Branch, and a King shall reign and prosper, and shall execute judgment and justice in the earth" (Je.23:5).

"The book of the generation of Jesus Christ, the son of David, the son of Abraham" (Mt.1:1).

"Men *and* brethren, let me freely speak unto you of the patriarch David, that he is both dead and buried, and his sepulchre is with us unto this day. Therefore being a prophet, and knowing that God had sworn with an oath to him, that of the fruit of his loins, according to the flesh, he would raise up Christ to sit on his throne" (Ac.2:29-30).

"Paul, a servant of Jesus Christ, called *to be* an apostle, separated unto the gospel of God, (Which he had promised afore by his prophets in the holy scriptures,) Concerning his Son Jesus Christ our Lord, which was made of the seed of David according to the flesh" (Ro.1:1-3).

"And I wept much, because no man was found worthy to open and to read the book, neither to look thereon. And one of the elders saith unto me, Weep not: behold, the Lion of the tribe of Juda, the Root of David, hath prevailed to open the book, and to loose the seven seals thereof" (Re.5:4-5).

2 (11:2) **Jesus Christ, Qualifications of, God's Spirit—Savior, Qualifications of—Holy Spirit, Work of, to Rest on Christ—Messiah, Qualifications of—Wisdom, Meaning—Understanding, Meaning—Counsel, Meaning of—Might, Meaning of—Power, Meaning of—Knowledge, Meaning of—Fear of the LORD, Meaning of**: the Savior will be imminently qualified to establish God's kingdom on earth, for He will be filled with all the fullness of God's Spirit. The *Spirit of the LORD* will rest on Him, fully equipping Him to fulfill His task. Throughout history, other people had been endowed with God's Spirit, including Isaiah. But in every case the person was a mere human being, therefore, the power of the Spirit was limited. But not so with the Savior. The Spirit of the LORD indwelt Him in *all the fullness of God Himself* (Col.1:19; 2:9). He was able to fulfill the works of God with the full power of God. Jesus Christ began His preaching ministry by proclaiming that the fullness of God's Spirit was upon Him (Lu.4:18). In the present passage Isaiah says that six very special gifts of the Spirit will rest upon the Messiah[3]:

a. There will be the gift of *wisdom (chokmah),* which means to be skillful; to have good sense; to act wisely.[4] It is practical wisdom, practical insight that enables a person to know what to do and how to do it. A person is able to act wisely, to carry out his project or task successfully.

b. There will be the gift of *understanding (biynah* or *binah),* which means to have the ability to grasp facts or knowledge that lead to understanding. A person with understanding can discern between various possibilities. He has the ability to solve problems.[5]

c. There will be the gift of *counsel (etsah),* which means advice, purpose, or plan. The Savior Jesus Christ will be filled with the *Spirit of Counsel*, the ability to see into a situation and to devise plans to handle the situation. Jesus Christ would be able to deal with all situations no matter how complex. By being filled with the "Spirit of Counsel" the Messiah is able to empathize with the sufferings of all people and to counsel them about how to cope with and manage their sufferings (He.4:15-16).

d. There will be also the gift of *might* or *power (gebuwrah or geburah),* which means to possess strength; to act mightily with force or valor; to be strong and prevail; to take heroic action. By possessing the *Spirit of Power* the Savior Jesus Christ was able to accomplish every task He undertook and to gain the victory over every obstacle, opposition, and enemy.

e. There will be the gift of *knowledge (daath),* which means to know and fully understand; to be deeply aware; to perceive with full comprehension. The idea is a deep knowledge, an embracing knowledge that fully comprehends. It is the kind of knowledge that takes hold of what is known, that experiences what is known. For example, the Savior Jesus Christ possessed the very knowledge of God Himself. His knowledge ran deep, embracing a full understanding of God. Thus the Savior possesses a full knowledge of every person, thing, and event, not only in the past and present but also in the future. The

---

3 The following definition of the six gifts is gleaned from *Strong's Exhaustive Concordance of the Bible; The NIV Exhaustive Concordance; The Old Testament Hebrew-English Dictionary of the Complete Biblical Library; The New Brown-Driver-Briggs-Gesenius Hebrew and English Lexicon; The Theological Word Book of the Old Testament;* and the commentaries listed in the bibliographies.

4 *The New Strong's Exhaustive Concordance*, #2451; also see #2449.

5 H.C. Leupold. *Exposition of Isaiah,* Vol. 1, p.217.

Spirit of Knowledge that rests upon Him is naturally the knowledge of God Himself. His knowledge is a great comfort to all believers, for He knows our every need. He can meet our need because of the *Spirit of Power* that He possesses.

f. There will be the gift of *fear*, the *fear of the LORD*. The word *fear* (*yirah*) means to have a reverential awe or dread; to experience great apprehension or show profound reverence. The idea is that a person humbly walks before God in reverence, trust, obedience and worship. Note that the Savior will take *great delight,* great joy and rejoicing, in the fear of the LORD (v.3). The idea is that He will totally yield Himself to the will of God. Carrying out the will of God will not be a burden to Him but, rather, a joy and a delight.

The task of the Savior was to be an enormous undertaking. He was to provide redemption for the sinful and to establish God's kingdom on earth. To equip Him for this awesome task, the *Spirit of the LORD* rested upon Him in all the fullness of God. This was the clear prophecy predicted by Isaiah the prophet.

OUTLINE	SCRIPTURE
2. The qualification of the Savior: God's Spirit rests on Him a. In wisdom & in understanding b. In counsel & in power c. In knowledge & in the fear of God	2 And the spirit of the LORD shall rest upon him, the spirit of wisdom and understanding, the spirit of counsel and might, the spirit of knowledge and of the fear of the LORD;

Thought 1. Isaiah predicted that the *Spirit of the LORD* will rest on the *Branch* that grew from the stump of Jesse (vv.1-2). Jesus Christ is unquestionably this Branch upon whom the Spirit of God rested. Christ fulfilled the prophecy of Isaiah:

"And the spirit of the LORD shall rest upon him, the spirit of wisdom and understanding, the spirit of counsel and might, the spirit of knowledge and of the fear of the LORD" (Is.11:2).

"Behold my servant, whom I uphold; mine elect, *in whom* my soul delighteth; I have put my spirit upon him: he shall bring forth judgment to the Gentiles" (Is.42:1).

"The Spirit of the Lord GOD *is* upon me; because the LORD hath anointed me to preach good tidings unto the meek; he hath sent me to bind up the brokenhearted, to proclaim liberty to the captives, and the opening of the prison to *them that are* bound" (Is.61:1).

"And Jesus, when he was baptized, went up straightway out of the water: and, lo, the heavens were opened unto him, and he saw the Spirit of God descending like a dove, and lighting upon him" (Mt.3:16).

"And John bare record, saying, I saw the Spirit descending from heaven like a dove, and it abode upon him" (Jn.1:32).

"How God anointed Jesus of Nazareth with the Holy Ghost and with power: who went about doing good, and healing all that were oppressed of the devil; for God was with him" (Ac.10:38).

Thought 2. Once we accept Christ as our Savior, the Spirit of God comes and lives within our lives. Listen to some of the amazing things the Spirit of God does for us:
(1) He bears witness that we are the adopted children of Israel.

"The Spirit itself beareth witness with our spirit, that we are the children of God" (Ro.8:16).

"But when the fulness of the time was come, God sent forth his Son, made of a woman, made under the law, To redeem them that were under the law, that we might receive the adoption of sons. And because ye are sons, God hath sent forth the Spirit of his Son into your hearts, crying, Abba, Father" (Ga.4:4-6).

"In whom ye also *trusted,* after that ye heard the word of truth, the gospel of your salvation: in whom also after that ye believed, ye were sealed with that holy Spirit of promise, Which is the earnest of our inheritance until the redemption of the purchased possession, unto the praise of his glory" (Ep.1:13-14).

"And he that keepeth his commandments dwelleth in him, and he in him. And hereby we know that he abideth in us, by the Spirit which he hath given us" (1 Jn.3:24).

"Hereby know we that we dwell in him, and he in us, because he hath given us of his Spirit" (1 Jn.4:13).

"This is he that came by water and blood, *even* Jesus Christ; not by water only, but by water and blood. And it is the Spirit that beareth witness, because the Spirit is truth" (1 Jn.5:6).

(2) He guides us as we walk day by day.

"Howbeit when he, the Spirit of truth, is come, he will guide you into all truth: for he shall not speak of himself; but whatsoever he shall hear, *that* shall he speak: and he will show you things to come" (Jn.16:13).

"And he that keepeth his commandments dwelleth in him, and he in him. And hereby we know that he abideth in us, by the Spirit which he hath given us" (1 Jn.3:24).

"For as many as are led by the Spirit of God, they are the sons of God" (Ro.8:14)

"And thine ears shall hear a word behind thee, saying, This *is* the way, walk ye in it, when ye turn to the right hand, and when ye turn to the left" (Is.30:21).

(3) He teaches us both the Word of God and how to walk through life.

> **"For the Holy Ghost shall teach you in the same hour what ye ought to say" (Lu.12:12).**
> **"But the Comforter, *which is* the Holy Ghost, whom the Father will send in my name, he shall teach you all things, and bring all things to your remembrance, whatsoever I have said unto you" (Jn.14:26).**
> **"Which things also we speak, not in the words which man's wisdom teacheth, but which the Holy Ghost teacheth; comparing spiritual things with spiritual" (1 Co.2:13).**
> **"But the anointing which ye have received of him abideth in you, and ye need not that any man teach you: but as the same anointing teacheth you of all things, and is truth, and is no lie, and even as it hath taught you, ye shall abide in him" (1 Jn.2:27).**

(4) The Spirit of God gives life to our mortal bodies.

> **"For the bread of God is he which cometh down from heaven, and giveth life unto the world" (Jn.6:33).**
> **"But if the Spirit of him that raised up Jesus from the dead dwell in you, he that raised up Christ from the dead shall also quicken your mortal bodies by his Spirit that dwelleth in you" (Ro.8:11).**
> **"Who also hath made us able ministers of the new testament; not of the letter, but of the spirit: for the letter killeth, but the spirit giveth life" (2 Co.3:6).**
> **"For Christ also hath once suffered for sins, the just for the unjust, that he might bring us to God, being put to death in the flesh, but quickened by the Spirit" (1 Pe.3:18).**

(5) The Spirit of God comforts us as He dwells within us.

> **"And I will pray the Father, and he shall give you another Comforter, that he may abide with you for ever" (Jn.14:16).**
> **"*Even* the Spirit of truth; whom the world cannot receive, because it seeth him not, neither knoweth him: but ye know him; for he dwelleth with you, and shall be in you" (Jn.14:17).**
> **"But the Comforter, *which is* the Holy Ghost, whom the Father will send in my name, he shall teach you all things, and bring all things to your remembrance, whatsoever I have said unto you" (Jn.14:26).**
> **"But when the Comforter is come, whom I will send unto you from the Father, *even* the Spirit of truth, which proceedeth from the Father, he shall testify of me" (Jn.15:26).**

(6) The Savior convicts us of sin.

> **"Nevertheless I tell you the truth; It is expedient for you that I go away: for if I go not away, the Comforter will not come unto you; but if I depart, I will send him unto you. And when he is come, he will reprove the world of sin, and of righteousness, and of judgment" (Jn.16:7-8).**

3 (11:3-16) **Messiah, Work of—Savior, Work of—Jesus Christ, Work of—Kingdom, Messianic, Nature of—Messiah, Kingdom of, Life Within—Remnant, Promised—Christ, Prophecy Concerning, to Establish God's Kingdom—Prophecies, Concerning Messiah's Kingdom; Concerning a Restored Creation; Concerning the Remnant; Concerning Israel's Salvation—Millennium, Discussed—Millennium, Founded – Ushered in, by Christ**: the future work of the Savior will involve a great task. The Savior will establish the kingdom of God on earth. This will be a period of history commonly known as the Messianic Kingdom or the Millennium (see DEEPER STUDY #2—Is.2:1-5 for more discussion). What follows is a captivating description of the Messiah's kingdom:

OUTLINE	SCRIPTURE	SCRIPTURE	OUTLINE
3. The future work of the Savior a. He will establish true righteousness & justice on the earth 1) He will not judge by appearance or hearsay 2) He will execute perfect righteousness & justice for the poor & the meek (the needy & oppressed) 3) He will execute judgment against the wicked, slay-	3 And shall make him of quick understanding in the fear of the LORD: and he shall not judge after the sight of his eyes, neither reprove after the hearing of his ears: 4 But with righteousness shall he judge the poor, and reprove with equity for the meek of the earth: and he shall smite the earth with the rod of his mouth, and with	the breath of his lips shall he slay the wicked. 5 And righteousness shall be the girdle of his loins, and faithfulness the girdle of his reins. 6 The wolf also shall dwell with the lamb, and the leopard shall lie down with the kid; and the calf and the young lion and the fatling together; and a little child shall lead them.	ing them with the breath of His mouth, Re.19:15 4) He will wear righteousness & faithfulness as a belt b. He will restore creation itself & bring peace to the earth, 30:23-26; 65:25; Eze.34:25-29; Ho.2:20-22 1) The nature of animals will be radically changed: From wild & ferocious to

OUTLINE	SCRIPTURE	SCRIPTURE	OUTLINE
tame & peaceful	7 And the cow and the bear shall feed; their young ones shall lie down together: and the lion shall eat straw like the ox.	assemble the outcasts of Israel, and gather together the dispersed of Judah from the four corners of the earth.	over the earth: To free them from their bondage & exile
2) The nature of man—even that of a child—will be totally changed: Fear & danger will be erased	8 And the sucking child shall play on the hole of the asp, and the weaned child shall put his hand on the cockatrice' den.	13 The envy also of Ephraim shall depart, and the adversaries of Judah shall be cut off: Ephraim shall not envy Judah, and Judah shall not vex Ephraim.	3) He will heal the division between Israel & Judah, Eze.37:15-28; Ho.1:11 • They will no longer be jealous or hostile to one another
3) The destruction of life & property will cease: Because the knowledge of God (His love & peace) will fill the earth c. He will save the Gentiles 1) He will be a *banner* to rally all people, 49:22 2) He will live in a glorious place of *rest*	9 They shall not hurt nor destroy in all my holy mountain: for the earth shall be full of the knowledge of the LORD, as the waters cover the sea. 10 And in that day there shall be a root of Jesse, which shall stand for an ensign of the people; to it shall the Gentiles seek: and his rest shall be glorious.	14 But they shall fly upon the shoulders of the Philistines toward the west; they shall spoil them of the east together: they shall lay their hand upon Edom and Moab; and the children of Ammon shall obey them.	• They will unite, defeat, & be victorious over all their enemies
d. He will save a remnant of Jewish believers, free His people for a second time (see v.16; Ex.12:1–13:16 for the first Exodus) 1) He will bring His people back from all nations	11 And it shall come to pass in that day, *that* the Lord shall set his hand again the second time to recover the remnant of his people, which shall be left, from Assyria, and from Egypt, and from Pathros, and from Cush, and from Elam, and from Shinar, and from Hamath, and from the islands of the sea.	15 And the LORD shall utterly destroy the tongue of the Egyptian sea; and with his mighty wind shall he shake his hand over the river, and shall smite it in the seven streams, and make *men* go over dryshod. 16 And there shall be an highway for the remnant of his people, which shall be left, from Assyria; like as it was to Israel in the day that	4) He will remove all obstacles that hinder the return of His people to the promised land • He will carry out a second Exodus, drying the Gulf of Suez & breaking up the great Euphrates River into seven shallow streams, Ex.14:21-22
2) He will raise a *banner* to rally His people from all	12 And he shall set up an ensign for the nations, and shall	he came up out of the land of Egypt.	• He will make a great highway for His people to leave Assyria, their enslavers

a. As world ruler, the Savior will establish true righteousness and justice on earth (vv.3-5). But He will not be like an ordinary judge who has to give opinions based upon imperfect knowledge. He will not judge by what appears to be true or false nor by the statements given by witnesses. And He certainly will not be a judge who can be bribed or who bases His decisions upon public opinion. To the contrary, there will be no favoritism or partiality in any of the Messiah's decisions. Every decision will be based upon true justice, in particular for the poor and meek, the needy and oppressed. Furthermore, He will execute justice against the wicked, slaying them with the very breath of His mouth (see Re.19:15).

In a marvelous way the Savior will wear righteousness and faithfulness as a belt. His righteousness and faithfulness will keep the loose clothing of injustice and oppression from affecting His decisions. Nothing will keep Him from executing perfect justice among the people of the earth.

Thought 1. Society today is anything but righteous. A quick glance at any form of news media sadly exposes this fact. Our society is gripped with a spirit of lawlessness and wicked behavior. Nevertheless, we as believers are to do all we can to establish a moral and just society, to bring God's kingdom to earth. His kingdom is the rule of righteousness, love, joy, and peace—peace among nations and peace within the human heart. Thus we can make no greater contribution to society than to live and teach righteousness, for in so doing we bring peace to the earth. Listen to God's Holy Word:

"For I say unto you, That except your righteousness shall exceed *the righteousness* of the scribes and Pharisees, ye shall in no case enter into the kingdom of heaven" (Mt.5:20).

"Awake to righteousness, and sin not; for some have not the knowledge of God: I speak *this* to your shame" (1 Co.15:34).

"Wherefore take unto you the whole armour of God, that ye may be able to withstand in the evil day, and having done all, to stand. Stand therefore, having your loins girt about with truth, and having on the breastplate of righteousness" (Ep.6:13-14).

"And this I pray, that your love may abound yet more and more in knowledge and *in* all judgment; That ye may approve things that are excellent; that ye may be sincere and without offence till the day of Christ; Being filled with the fruits of righteousness, which are by Jesus Christ, unto the glory and praise of God" (Ph.1:9-11).

"But thou, O man of God, flee these things; and follow after righteousness, godliness, faith, love, patience, meekness. Fight the good fight of faith, lay hold on eternal life, whereunto thou art also called, and hast professed a good profession before many witnesses" (1 Ti.6:11-12).

"Teaching us that, denying ungodliness and worldly lusts, we should live soberly, righteously, and godly, in this present world; Looking for that blessed hope, and the glorious appearing of the great God and our Saviour Jesus Christ; " (Tit.2:12-13).

"But the day of the Lord will come as a thief in the night; in the which the heavens shall pass away with a great noise, and the elements shall melt with fervent heat, the earth also and the works that are therein shall be burned up. *Seeing* then *that* all these things shall be dissolved, what manner *of persons* ought ye to be in *all* holy conversation [behavior] and godliness, Looking for and hasting unto the coming of the day of God, wherein the heavens being on fire shall be dissolved, and the elements shall melt with fervent heat? Nevertheless we, according to his promise, look for new heavens and a new earth, wherein dwelleth righteousness. Wherefore, beloved, seeing that ye look for such things, be diligent that ye may be found of him in peace, without spot, and blameless" (2 Pe.3:10-14).

"In righteousness shalt thou be established: thou shalt be far from oppression; for thou shalt not fear: and from terror; for it shall not come near thee" (Is.54:14).

"Sow to yourselves in righteousness, reap in mercy; break up your fallow ground: for *it is* time to seek the Lord, till he come and rain righteousness upon you" (Ho.10:12).

b.   Amazingly, the Savior will restore creation itself and bring peace to the earth (vv.6-9). A radical change will take place in the nature of animals. No longer will animals be wild and ferocious but, rather, tame and peaceful (vv.6-7). Wild animals such as the wolf, leopard, lion, and bear will live with the lamb, goat, calf, cow, and ox. A little child will even be safe in the presence of wild animals (Is.11:8). All fear and danger will be erased. A child will no longer fear a cobra and will easily put his hand into the vipers nest. Also, the very nature of man will be changed. Hostility, conflict, divisiveness, and discrimination will no longer fill the hearts of people. Destruction of life and property will cease (v.9). The knowledge of the Lord will fill the earth as the waters cover the sea. The message of the gospel, of a personal and saving knowledge of the Lord, will be everywhere.

As stated above, righteousness will sweep the earth. People will obey the laws of the Lord. His holy commandments will be kept. The Savior will save the Gentiles, as well as the Jews (v.10). The Savior will actually be a *banner* around which all the people and nations of the earth will rally (Is.49:22). While Christ was on earth, He clearly taught that many people would come from all the nations of the earth to sit down in the kingdom of God (Lu.13:29). This promise was even given to Abraham when God promised that his (Abraham's) descendants would bless all the people on earth (Ge.12:3).[6]

When the Savior returns to rule over the earth, His place of rest (home) will be the restored Jerusalem. Jerusalem will be glorious. Of course, its glory will be due to the majestic holiness and glory of the Savior Himself, the Lord Jesus Christ. Because of Christ's glory and that of Jerusalem, the nations of the earth will flood to the Lord's kingdom (see outline and note—Is.2:1-5 for more discussion).

Thought 1. The Lord Jesus will restore creation and bring peace to the earth.

"For I reckon that the sufferings of this present time *are* not worthy *to be compared* with the glory which shall be revealed in us. For the earnest expectation of the creature waiteth for the manifestation of the sons of God. For the creature was made subject to vanity, not willingly, but by reason of him who hath subjected *the same* in hope, Because the creature itself also shall be delivered from the bondage of corruption into the glorious liberty of the children of God. For we know that the whole creation groaneth and travaileth in pain together until now" (Ro.8:18-22).

"And it shall come to pass in the day that the Lord shall give thee rest from thy sorrow, and from thy fear, and from the hard bondage wherein thou wast made to serve" (Is.14:3).

"Moreover the light of the moon shall be as the light of the sun, and the light of the sun shall be sevenfold, as the light of seven days, in the day that the Lord bindeth up the breach of his people, and healeth the stroke of their wound" (Is.30:26).

"The wolf and the lamb shall feed together, and the lion shall eat straw like the bullock: and dust *shall be* the serpent's meat. They shall not hurt nor destroy in all my holy mountain, saith the Lord" (Is.65:25).

"I will feed them in a good pasture, and upon the high mountains of Israel shall their fold be: there shall they lie in a good fold, and in a fat pasture shall they feed upon the mountains of Israel" (Eze.34:14).

"And I will make them and the places round about my hill a blessing; and I will cause the shower to come down in his season; there shall be showers of blessing. And the tree of the field shall yield her fruit, and the earth shall yield her increase, and they shall be safe in their land, and shall know that I *am* the Lord, when I have broken the bands of their yoke, and delivered them out of the hand of those that served themselves of them….And I will raise up for them a plant of renown, and they shall be no more consumed with hunger in the land, neither bear the shame of the heathen any more" (Eze.34:26-27, 29).

"The remnant of Israel shall not do iniquity, nor speak lies; neither shall a deceitful tongue be found in their mouth: for they shall feed and lie down, and none shall make *them* afraid" (Zep.3:13).

"In that day it shall be said to Jerusalem, Fear thou not: *and to* Zion, Let not thine hands be slack" (Zep.3:16).

c.   The Savior will preserve a remnant of Jewish believers, freeing His people for a second time (vv.11-16, esp.v.16; Ex.12:1–13:16 for the first Exodus). Just as God freed the Israelites from Egypt under the leadership of Moses, so He will

---

6   John F. Walvoord and Roy B. Zuck, Editors. *The Bible Knowledge Commentary,* p.1057.

bring the Jews back from all nations under the leadership of the Messiah, the Lord Jesus Christ. Christ the Savior will raise a *banner* to rally His chosen people from all over the earth (v.12). Then all Jewish exiles will be set free from their bondage to return to the promised land, which will be restored under the rule of the Savior.

Note this fact: the division existing between Israel and Judah will be healed by the Savior (vv.13-14; Eze.37:15-28; Ho.1:11). Remember that Ephraim was the largest tribe of the Northern Kingdom of Israel; therefore Israel was often referred to as Ephraim. The jealousy and hostility between the Northern and Southern Kingdoms will be done away with. All the Jews will unite under the banner of the Savior. Through Him they will be victorious over all those who had persecuted them down through the ages. The traditional enemies of Israel—the Philistines, Edomites, Moabites, and Ammonites—probably represent all the enemies who will oppose the Messiah and the establishment of His kingdom on earth. All these enemies will be subjected under the rule of the Savior and His people.

Thought 1. When Christ returns for a second time, He will establish His kingdom on earth, the Messianic Kingdom. It will be the Lord Jesus Christ Himself who is lifted up before the world, the *banner* to whom all people will look for salvation. To Him and Him alone will the nations turn for peace and unity. Yet today neither the nations nor most of the people look to God. To the contrary, most people reject Him, and many even deny that He is the Savior of the world. Nevertheless since His coming, the door of salvation has been thrown wide open. God has loved the world and sent His Son into the world to offer salvation to anyone who will call upon Him.

(1) Note what Scripture says about the conversion of the Gentiles when Christ returns to establish God's kingdom on earth.

"I say then, Have they stumbled that they should fall? God forbid: but *rather* through their fall salvation *is come* unto the Gentiles, for to provoke them to jealousy. Now if the fall of them *be* the riches of the world, and the diminishing of them the riches of the Gentiles; how much more their fulness?" (Ro.11:11-12).

"That the Gentiles should be fellowheirs, and of the same body, and partakers of his promise in Christ by the gospel" (Ep.3:6).

"And in thy seed shall all the nations of the earth be blessed; because thou hast obeyed my voice" (Ge.22:18).

"All the ends of the world shall remember and turn unto the LORD: and all the kindreds of the nations shall worship before thee" (Ps.22:27).

"All nations whom thou hast made shall come and worship before thee, O Lord; and shall glorify thy name" (Ps.86:9).

"The people that walked in darkness have seen a great light: they that dwell in the land of the shadow of death, upon them hath the light shined" (Is.9:2).

"They shall not hurt nor destroy in all my holy mountain: for the earth shall be full of the knowledge of the LORD, as the waters cover the sea" (Is.11:9).

"Behold my servant, whom I uphold; mine elect, *in whom* my soul delighteth; I have put my spirit upon him: he shall bring forth judgment to the Gentiles" (Is.42:1).

"And he said, It is a light thing that thou shouldest be my servant to raise up the tribes of Jacob, and to restore the preserved of Israel: I will also give thee for a light to the Gentiles, that thou mayest be my salvation unto the end of the earth" (Is.49:6).

"Behold, thou shalt call a nation *that* thou knowest not, and nations *that* knew not thee shall run unto thee because of the LORD thy God, and for the Holy One of Israel; for he hath glorified thee" (Is.55:5).

"And the Gentiles shall come to thy light, and kings to the brightness of thy rising" (Is.60:3).

"And there was given him dominion, and glory, and a kingdom, that all people, nations, and languages, should serve him: his dominion *is* an everlasting dominion, which shall not pass away, and his kingdom *that* which shall not be destroyed" (Da.7:14).

"And I will sow her unto me in the earth; and I will have mercy upon her that had not obtained mercy; and I will say to *them which were* not my people, Thou *art* my people; and they shall say, *Thou art* my God" (Ho.2:23).

"For from the rising of the sun even unto the going down of the same my name *shall be* great among the Gentiles; and in every place incense *shall be* offered unto my name, and a pure offering: for my name *shall be* great among the heathen, saith the LORD of hosts" (Mal.1:11).

(2) Since the coming of Christ, the doors of salvation have been thrown wide open to the Gentiles. Listen to what God's Holy Word says;

"And he [Jesus Christ] said unto them, Go ye into all the world, and preach the gospel to every creature" (Mk.16:15).

"For God so loved the world, that he gave his only begotten Son, that whosoever believeth in him should not perish, but have everlasting life" (Jn.3:16).

"Then Peter opened *his* mouth, and said, Of a truth I perceive that God is no respecter of persons: But in every nation he that feareth him, and worketh righteousness, is accepted with him" (Ac.10:34-35).

"That if thou shalt confess with thy mouth the Lord Jesus, and shalt believe in thine heart that God hath raised him from the dead, thou shalt be saved. For with the heart man believeth unto righteousness; and with the mouth confession is made unto salvation. For the scripture saith, Whosoever believeth on him shall not be ashamed. For there is no difference between the Jew and the

Greek: for the same Lord over all is rich unto all that call upon him. For whosoever shall call upon the name of the Lord shall be saved" (Ro.10:9-13).

"And the Spirit and the bride say, Come. And let him that heareth say, Come. And let him that is athirst come. And whosoever will, let him take the water of life freely" (Re.22:17).

d. The Savior will remove all obstacles that hinder the return of His people to the promised land (vv.15-16). A second exodus will actually take place. Interestingly, Isaiah predicted that the Gulf of Suez will be dried up and the great Eu-phrates River will become so dry that it will be divided into seven shallow streams (see Ex.14:21-22). *In that day* no obstacle will be able to prevent the return of the Jewish remnant back to the promised land (v.11). The Savior will actually make a great highway for His people to leave the land of Assyria, their brutal enslavers (v.16). Keep in mind that the land of Assyria was eventually conquered by Babylon and Persia and that the Jews were freed by Persia. This great *highway* symbolizes the absolute certainty of the Jews' return to the promised land. Absolutely nothing will be able to stop their return.

Thought 1. When Jesus Christ returns to earth, there will be a movement of God's Spirit among the Jews. There will be a remnant of believers who will be saved. From every nation of the world there will be a stream of Jewish believers turning to the Lord as the true Messiah, the Savior who was promised to their father Abraham (see outlines and notes—Ro.11:1-36 for more discussion).

"Esaias also crieth concerning Israel, Though the number of the children of Israel be as the sand of the sea, a remnant shall be saved" (Ro.9:27).

"Even so then at this present time also there is a remnant according to the election of grace" (Ro.11:5).

"And I will restore thy judges as at the first, and thy counsellors as at the beginning: afterward thou shalt be called, The city of righteousness, the faithful city" (Is.1:26).

"In that day shall the branch of the LORD be beautiful and glorious, and the fruit of the earth *shall be* excellent and comely for them that are escaped of Israel. And it shall come to pass, *that he that is* left in Zion, and *he that* remaineth in Jerusalem, shall be called holy, *even* every one that is written among the living in Jerusalem: When the Lord shall have washed away the filth of the daughters of Zion, and shall have purged the blood of Jerusalem from the midst thereof by the spirit of judgment, and by the spirit of burning. And the LORD will create upon every dwelling place of mount Zion, and upon her assemblies, a cloud and smoke by day, and the shining of a flaming fire by night: for upon all the glory *shall be* a defence. And there shall be a tabernacle for a shadow in the daytime from the heat, and for a place of refuge, and for a covert from storm and from rain" (Is.4:2-6).

"And he shall set up an ensign for the nations, and shall assemble the outcasts of Israel, and gather together the dispersed of Judah from the four corners of the earth" (Is.11:12).

"And it shall come to pass in that day, *that* the great trumpet shall be blown, and they shall come which were ready to perish in the land of Assyria, and the outcasts in the land of Egypt, and shall worship the LORD in the holy mount at Jerusalem" (Is.27:13).

"Look upon Zion, the city of our solemnities: thine eyes shall see Jerusalem a quiet habitation, a tabernacle *that* shall not be taken down; not one of the stakes thereof shall ever be removed, neither shall any of the cords thereof be broken" (Is.33:20).

"Comfort ye, comfort ye my people, saith your God. Speak ye comfortably to Jerusalem, and cry unto her, that her warfare is accomplished, that her iniquity is pardoned: for she hath received of the LORD's hand double for all her sins. The voice of him that crieth in the wilderness, Prepare ye the way of the LORD, make straight in the desert a highway for our God. Every valley shall be exalted, and every mountain and hill shall be made low: and the crooked shall be made straight, and the rough places plain: And the glory of the LORD shall be revealed, and all flesh shall see *it* together: for the mouth of the LORD hath spoken *it*" (Is.40:1-5).

"Thus saith the Lord GOD, Behold, I will lift up mine hand to the Gentiles, and set up my standard to the people: and they shall bring thy sons in *their* arms, and thy daughters shall be carried upon *their* shoulders" (Is.49:22).

"And the sons of strangers shall build up thy walls, and their kings shall minister unto thee: for in my wrath I smote thee, but in my favour have I had mercy on thee. Therefore thy gates shall be open continually; they shall not be shut day nor night; that *men* may bring unto thee the forces of the Gentiles, and *that* their kings *may be* brought" (Is.60:10-11).

"And I will gather the remnant of my flock out of all countries whither I have driven them, and will bring them again to their folds; and they shall be fruitful and increase. And I will set up shepherds over them which shall feed them: and they shall fear no more, nor be dismayed, neither shall they be lacking, saith the LORD. Behold, the days come, saith the LORD, that I will raise unto David a righteous Branch, and a King shall reign and prosper, and shall execute judgment and justice in the earth. In his days Judah shall be saved, and Israel shall dwell safely: and this *is* his name whereby he shall be called, THE LORD OUR RIGHTEOUSNESS. Therefore, behold, the days come, saith the LORD, that they shall no more say, The LORD liveth, which brought up the children of Israel out of the land of Egypt; But, The LORD liveth, which brought up and which led the seed of the house of Israel out of the north country, and from all countries whither I had driven them; and they shall dwell in their own land" (Je.23:3-8).

"At the same time, saith the LORD, will I be the God of all the families of Israel, and they shall be my people....For there shall be a day, *that* the watchmen upon the mount Ephraim shall cry, Arise ye, and let us go up to Zion unto the LORD our God. For thus saith the LORD; Sing with gladness for Jacob, and shout among the chief of the nations: publish ye, praise ye, and say, O LORD, save thy people, the remnant of Israel. Behold, I will bring them from the north country, and gather them from the coasts of the earth, *and* with them the blind and the lame, the woman with child and her that travaileth with child together: a great company shall return thither" (Je.31:1, 6-8).

"For in mine holy mountain, in the mountain of the height of Israel, saith the Lord GOD, there shall all the house of Israel, all of them in the land, serve me: there will I accept them, and there will I require your offerings, and the firstfruits of your oblations, with all your holy things" (Eze.20:40).

"But ye, O mountains of Israel, ye shall shoot forth your branches, and yield your fruit to my people of Israel: for they are at hand to come. For, behold, I *am* for you, and I will turn unto you, and ye shall be tilled and sown: And I will multiply men upon you, all the house of Israel, *even* all of it: and the cities shall be inhabited, and the wastes shall be builded" (Eze.36:8-10).

"I will surely assemble, O Jacob, all of thee; I will surely gather the remnant of Israel" (Mi.2:12).

"Therefore thus saith the LORD; I am returned to Jerusalem with mercies: my house shall be built in it, saith the LORD of hosts, and a line shall be stretched forth upon Jerusalem. Cry yet, saying, Thus saith the LORD of hosts; My cities through prosperity shall yet be spread abroad; and the LORD shall yet comfort Zion, and shall yet choose Jerusalem" (Zec.1:16-17).

"And I will strengthen the house of Judah, and I will save the house of Joseph, and I will bring them again to place them; for I have mercy upon them: and they shall be as though I had not cast them off: for I *am* the LORD their God, and will hear them....And I will sow them among the people: and they shall remember me in far countries; and they shall live with their children, and turn again. I will bring them again also out of the land of Egypt, and gather them out of Assyria; and I will bring them into the land of Gilead and Lebanon; and *place* shall not be found for them....And I will strengthen them in the LORD; and they shall walk up and down in his name, saith the LORD" (Zec.10:6, 9-10, 12).

"And the LORD shall be king over all the earth: in that day shall there be one LORD, and his name one....And *men* shall dwell in it, and there shall be no more utter destruction; but Jerusalem shall be safely inhabited" (Zec.14:9, 11).

---

4 **(12:1-6) Savior, Duty Toward, to Praise—Praise, Reasons for—Messiah, Kingdom of, Songs About—Millennium, Songs About, the Savior—Kingdom, of Christ or Messiah, Songs of Praise**: a very special song of praise will be sung in the Savior's kingdom. The citizens of His kingdom will be filled with joy and thanksgiving for what the Savior has done for them. Note that this song will be sung by the Jews. But its praise is applicable to every believer, so probably all the redeemed will lift up their voices in singing this wonderful song of praise. It is divided into two stanzas, and each is introduced by the words "in that day you will say [sing]" (v.1, 4).

OUTLINE	SCRIPTURE	SCRIPTURE	OUTLINE
4. The song of praise for the Savior: True reasons to praise the LORD *in that day*	And in that day thou shalt say, O LORD, I will praise thee: though thou wast angry	wells of salvation.	necessities of life
a. God will turn away from wrath & comfort His people	with me, thine anger is turned away, and thou comfortedst me.	4 And in that day shall ye say, Praise the LORD, call upon his name, declare his doings among the people, make	b. God will flood His people with joy & a desire to proclaim His name
1) Because God is their salvation, strength, & song	2 Behold, God *is* my salvation; I will trust, and not be afraid: for the LORD JEHOVAH *is* my strength and *my* song;	mention that his name is exalted.	1) To share with the nations what He has done for them, see 11:11-16
	he also is become my salvation.	5 Sing unto the LORD; for he hath done excellent things: this *is* known in all the earth.	2) To exalt His name
			3) To make known all His glorious works
2) Because God will provide water, that is, the basic	3 Therefore with joy shall ye draw water out of the	6 Cry out and shout, thou inhabitant of Zion: for great *is* the Holy One of Israel in the midst of thee.	c. God—the Holy One of Israel—will dwell among them

a. The first stanza praises God because He had turned away from wrath and comforted His people. Down through the centuries their rebellion and hostility toward God had aroused His anger and brought His hand of judgment upon them. As a result, they had suffered every hardship and misfortune imaginable. Eventually they had been dispersed among the nations of the world. But then God turned away from His wrath and sent the promised Messiah back to earth to rescue them. God became their salvation, delivering them from their captivity. His promise of a remnant being saved was fulfilled. And there they stood, having been brought back to the promised land (11:11-16). Praise will be lifted up to the LORD because God is no longer their judge or avenger but their Savior. Therefore they will trust Him and no longer be afraid (v.2). No longer will they put their trust in men or in the military power of nations. Their source of strength is the LORD who has saved them.

God's salvation includes far more than just being delivered from the bondages of this earth. It includes His provision of the basic necessities of life, His meeting every need people have. In the kingdom of the Savior, citizens will draw water from the wells of salvation (v.3). In a dry land such as Israel, water was a scarcity. Thus the picture is that of the LORD providing all the basic necessities of life in the glorious day of His kingdom.

b. In the second stanza the emphasis shifts to giving thanks and to proclaiming the Name of the LORD among all the nations of the earth (vv.4-5). *In that day* of the Messiah's kingdom, the Jews will have a burning desire to let the whole world know what the LORD has done for them. With hearts bursting with joy over God's wonderful salvation, they will be shouting and encouraging one another to praise the LORD. They will call upon the nations to join them in exalting the LORD's Name, for great is the Holy One of Israel who was now living among them. Keep in mind that this is a picture of the Messiah, the

Lord Jesus Christ, who has returned to establish God's kingdom on earth. Christ is sitting in Jerusalem as the ruler of the world.

Thought 1. Jesus Christ deserves our praise. Through His death upon the cross, He has saved us and forgiven our sins. No longer are we held in the bondage of guilt nor enslaved by sin and death. Christ has set us free from sin, death, and the coming judgment of hell. Our souls have been released from all the bondages of this life, and we have been given eternal life. When we take our last breath on earth—quicker than the eye can blink—the LORD will snatch us out of the physical world and bring us into the spiritual world, into His very presence.

In addition to giving us eternal life, the LORD comforts us as we walk day by day. He guides and delivers us *through* all the trials and temptations of this life. By His Spirit He strengthens us to endure the hardships and misfortunes of life, teaching us to walk victoriously over all the difficult circumstances that confront us.

Our praise and thanksgiving are to be lifted up to the LORD. He has done so much for us that our voices should never be silenced. Shouts of joy should be sounded around the world, for the LORD has saved us. He has delivered us from sin and death and given us eternal life. How can we keep silent? An hour should never pass that we do not give thanks to Him for the great things He has done.

> "Let your light so shine before men, that they may see your good works, and glorify your Father which is in heaven" (Mt.5:16).

> "Herein is my Father glorified, that ye bear much fruit; so shall ye be my disciples" (Jn.15:8).

> "Now the God of patience and consolation grant you to be likeminded one toward another according to Christ Jesus: That ye may with one mind *and* one mouth glorify God, even the Father of our Lord Jesus Christ" (Ro.15:5-6).

> "For ye are bought with a price: therefore glorify God in your body, and in your spirit, which are God's" (1 Co.6:20).

> "By him therefore let us offer the sacrifice of praise to God continually, that is, the fruit of *our* lips giving thanks to his name" (He.13:15).

> "But ye *are* a chosen generation, a royal priesthood, an holy nation, a peculiar people; that ye should show forth the praises of him who hath called you out of darkness into his marvellous light" (1 Pe.2:9).

> "Sing praises to the LORD, which dwelleth in Zion: declare among the people his doings" (Ps.9:11).

> "Ye that fear the LORD, praise him; all ye the seed of Jacob, glorify him; and fear him, all ye the seed of Israel" (Ps.22:23).

> "Praise the LORD with harp: sing unto him with the psaltery *and* an instrument of ten strings" (Ps.33:2).

> "Let the people praise thee, O God; let all the people praise thee" (Ps.67:3).

> "Let them give glory unto the LORD, and declare his praise in the islands" (Is.42:12).

DIVISION II

THE PROPHECIES CONCERNING GOD'S JUDGMENT OF THE NATIONS AND HIS TRIUMPH OVER THE WORLD, 13:1–27:13

(13:1–27:13) **DIVISION OVERVIEW**: in these prophecies, one nation after another received scathing rebukes for their rebellion against God and their sinful lifestyles. Instead of trusting in the LORD, people placed their trust in the military power and economies of nations. But in the day of judgment, these worldly securities will be useless. Rebellion against God and sinful behavior will bring terrible judgment upon nations and individuals.

But within the prophecies of certain judgment preached by Isaiah, the main theme of God's message comes shining through: the LORD saves. Hope for salvation is found in repentance and in turning to God. The LORD will defeat all enemies who oppose Him and His people. He will establish His kingdom on earth. Furthermore, His kingdom will usher in a world of peace and protection for His people. The day is coming soon when God will nurture and shelter His people, arousing the whole world to establish a right relationship with Him. That day will be when Jesus Christ returns to set up His kingdom on earth. All who are willing to turn to the LORD to worship Him alone will escape the coming wrath.

THE PROPHECIES CONCERNING GOD'S JUDGMENT OF THE NATIONS AND HIS TRIUMPH OVER THE WORLD, 13:1–27:13

A. God's Judgment of Babylon: A Picture of God's Judgment upon Evil Governments, 13:1–14:23

B. God's Judgment of Assyria, Philistia, and Moab: A Picture of God's Plan for Judgment and of His Protection and Compassion, 14:24–16:14

C. God's Judgment of Damascus (Syria), Ephraim (Israel), and Ethiopia: A Picture of Distrust and of Hope in the Face of Judgment, 17:1–18:7

D. God's Judgment of Egypt: A Picture of God's Just Punishment, His Enduring Mercy, and His Clear Warning, 19:1–20:6

E. God's Judgment of Babylon (the Persian Gulf Region), Edom, and Arabia: A Need to Watch, Repent, and Turn to the LORD, 21:17

F. God's Judgment of Judah and Jerusalem: A Picture of God's Coming Judgment and Grace, 22:1-25

G. God's Judgment of Tyre (Phoenicia): A Picture of the Proud Being Humbled Yet Given Hope, 23:1-18

H. God's Judgment of the Whole World, His Universal Judgment: A Time of Great Tribulation, 24:1-23

I. God's Plan for the Whole World and for His People: God's Seven-Step Plan for the World, 25:1-12

J. God's Works and the Protection of His Vineyard, His People: God's Great Care for His People, 26:1–27:13

AN OVERVIEW OF THE PROPHECIES OF ISAIAH AGAINST THE NATIONS

The prophecies in Isaiah 13–23 were not just for people living centuries ago. Far from it! The prophecies of Isaiah are for every person of every age. Every person is confronted with the choice either to heed the message of prophecy or be doomed in the day of judgment. A day of judgment is coming, a time so terrifying that every effort must be made to escape it. And a person can escape the coming judgment. Throughout these prophecies, the LORD continually offers the promise of salvation to all who truly turn to Him, repenting of their sins and living righteously. The Word of God—with all its prophecies, principles, and applications—is not bound by time or circumstance (1 Ti.3:16; Ro.15:4; 1 Co.10:11).

NATION	MAIN PROPHECY	REASON JUDGED	APPLICATION
ARABIA *(21:13-17)* In the southern part of Arabia lived a tribe of traders from Dedan, called Dedanites.	Dedan would be wiped out in a year, but the day and the hour would not be known. The people would be forced to flee before the terrible army of the Assyrians. Only a few would survive.	Arabia was defiant and refused to acknowledge God.	We do not know the hour of our death. Therefore, we must be alert and prepared to meet the Lord. **"Repent ye therefore, and be converted, that your sins may be blotted out, when the times of refreshing shall come from the presence of the Lord" (Ac.3:19).**
ASSYRIA *(14:24-27)* Assyria was a much feared power from the north who launched a massive military campaign to take over the entire Middle East.	God would crush the Assyrians, freeing His people from their oppressive yoke of bondage.	God judged the Assyrians because of their pride. But He used their judgment to set His people free.	God will set free all who truly trust Him. He is going to create a new heaven and earth where there will be no wickedness or oppression. **"Nevertheless we, according to his promise, look for new heavens and a new earth, wherein dwelleth righteousness" (2 Pe.3:13).**
BABYLON *(13:1-14:23; 21:1-10)* Babylon was a massive kingdom from the north beyond the Euphrates. They were the strongest empire on earth until their arch-enemy, the Assyrians, finally gained supremacy. Babylon has always represented the corrupt world system. It has stood as a prideful tribute to man and as a rebellious defiance of God.	An army would be stirred, inflicting great terror and wrath upon Babylon. The destruction of Babylon would be like Sodom and Gomorrah—complete and final.	In Old Testament time, Isaiah's prophecy concerning Babylon revealed that God would deliver His people from captivity. In the final days, He will judge the evil world system of Babylon and put an end to all rebellion. He will punish all who defy the only true and living God, and His punishment will be eternal. He will deliver His people from a world of sin and persecution. After the defeat of Babylon in the end times, the evil world system will never rise again.	There will be a final judgment, a time when every nation, government, civilization, culture, society, city, community, and individual will face God. *In that day*, we must be prepared to meet God face-to-face and to give an answer for everything we have done, good or bad. **"Because he hath appointed a day, in the which he will judge the world in righteousness" (Ac.17:31).**
CUSH *(18:1-7)* More commonly referred to as Ethiopia, Cush was the powerful African nation that conquered and controlled Egypt from 714 to 633 B.C.	Despite constant attempts to form a strong military alliance, Cush would be destroyed before the harvest came. There would be so many dead, there would be no place for all the bodies to be buried.	In order to stir some to cry out to Him for salvation, God sent a message of the coming devastation. Isaiah also prophesied that the few survivors left would turn to the LORD in the end times.	Even in the face of judgment there is always hope for salvation. God gave the people of Cush ample warning of the coming devastation. They had one last opportunity to turn to the LORD, to cry out in repentance, yet they did not. Likewise, we have heard the warning about evil associations. We have heard that judgment is coming. Thus we still have time to call upon the LORD for deliverance. The gift of salvation is there for the taking, but *we* must step forward to receive it! **"For whosoever shall call upon the name of the Lord shall be saved" (Ro.10:13).**

NATION	MAIN PROPHECY	REASON JUDGED	APPLICATION
DAMASCUS OR SYRIA *(17:1-14)* Syria was the neighbor to the north and east of the Northern Kingdom of Israel. After Israel unwisely formed an alliance with Syria, Syria fortified Damascus as the capital in order to subject Israel and force the nations and citizens to pay tribute.	All fortified cities would be destroyed and abandoned. God would rebuke all invaders and they would flee from His land. Israel would suffer right along with the Syrian because of their close association with them. This alliance was forbidden by the Law and warned against by many prophets down through the centuries.	Israel would no longer forget the LORD but would have respect for the Holy One of Israel. God did not want Israel to form evil alliances in the first place. But through His judgment, God would force Israel to see that He was their Rock and Fortress of protection.	If we forget God, we are doomed to judgment. God is the supreme Creator and Sustainer of all that is. We must never carry on our daily business pretending that God has no part in it. We must acknowledge God in all our ways. "The wicked shall be turned into hell, *and* all the nations that forget God" (Ps.9:17). "In all thy ways acknowledge him, and he shall direct thy paths" (Pr.3:6).
EDOM *(21:11-12)* The Edomites were a very proud people, descendants of Esau and dwellers in the regions south and east of the Dead Sea.	Edom was called Dumah (meaning *silence*) by the prophet Isaiah, to emphasize the complete judgment to come. Despite the natural protection and difficult access to their land, a conqueror would come and prevail against the Edomites.	Isaiah's prophecies were given in order to spur Edom to repentance. The LORD offered help and hope to the Edomites, yet they would need to ask Him for deliverance. Edom would have to decide whether to put aside their pride or be destroyed.	Christ paid the ransom for our souls. Like the Edomites, every one of us stands one step away from the door of salvation. If we will only ask, the Lord will save us and set us free from the coming doom of judgment. "Let the wicked forsake his way, and the unrighteous man his thoughts: and let him return unto the LORD, and he will have mercy upon him; and to our God, for he will abundantly pardon" (Is.55:7).
EGYPT *(19:1–20:6)* Egypt was a great power for centuries. Located in the lower delta of the Nile River, the nation has a very rich history. Sadly, however, the Egyptians were also well-known for their worship of many false gods.	An intense eightfold prophecy would bring complete upheaval to Egypt. But all the false gods Egypt had trusted in would fail. They would be attacked and destroyed. Even the Nile River would dry up. But God would also offer salvation to Egypt. Eventually even Egypt, a type of the world, would come to the LORD and genuinely worship Him.	Everything the Egyptians did was ascribed to the care of one of Egypt's false gods. It was for this reason that Egypt would be judged. Thus Isaiah's prophecy concerning Egypt would prove that the Egyptian gods were false. Nevertheless, the idolatry was an abomination to the LORD.	Everyone will eventually face the judgment of God. All who have rejected Christ will be held accountable. All who deny God will be punished. But God is merciful. He extends the gift of salvation to all people of all times. "And these shall go away into everlasting punishment: but the righteous into life eternal" (Mt.25:46).
MOAB *(15:1–16:14)* The Moabites were herdsmen who lived east of the Dead Sea. They were descendants of Lot.	Within three years, the splendor of the once proud nation of Moab would come to an end. Only a few would survive.	Extreme pride and arrogance would be the reason for the certain doom of the Moabites. Down through the centuries, the Moabites had exalted themselves highly while continually rebelling against the LORD and refusing to bow to Him.	The Lord always executes justice perfectly. At the judgment, every individual will receive exactly what he deserves. But God never wants to condemn anyone. The heart of God is full of compassion, even for the doomed. In His great plan for the world, His constant desire is that the lost will choose to love Him by accepting His Son, Jesus Christ, before it is too late. "But he, being full of compassion, forgave their iniquity, and destroyed them not: yea, many a time turned he his anger away, and did not stir up all his wrath" (Ps.78:38).

NATION	MAIN PROPHECY	REASON JUDGED	APPLICATION
PHILISTIA *(14:28-32)* The Philistines are traditionally thought to be a sea people who migrated to the east coast of the Mediterranean. Long time enemies of Israel and Judah, the pagan and idolatrous Philistines fought against the two nations all their days.	Isaiah gave Philistia a strong warning. They were not to rejoice over the death of Assyria's king because they (the Philistines) would still be destroyed by famine and war.	This prophecy was given to demonstrate the practical difference between believers and unbelievers in life. While the Philistines were being destroyed, the people of God, under Hezekiah's leadership, would be protected without the help of other nations.	God is our refuge, protector, shield, and defender. No matter who the enemy is or how powerful he may be, the LORD will shelter us if we flee to Him for protection. All others are subject to the harsh realities of the world, with nowhere to run in the face of con-querors. **"The eternal God is thy refuge, and underneath are the everlasting arms: and he shall thrust out the enemy from before thee; and shall say, Destroy them" (De.33:27).**
TYRE *(23:1-18)* Tyre was a Phoenician seaport enjoying success and wealth beyond imagination. Tyre was the icon of trade, wealth, and luxury.	Tyre would be entirely destroyed. Every nation of the world would mourn its demise. Because of the great loss, the economy of the entire world would be shaken to the core.	Initially, Isaiah prophesied against Tyre to predict the humiliating end of the city's corruption and the people's rank immorality. In the end times, however, Tyre will be restored and established for the glory of the LORD.	God despises sinful pride. If we refuse to humble ourselves before Him, He will humble us Himself. Every person will either bow before Christ now, or bow on the day of judgment and be separated from God's presence forever. **"He that believeth on the Son hath everlasting life: and he that believeth not the Son shall not see life; but the wrath of God abideth on him" (Jn.3:36).**

CHAPTER 13

II. THE PROPHECIES CONCERNING GOD'S JUDGMENT OF THE NATIONS & HIS TRIUMPH OVER THE WORLD, 13:1–27:13

A. God's Judgment of Babylon: A Picture of God's Judgment upon Evil Governments, 13:1–14:23

1. God's destruction of Babylon predicted: A picture of God's coming judgment

a. The stirring of an army to execute God's judgment
  1) The summons would be issued
    • A banner would be raised
    • A command would be given by God to set apart a number of warriors, an army, to carry out His wrath
  2) The warriors would respond
    • A great number of nations would be mobilized
    • A great number would join forces from far away—from the very ends of heaven—to be the weapons of God's wrath

b. The terrifying description of God's judgment: The day of the LORD

  1) A day of terror
    • Weakened hands
    • Melting hearts
    • Paralyzing fear
    • Agonizing pain (like a woman in labor)
    • Utter horror, helplessness

  2) A day of God's wrath & fierce anger
  3) A day of devastation: The destruction of the earth & of sinners

  4) A day of astronomical changes: The heavens—sun, moon, & stars—would be dark, not show their light

  5) A day of punishment for

The burden of Babylon, which Isaiah the son of Amoz did see.

2 Lift ye up a banner upon the high mountain, exalt the voice unto them, shake the hand, that they may go into the gates of the nobles.

3 I have commanded my sanctified ones, I have also called my mighty ones for mine anger, *even* them that rejoice in my highness.

4 The noise of a multitude in the mountains, like as of a great people; a tumultuous noise of the kingdoms of nations gathered together: the LORD of hosts mustereth the host of the battle.

5 They come from a far country, from the end of heaven, *even* the LORD, and the weapons of his indignation, to destroy the whole land.

6 Howl ye; for the day of the LORD *is* at hand; it shall come as a destruction from the Almighty.

7 Therefore shall all hands be faint, and every man's heart shall melt:

8 And they shall be afraid: pangs and sorrows shall take hold of them; they shall be in pain as a woman that travaileth: they shall be amazed one at another; their faces *shall be as* flames.

9 Behold, the day of the LORD cometh, cruel both with wrath and fierce anger, to lay the land desolate: and he shall destroy the sinners thereof out of it.

10 For the stars of heaven and the constellations thereof shall not give their light: the sun shall be darkened in his going forth, and the moon shall not cause her light to shine.

11 And I will punish the world for *their* evil, and the wicked for their iniquity; and I will cause the arrogancy of the proud to cease, and will lay low the haughtiness of the terrible.

12 I will make a man more precious than fine gold; even a man than the golden wedge of Ophir.

13 Therefore I will shake the heavens, and the earth shall remove out of her place, in the wrath of the LORD of hosts, and in the day of his fierce anger.

14 And it shall be as the chased roe, and as a sheep that no man taketh up: they shall every man turn to his own people, and flee every one into his own land.

15 Every one that is found shall be thrust through; and every one that is joined *unto them* shall fall by the sword.

16 Their children also shall be dashed to pieces before their eyes; their houses shall be spoiled, and their wives ravished.

17 Behold, I will stir up the Medes against them, which shall not regard silver; and *as for* gold, they shall not delight in it.

18 *Their* bows also shall dash the young men to pieces; and they shall have no pity on the fruit of the womb; their eye shall not spare children.

19 And Babylon, the glory of kingdoms, the beauty of the Chaldees' excellency, shall be as when God overthrew Sodom and Gomorrah.

20 It shall never be inhabited, neither shall it be dwelt in from generation to generation: neither shall the Arabian pitch tent there; neither shall the shepherds make their fold there.

21 But wild beasts of the desert shall lie there; and their houses shall be full of doleful creatures; and owls shall dwell there, and satyrs shall dance there.

22 And the wild beasts of the islands shall cry in their desolate houses, and dragons in *their* pleasant palaces: and her time *is* near to come, and her days shall not be prolonged.

the whole world
    • The wicked for their sin
    • The proud for their arrogance
    • The ruthless for their haughtiness
  6) A day of few survivors

  7) A day of shaking the whole universe—both heaven & earth—from its place: Perhaps referring to storms & earthquakes, 2 Pe.3:10-13
  8) A day of flight & of savage brutality
    • People would flee, seeking safety

    • All the captured would be killed

    • Children & infants alike would be slaughtered
    • Property would be looted
    • Women would be raped

c. The agent used to enforce God's wrath on Babylon: The Medes
  1) They would seek revenge, not wealth
  2) They would show no mercy, not even to the infants or children

d. The total destruction of Babylon, a symbol of the evil & wickedness of this world
  1) Babylon would be destroyed: Like Sodom & Gomorrah
  2) Babylon would never rise again, never be lived in by people again

  3) Babylon would be inhabited only by wild animals

  4) Babylon's days would be numbered: Its destruction was near

158

2. God's purpose for destroying Babylon: To deliver His people from captivity

a. God would have mercy: Restore, give His people *rest* in the promised land

b. Foreigners would join Israel

c. Nations would be God's agents to free & return His people to the promised land

d. All nations would voluntarily submit to Israel: A picture of the Messiah's kingdom

3. God's punishment of Babylon's king: A picture of Satan's fall, Lu.10:15, 18; Re.12:9; Eze.28:11-19

a. The king would be taunted: By all who had been delivered

b. The oppressor's brutality & rule would be ended by the awesome power of God

1) God would break the rod & rule of the wicked king

• Due to his aggressive conquests of nations

• Due to his governing people in brutality, not justice

2) God would give rest to the whole earth

• The earth itself would sing

• The trees—a symbol of oppressed multitudes—would rejoice over the tyrant's fall

3) God would doom the wicked one to Sheol (the grave, hell)*DS1*

• The departed spirits who were awaiting judgment—especially other rulers—would become excited over his arrival in hell

• The departed spirits would scoff at his fall & his doom to hell: In the end, he was as weak & as doomed as they were

• The wicked ruler would lose his glory, wealth, & power, & his beloved music: Maggots & worms would cover his body

CHAPTER 14

For the LORD will have mercy on Jacob, and will yet choose Israel, and set them in their own land: and the strangers shall be joined with them, and they shall cleave to the house of Jacob.

2 And the people shall take them, and bring them to their place: and the house of Israel shall possess them in the land of the LORD for servants and handmaids: and they shall take them captives, whose captives they were; and they shall rule over their oppressors.

3 And it shall come to pass in the day that the LORD shall give thee rest from thy sorrow, and from thy fear, and from the hard bondage wherein thou wast made to serve,

4 That thou shalt take up this proverb against the king of Babylon, and say, How hath the oppressor ceased! the golden city ceased!

5 The LORD hath broken the staff of the wicked, *and* the sceptre of the rulers.

6 He who smote the people in wrath with a continual stroke, he that ruled the nations in anger, is persecuted, *and* none hindereth.

7 The whole earth is at rest, *and* is quiet: they break forth into singing.

8 Yea, the fir trees rejoice at thee, *and* the cedars of Lebanon, *saying,* Since thou art laid down, no feller is come up against us.

9 Hell from beneath is moved for thee to meet *thee* at thy coming: it stirreth up the dead for thee, *even* all the chief ones of the earth; it hath raised up from their thrones all the kings of the nations.

10 All they shall speak and say unto thee, Art thou also become weak as we? art thou become like unto us?

11 Thy pomp is brought down to the grave, *and* the noise of thy viols: the worm is spread under thee, and the worms cover thee.

12 How art thou fallen from heaven, O Lucifer, son of the morning! *how* art thou cut down to the ground, which didst weaken the nations!

13 For thou hast said in thine heart, I will ascend into heaven, I will exalt my throne above the stars of God: I will sit also upon the mount of the congregation, in the sides of the north:

14 I will ascend above the heights of the clouds; I will be like the most High.

15 Yet thou shalt be brought down to hell, to the sides of the pit.

16 They that see thee shall narrowly look upon thee, *and* consider thee, *saying, Is* this the man that made the earth to tremble, that did shake kingdoms;

17 *That* made the world as a wilderness, and destroyed the cities thereof; *that* opened not the house of his prisoners?

18 All the kings of the nations, *even* all of them, lie in glory, every one in his own house.

19 But thou art cast out of thy grave like an abominable branch, *and as* the raiment of those that are slain, thrust through with a sword, that go down to the stones of the pit; as a carcase trodden under feet.

20 Thou shalt not be joined with them in burial, because thou hast destroyed thy land, *and* slain thy people: the seed of evildoers shall never be renowned.

21 Prepare slaughter for his children for the iniquity of their fathers; that they do not rise, nor possess the land, nor fill the face of the world with cities.

22 For I will rise up against them, saith the LORD of hosts, and cut off from Babylon the name, and remnant, and son, and nephew, saith the LORD.

23 I will also make it a possession for the bittern, and pools of water: and I will sweep it with the besom of destruction, saith the LORD of hosts.

c. The fall of Lucifer, the morning star, from heaven, Lu.10:15, 18; Jn.3:8; Eze.28:11-19

1) His judgment: Had been cast from his exalted position

2) His sin: Pride—sought to ascend to heaven

• To raise his throne above God's stars

• To be the one worshipped on the sacred mountain (God's temple)

• To exalt himself above the clouds, becoming like the Most High (God Himself)

3) His fate: Would be brought down to hell, the very pit of hell, to its lowest depths

4) His shameful end: People would gaze upon & mock him because of who he was

• The one who had caused nations to tremble

• The one who had devastated the world & its cities & enslaved its people

5) His dishonorable burial: His body would not lie in state like other kings

• His body would be cast into a mass grave with slain soldiers—like a discarded branch

• His body would be trampled underfoot because of his destructive & cruel nature

6) His offspring & their fate

• Would not be mentioned again

• Would be doomed because of their forefather's sins

• Would not be allowed to inherit the land nor to build cities

7) His Babylonian empire: Would be utterly destroyed by God Himself: A picture of the evil world system

• To have its name, survivors, children, & descendants cut off

• To be a desolate place, a place for porcupines

• To be a swampland

• To be swept with the broom of destruction

DIVISION II

THE PROPHECIES CONCERNING GOD'S JUDGMENT OF THE NATIONS AND HIS TRIUMPH OVER THE WORLD, 13:1–27:13

A.   God's Judgment of Babylon: A Picture of God's Judgment upon Evil Governments, 13:1–14:23

(13:1–14:23) **Introduction**: all evil governments and every wicked person who has ever lived will face the coming judgment of God. No matter who a person is, a leader in government or an ordinary citizen, each will stand before God to give an account for what he or she has done. If a government or person has practiced wickedness, that government or individual will be condemned by the LORD. If either one fails to honor and obey the righteous laws of the LORD, punishment will be determined accordingly. God expects nations to promote the honor of the LORD, the only living and true God, and to care for the welfare of its citizens. When dealing with individuals, the LORD expects each person to love and worship Him with all his heart and to love his neighbor as himself. Any nation or person who fails to honor and bear testimony to the love of God will bear the punishment of God's judgment.

In the present Scripture God's judgment falls upon Babylon, for Babylon had denied the only living and true God, the LORD Himself (Jehovah, Yahweh). An inflated, puffed-up pride that exalted itself above all other peoples and nations was the great sin of Babylon. It was the sin from which all the other wicked behavior of Babylon evolved. Babylon's self-exalting pride aroused its citizens to become world conquerors in an attempt to build a worldwide empire. Other nations were subjected through acts of horrible cruelty and brutality. And the people were held in subjection through the most terrorizing means possible, all for the purpose of erasing national identities. Babylon adopted the policy of deporting the populations of conquered nations to other countries. Through this policy it was hoped that a person would become attached to a foreign culture, thereby losing all identity and attachment to his homeland. Uprisings and revolts were quickly and brutally crushed so as to leave the message that rebellion would not be tolerated.

From the beginning of human history, ever since the Tower of Babel (Ge.11:9), Babylon has represented civilization, the world system that man builds in defiance of God. The wicked, oppressive pride of governments and nations is sym-bolized in the name Babylon. Babylon is a type of the worst of human government. Babylon represents the power of darkness that seeks to enslave and oppress people. Any world power that rises up in defiance of God is following in the footsteps of Babylon. The great city of Babylon was characterized by its arrogance and hostility toward God and its brutal oppression of other people. Even when the end time comes and Babylon is once again rebuilt, it will stand as a symbol of rebellion and enmity against the LORD. Babylon will be the capital of an apostate or traitorous civilization that treats the LORD with contempt (see outline and notes—Re.14:8; 17:1–18:24 for more discussion). Consequently the destruction of Babylon in this passage is a picture of God's final judgment that is coming upon the civilizations of this world. God's final judgment will be against the political, economic, and religious centers of a godless society. This is, *God's Judgment of Babylon: A Picture of God's Judgment upon Evil Governments*, 13:1–14:23.

1. God's destruction of Babylon predicted: a picture of God's coming judgment (13:1-22).
2. God's purpose for destroying Babylon: to deliver His people from captivity (14:1-2).
3. God's punishment of Babylon's king: a picture of Satan's fall, Lu.10:15, 18; Re.12:9; Eze.28:11-19 (14:3-23).

1 (13:1-22) **Judgment, Prophecy Concerning, Babylon; the World; the Nations—Judgment, Executed by, God— God, Sovereignty of, Uses Nations as Agents—Day of the Lord, Described, Events of—Babylon, Destruction of, Predicted—Babylon, Symbol of, Evil Governments; the World System—World, System of, Symbolized by Babylon**: Babylon's destruction was predicted by God's prophet Isaiah. What he foresaw weighed ever so heavily upon his heart. He called Babylon's destruction a *burden* or *oracle* (*massa*), which means something lifted up or carried. It has the idea of carrying a heavy load or burden. This message of judgment was weighing heavily upon Isaiah's heart. It is difficult for any man of God to preach on judgment, but especially when he has to warn his own friends and neighbors to repent or else face the judgment of God. Although this particular message was directed toward the Babylonians, it stood as a warning to the people of Judah and Jerusalem. Any person will face the hand of God's judgment if they rebel against Him and live wickedly. Keep in mind that Babylon symbolizes the evil governments and systems of this world. Therefore, any prediction concerning Babylon should be closely observed by every generation of people. A frightful, graphic description is painted of Babylon's destruction:

OUTLINE	SCRIPTURE	SCRIPTURE	OUTLINE
1. God's destruction of Babylon predicted: A picture of God's coming judgment a. The stirring of an army to execute God's judgment 1) The summons would be issued • A banner would be raised • A command would be given by God to set apart a number of	The burden of Babylon, which Isaiah the son of Amoz did see. 2 Lift ye up a banner upon the high mountain, exalt the voice unto them, shake the hand, that they may go into the gates of the nobles. 3 I have commanded my sanctified ones, I have also called my mighty ones for	mine anger, *even* them that rejoice in my highness. 4 The noise of a multitude in the mountains, like as of a great people; a tumultuous noise of the kingdoms of nations gathered together: the LORD of hosts mustereth the host of the battle. 5 They come from a far country, from the end of heaven, *even* the LORD,	warriors—an army—to carry out His wrath 2) The warriors would respond • A great number of nations would be mobilized • A great number would join forces from far away—from the very ends of heaven—to be the weapons of God's

OUTLINE	SCRIPTURE	SCRIPTURE	OUTLINE
wrath	and the weapons of his indignation, to destroy the whole land.	shall every man turn to his own people, and flee every one into his own land.	seeking safety
b. The terrifying description of God's judgment: The day of the LORD	6 Howl ye; for the day of the LORD *is* at hand; it shall come as a destruction from the Almighty.	15 Every one that is found shall be thrust through; and every one that is joined *unto them* shall fall by the sword.	• All the captured would be killed
1) A day of terror • Weakened hands • Melting hearts • Paralyzing fear • Agonizing pain (like a woman in labor) • Utter horror, helplessness	7 Therefore shall all hands be faint, and every man's heart shall melt: 8 And they shall be afraid: pangs and sorrows shall take hold of them; they shall be in pain as a woman that travaileth: they shall be amazed one at another; their faces *shall be as* flames.	16 Their children also shall be dashed to pieces before their eyes; their houses shall be spoiled, and their wives ravished. 17 Behold, I will stir up the Medes against them, which shall not regard silver; and *as for* gold, they shall not delight in it.	• Children & infants alike would be slaughtered • Property would be looted • Women would be raped c. The agent used to enforce God's wrath on Babylon: The Medes 1) They would seek revenge, not wealth 2) They would show no mercy, not even to the infants or children
2) A day of God's wrath & fierce anger 3) A day of devastation: The destruction of the earth & of sinners	9 Behold, the day of the LORD cometh, cruel both with wrath and fierce anger, to lay the land desolate: and he shall destroy the sinners thereof out of it.	18 *Their* bows also shall dash the young men to pieces; and they shall have no pity on the fruit of the womb; their eye shall not spare children.	
4) A day of astronomical changes: The heavens—sun, moon, & stars—would be dark, not show their light	10 For the stars of heaven and the constellations thereof shall not give their light: the sun shall be darkened in his going forth, and the moon shall not cause her light to shine.	19 And Babylon, the glory of kingdoms, the beauty of the Chaldees' excellency, shall be as when God overthrew Sodom and Gomorrah.	d. The total destruction of Babylon, a symbol of the evil & wickedness of this world 1) Babylon would be destroyed: Like Sodom & Gomorrah
5) A day of punishment for the whole world • The wicked for their sin • The proud for their arrogance • The ruthless for their haughtiness 6) A day of few survivors	11 And I will punish the world for *their* evil, and the wicked for their iniquity; and I will cause the arrogancy of the proud to cease, and will lay low the haughtiness of the terrible. 12 I will make a man more precious than fine gold; even a man than the golden wedge of Ophir.	20 It shall never be inhabited, neither shall it be dwelt in from generation to generation: neither shall the Arabian pitch tent there; neither shall the shepherds make their fold there. 21 But wild beasts of the desert shall lie there; and their houses shall be full of doleful creatures; and owls shall dwell there, and satyrs shall dance there.	2) Babylon would never rise again, never be lived in by people again 3) Babylon would be inhabited only by wild animals
7) A day of shaking the whole universe—both heaven & earth—from its place: Perhaps referring to storms & earthquakes, 2 Pe.3:10-13 8) A day of flight & of savage brutality • People would flee,	13 Therefore I will shake the heavens, and the earth shall remove out of her place, in the wrath of the LORD of hosts, and in the day of his fierce anger. 14 And it shall be as the chased roe, and as a sheep that no man taketh up: they	22 And the wild beasts of the islands shall cry in their desolate houses, and dragons in *their* pleasant palaces: and her time *is* near to come, and her days shall not be prolonged.	4) Babylon's days would be numbered: Its destruction was near

a. An army was to be aroused by God Himself to execute judgment upon the wicked Babylonians (vv.1-5). This army was to be the Medes, who are clearly identified (v.17). In 612–609 B.C., the Medes joined the Babylonians in defeating the Syrians. However, in 539 B.C., the Medes formed an alliance with King Cyrus of Persia to conquer Babylon (see Je.51:11, 28; Da.5:31; 6:28).[1] In His sovereign power, the LORD stirs nations and people to be His agents on earth. When the LORD wants a task carried out, He arouses either a person or a nation to accomplish this task. In dealing with Babylon, the LORD would arouse the Medes to raise a *banner* for war. A loud shout and a vigorous waving of the hand would summon the armies from far distances to quickly mobilize. They were being brought together to attack the gates (palaces) of the nobles, the high and mighty Babylonians.

Behind the scenes of world history the LORD Himself was commanding the Medes to assemble and unite their armies. They were being *appointed* as God's warriors, set apart to execute His wrath against Babylon. However, the Medes' army was *sanctified* or *holy* only in the sense of being *set apart* as God's agents. In this case, God's appointment of the Medes had nothing to do with purity, righteousness, or morality.

Isaiah predicted that a great number of nations would be mobilized (vv.4-5). Again, it was the LORD of hosts mustering these forces for war. This army would be God's agent to execute His judgment. Coming from far away lands, the army of the

---

1 *The NIV Study Bible.* (Grand Rapids, MI: Zondervan Publishing House, 1985), Is.13:17.

Medes would be a mighty war machine. They would destroy the whole country of Babylon (v.5). Once more, the army is said to be the weapon of God's anger and wrath. Of course, as would be the case with most unbelievers, the Medes did not recognize that they were agents of God, His appointed instrument to carry out His judgment.

b. The terrifying description of the judgment is now given (vv.6-16). Note that it is referred to as the *Day of the LORD*. Remember, the *Day of the LORD* is a time when the LORD's judgment falls on the wicked and He delivers His people, pouring out His blessings upon them (see Zep.1:14–2:3. Also see **DEEPER STUDY #3**—Is.2:6–4:1 for more discussion.) The LORD's wrath upon Babylon was near, and it was coming from the LORD of hosts, the sovereign Creator and Majesty of the universe (v.6). Warren W. Wiersbe gives an excellent summary of what happened to the city of Babylon as well as pointing out that this passage refers to God's judgment in the last days of human history:

> The city of Babylon was completely destroyed in 689 B.C. by Sennacherib and the Assyrian army, but it was rebuilt by Sennacherib's son. In 539 B.C., Darius the Mede captured the city (Da.5:31), but he did not destroy it. In the centuries that followed, Babylon had its "shining moments," but after the death of its last great conqueror, Alexander the Great, the city declined and soon was no more. Isaiah's prophecy was fulfilled, for the city was not rebuilt.
>
> But it is clear that Isaiah's prophecy describes something more significant than the ups and downs of an ancient city. The prophets often began a message by focusing on local events, but then enlarged their vision to reveal something greater. Isaiah saw in the fall of Babylon a picture of "the Day of the LORD" (Isa.13:6, 9, 13), that time when God will pour out His wrath on the whole world (v.11). The image of the woman in travail is used in Scripture to describe a time of judgment (v.8; 21:3; 26:17; Jer.6:24; Micah 4:9-10; Matt.24:8, where "sorrows" is "birth pains"; 1 Thes.5:3). Isaiah looked beyond that day to the day when the Babylonian world system would be destroyed (Rev.17–18). Compare Isaiah 13:10 with Matthew 24:29; Joel 2:10; and Revelation 6:12-14; and see Jeremiah 50–51.[2]

The people of Babylon would cry out and scream in utter terror when the *Day of the LORD* approached. It would be the Day of the LORD's execution of true justice, a day that would bring about violent destruction. The people would not be able to prevent God's judgment nor could they endure it. Keep in mind that this prophecy has a double meaning, applying both to the destruction of Babylon in Isaiah's day and to the inevitable judgment that is to come at the end of human his-tory (see outlines and notes—Mt.24:1-31).

1) When the *Day of the LORD* strikes, it will be a time of paralyzing terror (vv.7-8). All hands will be weakened and fall limp; all hearts will melt. People will be overwhelmed with fear and gripped by agonizing pain, like the pain of a woman in labor. Looking aghast at each other, people will sense the horror and utter helplessness of their situation.

2) Note that the *Day of the LORD* is again mentioned by Isaiah. It is to be a day of God's wrath and fierce anger (v.9). God is going to execute His justice against all the unjust who have mistreated others. His judgment is going to fall upon all the evil and wicked of the earth.

3) God's day will be a day of destruction, a day when both the earth and sinners will be destroyed. Keep in mind the double application of this passage, applying to the final judgment as well as to the immediate destruction of Babylon. In the words of H.C. Leupold, "though the emphasis seems to lie on the worldwide aspect of what transpires, in the last analysis what befalls Babylon is under consideration."[3]

4) The LORD's *Day of Judgment* will involve some astronomical changes (v.10). The heavens—the sun, moon, and stars—will be darkened. Their lights will not shine in the sky, neither by day nor by night. Of course, this refers to God's judgment in the end times.

5) God's day will be a day of punishment for the whole world (v.11). In this particular verse, God's judgment is definitely stretched beyond Babylon to include the whole world. The wicked will be judged for their sins, the proud for their arrogance, and the ruthless for their haughtiness.

6) God's *Day of Judgment* will leave few survivors (v.12). Leupold points out that two words are used in this verse for *man*. The first refers to the average person, and the second to important persons throughout the community.[4] The once populous Babylon will have few citizens left. And after the judgment of the last days, only believers will survive.

7) The *Day of the LORD* will be a day of shaking the entire universe (v.13). The heavens themselves will shake as well as the earth. Perhaps this is a reference to violent storms or earthquakes, although it could mean there will be sudden and terrifying catastrophes in the atmosphere in the last days (see 2 Pe.3:1-12).

8) The LORD's *day* will be a day of flight and of savage brutality (v.14). Like a hunted gazelle, known for its speed, or a sheep wandering without a shepherd, people will flee and seek safety from the coming destruction. But those of Babylon who are captured will be killed. In utter horror the citizens of Babylon will witness their children being brutally slaughtered, their property looted of all valuables, and their wives and daughters being raped.

c. Remember that the agent of God's wrath on Babylon would be the Medes (vv.17-18). Therefore Isaiah stressed this fact again. Note that the Medes had no interest in wealth. The idea conveyed is that they were a wild, uncivilized, brutal people. They were motivated more by revenge for what they had suffered under the Babylonians than by a desire for great riches. Plundering the wealth of the Babylonians was of secondary interest to them.[5] When they attacked Babylon, they showed no mercy whatsoever, not even to the infants or children. They were showing themselves to be just as depraved as the Babylonians had been.

d. The destruction of Babylon would be total and permanent (vv.19-22). Keep in mind that Babylon is a symbol of the evil and wickedness of this world, a symbol of the prideful and hostile, the enemies of God and the dark powers of this

---

2 Warren W. Wiersbe. *Be Comforted*, pp.44-45.
3 H.C. Leupold. *Exposition of Isaiah*, Vol.1, p.244.
4 ibid., p.245.
5 ibid., p247.

world. Babylon symbolizes the evil governments and civilizations of the world, the world systems that people build in their defiance and rebellion against God. Babylon was an evil empire, as evil as Sodom and Gomorrah (v.19). For this reason, Babylon, the most glorious of all kingdoms in whom the world's citizens took great pride, was to be totally destroyed. And note: Babylon would never again rise, never be inhabited or lived in again. It should be noted that the Hebrew in this verse (13:20ª) can be translated, "She will not be inhabited for a long time and she will not be lived in for generation after generation."[6] In the last days, Babylon will be rebuilt and then destroyed by God for a final time (see outline and notes—Re.18:1-24 for more discussion; also see Je.50:1–51:58). After Babylon's destruction, only wild animals will live in the area. In closing out his prophetic message, Isaiah declared that Babylon's days would be numbered. Its destruction would not be prolonged.

Thought 1. The world is going to face a day of final judgment. All nations, governments, civilizations, cultures, societies, cities, communities, and people will face God. God is going to execute justice upon this earth, avenging all the injustices and evil deeds that have ever been done. No mistreatment of other people has ever escaped the eye of God. Every thought, word, and deed has been seen and heard by God. Scripture even declares that a record is being kept of every word and thought ever spoken or conceived by a person (Mt.12:36; 2 Co.10:3-5). Everything we have ever done, whether in our bodies or outside our bodies, will face the judgment of God. Just as God's predicted judgment fell upon Babylon, so it will fall upon this earth and upon every human being who has lived upon this earth.

"For the Son of man shall come in the glory of his Father with his angels; and then he shall reward every man according to his works" (Mt.16:27).

"When the Son of man shall come in his glory, and all the holy angels with him, then shall he sit upon the throne of his glory: And before him shall be gathered all nations: and he shall separate them one from another, as a shepherd divideth *his* sheep from the goats: And he shall set the sheep on his right hand, but the goats on the left" (Mt.25:31-33).

"For we must all appear before the judgment seat of Christ; that every one may receive the things *done* in *his* body, according to that he hath done, whether *it be* good or bad" (2 Co.5:10).

"And as it is appointed unto men once to die, but after this the judgment" (He.9:27).

"The Lord knoweth how to deliver the godly out of temptations, and to reserve the unjust unto the day of judgment to be punished" (2 Pe.2:9).

"But the heavens and the earth, which are now, by the same word are kept in store, reserved unto fire against the day of judgment and perdition of ungodly men" (2 Pe.3:7).

"And Enoch also, the seventh from Adam, prophesied of these, saying, Behold, the Lord cometh with ten thousands of his saints, To execute judgment upon all, and to convince all that are ungodly among them of all their ungodly deeds which they have ungodly committed, and of all their hard *speeches* which ungodly sinners have spoken against him" (Jude 1:14-15).

"And I saw a great white throne, and him that sat on it, from whose face the earth and the heaven fled away; and there was found no place for them. And I saw the dead, small and great, stand before God; and the books were opened: and another book was opened, which is *the book* of life: and the dead were judged out of those things which were written in the books, according to their works. And the sea gave up the dead which were in it; and death and hell delivered up the dead which were in them: and they were judged every man according to their works. And death and hell were cast into the lake of fire. This is the second death. And whosoever was not found written in the book of life was cast into the lake of fire" (Re.20:11-15).

"Also unto thee, O Lord, *belongeth* mercy: for thou renderest to every man according to his work" (Ps.62:12).

"I the LORD search the heart, *I* try the reins, even to give every man according to his ways, *and* according to the fruit of his doings" (Je.17:10).

2 (14:1-2) **Captivity, Deliverance from—Captivity, of Israel, Freed from—Deliverance, from Captivity, God's People—Believers, Freed from Captivity, Example of—Babylon, Destruction of, Reasons for—Israel, Return to the Promised Land, Promised—Prophecy, Concerning Israel, Restoration**: God's purpose for destroying Babylon was to deliver His people from captivity. Time and again Isaiah had warned the Jews that they would be led into captivity by Babylon (5:13; 6:11-12; 11:11 [Shinar refers to Babylon]; 39:6). The prophet Jeremiah had also warned the people for over 40 years (Je.20:4-6; 21:7-10). But the people had refused to listen to the warnings of the prophets. As a result, Babylon overran Judah and laid siege to the capital Jerusalem. In 586 B.C., the Babylonians utterly destroyed Jerusalem and took the surviving Jews into captivity. Babylon scattered the Jews throughout the empire in an attempt to destroy their identity with their homeland. But 70 years later, almost immediately after the Persian conquest of Babylon, the Persian king Cyrus allowed any Jew who wished to do so to return to his homeland (see outline and notes—Ezr.1:1–2:70 for more discussion. Also see Je.25:1-14.) In the present passage, Isaiah is predicting that God's people would be set free from their captivity. Once again, the LORD would have mercy upon them. He would choose them to be His people and to give them *rest* (a home, security, peace, prosperity) in the promised land (v.1). Centuries earlier the LORD had chosen Israel to be His *holy people* (De.7:6-11). Now, He would return them to the promised land for this very same purpose: to be His *holy people*, a people who would obey His commandments and be a strong testimony to the unbelievers of the world. Note that some foreigners would join the Jews in returning to the promised land, indicating that they had become true believers in the only living and true God.

---

6 John F. Walvoord and Roy B. Zuck, Editors. *The Bible Knowledge Commentary*, p.1060.

The nations who would set God's people free refer to all the independent nations within the Persian Empire (v.2). Perhaps it is also a reference to the end time when all nations will help transport the returning Jewish captives to Israel (2:3; 14:2; 43:6; 60:9). Note that Israel will possess the nations in that day. Nations will voluntarily serve Israel (v.2). Most likely this is a picture of the Messiah's coming kingdom (2:1-5; 14:2; 25:9-10; 49:23; 60:12).

OUTLINE	SCRIPTURE	SCRIPTURE	OUTLINE
2. God's purpose for destroying Babylon: To deliver His people from captivity a. God would have mercy: Restore, give His people *rest* in the promised land b. Foreigners would join Israel c. Nations would be God's	For the LORD will have mercy on Jacob, and will yet choose Israel, and set them in their own land: and the strangers shall be joined with them, and they shall cleave to the house of Jacob. 2 And the people shall take	them, and bring them to their place: and the house of Israel shall possess them in the land of the LORD for servants and handmaids: and they shall take them captives, whose captives they were; and they shall rule over their oppressors.	agents to free & return His people to the promised land d. All nations would voluntarily submit to Israel: A picture of the Messiah's kingdom

Thought 1. Israel's deliverance from captivity is a clear picture of our deliverance from sin and death. God liberates us from the bondages of this wicked and depraved earth. However, no person is sinless, and no person can keep from sinning. We were born with a sinful human nature, a depraved nature that lusts after forbidden fruit. Furthermore, not only can we not keep from sinning, but we cannot prevent death. We all die.

No matter how much we may try, we cannot escape sin or death. We are held captive, sentenced to spend our lives in the prison of sin and doomed to die. But there is wonderful news: the LORD will have mercy upon us. He will set us free from the enslavements of this corrupt world. No longer do we have to remain in captivity. The LORD has taken the doors of imprisonment and swung them wide open for us to escape. We can now be set free from sin and death. Victory over both can be ours through the Lord Jesus Christ. He took all our sins upon Himself and paid the penalty that was due us, even the penalty of death. Through Christ we can be set free, become acceptable to God and live eternally with Him. Listen to what God's Holy Word says:

> "And ye shall know the truth, and the truth shall make you free" (Jn.8:32).
>
> "Know ye not, that to whom ye yield yourselves servants to obey, his servants ye are to whom ye obey; whether of sin unto death, or of obedience unto righteousness? But God be thanked, that ye were the servants of sin, but ye have obeyed from the heart that form of doctrine which was delivered you. Being then made free from sin, ye became the servants of righteousness" (Ro.6:16-18).
>
> "But now being made free from sin, and become servants to God, ye have your fruit unto holiness, and the end everlasting life. For the wages of sin *is* death; but the gift of God *is* eternal life through Jesus Christ our Lord" (Ro.6:22-23).
>
> "There *is* therefore now no condemnation to them which are in Christ Jesus, who walk not after the flesh, but after the Spirit. For the law of the Spirit of life in Christ Jesus hath made me free from the law of sin and death" (Ro.8:1-2).
>
> "For I delivered unto you first of all that which I also received, how that Christ died for our sins according to the scriptures; And that he was buried, and that he rose again the third day according to the scriptures" (1 Co.15:3-4).
>
> "Who gave himself for our sins, that he might deliver us from this present evil world, according to the will of God and our Father" (Ga.1:4).
>
> "Who his own self bare our sins in his own body on the tree, that we, being dead to sins, should live unto righteousness: by whose stripes ye were healed" (1 Pe.2:24).
>
> "And he is the propitiation for our sins: and not for ours only, but also for *the sins of* the whole world" (1 Jn.2:2).
>
> "Unto him that loved us, and washed us from our sins in his own blood" (Re.1:5).

3 (14:3-23) **Babylon, King of, Judgment and Punishment—Judgment, Who Is to Be Judged, Babylon's King—Satan, Fall of, Pictured—Babylon, King of, Symbol of Satan's Fall**: God would judge and punish the king of Babylon. Throughout this passage the king of Babylon seems to be separated from the rest of mankind, destined for a very distinct judgment, one that seems far worse than that suffered by anyone else. His judgment is severe because his sins appear to have arisen from the depths of hell itself. Babylon's king was a powerful ruler who was so gripped by pride that he exalted himself above the very *stars* of God (v.13). He sought to be accepted as an equal to the most high God Himself. In addition to his terrible sins of pride and arrogance, he was the most cruel, wicked tyrant imaginable. Due to his appalling evil, he was doomed to suffer the terrifying judgment of God.

The excellent Lutheran commentator H.C. Leupold points out that this passage actually has three possible interpretations: first, it could refer to a specific king of Babylon, an actual historical figure. Or, second, it could be describing the imperial power of Babylon. Or, third, the king could be a symbol of the hostile forces who rebel against God and persecute His people.[7] Mr. Leupold says that he leans to the last of these interpretations, which is also the position taken in the excellent commentary *Jamieson, Fausset, and Brown*. Warren W. Wiersbe says this:

> The picture in Isaiah 14:1-23 is that of a mighty monarch whose pride brought him to destruction. This is what happened to Belshazzar when Darius the Mede captured Babylon in 539 B.C. (Dan.5). Isaiah described the king's

---

7 H.C. Leupold. *Exposition of Isaiah*, Vol. 1, pp.254-255.

arrival in Sheol, the world of the dead, where the kings wealth, glory, and power vanished. The dead kings already in Sheol stood in tribute to him (Isa.14:9), but it was all a mockery. Death is the great leveler; there are no kings in the world of the dead. "Lucifer" (v.12) is Latin for "morning star" and suggests that this king's glory did not last very long. The morning star shines but is soon swallowed up by the light of the sun.

The prophet saw in this event something far deeper than the defeat of an empire. In the fall of the king of Babylon, he saw the defeat of Satan, the "prince of this world," who seeks to energize and motivate the leaders of nations (Jn.12:31; Eph.2:1-3). Daniel 10:20 indicates that Satan has assigned "princes" (fallen angels) to the various nations so that he can influence leaders to act contrary to the will of God.

This highest of God's angels tried to usurp the throne of God and capture for himself the worship that belongs only to God (Matt.4:8-10). The name "Lucifer" ('morning star') indicates that Satan tries to imitate Jesus Christ who is the "the bright and morning star" (Rev.22:16). "I will be like the Most High" reveals his basic strategy, for he is an imitator (Isa.14:14; 2 Cor.11:13-15). Like the king of Babylon, Satan will one day be humiliated and defeated. He will be cast out of heaven (Rev.12) and finally cast into hell (20:10). Whether God is dealing with kings or angels, Proverbs 16:18 is still true: "Pride goes before destruction, and a haughty spirit before a fall" (NKJV).[8]

Since the king of Babylon seems to be the ultimate personification or representation of pride, many commentators feel that he is a clear type of Satan. The first to hold this view were Tertullian (about 160–230 A.D.) and Gregory the Great (about 540–604 B.C.).[9] Yet no matter what position a person may hold, this passage would certainly apply to anyone who exalts himself in prideful rebellion against God and lives such a cruel, wicked life. This sort of person will be doomed to hell, perhaps not to the lowest depth of hell as the king of Babylon was; but nevertheless, he will be doomed to hell. In addition to this passage, there are several others that point to the sin and fall of Satan:

"I beheld Satan as lightning fall[s] from heaven" (Lu.10:18).

"He that committeth sin is of the devil; for the devil sinneth from the beginning. For this purpose the Son of God was manifested, that he might destroy the works of the devil" (1 Jn.3:8).

"And there was war in heaven: Michael and his angels fought against the dragon; and the dragon fought and his angels, And prevailed not; neither was their place found any more in heaven. And the great dragon was cast out, that old serpent, called the Devil, and Satan, which deceiveth the whole world: he was cast out into the earth, and his angels were cast out with him" (Re.12:7-9).

"How art thou fallen from heaven, O Lucifer, son of the morning! how art thou cut down to the ground, which didst weaken the nations! For thou hast said in thine heart, I will ascend into heaven, I will exalt my throne above the stars of God: I will sit also upon the mount of the congregation, in the sides of the north: I will ascend above the heights of the clouds; I will be like the most High. Yet thou shalt be brought down to hell, to the sides of the pit. " (Is.14:12-15).

"Moreover the word of the LORD came unto me, saying, Son of man, take up a lamentation upon the king of Tyrus, and say unto him, Thus saith the Lord GOD; Thou sealest up the sum, full of wisdom, and perfect in beauty. Thou hast been in Eden the garden of God; every precious stone *was* thy covering, the sardius, topaz, and the diamond, the beryl, the onyx, and the jasper, the sapphire, the emerald, and the carbuncle, and gold: the workmanship of thy tabrets and of thy pipes was prepared in thee in the day that thou wast created. Thou *art* the anointed cherub that covereth; and I have set thee *so:* thou wast upon the holy mountain of God; thou hast walked up and down in the midst of the stones of fire. Thou *wast* perfect in thy ways from the day that thou wast created, till iniquity was found in thee. By the multitude of thy merchandise they have filled the midst of thee with violence, and thou hast sinned: therefore I will cast thee as profane out of the mountain of God: and I will destroy thee, O covering cherub, from the midst of the stones of fire. Thine heart was lifted up because of thy beauty, thou hast corrupted thy wisdom by reason of thy brightness: I will cast thee to the ground, I will lay thee before kings, that they may behold thee. Thou hast defiled thy sanctuaries by the multitude of thine iniquities, by the iniquity of thy traffick; therefore will I bring forth a fire from the midst of thee, it shall devour thee, and I will bring thee to ashes upon the earth in the sight of all them that behold thee. All they that know thee among the people shall be astonished at thee: thou shalt be a terror, and never *shalt* thou *be* any more" (Eze.28:11-19).

In looking at these Scriptures together, there seems to be some indication that Satan fell from his exalted position due to sin, especially the sin of prideful rebellion. He fell just as mankind has fallen. And, since mankind is doomed to hell because of its sin, naturally Satan would have been doomed to hell because of his sin. Again, what is being said here could be said about many people who have lived down through history. But the king of Babylon was evidently the very embodiment of pride and wickedness. Thus, if he was the embodiment of sin, there is only one who would be ranked a greater sinner than he: Satan himself. It seems only natural to see a picture of Satan's sin and fall in these verses. Note this fact while reading the Scripture and outline:

OUTLINE	SCRIPTURE	SCRIPTURE	OUTLINE
3. God's punishment of the king of Babylon: A picture of Satan's fall, Lu.10:15, 18;	3 And it shall come to pass in the day that the LORD shall give thee rest from thy sor-	row, and from thy fear, and from the hard bondage wherein thou wast made to serve,	Re.12:9; Eze.28:11-19

8 Warren W. Wiersbe. *Be Comforted*, pp.45-46.
9 John F. Walvoord and Roy B. Zuck, Editors. *The Bible Knowledge Commentary*, p.1061.

OUTLINE	SCRIPTURE	SCRIPTURE	OUTLINE
a. The king would be taunted: By all who had been delivered b. The oppressor's brutality & rule would be ended by the awesome power of God 1) God would break the rod & rule of the wicked king • Due to his aggressive conquests of nations • Due to his governing people in brutality, not justice 2) God would give rest to the whole earth • The earth itself would sing • The trees—a symbol of oppressed multitudes—would rejoice over the tyrant's fall 3) God would doom the wicked one to Sheol (the grave, hell)**DS1** • The departed spirits who were awaiting judgment—especially other rulers—would become excited over his arrival in hell • The departed spirits would scoff at his fall & his doom to hell: In the end, he was as weak & as doomed as they were • The wicked ruler would lose his glory, wealth, & power, & his beloved music: Maggots & worms would cover his body c. The fall of Lucifer, the morning star, from heaven, Lu.10:15, 18; Jn.3:8; Eze.28:11-19 1) His judgment: Had been cast from his exalted position 2) His sin: Pride—sought to ascend to heaven • To raise his throne above God's stars • To be the one worshipped on the sacred mountain (God's temple)	4 That thou shalt take up this proverb against the king of Babylon, and say, How hath the oppressor ceased! the golden city ceased! 5 The LORD hath broken the staff of the wicked, *and* the sceptre of the rulers. 6 He who smote the people in wrath with a continual stroke, he that ruled the nations in anger, is persecuted, *and* none hindereth. 7 The whole earth is at rest, *and* is quiet: they break forth into singing. 8 Yea, the fir trees rejoice at thee, *and* the cedars of Lebanon, *saying,* Since thou art laid down, no feller is come up against us. 9 Hell from beneath is moved for thee to meet *thee* at thy coming: it stirreth up the dead for thee, *even* all the chief ones of the earth; it hath raised up from their thrones all the kings of the nations. 10 All they shall speak and say unto thee, Art thou also become weak as we? art thou become like unto us? 11 Thy pomp is brought down to the grave, *and* the noise of thy viols: the worm is spread under thee, and the worms cover thee. 12 How art thou fallen from heaven, O Lucifer, son of the morning! *how* art thou cut down to the ground, which didst weaken the nations! 13 For thou hast said in thine heart, I will ascend into heaven, I will exalt my throne above the stars of God: I will sit also upon the mount of the congregation, in the sides of the north:	14 I will ascend above the heights of the clouds; I will be like the most High. 15 Yet thou shalt be brought down to hell, to the sides of the pit. 16 They that see thee shall narrowly look upon thee, *and* consider thee, *saying, Is* this the man that made the earth to tremble, that did shake kingdoms; 17 *That* made the world as a wilderness, and destroyed the cities thereof; *that* opened not the house of his prisoners? 18 All the kings of the nations, *even* all of them, lie in glory, every one in his own house. 19 But thou art cast out of thy grave like an abominable branch, *and as* the raiment of those that are slain, thrust through with a sword, that go down to the stones of the pit; as a carcase trodden under feet. 20 Thou shalt not be joined with them in burial, because thou hast destroyed thy land, *and* slain thy people: the seed of evildoers shall never be renowned. 21 Prepare slaughter for his children for the iniquity of their fathers; that they do not rise, nor possess the land, nor fill the face of the world with cities. 22 For I will rise up against them, saith the LORD of hosts, and cut off from Babylon the name, and remnant, and son, and nephew, saith the LORD. 23 I will also make it a possession for the bittern, and pools of water: and I will sweep it with the besom of destruction, saith the LORD of hosts.	• To exalt himself above the clouds, becoming like the Most High (God Himself) 3) His fate: Would be brought down to hell, the very pit of hell, to its lowest depths 4) His shameful end: People would gaze upon & mock him because of who he is • The one who had caused nations to tremble • The one who had devastated the world & its cities & had enslaved its people 5) His dishonorable burial: His body would not lie in state like other kings • His body would be cast into a mass grave with slain soldiers—like a discarded branch • His body would be trampled underfoot because of his destructive & cruel nature 6) His offspring & their fate • Would not be mentioned again • Would be doomed because of their forefather's sins • Would not be allowed to inherit the land nor to build cities 7) His Babylonian empire: Would be utterly destroyed by God Himself: A picture of the evil world system • To have its name, survivors, children, & descendants cut off • To be a desolate place, a place for porcupines • To be a swampland • To be swept with the broom of destruction

a. After the fall of Babylon, the people of God would be set free. Once liberated, they would taunt the king of Babylon due to the depths to which he had fallen. Remember all the suffering and turmoil and cruel bondage to which the king had subjected them. But now Babylon's king was to be cast from his exalted throne, utterly defeated. And through his defeat God's people would be set free. If there had ever been a day when their cruel enemy could be taunted, it was the day of their freedom and his doom.

b. It was God Himself—His awesome power—who ended the oppressor's brutality and rule (vv.4-11). Filled with malice and a vicious rage, the king had oppressed the nations of the world. But now his cruelty had come to a stunning halt.

    1) God snapped the rod and rule of this wicked king (vv.5-6). The LORD executed judgment against him…
- because of his aggressive conquest of nations
- because of his governing people in brutality, striking them down with endless blows

    Instead of ruling the nations in compassion and justice, the king had placed the people under his thumb, ruling them with an iron fist. But now the LORD had broken his power and cast the king off of his exalted throne. This wicked leader would rule no more.

2) By defeating the wicked king, the LORD gave rest and peace to the whole world (vv.7-8). The people broke into singing. Even the trees (all of nature) rejoiced over the tyrant's fall (see Ro.8:19-23). Some expositors hold that the trees represent the oppressed people who broke out in singing.

3) God doomed this wicked king to hell (Sheol) (vv.9-11; see DEEPER STUDY #1—Is.14:9 for more discussion). Keep in mind that *Sheol* can mean either the grave or the place of torment. Obviously the latter is the meaning here. As soon as the king of Babylon died on earth, he is pictured entering hell. His arrival aroused the spirits of the departed, apparently causing a great deal of commotion. Note that everyone still had their own personal, individual identity and that they recognized one another. No sooner had the king of Babylon arrived in hell than its inhabitants began to taunt him and scoff at his fall and doom (v.10). Although the king had been the most powerful leader on earth, in the end he was as weak and as doomed as they were. He was stripped of all power and position even as they were. His glory and wealth, his power and the music he loved—all had been lost by this condemned ruler. Now maggots and worms were covering his body as it lay decaying on earth. And his wicked soul was doomed to spend eternity in hell. (See DEEPER STUDY #1—Is.14:9 for more discussion.)

c. Lucifer's fall from heaven now takes place (vv.12-23). In the Hebrew, *Lucifer* literally means *day star* or *morning star.* Ezekiel says that Lucifer was the highest being ever created by God (Eze.28:12-15).

1) This morning star was cast from his exalted position from the heights of heaven itself (v.12). As will be seen in just a moment, Lucifer sought to climb to the height of heaven. Therefore, from that height he was cast down to the earth. Note who he is: he is the one who has weakened, subjected, and dominated the nations. Thus he was doomed to suffer the greatest conceivable overthrow: that of falling from the heights of heaven to the depths of hell.[10]

2) What was the sin that caused such a terrible fall, especially for one who had held such a prominent position and had been exalted so highly? His great sin was pride. In his innermost thoughts, Lucifer had set his heart upon exalting himself as high as the heavens. He was consumed with selfish ambition...

- to exalt his throne, his position above all the stars of God (v.13; see Ge.11:3-4)
- to be the very one worshipped on the sacred mountain
- to exalt himself above the clouds, to be like the Most High God Himself (v.14)

Note the five "I wills" of Lucifer in these verses. Within his innermost thoughts, he was exalting himself above God. Just as people down through history have exalted themselves, ignoring and even denying the LORD, so this morning star was ignoring the LORD and exalting himself. His personal will and ambition were set against God.

3) Lucifer's fate was sealed: he was brought down to the very pit of hell, that is, to its lowest depths (v.15). His prideful defiance of the LORD challenged the LORD to act. Hence the LORD did to Lucifer just as He will do to all who are prideful and defiant.

4) Lucifer's end will be most shameful and humiliating (vv.16-17). People will gaze at him and mock him, reflecting upon his astronomical fall. They will be wondering...

- Is this the one who had caused nations and kingdoms to tremble?
- Is this the one who had so long devastated the world and its cities and enslaved its people?

Because he will have fallen so low from such a high position, all will wonder how this could have happened. How could this be the person who had possessed such immense power and been able to move across the earth so ruthlessly without being stopped?

5) This morning star will have a dishonorable burial, for his body will not lie in state like other kings (vv.18-20). Instead, his body will be cast into a mass grave with slain soldiers, be discarded like a rejected branch or like the bloody clothing of dead soldiers. Once he has departed the earth, people will block out all memory of him...

- because of his destructive and brutal nature
- because he swept across the earth dominating and oppressing them

6) Even the king's offspring will never be mentioned again (v.20). None of his sons will succeed him upon the throne. Rather, they will all be doomed because of the sins of their forefathers and the influence of these sins upon their lives (v.21). They will never again be allowed to rise up and conquer land or to rebuild and fill the cities of the world.

7) The king's empire will be utterly destroyed by God Himself (vv.22-23). Babylon will be overthrown and punished for its terrible evil. Even its name will be cut off, as will any who survive, including their children and descendants (v.22). Babylon will become a desolate place, a place inhabited only by animals. It will be a swamp land, swept over with the broom of destruction (v.23).

Thought 1. The Lord Jesus Christ has destroyed the power of the devil. Satan's power has been broken. No longer are we doomed to be held in the grip of his enslavements. All bondages can now be broken through the power of Christ, bondages such as...

- greed and overindulgence
- smoking, drinking, and abusing drugs
- profanity and taking the Lord's name in vain
- illicit sex and pornography
- sensual pleasures and fleshly passions
- shoplifting and other forms of stealing
- laziness and indifference

No matter what bondage may hold us in its grip, this bondage can be broken through the power of the Savior. Christ has broken the power of sin, the power that Satan had over this earth and its people. Listen to what God's Word says:

---

10 H.C. Leupold. *Exposition of Isaiah,* Vol. 1, p.259.

"Jesus answered and said, This voice came not because of me, but for your sakes. Now is the judgment of this world: now shall the prince of this world be cast out" (Jn.12:30-31).

"Hereafter I will not talk much with you: for the prince of this world cometh, and hath nothing in me" (Jn.14:30).

"These things I have spoken unto you, that in me ye might have peace. In the world ye shall have tribulation: but be of good cheer; I have overcome the world" (Jn.16:33).

"Nay, in all these things we are more than conquerors through him that loved us" (Ro.8:37).

"Now thanks *be* unto God, which always causeth us to triumph in Christ, and maketh manifest the savour of his knowledge by us in every place" (2 Co.2:14).

"For though we walk in the flesh, we do not war after the flesh: (For the weapons of our warfare *are* not carnal, but mighty through God to the pulling down of strong holds;) Casting down imaginations, and every high thing that exalteth itself against the knowledge of God, and bringing into captivity every thought to the obedience of Christ" (2 Co.10:3-5).

"And he said unto me, My grace is sufficient for thee: for my strength is made perfect in weakness. Most gladly therefore will I rather glory in my infirmities, that the power of Christ may rest upon me" (2 Co.12:9).

"That he would grant you, according to the riches of his glory, to be strengthened with might by his Spirit in the inner man" (Ep.3:16).

"Now unto him that is able to do exceeding abundantly above all that we ask or think, according to the power that worketh in us" (Ep.3:20).

"Forasmuch then as the children are partakers of flesh and blood, he also himself likewise took part of the same; that through death he might destroy him that had the power of death, that is, the devil; And deliver them who through fear of death were all their lifetime subject to bondage" (He.2:14-15).

"Be sober, be vigilant; because your adversary the devil, as a roaring lion, walketh about, seeking whom he may devour: Whom resist stedfast in the faith, knowing that the same afflictions are accomplished in your brethren that are in the world. But the God of all grace, who hath called us unto his eternal glory by Christ Jesus, after that ye have suffered a while, make you perfect, stablish, strengthen, settle *you*" (1 Pe.5:8-10).

"He that committeth sin is of the devil; for the devil sinneth from the beginning. For this purpose the Son of God was manifested, that he might destroy the works of the devil" (1 Jn.3:8).

"For whatsoever is born of God overcometh the world: and this is the victory that overcometh the world, *even* our faith. Who is he that overcometh the world, but he that believeth that Jesus is the Son of God?" (1 Jn.5:4-5).

DEEPER STUDY # 1

(14:9) **Grave (Sheol):** the place where the dead go. The Hebrew word *sheol* is the same as the Greek word *Hades* (see DEEPER STUDY #3—Lu.16:23). Several facts should be noted about *sheol*, the place of the dead.

1. *Sheol* or *hell* does not always refer to the place of the damned, where the wicked of the earth suffer in an eternal fire. This is an inaccurate understanding of *sheol*.

    a. *Sheol* means grave or pit. This fact is clearly shown by many Scriptures.

> "And all his sons and all his daughters rose up to comfort him; but he refused to be comforted; and he said, For I will go down into the grave unto my son mourning. Thus his father wept for him" (Ge.37:35).

> "Do therefore according to thy wisdom, and let not his hoar [gray, aged] head go down to the grave in peace....Now therefore hold him not guiltless: for thou *art* a wise man, and knowest what thou oughtest to do unto him; but his hoar head bring thou down to the grave with blood" (1 K.2:6,9).

> "Like sheep they are laid in the grave; death shall feed on them; and the upright shall have dominion over them in the morning; and their beauty shall consume in the grave from their dwelling" (Ps.49:14).

> "Let us swallow them up alive as the grave; and whole, as those that go down into the pit" (Pr.1:12).

> "I said in the cutting off of my days, I shall go to the gates of the grave: I am deprived of the residue of my years...For the grave cannot praise thee, death can *not* celebrate thee: they that go down into the pit cannot hope for thy truth" (Is.38:10, 18. Also see Ge.42:38; 44:29; Jb.7:9; 14:13; 17:13; 21:13; 24:19; Ps.6:5; 30:3; 31:17; 49:14, 15; 88:3; 89:48; 141:7; Pr.30:16; Ecc.9:10; Song of S.8:6).

    b. The godly Jacob said he was going down into *sheol*, the grave. He was certainly not expecting to go down into hell.

> "And all his sons and all his daughters rose up to comfort him; but he refused to be comforted; and he said, For I will go down into the grave unto my son mourning. Thus his father wept for him" (Ge.37:35).

c. The Levite Heman who wrote Psalm 88 was not expecting to enter hell at death, but the grave. So was the Levite Ethan who wrote Psalm 89.

> "For my soul is full of troubles: and my life draweth nigh unto the grave" (Ps.88:3).
> "Remember how short my time is: wherefore hast thou made all men in vain? What man *is he that* liveth, and shall not see death? shall he deliver his soul from the hand of the grave? Selah" (Ps.89:47-48).

2. *Sheol* sometimes has the idea of *hell*, the place where the sinful are sent and where they suffer punishment, pain, and agony. The following Scriptures will serve as examples:

a. Korah and his rebels were sent into the pit (sheol) alive. Of course, this does not mean they were sent into the grave alive. Rather, they were sent into *hell* (*sheol*)—the place where they would be punished for their wickedness.

> "And it came to pass, as he [Moses] had made an end of speaking all these words, that the ground clave asunder that *was* under them: And the earth opened her mouth, and swallowed them up, and their houses, and all the men that *appertained* unto Korah, and all *their* goods. They, and all that *appertained* to them, went down alive into the pit, and the earth closed upon them: and they perished from among the congregation. And all Israel that *were* round about them fled at the cry of them: for they said, Lest the earth swallow us up *also*. And there came out a fire from the LORD, and consumed the two hundred and fifty men that offered incense" (Nu.16:31-35).

b. In pronouncing judgment on the Israelites, the LORD said that the *fire* of His anger…"shall burn unto the lowest hell (sheol)." The lowest part of *sheol* must be *hell*, a place where God's anger burns in judgment against those who have lived wicked lives.

> "For a fire is kindled in mine anger, and shall burn unto the lowest hell, and shall consume the earth with her increase, and set on fire the foundations of the mountains" (De.32:22).

c. Scripture clearly shows that *sheol* includes *hell*, a place of punishment, pain, and anguish.

> "But if the LORD make a new thing, and the earth open her mouth, and swallow them up, with all that *appertain* unto them, and they go down quick into the pit; then ye shall understand that these men have provoked the LORD.…They, and all that *appertained* to them, went down alive into the pit, and the earth closed upon them: and they perished from among the congregation" (Nu.16:30, 33).
> "For a fire is kindled in mine anger, and shall burn unto the lowest hell, and shall consume the earth with her increase, and set on fire the foundations of the mountains" (De.32:22).
> "Do therefore according to thy wisdom, and let not his hoar [gray, aged] head go down to the grave in peace.…Now therefore hold him not guiltless: for thou *art* a wise man, and knowest what thou oughtest to do unto him; but his hoar head bring thou down to the grave [the pit of hell] with blood" (1 K.2:6, 9).
> "Before I go *whence* I shall not return, *even* to the land of darkness and the shadow of death" (Jb.10:21).
> "They spend their days in wealth, and in a moment go down to the grave [hell]" (Jb.21:13).
> "The wicked shall be turned into hell, *and* all the nations that forget God. For the needy shall not alway be forgotten: the expectation of the poor shall *not* perish for ever" (Ps.9:17-18).
> "Like sheep they are laid in the grave; death shall feed on them; and the upright shall have dominion over them in the morning; and their beauty shall consume in the grave from their dwelling. But God will redeem my soul from the power of the grave [hell]: for he shall receive me. Selah" (Ps.49:14-15).
> "Her feet go down to death; her steps take hold on hell" (Pr.5:5).
> "But he knoweth not that the dead *are* there; *and that* her guests *are* in the depths of hell" (Pr.9:18).
> "Thou shalt beat him with the rod, and shalt deliver his soul from hell" (Pr.23:14).
> "Therefore hell hath enlarged herself, and opened her mouth without measure: and their glory, and their multitude, and their pomp, and he that rejoiceth, shall descend into it" (Is.5:14).

3. The Hebrew word *sheol* is the same as the Greek word *Hades*. The picture of *hades* or *sheol* revealed by Jesus Christ is that of the other world, which is the unseen world, the spiritual world, the spiritual dimension of being. Jesus says it is a place divided into two huge areas (sections or compartments). The two areas are separated by a great gulf that is impassible (Lu.16:26). One area is hell, the place of sorrow and torment (Lu.16:23-24, 28). The other area is the place of Paradise, the place of glory where believers go. In the Old Testament when a person died, he went to *Hades*, the other world. Jesus said both places actually exist. (See outline and notes—Lu.16:19-31; see DEEPER STUDY # 4—Lu.16:24; Mt.27:52-53; Ep.4:8-10; DEEPER STUDY # 1—1 Pe.3:19-20.)

People have different opinions about hell. But one fact needs to be remembered: what we think cannot annul or do away with the truth. If we deny hell, our denial will not make hell cease to exist. Denial does not void truth, no matter how much we may ignore or deny a fact. The world is round and will always be round, no matter how many people of former generations said it was flat. So it is with hell. Since hell exists, it will always exist, no matter how many people deny it. Our denial of hell does not keep it from being real.

The natural man views *hell* in one of three ways:
- ⇒ Some people believe the Christian teaching about hell, that hell is a place of life and punishment. But they do not believe strongly enough to give their hearts and lives to Jesus Christ, nor do they think that God will condemn them to hell, not in the final analysis. They think they will be accepted by God when all things are said and done.
- ⇒ Some people believe there is a place where people will be in a semi-conscious state or sleep when they die. They think they will have some sense of euphoria or sorrow or neither.
- ⇒ Other people believe in nothing beyond the grave. They think life ceases at death, that the grave is the end.

The spiritual man believes in life after death. He believes in eternal life, that is, that life continues on just as Christ taught and the Bible says. Thus, the spiritual man believes that *sheol* or *hell* is real just as the Scripture teaches (see note—Lu.16:23 for more discussion).

1. God's judgment of Assyria: A picture of God's plan for judgment—to set His people free, 10:5-19

a. God's plan for judgment ratified, sworn by on oath
  1) He will break, crush Assyria *in Israel*, 37:36-37; 2 K.19:35
  2) He will free His people from the yoke of Assyrian bondage

b. God's plan for judgment applied to the whole world, all evil nations: His purpose—to set His people free

  1) No person can stop God's plan for judgment
  2) No person can change God's plans

2. God's judgment of Philistia: A picture of God's refuge, of deliverance found only in Him

a. The warning to Philistia
  1) Must not rejoice over the Assyrian king's death
  2) Must know that the king's root, his son, will be like a venomous snake

b. The assurance of God's deliverance given to Judah: Will be safe & have food

c. The pronouncement of God's judgment upon Philistia
  1) To be destroyed by famine & war
  2) To wail because a powerful army from the north (Assyria) was coming like uncontrollable smoke

d. The answer of Judah to the threat of envoys from Assyria
  1) The LORD had established Jerusalem
  2) The LORD & His city were their refuge

3. God's judgment of Moab: A picture of God's compassion, of His weeping over the doomed

a. Moab's destruction by Assyria
  1) The two major cities will fall in a night
  2) The people will flee to their temples & gods for help

B. God's Judgment of Assyria, Philistia, & Moab: A Picture of God's Plan for Judgment & of His Protection & Compassion, 14:24–16:14

24 The LORD of hosts hath sworn, saying, Surely as I have thought, so shall it come to pass; and as I have purposed, *so* shall it stand:
25 That I will break the Assyrian in my land, and upon my mountains tread him under foot: then shall his yoke depart from off them, and his burden depart from off their shoulders.
26 This *is* the purpose that is purposed upon the whole earth: and this *is* the hand that is stretched out upon all the nations.
27 For the LORD of hosts hath purposed, and who shall disannul *it?* and his hand *is* stretched out, and who shall turn it back?
28 In the year that king Ahaz died was this burden.
29 Rejoice not thou, whole Palestina, because the rod of him that smote thee is broken: for out of the serpent's root shall come forth a cockatrice, and his fruit *shall be* a fiery flying serpent.
30 And the firstborn of the poor shall feed, and the needy shall lie down in safety: and I will kill thy root with famine, and he shall slay thy remnant.
31 Howl, O gate; cry, O city; thou, whole Palestina, *art* dissolved: for there shall come from the north a smoke, and none *shall be* alone in his appointed times.
32 What shall *one* then answer the messengers of the nation? That the LORD hath founded Zion, and the poor of his people shall trust in it.

CHAPTER 15

The burden of Moab. Because in the night Ar of Moab is laid waste, *and* brought to silence; because in the night Kir of Moab is laid waste, *and* brought to silence;
2 He is gone up to Bajith, and to Dibon, the high places, to weep: Moab shall howl

---

over Nebo, and over Medeba: on all their heads *shall be* baldness, *and* every beard cut off.
3 In their streets they shall gird themselves with sackcloth: on the tops of their houses, and in their streets, every one shall howl, weeping abundantly.
4 And Heshbon shall cry, and Elealeh: their voice shall be heard *even* unto Jahaz: therefore the armed soldiers of Moab shall cry out; his life shall be grievous unto him.
5 My heart shall cry out for Moab; his fugitives *shall flee* unto Zoar, an heifer of three years old: for by the mounting up of Luhith with weeping shall they go it up; for in the way of Horonaim they shall raise up a cry of destruction.
6 For the waters of Nimrim shall be desolate: for the hay is withered away, the grass faileth, there is no green thing.
7 Therefore the abundance they have gotten, and that which they have laid up, shall they carry away to the brook of the willows.
8 For the cry is gone round about the borders of Moab; the howling thereof unto Eglaim, and the howling thereof unto Beer-elim.
9 For the waters of Dimon shall be full of blood: for I will bring more upon Dimon, lions upon him that escapeth of Moab, and upon the remnant of the land.

CHAPTER 16

Send ye the lamb to the ruler of the land from Sela to the wilderness, unto the mount of the daughter of Zion.
2 For it shall be, *that,* as a wandering bird cast out of the nest, so the daughters of Moab shall be at the fords of Arnon.
3 Take counsel, execute judgment; make thy shadow as the night in the midst of the noonday; hide the outcasts; bewray not him that wandereth.
4 Let mine outcasts dwell with thee, Moab; be thou a covert to them from the face

---

3) The people will mourn & weep bitterly as city after city falls

4) The soldiers & armed citizens will be fainthearted, cry out & tremble in fear

b. Moab's refugees
  1) They are wept over by God & His prophet Isaiah
  2) They—the refugees—will weep as they flee to Zoar

3) They will weep because of the utter destruction of their water & land: Will become like a desert

4) They will weep because they will lose all of their possessions except what little they can carry as they flee
5) They will weep all across the land as they flee from one end to the other

- Because of the slaughter, the waters will be stained with blood
- Because the Assyrian attack will be relentless, like the pursuit of a lion

c. Moab's plea to Jerusalem: The people will send a tribute to Zion (Jerusalem) appealing for asylum
  1) Because the female refugees will be helpless, fleeing their houses like homeless birds

2) Because the only hope for the refugees will be to beg the Jerusalem officials for shelter, a safe haven

d. Moab's only hope
  1) A great promise: All oppressors & aggressors will

meet their end—be banished from the land

2) The LORD's love: He will act in love & send a King to sit on David's throne—One who will execute justice & righteousness on earth: A promise of the coming Savior, Jesus Christ, 9:6; 11:1-10; Am.9:11-12

e. Moab's sin: Extreme pride, arrogance, haughtiness, & boastful talk

1) Will result in the destruction of Moab: The people will wail over the slaughtered men (soldiers)

2) Will result in the devastation of the nation's vineyards & its chief crop, grapes

f. Moab's fate wept over by God & His prophet Isaiah
1) Because the joy of the

of the spoiler: for the extortioner is at an end, the spoiler ceaseth, the oppressors are consumed out of the land.
5 And in mercy shall the throne be established: and he shall sit upon it in truth in the tabernacle of David, judging, and seeking judgment, and hasting righteousness.
6 We have heard of the pride of Moab; *he is* very proud: *even* of his haughtiness, and his pride, and his wrath: *but* his lies *shall not be* so.
7 Therefore shall Moab howl for Moab, every one shall howl: for the foundations of Kir-hareseth shall ye mourn; surely *they are* stricken.
8 For the fields of Heshbon languish, *and* the vine of Sibmah: the lords of the heathen have broken down the principal plants thereof, they are come *even* unto Jazer, they wandered *through* the wilderness: her branches are stretched out, they are gone over the sea.
9 Therefore I will bewail with the weeping of Jazer the vine of Sibmah: I will water

thee with my tears, O Heshbon, and Elealeh: for shouting for thy summer fruits and for thy harvest is fallen.
10 And gladness is taken away, and joy out of the plentiful field; and in the vineyards there shall be no singing, neither shall there be shouting: the treaders shall tread out no wine in *their* presses; I have made *their vintage* shouting to cease.
11 Wherefore my bowels shall sound like an harp for Moab, and mine inward parts for Kir-haresh.
12 And it shall come to pass, when it is seen that Moab is weary on the high place, that he shall come to his sanctuary to pray; but he shall not prevail.
13 This *is* the word that the LORD hath spoken concerning Moab since that time.
14 But now the LORD hath spoken, saying, Within three years, as the years of an hireling, and the glory of Moab shall be contemned, with all that great multitude; and the remnant *shall be* very small *and* feeble.

people & the fruitfulness of the land will be destroyed

2) Because God will be forced to put an end to their harvests & their joy

3) Because the very heart of God will feel their pain & weep over their desperate plight
4) Because Moab will seek deliverance through their worship of false gods

g. Moab's judgment set: To be within three years

1) Moab's splendor will end

2) Moab's people will be despised
3) Moab's survivors will be few

DIVISION II

THE PROPHECIES CONCERNING GOD'S JUDGMENT OF THE NATIONS AND HIS TRIUMPH OVER THE WORLD, 13:1–27:13

B. God's Judgment of Assyria, Philistia, and Moab: A Picture of God's Plan for Judgment and of His Protection and Compassion, 14:24–16:14

(14:24–16:14) **Introduction**: judgment is a subject that is seldom preached or taught today. However, it is a subject people desperately need to hear.

One of the basic principles of judgment is this: whatever we sow, we will reap. If we become intoxicated and then drive an automobile, get into an accident, and injure ourselves—we reap what we have sown. For instance, if we sow adultery, we reap conflict in our marriages, which often leads to divorce. And we cause our children tremendous pain and suffering. Another principle of judgment is this: whatever we measure will be measured back to us (Lu.6:38). If we are friendly and kind to others, most people will be friendly and kind to us. If we are helpful to others, most of them will help us. If we turn to Christ and love and worship Him, God says He will turn to us and love and accept us. These are just two of the basic principles of judgment that God has put in place.

Messages of judgment are not intended to frighten us. They are warning flags meant to protect us and teach us how to live fruitful, productive lives on earth. The LORD wants us to walk victoriously in the world, conquering all the trials and difficulties of life. But as we walk, there are obstacles and potholes that we must avoid, or else we run the risk of harming ourselves and others. This is the reason God warns us about the coming day of judgment.

One day all human beings will give an account of their lives to God. Judgment is a warning that if we walk through life without Him, we will continue without Him for eternity. Alienation from God in this life means alienation from God in the next life. Knowing that the Day of Judgment is coming warns us that we must stop rebelling against God and turn to Him now if we wish to live with Him throughout eternity.

The prophecies of God's judgment against the nations of the world continue. This is, *God's Judgment of Assyria, Philistia, and Moab: A Picture for God's Plan of Judgment and of His Protection and Compassion*, 14:24–16:14.

1. God's judgment of Assyria: a picture of God's plan for judgment—to set His people free (14:24-27).
2. God's judgment of Philistia: a picture of finding refuge only in God (14:28-32).
3. God's judgment of Moab: a picture of God's compassion, of His weeping over the doomed (15:1–16:14).

1 (14:24-27) **Judgment, Plan for, Unstoppable; Surety of; Sworn by God's Oath—Oath, of God, Concerning Judgment—World, Judgment of, Surety—Assyria, Judgment of, Unstoppable—Judgment, Purpose of, to God's People**: God Himself planned the judgment of Assyria. He made a definite plan and swore by His own oath to carry it out (v.24). Therefore, it was certain that Assyria's power would be broken. Note where this was going to take place: in Israel, in the land of Judah. Very soon after Isaiah announced this prophecy, Assyria launched a military campaign against the western world of that time, which included all the cities of Judah. According to Assyrian historical records, King Sennacherib conquered 46 fortified cities and numerous small towns of Judah. He also took captive more than 200,000 people and threw up a siege around Jerusalem, trapping King Hezekiah "like a caged bird."[1]

With the massive Assyrian army camped within eyesight of the city gates, the situation looked utterly hopeless for Hezekiah and the citizens of Jerusalem. But Isaiah visited the king and assured him that this prophecy would be fulfilled: the LORD Himself would set His people free from the yoke of Assyrian bondage. Historically, the event happened just as predicted. That very night the angel of the LORD went into the Assyrian camp and put to death 185,000 of Sennacherib's soldiers.

Not understanding what had happened, the shocked survivors broke camp and returned to Nineveh. Soon afterward, Sennacherib was assassinated in the temple of his false god Nishroch. Having lost most of its army and its king, Assyria's domination was broken. The LORD Himself had executed this judgment upon the cruel, wicked Assyrians. (See outline and notes—Is.36:1–37:38; 2 K.18:17–35; 2 Chr.32:9–19 for more discussion.)

Now note a very significant point: God not only had a plan to judge Assyria, but He also has a plan to judge the entire world (vv.26–27). Scripture clearly says that His plan of judgment includes the whole world and that His hand of judgment is stretched out over all nations. No person or nation can change God's plan or stop Him from carrying it out. He has already determined exactly when and how He will judge the world, the order in which individuals and nations will be called to stand before Him, and the very day and hour when they will be judged. On Judgment Day, God Himself will exercise true justice and execute judgment.

OUTLINE	SCRIPTURE	SCRIPTURE	OUTLINE

1. God's judgment of Assyria: A picture of God's plan for judgment—to set free His people, 10:5-19
a. God's plan for judgment ratified, sworn by on oath
  1) He will break, crush Assyria *in Israel*, 37:36-37; 2 K.19:35
  2) He will free His people from the yoke of Assyrian bondage
	24 The LORD of hosts hath sworn, saying, Surely as I have thought, so shall it come to pass; and as I have purposed, *so* shall it stand: 25 That I will break the Assyrian in my land, and upon my mountains tread him under foot: then shall his yoke depart from off them, and his burden depart from off their	shoulders. 26 This *is* the purpose that is purposed upon the whole earth: and this *is* the hand that is stretched out upon all the nations. 27 For the LORD of hosts hath purposed, and who shall disannul *it?* and his hand *is* stretched out, and who shall turn it back?	b. God's plan for judgment applied to the whole world, all evil nations: His purpose—to set His people free
			
			  1) No person can stop God's plan for judgment
			  2) No person can change God's plans

Thought 1. Just as the LORD delivered His people from the yoke of Assyrian bondage, so He will set free all who truly trust Him. He will set His people free from all the wickedness and evil of this earth—from every enslavement, oppression, persecution, temptation, trial. And after He has judged the earth and everyone who has ever lived upon it, He is going to create a new heaven and earth, a perfect universe. This perfect universe will be the home of all believers of all generations and of all the angelic hosts. The LORD will free His people from the yoke of all bondages. This is the clear promise of His Holy Word:

"The Spirit itself beareth witness with our spirit, that we are the children of God: And if children, then heirs; heirs of God, and joint-heirs with Christ; if so be that we suffer with *him,* that we may be also glorified together. For I reckon that the sufferings of this present time *are* not worthy *to be compared* with the glory which shall be revealed in us. For the earnest expectation of the creature waiteth for the manifestation of the sons of God. For the creature was made subject to vanity, not willingly, but by reason of him who hath subjected *the same* in hope, Because the creature itself also shall be delivered from the bondage of corruption into the glorious liberty of the children of God. For we know that the whole creation groaneth and travaileth in pain together until now. And not only *they,* but ourselves also, which have the firstfruits of the Spirit, even we ourselves groan within ourselves, waiting for the adoption, *to wit,* the redemption of our body" (Ro.8:16-23).

"For our conversation [behavior, conduct] is in heaven; from whence also we look for the Saviour, the Lord Jesus Christ: Who shall change our vile body, that it may be fashioned like unto his glorious body, according to the working whereby he is able even to subdue all things unto himself" (Ph.3:20-21).

"When Christ, *who is* our life, shall appear, then shall ye also appear with him in glory" (Col.3:4).

"But the day of the Lord will come as a thief in the night; in the which the heavens shall pass away with a great noise, and the elements shall melt with fervent heat, the earth also and the works that are therein shall be burned up. *Seeing* then *that* all these things shall be dissolved, what manner *of persons* ought ye to be in *all* holy conversation and godliness, Looking for and hasting unto the coming of the day of God, wherein the heavens being on fire shall be dissolved, and the elements shall melt with fervent heat? Nevertheless we, according to his promise, look for new heavens and a new earth, wherein dwelleth righteousness" (2 Pe.3:10-13).

[1] Daniel David Luckenbill. *Ancient Records of Assyria and Babylonia*, p.120.

"And I saw a new heaven and a new earth: for the first heaven and the first earth were passed away; and there was no more sea....And God shall wipe away all tears from their eyes; and there shall be no more death, neither sorrow, nor crying, neither shall there be any more pain: for the former things are passed away....He that overcometh shall inherit all things; and I will be his God, and he shall be my son. But the fearful, and unbelieving, and the abominable, and murderers, and whoremongers, and sorcerers, and idolaters, and all liars, shall have their part in the lake which burneth with fire and brimstone: which is the second death....And had a wall great and high, *and* had twelve gates, and at the gates twelve angels, and names written thereon, which are *the names* of the twelve tribes of the children of Israel....And there shall be no more curse: but the throne of God and of the Lamb shall be in it; and his servants shall serve him: And they shall see his face; and his name *shall be* in their foreheads. And there shall be no night there; and they need no candle, neither light of the sun; for the Lord God giveth them light: and they shall reign for ever and ever" (Re.21:1, 4, 7-8, 12; 22:3-5).

2 (14:28-32) **Judgment, Concerning the Philistines—Philistines, Judgment of—Refuge, Source of, the LORD—God, Protection, Promised—Judah, Example of, Trust in God:** Isaiah declared the prophecy concerning God's judgment of Philistia in the year King Ahaz died (715 B.C.) At that time in history, the nations of the world were in constant upheaval, and feelings of helplessness and terror swept over the people like a flooding river. The Assyrians, who dominated the world, were one of the cruelest and most oppressive people ever to live upon the earth. Their king, Shalmaneser, launched an invasion of the Northern Kingdom of Israel, but he died before he could capture the capital, Sa-maria. His son Sargon ascended to the throne of Assyria, conquered the Northern Kingdom, and deported the survivors.

Right after the conquest (722 B.C.), Sargon had to rush to the other end of his kingdom to put down several revolts, but he suffered a defeat when he tried to conquer Babylon. It looked like a good time for other repressed people to throw off the yoke of Assyria.[2] Grasping the opportunity to free themselves, the Syrians and the Philistines formed an alliance and revolted against their Assyrian oppressors. In the midst of these events, Isaiah prophesied against the Philistines. Note the Scripture and outline:

OUTLINE	SCRIPTURE	SCRIPTURE	OUTLINE
2. God's judgment of Philistia: A picture of God's refuge, of deliverance found only in Him	28 In the year that king Ahaz died was this burden.	and he shall slay thy remnant.	judgment upon Philistia
a. The warning to Philistia	29 Rejoice not thou, whole Palestina, because the rod of	31 Howl, O gate; cry, O city; thou, whole Palestina, *art* dissolved: for there shall	1) To be destroyed by famine & war
1) Must not rejoice over the Assyrian king's death	him that smote thee is broken: for out of the serpent's	come from the north a smoke, and none *shall be* alone in his	2) To wail because a powerful army from the north (Assyria) was coming like
2) Must know that the king's root, his son, will be like a venomous snake	root shall come forth a cockatrice, and his fruit *shall be* a fiery flying serpent.	appointed times. 32 What shall *one* then answer the messengers of	uncontrollable smoke d. The answer of Judah to the threat of envoys from Assyria
b. The assurance of God's deliverance given to Judah: Will be safe & have food	30 And the firstborn of the poor shall feed, and the needy shall lie down in safety: and I	the nation? That the LORD hath founded Zion, and the poor of his people shall trust	1) The LORD had established Jerusalem 2) The LORD & His city
c. The pronouncement of God's	will kill thy root with famine,	in it.	were their refuge

Remember that God gave this prophecy for the benefit of His people. Down through the centuries, the Philistines had caused terrible suffering for Judah and Jerusalem, and now the LORD was ready to pronounce judgment upon them. Isaiah told the Philistines that they were foolish to rejoice over the death of Shalmaneser because they had rebelled without considering what the new ruler would be like. In fact, the son of the serpent Shalmaneser would be far worse. Sargon would be like a venomous snake, ready to strike any rebellion with a deadly poison.

Note the sharp contrast between the dark future of the Philistines and the bright future of the citizens of Judah. God's people would not face the wrath of God's judgment. Their experience would be just the opposite. When the Assyrians swept into the land to put down the revolt of the Philistines, God's people would be safe and still have plenty of food to eat.

Keep in mind that the LORD was using Assyria as His agent to execute judgment on other evil, oppressive nations. Isaiah declared that when Assyria attacked the Philistines (vv.30–31), they would be destroyed by war and famine. He described the impending calamity in graphic language: the Philistines would howl when the gates of their city fell, and they would melt in fear. Soon the powerful Assyrian war machine would sweep down upon them from the north like uncontrollable smoke (v.31).

But God held the fate of His people in His own hands, and it would be totally different from that of the Philistines (v.32). When envoys from Assyria came to Jerusalem and threatened God's people, King Hezekiah would have a straightforward answer for them. Since the LORD was their protector, they did not need alliances with other nations. The LORD had established Zion (Jerusalem), and His city was their refuge. Although God's people seemed weak and helpless against the mighty power of Assyria, even the weakest and poorest among them would find refuge in the LORD in Zion.

Thought 1. God is our refuge and shield, our protector and defender. No matter who or how powerful the enemy is, the LORD will shelter us if we flee to Him for protection. God loves us and wants to embrace us when people mistreat us. When they humiliate, scorn, curse, or assault us, the LORD will take us under the shadow of His wings. The LORD also wants to shelter us when life is hard. When we suffer from disease, disaster, divorce, or the death of a loved

---

2 Stanley M. Horton. *Isaiah, The Old Testament Study Bible*, p.127.

one—whatever the misfortune may be—He will embrace us and be a refuge to us. But we must come to Him in faith, trusting Christ to be our deliverer through all the trials and temptations of life. If we surrender our lives to Him, His overshadowing love and care will guard us. He will infuse us with the strength to conquer all the difficult circumstances of life. Listen to His Holy Word:

"**O Jerusalem, Jerusalem, *thou* that killest the prophets, and stonest them which are sent unto thee, how often would I have gathered thy children together, even as a hen gathereth her chickens under *her* wings, and ye would not!**" (Mt.23:37).

"**The eternal God *is thy* refuge, and underneath *are* the everlasting arms: and he shall thrust out the enemy from before thee; and shall say, Destroy *them***" (De.33:27).

"**For the eyes of the LORD run to and fro throughout the whole earth, to show himself strong in the behalf of *them* whose heart *is* perfect toward him**" (2 Chr.16:9).

"**For in the time of trouble he shall hide me in his pavilion: in the secret of his tabernacle shall he hide me; he shall set me up upon a rock**" (Ps.27:5).

"**Thou shalt hide them in the secret of thy presence from the pride of man: thou shalt keep them secretly in a pavilion from the strife of tongues**" (Ps.31:20).

"**Our soul waiteth for the LORD: he *is* our help and our shield**" (Ps.33:20).

"**The angel of the LORD encampeth round about them that fear him, and delivereth them**" (Ps.34:7).

"**God *is* our refuge and strength, a very present help in trouble**" (Ps.46:1).

"**Be merciful unto me, O God, be merciful unto me: for my soul trusteth in thee: yea, in the shadow of thy wings will I make my refuge, until *these* calamities be overpast**" (Ps.57:1).

"**Be thou my strong habitation, whereunto I may continually resort: thou hast given commandment to save me; for thou *art* my rock and my fortress**" (Ps.71:3).

"**For the LORD God *is* a sun and shield: the LORD will give grace and glory: no good *thing* will he withhold from them that walk uprightly**" (Ps.84:11).

"**He shall cover thee with his feathers, and under his wings shalt thou trust: his truth *shall be thy* shield and buckler**" (Ps.91:4).

"**O Israel, trust thou in the LORD: he *is* their help and their shield**" (Ps.115:9).

"**As the mountains *are* round about Jerusalem, so the LORD *is* round about his people from henceforth even for ever**" (Ps.125:2).

"**In the fear of the LORD *is* strong confidence: and his children shall have a place of refuge**" (Pr.14:26).

"**The name of the LORD *is* a strong tower: the righteous runneth into it, and is safe**" (Pr.18:10).

"**For thou hast been a strength to the poor, a strength to the needy in his distress, a refuge from the storm, a shadow from the heat, when the blast of the terrible ones *is* as a storm *against* the wall**" (Is.25:4).

"**And I have put my words in thy mouth, and I have covered thee in the shadow of mine hand, that I may plant the heavens, and lay the foundations of the earth, and say unto Zion, Thou *art* my people**" (Is.51:16).

---

3 (15:1–16:14) **Judgment, Attitude of God, Compassion—Compassion, of God, for the Doomed—God, Weeping, Over the Doomed—Attitude, of God, Toward the Doomed; Judgment—Moab, Judgment of**: Isaiah's announcement of the judgment against Moab reveals the very heart of God, opening it up for the world to see. The picture is touching, for it is contrary to what most people think when they hear a message on judgment. God's attitude toward judgment is one of compassion, even weeping. It is not His will for anyone to perish (2 Pe.3:9). He longs for all people to repent of their sins, be saved, and live with Him eternally. But He also longs for us to worship Him freely, not mechanically like robots. Therefore, God allows us to choose either to love Him or deny Him. Although God gives us this choice (free will), His heart breaks when we reject Him and doom ourselves to live apart from Him forever. God's compassion flows out from His heart, urging all people to repent of their sins. He longs for all to love and worship Him. And so, in the midst of God's pronounced judgment upon Moab, Isaiah gives us a touching picture of the LORD's compassion for those who are doomed. Note the Scripture and outline:

OUTLINE	SCRIPTURE	SCRIPTURE	OUTLINE

3. God's judgment of Moab: A picture of God's compassion, of His weeping over the doomed
a. Moab's destruction by Assyria
  1) The two major cities will fall in a night
  2) The people will flee to their temples & gods for help
  3) The people will mourn & weep bitterly as city after
	The burden of Moab. Because in the night Ar of Moab is laid waste, *and* brought to silence; because in the night Kir of Moab is laid waste, *and* brought to silence;
	2 He is gone up to Bajith, and to Dibon, the high places, to weep: Moab shall howl over Nebo, and over Medeba: on all their heads *shall be* baldness, *and* every beard cut
		off.
		3 In their streets they shall gird themselves with sackcloth: on the tops of their houses, and in their streets, every one shall howl, weeping abundantly.
		4 And Heshbon shall cry, and Elealeh: their voice shall be heard *even* unto Jahaz: therefore the armed soldiers of Moab shall cry out; his life
			city falls
			
			4) The soldiers & armed citizens will be fainthearted, cry out & tremble in fear

OUTLINE	SCRIPTURE	SCRIPTURE	OUTLINE
b. Moab's refugees 1) They are wept over by God & His prophet Isaiah 2) They—the refugees—will weep as they flee to Zoar 3) They will weep because of the utter destruction of their water & land: Will become like a desert 4) They will weep because they will lose all of their possessions except what little they can carry as they flee 5) They will weep all across the land as they flee from one end to the other • Because of the slaughter, the waters will be stained with blood • Because the Assyrian attack will be relentless, like the pursuit of a lion c. Moab's plea to Jerusalem: The people will send a tribute to Zion (Jerusalem) appealing for asylum 1) Because the female refugees will be helpless, fleeing their houses like homeless birds 2) Because the only hope for the refugees will be to beg the Jerusalem officials for shelter, a safe haven d. Moab's only hope 1) A great promise: All oppressors & aggressors will meet their end—be banished from the land 2) The LORD's love: He will act in love & send a King to sit on David's throne—One who will execute	shall be grievous unto him. 5 My heart shall cry out for Moab; his fugitives *shall flee* unto Zoar, an heifer of three years old: for by the mounting up of Luhith with weeping shall they go it up; for in the way of Horonaim they shall raise up a cry of destruction. 6 For the waters of Nimrim shall be desolate: for the hay is withered away, the grass faileth, there is no green thing. 7 Therefore the abundance they have gotten, and that which they have laid up, shall they carry away to the brook of the willows. 8 For the cry is gone round about the borders of Moab; the howling thereof unto Eglaim, and the howling thereof unto Beer-elim. 9 For the waters of Dimon shall be full of blood: for I will bring more upon Dimon, lions upon him that escapeth of Moab, and upon the remnant of the land. **CHAPTER 16** Send ye the lamb to the ruler of the land from Sela to the wilderness, unto the mount of the daughter of Zion. 2 For it shall be, *that,* as a wandering bird cast out of the nest, so the daughters of Moab shall be at the fords of Arnon. 3 Take counsel, execute judgment; make thy shadow as the night in the midst of the noonday; hide the outcasts; bewray not him that wandereth. 4 Let mine outcasts dwell with thee, Moab; be thou a covert to them from the face of the spoiler: for the extortioner is at an end, the spoiler ceaseth, the oppressors are consumed out of the land. 5 And in mercy shall the throne be established: and he shall sit upon it in truth in the tabernacle of David, judging, and seeking judgment, and	hasting righteousness. 6 We have heard of the pride of Moab; *he is* very proud: *even* of his haughtiness, and his pride, and his wrath: *but* his lies *shall* not *be* so. 7 Therefore shall Moab howl for Moab, every one shall howl: for the foundations of Kir-hareseth shall ye mourn; surely *they are* stricken. 8 For the fields of Heshbon languish, *and* the vine of Sibmah: the lords of the heathen have broken down the principal plants thereof, they are come *even* unto Jazer, they wandered *through* the wilderness: her branches are stretched out, they are gone over the sea. 9 Therefore I will bewail with the weeping of Jazer the vine of Sibmah: I will water thee with my tears, O Heshbon, and Elealeh: for the shouting for thy summer fruits and for thy harvest is fallen. 10 And gladness is taken away, and joy out of the plentiful field; and in the vineyards there shall be no singing, neither shall there be shouting: the treaders shall tread out no wine in *their* presses; I have made *their vintage* shouting to cease. 11 Wherefore my bowels shall sound like an harp for Moab, and mine inward parts for Kir-haresh. 12 And it shall come to pass, when it is seen that Moab is weary on the high place, that he shall come to his sanctuary to pray; but he shall not prevail. 13 This *is* the word that the LORD hath spoken concerning Moab since that time. 14 But now the LORD hath spoken, saying, Within three years, as the years of an hireling, and the glory of Moab shall be contemned, with all that great multitude; and the remnant *shall be* very small *and* feeble.	justice & righteousness on earth: A promise of the coming Savior, Jesus Christ, 9:6; 11:1-10; Am.9:11-12 e. Moab's sin: Extreme pride, arrogance, haughtiness, & boastful talk 1) Will result in the destruction of Moab: The people will wail over the slaughtered men (soldiers) 2) Will result in the devastation of the nation's vineyards & its chief crop, grapes f. Moab's fate wept over by God & His prophet Isaiah 1) Because the joy of the people & the fruitfulness of the land will be destroyed 2) Because God will be forced to put an end to their harvests & their joy 3) Because the very heart of God will feel their pain & weep over their desperate plight 4) Because Moab will seek deliverance through their worship of false gods g. Moab's judgment set: To be within three years 1) Moab's splendor will end 2) Moab's people will be despised 3) Moab's survivors will be few

a. Assyria would not completely annihilate the Moabites, for Jeremiah later predicted that someday Nebuchadnezzar would sweep across Moab and utterly devastate it (Je.48:1–47). One of two historical events can account for this earlier destruction of Edom.

In 715 B.C., King Sargon of Assyria apparently launched a major campaign against the Arabians. Coming from the north, his army had to march through Moab. As was typical of the Assyrian troops, they conquered, murdered, and plundered as they advanced. However, it could be that in 713 B.C., Moab joined forces with the Philistines against the Assyrians, in which case, Assyria would have invaded Moab.[3]

Whatever the reason for Assyria's action, Isaiah predicted that they would destroy Moab and that the destruction would be swift. Moab's two major cities, Ar and Kir, would be destroyed in one night. And the people, knowing that their fate was sealed, would flee to their temples to seek supernatural help from their gods (v.2). But no matter how much they called upon their gods, there would be no help for the Moabites as city after city fell—Nebo, Medba, Heshbon, Elealeh, Jahaz. Following the custom of that day, amid mourning and bitter weeping, the people would shave their heads, cut their beards, and put on sackcloth. Trembling in fear, their hearts would faint, even the hearts of the armed militia (v.4).

b. A mass of refugees would stream along the road of Moab, fleeing for their lives from the wrath of the onrushing Assyrian army. Seeing the refugees in a vision, Isaiah sensed God's heart and wept over their terrible plight (vv.5–9). God's compassion was flowing through His prophet, demonstrating how His heart flows out to all of suffering humanity. Even in the midst of judgment, God's heart weeps in compassion for those who reject and rebel against Him.

The destination of the refugees would be the little town of Zoar, which had escaped the flames that destroyed Sodom (Ge.19:21–22). Moab's survivors would pass through other cities destined to be crushed—Eglath-shelishiya, Luhith, Horonain—on their way to the abundant waters and fertile farmland of Nimrim. But they would reach the city only to find the waters dried up and the grass withered. The Assyrians would already have laid waste to the land, and it would be like a desert, utterly ruined (v.6).

Isaiah also predicted that the Moabite refugees would weep because they would lose all their possessions except for the little they could carry (v.7). Their outcry would echo across the land as they fled from one end of Moab to the other (vv.8–9). So much blood would be spilled that the waters of the brooks would be stained red. Although the brutal Assyrians would be as relentless in their attack as a lion in pursuit of its prey, a few Moabites would survive the assault and remain in the land. The LORD clearly says that He would bring more judgment upon this remnant in the future (Je.14).

c. Isaiah predicted that in the Moabites' desperate flight from the Assyrian invaders, the refugees would send tribute to Jerusalem and make an urgent plea to the King of Judah for asylum (16:1–5). Only the women are mentioned as refugees because most of the men would be fighting to protect their homeland.

Keep in mind the history of relations between Moab and Israel down through the centuries. The Moabites were descendants of Lot, Abraham's nephew (Ge.19:30–38), but from their earliest history they had been a thorn in the side of Israel. In an attempt to destroy Israel, Moabite women had enticed its men to commit immoral acts and worship false gods (see outline and note—Nu.31:14–18); and in succeeding generations, Moab oppressed Israel. Under King Saul's leadership, the Israelites were able to stand against Moab, and finally King David made it a vassal state of Israel. This meant that the Moabites had to pay tribute to Israel, a tax that was usually paid in lambs (1 S.14:47; see outline and note—2 S.8:1-18, esp.vv.2, 12, for more discussion). Solomon allowed his wives to build an altar to Chemosh, the major idol worshipped by the Moabites (1 K.11:7–8). Soon thereafter the Philistines broke the yoke of Israel's domination. Decades later King Ahaz of Judah again subjected Moab and made it a vassal state of (2 K.3:4). After Ahab's death, Moab rebelled, and the conflict between the two nations began again (see outline and notes—2 K.3:4-27 for more discussion).

Now, like fluttering, homeless baby birds, the women of Moab would be fleeing for their lives; and they would send tribute to King Hezekiah, begging him for protection. Clearly, they would consider this their only hope.

d. Moab's only true hope, however, lay in the future (vv.4–5). Isaiah prophesied that one day all oppressors would come to an end (v.4). In that day, the LORD would demonstrate His love for all people by sending a king to sit on David's throne, one who would execute justice and righteousness on earth (v.5). This is a clear prediction of the coming Messiah, the Lord Jesus Christ. It is as though Isaiah was telling Moab, "You will come to the Jews for help in that awful day of judgment, and we will give you help. We will share with you the wonderful promise and hope of the coming Messiah" (Is.9:6; 11:1-10).

Remember, this judgment was a future event; therefore, Isaiah was urging the Moabites to become true believers in the LORD. Through the years perhaps some Moabites responded to this bold witness, for Amos predicted that a small number of them would be saved (Am.9:11–12). Whatever the case, note the emphasis upon God's love in sending the Savior and future king.

e. Moab was being judged because of its terrible sin of extreme pride and arrogance (vv.6–8). Down through the centuries, the Moabites had exalted themselves and rebelled against the LORD. They refused to turn to Him as the only living and true God. In their pride, they had used their power to oppress other peoples whenever they could. Because of this terrible sin of pride, the sin from which all other sins arise, God would use Assyria to destroy Moab. The Moabites would grieve over their slaughtered soldiers and weep over the utter devastation of the nation's vineyards (v.7).

f. But note God's deep compassion for those who suffer such terrible devastation (vv.9–12). Through His prophet Isaiah, the LORD cries out in grief and weeps for them. Note why:
⇒ Because the people's harvests would fail and their joy cease.
⇒ Because the LORD would be forced to put an end to their harvest and joy (v.10).
⇒ Because God's heart would feel the people's pain (v.11).
⇒ Because Moab would seek deliverance from false gods, to no avail.

h. Though it broke God's heart, Moab's judgment was set due to its wickedness (vv.13–14). Within three years, the splendor of that once proud nation would come to an end. Only a few Moabites would survive, and Moab would be held in contempt.

Thought 1. What a picture of God's innermost being! Even in judgment, the LORD's heart flows out in love and compassion for the doomed. When He executes judgment, He does not lose control of His emotions and act out of anger. He exercises His judgments with perfect justice, so that all people receive exactly what they deserve. On earth we often

---

3 H.P. Leupold. *Exposition of Isaiah*, Vol.1, p.274.

suffer for things we have not done, but divine justice never makes a mistake. God will never declare us guilty of an offense we have not committed.

God's judgment is executed not only in justice, but also in love and compassion. His heart flows out to us when He is correcting us. Every chastisement, every discipline is meant to correct us and turn us back to Him. No matter what the judgment or discipline may be, God's motive is to correct His people in love. Even in the terrifying judgment of the end times, the heart of God will be full of love and compassion for the doomed. His greatest desire will always be that the lost will choose to love and worship Him. Listen to what God's Holy Word says about His love, mercy, and compassion:

"But when he saw the multitudes, he was moved with compassion on them, because they fainted, and were scattered abroad, as sheep having no shepherd" (Mt.9:36).

"And Jesus went forth, and saw a great multitude, and was moved with compassion toward them, and he healed their sick" (Mt.14:14).

"Then Jesus called his disciples *unto him,* and said, I have compassion on the multitude, because they continue with me now three days, and have nothing to eat: and I will not send them away fasting, lest they faint in the way" (Mt.15:32).

"So Jesus had compassion *on them,* and touched their eyes: and immediately their eyes received sight, and they followed him" (Mt.20:34).

"O Jerusalem, Jerusalem, *thou* that killest the prophets, and stonest them which are sent unto thee, how often would I have gathered thy children together, even as a hen gathereth her chickens under *her* wings, and ye would not!" (Mt.23:37).

"And Jesus, moved with compassion, put forth *his* hand, and touched him, and saith unto him, I will; be thou clean" (Mk.1:41).

"And when the Lord saw her, he had compassion on her, and said unto her, Weep not" (Lu.7:13).

"For God so loved the world, that he gave his only begotten Son, that whosoever believeth in him should not perish, but have everlasting life" (Jn.3:16).

"Jesus wept. Then said the Jews, Behold how he loved him!" (Jn.11:35-36).

"But God commendeth his love toward us, in that, while we were yet sinners, Christ died for us" (Ro.5:8).

"But God, who is rich in mercy, for his great love wherewith he loved us, Even when we were dead in sins, hath quickened us together with Christ, (by grace ye are saved;)" (Ep.2:4-5).

"Not by works of righteousness which we have done, but according to his mercy he saved us, by the washing of regeneration, and renewing of the Holy Ghost; Which he shed on us abundantly through Jesus Christ our Saviour; That being justified by his grace, we should be made heirs according to the hope of eternal life" (Tit.3:5-7).

"Seeing then that we have a great high priest, that is passed into the heavens, Jesus the Son of God, let us hold fast *our* profession. For we have not an high priest which cannot be touched with the feeling of our infirmities; but was in all points tempted like as *we are, yet* without sin. Let us therefore come boldly unto the throne of grace, that we may obtain mercy, and find grace to help in time of need" (He.4:14-16).

"Behold, what manner of love the Father hath bestowed upon us, that we should be called the sons of God: therefore the world knoweth us not, because it knew him not" (1 Jn.3:1).

"And the LORD said, I have surely seen the affliction of my people which *are* in Egypt, and have heard their cry by reason of their taskmasters; for I know their sorrows" (Ex.3:7).

"That then the LORD thy God will turn thy captivity, and have compassion upon thee, and will return and gather thee from all the nations, whither the LORD thy God hath scattered thee" (De.30:3).

"But he, *being* full of compassion, forgave *their* iniquity, and destroyed *them* not: yea, many a time turned he his anger away, and did not stir up all his wrath" (Ps.78:38).

"But thou, O Lord, *art* a God full of compassion, and gracious, longsuffering, and plenteous in mercy and truth" (Ps.86:15).

"Like as a father pitieth *his* children, *so* the LORD pitieth them that fear him" (Ps.103:13).

"For thy mercy *is* great above the heavens: and thy truth *reacheth* unto the clouds" (Ps.108:4).

"In all their affliction he was afflicted, and the angel of his presence saved them: in his love and in his pity he redeemed them; and he bare them, and carried them all the days of old" (Is.63:9).

"*It is of* the LORD's mercies that we are not consumed, because his compassions fail not. *They are* new every morning" (La.3:22-23).

"But though he cause grief, yet will he have compassion according to the multitude of his mercies" (La.3:32).

"Who *is* a God like unto thee, that pardoneth iniquity, and passeth by the transgression of the remnant of his heritage? he retaineth not his anger for ever, because he delighteth *in* mercy" (Mi.7:18).

CHAPTER 17

C. God's Judgment of Damascus (Syria), Ephraim (Israel), & Ethiopia: A Picture of Distrust & of Hope in the Face of Judgment, 17:1–18:7

1. God's judgment of Syria & Israel: The certainty of judgment due to forgetting God
a. The fate of both predicted
   1) Damascus: To be destroyed
   2) Aroer, the southern border town: To be deserted & left to flocks

   3) Ephraim's fortified cities: Will be destroyed
   4) Syria's power: Will end
   5) Aram's (Syria's) survivors: Will suffer a defeated glory—just like the Israelites
b. The fate of Israel's glory *in that day*: Will fade, waste away like a starving man

   1) The effects: Like the harvesting of crops
      • The economy will be stripped

      • The population will almost be wiped out

      • The survivors will be few

   2) The return of some to the LORD: A great hope

      • Some will turn from their false worship & idolatry
      • Some will seek the LORD *in that day*

c. The cause of Israel's desolation: Forgetting the LORD
   1) The fact: The cities will be deserted & taken over by thickets & undergrowth
   2) The reason: They had forgotten the God of salvation, that He alone is their Rock, their only solid

The burden of Damascus. Behold, Damascus is taken away from *being* a city, and it shall be a ruinous heap.
2 The cities of Aroer *are* forsaken: they shall be for flocks, which shall lie down, and none shall make *them* afraid.
3 The fortress also shall cease from Ephraim, and the kingdom from Damascus, and the remnant of Syria: they shall be as the glory of the children of Israel, saith the LORD of hosts.
4 And in that day it shall come to pass, *that* the glory of Jacob shall be made thin, and the fatness of his flesh shall wax lean.
5 And it shall be as when the harvestman gathereth the corn, and reapeth the ears with his arm; and it shall be as he that gathereth ears in the valley of Rephaim.
6 Yet gleaning grapes shall be left in it, as the shaking of an olive tree, two *or* three berries in the top of the uppermost bough, four *or* five in the outmost fruitful branches thereof, saith the LORD God of Israel.
7 At that day shall a man look to his Maker, and his eyes shall have respect to the Holy One of Israel.
8 And he shall not look to the altars, the work of his hands, neither shall respect *that* which his fingers have made, either the groves, or the images.
9 In that day shall his strong cities be as a forsaken bough, and an uppermost branch, which they left because of the children of Israel: and there shall be desolation.
10 Because thou hast forgotten the God of thy salvation, and hast not been mindful of the rock of thy strength,

therefore shalt thou plant pleasant plants, and shalt set it with strange slips:
11 In the day shalt thou make thy plant to grow, and in the morning shalt thou make thy seed to flourish: *but* the harvest *shall be* a heap in the day of grief and of desperate sorrow.
12 Woe to the multitude of many people, *which* make a noise like the noise of the seas; and to the rushing of nations, *that* make a rushing like the rushing of mighty waters!
13 The nations shall rush like the rushing of many waters: but *God* shall rebuke them, and they shall flee far off, and shall be chased as the chaff of the mountains before the wind, and like a rolling thing before the whirlwind.
14 And behold at eveningtide trouble; *and* before the morning he *is* not. This *is* the portion of them that spoil us, and the lot of them that rob us.

CHAPTER 18

Woe to the land shadowing with wings, which *is* beyond the rivers of Ethiopia:
2 That sendeth ambassadors by the sea, even in vessels of bulrushes upon the waters, *saying,* Go, ye swift messengers, to a nation scattered and peeled, to a people terrible from their beginning hitherto; a nation meted out and trodden down, whose land the rivers have spoiled!
3 All ye inhabitants of the world, and dwellers on the earth, see ye, when he lifteth up an ensign on the mountains; and when he bloweth a trumpet, hear ye.
4 For so the LORD said unto me, I will take my rest, and I will consider in my dwelling place like a clear heat upon herbs, *and* like a cloud of dew in the heat of harvest.
5 For afore the harvest, when the bud is perfect, and the sour grape is ripening in the flower, he shall both cut off the sprigs with pruninghooks, and take away *and* cut down the branches.
6 They shall be left together

ground or protection

   3) The result: All their efforts to improve their land & crops will be futile, as nothing in *the day* of grief & desperate sorrow

d. The collapse of the invader Assyria: After conquering Damascus & Ephraim & attacking Judah, 37:36-38
   1) The invaders will rage like a roaring sea

   2) The LORD will silence the invaders—stop the roaring waves of their rushing army

   3) The LORD—in one evening—will wipe out the invaders
   4) The enemies—robbers & plunderers—of God's people will be doomed

2. God's judgment of Ethiopia (Cush): The hope for salvation in the face of judgment
a. The situation in Ethiopia
   1) Ethiopia was a powerful, hostile nation
   2) Ethiopia is pictured as sending envoys far and wide to seek alliances: To stand against the onrushing Assyrian army

b. The judgment of Ethiopia
   1) The people of Ethiopia & of the world will know judgment is at hand when the war banner is raised & the trumpet blown
   2) The LORD will remain quiet & patient but strong & persistent in executing judgment—as quiet as the rising heat of the sun & the forming dew of the morning
   3) The LORD will judge & cut off the Ethiopians—just like sprigs are cut off with pruning shears
   4) The Ethiopians will suffer

innumerable deaths: Birds & wild animals will be able to feed upon the corpses all summer & winter	unto the fowls of the mountains, and to the beasts of the earth: and the fowls shall summer upon them, and all the beasts of the earth shall winter upon them.	scattered and peeled, and from a people terrible from their beginning hitherto; a nation meted out and trodden under foot, whose land the rivers have spoiled, to	1) The time will come when they will bring gifts to the LORD of hosts
c. The promise of future salvation for Ethiopia: A picture of the Messiah's Kingdom	7 In that time shall the present be brought unto the LORD of hosts of a people	the place of the name of the LORD of hosts, the mount Zion.	2) The time will come when they will worship the LORD at Mount Zion

DIVISION II

THE PROPHECIES CONCERNING GOD'S JUDGMENT OF THE NATIONS AND HIS TRIUMPH OVER THE WORLD, 13:1–27:13

C. God's Judgment of Damascus (Syria), Ephraim (Israel), and Ethiopia: A Picture of Distrust and of Hope in the Face of Judgment, 17:1–18:7

(17:1–18:7) **Introduction**: distrust is a very disturbing condition that can keep the human mind in turmoil. When we distrust people, we either withdraw from them or we treat them with suspicion. We wonder if we can depend upon them or if they are plotting some evil scheme against us.

⇒ Think of husbands and wives who cannot trust each other, the disturbance of mind and the pain of soul they suffer.
⇒ Think of employers who must watch employees they do not trust, having to pay close attention to see that these employees do their work, do not steal, and do not disturb relationships with fellow workers.
⇒ Think what distrust does to friendships, often ripping them apart due to broken promises.

Now think about what happens when we distrust God. It creates a huge gulf between God and us, one so wide that no human being can cross it. Only the cross of Christ can bridge the gulf of alienation, and we can cross the bridge only by trusting Christ. If we turn to Christ and trust Him, we can approach God and be accepted by Him. But if we do not approach God through Christ, we will face His judgment. As long as we are still alive on earth, we can repent and turn to the LORD in trust. Distrust and hope in the face of judgment are the two subjects of the present Scripture. This is, *God's Judgment of Damascus (Syria), Ephraim (Israel), and Ethiopia: A Picture of Distrust and of Hope in the Face of Judgment,* 17:1–18:7.

1. God's judgment of Syria and Israel: the certainty of judgment due to forgetting God (17:1-14).
2. God's judgment of Ethiopia (Cush): the hope for salvation in the face of judgment (18:1-7).

[1] (17:1-14) **Judgment, of Damascus, Predicted—Israel, Judgment of, Predicted—Distrust, Results, Judgment—Forsaking God, Results, Judgment—Unbelief, Results, Judgment—Idolatry, Results, Judgment—Repentance, Stirred by, Judgment—Syria, Judgment of, Predicted—Forgetting God, Results, Judgment—Assyria, Deliverance, Promised—Judah, Deliverance, Promised**: the LORD's prophet Isaiah now pronounces judgment on Syria and Israel. Damascus was the capital of Syria (Aram), and Ephraim, the largest tribe of the Northern Kingdom, is often used in Scripture to refer to Israel.

Looming on the horizon was a very serious threat from the Assyrians, a cruel people bent on dominating the world and building a worldwide empire. To withstand the onslaught of their brutal war machine, Syria and the Northern Kingdom of Israel had formed an alliance. Apparently, they asked Judah to join them, but King Ahaz refused. As a result, the allies marched against Jerusalem in an attempt to overthrow Ahaz and replace him with a Syrian puppet king who would support the alliance. Although their attempt to conquer Jerusalem failed, they inflicted heavy losses on Judah (see outline and notes—Is.7:1–9; 2 Chr.28:5–15 for more discussion). Now because of their brutal attack on God's people and their terrible wickedness down through the centuries, Syria and Israel were about to face the judgment of God.

OUTLINE	SCRIPTURE	SCRIPTURE	OUTLINE
1. God's judgment of Syria & Israel: The certainty of judgment due to forgetting God	The burden of Damascus. Behold, Damascus is taken away from *being* a city, and it shall be a ruinous heap.	shall be as the glory of the children of Israel, saith the LORD of hosts.	vors: Will suffer a defeated glory—just like the Israelites
a. The fate of both predicted	2 The cities of Aroer *are* forsaken: they shall be for	4 And in that day it shall come to pass, *that* the glory	b. The fate of Israel's glory *in that day*: Will fade, waste away like a starving man
1) Damascus: To be destroyed	flocks, which shall lie down, and none shall make *them*	of Jacob shall be made thin, and the fatness of his flesh	
2) Aroer, the southern border town: To be deserted & left to flocks	afraid.	shall wax lean.	
3) Ephraim's fortified cities: Will be destroyed	3 The fortress also shall cease from Ephraim, and the	5 And it shall be as when the harvestman gathereth the	1) The effects: Like the harvesting of crops
4) Syria's power: Will end	kingdom from Damascus, and	corn, and reapeth the ears	• The economy will be stripped
5) Aram's (Syria's) survi-	the remnant of Syria: they	with his arm; and it shall be as he that gathereth ears in	• The population will

OUTLINE	SCRIPTURE	SCRIPTURE	OUTLINE
almost be wiped out • The survivors will be few	the valley of Rephaim. 6 Yet gleaning grapes shall be left in it, as the shaking of an olive tree, two *or* three berries in the top of the uppermost bough, four *or* five in the outmost fruitful branches thereof, saith the LORD God of Israel.	pleasant plants, and shalt set it with strange slips: 11 In the day shalt thou make thy plant to grow, and in the morning shalt thou make thy seed to flourish: *but* the harvest *shall be* a heap in the day of grief and of desperate sorrow.	ground or protection 3) The result: All their efforts to improve their land & crops will be futile, as nothing in *the day* of grief & desperate sorrow
2) The return of some to the LORD: A great hope • Some will turn from their false worship & idolatry • Some will seek the LORD *in that day*	7 At that day shall a man look to his Maker, and his eyes shall have respect to the Holy One of Israel. 8 And he shall not look to the altars, the work of his hands, neither shall respect *that* which his fingers have made, either the groves, or the images.	12 Woe to the multitude of many people, *which* make a noise like the noise of the seas; and to the rushing of nations, *that* make a rushing like the rushing of mighty waters! 13 The nations shall rush like the rushing of many waters: but *God* shall rebuke them,	d. The collapse of the invader Assyria: After conquering Damascus & Ephraim & attacking Judah, 37:36-38 1) The invaders will rage like a roaring sea 2) The LORD will silence the invaders—stop the roaring waves of their rushing army
c. The cause of Israel's desolation: Forgetting the LORD 1) The fact: The cities will be deserted & taken over by thickets & undergrowth 2) The reason the judgment will come: They had forgotten the God of salvation, that He alone is their Rock, their only solid	9 In that day shall his strong cities be as a forsaken bough, and an uppermost branch, which they left because of the children of Israel: and there shall be desolation. 10 Because thou hast forgotten the God of thy salvation, and hast not been mindful of the rock of thy strength, therefore shalt thou plant	and they shall flee far off, and shall be chased as the chaff of the mountains before the wind, and like a rolling thing before the whirlwind. 14 And behold at eveningtide trouble; *and* before the morning he *is* not. This *is* the portion of them that spoil us, and the lot of them that rob us.	3) The LORD—in one evening—will wipe out the invaders 4) The enemies—robbers & plunderers—of God's people will be doomed

a. Isaiah predicted the fate of both Syria and Israel. As allies, they would share the same fate: the Assyrian war machine would destroy both nations.
1) Damascus, the capital of Syria, would be destroyed (v.1). Damascus was the seat of government, where the king and royal officials of the nation resided. The Assyrian attack would leave the city a heap of ruins.
2) Continuing to march across the country, the Assyrian army would overthrow all the cities, including Aroer, the most distant town on Syria's southern border (v.2). Syrians fleeing for their lives would abandon even this border town, leaving it for the sheep and wild animals to inhabit. Not a single person would be there to run the animals off.
3) All the fortified cities of Ephraim (Israel) would also be utterly destroyed. No fortress within Israel, whether a small military outpost or a major city, would be left standing. The onrushing Assyrian army would demolish all of Israel's military defenses.
4) The kingdom of Syria would come to an end. No longer would Damascus be a seat of royal power within the worldwide empire of Assyria.
5) The glory of both Syria and Israel would be a thing of the past (v.3). Both nations would suffer the loss of their honor and prestige.

b. The fate that lay in store for Israel was tragic, for God had given the ten tribes of the Northern Kingdom every opportunity to become a great nation. Time and again the LORD had assured them of His love, presence, and power. With the LORD on their side, they could have lived the most fruitful lives imaginable, but the Israelites repeatedly rejected the LORD. They turned away from Him and forgot His commandments. Consequently, Isaiah announced that the glory of Israel would fade.
When the Assyrians came against the Northern Kingdom, they would decimate the population, and Ephraim would waste away like a starving person (vv.4–8). They would strip the nation's economy as if they were harvesting grain in the most fruitful valley imaginable (the Valley of Rephaim). Just like the few heads of grain or the few stray olives that remain after the harvest, only a few Israelites would be left after God's hand of judgment fell upon the nation.
The LORD was using the Assyrians to execute His judgment upon the wicked nations of that day, including the Israelites. But note a most wonderful fact: in the midst of judgment some Israelites would return to the LORD. The phrase *in that day* (v.7) refers to the day of God's judgment. His judgment would cause some Israelites to abandon their idols, return to their Creator, and begin to worship the Holy One of Israel. They would turn from their false worship and acknowledge that their gods were merely the creations of their imaginations and the works of their hands.
Asherah poles (v.8) were wooden symbols of the goddess considered to be the mate of the god Baal. Under King Ahaz and the infamous Jezebel, almost the entire population of the Northern Kingdom had become loyal worshippers of Baal and Asherah. But now Isaiah predicts that when God's judgment falls, some Israelites, would realize that they could soon be face-to-face with their Creator. Therefore, they would repent of their sins and return to the LORD.
c. Again note the phrase *in that day*. This is the third time the phrase has been used in this passage (vv.4, 7, 9). *In that day*, God's hand of judgment would fall; but there is a reason why it would fall, and this reason needs to be heeded. God was going to judge His people because they had forsaken Him, their Savior and protector (vv.9–11). *In that day*, Israel's cities would be completely deserted. After the citizens were deported and scattered in foreign nations throughout the Assyrian Empire, their cities would be taken over by thickets, undergrowth, and wild animals.

But the judgment never had to happen. God's hand of judgment was falling because the Israelites had forgotten that He was their Rock, the only solid ground upon which they could build their lives. Having abandoned their Rock, they had built their lives on sand, which would quickly wash away in the downpour of judgment. The false gods they worshipped would be totally useless in the hour of crisis. All their efforts to improve their land, build a strong economy, and lead fruitful lives of comfort and plenty would prove futile. The Day of Judgment was coming, and it would be a day of deprivation, disease, and utter despair. Keep in mind, however, that those who turned back to the LORD could be assured of His faithfulness.

d. The Assyrians themselves would eventually face God's judgment for their wickedness and savage treatment of other nations (vv.12–14). Raging like the roaring seas, the Assyrians would soon launch an attack against Judah, but the LORD would silence them (37:35–38). In one night, He would stop the onrushing army by slaying 185,000 Assyrian soldiers. Such would be the fate of those who robbed and plundered God's people (v.14). This event took place during the reign of Hezekiah, just as Isaiah predicted. The backbone of the Assyrian war machine was broken, and King Sennacherib was assassinated by his own sons while he was worshipping his false gods (37:35–38).

Thought 1. Damascus and Israel were doomed to God's judgment because they forgot God. If we forget God, we will also feel His hand of judgment. The person who forgets God naturally turns his back upon Him and walks through life seldom, if ever, thinking about Him. The LORD will never tolerate the haughtiness and pride that prompt people to dismiss Him, to consign Him to oblivion, to a meaningless position of unimportance or insignif-icance.

Above all beings in the universe, the LORD is anything but meaningless. He is supreme, the great Creator and Sustainer of all that is, the majestic LORD who rules and reigns over all. Every good and perfect gift on this earth has come from the hand of the LORD God Himself (Ja.1:17). For this reason, there is no possibility that He will ever allow a person to dismiss Him. If a person forgets God and walks throughout life with his back to God, then he will continue to walk right on through eternity with his back to God. The person will be alienated from God eternally because he never turned around and faced God, never humbled himself and acknowledged God as the LORD of the universe. Listen to what God's Holy Word says about forgetting Him:

> **"He that believeth on the Son hath everlasting life: and he that believeth not the Son shall not see life; but the wrath of God abideth on him" (Jn.3:36).**
>
> **"I said therefore unto you, that ye shall die in your sins: for if ye believe not that I am** *he,* **ye shall die in your sins" (Jn.8:24).**
>
> **"Therefore we ought to give the more earnest heed to the things which we have heard, lest at any time we should let** *them* **slip. For if the word spoken by angels was stedfast, and every transgression and disobedience received a just recompence of reward; How shall we escape, if we neglect so great salvation; which at the first began to be spoken by the Lord, and was confirmed unto us by them that heard** *him***" (He.2:1-3).**
>
> **"Take heed, brethren, lest there be in any of you an evil heart of unbelief, in departing from the living God. But exhort one another daily, while it is called To day; lest any of you be hardened through the deceitfulness of sin. For we are made partakers of Christ, if we hold the beginning of our confidence stedfast unto the end; While it is said, To day if ye will hear his voice, harden not your hearts, as in the provocation. For some, when they had heard, did provoke: howbeit not all that came out of Egypt by Moses. But with whom was he grieved forty years?** *was it* **not with them that had sinned, whose carcases fell in the wilderness? And to whom sware he that they should not enter into his rest, but to them that believed not? So we see that they could not enter in because of unbe-lief" (He.3:12-19).**
>
> **"Only take heed to thyself, and keep thy soul diligently, lest thou forget the things which thine eyes have seen, and lest they depart from thy heart all the days of thy life: but teach them thy sons, and thy sons' sons" (De.4:9).**
>
> **"And it shall be, when the LORD thy God shall have brought thee into the land which he sware unto thy fathers, to Abraham, to Isaac, and to Jacob, to give thee great and goodly cities, which thou buildedst not, And houses full of all good** *things,* **which thou filledst not, and wells digged, which thou diggedst not, vineyards and olive trees, which thou plantedst not; when thou shalt have eaten and be full;** *Then* **beware lest thou forget the LORD, which brought thee forth out of the land of Egypt, from the house of bondage" (De.6:10-12).**
>
> **"The wicked shall be turned into hell,** *and* **all the nations that forget God" (Ps.9:17).**
>
> **"Now consider this, ye that forget God, lest I tear** *you* **in pieces, and** *there be* **none to deliver" (Ps.50:22).**
>
> **"And [they] forgat his works, and his wonders that he had showed them....Therefore the LORD heard** *this,* **and was wroth: so a fire was kindled against Jacob, and anger also came up against Israel; Because they believed not in God, and trusted not in his salvation" (Ps.78:11, 21-22).**
>
> **"And forgettest the LORD thy maker, that hath stretched forth the heavens, and laid the foundations of the earth?" (Is.51:13).**
>
> **"A voice was heard upon the high places, weeping** *and* **supplications of the children of Israel: for they have perverted their way,** *and* **they have forgotten the LORD their God. Return, ye backsliding children,** *and* **I will heal your backslidings. Behold, we come unto thee; for thou** *art* **the LORD our God" (Je.3:21-22).**

[2] (18:1-7) **Judgment, Predicted, Against Cush or Ethiopia—Messiah, Promises Concerning, Kingdom of— Kingdom, of the Messiah, Promised—Judgment, Deliverance from, Hope of Salvation**: Isaiah also prophesied

judgment against the ancient nation Ethiopia, which was located south of Egypt. In Scripture, Ethiopia is called *Cush*. Somewhere around 714 B.C., King So or Shabako (2 K.17:4) conquered and established the Twenty-Fifth Dynasty.[1] Ethiopia maintained its control over Egypt until 633 B.C., when the Egyptian Psammetichus recaptured the throne and put an end to Ethiopian domination.[2]

In addressing Ethiopia, Isaiah refers to Cush as the land of whirling or buzzing wings. This refers either to the large number of insects that infested the land or to the buzzing of frantic diplomatic activity as the government sought to form alliances with other nations. Assyria's quest for world domination would extend into Africa, reaching the nation of Ethiopia. Thus that nation would feel the wrath of God's judgment just as much as the other wicked nations of the world.

OUTLINE	SCRIPTURE	SCRIPTURE	OUTLINE

2. God's judgment of Ethiopia (Cush): The hope for salvation in the face of judgment
a. The situation in Ethiopia
  1) Ethiopia was a powerful, hostile nation
  2) Ethiopia is pictured as sending envoys far and wide to seek alliances: To stand against the onrushing Assyrian army
 	
b. The judgment of Ethiopia
  1) The people of Ethiopia & of the world will know judgment is at hand when the war banner is raised & the trumpet blown
  2) The LORD will remain quiet & patient but strong & persistent in executing judgment—as quiet as the rising heat of the sun & the forming dew of the
	Woe to the land shadowing with wings, which *is* beyond the rivers of Ethiopia:
	2 That sendeth ambassadors by the sea, even in vessels of bulrushes upon the waters, *saying,* Go, ye swift messengers, to a nation scattered and peeled, to a people terrible from their beginning hitherto; a nation meted out and trodden down, whose land the rivers have spoiled!
	3 All ye inhabitants of the world, and dwellers on the earth, see ye, when he lifteth up an ensign on the mountains; and when he bloweth a trumpet, hear ye.
	4 For so the LORD said unto me, I will take my rest, and I will consider in my dwelling place like a clear heat upon herbs, *and* like a cloud of dew in the heat of harvest.
		5 For afore the harvest, when the bud is perfect, and the sour grape is ripening in the flower, he shall both cut off the sprigs with prupinghooks, and take away *and* cut down the branches.
		6 They shall be left together unto the fowls of the mountains, and to the beasts of the earth: and the fowls shall summer upon them, and all the beasts of the earth shall winter upon them.
		7 In that time shall the present be brought unto the LORD of hosts of a people scattered and peeled, and from a people terrible from their beginning hitherto; a nation meted out and trodden under foot, whose land the rivers have spoiled, to the place of the name of the LORD of hosts, the mount Zion.
			morning
			3) The LORD will judge & cut off the Ethiopians— just like sprigs are cut off with pruning shears
			
			4) The Ethiopians will suffer innumerable deaths: Birds & wild animals will be able to feed upon the corpses all summer & winter
			
			c. The promise of future salvation for Ethiopia: A picture of the Messiah's Kingdom
			  1) The time will come when they will bring gifts to the LORD of hosts
			  2) The time will come when they will worship the LORD at Mount Zion

a. Isaiah began his prophecy by describing the situation in Ethiopia. Ethiopia was a powerful nation, but it was hostile in that it sought to conquer other countries and lands. (v.2). He described the Ethiopians as a tall, smooth-skinned people who were feared everywhere because of the aggressiveness of their nation. His reference to the fact that they spoke a foreign language indicates that their conquest had extended far and wide. The Nile River ran through their nation, which meant that their land was fertile and productive, providing a strong economy for the people.

Isaiah pictured the Ethiopian envoys traveling by sea (perhaps the Nile River) in search of alliances. Using boats made from the famous papyrus reed, these envoys were running to and fro from nation to nation. Why? Because the Ethiopians, too, would soon face the onrushing Assyrian war machine. But note God's message to the envoys: they should go, but then swiftly return to their own people. The implication is that alliances would not help them. Therefore, they needed to return home to take a stand with their own people when the coming judgment swept down upon their nation.

It is possible that the Ethiopian envoys visited Judah in the hope of securing an alliance with them. Judah's location would certainly provide a barrier between the Ethiopians and the Assyrians. If the envoys actually did reach Judah, perhaps Isaiah was announcing this prophecy to them personally.

b. Whatever the case, the prophet described the impending judgment of Ethiopia (vv.3–6). He was also addressing the entire world, warning all people everywhere about the coming day of judgment. God had chosen the Assyrians to execute His judgment, and Isaiah predicted that everyone would know that judgment was at hand when the war banner was raised and the trumpet blown (v.3). In other words, when Assyria mobilized its army and began to march, the peoples of the world would know that the sinful, oppressive nations of the earth were about to feel the wrath of God's judgment. The judgment of Ethiopia occurred just as Isaiah said it would, just as it will occur in the future when God's judgment falls upon the entire world.

Isaiah said that during the judgment, the LORD would watch quietly from His dwelling place. His judgment would be as patient and persistent as the heat shimmering in the sunshine and the dew forming in the heat of harvest (v.4). But it would be felt as much as the heat of the sun that rises in the morning and melts the dew off the harvest. And the judgment was right around the corner. Before the harvest season, the LORD would cut off the Ethiopians like sprigs are cut off with pruning shears (v.5). So many Ethiopians would be killed that the birds would feed on their corpses all summer, and the wild animals would feed on them all winter (v. 6).

c. Still, as with any generation, there was wonderful news for the Ethiopians. They could turn to the LORD of hosts, bring gifts and worship Him (v.7). Apparently, Isaiah is predicting that some Ethiopians would turn to the LORD when the

---

[1] *NIV Study Bible,* 18:1.
[2] H. C. Leupold. *Exposition of Isaiah,* Vol.1, p.301.

judgment came. When news of Assyria's early conquests reached them, apparently some Ethiopians began to turn their thoughts to the LORD worshipped by Hezekiah and his people.

Remember that Hezekiah was a godly king who ruled for almost 30 years (2 Chr.29:1). During his reign, his testimony for the LORD was so strong that many nations sent envoys to him, seeking to learn the secret of his power with the LORD (see outline and note—2 Chr.32:20–23 for more discussion). It is not known whether Ethiopia was one of these nations, but according to Isaiah's prediction, some Ethiopians would turn to the LORD and bring gifts to Mount Zion, which is Jerusalem.

Note that this verse is also a prediction of the Messiah's kingdom, which Jesus Christ will set up when He returns to earth in the last days of human history. At that time, Ethiopia will apparently still exist as a nation and will bring gifts to the LORD, who will be ruling from Jerusalem, the Holy City of God.

Thought 1. Even in the face of judgment there is always hope for salvation. Remember that all trials are not necessarily judgments from God. Carelessness causes some hardships, while other misfortunes are the natural result of living in a fallen world. In this corrupt world we are subject to all kinds of accidents and diseases. But when we deliberately sin, God will judge us. He will discipline us in order to correct us and keep us from harming ourselves or injuring other people. Because God loves us, He will do all He can to keep us from continuing in sin and darkness and shame.

When we sin, we will suffer as a result of it. We will bear some trial, some pain, some suffering. But in the midst of judgment there is hope. Even while we are suffering the judgment of God, He will deliver us if we will turn back to Him. As Scripture says, if we will judge ourselves, we will not be judged. If we will confess our sins, He will forgive and cleanse us. He will accept us back into His favor and restore the joy of our salvation. He will once again empower us to live fruitful and victorious lives. Infusing us with His presence and strength, He will enable us to overcome all the trials and temptations that confront us. Listen to the wonderful hope promised by God's Holy Word:

"And it shall come to pass, *that* whosoever shall call on the name of the Lord shall be saved" (Ac.2:21).

"For we are saved by hope: but hope that is seen is not hope: for what a man seeth, why doth he yet hope for?" (Ro.8:24).

"For whosoever shall call upon the name of the Lord shall be saved" (Ro.10:13).

"For whatsoever things were written aforetime were written for our learning, that we through patience and comfort of the scriptures might have hope" (Ro.15:4).

"For the hope which is laid up for you in heaven, whereof ye heard before in the word of the truth of the gospel" (Col.1:5).

"Teaching us that, denying ungodliness and worldly lusts, we should live soberly, righteously, and godly, in this present world; Looking for that blessed hope, and the glorious appearing of the great God and our Saviour Jesus Christ" (Tit.2:12-13).

"That by two immutable things, in which *it was* impossible for God to lie, we might have a strong consolation, who have fled for refuge to lay hold upon the hope set before us: Which *hope* we have as an anchor of the soul, both sure and stedfast, and which entereth into that within the veil" (He.6:18-19).

"Wherefore lay apart all filthiness and superfluity of naughtiness, and receive with meekness the engrafted word, which is able to save your souls" (Js.1:21).

"Blessed *be* the God and Father of our Lord Jesus Christ, which according to his abundant mercy hath begotten us again unto a lively hope by the resurrection of Jesus Christ from the dead, To an inheritance incorruptible, and undefiled, and that fadeth not away, reserved in heaven for you" (1 Pe.1:3-4).

"Wherefore the rather, brethren, give diligence to make your calling and election sure: for if ye do these things, ye shall never fall: For so an entrance shall be ministered unto you abundantly into the everlasting kingdom of our Lord and Saviour Jesus Christ" (2 Pe.1:10-11).

"But sanctify the Lord God in your hearts: and *be* ready always to *give* an answer to every man that asketh you a reason of the hope that is in you with meekness and fear" (1 Pe.3:15).

"And every man that hath this hope in him purifieth himself, even as he is pure" (1 Jn.3:3).

"Blessed *are* they that do his commandments, that they may have right to the tree of life, and may enter in through the gates into the city" (Re.22:14).

"The wicked is driven away in his wickedness: but the righteous hath hope in his death" (Pr.14:32).

CHAPTER 19

D. God's Judgment of Egypt: A Picture of God's Just Punishment, His Enduring Mercy, & His Clear Warning, 19:1–20:6

1. **An eightfold punishment executed by God Himself: A picture of coming judgment**
   a. The purpose: To prove that the Egyptian gods were false & the people's trust in them futile

   b. The eightfold punishment or judgment
      1) Civil strife, disorder, upheaval, rioting

      2) Despair & hopelessness
      3) Political confusion
      4) Empty, useless religion: Seeking help from false gods & from the world of the occult
      5) Subjection & captivity: Being conquered by a cruel master, a fierce king (perhaps Assyria)

      6) Drought: Drying up of the Nile River
         • Its canals would stink
         • Its streams would dry up
         • Its growth—reeds & rushes—would rot

      7) Economic devastation
         • The agriculture industry would be parched

         • The fishing industry would die

         • The clothing industry would collapse

         • The wage earners all across the nation would be hopeless, sick at heart
      8) Unwise counselors & foolish wisdom
         • The officials of Zoan would be fools

The burden of Egypt. Behold, the LORD rideth upon a swift cloud, and shall come into Egypt: and the idols of Egypt shall be moved at his presence, and the heart of Egypt shall melt in the midst of it.
2 And I will set the Egyptians against the Egyptians: and they shall fight every one against his brother, and every one against his neighbour; city against city, *and* kingdom against kingdom.
3 And the spirit of Egypt shall fail in the midst thereof; and I will destroy the counsel thereof: and they shall seek to the idols, and to the charmers, and to them that have familiar spirits, and to the wizards.
4 And the Egyptians will I give over into the hand of a cruel lord; and a fierce king shall rule over them, saith the Lord, the LORD of hosts.
5 And the waters shall fail from the sea, and the river shall be wasted and dried up.
6 And they shall turn the rivers far away; *and* the brooks of defence shall be emptied and dried up: the reeds and flags shall wither.
7 The paper reeds by the brooks, by the mouth of the brooks, and every thing sown by the brooks, shall wither, be driven away, and be no *more.*
8 The fishers also shall mourn, and all they that cast angle into the brooks shall lament, and they that spread nets upon the waters shall languish.
9 Moreover they that work in fine flax, and they that weave networks, shall be confounded.
10 And they shall be broken in the purposes thereof, all that make sluices *and* ponds for fish.
11 Surely the princes of Zoan *are* fools, the counsel of the wise counsellors of Pharaoh is become brutish:

how say ye unto Pharaoh, I *am* the son of the wise, the son of ancient kings?
12 Where *are* they? where *are* thy wise *men?* and let them tell thee now, and let them know what the LORD of hosts hath purposed upon Egypt.
13 The princes of Zoan are become fools, the princes of Noph are deceived; they have also seduced Egypt, *even they that are* the stay of the tribes thereof.
14 The LORD hath mingled a perverse spirit in the midst thereof: and they have caused Egypt to err in every work thereof, as a drunken *man* staggereth in his vomit.
15 Neither shall there be *any* work for Egypt, which the head or tail, branch or rush, may do.
16 In that day shall Egypt be like unto women: and it shall be afraid and fear because of the shaking of the hand of the LORD of hosts, which he shaketh over it.
17 And the land of Judah shall be a terror unto Egypt, every one that maketh mention thereof shall be afraid in himself, because of the counsel of the LORD of hosts, which he hath determined against it.
18 In that day shall five cities in the land of Egypt speak the language of Canaan, and swear to the LORD of hosts; one shall be called, The city of destruction.
19 In that day shall there be an altar to the LORD in the midst of the land of Egypt, and a pillar at the border thereof to the LORD.
20 And it shall be for a sign and for a witness unto the LORD of hosts in the land of Egypt: for they shall cry unto the LORD because of the oppressors, and he shall send them a saviour, and a great one, and he shall deliver them.
21 And the LORD shall be known to Egypt, and the Egyptians shall know the LORD in that day, and shall do sacrifice and oblation; yea, they shall vow a vow unto the LORD, and perform *it.*

• The wise counselors of Pharaoh would give worthless advice
• The advisors would be confounded, totally ignorant of the LORD & His plan

• The officials throughout Egypt—from Zoan (north) to Memphis (south)—would be deceived: They would lead Egypt astray
• The LORD would send a troubling spirit among the Egyptians, a spirit of warped judgment: Would cause Egypt to stagger like a drunkard
• The Egyptians would be powerless: No leader or citizen would be able to help

2. **A sixfold promise of future salvation for Egypt: A promise of God's mercy**
   a. *In that day* (of the Messiah) Egypt will fear the LORD
      1) They will fear His uplifted hand of power
      2) They will recognize that it was the God worshipped by Judah who executed judgment

   b. *In that day* some Egyptians will be converted to the LORD: Five cities in particular will institute true worship in the nation

   c. *In that day* the Egyptians will institute true worship in the land
      1) They will build an altar & monument to the LORD
      2) They will bear strong witness to the LORD
      3) They will cry out for deliverance from oppressors
   d. *In that day* the LORD will send a Savior to deliver the Egyptians

      1) The LORD will make Himself known to the Egyptians
      2) The Egyptians will acknowledge the LORD: They will worship & make genuine commitments to Him

185

3) The LORD will use His judgment to arouse their belief—stirring them to turn to Him

e. *In that day* peace will be established on earth & people will worship the LORD alone: A highway will be built between the empires of Egypt & Assyria

f. *In that day* Israel will be a major power—just as Egypt & Assyria were
1) Israel will be a blessing
2) God will bless & call them...
   • *Egypt My people*
   • *Assyria My handiwork*
   • *Israel My inheritance*

3. **A warning to Judah against following Egypt & Ethiopia: A warning against evil associations**
a. The situation: Assyria captured Ashdod of Philistia
b. The warning symbolized:

22 And the LORD shall smite Egypt: he shall smite and heal *it:* and they shall return *even* to the LORD, and he shall be intreated of them, and shall heal them.
23 In that day shall there be a highway out of Egypt to Assyria, and the Assyrian shall come into Egypt, and the Egyptian into Assyria, and the Egyptians shall serve with the Assyrians.
24 In that day shall Israel be the third with Egypt and with Assyria, *even* a blessing in the midst of the land:
25 Whom the LORD of hosts shall bless, saying, Blessed *be* Egypt my people, and Assyria the work of my hands, and Israel mine inheritance.

CHAPTER 20

In the year that Tartan came unto Ashdod, (when Sargon the king of Assyria sent him,) and fought against Ashdod, and took it;
2 At the same time spake

the LORD by Isaiah the son of Amoz, saying, Go and loose the sackcloth from off thy loins, and put off thy shoe from thy foot. And he did so, walking naked and barefoot.
3 And the LORD said, Like as my servant Isaiah hath walked naked and barefoot three years *for* a sign and wonder upon Egypt and upon Ethiopia;
4 So shall the king of Assyria lead away the Egyptians prisoners, and the Ethiopians captives, young and old, naked and barefoot, even with *their* buttocks uncov-ered, to the shame of Egypt.
5 And they shall be afraid and ashamed of Ethiopia their expectation, and of Egypt their glory.
6 And the inhabitant of this isle shall say in that day, Behold, such *is* our expectation, whither we flee for help to be delivered from the king of Assyria: and how shall we escape?

1) God told Isaiah to strip off his outer clothes & walk barefoot—for three years
2) Isaiah obeyed

c. The explanation
1) The prophet was a sign against following & forming alliances with Egypt & Ethiopia (the worldly unbelievers)
2) The Assyrians would conquer Egypt & Ethiopia: Take the people captive & lead them into exile, stripped & barefoot

d. The warning issued to Israel & others
1) All who trusted in Egypt & Ethiopia (the worldly unbelievers) would suffer fear & shame: They would see Ethiopia collapse
2) All who trusted worldly alliances would suffer despair: Would know they could not escape

DIVISION II

THE PROPHECIES CONCERNING GOD'S JUDGMENT OF THE NATIONS AND HIS TRIUMPH OVER THE WORLD, 13:1–27:13

D. God's Judgment of Egypt: A Picture of God's Just Punishment, His Enduring Mercy, and His Clear Warning, 19:1–20:6

(19:1–20:6) **Introduction**: there are many types of guides or instructions in life. For example, there are meters or signs that tell us where we are going, the distance and the speed necessary to reach the destination within a certain time. There are instruction guides that tell us how to grow and prepare food, to operate and repair machinery, when to prepare taxes, pay bills, undertake, and accomplish a task, report an assignment, and a host of other activities that control much of our lives. But some of the most important information ever given us is that of warnings. A warning protects us against harming ourselves or someone else. A warning attempts to arouse us to avoid or to be aware of dangerous situations—whether financial, spiritual, physical, or otherwise. The consequences of ignoring these warnings can range from minor problems to serious accidents or death.

The present Scripture deals with God's warning issued to Egypt. A just punishment was coming upon the nation due to the Egyptians' defiance and rejection of the LORD. They disobeyed God's holy commandments and lived wicked lives. In the days of Isaiah, there was a pro-Egyptian party that wanted to join the Egyptians in resisting Assyria, the world empire of that day. Assyria dominated the world, insisting on the prompt payment of taxes from all citizens throughout the empire. Taxes were heavy and the passion for freedom burned within the souls of many. Consequently, pockets of resistance arose all over the nation. There were those who were so opposed to the heavy taxation that they attempted to form a coalition with other nations to rebel against Assyria. The present Scripture is a warning to King Hezekiah and the Jews against joining such an alliance. God's people were not to place their trust in worldly power and alliances. They were to put their trust in the LORD. Only the LORD could deliver them from so great a power as the Assyrian war machine. This is, *God's Judgment of Egypt: A Picture of God's Just Punishment, His Enduring Mercy, and His Clear Warning*, 19:1–20:6.

1. An eightfold punishment executed by God Himself: a picture of coming judgment (19:1-15).
2. A sixfold promise of future salvation for Egypt: a promise of God's mercy (19:16-25).
3. A warning to Judah against following Egypt and Ethiopia: a warning against evil associations (20:1-6).

1 (19:1-15) **Judgment, of Egypt, Prophecy Concerning—Judgment, How God Judges, Eight Ways—Punishment, of Egypt, Purpose—Judgment, of Egypt, Purpose**: the hand of God's judgment was to fall upon Egypt. An eightfold punishment would be executed by God Himself. Note the Scripture and outline:

186

OUTLINE	SCRIPTURE	SCRIPTURE	OUTLINE

1. An eightfold punishment executed by God Himself: A picture of coming judgment
a. The purpose: To prove that the Egyptian gods are false & the people's trust in them futile
b. The eightfold punishment or judgment
  1) Civil strife, disorder, upheaval, rioting
 	
  2) Despair & hopelessness
  3) Political confusion
  4) Empty, useless religion: Seeking help from false gods & from the world of the occult
 	
  5) Subjection & captivity: Being conquered by a cruel master, a fierce king (perhaps Assyria)
 	
  6) Drought: Drying up of the Nile River
    • Its canals would stink
    • Its streams would dry up
    • Its growth—reeds & rushes—would rot
 	
  7) Economic devastation
    • The agriculture industry would be parched
	The burden of Egypt. Behold, the LORD rideth upon a swift cloud, and shall come into Egypt: and the idols of Egypt shall be moved at his presence, and the heart of Egypt shall melt in the midst of it.
	2 And I will set the Egyptians against the Egyptians: and they shall fight every one against his brother, and every one against his neighbour; city against city, *and* kingdom against kingdom.
	3 And the spirit of Egypt shall fail in the midst thereof; and I will destroy the counsel thereof: and they shall seek to the idols, and to the charmers, and to them that have familiar spirits, and to the wizards.
	4 And the Egyptians will I give over into the hand of a cruel lord; and a fierce king shall rule over them, saith the Lord, the LORD of hosts.
	5 And the waters shall fail from the sea, and the river shall be wasted and dried up.
	6 And they shall turn the rivers far away; *and* the brooks of defence shall be emptied and dried up: the reeds and flags shall wither.
	7 The paper reeds by the brooks, by the mouth of the brooks, and every thing sown by the brooks, shall wither, be driven away, and be no *more*.
		8 The fishers also shall mourn, and all they that cast angle into the brooks shall lament, and they that spread nets upon the waters shall languish.
		9 Moreover they that work in fine flax, and they that weave networks, shall be confounded.
		10 And they shall be broken in the purposes thereof, all that make sluices *and* ponds for fish.
		11 Surely the princes of Zoan *are* fools, the counsel of the wise counsellors of Pharaoh is become brutish: how say ye unto Pharaoh, I *am* the son of the wise, the son of ancient kings?
		12 Where *are* they? where *are* thy wise *men?* and let them tell thee now, and let them know what the LORD of hosts hath purposed upon Egypt.
		13 The princes of Zoan are become fools, the princes of Noph are deceived; they have also seduced Egypt, *even they that are* the stay of the tribes thereof.
		14 The LORD hath mingled a perverse spirit in the midst thereof: and they have caused Egypt to err in every work thereof, as a drunken *man* staggereth in his vomit.
		15 Neither shall there be *any* work for Egypt, which the head or tail, branch or rush, may do.
			• The fishing industry would die
			
			• The clothing industry would collapse
			
			• The wage earners all across the nation would be hopeless, sick at heart
			
			8) Unwise counselors & foolish wisdom
			• The officials of Zoan would be fools
			• The wise counselors of Pharoah would give worthless advice
			• The advisors would be confounded, totally ignorant of the LORD & His plan
			
			• The officials throughout Egypt—from Zoan (north) to Memphis (south)—would be deceived: They would lead Egypt astray
			• The LORD would send a troubling spirit among the Egyptians, a spirit of warped judgment: Would cause Egypt to stagger like a drunkard
			• The Egyptians would be powerless: No leader or citizen would be able to help

a. God's purpose for judging the Egyptians was to prove that their gods were false and that the people's trust in them was futile (v.1). Picture a judge with a long, flowing robe sweeping into a courtroom with stateliness and majesty; so it will be with the LORD. He, the judge of the world, will ride on a cloud in the splendor of His glory to judge Egypt. And He will come swiftly, riding far above the reach of all opposition and resistance. The root meaning of the word *idol* (eyiyl or elil) is *a nothing; something of no value; something vain, empty, worthless,* or *insufficient.* Although people think idols have some kind of existence, they do not. They are only a visible form or appearance that has no worth, no value, no substance. Therefore, any worship of them is meaningless, totally useless. The Egyptians had formed gods in their own minds and worshipped them, refusing to worship the only living and true God, the LORD Himself (Yahweh, Jehovah). Thus in their hour of trial the Egyptians found these gods to be utterly useless. When God's judgment fell upon Egypt, these false gods would tremble before the LORD. As the apostle James says:

> **"Thou believest that there is one God; thou doest well: the devils [demons] also believe, and tremble" (Js.2:19).**

With the hand of God's judgment falling upon them, the Egyptians would seek their false gods for help. But there would be no help, for the gods were lifeless, non-existent. They were only the imaginations and ideas of people. For that reason, there would be no help forthcoming to aid the Egyptians. Their hearts would melt like wax before the fire of God's judgment.[1] Down through history the Egyptians had rebelled and refused to worship the only living and true God. Consequently, when the judgment of God began to fall upon them, they would shrink back, showing no courage and no resolve to defend their country.

---

[1] *Matthew Henry's Commentary*, Vol.4, p.104.

b. Isaiah now predicts the details of God's coming judgment, eight specific catastrophes that would come upon Egypt due to their defiance of the LORD, the only true God. When the LORD began to execute justice upon the earth, no person or nation would be able to stand against His presence and power.

1) Egypt would be torn apart by civil strife, disorder, upheaval, and rioting. When the judgment begins to fall, families and entire neighborhoods would be ripped apart with everyone turning against one another. Brother would fight against brother, neighbor against neighbor, city against city, kingdom against kingdom.

2) Despair and hopelessness would grip people's hearts, demoralizing spirits (v.3). They would have no faith in the future, would feel as though all hope were gone. A deep sense of desperation would grip their hearts, for they would see no way to escape the judgment falling upon them.

3) Political confusion would grip the nation. When the politicians devised plans to handle the problems confronting them, they would find it impossible to agree on the plans. Utter confusion would prevail. Consequently, the leadership would be in chaos and the people would have no strong leaders to follow.

4) Empty religions would be totally unable to help the people (v.3). In their hour of desperate need, the people would turn to their false gods and to the world of the occult. But their so-called gods were useless; thus the people would receive no help. No charmers, mediums, spirits, psychics, or any other form of sorcery in the occult world would be able to deliver them from the judgment of God.

5) The next punishment to be carried out against the Egyptians would be that of subjection and captivity (v.4). The LORD would raise up cruel masters or fierce kings to conquer the Egyptians. Just who Isaiah was predicting is not known, but there was an Ethiopian named Piankha who conquered Egypt and took over the rule of the nation. Succeeding him in 715 B.C. was another Ethiopian, Shabako. Then in 670 B.C. the Assyrians conquered Egypt under the leadership of their king Esar-haddon. Later, in 633 B.C., Ashurbanipal conquered Thebes, the capital of Egypt.[2] From the moment of Isaiah's prophecy about God's coming judgment, the Egyptians would begin to experience a terrible period of subjection and captivity to foreign rulers.

6) Part of the judgment upon Egypt would be that of drought, the drying up of the Nile River (vv.5-6). As a result of the drought, the river's canals would stink, its streams dry up, and the growth around the river such as reeds and rushes would rot.

7) The drying up of the Nile River would be disastrous, for it would cause economic devastation throughout the nation (vv.7-10). The lack of irrigation would parch the land, devastating the agriculture and fishing industries. With the collapse of these two major industries, all other businesses throughout the nation, such as the production of clothing, would eventually go bankrupt. Wage earners all across the nation also suffer dramatically. A spirit of hopelessness—an utter sickness of heart—would grip the population of the nation.

8) Unwise counselors would rule the nation when God's judgment began to fall. The officials of the capital Zoan (also called Panis) would be fools (v.11). They would give bad advice. Being totally ignorant of the LORD, His righteousness, and His plan of judgment against the wicked, the advisers would not grasp what was happening. They would be utterly confounded by the sheer number of problems hitting them all at once.

Remember, there would be civil disorder, rioting, despair, and hopelessness among the people. Moreover, there would be continuous attacks by foreign nations, the drying up of the Nile River, and the collapse of the economy. For these and other reasons, the officials throughout Egypt—from the capital Zoan in the north to Memphis in the south—would be totally deceived. As a result, they would lead Egypt astray (v.13). Note the cause for their deception: the LORD would send a troubling spirit among the Egyptians, a spirit of warped judgment. This troubling spirit would cause the Egyptians to stagger like drunkards, rendering them totally powerless (v.15). There would be no leader (head or palm branch) or citizen (tail or reed) to help. No one would arise on the scene to help the Egyptians escape the judgment of God. Why? Because they had all forsaken the LORD, rebelled and turned against Him.

Thought 1. This is an excellent description showing the LORD's judgment upon a nation that denied and turned against Him. Quickly glance back to the Scripture and outline, noticing the eightfold punishment spelled out.

Every nation and citizen of this world will eventually face the judgment of God. And if we live wicked lives, denying and turning away from the LORD, we will face the *terrifying judgment* of God. Severe punishment will fall upon every nation and individual who denies God's existence and disobeys His Holy Word. How could the LORD of this universe—the sovereign Creator and Sustainer of all that is—do anything less? The LORD who sits upon the throne of the universe is perfectly *holy,* pure, and righteous. Therefore in righteousness He must execute justice upon this earth. All the nations and individuals who have done wrong against Him or His followers must be held accountable. In view of this fact, the execution of true justice upon earth is inescapable. The hand of God's judgment will fall upon all who are unjust and unrighteous. All who deny or turn against the LORD will be punished.

> **"Not every one that saith unto me, Lord, Lord, shall enter into the kingdom of heaven; but he that doeth the will of my Father which is in heaven. Many will say to me in that day, Lord, Lord, have we not prophesied in thy name? and in thy name have cast out devils? and in thy name done many wonderful works? And then will I profess unto them, I never knew you: depart from me, ye that work iniquity" (Mt.7:21-23).**

> **"When Jesus heard *it,* he marvelled, and said to them that followed, Verily I say unto you, I have not found so great faith, no, not in Israel. And I say unto you, That many shall come from the east and west, and shall sit down with Abraham, and Isaac, and Jacob, in the kingdom of heaven. But the children of the kingdom shall be cast out into outer darkness: there shall be weeping and gnashing of teeth" (Mt.8:10-12).**

---

2 Stanley M. Horton. *The Old Testament Study Bible, Isaiah,* p.147.

"As they went out, behold, they brought to him a dumb man possessed with a devil. And when the devil was cast out, the dumb spake: and the multitudes marvelled, saying, It was never so seen in Israel. But the Pharisees said, He casteth out devils through the prince of the devils. And Jesus went about all the cities and villages, teaching in their synagogues, and preaching the gospel of the kingdom, and healing every sickness and every disease among the people." (Mt.9:32-35).

"And fear not them which kill the body, but are not able to kill the soul: but rather fear him which is able to destroy both soul and body in hell" (Mt.10:28).

"The Son of man shall send forth his angels, and they shall gather out of his kingdom all things that offend, and them which do iniquity; And shall cast them into a furnace of fire: there shall be wailing and gnashing of teeth" (Mt.13:41-42).

"Then said the king to the servants, Bind him hand and foot, and take him away, and cast *him* into outer darkness; there shall be weeping and gnashing of teeth" (Mt.22:13).

"*Ye* serpents, *ye* generation of vipers, how can ye escape the damnation of hell?" (Mt.23:33).

"And shall cut him asunder, and appoint *him* his portion with the hypocrites: there shall be weeping and gnashing of teeth" (Mt.24:51).

"Then shall he say also unto them on the left hand, Depart from me, ye cursed, into everlasting fire, prepared for the devil and his angels" (Mt.25:41).

"And these shall go away into everlasting punishment: but the righteous into life eternal" (Mt.25:46).

"And if thy hand offend thee, cut it off: it is better for thee to enter into life maimed, than having two hands to go into hell, into the fire that never shall be quenched: And if thy foot offend thee, cut it off: it is better for thee to enter halt into life, than having two feet to be cast into hell, into the fire that never shall be quenched: Where their worm dieth not, and the fire is not quenched. And if thine eye offend thee, pluck it out: it is better for thee to enter into the kingdom of God with one eye, than having two eyes to be cast into hell fire: Where their worm dieth not, and the fire is not quenched." (Mk.9:43-48).

"And it came to pass, that the beggar died, and was carried by the angels into Abraham's bosom: the rich man also died, and was buried; And in hell he lift up his eyes, being in torments, and seeth Abraham afar off, and Lazarus in his bosom. And he cried and said, Father Abraham, have mercy on me, and send Lazarus, that he may dip the tip of his finger in water, and cool my tongue; for I am tormented in this flame" (Lu.16:22-24).

"He that believeth on the Son hath everlasting life: and he that believeth not the Son shall not see life; but the wrath of God abideth on him" (Jn.3:36).

"Of how much sorer punishment, suppose ye, shall he be thought worthy, who hath trodden under foot the Son of God, and hath counted the blood of the covenant, wherewith he was sanctified, an unholy thing, and hath done despite unto the Spirit of grace?" (He.10:29).

"For if God spared not the angels that sinned, but cast *them* down to hell, and delivered *them* into chains of darkness, to be reserved unto judgment; And spared not the old world, but saved Noah the eighth *person*, a preacher of righteousness, bringing in the flood upon the world of the ungodly....The Lord knoweth how to deliver the godly out of temptations, and to reserve the unjust unto the day of judgment to be punished" (2 Pe.2:4-5, 9).

"And whosoever was not found written in the book of life was cast into the lake of fire" (Re.20:15).

"But the fearful, and unbelieving, and the abominable, and murderers, and whoremongers, and sorcerers, and idolaters, and all liars, shall have their part in the lake which burneth with fire and brimstone: which is the second death" (Re.21:8).

---

2 (19:16-25) **Egypt, Promises to, Salvation—Mercy of God, Promised, to Egypt—Messiah, Kingdom of, Promise to Egypt—Millennium, Worship of the LORD, by Egyptians—Egypt, Conversion of, Promised**: the LORD gave Egypt a most wonderful promise, the promise of future salvation. This salvation would involve six very specific blessings. Note the phrase *in that day*, which refers not only to the coming day of God's judgment but also to the last days when Jesus Christ will set up His kingdom on earth. *In that day* of the Messiah, the LORD will pour out six very special blessings upon Egypt:

OUTLINE	SCRIPTURE	SCRIPTURE	OUTLINE

2. A sixfold promise of future salvation for Egypt: A promise of God's mercy
a. *In that day* (of the Messiah) Egypt will fear the LORD
 	
  1) They will fear His uplifted hand of power
  2) They will recognize that it was the God worshipped by Judah who executed judgment
	16 In that day shall Egypt be like unto women: and it shall be afraid and fear because of the shaking of the hand of the LORD of hosts, which he shaketh over it.
	17 And the land of Judah shall be a terror unto Egypt, every one that maketh mention thereof shall be afraid in himself, because of the counsel of the LORD of hosts, which he hath determined
		against it.
		18 In that day shall five cities in the land of Egypt speak the language of Canaan, and swear to the LORD of hosts; one shall be called, The city of destruction.
		19 In that day shall there be an altar to the LORD in the midst of the land of Egypt, and a pillar at the border thereof to the LORD.
		20 And it shall be for a sign
			b. *In that day* some Egyptians will be converted to the LORD: Five cities in particular will institute true worship in the nation
			
			c. *In that day* the Egyptians will institute true worship in the land
			  1) They will build an altar & monument to the LORD
			  2) They will bear strong wit-

OUTLINE	SCRIPTURE	SCRIPTURE	OUTLINE
ness to the LORD 3) They will cry out for deliverance from oppressors d. *In that day* the LORD will send a Savior to deliver the Egyptians 1) The LORD will make Himself known to the Egyptians 2) The Egyptians will acknowledge the LORD: They will worship & make genuine commitments to Him 3) The LORD will use His judgment to arouse their belief—stirring them to turn to Him	and for a witness unto the LORD of hosts in the land of Egypt: for they shall cry unto the LORD because of the oppressors, and he shall send them a saviour, and a great one, and he shall deliver them. 21 And the LORD shall be known to Egypt, and the Egyptians shall know the LORD in that day, and shall do sacrifice and oblation; yea, they shall vow a vow unto the LORD, and perform *it*. 22 And the LORD shall smite Egypt: he shall smite and heal *it:* and they shall return *even* to the LORD, and he shall be	intreated of them, and shall heal them. 23 In that day shall there be a highway out of Egypt to Assyria, and the Assyrian shall come into Egypt, and the Egyptian into Assyria, and the Egyptians shall serve with the Assyrians. 24 In that day shall Israel be the third with Egypt and with Assyria, *even* a blessing in the midst of the land: 25 Whom the LORD of hosts shall bless, saying, Blessed *be* Egypt my people, and Assyria the work of my hands, and Israel mine inheritance.	e. *In that day* peace will be established on earth & people will worship the LORD alone: A highway will be built between the empires of Egypt & Assyria f. *In that day* Israel will be a major power—just as Egypt & Assyria were 1) Israel will be a blessing 2) God will bless & call them... • *Egypt My people* • *Assyria My handiwork* • *Israel My inheritance*

a. *In that day* of the Messiah, Egypt will fear the LORD (v.16). When God's hand of judgment is uplifted against them, they will cower in fear and become as weak women (vv.1-17). Note that it will be the judgment of God that will arouse them to begin acknowledging the LORD (Jehovah, Yahweh), the God worshipped by the Jews.

b. *In that day* of the Messiah, some Egyptians will be converted to the LORD (v.18). Interestingly, five cities in particular will institute true worship within the nation. One of them will be called the City of Destruction, which is probably the city of Heliopis, *the city of the sun.* Heliopis was one of the major cities in southern Egypt, a city dedicated to the worship of the false sun god.[3] As a result of the terrible judgment taking place, many of these worshippers of false gods will turn to the LORD and become dynamic witnesses for Him. Filled with an insatiable hunger to know the LORD, a number of Egyptians will actually learn to read the Hebrew and Greek in order to study God's Word in its original language.

c. *In that day,* many of the converts will institute true worship in the land of Egypt (vv.19-20). They will even build an altar and monument to the LORD, with the worship center standing in Egypt as a strong testimony to the LORD of hosts. Because of the Egyptians' true faith and strong witness, the LORD will hear them when they cry out for deliverance from their enemies. He will deliver them from all oppressors. Most likely, this refers to the terrible oppression in the time of trial that is coming upon the earth during the last days, that is, the great tribulation (see outline and note—Mt.24:1-31 for more discussion).

d. In answer to the Egyptians' cry for deliverance, the LORD will send a Savior *in that day* to deliver them (vv.20-22). Of course when the Savior comes, all true believers will be delivered. The LORD will make Himself known to the Egyptians, and they will acknowledge Him as LORD (v.20-21). They will worship and make commitments (or vows) to Him, commitments that they will keep in the midst of judgment. Soldiers and refugees alike often make vows, promising to follow the LORD if He will just get them out of their present crises. Although many who make such vows during crises fail to follow through, the Egyptians *in that day* will be sincere. They will keep their vows. This will be the very reason the LORD will bring judgment upon them: to arouse their belief, stirring them to commit their lives to Him (v.22). Thus when they do repent and cry out to Him, the LORD will respond and heal them.

e. *In that day,* peace will be established on earth and the LORD alone will be worshipped throughout the world (v.23). When the Messiah Jesus Christ returns to earth, there will be a highway of peace built between the empires of Egypt and Assyria. That is, from all over the world people will travel freely to worship the LORD. Division, oppression, prejudice, and war will no longer separate people. Peace will flow like a river throughout the entire world, and all nations will worship the LORD, Him and Him alone. Of course, other Scriptures tell us that the LORD will establish the seat of His government in Jerusalem. Since Jerusalem will be the capital of the world, all nations will travel to Jerusalem to worship the LORD as well as to conduct business.

f. Since Jerusalem will be the capital of the world *in that day,* Israel will naturally be a major power along with Egypt and Assyria. Note that Israel will be a blessing on the whole earth. This will be due to the LORD's establishing Jerusalem as the seat of His government. These three nations will be greatly blessed by the LORD, so much so that He will call them...

• *Egypt My people*
• *Assyria the work of My hands*
• *Israel My inheritance*

Thought 1. The LORD had mercy upon the Egyptians. And He will have mercy upon any of us. But there is a condition: we must turn to the LORD, acknowledging Him as the only true LORD and Savior of the world. God loved the Egyptians, so He offered salvation to them. But He also loves us, so He offers salvation to all of us as well. However, when the gifts of God's mercy and salvation are offered, we must reach out to take them. No matter who may offer us a gift, it never becomes ours until we reach out to receive it. So it is with the gifts of God's mercy and salvation. We must reach out to receive them in order to be saved.

According to the present Scripture, the majority of Egyptians will not turn to the LORD until the days of great tribulation come to earth. It will be the judgment, the terrible trials, that will arouse the majority of Egyptians to turn to

---

3 John F. Walvoord and Roy B. Zuck, Editors. *The Bible Knowledge Commentary,* p.1067.

the LORD, the only living and true God. But God forbid that we wait until judgment comes to turn to Him. God help us all to turn to Him now. For when the war machines of this earth mobilize and begin their attack, far too often the hand of death snatches us before we can do anything, much less cry out to God for deliverance. War or disease or accident or even murderers can snatch us away at any time. As we all know, the youngest among us are sometimes snatched out of this world by the hand of death. Time to cry out for salvation is not always available. Today—right now, in this moment—the hand of God's mercy is extending the gift of salvation to us. But we must reach out to accept the gift in order to be saved. Listen to what God's Holy Word says about His mercy:

"And his mercy *is* on them that fear him from generation to generation" (Lu.1:50).

"But God, who is rich in mercy, for his great love wherewith he loved us, Even when we were dead in sins, hath quickened us together with Christ, (by grace ye are saved;) And hath raised *us* up together, and made *us* sit together in heavenly *places* in Christ Jesus: That in the ages to come he might show the exceeding riches of his grace in *his* kindness toward us through Christ Jesus. For by grace are ye saved through faith; and that not of yourselves: *it is* the gift of God" (Ep.2:4-8).

"Not by works of righteousness which we have done, but according to his mercy he saved us, by the washing of regeneration, and renewing of the Holy Ghost; Which he shed on us abundantly through Jesus Christ our Saviour; That being justified by his grace, we should be made heirs according to the hope of eternal life" (Tit.3:5-7).

"But the mercy of the LORD *is* from everlasting to everlasting upon them that fear him, and his righteousness unto children's children" (Ps.103:17).

"Praise ye the LORD. O give thanks unto the LORD; for *he is* good: for his mercy *endureth* for ever" (Ps.106:1).

"For thy mercy *is* great above the heavens: and thy truth *reacheth* unto the clouds" (Ps.108:4).

"The earth, O LORD, is full of thy mercy: teach me thy statutes" (Ps.119:64).

"*It is of* the LORD'S mercies that we are not consumed, because his compassions fail not. *They are* new every morning: great *is* thy faithfulness" (La.3:22-23).

"And rend your heart, and not your garments, and turn unto the LORD your God: for he *is* gracious and merciful, slow to anger, and of great kindness, and repenteth him of the evil" (Joel 2:13).

"Who *is* a God like unto thee, that pardoneth iniquity, and passeth by the transgression of the remnant of his heritage? he retaineth not his anger for ever, because he delighteth *in* mercy" (Mi.7:18).

3 **(20:1-6) Warning, Against Evil Associations—Egypt, Warning Against, Forming Alliances with—Ethiopia, Warning Against, Forming Alliances with—Evil Associations, Warnings Against—Believers, Warnings to, Against Evil Associations—Associations, Evil, Warnings Against—Fellowship, Evil, Warnings Against—Worldliness, Warnings Against, Evil Associations**: a strong warning was issued to Judah by the LORD, a warning against forming an alliance with Egypt and Ethiopia. Remember that Assyria was the dominant power during these days, holding most of the world under the thumb of its power. But there were pockets of resistance, anti-Assyrian movements who sought to overthrow the conqueror's domination. One of these movements was centered in Ashdod, one of the major cities of Philistia (v.1). This particular resistance had been encouraged by Egypt, who had promised its support in the event Assyria sought to put down the opposition. The Philistines even attempted to enlist Judah as well as Moab and Edom to form an alliance in the event of an attack (see outline and note—Is.15:28-32 for more discussion). The Assyrian king Sargon II, mentioned only here in the Old Testament, sent his commander-in-chief Tartan to put down the resistance in Ashdod. He conquered the city in 711 B.C. Considering that Ashdod was only 33 miles west of Jerusalem, the Assyrian army was naturally a threat to King Hezekiah and the Jews. However, there was a strong opponent or pro-Egyptian party in Jerusalem. Thus the threat of Assyria would become even more serious if this pro-Egyptian party gained control of the government.

Because of the looming danger to His people, the LORD instructed Isaiah to pronounce a severe warning to the Jews, and to do it in such a way that the people could not miss the point (v.2). The LORD told Isaiah to strip off his outer clothes or the sackcloth that he was wearing and to walk barefoot for three years. This meant that Isaiah was walking around wearing only a loin cloth in order to picture what would happen to the Jews if they formed an alliance with the Egyptians and Ethiopians. These two nations were unbelievers, people who had defied the LORD, the only living and true God. Therefore Isaiah was predicting that the Assyrians would conquer both Egypt and Ethiopia (v.4), and the survivors would be taken captive into exile, stripped and barefoot.

Through this symbolic action, the LORD used Isaiah to issue His strong warning (vv.5-6). All who put their trust in Egypt and Ethiopia would suffer fear and shame, for these two nations would collapse. Consequently, despair would grip the hearts of the people, for they would suddenly discover that they put their trust in the wrong place. They would know they could not possibly escape from the king of Assyria.

OUTLINE	SCRIPTURE	SCRIPTURE	OUTLINE
3. A warning to Judah against following Egypt & Ethiopia: A warning against evil associations a. The situation: Assyria captured Ashdod of Philistia b. The warning symbolized	In the year that Tartan came unto Ashdod, (when Sargon the king of Assyria sent him,) and fought against Ashdod, and took it; 2 At the same time spake	the LORD by Isaiah the son of Amoz, saying, Go and loose the sackcloth from off thy loins, and put off thy shoe from thy foot. And he did so, walking naked and barefoot.	1) God told Isaiah to strip off his outer clothes & walk barefoot—for three years 2) Isaiah obeyed c. The explanation

OUTLINE	SCRIPTURE	SCRIPTURE	OUTLINE
1) The prophet was a sign against following & forming alliances with Egypt & Ethiopia (the worldly unbelievers) 2) The Assyrians would conquer Egypt & Ethiopia: Take the people captive & lead them into exile, stripped & barefoot d. The warning issued to Israel	3 And the LORD said, Like as my servant Isaiah hath walked naked and barefoot three years *for* a sign and wonder upon Egypt and upon Ethiopia; 4 So shall the king of Assyria lead away the Egyptians prisoners, and the Ethiopians captives, young and old, naked and barefoot, even with *their* buttocks uncovered, to	the shame of Egypt. 5 And they shall be afraid and ashamed of Ethiopia their expectation, and of Egypt their glory. 6 And the inhabitant of this isle shall say in that day, Behold, such *is* our expectation, whither we flee for help to be delivered from the king of Assyria: and how shall we escape?	& others 1) All who trusted in Egypt & Ethiopia (the worldly unbelievers) would suffer fear & shame: They would see Ethiopia collapse 2) All who trusted worldly alliances would suffer despair: Would know they could not escape

Thought 1. This is a clear warning against evil associations. Forming alliances or getting involved with evil people will lead to catastrophe. If we associate with evil people, they will encourage us to join them in their sinful be-havior. And if we continue to associate with them, eventually we will cave in to their seduction. We cannot resist the lust of the flesh continually. Eventually we want a second helping of pie or cake, and if a young lady continues to date an immoral young man, eventually she caves in to the lust of the flesh and commits immorality. If a person associates with thieves, eventually he will join in the stealing. The same is true with those who smoke, take drugs, drink alcoholic beverages, look at pornographic material, or commit a host of other sins and misbehaviors. If a person associates with the disobedient and sinful of this world, eventually the person will join in the forbidden behav-ior. Consequently, the hand of God's judgment will fall upon him. God's hand is raised against all sin, against all evil associations. Listen to God's Holy Word:

"I wrote unto you in an epistle not to company with fornicators: Yet not altogether with the fornicators of this world, or with the covetous, or extortioners, or with idolaters; for then must ye needs go out of the world. But now I have written unto you not to keep company, if any man that is called a brother be a fornicator, or covetous, or an idolater, or a railer, or a drunkard, or an extortioner; with such an one no not to eat" (1 Co.5:9-11).

"Be not deceived: evil communications [companionships] corrupt good manners" (1 Co.15:33).

"Be ye not unequally yoked together with unbelievers: for what fellowship hath righteousness with unrighteousness? and what communion hath light with darkness? And what concord hath Christ with Belial? or what part hath he that believeth with an infidel? And what agreement hath the temple of God with idols? for ye are the temple of the living God; as God hath said, I will dwell in them, and walk in *them;* and I will be their God, and they shall be my people" (2 Co.6:14-16).

"And have no fellowship with the unfruitful works of darkness, but rather reprove *them.*" (Ep.5:11).

"Now we command you, brethren, in the name of our Lord Jesus Christ, that ye withdraw yourselves from every brother that walketh disorderly, and not after the tradition which he received of us." (2 Th.3:6).

"Thou shalt not follow a multitude to *do* evil; neither shalt thou speak in a cause to decline after many to wrest *judgment*" (Ex.23:2).

"Take heed to thyself, lest thou make a covenant with the inhabitants of the land whither thou goest, lest it be for a snare in the midst of thee" (Ex.34:12).

"Blessed *is* the man that walketh not in the counsel of the ungodly, nor standeth in the way of sinners, nor sitteth in the seat of the scornful" (Ps.1:1).

"Enter not into the path of the wicked, and go not in the way of evil *men*" (Pr.4:14).

"Be not thou envious against evil men, neither desire to be with them." (Pr.24:1).

"Depart ye, depart ye, go ye out from thence, touch no unclean *thing;* go ye out of the midst of her; be ye clean, that bear the vessels of the LORD." (Is.52:11).

"Eat thou not the bread of *him that hath* an evil eye, neither desire thou his dainty meats: For as he thinketh in his heart, so *is* he: Eat and drink, saith he to thee; but his heart *is* not with thee" (Pr.23:6-7).

"My son, if sinners entice thee, consent thou not....My son, walk not thou in the way with them; refrain thy foot from their path" (Pr.1:10, 15).

CHAPTER 21

E. God's Judgment of Babylon (the Persian Gulf Region), Edom, & Arabia: A Need to Watch, Repent, & Turn to the LORD, 21:1-17

1. God's judgment of Babylon foretold: A need to watch, be prepared
  a. The disaster: An invader would sweep upon Babylon like a desert storm, see v.9
    1) Babylon would suffer betrayal & looting
    2) Babylon would be attacked by Elam (Persia) & Media
    3) Babylon's brutality would end
  b. The reaction of Isaiah to foreseeing Babylon's fall: Experienced intense distress
    1) Isaiah suffered pain like a woman giving birth

    2) Isaiah suffered a weakened heart, trembling fear, & sleepless nights

  c. The attitude of the Babylonians that led to their destruction: Were lethargic pleasure-seekers, unprepared, 22:13
  d. The exhortation to Isaiah & God's people: To post a watchman to report the event when it happened (Babylon would fall)
    1) To stay fully alert for the invading army attacking Babylon

    2) To be faithful in looking for the event, the prophecy's fulfillment

The burden of the desert of the sea. As whirlwinds in the south pass through; *so* it cometh from the desert, from a terrible land.
2 A grievous vision is declared unto me; the treacherous dealer dealeth treacherously, and the spoiler spoileth. Go up, O Elam: besiege, O Media; all the sighing thereof have I made to cease.
3 Therefore are my loins filled with pain: pangs have taken hold upon me, as the pangs of a woman that travaileth: I was bowed down at the hearing *of it;* I was dismayed at the seeing *of it.*
4 My heart panted, fearfulness affrighted me: the night of my pleasure hath he turned into fear unto me.
5 Prepare the table, watch in the watchtower, eat, drink: arise, ye princes, *and* anoint the shield.
6 For thus hath the Lord said unto me, Go, set a watchman, let him declare what he seeth.
7 And he saw a chariot *with* a couple of horsemen, a chariot of asses, *and* a chariot of camels; and he hearkened diligently with much heed:
8 And he cried, A lion: My lord, I stand continually upon the watchtower in the

daytime, and I am set in my ward whole nights:
9 And, behold, here cometh a chariot of men, *with* a couple of horsemen. And he answered and said, Babylon is fallen, is fallen; and all the graven images of her gods he hath broken unto the ground.
10 O my threshing, and the corn of my floor: that which I have heard of the LORD of hosts, the God of Israel, have I declared unto you.
11 The burden of Dumah. He calleth to me out of Seir, Watchman, what of the night? Watchman, what of the night?
12 The watchman said, The morning cometh, and also the night: if ye will enquire, enquire ye: return, come.
13 The burden upon Arabia. In the forest in Arabia shall ye lodge, O ye travelling companies of Dedanim.
14 The inhabitants of the land of Tema brought water to him that was thirsty, they prevented with their bread him that fled.
15 For they fled from the swords, from the drawn sword, and from the bent bow, and from the grievousness of war.
16 For thus hath the Lord said unto me, Within a year, according to the years of an hireling, and all the glory of Kedar shall fail:
17 And the residue of the number of archers, the mighty men of the children of Kedar, shall be diminished: for the LORD God of Israel hath spoken it.

    3) To shout out the wonderful news when it occurred
      • That Babylon had fallen, Je.51:8; Re.14:8; 18:2
      • That Babylon's false gods were helpless in defending them, 41:22
  e. The deliverance of Judah
    1) They were being crushed under Babylonian captivity
    2) But they could take hope in Isaiah's vision
2. God's judgment of Edom foretold: A need to repent
  a. Edom's cry to the watchman: How much longer would it be dark, would they be oppressed?
  b. Edom's doom: Deliverance was coming, but also another darkness (oppression)
  c. Edom's only hope: Repentance, asking & turning to the LORD
3. God's judgment of Arabia foretold: A need to turn to the LORD
  a. The swift judgment

    1) Caravans would be forced to hide
    2) Fugitives would be forced to flee without adequate supplies of water or food
    3) All—both soldiers & citizens—would flee from the slaughter

  b. The brief delay of the judgment: To take place within a year, but the delay would give time for the unbelievers to turn to the LORD
  c. The few survivors of the judgment: Few citizens & few soldiers would survive

DIVISION II

THE PROPHECIES CONCERNING GOD'S JUDGMENT OF THE NATIONS AND HIS TRIUMPH OVER THE WORLD, 13:1–27:13

E. God's Judgment of Babylon (the Persian Gulf Region), Edom, and Arabia: A Need to Watch, Repent, and Turn to the LORD, 21:1-17

(21:1-17) **Introduction**: life is full of pitfalls, stumbling blocks, and dangers. Keeping a watchful eye and being prepared to face the potential problems of life is necessary. If people are sleepy while driving, they can easily cause an accident. If they fail to concentrate at work, they can lose their job. If they do not pay attention to their families, they could end up with broken relationships that all too often lead to divorce. If they do not keep a watchful eye on their finances, they can end up in financial difficulty or even bankruptcy. Being watchful, alert, and even vigilant prepares us to protect ourselves amid the perils of life. Being watchful and prepared is the practical subject of the present Scripture. Above all else, we must be alert and prepared for the coming judgment of God. If we do not know the LORD, we must repent and turn to Him.

Remember that Babylon is a picture of a wicked and prideful government, of any society or civilization that defies and turns away from the LORD (Yahweh, Jehovah). Throughout all of Scripture, from the building of the Tower of Babel

(Ge.11:1-9) to the godless state of Babylon in the last days of human history (Re.14:8; chs.17–18), Babylon represents all the evil systems and institutions of this world. For this reason, Babylon's destruction is emphasized for a second time.

Babylon represents the world system—the political, economic, military, social, and religious world system of darkness that stands opposed to the LORD Himself. In his pride and self-esteem, man exalts himself above God and walks in the darkness of this world, completely ignorant of the only living and true God. But no matter what he builds—a simple community or a worldwide empire—when he exalts himself, defies the LORD, and walks in darkness, he dooms himself. Every generation of God's people must stand watch and be prepared for the coming judgment. For the last days of human history are coming, and the godless state of Babylon, both religious and political, will fall (see outline and notes—Re.14:8; 17:1–18:24 for more discussion).

This passage of Scripture shows that the believers of Isaiah's day desperately needed to look ahead to the day God would deliver His people from oppression and the threat of constant attack. They needed to guard against trusting other nations to protect them and to trust in the LORD and Him alone. Thus, Isaiah warned the people of Judah not to sign treaties with the surrounding nations. This is, *God's Judgment of Babylon (the Persian Gulf Region), Edom, and Arabia: A Need to Watch, Repent, and Turn to the LORD*, 21:1-17.

1. God's judgment of Babylon foretold: a need to watch, be prepared (vv.1-10).
2. God's judgment of Edom foretold: a need to repent (vv.11-12).
3. God's judgment of Arabia foretold: a need to turn to the LORD (vv.13-17).

1 (21:1-10) **Babylon, Persian Gulf Region, Judgment of—Persian Gulf Region, Judgment of, Prophesied—Watchman, Duty, to Look for Prophetic Fulfillment—Believers, Duty, to Watch and Be Prepared—Judah, Exhortations to, Watch for Prophetic Fulfillment**: once again, God's judgment of Babylon is foretold, in particular the judgment that was coming upon the Persian Gulf region (13:1–14:23). Note the Scripture and outline:

OUTLINE	SCRIPTURE	SCRIPTURE	OUTLINE

1. God's judgment of Babylon foretold: A need to watch, be prepared
a. The disaster: An invader would sweep upon Babylon like a desert storm, see v.9
  1) Babylon would suffer betrayal & looting
  2) Babylon would be attacked by Elam (Persia) & Media
  3) Babylon's brutality would end
b. The reaction of Isaiah to foreseeing Babylon's fall: Experienced intense distress
  1) Isaiah suffered pain like a woman giving birth
 	
  2) Isaiah suffered a weakened heart, trembling fear, & sleepless nights
 	
c. The attitude of the Babylonians that led to their destruction: Were lethargic pleasure-
	The burden of the desert of the sea. As whirlwinds in the south pass through; *so it* cometh from the desert, from a terrible land.
	2 A grievous vision is declared unto me; the treacherous dealer dealeth treacherously, and the spoiler spoileth. Go up, O Elam: besiege, O Media; all the sighing thereof have I made to cease.
	3 Therefore are my loins filled with pain: pangs have taken hold upon me, as the pangs of a woman that travaileth: I was bowed down at the hearing *of it;* I was dismayed at the seeing *of it.*
	4 My heart panted, fearfulness affrighted me: the night of my pleasure hath he turned into fear unto me.
	5 Prepare the table, watch in the watchtower, eat, drink: arise, ye princes, *and* anoint
		the shield.
		6 For thus hath the Lord said unto me, Go, set a watchman, let him declare what he seeth.
		7 And he saw a chariot *with* a couple of horsemen, a chariot of asses, *and* a chariot of camels; and he hearkened diligently with much heed:
		8 And he cried, A lion: My lord, I stand continually upon the watchtower in the daytime, and I am set in my ward whole nights:
		9 And, behold, here cometh a chariot of men, *with* a couple of horsemen. And he answered and said, Babylon is fallen, is fallen; and all the graven images of her gods he hath broken unto the ground.
		10 O my threshing, and the corn of my floor: that which I have heard of the LORD of hosts, the God of Israel, have I declared unto you.
			seekers, unprepared, 22:13
			d. The exhortation to Isaiah & God's people: To post a watchman to report as the event happened (Babylon would fall)
			  1) To stay fully alert for the invading army attacking Babylon
			  2) To be faithful in looking for the event, the prophecy's fulfillment
			
			  3) To shout out the wonderful news when it occurred
			  • That Babylon had fallen, Je.51:8; Re.14:8; 18:2
			  • That Babylon's false gods were helpless in defending them, 41:22
			e. The deliverance of Judah
			  1) They were being crushed under Babylonian captivity
			  2) But they could take hope in Isaiah's vision

a. Disaster was to fall upon Babylon, in particular the desert region by the sea, or the Persian Gulf region of the empire. Isaiah predicted that an invader would sweep down upon Babylon like a whirlwind from a land of terror in the desert (vv.1-2). Who was this invader? Commentators differ as to its identity.

During Isaiah's day, Assyria was the dominant power—the one that controlled Syria and Palestine—so these verses could refer to Sennacherib's destruction of Babylon in 689 B.C. However, in 722 B.C. a Persian ruler named Marduk-apal-iddina (called Merodach-baladan in Is.39:1) revolted against Assyria and conquered Babylon. Elam, which is mentioned in verse 2, supported his revolt. In 710 B.C. the Assyrian king Sargon reconquered Babylon, but after Sargon's death, Marduk-apal-iddina and Elamite troops again revolted and were not finally defeated until Sennacherib destroyed the Persian Gulf region in 702 B.C.[1]

---

1 John F. Walvoord and Roy B. Zuck. *Bible Knowledge Commentary*, pp.1067-1068.

Although any of the above could have been the invader who destroyed Babylon during the days of Isaiah, H. C. Leupold points out that the Media-Persian ruler Cyrus fits the description given in this passage better than any other conqueror of Babylon.[2] Note three facts.

⇒ First, the two nations of Media and Elam, a major part of Persia, are mentioned (v.2), and the Media-Persian Empire conquered Babylon in 539 B.C.

⇒ Second, in describing the attitude of the Babylonians that would lead to their destruction, Isaiah said that they would be pleasure seekers who were totally unprepared for the invasion. In fact, he described them as sitting at a banquet, eating and drinking when they should have been grabbing their weapons to defend themselves. (v.5). This description is exactly what took place when Cyrus conquered the city of Babylon. Belshazzar, the king of Babylon, was throwing a great feast for one thousand of his officials. While they were feasting and drinking, Cyrus conquered the city with a minimum of effort (Da.5:1-31).

⇒ Third, although Isaiah predicted that God's people would be crushed in captivity (v.10), they should take hope, for Babylon was going to be destroyed (see outline and notes—2 K.25:1-30 for more discussion).

In light of these three facts, there is strong reason to believe that Isaiah was predicting the fall of Babylon to the Persian ruler Cyrus in 539 B.C. But no matter who the invader was, the meaning of the passage is clear. When the invader swept down upon Babylon, the nation would be betrayed and its wealth would be plundered (v.2). In any war, there are people who betray their own country. Every nation has its traitors, and so would Babylon.

Isaiah said that Media and Elam (Persia) would be the nations who would attack Babylon, but note who would destroy it: the LORD Himself. It would be the LORD Himself who would end the sufferings of the people Babylon had crushed. God would execute justice upon the Babylonians and punish them for their cruelty.

b. When Isaiah received this vision from the LORD, he experienced intense distress (vv.3–4). He suffered pain and anguish like a woman giving birth. He even says that his heart faltered, that he was gripped with a fear that made him tremble, and that he experienced sleepless nights. The fact that so many people on earth were to suffer so much war and death would weigh on the heart and mind of any person. Thus when Isaiah saw the future destruction of nation after nation, he felt tremendous strain and deep anguish of soul.

c. But whereas Isaiah was broken over the Babylonians' defiance of God and the coming judgment upon them, the Babylonians themselves were focused upon enjoying the pleasures of the flesh (v.5). Isaiah foresaw them spreading out their carpets to eat and drink and to enjoy immoral entertainment. Remember that this was exactly what happened on the night that Cyrus conquered the city of Babylon. King Belshazzar and one thousand of his royal officials were partying at a royal feast (Da.5:1-31).

d. The LORD exhorted Isaiah and the people of Judah to post a lookout on the wall of Jerusalem so they would know when Babylon fell (vv.6-9). This is God's exhortation to His people down through the centuries. Every generation is to watch for His coming judgment.

The watchman was to stay alert and scan the horizon for the invading army (v.7). No matter how long it took, he was to faithfully look for the event, for the prophecy would be fulfilled. He was to stand watch day after day, night after night, and never leave his post until he saw the invading army marching against Babylon. When he spotted the invasion, he was to shout out the wonderful news: *Babylon is fallen, is fallen.*

Keep in mind that Babylon is a symbol of all the ungodly religious, social, and political systems of the world and that this same event will take place in the last days of human history (Je.51:8; Re.14:8; 18:2). All the false gods of Babylon—and all the other godless, secular governments—will be unable to defend Babylon in that day (41:22; see outline and notes—Re.17:1–18:24 for more discussion).

e. But the fall of Babylon would mean the deliverance of Judah (v.10). Judah would be crushed like grain on the threshing floor in the Babylonian Captivity, but God's people could take great hope in Isaiah's vision, which predicted the destruction of Babylon and thus their eventual freedom from bondage (see outlines and notes—2 K.25:1-30; Ezr.1:1–2:70 for more discussion).

Thought 1. We must watch and be prepared for the fulfillment of the predictions in God's Holy Word. Christ Himself instructed us to stand watch and be alert for His return to earth. He is coming back, and He could come back at any time, so we must be prepared. We must also be prepared for death because we could die at any moment. And when we die, we will immediately come face-to-face with the LORD to give an account of whether we accepted Christ as our Savior or defied and turned against Him. By watching and being prepared to meet the LORD, we keep ourselves focused upon Him and His Holy Word. Listen to what God's Word says about watching and being prepared:

"**Watch therefore, for ye know neither the day nor the hour wherein the Son of man cometh**" (**Mt.25:13**).

"**Watch and pray, that ye enter not into temptation: the spirit indeed *is* willing, but the flesh *is* weak**" (**Mt.26:41**).

"**Blessed *are* those servants, whom the lord when he cometh shall find watching: verily I say unto you, that he shall gird himself, and make them to sit down to meat, and will come forth and serve them**" (**Lu.12:37**).

"**Therefore watch, and remember, that by the space of three years I ceased not to warn every one night and day with tears**" (**Ac.20:31**).

"**Wherefore let him that thinketh he standeth take heed lest he fall**" (**1 Co.10:12**).

"**Watch ye, stand fast in the faith, quit you like men, be strong**" (**1 Co.16:13**).

---

2 H.C. Leupold. *Exposition of Isaiah*, Vol.1, p.331.

"Continue in prayer, and watch in the same with thanksgiving" (Col.4:2).

"Ye are all the children of light, and the children of the day: we are not of the night, nor of darkness. Therefore let us not sleep, as *do* others; but let us watch and be sober" (1 Th.5:5-6).

"Teaching us that, denying ungodliness and worldly lusts, we should live soberly, righteously, and godly, in this present world; Looking for that blessed hope, and the glorious appearing of the great God and our Saviour Jesus Christ" (Tit.2:12-13).

"Be sober, be vigilant; because your adversary the devil, as a roaring lion, walketh about, seeking whom he may devour: Whom resist stedfast in the faith, knowing that the same afflictions are accomplished in your brethren that are in the world" (1 Pe.5:8-9).

"Be watchful, and strengthen the things which remain, that are ready to die: for I have not found thy works perfect before God. Remember therefore how thou hast received and heard, and hold fast, and repent. If therefore thou shalt not watch, I will come on thee as a thief, and thou shalt not know what hour I will come upon thee" (Re.3:2-3).

"Behold, I come quickly: hold that fast which thou hast, that no man take thy crown" (Re.3:11).

"Behold, I come as a thief. Blessed *is* he that watcheth, and keepeth his garments, lest he walk naked, and they see his shame" (Re.16:15).

2 (21:11-12) **Edom, Judgment of, Prophecy Concerning—Judgment, of Edom, Prophecy Concerning—Edom, Needs of, to Repent**: Edom was also about to face the judgment of God. Seir is another name for Edom, while Dumah is a symbolic name for it. *Dumah* means silence, which is what hangs over a city that has been completely destroyed. Thus, Isaiah's prophecy has to do with the destruction of Edom.

In the middle of a dark night a voice penetrated the silence, crying out to a watchman on the wall of Edom. The voice wanted to know how much longer it would be dark, for that was how much longer Edom would have to suffer under Assyrian oppression. Note that the voice cried out twice, emphasizing the deep distress of the Edomites who were desperate for deliverance. Sadly, the watchman offered the Edomites little hope. Although morning (deliverance from Assyria) was coming, there would soon be another night, a new conqueror, lying right over the horizon. Most likely this referred to Babylon.

Edom's only hope in the period between the two darknesses (conquerors) was to repent and turn to the LORD. They could ask repeatedly how much longer the darkness would last, but the answer would always be the same. They did not need to know when the judgment would fall; they needed to repent. If they repented, they could count on the LORD's presence to help them through whatever trial came.

OUTLINE	SCRIPTURE	SCRIPTURE	OUTLINE
2. God's judgment of Edom foretold: A need to repent a. Edom's cry to the watchman: How much longer would it be dark, would they be oppressed?	11 The burden of Dumah. He calleth to me out of Seir, Watchman, what of the night? Watchman, what of the night?	12 The watchman said, The morning cometh, and also the night: if ye will enquire, enquire ye: return, come.	b. Edom's doom: Deliverance was coming, but also another darkness (oppression) c. Edom's only hope: Repentance, asking & turning to the LORD

Thought 1. The LORD is the only hope for any of us to escape judgment. Instead of ignoring, denying, or defying Him, we should turn away from sin and ask Him to accept us in Christ. Only then will we escape the terrifying judgment of God. Christ has paid the penalty for our sins, which is death, hell, and eternal separation from God. When Christ paid the ransom for our souls, He set us free from the judgment to come. Through Him we are made acceptable to the LORD. Thus, our great need is to repent, to turn away from our sins and to the LORD.

"I tell you, Nay: but, except ye repent, ye shall all likewise perish" (Lu.13:3).

"Repent therefore of this thy wickedness, and pray God, if perhaps the thought of thine heart may be forgiven thee" (Ac.8:22).

"If my people, which are called by my name, shall humble themselves, and pray, and seek my face, and turn from their wicked ways; then will I hear from heaven, and will forgive their sin, and will heal their land" (2 Chr.7:14).

"Let the wicked forsake his way, and the unrighteous man his thoughts: and let him return unto the LORD, and he will have mercy upon him; and to our God, for he will abundantly pardon" (Is.55:7).

"And now, because ye have done all these works, saith the LORD, and I spake unto you, rising up early and speaking, but ye heard not; and I called you, but ye answered not; Therefore will I do unto *this* house, which is called by my name, wherein ye trust, and unto the place which I gave to you and to your fathers, as I have done to Shiloh. And I will cast you out of my sight, as I have cast out all your brethren, *even* the whole seed of Ephraim. Therefore pray not thou for this people, neither lift up cry nor prayer for them, neither make intercession to me: for I will not hear thee" (Je.7:13-16).

"But if the wicked will turn from all his sins that he hath committed, and keep all my statutes, and do that which is lawful and right, he shall surely live, he shall not die" (Eze.18:21).

"Take with you words, and turn to the LORD: say unto him, Take away all iniquity, and receive *us* graciously: so will we render the calves of our lips" (Ho.14:2).

3 (21:13-17) **Arabia, Judgment of, Prophesied—Caravans, Prophecy Concerning—Judgment, of Arabia, Prophecy Concerning**: Isaiah predicted that God's judgment would fall upon Arabia and that the judgment would be swift. God was going to use the Assyrian army to execute judgment on the Arabians because of their defiance and refusal to acknowledge Him as the only living and true LORD (Jehovah, Yahweh).

The Dedanites were a tribe of important traders from southern Arabia. Note that the judgment coming upon Arabia was to be so swift that the caravans of the Dedanites would be forced to hide in the thickets of Arabia (v.13). Their caravans would be no match for the Assyrian cavalry as it swept across the Arabian Desert. The people would be forced to flee for their lives without adequate supplies of water and food. In compassion, the LORD used His prophet to cry out to the Arabians in Tema, an oasis in northwestern Arabia, to take water and supplies to the fugitives. This rescue mission would be essential, for all the Arabians—both soldiers and citizens—would be fleeing from the rampaging Assyrian army.

There would be a brief delay before the judgment of God fell (v.16). It would take place within a year of Isaiah's prophecy, but there would be enough time for the pagan Arabians to turn to the LORD (v.16). When the judgment came, most of the population would be wiped out and never again have the opportunity to repent. Only a few Arabians—few citizens and few soldiers—would survive the slaughter.

OUTLINE	SCRIPTURE	SCRIPTURE	OUTLINE
3. God's judgment of Arabia foretold: A need to turn to the LORD a. The swift judgment 1) Caravans would be forced to hide 2) Fugitives would be forced to flee without adequate supplies of water or food 3) All—both soldiers & citizens—would flee from	13 The burden upon Arabia. In the forest in Arabia shall ye lodge, O ye travelling companies of Dedanim. 14 The inhabitants of the land of Tema brought water to him that was thirsty, they prevented with their bread him that fled. 15 For they fled from the swords, from the drawn sword, and from the bent bow, and	from the grievousness of war. 16 For thus hath the Lord said unto me, Within a year, according to the years of an hireling, and all the glory of Kedar shall fail: 17 And the residue of the number of archers, the mighty men of the children of Kedar, shall be diminished: for the LORD God of Israel hath spoken *it*.	the slaughter b. The brief delay of the judgment: To take place within a year, but the delay would give time for the unbelievers to turn to the LORD c. The few survivors of the judgment: Few citizens & few soldiers would survive

Thought 1. There is still time to turn to the LORD. Any person reading or hearing about the judgment of Arabia still has time to escape the coming judgment. None of us have yet been snatched from this world. We are still living, and God's hand of mercy is still reaching out to us. If we are sinking into the depths of sin and shame, darkness and doom, hearing this message may be our last hope. The Arabians had only a year before most of them would die. All of us must die, and for some of us death is just over the horizon, perhaps even within the next 24 hours. Most of us will never know the hour or day we are destined to leave the world. Thus, being alert, standing watch, and being prepared to meet the LORD is an urgent need for many of us. If we have never turned to Him, we must turn to Him today, right now, for our own protection. When we turn to Him, He immediately reaches out and accepts us. Listen to what His Holy Word says:

"I will arise and go to my father, and will say unto him, Father, I have sinned against heaven, and before thee, And am no more worthy to be called thy son: make me as one of thy hired servants. And he arose, and came to his father. But when he was yet a great way off, his father saw him, and had compassion, and ran, and fell on his neck, and kissed him" (Lu.15:18-20).

"Repent ye therefore, and be converted, that your sins may be blotted out, when the times of refreshing shall come from the presence of the Lord" (Ac.3:19).

"For ye were as sheep going astray; but are now returned unto the Shepherd and Bishop of your souls" (1 Pe.2:25).

"If we confess our sins, he is faithful and just to forgive us *our* sins, and to cleanse us from all unrighteousness" (1 Jn.1:9).

"If my people, which are called by my name, shall humble themselves, and pray, and seek my face, and turn from their wicked ways; then will I hear from heaven, and will forgive their sin, and will heal their land" (2 Chr.7:14).

"He looketh upon men, and *if any* say, I have sinned, and perverted *that which was* right, and it profited me not. He will deliver his soul from going into the pit, and his life shall see the light." (Jb.33:27-28).

"He that covereth his sins shall not prosper: but whoso confesseth and forsaketh *them* shall have mercy" (Pr.28:13).

"For thus saith the Lord GOD, the Holy One of Israel; In returning and rest shall ye be saved; in quietness and in confidence shall be your strength: and ye would not" (Is.30:15).

"Let the wicked forsake his way, and the unrighteous man his thoughts: and let him return unto the LORD, and he will have mercy upon him; and to our God, for he will abundantly pardon" (Is.55:7).

"Only acknowledge thine iniquity, that thou hast transgressed against the LORD thy God, and hast scattered thy ways to the strangers under every green tree, and ye have not obeyed my voice, saith the LORD" (Je.3:13).

"But if the wicked will turn from all his sins that he hath committed, and keep all my statutes, and do that which is lawful and right, he shall surely live, he shall not die" (Eze.18:21).

"Come, and let us return unto the LORD: for he hath torn, and he will heal us; he hath smitten, and he will bind us up" (Ho.6:1).

"O Israel, return unto the LORD thy God; for thou hast fallen by thine iniquity" (Ho.14:1).

"Therefore also now, saith the LORD, turn ye *even* to me with all your heart, and with fasting, and with weeping, and with mourning" (Joel 2:12).

"Even from the days of your fathers ye are gone away from mine ordinances, and have not kept *them.* Return unto me, and I will return unto you, saith the LORD of hosts. But ye said, Wherein shall we return?" (Mal.3:7).

CHAPTER 22

F. God's Judgment of Judah & Jerusalem: A Picture of God's Coming Judgment & Grace, 22:1-25

1. The judgment—an attack & siege by a cruel enemy: A picture of coming judgment

a. The alarm of the people
1) The city was filled with commotion & business, revelry & partying
2) The people would die from famine & disease due to the siege
3) The leaders would flee like cowards, refusing to fight in honor
4) The escapee would be captured

b. The compassion of Isaiah (representing the LORD): Wept bitterly

c. The description of the judgment, the day of the LORD, 2:11-12; 3:7,18; 4:1-2
1) A day appointed by God
2) A day of terror
3) A day of destruction
4) A day of crying & grief
5) A day of fierce attack by a coalition of forces: Elam & Kir (either Media or a province near Media)
6) A day of facing a well-equipped enemy

2. The reasons for the judgment

a. They were self-sufficient
1) Trusted their weapons
2) Inspected their defenses
3) Stored water
4) Strengthened their defenses & the city's wall
5) Built an additional water reservoir

b. They failed to trust the LORD, the Creator
1) He made the water that is so necessary
2) He is to be the first One trusted, called upon

c. They failed to repent, failed to turn to the LORD

The burden of the valley of vision. What aileth thee now, that thou art wholly gone up to the housetops? 2 Thou that art full of stirs, a tumultuous city, a joyous city: thy slain *men are* not slain with the sword, nor dead in battle. 3 All thy rulers are fled together, they are bound by the archers: all that are found in thee are bound together, *which* have fled from far. 4 Therefore said I, Look away from me; I will weep bitterly, labour not to comfort me, because of the spoiling of the daughter of my people. 5 For *it is* a day of trouble, and of treading down, and of perplexity by the Lord GOD of hosts in the valley of vision, breaking down the walls, and of crying to the mountains. 6 And Elam bare the quiver with chariots of men *and* horsemen, and Kir uncovered the shield. 7 And it shall come to pass, *that* thy choicest valleys shall be full of chariots, and the horsemen shall set themselves in array at the gate. 8 And he discovered the covering of Judah, and thou didst look in that day to the armour of the house of the forest. 9 Ye have seen also the breaches of the city of David, that they are many: and ye gathered together the waters of the lower pool. 10 And ye have numbered the houses of Jerusalem, and the houses have ye broken down to fortify the wall. 11 Ye made also a ditch between the two walls for the water of the old pool: but ye have not looked unto the maker thereof, neither had respect unto him that fashioned it long ago. 12 And in that day did the Lord GOD of hosts call to

weeping, and to mourning, and to baldness, and to girding with sackcloth: 13 And behold joy and gladness, slaying oxen, and killing sheep, eating flesh, and drinking wine: let us eat and drink; for to morrow we shall die. 14 And it was revealed in mine ears by the LORD of hosts, Surely this iniquity shall not be purged from you till ye die, saith the Lord GOD of hosts. 15 Thus saith the Lord GOD of hosts, Go, get thee unto this treasurer, *even* unto Shebna, which *is* over the house, *and say,* 16 What hast thou here? and whom hast thou here, that thou hast hewed thee out a sepulchre here, *as* he that heweth him out a sepulchre on high, *and* that graveth an habitation for himself in a rock? 17 Behold, the LORD will carry thee away with a mighty captivity, and will surely cover thee. 18 He will surely violently turn and toss thee *like* a ball into a large country: there shalt thou die, and there the chariots of thy glory *shall be* the shame of thy lord's house. 19 And I will drive thee from thy station, and from thy state shall he pull thee down. 20 And it shall come to pass in that day, that I will call my servant Eliakim the son of Hilkiah: 21 And I will clothe him with thy robe, and strengthen him with thy girdle, and I will commit thy government into his hand: and he shall be a father to the inhabitants of Jerusalem, and to the house of Judah. 22 And the key of the house of David will I lay upon his shoulder; so he shall open, and none shall shut; and he shall shut, and none shall open. 23 And I will fasten him as a nail in a sure place; and he shall be for a glorious throne to his father's house. 24 And they shall hang upon him all the glory of his father's house, the offspring and the issue, all vessels of small quantity, from the vessels of cups, even to all the vessels of flagons.

d. They lived by the worldly philosophy of pleasure: "Let us eat & drink, for tomorrow we die!"

e. They became hard-hearted: Sinned beyond the point of ever repenting & receiving forgiveness of sin

f. They had unfaithful leaders: The example of Shebna
1) He was second only to the king in authority & power: The Prime Minister
2) He used his authority & wealth pridefully & unwisely: Built a large tomb as a monument to himself so that he would always be remembered
3) He was forewarned by the LORD through Isaiah: He would be seized & cast away
• Would be thrown "like a ball" into captivity
• Would die in captivity leaving behind all his chariots (wealth & power)
• Would die a disgrace, having lost his office & position of power

3. The grace of God in raising up the godly leader Eliakim: A type of Jesus Christ

a. He would replace Shebna as government administrator, 36:3
1) Would be clothed with all the authority of the minister
2) Would be made a father—the head—of the people
3) Would be given the key to the house of David—the very power of the throne itself: A picture of Jesus Christ, Re.3:7

b. He would be like a well-driven peg in the nation, one of the key persons who helps hold the nation together

c. He would bear heavy responsibility & bring honor to his family

d. He would, however, be unable to stop God's judgment: The fall of Jerusalem 1) He was only a peg, a man	25 In that day, saith the LORD of hosts, shall the nail that is fastened in the sure place be removed, and be cut	down, and fall; and the burden that *was* upon it shall be cut off: for the LORD hath spoken *it*.	2) He would be sheared off (die): All who were supported by the peg would collapse

DIVISION II

THE PROPHECIES CONCERNING GOD'S JUDGMENT OF THE NATIONS AND HIS TRIUMPH OVER THE WORLD, 13:1–27:13

F. God's Judgment of Judah and Jerusalem: A Picture of God's Coming Judgment and Grace, 22:1-25

(22:1-25) **Introduction**: judgment is not a pleasant subject. No one enjoys thinking about being punished, especially being punished eternally by God in a place called *hell*. Many of us deny the coming judgment, the fact that God will ever punish people. Yet we must always remember: denying the truth never voids the truth. Truth cannot be invalidated, for a truth is fact. Therefore, because God *cannot lie*, His pronouncements of judgment, punishment, and hell are indisputable truths. But because God loves us, He warns us of the dangerous pitfalls lying out in the future, pitfalls that we must avoid. If a person continues to walk in defiance of God, denying His very existence, that person is dooming himself. Some day God will judge the world, punish all who have denied and defied Him. Thus, all who rebel against God will be doomed to a special place He has prepared, the place called *hell*.

Yet even in the midst of pronouncing judgment, God pours out His grace upon us by making a way for us to escape it. The way is Jesus Christ, the Savior of the world. This is the practical message of the present passage in which Isaiah describes God's coming judgment and the wonderful grace He extends to us. This is, *God's Judgment of Judah and Jerusalem: A Picture of God's Coming Judgment and Grace*, 22:1-25.

1. The judgment—an attack and siege by a cruel enemy: a picture of coming judgment (vv.1-7).
2. The reasons for the judgment (vv.8-19).
3. The grace of God in raising up the godly leader Eliakim: a type of Jesus Christ (vv.20-25).

[1] (22:1-7) **Judgment, of Judah, Prophesied—Jerusalem, Judgment of, Prophesied—Worldliness, Example of, Jews—God, Compassion of, for His People—Weeping, of God, Over His People**: God executed judgment on Judah and Jerusalem through the siege of a cruel enemy. Who was this enemy? Most commentators suggest that it was the Assyrians, specifically Sennacherib, who laid siege to Jerusalem in 701 B.C. (see outline and notes—Is.36:1–37:38 for more discussion). But note four facts.

First, verse 2 clearly indicates that the predicted siege lasted a long time—long enough for the city to collapse from a famine brought on by an extended siege. The Assyrian siege, however, was brief. Remember that the LORD struck the Assyrian army soon after it laid siege to Jerusalem and that it immediately withdrew and returned home (Is.37:36-38). Also, Jerusalem's citizens were not killed by the sword, which means they died from famine, starvation, or disease due to a siege. This points to Babylon as the invader.

Second, verse 3 suggests that a large number of leaders who tried to flee during the siege were captured. The description of the Assyrian siege does not mention this fact. To the contrary, immediately after it began, the principal leaders of King Hezekiah's government began to negotiate with the Assyrians. This, too, seems to indicate that the enemy in view in this passage is Babylon.

Third, verse 6 calls the invaders Elam (probably Persia) and Kir, which was either Media or a province near it. Since both of these nations became part of the Babylonian Empire, this reference indicates either that they represented Babylon or that they were special forces in the Assyrian army. Since Assyria is not mentioned in the passage, it seems more logical to assume the former.

Fourth, verse 15 mentions that Shebna, one of Hezekiah's chief officials, negotiated with the Assyrians when they besieged Jerusalem (36:3; 2 K.18:17-18). This, of course, suggests that Assyria was the invader.

Taking all these facts into consideration, it does not seem wise to assume that this passage refers *only* to one invader and one siege. It seems more logical to conclude that the prophecy applies to the long history of Jerusalem from Isaiah's day forward. Isaiah was predicting what would happen whenever God's people turned from the LORD. His hand of judgment would fall; and when the judgment began, a few would turn back to Him as Hezekiah had done during the Assyrian siege.

However, the impending judgment would not cause a significant or lasting change in the majority of people. Most would just carry on business as usual and keep on partying (v.2). Unwilling to give up their worldly pleasures, they would continue to live by the philosophy of pleasure that had always characterized their lives: "let us eat and drink, for tomorrow we die" (v.13). This was true during Hezekiah's reign, and it would continue to be true right up to the Babylonian siege and exile under Nebuchadnezzar (see outline and notes—2 K.25:1-30). In the words of Edward J. Young:

> It seems best to interpret the passage in a generic sense, as a description of the oncoming of an enemy and of the terrible worldliness and paganism found in the city of Jerusalem when that enemy comes. That enemy is really Babylon. In appealing to Tiglath-Pileser, Ahaz (Hezekiah's father) had in reality appealed to the spirit of Babylon, for the Assyrian king was the first great representative of that human power represented in Daniel's head of gold and in the lion with eagles' wings (Daniel 2 and 7). In the present chapter we are given phases of the warfare with the Mesopotamian power [Assyria] brought against the city of God. It was a necessary warfare, for the city must be

purged of its pagan elements. Such warfare may have led to temporary conversion and returns to the LORD, as in the case of Hezekiah. It did not, however, produce any lasting change in the city, and finally the Babylonian power came in the person of Nebuchadnezzar. When the city of God seeks help from the city of paganism, she will soon be controlled by the city of paganism. Verses 2 and 3 depict the final outcome of this struggle, whereas some of the succeeding verses picture certain previous phases thereof. In reality, however, it is a generic prophecy that we have before us; and it is this explanation that best accounts for references of various phases of the long struggle between the city of peace and light (Jerusalem) and the city of paganism and darkness (Babylon), a struggle that saw the climax of its first great stage and the deportation of the inhabitants of Jerusalem to Babylonia.[1]

(See outline and notes for Ahaz's appeal to Assyria—2 Chr.28:16-27.)

OUTLINE	SCRIPTURE	SCRIPTURE	OUTLINE

1. The judgment—an attack & siege by a cruel enemy: A picture of coming judgment
a. The alarm of the people
  1) The city was filled with commotion & business, revelry & partying
  2) The people would die from famine & disease due to the siege
  3) The leaders would flee like cowards, refusing to fight in honor
  4) The escapee would be captured
b. The compassion of Isaiah (representing the LORD): Wept bitterly
	The burden of the valley of vision. What aileth thee now, that thou art wholly gone up to the housetops?
	2 Thou that art full of stirs, a tumultuous city, a joyous city: thy slain *men are* not slain with the sword, nor dead in battle.
	3 All thy rulers are fled together, they are bound by the archers: all that are found in thee are bound together, *which* have fled from far.
	4 Therefore said I, Look away from me; I will weep bitterly, labour not to comfort
		me, because of the spoiling of the daughter of my people.
		5 For *it is* a day of trouble, and of treading down, and of perplexity by the Lord GOD of hosts in the valley of vision, breaking down the walls, and of crying to the mountains.
		6 And Elam bare the quiver with chariots of men *and* horsemen, and Kir uncovered the shield.
		7 And it shall come to pass, *that* thy choicest valleys shall be full of chariots, and the horsemen shall set themselves in array at the gate.
			c. The description of the judgment, the day of the LORD, 2:11-12; 3:7,18; 4:1-2
			  1) A day appointed by God
			  2) A day of terror
			  3) A day of destruction
			  4) A day of crying & grief
			  5) A day under fierce attack by a coalition of forces: Elam & Kir (either Media or a province near Media)
			  6) A day of facing a well-equipped enemy

a. The people would naturally be alarmed when the invader quickly conquered the cities of Judah and then laid siege to Jerusalem. Terrified, they would rush up to their rooftops to look out upon the enemy surrounding the city. Note how Isaiah described the city: it was full of commotion and revelry. For centuries, Jerusalem had been the nation's most important commercial center, the chief support of its economy, as well as the seat of government. But it had also been the center of worldly pleasure, of partying and feasting, drinking and dancing, sensuality and immorality. Thus it was the hub of activity in both legitimate and illegitimate business and pleasure.

When God's hand of judgment fell upon Jerusalem, its citizens would not die by the sword; they would die from starvation and disease, the results of the famine caused by the siege. Their cowardly leaders would refuse to fight and die honorable deaths. Instead, they would flee, only to be captured (v.3; 2 K.25:1-7).

b. Even though the destruction of the Jews lay in the future, Isaiah's heart broke when he saw their suffering in a vision. In deep distress, he wept bitterly. Remember that the prophet was representing the LORD and that God was revealing through the prophet His heart of compassion for His people. The LORD Himself must have been weeping over their defiant refusal to repent. Despite the judgment they would face, they would not turn back to Him. Even though He was brokenhearted, God had no choice but to execute justice upon them.

c. Isaiah painted a vivid picture of the coming judgment (vv.5-7). Note the double emphasis on who is carrying out the judgment: it is the "LORD God of hosts" (LORD Almighty). God's day of judgment was coming. What kind of day would it be? Isaiah gave a sixfold description:

⇒ It would be a day appointed by the LORD Almighty Himself (v.5).
⇒ It would be a day of terror.
⇒ It would be a day of destruction.
⇒ It would be a day of grief and crying.
⇒ It would be a day of fierce attack by a coalition of forces.
⇒ It would be a day of facing a large, well-equipped army camped right outside the gates of Jerusalem.

Thought 1. What a terrifying picture of impending judgment! And it is one that applies to every generation. God's judgment lies right over the horizon for all of us. We will face the LORD, either when we die or when Christ returns for us. No matter how hard we try to refute the facts, denying that God exists or that His judgment is coming does not change the truth. God does exist and He Himself plainly declares that a day of judgment is coming. Everyone will give an account for what he has done, whether he has obeyed the commandments of God or not. When we deny the truth, we only deceive and doom ourselves. We miss the truth and bring the consequences down on our own heads. The day of judgment is coming:

---

[1] Edward J. Young. *The Book of Isaiah*, Vol.2, p.89.

"Not every one that saith unto me, Lord, Lord, shall enter into the kingdom of heaven; but he that doeth the will of my Father which is in heaven. Many will say to me in that day, Lord, Lord, have we not prophesied in thy name? and in thy name have cast out devils? and in thy name done many wonderful works? And then will I profess unto them, I never knew you: depart from me, ye that work iniquity" (Mt.7:21-23).

"When Jesus heard *it*, he marvelled, and said to them that followed, Verily I say unto you, I have not found so great faith, no, not in Israel. And I say unto you, That many shall come from the east and west, and shall sit down with Abraham, and Isaac, and Jacob, in the kingdom of heaven. But the children of the kingdom [people who have a false profession] shall be cast out into outer darkness: there shall be weeping and gnashing of teeth" (Mt.8:10-12).

"And then shall appear the sign of the Son of man in heaven: and then shall all the tribes of the earth mourn, and they shall see the Son of man coming in the clouds of heaven with power and great glory" (Mt.24:30).

"When the Son of man shall come in his glory, and all the holy angels with him, then shall he sit upon the throne of his glory: And before him shall be gathered all nations: and he shall separate them one from another, as a shepherd divideth *his* sheep from the goats: And he shall set the sheep on his right hand, but the goats on the left....Then shall he say also unto them on the left hand, Depart from me, ye cursed, into everlasting fire, prepared for the devil and his angels" (Mt.25:31-33, 41).

"Marvel not at this: for the hour is coming, in the which all that are in the graves shall hear his voice, And shall come forth; they that have done good, unto the resurrection of life; and they that have done evil, unto the resurrection of damnation" (Jn.5:28-29).

"But unto them that are contentious, and do not obey the truth, but obey unrighteousness, indignation and wrath" (Ro.2:8).

"And to you who are troubled rest with us, when the Lord Jesus shall be revealed from heaven with his mighty angels, In flaming fire taking vengeance on them that know not God, and that obey not the gospel of our Lord Jesus Christ" (2 Th.1:7-8).

"And as it is appointed unto men once to die, but after this the judgment" (He.9:27).

"Of how much sorer punishment, suppose ye, shall he be thought worthy, who hath trodden under foot the Son of God, and hath counted the blood of the covenant, wherewith he was sanctified, an unholy thing, and hath done despite unto the Spirit of grace?" (He.10:29).

"The Lord knoweth how to deliver the godly out of temptations, and to reserve the unjust unto the day of judgment to be punished" (2 Pe.2:9).

"But the heavens and the earth, which are now, by the same word are kept in store, reserved unto fire against the day of judgment and perdition of ungodly men" (2 Pe.3:7).

"Behold, the Lord cometh with ten thousands of his saints, To execute judgment upon all, and to convince all that are ungodly among them of all their ungodly deeds which they have ungodly committed, and of all their hard *speeches* which ungodly sinners have spoken against him" (Jude 1:14-15).

2 (22:8-19) **Judgment, Reasons for, Six Reasons—Self-Sufficiency, Results, Judgment—Distrust, Consequences, Judgment—Unrepentance, Consequences, Judgment—Worldly Pleasure, Consequences, Judgment—Philosophy, of Pleasure, Example of—Pleasure, Philosophy of, Example—Worldliness, Philosophy, of Pleasure—Hard-hearted, Example of, Jews—Leaders, Unfaithful, Example of:** Isaiah spelled out the reasons for God's coming judgment upon the Jews. He gave six reasons.

OUTLINE	SCRIPTURE	SCRIPTURE	OUTLINE
2. The reasons for the judgment	8 And he discovered the covering of Judah, and thou didst look in that day to the armour of the house of the forest.	Lord GOD of hosts call to weeping, and to mourning, and to baldness, and to girding with sackcloth:	c. They failed to repent, failed to turn to the LORD
a. They were self-sufficient			
1) Trusted their weapons			
2) Inspected their defenses	9 Ye have seen also the breaches of the city of David, that they are many: and ye gathered together the waters of the lower pool.	13 And behold joy and gladness, slaying oxen, and killing sheep, eating flesh, and drinking wine: let us eat and drink; for to morrow we shall die.	d. They lived by the worldly philosophy of pleasure: "Let us eat & drink, for tomorrow we die!"
3) Stored water			
4) Strengthened their defenses & the city's wall	10 And ye have numbered the houses of Jerusalem, and the houses have ye broken down to fortify the wall.	14 And it was revealed in mine ears by the LORD of hosts, Surely this iniquity shall not be purged from you till ye die, saith the Lord GOD of hosts.	e. They became hard-hearted: Sinned beyond the point of ever repenting & receiving forgiveness of sin
5) Built an additional water reservoir	11 Ye made also a ditch between the two walls for the water of the old pool: but ye	15 Thus saith the Lord GOD of hosts, Go, get thee unto this treasurer, *even* unto She-	f. They had unfaithful leaders: The example of Shebna
b. They failed to trust the LORD, the Creator	have not looked unto the maker thereof, neither had respect unto him that fashioned	bna, which *is* over the house, *and say,*	1) He was second only to the king in authority & power: The Prime Minister
1) He made the water that is so necessary	it long ago.	16 What hast thou here? and	2) He used his authority &
2) He is to be the first One trusted, called upon	12 And in that day did the		

ISAIAH 22:1-25

OUTLINE	SCRIPTURE	SCRIPTURE	OUTLINE
wealth pridefully & un-wisely: Built a large tomb as a monument to himself so that he would always be remembered	whom hast thou here, that thou hast hewed thee out a sepulchre here, *as* he that heweth him out a sepulchre on high, *and* that graveth an habitation for himself in a rock?	surely cover thee. 18 He will surely violently turn and toss thee *like* a ball into a large country: there shalt thou die, and there the chariots of thy glory *shall be* the shame of thy lord's house.	cast away • Would be thrown "like a ball" into captivity • Would die in captivity leaving behind all his chariots (wealth & power)
3) He was forewarned by the LORD through Isaiah: He would be seized &	17 Behold, the LORD will carry thee away with a mighty captivity, and will	19 And I will drive thee from thy station, and from thy state shall he pull thee down.	• Would die a disgrace, having lost his office & position of power

a. *They were self-sufficient* (vv.8-11). Down through their history when the Jews confronted an enemy, they placed their trust in their military might and their own resources. In this instance, they strengthened their defenses and stored up water. They even built an additional reservoir (v.11).

Thought 1. We should be self-sufficient, but not to the point of ignoring the LORD and other people. Unless we are careful, self-sufficiency can lead us to be conceited and to act as though we do not need anyone else. No person is an island unto himself, and no nation stands alone in this world. The world is a community of nations, and every society is a community of people who need one another. Although we should be self-sufficient in many areas of life, we must guard against a sinful, self-centered sufficiency. Listen to what God's holy Word says:

"Peter answered and said unto him, Though all *men* shall be offended because of thee, *yet* will I never be offended. Jesus said unto him, Verily I say unto thee, That this night, before the cock crow, thou shalt deny me thrice. Peter said unto him, Though I should die with thee, yet will I not deny thee. Likewise also said all the disciples" (Mt.26:33-35).
"And he spake this parable unto certain which trusted in themselves that they were righteous, and despised others" (Lu.18:9).
"Wherefore let him that thinketh he standeth take heed lest he fall" (1 Co.10:12).
"He that trusteth in his own heart is a fool: but whoso walketh wisely, he shall be delivered" (Pr.28:26).
"The pride of thine heart hath deceived thee, thou that dwellest in the clefts of the rock, whose habitation *is* high; that saith in his heart, Who shall bring me down to the ground?" (Ob.1:3).

b. *They failed to look to their Creator* (v.11). Although God was the One who made the water that was so crucial to their survival, the Jews did not trust Him. They failed to look to Him as the source of their strength and deliverance. When they confronted hardships and enemies, a spirit of unbelief and distrust gripped them.

Thought 1. Unbelief and distrust are sins that will always condemn us. They will bring God's judgment down upon us. If we do not believe in the LORD, we are doomed. If we trust only in our own strength to pull us through when we face trials or hardship, we will have no power greater than our own to help us. We will be completely on our own. Just as all flesh ages, dies, and decays in the ground, so we too will eventually falter and fail, dooming ourselves to eternal judgment. Listen to God's warning against unbelief and distrust:

"He that believeth on the Son hath everlasting life: and he that believeth not the Son shall not see life; but the wrath of God abideth on him" (Jn.3:36).
"I said therefore unto you, that ye shall die in your sins: for if ye believe not that I am *he,* ye shall die in your sins" (Jn.8:24).
"And when he is come, he will reprove the world of sin, and of righteousness, and of judgment: Of sin, because they believe not on me" (Jn.16:8-9).
"Take heed, brethren, lest there be in any of you an evil heart of unbelief, in departing from the living God. But exhort one another daily, while it is called To day; lest any of you be hardened through the deceitfulness of sin. For we are made partakers of Christ, if we hold the beginning of our confidence stedfast unto the end; While it is said, To day if ye will hear his voice, harden not your hearts, as in the provocation. For some, when they had heard, did provoke: howbeit not all that came out of Egypt by Moses. But with whom was he grieved forty years? *was it* not with them that had sinned, whose carcases fell in the wilderness? And to whom sware he that they should not enter into his rest, but to them that believed not? So we see that they could not enter in because of unbelief" (He.3:12-19).
"Let us labour therefore to enter into that rest, lest any man fall after the same example of unbelief" (He.4:11).
"I will therefore put you in remembrance, though ye once knew this, how that the Lord, having saved the people out of the land of Egypt, afterward destroyed them that believed not. And the angels which kept not their first estate, but left their own habitation, he hath reserved in everlasting chains under darkness unto the judgment of the great day. Even as Sodom and Gomorrha, and the cities about them in like manner, giving themselves over to fornication, and going after strange flesh, are set forth for an example, suffering the vengeance of eternal fire" (Jude 5-7).

c. *They failed to repent of sin* (v.12). Throughout history, God's judgment has fallen upon His people for a very specific purpose: to arouse them to weep in sorrow for their sins and to call upon Him for forgiveness. Through judgment the LORD calls upon His people to repent and to turn back to Him, the only living and true God.

Thought 1. When we sin, God chastises us. The purpose for His discipline is always to move us to repent before we harm ourselves or others. Sin always damages us and often leads us to injure others. Think, for example, about the injuries caused in accidents by drunken drivers. God loves us, and because He does, He disciplines us in order to correct us.

"For this cause many *are* weak and sickly among you, and many sleep. For if we would judge ourselves, we should not be judged. But when we are judged, we are chastened of the Lord, that we should not be condemned with the world" (1 Co.11:30-32).

"And ye have forgotten the exhortation which speaketh unto you as unto children, My son, despise not thou the chastening of the Lord, nor faint when thou art rebuked of him: For whom the Lord loveth he chasteneth, and scourgeth every son whom he receiveth" (He.12:5-6).

"As many as I love, I rebuke and chasten: be zealous therefore, and repent" (Re.3:19).

"Thou shalt also consider in thine heart, that, as a man chasteneth his son, *so* the LORD thy God chasteneth thee" (De.8:5).

"Blessed *is* the man whom thou chastenest, O LORD, and teachest him out of thy law" (Ps.94:12).

"My son, despise not the chastening of the LORD; neither be weary of his correction: For whom the LORD loveth he correcteth; even as a father the son *in whom* he delighteth" (Pr.3:11-12).

"O LORD, I know that the way of man *is* not in himself: *it is* not in man that walketh to direct his steps. O LORD, correct me, but with judgment; not in thine anger, lest thou bring me to nothing" (Je.10:23-24).

d. *They continued to pursue worldly pleasures* (v.13). Isaiah predicted that even when they were facing doom, the Jews would continue to "live it up." They would be consumed with a craving to satisfy their sensual desires. And they would encourage one another in the pursuit of worldly pleasures, saying, "Let us eat and drink, for tomorrow we shall die." When the enemy threatened them, they would make light of the situation, even joke about dying, and continue to pursue sensual pleasures. Down through the years, they would totally disregard the warnings of God's prophets.

"And that which fell among thorns are they, which, when they have heard, go forth, and are choked with cares and riches and pleasures of *this* life, and bring no fruit to perfection" (Lu.8:14).

"And I will say to my soul, Soul, thou hast much goods laid up for many years; take thine ease, eat, drink, *and* be merry. But God said unto him, *Thou* fool, this night thy soul shall be required of thee: then whose shall those things be, which thou hast provided? So *is* he that layeth up treasure for himself, and is not rich toward God" (Lu.12:19-21).

"For the heart of this people is waxed gross, and their ears are dull of hearing, and their eyes have they closed; lest they should see with *their* eyes, and hear with *their* ears, and understand with *their* heart, and should be converted, and I should heal them" (Ac.28:27).

"For they that are after the flesh do mind the things of the flesh; but they that are after the Spirit the things of the Spirit" (Ro.8:5).

"Now the works of the flesh are manifest, which are *these;* Adultery, fornication, uncleanness, lasciviousness, Idolatry, witchcraft, hatred, variance, emulations, wrath, strife, seditions, heresies, Envyings, murders, drunkenness, revellings, and such like: of the which I tell you before, as I have also told *you* in time past, that they which do such things shall not inherit the kingdom of God" (Ga.5:19-21).

"This I say therefore, and testify in the Lord, that ye henceforth walk not as other Gentiles walk, in the vanity of their mind, Having the understanding darkened, being alienated from the life of God through the ignorance that is in them, because of the blindness of their heart: Who being past feeling have given themselves over unto lasciviousness, to work all uncleanness with greediness" (Ep.4:17-19).

"Now the Spirit speaketh expressly, that in the latter times some shall depart from the faith, giving heed to seducing spirits, and doctrines of devils; Speaking lies in hypocrisy; having their conscience seared with a hot iron" (1 Ti.4:1-2).

"But she that liveth in pleasure is dead while she liveth" (1 Ti.5:6).

"And shall receive the reward of unrighteousness, *as* they that count it pleasure to riot in the daytime. Spots *they are* and blemishes, sporting themselves with their own deceivings while they feast with you" (2 Pe.2:13).

"Love not the world, neither the things *that are* in the world. If any man love the world, the love of the Father is not in him. For all that *is* in the world, the lust of the flesh, and the lust of the eyes, and the pride of life, is not of the Father, but is of the world" (1 Jn.2:15-16).

"He that loveth pleasure *shall be* a poor man: he that loveth wine and oil shall not be rich" (Pr.21:17).

e. *They were stiff-necked and hard-hearted* (v.14). The Jews were so stubborn that they would sin beyond the point of repentance, beyond the point where forgiveness was possible. The LORD God of hosts (LORD Almighty) told Isaiah that the Jews would continue to sin until the day they died. Because of their hard hearts there would be no atonement for them. What a tragic indictment of any people!

Thought 1. If we continue to commit sin after sin, we harden our hearts. This is a dangerous path to walk because we can harden our consciences to such a degree that we eventually call sin good and righteousness evil. Sin is so deceptive that it can lead us to…

- twist the truth
- persecute the righteous
- condone or ignore the wicked
- idolize the most depraved
- demean the most upright

God's Word warns us: we can become so stiff-necked and hard-hearted that we doom ourselves. We can actually sin beyond the point of being able to repent and thus be beyond forgiveness. Listen to God's holy Word:

> **"Ye stiffnecked and uncircumcised in heart and ears, ye do always resist the Holy Ghost: as your fathers *did*, so *do* ye" (Ac.7:51).**
> **"But after thy hardness and impenitent heart treasurest up unto thyself wrath against the day of wrath and revelation of the righteous judgment of God; Who will render to every man according to his deeds: To them who by patient continuance in well doing seek for glory and honour and immortality, eternal life: But unto them that are contentious, and do not obey the truth, but obey unrighteousness, indignation and wrath, Tribulation and anguish, upon every soul of man that doeth evil, of the Jew first, and also of the Gentile" (Ro.2:5-9).**
> **"Take heed, brethren, lest there be in any of you an evil heart of unbelief, in departing from the living God. But exhort one another daily, while it is called To day; lest any of you be hardened through the deceitfulness of sin" (He.3:12-13).**
> **"Yet he sent prophets to them, to bring them again unto the LORD; and they testified against them: but they would not give ear" (2 Chr.24:19).**
> **"Harden not your heart, as in the provocation, *and* as *in* the day of temptation in the wilderness: When your fathers tempted me, proved me, and saw my work. Forty years long was I grieved with *this* generation, and said, It *is* a people that do err in their heart, and they have not known my ways: Unto whom I sware in my wrath that they should not enter into my rest" (Ps.95:8-11).**
> **"Happy *is* the man that feareth alway: but he that hardeneth his heart shall fall into mischief" (Pr.28:14).**
> **"He, that being often reproved hardeneth *his* neck, shall suddenly be destroyed, and that without remedy" (Pr.29:1).**
> **"*As for* the word that thou hast spoken unto us in the name of the LORD, we will not hearken unto thee" (Je.44:16).**
> **"But they refused to hearken, and pulled away the shoulder, and stopped their ears, that they should not hear" (Zec.7:11).**

f. *Their leaders were unfaithful* (vv.15-19). In this particular instance, the LORD gave the specific example of Shebna, who was second only to Hezekiah in authority and power. Shebna's position was comparable to that of a vice-president. He was one of the royal officials who negotiated with the Assyrians when Sennacherib laid siege to Jerusalem in 701 B.C. At some point in his career, he began to use his authority and wealth pridefully and most unwisely. As a result, he stopped serving the people and began to serve himself. He built what was apparently a huge tomb as a monument to his name and sought the power and honor that belonged only to the king. Through Isaiah, the LORD warned Shebna that he must repent or else God would seize him like a ball and throw him into captivity where he would die. He would leave behind all his prized chariots, which indicates that he was a man of great wealth and power. But because of his pride and self-exaltation, he would lose everything and die a disgrace, bringing shame upon the king's house.

Thought 1. All people who are gripped by sinful pride and exalt themselves above others will face the judgment of God. This is especially true for leaders, who should be serving people, not neglecting or exploiting them. Listen to what God's Word says about those who in their pride exalt themselves above others:

> **"And whosoever shall exalt himself shall be abased; and he that shall humble himself shall be exalted" (Mt.23:12).**
> **"He hath put down the mighty from *their* seats, and exalted them of low degree" (Lu.1:52).**
> **"Look on every one *that is* proud, *and* bring him low; and tread down the wicked in their place" (Jb.40:12).**
> **"A man's pride shall bring him low: but honour shall uphold the humble in spirit" (Pr.29:23).**
> **"For the day of the LORD of hosts *shall be* upon every *one that is* proud and lofty, and upon every *one that is* lifted up; and he shall be brought low" (Is.2:12).**
> **"For thou hast said in thine heart, I will ascend into heaven, I will exalt my throne above the stars of God: I will sit also upon the mount of the congregation, in the sides of the north: I will ascend above the heights of the clouds; I will be like the most High. Yet thou shalt be brought down to hell, to the sides of the pit" (Is.14:13-15).**
> **"Son of man, say unto the prince of Tyrus, Thus saith the Lord GOD; Because thine heart *is* lifted up, and thou hast said, I *am* a God, I sit *in* the seat of God, in the midst of the seas; yet thou *art* a man, and not God, though thou set thine heart as the heart of God: Behold, thou *art* wiser than Daniel; there is no secret that they can hide from thee: With thy wisdom and with thine understanding thou hast**

gotten thee riches, and hast gotten gold and silver into thy treasures: By thy great wisdom *and* by thy traffick hast thou increased thy riches, and thine heart is lifted up because of thy riches: Therefore thus saith the Lord GOD; Because thou hast set thine heart as the heart of God; Behold, therefore I will bring strangers upon thee, the terrible of the nations: and they shall draw their swords against the beauty of thy wisdom, and they shall defile thy brightness. They shall bring thee down to the pit, and thou shalt die the deaths of *them that are* slain in the midst of the seas" (Eze.28:2-8).

"Though thou exalt *thyself* as the eagle, and though thou set thy nest among the stars, thence will I bring thee down, saith the LORD" (Ob.1:4).

"For, behold, the day cometh, that shall burn as an oven; and all the proud, yea, and all that do wickedly, shall be stubble: and the day that cometh shall burn them up, saith the LORD of hosts, that it shall leave them neither root nor branch" (Mal.4:1).

3 (22:20-25) **Society, Corrupt, Answer to, Godly Leaders—Leaders, Godly, Example—Eliakim, Godly Leader**: in His wonderful grace, the LORD chose a godly leader to replace Shebna. Hezekiah appointed Eliakim as the government administrator, and God clothed him with the authority that had once been Shebna's. Unlike Shebna who had exploited the people, Eliakim would be like a *father* to the people of Judah and would serve them faithfully. Note the LORD's wonderful promise: He would place on Eliakim's shoulder a key to the house of David, the very power of the throne itself. Sometime later the Messiah, the Lord Jesus Christ, would hold the keys to the house of David (Re.3:7). This means that Eliakim was a picture or type of the coming Messiah.

The LORD also promised that as prime minister, Eliakim would be like a well-driven peg in the nation, which meant that he would be the key person holding the nation together (v.23). And although he would bring honor to his family in that position, he would not be able to stop God's judgment, the fall of Jerusalem (v.25). For *in that day*, the day of God's judgment, he would be only a peg, only a man who would himself be cut down (that is, die), and the burden he was holding up would fall. No matter how trustworthy Eliakim was, the Jews should not put their ultimate trust in him; for he was only a man, and he would die along with the other Jews.

OUTLINE	SCRIPTURE	SCRIPTURE	OUTLINE

3. The grace of God in raising up the godly leader Eliakim: A type of Jesus Christ
 	
a. He would replace Shebna as government administrator, 36:3
  1) Would be clothed with all the authority of the minister
  2) Would be made a father—the head—of the people
  3) Would be given the key to the house of David—the very power of the throne itself: A picture of Jesus Christ, Re.3:7
b. He would be like a well-
	20 And it shall come to pass in that day, that I will call my servant Eliakim the son of Hilkiah:
	21 And I will clothe him with thy robe, and strengthen him with thy girdle, and I will commit thy government into his hand: and he shall be a father to the inhabitants of Jerusalem, and to the house of Judah.
	22 And the key of the house of David will I lay upon his shoulder; so he shall open, and none shall shut; and he shall shut, and none shall open.
	23 And I will fasten him as a
		nail in a sure place; and he shall be for a glorious throne to his father's house.
		24 And they shall hang upon him all the glory of his father's house, the offspring and the issue, all vessels of small quantity, from the vessels of cups, even to all the vessels of flagons.
		25 In that day, saith the LORD of hosts, shall the nail that is fastened in the sure place be removed, and be cut down, and fall; and the burden that *was* upon it shall be cut off: for the LORD hath spoken *it*.
			driven peg in the nation, one of the key persons who helps hold the nation together
			c. He would bear heavy responsibility & bring honor to his family
			
			d. He would, however, be unable to stop God's judgment: The fall of Jerusalem
			  1) He was only a peg, a man
			  2) He would be sheared off (die): All who were supported by the peg would collapse

Thought 1. The world desperately needs a Savior, someone who can bring peace and economic security to the world. Consider the hostility, conflict, pain, suffering, and all the other ills rampant in the world. Throughout history people have looked for a savior among their leaders, but they have always been sadly disappointed. No human being can bring true peace and prosperity to the world, for we are all unable to see into the future or control it, no matter how hard we try. Moreover, we are mortal and have only a few short years on earth. A savior who can bring lasting peace and economic security simply cannot be found among humankind. He must come from God.

This is the glorious gospel of the Lord Jesus Christ. God has demonstrated His grace to the world by sending His Son to bring peace to earth. Because of Him, there can be peace among people, peace between…

- husband and wife
- neighbors
- employers and employees
- church members
- races
- social classes
- nations and governments

Jesus Christ alone can bring peace and economic security to this world. He promises to richly bless all who trust in Him and to provide for all the necessities of life. In addition, He promises us full, purposeful, and victorious lives. He alone is the promised Messiah, the Savior of the world. Listen to what God's Holy Word says:

"But seek ye first the kingdom of God, and his righteousness; and all these things shall be added unto you" (Mt.6:33).

"Peace I leave with you, my peace I give unto you: not as the world giveth, give I unto you. Let not your heart be troubled, neither let it be afraid" (Jn.14:27).

"These things I have spoken unto you, that in me ye might have peace. In the world ye shall have tribulation: but be of good cheer; I have overcome the world" (Jn.16:33).

"The word which *God* sent unto the children of Israel, preaching peace by Jesus Christ: (he is Lord of all:)" (Ac.10:36).

"Therefore being justified by faith, we have peace with God through our Lord Jesus Christ" (Ro.5:1).

"For the kingdom of God is not meat and drink; but righteousness, and peace, and joy in the Holy Ghost" (Ro.14:17).

"But the fruit of the Spirit is love, joy, peace, longsuffering, gentleness, goodness, faith, Meekness, temperance: against such there is no law" (Ga.5:22-23).

"For he is our peace, who hath made both one, and hath broken down the middle wall of partition *between us*" (Ep.2:14).

"Be careful for nothing; but in every thing by prayer and supplication with thanksgiving let your requests be made known unto God. And the peace of God, which passeth all understanding, shall keep your hearts and minds through Christ Jesus" (Ph.4:6-7).

"But my God shall supply all your need according to his riches in glory by Christ Jesus" (Ph.4:19).

"And, having made peace through the blood of his cross, by him to reconcile all things unto himself; by him, *I say*, whether *they be* things in earth, or things in heaven" (Col.1:20).

"And let the peace of God rule in your hearts, to the which also ye are called in one body; and be ye thankful" (Col.3:15).

"O let the nations be glad and sing for joy: for thou shalt judge the people righteously, and govern the nations upon earth. Selah" (Ps.67:4).

"For he satisfieth the longing soul, and filleth the hungry soul with goodness" (Ps.107:9).

"And he shall judge among the nations, and shall rebuke many people: and they shall beat their swords into plowshares, and their spears into pruninghooks: nation shall not lift up sword against nation, neither shall they learn war any more" (Is.2:4).

"For unto us a child is born, unto us a son is given: and the government shall be upon his shoulder: and his name shall be called Wonderful, Counsellor, The mighty God, The everlasting Father, The Prince of Peace" (Is.9:6).

"But he *was* wounded for our transgressions, *he was* bruised for our iniquities: the chastisement of our peace *was* upon him; and with his stripes we are healed" (Is.53:5).

"Behold, the days come, saith the LORD, that the plowman shall overtake the reaper, and the treader of grapes him that soweth seed; and the mountains shall drop sweet wine, and all the hills shall melt" (Am.9:13).

CHAPTER 23

G. God's Judgment of Tyre (Phoenicia): A Picture of the Proud Being Humbled Yet Given Hope, 23:1-18

1. The destruction of Tyre's harbor predicted: A picture of being humbled by God
a. The anguish of the Mediterranean nations
  1) Felt by Tarshish, Spain
  2) Felt by Cyprus
  3) Felt by Sidon & the countries surrounding the Mediterranean Sea
  4) Felt deeply by Egypt (Sihor)
    • The problem: They could no longer trade the grain of the Nile
    • The reason: Tyre had been the marketplace of the world
  5) Felt deeply by Sidon: Thereafter the number of seamen from the city would be few
  6) Felt immensely by Egypt

b. The cry to Tyre's refugees: Flee to Spain because the ancient city of joy (revelry, partying) & wealthy trade would be destroyed

c. The agent of the judgment
  1) The question: Who planned the destruction of Tyre, a city so mighty & rich?

  2) The answer: The LORD of hosts
  3) The purpose: To humble the prideful

d. The extent of the destruction
  1) Would ruin the trade of

The burden of Tyre. Howl, ye ships of Tarshish; for it is laid waste, so that there is no house, no entering in: from the land of Chittim it is revealed to them.
2 Be still, ye inhabitants of the isle; thou whom the merchants of Zidon, that pass over the sea, have replenished.
3 And by great waters the seed of Sihor, the harvest of the river, is her revenue; and she is a mart of nations.
4 Be thou ashamed, O Zidon: for the sea hath spoken, even the strength of the sea, saying, I travail not, nor bring forth children, neither do I nourish up young men, nor bring up virgins.
5 As at the report concerning Egypt, so shall they be sorely pained at the report of Tyre.
6 Pass ye over to Tarshish; howl, ye inhabitants of the isle.
7 Is this your joyous city, whose antiquity is of ancient days? her own feet shall carry her afar off to sojourn.
8 Who hath taken this counsel against Tyre, the crowning city, whose merchants are princes, whose traffickers are the honourable of the earth?
9 The LORD of hosts hath purposed it, to stain the pride of all glory, and to bring into contempt all the honourable of the earth.
10 Pass through thy land as a river, O daughter of

Tarshish: there is no more strength.
11 He stretched out his hand over the sea, he shook the kingdoms: the LORD hath given a commandment against the merchant city, to destroy the strong holds thereof.
12 And he said, Thou shalt no more rejoice, O thou oppressed virgin, daughter of Zidon: arise, pass over to Chittim; there also shalt thou have no rest.
13 Behold the land of the Chaldeans; this people was not, til the Assyrian founded it for them that dwell in the wilderness: they set up the towers thereof, they raised up the palaces thereof; and he brought it to ruin.
14 Howl, ye ships of Tarshish: for your strength is laid waste.
15 And it shall come to pass in that day, that Tyre shall be forgotten seventy years, according to the days of one king: after the end of seventy years shall Tyre sing as an harlot.
16 Take an harp, go about the city, thou harlot that hast been forgotten; make sweet melody, sing many songs, that thou mayest be remembered.
17 And it shall come to pass after the end of seventy years, that the LORD will visit Tyre, and she shall turn to her hire, and shall commit fornication with all the kingdoms of the world upon the face of the earth.
18 And her merchandise and her hire shall be holiness to the LORD: it shall not be treasured nor laid up; for her merchandise shall be for them that dwell before the LORD, to eat sufficiently, and for durable clothing.

Spain by destroying the harbor of Tyre
  2) Would shake the economies of all the kingdoms of the sea
  3) Would destroy the defenses of the merchant nation Phoenicia or Canaan
  4) Would stop the revelry, drunkenness, & immorality of the people
  5) Would give no rest even to the refugees

  6) Would destroy Tyre just as Babylon had been destroyed by Assyria
    • To be inhabited by the wild animals
    • To be attacked, laid siege to, & utterly ruined
  7) Would cause the sailors of Spain (the world) to wail over the economic loss

2. The hope of Tyre's restoration predicted: A look ahead to the coming kingdom of Christ
a. Restoration would take place after 70 years, Je.25:11-12; 29:10

  1) After 70 years Tyre would be like an old prostitute seeking once again to ply her trade by singing songs to attract former customers

  2) After 70 years the LORD would revive Tyre: The city would commit fornication with other nations—carry on selfish, immoral, dishonest, & covetous dealings

b. Restoration would be fully realized in the future kingdom of Christ
  1) Tyre's wealth would be holy, set apart for the LORD
  2) Tyre's wealth would be for those who live for the LORD

DIVISION II

THE PROPHECIES CONCERNING GOD'S JUDGMENT OF THE NATIONS AND HIS TRIUMPH OVER THE WORLD, 13:1–27:13

G. God's Judgment of Tyre (Phoenicia): A Picture of the Proud Being Humbled, Yet Given Hope, 23:1-18

(23:1-18) **Introduction**: God despises sinful pride. There is a legitimate pride and an illegitimate pride. Pride in oneself is essential for a healthy personality and a productive, fruitful life. All people should esteem themselves—but not too highly, for every person has weaknesses that must be acknowledged in order to strengthen them. An unacknowledged weakness will grow into a greater weakness. And the greater a weakness is, the more it will eat away at a person's strength. For this reason we must never walk around arrogantly, exalting ourselves and denying our weaknesses.

When we are always looking at ourselves, thinking only of our own affairs, we are being self-centered. We are considering ourselves more important than others. To avoid this, we must give attention to the concerns of others. Walking humbly among others, acknowledging them, and being friendly with them pleases the LORD. No matter what our social position in life, no matter where we live or how much money we make, we are to acknowledge the dignity of all other human beings. Every human being is a living person with an immortal soul that is important to God. Therefore, we are to take an interest in and care for our fellow human beings. To esteem ourselves more highly than anyone else is sinful pride, and God despises it.

Sinful pride was the great offense of the ancient city of Tyre. In the days of Isaiah the prophet, Tyre was already an ancient city, having been founded more than two thousand years earlier. It was a great commercial and shipping center, one of the major market centers of the world. Remember the relationship that David had established with King Hiram, the ruler of Tyre, which lay only about one hundred miles north of Jerusalem (2 S.5:11). Because of the city's excellent seaport, the best quality materials were shipped there from all over the world. Interestingly, the infamous Jezebel was the daughter of the King of Sidon, the twin city of Tyre, which was located about 25 miles north of it. In the present Scripture, Isaiah is pronouncing God's judgment on Tyre. The great seaport city was to be destroyed due to its sinful pride and the wicked lives of its citizens. This is, *God's Judgment of Tyre (Phoenicia): A Picture of the Proud Being Humbled Yet Given Hope*, 23:1-18.

1. The destruction of Tyre's harbor predicted: a picture of being humbled by God (vv.1-14).
2. The hope of Tyre's restoration predicted: a look ahead to the coming kingdom of Christ (vv.15-18).

1 (23:1-14) **Judgment, of Tyre—Judgment, of Phoenicia—Destruction, Caused by, Judgment of Tyre—God, Judgments of, Against Tyre—Spain, Economy Ruined, Due to Judgment—Cyprus, Economy Ruined, Due to Judgment—Egypt, Economy Ruined, Due to Judgment—Sidon, Economy Ruined, Due to Judgment—Mediterranean, Countries Surrounding, Economy Ruined**: the coming destruction of Tyre was announced by God's prophet Isaiah. Part of this important commercial city had been built on an island that lay about a half-mile offshore from the main part of the city. In Isaiah's day, the Assyrian king Sargon conquered the city on the mainland but could not take the island port of Tyre. Some time later, both Shalmanezer and Nebuchadnezzar of Babylon attacked the city, but only Alexander the Great was able to conquer the offshore island (332 B.C.) He did this by building a roadway from the mainland to the island. After he reached the island, he utterly destroyed it and the harbor. Subsequently, the city was rebuilt, for the book of *Acts* says that a church was firmly established in Tyre (Ac.21:3-6). Yet from the time of Isaiah until the time it was rebuilt, the city was to be attacked time and again, suffering the judgment of God because of its people's defiance and rejection of the LORD. Note the Scripture and outline:

OUTLINE	SCRIPTURE	SCRIPTURE	OUTLINE
1. The destruction of Tyre's harbor predicted: A picture of being humbled by God a. The anguish of the Mediterranean nations 1) Felt by Tarshish, Spain 2) Felt by Cyprus 3) Felt by Sidon & the countries surrounding the Mediterranean Sea 4) Felt deeply by Egypt (Sihor) • The problem: They could no longer trade the grain of the Nile • The reason: Tyre had been the marketplace of the world 5) Felt deeply by Sidon: Thereafter the number of seamen from the city would be few 6) Felt immensely by Egypt b. The cry to Tyre's refugees: Flee to Spain because the ancient city of joy (revelry, partying) & wealthy trade would be destroyed	The burden of Tyre. Howl, ye ships of Tarshish; for it is laid waste, so that there is no house, no entering in: from the land of Chittim it is revealed to them. 2 Be still, ye inhabitants of the isle; thou whom the merchants of Zidon, that pass over the sea, have replenished. 3 And by great waters the seed of Sihor, the harvest of the river, is her revenue; and she is a mart of nations. 4 Be thou ashamed, O Zidon: for the sea hath spoken, even the strength of the sea, saying, I travail not, nor bring forth children, neither do I nourish up young men, nor bring up virgins. 5 As at the report concerning Egypt, so shall they be sorely pained at the report of Tyre. 6 Pass ye over to Tarshish; howl, ye inhabitants of the isle. 7 Is this your joyous city, whose antiquity is of ancient	days? her own feet shall carry her afar off to sojourn. 8 Who hath taken this counsel against Tyre, the crowning city, whose merchants are princes, whose traffickers are the honourable of the earth? 9 The LORD of hosts hath purposed it, to stain the pride of all glory, and to bring into contempt all the honourable of the earth. 10 Pass through thy land as a river, O daughter of Tarshish: there is no more strength. 11 He stretched out his hand over the sea, he shook the kingdoms: the LORD hath given a commandment against the merchant city, to destroy the strong holds thereof. 12 And he said, Thou shalt no more rejoice, O thou oppressed virgin, daughter of Zidon: arise, pass over to Chittim; there also shalt thou have no rest.	c. The agent of the judgment 1) The question: Who planned the destruction of Tyre, a city so mighty & rich? 2) The answer: The LORD of hosts 3) The purpose: To humble the prideful d. The extent of the destruction 1) Would ruin the trade of Spain by destroying the harbor of Tyre 2) Would shake the economies of all the kingdoms of the sea 3) Would destroy the defenses of the merchant nation Phoenicia or Canaan 4) Would stop the revelry, drunkenness, & immorality of the people 5) Would give no rest even to the refugees

OUTLINE	SCRIPTURE	SCRIPTURE	OUTLINE
6) Would destroy Tyre just as Babylon had been destroyed by Assyria • To be inhabited by the wild animals • To be attacked, laid	13 Behold the land of the Chaldeans; this people was not, *til* the Assyrian founded it for them that dwell in the wilderness: they set up the towers thereof, they	raised up the palaces thereof; *and* he brought it to ruin. 14 Howl, ye ships of Tarshish: for your strength is laid waste.	siege to, & utterly ruined 7) Would cause the sailors of Spain (the world) to wail over the economic loss

a. When the hand of God's judgment fell upon Tyre, deep sorrow gripped all the nations surrounding the Mediterranean Sea (vv.1-5). Due to its ideal harbor, Tyre had become a great trade center for all these countries. The very best materials from all over the world were shipped there. Even Solomon turned to Tyre in search of building materials for the temple in Jerusalem (see outline and notes—1 K.5:1-18 for more discussion). The city was a commercial capital, the hub for all shipping trade throughout the Mediterranean world. Consequently, the economy of all these nations would suffer drastically or even collapse if trade with Tyre were cut off. And the trade would be cut off when God's hand of judgment fell. Note the catastrophic impact its fall would have on the nations surrounding the Mediterranean Sea:

1) The sailors (ships) of Tarshish (Spain) would wail in sorrow, for the great seaport of Tyre would be completely destroyed. Not a single house would be left standing, and the harbor would be so devastated that no ship would be able to dock in the port.

2) The economy of Cyprus would be especially hurt. As an island it was totally dependent upon products shipped in from the mainland. Indeed, Cyprus would be the first nation to feel the impact of Tyre's destruction. Isaiah said that word of Tyre's fall would come from the land of Cyprus (v.1). Seamen would bring the news with them when they docked in Cyprus, and then the seamen who shipped out from Cyprus would carry news of the destruction to all the other Mediterranean countries.

3) When news of Tyre's collapse reached these countries, the usual loud noise heard in a port—all the hustle and bustle of doing business—would be silenced (v.2). There would be no loading or unloading of ships from Tyre, and shipping economies would be utterly devastated. Jobs would be lost, money would dry up, businesses would collapse, and great seaports would lose much, if not all, of their commercial traffic. All business that flowed from the international seaport of Tyre would come to a complete standstill. Sidon, the other major Phonecian city, would suffer complete economic collapse, for it was totally dependent upon the commercial traffic of Tyre. Apparently, Sidon's economy rested upon selling goods from Tyre to countries that lay inland.

4) Egypt's economy would also suffer greatly from Tyre's destruction. Egypt's economy was especially dependent upon the harbor at Tyre, for its leaders had arranged commercial contracts with countries all around the known world. The nation depended upon the merchants of Tyre to export its grain. Out of all the products shipped in that day, grain was probably the most important. However with Tyre destroyed, Egypt could no longer trade its immense harvest from the fertile land of the Nile River.

5) When Sidon saw its economy collapse, the city would hang its head in shame (v.4). All the import and export trade upon which the city depended would be lost. Therefore, the number of children from Sidon who would grow up to sail the seas would be few. There would be no port from which they could sail.

6) Again, Isaiah forewarned the Egyptians as well as the people of Judah and the world: Tyre's destruction would cause economic devastation. Egypt especially would be in agony due to the catastrophic impact upon its economy.

b. Isaiah strongly suggested that when the hand of God's judgment began to fall, the citizens of Tyre flee while they still could (vv.6-7). And they should flee far away, all the way to Spain if possible. Tyre, that city of joy, revelry, and wealth, was soon to be destroyed. In Isaiah's day, the city of Tyre was already over two thousand years old. Sadly, down through the years the citizens had turned away from the LORD. They had defied and rebelled against Him. Now, after two thousand years, the city was to suffer God's terrifying judgment. Thus, the prophet gave the wisest advice he could to any who would hear: flee the coming wrath of God.

c. Who planned this judgment of destruction upon Tyre, a city so mighty and rich (vv.8-14)? The LORD of hosts, the LORD Almighty planned it. He had a very specific purpose in mind—to humble all the powerful, proud nations of the earth. He would humble them by devastating their economies. Some, and perhaps most, would suffer financial collapse and the loss of all their possessions and wealth.

d. To stress how utterly destroyed Tyre would be, Isaiah gave a graphic, sevenfold description of the coming judgment (vv.10-14).

1) The trade of Spain would cease when the harbor of Tyre was destroyed (v.10). Spain's economy would become extremely weak.

2) All the kingdoms around the Mediterranean Sea would be shaken to their core (v.11). Their economies would either collapse or be on the verge of collapsing. Note why: because the LORD will have stretched out His hand over the Mediterranean Sea. He and He alone would ruin the economies of these countries as He executed judgment upon those who rejected and defied Him.

3) A definite command from the LORD Himself doomed the merchant nation Phoenicia and destroyed its defenses (11b). It should be noted that some versions of the Bible translate the Hebrew word here as Canaan; that is, the LORD commanded that Canaan be destroyed. From the surrounding context, the correct translation seems to be Phoenicia, but perhaps Isaiah was either thinking of Phoenicia's location within the promised land of Canaan, or saying that Canaan was to be destroyed by the same invading army that devastated the land of Phoenicia.

4) All the joy and revelry in Tyre would stop (v.12). As has been true with all major cities down through history, Tyre was a city of partying, drunkenness, and immorality. When the hand of God's judgment fell, all this wickedness would cease at once.

5) Even if refugees from Tyre fled to Cyprus, they would find no rest or escape from suffering, for the economy of Cyprus would collapse due to lack of trade with Tyre (v.12). Isaiah might also have been warning that the cruel Assyrians were going to conquer Cyprus, which they eventually did.

6) Tyre was going to be destroyed just as Babylon had been destroyed by Assyria (v.13). The ancient city would be attacked, sieged, and utterly ruined. Only wild animals would inhabit it.

7) Again, Tyre's destruction would cause the sailors of Spain, who represented the world, to weep over the economic loss (v.14). The word *strength* (or *fortress*) probably refers to the strong economy of Spain and perhaps other countries. Note that this section closes just as it opened, with a warning that Spain should howl because of the coming judgment and destruction of Tyre (v.1, 14).

Thought 1. When God's judgment fell upon Tyre, the known world of that day was humbled. The day is coming when our world will also be humbled. God forewarns us: the day of judgment is coming. Either we humble ourselves now, or God will humble us in that day. We will either bow the knee before Christ now, or we will bow the knee on Judgment Day. The choice is ours alone. If we reject or deny the LORD, defying His name in this world, He will humble us. No defiant person will escape. Any person who refuses to acknowledge God's Son, the Lord Jesus Christ, will be humbled. God loves His Son above all else, so much that He will never tolerate abuse of Christ's name. If a person walks through life defying and cursing the Lord's name, there is no chance this person will ever escape the hand of God's judgment. This person will come to the end of life and suddenly be snatched into the next life, still continuing in his defiance, unbelief, and cursing. And he will continue to be separated from God forever. God will reject the person because he never bowed the knee to humble himself and acknowledge Jesus Christ as God's Son, the Savior of the world. Listen to what God says about humbling ourselves and acknowledging the Lord:

"And whosoever shall exalt himself shall be abased; and he that shall humble himself shall be exalted" (Mt.23:12).

"Then began he to upbraid the cities wherein most of his mighty works were done, because they repented not: Woe unto thee, Chorazin! woe unto thee, Bethsaida! for if the mighty works, which were done in you, had been done in Tyre and Sidon, they would have repented long ago in sackcloth and ashes. But I say unto you, It shall be more tolerable for Tyre and Sidon at the day of judgment, than for you. And thou, Capernaum, which art exalted unto heaven, shalt be brought down to hell: for if the mighty works, which have been done in thee, had been done in Sodom, it would have remained until this day" (Mt.11:20-23).

"I tell you, Nay: but, except ye repent, ye shall all likewise perish" (Lu.13:3).

"For God sent not his Son into the world to condemn the world; but that the world through him might be saved. He that believeth on him is not condemned: but he that believeth not is condemned already, because he hath not believed in the name of the only begotten Son of God" (Jn.3:17-18).

"He that believeth on the Son hath everlasting life: and he that believeth not the Son shall not see life; but the wrath of God abideth on him" (Jn.3:36).

"For the wrath of God is revealed from heaven against all ungodliness and unrighteousness of men, who hold the truth in unrighteousness" (Ro.1:18).

"And being found in fashion as a man, he humbled himself, and became obedient unto death, even the death of the cross. Wherefore God also hath highly exalted him, and given him a name which is above every name: That at the name of Jesus every knee should bow, of *things* in heaven, and *things* in earth, and *things* under the earth; And *that* every tongue should confess that Jesus Christ *is* Lord, to the glory of God the Father" (Ph.2:8-11).

"Kiss the Son, lest he be angry, and ye perish *from* the way, when his wrath is kindled but a little. Blessed *are* all they that put their trust in him" (Ps.2:12).

"But if the wicked will turn from all his sins that he hath committed, and keep all my statutes, and do that which is lawful and right, he shall surely live, he shall not die" (Eze.18:21).

[2] **(23:15-18) Tyre, Promises to, Restoration—Tyre, Prophecies Concerning, Restoration—Prophecies, Concerning Tyre, to Be Restored—Messiah, Kingdom of, Prophecies Concerning—Kingdom, of the Messiah, Prophecies Concerning**: the hope of Tyre's restoration was prophesied by the prophet Isaiah. Once Tyre was destroyed, the city that had once been a commercial giant among nations would be forgotten. It would no longer be an international hub for shipping, trade, or business dealings. From the perspective of international business, the city would lie dormant for 70 years. From about 700–630 B.C., the Assyrians ruled over Tyre and refused to allow the city to recapture its former commercial glory.

But at the end of the 70 years, about the time Assyria's power began to decline, Isaiah predicted that Tyre would seek to arise from the ashes of economic devastation. Using pictorial language, he said that Tyre would be like an old prostitute who seeks once again to ply her trade by singing songs to attract former customers (v.16). No doubt Isaiah was also picturing a worn out but proud city seeking to regain its former glory. But note, it would be the LORD Himself stirring up Tyre to once more become a world-class economic center for commercial shipping.

Just like the old prostitute, Tyre would again commit fornication with other nations by carrying on selfish, immoral, and dishonest business dealings. Although not all business dealings are illegitimate, some are. When people with depraved hearts engage in any enterprise, they tarnish the undertaking with their sinful dealings. Thus it would be with Tyre. Many of its commercial dealings would be honest, but some would be corrupt.

However, note the wonderful promise God made to the citizens of Tyre. Looking way ahead, the LORD promised the city and its citizens full restoration. When? In the future kingdom of the promised Messiah, the Lord Jesus Christ (v.18). *In that day*, Tyre's wealth will be holy, set apart for the LORD. The most wonderful thing will happen when Christ rules upon the earth: wealth will no longer be hoarded. Wealth will be used to eliminate all poverty, hunger, homelessness, unemployment, disease, and lack of education all over the world. Wealth will be used in the most profitable way possible to make sure everyone can live a productive, fruitful life that is completely free of economic suffering. Tyre's wealth will be used to help meet the needs of the world.

OUTLINE	SCRIPTURE	SCRIPTURE	OUTLINE
2. The hope of Tyre's restoration predicted: A look ahead to the coming kingdom of Christ a. Restoration would take place after 70 years, Je.25:11-12; 29:10 1) After 70 years Tyre would be like an old prostitute seeking once again to ply her trade by singing songs to attract former customers 2) After 70 years the LORD would revive Tyre: The	15 And it shall come to pass in that day, that Tyre shall be forgotten seventy years, according to the days of one king: after the end of seventy years shall Tyre sing as an harlot. 16 Take an harp, go about the city, thou harlot that hast been forgotten; make sweet melody, sing many songs, that thou mayest be remembered. 17 And it shall come to pass after the end of seventy years,	that the LORD will visit Tyre, and she shall turn to her hire, and shall commit fornication with all the kingdoms of the world upon the face of the earth. 18 And her merchandise and her hire shall be holiness to the LORD: it shall not be treasured nor laid up; for her merchandise shall be for them that dwell before the LORD, to eat sufficiently, and for durable clothing.	city would commit fornication with other nations—carry on selfish, immoral, dishonest, & covetous dealings b. Restoration would be fully realized in the future kingdom of Christ 1) Tyre's wealth would be holy, set apart for the LORD 2) Tyre's wealth would be for those who live for the LORD

Thought 1. When Christ returns to earth, He will meet every need in the world. No person will lack anything. All needs will be met. But what about today? How about the needs that confront us now? Needs such as…

* sufficient finances
* gainful employment
* training or skills to secure adequate employment
* food, clothing, and housing
* adequate heat and shelter during extreme weather

An endless number of needs exist among people today. What can the Messiah, Christ our Lord, do to help meet these needs now? He gives us the most wonderful promise: if we will seek God and His kingdom first, He will help us meet our needs. If we will believe in Christ, turn our lives over to Him, and obey His Holy Word, He promises to provide us with the basic necessities of life. He will make sure we have food, clothing, and housing. This does not mean that we are to sit around lazily waiting for God to meet these needs. To the contrary, the LORD teaches that we are to work diligently at our jobs and be faithful in all our tasks. When we are faithful, He makes sure that our basic needs are met. If by chance we are unemployed but diligently trying to find jobs to provide for our families, He will provide for us—if we are genuine believers. The LORD must provide if we are faithful, for if He did not, He would be untrue to His Word. But we can rest assured that the LORD is not a deceiver. He never lies. He always fulfills His promises. If we are genuinely trusting Him and doing all we can to meet our needs, He will provide for us. This is the wonderful promise of His Word:

> **"But seek ye first the kingdom of God, and his righteousness; and all these things shall be added unto you" (Mt.6:33).**
> **"Jesus said unto him, If thou canst believe, all things *are* possible to him that believeth" (Mk.9:23).**
> **"And Jesus said unto them, I am the bread of life: he that cometh to me shall never hunger; and he that believeth on me shall never thirst" (Jn.6:35).**
> **"And we know that all things work together for good to them that love God, to them who are the called according to *his* purpose" (Ro.8:28).**
> **"For our light affliction, which is but for a moment, worketh for us a far more exceeding *and* eternal weight of glory" (2 Co.4:17).**
> **"And he said unto me, My grace is sufficient for thee: for my strength is made perfect in weakness. Most gladly therefore will I rather glory in my infirmities, that the power of Christ may rest upon me" (2 Co.12:9).**
> **"Now unto him that is able to do exceeding abundantly above all that we ask or think, according to the power that worketh in us" (Ep.3:20).**
> **"But my God shall supply all your need according to his riches in glory by Christ Jesus" (Ph.4:19).**
> **"For the oppression of the poor, for the sighing of the needy, now will I arise, saith the LORD; I will set *him* in safety *from him that* puffeth at him" (Ps.12:5).**
> **"*Oh* how great *is* thy goodness, which thou hast laid up for them that fear thee; *which* thou hast wrought for them that trust in thee before the sons of men!" (Ps.31:19).**
> **"Trust in the LORD, and do good; *so* shalt thou dwell in the land, and verily thou shalt be fed" (Ps.37:3).**
> **"But I *am* poor and needy; *yet* the Lord thinketh upon me: thou *art* my help and my deliverer; make no tarrying, O my God" (Ps.40:17).**
> **"The LORD will strengthen him upon the bed of languishing: thou wilt make all his bed in his sickness" (Ps.41:3).**

"And call upon me in the day of trouble: I will deliver thee, and thou shalt glorify me" (Ps.50:15).

"I will abundantly bless her provision: I will satisfy her poor with bread" (Ps.132:15).

"Though I walk in the midst of trouble, thou wilt revive me: thou shalt stretch forth thine hand against the wrath of mine enemies, and thy right hand shall save me" (Ps.138:7).

"*When* the poor and needy seek water, and *there is* none, *and* their tongue faileth for thirst, I the LORD will hear them, *I* the God of Israel will not forsake them" (Is.41:17).

"When thou passest through the waters, I *will be* with thee; and through the rivers, they shall not overflow thee: when thou walkest through the fire, thou shalt not be burned; neither shall the flame kindle upon thee" (Is.43:2).

1. The main facts about the coming judgment
a. God Himself will be the agent
b. God will execute a universal judgment
1) It will be totally impartial, Acts 10:34
2) It will be perfect justice: The same for the high & rich as for the low & poor
c. God will devastate the earth, remove everything
1) God's Word declares this fact, Re. chs.6–9; 15–16
2) God will scorch, dry up, & wither the earth: It & the haughty (unbelievers) will pass away

2. The cause of the judgment: Sin—defilement of the earth
a. Disobeyed God's commands
b. Changed His laws (Word)
c. Broke His covenant

3. The results of the judgment
a. A cursed earth, Ge.3:17-19; Ro.8:19-22
b. People doomed: Must pay the penalty, be burned up
c. Few people left: The saved
d. Agriculture devastation
1) The vine (crops) will wither
2) The partying, drinking, & joyous occasions will be stopped
e. Worldwide destruction
1) Cities will lie in ruins
2) Houses will be barred
f. A dismal, gloomy spirit
1) Because all wine is gone
2) Because all joy & gaiety are banished from earth
g. Insecurity & no protection: Due to the cities' lying in ruins

CHAPTER 24

H. God's Judgment of the Whole World, His Universal Judgment: A Time of Great Tribulation, 24:1-23

See Mt.24; Re.6:1–22:21

Behold, the LORD maketh the earth empty, and maketh it waste, and turneth it upside down, and scattereth abroad the inhabitants thereof.
2 And it shall be, as with the people, so with the priest; as with the servant, so with his master; as with the maid, so with her mistress; as with the buyer, so with the seller; as with the lender, so with the borrower; as with the taker of usury, so with the giver of usury to him.
3 The land shall be utterly emptied, and utterly spoiled: for the LORD hath spoken this word.
4 The earth mourneth *and* fadeth away, the world languisheth *and* fadeth away, the haughty people of the earth do languish.
5 The earth also is defiled under the inhabitants thereof; because they have transgressed the laws, changed the ordinance, broken the everlasting covenant.
6 Therefore hath the curse devoured the earth, and they that dwell therein are desolate: therefore the inhabitants of the earth are burned, and few men left.
7 The new wine mourneth, the vine languisheth, all the merryhearted do sigh.
8 The mirth of tabrets ceaseth, the noise of them that rejoice endeth, the joy of the harp ceaseth.
9 They shall not drink wine with a song; strong drink shall be bitter to them that drink it.
10 The city of confusion is broken down: every house is shut up, that no man may come in.
11 *There is* a crying for wine in the streets; all joy is darkened, the mirth of the land is gone.
12 In the city is left desolation, and the gate is smitten with destruction.

13 When thus it shall be in the midst of the land among the people, *there shall be* as the shaking of an olive tree, *and* as the gleaning grapes when the vintage is done.
14 They shall lift up their voice, they shall sing for the majesty of the LORD, they shall cry aloud from the sea.
15 Wherefore glorify ye the LORD in the fires, *even* the name of the LORD God of Israel in the isles of the sea.
16 From the uttermost part of the earth have we heard songs, *even* glory to the righteous. But I said, My leanness, my leanness, woe unto me! the treacherous dealers have dealt treacherously; yea, the treacherous dealers have dealt very treacherously.
17 Fear, and the pit, and the snare, *are* upon thee, O inhabitant of the earth.
18 And it shall come to pass, *that* he who fleeth from the noise of the fear shall fall into the pit; and he that cometh up out of the midst of the pit shall be taken in the snare: for the windows from on high are open, and the foundations of the earth do shake.
19 The earth is utterly broken down, the earth is clean dissolved, the earth is moved exceedingly.
20 The earth shall reel to and fro like a drunkard, and shall be removed like a cottage; and the transgression thereof shall be heavy upon it; and it shall fall, and not rise again.
21 And it shall come to pass in that day, *that* the LORD shall punish the host of the high ones *that are* on high, and the kings of the earth upon the earth.
22 And they shall be gathered together, *as* prisoners are gathered in the pit, and shall be shut up in the prison, and after many days shall they be visited.
23 Then the moon shall be confounded, and the sun ashamed, when the LORD of hosts shall reign in mount Zion, and in Jerusalem, and before his ancients gloriously.

h. Economic & military devastation: Little of anything will be left among the nations, including food

4. The response of the righteous (remnant) to God's judgment: A scene of perfect justice
a. They will praise God's majesty
1) From everywhere—the west, the east, & the islands of the sea—they will all praise the Name of the LORD
2) From the ends of the earth they will praise the execution of justice by the *Righteous One*
b. Isaiah, pondering the coming judgment, cried out in shock & grief: Because of the sin & treachery of people

5. The picture of the coming judgment: A scene of terror & punishment
a. Scene 1: No escape
1) People will be fleeing in terror
2) People will be caught as in a trap or pit, Re.6:15-17
b. Scene 2: Natural disasters
1) Violent storms
2) Earthquakes & volcanic eruptions: Will split the earth apart
c. Scene 3: The fall of the earth & of the present evil world system
1) It will be destroyed
2) It will never rise again: Due to its rebellion
d. Scene 4: The punishment of fallen angels & the rulers of the earth, Ep.6:11f; Jude 6; Re.12:7-9; 20:1-3, 7-10
1) They will be imprisoned
2) They will be punished after being in prison for a long time
e. Scene 5: The glory & reign of the LORD, Re.20:4-10
1) His glory: Brighter than the sun or moon
2) His reign: In Jerusalem

DIVISION II

THE PROPHECIES CONCERNING GOD'S JUDGMENT OF THE NATIONS AND HIS TRIUMPH OVER THE WORLD, 13:1–27:13

H. God's Judgment of the Whole World, His Universal Judgment: A Time of Great Tribulation, 24:1-23

(24:1-23) **Introduction**: the present Scripture is known as *Isaiah's Apocalypse*. After predicting God's coming judgment on the nations—eleven in all—the LORD now pronounces the final judgment on the whole world. The fact that judgment is coming on the entire world is clear. Isaiah used the word *earth* (*erets*) 16 times in this Scripture. Christ Himself referred to a coming period of human history known as the *Great Tribulation* (Mt.24:21 KJV; NKJV; RSV; Douay Version), a period of "great distress" (NIV), "a time of greater horror than anything the world has ever seen or ever will see again" (NLT). It will be a period of horrifying judgment upon the world.

Long before Christ came, the LORD warned people through His prophet Isaiah. Because of all the unrighteousness and ungodliness of people—because of their injustice, oppression, bribery, cruelty, lawlessness, violence, and immorality—the wrath of God is to fall upon the human race. A period of human history known as *The Great Tribulation* is going to come upon the earth. It will be a period of catastrophic devastation and destruction, of fear and terror. This is, *God's Judgment of the Whole World, His Universal Judgment: A Time of Great Tribulation*, 24:1-23.

1. The main facts about the coming judgment (vv.1-4).
2. The cause of the judgment: sin—defilement of the earth (v.5)
3. The results of the judgment (vv.6-13).
4. The response of the righteous (remnant) to God's judgment: a scene of perfect justice (vv.14-16).
5. The picture of the coming judgment: a scene of terror and punishment (vv.17-23).

1 (24:1-4) **Judgment, Facts About, Three Major Facts—Judgment, Who Is to Be Judged—Judgment, Prophecy Concerning—Earth, Judgment of, in the Last Days—Unbelievers, Judgment of, Described—End Times, Day of Judgment, Prophecy Concerning—End Times, Day of Judgment, Discussed**: Isaiah announced three major facts about the coming judgment. Although God's day of universal judgment lies out in the future, readers today still find these three facts deeply disturbing, even mind-boggling. No person will escape the judgment of God, and even the earth itself will be cleansed of its pollution and corruption.

OUTLINE	SCRIPTURE	SCRIPTURE	OUTLINE
1. The main facts about the coming judgment a. God Himself will be the agent b. God will execute a universal judgment 1) It will be totally impartial, Acts 10:34 2) It will be perfect justice: The same for the high & rich as for the low & poor	**B**ehold, the LORD maketh the earth empty, and maketh it waste, and turneth it upside down, and scattereth abroad the inhabitants thereof. 2　And it shall be, as with the people, so with the priest; as with the servant, so with his master; as with the maid, so with her mistress; as with the buyer, so with the seller; as with the lender, so with the	borrower; as with the taker of usury, so with the giver of usury to him. 3　The land shall be utterly emptied, and utterly spoiled: for the LORD hath spoken this word. 4　The earth mourneth *and* fadeth away, the world languisheth *and* fadeth away, the haughty people of the earth do languish.	c. God will devastate the earth, remove everything 1) God's Word declares this fact, Re. chs.6–9; 15–16 2) God will scorch, dry up, & wither the earth: It & the haughty (unbelievers) will pass away

a. Isaiah said that God Himself will be the agent of judgment (v.1). The LORD personally is going to summon all people to appear before Him. Everyone will give an account for what he or she has done. All sin, evil, and wickedness—the lawlessness, violence, destruction, and immorality man has brought to earth—will face the terrifying judgment of God. Even the earth itself, with all its pollution and corruption, will be emptied and made waste. All the inhabitants of earth will be scattered over the face of the earth. At long last the stream of human history will come to that inevitable day when everything that has been corrupted will face the LORD in all His perfection and glory.

b. When the LORD executes judgment, it will be universal (v.2). He is going to summon all people to appear before Him. And the judgment will be impartial, for God is no respecter of persons (Ac.10:34). He will execute perfect justice, showing no partiality whatsoever. The high and the low, the rich and the poor alike will receive perfect justice. Neither position nor power, neither wealth nor fame will provide an escape from the coming judgment of God. Note how Isaiah listed six classes of people grouped in pairs, ranging from one extreme to the other. No matter who they are, they will face the judgment of God. God's justice will be executed the same...

- for priests as for lay persons
- for masters as for servants
- for mistresses as for maids
- for sellers as for buyers
- for borrowers as for lenders
- for bankers as for debtors

c. Third, God's universal judgment will devastate the earth itself (vv.3-4). The earth will be completely emptied and totally plundered. Other Scriptures tell us that God's purpose is to create a new earth that will be free of pollution and the violent, destructive forces of nature. In the present Scripture, the subject is the terrifying judgment of God that is coming upon the whole earth. Just as the earth itself will be scorched and withered, so will haughty people. Those who exalt themselves above others will be stricken by the hand of God's judgment. They will languish, waste, and fade away. People who have based their lives upon power, wealth, and fame will be stripped of everything. The blazing holiness of God will scorch and dry them up.

Thought 1. A day of universal judgment is coming. All the secrets of men and women will be exposed by the blazing holiness of God's righteousness. *In that day*, all the injustice and oppression, lawlessness and violence, pollution and corruption, and the violent disorder of nature will be eliminated from the face of the earth. Listen to what God's Word says about the coming universal judgment:

"**And before him shall be gathered all nations: and he shall separate them one from another, as a shepherd divideth** *his* **sheep from the goats: And he shall set the sheep on his right hand, but the goats on the left....Then shall he say also unto them on the left hand, Depart from me, ye cursed, into everlasting fire, prepared for the devil and his angels**" (Mt.25:32-33, 41).
"**Because he hath appointed a day, in the which he will judge the world in righteousness by** *that* **man whom he hath ordained;** *whereof* **he hath given assurance unto all** *men,* **in that he hath raised him from the dead**" (Ac.17:31).
"**In the day when God shall judge the secrets of men by Jesus Christ according to my gospel**" (Ro.2:16).
"**So then every one of us shall give account of himself to God**" (Ro.14:12).
"**For we must all appear before the judgment seat of Christ; that every one may receive the things** *done* **in** *his* **body, according to that he hath done, whether** *it be* **good or bad**" (2 Co.5:10).
"**And I saw a great white throne, and him that sat on it, from whose face the earth and the heaven fled away; and there was found no place for them. And I saw the dead, small and great, stand before God; and the books were opened: and another book was opened, which is** *the book* **of life: and the dead were judged out of those things which were written in the books, according to their works. And the sea gave up the dead which were in it; and death and hell delivered up the dead which were in them: and they were judged every man according to their works. And death and hell were cast into the lake of fire. This is the second death. And whosoever was not found written in the book of life was cast into the lake of fire**" (Re.20:11-15).

2 (24:5) **Judgment, Caused by—Judgment, Consequences of, a Cursed Earth—Earth, Curse of, Caused by—Penalty, of Sin, Must Be Paid—Sin, Penalty of, to Be Burned Up**: God's judgment is coming due to the sin, wickedness, and unrighteousness of people. Their sins have defiled the entire earth.

OUTLINE	SCRIPTURE
2. The cause of the judgment: Sin—defilement of the earth a. Disobeyed God's commands b. Changed His laws (Word) c. Broke His covenant	5 The earth also is defiled under the inhabitants thereof; because they have transgressed the laws, changed the ordinance, broken the everlasting covenant.

Due to the selfishness and iniquity of people, the earth has been polluted and corrupted. The corruption is so severe that the very forces of nature have been affected. Despite the orderliness of nature, it has been thrown out of balance. All the forces of nature that can be so beautiful have become so destructive that they often kill innocent people and animals and destroy the land in all its natural beauty.

What causes the violent disorder of nature and the wickedness that sweeps the earth? Human beings—men and women who live selfish, sinful lives because they reject, deny, and defy God (Ro.8:20-21). Isaiah spelled out three reasons that judgment is coming:

a. Judgment is coming because people disobey God's commandments (v.5). When people obey God, they live lives of righteousness. Simply stated, righteous people do what is right. They treat other people as they themselves want to be treated, and they love and care for their neighbors. People who obey God's commandments live moral lives that honor both God and others. But disobedient people, those who do not keep God's commandments, mistreat their neighbors. They lie, deceive, cheat, steal, and covet more and more wealth and possessions. And often, they oppress people to secure even more money and things. People who disobey God turn away from the LORD. They either turn to false gods or to the world in search of riches, property, and fame.
b. Judgment is coming because people have sought to change God's Holy Word (v.5). Down through history...
  • some people have denied God's Word, just as they have denied His existence
  • some people have denied certain parts of God's Word, while claiming to accept others
  • some people have twisted the meaning of God's Word, seeking to justify their way of life

There have always been false teachers and those who violate God's Holy Word, both in the church and in society at large. People who live like they want to sometimes try to claim the approval of God in order to justify their

216

sinful behavior or ambitions. So they twist the meaning of God's Word. The LORD will judge this earth because people have attempted to change His laws and commandments.

c. Judgment is coming because people have broken God's "everlasting covenant" (v.5). This probably refers to either one or both of the following covenants:

⇒ The covenant God made with Noah and his sons after the Flood, when He instructed them to look after the earth. They were to establish a just government and true justice upon earth. They were to treat all people as they should be treated, protecting the life of every person (see outline and note—Ge.9:1-17 for more discussion).

⇒ The covenant of conscience, the inner sense of right and wrong that exists in the heart of every human being.

> **"For there is no respect of persons with God. For as many as have sinned without law shall also perish without law: and as many as have sinned in the law shall be judged by the law; (For not the hearers of the law *are* just before God, but the doers of the law shall be justified. For when the Gentiles, which have not the law, do by nature the things contained in the law, these, having not the law, are a law unto themselves: Which show the work of the law written in their hearts, their conscience also bearing witness, and *their* thoughts the mean while accusing or else excusing one another;) In the day when God shall judge the secrets of men by Jesus Christ according to my gospel" (Ro.2:11-16; also see Ro.1:18-32).**

Sadly, every human being violates these covenants. Just how often is clearly seen when each person honestly evaluates his or her own heart. *Honesty* is absolutely essential in any evaluation. Being honest with ourselves is the only way we can escape the judgment of God. Only a truthful evaluation of our lives will stir us to turn to Christ for salvation, and only Christ can save us from the coming judgment.

Two significant passages of Scripture clearly show...

- why God's universal judgment is coming upon the earth
- how desperately all people need to make an honest evaluation of their lives

> **"For the wrath of God is revealed from heaven against all ungodliness and unrighteousness of men, who hold the truth in unrighteousness; Because that which may be known of God is manifest in them; for God hath showed *it* unto them. For the invisible things of him from the creation of the world are clearly seen, being understood by the things that are made, *even* his eternal power and Godhead; so that they are without excuse: Because that, when they knew God, they glorified *him* not as God, neither were thankful; but became vain in their imaginations, and their foolish heart was darkened. Professing themselves to be wise, they became fools, And changed the glory of the uncorruptible God into an image made like to corruptible man, and to birds, and fourfooted beasts, and creeping things. Wherefore God also gave them up to uncleanness through the lusts of their own hearts, to dishonour their own bodies between themselves: Who changed the truth of God into a lie, and worshipped and served the creature more than the Creator, who is blessed for ever. Amen. For this cause God gave them up unto vile affections: for even their women did change the natural use into that which is against nature: And likewise also the men, leaving the natural use of the woman, burned in their lust one toward another; men with men working that which is unseemly, and receiving in themselves that recompence of their error which was meet. And even as they did not like to retain God in *their* knowledge, God gave them over to a reprobate mind, to do those things which are not convenient; Being filled with all unrighteousness, fornication, wickedness, covetousness, maliciousness; full of envy, murder, debate, deceit, malignity; whisperers, Backbiters, haters of God, despiteful, proud, boasters, inventors of evil things, disobedient to parents, Without understanding, covenantbreakers, without natural affection, implacable, unmerciful: Who knowing the judgment of God, that they which commit such things are worthy of death, not only do the same, but have pleasure in them that do them" (Ro.1:18-32).**

> **"What then? are we better *than they?* No, in no wise: for we have before proved both Jews and Gentiles, that they are all under sin; As it is written, There is none righteous, no, not one: There is none that understandeth, there is none that seeketh after God. They are all gone out of the way, they are together become unprofitable; there is none that doeth good, no, not one. Their throat *is* an open sepulchre; with their tongues they have used deceit; the poison of asps *is* under their lips: Whose mouth *is* full of cursing and bitterness: Their feet *are* swift to shed blood: Destruction and misery *are* in their ways: And the way of peace have they not known: There is no fear of God before their eyes. Now we know that what things soever the law saith, it saith to them who are under the law: that every mouth may be stopped, and all the world may become guilty before God" (Ro.3:9-19).**

3 (24:6-13) **Judgment, Caused by, Sin—Sin, Consequences of, Eightfold Judgment—Earth, Curse of, Caused by—Mankind, Sin of, Eightfold Consequence—Earth, Destruction of, Caused by:** the terrifying judgment that will fall upon the earth will be the consequence of sin. Eight very specific consequences are spelled out:

OUTLINE	SCRIPTURE	SCRIPTURE	OUTLINE
3. The results of the judgment a. A cursed earth, Ge.3:17-19; Ro.8:19-22 b. People doomed: Must pay	6 Therefore hath the curse devoured the earth, and they that dwell therein are desolate: therefore the inhabitants	of the earth are burned, and few men left. 7 The new wine mourneth, the vine languisheth, all the	the penalty, be burned up c. Few people left: The saved d. Agriculture devastation

OUTLINE	SCRIPTURE	SCRIPTURE	OUTLINE
1) The vine (crops) will wither 2) The partying, drinking, & joyous occasions will be stopped e. Worldwide destruction 1) Cities will lie in ruins 2) Houses will be barred	merryhearted do sigh. 8 The mirth of tabrets ceaseth, the noise of them that rejoice endeth, the joy of the harp ceaseth. 9 They shall not drink wine with a song; strong drink shall be bitter to them that drink it. 10 The city of confusion is broken down: every house is shut up, that no man may come in.	11 *There is* a crying for wine in the streets; all joy is darkened, the mirth of the land is gone. 12 In the city is left desolation, and the gate is smitten with destruction. 13 When thus it shall be in the midst of the land among the people, *there shall be* as the shaking of an olive tree, *and* as the gleaning grapes when the vintage is done.	f. A dismal, gloomy spirit 1) Because all wine is gone 2) Because all joy & gaiety are banished from earth g. Insecurity & no protection: Due to the cities lying in ruins h. Economic & military devastation: Little of anything will be left among the nations, including food

a. *Cursed earth* (v.6). The sin of the first man, Adam, forced God to put a curse on the earth (see outlines and notes—Ge.3:17-19; Ro.8:19-22 for more discussion). Why? Why would the earth have to suffer a curse when it was Adam who sinned? Because the earth was Adam's home and the home of the members of the human race who were to be his descendants. Adam and the earth were *interrelated*. After he sinned, he was a fallen creature, and God could not let imperfect Adam continue to live in a perfect world. The earth belonged to Adam, and Adam belonged to the earth; they were as closely related as they could be. Therefore, whatever fall Adam suffered, the earth had to suffer as well. Imperfection is not compatible with perfection, and they cannot live together. Imperfection and sin do not belong in a perfect and righteous world. Consequently, God had to curse the earth as part of His judgment upon Adam.

Think of all the pollution and contamination on earth that man's selfishness, greed, and wickedness have caused. Think of all the blood spilled upon the ground through violence, murder, and wars. There is a seed of chaos in nature that often causes nature to erupt in violent disorder and disease, consuming both vegetation and animal life on earth. Both man and nature are out of balance, polluted, corrupted, and gripped by a violent disorder at their very core. One of the consequences is a cursed earth.

b. *Doomed people* (v.6). Once people sin, they must bear the guilt and penalty for their sin. When God's day of judgment comes, the holiness of God will blaze forth like a consuming fire, burning up every person who has continued to walk in sin. God is just, holy, and righteous; therefore, He cannot allow sin to go unpunished. All the inhabitants of the earth who reject God and refuse to turn away from their sin will face the flaming fire of His judgment. They will be burned up. This is the clear warning of God's prophet Isaiah.

c. *Decimated population* (v.6). The third consequence of judgment is terrifying: after God's judgment, only a few people will be left on earth. These few will be those who have trusted God's Son, the Lord Jesus Christ, as their Savior (Jn.3:16-18).

d. *Agricultural ruin* (vv.7-9). The *vine* represents all the agricultural crops people produce. All the crops of earth will wither, and the joyful revelry and partying on earth will stop. No longer will the inhabitants of the earth be drinking or enjoying the joyful occasions they have so often celebrated. The blazing fire of God's holiness will scorch and wither—utterly devastate—all agricultural growth.

e. *Worldwide destruction* (v.10). Cities will lie in ruins. The houses on earth will either be destroyed or boarded up due to the devastation. No one seeking to escape the judgment will be able to enter any home.

f. *All-encompassing gloom* (v.11). A dismal, gloomy spirit will grip people's hearts during the days of God's coming judgment. All the joy and gaiety of people will be banished from the earth. The days of revelry and partying will be over. All happy social events—legitimate and illegitimate, righteous and wicked—will stop in that day of God's wrath.

g. *Insecurity* (v.12). Deep anxiety and uncertainty will also grip people's hearts. There will be no place for people to sleep, no place in the ruined buildings of cities and no rooms in houses whose entrances are barred.

h. *Economic and military devastation* (v.13). Little of anything will be left among the nations, including food. The earth will look like a tree after the fruit has been harvested. The judgment will be sweeping, thorough, complete. It will affect everything and everyone on earth. The entire earth will suffer the judgment at God's hand as the consequence of sin.

"Because he hath appointed a day, in the which he will judge the world in righteousness by *that* man whom he hath ordained; *whereof* he hath given assurance unto all *men*, in that he hath raised him from the dead" (Ac.17:31).

"Wherefore, as by one man sin entered into the world, and death by sin; and so death passed upon all men, for that all have sinned" (Ro.5:12).

"What fruit had ye then in those things whereof ye are now ashamed? for the end of those things *is* death" (Ro.6:21).

"For the wages of sin *is* death; but the gift of God *is* eternal life through Jesus Christ our Lord" (Ro.6:23).

"For such *are* false apostles, deceitful workers, transforming themselves into the apostles of Christ. And no marvel; for Satan himself is transformed into an angel of light. Therefore *it is* no great thing if his ministers also be transformed as the ministers of righteousness; whose end shall be according to their works" (2 Co.11:13-15).

"(For many walk, of whom I have told you often, and now tell you even weeping, *that they are* the enemies of the cross of Christ: Whose end *is* destruction, whose God *is their* belly, and *whose* glory *is* in their shame, who mind earthly things.)" (Ph.3:18-19).

"Therefore we ought to give the more earnest heed to the things which we have heard, lest at any time we should let *them* slip. For if the word spoken by angels was stedfast, and every transgression and disobedience received a just recompence of reward; How shall we escape, if we neglect so great salvation; which at the first began to be spoken by the Lord, and was confirmed unto us by them that heard *him*" (He.2:1-3).

"But that which beareth thorns and briers *is* rejected, and *is* nigh unto cursing; whose end *is* to be burned. But, beloved, we are persuaded better things of you, and things that accompany salvation, though we thus speak" (He.6:8-9).

"The Lord knoweth how to deliver the godly out of temptations, and to reserve the unjust unto the day of judgment to be punished" (2 Pe.2:9).

"But the heavens and the earth, which are now, by the same word are kept in store, reserved unto fire against the day of judgment and perdition of ungodly men" (2 Pe.3:7).

"And Enoch also, the seventh from Adam, prophesied of these, saying, Behold, the Lord cometh with ten thousands of his saints, To execute judgment upon all, and to convince all that are ungodly among them of all their ungodly deeds which they have ungodly committed, and of all their hard *speeches* which ungodly sinners have spoken against him" (Jude 1:14-15).

"But the fearful, and unbelieving, and the abominable, and murderers, and whoremongers, and sorcerers, and idolaters, and all liars, shall have their part in the lake which burneth with fire and brimstone: which is the second death" (Re.21:8).

"But the transgressors shall be destroyed together: the end of the wicked shall be cut off" (Ps.37:38).

"There is a way which seemeth right unto a man, but the end thereof *are* the ways of death" (Pr.14:12).

"He, that being often reproved hardeneth *his* neck, shall suddenly be destroyed, and that without remedy" (Pr.29:1).

"But your iniquities have separated between you and your God, and your sins have hid *his* face from you, that he will not hear" (Is.59:2).

"The soul that sinneth, it shall die" (Eze.18:4).

4 (24:14-16) **Judgment, of the Righteous, Described—Believers, Judgment of, Described—Justice, Perfect Justice, Described—Believers, Response of, to God's Judgment—Judgment, Response to, by Believers**: the response of righteous believers to God's judgment will be entirely different from that of unbelievers. Genuine believers will see God's judgment as the execution of perfect justice upon the earth. They will praise the name of the LORD from everywhere—in the west, east, and the islands of the seas. Why? Because God will erase all the pollution and corruption and remove all oppressors and persecutors of God's people from the earth. Only believers will remain. Although Isaiah does not mention the fact in this passage, the Messiah, the Lord Jesus Christ, will be ready to establish His kingdom on earth. Only those who truly trust the LORD will be left to live with Him and serve Him eternally (see 2:1-5; 4:2-6; 9:1-7; 11:1–12:6; 19:1-22; 25:1-12; 26:1–27:13). From the ends of the earth, true believers will praise the *Righteous One* for executing justice, for the earth will then be a righteous place, and justice will fill it.

But note Isaiah's surprising response as he pondered the vision of the coming judgment: he cried out in shock and grief (v.16). He realized that most people would continue in their sinful, wicked ways. Their dishonesty and deception would continue. People would not change their conduct. They would refuse to repent and turn back to the LORD. Consequently, they would become hard-hearted and suffer the terrifying judgment of God.

Isaiah was almost crushed under the weight of what he witnessed. He cringed inwardly from the burden of distress he felt in his heart. Crying out in deep grief, he exclaimed that an unbearable heaviness and pressure—a *woe*—afflicted him. Thus he was unable to join in the joyful occasion he saw awaiting God's people in the future. The vision of the coming judgment was too terrifying, too horrifying for him to lift his voice in joy. Most people would not heed his warning of coming judgment. Most would not repent and escape the terror that lay right over the horizon.

OUTLINE	SCRIPTURE	SCRIPTURE	OUTLINE
4. The response of the righteous (remnant) to God's judgment: A scene of perfect justice a. They will praise God's majesty 1) From everywhere—the west, the east, & the islands of the sea—they will all praise the Name	14 They shall lift up their voice, they shall sing for the majesty of the LORD, they shall cry aloud from the sea. 15 Wherefore glorify ye the LORD in the fires, *even* the name of the LORD God of Israel in the isles of the sea.	16 From the uttermost part of the earth have we heard songs, *even* glory to the righteous. But I said, My leanness, my leanness, woe unto me! the treacherous dealers have dealt treacherously; yea, the treacherous dealers have dealt very	of the LORD 2) From the ends of the earth they will praise the execution of justice by the *Righteous One* b. Isaiah, pondering the coming judgment, cried out in shock & grief: Because of the sin & treachery of people

Thought 1. True believers will not face the terrifying judgment of God, not what is known as the *Great White Throne* judgment. When the Lord Jesus Christ sits upon the Great White Throne, He will be executing judgment against those who continue to live in sin and shame. *In that day* the wicked—all who disobey God's holy commandments—will be cast from God's presence forever, separated from Him eternally.

But not genuine believers. Once a person places his trust in the Lord Jesus Christ, this person is saved. The person's sins are forgiven, cleansed through the blood of Jesus Christ. Christ died for the sins of the world. The penalty for sin has been paid by Christ; consequently, any person who truly trusts Christ will be forgiven his sins. He or she will be accepted in the righteousness of Christ. Standing in the righteousness of Christ, the person is counted perfect before God. The person becomes acceptable to God. So it is with any of us who have truly trusted Christ. Our sins are forgiven, and we are accepted by God. Consequently, we will never face the judgment of God, never be doomed to be separated from His presence. Listen to the wonderful promise of God's Holy Word.

"For God so loved the world, that he gave his only begotten Son, that whosoever believeth in him should not perish, but have everlasting life. For God sent not his Son into the world to condemn the world; but that the world through him might be saved. He that believeth on him is not condemned: but he that believeth not is condemned already, because he hath not believed in the name of the only begotten Son of God" (Jn.3:16-18).

"Verily, verily, I say unto you, He that heareth my word, and believeth on him that sent me, hath everlasting life, and shall not come into condemnation; but is passed from death unto life" (Jn.5:24).

"There *is* therefore now no condemnation to them which are in Christ Jesus, who walk not after the flesh, but after the Spirit" (Ro.8:1).

"Who *is* he that condemneth? *It is* Christ that died, yea rather, that is risen again, who is even at the right hand of God, who also maketh intercession for us. Who shall separate us from the love of Christ? *shall* tribulation, or distress, or persecution, or famine, or nakedness, or peril, or sword?...Nay, in all these things we are more than conquerors through him that loved us. For I am persuaded, that neither death, nor life, nor angels, nor principalities, nor powers, nor things present, nor things to come, Nor height, nor depth, nor any other creature, shall be able to separate us from the love of God, which is in Christ Jesus our Lord" (Ro.8:34-35, 37-39).

"Christ hath redeemed us from the curse of the law, being made a curse for us: for it is written, Cursed *is* every one that hangeth on a tree" (Ga.3:13).

"In whom we have redemption through his blood, the forgiveness of sins, according to the riches of his grace" (Ep.1:7).

"Who his own self bare our sins in his own body on the tree, that we, being dead to sins, should live unto righteousness: by whose stripes ye were healed" (1 Pe.2:24).

"For Christ also hath once suffered for sins, the just for the unjust, that he might bring us to God, being put to death in the flesh, but quickened by the Spirit" (1 Pe.3:18).

"I, *even* I, *am* he that blotteth out thy transgressions for mine own sake, and will not remember thy sins" (Is.43:25).

"Let the wicked forsake his way, and the unrighteous man his thoughts: and let him return unto the LORD, and he will have mercy upon him; and to our God, for he will abundantly pardon" (Is.55:7).

5 (24:17-23) **Judgment, Terror and Punishment of—Judgment, Picture of, Terror and Punishment—Punishment, of Judgment, Discussed**: the picture of the coming judgment is a frightening one. Isaiah describes scenes of terror and punishment taking place one right after the other. Note the Scripture and outline:

OUTLINE	SCRIPTURE	SCRIPTURE	OUTLINE

5. The picture of the coming judgment: A scene of terror & punishment
a. Scene 1: No escape
  1) People will be fleeing in terror
  2) People will be caught as in a trap or pit, Re.6:15-17
b. Scene 2: Natural disasters
  1) Violent storms
  2) Earthquakes & volcanic eruptions: Will split the earth apart
 	
c. Scene 3: The fall of the earth & of the present evil world system
  1) It will be destroyed
	17 Fear, and the pit, and the snare, *are* upon thee, O inhabitant of the earth.
	18 And it shall come to pass, *that* he who fleeth from the noise of the fear shall fall into the pit; and he that cometh up out of the midst of the pit shall be taken in the snare: for the windows from on high are open, and the foundations of the earth do shake.
	19 The earth is utterly broken down, the earth is clean dissolved, the earth is moved exceedingly.
	20 The earth shall reel to and fro like a drunkard, and shall be removed like a cottage; and the transgression thereof
		shall be heavy upon it; and it shall fall, and not rise again.
		21 And it shall come to pass in that day, *that* the LORD shall punish the host of the high ones *that are* on high, and the kings of the earth upon the earth.
		22 And they shall be gathered together, *as* prisoners are gathered in the pit, and shall be shut up in the prison, and after many days shall they be visited.
		23 Then the moon shall be confounded, and the sun ashamed, when the LORD of hosts shall reign in mount Zion, and in Jerusalem, and before his ancients gloriously.
			2) It will never rise again: Due to its rebellion
			d. Scene 4: The punishment of fallen angels & the rulers of the earth, Ep.6:11f; Jude 6; Re.12:7-9; 20:1-3, 7-10
			
			  1) They will be imprisoned
			  2) They will be punished after being in prison for a long time
			
			e. Scene 5: The glory & reign of the LORD, Re.20:4-10
			  1) His glory: Brighter than the sun or moon
			  2) His reign: In Jerusalem

a. The first scene of the terrible judgment to come shows that there is *no escape*. People will flee the coming wrath, but they will be caught like animals in a trap or pit. No matter how they try to climb out of the pit or free themselves from the trap, God's judgment is too deep and His power too strong for them to escape. The pit and trap are set for the wicked inhabitants of this earth (see outline and notes—Re.6:15-17 for more discussion).

b. The second scene of God's judgment depicts *natural disaster* (vv.18-19). The terror of violent storms, catastrophic earthquakes, and volcanic eruptions will strike the earth. There will be so many that it will seem as though the earth itself is splitting apart. Shaking back and forth, the earth will reel and tremble at the command of God (see outline and note—Re.6:12-17 for more discussion).

c. Scene three shows *the destruction of the earth and the present evil world system* (v.20). God will scorch the earth to cleanse it from all pollution, corruption, and the seed of violent disorder lying within nature (vv.3-6). In addition to the fall of the earth, the present evil world system will be destroyed. All the organizations and structures of society that have been built by the hands of sinful people—governments, businesses, institutions—will be destroyed, never to rise again.

d. As the fourth scene opens, we witness *the punishment of fallen angels and the evil rulers of the earth* (vv.21-22). God's judgment will affect not only the earth, but also all the powers throughout the universe. This is a direct reference to Satan and his demonic forces. These spiritual forces will face the judgment of God just as the rulers of the earth will. Since the beginning of human history, the devil has waged war against the LORD, attempting to break the heart of God by turning people away from Him. Tragically, he has succeeded in captivating the hearts of the majority. Most people live selfish, worldly, and sinful lives, ignoring and denying the LORD. Because of the terrible evil Satan has brought upon the earth and throughout the universe, he will bear the terrifying judgment of God. He and his demonic horde will be herded together like bound prisoners and shut up in a dungeon. After being held in prison for a long time, they will be punished forever in the *Lake of Fire* (see outline and notes—Re.20:1-3; 20:7-10; Ge.3:15; Is.14:1-23; Lu.10:18 for more discussion).

e. The final scene depicts *the glory and reign of the LORD,* which will begin after His judgment (v.23). As Christ Himself revealed, God's judgment will affect even the heavenly bodies (see outline and notes—Mt.24:29 for more discussion). Isaiah said that the moon and sun will be disgraced, ashamed at the terrifying judgment humanity has brought upon the earth. But the judgment will bring about a climactic moment: the revelation of God's glory. God's glory will shine brighter than the sun or moon, and the LORD will reign over the earth from the seat of His government, which will be established in Jerusalem.

Thought 1. The day of God's judgment will be a frightening time, a day of utter terror and horrific punishment. All people must pay the penalty for their sinful behavior. All who deny, ignore, and defy the LORD, all who rebel against Him and refuse to repent, must pay the penalty for their rebellion—eternal separation from God. Listen to what God's Holy Word says about the coming punishment of judgment:

"Not every one that saith unto me, Lord, Lord, shall enter into the kingdom of heaven; but he that doeth the will of my Father which is in heaven. Many will say to me in that day, Lord, Lord, have we not prophesied in thy name? and in thy name have cast out devils? and in thy name done many wonderful works? And then will I profess unto them, I never knew you: depart from me, ye that work iniquity" (Mt.7:21-23).

"When Jesus heard *it,* he marvelled, and said to them that followed, Verily I say unto you, I have not found so great faith, no, not in Israel. And I say unto you, That many shall come from the east and west, and shall sit down with Abraham, and Isaac, and Jacob, in the kingdom of heaven. But the children of the kingdom shall be cast out into outer darkness: there shall be weeping and gnashing of teeth" (Mt.8:10-12).

"The Son of man shall send forth his angels, and they shall gather out of his kingdom all things that offend, and them which do iniquity; And shall cast them into a furnace of fire: there shall be wailing and gnashing of teeth" (Mt.13:41-42).

"Then said the king to the servants, Bind him hand and foot, and take him away, and cast *him* into outer darkness; there shall be weeping and gnashing of teeth" (Mt.22:13).

"*Ye* serpents, *ye* generation of vipers, how can ye escape the damnation of hell?" (Mt.23:33).

"When the Son of man shall come in his glory, and all the holy angels with him, then shall he sit upon the throne of his glory: And before him shall be gathered all nations: and he shall separate them one from another, as a shepherd divideth *his* sheep from the goats: And he shall set the sheep on his right hand, but the goats on the left….Then shall he say also unto them on the left hand, Depart from me, ye cursed, into everlasting fire, prepared for the devil and his angels" (Mt.25:31-33, 41).

"And if thy hand offend thee, cut it off: it is better for thee to enter into life maimed, than having two hands to go into hell, into the fire that never shall be quenched: Where their worm dieth not, and the fire is not quenched. And if thy foot offend thee, cut it off: it is better for thee to enter halt into life, than having two feet to be cast into hell, into the fire that never shall be quenched: Where their worm dieth not, and the fire is not quenched. And if thine eye offend thee, pluck it out: it is better for thee to enter into the kingdom of God with one eye, than having two eyes to be cast into hell fire: Where their worm dieth not, and the fire is not quenched" (Mk.9:43-48).

"And it came to pass, that the beggar died, and was carried by the angels into Abraham's bosom: the rich man also died, and was buried; And in hell he lift up his eyes, being in torments, and seeth Abraham afar off, and Lazarus in his bosom. And he cried and said, Father Abraham, have mercy on me, and send Lazarus, that he may dip the tip of his finger in water, and cool my tongue; for I am tormented in this flame" (Lu.16:22-24).

"Marvel not at this: for the hour is coming, in the which all that are in the graves shall hear his voice, And shall come forth; they that have done good, unto the resurrection of life; and they that have done evil, unto the resurrection of damnation" (Jn.5:28-29).

"But unto them that are contentious, and do not obey the truth, but obey unrighteousness, indignation and wrath" (Ro.2:8).

"And to you who are troubled rest with us, when the Lord Jesus shall be revealed from heaven with his mighty angels, In flaming fire taking vengeance on them that know not God, and that obey not the gospel of our Lord Jesus Christ: Who shall be punished with everlasting destruction from the presence of the Lord, and from the glory of his power; When he shall come to be glorified in his saints, and to be admired in all them that believe (because our testimony among you was believed) in that day" (2 Th.1:7-10).

"The Lord knoweth how to deliver the godly out of temptations, and to reserve the unjust unto the day of judgment to be punished" (2 Pe.2:9).

"But the heavens and the earth, which are now, by the same word are kept in store, reserved unto fire against the day of judgment and perdition of ungodly men" (2 Pe.3:7).

"And whosoever was not found written in the book of life was cast into the lake of fire" (Re.20:15).

"But the fearful, and unbelieving, and the abominable, and murderers, and whoremongers, and sorcerers, and idolaters, and all liars, shall have their part in the lake which burneth with fire and brimstone: which is the second death" (Re.21:8).

CHAPTER 25

I. God's Plan for the Whole World & for His People: God's Seven-Step Plan for the World, 25:1-12

1. God's plan to establish a personal relationship with His people: To be "my God" to every individual believer
   a. To praise His name
   b. To declare His faithfulness

2. God's plan to establish His worship among all people (salvation of the Gentiles)
   a. God will destroy all the cities of the Gentiles (unbelievers)
   b. God will arouse the Gentiles to worship Him

3. God's plan to protect His people: To be a refuge & shelter for the needy
   a. His reason: Because of the oppression by the ruthless people & nations of the world
   b. His protection: Will subdue the roar of the ruthless & the oppressive

4. God's plan to provide a feast in the future for all of His people: To be held in Jerusalem (The Great Supper of God's

O LORD, thou *art* my God; I will exalt thee, I will praise thy name; for thou hast done wonderful *things; thy* counsels of old *are* faithfulness *and* truth.
2 For thou hast made of a city an heap; *of* a defenced city a ruin: a palace of strangers to be no city; it shall never be built.
3 Therefore shall the strong people glorify thee, the city of the terrible nations shall fear thee.
4 For thou hast been a strength to the poor, a strength to the needy in his distress, a refuge from the storm, a shadow from the heat, when the blast of the terrible ones *is* as a storm *against* the wall.
5 Thou shalt bring down the noise of strangers, as the heat in a dry place; *even* the heat with the shadow of a cloud: the branch of the terrible ones shall be brought low.
6 And in this mountain shall the LORD of hosts make unto all people a feast of fat things, a feast of wines on the lees, of fat things full of marrow, of wines on the lees well refined.
7 And he will destroy in this mountain the face of the covering cast over all people, and the vail that is spread over all nations.
8 He will swallow up death in victory; and the Lord GOD will wipe away tears from off all faces; and the rebuke of his people shall he take away from off all the earth: for the LORD hath spoken *it.*
9 And it shall be said in that day, Lo, this *is* our God; we have waited for him, and he will save us: this *is* the LORD; we have waited for him, we will be glad and rejoice in his salvation.
10 For in this mountain shall the hand of the LORD rest, and Moab shall be trodden down under him, even as straw is trodden down for the dunghill.
11 And he shall spread forth his hands in the midst of them, as he that swimmeth spreadeth forth *his hands* to swim: and he shall bring down their pride together with the spoils of their hands.
12 And the fortress of the high fort of thy walls shall he bring down, lay low, *and* bring to the ground, *even* to the dust.

Kingdom), Mt.8:11; 22:1-14; Lu.13:28-29; 14:15-24

5. God's plan to conquer death: To swallow up & remove the shadow of death forever
   a. He will wipe away all tears of sorrow & grief, Re.7:17; 21:4
   b. He will remove the mockery & persecution by enemies
   c. He guarantees the conquest of death by His Word

6. God's plan to arouse people to trust & rejoice in His salvation: To have God's people see the LORD *in that day* & know it has been worth it

7. God's plan to defeat all enemies: To assure His people of victorious lives
   a. Before God, all enemies will be as worthless straw
   b. Before God, all enemies will be like swimmers seeking to escape the cesspool of guilt & condemnation
   c. Before God, all the prideful people of the earth & the fortress cities in which they trusted will be brought low & destroyed

DIVISION II

THE PROPHECIES CONCERNING GOD'S JUDGMENT OF THE NATIONS AND HIS TRIUMPH OVER THE WORLD, 13:1–27:13

I. God's Plan for the Whole World and for His People: God's Seven-Step Plan for the World, 25:1-12

(25:1-12) **Introduction**: the preceding thirteen chapters of Isaiah have predicted that God's hand of judgment will fall on the nations of the world. God's universal judgment of the world was the prophecy discussed in the previous chapter.

Focusing on so much judgment can weigh heavily upon the hearts of people—and even cause them to shrink back from the message. But God's judgment is not haphazard or without purpose. When He executes judgment on the earth, He acts according to a *master plan,* a detailed course of action that He has devised for the world. All that happens on earth—even every evil, wicked deed—is twisted, turned, worked out, and used by God to fulfill His plan. God's plan for mankind and this world *will* be fulfilled.

In the prophecy of the present Scripture, Isaiah gives us a glimpse into God's plan. After the terrifying days of universal judgment known as the *Great Tribulation,* Jesus Christ will then establish the kingdom of God on earth. The King is coming just as John the Baptist and Christ proclaimed (Mt.3:2; 4:17). From the beginning of creation, God's purpose has been to bring His kingdom to earth, and He has a seven-step plan to accomplish His purpose. This is, *God's Plan for the Whole World and for His People: God's Seven-Step Plan for the World,* 25:1-12.

1. God's plan to establish a personal relationship with His people: to be "my God" to every individual believer (v.1).
2. God's plan to establish His worship among all people (salvation of the Gentiles) (vv.2-3).
3. God's plan to protect His people: to be a refuge and shelter for the needy (vv.4-5).
4. God's plan to provide a feast in the future for all of His people: to be held in Jerusalem (The Great Supper of God's Kingdom), Mt.8:11; 22:1-14; Lu.13:28-29; 14:15-24 (v.6).

5. God's plan to conquer death: to swallow up and remove the shadow of death forever (vv.7-8).
6. God's plan to arouse people to trust and rejoice in His salvation: To have God's people see the LORD *in that day* and know it has been worth it (v.9).
7. God's plan to defeat all enemies: to assure His people of victorious lives (vv.10-12).

1 **(25:1) Relationship, with God, Personal—Believers, Relationship with God, Personal—Faithfulness of God, Duty, To Praise—Praise, of God's Faithfulness—God, Plan for the World, to Praise Him; to Establish a Personal Relationship with People**: God's plan is to establish a personal relationship with His people. In addressing the LORD, Isaiah says "You are my God." He acknowledges the LORD in a very personal way, that a personal relationship exists between him and the LORD. A personal relationship is always the first thing God is after in seeking people. God longs to be the Father of every human being, for every man and woman to become an adopted son or daughter of His. This was His very purpose for choosing the Jews to be His people. As Scripture says:

"For thou *art* an holy people unto the LORD thy God, and the LORD hath chosen thee to be a peculiar [treasured] people unto himself, above all the nations that *are* upon the earth" (De.14:2).
"Doubtless thou *art* our father, though Abraham be ignorant of us, and Israel acknowledge us not: thou, O LORD, *art* our father, our redeemer; thy name *is* from everlasting" (Is.63:16).
"When Israel *was* a child, then I loved him, and called my son out of Egypt" (Ho.11:1).

OUTLINE	SCRIPTURE
1. God's plan to establish a personal relationship with His people: To be "my God" to every individual believer a. To praise his name b. To declare His faithfulness	O LORD, thou *art* my God; I will exalt thee, I will praise thy name; for thou hast done wonderful *things; thy* counsels of old *are* faithfulness *and* truth.

Some commentators actually say that it is Israel who is addressing the LORD in this passage (H.C. Leupold). Other commentators say that it is the remnant that God preserved during the *Day of the LORD* (Warren W. Wiersbe). Still others say that it is Isaiah who is offering up praise to the LORD, acknowledging that he has a personal relationship with Him (Stanley M. Horton; *Bible Knowledge Commentary;* Matthew Henry). Most likely it is Isaiah himself who is claiming a personal relationship with the LORD. He is describing the praise that will be lifted up to the LORD when the Messiah returns to establish His kingdom on earth.

The point to note is this: God's plan for establishing a personal relationship with His people is fulfilled in Isaiah and all other believers. Believers are just what their name suggests: they are people who truly believe in the LORD and address Him as "My God."

A personal relationship is established between God and His people for two purposes: so that people will praise God's name and declare His faithfulness throughout the earth. This is the very first praise Isaiah offered up to the LORD, a praise for God's faithfulness. Down through history the LORD had done some wonderful works, works that He had planned long ago. Isaiah recognized that the LORD was faithful to do exactly what He had always said. Whatever the LORD had planned or promised, He had always done and would always do. In the past, God had always fulfilled His plan and Word. In fact, much of what He planned has already taken place. For example, remember His Word to Abraham: trust me. Leave your country and go where I lead you, and I will give you the promised land and bless you richly. And you will be a blessing to all nations (see outline and notes—Ge.12:1-3 for more discussion). Abraham trusted the LORD, and the Jews grew into a great people that God has used for three great purposes:

⇒ To be the people through whom the world would inherit the promised land of heaven (see outline and note—Ge.12:1c for more discussion).
⇒ To be the people through whom He would give His Word to the world (see outline and note—Ge.12:3).
⇒ To be the people through whom He would send the Savior into the world (see outline and note—Ge.12:3 for more discussion).

An honest comparison of the prophesies in the Bible with historical events clearly shows that much of what God has planned for the world has already taken place. The Word of God has been given to the world through the Jews in the Holy Bible. Furthermore the Savior, the Lord Jesus Christ, has been sent into the world through the Jews. And through faith in Christ, many people have inherited the promised land of heaven.

But God's plan for the world includes far more that still lies out in the future. There are still many events of God's Holy Word yet to be fulfilled. But God is faithful. What He says will come to pass. Quickly glance at the seven steps of God's plan that are covered in this passage. When Isaiah wrote this passage, none of the steps had yet taken place. Today, however, steps one through three have been partially fulfilled. Their complete fulfillment will take place when Christ returns to set up His kingdom on earth. The point is that God is faithful. He will fulfill His plan for the world. We can trust His faithfulness. Just as Isaiah praised God's faithfulness, so we too can praise Him. For the LORD is faithful and He will fulfill His Word, all His promises, to the people.

"God *is* faithful, by whom ye were called unto the fellowship of his Son Jesus Christ our Lord" (1 Co.1:9).
"Wherein God, willing more abundantly to show unto the heirs of promise the immutability of his counsel, confirmed *it* by an oath: That by two immutable things, in which *it was* impossible for God to lie,

we might have a strong consolation, who have fled for refuge to lay hold upon the hope set before us" (He.6:17-18).

"Wherefore let them that suffer according to the will of God commit the keeping of their souls *to him* in well doing, as unto a faithful Creator" (1 Pe.4:19).

"Know therefore that the LORD thy God, he *is* God, the faithful God, which keepeth covenant and mercy with them that love him and keep his commandments to a thousand generations" (De.7:9).

"Blessed *be* the LORD, that hath given rest unto his people Israel, according to all that he promised: there hath not failed one word of all his good promise, which he promised by the hand of Moses his servant" (1 K.8:56).

"Thy mercy, O LORD, *is* in the heavens; *and* thy faithfulness *reacheth* unto the clouds" (Ps.36:5).

"I will sing of the mercies of the LORD for ever: with my mouth will I make known thy faithfulness to all generations" (Ps.89:1).

"He hath remembered his covenant for ever, the word *which* he commanded to a thousand generations" (Ps.105:8).

"Happy *is he* that *hath* the God of Jacob for his help, whose hope *is* in the LORD his God: Which made heaven, and earth, the sea, and all that therein *is*: which keepeth truth for ever" (Ps.146:5-6).

---

2 (25:2-3) **God, Plan for the World, to Establish True Worship—Worship, Prophecy Concerning, Worship of Gentiles—Plan, of God, Worship of Gentiles—Kingdom of Messiah, Events During, Salvation of Gentiles—Gentiles, Prophecy Concerning, Salvation—Worship, of Gentiles, Prophecy Concerning**: God's plan for the world includes a wonderful event: a day when all the Gentile nations will be saved and worship the LORD. Since the first coming of Christ, some people from all over the world have been turning to Him and trusting Him as their Savior. But when Christ returns to set up God's kingdom on earth, *all* the Gentiles from every nation in the world will turn to Him and worship Him and Him alone.

However, before that takes place, a terrifying judgment will fall on all the wicked of the earth. As these verses say, God will destroy all the cities of the Gentiles because of their unbelief, wickedness, and defiance of Him. The term *the city* is a generic term, referring to all the cities of the world. In Isaiah's day the cities of the world were centers of…

- worldly power and wealth
- godlessness and wickedness
- covetousness and greed

Down through history, the cities of the world have continued to reject and defy the LORD. The same spirit of rebellion against the only living and true God marches on. As a result, the day is coming when He will destroy them. These fortresses of defiance and centers of wickedness will become heaps of rubble, never to be rebuilt.

OUTLINE	SCRIPTURE
2. God's plan to establish His worship among all people (salvation of the Gentiles) a. God will destroy all the cities of the Gentiles (unbelievers) b. God will arouse the Gentiles to worship Him	2 For thou hast made of a city an heap; *of* a defenced city a ruin: a palace of strangers to be no city; it shall never be built. 3 Therefore shall the strong people glorify thee, the city of the terrible nations shall fear thee.

But there is also wonderful news in the LORD's coming judgment. Note God's purpose for destroying the cities of the world: to stir up the Gentiles to repent of their sins and worship Him. For those who repent, there will be salvation. The Father will accept them because they approach Him through His Son, the Lord Jesus Christ. But for those who reject Him, there will be only judgment. They will stand before the Lord Jesus Christ in judgment and bow the knee, acknowledging that He is truly the Son of the living God. After bowing the knee, they will face the judgment of God because of their defiance and refusal to repent. Note what other Scriptures say about the Gentile nations' being saved:

"And I say unto you, That many shall come from the east and west, and shall sit down with Abraham, and Isaac, and Jacob, in the kingdom of heaven" (Mt.8:11).

"And they shall come from the east, and *from* the west, and from the north, and *from* the south, and shall sit down in the kingdom of God" (Lu.13:29).

"For there is no difference between the Jew and the Greek: for the same Lord over all is rich unto all that call upon him. For whosoever shall call upon the name of the Lord shall be saved" (Ro.10:12-13).

"So then faith *cometh* by hearing, and hearing by the word of God. But I say, Have they not heard? Yes verily, their sound went into all the earth, and their words unto the ends of the world. But I say, Did not Israel know? First Moses saith, I will provoke you to jealousy by *them that are* no people, *and* by a foolish nation I will anger you. But Esaias is very bold, and saith, I was found of them that sought me not; I was made manifest unto them that asked not after me" (Ro.10:17-20).

"Wherefore God also hath highly exalted him, and given him a name which is above every name: That at the name of Jesus every knee should bow, of *things* in heaven, and *things* in earth, and *things* under the earth; And *that* every tongue should confess that Jesus Christ *is* Lord, to the glory of God the Father" (Ph.2:9-11).

"And it shall come to pass in the last days, *that* the mountain of the LORD'S house shall be established in the top of the mountains, and shall be exalted above the hills; and all nations shall flow unto it. And many people shall go and say, Come ye, and let us go up to the mountain of the LORD, to the house of the God of Jacob; and he will teach us of his ways, and we will walk in his paths: for out of Zion shall go forth the law, and the word of the LORD from Jerusalem" (Is.2:2-3).

"And in that day there shall be a root of Jesse, which shall stand for an ensign of the people; to it shall the Gentiles seek: and his rest shall be glorious" (Is.11:10).

"They shall lift up their voice, they shall sing for the majesty of the LORD, they shall cry aloud from the sea. Wherefore glorify ye the LORD in the fires, *even* the name of the LORD God of Israel in the isles of the sea. From the uttermost part of the earth have we heard songs, *even* glory to the righteous." (Is.24:14-16).

"And the Gentiles shall come to thy light, and kings to the brightness of thy rising. Lift up thine eyes round about, and see: all they gather themselves together, they come to thee: thy sons shall come from far, and thy daughters shall be nursed at *thy* side" (Is.60:3-4).

"I am sought of *them that* asked not *for me;* I am found of *them that* sought me not: I said, Behold me, behold me, unto a nation *that* was not called by my name" (Is.65:1).

3 (25:4-5) **Protection of God, a Refuge and Shelter—Refuge, of God, for the Poor and Needy—Shelter, of God, for the Poor and Needy—Believers, Protection of, by God:** concern for the oppressed has always filled God's heart. His plan for the world includes the protection of His people and everyone who is poor and needy. Down through history, God has been a refuge and shelter for all who call upon Him for help.

The powerful of this world have always oppressed God's people as well as the poor and needy. Isaiah compared their oppressive acts to the pelting rain of a storm driving against a wall and to the burning heat beating down upon the desert. God is planning a final, victorious day of deliverance for all the persecuted of this earth. Before that day comes, however, the LORD will strengthen and empower His people to endure the oppression of the ruthless. Throughout all of history believers have fled to the LORD as a refuge and shelter from such tyranny, and the LORD strengthened them. They were able to walk through the sufferings of the storm and the burning heat of persecution.

But the day is coming when the Messiah will establish His kingdom on earth. When He does, God will silence the roar of the ruthless forever and punish them for their wicked acts. Once they are removed from the earth, God's people will experience His perfect protection. *In that day,* the perfect refuge and shelter of God's presence will be the continued, unbroken experience of every believer.

The LORD is our hiding place from the stormy, fiery trials of this world. Listen to God's promise to all believers that He will be a refuge and shelter in time of trouble.

OUTLINE	SCRIPTURE	SCRIPTURE	OUTLINE
3. God's plan to protect His people: To be a refuge & shelter for the needy a. His reason: Because of the oppression by the ruthless people & nations of the world	4 For thou hast been a strength to the poor, a strength to the needy in his distress, a refuge from the storm, a shadow from the heat, when the blast of the terrible ones *is* as a storm	*against* the wall. 5 Thou shalt bring down the noise of strangers, as the heat in a dry place; *even* the heat with the shadow of a cloud: the branch of the terrible ones shall be brought low.	b. His protection: Will subdue the roar of the ruthless & the oppressive

"The eternal God *is thy* refuge, and underneath *are* the everlasting arms: and he shall thrust out the enemy from before thee; and shall say, Destroy *them*" (De.33:27).

"Keep me as the apple of the eye, hide me under the shadow of thy wings" (Ps.17:8).

"For in the time of trouble he shall hide me in his pavilion: in the secret of his tabernacle shall he hide me; he shall set me up upon a rock" (Ps.27:5).

"Thou shalt hide them in the secret of thy presence from the pride of man: thou shalt keep them secretly in a pavilion from the strife of tongues" (Ps.31:20).

"Thou *art* my hiding place; thou shalt preserve me from trouble; thou shalt compass me about with songs of deliverance." (Ps.32:7).

"God *is* our refuge and strength, a very present help in trouble" (Ps.46:1).

"Hide me from the secret counsel of the wicked; from the insurrection of the workers of iniquity" (Ps.64:2).

"Be thou my strong habitation, whereunto I may continually resort: thou hast given commandment to save me; for thou *art* my rock and my fortress" (Ps.71:3).

"Thou *art* my hiding place and my shield: I hope in thy word" (Ps.119:114).

"Deliver me, O LORD, from mine enemies: I flee unto thee to hide me" (Ps.143:9).

"In the fear of the LORD *is* strong confidence: and his children shall have a place of refuge" (Pr.14:26).

"The name of the LORD *is* a strong tower: the righteous runneth into it, and is safe" (Pr.18:10).

"For thou hast been a strength to the poor, a strength to the needy in his distress, a refuge from the storm, a shadow from the heat, when the blast of the terrible ones *is* as a storm *against* the wall" (Is.25:4).

4 (25:6) **Great Supper of God, Prophecy Concerning—Supper of God, Prophecy Concerning—God, Great Supper of, Prophecy Concerning—Kingdom of Messiah, Events of, Great Supper of God—Prophecy, Concerning Great Supper of God**: God's plan for the world includes a feast which is to be held in the future in Jerusalem. This feast is known as the Great Supper of God's kingdom. When Christ returns to set up His kingdom on earth, He will hold this great feast for all believers of the earth, for all the saved from every nation, tribe, people and language (Re.7:9). The guests at this great feast will be all people, both Jews and Gentiles who are genuine believers in the LORD (see note 2 above—Is.25:2 for more discussion). No longer will there be a separation between Jews and Gentiles. When Christ returns to hold this great feast, all believers will be present. This was stressed by the Lord Jesus Christ Himself. He clearly stated that the *Great Supper of God* will include guests from the highways and hedges of the world, not just Jews. Thus this prophecy of the *Great Supper of God* has a strong personal message for people everywhere: people are saved by trusting Jesus Christ as their Savior and by responding to God's invitation to attend the supper. But tragically, those who reject are lost, no matter what their excuse is.

Note this fact about the feast: only the best food—the choicest meats and the finest wines—will be served. The idea being conveyed is that believers will receive the richest and most wonderful blessings imaginable *in that day*. When Jesus Christ returns to earth, He will create a flawless world in which everything will be perfect. To inaugurate His kingdom on earth, the LORD will hold this Great Supper, and all believers will attend (see outline and notes—Mt.8:11; 22:1-14; Lu.13:28-29; 14:15-24 for more discussion).

OUTLINE	SCRIPTURE
4. God's plan to provide a feast in the future for all of His people: To be held in Jerusalem (The Great Supper of God's Kingdom), Mt.8:11; 22:1-14; Lu.13:28-29; 14:15-24	6 And in this mountain shall the LORD of hosts make unto all people a feast of fat things, a feast of wines on the lees, of fat things full of marrow, of wines on the lees well refined.

"And Jesus answered and spake unto them again by parables, and said, The kingdom of heaven is like unto a certain king, which made a marriage for his son, And sent forth his servants to call them that were bidden to the wedding: and they would not come. Again, he sent forth other servants, saying, Tell them which are bidden, Behold, I have prepared my dinner: my oxen and *my* fatlings *are* killed, and all things *are* ready: come unto the marriage. But they made light of *it*, and went their ways, one to his farm, another to his merchandise: And the remnant took his servants, and entreated *them* spitefully, and slew *them*. But when the king heard *thereof*, he was wroth: and he sent forth his armies, and destroyed those murderers, and burned up their city. Then saith he to his servants, The wedding is ready, but they which were bidden were not worthy. Go ye therefore into the highways, and as many as ye shall find, bid to the marriage. So those servants went out into the highways, and gathered together all as many as they found, both bad and good: and the wedding was furnished with guests" (Mt.22:1-10).

"And when one of them that sat at meat with him heard these things, he said unto him, Blessed *is* he that shall eat bread in the kingdom of God. Then said he unto him, A certain man made a great supper, and bade many: And sent his servant at supper time to say to them that were bidden, Come; for all things are now ready....And the servant said, Lord, it is done as thou hast commanded, and yet there is room. And the lord said unto the servant, Go out into the highways and hedges, and compel *them* to come in, that my house may be filled. For I say unto you, That none of those men which were bidden shall taste of my supper" (Lu.14:15-17, 22-24).

"And I heard as it were the voice of a great multitude, and as the voice of many waters, and as the voice of mighty thunderings, saying, Alleluia: for the Lord God omnipotent reigneth. Let us be glad and rejoice, and give honour to him: for the marriage of the Lamb is come, and his wife hath made herself ready. And to her was granted that she should be arrayed in fine linen, clean and white: for the fine linen is the righteousness of saints. And he saith unto me, Write, Blessed *are* they which are called unto the marriage supper of the Lamb. And he saith unto me, These are the true sayings of God" (Re.19:6-9).

5 (25:7-8) **Death, Conquered, by Christ—Conquest, of Death, by Christ—Shadow, of Death, Removed Forever—Plan, of God, to Conquer Death**: God's plan for the world includes removing the worst enemy of life—death. From the beginning of human history, death has always cast a covering of gloom over people. In Isaiah's day, untold thousands of people were dying due to the cruelty of the Assyrian conquerors. The tears of the people were flowing like a blinding rain due to the slaughter and captivity of their loved ones, and the sufferings of the people weighed heavily upon Isaiah's heart.

In this prophecy, the LORD gave Isaiah a vision of what lay ahead in the distant future. Death would be conquered. Even the very shadow of death would be removed forever. The day is coming when all tears of sorrow and grief will be wiped away. All the mockery and persecution by enemies will be removed, and the disgrace that God's people suffered at their hands will be forgotten. Note the surety of this promise: it is a promise given by the LORD God, the Sovereign LORD Himself. Note the emphasis on this promise: the LORD has spoken, has guaranteed it. Beyond any question, death will be conquered. Although it is not mentioned in this Scripture, Jesus Christ conquered death at the cross. When He returns to earth, death will be no more.

227

OUTLINE	SCRIPTURE	SCRIPTURE	OUTLINE
5. God's plan to conquer death: To swallow up & remove the shadow of death forever a. He will wipe away all tears	7 And he will destroy in this mountain the face of the covering cast over all people, and the vail that is spread over all nations. 8 He will swallow up death	in victory; and the Lord GOD will wipe away tears from off all faces; and the rebuke of his people shall he take away from off all the earth: for the LORD hath spoken *it*.	of sorrow & grief, Re.7:17; 21:4 b. He will remove the mockery & persecution by enemies c. He guarantees the conquest of death by His Word

"Forasmuch then as the children are partakers of flesh and blood, he also himself likewise took part of the same; that through death he might destroy him that had the power of death, that is, the devil; And deliver them who through fear of death were all their lifetime subject to bondage" (He.2:14-15).

"For God so loved the world, that he gave his only begotten Son, that whosoever believeth in him should not perish, but have everlasting life" (Jn.3:16).

"He that believeth on the Son hath everlasting life: and he that believeth not the Son shall not see life; but the wrath of God abideth on him" (Jn.3:36).

"Verily, verily, I say unto you, If a man keep my saying, he shall never see death" (Jn.8:51).

"And whosoever liveth and believeth in me shall never die. Believest thou this?" (Jn.11:26).

"To them who by patient continuance in well doing seek for glory and honour and immortality, eternal life" (Ro.2:7).

"The last enemy *that* shall be destroyed *is* death" (1 Co.15:26).

"In a moment, in the twinkling of an eye, at the last trump: for the trumpet shall sound, and the dead shall be raised incorruptible, and we shall be changed. For this corruptible must put on incorruption, and this mortal *must* put on immortality. So when this corruptible shall have put on incorruption, and this mortal shall have put on immortality, then shall be brought to pass the saying that is written, Death is swallowed up in victory. O death, where *is* thy sting? O grave, where *is* thy victory? The sting of death *is* sin; and the strength of sin *is* the law. But thanks *be* to God, which giveth us the victory through our Lord Jesus Christ" (1 Co.15:52-57).

"Who hath saved us, and called *us* with an holy calling, not according to our works, but according to his own purpose and grace, which was given us in Christ Jesus before the world began, But is now made manifest by the appearing of our Saviour Jesus Christ, who hath abolished death, and hath brought life and immortality to light through the gospel" (2 Ti.1:9-10).

"For the Lamb which is in the midst of the throne shall feed them, and shall lead them unto living fountains of waters: and God shall wipe away all tears from their eyes" (Re.7:17).

"And God shall wipe away all tears from their eyes; and there shall be no more death, neither sorrow, nor crying, neither shall there be any more pain: for the former things are passed away" (Re.21:4).

"There shall be no more thence an infant of days, nor an old man that hath not filled his days: for the child shall die an hundred years old; but the sinner *being* an hundred years old shall be accursed" (Is.65:20).

"And many of them that sleep in the dust of the earth shall awake, some to everlasting life, and some to shame *and* everlasting contempt" (Da.12:2).

"I will ransom them from the power of the grave; I will redeem them from death: O death, I will be thy plagues; O grave, I will be thy destruction: repentance shall be hid from mine eyes" (Ho.13:14).

6 (25:9) **Salvation, Rejoicing in, Prophecy Concerning—*In That Day*, Event During, Rejoicing in Salvation—Messiah, Kingdom of, Rejoicing in Salvation—Kingdom of God, Rejoicing in, Prophecy Concerning—Salvation, Rejoicing in, During Messiah's Kingdom—Believers, Prophecy Concerning, Rejoicing in Christ's Kingdom—Rejoicing, in Christ's Kingdom, Because of Salvation—Restoration, of the Jews, Prophecy Concerning—Remnant, of the Jews, Prophecy Concerning:** God's plan for the world includes stirring people to trust and rejoice in His salvation. When Jesus Christ returns to set up His kingdom on earth, the Jews and many others will trust Him as their Savior (Zec.12:10). The blindness of their hearts will be removed. They will see Christ and realize that He is the true Messiah, the Savior of the world. As a result, they will turn to Him. Furthermore, *in that day* all persecuted believers will see the LORD and know it has been worth all the suffering. *In that day* they will sing a beautiful song:

OUTLINE	SCRIPTURE
6. God's plan to arouse people to trust & rejoice in His salvation: To have God's people see the LORD *in that day* & know it has been worth it	9 And it shall be said in that day, Lo, this *is* our God; we have waited for him, and he will save us: this *is* the LORD; we have waited for him, we will be glad and rejoice in his salvation.

"Lo, this is our God; we have waited for Him, and He will save us: this is the LORD; we have waited for Him, we will be glad and rejoice in his salvation" (KJV).

"Surely this is our God; we trusted in Him, and he saved us. This is the Lord, we trusted in Him; let us rejoice and be glad in his salvation" (NIV).

"This is our God. We trusted in him, and he saved us. This is the LORD, in whom we trusted. Let us rejoice in the salvation he brings!" (NLT).

7 (25:10-12) **Enemies, Prophecies Concerning, to Be Defeated—Spiritual Enemies, Promises Concerning, to Be Defeated—Victory, Prophecies Concerning, All Enemies Conquered—Assurance, of Victory, Prophecy Concerning—Believers, Promises to, Conquest of All Enemies—Plan, of God, to Conquer All Enemies—God, Plan of, to Conquer All Enemies**: God's plan for the world ensures the defeat of all enemies who stand opposed to Him and His people. Moab in this passage represents all nations and people who oppose God. *In that day* when the Lord returns to earth, God's hand will fall upon all who have denied and defied Him. His enemies will be nothing more than worthless straw to be trampled under His foot. Isaiah declared that they would be like crushed straw left to rot in manure pits (v.10). All God's enemies will be like swimmers seeking to escape the cesspool of guilt and condemnation. But there will be no escape. God will destroy their pride and the evil works of their hands (v.11). Standing before God, all the proud people of earth, along with the fortress cities in which they trusted, will be brought low (v.12). Once all the enemies of God have been destroyed, there will be no opposition left. No longer will God's people be persecuted, mocked, attacked, or martyred. All the enemies who confront God's people will be defeated, utterly destroyed. Ultimately, God's people will be victorious.

OUTLINE	SCRIPTURE	SCRIPTURE	OUTLINE
7. **God's plan to defeat all enemies: To assure His people of victorious lives** a. Before God, all enemies will be as worthless straw b. Before God, all enemies will be like swimmers seeking to escape the cesspool of guilt	10 For in this mountain shall the hand of the LORD rest, and Moab shall be trodden down under him, even as straw is trodden down for the dunghill. 11 And he shall spread forth his hands in the midst of them, as he that swimmeth	spreadeth forth *his hands* to swim: and he shall bring down their pride together with the spoils of their hands. 12 And the fortress of the high fort of thy walls shall he bring down, lay low, *and* bring to the ground, *even* to the dust.	& condemnation c. Before God, all the prideful people of the earth & the fortress cities in which they trusted will be brought low & destroyed

"Behold, I give unto you power to tread on serpents and scorpions, and over all the power of the enemy: and nothing shall by any means hurt you" (Lu.10:19).

"These things I have spoken unto you, that in me ye might have peace. In the world ye shall have tribulation: but be of good cheer; I have overcome the world" (Jn.16:33).

"Who shall separate us from the love of Christ? *shall* tribulation, or distress, or persecution, or famine, or nakedness, or peril, or sword?...Nay, in all these things we are more than conquerors through him that loved us. For I am persuaded, that neither death, nor life, nor angels, nor principalities, nor powers, nor things present, nor things to come, Nor height, nor depth, nor any other creature, shall be able to separate us from the love of God, which is in Christ Jesus our Lord" (Ro.8:35, 37-39).

"Then *cometh* the end, when he shall have delivered up the kingdom to God, even the Father; when he shall have put down all rule and all authority and power" (1 Co.15:24).

"Now thanks *be* unto God, which always causeth us to triumph in Christ, and maketh manifest the savour of his knowledge by us in every place" (2 Co.2:14).

"For though we walk in the flesh, we do not war after the flesh: (For the weapons of our warfare *are* not carnal, but mighty through God to the pulling down of strong holds;) Casting down imaginations, and every high thing that exalteth itself against the knowledge of God, and bringing into captivity every thought to the obedience of Christ" (2 Co.10:3-5).

"And the Lord shall deliver me from every evil work, and will preserve *me* unto his heavenly kingdom: to whom *be* glory for ever and ever. Amen" (2 Ti.4:18).

"For whatsoever is born of God overcometh the world: and this is the victory that overcometh the world, *even* our faith. Who is he that overcometh the world, but he that believeth that Jesus is the Son of God?" (1 Jn.5:4-5).

"And I saw as it were a sea of glass mingled with fire: and them that had gotten the victory over the beast, and over his image, and over his mark, *and* over the number of his name, stand on the sea of glass, having the harps of God" (Re.15:2).

"Through thee will we push down our enemies: through thy name will we tread them under that rise up against us" (Ps.44:5).

1. God's works in behalf of His people: To be celebrated in song *in that day* (Christ's kingdom)

  a. God gives His people a city of salvation: The New Jerusalem
    1) Its gates will always be open
    2) Its citizens will be the righteous, Ps. 15:1-5
  b. God gives perfect peace to the person whose mind is fixed on Him, Ro.5:1; Ph.4:6-9
  c. God gives a strong foundation to the person who trusts in Him: He is a Rock, Ps.18:2
  d. God humbles the proud person & levels the arrogant city to the dust
    1) The arrogant city will be cast down
    2) The city's oppressed & poor will survive the judgment & trample the city underfoot
  e. God levels the path & smoothes the way for the righteous
    1) Those who obey God's law
    2) Those who wait on God
    3) Those who seek to glorify God
    4) Those who yearn for God morning & night
  f. God executes His judgments on earth: To teach people to live righteously

    1) He shows grace to the wicked, but they still refuse to learn righteousness: Even in an upright land they continue to do evil & refuse to honor the LORD
    2) He lifts His fist, warning the wicked, but they do not see the warning
    3) He shames & consumes them through judgment

  g. God establishes peace for His people & strengthens them to accomplish their tasks, 3; Jn.14:27; 16:33; Ph.2:13

CHAPTER 26

J. God's Works & the Protection of His Vineyard, His People: God's Great Care for His People, 26:1–27:13

In that day shall this song be sung in the land of Judah; We have a strong city; salvation will God appoint *for* walls and bulwarks.
2 Open ye the gates, that the righteous nation which keepeth the truth may enter in.
3 Thou wilt keep *him* in perfect peace, *whose* mind *is* stayed *on thee:* because he trusteth in thee.
4 Trust ye in the LORD for ever: for in the LORD JEHOVAH *is* everlasting strength:
5 For he bringeth down them that dwell on high; the lofty city, he layeth it low; he layeth it low, *even* to the ground; he bringeth it *even* to the dust.
6 The foot shall tread it down, *even* the feet of the poor, *and* the steps of the needy.
7 The way of the just *is* uprightness: thou, most upright, dost weigh the path of the just.
8 Yea, in the way of thy judgments, O LORD, have we waited for thee; the desire of *our* soul *is* to thy name, and to the remembrance of thee.
9 With my soul have I desired thee in the night; yea, with my spirit within me will I seek thee early: for when thy judgments *are* in the earth, the inhabitants of the world will learn righteousness.
10 Let favour be showed to the wicked, *yet* will he not learn righteousness: in the land of uprightness will he deal unjustly, and will not behold the majesty of the LORD.
11 LORD, *when* thy hand is lifted up, they will not see: *but* they shall see, and be ashamed for *their* envy at the people; yea, the fire of thine enemies shall devour them.
12 LORD, thou wilt ordain peace for us: for thou also hast wrought all our works in us.

13 O LORD our God, *other* lords besides thee have had dominion over us: *but* by thee only will we make mention of thy name.
14 *They are* dead, they shall not live; *they are* deceased, they shall not rise: therefore hast thou visited and destroyed them, and made all their memory to perish.
15 Thou hast increased the nation, O LORD, thou hast increased the nation: thou art glorified: thou hadst removed *it* far *unto* all the ends of the earth.
16 LORD, in trouble have they visited thee, they poured out a prayer *when* thy chastening *was* upon them.
17 Like as a woman with child, *that* draweth near the time of her delivery, is in pain, *and* crieth out in her pangs; so have we been in thy sight, O LORD.
18 We have been with child, we have been in pain, we have as it were brought forth wind; we have not wrought any deliverance in the earth; neither have the inhabitants of the world fallen.
19 Thy dead *men* shall live, *together with* my dead body shall they arise. Awake and sing, ye that dwell in dust: for thy dew *is as* the dew of herbs, and the earth shall cast out the dead.
20 Come, my people, enter thou into thy chambers, and shut thy doors about thee: hide thyself as it were for a little moment, until the indignation be overpast.
21 For, behold, the LORD cometh out of his place to punish the inhabitants of the earth for their iniquity: the earth also shall disclose her blood, and shall no more cover her slain.

CHAPTER 27

In that day the LORD with his sore and great and strong sword shall punish leviathan the piercing serpent, even leviathan that crooked serpent; and he shall slay the dragon that *is* in the sea.
2 In that day sing ye unto her, A vineyard of red wine.
3 I the LORD do keep it; I will water it every moment:

    1) The LORD delivered them from tyrants & oppressors: They now honored only Him
    2) The oppressors were now dead, never again to arise
      • The LORD punished & ruined them
      • The LORD even wiped out all memory of them
    3) The LORD honored & made the nation of His people great: He enlarged & extended its borders

  h. God disciplines His people because of their sin & failure

    1) His purpose: To arouse them to cry out to the LORD (return to Him), just as a woman giving birth cries out in pain

    2) Their sin & failure: Failed to be strong witnesses to the world; failed to give birth, deliverance to the world

  i. God has power over death
    1) The dead bodies of believers will rise from the dust
    2) The dead will be given life by God, as dew gives life to the herbs of the earth
  j. God warns His people to prepare themselves for His coming wrath
    1) They must secure themselves
    2) They must keep His judgment in mind
      • Because He is coming to punish the people of the earth for their sins
      • Because the earth will no longer hide murderers or any other person who commits secret sin

      • Because the LORD will punish the serpent Leviathan, that is, the enemies & nations who oppose God & His people, 30:7; 51:9; Eze.29:3

2. God's protection of His vineyard, Israel (His people)

  a. God's care for His vineyard— His people

1) He waters & guards the vineyard
2) He digs out & burns all briars & thorns (unbelievers)
3) He invites all briars & thorns (unbelievers) to make peace with Him
4) He makes sure that His people take root, bud, blossom, & fill the earth with fruit (righteousness)

b. God's discipline of His people
1) His discipline is limited
 • He does not destroy them but He does destroy their enemies
 • He disciplines them by warfare & exile

2) His discipline has a two-fold purpose
 • To stir His people to seek forgiveness, atonement, the purging away of sin
 • To eliminate all idolatry & false worship

lest *any* hurt it, I will keep it night and day.
4 Fury *is* not in me: who would set the briers *and* thorns against me in battle? I would go through them, I would burn them together.
5 Or let him take hold of my strength, *that* he may make peace with me; *and* he shall make peace with me.
6 He shall cause them that come of Jacob to take root: Israel shall blossom and bud, and fill the face of the world with fruit.
7 Hath he smitten him, as he smote those that smote him? *or* is he slain according to the slaughter of them that are slain by him?
8 In measure, when it shooteth forth, thou wilt debate with it: he stayeth his rough wind in the day of the east wind.
9 By this therefore shall the iniquity of Jacob be purged; and this *is* all the fruit to take away his sin; when he maketh all the stones of the altar as chalkstones that are beaten in sunder, the groves and images shall not stand

up.
10 Yet the defenced city *shall be* desolate, *and* the habitation forsaken, and left like a wilderness: there shall the calf feed, and there shall he lie down, and consume the branches thereof.
11 When the boughs thereof are withered, they shall be broken off: the women come, *and* set them on fire: for it *is* a people of no understanding: therefore he that made them will not have mercy on them, and he that formed them will show them no favour.
12 And it shall come to pass in that day, *that* the LORD shall beat off from the channel of the river unto the stream of Egypt, and ye shall be gathered one by one, O ye children of Israel.
13 And it shall come to pass in that day, *that* the great trumpet shall be blown, and they shall come which were ready to perish in the land of Assyria, and the outcasts in the land of Egypt, and shall worship the LORD in the holy mount at Jerusalem.

3) His discipline is thorough: Will destroy the fortified city (Jerusalem)
 • The city will be desolate & abandoned, inhabited only by wild animals
 • The people will be like the dead branches of a tree, gathered & burned
4) His discipline is just, showing no mercy or partiality: Because they had no understanding

c. God's restoration of His people
1) They will be gathered from the Euphrates to Egypt (the whole world)
2) They will hear a trumpet sound; A picture of the rapture, Ac.1:9-11; 1 Co. 15:50-58; 1 Th.4:13-18
3) They will be freed from exile & come to Jerusalem to worship the LORD

DIVISION II

THE PROPHECIES CONCERNING GOD'S JUDGMENT OF THE NATIONS AND HIS TRIUMPH OVER THE WORLD, 13:1–27:13

J. God's Works and the Protection of His Vineyard, His People: God's Great Care for His People, 26:1–27:13

(26:1–27:13) **Introduction**: genuinely caring for people is one of the marks of true greatness. Caring for people means to consider them, tend to them, and keep an eye on their welfare. It means to protect, provide for, and pay attention to them. But caring for people also means disciplining them when they need to be corrected, lest they harm themselves or others. A person who wants to be truly great will acknowledge others, respect them and care for them. He will naturally look after his own interests, but he will also look after the interests of others. He will highly respect himself, but he will also highly esteem others (Ph.2:3-4). So it is with the LORD.

The present Scripture consists of a song that will be sung *in that day*, the day the Messiah, the Lord Jesus Christ, establishes His kingdom on earth. Remember that the people of Isaiah's day were facing the constant threat of attack by the Assyrians. Consequently, it was a day of extreme distress and uncertainty. Thus the LORD longed to assure His people that He cared for them and would look after them. There was only one condition: they had to repent of their sins and turn back to Him. To encourage His people, the LORD inspired His prophet to lift up the hope of their future blessings. This is, *God's Works and the Protection of His Vineyard, His People: God's Great Care for His People*, 26:1–27:13.

1. God's works in behalf of His people to be celebrated in song *in that day* (Christ's kingdom) (26:1–27:1).
2. God's protection of His vineyard, Israel (His people) (27:2-13).

1 (26:1–27:1) **Works, of God, for His People—New Jerusalem, Described As, City of Salvation—Peace, Source - How One Secures—Rock, Symbol of, God—God, Symbolized by, a Rock—Judgment, Described As, Humbling the Prideful—God, Judgment of, Purpose, to Teach People to Live Righteously—Righteous, Blessings of, a Smooth Path—Peace, Source, the LORD—Deliverance, from Whom, Tyrants and Oppressors—Discipline, of God, Reasons—Resurrection, of Believers, Promised—Prophecy, of What, Believers' Resurrection—Warning, of Coming Judgment, Must Be Prepared**: God always acts for the benefit of His people, for those who truly believe in Him and live righteously. Because of His great love, the LORD is moving human history toward one climactic day, the day when the Messiah, the Lord Jesus Christ, will establish His kingdom on earth. *In that day* (v.1) all believers will offer up to the LORD the song of praise found in this Scripture. Note that this song spells out ten specific works God does in behalf of His people.

OUTLINE	SCRIPTURE	SCRIPTURE	OUTLINE

1. God's works in behalf of His people: To be celebrated in song *in that day* (Christ's kingdom)
a. God gives His people a city of salvation: The New Jerusalem
  1) Its gates will always be open
  2) Its citizens will be the righteous, Ps. 15:1-5
b. God gives perfect peace to the person whose mind is fixed on Him, Ro.5:1; Ph.4:6-9
c. God gives a strong foundation to the person who trusts in Him: He is a Rock, Ps.18:2
d. God humbles the proud person & levels the arrogant city to the dust
  1) The arrogant city will be cast down
  2) The city's oppressed & poor will survive the judgment & trample the city underfoot
e. God levels the path & smoothes the way for the righteous
  1) Those who obey God's law
  2) Those who wait on God
  3) Those who seek to glorify God
  4) Those who yearn for God morning & night
f. God executes His judgments on earth: To teach people to live righteously
 	
  1) He shows grace to the wicked, but they still refuse to learn righteousness: Even in an upright land they continue to do evil & refuse to honor the LORD
  2) He lifts His fist, warning the wicked, but they do not see the warning
  3) He shames & consumes them through judgment
g. God establishes peace for His people & strengthens them to accomplish their tasks, 3; Jn.14:27; 16:33; Ph.2:13
  1) The LORD delivered them from tyrants & oppressors: They now honored
	In that day shall this song be sung in the land of Judah; We have a strong city; salvation will *God* appoint *for* walls and bulwarks.
	2 Open ye the gates, that the righteous nation which keepeth the truth may enter in.
	3 Thou wilt keep *him* in perfect peace, *whose* mind *is* stayed *on thee:* because he trusteth in thee.
	4 Trust ye in the LORD for ever: for in the LORD JEHOVAH *is* everlasting strength:
	5 For he bringeth down them that dwell on high; the lofty city, he layeth it low; he layeth it low, *even* to the ground; he bringeth it *even* to the dust.
	6 The foot shall tread it down, *even* the feet of the poor, *and* the steps of the needy.
	7 The way of the just *is* uprightness: thou, most upright, dost weigh the path of the just.
	8 Yea, in the way of thy judgments, O LORD, have we waited for thee; the desire of *our* soul *is* to thy name, and to the remembrance of thee.
	9 With my soul have I desired thee in the night; yea, with my spirit within me will I seek thee early: for when thy judgments *are* in the earth, the inhabitants of the world will learn righteousness.
	10 Let favour be showed to the wicked, *yet* will he not learn righteousness: in the land of uprightness will he deal unjustly, and will not behold the majesty of the LORD.
	11 LORD, *when* thy hand is lifted up, they will not see: *but* they shall see, and be ashamed for *their* envy at the people; yea, the fire of thine enemies shall devour them.
	12 LORD, thou wilt ordain peace for us: for thou also hast wrought all our works in us.
	13 O LORD our God, *other* lords besides thee have had dominion over us: *but* by thee
		only will we make mention of thy name.
		14 *They are* dead, they shall not live; *they are* deceased, they shall not rise: therefore hast thou visited and destroyed them, and made all their memory to perish.
		15 Thou hast increased the nation, O LORD, thou hast increased the nation: thou art glorified: thou hadst removed *it* far *unto* all the ends of the earth.
		16 LORD, in trouble have they visited thee, they poured out a prayer *when* thy chastening *was* upon them.
		17 Like as a woman with child, *that* draweth near the time of her delivery, is in pain, *and* crieth out in her pangs; so have we been in thy sight, O LORD.
		18 We have been with child, we have been in pain, we have as it were brought forth wind; we have not wrought any deliverance in the earth; neither have the inhabitants of the world fallen.
		19 Thy dead *men* shall live, *together with* my dead body shall they arise. Awake and sing, ye that dwell in dust: for thy dew *is as* the dew of herbs, and the earth shall cast out the dead.
		20 Come, my people, enter thou into thy chambers, and shut thy doors about thee: hide thyself as it were for a little moment, until the indignation be overpast.
		21 For, behold, the LORD cometh out of his place to punish the inhabitants of the earth for their iniquity: the earth also shall disclose her blood, and shall no more cover her slain.
		
		CHAPTER 27
		
		In that day the LORD with his sore and great and strong sword shall punish leviathan the piercing serpent, even leviathan that crooked serpent; and he shall slay the dragon that *is* in the sea.
			only Him
			
			  2) The oppressors were now dead, never again to arise
			  • The LORD punished & ruined them
			  • The LORD even wiped out all the memory of them
			  3) The LORD honored & made the nation of His people great: He enlarged & extended its borders
			
			h. God disciplines His people because of their sin & failure
			
			  1) His purpose: To arouse them to cry out to the LORD (return to Him), just as a woman giving birth cries out in pain
			  2) Their sin & failure: Failed to be strong witnesses to the world; failed to give birth, deliverance to the world
			
			i. God has the power over death
			  1) The dead bodies of believers will rise from the dust
			  2) The dead will be given life by God, as dew gives life to the herbs of the earth
			j. God warns His people to prepare themselves for His coming wrath
			  1) They must secure themselves
			  2) They must keep His judgment in mind
			  • Because He is coming to punish the people of the earth for their sins
			  • Because the earth will no longer hide murderers or any other person who commits secret sin
			
			  • Because the LORD will punish the serpent Leviathan, that is, the enemies & nations who oppose God & His people, 30:7; 51:9; Eze.29:3

a. God gives His people a strong city, a city of salvation (vv.1-2). Here, the word *salvation* means God's deliverance and protection from all the evil and oppressive people of the world. When the Messiah's kingdom is set up on earth, Jerusalem will no longer be a city inhabited by sinful, wicked people (1:1-31). Nor will it be a city fought over and oppressed by the nations of the world, as it was in Isaiah's day and has been down through history. Instead, it will become the New Jerusalem, the capital of Christ's government on earth. Jerusalem will be known as the city of salvation, the city from which the Savior rules over the earth. *In that day* its gates will always be open so that the righteous can enter to worship Him. Note that Jerusalem's citizens will be the righteous, those who truly believe in God and obey His holy commandments. Only the righteous will enter and live with the Savior. Jerusalem will no longer be known as a city of division and conflict, but as the city of God, the city of salvation.

Thought 1. A person who trusts Jesus Christ as Savior will become a citizen of His kingdom. A genuine believer has the wonderful hope of living in a strong city, a city of salvation ruled over by Christ. *In that day* all believers will be delivered from all the evil of this world. All pain, heartache, and trouble will be erased. The citizens of the Lord's kingdom will never again experience grief, suffering, or oppression from the unbelievers and the wicked of the earth. Listen to the promise of God's Holy Word:

> **"By faith Abraham, when he was called to go out into a place which he should after receive for an inheritance, obeyed; and he went out, not knowing whither he went. By faith he sojourned in the land of promise, as *in* a strange country, dwelling in tabernacles with Isaac and Jacob, the heirs with him of the same promise: For he looked for a city which hath foundations, whose builder and maker *is* God" (He.11:8-10).**

> **"These all died in faith, not having received the promises, but having seen them afar off, and were persuaded of *them,* and embraced *them,* and confessed that they were strangers and pilgrims on the earth. For they that say such things declare plainly that they seek a country. And truly, if they had been mindful of that *country* from whence they came out, they might have had opportunity to have returned. But now they desire a better *country,* that is, an heavenly: wherefore God is not ashamed to be called their God: for he hath prepared for them a city" (He.11:13-16).**

> **"But ye are come unto mount Sion, and unto the city of the living God, the heavenly Jerusalem, and to an innumerable company of angels" (He.12:22).**

> **"For here have we no continuing city, but we seek one to come" (He.13:14).**

> **"And I John saw the holy city, new Jerusalem, coming down from God out of heaven, prepared as a bride adorned for her husband. And I heard a great voice out of heaven saying, Behold, the tabernacle of God *is* with men, and he will dwell with them, and they shall be his people, and God himself shall be with them, *and be* their God. And God shall wipe away all tears from their eyes; and there shall be no more death, neither sorrow, nor crying, neither shall there be any more pain: for the former things are passed away. And he that sat upon the throne said, Behold, I make all things new. And he said unto me, Write: for these words are true and faithful. And he said unto me, It is done. I am Alpha and Omega, the beginning and the end. I will give unto him that is athirst of the fountain of the water of life freely. He that overcometh shall inherit all things; and I will be his God, and he shall be my son" (Re.21:2-7).**

> **"And he carried me away in the spirit to a great and high mountain, and showed me that great city, the holy Jerusalem, descending out of heaven from God" (Re.21:10).**

> **"And if any man shall take away from the words of the book of this prophecy, God shall take away his part out of the book of life, and out of the holy city, and *from* the things which are written in this book" (Re.22:19).**

b. God gives His people *perfect peace*. But *perfect peace* is given only to the person whose mind or thoughts are fixed on Him (v.3). The word *peace* (*shalom*) means to be in harmony with God, experiencing *peace with God* and the *peace of God*. It means to be in such harmony with God that one is assured of having all needs met. Peace gives a person the assurance of health, wholeness, the absence of conflict and strife within and without his soul. *Peace* is the assurance of deliverance through hardship, accident, disease, and calamity. The *peace* given by God is a quiet, restful soul; a sense of purpose, contentment, fulfillment and completion. God's *peace* is the assurance of present and future security, deliverance and success. God's *peace* delivers a person through all the conflicts, strife, divisions, trials, and temptations of this life.

However, note this important fact: the person who has such peace is the person whose mind or thoughts stay fixed on the LORD. through all the turmoil of Isaiah's day, the prophet Isaiah clearly experienced what so many long for: the *perfect peace* of God—peace of heart and soul.

> **"Peace I leave with you, my peace I give unto you: not as the world giveth, give I unto you. Let not your heart be troubled, neither let it be afraid" (Jn.14:27).**

> **"These things I have spoken unto you, that in me ye might have peace. In the world ye shall have tribulation: but be of good cheer; I have overcome the world" (Jn.16:33).**

> **"Therefore being justified by faith, we have peace with God through our Lord Jesus Christ" (Ro.5:1).**

> **"Be careful for nothing; but in every thing by prayer and supplication with thanksgiving let your requests be made known unto God. And the peace of God, which passeth all understanding, shall keep your hearts and minds through Christ Jesus" (Ph.4:6-7).**

> **"Finally, brethren, whatsoever things are true, whatsoever things *are* honest, whatsoever things *are* just, whatsoever things *are* pure, whatsoever things *are* lovely, whatsoever things *are* of good report; if *there be* any virtue, and if *there be* any praise, think on these things. Those things, which ye have both learned, and received, and heard, and seen in me, do: and the God of peace shall be with you" (Ph.4:8-9).**

> **"And let the peace of God rule in your hearts, to the which also ye are called in one body; and be ye thankful. Let the word of Christ dwell in you richly in all wisdom; teaching and admonishing one another in psalms and hymns and spiritual songs, singing with grace in your hearts to the Lord" (Col.3:15-16).**

> **"Depart from evil, and do good; seek peace, and pursue it" (Ps.34:14).**

c. One of the great works of God in behalf of His people is to provide a solid foundation for life. As the rock of life, the LORD provides stability, security, support, and defense against all the stormy trials and temptations of life.

Thought 1. As we walk through life, we decide to build our lives either upon sinking sand or upon the solid rock of the Lord. Listen to what God's Holy Word says:

"Therefore whosoever heareth these sayings of mine, and doeth them, I will liken him unto a wise man, which built his house upon a rock: And the rain descended, and the floods came, and the winds blew, and beat upon that house; and it fell not: for it was founded upon a rock. And every one that heareth these sayings of mine, and doeth them not, shall be likened unto a foolish man, which built his house upon the sand: And the rain descended, and the floods came, and the winds blew, and beat upon that house; and it fell: and great was the fall of it" (Mt.7:24-27).

"*There is* none holy as the LORD: for *there is* none beside thee: neither *is there* any rock like our God" (1 S.2:2).

"For the eyes of the LORD run to and fro throughout the whole earth, to show himself strong in the behalf of *them* whose heart *is* perfect toward him. Herein thou hast done foolishly: therefore from henceforth thou shalt have wars" (2 Chr.16:9).

"The LORD *is* my rock, and my fortress, and my deliverer; my God, my strength, in whom I will trust; my buckler, and the horn of my salvation, *and* my high tower" (Ps.18:2).

"For who *is* God save the LORD? or who *is* a rock save our God? *It is* God that girdeth me with strength, and maketh my way perfect" (Ps.18:31-32).

"Unto thee will I cry, O LORD my rock; be not silent to me: lest, *if* thou be silent to me, I become like them that go down into the pit" (Ps.28:1).

"Truly my soul waiteth upon God: from him *cometh* my salvation. He only *is* my rock and my salvation; *he is* my defence; I shall not be greatly moved" (Ps.62:1-2).

"But the LORD is my defence; and my God *is* the rock of my refuge" (Ps.94:22).

d. On Judgment Day, God will humble the proud and bring down the arrogant to the dust (vv.5-6). All people, cities, and nations that exalt themselves at the expense of others will face the judgment of God. Down through history, the proud have used their position, power, and wealth to oppress and mistreat others. Far too often the prideful...

- mock and persecute the righteous
- rob and cheat people
- falsely accuse and threaten people to fulfill their own wicked lusts
- twist the law and use bribery to secure more position, power, and wealth
- deny and defy the LORD, the only living and true God

But the day is coming when God will level the arrogant cities of this world and humble all their proud rulers and citizens. Once the cities have been leveled, the poor and needy will trample down their ruins (v.6). In this Scripture, the term *poor and needy* refers to believers who have been oppressed and stripped of their possessions by the proud. But the day of God's judgment will bring a reversal of position, power, and wealth. The proud will be destroyed, and the poor and needy will be exalted. The LORD will elevate all who have truly trusted Him to positions of leadership and give them unimaginable wealth.

Thought 1. In this world, many of God's people are looked upon as insignificant and unimportant. Because of their righteous lives and witness for the Lord, they are usually considered a thorn in the side of society. For this reason, the unbelievers of the world oppress and persecute them. They are poor, needy, and powerless. But the day is coming when all proud unbelievers will be humbled and all arrogant cities will be leveled to the ground. *In that day* the poor and needy believers of the world will be exalted.

"And whosoever shall exalt himself shall be abased; and he that shall humble himself shall be exalted" (Mt.23:12).

"He hath put down the mighty from *their* seats, and exalted them of low degree" (Lu.1:52).

"And he said unto him, Well, thou good servant: because thou hast been faithful in a very little, have thou authority over ten cities" (Lu.19:17).

"Do ye not know that the saints shall judge the world? and if the world shall be judged by you, are ye unworthy to judge the smallest matters?" (1 Co.6:2).

"To him that overcometh will I grant to sit with me in my throne, even as I also overcame, and am set down with my Father in his throne" (Re.3:21).

"Because he hath set his love upon me, therefore will I deliver him: I will set him on high, because he hath known my name" (Ps.91:14).

"These six *things* doth the LORD hate: yea, seven *are* an abomination unto him: A proud look, a lying tongue, and hands that shed innocent blood, An heart that deviseth wicked imaginations, feet that be swift in running to mischief, A false witness *that* speaketh lies, and he that soweth discord among brethren" (Pr.6:16-19).

"Whoso privily [secretly] slandereth his neighbour, him will I cut off: him that hath an high look and a proud heart will not I suffer" (Ps.101:5).

"The LORD will destroy the house of the proud: but he will establish the border of the widow" (Pr.15:25).

"Pride *goeth* before destruction, and an haughty spirit before a fall" (Pr.16:18).

"A man's pride shall bring him low: but honour shall uphold the humble in spirit" (Pr.29:23).

"The lofty looks of man shall be humbled, and the haughtiness of men shall be bowed down, and the LORD alone shall be exalted in that day. For the day of the LORD of hosts *shall be* upon every *one that is* proud and lofty, and upon every *one that is* lifted up; and he shall be brought low" (Is.2:11-12).

"And the loftiness of man shall be bowed down, and the haughtiness of men shall be made low: and the LORD alone shall be exalted in that day" (Is.2:17).

"For, behold, the day cometh, that shall burn as an oven; and all the proud, yea, and all that do wickedly, shall be stubble: and the day that cometh shall burn them up, saith the LORD of hosts, that it shall leave them neither root nor branch" (Mal.4:1).

e. God levels the path and smoothes the way for the righteous (vv.7-9a). As the righteous walk through life, obstacles often appear in their paths. Some large hurdle or hazard confronts them—a serious trial, temptation, or difficult circumstance. Isaiah says that God will level the path and smooth the way for the righteous to continue their journey. Note how Isaiah addressed the LORD: he called Him *the Most Upright*. Because the LORD is upright (righteous, just), He will act in behalf of the righteous. He will make sure that nothing prevents the righteous from traveling the road He has appointed them to travel. But note who the righteous are:

⇒ people who obey the judgments or laws of the LORD
⇒ people who *wait (quavah* or *qawahl)* patiently on the LORD
⇒ people who diligently seek to glorify the name of the LORD
⇒ people who yearn for and seek the LORD

Righteous people are those who obey God's Word and eagerly wait on Him. They are those who yearn for the LORD morning and night and seek to glorify Him (v.9a). God will act in behalf of such people, leveling the path and smoothing the way they travel throughout life.

"Enter ye in at the strait gate: for wide *is* the gate, and broad *is* the way, that leadeth to destruction, and many there be which go in thereat: Because strait *is* the gate, and narrow *is* the way, which leadeth unto life, and few there be that find it." (Mt.7:13-14).

"And thou, child [Jesus Christ], shalt be called the prophet of the Highest: for thou shalt go before the face of the Lord to prepare his ways....To give light to them that sit in darkness and *in* the shadow of death, to guide our feet into the way of peace" (Lu.1:76, 79).

"Saying, I will declare thy name unto my brethren, in the midst of the church will I sing praise unto thee. And again, I will put my trust in him. And again, Behold I and the children which God hath given me" (He.2:12-13).

"Thou wilt show me the path of life: in thy presence *is* fulness of joy; at thy right hand *there are* pleasures for evermore" (Ps.16:11).

"He restoreth my soul: he leadeth me in the paths of righteousness for his name's sake" (Ps.23:3).

"All the paths of the LORD *are* mercy and truth unto such as keep his covenant and his testimonies" (Ps.25:10).

"Make me to go in the path of thy commandments; for therein do I delight" (Ps.119:35).

"For the LORD giveth wisdom: out of his mouth *cometh* knowledge and understanding. He layeth up sound wisdom for the righteous: *he is* a buckler to them that walk uprightly. He keepeth the paths of judgment, and preserveth the way of his saints. Then shalt thou understand righteousness, and judgment, and equity; *yea,* every good path" (Pr.2:6-9).

"I have taught thee in the way of wisdom; I have led thee in right paths" (Pr.4:11).

"But the path of the just *is* as the shining light, that shineth more and more unto the perfect day" (Pr.4:18).

"And many people shall go and say, Come ye, and let us go up to the mountain of the LORD, to the house of the God of Jacob; and he will teach us of his ways, and we will walk in his paths: for out of Zion shall go forth the law, and the word of the LORD from Jerusalem" (Is.2:3).

"That the LORD thy God may show us the way wherein we may walk, and the thing that we may do" (Je.42:3).

f. Another work of God is to execute His judgments on earth (v.9b-11). Note that the LORD has a very specific purpose for His judgments: to teach people to live righteously. When disaster strikes people, they tend to turn to the LORD, seeking His strength and deliverance. The LORD hears when the wicked cry for help, and though He often meets their need, they still refuse to learn His righteous ways. Even when they live in a so-called land of righteousness, they continue to live sinful lives, no matter how much kindness the LORD shows them or how many blessings He bestows upon them. Although the LORD lifts His fist to warn them of coming judgment, they refuse to see the disaster that lies right over the horizon. But a day of rude awakening will come. *In that day* of coming judgment, all the wicked will see God's zeal in saving His people and putting the wicked to shame. The fire God has reserved for His enemies will consume the wicked (v.11).

Thought 1. The wicked of the earth have no spiritual understanding of the LORD or His Word. They are dull of hearing. They have closed their minds and chosen to be ignorant of the LORD, the only living and true God. Likewise, they reject Him and His warning of coming judgment. Listen to what God says about the wicked having no understanding and being dull of hearing:

"*Ye* hypocrites, ye can discern the face of the sky and of the earth; but how is it that ye do not discern this time? Yea, and why even of yourselves judge ye not what is right?" (Lu.12:56-57).

"Jesus said unto them, If God were your Father, ye would love me: for I proceeded forth and came from God; neither came I of myself, but he sent me. Why do ye not understand my speech? *even* because ye cannot hear my word. Ye are of *your* father the devil, and the lusts of your father ye will do. He was a murderer from the beginning, and abode not in the truth, because there is no truth in him. When he speaketh a lie, he speaketh of his own: for he is a liar, and the father of it" (Jn.8:42-44).

"For the heart of this people is waxed gross, and their ears are dull of hearing, and their eyes have they closed; lest they should see with *their* eyes, and hear with *their* ears, and understand with *their* heart, and should be converted, and I should heal them" (Ac.28:27).

"As it is written, There is none righteous, no, not one: There is none that understandeth, there is none that seeketh after God" (Ro.3:10-11).

"This know also, that in the last days perilous times shall come. For men shall be lovers of their own selves, covetous, boasters, proud, blasphemers, disobedient to parents, unthankful, unholy, Without natural affection, trucebreakers, false accusers, incontinent, fierce, despisers of those that are good, Traitors, heady, highminded, lovers of pleasures more than lovers of God; Having a form of godliness, but denying the power thereof: from such turn away. For of this sort are they which creep into houses, and lead captive silly women laden with sins, led away with divers lusts, Ever learning, and never able to come to the knowledge of the truth" (2 Ti.3:1-7, esp.v.7).

"Of whom we have many things to say, and hard to be uttered, seeing ye are dull of hearing" (He.5:11).

"They know not, neither will they understand; they walk on in darkness: all the foundations of the earth are out of course" (Ps.82:5).

"O LORD, how great are thy works! *and* thy thoughts are very deep. A brutish man knoweth not; neither doth a fool understand this. When the wicked spring as the grass, and when all the workers of iniquity do flourish; *it is* that they shall be destroyed for ever: But thou, LORD, *art most* high for evermore. For, lo, thine enemies, O LORD, for, lo, thine enemies shall perish; all the workers of iniquity shall be scattered" (Ps.92:5-9).

"For my people *is* foolish, they have not known me; they *are* sottish children, and they have none understanding: they *are* wise to do evil, but to do good they have no knowledge" (Je.4:22).

"Hear now this, O foolish people, and without understanding; which have eyes, and see not; which have ears, and hear not" (Je.5:21).

"But they know not the thoughts of the LORD, neither understand they his counsel: for he shall gather them as the sheaves into the floor" (Mi.4:12).

g. God gives His people peace and He strengthens them (vv.12-15). As Isaiah looked back over the history of Israel, he remembered how often the LORD had delivered them from the oppressors of this earth. Because of the Israelites' sins down through the centuries, the LORD had used other nations to discipline them through oppression and captivity. These tyrants had included the pharaohs of Egypt, as well as the rulers of surrounding nations. In Isaiah's day, the rulers of Assyria were threatening Judah. But Isaiah knew that God had always strengthened the true believers in times of oppression. Thus the faithful among His people had continued to honor the name of the LORD (v.13).

Note what Isaiah said about the oppressors: they were dead, and their spirits would never again rise (vv.14-15). This is a startling prophecy, for Isaiah was contrasting the enemies of God with genuine believers who place their trust in God. In stating that the spirits of God's enemies would not rise again, he implied that the spirits of those who trust God would rise again.

When the LORD punishes His enemies, He will even wipe out all memory of them. By *memory*, Isaiah meant their honor. For example, although we know about the Pharaoh of Egypt during Moses' day, no one honors his memory today. His name is found only in the records of that period of history. But this is not true for God's people. In the coming day of the Messiah's kingdom on earth, the nation of Israel will be enlarged and honored. Its borders will be extended, and the nation will be greatly honored (v.15).

Thought 1. Note the wonderful promises of God:
(1) God promises to flood the hearts of His people with peace as they walk through life.

"Peace I leave with you, my peace I give unto you: not as the world giveth, give I unto you. Let not your heart be troubled, neither let it be afraid" (Jn.14:27).
"These things I have spoken unto you, that in me ye might have peace. In the world ye shall have tribulation: but be of good cheer; I have overcome the world" (Jn.16:33).
"Be careful for nothing; but in every thing by prayer and supplication with thanksgiving let your requests be made known unto God. And the peace of God, which passeth all understanding, shall keep your hearts and minds through Christ Jesus" (Ph.4:6-7).
"Great peace have they which love thy law: and nothing shall offend them" (Ps.119:165).
"Thou wilt keep *him* in perfect peace, *whose* mind *is* stayed *on thee:* because he trusteth in thee" (Is.26:3).
"O that thou hadst hearkened to my commandments! then had thy peace been as a river, and thy righteousness as the waves of the sea" (Is.48:18).

(2) God promises to strengthen His people in times of oppression.

"And God *is* able to make all grace abound toward you; that ye, always having all sufficiency in all *things,* may abound to every good work" (2 Co.9:8).
"That he would grant you, according to the riches of his glory, to be strengthened with might by his Spirit in the inner man" (Ep.3:16).
"For it is God which worketh in you both to will and to do of *his* good pleasure" (Ph.2:13).

"I can do all things through Christ which strengtheneth me" (Ph.4:13).

"And I thank Christ Jesus our Lord, who hath enabled me, for that he counted me faithful, putting me into the ministry" (1 Ti.1:12).

"For thou hast girded me with strength to battle: them that rose up against me hast thou subdued under me" (2 S.22:40).

"But they that wait upon the LORD shall renew *their* strength; they shall mount up with wings as eagles; they shall run, and not be weary; *and* they shall walk, and not faint" (Is.40:31).

"Fear thou not; for I *am* with thee: be not dismayed; for I *am* thy God: I will strengthen thee; yea, I will help thee; yea, I will uphold thee with the right hand of my righteousness" (Is.41:10).

h. Another work of God is to discipline His people (vv.16-18). When God's people sinned and failed to do what they should have done, the LORD disciplined them. As Isaiah reviewed the history of Israel, he saw that the LORD had disciplined the people so much that they were now bowed under the weight of the chastisement. But God had a very specific purpose for disciplining them: to cause them to cry out to Him. He longed for them to turn from their sins and return to Him. As a woman giving birth cries out in pain, so the Israelites suffering the discipline of God cried out in pain. Up until the time of Isaiah, the LORD had always heard their cry and delivered the faithful believers among them, but His deliverance had not produced permanent righteousness in the nation. The people failed to be the strong witnesses to the world that the LORD had planned for them to be. Sadly, Israel had failed to give birth to righteousness.

Thought 1. God disciplines His people when they sin and fail to be witnesses for Him. But remember why God disciplines us: to correct us, to stir us up to live as we should.

"Every branch in me that beareth not fruit he taketh away: and every *branch* that beareth fruit, he purgeth it, that it may bring forth more fruit" (Jn.15:2).

"For this cause many *are* weak and sickly among you, and many sleep. For if we would judge ourselves, we should not be judged. But when we are judged, we are chastened of the Lord, that we should not be condemned with the world" (1 Co.11:30-32).

"And ye have forgotten the exhortation which speaketh unto you as unto children, My son, despise not thou the chastening of the Lord, nor faint when thou art rebuked of him: For whom the Lord loveth he chasteneth, and scourgeth every son whom he receiveth" (He.12:5-6).

"As many as I love, I rebuke and chasten: be zealous therefore, and repent." (Re.3:19).

"Thou shalt also consider in thine heart, that, as a man chasteneth his son, *so* the LORD thy God chasteneth thee" (De.8:5).

"Blessed *is* the man whom thou chastenest, O LORD, and teachest him out of thy law" (Ps.94:12).

"My son, despise not the chastening of the LORD; neither be weary of his correction: For whom the LORD loveth he correcteth; even as a father the son *in whom* he delighteth" (Pr.3:11-12).

"O LORD, I know that the way of man *is* not in himself: *it is* not in man that walketh to direct his steps. O LORD, correct me, but with judgment; not in thine anger, lest thou bring me to nothing" (Je.10:23-24).

i. One of the most astounding works of God will be the raising of the dead from the dust of the ground (v.19). Amazingly Isaiah predicted that the dead followers of the LORD will live; their bodies will rise from the dust of the ground. Some commentators apply this to the restoration of Israel as a nation (see Eze.36–37). But the reference to *body* or *bodies* is just too personal, too individualistic to apply to a national group of people. It is the bodies of people, of genuine believers to whom Isaiah is referring. Through the inspiration of God's Spirit he is predicting the resurrection of believers when the LORD returns. In that glorious day the *rapture* of believers will take place: their dead bodies will arise from the dust of the earth. Therefore, all believers should wake up and shout for joy because of this wonderful promise. "As dew gives life to the herbs of the earth, so *in that day* the dead will be given life by God.

"Marvel not at this: for the hour is coming, in the which all that are in the graves shall hear his voice, And shall come forth; they that have done good, unto the resurrection of life; and they that have done evil, unto the resurrection of damnation" (Jn.5:28-29).

"And this is the will of him that sent me, that every one which seeth the Son, and believeth on him, may have everlasting life: and I will raise him up at the last day" (Jn.6:40).

"Jesus said unto her, I am the resurrection, and the life: he that believeth in me, though he were dead, yet shall he live: And whosoever liveth and believeth in me shall never die. Believest thou this?" (Jn.11:25-26).

"But this I confess unto thee, that after the way which they call heresy, so worship I the God of my fathers, believing all things which are written in the law and in the prophets: And have hope toward God, which they themselves also allow, that there shall be a resurrection of the dead, both of the just and unjust" (Ac.24:14-15).

"But now is Christ risen from the dead, *and* become the firstfruits of them that slept. For since by man *came* death, by man *came* also the resurrection of the dead. For as in Adam all die, even so in Christ shall all be made alive. But every man in his own order: Christ the firstfruits; afterward they that are Christ's at his coming" (1 Co.15:20-23).

"Now this I say, brethren, that flesh and blood cannot inherit the kingdom of God; neither doth corruption inherit incorruption. Behold, I show you a mystery; We shall not all sleep, but we shall all be changed, In a moment, in the twinkling of an eye, at the last trump: for the trumpet shall sound, and the dead shall be raised incorruptible, and we shall be changed. For this corruptible must put on incorruption, and this mortal *must* put on immortality" (1 Co.15:50-53).

"Knowing that he which raised up the Lord Jesus shall raise up us also by Jesus, and shall present *us* with you" (2 Co.4:14).

"Who shall change our vile body, that it may be fashioned like unto his glorious body, according to the working whereby he is able even to subdue all things unto himself" (Ph.3:21).

"But I would not have you to be ignorant, brethren, concerning them which are asleep, that ye sorrow not, even as others which have no hope. For if we believe that Jesus died and rose again, even so them also which sleep in Jesus will God bring with him. For this we say unto you by the word of the Lord, that we which are alive *and* remain unto the coming of the Lord shall not prevent them which are asleep. For the Lord himself shall descend from heaven with a shout, with the voice of the archangel, and with the trump of God: and the dead in Christ shall rise first: Then we which are alive *and* remain shall be caught up together with them in the clouds, to meet the Lord in the air: and so shall we ever be with the Lord. Wherefore comfort one another with these words" (1 Th.4:13-18).

"And *though* after my skin *worms* destroy this *body,* yet in my flesh shall I see God" (Jb.19:26).

"For thou wilt not leave my soul in hell; neither wilt thou suffer thine Holy One to see corruption" (Ps.16:10).

"But God will redeem my soul from the power of the grave: for he shall receive me. Selah" (Ps.49:15).

"*Thou,* which hast showed me great and sore troubles, shalt quicken me again, and shalt bring me up again from the depths of the earth" (Ps.71:20).

"And many of them that sleep in the dust of the earth shall awake, some to everlasting life, and some to shame *and* everlasting contempt" (Da.12:2).

"I will ransom them from the power of the grave; I will redeem them from death: O death, I will be thy plagues; O grave, I will be thy destruction: repentance shall be hid from mine eyes" (Ho.13:14).

j. One of the significant works of God is to warn people to prepare for the coming day of wrath (26:20–27:1). Isaiah and His people needed to prepare for the Assyrian oppression, and then later generations needed to prepare for the Babylonian invasion (see outline and notes—2 K.25:1-30 for more discussion). The LORD encouraged them to enter their rooms and shut the doors. Most likely, this referred to finding their refuge in Him, for He was their only hope of security. No matter what the trial or its potential threat, the LORD is the true refuge for believers.

In the present Scripture, the primary reference is to a day of future judgment and *great tribulation* that is coming upon the earth (see outline and notes—Mt.24:15-28 for more discussion). Believers of all generations must prepare themselves for *that day* of terrifying judgment. Although the judgment will last for only a little while, they must secure themselves. Isaiah gave three reasons why believers must be prepared.

1) Believers must be prepared because the LORD is coming to punish the people of the earth for their sins. The implication is that believers must not be participating in the wicked behavior of unbelievers.

2) Believers must be prepared because the earth will no longer hide murderers, no longer conceal the sins of those who attempt to hide their wicked deeds. *In that day* no sin will be hidden from God, no matter how long it has been kept secret. The blazing purity of God's holiness will expose all sin, whether major or minor. All believers who are committing secret sin will have their sin exposed.

3) Believers must be prepared because the LORD will punish the serpent Leviathan; that is, the nations who oppose God and His people (27:1; 30:7; 51:9; Eze.29:3). Mentioned in the myths of that day, Leviathan was probably a sea monster that became a symbol of cruel, wicked nations. Thus *in that day* of God's terrible judgment, the LORD's sword (His Word, Ep.6:17) will slay all the monsters of the earth and its seas—all the nations who have opposed God and His people.

Thought 1. We must heed the warning of the LORD: He is returning to judge the earth. He has given us strong and sufficient warning to turn our lives around. Listen to what God's Holy Word says:

"Watch therefore: for ye know not what hour your Lord doth come. But know this, that if the goodman of the house had known in what watch the thief would come, he would have watched, and would not have suffered his house to be broken up. Therefore be ye also ready: for in such an hour as ye think not the Son of man cometh" (Mt.24:42-44).

"Then shall the kingdom of heaven be likened unto ten virgins, which took their lamps, and went forth to meet the bridegroom. And five of them were wise, and five *were* foolish. They that *were* foolish took their lamps, and took no oil with them: But the wise took oil in their vessels with their lamps. While the bridegroom tarried, they all slumbered and slept. And at midnight there was a cry made, Behold, the bridegroom cometh; go ye out to meet him. Then all those virgins arose, and trimmed their lamps. And the foolish said unto the wise, Give us of your oil; for our lamps are gone out. But the wise answered, saying, *Not so;* lest there be not enough for us and you: but go ye rather to them that sell, and buy for yourselves. And while they went to buy, the bridegroom came; and they that were ready went in with him to the marriage: and the door was shut. Afterward came also the other virgins, saying, Lord, Lord, open to us. But he answered and said, Verily I say unto you, I know you not. Watch therefore, for ye know neither the day nor the hour wherein the Son of man cometh" (Mt.25:1-13).

"Watch and pray, that ye enter not into temptation: the spirit indeed *is* willing, but the flesh *is* weak" (Mt.26:41).

"Watch ye therefore: for ye know not when the master of the house cometh, at even, or at midnight, or at the cockcrowing, or in the morning" (Mk.13:35).

"Let your loins be girded about, and *your* lights burning; And ye yourselves like unto men that wait for their lord, when he will return from the wedding; that when he cometh and knocketh, they may open unto him immediately" (Lu.12:35-36).

"Watch ye, stand fast in the faith, quit you like men, be strong" (1 Co.16:13).

"Ye are all the children of light, and the children of the day: we are not of the night, nor of darkness. Therefore let us not sleep, as *do* others; but let us watch and be sober" (1 Th.5:5-6).

"Be sober, be vigilant; because your adversary the devil, as a roaring lion, walketh about, seeking whom he may devour: Whom resist stedfast in the faith, knowing that the same afflictions are accomplished in your brethren that are in the world" (1 Pe.5:8-9).

"Behold, I come quickly: hold that fast which thou hast, that no man take thy crown" (Re.3:11).

"Behold, I come as a thief. Blessed *is* he that watcheth, and keepeth his garments, lest he walk naked, and they see his shame" (Re.16:15).

"Let us be glad and rejoice, and give honour to him: for the marriage of the Lamb is come, and his wife hath made herself ready. And to her was granted that she should be arrayed in fine linen, clean and white: for the fine linen is the righteousness of saints. And he saith unto me, Write, Blessed *are* they which are called unto the marriage supper of the Lamb. And he saith unto me, These are the true sayings of God" (Re.19:7-9).

---

[2] (27:2-13) **Protection, of God, for His People—Vineyard, Symbol of, Israel—Care, of God, for His People—Discipline, of God, Four Facts About—Restoration, of Israel, Promised—Remnant, of Israel, Promised**: God promised to protect His vineyard, which is a symbol of Israel and of His people—all genuine believers down through the ages. Note again the words *in that day*, which are a direct reference to the future day when the Messiah will set up His kingdom on earth. God gave His people three wonderful promises:

OUTLINE	SCRIPTURE	SCRIPTURE	OUTLINE
2. God's protection of His vineyard, Israel (His people)	2 In that day sing ye unto her, A vineyard of red wine.	chalkstones that are beaten in sunder, the groves and images shall not stand up.	away of sin
a. God's care for His vineyard—His people	3 I the LORD do keep it; I will water it every moment: lest *any* hurt it, I will keep it night and day.	10 Yet the defenced city *shall be* desolate, *and* the habitation forsaken, and left like a wilderness: there shall	• To eliminate all idolatry & false worship
1) He waters & guards the vineyard			3) His discipline is thorough: Will destroy the fortified city (Jerusalem)
2) He digs out & burns all briars & thorns (unbelievers)	4 Fury *is* not in me: who would set the briers *and* thorns against me in battle? I would go through them, I would burn them together.	the calf feed, and there shall he lie down, and consume the branches thereof.	• The city will be desolate & abandoned, inhabited only by wild animals
3) He invites all briars & thorns (unbelievers) to make peace with Him	5 Or let him take hold of my strength, *that* he may make peace with me; *and* he shall make peace with me.	11 When the boughs thereof are withered, they shall be broken off: the women come, *and* set them on fire: for it *is* a people of no understanding:	• The people will be like the dead branches of a tree, gathered & burned
4) He makes sure that His people take root, bud, blossom, & fill the earth with fruit (righteousness)	6 He shall cause them that come of Jacob to take root: Israel shall blossom and bud, and fill the face of the world with fruit.	therefore he that made them will not have mercy on them, and he that formed them will show them no favour.	4) His discipline is just, showing no mercy or partiality: Because they had no understanding
b. God's discipline of His people	7 Hath he smitten him, as he smote those that smote him? or is he slain according to the slaughter of them that are slain by him?	12 And it shall come to pass in that day, *that* the LORD shall beat off from the channel of the river unto the stream of Egypt, and ye shall be gathered one by one, O ye children of Israel.	c. God's restoration of His people
1) His discipline is limited			1) They will be gathered from the Euphrates to Egypt (the whole world)
• He does not destroy them but He does destroy their enemies			
• He disciplines them by warfare & exile	8 In measure, when it shooteth forth, thou wilt debate with it: he stayeth his rough wind in the day of the east wind.	13 And it shall come to pass in that day, *that* the great trumpet shall be blown, and they shall come which were ready to perish in the land of Assyria, and the outcasts in the land of Egypt, and shall worship the LORD in the holy mount at Jerusalem.	2) They will hear a trumpet sound; A picture of the rapture (Ac.1:9-11; 1 Co. 15:50-58; 1 Th.4:13-18)
2) His discipline has a twofold purpose	9 By this therefore shall the iniquity of Jacob be purged; and this *is* all the fruit to take away his sin; when he maketh all the stones of the altar as		3) They will be freed from exile & come to Jerusalem to worship the LORD
• To stir His people to seek forgiveness, atonement, the purging			

a. God promised to care for His vineyard, His people (vv.2-6). Note that this is a song that will be sung in the Messiah's coming kingdom. The LORD Himself promises to watch over His vineyard, to guard it day and night so that no one can harm it. Imagine the stark contrast between the Israel of Isaiah's day and the Israel of the Messiah's kingdom. In Isaiah's day, Assyria was a constant threat, and Babylon would soon invade Judah and send the people into exile. But in the Messiah's day there will be no enemies to attack God's people. His presence will bring peace to earth, and no one will harm the righteous citizens of His kingdom.

When dealing with the people in His kingdom, the LORD will harbor no anger toward them in His heart. But if any briar or thorn—any enemy or unbeliever—arises in His kingdom, God's blazing holiness will set it on fire (v.4).

Even so, the LORD will appeal to His enemies to come to Him for refuge and to make peace with Him (v.5). Note the implication that people will still have *freedom of will* during the millennial reign of Jesus Christ on earth. Some people will reject Christ when He rules as king, just as some rejected Him when He first came to earth as the Savior. But when He rules upon earth, any who confront Him will be consumed with the fire of His burning holiness. However, He will first give them an opportunity to repent and make peace with Him. The LORD will make sure that His people take root, bud, blossom, and fill the earth with the fruit of righteousness. Only righteousness will be allowed in His kingdom.

Thought 1. God looks after and cares for His people. Day by day, He keeps an eye on every person who truly follows Him. As He watches over us, He knows every trial, temptation, and misfortune that confronts us. Like a shepherd, He reaches out to us in care and concern, and He provides whatever we need to live fruitful and victorious lives.

> **"(For after all these things do the Gentiles seek:) for your heavenly Father knoweth that ye have need of all these things. But seek ye first the kingdom of God, and his righteousness; and all these things shall be added unto you" (Mt.6:32-33).**
> **"But even the very hairs of your head are all numbered. Fear not therefore: ye are of more value than many sparrows" (Lu.12:7).**
> **"For the which cause I also suffer these things: nevertheless I am not ashamed: for I know whom I have believed, and am persuaded that he is able to keep that which I have committed unto him against that day" (2 Ti.1:12).**
> **"And the Lord shall deliver me from every evil work, and will preserve *me* unto his heavenly kingdom: to whom *be* glory for ever and ever. Amen" (2 Ti.4:18).**
> **"Casting all your care upon him; for he careth for you" (1 Pe.5:7).**
> **"And, behold, I *am* with thee, and will keep thee in all *places* whither thou goest, and will bring thee again into this land; for I will not leave thee, until I have done *that* which I have spoken to thee of" (Ge.28:15).**
> **"The eternal God *is thy* refuge, and underneath *are* the everlasting arms: and he shall thrust out the enemy from before thee; and shall say, Destroy *them*" (De.33:27).**
> **"The LORD hath been mindful of us: he will bless *us;* he will bless the house of Israel; he will bless the house of Aaron" (Ps.115:12).**
> **"Behold, he that keepeth Israel shall neither slumber nor sleep" (Ps.121:4).**
> **"Fear thou not; for I *am* with thee: be not dismayed; for I *am* thy God: I will strengthen thee; yea, I will help thee; yea, I will uphold thee with the right hand of my righteousness" (Is.41:10).**
> **"And *even* to *your* old age I *am* he; and *even* to hoar [gray] hairs will I carry *you:* I have made, and I will bear; even I will carry, and will deliver *you*" (Is.46:4).**

b. God has promised that His discipline will be limited (vv.7-11). The LORD's discipline does not destroy His people, for they are very special to Him. However, when dealing with enemies, the LORD does destroy them because of their stubborn, hard hearts and defiance. He will strike down all who continually reject and defy Him, but not those who truly believe and follow Him. When His true followers sin, He sometimes punishes them by allowing them to suffer from war or even exile. This is the kind of discipline that He would mete out soon after Isaiah's day, when the Babylonians destroyed Jerusalem and deported its citizens to other nations. But the Jews would not become extinct. Other nations would be wiped off the face of the earth, but not the Jews. Because of the promises of God, the righteous among the Jews would be saved. However, as long as the Jews continued to sin, they would continue to suffer the discipline of God. Note that His discipline has a twofold purpose.

First, God's discipline is to stir His people to seek His forgiveness through faith in the blood of an atoning sacrifice. Remember that atonement means being reconciled with God through the shed blood of a *substitute sacrifice*. The substitute sacrifice was the Lord Jesus Christ. Only His blood, the blood of God's very own Son, can secure atonement and reconciliation with God. When people genuinely seek and believe in the LORD's forgiveness, Christ's atoning sacrifice cleanses them from their sins.

Second, the LORD's discipline is to stir His people to cease all idolatry and false worship. There is only one true and living God, the LORD Himself (Yahweh, Jehovah). Therefore, His people are to worship and serve Him and Him alone. The Jews' idolatry and false worship forced the LORD to continually discipline them. When His hand of judgment fell, the people who were sincere in seeking forgiveness and atonement eliminated all their idols. They stopped participating in false worship and turned to the LORD in repentance.

Isaiah predicted that the LORD's discipline would be thorough and that the city of Jerusalem would be destroyed (vv.10-11a). Because of its continued sin and rejection of the LORD, Jerusalem would be left desolate. Wild animals would be its only inhabitants. Because of their sins, the people would be like dead tree branches that are gathered and burned. This was a clear prediction of the Babylonian destruction of Jerusalem in 586 B.C.

In the day of His terrifying judgment, God's discipline will be not only thorough but also just. He will show neither mercy nor partiality. Note why: because the people have no understanding, no spiritual insight into the truth of the LORD. Although He is their Maker and Creator, they continue to deny Him and to reject His claim on their lives. Because of their unbelief and defiance, He will show no compassion and no favor to them—not in His day of wrath and justice.

c. God has promised to restore Israel and His people (vv.12-13). *In that day* the LORD will gather His people from the Euphrates to Egypt, from one end of the world to the other (Ac.1:9-11; 1 Co.15:50-58; 1 Th.4:13-18). Isaiah predicted that the Jews would be set free from the Assyrian and Egyptian exile, as well as from the Babylonian captivity. But he is also pointing to a future gathering of God's people, which will take place at Christ's return. *In that day* the great trumpet will sound, and God's people will be set free from captivity to worship the LORD in the New Jerusalem.

"Jesus saith unto him, Thou hast said: nevertheless I say unto you, Hereafter shall ye see the Son of man sitting on the right hand of power, and coming in the clouds of heaven" (Mt.26:64).

"Be ye therefore ready also: for the Son of man cometh at an hour when ye think not" (Lu.12:40).

"In my Father's house are many mansions: if *it were* not so, I would have told you. I go to prepare a place for you. And if I go and prepare a place for you, I will come again, and receive you unto myself; that where I am, *there* ye may be also" (Jn.14:2-3).

"And when he had spoken these things, while they beheld, he was taken up; and a cloud received him out of their sight. And while they looked stedfastly toward heaven as he went up, behold, two men stood by them in white apparel; Which also said, Ye men of Galilee, why stand ye gazing up into heaven? this same Jesus, which is taken up from you into heaven, shall so come in like manner as ye have seen him go into heaven" (Ac.1:9-11).

"Now this I say, brethren, that flesh and blood cannot inherit the kingdom of God; neither doth corruption inherit incorruption. Behold, I show you a mystery; We shall not all sleep, but we shall all be changed, In a moment, in the twinkling of an eye, at the last trump: for the trumpet shall sound, and the dead shall be raised incorruptible, and we shall be changed. For this corruptible must put on incorruption, and this mortal *must* put on immortality. So when this corruptible shall have put on incorruption, and this mortal shall have put on immortality, then shall be brought to pass the saying that is written, Death is swallowed up in victory. O death, where *is* thy sting? O grave, where *is* thy victory? The sting of death *is* sin; and the strength of sin *is* the law. But thanks *be* to God, which giveth us the victory through our Lord Jesus Christ. Therefore, my beloved brethren, be ye stedfast, un-movable, always abounding in the work of the Lord, forasmuch as ye know that your labour is not in vain in the Lord" (1 Co.15:50-58).

"But I would not have you to be ignorant, brethren, concerning them which are asleep, that ye sorrow not, even as others which have no hope. For if we believe that Jesus died and rose again, even so them also which sleep in Jesus will God bring with him. For this we say unto you by the word of the Lord, that we which are alive *and* remain unto the coming of the Lord shall not prevent them which are asleep. For the Lord himself shall descend from heaven with a shout, with the voice of the archangel, and with the trump of God: and the dead in Christ shall rise first: Then we which are alive *and* remain shall be caught up together with them in the clouds, to meet the Lord in the air: and so shall we ever be with the Lord. Wherefore comfort one another with these words" (1 Th.4:13-18).

"Teaching us that, denying ungodliness and worldly lusts, we should live soberly, righteously, and godly, in this present world; Looking for that blessed hope, and the glorious appearing of the great God and our Saviour Jesus Christ" (Tit.2:12-13).

"Be ye also patient; stablish your hearts: for the coming of the Lord draweth nigh" (Js.5:8).

"And now, little children, abide in him; that, when he shall appear, we may have confidence, and not be ashamed before him at his coming" (1 Jn.2:28).

"Behold, I come quickly: hold that fast which thou hast, that no man take thy crown" (Re.3:11).

"Behold, I come as a thief. Blessed *is* he that watcheth, and keepeth his garments, lest he walk naked, and they see his shame" (Re.16:15).

DIVISION III

THE PROPHECIES OF WOE: GOD'S WARNING TO HIS PEOPLE, 28:1–35:10

(28:1–35:10) **DIVISION OVERVIEW**: at the close of the former division (chs.13-27), Isaiah predicted the wonderful restoration and salvation of all who turn to the LORD. It was important for the people to know that God longs for every person in the world to be saved. But the requirement for salvation is true repentance. A person must turn away from the ways of the world and turn to the ways of the LORD, obeying His commandments and living righteously.

In the present division, Isaiah continues his prophecies with a series of six extreme warnings. These prophecies to God's people concern the dangers of sin and rebellion. Sin and rebellion will doom a people, causing the hand of God's judgment to fall upon them. And God's judgment upon sin will be quick and complete. Therefore, people must know the destructive force of sin. Sin blinds rational thinking and causes people to act foolishly. Sin causes people:

⇒ to act violently
⇒ to trust in the powers of the world to save them
⇒ to misplace their trust
⇒ to focus on this temporary world
⇒ to forget that God's kingdom is eternal and will triumph over all

Because of the destructive force of sin, Isaiah presents six strong *woes*—scathing warnings to the people of his day as well as to the people of every generation.

But within the *woes* of judgment, Isaiah repeatedly gives hope by preaching that God is merciful. God offers the wonderful promises of salvation and restoration to those who truly turn to Him. In fact, the LORD leads Isaiah to close this part of the book with the promise of a glorious future for the world. The kingdom of God Himself—a world of perfection and joy—will be established on the earth.

THE PROPHECIES OF WOE: GOD'S WARNING TO HIS PEOPLE, 28:1–35:10

A. Woe—A Strong Warning to Ephraim and Judah: Sins That Destroy a Nation and Its People, 28:1-29

B. Woe—A Strong Warning to Ariel (Jerusalem): God's Unusual Dealings with Jerusalem, 29:1-24

C. Woe—A Strong Warning to the Rebellious, the Stubborn, and the Hard-Hearted: A Message to All Who Rebel Against God, 30:1-33

D. Woe—A Strong Warning to Those Who Ignore God and Place Their Trust in Egypt (the World): A Message to All Who Foolishly Misplace Their Trust, 31:1–32:20

E. Woe—A Strong Warning to the Destroyer: A Message to All Who Commit Acts of Violence, 33:1-24

F. Woe—A Strong Warning to the Whole World: The LORD's Day of Wrath and His Coming Kingdom, 34:1–35:10

CHAPTER 28

III. THE PROPHECIES OF WOE: GOD'S WARNING TO HIS PEOPLE, 28:1–35:10

A. Woe—A Strong Warning to Ephraim & Judah: Sins That Destroy a Nation & Its People, 28:1-29

1. God's warning to Ephraim, the Northern Kingdom: Had become a people of pride & drunkenness (revelry)

a. The sin: Abusing prosperity with arrogance & extravagant reckless living

b. The warning & judgment
 1) The Lord will send a mighty army to destroy the nation Assyria
  • Like a destructive hailstorm
  • Like a torrential rain
 2) The people will see the crown of their pride—their capital Samaria—waste away, be destroyed
  • Will be like a fading flower: Quickly fall to the ground
  • Will be like a ripe fig: Quickly plucked & eaten

c. The results of God's judgment
 1) Some of God's people will turn to the LORD as their crown (pride) & glory
 2) Some leaders will look to the LORD for a spirit of justice, & some soldiers will look to Him as the source of their strength

d. The guilt & perversions of the people
 1) Drunkenness: Even among the priests & prophets
  • Were staggering around drunk, even while giving counsel, De.21:18-21; Pr.20:1; 23:20-21, 29-35
  • Were indulging & carousing around tables filled with vomit
 2) Mockery & rejection of God's Word & His prophet
  • Ridiculed Isaiah: Asked who he was trying to teach & did he think they were children needing correction?
  • Ridiculed God's Word:

Woe to the crown of pride, to the drunkards of Ephraim, whose glorious beauty is a fading flower, which *are* on the head of the fat valleys of them that are overcome with wine!
2 Behold, the Lord hath a mighty and strong one, *which* as a tempest of hail *and* a destroying storm, as a flood of mighty waters overflowing, shall cast down to the earth with the hand.
3 The crown of pride, the drunkards of Ephraim, shall be trodden under feet:
4 And the glorious beauty, which is on the head of the fat valley, shall be a fading flower, *and* as the hasty fruit before the summer; which *when* he that looketh upon it seeth, while it is yet in his hand he eateth it up.
5 In that day shall the LORD of hosts be for a crown of glory, and for a diadem of beauty, unto the residue of his people,
6 And for a spirit of judgment to him that sitteth in judgment, and for strength to them that turn the battle to the gate.
7 But they also have erred through wine, and through strong drink are out of the way; the priest and the prophet have erred through strong drink, they are swallowed up of wine, they are out of the way through strong drink; they err in vision, they stumble *in* judgment.
8 For all tables are full of vomit *and* filthiness, *so that there is* no place *clean.*
9 Whom shall he teach knowledge? and whom shall he make to understand doctrine? *them that are* weaned from the milk, *and* drawn from the breasts.
10 For precept *must be* upon precept, precept upon pre-

cept; line upon line, line upon line; here a little, *and* there a little:
11 For with stammering lips and another tongue will he speak to this people.
12 To whom he said, This *is* the rest wherewith ye may cause the weary to rest; and this *is* the refreshing: yet they would not hear.
13 But the word of the LORD was unto them precept upon precept, precept upon precept; line upon line, line upon line; here a little, *and* there a little; that they might go, and fall backward, and be broken, and snared, and taken.
14 Wherefore hear the word of the LORD, ye scornful men, that rule this people which *is* in Jerusalem.
15 Because ye have said, We have made a covenant with death, and with hell are we at agreement; when the overflowing scourge shall pass through, it shall not come unto us: for we have made lies our refuge, and under falsehood have we hid ourselves:
16 Therefore thus saith the Lord GOD, Behold, I lay in Zion for a foundation a stone, a tried stone, a precious corner *stone,* a sure foundation: he that believeth shall not make haste.
17 Judgment also will I lay to the line, and righteousness to the plummet: and the hail shall sweep away the refuge of lies, and the waters shall overflow the hiding place.
18 And your covenant with death shall be disannulled, and your agreement with hell shall not stand; when the overflowing scourge shall pass through, then ye shall be trodden down by it.
19 From the time that it goeth forth it shall take you: for morning by morning shall it pass over, by day and by night: and it shall be a vexation only to understand the report.
20 For the bed is shorter than that *a man* can stretch himself *on it:* and the covering narrower than that he can wrap himself *in it.*
21 For the LORD shall rise up as *in* mount Perazim, he shall be wroth as *in* the

Mocked Isaiah's preaching time & again

e. The response of God to the people's mockery of His Word
 1) They will hear the strange words of a foreign oppressor
  • Because they rejected God's offer of *rest* (peace), 8:6-8
  • Because they refused to hear God's Word
 2) They will see the fulfillment of God's Word:
  • Will learn that every precept & line is true
  • Will go their own way, stumble backward & be injured

2. God's warning to Judah, the Southern Kingdom: Were placing their security in *worldly alliances* instead of in God

a. The sin
 1) Scoffing—rejecting God's Word, His warning, 14
 2) Distrust, unbelief: Had formed an alliance with Egypt, turning to them instead of God for help in time of trouble—trusted lies, fabrications, secret treaties

b. The offer of the Lord, 1 Pe.2:4-8
 1) His provision: He is placing a foundation stone in Jerusalem, Mk.12:10; Ro.9:33
 2) His offer: Whoever trusts this stone (Jesus Christ) will never be disappointed

c. The warning of doom
 1) The foundation of each person's life will be inspected: Measured by justice & righteousness
  • Their refuge—trust in man—will be swept away
  • Their treaty with Egypt—made to escape death—will be cancelled, 15
  • Their nation will be overrun & trampled underfoot by the scourge of Assyria: Invaded time & again until all the people are completely beaten down
 2) The truth of this warning will bring sheer terror
 3) The security blanket of Egypt was too short, too narrow to wrap around the people
 4) The LORD will rise up & do a strange work: Destroy His own people

whom He had earlier blessed & given victories • At Mt. Perazim • At the Valley of Gibeon 5) The final warning: Stop mocking God's Word • Because your punishment will be more severe • Because your judgment is set d. The word of hope & comfort: Must hear & heed this parable 1) The parable of a farmer • He does not plow endlessly • He eventually sows: Has hope of a fruitful harvest & future	valley of Gibeon, that he may do his work, his strange work; and bring to pass his act, his strange act. 22 Now therefore be ye not mockers, lest your bands be made strong: for I have heard from the Lord GOD of hosts a consumption, even determined upon the whole earth. 23 Give ye ear, and hear my voice; hearken, and hear my speech. 24 Doth the plowman plow all day to sow? doth he open and break the clods of his ground? 25 When he hath made plain the face thereof, doth he not cast abroad the fitches, and scatter the cummin, and cast in the principal wheat and the	appointed barley and the rie in their place? 26 For his God doth instruct him to discretion, *and* doth teach him. 27 For the fitches are not threshed with a threshing instrument, neither is a cart wheel turned about upon the cummin; but the fitches are beaten out with a staff, and the cummin with a rod. 28 Bread *corn* is bruised; because he will not ever be threshing it, nor break *it with* the wheel of his cart, nor bruise it *with* his horsemen. 29 This also cometh forth from the LORD of hosts, *which* is wonderful in counsel, *and* excellent in working.	• He learns from nature—God's creation—when & where to plant • He uses the right farming tools & instruments • He uses his knowledge & wisdom: To beat out the grain to grind it into meal, making sure he does not beat nor grind too much 2) The point: The LORD is the wise Farmer—knows how to handle crops—sowing & harvesting (judging), giving the hope for a remnant

DIVISION III

THE PROPHECIES OF WOE: GOD'S WARNING TO HIS PEOPLE, 28:1–35:10

A. Woe—A Strong Warning to Ephraim and Judah: Sins That Destroy a Nation and Its People, 28:1-29

(28:1-29) **Introduction**: war is a terrible evil that ravages human lives and destroys nations. Down through the centuries one nation after another has arisen to take over, occupy, invade, or conquer land that did not belong to them. And sooner or later war has wreaked havoc on every one of them. As each has confronted the brutality and slaughter of war, millions of people have lost their lives, and millions more families and friends have suffered the pain of losing their loved ones.

But war is not the only thing that can destroy nations. A nation's sins can also destroy it. The present Scripture discusses a few of the sins that caused the LORD to issue a strong warning—a *woe*—to His people. Hopefully, some would turn away from their sins and turn back to Him in repentance. Both the Southern and Northern Kingdoms were committing sins that would destroy their nations. Although Isaiah preached this message in Judah, God knew that the warning would soon spread to the Northern Kingdom, and He hoped that His people in both kingdoms would repent. This is, *Woe—A Strong Warning to Ephraim and Judah: Sins That Destroy a Nation and Its People*, 28:1-29.

    1. God's warning to Ephraim, the Northern Kingdom of Israel: had become a people of pride and drunkenness (revelry) (vv.1-13).
    2. God's warning to Judah, the Southern Kingdom: were placing their security in *worldly alliances* instead of in God (vv.14-29).

1 (28:1-13) **Pride, Warning Against, Will Be Judged—Drunkenness, Warning Against, Leads to Judgment—Revelry, Warning Against, Leads to Judgment—Carousing, Warning Against, Leads to Judgment—Ephraim, Represented Israel, Judgment Predicted—Northern Kingdom of Israel, Judgment of, Prophecy Concerning—Word of God, Rejection of, by Prideful Drunkards—Isaiah, Persecuted, by Prideful Drunkards**: Isaiah's first *woe* was God's strong warning to Ephraim. Because Ephraim was the name of the leading tribe in the Northern Kingdom of Israel, it was often used to refer to the kingdom itself. Soon after Isaiah announced this prophecy, the cruel Assyrians would conquer the Northern Kingdom and the capital, Samaria, would fall (722 B.C.). The LORD used Isaiah to warn Ephraim of the coming judgment. Even though Isaiah ministered in Judah, God knew that the warning would spread to the people of the Northern Kingdom. Furthermore, the coming judgment on Ephraim would serve as a warning of what lay ahead for the people of Judah and Jerusalem if they did not repent of their sins. The sins of the Northern Kingdom were drunkenness, pride, and contempt for God's Word. Note the Scripture and outline:

OUTLINE	SCRIPTURE	SCRIPTURE	OUTLINE
1. God's warning to Ephraim, the Northern Kingdom: Had become a people of pride & drunkenness (revelry) a. The sin: Abusing prosperity	Woe to the crown of pride, to the drunkards of Ephraim, whose glorious beauty is a fading flower, which *are* on the head of the fat valleys of	them that are overcome with wine! 2 Behold, the Lord hath a mighty and strong one, *which* as a tempest of hail *and* a de-	with arrogance & extravagant reckless living b. The warning & judgment 1) The Lord will send a mighty army to destroy

OUTLINE	SCRIPTURE	SCRIPTURE	OUTLINE
the nation Assyria • Like a destructive hailstorm • Like a torrential rain 2) The people will see the crown of their pride—their capital Samaria—waste away, be destroyed • Will be like a fading flower: Quickly fall to the ground • Will be like a ripe fig: Quickly plucked & eaten c. The results of God's judgment 1) Some of God's people will turn to the LORD as their crown (pride) & glory 2) Some leaders will look to the LORD for a spirit of justice, & some soldiers will look to Him as the source of their strength d. The guilt & perversions of the people 1) Drunkenness: Even among the priests & prophets • Were staggering around drunk, even while giving counsel,	stroying storm, as a flood of mighty waters overflowing, shall cast down to the earth with the hand. 3 The crown of pride, the drunkards of Ephraim, shall be trodden under feet: 4 And the glorious beauty, which is on the head of the fat valley, shall be a fading flower, *and* as the hasty fruit before the summer; which *when* he that looketh upon it seeth, while it is yet in his hand he eateth it up. 5 In that day shall the LORD of hosts be for a crown of glory, and for a diadem of beauty, unto the residue of his people, 6 And for a spirit of judgment to him that sitteth in judgment, and for strength to them that turn the battle to the gate. 7 But they also have erred through wine, and through strong drink are out of the way; the priest and the prophet have erred through strong drink, they are swallowed up of wine, they are out of the way through strong	drink; they err in vision, they stumble *in* judgment. 8 For all tables are full of vomit *and* filthiness, *so that there is* no place *clean.* 9 Whom shall he teach knowledge? and whom shall he make to understand doctrine? *them that are* weaned from the milk, *and* drawn from the breasts. 10 For precept *must be* upon precept, precept upon precept; line upon line, line upon line; here a little, *and* there a little: 11 For with stammering lips and another tongue will he speak to this people. 12 To whom he said, This *is* the rest *wherewith* ye may cause the weary to rest; and this *is* the refreshing: yet they would not hear. 13 But the word of the LORD was unto them precept upon precept, precept upon precept; line upon line, line upon line; here a little, *and* there a little; that they might go, and fall backward, and be broken, and snared, and taken.	De.21:18-21; Pr.20:1; 23:20-21, 29-35 • Were indulging & carousing around tables filled with vomit 2) Mockery & rejection of God's Word & His prophet • Ridiculed Isaiah: Asked who he was trying to teach & did he think they were children needing correction? • Ridiculed God's Word: Mocked Isaiah's preaching time & again e. The response of God to the people's mockery of His Word 1) They will hear the strange words of a foreign oppressor • Because they rejected God's offer of *rest* (peace), 7:4; 8:6-8 • Because they refused to hear God's Word 2) They will see the fulfillment of God's Word: • Will learn that every precept & line is true • Will go their own way, stumble backward & be injured

a. The sins of the Northern Kingdom were a result of their prosperity. At that time in history the land was fertile, so the Northern Kingdom had become economically strong. Samaria in particular was prosperous, and it was considered a beautiful *wreath* or *crown* set on a high hill above a lush valley (v.1). Looking up at the city from the lush valley below, the citizens of the Northern Kingdom saw a rich and mighty fortress in an ideal location. They took great pride in their wealth and military strength, and they placed their trust in their impregnable capital instead of in God.

But their sin was not only pride in their wealth and material prosperity; they were also guilty of drunkenness. Because of their prosperity, they had plenty of free time to engage in whatever they desired. Sadly, instead of using their free time for constructive projects, they allowed their *idle hands* to become the *devil's tools*. Many of the people became drunkards, indulging their flesh by continually partying and carousing. A spirit of revelry gripped the nation.

b. Because of their pride and drunkenness, the LORD issued the warning of coming judgment (vv.2-4). He was going to raise up a mighty army—the Assyrians—to destroy the Northern Kingdom. Like a destructive hailstorm or a torrential downpour, the Assyrians would sweep across the Northern Kingdom. The people would see their capital, their *crown of pride*, destroyed (vv.3-4). When the judgment of God fell, the mighty, wealthy city of Samaria would collapse as quickly as a fading flower that falls to the ground or as a ripe fig that is plucked from a tree and eaten.

c. God's judgment would achieve its purpose. It would cause some to repent and turn to Him (vv.5-6). In the terrible distress of war, some citizens of the Northern Kingdom would turn to the LORD. He, not the mighty city of Samaria, would be their crown (pride) and glory. Even some of the political leaders would look to the LORD for a spirit of justice, and some of the soldiers would look to Him as the source of their strength (v.6).

Note the term *in that day*. This means that these two verses have a double reference. They refer not only to the Israelites of Isaiah's day, but also to the Jews who will be living in the last days of human history. *In that day* is a term that often refers to the day when Christ will set up His kingdom on earth. Thus when He returns to earth, some Jews will turn to the LORD, and He will replace the mighty, wealthy cities of the world as their crown and glory.

d. The people of the Northern Kingdom bore a heavy burden of guilt because of their perversions (vv.7-10). The word *perversion* is the appropriate word to describe their sins. *To pervert* means to turn away from what is right or good; to corrupt; to act improperly; to be obstinate, stiff-necked, and stubborn in opposing what is right, reasonable, or accepted. The people of the Northern Kingdom had so perverted the truth of God's Word that they called evil good and good evil. The people were guilty of two terrible perversions.

First, most of the people were guilty of drunkenness, and even the priests and prophets considered drunkenness acceptable behavior. Going along with the society of their day, they staggered around drunk, even while carrying out the functions of their offices. Note exactly what Scripture says: they staggered while claiming to receive visions and while giving counsel (v.7).

The problem of drunkenness was so common that Isaiah used a graphic picture to describe how pervasive it had become: not a single table was free from the filth of vomit. Just imagine the scene: people indulging their flesh and carousing around tables covered with vomit. Drunkenness had become such acceptable behavior in Israel that even the priests and prophets of the nation were engaging in it.

The second perversion of the Northern Kingdom was mocking God's Word and His prophet (vv.9-10). When Isaiah preached, the people insulted, scorned, and challenged him. Sarcastically, they asked if he thought they were children who needed correction. The implication is that they considered themselves adults, capable of making their own decisions. No one had the right to tell them how to behave. They felt they alone had that right; thus they alone would exercise that right.

The people ridiculed not only God's prophet but also God's Word (v.10). They mocked Isaiah for preaching God's Word. They accused him of repeating the same message over and over in the halting vocabulary of a child instead of the fluent language of an adult. Both God's message of judgment and the way the prophet proclaimed the message displeased the citizens of the Northern Kingdom, so they mocked both the message and the messenger.

e. Accordingly, the LORD now had a very special message for the people of the Northern Kingdom. Because they rejected His Word, they would hear the strange words of a foreign oppressor (vv.11-12). Because they rejected God's offer of *rest* and *refreshing*, or *peace* and *repose* (Is.7:4; 8:6-8), they would face the terrifying judgment of invasion and war. Because they refused to hear God's Word, the preaching of the prophet Isaiah, they would see the fulfillment of God's Word (v.13). Very soon God's hand of judgment would fall upon them, and they would learn that every precept and line of His Word was true. The result of going their own way would be catastrophic: they would stumble backward and fall, be injured, snared, and captured.

Thought 1. Pride can be good as well as evil. In fact, a degree of pride is essential for self-confidence and self-esteem. Scripture says that we are to love our neighbors as ourselves (Mt.5:43; 19:19; 22:39). Loving ourselves, taking pride in who we are and what we do, is a sign of a healthy personality.

But pride can become evil. Pride is evil when we begin to elevate ourselves above others and think of ourselves more highly than we should. It is evil when we begin to think that we are superior or indispensable to others, or that we are more important or more deserving of attention and honor than they are. Any arrogant or haughty spirit that degrades others is evil.

Pride also becomes sinful when we look upon man's works as the foundation and security of our lives. For no matter what man constructs or develops—a building, business, city, nation, economic wealth, or military power—it is not permanent. It can be destroyed. Neither man nor the works of his hands offer lasting or satisfying security. The spirit of man cannot find long-term contentment or fulfillment in people or possessions. The human soul is restless until it rests in God. This was the message of the LORD to the Northern Kingdom of Israel, but they rejected the offer of God's rest and peace and, as a result, they faced His judgment.

If we walk through life in sinful pride, boasting and placing our security in ourselves and in the works of our hands, we too will face the judgment of God. Listen to what God's Holy Word says about sinful pride, about being arrogant and exalting ourselves above others:

"And whosoever shall exalt himself shall be abased; and he that shall humble himself shall be exalted" (Mt.23:12).

"And I will say to my soul, Soul, thou hast much goods laid up for many years; take thine ease, eat, drink, *and* be merry. But God said unto him, *Thou* fool, this night thy soul shall be required of thee: then whose shall those things be, which thou hast provided? So *is* he that layeth up treasure for himself, and is not rich toward God" (Lu.12:19-21).

"But he giveth more grace. Wherefore he saith, God resisteth the proud, but giveth grace unto the humble" (Js.4:6).

"Love not the world, neither the things *that are* in the world. If any man love the world, the love of the Father is not in him. For all that *is* in the world, the lust of the flesh, and the lust of the eyes, and the pride of life, is not of the Father, but is of the world" (1 Jn.2:15-16).

"The wicked in *his* pride doth persecute the poor: let them be taken in the devices that they have imagined" (Ps.10:2).

"These six *things* doth the LORD hate: yea, seven *are* an abomination unto him: A proud look, a lying tongue, and hands that shed innocent blood, An heart that deviseth wicked imaginations, feet that be swift in running to mischief, A false witness *that* speaketh lies, and he that soweth discord among brethren" (Pr.6:16-19).

"Pride *goeth* before destruction, and an haughty spirit before a fall" (Pr.16:18).

"An high look, and a proud heart, *and* the plowing of the wicked, *is* sin" (Pr.21:4).

"A man's pride shall bring him low: but honour shall uphold the humble in spirit" (Pr.29:23).

"He that is of a proud heart stirreth up strife: but he that putteth his trust in the LORD shall be made fat" (Pr.28:25).

"Woe unto *them that are* wise in their own eyes, and prudent in their own sight!" (Is.5:21).

"For thou hast said in thine heart, I will ascend into heaven, I will exalt my throne above the stars of God: I will sit also upon the mount of the congregation, in the sides of the north: I will ascend above the heights of the clouds; I will be like the most High. Yet thou shalt be brought down to hell, to the sides of the pit" (Is.14:13-15).

"Therefore hear now this, *thou that art* given to pleasures, that dwellest carelessly, that sayest in thine heart, I *am,* and none else beside me; I shall not sit *as* a widow, neither shall I know the loss of children: But these two *things* shall come to thee in a moment in one day, the loss of children, and widowhood: they shall come upon thee in their perfection for the multitude of thy sorceries, *and* for the great abundance of thine enchantments. For thou hast trusted in thy wickedness: thou hast said, None seeth me. Thy wisdom and thy knowledge, it hath perverted thee; and thou hast said in thine heart, I *am,* and none else beside me. Therefore shall evil come upon thee; thou shalt not know from whence it riseth: and mischief shall fall upon thee; thou shalt not be able to put if off: and desolation shall come upon thee suddenly, *which* thou shalt not know" (Is.47:8-11).

"Though thou exalt *thyself* as the eagle, and though thou set thy nest among the stars, thence will I bring thee down, saith the LORD" (Ob.1:4).

Thought 2. Alcohol, drugs, and drunkenness take a terrible toll upon human lives. When people drink to excess, they damage their bodies. And if the drinking continues on indefinitely, the damage can result in serious disease or even death. But even more tragic are the deaths of other people at the hands of the intoxicated. Think how many drunk people have been in accidents that injured or killed other human beings. Also think how often drunk people become violent and attack, injure, or even take the lives of other people. In addition to causing injuries and deaths, drunkenness can rip families apart. If honestly faced, the evil of drunkenness is obvious. Listen to the warning of God against drunkenness:

"And take heed to yourselves, lest at any time your hearts be overcharged with surfeiting, and drunkenness, and cares of this life, and so that day come upon you unawares" (Lu.21:34).

"Let us walk honestly, as in the day; not in rioting and drunkenness, not in chambering and wantonness, not in strife and envying" (Ro.13:13).

"Know ye not that the unrighteous shall not inherit the kingdom of God? Be not deceived: neither fornicators, nor idolaters, nor adulterers, nor effeminate, nor abusers of themselves with mankind, Nor thieves, nor covetous, nor drunkards, nor revilers, nor extortioners, shall inherit the kingdom of God" (1 Co.6:9-10).

"Now the works of the flesh are manifest, which are *these;* Adultery, fornication, uncleanness, lasciviousness, Idolatry, witchcraft, hatred, variance, emulations, wrath, strife, seditions, heresies, Envyings, murders, drunkenness, revellings, and such like: of the which I tell you before, as I have also told *you* in time past, that they which do such things shall not inherit the kingdom of God" (Ga.5:19-21).

"Wine *is* a mocker, strong drink *is* raging: and whosoever is deceived thereby is not wise" (Pr.20:1).

"Be not among winebibbers; among riotous eaters of flesh" (Pr.23:20).

"Who hath woe? who hath sorrow? who hath contentions? who hath babbling? who hath wounds without cause? who hath redness of eyes? They that tarry long at the wine; they that go to seek mixed wine. Look not thou upon the wine when it is red, when it giveth his colour in the cup, *when* it moveth itself aright" (Pr.23:29-31).

"Woe unto them that rise up early in the morning, *that* they may follow strong drink; that continue until night, *till* wine inflame them!" (Is.5:11).

"Woe unto him that giveth his neighbour drink, that puttest thy bottle to *him,* and makest *him* drunken also, that thou mayest look on their nakedness!" (Hab.2:15).

---

2 (28:14-29) **Warning, to Judah, Against Evil Alliances—Southern Kingdom of Judah, Warning to—Evil Associations, Warning Against, Given to Judah—Alliances, Evil, Warning Against—Stone, Symbol of, Christ—Cornerstone, Prophecy Concerning, a Sure Foundation—Jesus Christ, Prophecy Concerning, the Chief Cornerstone—Egypt, Treaties of, with Judah—Parable, of a Farmer, Represented the LORD**: God issued a second *woe* or strong warning to Judah, the Southern Kingdom. Judah was just as guilty of wicked behavior as the Northern Kingdom. Therefore, the hand of God's judgment was hanging over Judah and its capital Jerusalem just as it was over the Northern Kingdom. Although the Assyrians would not capture Jerusalem, the rest of the nation would be conquered. The people would suffer greatly at the hands of the cruel Assyrians. Note the force of God's warning in the Scripture and outline:

OUTLINE	SCRIPTURE	SCRIPTURE	OUTLINE
2. God's warning to Judah, the Southern Kingdom: Were placing their security in *worldly alliances* instead of in God a. The sin 1) Scoffing—rejecting God's Word, His warning, 14 2) Distrust, unbelief: Had formed an alliance with Egypt, turning to them instead of God for help in time of trouble—trusted lies, fabrications, secret treaties b. The offer of the Lord, 1 Pe.2:4-8 1) His provision: He is placing	14 Wherefore hear the word of the LORD, ye scornful men, that rule this people which *is* in Jerusalem. 15 Because ye have said, We have made a covenant with death, and with hell are we at agreement; when the overflowing scourge shall pass through, it shall not come unto us: for we have made lies our refuge, and under falsehood have we hid ourselves: 16 Therefore thus saith the Lord GOD, Behold, I lay in	Zion for a foundation a stone, a tried stone, a precious corner *stone,* a sure foundation: he that believeth shall not make haste. 17 Judgment also will I lay to the line, and righteousness to the plummet: and the hail shall sweep away the refuge of lies, and the waters shall overflow the hiding place. 18 And your covenant with death shall be disannulled, and your agreement with hell shall not stand; when the	a foundation stone in Jerusalem, Mk.12:10; Ro.9:33 2) His offer: Whoever trusts this stone (Jesus Christ) will never be disappointed c. The warning of doom 1) The foundation of each person's life will be inspected: Measured by justice & righteousness • Their refuge—trust in man—will be swept away • Their treaty with Egypt—made to escape death—will be cancelled, see 15

OUTLINE	SCRIPTURE	SCRIPTURE	OUTLINE
• Their nation will be overrun & trampled underfoot by the scourge of Assyria: Invaded time & again until all the people are completely beaten down	overflowing scourge shall pass through, then ye shall be trodden down by it. 19 From the time that it goeth forth it shall take you: for morning by morning shall it pass over, by day and by night: and it shall be a vexation only to understand the report.	24 Doth the plowman plow all day to sow? doth he open and break the clods of his ground? 25 When he hath made plain the face thereof, doth he not cast abroad the fitches, and scatter the cummin, and cast in the principal wheat and the appointed barley and rie in their place?	parable 1) The parable of a farmer • He does not plow endlessly • He eventually sows: Has hope of a fruitful harvest & future
2) The truth of this warning will bring sheer terror 3) The security blanket of Egypt was too short, too narrow to wrap around the people	20 For the bed is shorter than that a man can stretch himself on it: and the covering narrower than that he can wrap himself in it.	26 For his God doth instruct him to discretion, and doth teach him.	• He learns from nature—God's creation—when & where to plant • He uses the right farming tools & instruments
4) The LORD will rise up & do a strange work: Destroy His own people whom He had earlier blessed & given victories • At Mt. Perazim • At the Valley of Gibeon 5) The final warning: Stop mocking God's Word • Because your punishment will be more severe • Because your judgment is set d. The word of hope & comfort: Must hear & heed this	21 For the LORD shall rise up as in mount Perazim, he shall be wroth as in the valley of Gibeon, that he may do his work, his strange work; and bring to pass his act, his strange act. 22 Now therefore be ye not mockers, lest your bands be made strong: for I have heard from the Lord GOD of hosts a consumption, even determined upon the whole earth. 23 Give ye ear, and hear my voice; hearken, and hear my speech.	27 For the fitches are not threshed with a threshing instrument, neither is a cart wheel turned about upon the cummin; but the fitches are beaten out with a staff, and the cummin with a rod. 28 Bread corn is bruised; because he will not ever be threshing it, nor break it with the wheel of his cart, nor bruise it with his horsemen. 29 This also cometh forth from the LORD of hosts, which is wonderful in counsel, and excellent in working.	• He uses his knowledge & wisdom: To beat out the grain to grind it into meal, making sure he does not beat nor grind too much 2) The point: The LORD is the wise Farmer—knows how to handle crops—sowing & harvesting (judging), giving

a. God's indictment against Judah included two charges of serious sin (vv.14-15). First, they were just as guilty of mocking God's Word as the Northern Kingdom was. Therefore, Many of the leaders scoffed at Isaiah's warning of the coming judgment (v.14). A skeptical spirit gripped their hearts; thus they mocked the prophet and sneered at the warning of God.

Second, the leaders and people did not trust the LORD. The leaders were sharp enough to perceive the Assyrian threat, and they knew they needed to prepare in the event Assyria did attack. But in their preparation they ignored the LORD and their need for His presence and help. Instead of turning to Him, Judah's leaders turned to Egypt to form an alliance of mutual protection against Assyria. Note that Isaiah called this alliance a "covenant with death." By forming an alliance with Egypt, the leaders and their pro-Egyptian party were sentencing themselves to death. They were trusting Egypt to save them from Assyria, but the word of Egypt would prove to be false; therefore, Judah's trust was based upon a lie. Tragically, they trusted in Egypt and its word instead of in the LORD and His Word. Instead of turning to God for security, the leaders led the people to trust the arm of the flesh, the power of Egypt.

b. The LORD makes a most wonderful promise to any person who will trust Him. He is going to place a *foundation stone* in Jerusalem, a *cornerstone* that will serve as the foundation for any life built upon it. Whoever trusts this stone will be secure and never have to flee from the coming judgment of God (v.16). This stone is a clear reference to the coming Messiah, the LORD Jesus Christ. Christ is the One upon whom believers and the church are built (Mk.12:10; Ac.4:11-12; Ro.9:33; 10:11; 1 Co.3:11; Ep.2:20; 1 Pe.2:4-8). All who build their lives upon the foundation of Christ will no longer have to run here and there seeking protection from enemies. Christ is the foundation stone that supports His followers amid the stormy trials and temptations of this world.

c. At the same time, people must understand this fact: if they reject the foundation stone God offers, they will face judgment (vv.17-22). God will inspect the foundation of every person's life and measure it by the standard of His justice and righteousness. If they have based their security on Egypt (the world), they will be swept away by the flood of God's judgment. They will be guilty of ignoring the LORD and trusting in the arm, the power of the flesh.

The treaty Judah made with Egypt would be annulled (v.18), and the scourge of Assyria would overflow and trample their nation underfoot (vv.18-19). The nation would be invaded time and again until its people were swept away into exile. Note the impact that this message of coming judgment had upon those who understood it: it struck them with sheer terror.

Continuing his warning of judgment, Isaiah proclaimed that the security blanket of Egypt was too short and too narrow to wrap around the people (v.20). Neither Egypt nor any other nation had the power to give the people permanent security. The LORD Himself was going to rise up and do a "strange work," one that no one ever thought He would do. He would destroy His own people, the very people He had earlier led to victory over their enemies. This is a reference to the victory the LORD gave David and the Israelites over the Philistines at Mount Perazim and at the Valley of Gibeon (see outline and notes—2 S.5:17-25; 1 Chr.14:8-17 for more discussion). God was now going to destroy these same people He had once so richly blessed.

In light of the coming judgment, Isaiah warned the people to stop mocking God's Word (v.22). If they continued to scoff at it, their punishment would be even more severe. The coming judgment was set, decreed. Nothing could stop it. But the people must guard against heaping up wrath against themselves. Mocking God's Word and His prophet was sure to bring a far more terrible judgment upon them.

d. In closing this prophecy, Isaiah gave a wonderful word of hope and comfort. He told the people to listen to a parable about a farmer (vv.23-29). When a farmer plows, he does not plow endlessly. Eventually, he sows—dill, cumin, wheat, barley, and rye, each in its own field—in the hope of a fruitful harvest in the future. Learning from nature—God's creation—a farmer knows when and where to plant (v.26). And when harvest time comes, he uses the right farming tools and instruments (v.27). In addition, he uses his knowledge and wisdom to beat out the grain to grind it into meal, making sure he does not beat or grind too much (v.28).

The point of the parable is a much-needed lesson. The LORD is the wise farmer who knows how to handle crops. When dealing with mankind and His people, He knows when to sow and harvest the crop. His overriding objective is the same as the farmer's, to reap a harvest. In the very midst of this message of judgment, the LORD gives the wonderful promise of a great harvest, a small number of believers who will base their lives upon the foundation stone promised by God. Keep in mind that the foundation stone is the promise of the Messiah, the Lord Jesus Christ. Neither the Jews of Isaiah's day nor the people of succeeding generations could base their lives upon any other foundation and escape the judgment of God.

"Jesus saith unto them, Did ye never read in the scriptures, The stone which the builders rejected, the same is become the head of the corner: this is the Lord's doing, and it is marvellous in our eyes? Therefore say I unto you, The kingdom of God shall be taken from you, and given to a nation bringing forth the fruits thereof. And whosoever shall fall on this stone shall be broken: but on whomsoever it shall fall, it will grind him to powder" (Mt.21:42-44).

"And have ye not read this scripture; The stone which the builders rejected is become the head of the corner" (Mk.12:10).

"This is the stone which was set at nought of you builders, which is become the head of the corner. Neither is there salvation in any other: for there is none other name under heaven given among men, whereby we must be saved" (Ac.4:11-12).

"As it is written, Behold, I lay in Sion a stumblingstone and rock of offence: and whosoever believeth on him shall not be ashamed" (Ro.9:33).

"For other foundation can no man lay than that is laid, which is Jesus Christ. Now if any man build upon this foundation gold, silver, precious stones, wood, hay, stubble; Every man's work shall be made manifest: for the day shall declare it, because it shall be revealed by fire; and the fire shall try every man's work of what sort it is. If any man's work abide which he hath built thereupon, he shall receive a reward. If any man's work shall be burned, he shall suffer loss: but he himself shall be saved; yet so as by fire" (1 Co.3:11-15).

"Now therefore ye are no more strangers and foreigners, but fellowcitizens with the saints, and of the household of God; And are built upon the foundation of the apostles and prophets, Jesus Christ himself being the chief corner *stone*" (Ep.2:19-20).

"To whom coming, *as unto* a living stone, disallowed indeed of men, but chosen of God, *and* precious, Ye also, as lively stones, are built up a spiritual house, an holy priesthood, to offer up spiritual sacrifices, acceptable to God by Jesus Christ. Wherefore also it is contained in the scripture, Behold, I lay in Sion a chief corner stone, elect, precious: and he that believeth on him shall not be confounded. Unto you therefore which believe *he is* precious: but unto them which be disobedient, the stone which the builders disallowed, the same is made the head of the corner, And a stone of stumbling, and a rock of offence, *even to them* which stumble at the word, being disobedient: whereunto also they were appointed" (1 Pe.2:4-8).

"I will praise thee: for thou hast heard me, and art become my salvation. The stone *which* the builders refused is become the head *stone* of the corner. This is the LORD's doing; it *is* marvellous in our eyes" (Ps.118:21-23).

Thought 1. The people of Judah were placing their trust in the wealth and power of Egypt. They were not trusting God. What are we trusting for our security? What are we trusting to give us peace of heart and a life that is productive, satisfying, and victorious?

The world offers many *false trusts* upon which we can build our lives, but every one of them will fail. Nothing on this earth—not a single thing—can conquer the corruption and death that engulfs this world. Any life built upon the false trusts of wealth, position, power, fame, leaders, technology, or the military might of a nation will collapse. As necessary as some of these earthly supports are, none of them can give us permanent peace of heart and security or assure us a purposeful, fulfilled life.

The only sure, permanent, eternal trust is Jesus Christ Himself. When we seek security through Christ, God Himself takes care of us. The Lord infuses our bodies with His own strength, enabling us to conquer any trial that confronts us. When we are attacked, our duty is to look to Christ and place our trust in Him. When we walk day by day placing our trust in Him, He promises to give us power to conquer all that confronts us. The only *true trust* that can give us genuine security is the Lord Jesus Christ. Listen to what God's Holy Word says about the *false trusts* that make life insecure:

"Peter answered and said unto him, Though all *men* shall be offended because of thee, *yet* will I never be offended. Jesus said unto him, Verily I say unto thee, That this night, before the cock crow, thou shalt deny me thrice. Peter said unto him, Though I should die with thee, yet will I not deny thee. Likewise also said all the disciples" (Mt.26:33-35).

"And the disciples were astonished at his words. But Jesus answereth again, and saith unto them, Children, how hard is it for them that trust in riches to enter into the kingdom of God!" (Mk.10:24).

"But he [Peter] spake the more vehemently, If I should die with thee, I will not deny thee in any wise. Likewise also said they all" (Mk.14:31).

"And I will say to my soul, Soul, thou hast much goods laid up for many years; take thine ease, eat, drink, *and* be merry. But God said unto him, *Thou* fool, this night thy soul shall be required of thee: then whose shall those things be, which thou hast provided? So *is* he that layeth up treasure for himself, and is not rich toward God" (Lu.12:19-21).

"And he [Peter] said unto him, Lord, I am ready to go with thee, both into prison, and to death" (Lu.22:33).

"And he spake this parable unto certain which trusted in themselves that they were righteous, and despised others" (Lu.18:9).

"Wherefore let him that thinketh he standeth take heed lest he fall" (1 Co.10:12).

"Charge them that are rich in this world, that they be not highminded, nor trust in uncertain riches, but in the living God, who giveth us richly all things to enjoy" (1 Ti.6:17).

"Then said David to the Philistine, Thou comest to me with a sword, and with a spear, and with a shield: but I come to thee in the name of the LORD of hosts, the God of the armies of Israel, whom thou hast defied" (1 S.17:45).

"If I have made gold my hope, or have said to the fine gold, *Thou art* my confidence; If I rejoiced because my wealth *was* great, and because mine hand had gotten much...This also *were* an iniquity *to be punished by* the judge: for I should have denied the God *that is* above" (Jb.31:24-25, 28).

"For I will not trust in my bow, neither shall my sword save me" (Ps.44:6).

"Lo, *this is* the man *that* made not God his strength; but trusted in the abundance of his riches, *and* strengthened himself in his wickedness" (Ps.52:7).

"*It is* better to trust in the LORD than to put confidence in princes" (Ps.118:9).

"Put not your trust in princes, *nor* in the son of man, in whom *there is* no help" (Ps.146:3).

"He that trusteth in his riches shall fall: but the righteous shall flourish as a branch" (Pr.11;28).

"A wise *man* feareth, and departeth from evil: but the fool rageth, and is confident" (Pr.14:16).

"The rich man's wealth *is* his strong city, and as an high wall in his own conceit" (Pr.18:11).

"He that trusteth in his own heart is a fool: but whoso walketh wisely, he shall be delivered" (Pr.28:26).

"Cease ye from man, whose breath *is* in his nostrils: for wherein is he to be accounted of?" (Is.2:22).

"Woe to them that go down to Egypt for help; and stay on horses, and trust in chariots, because *they are* many; and in horsemen, because they are very strong; but they look not unto the Holy One of Israel, neither seek the LORD!" (Is.31:1).

"Therefore hear now this, *thou that art* given to pleasures, that dwellest carelessly, that sayest in thine heart, I *am,* and none else beside me; I shall not sit *as* a widow, neither shall I know the loss of children: But these two *things* shall come to thee in a moment in one day, the loss of children, and widowhood: they shall come upon thee in their perfection for the multitude of thy sorceries, *and* for the great abundance of thine enchantments. For thou hast trusted in thy wickedness: thou hast said, None seeth me. Thy wisdom and thy knowledge, it hath perverted thee; and thou hast said in thine heart, I *am,* and none else beside me. Therefore shall evil come upon thee; thou shalt not know from whence it riseth: and mischief shall fall upon thee; thou shalt not be able to put if off: and desolation shall come upon thee suddenly, *which* thou shalt not know" (Is.47:8-11).

"Thus saith the LORD; Cursed be the man that trusteth in man, and maketh flesh his arm, and whose heart departeth from the LORD" (Je.17:5).

"For because thou hast trusted in thy works and in thy treasures, thou shalt also be taken..." (Je.48:7).

"Wherefore gloriest thou in the valleys, thy flowing valley, O backsliding daughter? that trusted in her treasures, *saying,* Who shall come unto me?" (Je.49:4).

"Woe to them *that are* at ease in Zion, and trust in the mountain of Samaria, *which are* named chief of the nations, to whom the house of Israel came!" (Am.6:1).

"The pride of thine heart hath deceived thee, thou that dwellest in the clefts of the rock, whose habitation *is* high; that saith in his heart, Who shall bring me down to the ground?" (Ob.3).

"Ye have plowed wickedness, ye have reaped iniquity; ye have eaten the fruit of lies: because thou didst trust in thy way, in the multitude of thy mighty men" (Ho.10:13).

CHAPTER 29

B. Woe—A Strong Warning to Ariel (Jerusalem): God's Unusual Dealings with Jerusalem, 29:1-24

1. God's clear warning of coming distress & judgment
  a. The sin: Routine & hypocritical worship, year after year
  b. The judgment
    1) Distress & sorrow
    2) Slaughter: Ariel means an *altar hearth*
    3) A frightful, terrifying siege

    4) A humiliated & weakened people
      • They will not be utterly destroyed
      • They will be weakened: Their voices will be only a whisper

2. God's future deliverance: A picture of the battle of Armageddon, 63:1–64:12; Re.19:17-21
  a. The enemies & ruthless foes defeated suddenly, instantly: Will be the LORD Himself

    1) They will be like fine dust blown away by a storm
    2) They will be like chaff consumed by fire

  b. The enemies' dream of conquest: Will be to no avail

    1) They will be like a hungry man dreaming of eating: When he awakens (in hell), he is still hungry
    2) They will be like a thirsty man dreaming that he is drinking: When he awakens (in hell), he is still thirsty

3. God's three major indictments
  a. First, the people's spiritual stupor, insensitivity, & hard hearts
    1) They stagger, not from wine but from blind hearts
    2) They will face the judgment of God's perfect justice
      • They were put into

Woe to Ariel, to Ariel, the city *where* David dwelt! add ye year to year; let them kill sacrifices.

2 Yet I will distress Ariel, and there shall be heaviness and sorrow: and it shall be unto me as Ariel.

3 And I will camp against thee round about, and will lay siege against thee with a mount, and I will raise forts against thee.

4 And thou shalt be brought down, *and* shalt speak out of the ground, and thy speech shall be low out of the dust, and thy voice shall be, as of one that hath a familiar spirit, out of the ground, and thy speech shall whisper out of the dust.

5 Moreover the multitude of thy strangers shall be like small dust, and the multitude of the terrible ones *shall be* as chaff that passeth away: yea, it shall be at an instant suddenly.

6 Thou shalt be visited of the LORD of hosts with thunder, and with earthquake, and great noise, with storm and tempest, and the flame of devouring fire.

7 And the multitude of all the nations that fight against Ariel, even all that fight against her and her munition, and that distress her, shall be as a dream of a night vision.

8 It shall even be as when an hungry *man* dreameth, and, behold, he eateth; but he awaketh, and his soul is empty: or as when a thirsty man dreameth, and, behold, he drinketh; but he awaketh, and, behold, *he is* faint, and his soul hath appetite: so shall the multitude of all the nations be, that fight against mount Zion.

9 Stay yourselves, and wonder; cry ye out, and cry: they are drunken, but not with wine; they stagger, but not with strong drink.

10 For the LORD hath poured out upon you the spirit of deep sleep, and hath closed

your eyes: the prophets and your rulers, the seers hath he covered.

11 And the vision of all is become unto you as the words of a book that is sealed, which *men* deliver to one that is learned, saying, Read this, I pray thee: and he saith, I cannot; for it *is* sealed:

12 And the book is delivered to him that is not learned, saying, Read this, I pray thee: and he saith, I am not learned.

13 Wherefore the Lord said, Forasmuch as this people draw near *me* with their mouth, and with their lips do honour me, but have removed their heart far from me, and their fear toward me is taught by the precept of men:

14 Therefore, behold, I will proceed to do a marvellous work among this people, *even* a marvellous work and a wonder: for the wisdom of their wise *men* shall perish, and the understanding of their prudent *men* shall be hid.

15 Woe unto them that seek deep to hide their counsel from the LORD, and their works are in the dark, and they say, Who seeth us? and who knoweth us?

16 Surely your turning of things upside down shall be esteemed as the potter's clay: for shall the work say of him that made it, He made me not? or shall the thing framed say of him that framed it, He had no understanding?

17 *Is* it not yet a very little while, and Lebanon shall be turned into a fruitful field, and the fruitful field shall be esteemed as a forest?

18 And in that day shall the deaf hear the words of the book, and the eyes of the blind shall see out of obscurity, and out of darkness.

19 The meek also shall increase *their* joy in the LORD, and the poor among men shall rejoice in the Holy One of Israel.

20 For the terrible one is brought to nought, and the scorner is consumed, and all that watch for iniquity are cut off:

21 That make a man an offender for a word, and lay a

a deep spiritual sleep (even their prophets)

  • They could not understand the messages & warnings of God: His Word was like a sealed book for both the educated (v.11) & the uneducated, 12

  b. Second, the people's formal & hypocritical worship
    1) They professed God, but did not truly follow Him: Followed man-made rituals & rules

    2) The result: They will face God's judgment
      • He will show that human wisdom is foolish
      • He will hide understanding from them

  c. Third, the people's attempt to hide their evil behavior, acting secretly in the dark
    1) They questioned if God could see them

    2) They twisted the facts
      • Treated the Potter (Creator) as the clay (a mere man)
      • Denied God as the Creator who knows all & can do all (as omniscient & omnipotent)

4. God's promise of a glorious transformation in the future: The future kingdom of Christ
  a. The earth will be transformed
  b. The disabled will be healed

  c. The humble & poor will rejoice: Be exalted & provided for

  d. The truth of righteousness & justice will prevail
    1) The evildoers of this earth will be removed & judged

    2) The false witnesses & corrupt lawyers, judges &

leaders—all will be removed & punished	snare for him that reproveth in the gate, and turn aside the just for a thing of nought.	children, the work of mine hands, in the midst of him, they shall sanctify my name,	the LORD, that it is He who truly blesses them
e. The attitude of Israel (God's people) will be totally changed	22 Therefore thus saith the LORD, who redeemed Abraham, concerning the house of Jacob, Jacob shall not now be ashamed, neither shall his face now wax pale.	and sanctify the Holy One of Jacob, and shall fear the God of Israel.	3) They will live righteously & keep God's name holy
1) They will no longer be ashamed nor grow pale with fear		24 They also that erred in spirit shall come to understanding, and they that murmured shall learn doctrine.	4) They will worship the LORD
2) They will acknowledge	23 But when he seeth his		5) They will no longer go astray or complain but will accept the truth (God's Word) & grow in the LORD

DIVISION III

THE PROPHECIES OF WOE: GOD'S WARNING TO HIS PEOPLE, 28:1–35:10

B. Woe—A Strong Warning to Ariel (Jerusalem): God's Unusual Dealings with Jerusalem, 29:1-24

(29:1-24) **Introduction**: down through history the Jews have probably suffered as much if not more persecution than any other people on earth. Tyrant after tyrant has attempted to eradicate them. Yet despite the slaughter of millions, the Jews have survived the holocausts launched against them. There is a reason—a very specific reason—why they have survived. God! God has a plan for them. Way back in ancient history the LORD chose Abraham to give birth to the Jews for three very specific purposes:

⇒ to be the people through whom He would send the Messiah, the Lord Jesus Christ, to save the world.
⇒ to be the people through whom He would give His Word, the Holy Bible, to the world.
⇒ to be His witnesses to the unbelievers of the world, that the LORD Himself (Yahweh, Jehovah) is the only true and living God

Down through history the Jews failed in their calling to be strong witnesses for the LORD. Tragically, they even turned away from Him and worshipped false gods, the idols of this world. As a result, God's hand of judgment fell upon the Jews time and time again. God always executed judgment in the hope that the people would cry out to the Him for deliv-erance, repent of their sins, and renew their commitment to serve Him. Although the judgments did sometimes cause the Jews to return to the LORD, every recommitment was temporary. Tragically, the people soon returned to their sinful ways and false worship.

In the present Scripture, Isaiah once again warned the Jews of the coming judgment of God. But as usual, they ignored the warning. This is the second of five *woes* or strong warnings that God's prophet pronounces in chapters 28–33. In this particular warning, Isaiah gives a glimpse into the events of the end times, in particular the events of Armageddon and the glorious transformation that is to take place in the future kingdom of the Messiah, the Lord Jesus Christ. This is, *Woe—A Strong Warning to Ariel (Jerusalem): God's Unusual Dealings with Jerusalem, 29:1-24.*

1. God's clear warning of coming distress and judgment (vv.1-4).
2. God's future deliverance: a picture of the battle of Armageddon, 63:1–64:12; Re.19:17-21 (vv.5-8).
3. God's three major indictments (vv.9-16).
4. God's promise of a glorious transformation in the future: the future kingdom of Christ (vv.17-24).

1 (29:1-4) **Warning, of Judgment, Issued to Jerusalem—Worship, Hypocritical, Example of, Jerusalem—Jerusalem, Warned of Judgment**: God gave Ariel (Jerusalem) a strong warning—a woe—of coming distress and judgment. Ariel is the city where David lived; therefore, Isaiah was definitely giving this warning to the citizens of Jerusalem.

OUTLINE	SCRIPTURE	SCRIPTURE	OUTLINE

1. God's clear warning of coming distress & judgment
a. The sin: Routine & hypocritical worship, year after year
b. The judgment
  1) Distress & sorrow
  2) Slaughter: Ariel means an *altar hearth*
  3) A frightful, terrifying siege
	Woe to Ariel, to Ariel, the city *where* David dwelt! add ye year to year; let them kill sacrifices.
	2 Yet I will distress Ariel, and there shall be heaviness and sorrow: and it shall be unto me as Ariel.
	3 And I will camp against thee round about, and will lay siege against thee with a
		mount, and I will raise forts against thee.
		4 And thou shalt be brought down, *and* shalt speak out of the ground, and thy speech shall be low out of the dust, and thy voice shall be, as of one that hath a familiar spirit, out of the ground, and thy speech shall whisper out of the dust.
			4) A humiliated & weakened people
			• They will not be utterly destroyed
			• They will be weakened: Their voices will only be a whisper

The people were guilty of a terrible sin, that of routine and hypocritical worship. Instead of repenting of their sins and turning back to the LORD, they continued year after year in their hypocritical worship. Note what the LORD says: they could continue their routine worship, keep on performing their religious rituals and ceremonies, but they could not stop God's hand of judgment from falling upon them.

What was the particular judgment they were to suffer? Very soon after Isaiah's prophecy, the LORD would use the Assyrians to set up a siege around Jerusalem, a siege that took place in 701 B.C. However, the LORD would deliver the citizens of the capital from this particular siege by slaying more than 185,000 Assyrian troops in one night. His supernatural power would send the rest of the Assyrian soldiers scurrying back home as rapidly as they could march. Although the other cities of Judah fell to the Assyrians, Jerusalem was left standing.

In thankfulness to God, the people should have repented of their sins and turned to the LORD in sincere worship and praise. Instead, they persisted in their sinful behavior and continued their routine and hypocritical worship. Therefore, the discipline of God could not be removed from the Jews. Some future discipline was inevitable. Thus the pronouncement of this judgment refers not only to the Assyrian siege, but also to the Babylonian destruction of Jerusalem and the exile of its citizens that would take place in 586 B.C. In that year the LORD used the Babylonians to totally destroy the capital and to send the vast majority of Jews into captivity.

Note how Isaiah addressed Jerusalem: "Ariel, Ariel." The word means *an altar hearth*. The prophet apparently addressed Jerusalem as Ariel because the city was to become an altar of slaughter, a place where the fire of God's judgment would fall. Although the Assyrians and Babylonians were the ones who besieged Jerusalem, note that God Himself is the One working behind the scenes of human history. He would use these two nations to execute His judgment against the sinful, hypocritical worshippers of Jerusalem. Three different times the LORD says that He Himself would set up the siege (v.3). The Assyrians and Babylonians were only the human agents the LORD would use to execute His judgment.

The Jews were to be humiliated and brought low, but they would not be utterly destroyed (v.4). They would be deliv-ered from the Assyrian siege (see outline and notes—Is.36:1–37:38 for more discussion), and a small remnant would survive the Babylonian slaughter and captivity (see outline and notes—Ezr.1:1–2:70 for more discussion). But the judgment would severely weaken the Jews as a people. Many of them would be slaughtered, and the survivors would lose their authority as a nation. Their influence among the nations would amount to nothing more than the murmur (whisper) of a ghost attempting to speak from the grave.

Thought 1. The coming judgment of God will be very personal. Each of us will stand before Him and hear His verdict on what we have done. If we have trusted Christ—trusted that He has taken our sins upon Himself and borne the penalty for them in our behalf—the verdict will be wonderful news: "Not guilty." He will not find us guilty of sin, for Christ has already paid the penalty for us. When He died on the cross, He died for our sins. Trusting Christ makes us acceptable to God and frees us from the guilt of sin. But if we have not trusted Christ, we will stand before God bearing our own sin. We will hear the terrifying verdict:

⇒ "Guilty of rejecting God's Son, the Lord Jesus Christ"
⇒ "Guilty of refusing to accept the forgiveness God offers"
⇒ "Guilty of disobeying God's Holy commandments"
⇒ "Guilty of living selfish, unrighteous, and wicked lives"
⇒ "Guilty of worshiping in a routine, formal, and hypocritical way"
⇒ "Guilty of ignoring, rejecting, defying, and rebelling against God"

"For the Son of man shall come in the glory of his Father with his angels; and then he shall reward every man according to his works" (Mt.16:27).

"For we must all appear before the judgment seat of Christ; that every one may receive the things *done* in *his* body, according to that he hath done, whether *it be* good or bad" (2 Co.5:10).

"And if ye call on the Father, who without respect of persons judgeth according to every man's work, pass the time of your sojourning *here* in fear" (1 Pe.1:17).

"Behold, I will cast her into a bed, and them that commit adultery with her into great tribulation, except they repent of their deeds. And I will kill her children with death; and all the churches shall know that I am he which searcheth the reins and hearts: and I will give unto every one of you according to your works" (Re.2:22-23).

"And I saw a great white throne, and him that sat on it, from whose face the earth and the heaven fled away; and there was found no place for them. And I saw the dead, small and great, stand before God; and the books were opened: and another book was opened, which is *the book* of life: and the dead were judged out of those things which were written in the books, according to their works. And the sea gave up the dead which were in it; and death and hell delivered up the dead which were in them: and they were judged every man according to their works. And death and hell were cast into the lake of fire. This is the second death. And whosoever was not found written in the book of life was cast into the lake of fire" (Re.20:11-15).

"And, behold, I come quickly; and my reward *is* with me, to give every man according as his work shall be" (Re.22:12).

"Also unto thee, O Lord, *belongeth* mercy: for thou renderest to every man according to his work" (Ps.62:12).

"If thou forbear to deliver *them that are* drawn unto death, and *those that are* ready to be slain; If thou sayest, Behold, we knew it not; doth not he that pondereth the heart consider *it?* and he that keepeth thy soul, doth *not* he know *it?* and shall *not* he render to *every* man according to his works?" (Pr.24:11-12).

"Therefore I will judge you, O house of Israel, every one according to his ways, saith the Lord GOD. Repent, and turn *yourselves* from all your transgressions; so iniquity shall not be your ruin" (Eze.18:30).

"I the LORD search the heart, *I* try the reins, even to give every man according to his ways, *and* according to the fruit of his doings" (Je.17:10).

253

Isaiah 29:1-24

"Great in counsel, and mighty in work: for thine eyes *are* open upon all the ways of the sons of men: to give every one according to his ways, and according to the fruit of his doings" (Je.32:19).

2 (29:5-8) **Deliverance, from Judgment, Predicted—Armageddon, Prophecy Concerning—Jews, Deliverance of, Prophecy Concerning**: in the midst of judgment, God makes a most wonderful promise. He will pour out His mercy upon His people and deliver them from the ruthless foes who attack them. This passage has a double meaning. It clearly refers to the miraculous, sudden deliverance of Jerusalem from the Assyrian invasion and siege (37:36-38). But note the reference to a multitude of enemies and nations (vv.5, 7). Also note the reference to the thunderstorms, earthquakes, great noises, windstorms (tornados), and the flaming fire that consumes the enemies (v.6). All this points to something far more than the Lord's deliverance of Jerusalem during the Assyrian siege. This seems to be a clear prediction of the battle of Armageddon, which is to take place in the last days of human history (see outline and notes—Is.63:1–64:12; Re.14:14-20; 16:12-16; 19:11-21 for more discussion).

When ruthless foes attack the Lord's people, He promises to defeat them immediately (vv.5-6). Note that it will be the Lord of hosts, the Lord Almighty, who will destroy them. Using the forces of nature—thunderstorms, earthquakes, terrifying noises, and tornados—along with the flaming fire of His holiness, the Lord will utterly destroy the enemy (see outline and note—Re.19:20 for more discussion).

Scripture actually says that the Lord will use the spirit of His mouth to consume all the enemies who stand opposed to Him and His people (2 Th.2:8). What is the *spirit of His mouth*? It is the spirit of His Word, the flaming holiness of His person. *In that day* when the armies of the world march against Jerusalem and the Lord Jesus returns to earth, He will simply speak the word of destruction. The result will be shocking: all the armies of the world will be instantly destroyed. All the tyrants' dreams of conquest will die with them. Before the Lord's flaming Word, all ruthless enemies will be nothing more than fine dust blown away by a storm; nothing more than chaff consumed by fire. Anyone who dreams of conquering Mount Zion, the mountain of God, will be like a hungry man who dreams of eating; but when he awakens (in hell), he will still be hungry. He will be like a thirsty man dreaming that he is drinking, but when he awakens (in hell), he will still be thirsty.

OUTLINE	SCRIPTURE	SCRIPTURE	OUTLINE
2. God's future deliverance: A picture of the battle of Armageddon, 63:1–64:12; Re.19:17-21 a. The enemies & ruthless foes defeated suddenly, instantly: Will be the Lord Himself 1) They will be like fine dust blown away by a storm 2) They will be like chaff consumed by fire b. The enemies' dream of conquest: Will be to no avail	5 Moreover the multitude of thy strangers shall be like small dust, and the multitude of the terrible ones *shall be* as chaff that passeth away: yea, it shall be at an instant suddenly. 6 Thou shalt be visited of the Lord of hosts with thunder, and with earthquake, and great noise, with storm and tempest, and the flame of devouring fire. 7 And the multitude of all the nations that fight against Ariel, even all that fight	against her and her munition, and that distress her, shall be as a dream of a night vision. 8 It shall even be as when an hungry *man* dreameth, and, behold, he eateth; but he awaketh, and his soul is empty: or as when a thirsty man dreameth, and, behold, he drinketh; but he awaketh, and, behold, *he is* faint, and his soul hath appetite: so shall the multitude of all the nations be, that fight against mount Zion.	1) They will be like a hungry man dreaming of eating: When he awakens (in hell), he is still hungry 2) They will be like a thirsty man dreaming that he is drinking: When he awakens (in hell), he is still thirsty

Thought 1. The Lord is going to deliver us from all our enemies, from all who oppress and persecute us. Note the word *from*. The day is coming when all enemies will be removed from the earth, doomed to hell because of their defiance of God and their persecution of believers. Deliverance from all ruthless oppressors and persecutors is coming. This is the wonderful promise of God, the promise of a perfect world in which there will be no oppression, persecution, or ruthless behavior of any kind.

Yet the Lord gives us an equally wonderful promise of deliverance today. When people become our enemies and assail us because of our faith, the Lord promises to deliver us through the attack. Note the word *through*. It may be the Lord's will for us to suffer *through* ridicule, persecution, hostility, abuse, or assault. But the Lord will be with us and strengthen us through whatever attack the enemy unleashes against us. Even if we are robbed of life by some cruel enemy, quicker than the eye can blink the Lord will snatch us right into His presence. God will always deliver us through the attacks of all ruthless foes. Note the promises of God's Holy Word:

"There hath no temptation taken you but such as is common to man: but God *is* faithful, who will not suffer you to be tempted above that ye are able; but will with the temptation also make a way to escape, that ye may be able to bear *it*" (1 Co.10:13).
"For we would not, brethren, have you ignorant of our trouble which came to us in Asia, that we were pressed out of measure, above strength, insomuch that we despaired even of life: But we had the sentence of death in ourselves, that we should not trust in ourselves, but in God which raiseth the dead: Who delivered us from so great a death, and doth deliver: in whom we trust that he will yet deliver *us*" (2 Co.1:8-10).
"And the Lord shall deliver me from every evil work, and will preserve *me* unto his heavenly kingdom: to whom *be* glory for ever and ever. Amen" (2 Ti.4:18).

ISAIAH 29:1-24

"Forasmuch then as the children are partakers of flesh and blood, he also himself likewise took part of the same; that through death he might destroy him that had the power of death, that is, the devil; And deliver them who through fear of death were all their lifetime subject to bondage" (He.2:14-15).

"The Lord knoweth how to deliver the godly out of temptations, and to reserve the unjust unto the day of judgment to be punished" (2 Pe.2:9).

"And he said, The LORD *is* my rock, and my fortress, and my deliverer" (2 S.22:2).

"He shall deliver thee in six troubles: yea, in seven [the complete number] there shall no evil touch thee" (Jb.5:19).

"Surely he shall deliver thee from the snare of the fowler, *and* from the noisome pestilence" (Ps.91:3).

"They reel to and fro, and stagger like a drunken man, and are at their wit's end. Then they cry unto the LORD in their trouble, and he bringeth them out of their distresses. He maketh the storm a calm, so that the waves thereof are still. Then are they glad because they be quiet; so he bringeth them unto their desired haven. Oh that *men* would praise the LORD *for* his goodness, and *for* his wonderful works to the children of men!" (Ps.107:27-31).

"And *even* to *your* old age I *am* he; and *even* to hoar [gray] hairs will I carry *you:* I have made, and I will bear; even I will carry, and will deliver *you*" (Is.46:4).

"Be not afraid of their faces: for I *am* with thee to deliver thee, saith the LORD" (Je.1:8).

---

3 (29:9-16) **Judgment, Caused by, Threefold Cause—Indictment, Caused by, Threefold Indictment—Hard-hearted, Results of, Judgment—Spiritual Insensitivity, Results of, Judgment—Spiritual Stupor, Results of, Judgment—Worship, Formal and Routine, Results of, Judgment—Hypocrisy, of Worship, Results of, Judgment—Worship, Hypocritical, Results of, Judgment—Sins, Secret, Warning Against—Secret Sins, Warning Against—Behavior, Evil, Secrecy of, Warning Against—Sin, Secret, Warning Against**: God issued three major charges against Jerusalem that were to cause His hand of judgment to fall upon them. Apparently the message of judgment stunned and perplexed the people. Isaiah told them to *pause* and *wonder*, to question why the judgment of God was coming upon them. The charges can be summarized in one statement: their hearts were far from God (v.13). The specific charges of God's indictment against Jerusalem and its people are spelled out by Scripture:

OUTLINE	SCRIPTURE	SCRIPTURE	OUTLINE

3. God's three major indictments
a. First, the people's spiritual stupor, insensitivity, a hard heart
  1) They stagger, not from wine but from blind hearts
  2) They will face the judgment of God's perfect justice
  • They were put into a deep spiritual sleep, (even their prophets)
  • They could not understand the messages & warnings of God: His Word was like a sealed book for both the educated (v.11) & the uneducated, 12
 	
b. Second, the people's formal & hypocritical worship
  1) They professed God, but did not truly follow Him:
	9 Stay yourselves, and wonder; cry ye out, and cry: they are drunken, but not with wine; they stagger, but not with strong drink.
	10 For the LORD hath poured out upon you the spirit of deep sleep, and hath closed your eyes: the prophets and your rulers, the seers hath he covered.
	11 And the vision of all is become unto you as the words of a book that is sealed, which *men* deliver to one that is learned, saying, Read this, I pray thee: and he saith, I cannot; for it *is* sealed:
	12 And the book is delivered to him that is not learned, saying, Read this, I pray thee: and he saith, I am not learned.
	13 Wherefore the Lord said, Forasmuch as this people draw near *me* with their mouth, and with their lips do
		honour me, but have removed their heart far from me, and their fear toward me is taught by the precept of men:
		14 Therefore, behold, I will proceed to do a marvellous work among this people, *even* a marvellous work and a wonder: for the wisdom of their wise *men* shall perish, and the understanding of their prudent *men* shall be hid.
		15 Woe unto them that seek deep to hide their counsel from the LORD, and their works are in the dark, and they say, Who seeth us? and who knoweth us?
		16 Surely your turning of things upside down shall be esteemed as the potter's clay: for shall the work say of him that made it, He made me not? or shall the thing framed say of him that framed it, He had no understanding?
			Followed man-made rituals & rules
			
			  2) The result: They will face God's judgment
			  • He will show that human wisdom is foolish
			  • He will hide understanding from them
			
			c. Third, the people's attempt to hide their evil behavior, acting secretly in the dark
			  1) They questioned if God could see them
			
			  2) They twisted the facts
			  • Treated the Potter (Creator) as the clay (a mere man)
			  • Denied God as the Creator who knows all & can do all (as omniscient & omnipotent)

a. The first charge was a strong indictment: the people were spiritually insensitive. They had hard hearts (vv.9-12; see 6:10). Although they were attending worship services (v.1), they were only going through the motions, not focusing their minds upon the LORD and His Word. They were in a spiritual stupor, allowing their minds to wander all about, here and there. They were focused on their own personal interests not on the LORD. They were like drunk men staggering all about, not from wine but from blind hearts. Closing their eyes and ears to the LORD week after week and month after month only increased the hardness of their hearts.

Thus they were to face the judgment of God's perfect justice (vv.10-12). They would reap exactly what they had sown: closed eyes and ears, hard hearts, and a deep spiritual sleep. Shutting their minds and hearts to the LORD and His Word, they became even more blind and hard-hearted. Because of the depth of their insensitivity to spiritual matters, even the prophets

255

of their day would not be able to help them. The people would not be able to understand the messages and warnings of God. His Word would be like a book sealed shut for both the educated and the uneducated (vv.11-12).

Thought 1. The more we close our minds and hearts to the LORD, the more our minds and hearts become closed. We are creatures of conditioning. If we blind our eyes to spiritual truth, our eyes will become increasingly blind. If we shut our ears against the message of the LORD, our ears will become increasingly shut. If we harden our hearts toward the LORD, against following Him, our hearts will become increasingly hard. One of the principles of judgment established in the universe is that of *reciprocal judgment*, the *judicial judgment* of God. Stated in Scriptural terms, a person reaps what he sows. If we sow the seed of spiritual blindness, we will reap more spiritual blindness. If we respond to God with hard hearts, we will reap hard hearts. Listen to what God's Holy Word says:

"But if thine eye be evil, thy whole body shall be full of darkness. If therefore the light that is in thee be darkness, how great *is* that darkness!" (Mt.6:23).

"Give, and it shall be given unto you; good measure, pressed down, and shaken together, and running over, shall men give into your bosom. For with the same measure that ye mete withal it shall be measured to you again" (Lu.6:38).

"For the heart of this people is waxed gross, and their ears are dull of hearing, and their eyes have they closed; lest they should see with *their* eyes, and hear with *their* ears, and understand with *their* heart, and should be converted, and I should heal them" (Ac.28:27).

"In whom the god of this world hath blinded the minds of them which believe not, lest the light of the glorious gospel of Christ, who is the image of God, should shine unto them" (2 Co.4:4).

"But after thy hardness and impenitent heart treasurest up unto thyself wrath against the day of wrath and revelation of the righteous judgment of God; Who will render to every man according to his deeds: To them who by patient continuance in well doing seek for glory and honour and immortality, eternal life: But unto them that are contentious, and do not obey the truth, but obey unrighteousness, indignation and wrath, Tribulation and anguish, upon every soul of man that doeth evil, of the Jew first, and also of the Gentile" (Ro.2:5-9).

"Be not deceived; God is not mocked: for whatsoever a man soweth, that shall he also reap. For he that soweth to his flesh shall of the flesh reap corruption; but he that soweth to the Spirit shall of the Spirit reap life everlasting" (Ga.6:7-8).

"This I say therefore, and testify in the Lord, that ye henceforth walk not as other Gentiles walk, in the vanity of their mind, Having the understanding darkened, being alienated from the life of God through the ignorance that is in them, because of the blindness of their heart: Who being past feeling have given themselves over unto lasciviousness, to work all uncleanness with greediness" (Ep.4:17-19).

"Now the Spirit speaketh expressly, that in the latter times some shall depart from the faith, giving heed to seducing spirits, and doctrines of devils; Speaking lies in hypocrisy; having their conscience seared with a hot iron" (1 Ti.4:1-2).

"Take heed, brethren, lest there be in any of you an evil heart of unbelief, in departing from the living God. But exhort one another daily, while it is called To day; lest any of you be hardened through the deceitfulness of sin" (He.3:12-13).

"Even as I have seen, they that plow iniquity, and sow wickedness, reap the same" (Jb.4:8).

"Frowardness *is* in his heart, he deviseth mischief continually; he soweth discord" (Pr.6:14).

"Happy *is* the man that feareth alway: but he that hardeneth his heart shall fall into mischief" (Pr.28:14).

"Because sentence against an evil work is not executed speedily, therefore the heart of the sons of men is fully set in them to do evil. Though a sinner do evil an hundred times, and his *days* be prolonged, yet surely I know that it shall be well with them that fear God, which fear before him: But it shall not be well with the wicked, neither shall he prolong *his* days, *which are* as a shadow; because he feareth not before God" (Ecc.8:11-13).

b. The second charge was shocking: the people were guilty of formal, routine, and hypocritical worship (vv.13-14). They were professing to follow God and were attending worship regularly, but they did not truly walk with the LORD. They participated in the ceremonies and activities of religion, but they were honoring the LORD only with their lips. Their hearts were far from Him. Their religious worship consisted of man-made rituals, ceremonies, and rules. They did not obey God's commandments or the instructions in His Word. Because of their hypocrisy, they would face the hand of God's judgment (v.14). The LORD would expose the foolishness of their human wisdom and withdraw understanding from them. They would not know what action to take when they faced problems or crises.

Thought 1. Far too much worship is routine, ritualistic, formal, and hypocritical. How many worshippers are truly following the LORD, obeying His commandments, and living righteously? How many are daily seeking the LORD, studying His Word, and trusting Him to guide their steps as they walk throughout the day?

Many people sit in worship services with their minds elsewhere, not listening to the Word of God being preached. They simply go through the motions of worship, participating in the rituals and ceremonies while their thoughts are elsewhere. To them, worship is no more than a custom, a practice or tradition they must observe. When they walk out of worship services, they do what they please instead of obeying God. Listen to what God's Holy Word says about hypocrites who profess to follow the LORD but only go through the motions of worship:

"And why beholdest thou the mote that is in thy brother's eye, but considerest not the beam that is in thine own eye?" (Mt.7:3).

"Not every one that saith unto me, Lord, Lord, shall enter into the kingdom of heaven; but he that doeth the will of my Father which is in heaven. Many will say to me in that day, Lord, Lord, have we not prophesied in thy name? and in thy name have cast out devils? and in thy name done many wonderful works? And then will I profess unto them, I never knew you: depart from me, ye that work iniquity" (Mt.7:21-23).

"Woe unto you, scribes and Pharisees, hypocrites! for ye devour widows' houses, and for a pretence make long prayer: therefore ye shall receive the greater damnation" (Mt.23:14).

"Woe unto you, scribes and Pharisees, hypocrites! for ye pay tithe of mint and anise and cummin, and have omitted the weightier *matters* of the law, judgment, mercy, and faith: these ought ye to have done, and not to leave the other undone" (Mt.23:23).

"Even so ye also outwardly appear righteous unto men, but within ye are full of hypocrisy and iniquity" (Mt.23:28).

"He answered and said unto them, Well hath Esaias prophesied of you hypocrites, as it is written, This people honoureth me with *their* lips, but their heart is far from me" (Mk.7:6).

"And why call ye me, Lord, Lord, and do not the things which I say?" (Lu.6:46).

"In the mean time, when there were gathered together an innumerable multitude of people, insomuch that they trode one upon another, he began to say unto his disciples first of all, Beware ye of the leaven of the Pharisees [the religionists], which is hypocrisy" (Lu.12:1).

"If a man on the sabbath day receive circumcision, that the law of Moses should not be broken; are ye angry at me, because I have made a man every whit whole on the sabbath day?" (Jn.7:23).

"Therefore thou art inexcusable, O man, whosoever thou art that judgest: for wherein thou judgest another, thou condemnest thyself; for thou that judgest doest the same things" (Ro.2:1).

"Thou therefore which teachest another, teachest thou not thyself? thou that preachest a man should not steal, dost thou steal?" (Ro.2:21).

"Thou that makest thy boast of the law, through breaking the law dishonourest thou God? For the name of God is blasphemed among the Gentiles through you, as it is written" (Ro.2:23-24).

"For the kingdom of God is not meat and drink; but righteousness, and peace, and joy in the Holy Ghost" (Ro.14:17).

"But when I saw that they walked not uprightly according to the truth of the gospel, I said unto Peter before *them* all, If thou, being a Jew, livest after the manner of Gentiles, and not as do the Jews, why compellest thou the Gentiles to live as do the Jews?" (Ga.2:14).

"Now the Spirit speaketh expressly, that in the latter times some shall depart from the faith, giving heed to seducing spirits, and doctrines of devils; Speaking lies in hypocrisy; having their conscience seared with a hot iron" (1 Ti.4:1-2).

"This know also, that in the last days perilous times shall come. For men shall be lovers of their own selves, covetous, boasters, proud, blasphemers, disobedient to parents, unthankful, unholy, Without natural affection, trucebreakers, false accusers, incontinent, fierce, despisers of those that are good, Traitors, heady, highminded, lovers of pleasures more than lovers of God; Having a form of godliness, but denying the power thereof: from such turn away" (2 Ti.3:1-5, esp. v.5).

"They profess that they know God; but in works they deny *him*, being abominable, and disobedient, and unto every good work reprobate" (Tit.1:16).

"If a brother or sister be naked, and destitute of daily food, And one of you say unto them, Depart in peace, be ye warmed and filled; notwithstanding ye give them not those things which are needful to the body; what *doth it* profit?" (Js.2:15-16).

"Out of the same mouth proceedeth blessing and cursing. My brethren, these things ought not so to be" (Js.3:10).

"And Samuel said, Hath the LORD *as great* delight in burnt offerings and sacrifices, as in obeying the voice of the LORD? Behold, to obey *is* better than sacrifice, *and* to hearken than the fat of rams" (1 S.15:22).

"And they remembered that God *was* their rock, and the high God their redeemer. Nevertheless they did flatter him with their mouth, and they lied unto him with their tongues" (Ps.78:35-36).

"Bring no more vain oblations; incense is an abomination unto me; the new moons and sabbaths, the calling of assemblies, I cannot away with; *it is* iniquity, even the solemn meeting" (Is.1:13).

"Hear ye this, O house of Jacob, which are called by the name of Israel, and are come forth out of the waters of Judah, which swear by the name of the LORD, and make mention of the God of Israel, *but* not in truth, nor in righteousness" (Is.48:1).

"Keep thy foot when thou goest to the house of God, and be more ready to hear, than to give the sacrifice of fools: for they consider not that they do evil" (Ecc.5:1).

"And they come unto thee as the people cometh, and they sit before thee as my people, and they hear thy words, but they will not do them: for with their mouth they show much love, *but* their heart goeth after their covetousness. And, lo, thou *art* unto them as a very lovely song of one that hath a pleasant voice, and can play well on an instrument: for they hear thy words, but they do them not" (Eze.33:31-32).

c. The third charge was an eye opener: the people were attempting to hide their evil behavior. Some tried to hide their sin from the public by committing their wickedness under the cover of darkness. Others did what they wanted, ignoring the LORD and refusing to seek His counsel. Most likely, this is a reference to the leaders' seeking an alliance with Egypt in an attempt to withstand the Assyrian threat. Placing their trust in Egypt and its military power, they totally ignored God and never sought His counsel. Instead of trusting the LORD, they trusted Egypt. Scheming to hide their evil alliance from the eyes of the LORD's prophet Isaiah, they apparently conducted the investigation in total secrecy.

Remember that Isaiah had preached against the treaty (28:14-15, 17-22). By hiding the negotiations from Isaiah, the leaders felt the LORD would not see their evil plans or else would ignore their disobedient behavior. They twisted the facts in their minds and reached the false conclusion that the LORD either did not know or did not care what was going on.

Note that Isaiah charges the leaders and people with stupidity. They were treating the Potter as though He were the clay, treating the Creator as though He were a mere man. In essence, they were denying that God is the Creator who knows all and can do all. Any attempt to hide evil behavior from the LORD is stupid. It is like a clay pot saying to the potter, "You did not make me" or "You know nothing about my sinful, disobedient behavior."

Thought 1. No matter what we do in secret, the LORD always knows. No sinful behavior is hidden from His piercing eyes. God sees and knows all, both the good and evil that we do. God is omniscient; He knows everything that happens throughout the entire universe. Whether we lie, steal, cheat, overeat, smoke, become drunk, commit immorality, fail to worship Him daily, or disobey and break His holy commandments—God knows. He sees exactly what we do. Nothing can be done in secret or hidden from His all-seeing eyes. Listen to what God's Holy Word says:

"For there is nothing covered, that shall not be revealed; neither hid, that shall not be known" (Lu.12:2).

"Therefore judge nothing before the time, until the Lord come, who both will bring to light the hidden things of darkness, and will make manifest the counsels of the hearts: and then shall every man have praise of God" (1 Co.4:5).

"But if ye will not do so, behold, ye have sinned against the LORD: and be sure your sin will find you out" (Nu.32:23).

"If I sin, then thou markest me, and thou wilt not acquit me from mine iniquity" (Jb.10:14).

"For now thou numberest my steps: dost thou not watch over my sin?" (Jb.14:16).

"The heaven shall reveal his iniquity; and the earth shall rise up against him" (Jb.20:27).

"He that hateth dissembleth with his lips, and layeth up deceit within him; When he speaketh fair, believe him not: for *there are* seven abominations in his heart. *Whose* hatred is covered by deceit, his wickedness shall be showed before the *whole* congregation" (Pr.26:24-26).

"For God shall bring every work into judgment, with every secret thing, whether *it be* good, or whether *it be* evil" (Ecc.12:14).

"Woe to the rebellious children, saith the LORD, that take counsel, but not of me; and that cover with a covering, but not of my spirit, that they may add sin to sin" (Is.30:1).

"And the Spirit of the LORD fell upon me, and said unto me, Speak; Thus saith the LORD; Thus have ye said, O house of Israel: for I know the things that come into your mind, *every one of* them" (Eze.11:5).

"For though thou wash thee with nitre, and take thee much sope, *yet* thine iniquity is marked before me, saith the Lord GOD" (Je.2:22).

"For mine eyes *are* upon all their ways: they are not hid from my face, neither is their iniquity hid from mine eyes" (Je.16:17).

"And they consider not in their hearts *that* I remember all their wickedness: now their own doings have beset them about; they are before my face" (Ho.7:2).

"For I know your manifold transgressions and your mighty sins: they afflict the just, they take a bribe, and they turn aside the poor in the gate *from their right*" (Am.5:12).

4 (29:17-24) **Prophecy, Concerning Israel, a Glorious Transformation—Kingdom of Christ, Described, Fivefold Description—Transformation, of the World, Prophecy Concerning—Jews, Prophecy Concerning, a Glorious Transformation**: God gave His people the promise of a glorious future. Note the phrases "in a very short time" and "in that day" (vv.17-18). These terms point to the Messiah's kingdom, to the time when Jesus Christ will return to earth to establish His kingdom. The glorious transformation described in these verses could not take place on earth apart from God's direct intervention. Isaiah is predicting a future transformation of the earth and of the hearts of God's people. Note the specific details of this glorious renovation:

OUTLINE	SCRIPTURE	SCRIPTURE	OUTLINE
4. God's promise of a glorious transformation in the future: The future kingdom of Christ a. The earth will be transformed b. The disabled will be healed c. The humble & poor will re-	17 *Is* it not yet a very little while, and Lebanon shall be turned into a fruitful field, and the fruitful field shall be esteemed as a forest? 18 And in that day shall the deaf hear the words of the book, and the eyes of the blind shall see out of obscurity, and out of darkness. 19 The meek also shall in-	crease *their* joy in the LORD, and the poor among men shall rejoice in the Holy One of Israel. 20 For the terrible one is brought to nought, and the scorner is consumed, and all that watch for iniquity are cut off: 21 That make a man an offender for a word, and lay a	joice: Be exalted & provided for d. The truth of righteousness & justice will prevail 1) The evildoers of this earth will be removed & judged 2) The false witnesses & corrupt lawyers, judges &

OUTLINE	SCRIPTURE	SCRIPTURE	OUTLINE
leaders—all will be re-moved & punished e. The attitude of Israel (God's people) will be totally changed 1) They will no longer be ashamed nor grow pale with fear 2) They will acknowledge	snare for him that reproveth in the gate, and turn aside the just for a thing of nought. 22 Therefore thus saith the LORD, who redeemed Abraham, concerning the house of Jacob, Jacob shall not now be ashamed, neither shall his face now wax pale. 23 But when he seeth his	children, the work of mine hands, in the midst of him, they shall sanctify my name, and sanctify the Holy One of Jacob, and shall fear the God of Israel. 24 They also that erred in spirit shall come to under-standing, and they that mur-mured shall learn doctrine.	the LORD, that it is He who truly blesses them 3) They will live righteously & keep God's name holy 4) They will worship the LORD 5) They will no longer go astray or complain but will accept the truth (God's Word) & grow in the LORD

a. The earth will be transformed (v.17). Lebanon, which had been devastated by the Assyrians, will be turned into a fertile field. And the fertile fields that had been devastated will grow huge forests. Simply stated, the earth will be turned into a paradise for both people and animals.

b. The disabled will be healed (v.18). For the first time, the deaf will be able to hear the Word of God as it is read. The eyes of the blind will be opened, and they will be able to see.

c. The humble and poor will rejoice in the LORD (v.19). The humble will be exalted, and the poor will have all their needs met. God will generously provide His people with housing, food, clothing, and all the other necessities of life (Mt.6:33).

d. The ruthless will be taken away. All the false witnesses and dishonest lawyers, judges, leaders, and all others who are corrupt will face the terrifying judgment of God. They will be punished and removed from earth. Righteousness and justice will rule over all the earth (vv.20-21).

e. Another marvelous change that the Messiah's kingdom will bring is a change of attitude. The mind set of God's chosen people will be totally transformed (vv.22-24). Five specific changes will take place in the Jews:

1) They will no longer be shamed by those who mock, ridicule, abuse, persecute, or oppress them. No evil person will be left on earth to strike fear in the hearts of those who truly follow the LORD. No longer will their faces grow pale in fear, for they will be redeemed just as the LORD redeemed Abraham.

2) They will finally acknowledge that it is the LORD who truly blesses them (v.23a). Witnessing the phenomenal transformation taking place on earth, they will realize that they themselves are the work of God's hands. He had truly chosen them to be the channel through whom He would send His Word and the Messiah into the world. Thus they will turn to the Lord, acknowledging Christ as the true Messiah.

3) They will join all other believers in living righteously and keeping God's name holy (v.23b). No longer will they be selfish or give in to their lustful desires. They will acknowledge the Holy One of Jacob and surrender their lives to the LORD.

4) They will genuinely worship the LORD and be faithful in their worship.

5) They will no longer go astray or complain. They will accept the truth of God's Word (v.24). They will obey His Word and grow in their knowledge and understanding of Him.

Thought 1. The amazing changes described in Scripture could not take place on earth or in people apart from the direct intervention of God. But the wonderful promise of the LORD is this: He *will* intervene! A glorious transformation will take place in the future. Both the earth and the hearts of people will be transformed. All evil, lawlessness, violence, immorality, and injustice will be erased from the face of the earth. All sinful, wicked people who reject God and oppress His people—all unbelievers—will be removed from the face of the earth. *In that day*, the day when the Lord Jesus returns to set up His kingdom, a magnificent change will sweep the entire earth. Listen to some of the wonderful transformations that will take place *in that day* (see DEEPER STUDY #2—Is.2:1-5 for more discussion):

"[Christ] Whom the heaven must receive until the times of restitution of all things, which God hath spoken by the mouth of all his holy prophets since the world began" (Ac.3:21).

"And ye shall serve the LORD your God, and he shall bless thy bread, and thy water; and I will take sickness away from the midst of thee. There shall nothing cast their young, nor be barren, in thy land: the number of thy days I will fulfil" (Ex.23:25-26).

"And I will give peace in the land, and ye shall lie down, and none shall make *you* afraid: and I will rid evil beasts out of the land, neither shall the sword go through your land" (Le.26:6).

"And it shall come to pass in the day that the LORD shall give thee rest from thy sorrow, and from thy fear, and from the hard bondage wherein thou wast made to serve" (Is.14:3).

"He will swallow up death in victory; and the Lord GOD will wipe away tears from off all faces; and the rebuke of his people shall he take away from off all the earth: for the LORD hath spoken *it*" (Is.25:8).

"Then the eyes of the blind shall be opened, and the ears of the deaf shall be unstopped. Then shall the lame *man* leap as an hart, and the tongue of the dumb sing: for in the wilderness shall waters break out, and streams in the desert" (Is.35:5-6).

"Violence shall no more be heard in thy land, wasting nor destruction within thy borders; but thou shalt call thy walls Salvation, and thy gates Praise" (Is.60:18).

"The remnant of Israel shall not do iniquity, nor speak lies; neither shall a deceitful tongue be found in their mouth: for they shall feed and lie down, and none shall make *them* afraid" (Zep.3:13).

"The LORD hath taken away thy judgments, he hath cast out thine enemy: the king of Israel, *even* the LORD, *is* in the midst of thee: thou shalt not see evil any more" (Zep.3:15).

CHAPTER 30

C. Woe—A Strong Warning to the Rebellious, the Stubborn, & the Hard-Hearted: A Message to All Who Rebel Against God, 30:1-33

1. God's pronouncement of judgment on the rebellious: A result of rejecting God & His help

a. The sign of a rebellious heart: Made an evil alliance with Egypt (symbolizes the world)
  1) They failed to seek, consult the Lord
  2) They trusted the help of man instead of God

b. The consequences of rebellion: Would be shamed & disgraced

  1) They would be shamed because they sent envoys to Zoan & Hanes seeking help: The Egyptian cities were weak, a crumbling empire
    • Would prove to be useless
    • Would not help Judah, not honor the treaty
  2) They would be disgraced because money & wealth were just being thrown away
    • They had risked their lives to buy Egypt's help by traveling through the Negev—a very difficult & dangerous trip
    • Their search for help was futile: Egypt was a "Do-Nothing" nation

c. The legal charges against those who rebel: Recorded forever as a witness against the obstinate, the rebellious

  1) They were liars, deceivers: Did not keep their commitments to God or others
  2) They rejected God's Word
  3) They rejected God's prophets
    • Did not want to hear God's righteous demands
    • Wanted flattering, undisturbing messages, Je.6:13-14; 8:11
  4) They rejected the Holy One, God Himself, & His

Woe to the rebellious children, saith the LORD, that take counsel, but not of me; and that cover with a covering, but not of my spirit, that they may add sin to sin:
2 That walk to go down into Egypt, and have not asked at my mouth; to strengthen themselves in the strength of Pharaoh, and to trust in the shadow of Egypt!
3 Therefore shall the strength of Pharaoh be your shame, and the trust in the shadow of Egypt *your* confusion.
4 For his princes were at Zoan, and his ambassadors came to Hanes.
5 They were all ashamed of a people *that* could not profit them, nor be an help nor profit, but a shame, and also a reproach.
6 The burden of the beasts of the south: into the land of trouble and anguish, from whence *come* the young and old lion, the viper and fiery flying serpent, they will carry their riches upon the shoulders of young asses, and their treasures upon the bunches of camels, to a people *that* shall not profit *them*.
7 For the Egyptians shall help in vain, and to no purpose: therefore have I cried concerning this, Their strength *is* to sit still.
8 Now go, write it before them in a table, and note it in a book, that it may be for the time to come for ever and ever:
9 That this *is* a rebellious people, lying children, children *that* will not hear the law of the LORD:
10 Which say to the seers, See not; and to the prophets, Prophesy not unto us right things, speak unto us smooth things, prophesy deceits:
11 Get you out of the way, turn aside out of the path, cause the Holy One of

Israel to cease from before us.
12 Wherefore thus saith the Holy One of Israel, Because ye despise this word, and trust in oppression and perverseness, and stay thereon:
13 Therefore this iniquity shall be to you as a breach ready to fall, swelling out in a high wall, whose breaking cometh suddenly at an instant.
14 And he shall break it as the breaking of the potters' vessel that is broken in pieces; he shall not spare: so that there shall not be found in the bursting of it a sherd to take fire from the hearth, or to take water *withal* out of the pit.
15 For thus saith the Lord GOD, the Holy One of Israel; In returning and rest shall ye be saved; in quietness and in confidence shall be your strength: and ye would not.
16 But ye said, No; for we will flee upon horses; therefore shall ye flee:' and, We will ride upon the swift; therefore shall they that pursue you be swift.
17 One thousand *shall flee* at the rebuke of one; at the rebuke of five shall ye flee: till ye be left as a beacon upon the top of a mountain, and as an ensign on an hill.
18 And therefore will the LORD wait, that he may be gracious unto you, and therefore will he be exalted, that he may have mercy upon you: for the LORD *is* a God of judgment: blessed *are* all they that wait for him.
19 For the people shall dwell in Zion at Jerusalem: thou shalt weep no more: he will be very gracious unto thee at the voice of thy cry; when he shall hear it, he will answer thee.
20 And *though* the Lord give you the bread of adversity, and the water of affliction, yet shall not thy teachers be removed into a corner any more, but thine eyes shall see thy teachers:
21 And thine ears shall hear a word behind thee, saying, This *is* the way, walk ye in it, when ye turn to the right

d. The judgment of those who rebel: Foretold by God
  1) The reason
    • Had rejected God's Word
    • Had trusted in oppression & lies
  2) The consequences
    • Their seeking power & peace through oppression & lies would be futile
    • Their lives & nation would be completely shattered—just like pieces of pottery: Not a fragment would be left

2. God's invitation to the rebellious, those who reject Him

a. The twofold invitation
  1) To repentance & rest: Would lead to salvation
  2) To quietness & trust: Would strengthen them

b. The people's tragic response
  1) They rejected God's invitation
  2) They trusted the strength of man (an alliance with Egypt)

c. The sad consequences: Judgment—a quick & total defeat

3. God's wonderful promise to the rebellious & all others who repent: A glimpse into Christ's kingdom

a. God's heart: Longs to show grace & compassion

b. God's promises of salvation
  1) Comfort: They will weep no more
  2) Answered prayers

  3) Deliverance from affliction & the gift of godly teachers

  4) His very own presence & guidance

	hand, and when ye turn to the left.	fire:	
5) True worship: He will arouse the people to destroy all idols, to turn away from all false worship	22 Ye shall defile also the covering of thy graven images of silver, and the ornament of thy molten images of gold: thou shalt cast them away as a menstruous cloth; thou shalt say unto it, Get thee hence.	28 And his breath, as an overflowing stream, shall reach to the midst of the neck, to sift the nations with the sieve of vanity: and *there shall be* a bridle in the jaws of the people, causing *them* to err.	• Will breathe judgment like a flooding stream • Will shake the people in a sieve, battering them to death • Will put a bridle on them to lead them to destruction
6) Prosperity: *In that day*, the day of the Messiah's kingdom • The land will be restored & fruitful • The pasture for livestock will be rich & abundant & of excellent quality • The grain for livestock will be plentiful	23 Then shall he give the rain of thy seed, that thou shalt sow the ground withal; and bread of the increase of the earth, and it shall be fat and plenteous: in that day shall thy cattle feed in large pastures. 24 The oxen likewise and the young asses that ear the ground shall eat clean provender, which hath been winnowed with the shovel and with the fan.	29 Ye shall have a song, as in the night *when* a holy solemnity is kept; and gladness of heart, as when one goeth with a pipe to come into the mountain of the LORD, to the mighty One of Israel. 30 And the LORD shall cause his glorious voice to be heard, and shall show the lighting down of his arm, with the indignation of *his* anger, and *with* the flame of a devouring fire, *with* scattering, and tempest, and hailstones.	2) God will cause His people to rejoice & worship Him 3) God will cause men to witness His awesome power & justice • His majestic voice • His judgment of thunder & hailstorm
7) A paradise of peace (flowing streams): After "the day of great slaughter"—Armageddon, 29:5-8; 63:1–64:12; Re.14:17-20; 16:16; 19:11-21 8) A brighter universe filled with light: The sun & moon will shine brighter than ever, 13:10; 24:23; Re.21:23; 22:5 9) Healing & health: Their broken hearts, lives, & bodies will be healed	25 And there shall be upon every high mountain, and upon every high hill, rivers *and* streams of waters in the day of the great slaughter, when the towers fall. 26 Moreover the light of the moon shall be as the light of the sun, and the light of the sun shall be sevenfold, as the light of seven days, in the day that the LORD bindeth up the breach of his people, and healeth the stroke of their wound.	31 For through the voice of the LORD shall the Assyrian be beaten down, *which* smote with a rod. 32 And *in* every place where the grounded staff shall pass, which the LORD shall lay upon him, *it* shall be with tabrets and harps: and in battles of shaking will he fight with it.	4) God will strike & shatter Assyria • With His voice (Word) • With His scepter (power) • With punishing strokes of justice, causing great joy & rejoicing among God's people
c. God's assurance of deliverance & rescue from all enemies 1) God will come full of wrath, speaking words of consuming fire	27 Behold, the name of the LORD cometh from far, burning *with* his anger, and the burden *thereof is* heavy: his lips are full of indignation, and his tongue as a devouring	33 For Tophet *is* ordained of old; yea, for the king it is prepared; he hath made *it* deep *and* large: the pile thereof *is* fire and much wood; the breath of the LORD, like a stream of brimstone, doth kindle it.	5) God will doom the evil king & his followers • Doom them to Topheth, a place of burning • Doom them to the volcanic breath (Word) of God: A picture of torment in the lake of Fire, Re.20:15; 21:8

DIVISION III

THE PROPHECIES OF WOE: GOD'S WARNING TO HIS PEOPLE, 28:1–35:10

C. Woe—A Strong Warning to the Rebellious, the Stubborn, and the Hard-Hearted: A Message to All Who Rebel Against God, 30:1-33

(30:1-33) **Introduction**: nothing cuts the human heart more than rejection. And nothing damages a group of people more than rebellion. Rejection and rebellion are two of the most destructive forces on earth. If one person in a family rebels, rejecting the other family members, the inevitable result is suffering. Sometimes the result is even divorce, a division that rips a family apart and causes unbearable pain, especially for children.

Rebellion within a nation often has tragic consequences: injury, bloodshed, and sometimes the slaughter of untold thousands. In addition, rebellion often causes unbelievable suffering through destruction of property, rape, and theft. Due to the violence and cruelty of many who rebel against governments, thousands are often forced to leave their homes and flee for their lives. Television reports of the wars around the world routinely depict scenes of fleeing refugees.

The subject of this important Scripture is the result of rebellion *against the LORD*. In fact, the great book of *Isaiah* begins and ends with the prophet levying the serious charge of rebellion against all who continually disobey and reject God.

> "Hear, O heavens, and give ear, O earth: for the LORD hath spoken, I have nourished and brought up children, and they have rebelled against me" (Is.1:2).
> "But if ye refuse and rebel, ye shall be devoured with the sword: for the mouth of the LORD hath spoken *it*" (Is.1:20).
> "Thy princes *are* rebellious, and companions of thieves: every one loveth gifts, and followeth after rewards: they judge not the fatherless, neither doth the cause of the widow come unto them" (Is.1:23).

261

"But they rebelled, and vexed his holy Spirit: therefore he was turned to be their enemy, *and* he fought against them" (Is.63:10).
"I have spread out my hands all the day unto a rebellious people, which walketh in a way *that was* not good, after their own thoughts" (Is.65:2).

The Jews of Isaiah's day were facing a critical problem, the threat of an Assyrian invasion. Assyria's evil ambition was to build an empire and subject the nations of the world to its authority. To meet this threat, some of the leaders of Judah wanted to form an alliance with Egypt. Instead of turning to the LORD, they chose to turn to a nation of unbelievers who had always engaged in wickedness and false worship. Within Judah there was a strong Egyptian faction, a large number of leaders who felt that the nation's only hope lay with Egypt. But the LORD continually warned the Jews against forming such an alliance. They needed to repent of their sins and trust Him, not the military power of Egypt. This is, *Woe— A Strong Warning to the Rebellious, the Stubborn, and the Hard-Hearted: A Message to All Who Rebel Against God*, 30:1-33.

1. God's pronouncement of judgment on the rebellious: a result of rejecting God and His help (vv.1-14).
2. God's invitation to the rebellious, those who reject Him (vv.15-17).
3. God's wonderful promise to the rebellious and all others who repent: a glimpse into Christ's kingdom (vv.18-33).

1 (30:1-14) **Obstinate, Results of, Judgment—Rebellion, Results of, Judgment—Obstinate, Example of, Leaders of Judah—Judgment, Predicted, to Fall on Judah—Indictments, Against the Obstinate, Fourfold—Rebellion, Indictments Against, Fourfold—Egypt, Alliances of, with Judah—Judah, Alliances of, Sometimes Called Evil**: God pronounced a strong warning of judgment—a *woe*—on the rebellious citizens of Judah because they continued to refuse God's help. Rejecting God time and again, their hearts became harder and more set against Him. This passage of Scripture is an excellent study of rebellion. It discusses...

- the sign of Judah's rebellious heart (vv.1-2)
- the consequences of Judah's rebellion (vv.3-7)
- the legal charges against those who rebel against God (vv.8-11)
- the judgment upon those who rebel against God (vv.13-14)

OUTLINE	SCRIPTURE	SCRIPTURE	OUTLINE

1. God's pronouncement of judgment on the rebellious: A result of rejecting God & His help
a. The sign of a rebellious heart: Made an evil alliance with Egypt (symbolizes the world)
  1) They failed to seek, consult the LORD
  2) They trusted the help of man instead of God
 	
b. The consequences of rebellion: Would be shamed & disgraced
 	
  1) They would be shamed because they sent envoys to Zoan & Hanes seeking help: The Egyptian cities were weak, a crumbling empire
  • Would prove to be useless
  • Would not help Judah, not honor the treaty
  2) They would be disgraced because money & wealth were just being thrown away
  • They had risked their lives to buy Egypt's help by traveling through the Negev—a very difficult & dangerous trip
 	
  • Their search for help was futile: Egypt was a "Do-Nothing" nation
	Woe to the rebellious children, saith the LORD, that take counsel, but not of me; and that cover with a covering, but not of my spirit, that they may add sin to sin: 2 That walk to go down into Egypt, and have not asked at my mouth; to strengthen themselves in the strength of Pharaoh, and to trust in the shadow of Egypt! 3 Therefore shall the strength of Pharaoh be your shame, and the trust in the shadow of Egypt *your* confusion. 4 For his princes were at Zoan, and his ambassadors came to Hanes. 5 They were all ashamed of a people *that* could not profit them, nor be an help nor profit, but a shame, and also a reproach. 6 The burden of the beasts of the south: into the land of trouble and anguish, from whence *come* the young and old lion, the viper and fiery flying serpent, they will carry their riches upon the shoulders of young asses, and their treasures upon the bunches of camels, to a people *that* shall not profit *them*. 7 For the Egyptians shall help in vain, and to no purpose: therefore have I cried concerning this, Their	strength *is* to sit still. 8 Now go, write it before them in a table, and note it in a book, that it may be for the time to come for ever and ever: 9 That this *is* a rebellious people, lying children, children *that* will not hear the law of the LORD: 10 Which say to the seers, See not; and to the prophets, Prophesy not unto us right things, speak unto us smooth things, prophesy deceits: 11 Get you out of the way, turn aside out of the path, cause the Holy One of Israel to cease from before us. 12 Wherefore thus saith the Holy One of Israel, Because ye despise this word, and trust in oppression and perverseness, and stay thereon: 13 Therefore this iniquity shall be to you as a breach ready to fall, swelling out in a high wall, whose breaking cometh suddenly at an instant. 14 And he shall break it as the breaking of the potters' vessel that is broken in pieces; he shall not spare: so that there shall not be found in the bursting of it a sherd to take fire from the hearth, or to take water *withal* out of the pit.	c. The legal charges against those who rebel: Recorded forever as a witness against the obstinate, the rebellious
			  1) Were liars, deceivers: Did not keep their commitments to God or others
			  2) Rejected God's Word
			  3) Rejected God's prophets
			  • Did not want to hear God's righteous demands
			  • Wanted flattering, undisturbing messages, Je.6:13-14; 8:11
			  4) Rejected the Holy One, God Himself, & His life of righteousness
			
			d. The judgment of those who rebel: Foretold by God
			  1) The reason
			  • Had rejected God's Word
			  • Had trusted in oppression & lies
			  2) The consequences
			  • Their seeking power & peace through oppression & lies would be futile
			
			  • Their lives & nation would be completely shattered—just like pieces of pottery: Not a fragment would be left

a. The sign of Judah's rebellious heart was the evil alliance it formed with the unbelievers of Egypt. In the Bible, Egypt is a symbol of the world so the application is clear: believers must not form evil associations with the unbelievers of the world. In Judah's case, the Jews were facing the threat posed by Assyria's ambition to build a world empire. The Assyrian war machine lay right over the horizon, ready to invade. Some of the leaders of Judah thought that the nation's only hope was to form an alliance with Egypt, even though God's prophet Isaiah had continually warned them against it. Judah's hope was not to be found in the military might of Egypt but, rather, in the power of the LORD.

However, the leadership refused to heed Isaiah's warning and failed to consult the LORD. Ignoring Him, they chose to trust the help of man instead of God. Instead of turning to the LORD, they turned to the Egyptians, to the unbelievers of the world. They should have sought refuge in the shadow of the LORD'S presence and power, but they chose to seek refuge in the shadow of Egypt, in their might and power.

Note what happened as a result: they heaped sin upon sin (v.1). The more they rebelled and rejected the LORD, the more stubborn and hard-hearted they became. As they continued to walk in rebellion day by day, they committed more sin and added more and more to their load of guilt. Ignoring God brought them to the point that they no longer even thought about Him. The terrible tragedy of sin is that people's hearts can become so hard that they seldom if ever think about God. The leaders of Judah made a deliberate decision to form an alliance with Egypt (the world) instead of trusting God to be their protection, and the results were tragic.

"But now I have written unto you not to keep company, if any man that is called a brother be a fornicator, or covetous, or an idolater, or a railer, or a drunkard, or an extortioner; with such an one no not to eat" (1 Co.5:11).

"Be ye not unequally yoked together with unbelievers: for what fellowship hath righteousness with unrighteousness? and what communion hath light with darkness? And what concord hath Christ with Belial? or what part hath he that believeth with an infidel? And what agreement hath the temple of God with idols? for ye are the temple of the living God; as God hath said, I will dwell in them, and walk in *them;* and I will be their God, and they shall be my people" (2 Co.6:14-16).

"Take heed to thyself, lest thou make a covenant with the inhabitants of the land whither thou goest, lest it be for a snare in the midst of thee" (Ex.34:12).

"Blessed *is* the man that walketh not in the counsel of the ungodly, nor standeth in the way of sinners, nor sitteth in the seat of the scornful" (Ps.1:1).

"Enter not into the path of the wicked, and go not in the way of evil *men*" (Pr.4:14).

b. The consequences of Judah's rebellion would be shame and disgrace (vv.3-7). The rebellious Jews were seeking protection and shelter from Egypt, but they found neither. Although they would send envoys to seek help from two of the major cities of Egypt, Zoan and Hanes (vv.4-5), all their diplomatic efforts would be shamefully wasted, for Egypt was no longer a powerful empire. It was a weak, crumbling kingdom, sustained only by its past reputation. Seeking the help of Egypt would prove useless, for the Egyptians would not be able to help Judah in their hour of need. They would not honor their treaty.

The leaders of Judah would also disgrace themselves by throwing money away in their pursuit for help from the Egyptians (vv.6-7). They would actually risk their lives to buy Egypt's help by making the very difficult and dangerous journey through the wilderness of the Negev. The Negev was an area inhabited by lions and other wild animals, poisonous snakes, scorpions, and marauding gangs of robbers. Endangering their lives on such a hazardous trip and spending their nation's money to seek help from a weak associate were both foolish acts. Their recklessness could only bring them disgrace and shame. In the end, all of their efforts to secure help from Egypt would prove utterly futile. In the day of crisis, Egypt would sit still. It would do nothing and be of no help at all.

Thought 1. Turning away from the LORD and trusting this world will bring shame upon anyone. Sin—whether it be lying, stealing, cheating, adultery, or any other violation of God's commandments—is always detestable and disgraceful to God. If our secret sins of distrust and disobedience are not uncovered in this life, they will be when we come face-to-face with the LORD. Listen to what God's Word says about shame and disgrace:

"Thou that makest thy boast of the law, through breaking the law dishonourest thou God? For the name of God is blasphemed [disgrace] among the Gentiles through you, as it is written" (Ro.2:23-24).

"But there were false prophets also among the people, even as there shall be false teachers among you, who privily shall bring in damnable heresies, even denying the Lord that bought them, and bring upon themselves swift destruction. And many shall follow their pernicious ways; by reason of whom the way of truth shall be evil spoken of [disgraced]" (2 Pe.2:1-2).

"And he said, I heard thy voice in the garden, and I was afraid, because I *was* naked; and I hid myself" (Ge.3:10).

"And said, O my God, I am ashamed and blush to lift up my face to thee, my God: for our iniquities are increased over *our* head, and our trespass is grown up unto the heavens" (Ezr.9:6).

"Yea, let none that wait on thee be ashamed: let them be ashamed which transgress without cause" (Ps.25:3).

"My confusion *is* continually before me, and the shame of my face hath covered me" (Ps.44:15).

"The wise shall inherit glory: but shame shall be the promotion of fools" (Pr.3:35).

"He that gathereth in summer *is* a wise son: *but* he that sleepeth in harvest *is* a son that causeth shame" (Pr.10:5).

"*When* pride [rebellion, distrust] cometh, then cometh shame: but with the lowly *is* wisdom" (Pr.11:2).

"The rod and reproof give wisdom: but a child left *to himself* bringeth his mother to shame" (Pr.29:15).

"They shall be ashamed, and also confounded, all of them: they shall go to confusion together *that are* makers of idols" (Is.45:16).

"Look unto me, and be ye saved, all the ends of the earth: for I *am* God, and *there is* none else. I have sworn by myself, the word is gone out of my mouth *in* righteousness, and shall not return, That unto me every knee shall bow, every tongue shall swear. Surely, shall *one* say, in the LORD have I righteousness and strength: *even* to him shall *men* come; and all that are incensed against him shall be ashamed" (Is.45:22-24).

"And I will bring an everlasting reproach upon you, and a perpetual shame, which shall not be forgotten [due to sin]" (Je.23:40).

"And when they entered unto the heathen, whither they went, they profaned [disgraced] my holy name, when they said to them, These *are* the people of the LORD, and are gone forth out of his land. But I had pity for mine holy name, which the house of Israel had profaned [disgraced] among the heathen, whither they went" (Eze.36:20-21).

c. Four legal charges were made against those with rebellious hearts (vv.8-11). Note that these were recorded forever as a witness against stubborn, hard-hearted rebels who reject God. These charges are so serious that the LORD instructed Isaiah to write them in two forms: both on a tablet and on a scroll, or in a book. It was to be a part of God's Word forever, passed down as a warning to every generation.

1) First, the rebellious were liars, deceivers (v.9ᵃ). They did not keep their promises to God. Remember that the Jews professed to be committed to God, but they did not truly follow Him. They were faithful in their worship, but their worship was routine, ritualistic, and hypocritical (29:1; 13-14). As soon as they left their worship services, they did what they wanted. They were liars and hypocrites.

"Having a form of godliness, but denying the power thereof: from such turn away" (2 Ti.3:5).

"But the fearful, and unbelieving, and the abominable, and murderers, and whoremongers, and sorcerers, and idolaters, and all liars, shall have their part in the lake which burneth with fire and brimstone: which is the second death" (Re.21:8).

"Thou shalt destroy them that speak leasing [lying]: the LORD will abhor the bloody and deceitful man" (Ps.5:6).

"The mouth of them that speak lies shall be stopped" (Ps.63:11).

"He that worketh deceit shall not dwell within my house: he that telleth lies shall not tarry in my sight" (Ps.101:7).

"Lying lips *are* abomination to the LORD: but they that deal truly *are* his delight" (Pr.12:22).

"The getting of treasures by a lying tongue *is* a vanity tossed to and fro of them that seek death" (Pr.21:6).

"A false witness shall not be unpunished, and *he that* speaketh lies shall not escape" (Pr.19:5).

2) Second, the rebellious rejected God's Word and refused to heed His instructions. They were unwilling to hear God's Word or to pay attention to His holy commandments. God's instructions to the leaders of Judah were clear: they were to place their trust in the LORD, not in Egypt. But they refused to heed God's instructions proclaimed by Isaiah. Spurning God's Word, they went ahead and did what they wanted.

"And he said unto them, Full well ye reject the commandment of God, that ye may keep your own tradition" (Mk.7:9).

"The fear of the LORD *is* the beginning of knowledge: *but* fools despise wisdom and instruction" (Pr.1:7).

"And say, How have I hated instruction, and my heart despised reproof" (Pr.5:12).

"Thus saith the LORD; For three transgressions of Judah, and for four, I will not turn away *the punishment* thereof; because they have despised the law of the LORD, and have not kept his commandments, and their lies caused them to err, after the which their fathers have walked" (Am.2:4).

3) Third, the rebellious rejected God's prophets (v.10). When Isaiah proclaimed God's instructions, the people refused to hear. They shut their ears and hardened their hearts. They wanted nothing to do with God's righteous demands and His warning of coming judgment. Instead, they wanted to hear pleasant, flattering messages that would allow them to continue to live as they wished.

"Preach the word; be instant in season, out of season; reprove, rebuke, exhort with all longsuffering and doctrine. For the time will come when they will not endure sound doctrine; but after their own lusts shall they heap to themselves teachers, having itching ears; And they shall turn away *their* ears from the truth, and shall be turned unto fables. But watch thou in all things, endure afflictions, do the work of an evangelist, make full proof of thy ministry" (2 Ti.4:2-5).

"But they mocked the messengers of God, and despised his words, and misused his prophets, until the wrath of the LORD arose against his people, till *there was* no remedy" (2 Chr.36:16).

"But unto the wicked God saith, What hast thou to do to declare my statutes, or *that* thou shouldest take my covenant in thy mouth? Seeing thou hatest instruction, and castest my words behind thee. When thou sawest a thief, then thou consentedst with him, and hast been partaker with adulterers. Thou givest thy mouth to evil, and thy tongue frameth deceit. Thou sittest *and* speakest against thy brother; thou slanderest thine own mother's son. These *things* hast thou done, and I kept silence; thou thoughtest that I was altogether *such an one* as thyself: *but* I will reprove thee, and set *them* in order before thine eyes. Now consider this, ye that forget God, lest I tear *you* in pieces, and *there be* none to deliver. Whoso offereth praise glorifieth me: and to him that ordereth *his* conversation *aright* will I show the salvation of God" (Ps.50:16-23).

"To whom shall I speak, and give warning, that they may hear? behold, their ear *is* uncircumcised, and they cannot hearken: behold, the word of the LORD is unto them a reproach; they have no delight in it" (Je.6:10).

"Therefore as the fire devoureth the stubble, and the flame consumeth the chaff, *so* their root shall be as rottenness, and their blossom shall go up as dust: because they have cast away the law of the LORD of hosts, and despised the word of the Holy One of Israel" (Is.5:24).

"Yea, they made their hearts *as* an adamant stone, lest they should hear the law, and the words which the LORD of hosts hath sent in his spirit by the former prophets: therefore came a great wrath from the LORD of hosts" (Zec.7:12).

4) Finally, the rebellious rejected the Holy One, God Himself, and His righteousness (v.11). The leaders actually demanded that Isaiah leave them alone and stop confronting them with the message of the Holy One of Israel. They did not want to hear about righteous living or the warning of judgment that Isaiah was preaching. In no uncertain terms, they insisted that he change his message or face their wrath. But in threatening Isaiah, the leaders were overlooking one important fact: attacking the prophet of God was the same as attacking the Holy One Himself. Those who persecuted God's prophet would face the wrath of God Himself.

"Behold, I send you forth as sheep in the midst of wolves: be ye therefore wise as serpents, and harmless as doves. But beware of men: for they will deliver you up to the councils, and they will scourge you in their synagogues; And ye shall be brought before governors and kings for my sake, for a testimony against them and the Gentiles. But when they deliver you up, take no thought how or what ye shall speak: for it shall be given you in that same hour what ye shall speak. For it is not ye that speak, but the Spirit of your Father which speaketh in you. And the brother shall deliver up the brother to death, and the father the child: and the children shall rise up against *their* parents, and cause them to be put to death. And ye shall be hated of all *men* for my name's sake: but he that endureth to the end shall be saved" (Mt.10:16-22).

"Remember the word that I said unto you, The servant is not greater than his lord. If they have persecuted me, they will also persecute you; if they have kept my saying, they will keep yours also" (Jn.15:20).

"Yea, and all that will live godly in Christ Jesus shall suffer persecution" (2 Ti.3:12).

"Therefore thus saith the LORD of the men of Anathoth, that seek thy life, saying, Prophesy not in the name of the LORD, that thou die not by our hand: Therefore thus saith the LORD of hosts, Behold, I will punish them: the young men shall die by the sword; their sons and their daughters shall die by famine" (Je.11:21-22).

"But ye gave the Nazarites wine to drink; and commanded the prophets, saying, Prophesy not" (Am.2:12).

"For thus Amos saith, Jeroboam shall die by the sword, and Israel shall surely be led away captive out of their own land. Also Amaziah said unto Amos, O thou seer, go, flee thee away into the land of Judah, and there eat bread, and prophesy there: But prophesy not again any more at Bethel: for it *is* the king's chapel, and it *is* the king's court" (Am.7:11-13).

"Prophesy ye not, *say they to them that* prophesy: they shall not prophesy to them, *that* they shall not take shame" (Mic.2:6).

d. God Himself spelled out the judgment upon those who rebelled against Him (vv.12-14). The people had rebelled against the Holy One of Israel, so the Holy One of Israel confronted them. They were...
- guilty of rejecting His message, His Holy Word
- guilty of using oppression to raise the money to secure Egypt's help
- guilty of trusting the lying, deceitful unbelievers in Egypt

The people's sins would doom them. Suddenly, in a moment's time, the hand of God's judgment would fall upon them. Their distrust of the LORD would be like a crack in a high wall that causes the wall to bulge out and suddenly collapse. Their lives and their nation would shatter like pieces of pottery. Not a fragment of pottery would be big enough to carry coals from a fireplace or scoop water out of a well. Their continued rebellion against the LORD would be the cause of this severe judgment. This was God's message to the leaders and people of Judah, and it is His Word to every generation. Judgment lies just over the horizon for every person who rebels against the LORD.

"But after thy hardness and impenitent heart treasurest up unto thyself wrath against the day of wrath and revelation of the righteous judgment of God...But unto them that are contentious, and do not obey the truth, but obey unrighteousness, indignation and wrath" (Ro.2:5, 8).

"And to you who are troubled rest with us, when the Lord Jesus shall be revealed from heaven with his mighty angels, In flaming fire taking vengeance on them that know not God, and that obey not the gospel of our Lord Jesus Christ: Who shall be punished with everlasting destruction from the presence of the Lord, and from the glory of his power" (2 Th.1:7-9).

"But fornication, and all uncleanness, or covetousness, let it not be once named among you, as becometh saints; Neither filthiness, nor foolish talking, nor jesting, which are not convenient: but rather giving of thanks. For this ye know, that no whoremonger, nor unclean person, nor covetous man, who is an idolater, hath any inheritance in the kingdom of Christ and of God. Let no man deceive you with vain words: for because of these things cometh the wrath of God upon the children of disobedience" (Ep.5:3-6).

"For if the word spoken by angels was stedfast, and every transgression and disobedience received a just recompence of reward; How shall we escape, if we neglect so great salvation; which at the first began to be spoken by the Lord, and was confirmed unto us by them that heard *him*" (He.2:2-3).

"Take heed, brethren, lest there be in any of you an evil heart of unbelief, in departing from the living God. But exhort one another daily, while it is called To day; lest any of you be hardened through the deceitfulness of sin" (He.3:12-13).

"But if ye will not obey the voice of the LORD, but rebel against the commandment of the LORD, then shall the hand of the LORD be against you, as *it was* against your fathers" (1 S.12:15).

"But my people would not hearken to my voice; and Israel would none of me. So I gave them up unto their own hearts' lust: *and* they walked in their own counsels. Oh that my people had hearkened unto me, *and* Israel had walked in my ways! I should soon have subdued their enemies, and turned my hand against their adversaries. The haters of the LORD should have submitted themselves unto him: but their time should have endured for ever. He should have fed them also with the finest of the wheat: and with honey out of the rock should I have satisfied thee" (Ps.81:11-16).

"He, that being often reproved hardeneth *his* neck, shall suddenly be destroyed, and that without remedy" (Pr.29:1).

"Woe to the rebellious children, saith the LORD, that take counsel, but not of me; and that cover with a covering, but not of my spirit, that they may add sin to sin" (Is.30:1).

2 (30:15-17) **Rebellious, the, Invitation to—Rejection, of the LORD, Invitation to—Invitation, to the Rebellious—Repentance, Who Needs, the Rebellious; the Disobedient—Spiritual Rest, Invitation to—Trust, Invitation to**: God gave a wonderful invitation to the rebellious Jews, an invitation that offered them the great hope of deliverance. What was the invitation? It was twofold:

⇒ to repent, return to the LORD, and find their rest (security) in Him
⇒ to seek quietness and confidence in the LORD

If the people would repent and seek their rest, quietness, and confidence in the LORD, He would deliver them from the Assyrian threat. He would strengthen their hearts and give them peace and assurance.

Tragically, the Jews rejected the LORD's invitation. Refusing to trust the LORD, they trusted instead in Egypt's military strength—the swiftness of their horses, weapons, and war machine. Thus Isaiah warned them: their enemies would be even swifter, so swift that a thousand Israelites would flee at the threat of one Assyrian soldier. And the threat of five enemy soldiers would cause all of them to flee. After the Assyrians attacked, the army of Israel would be like a lonely military banner flapping in the wind on a hill (v.17). Isaiah was predicting how devastating God's judgment would be because of Judah's rebellion. The Assyrians would conquer all of the nation except Jerusalem, and later the Babylonians would utterly destroy the capital city.

OUTLINE	SCRIPTURE	SCRIPTURE	OUTLINE

2. God's invitation to the rebellious, those who reject Him
a. The twofold invitation
  1) To repentance & rest: Would lead to salvation
  2) To quietness & trust: Would strengthen them
b. The people's tragic response
  1) They rejected God's invitation
	15 For thus saith the Lord GOD, the Holy One of Israel; In returning and rest shall ye be saved; in quietness and in confidence shall be your strength: and ye would not. 16 But ye said, No; for we will flee upon horses; therefore shall ye flee: and, We	will ride upon the swift; therefore shall they that pursue you be swift. 17 One thousand *shall flee* at the rebuke of one; at the rebuke of five shall ye flee: till ye be left as a beacon upon the top of a mountain, and as an ensign on an hill.	2) They trusted the strength of man (an alliance with Egypt)
			c. The sad consequences: Judgment—a quick & total defeat

Thought 1. The LORD gives the same invitation to the rebellious today that he extended to the rebellious citizens of Judah. Only the LORD can meet the needs of the human heart. The rebellious can find the rest, quietness, and confidence they seek in Him and Him alone. He is the only answer to lack of purpose, fulfillment, and assurance about the future. He alone is the cure for emptiness, loneliness, insecurity, and fear.

God made our hearts to be restless until they find rest in Him. It is this restlessness that arouses us to seek Him, to acknowledge and have fellowship with Him. When we are in fellowship with God, we can worship, share, and talk with Him day by day. But before the LORD will accept and fellowship with us, before He will give us peace and assurance, we must repent of our sins and turn back to Him. Listen to what God's Holy Word says about repentance:

"Then Peter said unto them, Repent, and be baptized every one of you in the name of Jesus Christ for the remission of sins, and ye shall receive the gift of the Holy Ghost" (Ac.2:38).

"Repent ye therefore, and be converted, that your sins may be blotted out, when the times of refreshing shall come from the presence of the Lord" (Ac.3:19).

"If my people, which are called by my name, shall humble themselves, and pray, and seek my face, and turn from their wicked ways; then will I hear from heaven, and will forgive their sin, and will heal their land" (2 Chr.7:14).

"The LORD *is* nigh unto them that are of a broken heart; and saveth such as be of a contrite spirit" (Ps.34:18).

"Let the wicked forsake his way, and the unrighteous man his thoughts: and let him return unto the LORD, and he will have mercy upon him; and to our God, for he will abundantly pardon" (Is.55:7).

"Return, ye backsliding children, *and* I will heal your backslidings. Behold, we come unto thee; for thou *art* the LORD our God" (Je.3:22).

"Cast away from you all your transgressions, whereby ye have transgressed; and make you a new heart and a new spirit: for why will ye die, O house of Israel?" (Eze.18:31).

3 (30:18-33) **Rebellious, the, Result of Repentance, Wonderful Blessings—Blessings, of Christ's Kingdom, Ninefold—Promises, of Salvation, Ninefold—Messiah, Kingdom of, Blessings of—Kingdom, of Christ, Blessings of—Repentance, Results of, Ninefold**: God makes some wonderful promises to the rebellious who truly repent. Even while God's people are rebelling against Him, He reaches out in mercy to them, longing to pour out His blessings upon them. Note how many of these blessings cannot be completely fulfilled in this present, corrupted world. They can be partially fulfilled, but this passage refers primarily to the Messiah's kingdom, that period of history lying in the future when the Lord Jesus Christ will return to establish His kingdom on earth. These wonderful promises of salvation were given to the Jews who truly trusted the LORD in Isaiah's day. However, keep in mind that they were also given to encourage true believers of every generation, whether Jew or Gentile.

OUTLINE	SCRIPTURE	SCRIPTURE	OUTLINE
3. God's wonderful promise to the rebellious & all others who repent: A glimpse into Christ's kingdom	18 And therefore will the LORD wait, that he may be gracious unto you, and therefore will he be exalted, that	the earth, and it shall be fat and plenteous: in that day shall thy cattle feed in large pastures.	stored & fruitful • The pasture for livestock will be rich & abundant & of excellent quality
a. God's heart: Longs to show grace & compassion	he may have mercy upon you: for the LORD *is* a God of judgment: blessed *are* all they that wait for him.	24 The oxen likewise and the young asses that ear the ground shall eat clean provender, which hath been winnowed with the shovel and with the fan.	• The grain for livestock will be plentiful
b. God's promises of salvation 1) Comfort: They will weep no more 2) Answered prayers	19 For the people shall dwell in Zion at Jerusalem: thou shalt weep no more: he will be very gracious unto thee at the voice of thy cry; when he shall hear it, he will answer thee.	25 And there shall be upon every high mountain, and upon every high hill, rivers *and* streams of waters in the day of the great slaughter, when the towers fall.	7) A paradise of peace (flowing streams): After "the day of great slaughter"—Armageddon, 29:5-8; 63:1–64:12; Re.16:16; 19:11-21
3) Deliverance from affliction & the gift of godly teachers	20 And *though* the Lord give you the bread of adversity, and the water of affliction, yet shall not thy teachers be removed into a corner any more, but thine eyes shall see thy teachers:	26 Moreover the light of the moon shall be as the light of the sun, and the light of the sun shall be sevenfold, as the light of seven days, in the day that the LORD bindeth up the breach of his people, and healeth the stroke of their wound.	8) A brighter universe filled with light: The sun & moon will shine brighter than ever, 13:10; 24:23; Re.21:23; 22:5
4) His very own presence & guidance	21 And thine ears shall hear a word behind thee, saying, This *is* the way, walk ye in it, when ye turn to the right hand, and when ye turn to the left.	27 Behold, the name of the LORD cometh from far, burning *with* his anger, and the burden *thereof is* heavy: his lips are full of indignation, and his tongue as a devouring fire:	9) Healing & health: Their broken hearts, lives, & bodies will be healed c. God's assurance of deliverance & rescue from all enemies
5) True worship: He will arouse the people to destroy all idols, to turn away from all false worship	22 Ye shall defile also the covering of thy graven images of silver, and the ornament of thy molten images of gold: thou shalt cast them away as a menstruous cloth; thou shalt say unto it, Get thee hence.	28 And his breath, as an overflowing stream, shall reach to the midst of the neck, to sift the nations with the sieve of vanity: and *there shall be* a bridle in the jaws	1) God will come full of wrath, speaking words of consuming fire • Will breathe judgment like a flooding stream • Will shake the people in a sieve, battering them to death
6) Prosperity: *In that day*, the day of the Messiah's kingdom • The land will be re-	23 Then shall he give the rain of thy seed, that thou shalt sow the ground withal; and bread of the increase of	of the people, causing *them* to err.	• Will put a bridle on them to lead them to destruction

OUTLINE	SCRIPTURE	SCRIPTURE	OUTLINE
2) God will cause His people to rejoice & worship Him	29 Ye shall have a song, as in the night *when* a holy solemnity is kept; and gladness of heart, as when one goeth with a pipe to come into the mountain of the LORD, to the mighty One of Israel.	be beaten down, *which* smote with a rod. 32 And *in* every place where the grounded staff shall pass, which the LORD shall lay upon him, *it* shall be with tabrets and harps: and in battles of shaking will he fight with it.	• With His voice (Word) • With His scepter (power) • With punishing strokes of justice, causing great joy & rejoicing among God's people
3) God will cause men to witness His awesome power & justice • His majestic voice • His judgment of thunder & hailstorm	30 And the LORD shall cause his glorious voice to be heard, and shall show the lighting down of his arm, with the indignation of *his* anger, and *with* the flame of a devouring fire, *with* scattering, and tempest, and hailstones.	33 For Tophet *is* ordained of old; yea, for the king it is prepared; he hath made *it* deep *and* large: the pile thereof *is* fire and much wood; the breath of the LORD, like a stream of brimstone, doth kindle it.	5) God will doom the evil king & his followers • Doom them to Topheth, a place of burning • Doom them to the volcanic breath (Word) of God: A picture of torment in the lake of Fire, Re.20:15; 21:8
4) God will strike & shatter Assyria	31 For through the voice of the LORD shall the Assyrian		

a. God's heart reaches out to all who reject and rebel against Him (v.18). The LORD longs to show mercy. It is true that God is just, a God who will execute justice and judgment against all who continue in rebellion. But it is also true that He is a God of grace and compassion, a God who will show mercy to all who *wait* for Him. To wait for God means to trust Him for salvation and for deliverance from all the enemies and trials of life. As the psalmist says:

> "Kiss the Son, lest he be angry, and ye perish *from* the way, when his wrath is kindled but a little. Blessed *are* all they that put their trust in him" (Ps.2:12).

b. God's promises of salvation will be given to all those who trust Him (vv.19-26). The LORD stirred Isaiah to proclaim the promises of salvation to the Jews of his day. Obviously, the LORD had the hope that the promises would appeal to the hearts of some. Perhaps they would be moved to repent and trust Him as their Savior. Imagine how reassuring these promises must have been to the few who already believed and trusted in the LORD. The prophet declared that a day was coming when God would pour out His richest blessings upon all who repented of their rebellion against the LORD. Nine blessings of salvation were spelled out by the prophet.

1) Comfort is the *first* blessing of salvation (v.19). When the Messiah sets up His kingdom on earth, there will be no more weeping, sorrow, or grief whatsoever. God's people will never again weep. Keep in mind, however, that God also promises to comfort His people while they are still living on earth.

> "Let not your heart be troubled: ye believe in God, believe also in me. In my Father's house are many mansions: if *it were* not so, I would have told you. I go to prepare a place for you" (Jn.14:1-2).
> "Blessed *be* God, even the Father of our Lord Jesus Christ, the Father of mercies, and the God of all comfort; Who comforteth us in all our tribulation, that we may be able to comfort them which are in any trouble, by the comfort wherewith we ourselves are comforted of God" (2 Co.1:3-4).
> "Forasmuch then as the children are partakers of flesh and blood, he also himself likewise took part of the same; that through death he might destroy him that had the power of death, that is, the devil; And deliver them who through fear of death were all their lifetime subject to bondage" (He.2:14-15).
> "Casting all your care upon him; for he careth for you" (1 Pe.5:7).
> "And God shall wipe away all tears from their eyes; and there shall be no more death, neither sorrow, nor crying, neither shall there be any more pain: for the former things are passed away" (Re.21:4).

2) Answered prayer is the *second* promise of salvation (v.19). In the Messiah's kingdom, the prayers of believers will be answered immediately. But even today when genuine believers need the LORD's help, all they have to do is cry for help. The LORD always hears their cry and meets their needs.

> "And I say unto you, Ask, and it shall be given you; seek, and ye shall find; knock, and it shall be opened unto you" (Lu.11:9).
> "If ye abide in me, and my words abide in you, ye shall ask what ye will, and it shall be done unto you" (Jn.15:7).
> "He shall call upon me, and I will answer him: I *will be* with him in trouble; I will deliver him, and honour him" (Ps.91:15).
> "And it shall come to pass, that before they call, I will answer; and while they are yet speaking, I will hear" (Is.65:24).
> "Then shalt thou call, and the LORD shall answer; thou shalt cry, and he shall say, Here I *am*" (Is.58:9).
> "Call unto me, and I will answer thee, and show thee great and mighty things, which thou knowest not." (Je.33:3).

3) The *third* promise is twofold: the deliverance from adversity and the gift of godly teachers (v.20). In this evil world believers suffer adversity and affliction. Sometimes the prophets of God are persecuted and forced to flee for safety. When the prophets are forced to flee, the people lose their teachers who instruct and guide them in the ways of the LORD. But in the day of the Messiah's kingdom, all believers—layperson and prophet alike—will be delivered from all trouble. God's people will no longer be persecuted, never again have to fear the threats of evil oppressors nor the loss of godly teachers.

"For we would not, brethren, have you ignorant of our trouble which came to us in Asia, that we were pressed out of measure, above strength, insomuch that we despaired even of life: But we had the sentence of death in ourselves, that we should not trust in ourselves, but in God which raiseth the dead: Who delivered us from so great a death, and doth deliver: in whom we trust that he will yet deliver *us*" (2 Co.1:8-10).

"There hath no temptation taken you but such as is common to man: but God *is* faithful, who will not suffer you to be tempted above that ye are able; but will with the temptation also make a way to escape, that ye may be able to bear *it*" (1 Co.10:13).

"And the Lord shall deliver me from every evil work, and will preserve *me* unto his heavenly kingdom: to whom *be* glory for ever and ever. Amen" (2 Ti.4:18).

"The Lord knoweth how to deliver the godly out of temptations, and to reserve the unjust unto the day of judgment to be punished" (2 Pe.2:9).

"Fear none of those things which thou shalt suffer: behold, the devil shall cast *some* of you into prison, that ye may be tried; and ye shall have tribulation ten days: be thou faithful unto death, and I will give thee a crown of life" (Re.2:10).

"O Lord my God, in thee do I put my trust: save me from all them that persecute me, and deliver me" (Ps.7:1).

"He that dwelleth in the secret place of the most High shall abide under the shadow of the Almighty" (Ps.91:1).

"Many *are* my persecutors and mine enemies; *yet* do I not decline from thy testimonies" (Ps.119:157).

"Princes have persecuted me without a cause: but my heart standeth in awe of thy word" (Ps.119:161).

"Be not afraid of their faces: for I *am* with thee to deliver thee, saith the LORD" (Je.1:8).

4) A *fourth* promise of salvation is that of God's personal presence and guidance (v.21). This is an obvious reference to the Spirit of God speaking to the hearts of believers, guiding and leading them as they go about their daily affairs. In the Messiah's kingdom believers will be able to hear the voice of God's Spirit more clearly. When the wicked are taken out of the way, nothing will hinder the clear sounds of the Holy Spirit's voice. But even in this corrupt world today, those who study God's Word and walk in constant communion with Him can hear the voice of God's Spirit.

"But the Comforter, *which is* the Holy Ghost, whom the Father will send in my name, he shall teach you all things, and bring all things to your remembrance, whatsoever I have said unto you" (Jn.14:26).

"Howbeit when he, the Spirit of truth, is come, he will guide you into all truth: for he shall not speak of himself; but whatsoever he shall hear, *that* shall he speak: and he will show you things to come" (Jn.16:13).

"For as many as are led by the Spirit of God, they are the sons of God" (Ro.8:14).

"The Spirit itself beareth witness with our spirit, that we are the children of God: And if children, then heirs; heirs of God, and joint-heirs with Christ; if so be that we suffer with *him*, that we may be also glorified together" (Ro.8:16-17).

"Now we have received, not the spirit of the world, but the spirit which is of God; that we might know the things that are freely given to us of God. Which things also we speak, not in the words which man's wisdom teacheth, but which the Holy Ghost teacheth; comparing spiritual things with spiritual" (1 Co.2:12-13).

"And because ye are sons, God hath sent forth the Spirit of his Son into your hearts, crying, Abba, Father" (Ga.4:6).

"And he that keepeth his commandments dwelleth in him, and he in him. And hereby we know that he abideth in us, by the Spirit which he hath given us" (1 Jn.3:24).

"Hereby know we that we dwell in him, and he in us, because he hath given us of his Spirit" (1 Jn.4:13).

5) Genuine worship is the *fifth* promise of God's salvation (v.22). In the Messiah's kingdom every citizen will be a true worshipper of the LORD. All idols and false gods will be cast away and purged from the minds and hearts of the people. Only the LORD, the one living and true God (Yahweh, Jehovah), will be worshipped.

"Then saith Jesus unto him, Get thee hence, Satan: for it is written, Thou shalt worship the Lord thy God, and him only shalt thou serve" (Mt.4:10).

"Ye worship ye know not what: we know what we worship: for salvation is of the Jews. But the hour cometh, and now is, when the true worshippers shall worship the Father in spirit and in truth: for the Father seeketh such to worship him" (Jn.4:22-23).

"For we are not as many, which corrupt the word of God: but as of sincerity, but as of God, in the sight of God speak we in Christ" (2 Co.2:17).

"Therefore let us keep the feast, not with old leaven, neither with the leaven of malice and wickedness; but with the unleavened *bread* of sincerity and truth" (1 Co.5:8).

"*And* we know that the Son of God is come, and hath given us an understanding, that we may know him that is true, and we are in him that is true, *even* in his Son Jesus Christ. This is the true God, and eternal life. Little children, keep yourselves from idols. Amen" (1 Jn.5:20-21).

"Thou shalt have no other gods before me. Thou shalt not make unto thee any graven image, or any likeness *of any thing* that *is* in heaven above, or that *is* in the earth beneath, or that *is* in the water under the earth: Thou shalt not bow down thyself to them, nor serve them: for I the LORD thy God *am* a jealous God, visiting the iniquity of the fathers upon the children unto the third and fourth *generation* of them that hate me; And showing mercy unto thousands of them that love me, and keep my commandments" (Ex.20:3-6).

"Take heed to yourselves, that your heart be not deceived, and ye turn aside, and serve other gods, and worship them" (De.11:16).

"Now therefore fear the LORD, and serve him in sincerity and in truth: and put away the gods which your fathers served on the other side of the flood, and in Egypt; and serve ye the LORD" (Jos.24:14).

"O worship the LORD in the beauty of holiness: fear before him, all the earth" (Ps.96:9).

"I *am* the LORD: that *is* my name: and my glory will I not give to another, neither my praise to graven images" (Is.42:8).

6) Prosperity is the *sixth* promise of salvation in the Messiah's kingdom (vv.23-24). In this present evil world, believers may be called upon to suffer adversity, affliction, and financial poverty. But in the coming day of Christ's kingdom, everyone will be prosperous and have food, water, clothing, housing, and all the other necessities of life. The land itself will be restored and become fruitful, which means there will be plenty of pasture and grain for livestock. But note the wonderful promises given to believers who live in this present evil world:

"But seek ye first the kingdom of God, and his righteousness; and all these things shall be added unto you" (Mt.6:33. Also see Mt.6:25-34).

"But my God shall supply all your need according to his riches in glory by Christ Jesus" (Ph.4:19).

"And ye shall serve the LORD your God, and he shall bless thy bread, and thy water; and I will take sickness away from the midst of thee" (Ex.23:25).

"Blessed *be* the Lord, *who* daily loadeth us *with benefits, even* the God of our salvation" (Ps.68:19).

"Bring ye all the tithes into the storehouse, that there may be meat in mine house, and prove me now herewith, saith the LORD of hosts, if I will not open you the windows of heaven, and pour you out a blessing, that *there shall* not *be room* enough *to receive it*" (Mal.3:10).

7) God's *seventh* promise is that the earth will become a peaceful paradise during the Messiah's kingdom (v.25). Note the reference to *the day of great slaughter*. This is a clear reference to Armageddon, the day when the Lord will return to execute judgment against all the rebellious nations and people of this earth (29:5-8; 63:1—64:12; see outline and notes—Re.14:17-20; 16:16-21; 19:11-21 for more discussion). But after the terrifying day of Armageddon, the Lord will turn the earth into a glorious paradise.

Streams of water will flow from every high mountain and hill on the earth. The term *streams of water* is a picture of peace and rest—being free from all pressure, distress, grief, oppression, lawlessness, violence, and wicked behavior. It is a picture of paradise, where only peace and tranquility will be experienced. Yet even in this present evil world where believers must walk through the trials and temptations of this life, the LORD promises us the wonderful gift of His peace.

"But the Comforter, *which is* the Holy Ghost, whom the Father will send in my name, he shall teach you all things, and bring all things to your remembrance, whatsoever I have said unto you" (Jn.14:26).

"These things I have spoken unto you, that in me ye might have peace. In the world ye shall have tribulation: but be of good cheer; I have overcome the world" (Jn.16:33).

"Be careful for nothing; but in every thing by prayer and supplication with thanksgiving let your requests be made known unto God. And the peace of God, which passeth all understanding, shall keep your hearts and minds through Christ Jesus" (Ph.4:6-7).

"The LORD will give strength unto his people; the LORD will bless his people with peace" (Ps.29:11).

"Great peace have they which love thy law: and nothing shall offend them" (Ps.119:165).

"Thou wilt keep *him* in perfect peace, *whose* mind *is* stayed *on thee*: because he trusteth in thee. Trust ye in the LORD for ever: for in the LORD JEHOVAH *is* everlasting strength" (Is.26:3-4).

8) The *eighth* promise of the Messiah's kingdom is astounding: the universe will be filled with the splendor of a far greater light than that of the sun (v.26). Both the sun and moon will shine far more brightly than they ever

have. In fact, Isaiah declares that the moon will shine as brightly as the sun and that the sun will be seven times brighter than usual, as bright as seven full days of light. Will this be literally fulfilled? Unquestionably. Just picture the blazing glory of the Holy One who created the entire universe and any other universes that may exist. Imagine the splendor and brilliance of His holiness. Scripture makes this astonishing declaration: *in that day* people will not need the light of the sun to give them daylight. The glory of God will provide the light for day, and there will be no more night.

> "This then is the message which we have heard of him, and declare unto you, that God is light, and in him is no darkness at all" (1 Jn.1:5).
> "And there shall be no night there; and they need no candle, neither light of the sun; for the Lord God giveth them light: and they shall reign for ever and ever" (Re.22:5).
> "Then the moon shall be confounded, and the sun ashamed, when the LORD of hosts shall reign in mount Zion, and in Jerusalem, and before his ancients gloriously" (Is.24:23).
> "Thy sun shall no more go down; neither shall thy moon withdraw itself: for the LORD shall be thine everlasting light, and the days of thy mourning shall be ended" (Is.60:20).

9) Healing and health will be the *ninth* blessing of the Messiah's kingdom (v.26). In Isaiah's day most people suffered illness due to hardship, poverty, disease, and a host of other causes. Both heart and body were often broken and in need of healing. In the coming days of the Messiah's kingdom, the Lord will heal all wounds and diseases. But now, even in this present evil world, the LORD promises to strengthen His people. He either heals them directly or gives them the power to walk through the suffering.

> "The Spirit of the Lord is upon me, because he hath anointed me to preach the gospel to the poor; he hath sent me to heal the brokenhearted, to preach deliverance to the captives, and recovering of sight to the blind, to set at liberty them that are bruised" (Lu.4:18).
> "Now no chastening [discipline, trials] for the present seemeth to be joyous, but grievous: nevertheless afterward it yieldeth the peaceable fruit of righteousness unto them which are exercised thereby" (He.12:11).
> "Wherein ye greatly rejoice, though now for a season, if need be, ye are in heaviness through manifold temptations: That the trial of your faith, being much more precious than of gold that perisheth, though it be tried with fire, might be found unto praise and honour and glory at the appearing of Jesus Christ" (1 Pe.1:6-7).
> "Beloved, think it not strange concerning the fiery trial which is to try you, as though some strange thing happened unto you: But rejoice, inasmuch as ye are partakers of Christ's sufferings; that, when his glory shall be revealed, ye may be glad also with exceeding joy" (1 Pe.4:12-13).
> "In the midst of the street of it, and on either side of the river, *was there* the tree of life, which bare twelve *manner* of fruits, *and* yielded her fruit every month: and the leaves of the tree *were* for the healing of the nations" (Re.22:2).
> "The LORD *is* my strength and my shield; my heart trusted in him, and I am helped: therefore my heart greatly rejoiceth; and with my song will I praise him" (Ps.28:7).
> "But I *am* poor and needy; *yet* the Lord thinketh upon me: thou *art* my help and my deliverer; make no tarrying, O my God" (Ps.40:17).
> "Fear thou not; for I *am* with thee: be not dismayed; for I *am* thy God: I will strengthen thee; yea, I will help thee; yea, I will uphold thee with the right hand of my righteousness" (Is.41:10).
> "Behold, I have refined thee, but not with silver; I have chosen thee in the furnace of affliction" (Is.48:10).
> "And I looked, and *there was* none to help; and I wondered that *there was* none to uphold: therefore mine own arm brought salvation unto me; and my fury, it upheld me" (Is.63:5).
> "Come, and let us return unto the LORD: for he hath torn, and he will heal us; he hath smitten, and he will bind us up" (Ho.6:1).

c. There is yet another promise of God's salvation that will be a blessing to some and a curse to others. That promise is the assurance of victory over all enemies. During the Messiah's kingdom, there will be complete victory over all who rebel against the LORD and persecute His people (vv.27-33).

1) The LORD will return to earth full of wrath, speaking words of consuming fire (v.27). Note the reference to *the name of the LORD*, which always indicates that a full revelation of the LORD is about to take place.[1] This is a clear reference to the return of the Messiah, the Lord Jesus Christ. When He returns to execute justice and to establish His kingdom on earth, He will descend from the sky radiating all the glory and holiness of His deity. He will simply speak the words of judgment, and the consuming power of His Word will sweep the earth like a flooding stream (vv.27-28). He will shake the unbelievers of the world as if they were in a large sieve, battering them to death. It will be as though He put a bridle on them to lead them to destruction.

2) Once the wicked have been judged and removed from the earth, God's people will rejoice and worship Him (v.29). They will go up to the mountain of the LORD (Jerusalem) to worship the Rock of Israel, the foundation and security of their lives.

---

[1] H.C. Leupold. *Exposition of Isaiah,* Vol.1, p.480.

3) In the day of coming judgment the LORD will demonstrate His awesome power and justice (v.30). The people will hear His majestic voice and witness the raging anger and consuming fire of His power. His judgment will strike with devastating force, hammering the earth with terrifying thunderstorms and fierce hailstorms.

4) The LORD promised to shatter the cruel Assyrians through the sheer might of His voice (vv.31-32). With the scepter of His power, He would strike them down with punishing strokes of justice. The execution of His justice would cause great joy and rejoicing among God's people.

5) God promised that He would doom the evil king of Assyria and his followers (v.33). Note that a specific place was prepared for them, a place called Tophet or Topheth. This was a site in the Valley of Hinnom just south of Jerusalem where the worshippers of the false god Molech sacrificed their children. This particular site became the garbage dump for Jerusalem and was named *Gehenna*. In the New Testament *Gehenna* means hell, a place of burning fire. The breath of the LORD, like a stream of brimstone, would set this site aflame. This is a clear picture of torment in the lake of fire, the destiny of all who reject and rebel against the LORD (Re.20:15).

"I indeed baptize you with water unto repentance: but he that cometh after me is mightier than I, whose shoes I am not worthy to bear: he shall baptize you with the Holy Ghost, and *with* fire: Whose fan *is* in his hand, and he will throughly purge his floor, and gather his wheat into the garner; but he will burn up the chaff with unquenchable fire" (Mt.3:11-12).

"The Son of man shall send forth his angels, and they shall gather out of his kingdom all things that offend, and them which do iniquity; And shall cast them into a furnace of fire: there shall be wailing and gnashing of teeth" (Mt.13:41-42).

"Wherefore if thy hand or thy foot offend thee, cut them off, and cast *them* from thee: it is better for thee to enter into life halt or maimed, rather than having two hands or two feet to be cast into everlasting fire" (Mt.18:8).

"Then shall he say also unto them on the left hand, Depart from me, ye cursed, into everlasting fire, prepared for the devil and his angels" (Mt.25:41).

"And I saw a great white throne, and him that sat on it, from whose face the earth and the heaven fled away; and there was found no place for them. And I saw the dead, small and great, stand before God; and the books were opened: and another book was opened, which is *the book* of life: and the dead were judged out of those things which were written in the books, according to their works. And the sea gave up the dead which were in it; and death and hell delivered up the dead which were in them: and they were judged every man according to their works. And death and hell were cast into the lake of fire. This is the second death. And whosoever was not found written in the book of life was cast into the lake of fire" (Re.20:11-15).

"But the fearful, and unbelieving, and the abominable, and murderers, and whoremongers, and sorcerers, and idolaters, and all liars, shall have their part in the lake which burneth with fire and brimstone: which is the second death" (Re.21:8).

"And they shall go forth, and look upon the carcases of the men that have transgressed against me: for their worm shall not die, neither shall their fire be quenched; and they shall be an abhorring unto all flesh" (Is.66:24).

CHAPTER 31

D. Woe—A Strong Warning to Those Who Ignore God & Place Their Trust in Egypt (the World): A Message to All Who Foolishly Misplace Their Trust, 31:1–32:20

1. **God's warning to those who ignore Him & trust the military power of Egypt (a symbol of the world): A picture of trusting men instead of God**
   a. God's indictment
      1) They did not trust Him, the Holy One
      2) They did not seek His help
   b. God's strong warning
      1) He is the One who is truly wise & should be trusted
      2) He keeps His Word: All evildoers will be judged

      3) He will destroy both Egypt & those who trust Egypt (the world)
         • They are mere men, not God: They are helpless before God & will perish

         • The LORD is as a great lion that is able to consume its prey: He is unafraid of the shepherds who oppose Him

      4) He will return to Mount Zion to fight against those who oppose Him & His people
      5) He will shield & deliver Jerusalem: He will save a remnant of believers in the city

2. **God's invitation to those who ignore & rebel against Him: A call to repent, turn back to Him**
   a. The evidence of repentance: They will turn away from idolatry & worshiping the LORD alone
   b. The assurance of God's deliverance: He will destroy Assyria
      1) They will not fall by the sword of mere mortals, but of God
         • Will panic & flee
         • Will be terrorized
      2) They will even see their commanders terrorized,

Woe to them that go down to Egypt for help; and stay on horses, and trust in chariots, because *they are* many; and in horsemen, because they are very strong; but they look not unto the Holy One of Israel, neither seek the LORD!

2 Yet he also *is* wise, and will bring evil, and will not call back his words: but will arise against the house of the evildoers, and against the help of them that work iniquity.

3 Now the Egyptians *are* men, and not God; and their horses flesh, and not spirit. When the LORD shall stretch out his hand, both he that helpeth shall fall, and he that is holpen shall fall down, and they all shall fail together.

4 For thus hath the LORD spoken unto me, Like as the lion and the young lion roaring on his prey, when a multitude of shepherds is called forth against him, *he* will not be afraid of their voice, nor abase himself for the noise of them: so shall the LORD of hosts come down to fight for mount Zion, and for the hill thereof.

5 As birds flying, so will the LORD of hosts defend Jerusalem; defending also he will deliver *it; and* passing over he will preserve *it.*

6 Turn ye unto *him from* whom the children of Israel have deeply revolted.

7 For in that day every man shall cast away his idols of silver, and his idols of gold, which your own hands have made unto you *for* a sin.

8 Then shall the Assyrian fall with the sword, not of a mighty man; and the sword, not of a mean man, shall devour him: but he shall flee from the sword, and his young men shall be discomfited.

9 And he shall pass over to his strong hold for fear, and

his princes shall be afraid of the ensign, saith the LORD, whose fire *is* in Zion, and his furnace in Jerusalem.

CHAPTER 32

Behold, a king shall reign in righteousness, and princes shall rule in judgment.

2 And a man shall be as an hiding place from the wind, and a covert from the tempest; as rivers of water in a dry place, as the shadow of a great rock in a weary land.

3 And the eyes of them that see shall not be dim, and the ears of them that hear shall hearken.

4 The heart also of the rash shall understand knowledge, and the tongue of the stammerers shall be ready to speak plainly.

5 The vile person shall be no more called liberal, nor the churl said *to be* bountiful.

6 For the vile person will speak villany, and his heart will work iniquity, to practise hypocrisy, and to utter error against the LORD, to make empty the soul of the hungry, and he will cause the drink of the thirsty to fail.

7 The instruments also of the churl *are* evil: he deviseth wicked devices to destroy the poor with lying words, even when the needy speaketh right.

8 But the liberal deviseth liberal things; and by liberal things shall he stand.

9 Rise up, ye women that are at ease; hear my voice, ye careless daughters; give ear unto my speech.

10 Many days and years shall ye be troubled, ye careless women: for the vintage shall fail, the gathering shall not come.

11 Tremble, ye women that are at ease; be troubled, ye careless ones: strip you, and make you bare, and gird *sackcloth* upon *your* loins.

12 They shall lament for the teats, for the pleasant fields, for the fruitful vine.

13 Upon the land of my people shall come up thorns *and* briers; yea, upon all the houses of joy *in* the joyous city:

14 Because the palaces shall

fleeing in panic
3) They will suffer the consuming fire of God's holy presence

3. **God's promise of triumph: A coming king, Jesus Christ**
   a. His righteous kingdom
      1) He will set up just leaders
      2) He will protect & provide for the people
         • Shelter them from trouble
         • Water their thirsty souls
         • Cast His shadow over the afflicted & dying
      3) He will enable everyone to see & hear the truth
         • The spiritually blind & deaf: The hard-hearted
         • The rash: The careless, reckless, & scornful
         • The stammerers: The hesitant, the uncertain

      4) He will right all wrongs: Fools & scoundrels will no longer be respected
         • Because they talk about & focus on evil
         • Because they live ungodly lives & spread error about the LORD
         • Because they ignore the needs of others

         • Because they use evil methods to take advantage of people: Scheming & lying to get their way & to fulfill their desires
      5) He will allow only the noble & generous to stand & live in His kingdom
   b. His coming kingdom stands as a warning to complacent, careless women, 3:16–4:1
      1) They must listen
         • Because judgment is to begin soon: Within a year
         • Because their security is false: A day of siege & famine is coming
      2) They will tremble & mourn

         • Because the land will be devastated & overgrown with thorns & briars
         • Because their happy homes & city revelry will be destroyed

         • Because the palace &

the noisy, bustling capital will be deserted • Because the cities of Judah will become nothing but dens for animals c. His coming kingdom will bring great blessings: A picture of the Millennium 1) His Spirit, 44:3; Eze.36:21-27; 39:29; Joel 2:28; Zec.12:10 2) A restored, fruitful land 3) Justice & righteousness 4) Peace, quietness, &	be forsaken; the multitude of the city shall be left; the forts and towers shall be for dens for ever, a joy of wild asses, a pasture of flocks; 15 Until the spirit be poured upon us from on high, and the wilderness be a fruitful field, and the fruitful field be counted for a forest. 16 Then judgment shall dwell in the wilderness, and righteousness remain in the fruitful field. 17 And the work of righ-	teousness shall be peace; and the effect of righteousness quietness and assurance for ever. 18 And my people shall dwell in a peaceable habitation, and in sure dwellings, and in quiet resting places; 19 When it shall hail, coming down on the forest; and the city shall be low in a low place. 20 Blessed *are* ye that sow beside all waters, that send forth *thither* the feet of the ox and the ass.	assurance 5) Secure homes—undisturbed & free from trouble 6) A restored land & city—restored from utter devastation • Will have abundant farmland & water • Will allow animals to roam freely

DIVISION III

THE PROPHECIES OF WOE: GOD'S WARNING TO HIS PEOPLE, 28:1–35:10

D. Woe—A Strong Warning to Those Who Ignore God and Place Their Trust in Egypt (the World): A Message to All Who Foolishly Misplace Their Trusts, 31:1–32:20

(31:1–32:20) **Introduction**: misplacing our trust—whether in an individual, a religion, technology, a machine, or even directions—can have disastrous consequences. It is every person's responsibility to find out who is or is not trustworthy before taking any major step or making an important decision. Why? Because failure to do so can result in any number of problems:
⇒ being shamed or embarrassed
⇒ failing a test
⇒ getting fired
⇒ going bankrupt
⇒ losing your home
⇒ hurting your family
⇒ getting sick or injured
⇒ being conned or deceived
⇒ losing your life or causing the death of someone else

The list could go on. But simply put, the *object of our trust* must be trustworthy for our efforts to achieve something or to be successful.

True believers know that only the LORD can meet the permanent longing and needs of the human heart. Thus it is the LORD who should be trusted, not men. And because the LORD is totally trustworthy, He is the One who should be honored and respected, trusted and obeyed.

The present Scripture is a strong warning to both the leaders and people of Isaiah's day. They all professed to know the LORD, but they ignored Him and His Word. They refused to do what He said. Instead of trusting God, they placed their trust in Egypt (the world). But sadly, the world will eventually fail all who put their trust in it.

This present warning is the fourth *woe* issued by the LORD to His people. Like the previous warning, this *woe* is also directed at the pro-Egyptian group within Judah. Remember that some of the leaders were seeking to form an alliance with Egypt in order to withstand the Assyrian threat that lay just over the horizon. But the LORD had warned the leaders against forming a partnership with the unbelieving, wicked Egyptians. Nevertheless, in defiance of God these leaders disregarded the LORD and His warning. They formed the alliance and placed their trust in Egypt, that is, the world. This is, *Woe—A Strong Warning to Those Who Ignore God and Place Their Trust in Egypt (the World): A Message to All Who Foolishly Misplace Their Trust*, 31:1–32:20.

1. God's warning to those who ignore Him and trust the military power of Egypt (a symbol of the world): a picture of trusting men instead of God (31:1-5).
2. God's invitation to those who ignore and rebel against Him: a call to repent, turn back to Him (31:6-9).
3. God's promise of triumph: a coming king, Jesus Christ (32:1-20).

1 (31:1-5) **Distrust, in God, Trusting Men Instead—Trust, in Men, Instead of God—Power, Trust in, Instead of God—Military, Trust in, Instead of God—Judah, Trust of, in Egypt Instead of God—Egypt, Trust in, Instead of God—World, Trust in, Instead of God—Man, Trust in, Instead of God—Humankind, Trust in, Instead of God—Warning, Against Ignoring God—Warning, Against Trusting Men Instead of God**: God gave a strong warning—a *woe*—to those who ignored Him and trusted the military power of Egypt. Remember that Egypt is a symbol of the world, of ungodly and wicked societies who totally ignore the only living and true God.

King Hezekiah of Judah and his people were facing a terrible crisis. The Assyrians, the most powerful nation on earth at that time, were a cruel people who sought world domination. Their war machine was unstoppable, and Judah lay right in its path. Isaiah warned Hezekiah and the leadership against forming alliances with surrounding nations to withstand the Assyrian forces. Instead of trusting the *arm of the flesh,* the power of other nations, they needed to trust the LORD. But a strong pro-Egyptian party in Judah wanted to form an alliance with Egypt, and they were successful. They formed an alliance with Egypt in an attempt to discourage the Assyrians from attacking either nation. What follows is a clear picture of people placing a far greater value in the wisdom and power of men instead of in the LORD, the only living and true God.

OUTLINE	SCRIPTURE	SCRIPTURE	OUTLINE
1. God's warning to those who ignore Him & trust the military power of Egypt (a symbol of the world): A picture of trusting men instead of God a. God's indictment 1) They did not trust Him, the Holy One 2) They did not seek His help b. God's strong warning 1) He is the One who is truly wise & should be trusted 2) He keeps His Word: All evildoers will be judged 3) He will destroy both Egypt & those who trust Egypt (the world) • They are mere men, not God: They are helpless	Woe to them that go down to Egypt for help; and stay on horses, and trust in chariots, because *they are* many; and in horsemen, because they are very strong; but they look not unto the Holy One of Israel, neither seek the LORD! 2 Yet he also *is* wise, and will bring evil, and will not call back his words: but will arise against the house of the evildoers, and against the help of them that work iniquity. 3 Now the Egyptians *are* men, and not God; and their horses flesh, and not spirit. When the LORD shall stretch out his hand, both he	that helpeth shall fall, and he that is holpen shall fall down, and they all shall fail together. 4 For thus hath the LORD spoken unto me, Like as the lion and the young lion roaring on his prey, when a multitude of shepherds is called forth against him, *he* will not be afraid of their voice, nor abase himself for the noise of them: so shall the LORD of hosts come down to fight for mount Zion, and for the hill thereof. 5 As birds flying, so will the LORD of hosts defend Jerusalem; defending also he will deliver *it; and* passing over he will preserve *it.*	before God & will perish • The LORD is as a great lion that is able to consume its prey: He is unafraid of the shepherds who oppose Him 4) He will return to Mount Zion to fight against those who oppose Him & His people 5) He will shield & deliver Jerusalem: He will save a remnant of believers in the city

a. God issued a twofold indictment against the people of Judah, in particular against King Hezekiah and the pro-Egyptian party (v.1). First, they did not trust Him, the Holy One. He alone is holy, *set apart and above* His creation, and He alone is righteous. Sitting above the universe, He knows exactly what should be done, and He has the power to deliver those who trust Him *through* the crises of life. Judah's only hope of deliverance from the Assyrian threat was the LORD, but the Jews totally ignored Him.

Second, the people of Judah did not seek the LORD's help. Instead, they looked to Egypt and relied on its military power to help them. Although Egypt was a fading power on the world scene, it apparently still had a large, well-equipped army, with a large cavalry and a huge number of chariots (1 K.10:28-29). Based solely on human observation, an alliance with Egypt seemed to be the only possible way to secure Judah against the Assyrian threat. But this was in direct violation of the LORD's Word. God's people were not to place their trust in horses or in Egypt, that is, in military power or in the wicked, godless nations of the world. But sadly, this was exactly what King Hezekiah and the people of Judah did. Ignoring the LORD, they sought the help of Egypt. Instead of placing their confidence in the LORD, they trusted the armies and weapons of unbelievers and the swiftness of their own horses.

b. God issued a strong warning to Judah, in particular to the pro-Egyptian politicians who ignored the LORD and sought the help of Egypt (vv.2-5). His warning was fivefold.

1) The LORD would prove that His wisdom far exceeds the wisdom of politicians. The LORD is the One who is truly wise and therefore should be trusted (v.2). The leaders of Judah felt that the only wise course was to seek an alliance with Egypt, but in His wisdom the LORD knew better. And through His prophet Isaiah, God warned the leaders not to seek the help of Egypt (30:1-14). Just as Isaiah predicted, if they sought an alliance with Egypt, disaster would come. The LORD's wise prediction would be fulfilled.

2) The LORD would keep His Word: all evildoers would be judged (v.2). As He had warned centuries earlier through Moses, so it would now be: all who disobeyed His Holy Word would face His judgment.

3) The LORD would destroy the wicked in Judah and all their allies (vv.2-4). The armies of both Judah and Egypt were mere men. Their horses were mere flesh, and their chariots mere machines. When the LORD stretched out His hand of judgment, He would utterly destroy both men and their weapons. Like a great lion, the LORD is able to consume the prey (v.4). Even though a band of shepherds oppose the lion, shouting and making as much noise as possible, they cannot frighten the lion.

4) The LORD would return to Mount Zion (Jerusalem) to fight His enemies when they gathered to destroy His people (v.4b). All who opposed the LORD and His people would face the LORD Himself and His hand of judgment. This is a direct reference to the Assyrian army, which would soon set up a siege against Jerusalem (Is.36:1-37:38).

5) Like birds who hover overhead, the LORD would shield and deliver Jerusalem (v.5). He would save a remnant of believers through whom he would fulfill all His promises. It was necessary to save a remnant through whom He could send the Savior and His Word to the world.

Thought 1. As we carry out our tasks throughout the day, how many of us ignore God, trusting only human power—our own abilities, wisdom, and technology—to accomplish the tasks? Think about these questions for a moment:

⇒ How many CEO's fail to base their business practices on the principles laid down in God's Word?

⇒ How many managers ignore the LORD'S instructions about how to lead people?

⇒ How many doctors, nurses, and medical technicians depend only upon their own abilities, wisdom, and the latest technology to heal?

⇒ How many politicians and government officials carry out their daily tasks without seeking God's will in the decisions they make?

⇒ How many of *us* act as if our fate is in our own hands?

Obviously, we are to use what wisdom we have and the technology we can develop to lessen the impact of nature's catastrophic forces as well as the diseases and the aging process of the human body. In fact, when God created man and woman, He instructed them to multiply on the earth and to subdue it, which implies that we are to control all the disorderly forces of nature as much as possible (Ge.1:28; Ps.8:6; He.2:8).

But as we go about our daily tasks on earth, we are to acknowledge the LORD and trust Him. Since the LORD created the universe and gave us the intelligence and abilities we have, we are to acknowledge Him as the Giver of life and of every good and perfect gift. In addition, situations arise in life that we cannot handle, no matter how wise we are or how sophisticated our technology. At such times only the LORD can deliver us. If we place our trust only in ourselves, we will collapse when catastrophe strikes. It will crush us. However, if we trust the LORD, He will give us the strength to *walk through and conquer* the crises, even death itself. Listen to what God's Holy Word says about the danger of trusting only in the power and ability of man:

"Peter answered and said unto him, Though all *men* shall be offended because of thee, *yet* will I never be offended. Jesus said unto him, Verily I say unto thee, That this night, before the cock crow, thou shalt deny me thrice. Peter said unto him, Though I should die with thee, yet will I not deny thee. Likewise also said all the disciples" (Mt.26:33-35).

"And the disciples were astonished at his words. But Jesus answereth again, and saith unto them, Children, how hard is it for them that trust in riches to enter into the kingdom of God!" (Mk.10:24).

"And I will say to my soul, Soul, thou hast much goods laid up for many years; take thine ease, eat, drink, *and* be merry. But God said unto him, *Thou* fool, this night thy soul shall be required of thee: then whose shall those things be, which thou hast provided? So *is* he that layeth up treasure for himself, and is not rich toward God" (Lu.12:19-21).

"And he spake this parable unto certain which trusted in themselves that they were righteous, and despised others: Two men went up into the temple to pray; the one a Pharisee, and the other a publican. The Pharisee stood and prayed thus with himself, God, I thank thee, that I am not as other men *are*, extortioners, unjust, adulterers, or even as this publican. I fast twice in the week, I give tithes of all that I possess. And the publican, standing afar off, would not lift up so much as *his* eyes unto heaven, but smote upon his breast, saying, God be merciful to me a sinner. I tell you, this man went down to his house justified *rather* than the other: for every one that exalteth himself shall be abased; and he that humbleth himself shall be exalted" (Lu.18:9-14).

"Wherefore let him that thinketh he standeth take heed lest he fall" (1 Co.10:12).

"Charge them that are rich in this world, that they be not highminded, nor trust in uncertain riches, but in the living God, who giveth us richly all things to enjoy" (1 Ti.6:17).

"If I have made gold my hope, or have said to the fine gold, *Thou art* my confidence; If I rejoiced because my wealth *was* great, and because mine hand had gotten much...This also *were* an iniquity *to be punished by* the judge: for I should have denied the God *that is* above" (Jb.31:24-25, 28).

"Lo, *this is* the man *that* made not God his strength; but trusted in the abundance of his riches, *and* strengthened himself in his wickedness" (Ps.52: 7).

"The name of the LORD *is* a strong tower: the righteous runneth into it, and is safe. The rich man's wealth *is* his strong city, and as an high wall in his own conceit" (Pr.18:10-11).

"He that trusteth in his own heart is a fool: but whoso walketh wisely, he shall be delivered" (Pr.28:26).

"Cease ye from man, whose breath *is* in his nostrils: for wherein is he to be accounted of?" (Is.2:22).

"Woe to the rebellious children, saith the Lord, that take counsel, but not of me; and that cover with a covering, but not of my spirit, that they may add sin to sin: That walk to go down into Egypt, and have not asked at my mouth; to strengthen themselves in the strength of Pharaoh, and to trust in the shadow of Egypt! Therefore shall the strength of Pharaoh be your shame, and the trust in the shadow of Egypt *your* confusion." (Is.30:1-3).

"Woe to them that go down to Egypt for help; and stay on horses, and trust in chariots, because *they are* many; and in horsemen, because they are very strong; but they look not unto the Holy One of Israel, neither seek the LORD! Yet he also *is* wise, and will bring evil, and will not call back his words: but will arise against the house of the evildoers, and against the help of them that work iniquity. Now the Egyptians *are* men, and not God; and their horses flesh, and not spirit. When the LORD shall stretch out his hand, both he that helpeth shall fall, and he that is holpen shall fall down, and they all shall fail together" (Is.31:1-3).

"Therefore hear now this, *thou that art* given to pleasures, that dwellest carelessly, that sayest in thine heart, I *am*, and none else beside me; I shall not sit *as* a widow, neither shall I know the loss of children: But these two *things* shall come to thee in a moment in one day, the loss of children, and widowhood: they shall come upon thee in their perfection for the multitude of thy sorceries, *and* for the great abundance of thine enchantments. For thou hast trusted in thy wickedness: thou hast said, None seeth me. Thy wisdom and thy knowledge, it hath perverted thee; and thou hast said in thine heart, I *am,* and none else beside me. Therefore shall evil come upon thee; thou shalt not know from whence it riseth: and mischief shall fall upon thee; thou shalt not be able to put if off: and desolation shall come upon thee suddenly, *which* thou shalt not know" (Is.47:8-11).

"Thus saith the LORD; Cursed be the man that trusteth in man, and maketh flesh his arm, and whose heart departeth from the LORD" (Je.17:5).

"When Ephraim saw his sickness, and Judah *saw* his wound, then went Ephraim to the Assyrian, and sent to king Jareb: yet could he not heal you, nor cure you of your wound" (Ho.5:13).

"Ye have plowed wickedness, ye have reaped iniquity; ye have eaten the fruit of lies: because thou didst trust in thy way, in the multitude of thy mighty men" (Ho.10:13).

"The pride of thine heart hath deceived thee, thou that dwellest in the clefts of the rock, whose habitation *is* high; that saith in his heart, Who shall bring me down to the ground? Though thou exalt *thyself* as the eagle, and though thou set thy nest among the stars, thence will I bring thee down, saith the LORD" (Ob.1:3-4).

2 (31:6-9) **Invitation, to Whom, Those Who Ignore God—Invitation, to Whom, Those Who Rebel—Repentance, Evidence of, Turning from Idolatry; Turning from False Worship—Assyria, Destruction of, Predicted—Jerusalem, Deliverance of, Predicted—Prophecy, Concerning Jerusalem, Deliverance of:** God extends an invitation to those who ignore and rebel against Him. Note what Isaiah said about the person who rebels: he is gripped by a *deep* or *great* rebellion. This indicates that God excludes no one from His invitation. He is willing to save from His coming judgment even those who have *greatly rebelled* against Him.

What is the invitation God extends? It is to repent, to turn back to the LORD. Since God saves His people from their enemies, all who are in rebellion should repent and return to Him. God's salvation is so wonderful that anyone who does not turn back to the LORD is a fool (Ps.14:1-7; 53:1-6).

The *evidence* of repentance is obvious. People who truly repent turn away from idolatry and worship the LORD alone. Note the phrase *in that day,* which refers to the latter days of human history when Christ sets up His kingdom on earth. *In that day* all idols will be cast down, false worship will cease, and the LORD alone will be worshipped. Isaiah's message was forceful: since the glorious day of the LORD's exaltation and worship is coming, everyone should renounce idolatry *now.* They should reject all idols and false worship *now.* The LORD is the only living and true God, so He should be the only object of man's worship *now.* There should be a total renunciation of idolatry and false worship and a total recommitment to worship the LORD alone.

But there is another reason for repenting and turning back to the LORD: He promises to deliver His people from their enemies (vv.8-9). Although the Jews would suffer the judgment of God's hand, and the Assyrian army would slaughter many of them, God would save a remnant of Jews. Although all the other cities of Judah would be destroyed, God would save Jerusalem. God Himself would destroy the Assyrian army. Its soldiers would not fall by the sword of mere mortals, but by the sword of God (v.8). When God wielded His sword, the Assyrian army, including its commanders, would panic and flee in terror for their lives. The enemies of God and His people would suffer the consuming fire of God's Holy presence. Note that this is the clear declaration of the LORD. Therefore, because of God's wonderful promise of deliverance, the people should repent and turn back to Him.

OUTLINE	SCRIPTURE	SCRIPTURE	OUTLINE

2. **God's invitation to those who ignore & rebel against Him: A call to repent, turn back to Him**
a. The evidence of repentance: They will turn away from idolatry & worshiping the LORD alone
 	
b. The assurance of God's deliverance: He will destroy Assyria
	6 Turn ye unto *him from* whom the children of Israel have deeply revolted.
	7 For in that day every man shall cast away his idols of silver, and his idols of gold, which your own hands have made unto you *for* a sin.
	8 Then shall the Assyrian fall with the sword, not of a mighty man; and the sword,
		not of a mean man, shall devour him: but he shall flee from the sword, and his young men shall be discomfited.
		9 And he shall pass over to his strong hold for fear, and his princes shall be afraid of the ensign, saith the LORD, whose fire *is* in Zion, and his furnace in Jerusalem.
			1) They will not fall by the sword of mere mortals, but of God
			  • Will panic & flee
			  • Will be terrorized
			2) They will even see their commanders terrorized,

Thought 1. God calls on all people everywhere to repent. Even if we have ignored and denied the LORD all our lives, the LORD extends an invitation to us: repent and turn back to Him. Repentance is absolutely essential if we are to escape the judgment that is coming upon the earth. If we fail to repent, we will face the terrifying judgment of God. Life is uncertain. No person is guaranteed another day of life. God's Spirit does not always convict and draw people to Him; that is, He will not strive with people continuously, endlessly (Ge.6:3). Man can reach a point of no return. Therefore, when God's Spirit convicts us of sin and of failing to trust the LORD, we must confess and repent. We must turn back to Him. If we confess our sins and distrust, He will cleanse us and give us a deep sense of assurance that we have been forgiven. The assurance of His acceptance and favor will flood our souls. God extends His great invitation to every human being: repent and turn back to Him.

"I tell you, Nay: but, except ye repent, ye shall all likewise perish" (Lu.13:3).

"Then Peter said unto them, Repent, and be baptized every one of you in the name of Jesus Christ for the remission of sins, and ye shall receive the gift of the Holy Ghost" (Ac.2:38).

"And the times of this ignorance God winked at; but now commandeth all men every where to repent" (Ac.17:30).

"Cast away from you all your transgressions, whereby ye have transgressed; and make you a new heart and a new spirit: for why will ye die, O house of Israel?" (Eze.18:31).

"Let the wicked forsake his way, and the unrighteous man his thoughts: and let him return unto the LORD, and he will have mercy upon him; and to our God, for he will abundantly pardon" (Is.55:7).

3 (32:1-20) **Age, Messianic, Discussed—Messiah, Kingdom of, Discussed—Christ, Kingdom of, Discussed—Women, Warning to, Against Being Complacent; Against Carelessness—Warning, to Women, Against Complacency; Against Carelessness—Complacency, Warning Against, to Women—Kingdom, of Christ, Blessings of:** God made a wonderful promise to those who repented: they would triumph over all their enemies through the leadership of a coming king. This is a clear reference to the promised descendant of David, the promised Messiah-King who will establish God's kingdom on earth. Jesus Christ is the Messiah-King who will return to earth to set up God's kingdom (Is.7:14; 9:6-7; 11:1-12:6; 16:5; 28:16; 33:17, 22; see outline and notes—Mt.22:41-46 for more discussion).

Note that Isaiah refers to the promised king as "a king" (32:1), then as "the king" (33:17), and finally as "our king" (33:22). Warren Wiersbe points out that it is not enough to claim that Jesus Christ is "a king" or "the king."[1] We must open our hearts to the Lord Jesus Christ and allow Him to be *our* king—the king of our lives.

OUTLINE	SCRIPTURE	SCRIPTURE	OUTLINE

3. God's promise of triumph: A coming king, Jesus Christ
a. His righteous kingdom
 1) He will set up just leaders
 2) He will protect & provide for the people
  • Shelter them from trouble
  • Water their thirsty souls
  • Cast His shadow over the afflicted & dying
 3) He will enable everyone to see & hear the truth
  • The spiritually blind & deaf: The hard-hearted
  • The rash: The careless, reckless, & scornful
  • The stammerers: The hesitant, the uncertain
 4) He will right all wrongs: Fools & scoundrels will no longer be respected
  • Because they talk about & focus on evil
  • Because they live ungodly lives & spread error about the LORD
  • Because they ignore the needs of others
  • Because they use evil methods to take advantage of people: Scheming & lying to get their way & to fulfill their desires
 5) He will allow only the noble & generous to stand & live in His kingdom
b. His coming kingdom stands as a warning to complacent, careless women, 3:16–4:1
 1) They must listen
  • Because judgment is to begin soon: Within a year
	Behold, a king shall reign in righteousness, and princes shall rule in judgment. 2 And a man shall be as an hiding place from the wind, and a covert from the tempest; as rivers of water in a dry place, as the shadow of a great rock in a weary land. 3 And the eyes of them that see shall not be dim, and the ears of them that hear shall hearken. 4 The heart also of the rash shall understand knowledge, and the tongue of the stammerers shall be ready to speak plainly. 5 The vile person shall be no more called liberal, nor the churl said *to be* bountiful. 6 For the vile person will speak villany, and his heart will work iniquity, to practise hypocrisy, and to utter error against the LORD, to make empty the soul of the hungry, and he will cause the drink of the thirsty to fail. 7 The instruments also of the churl *are* evil: he deviseth wicked devices to destroy the poor with lying words, even when the needy speaketh right. 8 But the liberal deviseth liberal things; and by liberal things shall he stand. 9 Rise up, ye women that are at ease; hear my voice, ye careless daughters; give ear unto my speech. 10 Many days and years shall ye be troubled, ye careless women: for the vintage shall fail, the gathering shall	not come. 11 Tremble, ye women that are at ease; be troubled, ye careless ones: strip you, and make you bare, and gird *sackcloth* upon *your* loins. 12 They shall lament for the teats, for the pleasant fields, for the fruitful vine. 13 Upon the land of my people shall come up thorns *and* briers; yea, upon all the houses of joy *in* the joyous city: 14 Because the palaces shall be forsaken; the multitude of the city shall be left; the forts and towers shall be for dens for ever, a joy of wild asses, a pasture of flocks; 15 Until the spirit be poured upon us from on high, and the wilderness be a fruitful field, and the fruitful field be counted for a forest. 16 Then judgment shall dwell in the wilderness, and righteousness remain in the fruitful field. 17 And the work of righteousness shall be peace; and the effect of righteousness quietness and assurance for ever. 18 And my people shall dwell in a peaceable habitation, and in sure dwellings, and in quiet resting places; 19 When it shall hail, coming down on the forest; and the city shall be low in a low place. 20 Blessed *are* ye that sow beside all waters, that send forth *thither* the feet of the ox and the ass.	• Because their security is false: A day of siege & famine is coming
			
			2) They will tremble & mourn
			
			• Because the land will be devastated & overgrown with thorns & briars
			• Because their happy homes & city revelry will be destroyed
			• Because the palace & the noisy, bustling capital will be deserted
			• Because the cities of Judah will become nothing but dens for animals
			
			c. His coming kingdom will bring great blessings: A picture of the Millennium
			 1) His Spirit, 44:3; Eze.36:21-27; 39:29; Joel 2:28; Zec.12:10
			 2) A restored, fruitful land
			 3) Justice & righteousness
			 4) Peace, quietness, & assurance
			 5) Secure homes—undisturbed & free from trouble
			
			6) A restored land & city—restored from utter devastation
			
			• Will have abundant farmland & water
			• Will allow animals to roam freely

1 Warren Wiersbe. *Be Comforted*, p.82.

a. The coming king will establish a righteous kingdom on earth. In contrast to the corrupt rulers of Isaiah's day—rulers who oppressed the people through unjust laws and greed—the promised king (the Messiah) will rule in righteousness and justice (vv.1-8; 16: 9:7; 11:3-5; 16:5; 28:16-17; 33:5).

1) The promised king will be a good, noble ruler who will establish His government on the basic principle of righteousness. Moreover all His officials—from those at the highest levels of government down to the most minor—will rule in true justice (v.1). In the society of the coming king, the standard of all behavior will be the perfect righteousness and justice of the Messiah. He will fill all the positions of leadership throughout the land with good, noble, and just leaders.

2) The promised king will protect and provide for the people (v.2). When the storm of trial or hardship strikes His people, the Messiah will be a shelter and refuge for them. When they become thirsty, either physically or spiritually, He will provide water for their bodies or souls. When they suffer under the scorching sun of affliction, He will cast His shadow over them like the shade of a huge rock.

3) The promised king will make radical changes when He establishes His kingdom on earth. He will enable everyone to see and hear the truth (vv.3-4). He will open the eyes and ears of the spiritually blind and deaf. He will make the hearts of the insensitive and stubborn soft and tender, open to receive the Word of God. Those who have stammering tongues—who are uncertain and hesitant to confess and speak up for the LORD—will be bold, fluent, and clear in bearing strong testimony to Him. Even the rash—those who are reckless in their relationship with God and sometimes mock the LORD and His people—will know and understand the truth *in that day*.

4) The promised king will right all wrongs that have taken place down through history (vv.5-7). Worldly society often honors the fools and scoundrels of society, people who live wicked, evil, and godless lives. They receive honor because they are famous, powerful, or wealthy. But the day is coming when wealth, power, and fame will not matter. The only thing that will matter will be what God values, and all fools and scoundrels—all who ignored, denied, and defamed the LORD's name, living sinful lives—will no longer be respected or honored. Isaiah gives four reasons for the judgment that is coming upon fools and scoundrels:

⇒ They talked about and focused their minds on evil (v.6).
⇒ They lived ungodly lives and misled others concerning the LORD (v.6).
⇒ They ignored the needs of others, even when people were suffering desperately (v.6).
⇒ They used evil methods to take advantage of people, scheming and lying to get their way and to fulfill their own lusts (v.7).

Fools and scoundrels often oppress people to increase their own wealth, positions, authority, power, or fame. Sometimes they even lie, steal, or cheat the poor and needy in order to satisfy their selfish lust for more and more. All that is going to change.

5) The promised King will ensure that only the noble and generous will stand in His kingdom (v.8). *Noble* does not refer only to those in positions of leadership and authority. It includes all who trust and acknowledge the LORD, all who live godly and righteous lives.

b. The coming King will establish His kingdom as a warning to complacent, careless women (3:16–4:1). In Isaiah's day many women were living in wealth and luxury; they had become indifferent to sin and were ignoring the warnings of God. They were living at ease, enjoying the pleasures of the moment, not giving any thought to the LORD or the fact that things might change. Spiritual concerns seldom if ever crossed their minds. A spirit of lethargy and complacency gripped them. Isaiah issued a strong warning to these women:

1) They must arise and heed the warning of God because judgment would soon fall upon them (vv.9-10). Note that Isaiah predicted the time frame in which the judgment would come: within a year. Although they were living in pleasure and luxury with plenty of everything they wanted, their feelings of security were based upon a false premise. A day of siege and famine was coming, a day of utter disaster. Very soon they would have nothing, not even food.

2) Within the year the invading forces would make them tremble and mourn (vv.11-14). Therefore, the women should strip off their clothes, put on sackcloth, mourn, and prepare to suffer the consequences of their sins. These complacent, lethargic women who had ignored the LORD and His warning of judgment would soon find themselves in dire circumstances:

⇒ The land would be devastated and overgrown with thorns and briars (vv.12-13a).
⇒ Their houses and cities—the central places of their joy and revelry—would be destroyed (v.13).
⇒ The palace and the noisy, bustling capital of Jerusalem would be deserted (v.14).

Note that this prediction is a reference to the Babylonian destruction of Jerusalem in 586 B.C., which took place 115 years after Isaiah made this prophecy. Although the Assyrian invasion and destruction of Judah's other cities would take place within a year, the LORD was warning the people of the future judgment that would fall upon the capital under the Babylonians. In that day the city of Jerusalem would become a wasteland inhabited only by animals.

c. When the promised king establishes His kingdom on earth, He will pour blessing after blessing upon its citizens. These blessings will be entirely different from the blessings of salvation described in chapter 30. This is a clear picture of the Messiah's kingdom and what life will be like when Christ rules upon earth during His millennial reign (vv.15-20). He will give the believers in His kingdom six of the most glorious blessings imaginable.

1) The Messiah will pour out His spirit upon all believers (v.15; 44:3; Eze.36:26-27; 39:29; Joel 2:28; Zec.12:10). God's Spirit will teach and lead the redeemed, guiding them as they walk day by day serving the Messiah. The redeemed will have a strong desire in their hearts to obey the LORD, a longing to accomplish the task He assigns them to do. Due to the Messiah's presence on earth, the work of the Spirit will flow far more freely and be far more evident than it is today. He will demonstrate His power much more clearly.

2) In the Messiah's kingdom the land itself will be transformed. The desert will become fertile, and the fertile fields will seem like forests (v.15). Nature itself will be redeemed, brought completely under control by the Messiah (see outline and note—Ro.8:18-27 for more discussion). The earth will become another "Garden of Eden."

3) Justice and righteousness will sweep the earth from one end to the other (v.16). People will live righteously, obeying both the commandments of God and the laws of the land. No longer will lawlessness, immorality, and violence blanket the earth. To the contrary, people will rejoice in righteousness and justice and hold great respect for God and His commandments and the rights of others.

4) Due to the rule of righteousness and justice, peace will descend on earth (v.17). All the redeemed in the Messiah's kingdom will experience a spirit of quietness, assurance, and security. No longer will a spirit of restlessness, insecurity, fear, anxiety, and purposelessness grip the souls of people. Instead, people's hearts will be filled with a deep sense of serenity and confidence.

5) The Messiah will provide a secure dwelling place for all the redeemed in His kingdom (v.18). All people will live in their own homes undisturbed and completely free from trouble.

6) In the Messiah's kingdom both the cities and countries will be transformed (vv.19-20). Though the cities were leveled to the ground in the past and all the lands completely ruined, they will not remain so. Even in this present evil world both can be devastated, but the day is coming when both will be restored and transformed. *In that day* there will be an abundance of farmland and water for every citizen. The land will be so fruitful that the animals will be allowed to roam freely.

Thought 1. The Word of God assures us: Christ will give the redeemed the most wonderful blessings imaginable when He returns to earth. But we must always remember this sad fact: not everyone is going to receive these blessings. People who reject the LORD and refuse to obey His commandments will be cut off from God. He will not bless them. Because they rejected Him, He will reject them. But again, this will not be the fate of the redeemed, the people who truly follow the LORD and seek to obey His holy commandments. They will be blessed beyond measure when Christ returns.

"But lay up for yourselves treasures in heaven, where neither moth nor rust doth corrupt, and where thieves do not break through nor steal" (Mt.6:20).

"Let not your heart be troubled: ye believe in God, believe also in me. In my Father's house are many mansions: if *it were* not so, I would have told you. I go to prepare a place for you" (Jn.14:1-2).

"The Spirit itself beareth witness with our spirit, that we are the children of God: And if children, then heirs; heirs of God, and joint-heirs with Christ; if so be that we suffer with *him,* that we may be also glorified together. For I reckon that the sufferings of this present time *are* not worthy *to be compared* with the glory which shall be revealed in us" (Ro.8:16-18).

"So when this corruptible shall have put on incorruption, and this mortal shall have put on immortality, then shall be brought to pass the saying that is written, Death is swallowed up in victory" (1 Co.15:54).

"For we know that if our earthly house of *this* tabernacle were dissolved, we have a building of God, an house not made with hands, eternal in the heavens" (2 Co.5:1).

"For our conversation [citizenship] is in heaven; from whence also we look for the Saviour, the Lord Jesus Christ: Who shall change our vile body, that it may be fashioned like unto his glorious body, according to the working whereby he is able even to subdue all things unto himself" (Ph.3:20-21).

"When Christ, *who is* our life, shall appear, then shall ye also appear with him in glory" (Col.3:4).

"And the Lord make you to increase and abound in love one toward another, and toward all *men,* even as we *do* toward you: To the end he may stablish your hearts unblameable in holiness before God, even our Father, at the coming of our Lord Jesus Christ with all his saints" (1 Th.3:12-13).

"For the Lord himself shall descend from heaven with a shout, with the voice of the archangel, and with the trump of God: and the dead in Christ shall rise first: Then we which are alive *and* remain shall be caught up together with them in the clouds, to meet the Lord in the air: and so shall we ever be with the Lord. Wherefore comfort one another with these words" (1 Th.4:16-18).

"Henceforth there is laid up for me a crown of righteousness, which the Lord, the righteous judge, shall give me at that day: and not to me only, but unto all them also that love his appearing" (2 Ti.4:8).

"By faith Abraham, when he was called to go out into a place which he should after receive for an inheritance, obeyed; and he went out, not knowing whither he went. By faith he sojourned in the land of promise, as *in* a strange country, dwelling in tabernacles with Isaac and Jacob, the heirs with him of the same promise: For he looked for a city which hath foundations, whose builder and maker *is* God" (He.11:8-10).

"These all died in faith, not having received the promises, but having seen them afar off, and were persuaded of *them,* and embraced *them,* and confessed that they were strangers and pilgrims on the earth. For they that say such things declare plainly that they seek a country. And truly, if they had been mindful of that *country* from whence they came out, they might have had opportunity to have returned. But now they desire a better *country,* that is, an heavenly: wherefore God is not ashamed to be called their God: for he hath prepared for them a city" (He.11:13-16).

"Blessed *be* the God and Father of our Lord Jesus Christ, which according to his abundant mercy hath begotten us again unto a lively hope by the resurrection of Jesus Christ from the dead, To an inheritance incorruptible, and undefiled, and that fadeth not away, reserved in heaven for you, Who are kept by the power of God through faith unto salvation ready to be revealed in the last time" (1 Pe.1:3-5).

"And when the chief Shepherd shall appear, ye shall receive a crown of glory that fadeth not away" (1 Pe.5:4).

"Beloved, now are we the sons of God, and it doth not yet appear what we shall be: but we know that, when he shall appear, we shall be like him; for we shall see him as he is" (1 Jn.3:2).

"They shall hunger no more, neither thirst any more; neither shall the sun light on them, nor any heat. For the Lamb which is in the midst of the throne shall feed them, and shall lead them unto living fountains of waters: and God shall wipe away all tears from their eyes" (Re.7:16-17).

"And God shall wipe away all tears from their eyes; and there shall be no more death, neither sorrow, nor crying, neither shall there be any more pain: for the former things are passed away" (Re.21:4).

CHAPTER 33

E. Woe—A Strong Warning to the Destroyer: A Message to All Who Commit Acts of Violence, 33:1-24

1. The surety of God's judgment on the violent oppressors & betrayers of this earth

a. The clear pronouncement: The destroyer & the traitor (Assyria) will reap exactly what they have sown—be destroyed & betrayed, Ga.6:7

b. The cry of the believers for God's deliverance: His grace, strength, & salvation
  1) They should pray because of the LORD's power
    • His power to scatter the enemy's army

    • His power to plunder the nations

  2) They should pray because of the LORD's exaltation
    • He will rule in justice & righteousness

    • He will be their foundation: Their salvation, wisdom, & knowledge

  3) They should pray because the source of God's treasure is the fear of the LORD

c. The pitiful state caused by the destructive judgment
  1) Soldiers & envoys will weep: As cities fall & peace fails
  2) Highways will be deserted
  3) Treaties will be broken & leaders despised
  4) Life will be cheap

  5) Crops & land will be ruined

d. The description of the coming judgment on the destroyer (Assyria): Because they make bold, cruel plans
  1) They will be nothing more than chaff & straw: Will be consumed
  2) They will be thoroughly burned: As though burned to lime or set ablaze like dry cut thorn bushes

Woe to thee that spoilest, and thou *wast* not spoiled; and dealest treacherously, and they dealt not treacherously with thee! when thou shalt cease to spoil, thou shalt be spoiled; *and* when thou shalt make an end to deal treacherously, they shall deal treacherously with thee.

2 O LORD, be gracious unto us; we have waited for thee: be thou their arm every morning, our salvation also in the time of trouble.

3 At the noise of the tumult the people fled; at the lifting up of thyself the nations were scattered.

4 And your spoil shall be gathered *like* the gathering of the caterpiller: as the running to and fro of locusts shall he run upon them.

5 The LORD is exalted; for he dwelleth on high: he hath filled Zion with judgment and righteousness.

6 And wisdom and knowledge shall be the stability of thy times, *and* strength of salvation: the fear of the LORD *is* his treasure.

7 Behold, their valiant ones shall cry without: the ambassadors of peace shall weep bitterly.

8 The highways lie waste, the wayfaring man ceaseth: he hath broken the covenant, he hath despised the cities, he regardeth no man.

9 The earth mourneth *and* languisheth: Lebanon is ashamed *and* hewn down: Sharon is like a wilderness; and Bashan and Carmel shake off *their fruits.*

10 Now will I rise, saith the LORD; now will I be exalted; now will I lift up myself.

11 Ye shall conceive chaff, ye shall bring forth stubble: your breath, *as* fire, shall devour you.

12 And the people shall be as the burnings of lime: *as* thorns cut up shall they be burned in the fire.

13 Hear, ye *that are* far off, what I have done; and, ye *that are* near, acknowledge my might.

14 The sinners in Zion are afraid; fearfulness hath surprised the hypocrites. Who among us shall dwell with the devouring fire? who among us shall dwell with everlasting burnings?

15 He that walketh righteously, and speaketh uprightly; he that despiseth the gain of oppressions, that shaketh his hands from holding of bribes, that stoppeth his ears from hearing of blood, and shutteth his eyes from seeing evil;

16 He shall dwell on high: his place of defence *shall be* the munitions of rocks: bread shall be given him; his waters *shall be* sure.

17 Thine eyes shall see the king in his beauty: they shall behold the land that is very far off.

18 Thine heart shall meditate terror. Where *is* the scribe? where *is* the receiver? where *is* he that counted the towers?

19 Thou shalt not see a fierce people, a people of a deeper speech than thou canst perceive; of a stammering tongue, *that thou canst* not understand.

20 Look upon Zion, the city of our solemnities: thine eyes shall see Jerusalem a quiet habitation, a tabernacle *that* shall not be taken down; not one of the stakes thereof shall ever be removed, neither shall any of the cords thereof be broken.

21 But there the glorious LORD *will be* unto us a place of broad rivers *and* streams; wherein shall go no galley with oars, neither shall gallant ship pass thereby.

22 For the LORD *is* our judge, the LORD *is* our lawgiver, the LORD *is* our king; he will save us.

23 Thy tacklings are loosed; they could not well strengthen their mast, they could not spread the sail: then is the prey of a great spoil divided; the lame take the prey.

24 And the inhabitant shall not say, I am sick: the people that dwell therein *shall be* forgiven *their* iniquity.

e. The lesson of God's judgment
  1) The world must acknowledge God's power
  2) The hypocrites & godless will be stricken with fear: Terrorized by the eternal fire of God's judgment, Is.10:17; He.12:29

2. The surety of God's deliverance of the righteous: A picture of the Messiah's kingdom

a. The righteous delivered
  1) Because he speaks the truth
  2) Because he takes no part in extortion or bribes
  3) Because he does not murder
  4) Because he shuts his eyes to evil

b. The righteous blessed
  1) The righteous will dwell on high, live with the LORD
  2) The righteous will be secure & fed, need nothing
  3) The righteous will see the king, the LORD in His glory, ruling over all the land
  4) The righteous will be freed from the terror of oppressors & destroyers, (know universal peace)
    • The evil military officers & political leaders
    • The arrogant of the earth (symbolized in the Assyrians)
  5) The righteous will see Jerusalem as the center of worship, a secure & peaceful place to live
    • It will never be moved, unlike a tent: A permanent place

    • It will be ruled over by the LORD Himself—in all His glory
    • It will be defended by the LORD Himself: Given undisturbed peace
  6) The righteous will be governed by the LORD: *Our* Judge, *our* Lawgiver, *our* King
  7) The righteous will be brought through the storm of life, even death itself—despite almost sinking
  8) The righteous will be given the enemy's spoils, his wealth & possessions
  9) The righteous will never again be sick
  10) The righteous will be forgiven all sin

DIVISION III

THE PROPHECIES OF WOE: GOD'S WARNING TO HIS PEOPLE, 28:1–35:10

E. Woe—A Strong Warning to the Destroyer: A Message to All Who Commit Acts of Violence, 33:1-24

(33:1-24) **Introduction**: the earth is full of violent people, people who use extreme force to impose their wills and desires on others. Violence is always destructive, hurting people or property and causing pain. Violence attacks people, assaulting, abusing, or coercing them. Violence is malicious and cruel, an act of unrestrained, brutal behavior. And violence often results in serious injury or death.

This present Scripture is a strong warning to those who destroy and commit acts of violence. God's hand of judgment will without question fall upon them. The particular destroyer being addressed in this Scripture was Assyria, the nation that was ruled by King Sennacherib. Seeking to build a world empire, the Assyrians had invaded nation after nation, subjecting them under the rule of Assyrian domination. The Assyrians were a cruel, brutal, savage, and vicious people with a reputation for violence and bloodshed. Using them as an example, the LORD describes the terrifying judgment that is to fall upon all the destroyers and the violent of earth. This is, *Woe—A Strong Warning to the Destroyer: A Message to All Who Commit Acts of Violence*, 33:1-24.

1. The surety of God's judgment on the violent oppressors and betrayers of this earth (vv.1-14).
2. The surety of God's deliverance of the righteous: a picture of Messiah's kingdom (vv.15-24).

1 (33:1-14) **Judgment, Surety of—Violence, Judgment of, Surety of—Betrayal, Judgment of, Surety of—Traitors, Judgment of, Surety of—Destroyers, Judgment of, Surety of—Reaping and Sowing, Principle of, Seen in Judgment—Assyria, Judgment of, Predicted—Deliverance, Source of, God**: God pronounces a strong warning—a *woe*—to those who deal treacherously with other people and nations, who are violent and who betray God's people. God's judgment is sure to fall on all who commit acts of cruelty and brutality, assaulting and attacking others. His judgment will fall also on all who betray His people. This is the clear teaching of this Scripture:

OUTLINE	SCRIPTURE	SCRIPTURE	OUTLINE
1. The surety of God's judgment on the violent oppressors & betrayers of this earth a. The clear pronouncement: The destroyer & the traitor (Assyria) will reap exactly what they have sown—be destroyed & betrayed, Ga.6:7 b. The cry of the believers for God's deliverance: His grace, strength, & salvation 1) They should pray because of the LORD's power • His power to scatter the enemy's army • His power to plunder the nations 2) They should pray because of the LORD's exaltation • He will rule in justice & righteousness •He will be their foundation: Their salvation, wisdom, & knowledge 3) They should pray because the source of God's treasure is the fear of the LORD c. The pitiful state caused by the destructive judgment	Woe to thee that spoilest, and thou *wast* not spoiled; and dealest treacherously, and they dealt not treacherously with thee! when thou shalt cease to spoil, thou shalt be spoiled; *and* when thou shalt make an end to deal treacherously, they shall deal treacherously with thee. 2 O LORD, be gracious unto us; we have waited for thee: be thou their arm every morning, our salvation also in the time of trouble. 3 At the noise of the tumult the people fled; at the lifting up of thyself the nations were scattered. 4 And your spoil shall be gathered *like* the gathering of the caterpiller: as the running to and fro of locusts shall he run upon them. 5 The LORD is exalted; for he dwelleth on high: he hath filled Zion with judgment and righteousness. 6 And wisdom and knowledge shall be the stability of thy times, *and* strength of salvation: the fear of the LORD *is* his treasure. 7 Behold, their valiant ones shall cry without: the ambas-	sadors of peace shall weep bitterly. 8 The highways lie waste, the wayfaring man ceaseth: he hath broken the covenant, he hath despised the cities, he regardeth no man. 9 The earth mourneth *and* languisheth: Lebanon is ashamed *and* hewn down: Sharon is like a wilderness; and Bashan and Carmel shake off *their fruits*. 10 Now will I rise, saith the LORD; now will I be exalted; now will I lift up myself. 11 Ye shall conceive chaff, ye shall bring forth stubble: your breath, *as* fire, shall devour you. 12 And the people shall be as the burnings of lime: *as* thorns cut up shall they be burned in the fire. 13 Hear, ye *that are* far off, what I have done; and, ye *that are* near, acknowledge my might. 14 The sinners in Zion are afraid; fearfulness hath surprised the hypocrites. Who among us shall dwell with the devouring fire? who among us shall dwell with everlasting burnings?	1) Soldiers & envoys will weep: As cities fall & peace fails 2) Highways will be deserted 3) Treaties will be broken & leaders despised 4) Life will be cheap 5) Crops & land will be ruined d. The description of the coming judgment on the destroyer (Assyria): Because they make bold, cruel plans 1) They will be nothing more than chaff & straw: Will be consumed 2) They will be thoroughly burned: As though burned to lime or set ablaze like dry cut thorn bushes e. The lesson of God's judgment 1) The world must acknowledge God's power 2) The hypocrites & godless will be stricken with fear: Terrorized by the eternal fire of God's judgment, Is.10:17; He.12:29

a. The pronouncement of God's Word is unquestionable. Destroyers and betrayers will reap exactly what they sow: they will be destroyed and betrayed. Who is the particular adversary to whom this *woe* is directed? Assyria. But keep in mind that Assyria represents all the evil, cruel nations and peoples of the earth. So the warning is directed equally to all who commit acts of violence and betrayal.

When the Assyrian ruler Sennacherib invaded Judah, King Hezekiah paid a huge ransom to buy off the Assyrians and secure peace with them. Sennacherib accepted the ransom and withdrew his forces, but only temporarily. He later betrayed Hezekiah, broke the peace agreement, and invaded Judah again. He destroyed all the cities and laid siege to Jerusalem (see outline and notes—2 K.18:13-37 for more discussion). This cruel tyrant betrayed those who had trusted his promise of peace, and for that he would suffer the retribution of God.

Sennacherib would reap exactly what he had sown. Isaiah announced that he would be betrayed and suffer a violent death. And he did. Soon after Sennacherib withdrew his army and returned to Nineveh, two of his own sons betrayed and assassinated him (Is.37:37-38). The violent king who had betrayed and slaughtered so many reaped exactly what he had sown.

b. When Assyria launched its invasion of Judah, a small number of righteous believers began to cry out to the LORD for help (vv.2-6). As the Assyrian army marched across Judah, conquering city after city, the situation looked more and more hopeless. Although Isaiah and the rest of the righteous continued to pray for deliverance, the Assyrian army marched right up to the gates of Jerusalem and set up a siege around the city that prevented anyone from escaping. The capital was doomed, and the Assyrians would treat its citizens just as brutally as they had the citizens of the other cities. They would either slaughter them or deport them to some foreign nation.

Despite the hopelessness of the situation, the true believers continued to seek the LORD for deliverance from their distress. Knowing that they were guilty of sin and undeserving of God's mercy, they nevertheless asked the LORD to shower His grace—His undeserved favor—upon them. They needed special strength to bear up under the daily strain and terror of the threatening Assyrians: thus day after day they asked the LORD to be their strength and their salvation. Isaiah listed three reasons why the small remnant of righteous believers should seek the LORD:

1) The remnant of righteous believers should pray because of the LORD's power (v.3). As the LORD God of the universe, He has the power to scatter any army who opposes Him or His people. All He has to do is speak, and the thunder of His voice will cause the enemy to flee for their lives. God's omnipotent power is far greater than the power of any man or nation. No matter how powerful a nation's military may be, the LORD can plunder, or strip it of its power as quickly as a swarm of locusts can strip a nation's crops. And that was exactly what happened to the Assyrian army when it besieged Jerusalem. The LORD Himself struck them. Thousands of them died; the rest retreated in panic and returned home. As the soldiers fled in terror from the hand of God's judgment, they abandoned all the wealth they had plundered. As a result, the surviving Jews swarmed down upon the Assyrian camp and recovered the wealth for themselves (see outline and notes—2 K.19:14-37; Is.37:14-38 for more discussion).

2) The remnant of righteous believers should pray because of the LORD's exaltation (vv.5-6). The LORD is exalted in the splendor of His glory and majesty, in the blazing light of His holiness. He is exalted far beyond what humans can imagine, higher than any creatures in any world or dimension of being. He lives in the spiritual world of heaven itself. Because of *who He is*, the day is coming when He will rule as LORD of the earth.

First, the LORD will establish His throne in Zion, the New Jerusalem, and He will rule on earth with justice and righteousness. Oppression, discrimination, greed, immorality—all acts of lawlessness and violence—will be erased throughout the world. Only the righteous will live on earth, and they will live in a world governed by God's laws. The LORD's justice and righteousness will reign on earth, for He is the exalted LORD of the universe.

Second, *in that day* the LORD Himself will be the stability of His people, the foundation upon which they stand. He Himself will be their salvation and security, wisdom and knowledge day by day. No longer will people lack understanding or be indecisive. No longer will they be ignorant of how they should live or of what steps they should take. They will be filled with the wisdom of God Himself and will know how to live and exactly what to do when problems confront them.

3) The remnant of righteous believers should pray because of the source of God's blessings: the fear of the LORD (v. 6b). When people truly seek the LORD in prayer, they demonstrate a *fear of the LORD*. The word *fear* means reverence, a deep-seated trust that acknowledges the LORD as the only living and true God who can answer prayer. When people truly fear the LORD, they possess a wonderful treasure, for the fear of the LORD assures them of the presence of God Himself. When God is present with His people, He blesses them and guides their every step. Thus prayer was the key to the Jews' deliverance from the Assyrian threat.

c. Seeing into the future made Isaiah's heart heavy, for he saw the grim devastation the Assyrians would cause. Remember that God was allowing the Assyrian invasion because of the Jews' terrible sins and unbelief. Their peace treaty with Egypt crumbled, for it was an alliance with unbelievers (30:1-14). Isaiah says that Judah's soldiers and envoys would weep openly as the nation's cities fell. No doubt the diplomats who had carried on negotiations with the Assyrian ambassadors would be among the weeping envoys mentioned here (36:2-22).

d. Once the Assyrians launched their invasion of Judah, the highways would be deserted. Because of the danger, the people would be too afraid to travel. When Egypt broke the treaty with Judah, the people would despise their leaders for bringing this destruction upon them. The cruel Assyrians had no regard for human life and would slaughter thousands. Furthermore, they would deliberately ravage the land (v.9). Once the Assyrian war machine struck, no matter where people looked, they would see only the sad, tragic spectacle of devastation. No longer would Lebanon be a land of beautiful mountains and forests, or Sharon a fertile land, or the fields of Bashan and Carmel fruitful. The Assyrian army would utterly devastate all these lands.

e. But the day of atrocities would come to an end, for the LORD Himself would execute judgment on the Assyrians (vv.10-12). The violent *destroyer* and *betrayer* will be destroyed (see v.1). Although Assyria had dreams of grandeur and plans for world conquest, their dreams and plans were nothing more than chaff. When the LORD rose against them, He would consume their dreams and plans as quickly as fire consumes straw. He would set the cruel Assyrians ablaze. Note this fact: God's judgment would be like an intense fire that would burn them until there was nothing left but lime, or dust, and it would burn them as quickly as if He were burning cut, dried thornbushes. God's judgment upon the Assyrian army was just as Isaiah predicted, thorough and quick. During one night's time, probably within a few minutes, the angel of the LORD appeared in the Assyrian camp surrounding Jerusalem and slew 185,000 soldiers. When the surviving soldiers arose the next morning and saw all the dead bodies lying around, they fled for their lives, bewildered and terrified (37:36-37).

God's judgment is to teach a lesson (vv.13-14), one that all people—both far and near—must heed. Throughout history the LORD's judgment has fallen upon the Assyrians, the Jews, and other nations of the world for a very specific purpose: so they would acknowledge His power. The LORD is the Creator and Sovereign of the universe; therefore, all must acknowledge Him as the LORD God, the only living and true God. Even the sinners in Zion—the hypocrites who profess the LORD but live wickedly—must tremble in fear before Him. The LORD is a consuming fire (Is.10:17; He.12:29); no person can stand in the presence of His blazing holiness. Therefore, God's presence and His coming judgment should terrify all hypocrites.

Thought 1. God's judgment is sure. It is definitely coming. Nothing can stop His hand of judgment from falling upon earth. His day of judgment is fixed, already determined and set. When that day and hour come, Christ will rend the skies above and strike this earth in judgment. Every one of us will face the wrath of God, and the LORD will be unwavering in executing judgment against us unless we have accepted His Son, the Lord Jesus Christ, and been forgiven our sins.

"When the Son of man shall come in his glory, and all the holy angels with him, then shall he sit upon the throne of his glory: And before him shall be gathered all nations: and he shall separate them one from another, as a shepherd divideth *his* sheep from the goats: And he shall set the sheep on his right hand, but the goats on the left...Then shall he say also unto them on the left hand, Depart from me, ye cursed, into everlasting fire, prepared for the devil and his angels" (Mt.25:31-33, 41).

"And there shall be signs in the sun, and in the moon, and in the stars; and upon the earth distress of nations, with perplexity; the sea and the waves roaring; Men's hearts failing them for fear, and for looking after those things which are coming on the earth: for the powers of heaven shall be shaken. And then shall they see the Son of man coming in a cloud with power and great glory. And when these things begin to come to pass, then look up, and lift up your heads; for your redemption draweth nigh" (Lu.21:25-28).

"And to you who are troubled rest with us, when the Lord Jesus shall be revealed from heaven with his mighty angels, In flaming fire taking vengeance on them that know not God, and that obey not the gospel of our Lord Jesus Christ" (2 Th.1:7-8).

"The Lord knoweth how to deliver the godly out of temptations, and to reserve the unjust unto the day of judgment to be punished" (2 Pe.2:9).

"But the heavens and the earth, which are now, by the same word are kept in store, reserved unto fire against the day of judgment and perdition of ungodly men. But, beloved, be not ignorant of this one thing, that one day *is* with the Lord as a thousand years, and a thousand years as one day. The Lord is not slack concerning his promise, as some men count slackness; but is longsuffering to us-ward, not willing that any should perish, but that all should come to repentance. But the day of the Lord will come as a thief in the night; in the which the heavens shall pass away with a great noise, and the elements shall melt with fervent heat, the earth also and the works that are therein shall be burned up" (2 Pe.3:7-10).

"And Enoch also, the seventh from Adam, prophesied of these, saying, Behold, the Lord cometh with ten thousands of his saints, To execute judgment upon all, and to convince all that are ungodly among them of all their ungodly deeds which they have ungodly committed, and of all their hard *speeches* which ungodly sinners have spoken against him" (Jude 1:14-15).

"Behold, he cometh with clouds; and every eye shall see him, and they *also* which pierced him: and all kindreds of the earth shall wail because of him. Even so, Amen" (Re.1:7).

2 (33:15-24) **Kingdom, of Messiah, Blessings of—Deliverance, Surety of, for the Righteous—Righteous, the, Traits of; Blessings of—Blessings, of the Righteous, in Messiah's Kingdom—Millennium, Blessings of**: God gave a strong promise to the righteous of the earth, those who truly believe in the LORD and follow Him: He will deliver them from the violent oppressors and betrayers of earth. A glorious day of salvation is coming for God's people, a day when the Messiah will set up His kingdom on earth and rule in righteousness. Isaiah painted a graphic picture of what life will be like in the Messiah's kingdom. Although *some* of what he described could possibly apply to the Jews after the withdrawal of the Assyrian forces, most of his description could not apply to life in a corruptible world. Thus, Isaiah is definitely describing the future kingdom of the Messiah.

OUTLINE	SCRIPTURE	SCRIPTURE	OUTLINE
2. The surety of God's deliverance of the righteous: A picture of the Messiah's kingdom	15 He that walketh righteously, and speaketh uprightly; he that despiseth the gain of oppressions, that shaketh his hands from holding of bribes, that stoppeth his ears from hearing of blood, and shut-	teth his eyes from seeing evil;	4) Because he shuts his eyes to evil
a. The righteous delivered		16 He shall dwell on high: his place of defence *shall be* the munitions of rocks: bread shall be given him; his waters *shall be* sure.	b. The righteous blessed
1) Because he speaks the truth			1) The righteous will dwell on high, live with the LORD
2) Because he takes no part in extortion or bribes			2) The righteous will be secure & fed, need nothing
3) Because he does not murder		17 Thine eyes shall see the	3) The righteous will see the

ISAIAH 33:1-24

OUTLINE	SCRIPTURE	SCRIPTURE	OUTLINE
king, the LORD in His glory, ruling over all the land 4) The righteous will be freed from the terror of oppressors & destroyers, (know universal peace) • The evil military officers & political leaders • The arrogant of the earth (symbolized in the Assyrians) 5) The righteous will see Jerusalem as the center of worship, a secure & peaceful place to live • It will never be moved, unlike a tent: A permanent place	king in his beauty: they shall behold the land that is very far off. 18 Thine heart shall meditate terror. Where is the scribe? where is the receiver? where is he that counted the towers? 19 Thou shalt not see a fierce people, a people of a deeper speech than thou canst perceive; of a stammering tongue, *that thou canst* not understand. 20 Look upon Zion, the city of our solemnities: thine eyes shall see Jerusalem a quiet habitation, a tabernacle *that* shall not be taken down; not one of the stakes thereof shall ever be removed, neither shall any of the cords thereof	be broken. 21 But there the glorious LORD *will be* unto us a place of broad rivers *and* streams; wherein shall go no galley with oars, neither shall gallant ship pass thereby. 22 For the LORD *is* our judge, the LORD *is* our lawgiver, the LORD *is* our king; he will save us. 23 Thy tacklings are loosed; they could not well strengthen their mast, they could not spread the sail: then is the prey of a great spoil divided; the lame take the prey. 24 And the inhabitant shall not say, I am sick: the people that dwell therein *shall be* forgiven *their* iniquity.	• It will be ruled over by the LORD Himself—in all His glory • It will be defended by the LORD Himself: Given undisturbed peace 6) The righteous will be governed by the LORD: *Our* Judge, *our* Lawgiver, *our* King 7) The righteous will be brought through the storm of life, even death itself—despite almost sinking 8) The righteous will be given the enemy's spoils, his wealth & possessions 9) The righteous will never again be sick 10) The righteous will be forgiven all sin

a. The citizens of the kingdom will be the righteous of this earth (v.15). Only the righteous will be delivered from the tyranny of those who persecute God's people. Who are the righteous? Isaiah leaves no doubt about their identity. They are the people who believe and follow the LORD and walk uprightly before Him. They obey God's commandments, His Holy Word. Specifically, the righteous...
• speak the truth, never lying to or deceiving people
• do not seek gain through oppression or extortion and do not accept bribes
• refuse to listen to or take part in plots of murder or any other evil act that would harm people
• shut their eyes to all the seductions and enticements to do evil

God will greatly bless people who truly believe the LORD, who walk righteously day by day and seek to follow the commandments of God. Isaiah spelled out eleven very specific blessings. These blessings describe what life will be like when Christ returns to establish God's kingdom on earth.
1) The righteous will dwell on high with the LORD Himself (v.16). "On high" means the place where God lives, the place of His residence or dwelling. Once Christ returns to earth, righteous believers will live with Him forever. They will never again be separated from Him. This is one of God's great promises to righteous believers:

"Let not your heart be troubled: ye believe in God, believe also in me. In my Father's house are many mansions: if *it were* not so, I would have told you. I go to prepare a place for you. And if I go and prepare a place for you, I will come again, and receive you unto myself; that where I am, *there* ye may be also" (Jn.14:1-3).
"For our conversation [citizenship] is in heaven; from whence also we look for the Saviour, the Lord Jesus Christ: Who shall change our vile body, that it may be fashioned like unto his glorious body, according to the working whereby he is able even to subdue all things unto himself" (Ph.3:20-21).
"Blessed *be* the God and Father of our Lord Jesus Christ, which according to his abundant mercy hath begotten us again unto a lively hope by the resurrection of Jesus Christ from the dead, To an inheritance incorruptible, and undefiled, and that fadeth not away, reserved in heaven for you" (1 Pe.1:3-4).
"And there shall in no wise enter into it [New Jerusalem] any thing that defileth, neither *whatsoever* worketh abomination, or *maketh* a lie: but they which are written in the Lamb's book of life" (Re.21:27).

2) The righteous will be secure and well fed, lacking nothing (v.16). All necessities of life will be met with an inexhaustible supply of provisions to meet every need. Furthermore, the Messiah's kingdom will be a refuge providing perfect security, a place far more secure than a mountain fortress. This is God's wonderful promise to righteous believers:

"But seek ye first the kingdom of God, and his righteousness; and all these things shall be added unto you" (Mt.6:33).
"I can do all things through Christ which strengtheneth me" (Ph.4:13).
"For we have not an high priest which cannot be touched with the feeling of our infirmities; but was in all points tempted like as *we are,* yet without sin. Let us therefore come boldly unto the throne of grace, that we may obtain mercy, and find grace to help in time of need" (He.4:15-16).

"The LORD *is* my rock, and my fortress, and my deliverer; my God, my strength, in whom I will trust; my buckler, and the horn of my salvation, *and* my high tower" (Ps.18:2).

"As the mountains *are* round about Jerusalem, so the LORD *is* round about his people from henceforth even for ever" (Ps.125:2).

"*Oh* how great *is* thy goodness, which thou hast laid up for them that fear thee; *which* thou hast wrought for them that trust in thee before the sons of men! Thou shalt hide them in the secret of thy presence from the pride of man: thou shalt keep them secretly in a pavilion from the strife of tongues. Blessed *be* the LORD: for he hath showed me his marvellous kindness in a strong city" (Ps.31:19-21).

3) The righteous will see the King, the LORD, in all His glory and splendor. They will live with Him as He rules over all the land that stretches across the face of the earth (v.17; also see v.22; Mt.5:8). Righteous believers could have no greater privilege than to see the LORD face-to-face and to be allowed to live with, worship, and serve Him. This is one of the great promises God gives the righteous:

"Blessed *are* the pure in heart: for they shall see God" (Mt.5:8).

"Beloved, now are we the sons of God, and it doth not yet appear what we shall be: but we know that, when he shall appear, we shall be like him; for we shall see him as he is. And every man that hath this hope in him purifieth himself, even as he is pure" (1 Jn.3:2-3).

"As for me, I will behold thy face in righteousness: I shall be satisfied, when I awake, with thy likeness" (Ps.17:15).

"Thine eyes shall see the king in his beauty: they shall behold the land that is very far off" (Is.33:17).

"Father, I will that they also, whom thou hast given me, be with me where I am; that they may behold my glory, which thou hast given me: for thou lovedst me before the foundation of the world" (Jn.17:24).

"For now we see through a glass, darkly; but then face to face: now I know in part; but then shall I know even as also I am known" (1 Co.13:12).

"And there shall be no more curse: but the throne of God and of the Lamb shall be in it [New Jerusalem]; and his servants shall serve him: And they shall see his face; and his name *shall be* in their foreheads" (Re.22:3-4).

"And while they looked stedfastly toward heaven as he went up, behold, two men stood by them in white apparel; Which also said, Ye men of Galilee, why stand ye gazing up into heaven? this same Jesus, which is taken up from you into heaven, shall so come in like manner as ye have seen him go into heaven" (Ac.1:10-11).

"According to my earnest expectation and *my* hope, that in nothing I shall be ashamed, but *that* with all boldness, as always, *so* now also Christ shall be magnified in my body, whether *it be* by life, or by death. For to me to live *is* Christ, and to die *is* gain" (Ph.1:20-21).

"For the Lord himself shall descend from heaven with a shout, with the voice of the archangel, and with the trump of God: and the dead in Christ shall rise first: Then we which are alive *and* remain shall be caught up together with them in the clouds, to meet the Lord in the air: and so shall we ever be with the Lord. Wherefore comfort one another with these words" (1 Th.4:16-18).

4) The righteous will be forever free from the terror of oppressors and destroyers (vv.18-19). Universal peace will sweep the earth because of the government of the Messiah. The righteous will remember the terror of evil military officers and political leaders, but those evil, arrogant people will no longer be present to oppress them. Note that Isaiah contrasted the terror of the Assyrian siege with the universal peace that will exist in the Messiah's kingdom. In His kingdom, officers will no longer plot to attack the towers of the city or estimate how much wealth they can plunder after they conquer it. No longer will foreign invaders speak in a strange, unknown language. The LORD will remove all evil oppressors from the earth, and there will finally be universal peace.

"He maketh wars to cease unto the end of the earth; he breaketh the bow, and cutteth the spear in sunder; he burneth the chariot in the fire" (Ps.46:9).

"And he shall judge among the nations, and shall rebuke many people: and they shall beat their swords into plowshares, and their spears into pruninghooks: nation shall not lift up sword against nation, neither shall they learn war any more" (Is.2:4).

"Of the increase of *his* government and peace *there shall be* no end, upon the throne of David, and upon his kingdom, to order it, and to establish it with judgment and with justice from henceforth even for ever. The zeal of the LORD of hosts will perform this" (Is.9:7).

"They shall not hurt nor destroy in all my holy mountain: for the earth shall be full of the knowledge of the LORD, as the waters cover the sea" (Is.11:9).

"But they shall sit every man under his vine and under his fig tree; and none shall make *them* afraid: for the mouth of the LORD of hosts hath spoken *it*" (Mi.4:4).

"And I will cut off the chariot from Ephraim, and the horse from Jerusalem, and the battle bow shall be cut off: and he shall speak peace unto the heathen: and his dominion *shall be* from sea *even* to sea, and from river *even* to the ends of the earth" (Zec.9:10).

5) The righteous will worship in Jerusalem, which will be a secure, quiet, and peaceful place (vv.20-21). Jerusalem will be a center of worship, not a center of terrorist attacks or war. It will never again know trouble or unrest.

During the Messiah's reign, peace will blanket the city like a tent whose stakes cannot be pulled up nor any of its ropes cut or moved. The LORD Himself, the Mighty One, will rule over the city, and He will be like a wide river that protects the city from all enemies (v.21). Peace and protection are two of the great promises the LORD gives to righteous believers.

"But there shall not an hair of your head perish" (Lu.21:18).
"Peace I leave with you, my peace I give unto you: not as the world giveth, give I unto you. Let not your heart be troubled, neither let it be afraid" (Jn.14:27).
"These things I have spoken unto you, that in me ye might have peace. In the world ye shall have tribulation: but be of good cheer; I have overcome the world" (Jn.16:33).
"Then *cometh* the end, when he shall have delivered up the kingdom to God, even the Father; when he shall have put down all rule and all authority and power. For he must reign, till he hath put all enemies under his feet" (1 Co.15:24-25).
"Be careful for nothing; but in every thing by prayer and supplication with thanksgiving let your requests be made known unto God. And the peace of God, which passeth all understanding, shall keep your hearts and minds through Christ Jesus" (Ph.4:6-7).
"As the mountains *are* round about Jerusalem, so the LORD *is* round about his people from henceforth even for ever" (Ps.125:2).

6) The LORD will govern the righteous, for He is our Judge, Lawgiver, and King (v.22). It is He and He alone who will save us. As our Judge, the LORD will accept us into His kingdom if we have truly trusted Him and lived righteous lives. As our Lawgiver, the LORD expects us to obey His holy commandments and live under His government. As our King, He expects us to serve Him by working diligently and making the greatest contribution we can to His kingdom. Note that all the functions of government are covered in this threefold title of the LORD: the judicial, the legislative, and the executive.[1]
7) The righteous will be brought through the storm of life despite almost sinking (v.23). Life is so fragile that it is like a sailboat caught in a severe storm—its riggings hanging loose, its masts insecure, and its sail not yet spread—ready to sink at any moment. But the LORD will save the righteous from the storms of life and usher them into His wonderful kingdom.

"And Jesus said unto him, Verily I say unto thee, To day shalt thou be with me in paradise" (Lu.23:43).
"If any man serve me, let him follow me; and where I am, there shall also my servant be: if any man serve me, him will *my* Father honour" (Jn.12:26).
"In my Father's house are many mansions: if *it were* not so, I would have told you. I go to prepare a place for you. And if I go and prepare a place for you, I will come again, and receive you unto myself; that where I am, *there* ye may be also" (Jn.14:2-3).
"For the Lord himself shall descend from heaven with a shout, with the voice of the archangel, and with the trump of God: and the dead in Christ shall rise first: Then we which are alive *and* remain shall be caught up together with them in the clouds, to meet the Lord in the air: and so shall we ever be with the Lord" (1 Th.4:16-17).
"And the Lord shall deliver me from every evil work, and will preserve *me* unto his heavenly kingdom: to whom *be* glory for ever and ever. Amen" (2 Ti.4:18).
"Thou shalt guide me with thy counsel, and afterward receive me *to* glory" (Ps.73:24).

8) The righteous will receive the spoils—the wealth and possessions—of their enemies (v.23). Just as the Jews recovered all the plunder the Assyrian army left behind when the soldiers fled, so believers will inherit all the riches of both heaven and earth. This is the wonderful promise of the LORD.

"But lay up for yourselves treasures in heaven, where neither moth nor rust doth corrupt, and where thieves do not break through nor steal" (Mt.6:20).
"Whether Paul, or Apollos, or Cephas, or the world, or life, or death, or things present, or things to come; all are yours" (1 Co.3:22).
"By faith Moses, when he was come to years, refused to be called the son of Pharaoh's daughter; Choosing rather to suffer affliction with the people of God, than to enjoy the pleasures of sin for a season; Esteeming the reproach of Christ greater riches than the treasures in Egypt: for he had respect unto the recompence of the reward" (He.11:24-26).
"Hearken, my beloved brethren, Hath not God chosen the poor of this world rich in faith, and heirs of the kingdom which he hath promised to them that love him?" (Js.2:5).
"I counsel thee to buy of me gold tried in the fire, that thou mayest be rich; and white raiment, that thou mayest be clothed, and *that* the shame of thy nakedness do not appear; and anoint thine eyes with eyesalve, that thou mayest see" (Re.3:18).
"I have seen his ways, and will heal him: I will lead him also, and restore comforts unto him and to his mourners. I create the fruit of the lips; Peace, peace to *him that is* far off, and to *him that is* near, saith the LORD; and I will heal him" (Is.57:18-19).

---

1 *The New Scofield Reference Bible.* Edited by C.I. Scofield. (New York, NY: Oxford University Press, 1967), Isaiah 33:22.

"Then shall thy light break forth as the morning, and thine health shall spring forth speedily: and thy righteousness shall go before thee; the glory of the LORD shall be thy rereward" (Is.58:8).

"Behold, I will bring it health and cure, and I will cure them, and will reveal unto them the abundance of peace and truth" (Je.33:6).

9) The righteous will never again be sick or unhealthy (v.24). The LORD will do away with all disease and sickness when He establishes His kingdom on earth. No longer will the righteous shed tears due to sickness and disease.

"For the Lamb which is in the midst of the throne shall feed them, and shall lead them unto living fountains of waters: and God shall wipe away all tears from their eyes" (Re.7:17).

"And God shall wipe away all tears from their eyes; and there shall be no more death, neither sorrow, nor crying, neither shall there be any more pain: for the former things are passed away" (Re.21:4).

"He will swallow up death in victory; and the Lord GOD will wipe away tears from off all faces; and the rebuke of his people shall he take away from off all the earth: for the LORD hath spoken *it*" (Is.25:8).

"Therefore the redeemed of the LORD shall return, and come with singing unto Zion; and everlasting joy *shall be* upon their head: they shall obtain gladness and joy; *and* sorrow and mourning shall flee away" (Is.51:11).

"Thy sun shall no more go down; neither shall thy moon withdraw itself: for the LORD shall be thine everlasting light, and the days of thy mourning shall be ended" (Is.60:20).

"And I will rejoice in Jerusalem, and joy in my people: and the voice of weeping shall be no more heard in her, nor the voice of crying. There shall be no more thence an infant of days, nor an old man that hath not filled his days: for the child shall die an hundred years old; but the sinner *being* an hundred years old shall be accursed" (Is.65:19-20).

"Therefore they shall come and sing in the height of Zion, and shall flow together to the goodness of the LORD, for wheat, and for wine, and for oil, and for the young of the flock and of the herd: and their soul shall be as a watered garden; and they shall not sorrow any more at all" (Je.31:12).

10) The righteous will be forgiven all their sins in the Messiah's kingdom. All the citizens of His kingdom will be cleansed from every evil thought that has crossed their minds and from every sinful act they have ever committed. They will be counted righteous and accepted by the Lord.

"And said unto them, Thus it is written, and thus it behoved Christ to suffer, and to rise from the dead the third day: And that repentance and remission of sins should be preached in his name among all nations, beginning at Jerusalem" (Lu.24:46-47).

"Be it known unto you therefore, men *and* brethren, that through this man is preached unto you the forgiveness of sins" (Ac.13:38).

"The God of our fathers raised up Jesus, whom ye slew and hanged on a tree. Him hath God exalted with his right hand *to be* a Prince and a Saviour, for to give repentance to Israel, and forgiveness of sins. And we are his witnesses of these things; and *so is* also the Holy Ghost, whom God hath given to them that obey him" (Ac.5:30-32).

"*There is* therefore now no condemnation to them which are in Christ Jesus, who walk not after the flesh, but after the Spirit [in the righteousness of Christ]" (Ro.8:1).

"In whom we have redemption through his blood, the forgiveness of sins, according to the riches of his grace" (Ep.1:7).

"If we confess our sins, he is faithful and just to forgive us *our* sins, and to cleanse us from all unrighteousness" (1 Jn.1:9).

"Let the wicked forsake his way, and the unrighteous man his thoughts: and let him return unto the LORD, and he will have mercy upon him; and to our God, for he will abundantly pardon" (Is.55:7).

"And they shall teach no more every man his neighbour, and every man his brother, saying, Know the LORD: for they shall all know me, from the least of them unto the greatest of them, saith the LORD; for I will forgive their iniquity, and I will remember their sin no more" (Je.31:34).

"And I will cleanse them from all their iniquity, whereby they have sinned against me; and I will pardon all their iniquities, whereby they have sinned, and whereby they have transgressed against me" (Je.33:8).

"It may be that the house of Judah will hear all the evil which I purpose to do unto them; that they may return every man from his evil way; that I may forgive their iniquity and their sin" (Je.36:3).

"In those days, and in that time, saith the LORD, the iniquity of Israel shall be sought for, and *there shall be* none; and the sins of Judah, and they shall not be found: for I will pardon them whom I reserve" (Je.50:20).

CHAPTER 34

F. Woe—A Strong Warning & a Glorious Promise to the Whole World: The LORD's Day of Wrath & His Coming Kingdom, 34:1–35:10

1. God's warning of a final judgment on this sinful, corrupt world: His day of wrath

a. The summons to the whole world: Hear the warning
1) It will be a day of the LORD's anger: He will destroy all nations & armies, (see outline on Armageddon, 63:1-6; Re.19:11-21)
2) It will be a day of horrifying death
   • Bodies will stink, lie unburied
   • Blood will soak the ground
3) It will be a day of catastrophic events in the sky, Joel 2:10, 30-31; 3:15; Ze. 14:6-7; Mt.24:29; 2 Pe.3:8-14; Re.6:12-14; 21:1
   • The heavens will melt
   • The stars will fall like leaves or shriveled figs

b. The coming wrath on all nations: Seen in the example of Edom, 63:1-6
1) The people will be cursed, doomed—totally destroyed
   • As lambs & goats are sacrificed, so the common citizens of the nation will be slain

   • As wild oxen & bulls are slaughtered, so the strong supporters & leaders of the nation(s) will be slain

2) The LORD's purpose will be executed—justice in behalf of Zion, His people
3) The land will be utterly devastated—just as Sodom & Gomorrah were, Ge.19:23-26
   • Waters will be polluted
   • Land will be set ablaze & ruined forever
   • Land will lie desolate, never again to be inhabited by people

Come near, ye nations, to hear; and hearken, ye people: let the earth hear, and all that is therein; the world, and all things that come forth of it.
2 For the indignation of the LORD *is* upon all nations, and *his* fury upon all their armies: he hath utterly destroyed them, he hath delivered them to the slaughter.
3 Their slain also shall be cast out, and their stink shall come up out of their carcases, and the mountains shall be melted with their blood.
4 And all the host of heaven shall be dissolved, and the heavens shall be rolled together as a scroll: and all their host shall fall down, as the leaf falleth off from the vine, and as a falling *fig* from the fig tree.
5 For my sword shall be bathed in heaven: behold, it shall come down upon Idumea, and upon the people of my curse, to judgment.
6 The sword of the LORD is filled with blood, it is made fat with fatness, *and* with the blood of lambs and goats, with the fat of the kidneys of rams: for the LORD hath a sacrifice in Bozrah, and a great slaughter in the land of Idumea.
7 And the unicorns shall come down with them, and the bullocks with the bulls; and their land shall be soaked with blood, and their dust made fat with fatness.
8 For *it is* the day of the LORD's vengeance, *and* the year of recompences for the controversy of Zion.
9 And the streams thereof shall be turned into pitch, and the dust thereof into brimstone, and the land thereof shall become burning pitch.
10 It shall not be quenched night nor day; the smoke thereof shall go up for ever: from generation to generation it shall lie waste; none shall pass through it for ever and ever.

11 But the cormorant and the bittern shall possess it; the owl also and the raven shall dwell in it: and he shall stretch out upon it the line of confusion, and the stones of emptiness.
12 They shall call the nobles thereof to the kingdom, but none *shall be* there, and all her princes shall be nothing.
13 And thorns shall come up in her palaces, nettles and brambles in the fortresses thereof: and it shall be an habitation of dragons, *and a* court for owls.
14 The wild beasts of the desert shall also meet with the wild beasts of the island, and the satyr shall cry to his fellow; the screech owl also shall rest there, and find for herself a place of rest.
15 There shall the great owl make her nest, and lay, and hatch, and gather under her shadow: there shall the vultures also be gathered, every one with her mate.
16 Seek ye out of the book of the LORD, and read: no one of these shall fail, none shall want her mate: for my mouth it hath commanded, and his spirit it hath gathered them.
17 And he hath cast the lot for them, and his hand hath divided it unto them by line: they shall possess it for ever, from generation to generation shall they dwell therein.

CHAPTER 35

The wilderness and the solitary place shall be glad for them; and the desert shall rejoice, and blossom as the rose.
2 It shall blossom abundantly, and rejoice even with joy and singing: the glory of Lebanon shall be given unto it, the excellency of Carmel and Sharon, they shall see the glory of the LORD, *and* the excellency of our God.
3 Strengthen ye the weak hands, and confirm the feeble knees.
4 Say to them *that are* of a fearful heart, Be strong, fear not: behold, your God will come *with* vengeance, *even* God *with* a recompence; he will come and save you.
5 Then the eyes of the blind shall be opened, and the ears

   • Only inhabitants will be wild animals
   • Chaos & emptiness will be sealed: By the measurement of God's justice
   • Kingdom (government) & leaders will be gone

   • Palaces, fortresses, cities—all military defenses & strongholds—will be overgrown by thorns & overrun by wild animals

c. The surety of the coming wrath: The *book of the LORD* declares it
1) God has declared the coming wrath & will execute it by His Spirit
2) God will judge Edom: Give the land to wild animals forever

2. God's promise of a glorious future for this world: His coming kingdom of perfection & joy

a. The land will be restored: The desert & parched land will undergo a dramatic change, will blossom & rejoice, Ps.55:12-13; 96:11-13; 98:7-9; Ro.8:19-22
b. The glory & splendor of God will be seen
c. The guarantee of God's salvation will be given to weak & fearful believers
1) To be strong
2) To be assured: The LORD will come to execute justice & to save believers

d. The disabled believers will be healed, restored to health

OUTLINE	SCRIPTURE	SCRIPTURE	OUTLINE
1) The blind & deaf 2) The crippled & mute e. The parched land will be changed into well-watered, fertile soil 1) Water will flow in the wilderness & desert 2) Pools will replace desert sand & springs will bubble up out of thirsty ground 3) Vegetation will grow on the once ruined land f. The kingdom will have a very special highway: Named *The Way of Holiness*	of the deaf shall be unstopped. 6 Then shall the lame *man* leap as an hart, and the tongue of the dumb sing: for in the wilderness shall waters break out, and streams in the desert. 7 And the parched ground shall become a pool, and the thirsty land springs of water: in the habitation of dragons, where each lay, *shall be* grass with reeds and rushes. 8 And an highway shall be there, and a way, and it shall be called The way of holi-	ness; the unclean shall not pass over it; but it *shall be* for those: the wayfaring men, though fools, shall not err *therein.* 9 No lion shall be there, nor *any* ravenous beast shall go up thereon, it shall not be found there; but the redeemed shall walk *there:* 10 And the ransomed of the LORD shall return, and come to Zion with songs and everlasting joy upon their heads: they shall obtain joy and gladness, and sorrow and sighing shall flee away.	1) Its travelers: No unclean or wicked person, only those who follow God 2) Its safety • No wild beast will be a threat • No thief will travel on the highway, only the redeemed 3) Its purpose • To be the road for the ransomed to return to the LORD • To be the road leading to Zion, where people will worship God

DIVISION III

THE PROPHECIES OF WOE: GOD'S WARNING TO HIS PEOPLE, 28:1–35:10

F. Woe—A Strong Warning and a Glorious Promise to the Whole World: The LORD's Day of Wrath and His Coming Kingdom, 34:1–35:10

(34:1–35:10) **Introduction**: warnings that notify us of some danger or evil are absolutely essential in life. Warnings can range all the way from minor cautions (Step Down Please) to notification of a life-threatening danger (Caution: Live Electrical Wires). To prevent catastrophic results, people have devised all kinds of warning signals. Fire alarms, house alarms, car alarms, S.O.S. signals, distress signals, and Mayday alerts have all been devised to protect us from imminent danger.

On the other hand, there are many encouraging signs in life. Picture the millions of travelers on the highways and byways across the nation. When we are running low on fuel and see a road sign for gas one mile away, we feel blessed. When we are thirsty or hungry and spot a listing of restaurants up ahead, we feel energized. When we are too weary to travel on and spot a hotel billboard, we are relieved. And when we finally arrive at our destination due to a good map and accurate road markers, we are excited and feel a sense of accomplishment. At that point, we consider that the journey was worthwhile.

In the present Scripture the LORD issues a strong warning to the whole world (28:1-35:10). This warning is the climactic close to the *woes*, the strong warnings to the various nations of the earth. But it is also a glorious promise of the LORD's coming kingdom, a promise to all who *travel* the *highway of holiness*. This is, *Woe—A Strong Warning and a Glorious Promise to the Whole World: The LORD's Day of Wrath and His Coming Kingdom*, 34:1–35:10.

    1. God's warning of a final judgment on this sinful, corrupt world: His day of wrath (34:1-17).
    2. God's promise of a glorious future for this world: His coming kingdom of perfection and joy (35:1-10).

1 (34:1-17) **World, Judgment of, in the End Time—Judgment, of the World, in the End Time—Wrath, Day of, Predicted—God, Wrath of, in the End Time—Judgment, in the End Time, Catastrophic Events—End Times, Judgment During, Catastrophic Events—Armageddon, Predicted**: God *issued* a stunning warning to all people and all nations of the earth: a day of final judgment is coming on this sinful, corrupt world. Due to people's ungodliness and unrighteousness and the seed of corruption within nature, God's wrath is to be poured out upon the earth. What follows is a shocking, graphic description of the last days of human history in this wicked and depraved world:

OUTLINE	SCRIPTURE	SCRIPTURE	OUTLINE
1. God's warning of a final judgment on this sinful, corrupt world: His day of wrath a. The summons to the whole world: Hear the warning 1) It will be a day of the LORD's anger: He will destroy all nations & armies, (see outline of Armageddon, 63:1-6; Re.19:11-21) 2) It will be a day of horrifying death • Bodies will stink, lie	Come near, ye nations, to hear; and hearken, ye people: let the earth hear, and all that is therein; the world, and all things that come forth of it. 2 For the indignation of the LORD *is* upon all nations, and *his* fury upon all their armies: he hath utterly destroyed them, he hath delivered them to the slaughter. 3 Their slain also shall be cast out, and their stink shall come up out of their	carcases, and the mountains shall be melted with their blood. 4 And all the host of heaven shall be dissolved, and the heavens shall be rolled together as a scroll: and all their host shall fall down, as the leaf falleth off from the vine, and as a falling *fig* from the fig tree. 5 For my sword shall be bathed in heaven: behold, it shall come down upon	unburied • Blood will soak the ground 3) It will be a day of catastrophic events in the sky, Joel 2:10, 30-31; 3:15; Ze.14:6-7; Mt.24:29; 2 Pe.3:8-14; Re.6:12-14 • The heavens will melt • The stars will fall like leaves or shriveled figs b. The coming wrath on all nations: Seen in the example of Edom, 63:1-6

291

OUTLINE	SCRIPTURE	SCRIPTURE	OUTLINE
1) The people will be cursed, doomed—totally destroyed • As lambs & goats are sacrificed, so the common citizens of the nation will be slain • As wild oxen & bulls are slaughtered, so the strong supporters & leaders of the nation(s) will be slain 2) The LORD's purpose will be executed—justice in behalf of Zion, His people 3) The land will be utterly devastated—just as Sodom & Gomorrah were, Ge.19:23-26 • Waters will be polluted • Land will be set ablaze & ruined forever • Land will lie desolate, never again to be inhabited by people • Only inhabitants will be wild animals • Chaos & emptiness will be sealed: By the measurement of God's	Idumea, and upon the people of my curse, to judgment. 6 The sword of the LORD is filled with blood, it is made fat with fatness, *and* with the blood of lambs and goats, with the fat of the kidneys of rams: for the LORD hath a sacrifice in Bozrah, and a great slaughter in the land of Idumea. 7 And the unicorns shall come down with them, and the bullocks with the bulls; and their land shall be soaked with blood, and their dust made fat with fatness. 8 For *it is* the day of the LORD'S vengeance, *and* the year of recompences for the controversy of Zion. 9 And the streams thereof shall be turned into pitch, and the dust thereof into brimstone, and the land thereof shall become burning pitch. 10 It shall not be quenched night nor day; the smoke thereof shall go up for ever: from generation to generation it shall lie waste; none shall pass through it for ever and ever. 11 But the cormorant and the bittern shall possess it; the owl also and the raven shall dwell in it: and he shall stretch out upon it the line of	confusion, and the stones of emptiness. 12 They shall call the nobles thereof to the kingdom, but none *shall be* there, and all her princes shall be nothing. 13 And thorns shall come up in her palaces, nettles and brambles in the fortresses thereof: and it shall be an habitation of dragons, *and* a court for owls. 14 The wild beasts of the desert shall also meet with the wild beasts of the island, and the satyr shall cry to his fellow; the screech owl also shall rest there, and find for herself a place of rest. 15 There shall the great owl make her nest, and lay, and hatch, and gather under her shadow: there shall the vultures also be gathered, every one with her mate. 16 Seek ye out of the book of the LORD, and read: no one of these shall fail, none shall want her mate: for my mouth it hath commanded, and his spirit it hath gathered them. 17 And he hath cast the lot for them, and his hand hath divided it unto them by line: they shall possess it for ever, from generation to generation shall they dwell therein.	justice • Kingdom (government) & leaders will be gone • Palaces, fortresses, cities—all military defenses & strongholds—will be overgrown by thorns & overrun by wild animals c. The surety of the coming wrath: The *book of the LORD* declares it 1) God has declared the coming wrath & will execute it by His Spirit 2) God will judge Edom: Give the land to wild animals forever

a. God summons the whole world to listen to His warning of the coming day of wrath (vv.1-3). All nations and peoples of the earth are to hear the warning. Even the earth itself and everything in it is summoned to hear the warning of God. His wrath will fall not only upon people but also upon the world of animals and vegetation. The earth and the entire universe will be affected when the LORD's *day of wrath* comes. Three shocking pictures are given that show the terror of that day.

1) On the day of God's wrath, His anger will destroy all the unrighteous nations and armies of this world (v.2). Through the ages the LORD's wrath has been building up against them. But one day in the future His wrath and fury will be filled to the full, reaching its full limit. No longer will He restrain His wrath. His judgment will explode against all the evil and ungodly nations and military forces. They will all be slaughtered, totally destroyed. This is a clear, vivid description of Armageddon, the final bloody, hellish war that will be fought in the last days of human history (see outline and notes—Is.63:1-6; Re.19:11-21 for more discussion).
2) The day of God's wrath will be a day of horrifying death (v.3). So many soldiers will be killed, there will not be enough men left to bury the dead. As the dead bodies lie openly on the ground unburied, they will decompose and a terrible smell will fill the air. It will be a gory, gruesome scene. So many soldiers will be slaughtered that the very ground itself will be soaked with blood. And when the rains come, it will appear as though the mountains themselves were flowing with blood.
3) The day of God's wrath will be a day of cosmic, catastrophic events in the sky (v.4). Shockingly, Isaiah predicted that the very stars of the sky will be burned up and dissolved. They will disappear just like a scroll that is rolled up and put away, completely out of sight. The stars will fall from their place like shriveled leaves or ripened fruit from a tree. Keep in mind that the destruction of the universe will take place to prepare for the new heavens and earth (Mt.24:29; 2 Pe.3:8-14; Re.6:12-14; Re.21:1; Joel 2:10, 30-31; 3:15; Zec.14:6-7).

b. The coming day of God's wrath is now pictured for the reader. The nation of Edom is chosen to show how God's wrath will fall upon all the nations of the earth. Edom is an example, a representative, a symbolic picture of all the enemies of God's people (vv.5-17; 63:1-6). The Edomites were the descendants of Esau, and down through history they had been the bitter enemies of Israel. A spirit of hatred, animosity, and hostility continually stirred the Edomites to oppose Israel. In the last days of human history, the LORD's wrath will focus on the enemies of God's people. Three facts are to be noted about the judgment that will fall upon Edom.

1) The people of Edom will be cursed, doomed—totally crushed (vv.5-7). The LORD's sword of judgment will be bathed in blood. As lambs and goats are sacrificed by the shedding of their blood, so the common citizens of the nation(s) will be slain. The "lambs and goats" probably refer to the common citizens of the world. Whatever the case,

the lives of the Edomites will be sacrificed to the LORD in their capital Bozrah and throughout their nation. A great slaughter will take place throughout the entire land of Edom. God's sword of wrath will execute His justice upon the nation. As wild oxen and bulls are slaughtered, so the strong and the leaders of the nation(s) will be slain. The land of Edom will be soaked with blood, and the dust of the ground will be covered with the fat oozing out from the carcasses (v.7).

2) The *LORD's day of wrath* has a very specific purpose: to execute justice in behalf of Zion, His people (v.8). God will take vengeance against Edom and the other nations because of their mistreatment and persecution of His people. It will be the year for retribution, the year when Edom and the other nations of the world will be paid back for their defiance of the LORD and their mistreatment of true believers.

3) The land of Edom (and of the nations) will be utterly devastated—just like the land of Sodom and Gomorrah (see outline and note—Ge.19:23-26 for more discussion). Its waters will be polluted; its ground will be set ablaze like burning sulfur and be ruined forever. Edom's land will lie desolate, never again to be inhabited by people (v.10). Only wild animals will inhabit the land (v.11). God's justice will be measured out over the land, and its chaos and emptiness will be sealed forever. Both its kingdom and leaders—the entire political structure with all its officials—will vanish away and be gone forever (v.12). The nation's palaces, fortresses, and cities, along with all its military defenses and forts, will be overgrown with thorns and overrun by wild animals (vv.13-15).

c. The *LORD's day of wrath* is sure to come. It cannot be stopped. The time is set, fixed once and for all by the LORD. The *book of the LORD* declares it (vv.16-17). And every living person is commanded to read the warning of God in the *book of the LORD*. Not a single detail of His warning will be omitted in that day, not even one of the birds or animals mentioned in these verses will be missing or lack a mate in that day. The LORD Himself has spoken the Word concerning the coming day of wrath, and He will execute that day by His Spirit. God's Spirit will carry out the orders, make everything happen just as God has declared. God will judge Edom and give the land to wild animals forever (v.17).

Thought 1. Remember, the warning about the *LORD's day of wrath* was not given just to the people of Isaiah's day. It was given to all people of all generations. The *LORD's day of wrath* is coming to this world. It cannot be hindered or prevented. The day is fixed, set forever by the plan and Word of God Himself. All unbelievers—all who have defied, cursed, and rebelled against God; all who have mistreated God's people; all the ungodly and unrighteous of this earth—will face the wrath of God. They will face the terrifying day of judgment. And there will be no escape.

(1) Listen to what God's Holy Word says about the *LORD's day of wrath*:

"He that believeth on the Son hath everlasting life: and he that believeth not the Son shall not see life; but the wrath of God abideth on him" (Jn.3:36).

"For the wrath of God is revealed from heaven against all ungodliness and unrighteousness of men, who hold the truth in unrighteousness" (Ro.1:18).

"But unto them that are contentious, and do not obey the truth, but obey unrighteousness, indignation and wrath, Tribulation and anguish, upon every soul of man that doeth evil, of the Jew first, and also of the Gentile" (Ro.2:8-9).

"But fornication, and all uncleanness, or covetousness, let it not be once named among you, as becometh saints; Neither filthiness, nor foolish talking, nor jesting, which are not convenient: but rather giving of thanks. For this ye know, that no whoremonger, nor unclean person, nor covetous man, who is an idolater, hath any inheritance in the kingdom of Christ and of God. Let no man deceive you with vain words: for because of these things cometh the wrath of God upon the children of disobedience" (Ep.5:3-6).

"For if we sin wilfully after that we have received the knowledge of the truth, there remaineth no more sacrifice for sins, But a certain fearful looking for of judgment and fiery indignation, which shall devour the adversaries" (He.10:26-27).

"And the third angel followed them, saying with a loud voice, If any man worship the beast and his image, and receive *his* mark in his forehead, or in his hand, The same shall drink of the wine of the wrath of God, which is poured out without mixture into the cup of his indignation; and he shall be tormented with fire and brimstone in the presence of the holy angels, and in the presence of the Lamb" (Re.14:9-10).

"Kiss the Son, lest he be angry, and ye perish *from* the way, when his wrath is kindled but a little. Blessed *are* all they that put their trust in him" (Ps.2:12).

"Behold, the name of the LORD cometh from far, burning *with* his anger, and the burden *thereof is* heavy: his lips are full of indignation, and his tongue as a devouring fire" (Is.30:27).

"But the LORD *is* the true God, he *is* the living God, and an everlasting king: at his wrath the earth shall tremble, and the nations shall not be able to abide his indignation" (Je.10:10).

(2) The coming of the *LORD's day of wrath* is inevitable. There will be no escape for the unbelievers, the ungodly, and the unrighteous of the world.

"When the Son of man shall come in his glory, and all the holy angels with him, then shall he sit upon the throne of his glory: And before him shall be gathered all nations: and he shall separate them one from another, as a shepherd divideth *his* sheep from the goats: And he shall set the sheep on his right hand, but the goats on the left….Then shall he say also unto them on the left hand, Depart from me, ye cursed, into everlasting fire, prepared for the devil and his angels:" (Mt.25:31-33, 34).

"Being filled with all unrighteousness, fornication, wickedness, covetousness, maliciousness; full of envy, murder, debate, deceit, malignity; whisperers, Backbiters, haters of God, despiteful, proud, boasters, inventors of evil things, disobedient to parents, Without understanding, covenantbreakers, without natural affection, implacable, unmerciful: Who knowing the judgment of God, that they which commit such things are worthy of death, not only do the same, but have pleasure in them that do them. Therefore thou art inexcusable, O man, whosoever thou art that judgest: for wherein thou judgest another, thou condemnest thyself; for thou that judgest doest the same things. But we are sure that the judgment of God is according to truth against them which commit such things. And thinkest thou this, O man, that judgest them which do such things, and doest the same, that thou shalt escape the judgment of God?" (Ro.1:29–2:3).

"For when they shall say, Peace and safety; then sudden destruction cometh upon them, as travail upon a woman with child; and they shall not escape" (1 Th.5:3).

"Therefore we ought to give the more earnest heed to the things which we have heard, lest at any time we should let *them* slip. For if the word spoken by angels was stedfast, and every transgression and disobedience received a just recompence of reward; How shall we escape, if we neglect so great salvation; which at the first began to be spoken by the Lord, and was confirmed unto us by them that heard *him*" (He.2:1-3).

"See that ye refuse not him that speaketh. For if they escaped not who refused him that spake on earth, much more *shall not* we *escape,* if we turn away from him that *speaketh* from heaven" (He.12:25).

"*Though* hand *join* in hand, the wicked shall not be unpunished: but the seed of the righteous shall be delivered" (Pr.11:21).

"Therefore thus saith the LORD, Behold, I will bring evil upon them, which they shall not be able to escape; and though they shall cry unto me, I will not hearken unto them" (Je.11:11).

"Woe unto you that desire the day of the LORD! to what end *is* it for you? the day of the LORD *is* darkness, and not light. As if a man did flee from a lion, and a bear met him; or went into the house, and leaned his hand on the wall, and a serpent bit him. *Shall* not the day of the LORD *be* darkness, and not light? even very dark, and no brightness in it?" (Am.5:18-20).

"Though they dig into hell, thence shall mine hand take them; though they climb up to heaven, thence will I bring them down" (Am.9:2).

---

2 (35:1-10) **World, Prophecy Concerning, to Be Perfected—Earth, Prophecy Concerning, to Be Perfected—Future, Prophecy Concerning, Earth Perfected—Kingdom, Messianic, Prophecy Concerning**: God issued a wonderful, astounding promise: some day in the future the earth will be transformed, perfected, and filled with joy. This is a glorious description of the Messiah's kingdom, what is known as the millennial reign of Christ on earth. One day the Lord Jesus Christ will return to earth to establish God's kingdom. The future of the earth is bright, hopeful, promising, and encouraging. The LORD is going to change this evil world back into a Garden of Eden. What follows is a vivid portrayal of the transformation that will take place:

OUTLINE	SCRIPTURE	SCRIPTURE	OUTLINE

2. God's promise of a glorious future for this world: His coming kingdom of perfection & joy
 	
a. The land will be restored: The desert & parched land will undergo a dramatic change, will blossom & rejoice, Ps.55:12-13; 96:11-13; 98:7-9; Ro.8:19-22
b. The glory & splendor of God will be seen
c. The guarantee of God's salvation will be given to weak & fearful believers
  1) To be strong
  2) To be assured: The LORD will come to execute justice & to save believers
 	
d. The disabled believers will be healed, restored to health
  1) The blind & deaf
	The wilderness and the solitary place shall be glad for them; and the desert shall rejoice, and blossom as the rose.
	2 It shall blossom abundantly, and rejoice even with joy and singing: the glory of Lebanon shall be given unto it, the excellency of Carmel and Sharon, they shall see the glory of the LORD, *and the* excellency of our God.
	3 Strengthen ye the weak hands, and confirm the feeble knees.
	4 Say to them *that are* of a fearful heart, Be strong, fear not: behold, your God will come *with* vengeance, *even* God *with* a recompence; he will come and save you.
	5 Then the eyes of the blind shall be opened, and the ears of the deaf shall be unstopped.
		6 Then shall the lame *man* leap as an hart, and the tongue of the dumb sing: for in the wilderness shall waters break out, and streams in the desert.
		7 And the parched ground shall become a pool, and the thirsty land springs of water: in the habitation of dragons, where each lay, *shall be* grass with reeds and rushes.
		8 And an highway shall be there, and a way, and it shall be called The way of holiness; the unclean shall not pass over it; but it *shall be* for those: the wayfaring men, though fools, shall not err *therein.*
		9 No lion shall be there, nor *any* ravenous beast shall go up thereon, it shall not be found there; but the redeemed shall walk
			2) The crippled & mute
			e. The parched land will be changed into well-watered, fertile soil
			  1) Water will flow in the wilderness & desert
			  2) Pools will replace desert sand & springs will bubble up out of thirsty ground
			  3) Vegetation will grow on the once ruined land
			
			f. The kingdom will have a very special highway: Named *The Way of Holiness*
			  1) Its travelers: No unclean or wicked person, only those who follow God
			
			  2) Its safety
			   • No wild beast will be a threat
			   • No thief will travel on the highway, only the

OUTLINE	SCRIPTURE	SCRIPTURE	OUTLINE

redeemed
3) Its purpose
  • To be the road for the
    ransomed to return to
	there:
	10 And the ransomed of the
	LORD shall return, and come
	to Zion with songs and ever-
		lasting joy upon their heads:
		they shall obtain joy and
		gladness, and sorrow and
		sighing shall flee away.
			the LORD
			  • To be the road leading
			    to Zion, where people
			    will worship God

a. The land will be completely restored, transformed into a Garden of Eden (vv.1-2). The desert and parched land of the earth will undergo a dramatic change. The soil will be filled with rich nutrients, and the vegetation will blossom so much that it will seem to break forth in shouts of joy and rejoicing (Ps.55:12-13; 96:11-13; 98:7-9; see outline and note—Ro.8:19-22 for more discussion).

The glory of Lebanon is a reference to the fragrant cedar forest of the land. Carmel was known for its mighty oaks, and Sharon for its beautiful pastures and lush, green pastureland. [1]

b. *In that day*, the glory and splendor of God will be seen by all the people of the earth (v.2). As a result of the total transformation, the whole earth will be filled with the beauty of nature, with the radiance and majesty of God. All the citizens of the earth will witness God's glory in nature. But even more incredible, they will be able to see the Lord living upon earth as their Ruler and King (33:17).

c. Down through the centuries, God has given weak and fearful believers the wonderful guarantee of God's salvation. Isaiah now says that the weak and fearful should look ahead to the glorious future promised by God. They should strengthen themselves in the promise of God's Word. When they become weak, they need to strengthen their weak hands and steady their feeble knees. They need to live strong and righteous lives, keeping the commandments of God. Furthermore, they need to be courageous witnesses for the LORD. Fear should never be allowed to take over their hearts, turning them into cowards. God's people are to keep their eyes on the glorious future promised by the LORD. The LORD will come to carry out perfect justice and judgment upon this earth. He will come to save His people from their enemies, those who ridicule, mock, and persecute them (v.4).

d. When the glorious transformation of the earth takes place, all disabled believers will be healed and restored to health (v.5). All the blind will be able to see, and all the deaf will be able to hear. Crippled believers will leap like deer, and the mute—those who cannot speak—will shout out for joy.

e. All land that had been ruined and parched will be transformed, changed into fertile soil that is well watered (v.6). Water will flow both in the wilderness and in the desert. Streams and rivers will flow abundantly across the face of the earth. Pools will replace desert sand, and springs will bubble up out of ground that had lacked rain (v.7). Vegetation will grow everywhere, on all land that had formerly been ruined or barren.

f. The Messiah's kingdom will have a very special highway running through the midst of it, a highway that will be known as the *Way of Holiness* (vv.8-10; 11:16; 19:23; 40:3; 62:10). In Isaiah's day traveling along the roads was often dangerous. The danger was due to ferocious animals, thieves, and natural obstacles such as deep ravines and narrow paths on the sides of hills. But in the Messiah's kingdom, the *highway of holiness* will be perfectly safe. There will be no unclean or wicked person or ferocious animal to endanger the life of the traveler. All the unclean and wicked of the world will have been removed from the earth. Only the righteous—the holy and obedient who have kept God's commandments—will be living upon earth. Therefore traveling the *highway of holiness* will pose no threat to anyone. Only the redeemed will travel this path.

Note the purpose for the highway: it is to be the road by which the ransomed of the LORD return to Him (v.10). If a person is to return to the LORD, he must first be redeemed by the LORD. When the LORD calls individuals to the promised land from their captivity (to sin, evil, and wickedness), they must respond. They must return to the LORD by traveling along the *Way of Holiness*. This path is the only road by which a person can return to the LORD. In the Messiah's kingdom, the *highway of holiness* will be the road that leads to Zion or Jerusalem, the capital of the Messiah's government. In the present Scripture the people of the Messiah's kingdom are pictured traveling the *Way of Holiness* in order to worship the LORD in Jerusalem.

Thought 1. God gives the wonderful promise of a climactic change of the earth. He will cleanse the earth of its sinful, corrupt condition and transform it into a new Garden of Eden. The kingdom of God is coming to this earth, and when it does, the earth will become a perfect utopia. Listen to what God's Holy Word says:
(1) The present heavens and earth will be recreated into a new heavens and earth.

> **"Heaven and earth shall pass away, but my words shall not pass away" (Mt.24:35).**
> **"But the heavens and the earth, which are now, by the same word are kept in store, reserved unto fire against the day of judgment and perdition of ungodly men. But, beloved, be not ignorant of this one thing, that one day *is* with the Lord as a thousand years, and a thousand years as one day. The Lord is not slack concerning his promise, as some men count slackness; but is longsuffering to us-ward, not willing that any should perish, but that all should come to repentance. But the day of the Lord will come as a thief in the night; in the which the heavens shall pass away with a great noise, and the elements shall melt with fervent heat, the earth also and the works that are therein shall be burned up. *Seeing* then *that* all these things shall be dissolved, what manner *of persons* ought ye to be in *all* holy conversation and godliness, Looking for and hasting unto the coming of the day of God, wherein the heavens being on fire shall be dissolved, and the elements shall melt with fervent heat? Nevertheless we, according to his promise, look for new heavens and a new earth, wherein dwelleth righteousness" (2 Pe.3:7-13).**

---

[1] H.C.Leupold. *Exposition of Isaiah*, Vol.1, p.547.

"Of old hast thou laid the foundation of the earth: and the heavens *are* the work of thy hands. They shall perish, but thou shalt endure: yea, all of them shall wax old like a garment; as a vesture shalt thou change them, and they shall be changed" (Ps.102:25-26).

"And I saw a new heaven and a new earth: for the first heaven and the first earth were passed away; and there was no more sea" (Re.21:1).

"And all the host of heaven shall be dissolved, and the heavens shall be rolled together as a scroll: and all their host shall fall down, as the leaf falleth off from the vine, and as a falling *fig* from the fig tree" (Is.34:4).

"Lift up your eyes to the heavens, and look upon the earth beneath: for the heavens shall vanish away like smoke, and the earth shall wax old like a garment, and they that dwell therein shall die in like manner: but my salvation shall be for ever, and my righteousness shall not be abolished" (Is.51:6).

"For, behold, I create new heavens and a new earth: and the former shall not be remembered, nor come into mind" (Is.65:17).

"For as the new heavens and the new earth, which I will make, shall remain before me, saith the LORD, so shall your seed and your name remain" (Is.66:22).

(2) No people will enter the Messiah's kingdom or live in the new heavens and earth unless they have been redeemed by the Lord and live holy lives.

"For all have sinned, and come short of the glory of God; Being justified freely by his grace through the redemption that is in Christ Jesus" (Ro.3:23-24).

"Having therefore these promises, dearly beloved, let us cleanse ourselves from all filthiness of the flesh and spirit, perfecting holiness in the fear of God" (2 Co.7:1).

"Christ hath redeemed us from the curse of the law, being made a curse for us: for it is written, Cursed *is* every one that hangeth on a tree" (Ga.3:13).

"In whom we have redemption through his blood, the forgiveness of sins, according to the riches of his grace" (Ep.1:7).

"That ye put off concerning the former conversation [conduct, behavior] the old man, which is corrupt according to the deceitful lusts; And be renewed in the spirit of your mind; And that ye put on the new man, which after God is created in righteousness and true holiness" (Ep.4:22-24).

"In whom we have redemption through his blood, *even* the forgiveness of sins" (Col.1:14).

"Who gave himself for us, that he might redeem us from all iniquity, and purify unto himself a peculiar people, zealous of good works" (Tit.2:14).

"Neither by the blood of goats and calves, but by his own blood he entered in once into the holy place, having obtained eternal redemption *for us.* For if the blood of bulls and of goats, and the ashes of an heifer sprinkling the unclean, sanctifieth to the purifying of the flesh: How much more shall the blood of Christ, who through the eternal Spirit offered himself without spot to God, purge your conscience from dead works to serve the living God?" (He.9:12-14).

"Follow peace with all *men,* and holiness, without which no man shall see the Lord" (He.12:14).

"But as he which hath called you is holy, so be ye holy in all manner of conversation; Because it is written, Be ye holy; for I am holy" (1 Pe.1:15-16).

"Forasmuch as ye know that ye were not redeemed with corruptible things, *as* silver and gold, from your vain conversation [conduct, behavior] *received* by tradition from your fathers; But with the precious blood of Christ, as of a lamb without blemish and without spot" (1 Pe.1:18-19).

"*Seeing* then *that* all these things shall be dissolved, what manner *of persons* ought ye to be in *all* holy conversation and godliness, Looking for and hasting unto the coming of the day of God, wherein the heavens being on fire shall be dissolved, and the elements shall melt with fervent heat? Nevertheless we, according to his promise, look for new heavens and a new earth, wherein dwelleth righteousness. Wherefore, beloved, seeing that ye look for such things, be diligent that ye may be found of him in peace, without spot, and blameless" (2 Pe.3:11-14).

RESOURCES

ISAIAH

PRACTICAL BIBLE HELPS AND RESOURCES – ISAIAH   PAGE

    MAP 1: The Assyrian Empire   298

    MAP 2: The Babylonian Empire   299

    CHART 1: A Timeline of Kings, Prophets, and History   300

    CHART 2: Sacred Days in the Hebrew Calendar   302

    CHART 3: The Prophets: Their Message—Then and Now   304

       ➤ Chronological Listing of the Prophets   305

       ➤ Alphabetical Listing of the Prophets   306

       ➤ The Prophets   307

TYPES IN ISAIAH

       ➤ Alphabetical Outline   375

       ➤ Chronological Outline   377

OUTLINE AND SUBJECT INDEX: ISAIAH   379

THE ASSYRIAN EMPIRE

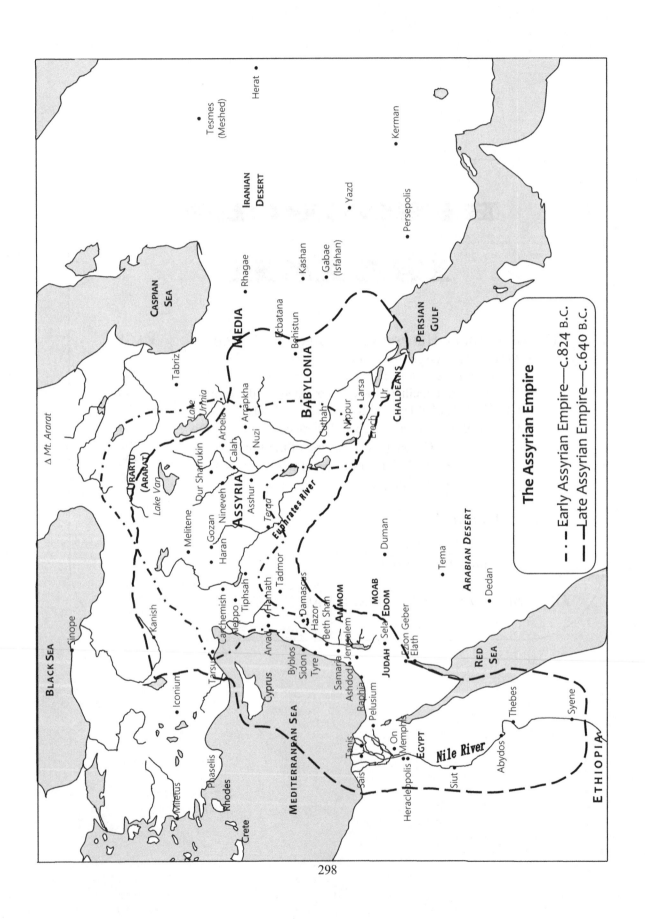

The Assyrian Empire

- - - Early Assyrian Empire—c.824 B.C.
——— Late Assyrian Empire—c.640 B.C.

BLACK SEA

CASPIAN SEA

MEDITERRANEAN SEA

PERSIAN GULF

RED SEA

ARABIAN DESERT

IRANIAN DESERT

MEDIA

BABYLONIA

CHALDEANS

ASSYRIA

URARTU (ARARAT)

EGYPT

ETHIOPIA

JUDAH

EDOM

MOAB

AMMON

Nile River

Euphrates River

Terqa

△ Mt. Ararat

Lake Van

Lake Urmia

Herat
Tesmes (Meshed)
Kerman
Yazd
Persepolis
Kashan
Gabae (Isfahan)
Rhagae
Ecbatana
Behistun
Tabriz
Arrapkha
Larsa
Erech
Ur
Nippur
Cuthah
Arbela
Nuzi
Calah
Dur Sharrukin
Asshur
Nineveh
Melitene
Gozan
Haran
Duman
Tema
Dedan
Kanish
Carchemish
Aleppo
Tiphsah
Hamath
Tadmor
Damascus
Hazor
Beth Shan
Arvad
Byblos
Sidon
Tyre
Samaria
Ashdod
Raphia
Jerusalem
Sela
Ezion Geber
Elath
Sinope
Iconium
Tarsus
Cyprus
Pelusium
Tanis
Sais
On
Memphis
Heracleopolis
Siut
Abydos
Thebes
Syene
Phaselis
Rhodes
Miletus
Crete

298

THE BABYLONIAN–MEDIAN EMPIRE

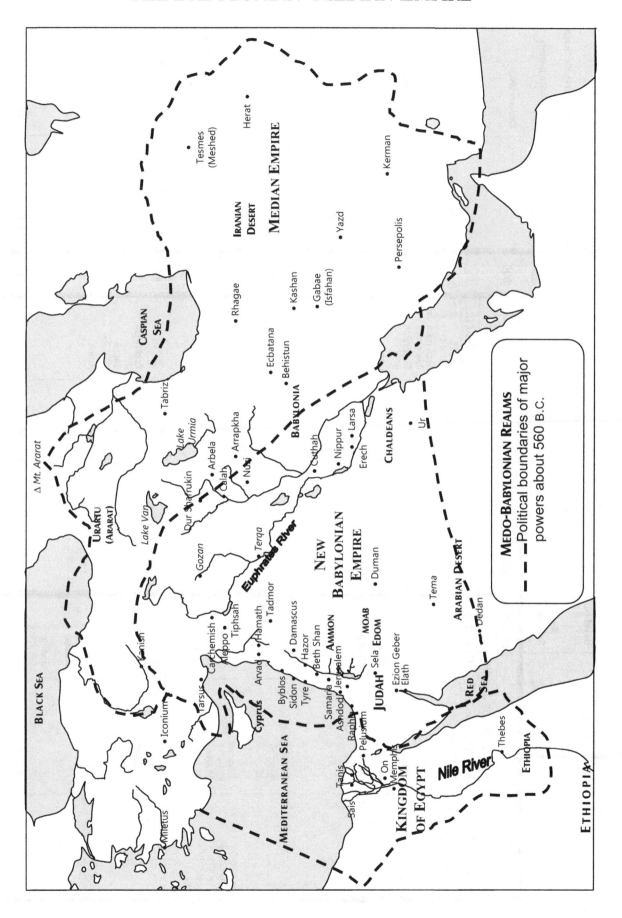

MEDO-BABYLONIAN REALMS
Political boundaries of major
powers about 560 B.C.

MEDIAN EMPIRE

Tesmes
(Meshed)

Herat

Kerman

IRANIAN
DESERT

Yazd

Persepolis

Kashan

Gabae
(Isfahan)

Rhagae

Ecbatana
Behistun

CASPIAN
SEA

BABYLONIA

Tabriz

Lake
Irmia

Arbela

Arrapkha

Nuzi

Cuthah

Nippur

Larsa

Erech

CHALDEANS

Ur

Calah

Dur Sharrukin

Lake Van

△ Mt. Ararat

URARTU
(ARARAT)

Gozan

Terqa

Euphrates River

NEW
BABYLONIAN
EMPIRE

Duman

Tema

ARABIAN DESERT

Dedan

Kanish

Tiphsah

Tadmor

Carchemish

Aleppo

Hamath

Damascus

Hazor

Beth Shan

AMMON

MOAB

Sela EDOM

BLACK SEA

Tarsus

Iconium

Arvad

Byblos

Sidon

Tyre

Cyprus

Samaria

Ashdod

Jerusalem

Raphia

JUDAH

Ezion Geber
Elath

RED SEA

Miletus

Pelusium

Tanis

Sais

On

Memphis

Thebes

ETHIOPIA

Nile River

MEDITERRANEAN SEA

KINGDOM
OF EGYPT

ETHIOPIA

TIMELINE OF KINGS, PROPHETS AND HISTORY*

HISTORY

Date BC	Foreign Kings	World Events
1000	Ashur-Rabi II (1010–970) (Assyria); Hiram (1003–966) (Tyre)	David captures Jerusalem (1004)
950	Tiglath-Pileser II (960–935) (Assyria); Shishak I (945–924) (Egypt)	Foundation for the Temple (966); 22nd Egyptian Dynasty (945)
930		Kingdom Divided (930)
900	Ben-Hadad I (900) (Syria); Eth-Baal (887–856) (Sidon)	Assyria makes peace with Babylon (915); Jehoshaphat leads a revival (865)
850	Hazael (840) (Syria)	Elijah's contest with prophets of Baal (857); Elijah's mantle passed to Elisha (845)
800	Ben-Hadad II (798) (Syria); Ben-Hadad III (773) (Syria)	Carthage established (814); Joash repairs Temple (812); 23rd Egyptian dynasty (800)
750	Rezin (750) (Syria)	Olympic games begin (776); Rome founded (753); Babylonian and Chinese calendar (750)

THE UNITED KINGDOM

Bible Ref.	Kings (Years Reigned)	Prophets
1 S.16:1-1 K:2:11; 1 Chr.11:1-30	David (40) (1011–971)	Samuel (1095–1015); Gad (1015–950); Asaph (1004); Nathan (1003–931); Heman (971)
1 K.2:12-11:43; 1 Chr.28:1-2 Chr.9:31	Solomon (40) (971–931)	

THE DIVIDED KINGDOM

NORTHERN KINGDOM OF ISRAEL

Prophets	Kings (Years Reigned)	Bible Ref.
Ahijah (931–910); Man from Judah (930); Shemaiah (927)	Jeroboam I (22) (931–910)	1 K.12:1-24; 12:25-14:20; 2 Chr.10:1-16
Jehu (886)	Nadab (2) (910–909); Baasha (24) (909–886); Elah (2) (886–885)	1 K.15:25-31; 1 K.15:16-16:7; 2 Chr.16:1-6; 1 K.16:6-14
Hanani (870)	Zimri (7 days) (885); Omri (12) (885–874)	1 K.16:9-20; 1 K.16:21-28
Elijah (860–845); Micaiah (853); Elisha (850–795); Eliezer (849–48)	Ahab (22) (874–853); Ahaziah (2) (853–852); Joram/Jehoram (12) (852–841)	1 K.16:28-22:40; 2 Chr.18:1-34; 1 K.22:49-51; 2 K.1:1-18; 2 Chr.20:35-37; 22:1-11; 2 K.1:17; 3:1-8:15
Zechariah (797); Jonah (780–765); Amos (750)	Jehu (28) (841–814); Jehoahaz (17) (814–798); Jehoash (16) (798–782); Jeroboam II (41) (793–753); Zechariah (6 mos) (753); Shallum (1 mo) (752); Menahem (10) (752–742)	2 K.9:1-10:36; 2 Chr.22:7-9; 2 K.13:1-9; 2 K.13:9-25; 14:8-16; 2 K.14:23-29; 2 K.15:8-12; 2 K.15:13-15; 2 K.15:16-22

SOUTHERN KINGDOM OF JUDAH

Bible Ref.	Kings (Years Reigned)	Prophets
1 K.12:1-24; 14:21-31; 2 Chr.9:31-12:16; 1 K.15:1-8; 2 Chr.12:16-14:1; 1 K.15:9-24; 2 Chr.14:1-16:14	Rehoboam (17) (931–913); Abijah (3) (913–911); Asa (3) (911–870)	Iddo (910); Azariah (896)
1 K.22:41-50; 2 K.3:6-14; 2 Chr.17:1-21:1	Jehoshaphat (25) (873–848)	Obadiah (845)
2 K.8:16-24; 2 Chr.21:1-20; 2 K.8:25-29; 9:27-29; 2 Chr.22:1-10; 2 K.11:1-16; 2 Chr.22:10-23:21; 2 K.11:17-12:21; 2 Chr.22:11-12; 24:1-27	Jehoram (8) (853–841); Ahaziah (2) (841); Athaliah (7) (841–835); Joash/Jehoash (40) (835–796)	Joel (830)
2 K.14:1-20; 2 Chr.24:27-25:28; 2 K.14:21-22; 15:1-7; 2 Chr.26:1-23; 2 K.15:32-38; 2 Chr.26:23-27:9	Amaziah (29) (796–767); Azariah/Uzziah (52) (792–740); Jotham (16) (750–731)	Hosea (788–723); Jonah (780–765)

THE DIVIDED KINGDOM

SOUTHERN KINGDOM OF JUDAH			NORTHERN KINGDOM OF ISRAEL			DATE BC	HISTORY	
BIBLE REF.	KINGS (YEARS REIGNED)	PROPHETS	PROPHETS	KINGS (YEARS REIGNED)	BIBLE REF.		FOREIGN KINGS	WORLD EVENTS
				Pekahiah (2) (742–740)	2 K.15:23-26		Tiglath-Pil[n]eser III [or Pul] (745–727) (Assyria)	Assyria takes control of Northern Kingdom (745–627)
2 K.15:38-16:20; 2 Chr.27:9-27: Is.7:1-9:1	Ahaz (16) (735–715)	Isaiah (740–690)		Pekah (20) (752–732) .(752–740) (ruled only in Gilead) (740–732) (ruled in Samaria)	2 K.15:27-31		Shalmaneser V (727–722) (Assyria)	Assyria invades Northern Israel (732)
		Micah (735–725), Oded (733)		Hoshea (9) (732–722)	2 K.17:1-23		So (727–716) (Egypt), Sargon II (710–705) (Assyria)	Fall of Northern Kingdom (722)
2 K.18:1-20:21; 2 Chr.28:27-32:33; Pr.25:1; Is.36:1-39:8	Hezekiah (29) (729–686)					700	Sennacherib (705–681) (Assyria), Merodach-Baladan (721–710, 705–704) (Assyria)	Sennacherib defeats Egypt (701), Hezekiah's tunnel (701)
							Tirhakah (690–664) (Egypt)	185,000 Assyrians killed by God (701)
2 K.20:21-21:18; 2 Chr.32:33-33:20	Manasseh (55) (696–642)	Nahum (663–612)				650	Esarhaddon (681–669) (Assyria)	Sennacherib destroys Babylon (689)
2 K.21:18-26; 2 Chr.33:20-25	Amon (2) (642–640)						Nabopolassar (626–605) (Assyria)	Josiah's reform (621), Nineveh destroyed (612)
2 K.21:26-23:30; 2 Chr.33:25-35:27	Josiah (31) (640–609)	Zephaniah (640–609), Jeremiah (627–562)					Neco (610–595) (Egypt)	Battle of Carchemish (605), 1st group of exiles from Judah taken to Babylon (605)
2 K.23:31-33; 2 Chr.36:1-4	Jehoaz/Jehoahaz (3 mos) (609)							
2 K.23:34-24:7; 2 Chr.36:5-8	Jehoiakim (11) (608–598)	Habakkuk (615–598)				600	Nebuchadnezzar II (605–562) (Babylon)	2nd group of exiles from Judah taken to Babylon (597)
2 K.24:8-17; 25:27-30; 2 Chr.36:8-10;	Jehoiachin (3 mos) (598–597)	Daniel (605–535)						Fall of Judah—Third group of exiles from Judah taken to Babylon (586)
2 K.24:18-25:21; Je.21:1-52:11	Zedekiah/Mattaniah (11) (597–586)	Ezekiel (593–571)						
2 K.25:22-26; Je.40:5-41:18	Gedaliah (2 mos) (Appointed by Nebuchadnezzar) (586)					550	Evil-Merodach (562–560) (Babylon), Cyrus II (559–530) (Medo-Persia)	Fall of Babylon to Medo-Persian Empire (539)
							Belshazzar (552–539) (Babylon)	Cyrus II decrees that the Jews may return to the Holy Land (538), 1st exiles return to Holy Land with Zerubbabel (537)
		Haggai (520), Zechariah (520–518)				500	Darius I (521–486) (Medo-Persia)	1st Temple foundation laid (536), 2nd Temple foundation laid (520), Temple completed (516), Republic of Rome est. (509)
						450	Artaxerxes (465–425) (Persia)	2nd return under Ezra (458), 3rd return under Nehemiah (445)
		Malachi (430)						

*Some dates are approximate.

The resources used for the timeline in addition to the Bible are as follows:

1 Archer, Gleason L. Encyclopedia of Bible Difficulties. (Grand Rapids, Michigan: Zondervan Publishing House), 1982.
2 Freedman, David Noel, ed., et. al. The Anchor Bible Dictionary. (New York: Doubleday), 1992.
3 Grun, Bernard. The Timetables of History. 3rd ed. (New York: Simon & Schuster), 1991.
4 Kaiser, Walter C. A History of Israel. (Nashville, Tennessee: Broadman & Holman Publishers), 1998.
5 Silverman, David P., ed. Ancient Egypt. (New York: Oxford University Press), 1997.

SACRED DAYS IN THE HEBREW CALENDAR
AND THEIR PROPHETIC SYMBOLISM

NAME OF FEAST OR EVENT	OLD TESTAMENT PURPOSE	NEW TESTAMENT SYMBOLISM	CALENDAR TIME	FARM SEASON (Crops/Weather)
The Festival of Passover	To remember God's judgment and deliverance from Egyptian bondage. (Le.23:6; Nu.9:5; Jos. 5:10; 2 K.23:22; 2 Chr.35:1)	A symbol of Christ our Passover who was sacrificed to deliver us from the judgment of God. (Mt.26:17; Lu.2:41; Lu.22:15; He.11:28)	*Hebrew Time*: The 1st Month [Abib or Nisan], 14th Day *Secular Equivalent*: March - April	Harvesting barley and flax; Later Spring rains***
The Festival of Unleavened Bread	To recall the need and urgency to leave Egypt (a symbol of the world). (Ex.12:17-18; Ex.13:6-7; Ex.23:15; Ex.34:18; Le.23:6; Nu.28:17; De.16:3; De.16:16; 2 Chr.8:13; 2 Chr.30:13)	A symbol of the urgency for God's people to escape the enslavement of the world and immediately begin their march to the promised land of heaven (Mt.26:17; Mk.14:1)	*Hebrew Time*: The 1st Month [Abib or Nisan], 15th thru the 21st Day *Secular Equivalent*: March - April	Harvesting barley and flax; Later Spring rains
The Festival of Firstfruits	To thank God for the crops, the first harvest of the season that sustained life. (Ex.34:22; Le. 23:10; Nu.28:26)	A symbol of Christ's resurrection and of the believers hope: Christ is the first of the harvest, the first to arise from the dead. (Ro.8:23; 1 Co.15:23)	*Hebrew Time*: The 1st Month [Abib or Nisan], 16th Day *Secular Equivalent*: March - April	Harvesting barley and flax; Later Spring rains
The Festival of Pentecost or Harvest or Weeks	To give thanks for the harvest and to dedicate one's life anew to God. This festival took place fifty days after the Festival of Firstfruits. (Ex.23:16; Ex.34:22; Le.23:16; Nu.28:26; De.16:10)	A symbol of Pentecost... • of the great harvest of souls • of people giving their lives to God • of the coming of the Holy Spirit and the birth of the church (Ac.2:1-47; Ac.20:16; 1 Co. 16:8)	*Hebrew Time*: The 3rd Month [Sivan], the 6th Day *Secular Equivalent*: May - June	Wheat harvest; other crops—grapes and almonds begin to open
The Festival of Trumpets	To focus upon God, learning to trust God more and more and to proclaim the message of joy over the atonement or reconciliation with God. (Le.23:24; Nu.29:1; Neh.8:2)	A symbol of salvation and of the rapture, the glorious day when Christ will return and take believers—both the living and the dead—to be with Him forever.	*Hebrew Time*: 7th Month, [Ethanim or Tishri **], the 1st Day *Secular Equivalent* September - October	Plowing of the fields: Early autumn rains
The Day of Atonement	To focus upon the only way to approach God and be forgiven—through the shed blood of the atoning sacrifice. Celebrated yearly, it was a national day of repentance. (Ex.30:10; Le.16:30; Le.23:27; Nu.29:7)	A symbol of being reconciled with God through the atonement, through the substitute sacrifice of Christ. (He.9:7)	*Hebrew Time*: 7th Month, [Ethanim or Tishri **], the 10th Day *Secular Equivalent*: September - October	Plowing of the fields: Early autumn rains
The Feast of Tabernacles or Booths	To celebrate the wilderness wanderings when the people lived in tents on their way to the promised land and to thank God for the harvest. (Le.23:34, 39; Nu.29:12; De.16:13; 2 Chr.8:13; Ezr.3:4; Neh.8:14; Zec.14:16)	A symbol of the believer's march through this world to heaven, a symbol of how temporary our world is as believers march to heaven (Jn.7:2)	*Hebrew Time*: 7th Month, [Ethanim or Tishri **], the 15th thru the 21st Day *Secular Equivalent*: September - October	Plowing of the fields: Early autumn rains
The Feast of Purim	To remember God's deliverance from Israel's enemies during the time of Esther. Purim was a time of sharing with one's neighbor and with the poor. (Est.9:18-32)	Not mentioned in the New Testament	*Hebrew Time*: The 12th Month [Adar *], the 14th & 15th Day *Secular Equivalent*: February - March	Blooming of almond trees; Harvesting of citrus fruit; the later rains begin.

---

*   Note: An additional month (Second Adar or Adar Sheni or Veadar) was added to the Hebrew calendar about every three years. This was how the lunar calendar corresponded to the solar year.

**   Hebrew names of the month that are not in the Bible are marked with two stars (**). These are known as "Post-exilic" names, from the period of history known as "The Babylonian Exile."

*** The idea for listing the Farm Seasons was stirred by the *NIV Study Bible*, Grand Rapids, MI: Zondervan Bible Publishers, 1985, pp.102-103.

OTHER SACRED DAYS IN THE HEBREW CALENDAR

NAME OF FEAST OR EVENT	OLD TESTAMENT PURPOSE	NEW TESTAMENT SYMBOLISM	CALENDAR TIME	FARM SEASON (Crops/ Weather)
The Sabbath Day	To have a day of rest and worship (Ex.20:8-11; Ex.31:12-17; Le.23:3; De.5:12-15)	The Sabbath is a symbol of the spiritual rest that God promises to those who believe and follow him. The Sabbath rest is a symbol of redemption, of God's deliverance from the heavy burdens and trials of this life. (Mt.12:1-14; Mt.28:1; Lu. 4:16; Jn.5:9; Ac.13:42; Col.2:16; He.4:1-11)	*Hebrew Time*: Celebrated on the seventh day of each week *Secular Equivalent*: Same as above	Not Applicable
The Sabbatical Year	The Sabbatical Year was celebrated every seven years. During the seventh year the land was given rest from agricultural use and debts were forgiven (Ex.23:10-11; Le. 25:1-7; De.15:1)	Not mentioned in the New Testament	*Hebrew Time*: Celebrated every seven years *Secular Equivalent*: Same as above	Not Applicable
The Year of Jubilee	The Year of Jubilee was celebrated at the end of every forty-ninth year on the Day of Atonement. On this special day, the trumpet would sound out the message of freedom to all the inhabitants of the land who had been held in bondage. In addition, all property was to be returned to the original owners who had been forced to sell because of poverty. This meant that all prices in the economy throughout the forty-nine years were to be fairly adjusted according to the closeness to The Year of Jubilee. (Le.25:8-17; Le. 27:17-24; Nu.36:4)	Not mentioned in the New Testament	*Hebrew Time*: Celebrated at the end of every forty-ninth year on the Day of Atonement. *Secular Equivalent*: Same as above	Not Applicable
The Sacred Assembly	To celebrate the end of the final feast. The sacred assembly was a day of sacrifice and then rest. (Le.23:36; Nu.29:35-38)	Not mentioned in the New Testament	*Hebrew Time*: The 7th Month [Ethanim or Tishri **], on the 22nd Day *Secular Equivalent:* September - October	Plowing of the fields; early autumn rains.

THE PROPHETS: THEIR MESSAGE—THEN AND NOW

The prophets were called and chosen by God to do two things:
> ➤ to proclaim God's salvation to the world
> ➤ to prophesy and predict how God was going to save humanity

Both functions were necessary. The prophet had to proclaim salvation to the people of his own generation and to predict how God was going to save the people of all generations. But note: the predictions of the future salvation were not the prophet's own predictions. He had not been called to proclaim his own ideas or message; he had been called to proclaim the salvation of God Himself. He was a man given a very special call, a call to the most important task in all the world: the task of proclaiming the glory and wonder of God's salvation. God was making it possible for man to be saved and to live eternally.

The prophet conveyed the salvation of God…

- by pointing out the sins of the people
- by warning the people about the terrible and certain consequences of sin, the discipline and judgment of God
- by encouraging the people to repent by wholeheartedly turning back to God, worshipping Him and Him alone
- by proclaiming God's eternal plan of salvation and blessings to those who would believe

Speaking of the prophets, Peter Adams writes, "To respond to God's words is to respond to God."[1]

"But those things, which God before had showed by the mouth of all his prophets, that Christ should suffer, he hath so fulfilled. Repent ye therefore, and be converted, that your sins may be blotted out, when the times of refreshing shall come from the presence of the Lord; And he shall send Jesus Christ, which before was preached unto you: Whom the heaven must receive until the times of restitution of all things, which God hath spoken by the mouth of all his holy prophets since the world began. For Moses truly said unto the fathers, A prophet shall the Lord your God raise up unto you of your brethren, like unto me; him shall ye hear in all things whatsoever he shall say unto you. And it shall come to pass, that every soul, which will not hear that prophet, shall be destroyed from among the people. Yea, and all the prophets from Samuel and those that follow after, as many as have spoken, have likewise foretold of these days. Ye are the children of the prophets, and of the covenant which God made with our fathers, saying unto Abraham, And in thy seed shall all the kindreds of the earth be blessed. Unto you first God, having raised up his Son Jesus, sent him to bless you, in turning away every one of you from his iniquities" (Ac.3:18-26).

---

[1] Peter Adams. *Speaking God's Words.* (Downers Grove, IL: Inter-Varsity Press, 1996), pp.19-20.

THE PROPHETS

ALPHABETICAL LISTING OF THE PROPHETS

NAME	DATE
Abel	Right after creation
Abraham	2000 B.C.
Agabus	A.D. 43
Ahijah	931–910 B.C.
Amos	750 B.C.
Anna	4 B.C.
Asaph	1004 B.C.
Azariah	896 B.C.
Daniel	605–535 B.C.
David	1029–971 B.C.
Deborah	1220 B.C.
Eliezer	849–848 B.C.
Elijah	860–845 B.C.
Elisha	850–795 B.C.
Ezekiel	593–571 B.C.
Gad	1015–950 B.C.
Habakkuk	615–598 B.C.
Haggai	520 B.C.
Hanani	870 B.C.
Heman	971 B.C.
Hosea	788–723 B.C.
Huldah	623 B.C.
Iddo	910 B.C.
Isaiah	740–690 B.C.
Jacob/Israel	1858 B.C.
Jehu	886 B.C.
Jeremiah	627–562 B.C.
Joel	830 B.C.
John the Apostle	A.D. 95
John the Baptist	A.D. 26
Jonah	780–765 B.C.
Joseph	1900–1885 B.C.
Malachi	430 B.C.
Micah	735–725 B.C.
Micaiah	853 B.C.
Moses	1405 B.C.

NAME	DATE
Nahum	663–612 B.C.
Nathan	1003–931 B.C.
Noah	At least seven generations after Adam
Obadiah	845 B.C.
Oded	733 B.C.
Paul	A.D. 35–64
Shemaiah	926 B.C.
Unnamed prophet Prophesied a total victory over the Syrians	855 B.C.
Unnamed prophet Prophesied a victory over the Syrians	856 B.C.
Unnamed prophet Rebuked Eli and his house for profaning the temple	1085 B.C.
Unnamed prophet Rebuked Israel for fearing idols	1210 B.C.
Unnamed prophet Rebuked King Ahab for sparing the evil Ben-Hadad	855 B.C.
Unnamed prophet Rebuked King Amaziah for his idolatry	767 B.C.
Unnamed prophet Rebuked King Jeroboam I for his idolatry	931 B.C.
Unnamed prophet Warned King Amaziah not to hire Israel's army	767 B.C.
Urijah	608 B.C.
Zechariah, son of Jehoiada	797 B.C.
Zephaniah	640–609 B.C.

The Prophets

Chronological Listing of the Prophets[2]

Name	Date
Abel	Right after creation
Noah	At least seven generations after Adam
Abraham	2000 B.C.
Joseph	1900–1885 B.C.
Jacob/Israel	1858 B.C.
Moses	1405 B.C.
Deborah	1220 B.C.
Unnamed prophet Rebuked Israel for fearing idols	1210 B.C.
Samuel	1095–1015 B.C.
Unnamed prophet Rebuked Eli and his house for profaning the temple	1085 B.C.
David	1029–971 B.C.
Gad	1015–950 B.C.
Asaph	1004 B.C.
Nathan	1003-931 B.C.
Heman	971 B.C.
Unnamed prophet Rebuked King Jeroboam I for his idolatry	931 B.C.
Ahijah	931–910 B.C.
Shemaiah	926 B.C.
Iddo	910 B.C.
Azariah	896 B.C.
Jehu	886 B.C.
Hanani	870 B.C.
Elijah	860–845 B.C.
Unnamed prophet Prophesied a victory over the Syrians	856 B.C.
Unnamed prophet Prophesied total victory over the Syrians	855 B.C.
Unnamed prophet Rebuked King Ahab for sparing the evil Ben-Hadad	855 B.C.

Name	Date
Micaiah	853 B.C.
Elisha	850–795 B.C.
Eliezer	849–848 B.C.
Obadiah	845 B.C.
Joel	830 B.C.
Zechariah, son of Jehoiada	797 B.C.
Hosea	788–723 B.C.
Jonah	780–765 B.C.
Unnamed prophet Rebuked King Amaziah for his idolatry	767 B.C.
Unnamed prophet Warned King Amaziah not to hire Israel's army	767 B.C.
Amos	750 B.C.
Isaiah	740–690 B.C.
Micah	735–725 B.C.
Oded	733 B.C.
Nahum	663–612 B.C.
Zephaniah	640–609 B.C.
Jeremiah	627–562 B.C.
Huldah	623 B.C.
Habakkuk	615–598 B.C.
Urijah	608 B.C.
Daniel	605–535 B.C.
Ezekiel	593–571 B.C.
Haggai	520 B.C.
Zechariah, son of Berechiah	520–518 B.C.
Malachi	430 B.C.
Anna	4 B.C.
John the Baptist	A.D. 26
Paul	A.D. 35–64
Agabus	A.D. 43
John the Apostle	A.D. 95

[2] The list above serves as a timeline for all the prophets discussed in the following chart. The unnamed prophets are listed according to their message. (Also see the *Timeline of Kings, Prophets, and History* chart, pp.392-393.)

THE PROPHETS

PROPHET	TIME/PLACE GIVEN	MAIN MESSAGE	PRACTICAL APPLICATION
ABEL **(Breath)** **Known Facts** 1. Was the son of Adam (Ge.4:2). 2. Was called a prophet by Jesus Christ (Mt. 23:34-35; Lu. 11:50-51). 3. Kept the flocks of animals (Ge.4:2). 4. Brought an acceptable and pleasing sacrifice to God (Ge. 4:4). 5. Was murdered by his brother, Cain (Ge.4:8). 6. Was avenged by God (Ge.4:9-12). **Predictions and Messages** By example he taught that a person must approach God through the sacrifice of a substitute offering (Ge.4:4). **Scripture References** Ge.4:1-16; Mt.23:34-39; Lu.11:47-51; He.11:4; 12:24	**Time** *The first years after creation, when Adam was still alive.* **Place** *Outside the garden of Eden, where man first began to farm.*	Abel's message is seen in his worship. Note what Abel did: when he approached the LORD, he brought an animal, a blood sacrifice. Why? Because his father, Adam, had taught him to approach God through the sacrifice of an animal. God taught Adam… • that sin causes death • that an innocent substitute had to sacrificially die in order to clothe man's shame and guilt • that thereafter man could only approach God through the sacrificial death of an innocent substitute Thus Abel pointed forward to Christ, the perfect sacrifice. He may not have completely understood, but Abel did approach God through the blood sacrifice, just as his father had taught him. Abel had *faith*. He believed that God would forgive his sins and accept him through the sacrifice of an innocent life. And note the remarkable testimony Scripture gives about Abel's faith in the coming Savior: Abel even today, although dead, testifies of Christ (He.11:4). What a striking legacy Abel left to the world! **"And Abel, he also brought of the firstlings of his flock and of the fat thereof. And the LORD had respect unto Abel and to his offering" (Ge.4:4).** **"By faith Abel offered unto God a more excellent sacrifice than Cain, by which he obtained witness that he was righteous, God testifying of his gifts: and by it he being dead yet speaketh" (He.11:4).** **"And to Jesus the mediator of the new covenant, and to the blood of sprinkling, that speaketh better things than that of Abel" (He.12:24).**	No person can earn, win, or merit salvation. No person can approach God through his own works, energy, efforts, fruits, ways, religion, ceremony or ritual. The reason is clearly evident: no person is perfect. We have a sin problem and a death problem that has to be taken care of before we can ever become acceptable to God. God has taken care of this in the sacrifice of His Son for our sins. Jesus Christ took our sins upon Himself and died for them. This is what the sacrifice of the innocent life symbolized in the Old Testament. Just like Abel, we must believe God, believe that the death (the blood) of the sacrifice of Jesus Christ covers our sins. God accepts no person apart from Jesus Christ, the promised seed and Savior of the world. God has never accepted *any person* apart from the shedding of the blood of His dear Son. The blood of Christ had to be shed for all persons through all the generations of human history. Apart from Christ, apart from accepting His sacrifice, no person can be saved from sin. No person can escape the judgment of death and hell apart from Christ. **"Ye serpents, ye generation of vipers, how can ye escape the damnation of hell?" (Mt.23:33).** **"For when we were yet without strength, in due time Christ died for the ungodly" (Ro.5:6).** **"For I delivered unto you first of all that which I also received, how that Christ died for our sins according to the scriptures" (1 Co.15:3).** **"And walk in love, as Christ also hath loved us, and hath given himself for us an offering and a sacrifice to God for a sweetsmelling savour" (Ep.5:2).**

PROPHET	TIME/PLACE GIVEN	MAIN MESSAGE	PRACTICAL APPLICATION
AGABUS (Locust) **Known Facts** 1. Lived in Judea near Jerusalem (Ac.21:10). 2. Ministered among a company of prophets (Ac.11:27-28). 3. Prophesied with the words of the Holy Spirit (Ac.11:28; 21:11). 4. Spoke for the prophets (Ac.11:28). **Predictions and Messages** 1. A severe famine would come to the entire Roman world (Ac.11:28). 2. The Apostle Paul would be bound and taken prisoner, and eventually killed (Ac. 21:11-13). **Scripture References** Ac.11:27-30; 21:10-14	**Time** *A.D. 43, at the beginning of the terrible persecution of Agrippa.* **Place** *Antioch of Syria, where the followers of Jesus Christ were first called Christians.*	Agabus prophesied two future events by the Spirit of God. First, Agabus prophesied that a great famine would occur. The disciples accepted the message given and gathered funds and stores of food to be used for those in need. Note this fact: the disciples did not waste time questioning God; they simply acted immediately on the information given, doing what was necessary for the church to continue. Some time later, Agabus prophesied that the Gentiles (or Romans) would take the Apostle Paul prisoner. Despite the danger of suffering and persecution, and eventually death, Paul was unhindered in his mission to preach the gospel. Knowing the prophecy, the fire of devotion within Paul burned all the more. Why? Because Paul trusted God. He understood that nothing is out of God's control. He firmly believed that as long as he continued to do the will of the Lord, the Lord would richly bless his labor for the gospel. **"And in these days came prophets from Jerusalem unto Antioch. And there stood up one of them named Agabus, and signified by the Spirit that there should be great dearth throughout all the world" (Ac.11:27-28).** **"And as we tarried there many days, there came down from Judaea a certain prophet, named Agabus. And when he was come unto us, he took Paul's girdle, and bound his own hands and feet, and said, Thus saith the Holy Ghost, So shall the Jews at Jerusalem bind the man that owneth this girdle, and shall deliver him into the hands of the Gentiles" (Ac.21:10-11).**	1. Giving is essential. Believers must give to those in need. And they should practice regular giving, not waiting for some disaster to strike and then scrambling for a solution to the problem. Giving should be a regular habit of the believer so the mission of the church can be carried out, even in difficult times. 2. Believers will suffer. Believers suffer by: ➢ being ridiculed ➢ being mocked ➢ being assaulted ➢ being spoken evil of ➢ being gossiped about ➢ being slandered ➢ being reviled ➢ being insulted ➢ being scolded ➢ being falsely accused ➢ being put on trial ➢ even being murdered But suffering is necessary. First of all, believers must live out the calling given to them by the Lord no matter how unpleasant, no matter what the cost. Second, suffering prepares the believer to participate in the glory of Christ. It is the necessary condition for exaltation. Suffering and struggling are a refining process through which the believer must pass. It refines the believer by forcing him to expand his trust in God more and more. Suffering drives a believer to cast himself more and more upon the care of God; therefore, the believer moves closer and closer to the Lord praying, worshipping and fellowshipping with him more and more. God is in complete control of every situation. Sometimes He allows unpleasant trials to come our way, but this is all according to His will, according to His plan for our lives. We must trust God no matter what and do all we can to understand His will and to do it. **"Yea, and all that will live godly in Christ Jesus shall suffer persecution" (2 Ti.3:12).** **"For unto you it is given in the behalf of Christ, not only to believe on him, but also to suffer for his sake" (Ph.1:29).** **"Wherein ye greatly rejoice, though now for a season, if need be, ye are in heaviness through manifold temptations: That the trial of your faith, being much more precious than of gold that perisheth, though it be tried with fire, might be found unto praise and honour and glory at the appearing of Jesus Christ" (1 Pe.1:6-7).**

THE PROPHETS

PROPHET	TIME/PLACE GIVEN	MAIN MESSAGE	PRACTICAL APPLICATION
AHIJAH (Brother in Jehovah/Yahweh) **THE SHILONITE** **Known Facts** 1. Lived in Shiloh (1 K. 11:29). 2. Called to minister during the time of Solomon and Jeroboam (1 K.11:28-29). 3. Became blind in his old age (1 K.14:4). **Predictions and Messages** 1. The division of the nation of Israel into two kingdoms—the Northern Kingdom of Israel and the Southern Kingdom of Judah (1 K.11:31). 2. The death of Abijah, the son of King Jeroboam (1 K.14:9-13). 3. The destruction of the entire family of King Jeroboam (1 K. 14:10-13). 4. The captivity and exile of Israel to a foreign land (1 K. 14:14-16). **Scripture References** 1 K.11:29-39; 12:15; 14:4-16; 2 Chr.9:29	**Time** *The end of Solomon's reign, just before 931 B.C. until 910 B.C., near the end of the reign of Jeroboam I.* **Place** *Ahijah's first prophecy was given in the countryside, just outside Jerusalem.* *Later, after the division of the kingdom, Ahijah ministered in his hometown of Shiloh, preaching mainly to the Northern Kingdom of Israel.*	Israel was divided because the king and people had forsaken God, engaged in false worship, disobeyed God's commandments and refused to walk in the ways of the LORD. Jeroboam, Solomon's very own trusted servant, became king over the Northern Kingdom just as Ahijah predicted. But when King Jeroboam displayed a life of wickedness and idolatry, judgment fell on him and on his entire household, beginning with the immediate death of his own son. Eventually, all Israel would go into captivity, because they would not repent of their wickedness, nor turn from the state religion of idolatry and false worship instituted by Jerusalem. **"And he said to Jeroboam, Take thee ten pieces: for thus saith the LORD, the God of Israel, Behold, I will rend the kingdom out of the hand of Solomon, and will give ten tribes to thee" (1 K.11:31).** **"But [you] hast done evil above all that were before thee: for thou hast gone and made thee other gods, and molten images, to provoke me to anger, and hast cast me behind thy back: Therefore, behold, I will bring evil upon the house of Jeroboam,"...Arise thou therefore, get thee to thine own house: *and* when thy feet enter into the city, the child shall die. ...For the LORD shall smite Israel, as a reed is shaken in the water, and he shall root up Israel out of this good land, which he gave to their fathers, and shall scatter them beyond the river, because they have made their groves, provoking the LORD to anger" (1 K. 14:9-10, 12, 15).**	If we continue in sin and wickedness and become involved in false worship, we will face the judgment of God. God will chastise and discipline us in order to bring us back to Him. God is zealous for us and will not allow us to chase after worldly affections, not for long. If we refuse to repent, we will face the judgment of God's hand. Even future generations may suffer and bear the brunt of our sins, suffering the great and terrible consequences of God's wrath. **"The LORD knoweth how to deliver the godly out of temptations, and to reserve the unjust unto the day of judgment to be punished" (2 Pe.2:9).** **"Every branch in me that beareth not fruit he taketh away: and every branch that beareth fruit, he purgeth it, that it may bring forth more fruit" (Jn.15:2).** **"My son, despise not the chastening of the LORD; neither be weary of his correction: For whom the LORD loveth he correcteth; even as a father the son in whom he delighteth" (Pr. 3:11-12).** **"Thou shalt not bow down thyself to them, nor serve them: for I the LORD thy God am a jealous God, visiting the iniquity of the fathers upon the children unto the third and fourth generation of them that hate me; And showing mercy unto thousands of them that love me, and keep my commandments" (Ex.20:5-6).**

PROPHET	TIME/PLACE GIVEN	MAIN MESSAGE	PRACTICAL APPLICATION
AMOS **(Burden-bearer)** **Known Facts** 1. Lived in Tekoa, on the edge of the Judean desert (Am.1:1). 2. Worked as a shepherd and as a farmer of sycamore trees (Am.1:1; 7:14). 3. Wrote the book of *Amos*. 4. Preached fiery sermons and saw startling visions. **Predictions and Messages** 1. A sermon about God's coming judgment on sinful nations, including Israel (Am.1:1-4:13). 2. A sermon about the need for seeking God with the whole heart (Am.5:1-27). 3. A sermon warning the people not to be greedy (Am.6:4-14). 4. The vision of locusts—a picture of the crops being destroyed by the ferocious insects, but Amos interceded and God had mercy (Am.7:1-3). 5. The vision of fire—a picture of the fields being destroyed, but Amos interceded and God had mercy (Am.7:4-5). 6. The vision of a plumb line—a picture of the crookedness of Israel (Am.7:7-9). 7. The vision of a basket of fruit—a picture of the rottenness of Israel's sin (Am.8:1-3). 8. A sermon warning that God will severely judge those who treat the poor unfairly (Am.8:4-14). 9. The vision of the LORD standing on the altar, striking His own temple (Am.9:1-10). 10. The prophecy about the captivity and return of Israel (Am.9:9-15). **Scripture References** The book of *Amos*	**Time** *About 750 B.C., near the end of the rule of Jeroboam II in Israel and during the long reign of Uzziah in Judah.* *The time in which Amos preached was a very prosperous time economically and financially for the people of Israel, but not spiritually. Spiritually the hearts of the people were filled with greed, so much so that they oppressed the poor without mercy.* **Place** *Israel, the Northern Kingdom.*	God will judge sin wherever it is found. No sinner is exempt from judgment. Without genuine repentance, God's judgment will surely fall upon the sinner. Amos focused upon one theme, one subject: the coming judgment of God upon those who refused to turn from sin. Despite persecution and death threats, Amos faithfully continued to preach the messages given him by God, a series of blistering sermons against the sins of arrogance and pride. **"Therefore thus will I do unto thee, O Israel: and because I will do this unto thee, prepare to meet thy God, O Israel" (Am. 4:12).** **"Then answered Amos, and said to Amaziah, I was no prophet, neither was I a prophet's son; but I was an herdman, and a gatherer of sycamore fruit: And the LORD took me as I followed the flock, and the LORD said unto me, Go, prophesy unto my people Israel" (Am.7:14-15).**	Worldly gain, such as riches, social position, heritage, even religion will not save a person. Such things can be good if they are used to help the poor or advance God's kingdom. But when a person uses worldly gain just for the purpose of more worldly gain, God's judgment is sure to fall upon that person. At least two major applications can be seen in the prophecies of Amos. 1. Just think of the people gripped by greed who push aside the needs of others… • to make themselves more comfortable • to buy some luxury • to enjoy more leisure time • to hoard more riches Shockingly, some people are so gripped by greed, they even assault and murder in order to gain more and more. Unbelievably, they consider human life worthless if it stands in the way of their gaining more riches. 2. The minister of God must boldly preach the Word of God. He must not form his sermon based on what people want to hear, nor avoid certain subjects because he will not be popular. The messenger of the LORD must be unashamed and unswerving in his calling to preach the whole counsel of God. Even persecution, no matter how serious, must not prevent the minister from proclaiming the Word of God, declaring what God has anointed him to say. **"Charge them that are rich in this world, that they be not highminded, nor trust in uncertain riches, but in the living God, who giveth us richly all things to enjoy" (1 Ti.6:17).** **"I charge thee therefore before God, and the Lord Jesus Christ, who shall judge the quick [living] and the dead at his appearing and his kingdom; preach the word; be instant in season, out of season; reprove, rebuke, exhort with all longsuffering and doctrine" (2 Ti.1:3-4).**

PROPHET	TIME/PLACE GIVEN	MAIN MESSAGE	PRACTICAL APPLICATION
ANNA **(Gracious)** **Known Facts** 1. Served in the temple as a woman prophet (Lu.2:36). 2. Appeared as the first prophet since Malachi, a space of over 300 years. 3. Descended from the tribe of Asher (Lu. 2:36). 4. Widowed for many years (Lu.2:36). 5. Fasted and prayed continually (Lu.2:37). 6. Loved and hoped in God, therefore she was blessed (Lu.2:37). 7. Pointed out Christ to others (Lu.2:38). **Predictions and Messages** Jesus is the Christ, the Savior of the world (Lu.2:38). **Scripture References** Lu.2:36-38	**Time** *About 4 B.C., eight days after the birth of Jesus Christ.* **Place** *At the temple in Jerusalem.*	Anna's message was the greatest of all messages: Jesus Christ is the Redeemer, the promised Messiah Who brings redemption to all who ask for God's salvation. Anna shared this good news with anyone looking for redemption in Jerusalem. **"And she coming in that instant gave thanks likewise unto the Lord, and spake of him [the Christ child] to all them that looked for redemption in Jerusalem" (Lu.2:38).**	1. God will greatly bless the person who places his entire hope in Him. God will always bless the person who trusts in Him. We must rely on God for our salvation, rely on Him with our whole heart, holding nothing back, seeking Him continually. For there is no other person, no other place, no other source to whom we can turn for the salvation of our soul. Salvation is in Christ, and Christ alone. 2. Believers should be busy talking to everyone about Jesus Christ, for Jesus Christ came to earth to redeem us from our sins. And He will grant forgiveness to anyone who seeks for it, to anyone who will place his entire hope in the Lord. **"Behold the eye of the Lord is upon them that fear him, upon them that hope in his mercy" (Ps.33:18).** **"Being justified freely by his grace through the redemption that is in Christ Jesus" (Ro.3:24).**
ASAPH **(Gathering)** **Known Facts** 1. Was the son of Berechiah (1 Chr.6:39). 2. Descended from the tribe of Levi and the clan of Kohathites (1 Chr.6:33, 39). 3. Appointed by David as a musician, Asaph played the cymbals and sang (1 Chr. 6:31, 39). 4. Called a Seer (2 Chr. 29:30). 5. Wrote lyrics which were used many years after his death (2 Chr. 29:30). **Predictions and Messages** Sang and played music to praise and glorify the LORD. **Scripture References** 1 Chr.6:31-43; 15:17-19 2 Chr.29:30	**Time** *1004 B.C. Right after David was first crowned king in Hebron, he decided to bring the Ark of the Covenant from Kiriath-Jearim to Jerusalem. It was at this time that Asaph and the other musicians were appointed by King David to lead the people of Israel in worship, praising the LORD in songs of praise and celebration to the LORD.* **Place** *Jerusalem, the Holy City.*	Asaph was one of the leading musicians during the days of King David. Although there is not any specific message recorded by Asaph, he lived a life of praise and worship and greatly encouraged others to do so. Down through the years, Asaph's testimony was that of leading and encouraging the congregation in praising the LORD. **"So the Levites appointed Heman the son of Joel; and of his brethren, Asaph the son of Berechiah; and of the sons of Merari their brethren, Ethan the son of Kushaiah" (1 Chr.15:17).** **"Moreover Hezekiah the king and the princes commanded the Levites to sing praise unto the LORD with the words of David, and of Asaph the seer. And they sang praises with gladness, and they bowed their heads and worshipped" (2 Chr.29:30).**	The importance of praise and worship cannot be overstressed. As the Creator of the universe, the LORD expects us to praise and worship Him. It is the LORD Who has created life and Who sustains life. The air we breathe, the water we drink, the food we eat—every good and perfect gift we have comes from the hand of the LORD with Whom there is no changing. Because of all the richness and depth of all the blessings God pours out upon us—because of all the good and perfect gifts He so mercifully gives every day of our lives—the LORD expects, and rightly deserves, our worship and the praise of His holy name. **"Oh that men would praise the LORD for his goodness, and for his wonderful works to the children of men!" (Ps.107:8, 15, 21, 31).** **"Blessed be the Lord, who daily loadeth us with benefits, even the God of our salvation. Selah" (Ps.68:19).**

THE PROPHETS

PROPHET	TIME/PLACE GIVEN	MAIN MESSAGE	PRACTICAL APPLICATION
AZARIAH (Jehovah/Yahweh is my Helper) **Known Facts** 1. Was the son of Oded (2 Chr.15:1). 2. Ministered as the first of the prophets to the Southern King-dom of Judah after the division of the nation of Israel. **Predictions and Messages** Azariah instructed King Asa to extend the revival which had begun in the land. Asa was not to lose courage, but to continue to serve God with fervor (2 Chr.15:2-7). **Scripture References** 2 Chr.15:1-12	**Time** *896 B.C., during the reign of Asa, king of Judah, who stirred a great reformation and revival among the people.* **Place** *Jerusalem, the Holy City and capital of Judah.*	Revival was sweeping through the land of Judah resulting in changed lives and a reformation of worship. King Asa and his troops had just delivered a crushing defeat to the invading Ethiopians. But right afterward, Asa was tempted to rely on his own strength. So Azariah, the prophet, pressed the king and the people to seek the LORD more than ever before. He challenged them not to fall into a foolish and destructive attitude of pride and self-reliance. Azariah declared that the LORD wanted the people to be as strong spiritually as they had been in battle. King Asa responded to Azariah's message and continued to stir a strong reformation among the people. He removed the pagan images of idolatry as well as those in charge of their worship. Then, he made all false worship illegal, instituting the death penalty for all who practiced it. Committing himself totally to the LORD, he established the purity of true worship, the worship of the LORD God alone (Jehovah/Yahweh). **"Now the Spirit of God came on Azariah the son of Oded, and he went out to meet Asa and said to him, "Listen to me, Asa, and all Judah and Benjamin: the LORD is with you when you are with Him. And if you seek Him, He will let you find Him; but if you forsake Him, He will forsake you... be strong and do not lose courage, for there is reward for your work" (2 Chr.15:1-2, 7).**	Seeking the LORD is essential for every believer. We must seek Him with our whole heart, seek Him continually. Anything that could trap us in a deadly snare of sin must be removed. Placing God first in our lives, first in everything we do, must be our never-ending effort. We must draw close to the LORD, as close as we possibly can. We must continue to stoke the fire of revival in our hearts, to let it burn hotter and hotter. Why? Because we are always in need, in very desperate need, of God's help. Even when things seem to be going smoothly, we need God. We need Him… • for daily guidance • for spiritual strength • to escape temptation • for our daily food • to hold the world together • for our very next breath • for *all* our needs, *for every single need, every day of our lives* And remember this: God will *actively move in the behalf of the one who seeks Him*. Our labor is not in vain. There is a reward for serving God. God strongly supports those who wholeheartedly serve Him. **"And let us not be weary in well doing: for in due season we shall reap, if we faint not" (Ga.6:9).** **"But seek ye first the kingdom of God, and his righteousness; and all these things shall be added unto you" (Mt.6:33).** **"For the eyes of the Lord run to and fro throughout the whole earth to show himself strong in the behalf of them whose heart is perfect toward him" (2 Chr.16:9).**

336

PROPHET	TIME/PLACE GIVEN	MAIN MESSAGE	PRACTICAL APPLICATION
### DANIEL (God is my Judge) **Known Facts** 1. Was taken captive by the Babylonians and forced to live in Babylon (Da.1:1-2). 2. Prophesied to three major world powers— Israel, Babylon and Medo-Persia (Da.1:1-2; 5:31). 3. Possessed tremendous integrity (Da.1:8-10; 6:4; Eze.14:1). 4. Was given a Babylonian name (Belteshazzar) because he was highly favored among the exiles, and because he needed to conduct business in Babylon (Da.1:7). 5. Was able to understand all kinds of mysteries (Da.7:15-28; 8:15-27; 9:24-27; 10:1-14; Eze.28:3). 6. Was delivered miraculously from the den of lions (Da.6:19-23). 7. Saw strange and vivid visions about Israel's future, about the coming dominant world powers of human history, and about a future period of history known as the *Great Tribulation* and the end of the world (Da.7:1–12:13). 8. Wrote the book of *Daniel*. **Predictions and Messages** 1. The interpretation of King Nebuchadnezzar's dream of a great statue, which symbolizes the coming great world powers (Da.2:17-19). 2. The interpretation of King Nebuchadnezzar's dream of a great tree which predicted the coming judgment against Nebuchadnezzar due to his pride (Da.4:19-27). (Cont. on next page)	**Time** *605–535 B.C., during the Babylonian captivity of Judah and on into the first years of the Medo-Persian Empire. Daniel was just a young man, only about thirty years old when he was taken captive. He lived the rest of his days in Babylon, ministering to his people, serving as a statesman for Babylon and recording history, writing down his visions and prophecies of the future.* **Place** *Near the Tigris River during the last years of the Babylonian Empire and the first few years of the Medo-Persian Empire.*	The book of *Daniel* has one unmistakable message: God sets up kings and puts down kings. The powers of the world will struggle and struggle to gain domination, wealth, and control; but God is in control and overrules everything they do, working all things out for the good of genuine believers and accomplishing His will for the world. Only He can exalt or humble; only He can deliver or destroy. God is sovereign over all. He lifts up those who acknowledge His sovereignty and puts down those who become filled with pride and self-sufficiency. After the end of the Assyrian Empire, control passed mainly to Babylon, which had been firmly established by Nabopolassar. Nabopolassar's son (Nebuchadnezzar II, the king we read about in the book of *Daniel*) then took over. The first thing Nebuchadnezzar did was to export most of the Judeans to Babylon. This included Daniel and his three friends. But despite their new pagan surroundings, Daniel and his three friends became very successful and were highly esteemed by the Babylonians. This was due to God's guidance, for they remained faithful to the LORD and to Him alone. Daniel became a close advisor and statesman for Nebuchadnezzar. Through the interpretation of dreams, which God inflicted upon the king, Daniel was lifted to a very high position in the Babylonian kingdom. Years later, Nebuchadnezzar's grandson Belshazzar became king. He was prideful like his grandfather before him. But there was a difference. Nebuchadnezzar repented and acknowledged God as the Sovereign over the earth, but Belshazzar refused to do so. The last straw came when Belshazzar defiled the articles of the temple of God by using them at a drunken feast in honor of a false god. At this, God literally wrote on the wall with His finger, burning a permanent message of immediate doom upon the king and the Babylonian empire. Belshazzar was slain that night as the Medo-Persian soldiers stormed the capital and the palace, and the new empire was put in place.	➢ All the world is to praise God for His holiness. ➢ All the world is to praise God for His sovereignty and omnipotence. ➢ All the world is to praise God for His eternal existence. What an indictment against man! How little we praise and worship God—truly praise and worship Him. Think for a moment and imagine in your mind the four beings who surround the throne of God. They were created to worship God, and they worship Him day and night, never ceasing from worshipping Him. They cry out day and night the glorious praise: "Holy, holy, holy, Lord God Almighty, which was, and is, and is to come" (Re. 4:8). The very thought of such a scene should bring us to our knees in repentance, humility and worship of God and His Son, Jesus Christ, the King of kings and Lord of lords. What a lesson the book of *Daniel* has for us! For the LORD God Almighty dwells in glory and majesty, dominion, and power. We owe Him our lives, all we are and have. **"Exalt the LORD our God, and worship at his holy hill; for the LORD our God is holy" (Ps.99:9).** **"And one cried unto another, and said, Holy, holy, holy, is the LORD of hosts: the whole earth is full of his glory" (Is.6:3).** **"Who shall not fear thee, O Lord, and glorify thy name? for thou only art holy: for all nations shall come and worship before thee; for thy judgments are made manifest" (Re.15:4).** **"For I am the LORD that bringeth you up out of the land of Egypt, to be your God: ye shall therefore be holy, for I am holy" (Lev.11:45).** **"I know that thou canst do every thing, and that no thought can be withholden from thee" (Jb.42:2).** **"But our God is in the heavens: he hath done whatsoever he hath pleased" (Ps.115:3).** **"Yea, before the day was I am he; and there is none that can deliver out of my hand: I will work, and who shall let [hinder] it?" (Is.43:13).**

PROPHET	TIME/PLACE GIVEN	MAIN MESSAGE	PRACTICAL APPLICATION
DANIEL (cont.) 3. The message that God gives political power to whomever He wishes (Da.4:25). 4. The interpretation of the handwriting on the wall written to King Belshazzar by the finger of God Himself—the prediction of the soon coming judgment against Belshazzar and the end of the Babylonian Empire (Da.5:10-28). 5. The vision of the four beasts arising from the sea—a prophecy of the coming dominant world powers (Da.7:1-8). 6. The vision of Jesus Christ, the Ancient of Days (Da.7:9-10; Re. 4:4; Mt.19:28; 1 Co.6:3). 7. The vision of the fourth beast being destroyed—the prophecy about the defeat of the antichrist (Da.7:11-12). 8. The vision of Jesus Christ—One like the Son of Man (Da. 7:13-14). 9. The vision of the ram and the two horns—a prophecy of the end of the Medo-Persian Empire and the rise of the Greek Empire (Da.8:1-14). 10. The message from Gabriel about Jeremiah's seventy weeks—the prediction that the Messiah, Jesus Christ, the Savior of the world, would be rejected 483 years in the future (Da.9:24-26). 11. The message from Gabriel about Jeremiah's seventieth week—the prediction of the coming Tribulation, the desecration of the temple by the antichrist and the end of the world (Da.9:26-27; Mt.24:15-25; Mk. 13:14-23). (Cont. on next page)		But Daniel, who continued to give God honor and to remain humble, was quickly lifted up to a high rank in the government of the Medes. Both before and after the change in power, Daniel saw amazing visions and received many startling messages from angels about the powers of the world, both present and future, and about the end times. Daniel wrote down many of these, but was instructed to withhold others. In all of his writings, Daniel continually proclaimed the great majesty of God and the need to honor Him. **"This is the dream; and we will tell the interpretation thereof before the king. Thou, O king, art a king of kings: for the God of heaven hath given thee a kingdom, power, and strength, and glory. And wheresoever the children of men dwell, the beasts of the field and the fowls of the heaven hath he given into thine hand, and hath made thee ruler over them all. Thou art this head of gold. And after thee shall arise another kingdom inferior to thee, and another third kingdom of brass, which shall bear rule over all the earth. And the fourth kingdom shall be strong as iron: forasmuch as iron breaketh in pieces and subdueth all things: and as iron that breaketh all these, shall it break in pieces and bruise. And whereas thou sawest the feet and toes, part of potters' clay, and part of iron, the kingdom shall be divided; but there shall be in it of the strength of the iron, forasmuch as thou sawest the iron mixed with miry clay. And as the toes of the feet were part of iron, and part of clay, so the kingdom shall be partly strong, and partly broken. And whereas thou sawest iron mixed with miry clay, they shall mingle themselves with the seed of men: but they shall not cleave one to another, even as iron is not mixed with clay. And in the days of these kings shall the God of heaven set up a kingdom, which shall never be destroyed: and the kingdom shall not be left to other people, but it shall break in pieces and consume all these kingdoms, and it shall stand for ever. Forasmuch as thou sawest that the stone was cut out of the**	**"But Jesus beheld them, and said unto them, With men this is impossible; but with God all things are possible"** (Mt.19:26). **"Now to him that is of power to stablish you according to my gospel, and the preaching of Jesus Christ, according to the revelation of the mystery, which was kept secret since the world began"** (Ro.16:25). **"For I lift up my hand to heaven, and say, I live for ever"** (De.32:40). **"The eternal God is thy refuge, and underneath are the everlasting arms"** (De.33:27). **"Thy name, O LORD, endureth for ever; and thy memorial, O Lord, throughout all generations"** (Ps.135:13). **"I am Alpha and Omega, the beginning and the ending, saith the Lord, which is, and which was, and which is to come, the Almighty"** (Re.1:8). **"Thine, O LORD, is the greatness, and the power, and the glory, and the victory, and the majesty: for all that is in the heaven and in the earth is thine; thine is the kingdom, O LORD, and thou art exalted as head above all"** (1 Chr.29:11). **"The LORD reigneth, he is clothed with majesty; the LORD is clothed with strength, wherewith he hath girded himself: the world also is stablished, that it cannot be moved"** (Ps.93:1). **"I will speak of the glorious honour of thy majesty, and of thy wondrous works"** (Ps.145:5). **"And the seventh angel sounded; and there were great voices in heaven, saying, The kingdoms of this world are become the kingdoms of our Lord, and of his Christ; and he shall reign for ever and ever"** (Re.11:15).

PROPHET	TIME/PLACE GIVEN	MAIN MESSAGE	PRACTICAL APPLICATION
DANIEL (cont.) 12. The vision of the man dressed in linen standing by the Tigris River (Da.10:1-14). 13. The vision of the man who strengthened Daniel (Da.10:15-21). 14. The prophecy about the coming Greek Empire and Alexander the Great (Da.11:2-4). 15. The prophecies about the coming empires of Egypt and Syria and their struggle for world power (Da.11:5-35). 16. The prophecy of the distressing time at the end of the world—that those whose names are written in the Book of Life will be rescued (Da.12:1). 17. The prophecy of additional resurrections during the Tribulation (Da.12:2-3). **Scripture References** The book of *Daniel*		mountain without hands, and that it brake in pieces the iron, the brass, the clay, the silver, and the gold; the great God hath made known to the king what shall come to pass hereafter: and the dream is certain, and the interpretation thereof sure" (Da.2:36-45). "How great are his signs! and how mighty are his wonders! his kingdom is an everlasting kingdom, and his dominion is from generation to generation" (Da. 4:3). "And at the end of the days I Nebuchadnezzar lifted up mine eyes unto heaven, and mine understanding returned unto me, and I blessed the most High, and I praised and honoured him that liveth for ever, whose dominion is an everlasting dominion, and his kingdom is from generation to generation: And all the inhabitants of the earth are reputed as nothing: and he doeth according to his will in the army of heaven, and among the inhabitants of the earth: and none can stay his hand, or say unto him, What doest thou?" (Da.4:34-35). "And this is the writing that was written, MENE, MENE, TEKEL, UPHARSIN. This is the interpretation of the thing: MENE; God hath numbered thy kingdom, and finished it. TEKEL; Thou art weighed in the balances, and art found wanting. PERES; Thy kingdom is divided, and given to the Medes and Persians" (Da.5:25-28).	

THE PROPHETS

PROPHET	TIME/PLACE GIVEN	MAIN MESSAGE	PRACTICAL APPLICATION
DAVID (Loved) **Known Facts** 1. Was the son of Jesse and the youngest of eight sons (1 S.16:11; 17:12). 2. Lived in Bethlehem (1 S.16:1; 17:12). 3. Descended from the tribe of Judah (Mt. 1:1-6). 4. Served the first king of Israel, King Saul, by playing music for him and by serving in Saul's army (1 S.16:23; 18:5). 5. Defeated the giant Goliath as a youth (1 S.17). 6. Was anointed king over all Israel and reigned forty years (1 S.16:1, 11-13; 2 S.5:5). 7. Was promised by God that the Savior would come through his lineage (Mt.1:1-17). 8. Wrote 73 Psalms (Ps. 22:1; 23:1; 41:1; 110:1). 9. Played musical instruments in praise to the LORD (2 S.23:2). 10. Was a brilliant military leader and strategist. Led great military campaigns (1 S. 18:5-7). 11. Had a heart that was like the heart of God (1 S.13:14; Ac.13:22). **Predictions and Messages** 1. The Messiah, the Savior of the world, would be a priest after the order of Melchizedek (Ps.110:4; Mt. 27:50-51; Mk. 15:37-38; Lu.23:44-46; He.6:20). 2. The Messiah would be betrayed by a friend (Ps.41:9; Mt. 26:20-25; Mk.14:10-11; Lu.22:2-6; Jn. 13:1-2; 1 Co.11:23). 3. The Messiah's betrayer would be removed from office and replaced (Ps. 109:7-8; Ac.1:18-20). (Cont. on next page)	**Time** *1029–971 B.C. All his life, King David sang and wrote psalms (songs) to the LORD. In his times of rejoicing and in his time of despair, David cried out to God in beautiful songs of poetry.* **Place** *Many places throughout Judea and Samaria as well as southern Jerusalem, the City of David.*	David was a shining example of trust in God, of placing his life in the palm of God's hand. Whenever David was in trouble, he turned to God as His Savior, trusting the LORD completely for deliverance. And the LORD always saved, delivered David because of the saving acts of God and in his behalf, David was able to write many heartfelt Psalms that are recorded in the Holy Scripture. And God was able to use David to predict many of the prophecies about Jesus Christ hundreds of years before the Savior was born. **"Now these are the last words of David. David the son of Jesse declares, The man who was raised on high declares, The anointed of the God of Jacob, And the sweet psalmist of Israel, 'The Spirit of the Lord spoke by me, And His word was on my tongue'" (2 S.23:1-2).**	David trusted fully that God would do exactly as He had promised, that He would send the promised King and Savior to establish His throne forever in the world. The confessions of David's heart were made in simple trust, arising from a heart that was truly convinced that God does exactly what He says He will do. David's trust is a dynamic example for us, for it is simple trust God desires from man—nothing more and nothing less. We simply must rely on God. We must lean on Him with our whole heart, put our complete trust in the LORD to do exactly as He says. The LORD will save those who trust in Him. **"The God of my rock; in him will I trust: he is my shield, and the horn of my salvation, my high tower, and my refuge, my saviour; thou savest me from violence" (2 S.22:3).** **"But let all those that put their trust in thee rejoice: let them ever shout for joy, because thou defendest them: let them also that love thy name be joyful in thee" (Ps.5:11).** **"O LORD my God, in thee do I put my trust: save me from all them that persecute me, and deliver me" (Ps.7:1).** **"The LORD redeemeth the soul of his servants: and none of them that trust in him shall be desolate" (Ps.34:22).** **"Cause me to hear thy lovingkindness in the morning; for in thee do I trust: cause me to know the way wherein I should walk; for I lift up my soul unto thee" (Ps.143:8).**

PROPHET	TIME/PLACE GIVEN	MAIN MESSAGE	PRACTICAL APPLICATION
DAVID (cont.) 4. The Messiah, the Savior of the world, would be falsely accused (Ps. 27:12; 35:11; Mt. 26:59-62; Mk. 14:55-59). 5. The Messiah would be hated for no reason (Ps.69:4; Jn.15:23-25). 6. The Messiah's hands and feet would be pierced (Ps.22:16; Jn. 20:25-27). 7. The Messiah would bear the sins of the world (Ps.22:1; Mt. 27:45-46; Mk.15:33-34). 8. The Messiah would be mocked (Ps.22:6-8; Mt.27:39-40; Mk. 15:29-32; Lu. 23:35-37). 9. The Messiah would be given gall and vinegar (Ps.69:21; Mt. 27:48; Mk.15:36; Jn. 19:28-29). 10. The Messiah would pray for His enemies (Ps.109:4; Lu.23:34). 11. The Messiah's garments would be gambled for (Ps.22:18; Mt.27:35; Mk.15:24; Lu.23:34; Jn.19:23-25). 12. The Messiah would not have any broken bones (Ps.34:20; see Ex. 12:46; Jn.19:31-37). 13. The Messiah would be resurrected (Ps. 16:10; Mt.12:39-41; 16:4; 28:1-7; Mk. 16:1-8; Lu.11:29-32; 24:1-8; Jn.20:1-8). 14. The Messiah would ascend to heaven (Ps. 68:18; Mk.16:19-20; Lu.24:50-51; Ac.1:6-9; Ep.4:8-10). **Scripture References** 1 S.16–1 K. 2; Ps.16, 22, 27, 34, 41, 68, 69, 109, 110			

DEBORAH
(Honey bee)

Known Facts

1. Was married to Lapidoth (Jud.4:4).
2. Judged Israel, deciding civil cases for the people according to God's Word (Jud. 4:4).
3. Wrote a song of deliverance after the defeat of Sisera and the Canaanite army (Jud.5).

Predictions and Messages

1. Barak was to gather ten thousand men from Naphtali and Zebulun, and God would deliver Sisera into his hand (Jud.4:4-8).
2. Sisera would be killed by a woman because Barak refused to go without Deborah (Jud.4:9).

Scripture References
Jud.4-5

Time

Approximately 1220 B.C., during a time of oppression by King Jabin of the Canaanites. It was about 200 plus years before King David and about 200 plus after the Exodus.

Place

Between Ramah and Bethel, in the hill country of Ephraim.

The LORD is a mighty Deliverer, Who will deliver Israel from the Canaanite enemies. Through Deborah, God instructed Barak to mobilize ten thousand troops and to meet the enemy commander Sisera, at the Kishon River. Gripped by fear and feeling inadequate for the task, Barak refused to go without Deborah's help. Granting his request, God used both Deborah and Barak to soundly defeat the oppressing Canaanites in a tremendous victory. But because Barak refused to obey God, he was denied the honor of capturing the enemy commander Sisera. Instead, the honor of killing the dreaded enemy commander was given to a woman name Jael.

"Now she sent and summoned Barak the son of Abinoam from Kedesh-naphtali, and said to him, 'Behold, the LORD, the God of Israel, has commanded, "Go and march to Mount Tabor, and take with you ten thousand men from the sons of Naphtali and from the sons of Zebulun. I will draw out to you Sisera, the commander of Jabin's army, with his chariots and his many troops to the river Kishon, and I will give him into your hand."' Then Barak said to her, 'If you will go with me, then I will go; but if you will not go with me, I will not go.' She said, 'I will surely go with you; nevertheless, the honor shall not be yours on the journey that you are about to take, for the LORD will sell Sisera into the hands of a woman.' Then Deborah arose and went with Barak to Kedesh" (Jud.4:6-9).

The courage of Deborah stands as a dynamic example for us all. Just imagine—facing a massive army unarmed! Deborah courageously accepted this challenge, but not Barak. He was reluctant, fainthearted, fearful, and unbelieving. From this experience of Deborah and Barak, we must learn one lesson: there is no room in the service of God for being fainthearted, fearful, or unbelieving. God commands us to be courageous, to step forth and face the enemy with courage and boldness, No matter what the enemy or its power, we are to be courageous in standing against it. God promises to help us and to deliver us if we will confront the enemy courageously in His name.

"Have I not commanded thee? Be strong and of a good courage; be not afraid, neither be thou dismayed: for the LORD thy God is with thee whithersoever thou goest" (Jos.1:9).

"The wicked flee when no man pursueth, But the righteous are bold as a lion" (Pr.28:1).

"Fear thou not; for I am with thee: be not dismayed; for I am thy God: I will strengthen thee; yea, I will help thee; yea, I will uphold thee with the right hand of my righteousness" (Is.41:10).

THE PROPHETS

PROPHET	TIME/PLACE GIVEN	MAIN MESSAGE	PRACTICAL APPLICATION
ELIEZER (God is my Helper) **Known Facts** 1. Was the son of Doda-vahu (2 Chr. 20:37). 2. Lived in Mareshah (2 Chr.20:37). **Predictions and Messages** Rebuked King Jehosha-phat for forming an alli-ance with an evil king, King Ahaziah of the Northern Kingdom of Is-rael (2 Chr.20:37). **Scripture References** 2 Chr.20:35-37	**Time** *849-48 B.C., at the end of the reign of Jehosha-phat, king of Ju-dah.* **Place** *Jerusalem, the cap-ital of the South-ern Kingdom of Judah.*	Eliezer rebuked King Jehosha-phat of Judah for making an agree-ment with the evil King Ahaziah of the Northern Kingdom of Israel. Eliezer declared that God had caused their gold-seeking ships to be destroyed because God was so displeased with Jehoshaphat's ac-tions. **"And after this did Jehosha-phat king of Judah join himself with Ahaziah king of Israel, who did very wickedly: And he joined himself with him to make ships to go to Tarshish: and they made the ships in Eziongeber. Then Eliezer the son of Dodavah of Mareshah prophesied against Jehoshaphat, saying, Because thou hast joined thyself with Aha-ziah, the LORD hath broken thy works. And the ships were broken, that they were not able to go to Tarshish" (2 Chr.20:35-37).**	God warns the believer against compromising and forming worldly alliances with the unbelievers and wicked people of this world. God demands spiritual separation. For if we fellowship, closely associate with the sinful and wicked of this earth, eventually we will be seduced to join in and participate in their sin. Com-promise is forbidden by God. We are to live lives of spiritual separation, not compromising our commitment to God, not engaging in the sinful and wicked behavior of unbelievers. **"And take heed to yourselves, lest at any time your hearts be overcharged with surfeiting, and drunkenness, and cares of this life, and so that day come upon you unawares" (Lu.21:34).** **"I beseech you therefore, breth-ren, by the mercies of God, that ye present your bodies a living sacri-fice, holy, acceptable unto God, which is your reasonable service. And be not conformed to this world: but be ye transformed by the renewing of your mind, that ye may prove what is that good, and acceptable, and perfect, will of God" (Ro.12:1-2).** **"But now I have written unto you not to keep company, if any man that is called a brother be a fornicator, or covetous, or an idol-ater, or a railer, or a drunkard, or an extortioner; with such an one no not to eat" (1 Co.5:11).**

THE PROPHETS

PROPHET	TIME/PLACE GIVEN	MAIN MESSAGE	PRACTICAL APPLICATION
ELIJAH (Yahweh is God) **Known Facts** 1. Was from Tishbi (1 K.17:1). 2. Lived in Gilead (1 K.17:1). 3. Ministered to the Northern Kingdom of Israel (1 K.17:1). 4. Performed many miracles: ➤ Prevented rain for three years (1 K.17:1; Js.5:17). ➤ Multiplied flour and oil during the entire time of the drought (1 K.17:14). ➤ Raised a child from the dead (1 K.17:22). ➤ Called fire down from heaven (1 K.18:38; 2 K.1:10). ➤ Brought rain (1 K.18:41). ➤ Divided the Jordan River and crossed on dry ground (2 K.2:8). **Predictions and Messages** 1. A long, severe drought would come to Israel (1 K.17:1). 2. The flour and oil of the widow of Zarepath would multiply miraculously so that she would have an unending daily supply as long as the drought continued (1 K.17:14). 3. A torrential rain would come to end the long drought (1 K.18:41). 4. The blood of Ahab would be licked up by the dogs to avenge the blood of Naboth (1 K.21:19; 2 K.9:24-26). 5. The household of Ahab would be destroyed and come to a complete end (1 K.21:21-24). **Scripture References** 1 K.17–2 K.2	**Time** *860-845 B.C., during the reigns of Ahab, Ahaziah, and Jehoram, kings of Northern Israel.* **Place** *The Northern Kingdom of Israel.*	For over three years, Elijah predicted that it would not rain. Through this terrible drought, Elijah was able to warn the people time and again against the false worship of Baal. Baal was thought to be the god of the weather and fertility, and the worship of this false god was strongly encouraged by King Ahab and Queen Jezebel. But with fervor and stunning miracles, God called people to repentance through Elijah's ministry. Finally, a showdown was held between Elijah and the false prophets of Baal, a confrontation that was to prove once and for all who the real God was. Perhaps no scene in the Old Testament is more dramatic than when Elijah called down fire from heaven upon his sacrifice on Mt. Carmel. The spectacular, miraculous event proved once for all that Jehovah/Yahweh is the One True God, the only real and living God. Sadly, despite this tremendous display of God's power, Ahab and the people still did not repent. **"And Elijah the Tishbite, who was of the inhabitants of Gilead, said unto Ahab, As the Lord God of Israel liveth, before whom I stand, there shall not be dew nor rain these years, but according to my word" (1 K.17:1).** **"For thus saith the Lord God of Israel, The barrel of meal shall not waste, neither shall the cruse of oil fail, until the day that the Lord sendeth rain upon the earth" (1 K.17:14).** **"And Elijah said unto Ahab, Get thee up, eat and drink; for there is a sound of abundance of rain" (1 K.18:41).** **"And will make thine house like the house of Jeroboam the son of Nebat, and like the house of Baasha the son of Ahijah, for the provocation wherewith thou hast provoked me to anger, and made Israel to sin" (1 K.21:22).**	1. The LORD (Jehovah, Yahweh) is the One and only living and true God: there is no other God. All false gods are just this: false. They are nonexistent, not really living, not possessing life. They are powerless, unable to respond. Being lifeless, they cannot hear prayers, nor reach out to help us in our desperate hours of need. False gods are totally incapable of being present with us as we walk day by day. They are unable to guide us or to fulfill any promise ever made by a false prophet. All other so-called gods are false. They exist only in a person's imagination. 2. If a person refuses to believe God's Word, he will not believe nor follow the Lord, even if he sees a dramatic sign from heaven. **"I am Alpha and Omega, the beginning and the ending, saith the Lord, which is, and which was, and which is to come, the Almighty" (Re.1:8).** **"Fear ye not, neither be afraid: have not I told thee from that time, and have declared it? ye are even my witnesses. Is there a God beside me? yea, there is no God; I know not any" (Is.44:8).** **"Then the steward said within himself, What shall I do? for my lord taketh away from me the stewardship: I cannot dig; to beg I am ashamed" (Lu.16:31).**

PROPHET	TIME/PLACE GIVEN	MAIN MESSAGE	PRACTICAL APPLICATION
ELISHA (God is the Savior) **Known Facts** 1. Was the son of Shaphat (1 K.19:16). 2. Lived in Abel-Meholah (1 K.19:16). 3. Was anointed by Elijah to take his place, as God instructed (1 K.19:16). 4. Performed many miracles: ➤ Parted the Jordan River (2 K.2:14). ➤ Made bitter water sweet (2 K.2:19-22). ➤ Saved an army by causing water to appear in ditches (2 K.3:13-20). ➤ Multiplied the widow's oil (2 K.4:1-7). ➤ Raised a child from the dead (2 K.4:32-37). ➤ Purified a pot of food from poison (2 K.4:38-41). ➤ Multiplied bread and grain to feed one hundred men (2 K.4:42-44). ➤ Healed a leper (2 K.5:1-14). ➤ Caused an ax head to float in the Jordan River (2 K.6:1-7). ➤ Raised a man from the dead, when the man came in contact with Elisha's bones (2 K.13:21). 5. Prophesied in the Northern Kingdom (2 K. 2:2). 6. Saw Elijah transported to heaven (2 K.2:9-13). 7. Was the model of a spiritual leader (1 K. 19:19-21; 2 K.5:16). (Cont. on next page)	**Time** *850–795 B.C., during the reigns of Jehoram, Jehu, Jehoahaz, and Jehoash, kings of Northern Israel.* **Place** *Israel, The Northern Kingdom of Israel.*	God will save those who have faith in Him. Time and time again, in both the words and deeds of Elisha, this message of salvation was demonstrated. Elisha had strong faith in God and faithfully followed God. But he not only followed, he demonstrated an iron determination in living a godly, righteous life. Elisha's life was a beacon, a bright example to everyone he met. Persevering to his very last day on earth, he repeatedly demonstrated the saving, miraculous power of God. **"And he went forth unto the spring of the waters, and cast the salt in there, and said, Thus saith the LORD, I have healed these waters; there shall not be from thence any more death or barren land" (2 K.2:21).** **"For thus saith the LORD, Ye shall not see wind, neither shall ye see rain; yet that valley shall be filled with water, that ye may drink, both ye, and your cattle, and your beasts" (2 K.3:17).** **"And his servitor said, What, should I set this before an hundred men? He said again, Give the people, that they may eat: for thus saith the LORD, They shall eat, and shall leave thereof" (2 K.4:43).** **"And he said unto him, Went not mine heart with thee, when the man turned again from his chariot to meet thee? Is it a time to receive money, and to receive garments, and oliveyards, and vineyards, and sheep, and oxen, and menservants, and maidservants? The leprosy therefore of Naaman shall cleave unto thee, and unto thy seed for ever. And he went out from his presence a leper as white as snow" (2 K.5:26-27).** **"Then Elisha said, Hear ye the word of the LORD; Thus saith the LORD, To morrow about this time shall a measure of fine flour be sold for a shekel, and two measures of barley for a shekel, in the gate of Samaria. Then a lord on whose hand the king leaned answered the man of God, and said, Behold, if the LORD would make windows in heaven, might this thing be? And**	Far too often men and women demonstrate traits of weak character, traits such as insincerity, deception, impurity, dishonesty, corruption and wickedness. Whereas they should be living lives of honor, goodness, purity, morality, & sincerity. This is not the way any of us should be living. We should be men and women of honor and uprightness, holding ever so high the principles of morality, righteousness and justice for all people everywhere. We should be followers of Christ, and we should persevere, be steadfast in our faith. Once we profess Christ, we must continue to profess and follow after Him. *Continuing on* is the evidence of our faith. When people see us continuing to follow Christ, they know that our profession is true. But if we profess to be a follower of the LORD and then refuse to live like He says, people know that we are making a false profession. We must *continue on,* being steadfast, enduring, persevering in following Christ—this assures our salvation, that our profession is true, that our life demonstrates what we say. **"Awake to righteousness, and sin not; for some have not the knowledge of God: I speak this to your shame" (1 Co.15:34).** **"Knowing that whatsoever good thing any man doeth, the same shall he receive of the Lord, whether he be bond or free" (Ep.6:8).** **"But thou, O man of God, flee these things; and follow after righteousness, godliness, faith, love, patience, meekness. Fight the good fight of faith, lay hold on eternal life, whereunto thou art also called, and hast professed a good profession before many witnesses" (1 Ti.6:11-12).** **"Teaching us that, denying ungodliness and worldly lusts, we should live soberly, righteously, and godly, in this present world; Looking for that blessed hope, and the glorious appearing of the great God and our Saviour Jesus Christ" (Tit.2:12-13).** **"And ye shall serve the Lord your God, and he shall bless thy bread, and thy water; and I will take sickness away from the midst of thee" (Ex.23:25).**

PROPHET	TIME/PLACE GIVEN	MAIN MESSAGE	PRACTICAL APPLICATION
ELISHA (cont.) **Predictions and Messages** 1. The water of a spring would be purified, will be sweet (2 K. 2:21). 2. Water would miraculously appear in some trenches especially prepared by faith to catch the water (2 K.3:17). 3. Food would be multiplied (2 K.4:43). 4. Gehazi and his descendants would be struck with leprosy (2 K.5:26-27). 5. A great famine would end in one day (2 K.7:1). 6. The king's attendant would see the end of the famine, but would not eat any of the food because he did not believe the Word of the LORD (2 K. 7:2). 7. Jehu would become king and kill the entire family of Ahab (2 K.9:6-8). 8. The prediction that Israel would have three victories over Syria (2 K.13:14-19). **Scripture References** 1 K.19:16-19; 2 K.2–13		he said, Behold, thou shalt see it with thine eyes, but shalt not eat thereof" (2 K.7:1-2). "And he arose, and went into the house; and he poured the oil on his head, and said unto him, Thus saith the LORD God of Israel, I have anointed thee king over the people of the Lord, even over Israel. And thou shalt smite the house of Ahab thy master, that I may avenge the blood of my servants the prophets, and the blood of all the servants of the LORD, at the hand of Jezebel. For the whole house of Ahab shall perish: and I will cut off from Ahab him that pisseth against the wall, and him that is shut up and left in Israel" (2 K.9:6-8).	"He withdraweth not his eyes from the righteous: but with kings are they on the throne; yea, he doth establish them for ever, and they are exalted" (Jb.36:7). "The eyes of the Lord are upon the righteous, and his ears are open unto their cry" (Ps.34:15). "I have been young, and now am old; yet have I not seen the righteous forsaken, nor his seed begging bread" (Ps.37:25).

PROPHET	TIME/PLACE GIVEN	MAIN MESSAGE	PRACTICAL APPLICATION
EZEKIEL **(God is strong)** **Known Facts** 1. Was the son of Buzi (Eze.1:3). 2. Served as a priest in the temple (Eze.1:3). 3. Wrote the book of *Ezekiel* (Eze.1:1-3). 4. Was taken captive into Babylon (Eze. 1:2; 2 K.24:11-16). 5. Called to be a watchman to the people of Israel (Eze. 3:17). 6. Called to be a sign or symbol to the people of Israel (Eze.12:6, 11; 24:21-27). **Predictions and Messages** 1. Visions of the glory of the LORD and Ezekiel's calling (Eze.1–3). 2. Prophecies concerning Judah and Jerusalem—that God would judge and send the people into captivity because they profaned the holy temple (Eze.4–24). 3. Prophecies concerning other nations—that God would judge their sin, especially Egypt, but Israel will be restored (Eze.25–32). 4. Prophecies concerning the restoring of Israel—that Israel would be restored when the people repented and turned back to the LORD (Eze.33–39). 5. A vision and a detailed description of the future temple and of heaven (Eze.40–48). **Scripture References** The book of *Ezekiel*	**Time** *593–571 B.C., before and during the final captivity and exile of Judah and Jerusalem in 586 B.C.* **Place** *Ezekiel first prophesied in Jerusalem, but later was taken captive into Babylon. In Babylon (or the land of the Chaldeans), Ezekiel was sitting next to the River Chebar when the Spirit of God revealed to him strange and wonderful visions of the glory of the LORD and of heaven (Eze.1:3).*	"Know that I am the LORD." This main message of Ezekiel occurs sixty-three times throughout the book of *Ezekiel*. Ezekiel's messages strongly emphasized the holiness of God, and the fact that God will judge sin. But the LORD will also forgive and restore those who repent and turn to Him. God is known by His judgment; but He is better known by His mercy. Throughout his ministry, Ezekiel was greatly persecuted and eventually killed for his straightforward preaching. But he stood fast, unswervingly preaching the messages the LORD laid upon his heart. **"For every one of the house of Israel, or of the stranger that sojourneth in Israel, which separateth himself from me, and setteth up his idols in his heart, and putteth the stumblingblock of his iniquity before his face, and cometh to a prophet to enquire of him concerning me; I the LORD will answer him by myself: And I will set my face against that man, and will make him a sign and a proverb, and I will cut him off from the midst of my people; and ye shall know that I am the LORD" (Eze.14:7-8).** **"And they shall know that I am the LORD, and that I have not said in vain that I would do this evil unto them" (Eze.6:10).** **"But if the wicked will turn from all his sins that he hath committed, and keep all my statutes, and do that which is lawful and right, he shall surely live, he shall not die" (Eze.18:21).** **"Say unto them, As I live, saith the Lord GOD, I have no pleasure in the death of the wicked; but that the wicked turn from his way and live: turn ye, turn ye from your evil ways; for why will ye die?" (Eze.33:11).**	Despite the love of God, people shockingly reject the LORD. This is why God judges and shows His wrath. Man is without excuse. Man has no defense, no answer, no reason that can justify his rebellion against God. Yet God is merciful to the person who repents. He gave His Son to die for us. We do not deserve it—we never have and we never will—but God loves us with an incomprehensible love. Therefore, He has given His Son to die *for* us, as our substitute, in our behalf. But a person must accept the gift of God's Son, accept Jesus Christ by true faith and repentance in order to receive God's mercy. **"Let the wicked forsake his way, and the unrighteous man his thoughts: and let him return unto the LORD, and he will have mercy upon him; and to our God, for he will abundantly pardon" (Is.55:7).** **"Therefore say thou unto them, Thus saith the LORD of hosts; Turn ye unto me, saith the LORD of hosts, and I will turn unto you, saith the LORD of hosts" (Zec. 1:3).**

PROPHET	TIME/PLACE GIVEN	MAIN MESSAGE	PRACTICAL APPLICATION
GAD **(Fortunate)** **Known Facts** 1. Recorded some of the history of King David (1 Chr.29:29-30). 2. Ministered as a prophet for many years. 3. Served by the side of King David and King Solomon as the king's seer (2 Chr.29:25). **Predictions and Messages** 1. Warned David to flee from Judah whenever Saul was about to find him (1 S.22:5). 2. Announced God's judgment for David's sin of numbering the people (2 S.24:10-15; 1 Chr.21:9-13). 3. Gave instructions to David for ending the severe plague of judgment on the people (2 S. 24:18-19; 1 Chr. 21:18-19). **Scripture References** 1 S.22:4; 2 S.24:11-19; 1 Chr.9-19; 2 Chr.29:25	**Time** *1015–950 B.C., before the division of the nation of Israel.* **Place** *Jerusalem and certain areas to the south, while he served by the side of King David and King Solomon.*	Our strength and security is in the LORD. No amount of human ability or might can keep us safe—only God can. So as we face the trials, temptations and enemies of life, we must remain humble before the LORD, never allowing ourselves to become puffed up with pride, thinking that we have some great ability or resource to conquer the hardships and sufferings of life. It is never by our own strength, but God's that we triumph in life. **"They dwelt with him all the while that David was in the hold. And the prophet Gad said unto David, Abide not in the hold; depart, and get thee into the land of Judah. Then David departed, and came into the forest of Hareth" (1 S.22:4-5).** **"The word of the LORD came unto the prophet Gad, David's seer, saying, Go and say unto David, Thus saith the LORD, I offer thee three things; choose thee one of them, that I may do it unto thee. So Gad came to David, and told him, and said unto him, Shall seven years of famine come unto thee in thy land? or wilt thou flee three months before thine enemies, while they pursue thee? or that there be three days' pestilence in thy land?...advise, and see what answer I shall return to him that sent me" (2 S.24:11-13).** **"Then the angel of the LORD commanded Gad to say to David, that David should go up, and set up an altar unto the LORD in the threshingfloor of Ornan the Jebusite. And David went up at the saying of Gad, which he spake in the name of the LORD....Then David said to Ornan, Grant me...this threshingfloor, that I may build an altar...unto the LORD:...that the plague may be stayed from the people" And David built there an altar unto the LORD, and offered burnt offerings and peace offerings, and called upon the LORD; and he answered him from heaven by fire upon the altar of burnt offering. And the LORD commanded the angel; and he put up his sword again into the sheath thereof" (1 Chr.21:18-19, 22, 26-27).**	A spirit of pride, conceit, and haughtiness is a terrible evil. For when we exalt ourselves, we walk around acting as though we are better, more capable, more deserving, more moral, more righteous than someone else. But note this inescapable truth: we reap what we sow. If we sow prideful sin and evil, we reap the consequences. So it is with any act of wickedness. This is a spiritual law set up by God for the purpose of divine judgment. A person may repent, but the wickedness will result in some consequence of suffering. **"Pride goeth before destruction, and an haughty spirit before a fall" (Pr.16:18).** **"Be not deceived; God is not mocked: for whatsoever a man soweth, that shall he also reap" (Ga.6:7).** **"With him is an arm of flesh; but with us is the LORD our God to help us, and to fight our battles" (2 Chr.32:8).** **"He that trusteth in his own heart is a fool: but whoso walketh wisely, he shall be delivered" (Pr.28:26).**

PROPHET	TIME/PLACE GIVEN	MAIN MESSAGE	PRACTICAL APPLICATION
HABAKKUK (Tightly embraced) **Known Facts** 1. Ministered to Judah, the Southern Kingdom. 2. Wrote the book of *Habakkuk* (Hab.1:1). **Predictions and Messages** 1. The oracle of the wickedness of the people (Hab.1:1-4). 2. The oracle of the shocking invasion of the Chaldeans (Hab. 1:5-17). 3. The answer of God to Habakkuk's plea— the wicked will be judged, but the righteous will live by faith (Hab.2:1-20). 4. The prayer of Habakkuk—the LORD is glorious and mighty (Hab.3:1-16). 5. The praise of Habakkuk—the LORD protects those who trust in Him even in the midst of trouble and distress (Hab.3:17-20). **Scripture References** The book of *Habakkuk*; Ro.1:17; Ga.3:11-12; He.10:37-38	**Time** *615-598 B.C., during the reigns of Jehoahaz and Jehoiakim, about 20 years before the captivity of Judah and Jerusalem.* **Place** *Judah, the Southern Kingdom.*	The heart of Habakkuk ached to the point of breaking. The prophet was in anguish for three reasons. First, Habakkuk saw the horrible wickedness of Israel, the deep sin of his own people. Second, he knew that the terrible judgment of God's hand was coming because of Israel's sin. Third, and what weighed most heavily on his soul, Habakkuk longed to be acceptable before the holy God Whom he served. In his book, Habakkuk recorded several question he asked of God and the LORD's answer to his questions. After humbly pleading and lamenting to the LORD, Habakkuk waited (for the prophet never presumed, not even for a moment, that God is unjust). He simply asked his questions and then waited for the LORD to change his heart, so that he could fully trust Him. Among the LORD's answer to Habakkuk is the vital message found in Hab.2:4. This important verse teaches us that we must guard against pride and trust in God. Habakkuk faithfully preached this message, longing for his people to listen and repent. **"Therefore the law is slacked, and judgment doth never go forth: for the wicked doth compass about the righteous; therefore wrong judgment proceedeth"** (Hab.1:4). **"For, lo, I raise up the Chaldeans, that bitter and hasty nation, which shall march through the breadth of the land, to possess the dwellingplaces that are not theirs"** (Hab.1:6). **"Behold, his soul which is lifted up is not upright in him: but the just shall live by his faith"** (Hab.2:4). **"God came from Teman, and the Holy One from mount Paran. Selah. His glory covered the heavens, and the earth was full of his praise"** (Hab.3:3). **"The LORD God is my strength, and he will make my feet like hinds' feet, and he will make me to walk upon mine high places"** (Hab.3:19).	God's chosen way for us to approach Him is that we "live by faith." After all, Scripture declares as clearly as it can: no man is justified by the law in the sight of God. God is perfect; He is perfectly righteous. No man can achieve perfection; therefore, no man can live in the presence of God. No matter how good he is or how much good he does, he cannot achieve perfection. The fact is evident, for if a man had achieved perfection, he would be perfect—living forever in a perfect state of being, even on this earth. But note this: What God does is take a person's faith and count that faith as righteousness. Therefore, a man is able to live in God's presence by faith or justification. The point is this: God's way for a man to approach Him is the way of faith: "The just shall live by faith." **"But without faith it is impossible to please him: for he that cometh to God must believe that he is, and that he is a rewarder of them that diligently seek him"** (He.11:6). **"Let the heavens be glad, and let the earth rejoice: and let men say among the nations, The LORD reigneth"** (1 Chr.16:31). **"God reigneth over the heathen: God sitteth upon the throne of his holiness"** (Ps.47:8). **"Let not thine heart envy sinners: but be thou in the fear of the LORD all the day long"** (Pr.23:17). **"I know that, whatsoever God doeth, it shall be for ever: nothing can be put to it, nor any thing taken from it: and God doeth it, that men should fear before him"** (Ec.3:14).

PROPHET	TIME/PLACE GIVEN	MAIN MESSAGE	PRACTICAL APPLICATION
HAGGAI (Feast of Yahweh) **Known Facts** 1. Ministered to Judah, the Southern Kingdom. 2. Wrote the book of *Haggai* (Hag.1:1). **Predictions and Messages** 1. The declaration that it is time to build the temple of the LORD (Hag.1:2). 2. A sermon about taking courage because the LORD is with you (Hag.2:4). 3. The foretelling of the future blessing of Israel by the LORD (Hag.2:19). 4. The prophecy that Zerubbabel will be lifted up as a leader (Hag.2:23). **Scripture References** The book of *Haggai*; Ezr.5:1; 6:14	**Time** *520 B.C., when the second foundation of the temple was to be laid.* **Place** *Jerusalem, the Holy City and place of the temple.*	Haggai's messages were given to encourage and strengthen the returned exiles of Jerusalem as they sought to rebuild their temple and nation. He taught that the Spirit of the LORD mightily dwells among those who reverence and honor Him. The citizens of Jerusalem at this time had just returned from captivity in Babylon. Although they were in their own land, it was new and unfamiliar because it was their ancestors, not them, who had been taken captive seventy years before. Naturally, the people were glad to be free. But they still felt somewhat discouraged, unsure of what to do next. They were a people without direction. Through the prophet Haggai, the LORD gave special direction and greatly encouraged the people. Haggai told of a bright future and promised a strong leader in Zerubbabel. Most of all, the Spirit of the LORD would be among the people if they would honor the LORD and give Him their true heartfelt worship. **"Thus speaketh the LORD of hosts, saying, This people say, The time is not come, the time that the LORD's house should be built" (Hag.1:2).** **"Yet now be strong, O Zerubbabel, saith the LORD; and be strong, O Joshua, son of Josedech, the high priest; and be strong, all ye people of the land, saith the LORD, and work: for I am with you, saith the LORD of hosts" (Hag.2:4).** **"Is the seed yet in the barn? yea, as yet the vine, and the fig tree, and the pomegranate, and the olive tree, hath not brought forth: from this day will I bless you" (Hag.2:19).** **"In that day, saith the LORD of hosts, will I take thee, O Zerubbabel, my servant, the son of Shealtiel, saith the LORD, and will make thee as a signet: for I have chosen thee, saith the LORD of hosts" (Hag.2:23).**	How many of us have little rituals, prayers, habits, ceremonies, and objects that we use to keep us religiously secure? So many of us seek religious security while at the same time we neglect the weightier matter of breaking God's Law. It is not the man-made place or the man-made ritual that saves a person. What saves a person is coming to God in true worship, bowing before Him, acknowledging Him as God, acknowledging that His Son, Jesus Christ, is the only way and the only hope of salvation. The place of worship is no longer the temple or any other particular location on earth. God's presence now dwells in the hearts and lives of His people. His people worship Him wherever they are, and they can worship Him every day all day long. True worship means that we focus on the object of worship, being sure that we are truly worshipping the Father, God Himself. A person may be in a fancy, expensive church or in a broom closet worshipping, and yet not be worshipping the Father. A man's whole being must be focused upon the only true and living God, worshipping Him and Him alone. God desires worship, for He created man to worship and fellowship with Him. Therefore, man needs to truly worship God. Man needs to worship God with the spiritual drive and ability of his soul, seeking the most intimate communion and fellowship with God. Man needs to worship God with the spiritual core of his life and being, trusting and resting in God's acceptance and love and care. **"Praise ye the LORD: for it is good to sing praises unto our God; for it is pleasant; and praise is comely" (Ps.147:1).** **"But thou art holy, O thou that inhabitest the praises of Israel" (Ps.22:3).** **"Let us be glad and rejoice, and give honour to him" (Re.19:7).** **"Praise ye the LORD. Sing unto the LORD a new song, and his praise in the congregation of saints" (Ps.149:1).** **"O magnify the LORD with me, and let us exalt his name together" (Ps.34:3).**

PROPHET	TIME/PLACE GIVEN	MAIN MESSAGE	PRACTICAL APPLICATION
HANANI **(Merciful)** **Known Facts** 1. Ministered to Judah, the Southern Kingdom (2 Chr.16:7). 2. Father of Jehu, the prophet (1 K.16:1-7). **Predictions and Messages** 1. The declaration that it was foolish for King Asa to rely on anyone other than the LORD (2 Chr.16:7-9). 2. The declaration that the LORD supports those who completely rely on Him (2 Chr. 16:9). **Scripture References** 2 Chr.16:7-10	**Time** *870 B.C., at the end of the reign of Asa, king of Judah, and just after King Asa made a treaty with the Arameans (Syrians).* **Place** *Jerusalem, in the palace of the king.*	We must rely totally on the LORD, and our dependence upon Him must not be passive. Rather, we must *actively seek* to trust the LORD more and more. For He searches the earth seeking people who are totally committed to Him. His eyes scan back and forth, looking for people who will place their lives fully into His hands. Furthermore, He longs to meet their needs and to strengthen and deliver them from all the hardships and temptations of life. But the people of Judah failed to actively trust and seek the Lord. Consequently, they were to suffer the judgment of God. **"And at that time Hanani the seer came to Asa king of Judah, and said unto him, Because thou hast relied on the king of Syria, and not relied on the LORD thy God, therefore is the host of the king of Syria escaped out of thine hand. Were not the Ethiopians and the Lubims a huge host, with very many chariots and horsemen? yet, because thou didst rely on the LORD, he delivered them into thine hand. For the eyes of the Lord run to and fro throughout the whole earth, to show himself strong in the behalf of them whose heart is perfect toward him. Herein thou hast done foolishly: therefore from henceforth thou shalt have wars" (2 Chr.16:7-9).**	Note the wonderful promise of Scripture: God works through the events of this world to meet the needs of His dear people, those who are fully committed to Him. No matter how terrible the trial or temptation, God moves within the event for one purpose and one purpose only: to deliver and to strengthen those who are fully committed to Him. A person who is fully committed can rest assured in this promise of the Lord. For the Lord will provide, protect and guide His dear people. Even in the moment of death, the Lord will transfer us into His presence—quicker than the eye can blink (2 Ti.4:18). **"Wait on the LORD: be of good courage, and he shall strengthen thine heart: wait, I say, on the LORD" (Ps.27:4).** **"And the Lord shall deliver me from every evil work, and will preserve me unto his heavenly kingdom: to whom be glory for ever and ever. Amen" (2 Ti.4:18).** **"Fear thou not; for I am with thee: be not dismayed; for I am thy God: I will strengthen thee; yea, I will help thee; yea, I will uphold thee with the right hand of my righteousness" (Is.41:10).** **"But the God of all grace, who hath called us unto his eternal glory by Christ Jesus, after that ye have suffered a while, make you perfect, stablish, strengthen, settle you" (1 Pe.5:10).**

THE PROPHETS

PROPHET	TIME/PLACE GIVEN	MAIN MESSAGE	PRACTICAL APPLICATION
HEMAN **(Faithful)** **Known Facts** 1. Was the son of Joel (1 Chr.15:17). 2. Served as the seer to King David (1 Chr. 25:5). 3. Appointed by David to lead the congregational music (1 Chr. 25:1). 4. Born into the tribe of Levi (1 Chr.24:31). 5. Prophesied along with his family through the music (1 Chr. 25:1-8). **Predictions and Messages** None recorded. Since he is called a *seer*, he must have sung some of the LORD's predictions through the music of worship, as well as advised David about the results of certain royal decisions. **Scripture References** 1 Chr.25:1-8	**Time** 971 B.C., *the last days of the life of King David. In these solemn times of final instructions from King David, Levites were assigned the task of making sure the worship of the LORD continued down through coming generations.* **Place** *Jerusalem, the Holy City.*	Heman praised the LORD with music and greatly encouraged the congregation of Israel in their worship of God. Leading music was his official position under King David. Heman prophesied while playing musical instruments. Just as Asaph, Heman's father, had faithfully served under King David, now Heman, Asaph's son, carried on the work. Heman carried on the legacy of his father, praising the LORD with music and spurring the people on in their devotion to the LORD. **"Moreover David and the captains of the host separated to the service of the sons of Asaph, and of Heman, and of Jeduthun, who should prophesy with harps, with psalteries, and with cymbals....Of Heman: the sons of Heman; Bukkiah, Mattaniah, Uzziel, Shebuel, and Jerimoth, Hananiah, Hanani, Eliathah, Giddalti, and Romamtiezer, Joshbekashah, Mallothi, Hothir, and Mahazioth: All these were the sons of Heman the king's seer in the words of God, to lift up the horn. And God gave to Heman fourteen sons and three daughters. All these were under the hands of their father for song in the house of the LORD, with cymbals, psalteries, and harps, for the service of the house of God, according to the king's order to Asaph, Jeduthun, and Heman" (1 Chr.25:1, 4-6).**	The importance of praise and worship cannot be overstressed. Because of all His good and perfect gifts—the LORD expects us to worship and praise His holy name. Music is one way, a very powerful way, to give praise to the Lord. We are to be talking about Christ, admonishing others in the Word of God and singing within our hearts the hymns of the church. We are to walk about rejoicing and praising the Lord within our hearts, being filled with the joy of the Lord and His Word, and bearing strong testimony for the Lord. **"Let the word of Christ dwell in you richly in all wisdom; teaching and admonishing one another in psalms and hymns and spiritual songs, singing with grace in your hearts to the Lord" (Col.3:16).**

PROPHET	TIME/PLACE GIVEN	MAIN MESSAGE	PRACTICAL APPLICATION
HOSEA (Salvation) **Known Facts** 1. Was the son of Beeri (Ho.1:1) 2. Prophesied for many years, his ministry extending through the reign of four kings (Ho.1:1). 3. Ministered to Israel, the Northern Kingdom (Ho.1:1). **Predictions and Messages** 1. The illustrated sermon about Hosea's unfaithful wife (Ho. 1:1–3:5). 2. The sermon about God's case against Israel, that they were full of sin and that they must repent (Ho.4:1–6:3). 3. The sermon about God's certain judgment of sin (Ho.6:4–10:15). 4. The sermon about God's love for Israel, even though they were rebellious (Ho. 11:1–13:16). 5. The prophecy that Christ would come out of Egypt (Ho. 11:1; Mt.2:15). 6. The sermon about God's call to repentance (Ho.14:1-3). 7. The promise of God's blessing coming upon the people (Ho.14:4-8). 8. The sermon about God's challenge to the wise listener (Ho.14:9). *Scripture References* The book of *Hosea*	**Time** *788–723* B.C., *during the reigns of four Judean kings: Uzziah, Jotham, Ahaz, and Hezekiah. His ministry spawned the reigns of the last six kings of the Northern Kingdom, but he did not name these rulers. His ministry ended just before the fall of Samaria in 722 B.C.* **Place** *Judah, the Southern Kingdom of Israel.*	Hosea had a hard life. He was given a very unusual command from God: to marry a prostitute. Hosea's life was an illustrated sermon of the unfaithfulness of the people, and how they had turned away from God. During the course of their marriage, Gomer (Hosea's wife) bore three children to Hosea, two of them fathered by someone else. Once, Hosea had to go to the public auction and buy his wife back from slavery. The shame of the situation was unbearable, which was the very message preached to the people. Israel should have been… • ashamed at the way they had been acting • ashamed at the way they had run away from the LORD • ashamed at the way they had gone after the lust of their flesh • ashamed at the way they had failed to serve God, in particular after all He had done for them Hosea preached bold, straightforward messages to the people, warning them that they must repent from their sin and seek the LORD. The people had been committing spiritual adultery against the LORD, running after the pleasures and the false gods of the world, pleasing their carnal nature. They needed to allow the LORD to break through the callousness of their hearts, for their souls were as unyielding as dry ground that had not been plowed. Otherwise, the hand of God's judgment would chastise them. But even in chastisement, God's people must remember that God disciplines His people. **"Come, and let us return unto the Lord: for he hath torn, and he will heal us; he hath smitten, and he will bind us up. After two days will he revive us: in the third day he will raise us up, and we shall live in his sight. Then shall we know, if we follow on to know the LORD: his going forth is prepared as the morning; and he shall come unto us as the rain, as the latter and former rain unto the earth" (Ho.6:1-3).**	God disciplines believers. He chastens, corrects, and rebukes believers. Now God does not cause bad and evil in life. God loves man. Therefore, God's concern is not to cause problems and pain for us; His concern is to deliver us through all the trouble and pain on earth and to save us for heaven and eternity. How does God do this? By chastising us. When we think of chastisement, we usually think of discipline and correction and it does mean this. But it also means to train and teach and instruct a person. Every true child of God knows the discipline of God's hand. His discipline differs with each of us, but each of us can recognize His discipline nevertheless. God stirs, guides, directs, teaches, trains, and instructs us all along the way, making us stronger and stronger in life and drawing us closer and closer to Him. **"I will be as the dew unto Israel: he shall grow as the lily, and cast forth his roots as Lebanon. His branches shall spread, and his beauty shall be as the olive tree, and his smell as Lebanon" (Ho.14:5-6).** **"That ye may be blameless and harmless, the sons of God without rebuke, in the midst of a crooked and perverse nation, among whom ye shine as lights in the world" (Ph.2:15).** **"Acquaint now thyself with him, and be at peace: thereby good shall come unto thee" (Jb.22:21).** **"I am crucified with Christ: nevertheless I live; yet not I, but Christ liveth in me: and the life which I now live in the flesh I live by the faith of the Son of God, who loved me, and gave himself for me" (Ga.2:20).**

(Cont. on next page)

PROPHET	TIME/PLACE GIVEN	MAIN MESSAGE	PRACTICAL APPLICATION
HOSEA (cont.)		"It is in my desire that I should chastise them; and the people shall be gathered against them, when they shall bind themselves in their two furrows. And Ephraim is as an heifer that is taught, and loveth to tread out the corn; but I passed over upon her fair neck: I will make Ephraim to ride; Judah shall plow, and Jacob shall break his clods. Sow to yourselves in righteousness, reap in mercy; break up your fallow ground: for it is time to seek the LORD, till he come and rain righteousness upon you. Ye have plowed wickedness, ye have reaped iniquity; ye have eaten the fruit of lies: because thou didst trust in thy way, in the multitude of thy mighty men" (Ho.10:10-13).	

PROPHET	TIME/PLACE GIVEN	MAIN MESSAGE	PRACTICAL APPLICATION
## HULDAH ### (Life) **Known Facts** 1. Was the wife of Shallum, the keeper of the wardrobe (2 K. 22:14). 2. Lived in the Second Quarter of Jerusalem (2 K.22:14). **Predictions and Messages** 1. The prophecy that God would judge Jerusalem for idolatry, for ignoring God's Word (2 K.22:14-17; 2 Chr.34:22-25). 2. The prophecy that God would be kind to King Josiah, because Josiah had humbled himself, recognizing the sin of the people and the importance of heeding God's Word (2 K.22:18-20; 2 Chr. 34:26-28). **Scripture References** 2 K.22:14-20; 2 Chr. 34:22-28	**Time** *623 B.C., the eighteenth year of Josiah's reign, when King Josiah decided to repair the temple and a copy of the Law of Moses was found during the renovations.* **Place** *Jerusalem, the capital of Judah, the Southern Kingdom of Israel.*	King Josiah gave specific instructions to repair the temple of the LORD. While the repairs were being made, a copy of the Law was found in the temple. King Josiah read the Word of God and was aghast at what he read, because he realized that the people had grossly neglected the law and disobeyed the LORD's commandments. Earnestly wanting to understand what he had read, he commissioned a delegation of officials to seek a prophet who could explain God's Word to him. The delegation went to Huldah the prophetess who gave the following explanation: the penalties for disobeying the laws found written in the Book were to be executed, because the people had forsaken the LORD, worshipped false gods, and provoked the LORD to anger. God was going to judge and destroy the city of Jerusalem. But despite the terrifying message of judgment spoken by Huldah, the LORD had a very special message for King Josiah. Josiah had grieved over the people's sin, and he had humbled himself before the LORD in prayer and personal repentance. Because Josiah's heart was tender and responsive to the Word of God, Josiah would not personally experience the terrible judgment. It would come after Josiah's death. **"Thus saith the LORD God of Israel, Tell the man that sent you to me, Thus saith the LORD, Behold, I will bring evil upon this place, and upon the inhabitants thereof, even all the words of the book which the king of Judah hath read: Because they have forsaken me, and have burned incense unto other gods, that they might provoke me to anger with all the works of their hands; therefore my wrath shall be kindled against this place, and shall not be quenched. But…because thine heart was tender, and thou hast humbled thyself before the LORD, when thou heardest what I spake against this place, and against the inhabitants thereof, that they should become a desolation and a curse, and hast rent thy clothes, and wept before me; I also have heard thee, saith the LORD Behold therefore, I will gather thee unto thy fathers, and thou shalt be gathered into thy grave in peace; and thine eyes shall not see all the evil which I will bring upon this place" (2 K.22:15-20).**	What a lesson for us! To Josiah and his people, the Word of God had been lost. To many of us, the Word of God is neglected and ignored, even denied and rejected. Some of us act as though we do not believe the Bible is the written Word of God. After all, if we truly believed that the Bible is God's Word, we would read, study and feast upon it. The Bible truly is what it claims to be, God's Word; and if we ignore it and neglect it, what will God say to us when we face Him? Above all that is to be feared in this life is the neglect or denial of God and His Holy Word. Nothing on this earth is as important as doing exactly what God's Word says, obeying Him and keeping His commandments. But before we can keep His commandments, we must know what His commandments are. And there is only one way to learn God's commandments: study His Holy Word. **"Search the scriptures; for in them ye think ye have eternal life: and they are they which testify of me" (Jn.5:39).** **"These were more noble than those in Thessalonica, in that they received the word with all readiness of mind, and searched the scriptures daily, whether those things were so" (Ac.17:11).** **"Study to show thyself approved unto God, a workman that needeth not to be ashamed, rightly dividing the word of truth" (2 Ti.2:15).**

PROPHET	TIME/PLACE GIVEN	MAIN MESSAGE	PRACTICAL APPLICATION
IDDO **(Appointed)** **Known Facts** 1. Recorded some history about Solomon, Rehoboam, and Abijah (2 Chr.9:29). 2. Called a seer by the Scripture, a seer to whom God gave special vision against the wickedness and false worship of Jeroboam I (2 Chr.9:29). 3. Kept genealogical records (2 Chr.12:15). 4. Was not the "Iddo" who was the father of Zechariah the prophet. **Predictions and Messages** Wrote about the rebuke of Jeroboam given by the unnamed prophet at Bethel (1 K.13:1-5). **Scripture References** 2 Chr.9:29; 12:15; 13:22	**Time** *910 B.C., after the close of the ministry of Ahijah, the Shilonite, and after the reign of Jeroboam I, who put the idols of the golden calves at Dan and Bethel.* **Place** *Judah, the Southern Kingdom of Israel.*	Iddo was appointed by God to keep a record of Jeroboam's terrible wickedness and false worship and of the unknown prophets who rebuked the king. How did Iddo know about these events? The Scripture expressly states that Iddo was given special visions concerning Jeroboam (2 Chr.9:29). It should be noted that the unnamed prophet who gave the rebuke to Jeroboam did not remain faithful. He forgot God's Word and went off on his own, doing what he thought was right instead of following God's clear instructions. Apparently, because of the prophet's unfaithfulness, God later raised up Iddo to record the event so the world would have a permanent warning against the wickedness and the false worship of Jeroboam I. The unnamed prophet who cursed the altar at Bethel could not have been Iddo the seer because the unnamed prophet was killed before returning home (1 K.13:24). **"Now the rest of the acts of Solomon, first and last, are they not written in the book of Nathan the prophet, and in the prophecy of Ahijah the Shilonite, and in the visions of Iddo the seer against [about] Jeroboam the son of Nebat?" (2 Chr.9:29).** **"Now the acts of Rehoboam, first and last, are they not written in the book of Shemaiah the prophet, and of Iddo the seer concerning genealogies?" (2 Chr.12:15).** **"And the rest of the acts of Abijah, and his ways, and his sayings, are written in the story of the prophet Iddo" (2 Chr.13:22).**	Accountability is clearly taught in Scripture. The Lord is coming; and when He comes, He will judge the works of His servant and followers. All works of the believer will be inspected by the Lord so that each believer may be rewarded in perfect justice, receiving exactly what is due, whether good or bad (2 Co. 5:10). **"Therefore be ye also ready: for in such an hour as ye think not the Son of man cometh. Who then is a faithful and wise servant, whom his lord hath made ruler over his household, to give them meat in due season? Blessed is that servant whom his lord when he cometh shall find so doing" (Mt.24:44-46).** **"Moreover it is required in stewards, that a man be found faithful" (1 Co.4:2).** **"As every man hath received the gift, even so minister the same one to another, as good stewards of the manifold grace of God" (1 Pe.4:10).** **"Therefore, my beloved brethren, be ye stedfast, unmoveable, always abounding in the work of the Lord, forasmuch as ye know that your labour is not in vain in the Lord" (1 Co.15:58).** **"Take heed unto thyself, and unto the doctrine; continue in them: for in doing this thou shalt both save thyself, and them that hear thee" (1 Ti.4:16).**

PROPHET	TIME/PLACE GIVEN	MAIN MESSAGE	PRACTICAL APPLICATION
ISAIAH **(Salvation is from the LORD)** **Known Facts** 1. Was the son of Amoz (Is.1:1). 2. Ministered alongside Hosea the prophet. 3. Saw a tremendous vision of the LORD (Is.6). 4. Prophesied more about the Messiah than any other prophet. **Predictions and Messages** 1. A holy group of people will remain after the captivity (Is.6:11-13). 2. Christ, the Savior of the world, will live among men on the earth (Is.7:13-16). 3. Foreign armies will quickly invade and smash Samaria (Is. 8:1-4). 4. Christ will be the Wonderful Counselor (Is.9:1-7). 5. The Savior will come from the family of David (Is.11:1-6). 6. Judgment will come on wicked nations (Is.13:1–20:6). 7. The Servant of the LORD will come on a mission of mercy (Is.42:1-9). 8. A remnant of God's people will be gathered back to the promised land (Is. 43:1–45:25). 9. King Cyrus, who would help Israel many years later to return to the promised land, is called by name (Is. 45:1-13). 10. Yahweh is the only Savior (Is.45:18-25). 11. Babylon will fall (Is.47:1–48:15). 12. Christ will be the Suffering Servant and die an atoning death (Is.52:13–53:12). 13. An everlasting covenant will be given to Israel (Is.55:3-5). (cont. in col.3) **Scripture References** The book of *Isaiah*, 2 K.18–20	**Time** *740–690 B.C., during the reigns of Uzziah, Jotham, Ahaz, and Hezekiah.* **Place** *Jerusalem, the capital city of Judah.*	Isaiah's prophecies and sermons centered on the holiness of God and His desire to save mankind from his sin. Spurred on by his dramatic and unforgettable vision of God's holy throne, he warned people of coming disaster. But he also had many words of comfort to say from the LORD. Most importantly, Isaiah prophesied of the coming Savior, Who would bear the punishment for the sins of the world. But the main message of Isaiah is the same as the meaning of his name: "Salvation is from the LORD." It is essential to understand this biblical truth. For it is not just that salvation comes from the LORD (Jehovah/Yahweh) the One True God; but that salvation *only* comes from the LORD. It *only* comes through Jesus Christ, the Son of God, the Messiah whom the Father sent into the world to give His life as a ransom for the world. There is no other that can save. Only the LORD can rescue man from his desperately sinful situation. **"Behold, God is my salvation; I will trust, and not be afraid: for the LORD JEHOVAH is my strength and my song; he also is become my salvation" (Is.12:2).** **"And it shall be said in that day, Lo, this is our God; we have waited for him, and he will save us: this is the LORD; we have waited for him, we will be glad and rejoice in his salvation" (Is.25:9).** **"Tell ye, and bring them near; yea, let them take counsel together: who hath declared this from ancient time? who hath told it from that time? have not I the LORD? and there is no God else beside me; a just God and a Saviour; there is none beside me. Look unto me, and be ye saved, all the ends of the earth: for I am God, and there is none else" (Is.45:21-22).** **"But he was wounded for our transgressions, he was bruised for our iniquities: the chastisement of our peace was upon him; and with his stripes we are healed" (Is.53:5).** **Predictions and Messages** (cont. from col.1) 14. A Messiah will come to save (Is.61:1-11). 15. A description of the Millenium (Is.66:14-24).	The way to God is through Jesus Christ Himself. Jesus Christ alone saves, for there is no other exalted Lord. Therefore, no man can be saved by any other name other than the Lord's name. No teacher is capable enough, no prophet is noble enough, no minister is good enough to save himself, much less anyone else. Therefore, no matter the claim and no matter the strength of a person's name, no man has the name by which God can save people. All men are mortal. Therefore, no man can make another man immortal. But the Name which God uses to save men is eternal, the Name of the Lord Jesus Christ, the Son of God Himself. **"Jesus saith unto him, I am the way, the truth, and the life: no man cometh unto the Father, but by me." (Jn.14:6).** **"Neither is there salvation in any other: for there is none other name under heaven given among men, whereby we must be saved" (Ac.4:12).**

PROPHET	TIME/PLACE GIVEN	MAIN MESSAGE	PRACTICAL APPLICATION
JACOB/ISRAEL (Deceiver/Contender with God) **Known Facts** 1. Was the son of Isaac, son of Abraham (Ge. 25:19-26). 2. Fathered twelve sons, who became the heads of the twelve tribes of Israel (Ex.1:1-7). 3. Tricked his brother, Esau, into giving him the birthright; thus, the Messiah, the Savior of the world, came through Jacob's family (Ge.25:27-34). 4. Tricked his father, Isaac, into giving him the blessing of the firstborn, taking it from his brother, Esau (Ge.27:30-40). **Predictions and Messages** Jacob prophesied about the future of his twelve sons. The most important of all these prophetic utterances is that the Messiah, the Savior of the world, would come from the tribe of Judah. **Scripture References** Ge.48–49	**Time** *1858 B.C., after Jacob and his sons had sojourned in Egypt 17 years and more than 400 years before the Exodus.* **Place** *Goshen, a territory in the land of Egypt that was ruled by Pharaoh Sunusret III.*	In the later years of Jacob's life, he predicted the future of his twelve sons. His sons were to become the twelve tribes of Israel; consequently, Jacob was predicting the future of the nation of Israel and ultimately of the Savior to come, Jesus Christ. Although Jacob was not ordinarily a prophet, while on his deathbed, Jacob was anointed by God's Spirit to prophesy. The most important part of what Jacob predicted had to do with his son Judah. Judah would be the tribe from which the Messiah would arise. **"The sceptre shall not depart from Judah, nor a lawgiver from between his feet, until Shiloh come; and unto him shall the gathering of the people be" (Ge.49:10).**	Just think of this wonderful fact: God had a plan to save us before the world was ever made. How marvelous is God's love. And so that there would be no mistake, God revealed His plan in His Holy Word. God outlined very specific facts about Jesus Christ so that it would be clear that He is the Messiah, Son of God, and Savior of the world. Note just six of the essential facts, facts that clearly teach that Jesus Christ is the promised Seed, the Savior of the world: ➤ Jesus Christ is "the Lion of the tribe of Judah" (Re.5:5). ➤ Jesus Christ is the Prince of peace (Is.9:6). ➤ Jesus Christ gives rest to the human soul (Mt.11:29). ➤ Jesus Christ came to the earth so that we might have life, abundant life (Jn.10:10). ➤ Jesus Christ is the Savior and lord of the world and all owe their obedience to Him (Is.45:22-23; Ph.2:9-11). ➤ Jesus Christ came and gave His life on the cross for the redemption of humankind, and He will return again to gather His people unto Himself (Mk.13:27; Jn.14:1-3; 1 Th.4:16-18). **"And one of the elders saith unto me, Weep not: behold, the Lion of the tribe of Juda, the Root of David, hath prevailed to open the book, and to loose the seven seals thereof" (Re.5:5).** **"Wherefore God also hath highly exalted him, and given him a name which is above every name: That at the name of Jesus every knee should bow, of things in heaven, and things in earth, and things under the earth; And that every tongue should confess that Jesus Christ is Lord, to the glory of God the Father" (Ph.2:9-11).**

THE PROPHETS

JAHAZIEL
(God sees me)

Known facts
1. Was a Levite (2 Chr. 20:14).
2. Was the son of Zechariah (not the prophet) (2 Chr.20:14).
3. Descended from the lineage of Asaph (2 Chr. 20:14).
4. Served during the reign of Jehoshaphat (2 Chr.20:15).

Predictions and Messages
Prophesied that the LORD Himself would defeat the foreign coalition that was coming to attack (2 Chr. 20:15-17).

Scripture References
2 Chr.20:14-18

Time
860 B.C., in the middle of the reign of Jehoshaphat and during the ministry of Elijah in the Northern Kingdom.

Place
Jerusalem, in the courtyard of the house of the LORD.

During the reign of King Jehoshaphat, a coalition of three nations joined together to attack Judah. Instead of turning to foreign alliances as he had done in the past, Jehoshaphat prayed to God for help. As he waited for an answer, the Spirit of the LORD came upon Jahaziel, a Levite standing in the courtyard. Jahaziel prophesied that the LORD Himself would defeat the enemy (2 Chr.20:15-17).

The next day when Judah went out to battle, they discovered the vast army of enemy soldiers lying dead all over the ground. During the night the LORD had apparently stirred the enemy soldiers to argue and fight among themselves. The result was catastrophic; and the enemy coalition, in a state of utter confusion, attacked and slaughtered each other. All Judah had to do was pick up the spoils. God had worked a wonderful miracle to rescue Judah and King Jehoshaphat (2 Chr.20:20-30).

"Then upon Jahaziel the son of Zechariah, the son of Benaiah, the son of Jeiel, the son of Mattaniah, a Levite of the sons of Asaph, came the Spirit of the Lord in the midst of the congregation; And he said, Hearken ye, all Judah, and ye inhabitants of Jerusalem, and thou king Jehoshaphat, Thus saith the Lord unto you, Be not afraid nor dismayed by reason of this great multitude; for the battle is not yours, but God's. To morrow go ye down against them: behold, they come up by the cliff of Ziz; and ye shall find them at the end of the brook, before the wilderness of Jeruel. Ye shall not need to fight in this battle: set yourselves, stand ye still, and see the salvation of the Lord with you, O Judah and Jerusalem: fear not, nor be dismayed; to morrow go out against them: for the Lord will be with you" (2 Chr.20:14-17).

The lesson for us is a much needed one on the importance of prayer and fasting. Jehoshaphat and his people faced an overwhelming crisis, a crisis that they stood no chance of getting through—at least not successfully. Within their own strength, they would have been crushed. Therefore, they did the only thing they could do: they turned to the LORD. In order to show the LORD how sincere and desperate they were, they set aside a full day for fasting and prayer. They showed the LORD the depth of their sincerity, that they were willing to repent, to turn away from their sins and recommit their lives to Him anew.

What a dynamic lesson for us! When we face a severe crisis, we too must seek to show the sincerity of our hearts and the depth of our need through fasting and prayer. We must commit ourselves to the LORD.

Simply stated, seeking God through prayer and fasting is the way to secure the presence and power of the LORD. When we face a crisis or are longing for more of God's blessings, we should fast and pray often, showing the depth of our sincerity.

"Watch and pray, that ye enter not into temptation: the spirit indeed is willing, but the flesh is weak" (Mt.26:41).

"But as for me, when they were sick, my clothing was sackcloth: I humbled my soul with fasting; and my prayer returned into mine own bosom" (Ps.35:13).

359

PROPHET	TIME/PLACE GIVEN	MAIN MESSAGE	PRACTICAL APPLICATION
JEHU **(Jehovah/Yahweh is He)** **Known Facts** 1. Was the son of Hanani the seer (1 K.16:1). 2. Was not the king whom Elijah and Elisha anointed to be king of Israel and to execute the LORD's vengeance upon the household of Ahab. 3. Recorded history about some of the kings of Israel (2 Chr.20:34). **Predictions and Messages** 1. The family of King Baasha would be completely destroyed because of his terrible idolatry (1 K.16:1-3). 2. The wrath of the LORD would be upon Jehoshaphat because of the evil alliance he had made with King Ahab. However, because Jehoshaphat had removed the wicked idols of Ashtoreth, the LORD also saw the good in Jehoshaphat's heart (2 Chr.19:2-3). **Scripture References** 1 K.16:1-3, 12; 2 Chr. 19:1-3	**Time** *886 B.C., at the end of the reign of Baasha, king of Israel, to 853 B.C., during the reign of Jehoshaphat, king of Judah—the year Jehoshaphat made an alliance with the evil King Ahab of Israel.* **Place** *Samaria, the northern capital, in 886 B.C.; Jerusalem, the southern capital in 853 B.C.*	Before Israel conquered the land of Canaan, the LORD had strongly given them two warnings. First, they were to drive out the Canaanites completely and without mercy so that the evil of idolatry would not creep into the pure worship of the LORD. Second, they were not to intermarry with the heathen nations. The message of Jehu rekindled the fire of God's warning that had been given down through the centuries. But as before, His warnings through Jehu were not heeded. King Baasha followed after the false gods of idolatry. And King Jehoshaphat intermarried with the family of Ahab and Jezebel in order to form an alliance. God was angry because these kings, the leaders of His people, had rejected and disobeyed His Holy Word. They had ignored God's written message, so God raised up Jehu the prophet to once again warn the leaders and people: they must obey God's Word or face the judgment of God. **"Then the word of the LORD came to Jehu the son of Hanani against Baasha, saying, Forasmuch as I exalted thee out of the dust, and made thee prince over my people Israel; and thou hast walked in the way of Jeroboam, and hast made my people Israel to sin, to provoke me to anger with their sins; Behold, I will take away the posterity of Baasha, and the posterity of his house; and will make thy house like the house of Jeroboam the son of Nebat" (1 K.16:1-3).** **"And Jehu the son of Hanani the seer went out to meet him, and said to king Jehoshaphat, Shouldest thou help the ungodly, and love them that hate the LORD? therefore is wrath upon thee from before the LORD. Nevertheless there are good things found in thee, in that thou hast taken away the groves out of the land, and hast prepared thine heart to seek God" (2 Chr.19:2-3).**	God expects His followers to love everyone, even the wicked and those who hate God and His followers (Mt.5:44). But while loving and reaching out to the unbelievers of the world, the believer must never compromise his testimony for the LORD. He must never act against God's Word, disobeying the commandments of the LORD. He must always live a life of spiritual separation, a life that does not fellowship or form alliances with unbelievers. The believer must always take a stand for righteousness against wickedness. **"But now I have written unto you not to keep company, if any man that is called a brother be a fornicator, or covetous, or an idolater, or a railer, or a drunkard, or an extortioner; with such an one no not to eat" (1 Co.5:11).** **"If there come any unto you, and bring not this doctrine, receive him not into your house, neither bid him God speed: For he that biddeth him God speed is partaker of his evil deeds" (2 Jn.10-11).** **"Take heed to thyself, lest thou make a covenant with the inhabitants of the land whither thou goest, lest it be for a snare in the midst of thee" (Ex.34:12).** **"Blessed is the man that walketh not in the counsel of the ungodly, nor standeth in the way of sinners, nor sitteth in the seat of the scornful" (Ps.1:1).**

PROPHET	TIME/PLACE GIVEN	MAIN MESSAGE	PRACTICAL APPLICATION

JEREMIAH
(Yahweh will rise up)

Known Facts
1. Known as *the weeping prophet.*
2. Lived in Anathoth (Je.1:1; 29:27).
3. Was the son of Hilkiah (Je.1:1).
4. Served as a priest in the line of Abiathar.
5. Called as a youth.
6. Is thought to have written a large portion of the Bible: *1 & 2 Kings, Jeremiah, Lamentations.*

Predictions and Messages
1. The vision of the almond branch (Je. 1:11-12).
2. The vision of the steaming pot (Je. 1:13-16).
3. The sermon about Israel's disobedience to God's Word and the coming judgment (Je. 2:1-6; 34:17; 35:17).
4. The sermon that Judah will be taken captive if they do not repent (Je.7:1-7; 26:1-7).
5. The prophecy that the house of the LORD will be made into a den of robbers (Je. 7:11; Mt.21:13).
6. The lesson of the linen waistband (Je. 13:1-10).
7. The prophecy of a great drought (Je.14:1-7).
8. The illustration of no comfort based upon the fact that Jeremiah remained unmarried (Je.16:1-6).
9. The sermon about observing the Sabbath (Je.17:20-27).
10. The illustration of the potter and the clay (Je.18:1-6).
11. The illustration of the broken jar (Je.19:1-6).
12. The sermon about administering righteous justice (Je.21:11-14).
13. The prophecy of the judgment against Jehoiachin (Je.22:29-30).

(Cont. on next page)

Time
627–562 B.C., after the fall of Samaria until long after the final captivity of Judah, from King Josiah to King Gedaliah.

Place
Jerusalem until he was forced to go to Egypt.

Many important prophecies and messages have been given to the world by the LORD through His prophet Jeremiah: Often the LORD aroused Jeremiah to use symbols or illustrated sermons to demonstrate the message of his prophecy.

Of all his prophecies (some foretelling, but most preaching), one overall message comes through loud and clear: The LORD will rise up. Over and over Jeremiah's messages pointed out that God arises in favor of those who truly serve Him, and in judgment of those who refuse to hear His Word.

God will arise and defend His faithful followers, delivering them from evil circumstances. God will even change His mind about judging a person if that person truly repents and then follows the LORD completely, trusting fully in His power to save.

"And the LORD hath sent unto you all his servants the prophets, rising early and sending them; but ye have not hearkened, nor inclined your ear to hear" (Je.25:4).

"Behold, as the clay is in the potter's hand, so are ye in mine hand, O house of Israel. At what instant I shall speak concerning a nation, and concerning a kingdom, to pluck up, and to pull down, and to destroy it; If that nation, against whom I have pronounced, turn from their evil, I will repent of the evil that I thought to do unto them. And at what instant I shall speak concerning a nation, and concerning a kingdom, to build and to plant it; If it do evil in my sight, that it obey not my voice, then I will repent of the good, wherewith I said I would benefit them" (Je.18:6-10).

"Therefore thus saith the LORD God of hosts, the God of Israel; Behold, I will bring upon Judah and upon all the inhabitants of Jerusalem all the evil that I have pronounced against them: because I have spoken unto them, but they have not heard; and I have called unto them, but they have not answered. And Jeremiah said unto the house of the Rechabites, Thus saith the LORD of hosts, the God of Israel; Because ye have obeyed the commandment of Jonadab your father, and kept

God is not some far away Being Who has no interest in what happens in the world. The LORD is the Creator of the earth and everything and everyone in it. He created every person for the purpose of worshiping Him, that men and women might have communion, a personal relationship, with Him. He is zealous for the souls of people. He rises up, calling for people to turn from sin and follow Him.

But God will not rise up in our behalf forever. Eventually the time of judgment comes. And when the instant comes for judgment, judgment will fall swiftly and justly. Every person will be placed on the scales of judgment. It is then that a person must be on the side of Jesus Christ, God's Son.

Always remember this unchanging fact: Without being on Christ's side, the scales of judgment will never tip in our favor, no matter what:
➤ No matter how much money we have given to the church or charity.
➤ No matter how many people we have helped.
➤ No matter how *good* we have been.
➤ No matter how much we have sacrificed.
➤ No matter how we die, even if we paid the supreme sacrifice of dying as a martyr.

The teaching of Scripture is definite. It is crystal clear. Even if a person were to give his life for another, it would not remove his sin nor make him acceptable to God. Christ is the only way to become acceptable to God.

"For I have no pleasure in the death of him that dieth, saith the Lord GOD: wherefore turn yourselves, and live ye" (Eze.18:32).

"Neither is there salvation in any other: for there is none other name under heaven given among men, whereby we must be saved" (Ac.4:12).

PROPHET	TIME/PLACE GIVEN	MAIN MESSAGE	PRACTICAL APPLICATION

JEREMIAH (cont.)

14. The prophecy that the righteous Messiah would be from the family line of King David (Je.23:5-6; 33:15).
15. The vision of the good and the bad figs (Je.24:1-10).
16. The prophecy that Judah will be taken to Babylon as captives (Je.25:8-9).
17. The sermon about the cup of God's wrath (Je.25:15-17).
18. The illustration of the yoke—a symbol of the power of Nebucadnazzar, king of Babylon, over other nations (Je.27:1-6).
19. The prediction that Hananiah, the false prophet, will die (Je.27:1-6).
20. The prediction of the public execution of the false prophets, Ahab and Zedekiah, by the hand of Nebuchadnezzar, the invading Babylonian king (Je.29:21-23).
21. The prediction of the destruction of the family of Shemaiah (Je.29:30).
22. The prophecy of promised restoration to Israel (Je.30:1-3; 31:10).
23. The prophecy of the slaughter of the infants in Bethlehem at the time of Christ (Je.31:15; Mt.2:17).
24. A prophecy of the new eternal covenant to be made with Israel (Je.31:31-34; He. 8:8-12).
25. The prediction that King Zedekiah will die in captivity (Je. 34:4-5).
26. The prediction that Jehoiakim's family will all die (Je.36:30).

Scripture References
The book of *Jeremiah*;
2 Chr.35:25; 36:12, 21-22

all his precepts, and done according unto all that he hath commanded you: Therefore thus saith the LORD of hosts, the God of Israel; Jonadab the son of Rechab shall not want a man to stand before me for ever" (Je.35:17-19).

PROPHET	TIME/PLACE GIVEN	MAIN MESSAGE	PRACTICAL APPLICATION
JESUS CHRIST (Jehovah is Salvation) **Known Facts** 1. Is God's Son, the King of kings and LORD of lords, the Messiah, the Savior of the world (Mt.14:33; Mk.1:1; Lu. 1:35; 1 Ti.6:15; Re. 17:14; 19:16). 2. Is proclaimed by the Scriptures from Genesis to Revelation. 3. Stands forever as Prophet, Priest, and King (De.18:18; He. 5:6; Re.19:16). 4. Is the subject of endless facts too numerous to mention. **Predictions and Messages** 1. The proclamation that God wants to save every person ever born in the world (Jn.3:16). 2. The prophecy that the people would ask for Him to perform miracles of healing (Lu. 4:23). 3. The declaration that anyone who does not follow His teaching will be destroyed (Mt. 7:24-27). 4. The prophecy of the destruction of Jerusalem in A.D. 70 (Mt. 24:2; Mk.13:2). 5. The prophecy that the end of the world would come and terrible judgment would fall (Mt.24:1–25:46). 6. The prediction that Peter would deny the LORD three times in one night (Mt.26:34; Mk.14:30; Lu.22:34; Jn.13:38). 7. The prophecy that Christ would be killed and rise again on the third day (Mt.12:40; 17:22-23; 20:18-19; Mk.8:31; 9:31; 10:33-34; Lu.18:32-33). (cont. in col. 3) **Scripture References** De.18:15-18; Mt.21:11; Lu.24:19; Ac.7:37	**Time** *During the years of Roman Oppression (A.D. 26-29) the Preeminent Prophet, the Son of God Himself was sent into the world in human flesh to save and set free all people of all generations.* **Place** *The nation of Israel under Roman rule.*	No greater prophet than Christ has ever lived—or ever will live—for no one else is perfect; no other prophet is God in the flesh. No greater message has ever been proclaimed—or ever will be—than the great gospel message, the good news of salvation. The good news is that Jesus Christ has come so that we can escape death and hell and have eternal life through Christ's death upon the cross and His resurrection from the grave. Through Him we will live with God in perfection forever and ever. What more can be said? **"For God so loved the world, that he gave his only begotten Son, that whosoever believeth in him should not perish, but have everlasting life" (Jn.3:16).** **Predictions and Messages** (cont. from col. 1) 8. The prophecy that Christ would ascend to the right hand of the Father in heaven (Jn.6:62; 14:2-3; 16:10). 9. The prophecy that Christ would come again to judge the world, rewarding the faithful and punishing the wicked (Mt.10:42; 16:27; 22:13; 25:21; Re.22:12). 10. The prophecy that the end of this age and world was coming, coming suddenly and unexpectedly (Mt.24:1–25:46).	God loves every man, not just the religious and the good. He does not love only the people who love Him. He loves everyone, even the unlovely and the unloving, the unbelieving and the obstinate, the selfish and the greedy, the spiteful and the vengeful. God wants man to know His love. He wants to reach everyone in the world with His love. So God demonstrated His love in the most perfect way possible: He sent His Son into the world to reveal the truth of life to man and to pay the penalty of sin for man, in "behalf of man." Through the death of His Son upon the cross, God poured out the very life blood of His Son for man. No greater love could ever be expressed; no greater act could ever be carried out to show the depth of perfect love. **"Ho, every one that thirsteth, come ye to the waters, and he that hath no money; come ye, buy, and eat; yea, come, buy wine and milk without money and without price" (Is.55:1).** **"The Lord is not slack concerning his promise, as some men count slackness; but is longsuffering to us-ward, not willing that any should perish, but that all should come to repentance" (2 Pe.3:9).** **"But God commendeth his love toward us, in that, while we were yet sinners, Christ died for us" (Ro.5:8).** **"Who needeth not daily, as those high priests, to offer up sacrifice, first for his own sins, and then for the people's: for this he did once, when he offered up himself" (He.7:27).**

THE PROPHETS

PROPHET	TIME/PLACE GIVEN	MAIN MESSAGE	PRACTICAL APPLICATION
JOEL (Yahweh is God) **Known Facts** 1. Was the son of Pethuel (Joel 1:1). 2. Wrote the book of *Joel* (Joel 1:1). 3. Prophesied in Judah for a short time during the ministry of Elisha. **Predictions and Messages** 1. The prophecy of the coming devastating locust invasion (Joel 1:1–2:20). 2. The prophecy that restoration will come to Israel in abundance (Joel 2:21-27). 3. The prophecy of the Day of Pentecost (Joel 2:28-32; Ac.2:1-24). 4. The prophecy that a remnant will escape the coming judgment because they will call upon the LORD (Joel 2:32). 5. The prophecy of God's judgment against evil nations (Joel 3:1-19). 6. The prophecy of God's greatness and the truth that Jerusalem is protected by God (Joel 3:16-21). **Scripture References** The book of *Joel*; Ac.2:16	**Time** *830 B.C., during the ministry of Elisha and during the reign of Joash, king of Judah* **Place** *Jerusalem and Judah, the Southern Kingdom.*	Joel predicted several national disasters. In particular, Joel predicted that a locust invasion was going to wipe out the land, one that would be talked about for generations. The plague would be so terrible that no harvest would be left, none whatsoever. But Joel also prophesied that the Spirit of God would come in a special way and that there would be tremendous days of refreshing for those who stay true to the Lord. The message of Joel teaches that those who call upon the Lord will be saved. Judgment will come because of sin, but it will not last forever. Blessing and restoration will also be sent by God, but only for those who are called by God's name, only for those who truly acknowledge the Lord as the only true and living God. **"And it shall come to pass, *that* whosoever shall call on the name of the LORD shall be delivered: for in mount Zion and in Jerusalem shall be deliverance, as the LORD hath said, and in the remnant whom the LORD shall call" (Joel 2:32).**	Man is self-centered and rebellious toward God. He likes to feel independent. Consequently, man is dead to God and resistant to the pulling call and quickening power of God. Both God and man have a part in salvation. God calls. He attracts, draws, pulls, and tugs at the heart of man to come. But note: God will not call forever. When a man senses the call and pull of God, he must act then and there. He must believe and make the decision to follow Christ. **"I will take the cup of salvation, and call upon the name of the LORD" (Ps.116:13).** **"For whosoever shall call upon the name of the Lord shall be saved" (Ro.10:13).** **"This is the day which the LORD hath made; we will rejoice and be glad in it" (Ps.118:24).** **"For he saith, I have heard thee in a time accepted, and in the day of salvation have I succoured thee: behold, now is the accepted time; behold, now is the day of salvation" (2 Co.6:2).**

PROPHET	TIME/PLACE GIVEN	MAIN MESSAGE	PRACTICAL APPLICATION
JOHN THE APOSTLE (Jehovah/Yahweh has been gracious) **Known Facts** 1. Was the son of Zebedee, the brother of James (Mt.10:2). 2. Called away from the fishing trade to follow Christ (Mt.4:21). 3. Followed Christ closely. 4. Wrote the *Gospel of John*, the *Epistles of 1, 2, 3 John*, and the book of *Revelation*. 5. Was the only one of the twelve apostles not to be martyred, although an attempt was made against his life. **Predictions and Messages** The book of *Revelation* **Scripture References** The book of *John*, the *Epistles of 1, 2, 3 John*, and the book of *Revelation*	**Time** *A.D. 95, near the end of John's life.* **Place** *The island of Patmos, where John was exiled after a failed attempt to kill him by boiling him in oil.*	All prophecy points to this undeniable fact: Jesus Christ is the King of kings and LORD of lords. The book of *Revelation* shows Christ in all His glory and splendor. Christ is the Righteous Judge, the Righteous Lamb and the Righteous King. *Revelation* teaches us that to overcome the world, we must be fully committed to following Christ, the One Who has already overcome the world. God's purpose in revealing to John the great revelation of Christ is to focus attention upon the Lamb, the Lord Jesus Christ Himself, and His ultimate triumph over the world and its ungodliness and evil. God's purpose is to show the great redemption that He is preparing for all those who truly believe and follow His Son. God's purpose is to show man that he can be saved from the terrible things that are coming upon the earth. **"The Revelation of Jesus Christ, which God gave unto him, to show unto his servants things which must shortly come to pass; and he sent and signified it by his angel unto his servant John" (Re.1:1).** **"These things saith he that holdeth the seven stars in his right hand, who walketh in the midst of the seven golden candlesticks" (Re.2:1).** **"And every creature which is in heaven, and on the earth, and under the earth, and such as are in the sea, and all that are in them, heard I saying, Blessing, and honour, and glory, and power, be unto him that sitteth upon the throne, and unto the Lamb for ever and ever" (Re.5:13).** **"For the great day of his wrath is come; and who shall be able to stand?" (Re.6:17).** **"The testimony of Jesus is the spirit of prophecy" (Re.19:10).** **"And he hath on his vesture and on his thigh a name written, KING OF KINGS, AND LORD OF LORDS" (Re.19:16).**	God has appointed a day to judge the world. The day of judgment is set, already determined. God demands that all men repent now, repent of their sin and idolatry, from the vain imaginations of the world. Every man has a *concept*, a thought about God. But we should *seek* and find the only living and true God as revealed in the Holy Bible. This we do by reading and obeying His Word. Every person is personally responsible for forsaking the idols of this world and for finding God. Man is now to repent. God wants people to know that they can be saved while there is still time for them to repent. It is God's purpose to lead people to repentance and salvation, to lead them to the glorious inheritance of the great redemption that is to be given to all true followers of the Lord Jesus Christ. **"O Jerusalem, wash thine heart from wickedness, that thou mayest be saved. How long shall thy vain thoughts lodge within thee?" (Je.4:14).** **"And the times of this ignorance God winked at; but now commandeth all men every where to repent" (Ac.17:30).** **"But the heavens and the earth, which are now, by the same word are kept in store, reserved unto fire against the day of judgment and perdition of ungodly men" (2 Pe.3:7).** **"Knowing that of the Lord ye shall receive the reward of the inheritance: for ye serve the Lord Christ" (Col.3:24).**

PROPHET	TIME/PLACE GIVEN	MAIN MESSAGE	PRACTICAL APPLICATION
JOHN THE BAPTIST (Jehovah/Yahweh has been gracious) **Known Facts** 1. Was the son of Zacharias the priest and Elisabeth, and the first cousin of Jesus Christ (Lu.1:5-63). 2. Was the forerunner of Jesus Christ (Mal. 4:4-6; Mt.11:12-15; 17:10-13). 3. Lived and preached in the countryside and desert places of Palestine (Mt. 3:1-4). 3. Was jailed and beheaded by Herod (Mk.6:24-28). **Predictions and Messages** The unmistakable declaration that Jesus of Nazareth is the Christ, the sacrificial Lamb of God, Who would take away the sin of the world (Jn.1:29). **Scripture References** Mal.4:5; Mt.11:9; Mk.11:32; Lu.7:26; Jn.20:6	**Time** *A.D. 26, at the beginning of the earthly ministry of Jesus Christ.* **Place** *The Jordan River, about 20 miles east of Jerusalem.*	Jesus Christ is "the Lamb of God Who takes away the sin of the world" (Jn.1:29). Christ declared an astonishing thing: John the Baptist was the greatest man ever born of a woman. John was neither a prince nor a king. He was not a man of wealth, fame, or power. Who was he? Why would Christ make such a striking statement about him? He was simply a man who believed in the Messiah and who totally committed his life to that belief. But notice: John was chosen for this special task because he was so dedicated, so committed to God. John lived a life of total dedication to the Lord and of self-denial. He rejected the carnal, fleshly pleasures of this world and the coveting of its possessions. **"The next day John seeth Jesus coming unto him, and saith, Behold the Lamb of God, which taketh away the sin of the world" (Jn.1:29).**	God does not value a man by his social status nor by how far he gets in this world, but by his commitment to Jesus Christ. Christ declared John's eminence over all men; and in John, we have a blazing example of humility, of self-denial and commitment to God. And Christ declared that those who humble themselves will be greater still in the kingdom of God. It is an astonishing thought! But that is how much God values commitment and humility. **"Verily I say unto you, Among them that are born of women there hath not risen a greater than John the Baptist: notwithstanding he that is least in the kingdom of heaven is greater than he" (Mt.11:11).** **"For thus saith the high and lofty One that inhabiteth eternity, whose name is Holy; I dwell in the high and holy place, with him also that is of a contrite and humble spirit, to revive the spirit of the humble, and to revive the heart of the contrite ones" (Is.57:15).** **"And whosoever shall exalt himself shall be abased; and he that shall humble himself shall be exalted" (Mt.23:12).** **"Humble yourselves in the sight of the Lord, and he shall lift you up" (Js.4:10).**

PROPHET	TIME/PLACE GIVEN	MAIN MESSAGE	PRACTICAL APPLICATION
JONAH (Dove) **Known Facts** 1. Was the son of Ammitai (2 K.14:25; Jona.1:1). 2. Wrote the book of *Jonah* (Jona.1:1). 3. Ministered to the Northern Kingdom of Israel (2 K.14:25). 4. Tried to resist obeying God's instructions to go to Nineveh (Jona.1:3). 5. Was called to a foreign nation (Jona.1:2). 6. Converted the entire city of Nineveh with his preaching (Jona. 3:5-10). 7. Lived in Gath-Hepher (2 K.14:25). 8. Quoted the Psalms repeatedly in his prayer for God to save him from the great fish (Jona.2:2-9) **Predictions and Messages** 1. Nineveh will be overthrown in forty days (Jona.3:4). 2. Israel's borders will be extended and restored to their original positions (2 K.14:25). **Scripture References** The book of *Jonah*; 2 K.14:25; Mt.12:39-41; 16:4	**Time** *780–765* B.C., *during the reign of Jeroboam II, king of Israel.* **Place** *Nineveh, the capital of Assyria, about 500 miles east of Israel.*	Jonah was called by God to preach to Nineveh, the capital city of the Assyrians. But Jonah did not want to go. He had a simple reason: The Assyrians were known for their cruelty to his people. Their war strategy was not only designed to take control of lands, but to instill absolute terror in the people they were conquering. The Assyrians wanted to make sure that the people would be so afraid of them that they would not ever try to avoid paying the demanded tribute each year. So Jonah tried to run away from God. Jonah got on a ship sailing in the opposite direction. But God sent a storm. Jonah knew why the storm had come. At Jonah's request, the men of the ship threw him overboard. But God was gracious. He had a great fish prepared to swallow Jonah. When Jonah repented, the fish threw Jonah up onto the land. After recovering from his ordeal, the repentant prophet went to Nineveh and preached. The city repented too, and they were saved from judgment. The book of *Jonah* clearly teaches that no matter how evil a person is, God will forgive him if he truly repents. No place represented self-exaltation and opposition to God more than Nineveh. God was so angry with the Ninevites that their total destruction was only forty days away. Yet, when they repented, God relented, forgave Nineveh and spared the city. **"But I will sacrifice unto thee with the voice of thanksgiving; I will pay that that I have vowed. Salvation is of the LORD" (Jona.2:9).** **"But let man and beast be covered with sackcloth, and cry mightily unto God: yea, let them turn every one from his evil way, and from the violence that is in their hands. Who can tell if God will turn and repent, and turn away from his fierce anger, that we perish not? And God saw their works, that they turned from their evil way; and God repented of the evil, that he had said that he would do unto them; and he did it not" (Jona.3:8-10).**	We can now obtain the mercy of God. We need God to have mercy upon us because we have sinned against Him. We have done everything imaginable against God... • ignored Him • neglected Him • rebelled against Him • disobeyed Him • rejected Him • denied Him • cursed Him God will forgive our sins; He will have mercy upon us. But we must come to the throne of grace and ask for mercy. We must humble ourselves and fully acknowledge that mercy comes only through Christ Jesus. **"Who is a God like unto thee, that pardoneth iniquity, and passeth by the transgression of the remnant of her heritage? he retaineth not his anger for ever, because he delighteth in mercy" (Mi.7:18).**

PROPHET	TIME/PLACE GIVEN	MAIN MESSAGE	PRACTICAL APPLICATION
JOSEPH (He has added) **Known Facts** 1. Was the son of Jacob (Ge.29:22-24). 2. Was persecuted and sold into slavery by his brothers (Ge.37:4; 23-28). 3. Was forced to live in Egypt, a slave to Potiphar, falsely accused by his master's wife (39:1-2; 11-17). 4. Remained faithful to God (39:21-23). 5. Raised up after many years in prison to the throne of Egypt, second only to Pharaoh (Ge.41:39-41). 6. Had a gift from God for interpreting dreams (Ge.40:6-22). **Predictions and Messages** 1. Pharaoh's butler would be restored to his position (Ge.40:9-13). 2. Pharaoh's baker would be executed (Ge. 40:16-19). 3. Seven years of bountiful harvest would come to Egypt, but they would be followed by seven years of terrible famine (Ge.41:25-32). **Scripture References** Ge.40:1-23; 41:1-32	**Time** *1900–1885 B.C., during Joseph's reign as secondary only to Pharaoh of Egypt.* **Place** *Ancient Egypt, during the time of the Pharaohs.*	God is in complete control, and He carries out His plan regardless of the evil intentions of mankind. Joseph had all kinds of evil done against him. He was… • hated and persecuted by his brothers • sold into slavery • reported dead to his father • tempted by an immoral woman • falsely accused of adultery • imprisoned for twenty years Despite all of these awful experiences, God's purpose for Joseph was not stopped, not even hindered. At just the right time, God lifted Joseph up to be the second highest ranking official in Egypt, second only to Pharaoh himself. Even then Joseph did not take credit for himself. He gave all honor and praise to God for the interpretation of the dreams of Pharaoh. Through dreams, God delivered Joseph out of all his troubles and used him in a mighty way to save lives of multiplied thousands. **"Yet within three days shall Pharaoh lift up thine head, and restore thee unto thy place and thou shalt deliver Pharaoh's cup into his hand, after the former manner when thou wast his butler" (Ge.40:13).** **"Yet within three days shall Pharaoh lift up thy head from off thee, and shall hang thee on a tree; and the birds shall eat thy flesh from off thee" (Ge.40:19).** **"Behold, there come seven years of great plenty throughout all the land of Egypt: And there shall arise after them seven years of famine; and all the plenty shall be forgotten in the land of Egypt; and the famine shall consume the land" (Ge.41:29-30).** **"And for that the dream was doubled unto Pharaoh twice; it is because the thing is established by God, and God will shortly bring it to pass" (Ge.41:32).** **"But as for you, ye thought evil against me; but God meant it unto good, to bring to pass, as it is this day, to save much people alive" (Ge.50:20).**	God's plans overrule man's opposition. God's counsel controls the evil of men, subjecting and using even the wickedness of men to work all things out for good and to achieve His will for the earth. Not even rulers, no matter how powerful they are, can stop or hinder the hand of God. People do all kinds of evil, trying to control situations, trying to rule over someone or to exert some authority beyond their position. Just think for a moment of the terrible evil things people in the world do every day. They … • hate • steal • murder • destroy • commit immorality • encourage others to sin • revile those who will not take part in their sin • persecute believers • even attempt to stamp out the gospel and the church But no matter what people do, they cannot stop the will of God and His plan. They will fail, for God has a plan and He will overrule and carry out His plan. Kings and rulers stand up and rally against God and His Christ, the Messiah. They stand against, stand in opposition to and in hostility toward Christ, foolishly thinking that they always have and always will overthrow God's plan. But they will fail. God's great plan of salvation will continue to march triumphantly down through the ages of history. Despite the railings of the devil and all his forces, God's church will go forward, will grow and conquer more and more. God rules and will continue to rule over all the evil plans of men. It is critical to know that God not only has a plan for the world, but for every person. The believer can rest assured that nothing can stop the plan God has for his life. **"The LORD bringeth the counsel of the heathen to nought: he maketh the devices of the people of none effect. The counsel of the LORD standeth for ever, the thoughts of his heart to all generations" (Ps.33:10-11).** **"Consider the work of God: for who can make that straight, which he hath made crooked?" (Ec.7:13).**

THE PROPHETS

PROPHET	TIME/PLACE GIVEN	MAIN MESSAGE	PRACTICAL APPLICATION
MALACHI **(My messenger)** **Known Facts** 1. Prophesied after the captivity in Judah. 2. Lived in the time of Nehemiah. 3. Was the last of the Old Testament writers. **Predictions and Messages** 1. The declaration that God has always loved Israel (Mal. 1:1-5). 2. The declaration that worship must be sincere (Mal.1:6-14). 3. The declaration that failing to honor the LORD results in a curse (Mal.2:1-9). 4. The declaration that marriage is holy before the LORD (Mal. 2:10-16). 5. The call to return to the LORD (Mal.2:17–3:7). 6. The declaration that a person must not rob God of His tithes and offering, not if the person wishes to be blessed by God. (Mal. 3:8-12). 7. The prophecy concerning the judgment of the wicked—they will not be spared (Mal.3:13-18). 8. The declaration that the righteous will triumph (Mal.4:1-3). 9. The prophecy that one like Elijah (John the Baptist) will come as a forerunner to the Messiah (Mal.4:4-6; Mt. 11:12-15; 17:10-13). **Scripture References** The book of *Malachi*	**Time** *430 B.C., about one hundred years after the Temple had been rebuilt under the direction of Haggai and Zechariah. Malachi was the last of the prophets to appear until Christ was born.* **Place** *Jerusalem, the capital city of the Southern Kingdom of Judah.*	Many of Malachi's listeners had participated in the great revivals of Ezra and Nehemiah and had fully committed their lives to the LORD. But now, just a few years later, they had slipped away from the LORD, turning back to a life of sin and neglecting the worship of the LORD and their duty to support the House of God (1:6-14; 3:6-12). The people were apathetic, complacent, only half-heartedly committed to the LORD. They needed to be called back to God. Thus God raised up Malachi to preach the utter necessity of repentance. In scathing sermon after scathing sermon, he pointed out the seriousness of Israel's sin. He called the people to return to the true worship of God. **"For from the rising of the sun even unto the going down of the same my name shall be great among the Gentiles; and in every place incense shall be offered unto my name, and a pure offering: for my name shall be great among the heathen, saith the LORD of hosts" (Mal.1:11).** **"Even from the days of your fathers ye are gone away from mine ordinances, and have not kept them. Return unto me, and I will return unto you, saith the LORD of hosts" (Mal.3:7).**	True worship means more than ceremony, ritual and form. True worship must be sincere in heart, completely genuine. True worship, worship which truly draws us closer to the LORD must be five things: ➤ Worshipping the only living and true God, the worship of Him and Him alone. ➤ Approaching and seeking God's acceptance exactly as He says through the substitute sacrifice of the Lord Jesus Christ. ➤ Living for God by following the Lord Jesus Christ and obeying His holy Word. ➤ Hoping in the resurrection and not holding on to this world, but looking to the next. ➤ Always seeking to have a pure conscience. This means… • struggling, even to the point of pain, to keep a pure conscience • struggling to be *void of offense*—to keep from stumbling and from causing others to stumble • struggling to have a clear conscience toward both God and men **"There shall no strange god be in thee; neither shalt thou worship any strange god" (Ps.81:9).** **"But the hour cometh, and now is, when the true worshippers shall worship the Father in spirit and in truth: for the Father seeketh such to worship him" (Jn.4:23).** **"That ye may approve things that are excellent; that ye may be sincere and without offence till the day of Christ" (Ph.1:10).**

PROPHET	TIME/PLACE GIVEN	MAIN MESSAGE	PRACTICAL APPLICATION
MICAH (Who is like Jehovah/Yahweh?) **Known Facts** 1. Lived in Moresheth (Mi.1:1). 2. Wrote the book of *Micah* (Mi.1:1). 3. Ministered only a few years, but prophesied to both the Northern and Southern Kingdom (Mi.1:1). 4. Prophesied with Isaiah (Mi.1:1; Je.26:18; see Is.36-39). **Predictions and Messages** 1. The prophecy of God's judgment against Samaria and Jerusalem for idolatry (Mi.1). 2. The prophecy that judgment will come against social injustice (Mi.2:1-11). 3. The prophecy that there will be restoration for those remaining (Mi.2:12-13). 4. The prophecy that wicked leaders will be judged (Mi.3). 5. The prophecy of the promise of peace and purity of worship (Mi.4:1-5). 6. The prophecy that Israel will be made strong (Mi.4:6–5:1). 7. The prophecy that Christ will be born in Bethlehem (Mi.5:2-6; Mt.2:5-6). 8. The prophecy that Israel will be pure from the idolatry of the world (Mi.5:7-15). 9. A sermon about what God requires of a person (Mi.6). 10. A sermon concerning the terrible corruption among the people (Mi.7:1-6). 11. A prayer of repentance (Mi.7:7-11). 12. The prophecy about Israel's future restoration (Mi.7:12-20). **Scripture References** The book of *Micah*; Je.26:18; Mt. 2:5-6	**Time** *735-725 B.C., during the reigns of Jotham, Ahaz, and Hezekiah.* **Place** *Judea, Jerusalem, and Samaria.*	In Micah's day, the Assyrians were just a few years away (722 B.C.) from conquering Samaria, the capital of the Northern Kingdom of Israel. The Assyrians would be within easy striking distance of Jerusalem. Although Micah sternly warned Judah that a terrible situation was coming for the nation, the religious leaders would not believe it. Micah preached that not even God's holy mountain would be spared. But the leaders assumed that since the temple and God's Holy Place was in Jerusalem, the foreign invasion was impossible. Their pride would lead to their downfall. Micah warned the people: The LORD absolutely requires justice, mercy and humility. No matter how much we do in the name of the LORD, without these three things, we cannot hope to be acceptable before God. Without living the way God requires, judgment will come, terrible judgment. But if we walk humbly before people, showing mercy and executing justice, and truly worshipping the LORD, the LORD will accept us. For He accepts all who obey His Word and walk humbly before Him. **"Wherewith shall I come before the LORD, and bow myself before the high God? shall I come before him with burnt offerings, with calves of a year old? Will the LORD be pleased with thousands of rams, or with ten thousands of rivers of oil? shall I give my firstborn for my transgression, the fruit of my body for the sin of my soul? He hath showed thee, O man, what is good; and what doth the LORD require of thee, but to do justly, and to love mercy, and to walk humbly with thy God? The LORD's voice crieth unto the city, and the man of wisdom shall see thy name: hear ye the rod, and who hath appointed it" (Mi.6:6-9).**	God is to be feared, for He resists and stands opposed to the proud. The very thing we do not want to be is prideful. For the only way to escape the judgment of God's hand is to humble ourselves under His mighty hand. If we stand up to His hand, we will be stricken down; but if we humble ourselves under His hand, we will be protected and lifted up, exalted forever and ever. God is going to exalt the humble. The day is coming when the humble will be exalted in all the glory and majesty of Christ. They will be exalted to live with Christ, ruling and reigning with Him and serving Him throughout the entire universe. They will be with Christ, worshipping and serving Him forever and ever. **"Humble yourselves therefore under the mighty hand of God, that he may exalt you in due time" (1 Pe.5:6).** **"Humble yourselves in the sight of the Lord, and he shall lift you up" (Js.4:10).** **"But thou, O God, shalt bring them down into the pit of destruction: bloody and deceitful men shall not live out half their days; but I will trust in thee" (Ps.55:23).**

THE PROPHETS

PROPHET	TIME/PLACE GIVEN	MAIN MESSAGE	PRACTICAL APPLICATION
MICAIAH **(Who is like Jehovah/Yahweh?)** **Known Facts** 1. Was the son of Imlah (1 K.22:8-9). 2. Suffered persecution for speaking the Word of the LORD (1 K. 22:24). **Predictions and Messages** 1. The prophecy that King Ahab of Israel and King Jehoshaphat of Judah would meet with disaster if they tried to battle the Aramean (Syrian) army (2 Chr.18:16). 2. The declaration that the LORD had allowed a lying spirit to influence the false prophets so that Ahab would be enticed into battle and to his doom (1 K.22:19-23; 2 Chr.18:18-22). **Scripture References** 1 K.22:1-37; 2 Chr.18:1-34	**Time** *853 B.C., at the end of the reign of King Ahab.* **Place** *Samaria, the capital of the Northern Kingdom.*	The battle at Ramoth-Gilead would be a disaster. Micaiah gave this prophetic message to King Ahab of Israel and King Jehoshaphat of Judah, who were planning to attack the Arameans (Syrians). Even though an attendant of the king warned Micaiah not to give a negative message to King Ahab, he advised that everyone go home and not fight the Arameans (Syrians) at this time. But the LORD had allowed a lying spirit to influence the false prophets to speak in unison so that Ahab would go against what the LORD had truly said. Because of his terribly wicked life and rule, God's longsuffering with Ahab had run its course. Now, it was time for Ahab to face the judgment of God. **"Then he said, I did see all Israel scattered upon the mountains, as sheep that have no shepherd: and the LORD said, These have no master; let them return therefore every man to his house in peace" (2 Chr.18:16).** **"Now therefore, behold, the LORD hath put a lying spirit in the mouth of all these thy prophets, and the LORD hath spoken evil concerning thee" (1 K.22:23).**	We must guard ourselves against false prophets and false teachers, for the world is full of both. Far too often, the pulpits of the world are filled with false prophets who preach a doctrine other than the doctrine of Christ and His Holy Word. Their focus is not the Word of God but some other religious literature or some feel-good message. Ignoring the truth of God's Word, they seek the approval of their congregations by tickling their ears with messages of positive thinking and self-esteem or by placing too much emphasis on healing and miracles or a particular spiritual gift. These subjects are important, for they are each a part of God's Word. But the whole counsel of God's Word is to be proclaimed—both negative and positive. False prophets seek merely to captivate or pacify us, giving us messages they feel will secure our approval and enhance their own honor and recognition. We must guard against false teachers, wherever they come from, whatever position they have. False teachers mislead us into half-truths, lies and serious doctrinal error, which will lead to destruction. **"Beware of false prophets, which come to you in sheep's clothing, but inwardly they are ravening wolves" (Mt.7:15).**

THE PROPHETS

PROPHET	TIME/PLACE GIVEN	MAIN MESSAGE	PRACTICAL APPLICATION
MOSES (Drawn out) **Known Facts** 1. Was the only prophet of Old Testament times with whom God spoke face-to-face (Ex.33:11). 2. Was born into the tribe of Levi (Ex. 6:16-20). 3. Was the son of Amram and Jochebed (Ex.6:20). 4. Was raised as an Egyptian (Ex.2:1-10; He.11:26-27). 5. Ran from Egypt to escape from a murder charge (Ex.2:11-15). 6. Heard God speak from the burning bush where God revealed His Name to him (Ex.3:1-14). 7. Led the people of Israel out of bondage (Ex.14:21-31). 8. Performed many miraculous signs (Ex. 4:30; 7:20; 8:6, 17; 9:10, 23; 10:13, 22; 14:21, 27). 9. Received the Law from God on Mt. Sinai (Ex.19:1–24:18). 10. Received the instructions for the Tabernacle from God on Mt. Sinai (Ex.25:1–31:18). 11. Was prevented from entering the promised land because he disobeyed God (De.34:4). 12. Wrote the Penteteuch, the first five books of the Bible. **Predictions and Messages** 1. The prophecy of the coming Messiah, the Savior of the world (De.18:15-18). 2. The Song of Moses: a prophecy concerning the future of Israel (De.32:1-43). 3. The Blessing of Moses: a prophecy concerning the future of each of the twelve tribes of Israel (De.33:1-29). (cont. on next page)	**Time** *1405 B.C., near the end of Moses' life.* **Place** *Across the Jordan from the promised land, in the Arabah, the dry desert land east of the Jordan River.*	Throughout his final forty years, Moses proclaimed the holiness and sovereignty of the LORD. During this time of leading the Israelites from the exodus from Egypt to the promised land of blessing, Moses wrote the first five books of the Bible (which is really one great book called *the Law* or *the Instruction* or *the Pentateuch*). In these Scriptures are found: 1. The beginnings of the world and the Israelite nation (*Genesis*). 2. The account of Israel's Exodus from Egypt, their escape from bondage: A type of escaping from the bondage of sin (*Exodus*). 3. The Law of God which Moses received on Mt. Sinai (*Exodus*). 4. The instructions for the Tabernacle, the place of worship: A picture of heaven (*Exodus*). 5. The instructions for the sacrifices, showing how man can approach God and be acceptable to God: The sacrifices foreshadowed Jesus Christ and His sacrifice as a sin offering. Through His sacrifice a person can be saved from sin, death and hell (*Leviticus*). 6. The journeys of the Israelite people: powerful lessons on following God (*Numbers*). 7. The sermons of Moses: the first studies concerning the nature and character of God and how people can follow and live for God (*Deuteronomy*). Thus the Mosaic Covenant, the law of God, lays the groundwork for all that follows in the Old Testament and in the Bible. For the Law points out that we need a Savior and that we must humbly come to God on His terms, offering the Sacrifice that He demands. The Law also points out that the believer must be separated from the world, refusing to live like the world and not being conformed to the world. The Law of Moses proclaims the very same message the entire Bible proclaims, that we need the salvation provided in Jesus Christ, God's Son. Moses preached his series of sermons (found in the book of *Deuteronomy*) as the children of Israel were getting ready to enter the promise Land. At the end of his life, he warned Israel not to forget the LORD, not to go astray as they had in the past.	The greatest commandment is clear: we must love God with all our heart, soul and strength. We must know that "the LORD our God is one LORD" (De.6:4). Note these three vital facts about this great declaration: ➤ God is the *only* living and true God, the only God Who can save, deliver and redeem. ➤ The Lord is our God. We have a personal relationship with the Lord. It is a daily experience. We are His people, the sheep of His pasture. Therefore, we should love, adore and worship Him. ➤ The Lord is one Lord. There is no other. The many false gods of the world exist only in the imaginations of people. Look at how great God is! No wonder the Scripture commands us to love God with our whole being, with all of our heart, soul, mind and strength. We are to love Him thoroughly, fully, completely—in every way for the rest of our lives. **"And he said unto them, Set your hearts unto all the words which I testify among you this day, which ye shall command your children to observe to do, all the words of this law. For it is not a vain thing for you; because it is your life: and through this thing ye shall prolong your days in the land, whither ye go over Jordan to possess it" (De.32:46-47).** **"For the law was given by Moses, but grace and truth came by Jesus Christ" (Jn.1:17).** **"Hear, O Israel: The LORD our God is one LORD: And thou shalt love the LORD thy God with all thine heart, and with all thy soul, and with all thy might" (De.6:4-5).**

PROPHET	TIME/PLACE GIVEN	MAIN MESSAGE	PRACTICAL APPLICATION
MOSES (cont.) **Scripture References** The books of *Genesis, Exodus, Leviticus, Numbers,* and *Deuteronomy;* Jos.8:31-32; 1 S.12:8; 1 K.8:56; 2 K.23:23-25; 1 Chr.22:13; Ps.90; Is.63:11-12; Mt.17:1-3		As he preached, Moses also broke out into song and prophesied of the future of Israel. Most importantly, Moses told of One Who would rise later, One Who would be similar to Moses. Moses spoke of the Messiah, Jesus Christ. Just as Moses spoke the words God gave him to speak so Jesus Christ spoke and did what the Father spoke and directed Him to do. Just as Moses delivered God's people from the bondage of Egypt so Christ delivers God's people from the bondage of sin. **"The Lord thy God will raise up unto thee a Prophet from the midst of thee, of thy brethren, like unto me; unto him ye shall hearken … I will raise them up a Prophet from among their brethren, like unto thee, and will put my words in his mouth; and he shall speak unto them all that I shall command him" (De.18:15, 18).** **"Give ear, O ye heavens, and I will speak; and hear, O earth, the words of my mouth. My doctrine shall drop as the rain, my speech shall distil as the dew, as the small rain upon the tender herb, and as the showers upon the grass: Because I will publish the name of the Lord: ascribe ye greatness unto our God" (De.32:1-3).** **"And this is the blessing, wherewith Moses the man of God blessed the children of Israel before his death. And he said, The Lord came from Sinai, and rose up from Seir unto them; he shined forth from mount Paran, and he came with ten thousands of saints: from his right hand went a fiery law for them. Yea, he loved the people; all his saints are in thy hand: and they sat down at thy feet; every one shall receive of thy words" (De.33:1-3).**	

THE PROPHETS

PROPHET	TIME/PLACE GIVEN	MAIN MESSAGE	PRACTICAL APPLICATION
NAHUM **(Comfort)** **Known Facts** 1. Lived in Elkosh (Na. 1:1). 2. Prophesied about Nineveh, just as Jonah did, but the Ninevites did not listen to Nahum, and they were destroyed (Na.2:8-13). 3. Wrote the book of *Nahum* (Na.1:1). **Predictions and Messages** 1. A poem about God's zeal for justice—His goodness and protection for those who take refuge in Him and His fierce wrath that falls upon the wicked (Na.1:2-8). 2. The doom of the Ninevites, who will be destroyed even though they have many weapons (Na.1:9-2:13). 3. A funeral poem about Nineveh, the greedy and violently wicked city (Na.3:1-19). **Scripture References** The book of *Nahum*; Is.52:7	**Time** *663–612 B.C., during the reign of Manasseh, Amon and Josiah.* **Place** *Judah, the Southern Kingdom and Nineveh, the capital city of Assyria, hundreds of miles from Jerusalem.*	The outcry of evil from Nineveh, the capital city of the Assyrians, reached up to God, calling out for judgment. And swift judgment was on the way. The Ninevites thought that they were unstoppable, too mighty to even be slowed down. For the small country of Judah, Nineveh personified the word terror. But Nahum had a message from God: the LORD is zealous, avenging His people and pouring out wrath upon His enemies. About one hundred years earlier, Nineveh had repented under conviction of Jonah's preaching to them. But now, the city had returned to its wicked and brutal ways, caring only about conquest and plunder, power and wealth. Nahum preached a message of total destruction. This time, the Ninevites did not repent and the judgment of God fell on the entire city. Tragically, the Ninevites had felt all powerful, so powerful that nothing or no one could harm their large fortified city. But when God pronounced judgment on them, nothing and no one could save them. Nineveh was destroyed in 663 B.C. **"God is jealous, and the LORD revengeth; the LORD revengeth, and is furious; the LORD will take vengeance on his adversaries, and he reserveth wrath for his enemies. The LORD is slow to anger, and great in power, and will not at all acquit the wicked: the LORD hath his way in the whirlwind and in the storm, and the clouds are the dust of his feet" (Na.1:2-3).** **"There is no healing of thy bruise; thy wound is grievous: all that hear the bruit [report] of thee shall clap the hands over thee: for upon whom hath not thy wickedness passed continually?" (Na.3:19).**	God is going to rectify all the injustices of the world. God's judgment is going to fall upon every person who has mistreated others. All unjust behavior of men will bear the terrible judgment of God, all the... • killing • stealing • mocking • fighting • cursing • prejudice • cheating • bitterness • abusing • hatred The list could go on and on, but the point is this: much of the world's behavior is evil and unjust. God *must judge* the world, for judgment is the righteous and just penalty for evil. All the injustices of the world must be corrected. God is going to judge the world. He is just and righteous Himself; therefore, His very nature demands that all the injustices and wrongs that men have inflicted upon others be judged and punished. God will execute justice and avenge His people. God sees the great need of His people, and God alone can meet their need. Therefore God, the just Judge of the universe, will avenge them of their adversaries (spiritual as well as human). Even now, when His people pray, continually bringing their case before God, He hears their plea, and He delivers them. And when the time comes, justice will be executed against the persecutors of His people. **"Shall not the Judge of all the earth do right?" (Ge.18:25).** **"And shall not God avenge his own elect, which cry day and night unto him, though he bear long with them? I tell you that he will avenge them speedily" (Lu.18:7-8).** **"So that a man shall say, Verily there is a reward for the righteous: verily he is a God that judgeth in the earth" (Ps.58:11).**

374

NATHAN
(He has given)

Known Facts

1. Ministered during the time of the united kingdom under King David and King Solomon (2 S.7:1-5; 1 Chr. 17:1-4).
2. Named David's son Jedidiah (who later became known as Solomon) (2 S.12:25).
3. Stood with David against Adonijah the rebel, helping establish Solomon on the throne (1 K.1:8-46).
4. Wrote the history of the kingship of David and Solomon (1 Chr. 9:29; 2 Chr.29:25).

Predictions and Messages

1. The prophecy that Israel would have a permanent dwelling place (2 S.7:4-10; 1 Chr.17:3-9).
2. The prophecy that God would establish David's family on the throne forever—that the Messiah, the King of kings, would come through David's family (2 S.7:11-17; 1 Chr.17:10-15).
3. The parable of the poor sheep owner—the exposure of David's sin of adultery (2 S.12:1-9; Ps.51:1).
4. The prophecy that David's household would be filled with death and violence (2 S.12:10).
5. The prophecy that David's secret sin of adultery would be punished by a public sin of adultery against him (2 S.12:11-12).

(Cont. on next page)
(Cont. on next page)

Time

1003-931 B.C., during the reigns of King David and King Solomon when the kingdom of Israel was still united and strong.

Place

Jerusalem, the capital of Israel and the city chosen by God to place the temple.

Through all the messages sent by God through Nathan the prophet, this one theme stands out: the LORD will greatly bless and defend all who honor Him.

King David had a burning desire to build a temple for the LORD. Nathan had encouraged David to build the temple; but that very night God corrected Nathan, reversing his counsel to David.

Nonetheless, God was very pleased with David and blessed David greatly because David honored Him with his whole heart. Note the tremendous blessings that Nathan predicted would be given to David by God:

➤ David would be given a position of astounding royalty and power.
➤ David would have the blessing of God's presence and guidance through the years.
➤ David would be given the power to conquer his enemies.
➤ David would be given an honorable name and reputation.
➤ David was assured that the promised land would be given to Israel.
➤ David was assured that he would receive future rest from all his enemies.
➤ David would receive a never ending dynasty.
➤ David would receive a Promise Seed raised up by God Himself.
➤ David would receive a kingdom established by God Himself.
➤ David was given the promise that the temple would be built by his son.
➤ David was given the promise of a descendant Who would be God's own Son.
➤ David was given the promise that the same descendant would be punished for sin.

Although David did not build the temple, he honored God by his burning desire to build it. God greatly blessed David because he had a heart that longed to give honor to God.

God is good, and His goodness is overwhelming. But we live in a wicked world, a world where evil men roam and commit acts of terror, violence and lawlessness. In addition to evil men, the world is full of misfortune and hardship, temptation and trial. Yet in the midst of all the difficulties and problems of life, God's goodness shines through. For if we trust the Lord, He promises to save and deliver us and to meet our every need. No matter what the terrible circumstance, God will pour out His goodness upon us, strengthening and helping us to walk through any problem or difficulty. God is good, and He longs for us to trust Him. And if we trust Him, His goodness pours out the riches promises to us, promises that assure us of the most victorious and fruitful life imaginable. This is the wonderful promise of the incredible goodness of God.

"And he said unto him, Why callest thou me good? there is none good but one, that is, God: but if thou wilt enter into life, keep the commandments" (Mt. 19:17).

"The LORD is my strength and my shield; my heart trusted in him, and I am helped: therefore my heart greatly rejoiceth; and with my song will I praise him" (Ps.28:7).

"Thou art good, and doest good; teach me thy statutes" (Ps.119:68).

"The LORD is good, a strong hold in the day of trouble; and he knoweth them that trust in him" (Na.1:7).

PROPHET	TIME/PLACE GIVEN	MAIN MESSAGE	PRACTICAL APPLICATION
NATHAN (cont.) 6. The declaration that God had seen David's repentance and had forgiven him of his adultery (2 S.12:13). 7. The prophecy that David and Bathsheba son, born from their adulterous relationship, would die (2 S. 12:14). **Scripture References** 2 S.7:1-17; 1 K.1; 1 Chr.17		"And it came to pass that night, that the word of the LORD came unto Nathan, saying, Go and tell my servant David, Thus saith the LORD, Shalt thou build me an house for me to dwell in? Whereas I have not dwelt in any house since the time that I brought up the children of Israel out of Egypt, even to this day, but have walked in a tent and in a tabernacle. In all the places wherein I have walked with all the children of Israel spake I a word with any of the tribes of Israel, whom I commanded to feed my people Israel, saying, Why build ye not me an house of cedar? Now therefore so shalt thou say unto my servant David, Thus saith the LORD of hosts, I took thee from the sheepcote, from following the sheep, to be ruler over my people, over Israel: And I was with thee whithersoever thou wentest, and have cut off all thine enemies out of thy sight, and have made thee a great name, like unto the name of the great men that are in the earth. Moreover I will appoint a place for my people Israel, and will plant them, that they may dwell in a place of their own, and move no more; neither shall the children of wickedness afflict them any more, as beforetime, And as since the time that I commanded judges to be over my people Israel, and have caused thee to rest from all thine enemies. Also the LORD telleth thee that he will make thee an house. And when thy days be fulfilled, and thou shalt sleep with thy fathers, I will set up thy seed after thee, which shall proceed out of thy bowels, and I will establish his kingdom. He shall build an house for my name, and I will stablish the throne of his kingdom for ever. I will be his father, and he shall be my son. If he commit iniquity, I will chasten him with the rod of men, and with the stripes of the children of men: But my mercy shall not depart away from him, as I took it from Saul, whom I put away before thee. And thine house and thy kingdom shall be established for ever before thee: thy throne shall be established for ever" (2 S.7:4-17).	

PROPHET	TIME/PLACE GIVEN	MAIN MESSAGE	PRACTICAL APPLICATION
NOAH **(Rest)** **Known Facts** 1. Was the son of Lamech (Ge.5:28-29). 2. Found favor in the sight of God (Ge. 6:5-8). 3. Was a righteous man (Ge.6:9). 4. Received instruction from God to build an ark to preserve his family and some of each living animal (Ge.6:13-21). 5. Entered into a covenant with God to be saved (Ge.6:18). 6. Built the ark (Ge. 6:22). 7. Called a preacher of righteousness by the Scripture (2 Pe.2:5). 8. Was saved by following God's instructions (Ge.7:1-24). **Predictions and Messages** 1. Preached righteousness to a wicked generation (2 Pe.2:5). 2. Prophesied about the future of his three sons and their descendants (Ge.9:25-27). **Scripture References** Ge.5–8	**Time** *Unknown, but at least seven generations after Adam.* **Place** *The center of civilization, before the tower of Babel.*	Noah was a preacher of righteousness, warning people that the judgment of God was coming upon the whole world. What did he preach? Simply what God had told him—there is a consequence for sin. God would eventually withdraw his Spirit: His Spirit would not always strive with man, not forever. If man did not repent, the consequences of his sin would come upon him. Through the preaching of Noah, the Spirit of God was doing just what He does with people today when they hear the Word of God preached and taught in the power of God. He was convicting them of sin and of coming judgment. But the people were resisting and quenching the convictions of the Spirit. They were not listening to the voice of God struggling within their hearts. They wanted to live like they wanted, to do their own thing. Consequently, God had no choice. God had to give man a final warning: if man did not repent, God would withdraw His Spirit and let judgment fall upon the ungodliness and unrighteousness of men. **"And the LORD said, My spirit shall not always strive with man, for that he also is flesh: yet his days shall be an hundred and twenty years....And the LORD said, I will destroy man whom I have created from the face of the earth" (Ge.6:3, 7).** **"And he said, Cursed be Canaan; a servant of servants shall he be unto his brethren. And he said, Blessed be the LORD God of Shem; and Canaan shall be his servant. God shall enlarge Japheth, and he shall dwell in the tents of Shem; and Canaan shall be his servant" (Ge.9:25-27).** **"[God] spared not the old world, but saved Noah the eighth person, a preacher of righteousness, bringing in the flood upon the world of the ungodly" (2 Pe. 2:5).**	Judgment for sin is coming. Yet, people act as if the world will go on undisturbed. People act as if tomorrow will be just like today. The world continues in sin, foolishly rushing here and there, living as if there is no consequence for sin. Think how much our society is like the first society of earth. Think of the cult of beauty and sex, the power given to the immoral, the sin that runs wild all through society. But it will not continue forever. Just like Noah's day, eventually God will withdraw His Spirit and judgment will fall. The terrible wrath of God will be made known to the sinner, either when he dies, or when the judgment of God falls upon the entire world. A person simply cannot live an immoral and wicked life and hope that God will not notice. There are consequences for sin, serious consequences. **"But as the days of Noe were, so shall also the coming of the Son of man be. For as in the days that were before the flood they were eating and drinking, marrying and giving in marriage, until the day that Noe entered into the ark, and knew not until the flood came, and took them all away; so shall also the coming of the Son of man be" (Mt.24:37-39).** **"Now the works of the flesh are manifest, which are these; Adultery, fornication, uncleanness, lasciviousness, Idolatry, witchcraft, hatred, variance, emulations, wrath, strife, seditions, heresies, Envyings, murders, drunkenness, revellings, and such like: of the which I tell you before, as I have also told you in time past, that they which do such things shall not inherit the kingdom of God" (Ga.5:19-21).**

PROPHET	TIME/PLACE GIVEN	MAIN MESSAGE	PRACTICAL APPLICATION
OBADIAH **(Servant of Jehovah/Yahweh)** **Known Facts** 1. Wrote the book of *Obadiah* (Ob.1). 2. Ministered to Judah, the Southern Kingdom of Israel (Ob.16-17). **Predictions and Messages** 1. The prophecy of the doom of the nation of Edom (Ob.1-16). 2. The prophecy that Judah will overpower Edom, taking away Edom's territory and ending the evil nation's violence against Judah (Ob.17-21). **Scripture References** The book of *Obadiah*; 2 K.8:20-22; 2 Chr.21:8-20	**Time** *845 B.C., during the reign of King Jehoram of Judah.* **Place** *Judah, the Southern Kingdom of Israel.*	Edom will be overthrown because of her pride, a pride which led to a lifestyle of wickedness, and savage brutality, and violence against the Israelites down through the centuries. The Edomites were the descendants of Esau and were actually related to Judah. Because of their ancient relationship, the Edomites should have been good neighbors to Judah, but instead they were hostile, brutal and savage. Now, God would make them pay for their arrogance. Edom would suffer one invasion after the other over the next several centuries. Eventually, just as predicted, in the second century B.C., the Maccabees, who were Jewish zealots, finally conquered the Edomites and subjected them under the heel of Judah's authority. **"The vision of Obadiah. Thus saith the Lord GOD concerning Edom; We have heard a rumour from the LORD, and an ambassador is sent among the heathen, Arise ye, and let us rise up against her in battle" (Ob.1).** **"Though thou exalt thyself as the eagle, and though thou set thy nest among the stars, thence will I bring thee down, saith the LORD" (Ob.4).** **"But thou shouldest not have looked on the day of thy brother in the day that he became a stranger; neither shouldest thou have rejoiced over the children of Judah in the day of their destruction; neither shouldest thou have spoken proudly in the day of distress" (Ob.12).** **"For the day of the LORD is near upon all the heathen: as thou hast done, it shall be done unto thee: thy reward shall return upon thine own head" (Ob.15).**	All boasting and arrogance, pride and conceit is wrong. It is wrong to elevate ourselves above others, to think that we are *better* or *higher* than anyone else. God will severely judge all pride. **"Therefore pride compasseth them about as a chain; violence covereth them as a garment" (Ps.73:6).** **"And he shall spread forth his hands in the midst of them, as he that swimmeth spreadeth forth his hands to swim: and he shall bring down their pride together with the spoils of their hands" (Is.25:11).**

The Prophets

PROPHET	TIME/PLACE GIVEN	MAIN MESSAGE	PRACTICAL APPLICATION
PAUL (Small, little) **Known Facts** 1. Lived in Tarsus (Ac. 9:11; 21:39). 2. Was an apostle "born out of due time" (1 Co.15:8). 3. Was originally named *Saul* (Ac.13:9). 4. Persecuted the Christians, fiercely persecuted them (Ac.8:1–9:2). 5. Was converted in a dramatic confrontation with Christ (Ac. 9:3-9). 6. Became just as zealous for Christ as he had been for Judaism (2 Co.12:15). 7. Made many missionary journeys, taking the gospel to the world (Ac.13:1–28:31). 8. Was taken prisoner by the Roman empire (Ac.21:11-13; 25:14). 9. Wrote much of the New Testament. 10. Was martyred for the cause of Christ (by Nero in A.D. 64, according to church history). **Predictions and Messages** 1. A prophecy given to Paul by an angel—that all on board the ship caught in a storm would live (Ac.27:12-26). 2. A prophecy that Christ will return to the earth (Ph.3:20; 1 Th. 4:16). 3. A prophecy that the world will become very evil in the last times, with some saints even falling away (2 Th.2:3; 2 Ti. 3:1-7). 4. A prophecy that the saints of God will be resurrected (1 Co. 15:50-57; Ph.3:21; 1 Th.4:13-18). (cont. on next page)	**Time** *A.D. 35–64, all the years of Paul's life after his conversion.* **Place** *Various churches, homes and prisons, north and east of the Mediterranean Sea.*	If the message of Paul can be summed up in a few words, it can only be done in his own words: **"For I am not ashamed of the gospel of Christ: for it is the power of God unto salvation to every one that believeth; to the Jew first, and also to the Greek. For therein is the righteousness of God revealed from faith to faith: as it is written, The just shall live by faith" (Ro.1:16-17).** **"For though I preach the gospel, I have nothing to glory of: for necessity is laid upon me; yea, woe is unto me, if I preach not the gospel!" (1 Co.9:16).** What greater example could be set before us than the life of Paul, other than the life of Christ? The Apostle Paul was the apex of dedication and service, surpassed only by Christ Himself. Paul exhausted himself preaching and teaching the gospel, finally giving his life as a martyr. In all the preaching and prophecies of Paul, there was one clear point, one unmistakable focus: the gospel of Jesus Christ, the good news that Christ paid the price for sin on Calvary. Every person who accepts this, calling on the name of the Lord, can be saved from his sins. This person can become acceptable to God and be given a wonderful entrance into heaven, the place of eternal reward and receive the Spirit of God into his heart and life. With the presence of God's Spirit in his life, the believer has the power to live a conquering triumphant life through all the trials and temptations of life. No matter what the believer faces—even if it is the terrible evil of the last days—God empowers the believer to be "more than a conqueror" (Ro.8:37-39). Think, when the believer comes face-to-face with death, quicker than the eye can blink, the Lord transfers him to heaven, the place of eternal reward.	The hope of salvation—the forgiveness of sins, a victorious and conquering life and the gift of eternal life—all this has been entrusted into the hands of Paul and to all other believers. Note exactly what the Bible teaches: God's Word and the teaching of God's Word have been committed to men by the commandment of God. God's Word and the preaching of His Word are not an option. God commands that we take care of His Word, that we be good stewards of the truth of the gospel, that we preach and teach it to the whole world. **"Go ye therefore, and teach all nations, baptizing them in the name of the Father, and of the Son, and of the Holy Ghost: Teaching them to observe all things whatsoever I have commanded you: and, lo, I am with you alway, even unto the end of the world" (Mt.28:19-20).** **"And he said unto them, Go ye into all the world, and preach the gospel to every creature" (Mk. 16:15).** **"Then said Jesus to them again, Peace be unto you: as my Father hath sent me, even so send I you" (Jn.20:21).**

379

PROPHET	TIME/PLACE GIVEN	MAIN MESSAGE	PRACTICAL APPLICATION
PAUL (cont.) 5. A prophecy of the antichrist—that the man of sin will be revealed in the end time (2 Th.2:1-5). 6. A prophecy that Christ will receive those who are His into heaven and their eternal reward (1 Co.1:8). 7. A prophecy that death will be destroyed (1 Co.15:24-26). **Scripture References** Ac.8:1–28:31; the books of *Romans, 1 & 2 Corinthians, Galatians, Ephesians, Philippians, Colossians, 1 & 2 Thessalonians, 1 & 2 Timothy, Titus, Philemon*		"Nay, in all these things we are more than conquerors through him that loves us. For I am persuaded, that neither death, nor life, nor angels, nor principalities, nor powers, nor things present, nor things to come, Nor height, nor depth, nor any other creature, shall be able to separate us from the love of God, which is in Christ Jesus our Lord" (Ro.8:37-39). "And the Lord shall deliver me from every evil work, and will preserve *me* unto his heavenly kingdom: to whom *be* glory for ever and ever. Amen" (2 Ti.4:18).	

PROPHET	TIME/PLACE GIVEN	MAIN MESSAGE	PRACTICAL APPLICATION
SAMUEL **(God hears)** **Known Facts** 1. Dedicated to God from birth (1 S.1:11; 2:18). 2. Was favored highly with God and man (1 S.2:26). 3. Was given prophecies from God even as a boy (1 S.3:1-18). 4. Was recognized as a prophet to all Israel (1 S.3:20). 5. Lived in Ramah (1 S. 7:17). 6. Appointed his sons as judges, but they were wicked (1 S.8:3). 7. Anointed Saul as king (1 S.10:1). 8. Recorded events of David's reign and the regulations to govern the king and control his power (1 S.10:25; 1 Chr.29:29). 9. Faithfully served as a judge all his days (1 S.12:1-5). 10. Called down rain and thunder during the dry season—a sign that Samuel was God's spokesman (1 S. 12:16-18). 11. Anointed David as king over Israel (1 S. 16:1, 13). **Predictions and Messages** 1. The prophecy that judgment would fall on the family of Eli, the priest, because of his evil sons (1 S. 3:11-14; 4:17-22). 2. The prophecy that if Israel would get rid of their false gods, the LORD would help Israel defeat the Philistines (1 S.7:3). 3. The prophecy that when Israel cried out to the LORD because of the severe rule of the king they had insisted on, the LORD would not hear them (1 S.8:10-18). (cont. on next page)	**Time** *1095-1015 B.C., about forty years before King Saul and during most of his reign.* **Place** *In the center regions of Israel, serving as judge to the entire nation. In order to hear all the cases and judge Israel rightly, Samuel traveled on a regular yearly circuit all his life from Bethel to Gilgal to Mizpeh and back to his home in Ramah (1 S. 7:15-17).*	The messages, ministry and life of Samuel the prophet can be summed up in three words: "Serve the LORD." With this simple message, Samuel guided and judged the people of Israel for eighty years. Samuel encouraged the people: 1. To serve the LORD with all their heart (1 S.12:20, 24). 2. To serve the LORD and not to turn aside (1 S.12:20). 3. To serve the LORD in truth (1 S.12:24). 4. To serve the LORD, considering what great things He had done for them (1 S.12:24). Samuel's testimony is one of the strongest records of faithfulness ever lived. In Samuel's lifetime, he witnessed some of the most horrifying evil and wickedness ever committed upon the face of the earth, even by the leadership of Israel. For example, Eli, the priest who reared and trained him, would not control his own wicked sons. They committed the most vile acts of immorality imaginable—at the very tabernacle itself, the worship center of Israel (1 S.2:22). Saul, whom God had raised up to serve as king, turned out to be a great disappointment. Despite Samuel's great trust in him, Saul disobeyed God time and time again, until God finally had to remove him from the kingship and instruct Samuel to anoint another (David). But Samuel was faithful, faithful to the end. Through all the years he stayed true to the LORD despite all the horrifying evil of society.	Just imagine the impact Samuel's life and ministry had. There was no one, not a single person who could accuse Samuel of wrongdoing. he had lived a righteous life and served faithfully throughout all the years, throughout all the days of his life. What a testimony! What a dynamic, living example for us. We must live righteous lives, keeping all the commandments of God, obeying Him in all that He says. We must be faithful and diligent in all that we do. This is the strong declaration of God's Holy Word: **"Moreover it is required in stewards, that a man be found faithful" (1 Co.4:2).** **"Therefore, my beloved brethren, be ye stedfast, unmoveable, always abounding in the work of the Lord, forasmuch as ye know that your labour is not in vain in the Lord" (1 Co.15:58).** **"As every man hath received the gift, even so minister the same one to another, as good stewards of the manifold grace of God" (1 Pe.4:10).** **"These shall make war with the Lamb, and the Lamb shall overcome them: for he is Lord of lords, and King of kings: and they that are with him are called, and chosen, and faithful" (Re.17:14).** **"Let your heart therefore be perfect with the LORD our God, to walk in his statutes, and to keep his commandments, as at this day" (1 K.8:61).**

PROPHET	TIME/PLACE GIVEN	MAIN MESSAGE	PRACTICAL APPLICATION
SAMUEL (cont.) 4. The declaration that Saul's donkeys had been found (1 S.9:20). 5. The prophecy that God would change Saul into a different man so that he could serve as king (1 S.10:6). 6. The sermon of the history of Israel—a strong message that God would be with Israel so long as they faithfully obeyed Him (1 S.12:6-15). 7. The prophecy that the LORD would take Israel out of the promised land if they did evil (1 S.12:24-25). 8. The declaration that God had rejected Saul and chosen another (David) to be king (1 S.13:13-14; 15:17-29; 28:16-17). 9. The message from God to Samuel, that God was sorry he had made Saul king, because Saul had been so disobedient (1 S.15:10-11). 10. The prophecy that Saul and Jonathan would die the next day in battle (1 S. 28:18-19). **Scripture References** 1 S.1:1-25:1; 28:8-20; Je.15:1		"If ye will fear the LORD, and serve him, and obey his voice, and not rebel against the commandment of the LORD, then shall both ye and also the king that reigneth over you continue following the LORD your God: But if ye will not obey the voice of the LORD, but rebel against the commandment of the LORD, then shall the hand of the LORD be against you, as it was against your fathers....And Samuel said unto the people, Fear not: ye have done all this wickedness: yet turn not aside from following the LORD, but serve the LORD with all your heart; And turn ye not aside: for then should ye go after vain things, which cannot profit nor deliver; for they are vain. For the LORD will not forsake his people for his great name's sake: because it hath pleased the LORD to make you his people. Moreover as for me, God forbid that I should sin against the LORD in ceasing to pray for you: but I will teach you the good and the right way: Only fear the LORD, and serve him in truth with all your heart: for consider how great things he hath done for you. But if ye shall still do wickedly, ye shall be consumed, both ye and your king" (1 S.12:14-15, 20-25). "And Samuel said, Hath the LORD as great delight in burnt offerings and sacrifices, as in obeying the voice of the LORD? Behold, to obey is better than sacrifice, and to hearken than the fat of rams. For rebellion is as the sin of witchcraft, and stubbornness is as iniquity and idolatry" (1 S.15:22-23).	

PROPHET	TIME/PLACE GIVEN	MAIN MESSAGE	PRACTICAL APPLICATION
SHEMAIAH (Jehovah/Yahweh hears) **Known Facts** 1. Recorded the history of Rehoboam (2 Chr. 11:15). 2. Ministered to Judah, the Southern Kingdom (1 K.12:22; 2 Chr.12:5). **Predictions and Messages** 1. The message to King Rehoboam that the rebellion of Jeroboam and the northern tribes of Israel was the will of God and that Rehoboam should not try to stop the uprising (1 K.12:22-24; 2 Chr.11:2-4). 2. The prophecy that Jerusalem would be given into the hand of Egypt's King Shi-shak because the people had been unfaithful, forsaking the Law of the LORD (2 Chr.12:5). 3. The prophecy that the people would become servants of Shishak, but Jerusalem would not be destroyed, because the people had repented at the LORD's first message (see #2; 2 Chr.12:7-8). **Scripture References** 1 K.12:22-24; 2 Chr.11:2-4; 12:5-8, 15	**Time** *926 B.C., the fifth year of the reign of Rehoboam, king of Judah.* **Place** *Jerusalem, the capital of Judah, the Southern kingdom of Israel.*	Shortly after the ten northern tribes had revolted and formed the Northern Kingdom, Rehoboam mobilized an army of 180,000 soldiers to put down the rebellion. His purpose was to invade the northern tribes and permanently subject them under his rule. But while marching north to attack, God's prophet Shemaiah confronted Rehoboam. God's prophet had a stark warning for the king and the leaders of Judah (vv.2-4). They were not to fight against their brothers, the Israelites. Rather they were to return home, for the ruptured, divided kingdom was of God, the work of His hands. Hearing this stern warning from the prophet, the king and the people obeyed the LORD and returned home. But five years later when the scene refocuses upon Rehoboam and Judah, tragic differences are seen in the life of the king and people. They have turned away from the LORD, disobeying His Word and committing apostasy against Him. The hearts of Rehoboam and the people have wandered away from the LORD. As a result Shemaiah, the prophet, had another message for the king and people: Shishak, the Egyptian king was going to destroy Jerusalem. Upon hearing this message, the leaders quickly humbled themselves before the LORD. Thus God sent Shemaiah back with an amended message: Shishak would still attack and some of the people would be taken away as slaves, but the city of Jerusalem would remain. Note: the more severe judgment of God was averted because the people repented, but they still suffered the consequences for their sin. **"But the word of God came unto Shemaiah the man of God, saying, Speak unto Rehoboam, the son of Solomon, king of Judah, and unto all the house of Judah and Benjamin, and to the remnant of the people, saying, Thus saith the LORD, Ye shall not go up, nor fight against your brethren the children of Israel: return every man to his house; for this thing is from me. They hearkened therefore to the word of the LORD, and returned to depart, according to the word of the Lord" (1 K.12:22-24).**	God demands obedience, a lifetime of obedience. We are to always obey God's Holy Word, His commandments. Obeying God today and disobeying Him tomorrow does not make us acceptable to God. A life of inconsistency—obeying this week and disobeying next week—exposes a heart of insincerity and hypocrisy, a heart of dishonesty before God. A true profession of Christ means that we keep God's Word, obey His holy commandments. When we keep some commandments now and break other commandments later and continue a path of inconsistency, this is a life of deception and duplicity. Professing to be a follower of the LORD and consistently breaking His commandments is living a double life. It is attempting to establish a relationship with the LORD that is phony, double-dealing, shifty—a fake life that professes to obey God by living an unfaithful, untruthful life—a hypocritical life. **"Not every one that saith unto me, Lord, Lord, shall enter into the kingdom of heaven; but he that doeth the will of my Father which is in heaven. Many will say to me in that day, Lord, Lord, have we not prophesied in thy name? and in thy name have cast out devils? and in thy name done many wonderful works? And then will I profess unto them, I never knew you: depart from me, ye that work iniquity" (Mt.7:21-23).** **"Ye are my friends, if ye do whatsoever I command you" (Jn.15:14).** **"O that there were such an heart in them, that they would fear me, and keep all my commandments always, that it might be well with them, and with their children for ever!" (De.5:29).** **"Draw nigh to God, and he will draw nigh to you. Cleanse your hands, ye sinners; and purify your hearts, ye double minded" (Js.4:8).**
(cont. on next page)			

PROPHET	TIME/PLACE GIVEN	MAIN MESSAGE	PRACTICAL APPLICATION
SHEMAIAH (cont.)		"Then came Shemaiah the prophet to Rehoboam, and to the princes of Judah, that were gathered together to Jerusalem because of Shishak, and said unto them, Thus saith the LORD, Ye have forsaken me, and therefore have I also left you in the hand of Shishak. Whereupon the princes of Israel and the king humbled themselves; and they said, The LORD is righteous. And when the LORD saw that they humbled themselves, the word of the LORD came to Shemaiah, saying, They have humbled themselves; therefore I will not destroy them, but I will grant them some deliverance; and my wrath shall not be poured out upon Jerusalem by the hand of Shishak. Nevertheless they shall be his servants; that they may know my service, and the service of the kingdoms of the countries" (2 Chr.12:5-8).	

PROPHET	TIME/PLACE GIVEN	MAIN MESSAGE	PRACTICAL APPLICATION
The **UNNAMED PROPHET** who prophesied total victory for King Ahab of Israel over the Arameans (Syrians) **Known Facts** Delivered a message from God to King Ahab (1 K. 20:28). **Predictions and Messages** The entire Aramean (Syrian) army would be given into the hand of King Ahab. **Scripture References** 1 K.20:26-30	**Time** *855 B.C., during the reign of Ahab of Israel and during the ministry of Elijah the prophet.* **Place** *Samaria, the capital of the Northern Kingdom of Israel.*	The LORD sent His prophet to King Ahab once more to announce that He would deliver the vast army of the Arameans (Syrians) into the hands of the Israelites. Through the victory Ahab was to learn a great truth: The LORD is sovereign; His power is not partial or limited, but absolute. The LORD was going to prove that He was not just one god among many, not just a god of the hills as the Syrians falsely believed. He alone is the LORD (Jehovah/Yahweh), the only true and living God. **"And there came a man of God, and spake unto the king of Israel, and said, Thus saith the LORD, Because the Syrians have said, The LORD is God of the hills, but he is not God of the valleys, therefore will I deliver all this great multitude into thine hand, and ye shall know that I am the LORD" (1 K.20:28).**	The lesson for us is a much needed one: The LORD's sovereignty (His power) is not limited or partial, but absolute. The LORD is sovereign everywhere, throughout the entire universe. He is sovereign over all nations and kingdoms upon earth and in heaven. No limitation whatsoever hampers God's sovereignty or power. God controls all events and all happenings. And His sovereign power will eventually end all evil. **"For he must reign, till he hath put all enemies under his feet" (1 Co.15:25).** **"The LORD shall reign for ever and ever" (Ex.15:18).** **"The LORD hath prepared his throne in the heavens; and his kingdom ruleth over all" (Ps. 103:19).**

385

PROPHET	TIME/PLACE GIVEN	MAIN MESSAGE	PRACTICAL APPLICATION
The UNNAMED PROPHET who prophesied a victory for King Ahab of Israel over the Arameans (Syrians) **Known Facts** Delivered two messages from God to King Ahab (1 K.20:13, 22). **Predictions and Messages** 1. The prophecy that the LORD would deliver the Arameans (Syrians) into the hand of King Ahab (1 K. 20:13-15). 2. The prophecy that the Arameans would attack again the next year (1 K.20:22). **Scripture References** 1 K.20:1-25	**Time** *856 B.C., during the reign of Ahab of Israel and during the ministry of Elijah the prophet.* **Place** *Samaria, the capital of the Northern Kingdom of Israel.*	The LORD sent His prophet to King Ahab with a very special message during a very difficult time. The massive Syrian army was surrounding Ahab's capital city of Samaria. The situation seemed utterly hopeless. But the LORD longed to reach the heart of Ahab, longed for Ahab to stop Jezebel's savage purge of God's prophets and the worship of the LORD. Thus the LORD sent an unnamed prophet to Ahab, announcing that God was going to give a miraculous victory to the king for one specific purpose: to prove that He alone is God, the only true and living God. Ahab followed the battle instructions given him and achieved a great victory. Later, after the battle, the prophet came again and warned Ahab that the Arameans would attack again the next year. Now note this fact: even this warning should have aroused Ahab to repent, for God was still reaching out to him in compassion, patiently longing for him to turn from his wickedness, to acknowledge the one and only true God. But Ahab's heart was stubborn and unyielding. "Thus saith the LORD, Hast thou seen all this great multitude? behold, I will deliver it into thine hand this day; and thou shalt know that I am the LORD. And Ahab said, By whom? And he said, Thus saith the LORD, Even by the young men of the princes of the provinces. Then he said, Who shall order the battle? And he answered, Thou. Then he numbered the young men of the princes of the provinces, and they were two hundred and thirty two: and after them he numbered all the people, even all the children of Israel, being seven thousand" (1 K.20:13-15). "Go, strengthen thyself, and mark, and see what thou doest: for at the return of the year the king of Syria will come up against thee" (1 K.20:22).	God's purpose for helping us in times of trouble is to prove that He alone is God. There is only one true and living God, only one Creator, only one Sovereign LORD and Majesty of the universe. All other gods are false, deceivers that mislead and entrap human beings and capture their loyalty. And the terrible tragedy is this: if we are deceived into following and worshipping false gods, we condemn and doom ourselves. When hardships and misfortunes fall upon us, there is no living God to help us; for we are following false gods that are lifeless and powerless to help. We must recognize the LORD, the only true God. We must trust in the only One Who can help us in time of trouble. "Thou, even thou, art LORD alone; thou hast made heaven, the heaven of heavens, with all their host, the earth, and all things that are therein, the seas, and all that is therein, and thou preservest them all; and the host of heaven worshippeth thee" (Neh.9:6). "Of old hast thou laid the foundation of the earth: and the heavens are the work of thy hands" (Ps.102:25). "I make a decree, That in every dominion of my kingdom men tremble and fear before the God of Daniel: for he is the living God, and stedfast for ever, and his kingdom that which shall not be destroyed, and his dominion shall be even unto the end" (Da.6:26). "But the salvation of the righteous is of the LORD: he is their strength in the time of trouble" (Ps.37:39).

PROPHET	TIME/PLACE GIVEN	MAIN MESSAGE	PRACTICAL APPLICATION
The UNNAMED PROPHET who rebuked Eli and his house for profaning the temple of the LORD **Known Facts** Delivered a message to Eli the priest (1 S.2:27-34). **Predictions and Messages** 1. The prophecy that each generation of Eli's family would be stricken so that all the men would die in the prime of life (1 S. 2:27-33; esp. v.31). 2. The prophecy that Eli's sons would both die in the same day—a sign that the prophecy concerning Eli's family would come true (1 S.2:34). 3. The prophecy that the LORD would raise up a faithful priest in place of Eli (1 S.2:35-36). **Scripture References** 1 S.2:12-36	**Time** *1085 B.C., when Eli, the priest, was an old man.* **Place** *Shiloh, the central place of worship in Israel prior to the rule of the kings.*	An unnamed prophet was sent by God to pronounce the terrifying judgment against the priestly family of Eli. All three of his sons who were priests, would soon die, and the priesthood of Eli's family was to be transferred to the family of a faithful priest. The unnamed prophet declared three things: 1. He challenged Eli and his sons to remember the history of the priesthood. He pointed out what a privilege it was for priests to approach God and present the offerings to him. For the offerings symbolized the redemption of God's people through the blood of the sacrifice. 2. He pronounced the charge of God against Eli and his sons—that they had scorned the holy things of God and committed immorality. 3. He pronounced the judgment of God against Eli and his sons. The wickedness of Eli and his sons had been so horrible that God was left with no choice. He had to cut them off as priests. **"And there came a man of God unto Eli, and said unto him, Thus saith the LORD,...Wherefore kick ye at my sacrifice and at mine offering, which I have commanded in my habitation; and honourest thy sons above me, to make yourselves fat with the chiefest of all the offerings of Israel my people? Wherefore the LORD God of Israel saith,...Behold, the days come, that I will cut off thine arm, and the arm of thy father's house, that there shall not be an old man in thine house....And this shall be a sign unto thee, that shall come upon thy two sons, on Hophni and Phinehas; in one day they shall die both of them. And I will raise me up a faithful priest, that shall do according to that which is in mine heart and in my mind: and I will build him a sure house; and he shall walk before mine anointed for ever. And it shall come to pass, that every one that is left in thine house shall come and crouch to him for a piece of silver and a morsel of bread, and shall say, Put me, I pray thee, into one of the priests' offices, that I may eat a piece of bread" (1 S.2:27, 29-31, 34-36).**	Judgment upon the immoral and wicked of this world will definitely take place. This is the strong prophetic message of God's Word. Just when the judgment of God is going to fall upon this world is unknown. Just when each of us is going to stand before God, even the minister, is unknown. But the day is definitely coming. The only sure thing that we know about our lives is this: we will die and after that will be the judgment. Judgment is sure, definite, and absolutely certain. Judgment is coming. **"And as it is appointed unto men once to die, but after this the judgment" (He.9:27).** **"When the Son of man shall come in his glory, and all the holy angels with him, then shall he sit upon the throne of his glory: And before him shall be gathered all nations: and he shall separate them one from another, as a shepherd divideth his sheep from the goats: And he shall set the sheep on his right hand, but the goats on the left" (Mt.25:31-33).**

PROPHET	TIME/PLACE GIVEN	MAIN MESSAGE	PRACTICAL APPLICATION
The UNNAMED PROPHET who rebuked Israel for fearing the false gods of the Amorites **Known Facts** Delivered a message to the Israelites (Jud.6:8-10). **Predictions and Messages** The message that Israel had been disobedient because they were in fear of the Amorites (Jud.6:8-10). **Scripture References** Jud.6:7-10	**Time** *Approximately 1210 B.C., during the oppression of the Israelites by the Amorites.* **Place** *The southern regions of Israel.*	The LORD raised up a prophet to rebuke the Israelites because the Israelites needed to be warned as never before. For generations, the Israelites had been failing God, turning back time and again to the sins and evil of their neighbors and engaging in their false worship. The prophet rebuked Israel for four specific sins or evils: ➤ The Israelites had forgotten God's salvation, His wonderful deliverance from Egyptian slavery. ➤ The Israelites had forgotten God's deliverance down through the centuries from their oppressors and forgotten His gift of the promised land. ➤ The Israelites had forsaken God, engaging in false worship or idolatry. ➤ The Israelites had refused to listen to God, disobeying Him and breaking His commandments. **"The LORD sent a prophet unto the children of Israel, which said unto them, Thus saith the LORD God of Israel, I brought you up from Egypt, and brought you forth out of the house of bondage; And I delivered you out of the hand of the Egyptians, and out of the hand of all that oppressed you, and drave them out from before you, and gave you their land; And I said unto you, I am the LORD your God; fear not the gods of the Amorites, in whose land ye dwell: but ye have not obeyed my voice" (Jud.6:8-10).**	If we continue in sin—walk day by day disobeying God—a strong rebuke and correction are needed. We need to be awakened, stirred, aroused out of our slumber and hardness of sin. When we sincerely confess our sins and repent, God will deliver us. But we need to learn one truth: we are not to return to our sin. The sin is to be forsaken or left behind, and we are to walk forward, growing more and more in the righteousness of God. If we return to the same sin time and again, continuing in sin, we deserve to be rebuked. **"And Jesus said unto him, No man, having put his hand to the plough, and looking back, is fit for the kingdom of God" (Lu. 9:62).** **"And have no fellowship with the unfruitful works of darkness, but rather reprove them" (Ep. 5:11).** **"Them that sin rebuke before all, that others also may fear" (1 Ti.5:20).**

PROPHET	TIME/PLACE GIVEN	MAIN MESSAGE	PRACTICAL APPLICATION
The UNNAMED PROPHET who rebuked **King Ahab of Israel for sparing Ben-Hadad, the evil king of Aram (Syria)** **Known Facts** 1. Belonged to the school of the prophets (1 K.20:35). 2. Delivered a message to King Ahab (1 K. 20:39-42). 3. Was known as a prophet (1 K.20:41). **Predictions and Messages** 1. The prophecy that a fellow prophet would be killed by a lion (1 K.20:36). 2. The message that King Ahab had done evil by sparing Ben-Hadad, the evil king of Aram (1 K.20:39-42). **Scripture References** 1 K.20:31-43	**Time** *855 B.C., during the reign of Ahab of Israel and during the ministry of Elijah the prophet.* **Place** *Samaria, the capital of the Northern Kingdom of Israel.*	Under God's instructions, an unnamed prophet sought to disguise himself in order to confront King Ahab. The unnamed prophet ordered a fellow prophet to strike him so that he would appear to be a wounded soldier when he confronted the king. But the fellow prophet refused. As a result, the unnamed prophet predicted the other prophet's death. The next man obeyed and struck the unnamed prophet, wounding him so that his disguise would not be questioned. Disguised as a wounded soldier, the unnamed prophet waited by the road for the king. When Ahab finally arrived and was passing by, the unnamed prophet cried out for a pardon. He told the king that he was in trouble because he had let a prisoner escape. Ahab demonstrated his hard heart by condemning the man. As soon as Ahab had issued his verdict, the prophet stripped off his disguise and pronounced God's condemnation upon Ahab for letting Ben-Hadad, the evil king of Syria, go free. Ahab's life would be demanded in place of the life of Ben-Hadad. **"Then said he unto him, Because thou hast not obeyed the voice of the LORD, behold, as soon as thou art departed from me, a lion shall slay thee. And as soon as he was departed from him, a lion found him, and slew him" (1 K.20:36).** **"And as the king passed by, he cried unto the king: and he said, Thy servant went out into the midst of the battle; and, behold, a man turned aside, and brought a man unto me, and said, Keep this man: if by any means he be missing, then shall thy life be for his life, or else thou shalt pay a talent of silver. And as thy servant was busy here and there, he was gone. And the king of Israel said unto him, So shall thy judgment be; thyself hast decided it" (1 K.20:39-40).**	The lesson we need to learn is that disobedience has consequences. If we disobey God, we stand condemned and will bear the hand of God's judgment. In giving the commandments, God intended good for us. The commandments tell us how to live good, honorable and productive lives that are victorious and conquering. Through obedience, we can live lives that prove to be successful and that bring a sense of fulfillment and satisfaction to the human heart. **"And to you who are troubled rest with us, when the Lord Jesus shall be revealed from heaven with his mighty angels, In flaming fire taking vengeance on them that know not God, and that obey not the gospel of our Lord Jesus Christ: Who shall be punished with everlasting destruction from the presence of the Lord, and from the glory of his power" (2 Th.1:7-9).** **"But if ye will not obey the voice of the LORD, but rebel against the commandment of the LORD, then shall the hand of the LORD be against you, as it was against your fathers" (1 S.12:15).** **"And a curse, if ye will not obey the commandments of the LORD your God, but turn aside out of the way which I command you this day, to go after other gods, which ye have not known" (De.11:28).**

PROPHET	TIME/PLACE GIVEN	MAIN MESSAGE	PRACTICAL APPLICATION
The **UNNAMED PROPHET** who rebuked **King Amaziah of Judah** for his idolatry **Known Facts** Delivered a message to King Amaziah of Judah. **Predictions and Messages** 1. The rebuke of King Amaziah for foolishly worshipping the gods of the Edomites (2 Chr.25:15). 2. The prophecy that King Amaziah would be destroyed because he would not listen to the message of the prophet (2 Chr.25:16). **Scripture References** 2 Chr.25:14-16	**Time** *767 B.C., the last year of the reign of King Amaziah of Judah.* **Place** *Jerusalem, the capital of the Southern Kingdom of Judah.*	Almost unbelievably and certainly tragically, Amaziah committed the terrible sin of false worship. As part of the plunder from his victory, the king brought back the idols of Edom, set them up and worshipped them. Why would King Amaziah commit such folly, turning away from the LORD to false idols? Perhaps King Amaziah began to think that he actually had the support of these false gods so he began to worship them in thanksgiving for the victory he had achieved. The anger of the LORD was aroused and burned against Amaziah. God sent a prophet to warn the king by asking him a question: why had the king worshipped false gods, gods that could not save their own people from the hand of Amaziah? Reacting in rage, the king rejected the prophetic warning and threatened the prophet if he continued issuing his message of rebuke. But fearlessly, the prophet issued a final warning: God would judge and destroy the king for his sin and for not heeding the warning. **"Wherefore the anger of the LORD was kindled against Amaziah, and he sent unto him a prophet, which said unto him, Why hast thou sought after the gods of the people, which could not deliver their own people out of thine hand? And it came to pass, as he talked with him, that the king said unto him, Art thou made of the king's counsel? forbear; why shouldest thou be smitten? Then the prophet forbare, and said, I know that God hath determined to destroy thee, because thou hast done this, and hast not hearkened unto my counsel" (2 Chr.25:15-16).**	Believers must guard and keep themselves from idols. What does this mean? An idol is anything that takes first place in a person's life, anything that a person puts before God. An idol is anything that consumes man's focus and concentration, anything that consumes his energy and efforts more than God. A person can make an idol out of anything in this world; a person can take anything and worship it before God; he can allow it to consume his mind and thoughts and life: ⇒ houses ⇒ cars ⇒ lands ⇒ boats ⇒ job ⇒ sports ⇒ position ⇒ money ⇒ spouse ⇒ comfort ⇒ children ⇒ television ⇒ sex ⇒ possessions ⇒ food ⇒ pleasures ⇒ power ⇒ recreation But idols are not gods, no matter what their worshipers may think. There is no other God but One. It is true that people call out to gods, but... • they are gods of their own minds and imaginations, ideas and notions. • they are gods of wood and stone. • they are gods and lords of their own creation. • they have no power to save or deliver. **"Little children, keep yourselves from idols" (1 Jo.5:21).** **"Professing themselves to be wise, they became fools, and changed the glory of the uncorruptible God into an image made like to corruptible man, and to birds, and four-footed beasts, and creeping things" (Ro.1:22-23).**

THE PROPHETS

PROPHET	TIME/PLACE GIVEN	MAIN MESSAGE	PRACTICAL APPLICATION
The UNNAMED PROPHET who rebuked **King Jeroboam I** for his idolatry **Known Facts** 1. Lived in Judah (1 K. 13:1). 2. Prayed for King Jeroboam and the king's withered hand was healed (1 K.13:6). 3. Commanded by God not to delay—not even to eat or drink—while on his mission (1 K. 13:9). 4. Broke the command of God by visiting and having a meal with an old prophet (1 K.13:19). 5. Was killed by a lion because he disobeyed God's command (1 K.13:24). **Predictions and Messages** 1. The prophecy that a king named Josiah would execute all the false prophets on the altar at Bethel which King Jeroboam had set up for idolatry (1 K.13:2). 2. The prophecy that the altar at Bethel would split apart (1 K.13:3). **Scripture References** 1 K.13:1-25; 2 K.23:15-20	**Time** *931 B.C., the first year of the reign of King Jeroboam I, when the country of Israel had just split into two nations, the Northern Kingdom of Israel and the Southern Kingdom of Judah.* **Place** *Bethel, just north of Jerusalem.*	Just as King Jeroboam was standing by the altar he had set up at Bethel, getting ready to present a false sacrifice, he was suddenly confronted by a young unnamed prophet. The young man prophesied against the altar of false worship established by Jeroboam. The altar and its priests would be destroyed by a future descendant of David named Josiah. To prove that this event would take place, the young prophet gave Jeroboam a sign. The altar would immediately be split apart by the power of God Himself and the ashes would pour out. And so it happened. Pointing to the young man, Jeroboam ordered his guards to arrest him. Instead, another shocking sign happened, which abruptly interrupted the arrest. Jeroboam's hand immediately withered. Terrified, Jeroboam pleaded with the prophet for help. The prophet prayed for the king and his hand was restored. **"And he cried against the altar in the word of the LORD, and said, O altar, altar, thus saith the LORD; Behold, a child shall be born unto the house of David, Josiah by name; and upon thee shall he offer the priests of the high places that burn incense upon thee, and men's bones shall be burnt upon thee. And he gave a sign the same day, saying, This is the sign which the LORD hath spoken; Behold, the altar shall be rent, and the ashes that are upon it shall be poured out" (1 K.13:2-3).**	The lesson for us is strikingly clear: idolatry and false worship do not please the LORD. God totally opposes idolatry and false worship. Idols are not just images made out of wood, stone, metal or some other material. We can make an idol out of anything, for idols are anything that captures our heart more than God. Whatever captivates our hearts, whatever the focus of our hearts is, whatever we give our hearts to, that person or thing becomes our god, our idol. For that person or thing possesses our hearts, our primary interest and attention. As a result, God is denied, ignored or forgotten. **"For the wrath of God is revealed from heaven against all ungodliness and unrighteousness of men, who hold the truth in unrighteousness;…Who changed the truth of God into a lie, and worshipped and served the creature more than the Creator, who is blessed for ever. Amen" (Ro. 1:18, 25).** **"Thou shalt not make unto thee any graven image, or any likeness of any thing that is in heaven above, or that is in the earth beneath, or that is in the water under the earth" (Ex.20:4).** **"Take heed to yourselves, that your heart be not deceived, and ye turn aside, and serve other gods, and worship them" (De.11:16).**

THE PROPHETS

PROPHET	TIME/PLACE GIVEN	MAIN MESSAGE	PRACTICAL APPLICATION
The **UNNAMED PROPHET** who warned **King Amaziah of Judah** not to hire the army of Israel **Known Facts** Delivered a message to King Amaziah. **Predictions and Messages** 1. The warning that King Amaziah of Judah will meet with disaster if he deploys the troops of Israel into battle (2 Chr. 25:7-8). 2. The message that God has the power to help or to bring defeat (2 Chr.25:8). 3. The message that God is able to supply far more than anything ever lost (2 Chr.25:9). **Scripture References** 2 Chr.25:5-10	**Time** *767 B.C., the last year of the reign of King Amaziah of Judah.* **Place** *Jerusalem, the capital of the Southern Kingdom of Judah.*	King Amaziah of Judah was preparing for war against the age-old enemy of Israel, the Edomites. Amaziah had just hired the armies of Israel to assist him in his battles. But before he could deploy these troops, Amaziah was confronted by a prophet of the LORD who issued a strong warning to the king. The prophet told King Amaziah that he must not allow Israel's mercenary troops to march with him. For the LORD was not with Israel. Living wicked lives and engaging in false worship, the people of the Northern Kingdom had rejected the LORD and were no longer placing their hope in the eternal covenant given to David. They had abandoned the LORD; consequently, the LORD had abandoned them. Still speaking to Amaziah, the prophet continued his warning. If the king marched into battle with the Israelite mercenary soldiers, he would be defeated. Even if he fought courageously against the Edomites, the LORD would make sure he was defeated. For the LORD has the power to help or to overthrow an army. The prophet further assured King Amaziah that God would provide far more plunder—more than enough—to cover his losses if he would just discharge the unbelieving troops. **"But there came a man of God to him, saying, O king, let not the army of Israel go with thee; for the LORD is not with Israel, to wit, with all the children of Ephraim. But if thou wilt go, do it, be strong for the battle: God shall make thee fall before the enemy: for God hath power to help, and to cast down. And Amaziah said to the man of God, But what shall we do for the hundred talents which I have given to the army of Israel? And the man of God answered, The LORD is able to give thee much more than this" (2 Chr.25:7-9).**	Believers are to turn away from evil associations. Close associations always influence us. If we fellowship with godly people, we will be influenced by godliness. But if we fellowship with ungodly people, their ungodliness will influence us. It is impossible to escape the influence of close associations. We all influence each other; and the more closely we are associated, the more we are influenced. If a believer associates with the wicked, eventually the wicked will encourage the believer to join him in his sinful behavior. A godly person is always pulled down, influenced negatively by close associations with those who smoke, take drugs, get drunk, or engage in immoral behavior. No matter who we are or how strong we may be, we will be strongly influenced to participate in the sinful behavior. For this reason the LORD commands us to live lives of *spiritual separation.* Believers are not to fellowship nor become closely associated with the wicked and evil of this earth. We are to be spiritually separated. Living upon the earth, we are to be friends with everyone, unbeliever as well as believer. And we are to be kind, caring, and helpful to everyone. But we are not to form close alliances, associations, or bonds with the wicked and evil of this earth. **"But now I have written unto you not to keep company, if any man that is called a brother be a fornicator, or covetous, or an idolater, or a railer, or a drunkard, or an extortioner; with such an one no not to eat" (1 Co.5:11).** **"Thou shalt not follow a multitude to do evil; neither shalt thou speak in a cause to decline after many to wrest judgment" (Ex.23:2).**

PROPHET	TIME/PLACE GIVEN	MAIN MESSAGE	PRACTICAL APPLICATION
URIJAH **(Jehovah/Yahweh is a Light)** **Known Facts** 1. Was the son of Shemaiah (Je.26:20). 2. Lived in Kiriath-Jearim (Je.26:20). 3. Prophesied in Judah (Je.26:20-21). 4. Fled to Egypt to escape execution by King Jehoiakim (Je.26:21). 5. Was brought back from Egypt by the king's men and slain (Je.26:22-23). 6. Given the burial of a common criminal (Je.26:23). **Predictions and Messages** Preached messages similar to those of Jeremiah the prophet (Je.26:20). **Scripture References** Je.26:20-23	**Time** *608 B.C., at the beginning of the reign of Jehoiakim, king of Judah.* **Place** *Jerusalem, the capital city of Judah, in the palace of the king.*	All that is known about the messages of Urijah is that they were similar to those of Jeremiah, the prophet. By this one fact, we can know something of what Urijah prophesied. First, Urijah was bound to be a true prophet, proclaiming the messages given him by God. He was not speaking the popular, conscience-soothing messages of the false prophets of that time. Second, Urijah was courageous, warning both king and citizen to repent of their wickedness and false worship or else face the judgment of God. Otherwise, why would the king be so angry and determined to have Urijah executed? Third, we can be sure that Urijah preached the truth of God's Word right up until the day of his martyrdom. **"And there was also a man that prophesied in the name of the LORD, Urijah the son of Shemaiah of Kirjathjearim, who prophesied against this city and against this land according to all the words of Jeremiah" (Je.26:20).**	The preacher must not compromise the Word of God. He must say exactly what God gives him to say. After all, the message is not his, but God's. It is not his to change or alter in the least. Even if it means death, the man of God must not give another message or a watered down version of the truth. He must not seek to say what is popular or more acceptable to his listeners. He must preach the whole counsel of God without regard to circumstances or popular opinion. He must say exactly what God gives him to say. **"And he said unto them, Go ye into all the world, and preach the gospel to every creature" (Mk. 16:15).** **"And daily in the temple, and in every house, they ceased not to teach and preach Jesus Christ" (Ac.5:42).** **"But we preach Christ crucified, unto the Jews a stumblingblock, and unto the Greeks foolishness" (1 Co.1:23).** **"For though I preach the gospel, I have nothing to glory of: for necessity is laid upon me; yea, woe is unto me, if I preach not the gospel! (1 Co.9:16).** **"Preach the word; be instant in season, out of season; reprove, rebuke, exhort with all longsuffering and doctrine" (2 Ti.4:2).**

PROPHET	TIME/PLACE GIVEN	MAIN MESSAGE	PRACTICAL APPLICATION
ZECHARIAH (Jehovah/Yahweh has brought to mind), the son of Jehoiada **Known Facts** 1. Was the son of Jehoiada, the priest (2 Chr.24:20). 2. Was stoned to death because of his message (2 Chr.24:21). **Predictions and Messages** The message that the LORD had forsaken the people of Judah because they had forsaken the LORD and his commandments by their false worship and idolatry (2 Chr. 24:20). **Scripture References** 2 Chr.24:17-22; Mt. 23:34-39; Lu.11:47-51	**Time** *797 B.C., a year before the death of Joash, king of Judah.* **Place** *Jerusalem, the capital city of Judah.*	After the death of Jehoiada, the priest, King Joash, who had led a tremendous revival and spiritual reformation in his younger years, slipped away from the LORD and committed terrible apostasy. Joash listened and gave in to wicked, influential leaders who were false worshipers. Because of their terrible apostasy of turning away to false worship, they stood guilty before the LORD and aroused His anger. God sent prophet after prophet to warn the king, but the king and people stubbornly rejected the prophets of God, refusing to listen to their warnings and refusing to repent. In mercy, however, the LORD made one last attempt to get Joash and the people to repent. The Spirit of the LORD came upon Zechariah with a very special message for the king and the people. They had disobeyed God's commandments and forsaken Him; consequently, the LORD had now forsaken them. But in the depth of their stubborn, stiff-necked rebellion, they still did not repent. Instead, they actually murdered the prophet Zechariah. Furious over the pronouncement of judgment against them, Joash ordered the prophet stoned to death in the very courtyard of the temple itself. Looking up into the eyes of the king as he lay dying, Zechariah pronounced a divine curse upon the king and the people. They were to soon face God's vengeance. The next year, the Arameans (Syrians) attacked and overran the countryside. Joash was killed in battle. **"And the Spirit of God came upon Zechariah the son of Jehoiada the priest, which stood above the people, and said unto them, Thus saith God, Why transgress ye the commandments of the LORD, that ye cannot prosper? because ye have forsaken the LORD, he hath also forsaken you" (2 Chr.24:20).**	How many people have a wonderful beginning in life but a terrible ending? Think of people who have walked through many years of life with upright characters, living honest, moral, and just lives. Yet in the latter years of their lives their character has declined, deteriorated. Some have become immoral and dishonest, even cheating other people. Others are no longer kind and gracious but, rather, unkind, mean-spirited, and reactionary, sometimes even cursing or assaulting those who love and care for them. Whereas they used to live righteous lives and profess to be followers of the LORD, they are now backsliding, living carnal, fleshly lives. They not only ignore the LORD but they also deny Him. They curse His name, use profanity, and tell off-colored jokes. They no longer worship the LORD or are faithful in church attendance. Instead of setting the example that we must listen to the Word of God being taught, they slip into immorality, tearing out the hearts of parents, wives, husbands, children, former pastors, and teachers. Far too many who begin with Christ eventually turn away from Him, committing terrible apostasy against Him. **"And because iniquity shall abound, the love of many shall wax cold" (Mt.24:12).** **"They on the rock *are they*, which, when they hear, receive the word with joy; and these have no root, which for a while believe, and in time of temptation fall away" (Lu.8:13).** **"But now, after that ye have known God, or rather are known of God, how turn ye again to the weak and beggarly elements, whereunto ye desire again to be in bondage" (Ga.4:9).** **"Harden not your hearts, as in the provocation, in the day of temptation in the wilderness: When your fathers tempted me, proved me, and saw my works forty years. Wherefore I was grieved with that generation, and said, They do alway err in their heart; and they have not known my ways. So I sware in my wrath, They shall not enter into my rest.) Take heed, brethren, lest there be in any of you an evil heart of unbelief, in departing from the living God" (He.3:8-12).**

PROPHET	TIME/PLACE GIVEN	MAIN MESSAGE	PRACTICAL APPLICATION
ZECHARIAH (Jehovah/Yahweh has brought to mind), the son of Berechiah **Known Facts** 1. Was the son of Berechiah, the priest (Zec. 1:1). 2. Was the grandson of Iddo, the priest (Ezr. 6:14). 3. Ministered at the same time as Haggai, the prophet (Ezr.5:1; 6:14). 4. Prophesied in Jerusalem after the return from captivity (Zec. 1:1; Ezr.6:16). 5. Helped to restore the temple (Ezr.6:14-15). 6. Saw startling visions of the end times (Zec. 1:7-6:8). **Predictions and Messages** 1. The sermon that the people needed to repent and turn to the LORD (Zec.1:2-6). 2. The vision of the horseman beside the myrtle trees—the promise of restoration of the temple and to Jerusalem (Zec.1:7-17). 3. The vision of the four horns and the four craftsmen—the prophecy of future world powers (Zec.1:18-21). 4. The vision of a man with a measuring line—the prophecy of divine protection for Jerusalem (Zec.2). 5. The vision of Joshua the High Priest being accused and slandered by Satan—a prophecy of the redemption for all Israel (Zec.3). 6. The prophecy of the Messiah, the Savior of the world, the Righteous Branch Who would take away the sins of the land and bring peace (Is.11:1; Zec.3:8-10; Mt.2:23). (cont. on next page)	**Time** *520-518 B.C., during the reign of Darius the Mede, when the Israelites had returned from captivity.* **Place** *Jerusalem, the capital city of the remnant of Israel.*	The people of Israel had just come out of foreign captivity and badly needed to have a strong sense of direction. Zechariah, along with Haggai, the prophet, immediately pointed them to God, greatly encouraging the people to restore the temple so that it might be worthy to be used to worship the LORD. Now it was not just a building project that Zechariah was leading. As a spiritual leader of thousands of exiles who had just returned from captivity, Zechariah realized the great importance of quickly calling the people to genuine worship. He had to ground them firmly in the LORD right away. And so Zechariah encouraged the people time and again to turn to the LORD with their whole heart, to worship the Great Shepherd of their souls. Zechariah helped to lead a very great revival. His many visions and prophecies emphasized the love of a sovereign God for His people, and His desire to uphold them and work in their behalf. For those who were determined to serve God wholeheartedly, they would be supported and sustained by the LORD. He would bring about marvelous things in their future. **"Therefore say thou unto them, Thus saith the LORD of hosts; Turn ye unto me, saith the LORD of hosts, and I will turn unto you, saith the LORD of hosts" (Zec.1:3).** **"Thus saith the LORD of hosts; Let your hands be strong, ye that hear in these days these words by the mouth of the prophets, which were in the day that the foundation of the house of the LORD of hosts was laid, that the temple might be built" (Zec.8:9).**	God is sovereign. He rules over the entire universe. But a person should not think that God is far off in outer space someplace. Coming out of terrible tragedy, it is easy for a person to feel that God is a billion miles away. After a tragedy, it is difficult to have a sense of direction. But it is during hardship that a person needs to seek God like never before and to draw close to Him for understanding, for God cares about our problems. We must always be aware that God is not an unconcerned observer of the world He created. He truly cares about every struggle we go through, and He longs to move in our lives to make the future better, much better than our past. God did not just create the world, wind it up and leave it on its own to fly throughout space with man making out the best he can. God is interested and concerned with the world—so much so that He came to earth in human flesh to show how vitally concerned He is. God would not leave man to grope and grasp in the dark. His call to repentance is not for the purpose of pushing man down but to bring him up, to show man that there is a bright future ahead for those who determine to wholeheartedly serve the LORD. **"Jesus saith unto him, I am the way, the truth, and the life: no man cometh unto the Father, but by me" (Jn.14:6).** **"In my distress I called upon the LORD, and cried to my God: and he did hear my voice out of his temple, and my cry did enter into his ears" (2 S.22:7).** **"When thou art in tribulation, and all these things are come upon thee, even in the latter days, if thou turn to the LORD thy God, and shalt be obedient unto his voice; (For the LORD thy God is a merciful God;) he will not forsake thee, neither destroy thee, nor forget the covenant of thy fathers which he sware unto them" (De.4:30-31).**

THE PROPHETS

PROPHET	TIME/PLACE GIVEN	MAIN MESSAGE	PRACTICAL APPLICATION
ZECHARIAH (cont.) 7. The vision of a golden lampstand and two olive trees—the prophecy of continual anointing for Zerubbabel, who was a type of Christ (Zec.4). 8. The vision of a flying scroll—a declaration that wickedness will be purged from the land (Zec.5:1-4). 9. The vision of a woman in a basket—the prophecy of the rebellion of Babylon in the end times (Zec. 5:5-11). 10. The vision of four chariots—the declaration of God's sovereignty over all nations (Zec.6:1-8). 11. A sermon about the proper attitude for religious ceremony (Zec. 7:4-7). 12. A sermon about loving your neighbor (Zec.7:8-14). 13. The prophecy of God's favor coming upon Jerusalem and Judah (Zec.8:1-17). 14. The prophecy of the salvation of the Gentiles (Zec.8:18-23). 15. The prophecy of God's judgment upon Judah's enemies (Zec. 9:1-10). 16. The prophecy of the Christ's kingly declaration—that the Messiah, the Savior of the world, would enter Jerusalem riding on a young donkey (Zec.9:9; Mt.21:1-11). (Cont. in col.3) **Scripture References** The book of *Zechariah*; Ezr.5:1; 6:14; 8:3, 11, 16		**Predictions and Messages** (cont. from col.1) 17. The prophecy of restoration to all Israel (Zec.9:11-10:12). 18. The illustration of two shepherds' staffs—a prophecy of the rejection of the Messiah, the Great Shepherd (Zec.11). 19. The prophecy that the Messiah, the Savior of the world, would be betrayed for thirty pieces of silver (Zec.11:13). 20. The prophecy that Israel will never again abandon the LORD (Zec.12:1-13:9). 21. The prophecy that the Jews will recognize Jesus Christ as the true Messiah, as their true Savior, in the last days (Zec.12:10-14). 22. The prophecy that in the end times, the LORD will be the only king on the earth (Zec.14).	

PROPHET	TIME/PLACE GIVEN	MAIN MESSAGE	PRACTICAL APPLICATION
ZEPHANIAH **(Jehovah/Yahweh is darkness or God hides)** **Known Facts** 1. Was the son of Cushi (Zep.1:1). 2. Was a descendant of the righteous King Hezekiah (Zep.1:1). 3. Prophesied to Judah, the Southern Kingdom, helping to lead the way for the religious reforms of Josiah (Zep.1:1). **Predictions and Messages** 1. The prophecy of the coming judgment against Judah and Jerusalem (Zep.1:2-18). 2. The sermon about seeking the LORD to escape His wrath (Zep. 2:1-3). 3. The prophecy of the coming judgment against the Philistines (Zep.2:4-7). 4. The prophecy of the coming judgment against Moab and Ammon (Zep.2:8-11). 5. The prophecy of the coming judgment against Cush (Zep. 2:12). 6. The prophecy of the coming judgment against Assyria (Zep. 2:13-15). 7. The prophecy of the coming judgment against Jerusalem (Zep.3:1-7). 8. The prophecy of the purity of Israel in the last days (Zep.3:8-13; Re.14:1-5). 9. The prophecy of the restoration of Israel and Jerusalem (Zep. 3:14-20). **Scripture References** The book of *Zephaniah*	**Time** *640-609 B.C., during the entire reign of Josiah, king of Judah, who led the last great revival before the fall of Jerusalem in 586 B.C.* **Place** *Judah, the Southern Kingdom of Israel and Jerusalem, the capital city.*	After Manasseh and Amon, two of the most wicked kings in all of Judah's history, God raised up a godly king—Josiah. It was at the tender age of eight that Josiah was crowned king. Obviously, some consistent and righteous believers had a strong, spiritual influence upon young Josiah, for he lived a righteous life in the sight of the LORD. In fact, Scripture says that he followed the godly example of David, never deviating from the righteous example set by the ancient king (2 K.22:2). During his reign, Josiah had one major concern: the restoration of the temple and the true worship of the LORD, the only living and true God (2 K.22:3-7). No doubt, the prophet Zephaniah was one of the people who had a strong spiritual influence on Josiah. Zephaniah called the people to repent and to turn back to God. They had acted no better than their evil neighbors, and the wrath of God was about to be poured out. But there was still a ray of hope if only the people would repent and change their evil ways. Scripture reveals to us that the nation did listen to Zephaniah and the other prophets of that time and that the invasion of Babylon was delayed because of their change of heart (2 Chr.34:27-28). As a result of the messages of Zephaniah and others, Josiah started one of the two great revivals in Israel's history. (The other was by Hezekiah, the ancestor of Zephaniah.) Zephaniah's message announced the coming terrible judgment of God, in very dark words. But there was also promised blessing and a bright future ahead for those who turned to God. **"Gather yourselves together, yea, gather together, O nation not desired; Before the decree bring forth, before the day pass as the chaff, before the fierce anger of the LORD come upon you, before the day of the LORD's anger come upon you. Seek ye the LORD, all ye meek of the earth, which have wrought his judgment; seek righteousness, seek meekness: it may be ye shall be hid in the day of the LORD's anger" (Zep.2:1-3)**	Deep concern for righteousness and for true worship should grip our hearts. For righteousness and true worship determine our destiny, both individually and corporately, as a society and nation. Righteousness builds a character of integrity within people, and righteous individuals build up a nation. If a person is righteous, he is honest, just, true, moral and law-abiding. He keeps the laws of the land and works diligently at his job in order to make a significant contribution to society. Righteousness builds the character of morality and integrity. And when there are enough of us with righteous characters, we build a nation of righteousness, a nation of enormous strength. This can be the experience of any of us. True worship also determines our destiny. If we truly worship the true and living God with a humble and repentant attitude, accepting the sacrifice of His Son, then He will accept us. Think about this glorious truth: The LORD God of the universe, Who sent His Son to die for our sins, is the true and living God who loves us. It is He who is to be worshipped, and He alone. There is a bright future for anyone who turns from sin, lives a righteous life, and truly worships God. **"Awake to righteousness, and sin not; for some have not the knowledge of God: I speak this to your shame" (1 Co.15:34).** **"Teaching us that, denying ungodliness and worldly lusts, we should live soberly, righteously, and godly, in this present world; Looking for that blessed hope, and the glorious appearing of the great God and our Saviour Jesus Christ" (Tit.2:12-13).** **"By the blessing of the upright the city is exalted: but it is overthrown by the mouth of the wicked" (Pr.11:11).**
(cont. on next page)			

PROPHET	TIME/PLACE GIVEN	MAIN MESSAGE	PRACTICAL APPLICATION
ZEPHANIAH (cont.)		"I will gather them that are sorrowful for the solemn assembly, who are of thee, to whom the reproach of it was a burden. Behold, at that time I will undo all that afflict thee: and I will save her that halteth, and gather her that was driven out; and I will get them praise and fame in every land where they have been put to shame. At that time will I bring you again, even in the time that I gather you: for I will make you a name and a praise among all people of the earth, when I turn back your captivity before your eyes, saith the LORD" (Zep.3:18-20).	

TYPES, SYMBOLS, AND PICTURES
THE BOOK OF ISAIAH
CHAPTERS 1-35

ALPHABETICAL OUTLINE

What is a biblical type or symbol? Simply put, a *biblical type* is a *foreshadowing* of what was to come at a later time in history. Through a person, place, or thing, a biblical type points toward a New Testament fulfillment.

In addition to biblical types, there are what we may call *biblical pictures*. A biblical picture is a lesson that we can see in the Scriptures *without distorting the truth*. The study of biblical types and pictures is a valuable tool in that it helps us apply the truth of the Scriptures in our lives. Scripture itself tells us this:

"Now all these things happened unto them for examples: and they are written for our admonition, upon whom the ends of the world are come" (1 Co.10:11).

"For whatsoever things were written aforetime were written for our learning, that we through patience and comfort of the scriptures might have hope" (Ro.15:4).

PERSON/PLACE/THING	SCRIPTURE, OUTLINE AND DISCUSSION
ASSYRIA. *Doom of. A picture of the sinner's doom and torment in the lake of fire*	Is.30:33
BABYLON. *A picture of the world's evil system.*	Is.13:1–14:23
A type of rebellion against God.	Is.13:1–14:23
King of. A type of Satan.	Is.14:1-23
Punishment of. By God. A picture of Satan's fall.	Is.14:3-23
BRANCH. *From the stump of Jesse. A symbol of Christ being from Nazareth.*	Is.11:1
CORNERSTONE. *Of Zion. A type of Christ.*	Is.28:16
CUSH. *Promise of future salvation. A picture of mercy to the repentant in the Messiah's kingdom.*	Is.18:7
DELIVERANCE. *By God. Of His people. Surety of. A picture of safety from all enemies in the Millennium.*	Is.33:15-24
EGYPT. *A symbol of the world.*	Is.30:2; 31:1
Alliance with. By Judah. A picture of trusting the world instead of God.	Is.31:1-5
ELIAKIM. *Godly leader of Judah. A type of Christ.*	Is.22:20-24
HOLY SPIRIT. *Poured out upon God's people. A picture of the blessing of God's Presence in the Millennium.*	Is.32:15-20
HOT COALS. *In Isaiah's vision.* *From the altar. Put on his lips. A symbol of burning away sin.*	Is.6:7
On the altar. A type of Christ, His sacrifice on the cross.	Is.6:5-7
INCENSE. *A symbol of prayer.*	Is.1:13
INDICTMENT. *By God. Of the leaders of Jerusalem. A picture of God holding leaders accountable.*	Is.3:13-15

TYPES, SYMBOLS, AND PICTURES
Alphabetical Outline

PERSON/PLACE/THING	SCRIPTURE, OUTLINE AND DISCUSSION
ISAIAH. *Family of*. A symbol of deliverance through spiritual separation.	Is.8:11-22
Son of. Name of. Maher-Shalal-Hash-Baz. Meaning. A symbol of deliverance from judgment through heeding God's Word.	Is.8:1-10
A symbol of soon-coming judgment.	Is.8:1-10
Stripping of clothing. A symbol of warning not to rely on Egypt.	Is.20:2-4
JERUSALEM. *Deliverance of*. A picture of God's protection of His people in the battle of Armageddon.	Is.29:5-8
JUDGMENT. *Of Assyria*. A picture of God's plan to set His people free.	Is.14:24-27
Of Babylon. A picture of God's judgment against evil governments.	Is.13:1–14:23
Of Damascus, Ephraim and Cush. A picture of distrust but also of hope in the face of judgment.	Is.17:1–18:7
Of Egypt. A picture of God's just punishment.	Is.19:1–20:6
Of Judah and Jerusalem. A picture of coming judgment.	Is.22:1-25
Of Moab. A picture of God's compassion: weeping over the doomed.	Is.15:1–16:14
Of Philistia. A picture of God's refuge, of deliverance found only in Him.	Is.14:28-32
Of Tyre. A picture of God humbling the proud.	Is.23:1-14
PRESENCE. *Of the Holy One in Zion*. A picture of Christ's millennial rule.	Is.12:6
PROMISED LAND. A type of heaven, the believer's personal inheritance throughout eternity.	Is.5:1
SUBMISSION. *Of nations*. *To Israel*. A picture of the Messiah's coming kingdom upon the earth.	Is.14:2
VINEYARD. A symbol of God's care and concern for His people, Israel.	Is.5:1-7; 27:2

376

TYPES, SYMBOLS, AND PICTURES
THE BOOK OF ISAIAH
CHAPTERS 1-35

CHRONOLOGICAL OUTLINE

What is a biblical type or symbol? Simply put, a *biblical type* is a *foreshadowing* of what was to come at a later time in history. Through a person, place, or thing, a biblical type points toward a New Testament fulfillment.

In addition to biblical types, there are what we may call *biblical pictures*. A biblical picture is a lesson that we can see in the Scriptures *without distorting the truth*. The study of biblical types and pictures is a valuable tool in that it helps us apply the truth of the Scriptures in our lives. Scripture itself tells us this:

"**Now all these things happened unto them for examples: and they are written for our admonition, upon whom the ends of the world are come**" (1 Co.10:11).

"**For whatsoever things were written aforetime were written for our learning, that we through patience and comfort of the scriptures might have hope**" (Ro.15:4).

PERSON/PLACE/THING	SCRIPTURE, OUTLINE AND DISCUSSION
INCENSE. A *symbol of prayer.*	Is.1:13
INDICTMENT. *By God. Of the leaders of Jerusalem. A picture of God holding leaders accountable.*	Is.3:13-15
PROMISED LAND. *A type of heaven.*	Is.5:1
VINEYARD. *A symbol of God's care and concern for His people, Israel.*	Is.5:1-7; 27:2
HOT COALS. *In Isaiah's vision.* *From the altar. Put on his lips. A symbol of burning away sin.*	Is.6:5-7
On the altar. A type of Christ, His sacrifice on the cross.	Is.6:7
ISAIAH. *Son of. Name of. Maher-Shalal-Hash-Baz. Meaning. A symbol of soon-coming judgment.*	Is.8:1-10
A symbol of deliverance from judgment through heeding God's Word.	Is.8:1-10
Family of. A symbol of deliverance through spiritual separation.	Is.8:11-22
BRANCH. *From the stump of Jesse. A symbol of Christ being from Nazareth.*	Is.11:1
PRESENCE. *Of the Holy One in Zion. A picture of Christ's millennial rule.*	Is.12:6
JUDGMENT. *Of Babylon. A picture of God's judgment against evil governments.*	Is.13:1–14:23
BABYLON. *A type of rebellion against God.*	Is.13:1–14:23
A picture of the world's evil system.	Is.13:1–14:23
King of. A type of Satan.	Is.14:1-23
SUBMISSION. *Of nations. To Israel. A picture of the Messiah's coming kingdom on earth.*	Is.14:2
BABYLON. *King of. Punishment of. By God. A picture of Satan's fall.*	Is.14:3-23

PERSON/PLACE/THING	SCRIPTURE, OUTLINE AND DISCUSSION
JUDGMENT. *Of Assyria*. A picture of God's plan to set His people free.	Is.14:24-27
Of Philistia. A picture of God's refuge, of deliverance found only in Him.	Is.14:28-32
Of Moab. A picture of God's compassion: weeping over the doomed.	Is.15:1–16:14
Of Damascus, Ephraim and Cush. A picture of distrust but also of hope in the face of judgment.	Is.17:1–18:7
CUSH. *Promise of future salvation*. A picture of mercy to the repentant in the Messiah's kingdom.	Is.18:7
JUDGMENT. *Of Egypt*. A picture of God's just punishment.	Is.19:1–20:6
ISAIAH. *Stripping of clothing*. A symbol of warning not to rely on Egypt.	Is.20:2-4
JUDGMENT. *Of Judah and Jerusalem*. A picture of coming judgment.	Is.22:1-25
ELIAKIM. *Godly leader of Judah*. A type of Christ.	Is.22:20-24
JUDGMENT. *Of Tyre*. A picture of God humbling the proud.	Is.23:1-14
CORNERSTONE. *Of Zion*. A type of Christ.	Is.28:16
JERUSALEM. *Deliverance of*. A picture of God's protection of His people in the battle of Armageddon.	Is.29:5-8
EGYPT. *A symbol of the world.*	Is.30:2; 31:1
ASSYRIA. *Doom of*. A picture of the sinner's doom and torment in the lake of fire.	Is.30:33
EGYPT. *Alliance with*. *By Judah*. A picture of trusting the world instead of God.	Is.31:1-5
HOLY SPIRIT. *Poured out upon God's people*. A picture of the blessing of God's Presence in the Millennium.	Is.32:15-20
DELIVERANCE. *By God*. *Of His people*. *Surety of*. A picture of safety from all enemies in the Millennium.	Is.33:15-24

OUTLINE & SUBJECT INDEX

REMEMBER: When you look up a subject and turn to the Scripture reference, you have not just the Scripture but also an outline and a discussion (commentary) of the Scripture and subject.

This is one of the GREAT FEATURES of *The Preacher's Outline & Sermon Bible*®. Once you have all the volumes, you will have not only what all other Bible indexes give you, that is, a list of all the subjects and their Scripture references, but in addition you will have...

- an outline of every Scripture and subject in the Bible
- a discussion (commentary) on every Scripture and subject
- every subject supported by other Scripture, already written out or cross referenced

DISCOVER THE UNIQUE VALUE for yourself. Quickly glance below to the following subject of the Index. It is:

> **APOSTASY**
> Example.
> Israel. 9:8-10:4
> Judah. 1:2-10
> The world. **A**. will grow worse and worse in the last days. 2:6-9
> Judgment of. 33:1-14
> Repentance from. By Israel. Promised. 10:20-23
> Result.
> Judgment. 17:1-14
> Shame. 30:1-14, Thgt.1

Turn to the first reference. Glance at the Scripture and the outline, then read the commentary. You will immediately see the TREMENDOUS BENEFIT of the INDEX of *The Preacher's Outline & Sermon Bible*®.

OUTLINE AND SUBJECT INDEX

AGE, Messianic (See **MILLENNIUM**)

AHAZ
King. Of Judah. 1:1; 6:1; 7:1
Reign of. Given in brief. 1:1

ALCOHOL (See **DRUNKENNESS**)

ALLIANCES (See **ASSOCIATIONS**)

APOSTASY
Example.
Israel. 9:8-10:4
Judah. 1:2-10
The world. **A**. will grow worse and worse in the last days. 2:6-9
Judgment of. 33:1-14
Repentance from. By Israel. Promised. 10:20-23
Result.
Judgment. 17:1-14
Shame. 30:1-14, Thgt.1

ARABIA
History. 18:13
Judgment of. Prophesied. 18:13-17

ARMAGEDDON
Prophecy concerning. 29:5-8; 34:1-17
Victory in. Over all the enemies of God. How it will be accomplished. 29:5-6

ARROGANCE (See **PRIDE**)

ASSOCIATIONS (Evil)
Avoiding. 2:6; 20:1-6

By Judah. With Egypt. A picture of trusting the world instead of God. 31:1-5
Danger of. Will encourage the believer to sin. 20:1-6, Thgt.1
Example. Israel and Syria. Against Judah. 7:4-6
Fact. Will be common in the last days. 2:6
Warning against.
Example. Not to make an **a**. with Egypt or Cush. 20:3-6
To Judah. Or else judgment will fall. 8:9; 28:14-29

ASSURANCE
Example. To King Ahaz and Judah. That God would prevent them from being attacked. 7:4-9
Of God's Word. That it does not fail. Discussed. 32:1-20, Thgt.1
Of victory. To God's people.
Over Assyria. 17:1-8
Over all spiritual enemies. 25:10-12

ASSYRIA
Deliverance through. Promised to Judah. 17:1-8
Destruction of. Prophesied. 31:6-9; 33:1-14
Doom of. A picture of the sinner's doom and torment in the lake of fire. 30:33
Enemy. Of Israel. 1:1
Fact. Were a brutal people. 1:1; 17:4-8

Judgment of.
Picture. Of God's plan to set His people free. 14:24-27, Thgt.1
Reasons. Listed and discussed. 10:6-15; 14:24-27
Kings of.
Sargon. 14:28
Shalmaneser. 14:28
Prophecies concerning. Being defeated by the LORD. 10:20-34
Sins of.
Greed for power. 10:7
Idolatry. 10:10-11
Pride. 10:9, 13-14
Used. By God. To punish Judah. 7:18-25; 22:1-7
Wars of. Summarized. 14:28-32

BABYLON
Judgment of.
Agent for. Medes. 13:17-18
A picture of God's judgment against evil governments. 13:1–14:23
Description of. 13:6-16; 21:1-5
Prophesied. 13:1-14:23; 21:1-10
Reason for.
Evil. 13:19-22
To deliver God's people. 14:1-2
To punish the king. 14:3-23
King of.
A type of Satan. 14:3-23
Punishment of. By God. A picture of Satan's fall. 14:3-23

Symbol.
Of the evil and wickedness of this world. 13:19-23; 21:1-17, Intro.
Of the evil system of the world. 13:1-22
Type. Of rebellion against God. 13:1-14:23, Intro.

BACKSLIDING (See **APOSTASY**)
BELIEVERS
Discipline of. By God.
Fact. May come by the hand of others, even by unbelievers. 10:20-34, Thgt.2
Reasons for. (See **DISCIPLINE**, Reason)
Duty. (See **WARNINGS**)
To God.
To avoid evil associations. 2:6; 20:1-6, Thgt.1
To be spiritually separated from the world. 2:22
To heed His Word. 1:2-4
To praise His Son, Jesus Christ. 12:1-6
To produce good fruit. 5:1-7, Thgt.1
To watch for judgment day. 21:1-17, Intro.
To worship Him. 1:5
To the church.
To fellowship. 1:5
To love each other. 1:5
To others.
To assure the righteous of their reward. 3:10
To treat them fairly. 5:1-7, Thgt.1
To warn unbelievers of the coming judgment. 3:11
Fact.
Have the Spirit within. 11:2, Thgt.2
Will be opposed by the unrepentant. 9:8-10:34, Intro.
False. How to identify. They reject God's Word. 31:1-32:20, Intro.
Judgment of. Described. 24:14-16, Thgt.1
Number of. Is always relatively few. Reasons. Discussed. 10:20-34, Thgt.1
Preparation of. For judgment day. Reasons it is so necessary. 26:20-27:1
Provisions to. By God.
Deliverance from enemies. 29:5-8, Thgt.1
Empowerment for service. 6:8-13, Thgt.1
For growth. Everything necessary is done. 5:1-2
Peace. 2:4; 26:1-27:1, pt.7, Thgt.1
Protection. 4:2-6, Thgt.1; 4:28-32, Thgt.1; 27:2-13, Thgt.1
Relationship with God. 25:1
Strength during persecution. 26:1-27:1, pt.7, Thgt.1
Resurrection of. Promised. 26:19

Vindication of. By God. Discussed. 26:1-27:1, pt.4, Thgt.1
Warnings to.
That God will judge all sin. 5:24-30
To avoid the occult. 8:19-22
To fear God only. 8:11-14
To trust in God alone. 31:1-5, Thgt.1
BETRAYAL (See **APOSTASY**)

BIBLE (See **WORD OF GOD**)

BLESSINGS OF GOD (See **GOD**, Blessings by)

BOASTING (See **PRIDE**)
Example. Assyria. Exalted themselves as God. 10:5-19
Result.
Certain judgment. 10:6-15
Demeaning others. 10:5-19, Thgt.1

BRANCH
From the stump of Jesse. A symbol of Christ's being from Nazareth. 11:1

BRIBERY
Definition of. Taking wealth in exchange for a right judgment. 5:22-23
Result.
Being uprooted and destroyed. 5:23
Oppression of the people. 5:22
Warning against. 5:22-23

CALL (of God)
Surrender to. Example. Isaiah. 6:8-13
To salvation. Fact. Is accepted only by a few. 6:1-13, Intro.
To the ministry.
Example. Isaiah. 6:1-4
Requirements.
Discussed. 6:1-4, Thgt.1

CALLOUSED (See **HARD-HEARTED**)

CAPTIVITY
Deliverance from. Of Israel. 14:1-2

CARE
By God. Condition for. Repentance. 26:1-27:13, Intro.
Fact. Is a mark of true greatness. 26:1-27:13, Intro.
Meaning. To protect and provide. 26:1-27:13, Intro.

CARELESSNESS (See **SLOTH**)

CAROUSING (See **DRUNKENNESS**)

CEREMONY (See **RITUAL**)

CHARGES
By God. Against Judah.
Fourfold indictment. Listed and explained. 30:8-11

In the prophecies of Isaiah. Was like a courtroom trial. 1:1-31
Injustice. 1:21-31
Rebellion. 1:2-10
Their worship was not sincere. 1:11-20
Threefold indictment. 29:9-16
Example. Of God's people. By the LORD Himself. 1:1-31

CHASTISEMENT (See **DISCIPLINE**)

CHRIST (See **JESUS CHRIST**)

CLEANSING (Spiritual)
Example of. Isaiah. 6:6-7
Need for. Example. Isaiah. 6:5
Steps to. 1:16-18

COMMISSION
Of Isaiah. 6:9-13

COMPASSION (See **GOD**, Compassion of)

COMPLACENCY (See **SLOTH**)

CONCEIT (See **PRIDE**)

CONFESSION
Example. Isaiah. 6:5
Need for. To received forgiveness. 6:5-7, Thgt.1

CONVICTION
Need for. To spur repentance. 6:5-7, Thgt.1
Of sin. Example. Isaiah. 6:5-7

CORNERSTONE
Of Zion. A type of Christ. 28:16

COUNSEL
Meaning. Discussed. 11:2

COVETOUSNESS (See **GREED**)

CREATION
Restoration of. By the Messiah. During the Millennium. 11:6-9

CUSH
History. Summary. 18:1:2
Judgment of.
Described. 18:3-6
Reason. That they might be saved in the future. 18:7
Promise to. Of future salvation. A picture of mercy to the repentant in the Messiah's kingdom. 18:7

DAMASCUS
Ally. Of Israel. 17:1
Enemy. Of Judah. 17:1
History. Summary. 17:1
Judgment of.
Described. 17:1-9
Reasons. Listed and discussed. 17:10-14

DARKNESS
Spiritual.
Definition. Ignorant of the truth about life. 9:1-2
Overcome. By Jesus Christ. 9:1-5

DAY OF THE LORD (See **JUDGMENT**)
Cause. 24:13
Deeper study on. 2:6-4:1
Described. 24:1-23
Facts
Cannot be stopped. 34:1-17, Thgt.1
Listed. 24:1-4
Reaction to. Terror and panic. 2:10-21; 13:7-14; 24:17-23
Reasons for. Listed and discussed. 2:6-9
Surety of. 2:6-4:1, Thgt. 1

DEATH
Conquered. Prophesied. 25:7-8
Fact. Will be removed forever by Jesus Christ. 25:7-8

DECEPTION
Definition of. Sinning to the point of spiritual blindness. 5:18-19
Result. Judgment will come unexpectedly. 5:19
Warning against. 5:18-19

DEDANITES (See **ARABIA**)

DELIVERANCE
By Assyria. Promised. To Judah. 17:1-8
By God.
Of His people. Surety of. A picture of safety from all enemies in the Millennium. 33:15-24
Of Jerusalem. A picture of God's protection of His people in the battle of Armageddon. 29:5-8
From captivity. Of God's people. 14:1-2
Source.
Fearing God only. 8:11-14
God. 9:1-7
God's presence. 7:10-25
God's promise. 7:1-9
Heeding God's Word. 8:1-10, Thgt.1
Jesus Christ. 7:14
Spiritual separation. 8:11-22
Way to. By trusting in God for mercy. 7:1-9, Thgt.1

DESPAIR (See **HOPE**)

DEVIL (See **SATAN**)

DISCIPLINE
Four facts about. 27:7-11
Upon all. Reason for.
Because God loves us. 10:20-34, Thgt.2

Rebellion. 1:5-9
To keep us from harm. 18:1-7, Thgt.1
To move us to repentance. 22:8-19, pt.3, Thgt.1
Upon believers.
Fact. May come by the hand of others, even unbelievers. 10:20-34, Thgt.2
Reason for. To teach us to act righteously. 26:8-10

DISGRACE (See **SHAME**)

DISOBEDIENCE (See **HARD-HEARTED**; **REBELLION**; **SIN**)

DISTRESS
Answer to. The light of God. 9:1-2
Deliverance from. Is found in Jesus Christ. 9:4-5

DISTRUST
Of God.
Reason. People simply trust someone else. 31:1-5
Result. Prevents repentance and salvation. 17:1-18:7, Intro.; 22:8-19, pt.2, Thgt.1
Pain of. Discussed. 17:1-18:7, Intro.

DRUGS (See **DRUNKENNESS**)

DRUNKENNESS
Definition of. Addiction to a self-destructive substance. 5:11-17
Problems caused by. Discussed. 28:1-13, Thgt.2
Result.
Hunger, thirst and humiliation. 5:13-17
Judgment. 28:3-4
Warning against. 5:11-17; 28:2-4

DUMAH (See **EDOM**)

EARTH (See **WORLD**)
Curse on. Cause. Judgment of God. 24:5
Devastation of.
During God's universal judgment. Described. 24:3-4
Reason. Sin of humankind. 24:6-13
Prophecy concerning. To be perfected. 35:1-10

ECONOMY
Of the nations. Ruined. By the destruction of Tyre. 23:4-9
Trust in. Vanity of. Discussed. 2:7

EDOM
History. 21:11
Judgment of. Prophesied. 21:11-12; 34:5-7
Names.
Dumah. Meaning. Silence. 18:11
Seir. 18:11

EGYPT
Alliance with. By Judah. A picture of trusting the world instead of God. 31:1-5
History. Summary. 19:1
Hope. Offered. By God. For mercy and salvation. 19:16-25
Judgment of.
A picture of God's just punishment. 19:1-20:6
Described. 19:1-15
Reason.
Because **E**. denied God and turned away from Him. 19:1-15, Thgt.1
To prove **E**. gods were false. 19:4-15
Salvation of. Prophesied. 19:16-25
Symbol. Of the world. 30:2; 31:1

ELIAKIM
Godly leader. Of Judah. Appointed by Hezekiah. 22:20
Type. Of Christ. 22:20-25

END TIMES (See **DAY OF THE LORD**; **JUDGMENT**; **MILLENNIUM**)

ENEMIES
Of believers.
Attacks by. Enduring. How to.
By calling out to God for help. 7:10-25, Thgt.1
By trusting in God for mercy. 7:1-9, Thgt.1
Deliverance from. Is promised. 29:5-8, Thgt.1
Of Israel. (See **ISRAEL**, Enemies)
Of Judah. (See **JUDAH**, Enemies)
Spiritual. Fact. Will all be defeated. 25:10-12

ETHIOPIA (See **CUSH**)

EXALTATION (See **GOD**, Glory of)

EXILE (See **CAPTIVITY**)

FALSE PROPHETS (See **PROPHETS**, False)

FALSE WORSHIP (See **WORSHIP**, False)

FEAR OF THE LORD (See **GOD**, Fear of)

FEAST (See **GOD**, Great Supper)

FORGIVENESS (See **MERCY**; **SALVATION**)
Offered. By God. 1:1-31, Intro.
Result. Living in the city of God. 1:1-31, Intro.
Source. God. 1:1-31, Intro.

FORSAKING (See **APOSTASY**)

FUTURE
Of the world. (See **WORLD**, Future of)
Visions about. Were given to Isaiah by God. 1:1

GALILEE
Prophecy concerning. To be honored. 9:1-4

GENTILES (See **NATIONS**)

GLOOM (See **DARKNESS**)

GLORY (See **GOD**, Glory of)

GOD
Blessings by. Fact. Are many to those who repent. 30:18-33
Call of.
Of Isaiah. 6:1-13
To salvation. Fact. Is rejected by most. 6:1-13, Intro.
Character of.
Gives hope. Even during rebuke. 1:1-31, Intro.
Loves at all times. 1:1-31, Intro.
Merciful. 7:1-9, Thgt.1
Charges by. Of Judah. Through the prophecies of Isaiah. 1:1-31, Intro.
City of. Facts.
Contains no evil or injustice. 1:1-31, Intro.
Is a righteous place. 1:1-31, Intro.
Is holy. 1:1-31, Intro.
Place where the people of **G**. will live. 1:1-31, Intro.
Compassion of.
For His people. Weeps when they are punished. 22:1-7
Weeps over the doomed. 15:1–16:14
Deliverance by.
Example. Of Judah. 17:1-8
Surety of. A picture of safety from all enemies in the Millennium. 33:15-24
Discipline by. (See **DISCIPLINE**)
Fear of. Meaning. Discussed. 11:2
Forsaking. Example. Judah. 1:2-10
Great Supper. In the last days.
Prophesied. 25:6
Represents the richest of blessings for the believer. 25:6
Holiness of.
Fact.
Is declared continually around the throne of **G**. 6:3
Is the most essential characteristic of **G**. 6:3
Reaction to. By Isaiah. Complete humility. 6:5-7
Judgment by.
Against enemies. Will be executed. 1:24
(See **JUDGMENT**)
Kingdom of. (See **KINGDOM** of God; **MILLENNIUM**)

Light of. Results. Overcomes the darkness of the world. 9:1-7
Names-Titles.
Creator. 17:1-14, Thgt.1; 22:11
Judge of the universe. 1:1-31, Intro.
Refuge. 25:4-5
Shelter. 25:4-5
Sustainer of all that is. 17:1-14, Thgt.1
Oaths of. To carry out His judgment. 14:24
People of.
Future of. An overview. 1:1-12:6
Indicted. By the **G**. himself. 1:1-31
Plan of.
Facts.
Much still lies in the future. 25:1
Will be fulfilled. 25:1
For the world. Seven steps of. Listed and discussed. 25:1-12
Promises by.
New Jerusalem. 1:27
Peace. 11:1-12:6, Intro.
Remnant of Israel. Will always be. 1:10; 7:1-9
Restoration.
Of Israel. 4:2-6
To Jerusalem. 1:26-31
Provisions by. To the believer.
Peace. 2:4
Protects. 4:2-6, Thgt.1; 25:4-5
(See **BELIEVER**, Provisions to)
Revelation by.
Example. To Isaiah the prophet. 1:1
Fact. Assures the believer of the truth. 2:1-4:6, Intro.
Service to. What is needed. Discussed. 6:1-13, Intro.
Sovereignty of. Uses nations as His agent. 10:5
Trust in. (See **TRUST**)
Warnings by. (See **WARNINGS**, By God)
Works of. For His people.
Disciplines His people. 26:16–27:1
Establishes peace. 26:12-15
Executes judgment. 26:9-11
Fact. He always acts for their benefit. 26:1
Humbles the prideful. 26:5
Makes smooth the path of the just. 26:6-7

GOVERNMENT
Evil.
Judgment of. Is certain. 13:1-14:23, Intro.
Problems of. Discussed. 13:1-14:23, Intro.
Requirements. By God.
To be kind. 13:1-14:23, Intro.
To honor God. 13:1-14:23, Intro.

GRAVE (See **SHEOL**)

GREAT SUPPER OF GOD (See **GOD**, Great Supper)

GREAT TRIBULATION (See **DAY OF THE LORD**; **JUDGMENT**)

GREAT WHITE THRONE JUDGMENT (See **JUDGMENT**, Of believers)

GREED
Definition of. Accumulating wealth for selfish reasons. 5:8-10
Result. All will be lost. 5:9-10
Warning against. 5:8-10

GUILT
Ignoring. Consequences of. Discussed. 5:1-30, Intro.
Of humankind. Fact. Is universal. 6:5; 29:1-4, Thgt.1
Purpose of. To help us correct our mistakes. 5:1-30, Intro.

HARDHEARTED (See **REBELLION**; **WORD OF GOD**, Rejection of)
Cause. Rejecting God's Word. 6:9-10; 29:9-16, pt.2, Thgt.1
Commonness of. Tragedy of. Discussed. 6:9-10
Example. Judah. Did not listen to Isaiah. 6:9-10; 22:8-19
Result.
Distorts right judgment. 22:8-19, pt.5, Thgt.1
Forgiveness is not possible. 22:14
Judgment. 29:9-12

HELL (See **SHEOL**)

HEZEKIAH
King. Of Judah. 1:1
Reign of. Given in brief. 1:1

HISTORY (See **WORLD**, History of)

HOLINESS
Of God. (See **GOD**, Holiness of)

HOLY SPIRIT
Names-Titles. Spirit of the LORD
Poured out. Upon God's people. A picture of the blessing of God's presence in the Millennium. 32:15-20
Work of.
In the life of the believer. Discussed. 11:2, Thgt.2
To point to the Messiah, Jesus Christ. 11:2

HOPE
Example. Of Judah and Jerusalem. Through Isaiah's prophecies. 1:1-12:6

Fact.

Is one of the strongest forces on earth. 7:1–9:7, Intro.

There is **h.** even in the face of judgment as long as a person is on the earth. 17:1-18:7, Intro.

Given.

To believers. Of a remnant. 7:1-9

To Judah.

By God's assurance of victory over the enemy. 9:8-10:34

By Isaiah. That God knows how to take care of Judah. 28:23-29

Pictured within. The judgment of Damascus, Ephraim and Cush. 19:1-20:6

Source.

Jesus Christ. 11:1-12:6

Love of God. 1:1-31, Intro.

Prophecy. 1:1-31, Intro.

HOPELESSNESS (See HOPE)

HUMANKIND

Guilt of. Fact. Is universal. 6:5

Repentance by. Need for. Fact. Is needed by everyone. 6:5-7, Thgt.1

IDOLATRY (See WORSHIP, False)

Folly of. Exposed. By God's judgment of Egypt. 19:4-15

Uselessness of. False gods do not deliver in time of trial. 19:1

IMMANUEL

Name. Meaning. God with us. 7:14

Prophesied. Of the Messiah. 7:14

INDICTMENT (See CHARGES)

INJUSTICE

Cause. Corrupt leaders and people. 1:21-31

Definition. To treat others unfairly. 1:21-31, Thgt.1

Fact. Involves all kinds of sin. 1:21-31, Thgt.1

Types of. Listed. 1:21-31, Thgt.1

INTOXICATION (See DRUNKENNESS)

INVITATION

By God. To the rebellious. To repent and enter God's rest. 30:15-17

To salvation. (See SALVATION)

ISAIAH

Call of.

Discussed. 6:1-3, Intro.

Recorded. 6:1-13

Vision of. Possible reasons for. 6:1-13

Family of. Were signs to Judah of what God would do. 7:4-9; 8:1-10; 8:18

Ministry of.

Difficulty of. Knew ahead of time that people would not listen. 6:9-10

Focus. On Judah and Jerusalem. 1:1

Time of.

During the reigns of Uzziah, Jotham, Ahaz and Hezekiah. 1:1

Were perilous. 1:1

Name.

Meaning. The LORD saves. 1:1-31, Intro.

Witness for the LORD. 8:18

Prophecies of. Main ones. List of.

About the whole world. 24:1-23; 35:1-10

Armageddon. 29:5-8

Assyria defeated by the LORD. 10:20-34; 31:6-9; 33:1-14

Attack of Israel and Syria would be stopped. 7:4-9

Egypt will come to the LORD in the end times. 19:16-25

Israel would be destroyed within 65 years. 7:8

Judgment of the nations. 13:1-27:13

Last days.

Of God's plan for the world. 25:1-13

Parallels the Book of Revelation. 24:17-23

List of accusations. Against God's people.

False worship. 1:11-20

Injustice. 1:21-31

Rebellion. 1:2-10

Messiah.

Born of a virgin. 7:14

From the family of King David. 11:1

Reign of. (See MILLENNIUM)

Parable. Of the farmer. 28:23-29

Rebuke and hope. 1:1-12:6

Received by special visions. 1:1

Remnant of Israel. Will survive. 1:10; 8:4; 10:20-34; 14:1-2; 25:9

Restoration. Of the Jews. In the end times. 25:9

Result. Brought rebuke and hope. 1:1-12:6

Saw the future. 1:1

Song. Of the vineyard. 5:1-7

Warning against evil associations with Egypt and Cush. 20:1-6

Prophet.

Given a special vision. 1:1

To Judah and Jerusalem. 1:1

Revelations to. By God. Listed. 1:1

Son. Of Amoz. 1:1

Song of. Comparing Israel to a vineyard. 5:1-7

Visions of.

Concerned the future of the world. 1:1

Of God's throne. At the time **I.** was called. 6:1-4

ISRAEL

Alliances of. Syria. 7:4-6

Deliverance of.

From Babylonian captivity. 14:1-2

Picture. Of the believer's deliverance from sin and death. 14:1-2, Thgt.1

Division. With Judah. Will be healed. 11:13-14

Enemies.

Assyria. 7:1–9:7; 17:1-14

Babylon. 13:1-14:23

Judah. But will be reunited. 7:1–9:7; 11:13-14

Will be subjected. 11:14

Judgment of.

By the hand of Assyria. 17:1-14

Reasons.

Forgot God. 17:9-11

Four. Listed and discussed. 9:8-10:4

Names-Titles.

Ephraim. 7:2-17; 9:9, 21; 11:13; 17:3; 28:1-3

God's vineyard. 5:1-7

Promises to.

Deliverance. From captivity. 14:1-2

Remnant. Will always be. 1:10; 8:4; 10:20-34; 27:12

Restoration. 4:2-6; 27:12-13

Return of. To the Promised Land. Prophesied. 14:1-2

Sins of.

Drunkenness. 28:7-13

Evil associations. 7:2-9

Listed and rebuked. 5:8-23; 9:8-10:4

Pride. 28:1-6

Symbols of. Vineyard. 5:1-7; 27:2-6

Warnings to. Six specific warnings. 5:8-23

JERUSALEM (See JUDAH)

Capital.

Of Judah. 1:1

Of the world. In the Millennium. 2:1-5

Deliverance of. A picture of God's protection of His people in the battle of Armageddon. 29:5-8

Hope. Inspired by. The prophecies of Isaiah. 1:1-12:6

Names-Titles.

Ariel. Meaning. Lion. 29:1

City of righteousness. 1:26

Zion. Meaning. Fortress. 1:27

New.

Description. City of salvation. 26:1

Facts.

Place where only the righteous live. 1:1-31, Intro.

Will be created by God. 1:1-31, Intro.

Rebuke of. By God. Through the prophecies of Isaiah. 1:1-12:6

Sins of.
Injustice. 1:21-31
Unfaithfulness. 1:21-22
Spiritual state of. Unjust and like a
harlot. 1:21-22

JESUS CHRIST (See also **MESSI-
AH**)
Blessings of. Fourfold. Discussed.
9:1-7
Duty toward. By His people. To
praise Him. 12:1-6
Facts.
Deserves our praise. 12:1-6,
Thgt.1
Never lies. 23:15-18, Thgt.1
Spirit rests in Him. 11:2
Genealogy of. From the dynasty of
King David. 4:2; 11:1
Kingdom of. (See **MILLENNIUM**)
Millennial reign of.
Purposes. Discussed. 2:3-4
(See **MILLENNIUM**)
Names-Titles of.
Banner of salvation. 11:3-16,
Thgt.1
Branch of the LORD. 4:2; 11:1
Cornerstone of Zion. 28:16
Exalted LORD of the universe.
6:1-4, Thgt.1
Immanuel. 7:14
Light. 9:1-2
Messiah. 9:1; 11:1; 22:20-25,
Thgt.1
Need for. Cannot have peace with-
out Him. 22:20-25, Thgt.1
Power of. To break the bondage of
Satan. 14:3-23, Thgt.1
Prophecies concerning. 9:1-7,
DS #3
Salvation by. For all who trust in
Him. 2:6-4:1, Thgt.1
Source.
Of deliverance from sin and
death. 14:1-2, Thgt.1
Of hope. 11:1-12:6
Of peace. 22:20-25, Thgt.1
Of security. 28:14-29, Thgt.1
Symbols of. A branch from Jesse.
11:1
Type of. Eliakim. 22:20-25
Vision of. Given to Isaiah. 6:1-4

JEWS (See **JERUSALEM; JUDAH**)
Deliverance of. Prophesied. 29:5-8
Failure of. To be strong witnesses
for the LORD. Is the great tragedy
of Jewish history. 29:1-24, Intro.
Glorious future of. Prophesied.
29:17-24
Persecution of. Discussed. 29:1-24,
Intro.
Purposes of. Listed. 29:1-24, Intro.

JOTHAM
King. Of Judah. 1:1; 7:1
Reign of. Given in brief. 1:1

JUDAH (See **JERUSALEM; GOD,**
People of)
Associations. Evil. With Egypt.
28:18-22; 30:1-3
Assurance. Given by God. That an
impending attack would be
stopped. 9:4-9
Deliverance of. From Israel and Syr-
ia. Promised. 17:1-8
Division. With Israel. Will be
healed. 11:13-14
Duty of. To witness.
Failure in. Reason. **J**. had become
rebellious themselves. 1:2-10
To the unbelieving nations. 1:1-
31, Intro.
Enemies. (See 13:1-27:13, Div.2 In-
tro.)
Assyria. 7:1–9:7; 30:1-14
Babylon. 13:1-14:23
Israel. But will be reunited. 7:1–
9:7; 11:13-14
Syria. 7:1–9:7
Will be subjected. 11:14
Hope. Inspired by. The prophecies
of Isaiah. 1:1-12:6; 28:23-29
Indictments against.
False worship. 1:11-20
Injustice. 1:21-31
Rebellion. 1:2-10
Judgment of.
Described. 22:1-7
Mercy promised. 22:20-25
Reasons for. 22:8-19
Kings of.
Ahaz. 1:1; 7:1-12; 14:28
Hezekiah. 1:1
Jotham. 1:1; 6:1
Uzziah. 1:1; 6:1; 7:1
Rebuke of. By God. Through the
prophecies of Isaiah. 1:1-12:6
Sins of.
Evil associations. 28:14-15
False worship. 1:11-20
Injustice. 1:21-31
Leaders were obstinate. 30:1
Mocking. 28:22-29
Not trusting in God alone. 28:16-21
Rebellion. 1:2-10
Trusted in worldly powers instead
of God. 31:1-5
Worldliness. 22:2
Warnings to. Against sins. (See Sins
of, above)

JUDGMENT (See **DAY OF THE
LORD**)
Attitude toward.
By believers. A burden of woe,
realizing that most will not re-
pent. 24:14-16
By God. Compassion and weep-
ing. 15:1-16:14
Cause. (See Reason for, below)
Consequences. A cursed earth. 24:5-
13
Deliverance from. By God.

Fact. Will only come through
heeding His Word. 8:1-10,
Thgt.1
For Jerusalem. Prophesied. 29:5-8
Described.
Courtroom scene. 1:1-31;
3:13-15
Events of. 13:6-16
Raging fire. 5:24-25
The Day of the LORD. 2:6-4:1;
24:6-13
Time of great terror and panic.
2:10-21; 13:7-14; 24:17-23
Escape from. Requirements for.
Repentance. 21:11-12
Turning to the LORD. 21:13-17
Watchfulness. 21:1-10
Execution of. Described. 33:1-14
Fact.
Is universal. (See Surety of, be-
low)
There is a point of no return.
6:10; 22:8-19, pt.5, Thgt.1
There is hope as long as a person
is on the earth. 17:1-14,
Thgt.1; 18:1-7, Thgt.1
Final. Pictured.
By Isaiah's descriptive prophecy.
24:17-23
By the j. of Babylon. 13:1-22
Oath concerning. By God Himself.
14:24
Of Israel. (See **ISRAEL**, Judgment
of)
Of Judah (See **JUDAH**, Judgment of)
Of the nations. (See 13:1-27:13,
Div.2 Intro.)
Of the righteous. Described. 24:14-
16, Thgt.1
Of the world. In the end times.
Events of. Described. 24:1-23;
34:1-17
Principle of. Sowing and Reaping.
31:1-14
Reason for.
Defilement. 24:5
Denying the truth of God's Word.
22:1-7, Thgt.1
Disobedience. 24:5
In the last days. Discussed. 2:6-9
Injustice. 10:1-4
Pride. 9:9-12
Rejecting God's Word. 5:24-25
Sin. 24:5-13
Stubbornness. 9:13-17
Threefold cause. Explained. 29:9-
16
To stir repentance. 17:7
To teach righteousness. 26:8-10
Wickedness. 9:18-21
Surety of. By God.
Against God's enemies. 1:24
Fact.
All will be **j**. 13:1-22, Thgt.1;
14:24-16:14, Intro.; 19:1-15,
Thgt.1; 23:1-14, Thgt.1;
24:2; 24:1-4, Thgt.1
Will be sudden and complete.
5:24; 33:1-14, Thgt.1

Upon violence. 33:1-14
Symbols of. Isaiah's child. 8:1-10
Terror and punishment of. Described. 24:17-23
Upon Assyria. Reasons. Listed and discussed. 10:6-15
Warnings of. By Isaiah. To Judah. Were many. 1:28; 5:24-30; 7:1-9; 8:3-6; 26:20-27:1; 29:1-4; 33:1-14; 34:1-35:10
Ways. How God renders **j**. Eight ways. 19:1-15

KINGDOM (of God)
Established on earth. (See **MILLENNIUM**)
Prophesied. 9:1-7; 11:1-12:6; 18:7
Purposes. 2:3-4
Nature of.
Life within. 11:3-16
Messianic. 11:3-16
Song of. In the Millennium. 12:1-6
Supremacy of. Will be exalted above all other kingdoms. 2:1-2

LAST DAYS (See **JUDGMENT**; **MILLENNIUM**)
Deeper study on. 2:1

LAZINESS (See **SLOTH**)

LEADERS
Godly. Example. Eliakim, a type of Christ. 22:20
Needs of. To seek clear insight. 1:1, Thgt.1
Sins of. Oppression. 3:12-15
Trust in. Is good, but still temporary. 22:20-25, Thgt.1
Unfaithful. Example. Of Judah. 22:15-19

LIGHT OF GOD (See **GOD**, Light of)

LORD (See **GOD**)

LOVE
Of God. Fact. Shines forth at all times. 1:1-31, Intro.

MAHER-SHALAL-HASH-BAZ
Name. Meaning. Swift destruction. 8:3-4
Sign. To Judah. 8:1-10
Son. Of Isaiah. 8:3

MAJESTY (See **GOD**, Glory of)

MEDES
Agent. Of judgment against Babylon. 13:17-18; 21:1-10
Character of. Depraved. 13:17-18

MERCY (See **SALVATION**)
Fact. There is hope for **m**. as long as a person is on the earth. 17:1-14, Thgt.1; 18:1-7, Thgt.1; 21:13-17, Thgt.1

Offered. By God. Example.
To Cush. 18:1-7
To Egypt. 19:16-25
Requirement for. Calling out to God, acknowledging Him as the only true LORD. 19:16-25, Thgt.1
Results.
Deliverance. 9:1-7
Salvation. 19:16-25

MESSIAH (See **JESUS CHRIST**)
Characteristics of. Discussed. 11:2
Fact.
Is the God-Man. 9:6
Is the manifest Presence of God. 4:5-6
Spirit rests in Him. 11:2
Millennial reign of. (See **MILLENNIUM**)
Names-Titles.
Everlasting Father. 9:6
Meaning of. Discussed. 9:6
Mighty God. 9:6
Prince of Peace. 9:6
Wonderful Counselor. 9:6
Prophecy concerning. (See 9:1-7, DS#3)
From the line of David. 11:1
Will bear fruit. 11:1
Provisions by. Described. 4:2-4
Song. Sung to. In the Millennium. 12:1-6; 25:1-12; 27:2-6
Symbols of. Branch of Jesse. 11:1
Triumph of. Over the world. Prophecies about. 13:1-27:13
Work of. For His people.
Brings peace. 9:5; 11:6-7
Delivers from bondage and oppression. 9:4
Discussed. 11:1
Establishes true righteousness and justice. 11:3-5
Gives joy. 9:3
Governs. 9:6-7; 11:3-16
Guides. 9:6
Protects. 9:3
Restores. 11:3-16
Saves. 11:11-16

MIGHT (See **POWER**)

MILITARY (See **POWER**)

MILLENNIUM
Blessings during.
Fact. Are beyond imagination. 32:1-20; 32:15-20, Thgt.1
Of the righteous. Listed and described. 33:16-24
Tenfold. Listed and discussed. 30:18-33
World will be perfected. 35:1-10
Deeper study on. 2:1-5
Description.
Called, "that day." 19:16-25
Every need will be met. 23:15-18, Thgt.1
Fivefold description. 29:17-24

Of the Messiah's rule. 9:6-7; 32:1-20
Of total peace. 11:6-9
Of worship. By other nations. 19:16-25
There will be a new heaven and a new earth. 35:1-10, Thgt.1
Will be ruled in righteousness. 33:15-24
Discussed. 2:2-4 (See 2:1-5, DS#1)
Establishment of. Will be by Christ. 9:6-7; 11:3-16
Songs of. 12:1-6; 25:1-12; 27:2-6

MINISTERS (See **LEADERS**; **MINISTRY**)

MINISTRY
Call to.
Example. Isaiah. 6:1-4
Requirements. Discussed. 6:1-4, Thgt. 1
Difficulty of. Described. 6:8-13
Empowerment for. Fact. Is promised by God. 6:8-13, Thgt.1

MOAB
Defeat of. By Assyria. Prophecy of. Detailed. 15:1-9
Enemy. Of Israel. 15:1-16:14
Judgment of.
Picture. Of God's compassion, weeping over the doomed. 15:1-16:14
Reasons. Listed and discussed. 16:6-14

MOCKERY
Definition of. Sinning to the point of blindness to the truth. 5:18-19
Result. Judgment will come unexpectedly. 5:19
Warning against. 5:18-19

NAPHTALI
Prophecy concerning. To be honored. 9:1-4

NATIONS (See by name of nation)
Economies of. Ruined. By the destruction of Tyre. 23:4-9
Fact. Are agents of God's will. 10:5; 13:4-5; 17:1-14
Judgment of. Prophecies about. 13:1-27:13, Div.2 Intro.
Salvation of. Prophesied. 25:2-3
Submission of. To Israel. A picture of the Messiah's coming kingdom upon the earth. 14:2
Worship by. Of God. Will occur during the Millennium. 25:2-3

NEEDS
Meeting. Source. Jesus Christ. 23:15-18, Thgt.1
Of the world. Fact. Are massive. 23:15-18

NEW EARTH (See **MILLENNIUM**)

NEW HEAVENS (See **MILLENNIUM**)

NEW JERUSALEM (See **JERUSALEM**, New)

NORTHERN KINGDOM (See **ISRAEL**)

OBSTINATE (See **REBELLION**)

OPPOSITION (See **PERSECUTION**)

PEACE
On earth. Promised. Will come through the reign of Christ. 2:4; 22:20-25, Thgt.1
Source.
Jesus Christ. 22:20-25, Thgt.1
Fixing our mind upon God. 26:3

PENALTY OF SIN (See **SIN**, Penalty for)

PEOPLE OF GOD (See **GOD**, People of)

PERSECUTION
Assurance concerning. God will give victory to the believer. 9:8-10:34, Intro.
Of believers.
Deliverance from. Promised. 29:5-8, Thgt.1
End of. 25:9
Reason. Because of the believer's testimony for Christ. 9:8–10:34, Intro.

PERVERSION
Definition of. Insensitive to moral values. 5:20
Result. Complete breakdown of morality and justice within society. 5:20
Warning against. 5:20

PHILISTIA
Enemy.
Of Assyria. 14:28-32
Of Israel. 14:28-32
Judgment of.
Picture. Of finding refuge only in God. 14:28-32, Thgt.1
Reasons. Listed and discussed. 14:28-32

PHOENICIA (See **TYRE**)

PLAN OF GOD (See **GOD**, Plan of)

POWER
Meaning. Discussed. 11:2
Military. Trust in. Vanity of. Discussed. 2:7; 31:1-5
Of Christ. (See **CHRIST**, Power of)
Of God. (See **GOD**, Glory of)

PRAISE (See **WORSHIP**)

PRIDE (See **BOASTING**)
Avoiding. How to. By being concerned for others. 23:1-18, Intro.
Definition of.
Exalting oneself over another. 10:5-19, Thgt.1; 22:8-19, pt.6, Thgt.1; 28:1-13, Thgt.1
Feeling no need for correction. 5:21
Example.
Assyria. 10:13-14
Israel. 5:21
Tyre. 23:1-3, 9
Fact. A measure of self-worth is needed. 23:1-18, Intro.; 28:1-13, Thgt.1
Legitimate. Definition. Not esteem oneself about another. 23:1-18, Intro.
Results.
A false, imagined religion. 5:21
Causes us to deny our weaknesses. 23:1-18, Intro.
Judgment. 10:13-14; 28:1-13
Sin of. Discussed. 28:1-13, Thgt.1
Warning against. 5:21

PROMISED LAND
Return to. By Israel. Prophesied. 14:1-2
Type. Of heaven. 5:1

PROMISES OF GOD (See **GOD**, Promises by)

PROPHECY
About the judgment of the nations. 13:1-27:13
About the whole world. 24:1-23; 35:1-10
By Isaiah. (See **ISAIAH**, Prophecies of)
Concerning Israel. A glorious transformation. 29:17-24
Of Israel's return to the Promised Land. 14:1-2
Of the Day of the LORD. Discussed. 2:6-9
Purposes of. Both to rebuke and to give hope. 1:1-31, Intro.

PROPHETS
Definition. One sent by God with a message. 1:1
False. Fact.
They are hypocrites. 9:17
They cause people to go astray. 9:16
They teach lies instead of God's Word. 9:15
They will be judged. 9:18
Isaiah. One of God's great **p**. 1:1

PROTECTION
By God. Fact. God **p**. every believer. 4:2-6, Thgt.1

PROVIDENCE (See **GOD**, Sovereignty of)

REBELLION (See **HARD-HEARTED**)
Answer to. Repentance. 30:15-17
Consequences. 1:2-10, Thgt.1; 30:1-33, Intro.
Definition. Disobeying God. 30:1-33, Intro.
Discussed. 1:2-10, Thgt.1
Example.
Israel. 1:2-10
Leaders of Judah. 30:1-14
Hope for. The **r**. must hear the Word of God and listen to His commandments. 1:10
Problems related to. Explained. 1:3-4
Results. Discussed. 1:2-10, Thgt.1

REBUKE
Example. Of Judah and Jerusalem. By Isaiah. 1:1-12:6

REDEMPTION (See **FORGIVENESS**; **SALVATION**)

REFUGE
For the poor and needy. Against oppression. Fact. God has helped those who have called out to Him. 25:4-5
Of God. For the poor and needy. Fact. Oppression will not exist during the Messiah's rule on earth. 25:4-5

REJECTION
Of God. Cause. Rebellion. 30:1-33, Intro.
Pain of. Discussed. 30:1-33, Intro.

RELATIONSHIP
With God. Personal. Is the desire of God for every person. 25:1

REMNANT
During Isaiah's day. Fact. There was a **r**. 3:8-9
Of believers. In the world. Discussed. 10:20-34, Thgt.1
Of Israel. Promised. 1:10; 8:4; 10:20-34; 25:9; 27:11

REPENTANCE
Attitude of. Must be one of humility. 17:1-14, Thgt.1
Call to. Fact. Is worldwide and continual. 31:6-9, Thgt.1
Lack of. Result. Judgment. 22:8-19; 31:6-9, Thgt.1
Required. By God. For salvation. 1:1-31, Intro.; 17:1-14, Thgt.1; 23:1-14, Thgt.1
Result. Wonderful blessings. 30:18-33
Stirred by. Judgment. 17:7

REST (See **SALVATION**)

RESTORATION
Of creation. By the Messiah. During the Millennium. 11:6-9
Of Israel. Promised. 4:2-6; 27:1-13

RESURRECTION
Of believers. Promised. 26:19

REVELRY (See **DRUNKENNESS**)

RIGHTEOUS (See **BELIEVERS**)

RITUAL
Danger of. Can become false worship if it is only a form. 1:11-20

SALVATION (See **MERCY**)
Defined. Set free from sin. 1:1-31, Intro.
Invitation. To accept.
Example. To the rebellious. 30:15-17
Fact. Is the same invitation God has always offered. 30:15-17, Thgt.1
Of the nations. Prophesied. 25:2-3
Offered.
By God.
To Cush. A picture of mercy to the repentant in the Messiah's kingdom. 18:7
To Judah. 1:1-31, Intro.
To the Gentiles as well as the Jews. 11:3-16, pt.3, Thgt.1
Requirements for.
Calling out to God, acknowledging Him as the only true LORD. 19:16-25, Thgt.1
Repentance and confession before the LORD. 1:16-18
Trusting in Jesus Christ. 2:6-4:1, Thgt.1; 29:1-4, Thgt.1
Turning to the LORD. 21:13-17, Thgt.1
Result. Living in the city of God. 1:1-31, Intro.
Source. God. 1:1-31, Intro.
Time of. Fact. Right now.
Because only then will we have God's protection. 21:13-17, Thgt.1
Because we do not know when we will die. 21:13-17, Thgt.1

SARGON
King. Of Assyria. 20:1
Wars of.
Against Ashdod. 20:1
Summarized. 14:28-32

SATAN
Fall of.
Discussed. 14:3-23
Pictured. By the judgment of God against the king of Babylon. 14:3-23
Reason. Pride. 14:12-15
Pictured. By the king of Babylon. 14:3-23

Power of. Fact. Has been broken by Christ. 14:3-23, Thgt.1

SAVIOR (See **JESUS CHRIST**; **MESSIAH**)

SCRIPTURE (See **WORD OF GOD**)

SECURITY
Fact. Is not found in the wealth and power of the world. 28:14-29, Thgt.1
Source. Jesus Christ. 28:14-29, Thgt.1

SEIR (See **EDOM**)

SELF-EXALTATION (See **BOASTING**)

SELF-SUFFICIENCY
Example. Judah. 22:8-19
Result. Judgment. 22:8-19, Thgt.1

SEPARATION
Spiritual.
Required. To escape the wrath of God. 2:22
Result. Deliverance. 8:11-22

SERVICE (See **MINISTRY**)

SHAME
Cause.
Sin and disobedience. 30:1-14, Thgt.1
Turning away from the LORD. 30:1-14, Thgt.1
Of sin. Discussed. 30:1-14, Thgt.1

SHEAR-JASHUB
Name. Meaning. A remnant will return. 7:4-9
Sign. To Judah. 7:1-9
Son. Of Isaiah. 7:3

SHELTER (See **REFUGE**)

SHEOL
Fact. Is real no matter what people believe. 14:9, DS#1
Meaning of. Discussed. 14:9, DS#1

SIGNS
To Judah. Isaiah's sons.
Maher-Shalal-Hash-Baz. A **s.** that Judah's attackers would quickly be destroyed. 7:10-17
Shear-Jeshub. A **s.** that remnant of Jews would always exist. 7:1-9
To the world. That a Messiah would be born of a virgin. 7:14

SIN (See **SALVATION**)
Attraction of.
Cause. Evil associations. 20:1-6, Thgt.1
Discussed. 10:20-34, Thgt.1

Confession of.
Example. Isaiah. 6:5
Need for. To received forgiveness. 6:5-7, Thgt.1
Consequences. (See Result, below)
Dangers of. Discussed. 22:8-19, pt.5, Thgt.1
Described as. Wild grapes. 5:4
Destructiveness of. Discussed. 28:1-29, Intro.
Fact.
Is very deceptive. 22:8-19, pt.5, Thgt.1
Is universal. 6:5-7, Thgt.1
There is a point of no return. 6:10; 22:8-19, pt.5, Thgt.1
Will all be judged. 24:1
Forgiveness of. Example. Isaiah. 6:6-7
Judgment of.
Fact. Is certain. 1:28; 5:24-30
(See **JUDGMENT**, Surety of)
Penalty for.
Fact. Must be paid. 24:5
To be burned. 24:5
Result.
Distorts right judgment. 22:8-19, pt.5, Thgt.1
It always damages. 22:8-19, pt.3, Thgt.1
Judgment. (See **JUDGMENT**)
Secret.
Folly of. Discussed. 29:9-16, pt.3, Thgt.1
Warning against. 29:15-16
Universal. Fact of. Discussed. 6:5-7, Tght.1

SLOTH
Dangers of. Discussed. 32:11-14
Warning against. 32:9-10

SOCIETY (See **WORLD**)
Corrupt. Answer to.
Jesus Christ, the Righteous Savior. 22:20-25, Thgt.1
Righteous leaders. 22:20
Longings of. Peace. 11:1-12:6, Intro.
Problems in.
Lawlessness. 11:3-16, Thgt.1
No peace. 11:1-12:6, Intro.
Not righteous. 11:3-16, Thgt.1
Rebellion and violence. 1:2-10, Thgt.1

SOUTHERN KINGDOM (See **JUDAH**)

SOVEREIGNTY (See **GOD**, Sovereignty of)

SOWING AND REAPING (See **JUDGMENT**, Surety of)

SPIRITUAL THINGS (See other, such as, for Spiritual separation, see **SEPARATION**, Spiritual.)

STIFF-NECKED (See **HARD-HEARTED**)

STONE
Foundation. Of Zion. Is Jesus Christ. 28:16
Symbol. Of Christ. 28:16

STRENGTH (See **POWER**)

STUBBORN (See **HARD-HEARTED**)

SURRENDER (To the LORD's call)
Example. By Isaiah. 6:8-13
Fact. Should be without reservation. 6:8
Required. To be able to serve the LORD. 6:8-13, Thgt.1

SYRIA (See **DAMASCUS**)

TEMPLE
Abuse of. By Judah. Their worship was not sincere. 1:11-20
Future. Promised. 1:2-3
Heavenly. Vision of. Given to Isaiah. 6:1-4

TEMPTATION
Avoiding. How to. By not associating closely with the world. 20:1-6, Thgt.1
Source. Evil associations. 20:1-6, Thgt.1

TRIBULATION, GREAT (See **DAY OF THE LORD**; **JUDGMENT**)

TRIUMPH (See **VICTORY**)

TRUST (in God)
Fact. Is the answer to impossible situations. 7:7-9
Invitation to. Given to the rebellious. 30:15-17
Lack of. Foolishness of. 31:1-5, Thgt.1
Misplaced. Consequences of. 31:1-32:20, Intro.
Need for. To escape the judgment. 5:24-25; 17:1-14, Thgt.1; 18:1-7, Thgt.1; 21:13-17; 28:14-29, Thgt.1
Required. To avoid destruction. 7:9
Result.
(See **SALVATION**)
Wonderful blessings. 30:18-33, Thgt.1
True and false. Discussed. 28:14-29, Thgt.1

TURNING AWAY (See **APOSTASY**)

TYRE
Appeal to. To repent. 23:4
City of. Major Phoenician seaport. 23:1-3

Judgment of.
A picture of God's humbling the proud. 23:1-14
Description of. 23:1-4, 10-14
Prophesied. 23:1-14
Reason. To humble the prideful. 23:9
Promise to. Restoration. 23:15-18

UNBELIEF
Reason. Forgetting God. 17:1-14, Thgt.1
Result. Judgment. 17:1-14

UNBELIEVERS
Fact.
They oppose believers. 9:8-10:34, Intro.
They reject the LORD. 8:11-22, Thgt.1
Judgment of. Facts about. 24:1-4
Way of.
Described. 8:11-22, Thgt.1
Warning against. To avoid. 8:11-22

UNDERSTANDING
Meaning. Discussed. 11:2

UNREPENTANCE (See **REPENTANCE**, Lack of)

UZZIAH
King. Of Judah. 1:1; 6:1; 7:1
Reign of. Given in brief. 1:1

VICTORY
Over all spiritual enemies. Prophesied. 25:10-12

VIGILANCE (See **WATCHFULNESS**)

VINEYARD
Song of. Parable about the unfruitfulness of Israel. 5:1-7
Symbol. Of God's people. 5:1-7; 27:2-6

VIOLENCE
Fact.
Is common in the world. 33:1-24, Intro.
Will be judged. 33:1-14
Problem of. Discussed. 33:1-24, Intro.

VIRGIN BIRTH
Deeper study on. 7:14
Prophecy concerning. Of the Messiah. 7:14

VISION
Definition. Revealed truth given by God. 1:1
Need for. Reason. To remove the blindness to spiritual truth. 1:1, Thgt.1
Of God's throne. When Isaiah was called. 6:1-4

Of the future. Example. Given to Isaiah by God. 1:1
What it is not. Does not come from human reasoning. 1:1

WARNINGS (By God)
Against.
Drunkenness. 28:2-4
Evil associations. 8:9; 20:3-6
Injustice. 10:1-4, Thgt.1
Pride. 28:1-13
Secret sin. 29:15-16
Sin and its fruit. 1:5-9; 5:1-7
Stubbornness. 9:13-17, Thgt.1
Wickedness. 9:18-21, Thgt.1
Need for. To save us from dangers. 34:1–35:10, Intro.
Not to trust in the ability of man. 31:1-5
Of coming judgment. 5:24-30; 13:1–27:13; 29:1-4 (See **JUDGMENT**)
To avoid.
The occult. 8:19-22
The path of unbelievers. 8:11-22
To be prepared for judgment. 26:20-27:1
To be spiritually separated from the world or face His terrible judgment. 2:22
To guard against pride. Is a strong **w**. in Scripture. 9:8-10:4, Thgt.1
To Israel. Six specific warnings. 5:8-23
To stop formal, insincere worship. 1:13-15
To turn from sin. 2:6-4:1, Thgt.1

WATCHFULNESS
For the coming judgment of God. Fact. Is most important of all. 21:1-17, Intro.
Need for. In life. Discussed. 21:1-17, Intro.

WEEPING (See **GOD**, Compassion of)

WICKEDNESS (See **SIN**)

WISDOM
Meaning. Discussed. 11:2

WITNESS
Duty to.
Example. Judah. 1:1-31, Intro.
Fact. **W**. is the duty of every follower of the LORD. 1:1-31, Intro.
Failure. Example. By Judah. They became rebellious themselves. 1:2-10
To the unbelieving nations. Fact. Is the duty of every follower of the LORD. 1:1-31, Intro.

WOMEN
Worldly. Judgment of. 3:16-4:1

WORD OF GOD
Fact.
  Is certain. 9:7
  Is the only sure word. 8:21-22
Need for. To be able to walk in righteousness, morality and justice. 2:3
Rejection of.
  By false teachers. Who teach what people want to hear. 24:5
  By prideful drunkards. Example. Israel. 28:9-10
  By the world. Fact. Will bring down the judgment of God. 2:9; 22:1-7, Thgt.1
  Fact. Reveals a false profession of Christianity. 31:1-32:20, Intro.
Result.
  Causes the heart to become hard. 6:9-10; 29:9-16, pt.1, Thgt.1
  Prohibits repentance. 2:9
Teaching of. In the Millennium. Fact. Will be taught to the whole world. 2:2-4

WORKS, Of God (See **GOD**, Works of)

WORLD (See **SOCIETY**; **UNBE-LIEVERS**)
End of. Deeper study on. 2:1
Future of.
  Christ will rule on earth. 2:1-5
  Day of judgment. 2:6-4:1
  Fact. It will all pass away. 2:22
  Restoration of Israel. 4:2-6
  Under Christ's rule.
    To be perfected. 35:1-10
    Will be glorious. 9:6-7

God's plan for. The seven steps. 25:1-12
Guilt of. Will be pronounced on Judgment Day. 29:1-4, Thgt.1
History of.
  Foreseen by Isaiah. 1:1
Judgment of. In the last days.
  Reasons and facts discussed. 2:6-4:1; 24:1-13
  The Great Tribulation. Prophesied. 24:1-23; 34:1-17
Philosophy of. To seek pleasure because pleasure is always good. 22:13
Problems of.
  Listed. 1:1, Thgt.1
  No peace. 11:1-12:6, Intro.
  Violent. 33:1-24, Intro.
Prophecy about. About the whole w. 24:1-23; 35:1-10
Sins of. In the last days. Listed and discussed. 2:6-9
System of. Symbolized. By Babylon. 13:1-22
Transformation of. In the Millennium. Prophesied. 29:17-24
Triumph over. By God. Prophecies about. 13:1-27:13
Trust in. Foolishness of. 31:1-5, Thgt.1

WORLDLINESS (See **SIN**)
Example. Judah. 22:8-19
Result. Judgment. 22:8-19, Thgt.1

WORSHIP
By the Gentile nations. Is part of the plan of God. 25:2-3

False.
  Example.
    Egypt. 19:1-3
    Jerusalem. 29:4
    Judah. 1:11-20
  Folly of. Exposed. By God's judgment of Egypt. 19:4-15
  Results.
    Discussed. 1:11-20, Thgt.1
    Judgment. 17:1-14
  Types of. Only following form and ritual. 1:11-20
Formal and routine. Results. Judgment. 29:13-14
Hypocritical.
  Example. Jerusalem. 29:1-4, 13-14
  Problem of. Discussed. 29:9-16, pt.2, Thgt.1
Of Jesus Christ. Fact. Is the duty of every believer. 12:1-6; 25:1
Reasons for.
  God is faithful. 25:1
  Personal relationship with God. 25:1
Requirements for. To abandon sin. 1:11-20, Thgt.1
Song of. Sung in the Millennium. 12:1-6

WRATH OF GOD (See **DAY OF THE LORD**; **JUDGMENT**)

YAHWEH (See **GOD**)

ZEBULON
Prophecy concerning. To be honored. 9:1-4

ZION (See **JERUSALEM**)

LEADERSHIP MINISTRIES WORLDWIDE

PURPOSE STATEMENT

LEADERSHIP MINISTRIES WORLDWIDE exists to equip ministers, teachers, and laypersons in their understanding, preaching, and teaching of God's Word by publishing and distributing worldwide *The Preacher's Outline & Sermon Bible*® and derivative works to reach & disciple all people for Jesus Christ.

MISSION STATEMENT

1. To make the Bible so understandable – its truth so clear and plain – that men and women everywhere, whether teacher or student, preacher or hearer, can grasp its message and receive Jesus Christ as Savior, and...

2. To place the Bible in the hands of all who will preach and teach God's Holy Word, verse by verse, precept by precept, regardless of the individual's ability to purchase it.

The Preacher's Outline & Sermon Bible and derivative works have been given to LMW as LMW Resources for printing and distribution worldwide at/below cost, by those who remain anonymous. One fact, however, is as true today as it was in the time of Christ:

THE GOSPEL IS FREE, BUT THE COST OF TAKING IT IS NOT

LMW depends on the generous gifts of believers with a heart for Him and a love for the lost. They help pay for the printing, translating, and distributing of LMW Resources into the hands of God's servants worldwide, who will present the Gospel message with clarity, authority, and understanding beyond their own.

LMW was incorporated in the state of Tennessee in July 1992 and received IRS 501 (c)(3) non-profit status in March 1994. LMW is an international, nondenominational mission organization. All proceeds from USA sales, along with donations from donor partners, go directly to underwrite translation and distribution projects of LMW Resources to preachers, church and lay leaders, and Bible students around the world.

LMW RESOURCES

This material, like similar works, has come from imperfect man and is thus susceptible to human error. We are nevertheless grateful to God for both calling us and empowering us through His Holy Spirit to undertake this task. Because of His goodness and grace, *The Preacher's Outline & Sermon Bible*® New Testament and the Old Testament volumes have been completed.

LMW Resources include *The Minister's Personal Handbook, The Believer's Personal Handbook,* and other helpful resources available in printed form as well as electronically on various digital platforms.

God has given the strength and stamina to bring us this far. Our confidence is that as we keep our eyes on Him and remain grounded in the undeniable truths of the Word, we will continue to produce other helpful resources for God's dear servants to use in their Bible study and discipleship.

We offer this material, first, to Him in whose name we labor and serve and for whose glory it has been produced and, second, to everyone everywhere who studies, preaches, and teaches the Word.

Our daily prayer is that each volume will lead thousands, millions, yes even billions, into a better understanding of the Holy Scriptures and a fuller knowledge of Jesus Christ the Incarnate Word, of whom the Scriptures so faithfully testify.

You will be pleased to know that Leadership Ministries Worldwide partners with Christian organizations, printers, and mission groups around the world to make LMW Resources available and affordable in many countries and foreign languages. It is our goal that *every* leader around the world, both clergy and lay, will be able to understand God's holy Word and present God's message with more clarity, authority, and understanding—all beyond his or her own power.

LEADERSHIP MINISTRIES WORLDWIDE
1928 Central Avenue • Chattanooga, TN 37408
1(800) 987-8790
Email: info@lmw.org
lmw.org

11/22

Product Listing

THE PREACHER'S OUTLINE & SERMON BIBLE® (POSB)   *Available in KJV (44 vols) & NIV (40 vols)*

OLD TESTAMENT

- Genesis I: Chs. 1–11
- Genesis II: Chs. 12–50
- Exodus I: Chs. 1–18
- Exodus II: Chs. 19–40
- Leviticus
- Numbers
- Deuteronomy
- Joshua
- Judges, Ruth
- 1 Samuel
- 2 Samuel
- 1 Kings
- 2 Kings
- 1 Chronicles
- 2 Chronicles
- Ezra, Nehemiah, Esther
- Job

- Psalms I: Chs. 1-41
- Psalms II: Chs. 42-106
- Psalms III: Chs. 107-150
- Proverbs
- Ecclesiastes, Song of Solomon
- Isaiah I: Chs. 1-35
- Isaiah II: Chs. 36-66
- Jeremiah I: Chs. 1-29
- Jeremiah II: Chs. 30-52, Lamentations
- Ezekiel
- Daniel, Hosea Joel, Amos, Obadiah, Jonah, Micah, Nahum
- Habakkuk, Zephaniah, Haggai, Zechariah, Malachi

NEW TESTAMENT

- Matthew I: Chs. 1–15
- Matthew II: Chs. 16–28
- Mark
- Luke
- John
- Acts
- Romans
- 1 & 2 Corinthians
- Galatians, Ephesians, Philippians, Colossians
- 1 & 2 Thessalonians, 1 & 2 Timothy, Titus, Philemon
- Hebrews, James
- 1 & 2 Peter, 1, 2, & 3 John, Jude
- Revelation
- Master Outline & Subject Index

Handbooks

- **What the Bible Says to the Believer** — The Believer's Personal Handbook
  11 Chapters. – Over 500 Subjects, 300 Promises, & 400 Verses Expounded - Gift leatherette or paperback options

- **What the Bible Says to the Minister** — The Minister's Personal Handbook
  12 Chapters. - 127 Subjects - 400 Verses Expounded - Gift leatherette or paperback options

- **What the Bible Says to the Business Leader**—The Business Leader's Personal Handbook
  12 Chapters – Over 100 topics plus hundreds of scriptural values for conducting business in a 21st-century world — Paperback

- **What the Bible Says About Series** — Various Subjects

everyWORD

Scripture, Outline, Commentary of the Gospels with ESV Scripture

- everyWORD: Matthew 1–16:12

- everyWORD: Matthew 16:13–28:20

- everyWORD: Mark

- everyWORD: Luke 1–13:21

- everyWORD: Luke 13:22–24:53

- everyWORD: John

- **The Teacher's Outline & Study Bible™** - Various New Testament Books
  Complete 30 - 45 minute lessons – with illustrations and discussion questions
- *Practical Illustrations — Companion to the POSB Arranged by topic and Scripture reference*
- *LMW Resources on various digital platforms Learn more on our website at lmw.org*
- *Contact for resources in other languages*

Contact Us

LEADERSHIP MINISTRIES WORLDWIDE
1928 Central Avenue • Chattanooga, TN 37408
1(800) 987-8790 • E-mail - info@lmw.org
Order online at lmw.org

Made in the USA
Columbia, SC
23 August 2024